NURSING AND INFORMATICS
for the 21st Century
An International Look at Practice,
Education and EHR Trends
Second Edition

Edited by
Charlotte A. Weaver
Connie White Delaney
Patrick Weber
Robyn L. Carr

American Medical
Informatics Association
The professional home for biomedical and health informatics

About the Editors

Charlotte Weaver, PhD, RN, MSPH, FHIMSS, is Senior Vice President and Chief Clinical Officer for Gentiva Health Services, Atlanta, GA, and serves as Adjunct Professor at the University of Kansas School of Nursing and the University of Minnesota School of Nursing. Previously, she was with Cerner Corporation from 1999 to 2008 where she served as the first Chief Nurse Officer in the IT industry until May 2007. Dr. Weaver then moved into the position of Vice President and Executive Director for Nursing Research—a new and uniquely created role to foster nursing research. Her informatics career started in academia at the University of Hawaii in 1981 and over the intervening three decades has covered every side of the industry—software supplier, consulting and provider in the United States, UK, Europe, Canada and Australia. Dr. Weaver has served as part of the TIGER Initiative (Technology Informatics Guiding Education Reform) since its inception in 2004. She has been a long standing AMIA and NIWG member and is currently NIWG chair. She has served as corporate member to the International Medical Informatics Association, Nursing Informatics Working Group (IMIA-NI) from 2004-2008; she currently chairs IMIA-NI's evidence-based nursing practice working group. Dr. Weaver is a HIMSS Fellow, a member of HIMSS' Nursing Informatics (NI) Community and served as NI Committee chair for 2007-2008. A frequent presenter at national and international conferences, Dr. Weaver is widely published in informatics, patient safety and quality, and evidence-based practice.

Connie White Delaney, PhD, RN, FAAN, FACMI, is Professor and Dean of the School of Nursing at the University of Minnesota. Dr. Delaney is the first nurse informatician Fellow in the American College of Medical Informatics to be selected as dean for a major university in the United States, a position she has held since August 2005. She also holds an appointment in the Institute for Health Informatics, University of Minnesota. Dr. Delaney has held a professorship at the University of Iceland, Faculty of Medicine and Faculty of Nursing, with focused activities in health informatics for 10 years. Prior to her deanship position, she held a full professor position at the University of Iowa, College of Nursing, where she led the nursing informatics graduate program, directed the Institute for Knowledge Discovery, and served as director/co-director of research teams; these teams included the International Nursing Minimum Data Set, USA Nursing Management Minimum Data Set, and USA Nursing Minimum Data Set. In addition, she led development of evidence-based nursing protocols translated to automated clinical information systems and data mining of large data sets. Dr. Delaney currently serves on numerous boards, including the LifeScience Alley, a Minnesota-based trade association in the Upper Midwest focused on the life sciences; the American Medical Informatics Association (AMIA), and the American Association of Colleges of Nursing, Premiere Quest National Advisory Panel. She serves as the U.S. Government Accountability Office (GAO) appointee to the Health Information Technology Policy Committee, which is charged with making policy recommendations related to the nation's health information technology infrastructure. Most recently, she co-edited the October 2008 special issue of *Nursing Outlook;* this issue focused on Nursing Informatics as a strategic initiative of the American Academy of Nursing.

Patrick Weber, MA, RN, is Director and Principal of Nice Computing in Lausanne, Switzerland. He has more than 30 years of healthcare experience, with more than 20 years in the field of health informatics. Mr. Weber has served as his country's national representative to IMIA-Nursing Informatics for over ten years and is a recognized informatics leader across Europe. He has been a pivotal leader in the European Federation for Medical Informatics

(EFMI) holding numerous offices in EFMI and in Switzerland's Nursing Association. Mr. Weber works extensively across Europe and is a frequent collaborator on informatics projects across the European Union countries. He has numerous publications in both English and French and is a frequent presenter at national and international conferences.

Robyn L. Carr, RGON, is Director of Informatics Project Contracting at IPC & Associates, Cambridge, New Zealand. Prior to starting her own IT consulting company in the Asia-Pacific Rim countries, Ms. Carr served in various clinical management and administrative positions in New Zealand Health Services for over 35 years. In her consulting business, she has served as an international consultant for IT initiatives in countries as far ranging as Taiwan and South Africa. She was a founding member of the Health Informatics New Zealand in 1991 and has been a member and active leader since that time. In addition, Ms. Carr has served as New Zealand's country representative into the International Medical Informatics Association (IMIA) Nursing Informatics – Special Interest Group for the past 15 years. Her leadership on the international level resulted in her winning host country bid for the International Nursing Informatics Congress of 2000, and holding numerous board positions within IMIA-NI-SIG, including chair (2006-09). Ms. Carr is widely networked and well respected internationally. Ms. Carr co-authored *NINZ the first 10 years,* published in 2000, and is co-editor of *"One Step Beyond: The Evolution of Technology and Nursing,"* the 7ᵗʰ International Congress Nursing Informatics Proceedings.

Contributors

Outi Ahonen, MNSc
Senior Lecturer
Department of Social Services, Health and
    Sports
Laurea University of Applied Sciences

**Suzanne Bakken, DNSc, RN, FAAN,
    FACMI**
Alumni Professor of Nursing
School of Nursing
Professor of Biomedical Informatics
Department of Biomedical Informatics
Columbia University

**Marion J. Ball, EdD, FACMI, FCHIME,
    FHIMSS, FAAN**
Senior Advisor
Healthcare and Life Sciences Institute
IBM Research
Professor Emerita
Johns Hopkins University School of
    Nursing

Cristina Barrios, BSN
Department of Nursing Direction
Favaloro Foundation – University Hospital

Claudia Bartz, PhD, RN, FAAN
Coordinator, International Classification for
    Nursing Practice (ICNP©)
International Council of Nurses (ICN)
College of Nursing
University of Wisconsin-Milwaukee

Lejo Bouma, RN
Department of Youth Health Care
CARE

**Suzanne Brown, MSc Health Informatics,
    BNS**
Assistant Nurse Coordinator, Computer
    Sciences
Department of Information Management
Mater Misericordiae University Hospital

**Claire Buchner, MSc Health Informatics,
    BSc(Hons) Nursing Studies**
Teaching Fellow
School of Nursing & Midwifery
Queens University Belfast

Laura J. Burke, PhD, RN, FAAN
Director
Department of System Nursing Research
    & Scientific Support, c/o Aurora Sinai
    Medical Center
Aurora Health Care

Helen K. Burns, PhD, MN, BSN, RN, FAAN
Associate Dean for Clinical Education
School of Nursing
University of Pittsburgh

Andrew F. Carlson, BS Systems Analysis
Strategic Program Manager
Department of Information Systems
Aurora Health Care

Anne Casey, MSc, RN, FRCN
Royal College of Nursing, UK

Mary Chambers, PhD, BED(Hons)
Professor of Mental Health Nursing
Faculty of Health and Social Care Sciences
St. Georges University of London/Kingston
    University

Polun Chang, PhD
Associate Professor
Institute of BioMedical Informatics
National Yang-Ming University

Insook Cho, PhD
Professor
Department of Nursing, School of Medicine
Inha University

Lynn M. Choromanski, MS, RN
Nursing Informatics Specialist
Department of Nursing Administration
Gillette Children's Specialty Healthcare

Thomas R. Clancy, PhD, MBA, RN
Clinical Professor
School of Nursing
University of Minnesota

Amy Coenen, PhD, RN, FAAN
Director, International Classification for
    Nursing Practice (ICNP©)
International Council of Nurses (ICN)
College of Nursing
University of Wisconsin-Milwaukee

Beverly J. Collins, MS, RN
Research Fellow
Institute for Health Informatics
University of Minnesota

Rita W. Collins, PhD, MEd, BNS, RN, RM
Lecturer
School of Nursing, Midwifery & Health
    Systems
University College Dublin

Jennifer Conner, BA
Engagement Leader, Consulting
Cerner Corporation

**Helen R. Connors, PhD, DrPS (Hon), RN,
    FAAN**
Executive Director
Center for Health Informatics
E. Jean M. Hill Professor
School of Nursing
University of Kansas

Robyn Cook, MBA, BBus, RN
Honorary Associate
Faculty of Nursing & Midwifery
University of Technology, Sydney

Karen L. Courtney, PhD, RN
Assistant Professor
Department of Health and Community
    Systems
University of Pittsburgh School of Nursing

**Grace T.M. Dal Sasso, Nursing Informatics
    PhD, RN**
Adjunct Professor
Department of Nursing
Federal University of Santa Catarina

Kelly Marie Damon, MAL, BSN, RN
Director
Department of Nursing
Oasis Hospital

Walter De Caro, MNs, DAI
Head, Nursing and Health Profession
    Service
Minister of Defense (Italy) – General Direc-
    torate Military Health Services
Public Health Department
University Sapienza Roma (Italy)

Elizabeth C. Devine, PhD, MSN, RN
Professor
College of Nursing
University of Wisconsin-Milwaukee

**Charles Docherty, PhD, MN, MBCS, BN,
    RN, RNT**
Royal College of Surgeons in Iceland (RCSI)

Beth A. Donahue, MA, BAN, RN-BC
Assistant Professor
School of Nursing
The College of St. Scholastica

Donna B. DuLong, BSN, RN

Nancy E. Dunton, PhD
Research Associate Professor
School of Nursing
University of Kansas Medical Center

**Nighat Ijaz Durrani, MPH(PAK), Dip in
    Administration & Teaching, Opthlamic
    Nursing UK, RN, RM**
Registrar
Pakistan Nursing Council

Patricia C. Dykes, DNSc, MA, RN
Corporate Manager, Nursing Informatics
    and Research
Department of Clinical Informatics
    Research and Development/Information
    Systems
Partners HealthCare

Margareta Ehnfors, PhD, Dipl NEd, RN
Professor
School of Health and Medicine
Orebro University

Anna Ehrenberg, PhD, RN
Associate Professor
School of Health and Social Sciences
Dalarna University

Scott W. Eising, BS
Director, Product Management
Department of Global Products and
 Services
Mayo Clinic

Anneli Ensio, PhD, RN
Research Director
Department of Health Policy and
 Management
University of Kuopio

Firdevs Erdemir, PhD, RN
Associate Professor
Department of Nursing
Baskent University

Sally K. Fauchald, PhD, RN
Associate Professor and Chair
Department of Graduate Nursing
The College of St. Scholastica

Myriam Martin Fernández, PhD, MSN, RN
IA, Nurse Leader
Spain Services
Cerner Iberia

Daniel Flemming, Dipl. Kaufmann, RN
Faculty of Business Management and
 Social Sciences
Health Informatics Research Group
University of Applied Sciences Osnabrueck

**Joanne Foster, GradDipCIEdn, MEdTech,
 DipAppSc (NsgEd), BN, RN**
School of Nursing
Queensland University of Technology

**Yoadis Cuesta Garcia, Master of Science
 in Health Informatics, Teacher in Health
 Informatics, BSN, BCN**
Department of Health, Education
Cybernetics Center Applied to Medicine
 (CECAM)

Ayala Gonen, PhD, RN
Nursing Informatics Manager
Department of Nursing
Tel Aviv Souraski Medical Center

William T.F. Goossen, PhD, RN
Director
Results 4 Care B.V.

A.T.M. Goossen-Baremans, MSN, RN
Results 4 Care B.V.

Brian Gugerty, DNS, MS, RN
Owner
Gugerty Consulting, LLC

Herdís Gunnarsdóttir, MSc, MBA, BSc, RN
Project Manager
Department of Development, Nursing
 Chief Executive Officer Office
Landspitali University Hospital

Kathryn J. Hannah, PhD, RN
Executive Project Leader
Canadian Health Outcomes for Better
 Information and Care
Health Informatics Advisor
Canadian Nurses Association

Nicholas R. Hardiker, PhD, RN
Senior Research Fellow
School of Nursing
University of Salford

Ellen Harper, MBA, RN
Senior Director, CNO Lighthouse
Cerner Corporation

Marceline Harris, PhD, RN
Nurse Administrator and Senior Associate
 Consultant
Department of Nursing and Health Sciences
 Research
Mayo Clinic

Colleen M. Hart, MS, RN
Research Assistant/PhD Student
School of Nursing
University of Minnesota

Nursing and Informatics for the 21st Century, Second Edition

Kristiina Hayrinen, MSc
Researcher
Department of Health Policy and
  Management
University of Kuopio

Maria Heimisdóttir, PhD, MD, MBA
Director
Division of Economics, Budgeting and
  Information
Landspitali University Hospital

Michelle LL Honey, PhD, MPhil (Nursing), RN, FCNA (NZ)
School of Nursing
University of Auckland

Mary L. Hook, PhD, RN, PHCNS-BC
Research Scientist
System Nursing Research
Aurora Health Care

Derek Hoy, MSc, BSc
SnowCloud

Ursula Hübner, PhD
Professor
Department of Business Management and
  Social Sciences
University of Applied Sciences

Susan C. Hull, MSN, BSN, RN
Vice President, Business Strategies
Clinical Practice Model Resource Center
Elsevier

Susan I. Hyndman, EdD, RN
Chair, Non-Traditional Nursing
  Department
Director, RNI BS Nursing Program
School of Nursing
College of St. Scholastica

Helena Ikonen, MSc
Project Manager
Laurea University of Applied Sciences

Rafat Jan, PhD, RN
School of Nursing
Aga Khan University Karachi

Melinda J. Jenkins, PhD, RN, FNP
Consultant, Primary Care and Consumer
  Informatics

Luis Cibanal Juan, PhD, BPsy, RN
Cateobatico – Escuela Universitaria
Enfermeria en Salud Mental
Universidad de Alicante

Alain Junger, MPA, RN
Department of Nursing Administration
CHUV

Premarani Kannusamy, PhD, RN
Department of Nursing
Institute of Mental Health

Karlene M. Kerfoot, PhD, RN, NEA-BC, FAAN
Vice President and Chief Clinical Officer
Department of Administration
Aurora Health Care

Karolyn Kerr, PhD Information Systems, MHSc, RN
Informatics Consult

Rosaleen Killalea, MSc Nursing, BNS, RN
Department of Information Management
  Services
Mater Misericordiae University Hospital

Hyeoneui Kim, PhD, MPH, BSN, RN
Informatician
UCSD

Tae Youn Kim, PhD
Assistant Professor
College of Nursing
University of Wisconsin-Milwaukee

Pirkko Kouri, PhD, PHN, RN
Principal Lecturer
Department of Health Professions, Kuopio
Savonia University of Applied Sciences

Margaret Ross Kraft, PhD, RN
Assistant Professor
Niehoff School of Nursing
Loyola University Chicago

Arusa Lakhani, MScN, BScN, RN, RM
Senior Instructor
School of Nursing
Aga Khan University

Norma M. Lang, PhD, RN, FAAN, FRCN
Wisconsin Regent Distinguished Professor
Aurora Distinguished Professor of
    Healthcare Quality Informatics
College of Nursing
University of Wisconsin-Milwaukee

Laura Heermann Langford, PhD, RN
Director, Nursing Informatics
Department of Medical Informatics
Intermountain Healthcare

Martin LaVenture, PhD, MPH
Director
Center for Health Informatics
Minnesota Department of Health

Carlos Hugo Leonzio, PhD(c), BSN
Department of Education and Research
Favaloro Foundation – University Hospital

**Nancy M. Lorenzi, PhD, MS, MA, AB,
    FACMI**
Assistant Vice Chancellor for Health Affairs
Informatics Center
Vanderbilt University Medical Center

**Sally P. Lundeen, PhD, MSN, BSN, RN,
    FAAN**
Dean and Professor
College of Nursing
University of Wisconsin-Milwaukee

Merete Lyngstad, MSN, RN
Special Adviser
Department of Policy Issues
Norwegian Nurses Organisation

**Shirley Eichenwald Maki, MBA, RHIA,
    FAHIMA**
Assistant Professor
Department of Healthcare Informatics and
    Information Management
The College of St. Scholastica

John Mantas, PhD, MSc, BSc (Hons),
Professor
Faculty of Nursing
University of Athens

**Heimar De Fatima Marin, PhD, MS, RN,
    FACMI**
Professor
Department of Nursing
Federal University of Sao Paulo

**Sana Daya Marini, PhD(c), BSN, BS, RN,
    HCC**
Clinical Assistant Professor
School of Nursing
American University of Beirut

Anna Rita Marucci, MsNs, BaNsc, RN
Head Nurse
Pediatric and Hemhatology Pediatric Ward
San Cahillo – Forlanini Hospital – Rome

Susan Matney, MSN, RN
Senior Content Engineer
Department of Health Sciences IT
University of Utah

**Nagendra Prakash Mattur, PhD, MA,
    M.Phil**
Professor
Manipal Institute of Management
Manipal University

Angela Barron McBride, PhD, RN, FAAN
Distinguished Professor-University Dean
    Emerita
School of Nursing
Indiana University

Mary N. Meyer, MSN, RN
Assistant Professor, Director of Clinical
    Learning Laboratory
School of Nursing
University of Kansas

**Susan Meyer, B.Soc.Sci (Nursing) Diploma
    Paediatrics**

Kathryn Møelstad, RN
Senior Adviser
Department of Policy Issues
Norwegian Nurses Organisation

David N. Mohr, MD, FACP
Chair, Information Technology Committee
Department of Internal Medicine
Mayo Clinic

Erika Mayela Caballero Munoz, MEd Instructional Design, RN-BC
Dean
San Sebastián University Nursing School
Vice President
Virtual Community of Infantile Health
Treasurer
Chilean Health Informatics Association

Judy Murphy, BSN, RN
Vice President, Information Services
Aurora Health Care

Peter J. Murray, PhD, MSc, RN
Director and Founding Fellow
Centre for Health Informatics Research and Development (CHIRAD)

Lynn M. Nagle, PhD, MScN, BN, RN
Assistant Professor
Laurence S. Bloomberg Faculty of Nursing
University of Toronto

Nancy C. Nelson, MS, BSN, RN
Data Manager
Intensive Medicine Clinical Program
Intermountain Healthcare

Elina Ora-Hyytiainen, PhD, MNSc, RN
Principal Lecturer
Laurea University of Applied Sciences

Mary E. Paden, MSN, RN, CPNP
TIP-NEP Program Coordinator
School of Nursing
Duke University

Hyeoun-Ae Park, PhD, RN
Associate Dean and Professor
College of Nursing
Seoul National University

Filipe Suares Pereira, ND (PhD), MNSc, BN, RN
Associate Professor
Oforto College of Nursing

Heloísa Helena Ciqueto Peres
Professor Doutor
Orientacao Profissional – ENO
Escola de Enfermagem da USP

Rutja Phuphaibul, DNS, RN
Professor
Department of Nursing, Faculty of Medicine
Ramathibodi Hospital, Mahidol University

Ratna Prakash, PhD, MSc, BSc, BScN, PG DH.Ed
Dean and Professor
College of Nursing
Manipal University

Vesna Prijatelj, MSc, RN
Consultant Director in the Field of Organization and Informatics
Department of Managament
General Hospital Celje

David Printy, MS
President and CEO
Oasis Hospital

Patricia Pruden, RN
Nurse Consultant
Children's Cancer Hospital Egypt Foundation 57357

Elina Rajalahti, MNSc
Senior Lecturer
Department of Social Services, Health and Sports
Laurea University of Applied Sciences

Sripriya Rajamani, PhD, MBBS, MPH
Senior Project Consultant
Center for Health Informatics
Minnesota Department of Health

Uroš Rajkovič, MSc
Faculty of Organizational Sciences
University of Maribor

Vladislav Rajkovič, PhD
Professor
Faculty of Organizational Sciences
University of Maribor

Roberto A. Rocha, PhD, MD
Senior Corporate Manager, Knowledge Management and Clinical Decision Support
Department of Clinical Informatics Research and Development (CIRD)
Partners HealthCare System, Inc.

April J. Roche, MBA, CPEHR
Project Manager
Center for Health Informatics
School of Nursing
University of Kansas

Julita Sansoni, PhD, MScN, RN
Professor
Nursing Area Department of Public Health
University "Sapienza" of Rome

Kaija Saranto, PhD, RN
Professor
Department of Health Policy and
　Management
University of Kuopio

Bjoern Sellemann, Dipl.-Pflegewirt, RN
Faculty of Business Management and Social
　Sciences
Health Informatics Research Group
University of Applied Sciences Osnabrueck

**Joyce Sensmeier, MS, RN-BC, CPHIMS,
　FHIMSS**
Vice President, Informatics
Healthcare Information and Management
　Systems Society

Walter Sermeus, PhD, RN
Professor
School of Public Health
Catholic University Leuven

**Abel Paiva e Silva, ND (PhD), MNSc,
　BN, RN**
Coordinator Professor
Oporto College of Nursing

Denise Tolfo Silveira, PhD, MS, RN
Professor
School of Nursing
Federal University of Rio Grande do Sul
　(UFRGS)

Roy L. Simpson, RN,C, DPNAP, FAAN
Vice President, Nursing
Cerner Corporation

Diane J. Skiba, PhD, FAAN
Professor and Coordinator of the Health
　Informatics Specialty
Department of Nursing
University of Colorado Denver

Deirdre M. Stewart, Dip HCI, RGN, RPN
Healthcare Executive
Cerner Middle East

**Heather Strachan, MSc, MBCS, Dip. N,
　RGN**
Clinical eHealth Lead (NMAHP)
eHealth Directorate
Scottish Government

Amarnath Subramanian, MD, MS
Medical Director, Pathology Informatics
Department of Pathology and Lab Medicine
Regions Hospital

Olga Šušteršič, PhD, RN
Associate Professor
Department of Nursing, Faculty of Health
　Sciences
University of Ljubljana

Francesco Tarantini, MSN, BSN, RN
Dott.
Transplant Operating Theatre
Fondazione IRCCS Ospedale Maggiore
　Policlinico, Mangiagalli e Regina Elena

Teri L. Thompson, PhD(c), RN, CPNP
Director, Pediatric Nurse Practitioner
　Program
School of Nursing
University of Missouri-Kansas City

Asta Thoroddsen, PhD(c), MSc, RN
Associate Professor and Academic Chair of
　Nursing Informatics
Department of Nursing
University of Iceland and Landspitali Uni-
　versity Hospital

Jane A. Timm, MS, RN
Informatics Nurse Specialist
Department of Nursing
Mayo Clinic

Barbara S. Turner, DNSc, RN, FAAN
Professor
School of Nursing
Duke University

Catherine E. Vanderboom, PhD, RN
Clinical Nurse Researcher
Department of Nursing
Mayo Clinic

Irene van Middelkoop, Hons. BA(Cur)
CAPRISA
University of KwaZula-Natal

Elmarie Venter, Mcom (Informatics), Bcur
SAP Research, Pretoria

Philipp Vetter, PhD
Head of Strategy
Health Authority of Abu Dhabi

Kanittha Volrathongchai, PhD (Nursing), RN
Assistant Professor
Faculty of Nursing
KhonKaen University Thailand

Janelle Wapola, MA, RHIA
Assistant Professor
Department of Healthcare Informatics and
    Information Management
The College of St. Scholastica

**Judith J. Warren, PhD, RN-BC, FAAN,
    FACMI**
Christine A. Hartley Centennial Professor
    and Director of Nursing Informatics,
    Center for Health Informatics
School of Nursing
University of Kansas

Tera J. Watkins, MS, RN
Senior Solution Designer, Lighthouse
Cerner Corporation

John M. Welton, PhD, RN
Associate Professor
College of Nursing
Medical University of South Carolina

**Lucy Westbrooke, GDipBus (Health
    Informatics), DipNg, RCpN**
Department of Information Management
    and Technology Services
Auckland District Health Board

Bonnie L. Westra, PhD, RN, FAAN
Assistant Professor
School of Nursing
University of Minnesota

Peggy White, MN, BA, RN
National Project Director
Canadian Health Outcomes for Better
    Information
Canadian Nurses Association
Care Project and Program Manager
Health Outcomes for Better Information
    and Care
Ontario Ministry of Health and Long-Term
    Care

Barbara J. Wills
Assistant Director
Division of Health Policy
Minnesota Department of Health

Marty Witrak, PhD, RN, FAAN
Professor and Dean
School of Nursing
The College of St. Scholastica

Dedication

This is for those life-long friends who have stayed in my life throughout the decades—Gail Mitchell, Ann Schmella and Mikelle Streicher—they are treasures beyond all measure. And as always—to my son, Kevin Kauth.

— Charlotte A. Weaver

To my family who unselfishly supports my professional focus and giving of time—especially son Jeremy & Jessica and granddaughters Ashley, Aana, Skye, & Storme Jade; Betty White, Sue, E. Clark, Lora & Randy, Loren & Wendy, Ann, and Chris and Pat; and my late father and brother, E. N. and Craig.

— Connie White Delaney

To my ever-supportive family—my wife, Marie-France, and my daughters, Delphine and Chloé, to all my friends and colleagues in Europe, and to Charlotte Weaver for having been a very helpful support.

— Patrick Weber

To my supportive husband Peter for his understanding of the English language and to my colleagues in Health Informatics New Zealand (HINZ).

— Robyn L. Carr

Acknowledgments

In preparing this book, we have incurred many debts. First and foremost, we would like to express our appreciation to Mary Kelly and Becky Thompson for their tireless editing and project management of the many moving parts that make up this book. Nancy Vitucci, our HIMSS editor, has worked through weekends and holidays burning the midnight oil with us as we have all pushed to narrow the window between authors' completion and time to print. From conception to "book on the street," this second edition has been produced in less than two years. This accomplishment is due primarily to HIMSS' commitment to supporting this body of work and demonstrated through the hard work of Mary, Becky and Nancy. To all three of you, we bow our heads in thanks!

Fran Perveiler, chief editor at HIMSS, is due our deep appreciation for having the vision and courage to publish this second edition just four years after the first edition. Fran recognized immediately the importance of continuing to capture the seismic changes that are happening in nursing, as countries' adoption of EHR technologies accelerates.

And finally, Charlotte Weaver would like to express her gratitude to her employer, Gentiva Health Services, for supporting this book initiative when, for all apparent purposes, it would not appear to have much relevancy to a U.S. home healthcare organization.

Charlotte A. Weaver
Connie White Delaney
Patrick Weber
Robyn L. Carr
Editors

Table of Contents

Section III
Innovation Through Applied Informatics

Section V
The Near Future and Nursing

Foreword

Those of us who have been involved with biomedical and health informatics for most of our professional lives are amazed and gratified by the growing recognition, support, and enthusiasm for our field. The pace of change has been particularly remarkable in the last decade, spurred on in the United States by a Secretary of Health and Human Services, Tommy Thompson, who made health information technology (IT) a key element in his strategy for addressing the problems with the U.S. healthcare system. Reflected also in frequent comments by President George W. Bush, support for health IT innovation and investment became even more evident in the administration of President Barack Obama, who worked with Congress to make health IT a key element in the American Recovery and Reinvestment Act of 2009. The Office of the National Coordinator for Health Information Technology (ONC), now formally codified in law, has new leadership and a large stimulus budget to invest heavily in a variety of programs intended to enhance the adoption, "meaningful use," and acceptance of electronic health records and related components of the health information infrastructure. Recognizing the dearth of trained professionals who understand both the technology and the cultural milieu into which health IT must be introduced, ONC is also investing in a variety of workforce development programs, ranging from certification courses and validation of competencies to degree programs in universities and professional schools.

Throughout the evolution of our field, the nursing community has provided remarkable leadership in defining the role of informatics in the nursing profession, in bringing informatics knowledge to nursing practitioners, and in building an international community of nursing educators and informaticians that has been a role model for the other health professions. The first edition of this volume, appearing only four years ago, has been a stimulus to the cohesion of the nursing community regarding informatics education, scholarship, and the effective application of the field's principles. Yet, as mentioned, those same four years have seen impressive change in the societal interest and investment in health information technology, and thus, it is now highly appropriate to update the volume with a second edition that reflects the current momentum and investment. Nursing itself is evolving, in part due to what is happening in the information management arena, and this volume reflects and enhances those changes as well.

As we pursue "meaningful use" of health information technology, a key element is clearly the extent to which health professionals understand and embrace the role of such systems in their work, while appreciating their limitations and the need for ongoing research and innovation. No health profession has been as effective as nursing in bringing a knowledge of informatics concepts and applications to the routine education of practitioners. Section II in this volume describes key elements in such educational programs for nurses, including evolving expectations, curricular components, and the competencies that graduates must demonstrate. Other schools in the health professions have much to learn from the extensive experience and success described in these pages.

But the rest of the book is inspiring as well. Using scenarios and case studies to make the concepts concrete, the editors and chapter authors have nicely demonstrated the wide ranging and international role that informatics is playing in nursing practice, as well as the important contributions of nursing informatics innovation. Those of us who have attended the triennial Nursing Informatics (NI) conferences (sponsored by the International Medical Informatics Association) can attest to the energy, enthusiasm, and accomplishment that is routinely demonstrated in the scientific sessions and policy panels. It is small wonder that an involvement with informatics is often identified as a key indicator of the intellectual rigor and pragmatic orientation of the leaders in the nursing profession, whether in academia or in practice settings.

This volume is also evidence of the recognized synergies between the American Medical Informatics Association, the professional home for those in biomedical and health informatics (including a strong component representing the nursing informatics community), and the Healthcare Information and Management Systems Society (HIMSS), the membership organization that focuses on providing global leadership for the optimal use of health IT. We at AMIA are delighted to be collaborating with HIMSS on the co-publication of the second edition of a volume that we know will continue to inform and inspire a generation of nurses and other professionals who turn to nursing for examples of excellence in informatics education, scholarship, and application.

— Edward H. Shortliffe, MD, PhD
President and Chief Executive Officer
American Medical Informatics Association
Bethesda, MD USA

Preface

Since the publication of this book's first edition in 2006, the fundamentals set out in the preface have not changed. Governments still struggle to balance available funding against optimum quality care, as evidence of value for money spent. Many governments, ever challenged to place funding for health against financial demands from education, social welfare infrastructure and, for some, defense, find additional squeezing of their budgets. This financial imperative brings with it a greater need for enhanced technical support in cross-discipline communications and care options to enhance quality, safety, access, and efficiency.

What has notably changed is that nursing informatics per se, originally with European and American initiatives, is now being practiced in an ever increasing number of countries on the Asian, Australasian, South American and African continents, although firm evidence of the latter is sparse. Therefore, in this edition, we have attempted to embrace qualitative evidence from a number of the more recent sources of informatics practices in the countries entering into the wider group. While some of these new entrants may be perceived to be in the embryonic stage of advancement, there is a common theme—the basic education of nurses must include informatics competencies and the capacity to prepare informatics specialists.

While this second edition has substantial changes in the content covered in comparison to the first edition, the essence of the international "snapshot" of current state remains the same. These past four years have brought such rapid change in information and communication technologies, governments' IT strategies and their implementations, that we felt it was imperative to capture the state of nursing internationally as we go into the second decade of the 21st century. Major geopolitical changes have also occurred over these intervening years. China and India have emerged on the international stage as major economic and geopolitical powers. The health indicators of both countries show a rapid ascent that parallels their economic rise and gains in standards of living. And importantly, the health indicators of China and India are now matching those of EU countries, indicating their full emergence status. While India is represented in the country case studies and Taiwan has been added, we were not able to secure a contributor from mainland China. This omission reflects a lack of professional integration with our Chinese counterparts through international collaborations such as the International Medical Informatics Association (IMIA). It is through the editors' networks made possible by IMIA-NI that the majority of authors have been recruited for this book. Given that together China and India's citizens account for about 2.5 billion of the world's near 7 billon population,[1] we recognize that any international trend analysis without both of these superpowers included is seriously remiss.

This second edition book is organized into five sections, and while it has a heavy U.S. perspective, each section and most chapters have international content and authors. Section I carries the same title as in the first edition: "Revolutionizing Nursing: Technology's Role." Dr. Angela McBride's opening Chapter 1 provides a penetrating overview of how extensively informatics has already permeated nursing practice in the United States. Dr. McBride poses the question to professional nursing as to how we will use the quantitative nursing data that emanates from EHR systems. Dr. McBride notes that EHR systems and their data allow nursing's contribution to outcomes to be visible for the first time in our history. The interesting twist in Dr. McBride's observations is that with this visibility comes accountability, and she counsels: "It can be scary to get what you wished for, but, most of all, it can be enormously energizing. Let us all move to seize the opportunities before us that will not come this way again." Dr. McBride's chapter is a ***must*** read for all nurses regardless of role or country.

There are four additional strong chapters included in Section I. DuLong and Ball's Chapter 2 is an up-to-date summary of the TIGER Collaborative, a grassroots initiative in the United

States originally formed to address nursing workforce competencies and educational reforms. In Chapter 3, Jenkins and colleagues address the emergence of person empowerment in self management enabled by new Internet technologies and government health policies. In Chapter 4, Marin and Lorenzi use their long-standing leadership involvement in international informatics circles to give an overview on key informatics initiatives currently in process. This is followed by Skiba, Connors, and Honey in Chapter 5, who present a powerful description of nursing education, IT competencies needed in core curriculum and document the rapid growth in nursing informatics programs occurring in different parts of the world. In the closing chapter, Dykes and colleagues report on a three-year survey study looking at international comparisons of nurses perspectives on the helpfulness of information technology in acute care settings.

Section II focuses on nursing education, including IT competencies in basic curriculum. The new topic introduced here is a description of formal programs for nursing faculty development in IT competencies being conducted in many countries today; the chapters and case studies explore examples from Italy, Finland, and the United States. Section III is dedicated to new developments in international standards for information management, terminologies, and minimum data base sets. This section also includes an update from the University of Wisconsin-Milwaukee, Aurora Health and Cerner Corporation's research team on their 6+ year project to develop and embed evidence-based nursing content into an automated nursing clinical documentation system with the generation of nursing outcomes.

Section IV presents the international overview on the current state of nursing and adoption of EHR technologies. Section IV entitled *EHR Initiatives Across the Globe* is the core of the book, with 6 chapters representing the following geographic regions: The Americas, The United Kingdom and Ireland, Europe, Middle East, South Africa, and Asia, Australasia, and the South Pacific. There are 35 country case studies under these six geographic chapters. And, as mentioned above, we have been able to include a number of new areas and countries in this edition. Chapter 17 focuses on the Middle East and includes case studies from Egypt, Israel, Lebanon, the United Arab Emirates, and Turkey. In Europe, we have added Portugal and a contribution from Slovenia for Eastern Europe. In Southeast Asia, we are very pleased to have been able to include new case studies from Thailand, Singapore, and Pakistan, in addition to India.

The final section is a single chapter written by the four editors and presents an overview on the current state of nursing and nursing informatics identifying common themes, structural indicators in nursing status within a country, and correlation of educational levels to professional autonomy. We close this critique with a projected vision for the near future that includes opportunities, challenges, and questions for nursing leaders to ponder.

This second version of *Nursing and Informatics for the 21ˢᵗ Century* is bringing brand new contributions. Each author, empowered by the success of the first edition, has given his or her best to provide the latest up-to-date information and to propose a realistic vision of the near future of information and informatics in the field of health and nursing. This book affords the widest view of the most recent developments in this field. The best known experts in the nursing informatics world have contributed to this volume. We hope it becomes one of your most used, referenced, read, and reread books over these next years.

Charlotte A. Weaver
Connie White Delaney
Patrick Weber
Robyn L. Carr
Editors

Reference

1.   Central Intelligence Agency. The World Factbook—China. https://www.cia.gov/library/publications/the-world-factbook/geos/ch.html. Accessed December 8, 2009.

Revolutionizing Nursing: Technology's Role

Section I

Introduction

By Charlotte A. Weaver, PhD, MSPH, RN, FHIMSS

The six chapters that make up Section I provide a framework for a current state assessment of the degree to which the use of information and communication technologies have permeated nursing practice, educational curricula, and nursing science. While coverage of recent developments in the United States dominates the content in most of these chapters, there is an international focus in five of the six chapters. We recognize that many countries are much further advanced in the adoption of electronic health record (EHR) technologies than the United States and have achieved automation that extends across all levels and venues of care, including to the home and the individual, e.g., Finland, Norway, and Denmark. The value provided from these international perspectives and authors is that it allows us to step back and see the common themes, the variations, and the significance of these factors for the status of professional nursing and its practice in a given country. The power of our ability to do these comparisons and contrasts is that they enable us to clearly identify the differentiators that allow nurses in one country to be included in their country's EHR strategies and to be recognized as professional members of the healthcare provider community, while in another country, nurses are excluded.

Today, we have tremendous variation in the professional status and level of nursing practice across nations. This variation is inevitably grounded in the historic beginnings of nursing, but the most telling predictor is whether the country is in control of its own university-based degree programs in nursing, with nursing faculty prepared at a master's and doctoral level. Where university-based nursing degree programs are just beginning, nursing tends to be on the outside looking in, as it pertains to national healthcare IT strategies. In our increasingly interconnected global village, this extensive variation does our citizens a disservice, and it is in all our best interests to narrow these differences within our developed countries and to extend our collective hands to our colleagues beyond the countries of North America and the European Union.

This second edition again opens with Angela McBride's chapter in which she chronicles the resolute march toward EHRs throughout the world and the dramatic developments in the United States being marshaled in under the American Recovery and Reinvestment Act (ARRA) of 2009.[1] McBride calls out some of the key areas of nursing's challenges and notes that while the "informatics revolution in process has the potential to deliver what nurses have historically wished for in their profession," she poses the question of "what will nurses do with this opportunity?" McBride's ability to outline such a piercing overview of nursing's opportunities and challenges as we stand on the threshold of possibilities enabled by this IT era, makes this chapter a "must read" for all nurses.

In Chapter 2, DuLong and Ball describe the work that has been completed under the umbrella of the TIGER Collaborative (Technology Informatics Guiding Education Reform) since its conception as a burning imperative in July 2004. The accomplishments of this grassroots initiative are chronicled through two working summits and nine collaborative work teams that focused on nursing workforce, faculty competencies, educational curricula, leadership, standards, usability, consumer empowerment, national health IT agenda, and development of a virtual demonstration center.

The rapidly developing area of consumer empowerment, self-management, and personal health record technologies is the focus of Chapter 3. Contrasting strategies between approaches being taken in Finland and the United States are described. Jenkins, Kouri, and Weaver also review the national health strategies of numerous countries to show the common trend toward patient empowerment and self-management enabled by new Internet technologies and online health information. The authors note that the focus of these national strategies especially target elderly populations and those with chronic illnesses, as countries struggle to contain costs by more effective care delivery.

In Chapter 4, Marin and Lorenzi give us an international overview on the state of nursing informatics from their positions as nursing leaders whose professional activities carry them across geographic boundaries. Chapter 5 chronicles the evolution, new developments, and current state of growth and maturity of nursing informatics as a recognized program specialty within nursing. Skiba, Connors, and Honey do a masterful job of capturing the progression of nursing informatics in the United States but also bring in new developments in Europe, South America, Australia, New Zealand, and Asia Pacific countries.

Chapter 6 is the summary report of a three-year, international collaborative study on the impact of health IT on nurses working in acute care settings. The work was funded under HIMSS and sponsored as an endorsed initiative of the International Medical Informatics Association, Nursing Informatics – Special Interest Group (IMIA-NI). Dr. Patricia Dykes' persistent leadership saw this complex research project through to completion. The findings are a reminder of the variation that exists between the United States and the rest of world in the way in which EHR adoption starts in acute care organizations and radiates outward. In other national IT strategies, countries have built their infrastructure from a community and primary care base. Within this chapter, each country's participating lead author is also the country representative into IMIA-NI, with the exception of Nicholas Hardiker who graciously led the effort for Great Britain.

Reference

1. American Recovery and Reinvestment Act. http://frwebgate.access.gpo.gov/cgi-bin/getdoc. cgi?dbname=111_cong_bills&docid=f:h1enr.pdf. Accessed November 20, 2009.

CHAPTER 1

Informatics and the Future of Nursing Practice

By Angela Barron McBride, PhD, RN, FAAN

Introduction

Around the world, significant movement is underway in processing and maintaining health-care information that makes this the Decade of Health Information Technology. Various governments are making billion-dollar investments in establishing electronic health networks. In the United States, this movement began in 2004, when then U.S. Secretary of Health and Human Services Tommy Thompson and David Brailer, MD, PhD, the country's first health information technology coordinator, unveiled a strategic plan with goals for adoption and diffusion of an electronic health record (EHR). The aim of implementing the EHR was seamless continuity of care across settings and clinicians, maximum informed consumer choice, and improved public health through timely incident reporting.[1] The American Recovery and Reinvestment Act (ARRA) of 2009, signed by President Barack Obama in February 2009, earmarked $19.2 billion for this purpose.[2] In April 2009, the U.S. Government Accountability Office (GAO) appointed a Health Information Technology Policy Committee to create a framework for development and adoption of such a nationwide infrastructure.[3] A nurse, Connie Delaney, was appointed to that effort. In the five years between the launching of a plan and concrete development in that direction, nurses have labored to be seen as key stakeholders in this defining movement.

A reformed healthcare system must include a nursing workforce prepared to wield the information and communication technology that will achieve quality, cost-effective outcomes.[4,5,6] And it is clear that no aspect of nursing and patient care will be untouched by the information revolution in process, yet most nurses remain dubious about the changes underway or feel unprepared for what is to come. Many have also struggled with whether informatics is yet another thing to learn or something much more profound. What is true in some U.S. Veterans Affairs Medical Centers may be true in most hospitals: information and communication technology that permits computerized patient records and decision support may generally be regarded as a positive development, particularly by administrators charged with facilitating system issues. But frontline clinicians are more likely to view computers and new ways of doing things as troublesome, adding to already-heavy workloads and interfering with existing workflow patterns.[7]

Informatics—used in this chapter to encompass the broad and evolving knowledge base concerned with all aspects of information literacy, not just computer competence[8,9]—is still not perceived as fundamental to nursing practice but only as an add-on. The American Nurses Association's (ANA's) *Nursing: Scope and Standards of Practice*[10] lists the profession's fundamentals as the core activities of assessment, diagnosis, planning, implementation, evaluation, and outcomes identification. Though all aspects of the nursing process can be transformed by information and communications technology, informatics as such is described as "a role specialty" not unlike others, such as education and research. This conceptualization, though true in a literal sense because informatics innovation is a specialty, is pernicious. It obscures the extent to which information and communication technology (ICT) is central to every aspect of the nursing profession.

Informatics does certainly exist as a specialty that integrates computer/information sciences and cognitive science with nursing science.[11] But it is important to understand that the long-established staples taught by schools of nursing—assessment, evaluation, documentation, communication problem solving, medication administration, patient education, and care coordination—require some familiarity with ICT and various informatics solutions.[12,13] Indeed, one can argue that nursing, particularly nursing administration, has long held goals—monitor needs of vulnerable populations, document clinical problems, foster continuous quality improvement, utilize research findings, evaluate achievement of desired outcomes, integrate clinical and financial data in strategic planning—that were never fully achievable before the advent of 21st century ICT.

Nursing has long prided itself on understanding patients within their environments—describing the phenomena of nursing as the interaction between and among the nurse, patient, health, and environment; yet, the emphasis in education and practice remains on nurses as direct providers of care in acute care hospitals. The "real" nurse is typically perceived as one who interacts on a one-to-one basis with patients and their families, and all that is and can be done to benefit them and facilitate care through ICT is given short shrift. All that nurses accomplish within community structures and in chronic or home care that can be enhanced by ICT is even more ignored.

The remainder of this chapter will elaborate on the informatics revolution that is underway and how it is inextricably tied to realizing the recommendations of the various quality reports issued by the Institute of Medicine (IOM) in the last decade. The paradigm is shifting for all healthcare professionals away from a single-minded emphasis on the provider-patient relationship and on to a systems approach that emphasizes the importance of a culture of safety, organizational structures, information at the point of decision making, continuity of care, and technologies that enable effectiveness by both the professional caregiver and the family caregiver.

The Informatics Revolution

The IOM's various quality initiatives have each linked ICT to the improvement of healthcare. The landmark report *Crossing the Quality Chasm*[14] did not just emphasize the importance of ICT in financial transactions and administrative processes but noted how crucial ICT is to all aspects of research, clinical decision making, consumer education, professional development, and delivery of population-based care. The 1st Annual Crossing the Quality Chasm Summit treated ICT as a strategy essential to all reform and one particularly important in expediting patient self-management in chronically ill patients.[15] "Utilizing informatics" has been described as a core competency all healthcare professionals will need in the 21st century because it is foundational to delivering patient-centered quality care that is evidence based.[16] And it is a competency that has international importance[17,18] because IOM's quality initiatives have become priorities around the world.[19]

"Utilizing informatics" may be a core competency all healthcare professionals will need in the 21st century, but most nurses, having insufficient knowledge, skills, and supports (training, time, and resources) in this area, remain unprepared for that future.[20] Almost all nurses are unsure about meeting new expectations when the EHR becomes the norm and makes possible easier data retrieval to turn information into knowledge that guides practice. Core informatics competencies have been identified at four levels of practice—beginning, experienced, specialist, and innovator—but these competencies have not been fully incorporated by educational level (undergraduate and graduate) into curriculum changes and performance appraisals.[21,22]

In 2006, the National League for Nursing conducted a survey[23] of more than 2,000 faculty and deans/directors and found that computer literacy (60%) was valued over information literacy (40%), with many failing to recognize a difference between educational technology (the ability to handle a Web-based course) and practice technology (the ability to use ICT to ensure best practices). Nursing faculty have been pioneers in the development of distance learning—moving from making didactic classes available via videotapes to two-way audio and video delivery to Web-based courses—but that is not the same as having the skills to integrate ICT into their practicum courses.[24,25]

Concerned that nurses would truly be prepared in the 21st century to integrate evidence and informatics into practice, the Technology Informatics Guiding Education Reform (TIGER) Initiative was launched. After a summit of stakeholders was held in 2006, action steps were drafted that lead to initiatives in nine areas, one of which was education and faculty development.[26] Influenced in part by TIGER's grassroots drive to not let informatics become the sole province of technology specialists, the Division of Nursing within the Health Service Resources Administration (HSRA) launched the Integrated Technology into Nursing Education and Practice Initiative.[27] Both the National League for Nursing and the American Association of Colleges of Nursing stepped up efforts to incorporate informatics education into nursing curricula.[28,29,30] The development of the new doctor of nursing practice (DNP) degree has even been touted as an opportunity to integrate informatics into the curriculum at the outset for the purpose of transforming practice.[31]

The gap between what is in place and what is needed remains wide, exacerbated by the fact that informatics is least likely to be integrated into the already-packed associate-degree curriculum, still the major entranceway into nursing.[23] Matters are further complicated by nursing faculty and students typically only having "guest" status as they rotate through a number of clinical and community agencies for their practicum experiences, so that they may not be familiar with the ICT systems in place in a particular institution, nor encouraged to use them. One attempt to bridge this divide was development of a simulated data system for academic purposes that mirrors a major system used by service settings.[32,33]

Nursing does not generally require students to use personal digital assistants (PDAs) as physicians now do, although use of PDAs is beginning to change, particularly in nurse practitioner programs.[34,35] The difference in the use of Internet linked-technologies is also reflected in the finding that nurses are less likely to make use of online evidence to support their work than are physicians.[36] Not only may nurses be constrained by lack of educational preparation but also by whether they think it is even their role to initiate information seeking related to patient care because they (and others around them) still view physicians as the major decision makers.[37] These limitations are exacerbated by the fact that many nurses have limited on-the-job access to computer features, such as e-mail, the Internet, or charting screens,[7] because they do not have personal desktop computers as do physicians and administrators.

The level of information literacy varies by year of graduation, with those graduating before 1990 typically having weaker computer skills,[38] yet these are the very individuals likely to be in leadership positions by virtue of their seniority. Because this group of veteran nurses is more likely to feel awkward and frustrated when new ICT expectations are added to their existing portfolio of responsibilities, they may be less likely to embrace such changes and to encourage others to do so.

In hospitals, the perception often exists that a few nurses with highly developed ICT skills are enough for the institution to function when new systems are adopted, but that attitude overlooks the fact that nurses serve as the primary interface between ICT systems and patients and their families. Physicians and administrators may assign "primary responsibility for patient safety" to nurses,[39] but may simultaneously omit their voices and opinions in the procurement, design, and implementation phases of ICT adoption when the framework for future nursing practice is being set in place. Nurse informaticians are prized, but they may spend most of their time getting physicians and others to use new ICT systems, rather than working on improving nursing practice.[40] This lack of ICT investment in support of clinical nursing has been identified by nurses as a major source of dissatisfaction in their work lives.[41]

Incorporating ICT into education and practice is now at the same developmental stage as was research in previous decades, when it was only incorporated into graduate research courses that actually had the word "research" in their titles. Now research is expected to be incorporated into all undergraduate and graduate courses because no aspect of nursing can be adequately discussed without some attention given to the classic studies that shaped what we now know. Nurses historically oversaw implementation of physicians' research protocols but did not focus on getting their own clinical questions answered.[42] Now, annuals and journals are full of studies that support the scientific basis for nursing care of individuals across the life span during illness and recovery. In similar fashion, ICT and informatics competencies must now be incorporated into all undergraduate and graduate courses, not just informatics courses, and nurse informaticians must focus more on improving nursing care.

There are a number of initiatives underway that are speeding progress in this direction. Various educational collaboratives have been funded to support faculty development.[43,44] Nurses are teaching to IOM reports.[45] The Robert Wood Johnson Foundation has funded Quality and Safety Education for Nurses (QSEN) to move forward the core competencies all healthcare professionals need.[46] That initiative spells out the knowledge, skills, and attitudes necessary to use informatics to communicate, manage knowledge, mitigate error, and support decision making,[47] and computational modeling is increasingly being used to support quality and safety.[48] Whole issues of journals have focused on informatics, such as the September/October 2008 issue of *Nursing Outlook*.[12] The most successful initiatives reinforce that ICT is not about the technology but about finally achieving the quality of care and continuity of care that have long been professional aspirations. This point is important because anxiety about correctly using new technology can easily cloud matters, grabbing attention away from the central reason for the changes.

Quality Practice

The ANA distinguishes between standards of *nursing* practice—assessment, diagnosis, planning, implementation, evaluation, and outcomes identification—and standards of *professional* practice—education, collegiality, collaboration, ethics, research, leadership, resource utilization, quality of practice, and practice evaluation.[10] The former emphasizes the critical thinking approach of the nursing process; the latter describes expectations for acting as a professional. As nurses go about using the nursing process, they should presumably aim for quality, keep up-to-date, act collaboratively and ethically, and integrate research findings into their practice.

The IOM quality initiatives focus on six aims—safety, effectiveness, patient-centeredness, timeliness, efficiency, and equity—that would largely be subsumed under "quality of practice" in the ANA's *Nursing: Scope and Standards of Practice*.[10] Both the ANA and the IOM statements expect the nurse to aim for quality, but there is a difference in how they approach the matter. In the former, quality practice is a standard each nurse must adhere to; indeed, the critical thinking approach of the nursing process is in service to quality. The IOM's quality initiatives, by contrast, move the emphasis away from the practice of individuals, believing that healthcare professionals can only practice at the highest level if system supports are in place.

This shift in emphasis, occasioned as it first was by the IOM's finding that most errors are the result of system failures and not individuals' mistakes,[49] should be a source of comfort to nurses because this approach requires nurses to speak out when conditions are not safe. There is no one in the nursing profession who has missed out on the experience of being responsible for what was beyond one's personal control, a situation that only promotes a feeling of helplessness, rather than encouraging competence. When the focus is on system supports, ICT ceases to be primarily an avenue of technical innovation and becomes instead a shift in paradigm, with the nurse truly becoming a knowledge worker[50] who uses information to deliver best practices.

One could be glib and say that nursing's decades-long emphasis on the nursing process had the unintended consequence of making nursing appear to be in a continual state of flux, never achieving outcomes. And there is some truth to that statement because all of the focus on process was skimpy on stipulating concrete outcomes. The thousands of outcomes nurses achieved on a daily basis in working with their patients consequently did not add up to summative data that others could easily see. Hopefully, that will dramatically change as nurses come to view ICT as a means to structure and aggregate their data to demonstrate results.

One would hope that all nurses would embrace ICT with enthusiasm if they fully understood how the informatics revolution will make it possible for them to achieve their goals, including the six aforementioned IOM aims. *Person-centered* is the one aim that nurses excel at already,[51] since they are constantly supporting consumer decision making. ICT has already enabled nurses to develop new ways of supporting patients and their families, e.g., teaching older adults to access patient education Web sites,[52,53] recommending asthma Web sites for parent education,[54] and helping families manage health information in households.[55]

The Internet has been used to support family caregivers of cancer patients, assisting them in dealing with the roller coaster of physical, emotional, and psychological demands.[56] Nursing, with its definitional emphasis on helping patients and their families do what they would do unaided if they knew what to do, has used ICT to promote patient and family self-management, e.g., e-mail discussion groups around back pain,[57] posthospitalization recovery from CABG (coronary artery bypass graft) surgery,[58] and continence health promotion.[59] Some nurses are working with engineers both to develop a personal robotic assistant for homebound patients and to realize the possibilities of smart technology that can unobtrusively monitor changes in a person's activities of daily living at a distance, thus permitting seniors to obtain watchful help without leaving their homes.[60]

Safety can be expedited by ICT in many ways, from the use of bar coding around the administration of medications to wearing near-hands-free communication devices to stay in real-time communication with colleagues who can provide back-up assistance. ICT makes seamlessness possible at points of transition—e.g., shift changes, moves between care settings, or release back home—when mistakes or omissions are most likely to happen.[61] Surveillance is a major nursing responsibility, and all sorts of "event monitoring" functions can be built with ICT to alert the nurse to changes in physiologic status and other predictors of problems. ICT also makes possible appropriate information sharing just before clinicians are about to make decisions, e.g., flashing cautions and contraindications before a procedure is undertaken.[62]

In our outcomes-oriented world, *effectiveness* has assumed new importance, if for no other reason than the likelihood that reimbursement will increasingly be linked to the achievement of best practices. Quality-improvement committees in every healthcare institution are tracking their progress using a range of indicators, e.g., Health Plan Employer Data and Information Set (HEDIS), Outcome and Assessment Information Set (OASIS), Centers for Medicare & Medicaid Services (CMS), Leapfrog, and National Surgery Quality Improvement Project (NSQIP). ICT makes online dissemination of constantly changing standards and policies possible and then permits benchmarking local outcomes against national averages for similar institutions.[63,64]

Although current benchmarking largely focuses on whether services are provided, e.g., ordering fasting blood glucose and A1c tests for patients with diabetes, the day is fast approaching when the emphasis will be on whether patients received, understood, and acted on the information that might change these laboratory values and achieve the desired glucose control. The quality of nursing will eventually be determined by that linkage between processes and outcomes, which will be good news for those who believed all along that the nursing process was supposed to begin with "assessment" then proceed to "evaluation."

ICT can facilitate *timeliness* in many ways, from improved arranging of appointments and work schedules to ensuring that a unit's inventory of supplies is automatically replenished. ICT permits continuous communication between patients and providers thus eliminating much of the need for "just in case" (as opposed to "just in time") interventions. The Veterans Health Administration's (VA's) new Care Coordination and My Health E Vet programs have eliminated most routine clinic visits, focusing instead on seeing patients when actually needed.[65]

Efficiency is an aim that can be greatly enhanced by ICT because so much time and money are wasted asking patients questions they have already answered many times before and repeating lab and imaging tests that have been lost from the paper record.[66] ICT makes possible targeted population-based interventions, e.g., the design of a computer-based system to support nicotine dependence treatment in primary care.[67] Limited resources can be strategically deployed, using geographic information systems (GIS) to provide care to the neediest customized by zip code.[68,69]

Equity can be realized through ICT in many ways, from providing some version of telecare to patients in rural settings to making sure that take-home information on discharge is printed in the patient's first language. Nurses have already provided end-of-life care over the lines via telehospice.[70,71] Since ICT programs offer the opportunity of mass customization, health information can be broadly disseminated but tailored in terms of the patient's age, gender, race, and reading level.[72] Nurses have already used these strategies successfully in cancer screening.[73]

All of the healthcare professions are being challenged by the enormity of the changes taking place. Both nursing and the field of medicine, in general, have been socialized to primarily think in terms of the provider-patient relationship, rather than in terms of the systems that need to be put in place to support individuals in doing their best. Most nurses would be inclined to agree that "All nursing practice, regardless of specialty, role, or setting, is fundamentally independent practice."[10] In context, the emphasis on independent practice is not meant to be read as a call for rugged individualism but as a reminder of the responsibilities each nurse bears in maintaining personal competence over a career lifetime. Nevertheless, the equation of nursing practice with independent practice, paralleling longstanding conceptualizations of medical practice as independent practice, signals how challenging it is likely to be for all concerned to harness so many individual impulses in service to the system changes ahead.

Achieving Nursing's Preferred Future

You can sound the clarion call, but change will not proceed apace unless it is viewed as a means of achieving what is really wanted by the key players. And one can argue that the informatics revolution in process has the potential to deliver what nurses have historically wished for in their profession.[74] Information system design can smooth progress in many areas heretofore insufficiently addressed, from orientation of temporary staff and participation in management to continuity of care and development of a learning environment.[75] Though nurse executives and nurse managers have long been charged with encouraging their staffs to be responsible for their practice, standardized measurements and outcomes (e.g., the National Database of Nursing Quality Indicators) did not exist until now to allow nurses to be accountable using accepted indicators of excellence.

The institutional data that historically existed in acute care settings largely focused on numbers of procedures and tests completed because physician-ordered diagnostics and interventions were the key to hospital reimbursement. In that calculation, nursing was regarded as a necessary cost, not as a value. That thinking is becoming dated with the current emphasis on achieving quality, cost-effective outcomes. CMS is strengthening the ties between payment for services and quality of care, no longer paying the cost of treating so-called "never events" that are reasonably preventable through proper care.[76] And nursing bears primary responsibility for avoiding many of those problems that should never happen, for example, certain types of falls, infections of various types, and pressure ulcers. The more nurses address these problems by designing ways to avoid them, the more nursing will be regarded as invaluable because level of reimbursement is now linked to nursing care.

Nurses began to describe themselves in recent years as "knowledge workers,"[77] in part because they wanted to buttress support for the importance of nursing research and in part because they wanted to counter stereotypical notions that all you needed to be a good nurse was a caring heart, strong back, and gentle hands. But the move to describe themselves as knowledge workers sometimes sounded self-serving and did not capture the attention of others (e.g., physicians, administrators) before the IOM quality initiatives and CMS guidelines. In 2004, IOM devoted an entire volume, *Keeping Patients Safe: Transforming the Work Environment of Nurses*,[78] to the proposition that nurses must function as knowledge workers, and their work environments must strive to display the hallmarks of a learning organization. This IOM report supports the importance of strong nurse leadership if quality and patient safety are to be realized and recommends additional education so nurses can meet new expectations, particularly around knowledge management and the design of work to reduce error. Publication of this report, because it honors the work of nursing as essential to quality care and urges that the work environment of nurses be improved to support the nursing staff, was a watershed event in that it elevated nursing leadership to a national priority.

Now, the question is what will nurses do with this opportunity? After years of feeling not fully appreciated for our contributions, nurses are being recognized as indispensable in areas that will only grow in importance as healthcare institutions seek to develop an organizational culture that continuously strengthens patient safety. Both the government's strategic plan for the development of the EHR and the various IOM reports emphasize delivery of consumer-centric and information-rich healthcare—areas at the center of nursing's self-definition as a profession. But do we fully recognize the opportunities before us? Are we mobilizing our strengths—a systems orientation, the ability to work collaboratively, creativity demonstrated in a long record of savvy workarounds—to take the lead at this crucial time?

In many ways, this chapter is meant to be a major reframing. Instead of nurses viewing the informatics revolution as an intrusion that gets in the way of one's real work with patients, it is important to appreciate the extent to which we are living in a time when nursing can fully come into its own as a discipline and be perceived that way by others. Surely there will be new skills to be learned on the part of students, faculty, clinicians, and executives, but that has always been true of the field. This time, the new skills to be learned serve to reinforce our own notion of ourselves as knowledge workers exerting leadership through the creation of learning organizations, and that is a vision worthy of our concerted best efforts.[79]

The development of one integrated EHR means that what nurses contribute will truly be seen by all other healthcare providers. And the telecare opportunities mean that nurses do not have to be limited by their venue, shifts, or place, as has so often been the experience of nurses working in traditional hospitals but can begin to think and act beyond the constraints of time and geography.[80] Can we seize these opportunities and assume primary responsibility for managing all key transitions (across levels of care, across developmental challenges)? Can we take the lead in managing chronicity and promoting functional ability, not constrained by disease-management standards but energized by new ways to touch base with patients on a daily basis? "Ask A Nurse" services have grown in recent times, and will only expand further in new directions. What will those new directions be?

To embrace the informatics revolution is to exert leadership. The early leadership research was dominated by a preoccupation with relations-oriented behaviors (Does the leader demonstrate caring and integrity?) and task-oriented behaviors (Does the leader clarify tasks to be performed and monitor progress?). Now, there is increasing emphasis on a third dimension, that is, the way leaders initiate change and encourage organizational innovation.[81,82] And one of the most important components of organizational innovation in nursing and patient care is developing an informatics vision that realizes our long-held values and goals.[83]

There are many efforts on the part of organized nursing to move such leadership forward. For example, the American Association of Critical-Care Nurses has published *Standards for Establishing and Sustaining Healthy Work Environments*.[84] That document reaffirmed that practice is driven by the needs of patients and their families but noted that the quality of nursing practice and patient outcomes are inextricably linked to the quality of the work environment. Six essential standards for a healthy work environment were identified, and several of them demonstrate the extent to which informatics is important even when the word is not used. Skilled communication is listed as the first standard, and skilled communicators are described as having access to appropriate communication technologies and being proficient in their use. Another standard is effective decision making, which is achieved when data are transformed into meaningful information that guides decisions, which can be subsequently evaluated as to their effectiveness. Yet another standard is authentic leadership, which is said to involve the design of systems.

Nursing has a long proud history of innovation, dating back to Florence Nightingale's founding of public health statistics and design of military hospitals, both of which promoted healthy environments as a means of achieving quality nursing practice. Nurses today are similarly called upon to make use of information design,[85] this time mindful of the importance of clinical data repositories and data warehouses in the identification of actionable knowledge.[86] Today's reengineering of nursing practice must involve the harnessing of new technologies to empower patients and their caregivers.[87,88] Nightingale would no doubt be pleased to think that data continue to serve the transforming role in care-giving that her mortality and morbidity figures once did.

I end this chapter not recalling Nightingale's work to be politically correct but to remind us of all she accomplished amidst chaos and scarcity by seizing the opportunities before her. She never lost sight of what was most important, the well-being of her patients, but she understood that you cannot effect system-wide change without aggregating data so patterns can emerge. She used the pie chart to effect, so others could see the reality of the situation and be engaged in policy changes. In seizing the opportunities of this moment in time, we have advantages that Nightingale did not have, not the least of which is a mandate from the IOM to exert the leadership that we always said we could. It can be scary to get what you wished for, but, most of all, it can be enormously energizing. Let us all move to seize the opportunities before us that will not come this way again.

References

1. Thompson TG, Brailer DJ. *The Decade of Health Information Technology: Delivering Consumer-centric and Information-rich Health Care. Framework for Strategic Action.* Washington, DC: Department of Health and Human Services; 2004.

2. Healthcare Information and Management Systems Society. *Economic Stimulus for the Healthcare IT Industry. What Will it Mean for You and the Industry?* http://www.himss.org/EconomicStimulus/. Accessed April 24, 2009.

3. Government Accountability Office. *GAO Announces Appointment to Health Information Technology Committee.* http://www.gao.gov/press/health_it_committee2009apr03.pdf. Accessed April 24, 2009.

4. Rother J, Lavizzo-Mourey R. Addressing the nursing workforce: A critical element for health reform. *Health Aff.* 2009;28:620-624.

5. Fuchs VR. Three "inconvenient truths" about health care. *NEJM.* 2008;359:1749-1751.

6. Roman C. Informatics is on the national agenda and nurses need to be informed and involved. *Nurs Outlook.* 2006;54:303-305.

7. Lyons SS, Tripp-Reimer T, Sorofman BA, et al. Information technology for clinical guideline implementation: Perceptions of multidisciplinary stakeholders. *J Am Med Inf Assoc.* 2005;12(1):64-71.

8. Kerfoot KM, Simpson R. Knowledge-driven care: Powerful medicine. *Reflections Nurse Leadership.* 2002;28(3):22-24, 44.

9. Saranto K, Hovenga EJS. Information literacy—what is it about? *Int J Med Inform.* 2004;73:503-513.

10. American Nurses Association. *Nursing: Scope and Standards of Practice.* Washington, DC: http://www.Nursesbooks.org; 2004. Accessed April 28, 2009.

11. American Nurses Association. *Nursing Informatics: Scope and Standards of Practice.* Silver Spring, MD: http://www.Nursesbooks.org; 2009. Accessed April 28, 2009.

12. McBride AB, Detmer DE. Using informatics to go beyond technologic thinking. *Nurs Outlook.* 2008;56:195-196.

13. Hendrich A, Chow M, Skierczynski BA, Lu Z. A 36-hospital time and motion study: How do medical-surgical nurses spend their time? *Permanente J.* 2008;12(3):25-34. http://xnet.kp.org/permanentejournal/. Accessed on Nov. 7, 2009.

14. Institute of Medicine. *Crossing the Quality Chasm. A New Health System for the 21st Century.* Washington, DC: The National Academies Press; 2001.

15. Institute of Medicine. *The 1st Annual Crossing the Quality Chasm Summit: A Focus on Communities.* Washington, DC: The National Academies Press; 2004.

16. Institute of Medicine. *Health Professions Education: A Bridge to Quality.* Washington, DC: The National Academies Press; 2003.

17. Murphy J, Stramer K, Clamp S, Grubb P, Gosland J, Davis S. Health informatics education for clinicians and managers—what's holding up progress? *Int J Med Inform.* 2004; 73: 205-213.

18. Marin HF. Nursing informatics: Advances and trends to improve health care quality. *Int J Med Inform.* 2007;76: S267-S269.

19. Van de Castle B, Kim J, Pedreira MLG, Paiva A, Goossen W, Bates DW. Information technology and patient safety in nursing practice: An international perspective. *Int J Med Inform*. 2004;73:607-614.

20. Hart MD. Informatics competency and development within the US nursing population workforce: A systematic literature review. *CIN*. 2008;26:320-329.

21. Staggers N, Gassert CA, Curran, C. Informatics competencies for nurses at four levels of practice. *J Nurs Educ*. 2001;40:303-316.

22. Gassert CA. Technical and informatics competencies. *Nurs Clin North Am*. 2008;43:507-521.

23. National League for Nursing. *Preparing the Next Generation of Nurses to Practice in a Technology-rich Environment: An Informatics Agenda*. http://www.nln.org/aboutnln/PositionStatements/informatics_052808.pdf. Accessed April 28, 2009.

24. Chastain AR. Are nursing faculty members ready to integrate information technology into the curriculum? *Nurse Edu Perspect*. 2002;23:187-190.

25. McNeil BJ, Elfrink VL, Bickford CJ, et al. Nursing information technology knowledge, skills, and preparation of student nurses, nursing faculty, and clinicians: A US survey. *J Nurs Educ*. 2003;42:341-349.

26. Weaver CA, Skiba D. TIGER initiative: Addressing information technology competencies in curriculum and workforce. *CIN*. 2006;24:175-176.

27. Technology Informatics Guiding Education Reform. *The TIGER Initiative. Collaborating to Integrate Evidence and Informatics into Nursing Practice and Education: An Executive Summary*. http://www.tigersummit.com/uploads/TIGER_Collaborative_Exec_Summary_040509.pdf. Accessed April 28, 2009.

28. Skiba DJ, Rizzolo MA. National League for Nursing's informatics agenda. *CIN*. 2009;27:66-68.

29. American Association of Colleges of Nursing. *The Essentials of Doctoral Education for Advanced Nursing Practice*. http://www.aacn.nche.edu/DNP/pdf/Essentials.pdf. Accessed April 28, 2009.

30. American Association of Colleges of Nursing. *The Essentials of Baccalaureate Education for Professional Nursing Practice*. http://www.aacn.nche.edu/Education/pdf/BaccEssentials08.pdf. Accessed April 28, 2009.

31. Jenkins M, Wilson M, Ozbolt J. Informatics in the Doctor of Nursing Practice Curriculum. *AMIA Annual Symposium Proceedings*. 2007;364-368. http://www.pubmedcentral.nih.gov/articlerender.fcgi?artid=2655779. Accessed April 28, 2009.

32. Connors HR, Weaver C, Warren J, Miller KL. An academic-business partnership for advancing clinical informatics. *Nurse Edu Perspect*. 2002;23:228-233.

33. Connors H, Warren J, Weaver C. HIT plants SEEDS in healthcare education. *J Nurs Adm Q*. 2007;31:129-133.

34. Huffstutler S, Wyatt TH, Wright CP. The use of handheld technology in nursing education. *J Nurs Educ*. 2002;27:271-275.

35. Bakken S, Cook SS, Curtis L, et al. Promoting patient safety through informatics-based nursing education. *Int J Med Inform*. 2004;73:581-589.

36. McCannon M, O'Neal PV. Results of a national survey indicating information technology skills needed by nurses at time of entry into the work force. *J Nurs Educ*. 2003;42:337-340.

37. Gosling AS, Westbrook JI, Spencer R. Nurses' use of online clinical evidence. *J Adv Nurs*. 2004;47:201-211.

38. Pravikoff D, Pierce S, Tanner A. Are nurses ready for evidence-based practice? *Amer J Nurs*. 2003;103(5):95-96.

39. Cook AF, Hoas H, Guttmannova K, Joyner JC. An error by any other name. *Amer J Nurs*. 2004;104(6):32-43.

40. Sensmeier J, West L, Horowitz JK. Survey reveals role, compensation of nurse informaticists. *CIN*. 2004;22:171, 178-81.

41. O'Neil E, Seago JA. Meeting the challenge of nursing and the nation's health. *JAMA*. 2002;288:2040-2041.

42. McBride AB. Nursing and the informatics revolution. *Nurs Outlook*. 2005;53:183-191.

43. Warren J, Connors H. Health information technology can and will transform nursing education. *Nurs Outlook*. 2007;55:58-60.

44. Skiba DJ, Connors HR, Jeffries PR. Information technologies and the transformation of nursing education. *Nurs Outlook*. 2008;56:225-230.

45. Finkelman A, Kenner C. *Teaching IOM: Implications of the Institute of Medicine reports for nursing education*. Silver Spring, MD: http://www.nursesbooks.org. Accessed April 28, 2009.

46. Cronenwett L, Sherwood G, Barnsteiner J, et al. Quality and safety education for nurses. *Nurs Outlook*. 2007;55:122-131.

47. QSEN. *Competency definitions*. http://www.qsen.org/competency_definitions.php. Accessed April 28, 2009.

48. Effken JA, Brewer BB, Lamb GS, Verran JA, Carley K. Using OrgAhead, a computational modeling program to improve patient care unit safety and quality outcomes. *Int J Med Inform*. 2005;74:605-613.

49. Institute of Medicine. *To Err is Human: Building a Safer Health System*. Washington, DC: The National Academies Press; 2000.

50. Snyder-Halpern R, Corcoran-Perry S, Narayan S. Developing clinical practice environments supportive of the knowledge work of nurses. *CIN*. 2001;19(1):17-23.

51. Mitchell PH. Patient-centered care—A new focus on a time-honored concept. *Nurs Outlook*. 2008;56:197-198.

52. Dauz E, Moore J, Smith CE, Puno F, Schaag H. Installing computers in older adults' homes and teaching them to access a patient education web site. *CIN*. 2004;22:266-272.

53. Nahm E-S, Preece J, Resnick B, Mills ME. Usability of health web sites for older adults. *CIN*. 2004;23:326-334.

54. Oermann MH, Gerich J, Ostosh L, Zaleski S. Evaluation of asthma websites for patient and parent education. *J Pediatr Nurs.* 2003;18:389-396.

55. Moen A, Brennan, PF. Health@Home: The work of Health Information Management in the Household (HIMH) - Implications for Consumer Health Informatics (CHI) innovations. *J Am Med Inform Assoc.* 2005;12:648-656.

56. Klemm P, Wheeler E. Cancer caregivers online. Hope, emotional roller coaster, and physical/emotional/psychological responses. *CIN.* 2005;23:38-45.

57. Lorig K, Laurent D, Deyo R, Marnell M, Minor M, Ritter P. Can a back pain e-mail discussion group improve health status and lower health costs? A randomized study. *Arch Intern Med.* 2002;162:792-796.

58. Brennan PF, Jones J, Moore SM, Visovsky C. A scalable technological solution to the challenges of posthospitalization recovery from CABG surgery. In: Nelson R and Ball MJ, eds. *Consumer Informatics. Applications and Strategies in Cyber Health Care.* New York: Springer-Verlag;2004:33-39.

59. Boyington AR, Widemuth BM, Dougherty MC, Hall EP. Development of a computer-based system for continence health promotion. *Nurs Outlook* 2004;52:241-247.

60. Alwan M, Aversano T, Matthews JT, Rosen MJ. Technology in the pipeline to help older adults. *Public Policy & Aging Report.* 2004;14(1):14-15.

61. Coleman EA, Berenson RA. Lost in transition: Challenges and opportunities for improving the quality of transitional care. *Ann Intern Med.* 2004;140:533-536.

62. Ball MJ, Weaver C, Abbott PA. Enabling technologies promise to revitalize the role of nursing in an era of patient safety. *Int J Med Inform.* 2004;69:29-38.

63. Bakken S, Cimino JJ, Hripcsak G. Promoting patient safety and enabling evidence-based practice through informatics. *Med Care.* 2004;42:II49-II56.

64. Brooten D, Youngblut JM, Kutcher J, Bobo C. Quality and the nursing workforce: APNs, patient outcomes and health care costs. *Nurs Outlook.* 2004;52:45-52.

65. Perlin JB, Roswell RH. Why do we need technology for caregiving of older adults in the US? *Public Policy & Aging Report* 2004;14(1):14-15.

66. Cowden S, Johnson LC. A process for consolidation of redundant documentation forms. *CIN.* 2004;22:90-93.

67. McDaniel AM, Benson PL, Roesener GH, Martindale J. An integrated computer-based system to support nicotine dependence treatment in primary care. *Nicotine Tob Res.* 2005;7:S57-S66.

68. Riner ME, Cunningham CJ, Johnson A. Public health education and practice using Geographic Information System technology. *Public Health Nurs.* 2004;21(1):57-65.

69. Endacott R, Kamel Boulos MN, Manning BR, Maramba I. Geographic information systems for healthcare organizations: A primer for nursing professions. *CIN.* 2009;27:50-56.

70. Whitten P, Doolittle G, Mackert M, Rush T. Telehospice: End-of-life care over the lines. *Nurs Manage.* 2003;34(11):36-39.

71. Buis LR. Emotional and informational support messages in an online hospice support community. *CIN.* 2008;26:358-367.

72. Park E-J, McDaniel A, Jung M-S. Computerized tailoring of health information. *CIN.* 2009;27:34-43.

73. Champion V, Foster JL, Menon U. Tailoring interventions for health behavior change in breast cancer screening. *Cancer Pract.* 1997;5:283-288.

74. McBride AB. Actually achieving our preferred future. *Reflections Nurse Leadership.* 2005;31(4):22-23, 28, 31.

75. Brennan PF, Anthony M, Jones J, Kahana E. Nursing practice models: Implications for information system design. *J Nurs Adm.* 1998;28(10), 26-31.

76. CMS. *ELIMINATING SERIOUS, PREVENTABLE, AND COSTLY MEDICAL ERRORS-NEVER EVENTS.* http://www.cms.hhs.gov/apps/media/press/release.asp?Counter=1863. Accessed June 19, 2009.

77. Sorrells-Jones J, Weaver D. Knowledge workers and knowledge-intense organizations. *J Nurs Adm.* 1999;29(7/8):12-18.

78. Institute of Medicine. *Keeping Patients Safe. Transforming the Work Environment of Nurses.* Washington, DC: The National Academies Press; 2004.

79. Mahoney R. Leadership and learning organisations. *The Learning Organisation.* 2000;7:241-244.

80. Prinz L, Cramer, M, Englund A. Telehealth: A policy analysis for quality, impact on patient outcomes, and political feasibility. *Nurs Outlook.* 2008;56:152-158.

81. Yukl G, Gordon A, Taber T. A hierarchical taxonomy of leadership behavior: Integrating a half century of behavior research. *J Leadership and Organ Stud.* 2002;9:15-32.

82. Scoble KB, Russell G. Vision 2020, Part 1. Profile of the future nurse leader. *J Nurs Adm.* 2003;33:324-330.

83. McCartney PR. Clinical issues. Leadership in nursing informatics. *JOGNN.* 2004;33:371-380.

84. American Association of Critical-Care Nurses. *AACN Standards for Establishing and Sustaining Healthy Work Environments. A Journey to Excellence.* http://www.aacn.org/WD/HWE/Docs/HWEStandards.pdf. Accessed April 29, 2009.

85. Brasseur L. Florence Nightingale's visual rhetoric in the rose diagrams. *Technical Communication Quarterly.* 2005;14:161-182.

86. Lang NM. The promise of simultaneous transformation of practice and research with the use of clinical information systems. *Nurs Outlook.* 2008; 56:232-236.

87. Bakken, S, Stone PW, Larson EL. A nursing informatics research agenda for 2008-18: Contextual influences and key components. *Nurs Outlook.* 2008;56:206-214.

88. McDaniel AM, Schutte DL, Keller LO. Consumer health informatics: From genomics to population health. *Nurs Outlook.* 2008;56:216-223.

## CHAPTER 2

TIGER: Technology Informatics Guiding Educational Reform—A Nursing Imperative

By Donna B. DuLong, BSN, RN; and Marion J. Ball, EdD, FACMI, FCHIME, FHIMSS, FAAN

Introduction

As the U.S. healthcare industry works toward the widespread adoption of EHRs by 2014, nursing must transform itself as a profession to make full use of the capabilities electronic records will provide. This transformation will require changes in nursing education and nursing practice to make informatics competencies part of every nurse's skill set. It will also require nursing organizations to work toward a shared vision. Above all, it will demand that the profession continue to be actively involved in advancing the national health IT agenda and the vision of patient-centered, knowledge-based care targeted by that agenda.[1]

Informatics and health IT are becoming as indispensable to the practicing nurse as the stethoscope was in the 20th century. As the IOM has emphasized in its quality reports, utilizing informatics is a core competency required of all healthcare professions. Yet today, most nurses lack the skills needed as professionals to seamlessly integrate health IT into their practice. Core informatics competencies have been identified and defined. Now they must be incorporated into education at every level and into daily practice through such means as accreditation standards, state board requirements, position descriptions, and performance appraisals. This dissemination not only requires a commitment across nursing but interdisciplinary collaboration as well. In the words of the IOM, "It is high time to embrace a collaborative approach to educational reform. The professions and, most important, patients will be the beneficiaries."[2]

Nurses in education and practice settings need the access to evidence-based knowledge that health IT can provide. As the IOM acknowledges, such access is often not available, resulting in the chasm between "the healthcare we have and the care we could have."[2] As EHRs become the national standard, nurses must have the tools they need to collect evidence at the bedside and apply the knowledge based on that evidence at the bedside, in the classroom, and in research.

The Technology Informatics Guiding Education Reform (TIGER) Initiative[3] aims to enable practicing nurses and nursing students to fully engage in the evolving digital era of healthcare. Through its agenda and action plans, TIGER is working to ensure that *all* nurses are educated in using informatics and are, thereby, empowered to deliver safer, higher-quality patient care. The challenge is clear: To support IT-enabled nursing practice in the future, nursing education must be redesigned to keep up with the rapidly changing technology environment.

Background

National attention on health IT has accelerated since 2004 when then President George W. Bush announced plans to support adoption of EHRs for all Americans. In January 2005, a small group of nursing leaders and advocates met and resolved to strengthen the voice of the nursing profession in the transformation of healthcare for the 21st century. This group organized the TIGER Initiative. The TIGER Initiative developed a charter at the first meeting to bring together nursing stakeholders to develop a shared vision, strategies, and specific actions

Allow informatics tools, principles, theories, and practices to be used by nurses to make healthcare safer and more effective, efficient, patient-centered, timely, and equitable.

Interweave enabling technologies transparently into nursing practice and education, making information technology the stethoscope for the 21st century.

TIGER VISION

"We must teach for the future. This means teaching to find rather than to know, question rather than answer, achieve rather than accomplish, inspire rather than inform."

Figure 2-1. *The TIGER Vision*

for improving nursing practice, education, and the delivery of patient care through the use of health IT. In 2006, the TIGER Initiative convened a summit of nursing stakeholders titled *Evidence and Informatics Transforming Nursing* to develop, publish, and commit to carrying out the action steps defined within this plan. The summary report titled *Evidence and Informatics Transforming Nursing: 3-Year Action Steps Toward a 10-Year Vision* is available at www.tigersummit.com.

The TIGER Summit

The 2006 TIGER Initiative summit gathered more than 100 leaders from the nation's nursing administration, practice, education, informatics, technology organizations, government agencies, and other key stakeholders to create *a vision for the future of nursing that bridges the quality chasm with information technology*. While many of the statements resonate with a wide range of interdisciplinary health professions, the initial focus of the agenda was nurses and the nursing profession.

The TIGER Vision

After two and a half days, the attendees developed a vision statement and action plan to be completed within the next three years. The vision is described in Figure 2-1.

The Action Plan

The action plan focused on seven components defined and ranked by the summit attendees using a wireless audience response system. Attendees concurred that essential components are interdependent. Together, all seven components act as pillars for the TIGER vision and provide the framework for TIGER's action plan. They acknowledged the importance of respect, trust, and openness in healthcare and confirmed that culture permeates all of the key action areas listed next.

1. **Management and Leadership.** The TIGER attendees envisioned *revolutionary leadership that drives, empowers, and executes the transformation of healthcare* as the highest priority of the TIGER Summit. To achieve this outcome, the attendees recommended that the industry identify strategies for increasing the power, influence, and presence of nursing through professional organizations and governmental and legal bodies. As national attention remains focused on healthcare reform enabled through the use of health IT, numerous activities are available in which nurses may lead and participate in public discussions, forums, and policy committees. To initiate this action, the attendees recommended publication and widespread dissemination of the TIGER Summit report to nursing leaders, especially through professional networking organizations. Another recommended strategy was to highlight educational programs for nursing leaders that emphasize informatics and information management competencies.

2. **Education.** Education reform, targeted at all levels of nursing preparation, remains the primary purpose of the TIGER Initiative. The participants described their vision for education as *collaborative learning communities that maximize the possibilities of technology toward knowledge development and dissemination, driving rapid deployment and implementation of best practices.* To accomplish these goals, the participants suggested numerous strategies starting with acquiring funding to develop and implement learning innovations, foster faculty development, and ensure necessary infrastructure. Faculty acceptance of technology, a critical success factor, will require incentives, education and training, and necessary support. Integrating computer competencies, information literacy, information management, and informatics will require nursing curriculum reform and the infusion of technologies for learning. New collaborative partnerships among public and private academic, service, and industry enterprises will be required to provide ongoing access to new technologies. In addition, the participants recommended that a national group be convened to develop strategies for the recruitment, retention, and training of current and future workforces in informatics education, practice, and research.

3. **Communication and Collaboration.** As nurses are central to communication and collaboration with other members of the healthcare team, the participants envisioned *standardized, person-centered, technology-enabled processes to facilitate teamwork and relationships across the continuum of care.* Nursing needs to work with all other stakeholders to establish, disseminate, and support a shared vision, core values, and goals related to the use of health IT. One of the best ways to achieve this objective is through the use of demonstration projects that model collaborative relationships across the continuum of care. Other examples are local TIGER teams or regional sharing among practice, education, and research teams. The industry would benefit from publication and dissemination of the successes and failures of these demonstration programs and would establish replicable models for others to follow.

4. **Informatics Design.** The TIGER Summit attendees acknowledged that the current state of health IT did not and today, does not fully support state-of-the-art-and-science nursing practice. However, they were able to describe their future health IT vision as "evidence-based, interoperable intelligence systems that support education and practice to foster quality care and safety." Nurses, by involving themselves in future informatics design, will have a crucial role in helping to realize this vision. In addition, it is necessary to include multidisciplinary end-users in the design and integration/incorporation of informatics, contributing the input to create design and integration that is intuitive, affordable, usable, responsive, and evidence-based across the continuum of care. Future health IT systems must be designed that promote the mining and use of data for analysis, clinical decision-making, and measurement to improve the quality of care. This achievement will require the creation and implementation of multidisciplinary, multilingual standards. Best practices can be shared with others by developing guidelines for integrating informatics infrastructure, including, but not limited, to intelligence systems, IT hardware architecture, data documentation and warehousing, universal database, and portals of knowledge.

5. **Information Technology.** A clear vision for health IT emerged as "smart, people-centered, affordable technologies that are universal, useable, useful, and standards-based." This vision demands the integration of interoperability IT standards to clinical standards in both practice and education. A strong need exists to educate practice and education communities on IT standards and establish hard deadlines for adoption. The need for security, privacy, and interoperable systems must drive the ongoing development and implementation of standards across all healthcare settings, and nurses must be at the table to prioritize, develop, and evaluate all standards development efforts.

6. **Policy.** The attendees envisioned policy needs related to health IT as consistent, incentives-based initiatives (organizational and governmental) that support advocacy and coalition-building, achieving and resourcing an ethical culture of safety. Above all, bringing these policy needs forward will require nurses' involvement in a national health IT agenda, congressional testimony, and participation in policy decisions at all levels toward technology that supports ethical, safe patient care. Nursing must have a strong, unified voice to endorse consistent, agreed-upon IT standards. Other priorities include obtaining funding for curriculum expansion, research, and practice in nursing informatics and health IT, as well as identifying incentives that support the adoption of innovative technologies. Finally, the attendees support the use of a PHR for every person in the United States.

7. **Culture.** In concluding the summit, which we defined as phase one of the TIGER initiative, attendees affirmed the critical role of culture in transforming an IT-enabled nursing profession. They envisioned a respectful, open system that leverages technology across disciplines and stressed the importance of trust in working toward a shared goal of high quality and safety. To achieve such a culture, technology needs to be integrated into the strategic plans, missions, and goals of nursing organizations.

Organization Commitment

More than 70 organizations participated in the TIGER Summit. Each agreed that nursing must integrate informatics technology into education and practice, and each pledged to incorporate the TIGER vision and action steps into their organization's strategic plans, fulfilling a critical role by distributing the TIGER Summit Summary Report within their network to build additional support for this agenda. A list of the participating organizations is available at http://www.tigersummit.com/Summit_Attendees.html.

From the TIGER Summit in 2006 until now, these organizations, together with hundreds of additional volunteers and industry experts, have collaborated to complete the action steps necessary toward achieving the TIGER vision. Articles and presentations at regional, national, and international conferences have brought TIGER activities to nursing colleagues. The TIGER Initiative remains focused on the need to engage nurses in the national effort to prepare the healthcare workforce toward *effective adoption of EHRs*.

TIGER's mission of reaching the three million nurses practicing in the United States required widespread and rapid dissemination and support of the vision, action steps, and ongoing work with the collaborative teams. One of the challenges to reaching nurses is that there is no one professional organization representing all nurses. Instead, nurses are organized by professional associations that represent their role or specialty and are also served by administrative, educational, and research organizations. By design, the TIGER Initiative comprised representatives from nursing specialty organizations that could work through the action plan within their own organizations. The support received from the practice specialties was timely and set a new industry precedent in raising awareness for TIGER in the broader nursing community. As the timeframe for completing the action steps for phase two of TIGER was three years, TIGER was intentionally structured as a program versus an organization. TIGER relied on the participating organizations to complete the action steps, recognizing that the organizations had the membership and existing mechanisms in place to organize activities and distribute information.

Table 2-1. TIGER Collaborative Teams

TIGER COLLABORATIVE TEAMS
1.   Standards & Interoperability
2.   National Health Information Technology (IT) Agenda
3.   Informatics Competencies
4.   Education & Faculty Development
5.   Staff Development
6.   Usability & Clinical Application Design
7.   Virtual Demonstration Center
8.   Leadership Development
9.   Consumer Empowerment & Personal Health Record (PHR)

A Collaborative Approach

Since the summit in 2006, hundreds of volunteers have joined the TIGER Initiative to continue the action steps defined at the summit. To accelerate their progress, nine collaborative teams were developed to help increase collaboration across the participating organizations. These teams were organized around nine strategic topics (see Table 2-1), and each was led by industry leaders and was open to any interested participant. More than 400 individuals responded to the open call for participation on the collaborative teams.

Each collaborative team researched their subject from the perspective of "What does every practicing nurse need to know about this topic?" The teams identified resources, references, gaps, and other areas that needed further development. They provided recommendations for the industry to accelerate the adoption of health IT for nursing. All teams started by building upon and recognizing the work of organizations, programs, research, and related initiatives in the academic, practice, and government sectors within their topic area.

Each of the nine collaborative teams developed its own wiki, similar to a Web site, to share information. The wikis were used as a project workspace and resource to communicate among the team, with other collaborative teams, and with the public. Most of the communication with the teams was done via webinars, or Web meetings, teleconferences, and e-mail lists. A TIGER Advisory Council, comprising collaborative leaders and the program director, met monthly to coordinate activities and review progress. By early 2009, more than 1,500 individuals had joined the TIGER effort and are helping to achieve the TIGER vision throughout the healthcare community. Most of this outreach was accomplished by the diverse communities that make up the TIGER Initiative. The results and recommendations of the TIGER Collaborative teams are published on the Web site at www.tigersummit.com.

Collaborative Results and Recommendations

After 15 months of virtual work, the nine collaborative teams developed recommendations focused on raising awareness with nursing stakeholders in three areas:[3]
1. Workforce development
2. Engagement of nurses in health IT policy discussions
3. Improved technology used by nurses

Nursing Workforce Development. The primary objective of the TIGER Initiative is to better prepare nurses to use technology to deliver safer, more efficient, timely, and patient-centered care. This means developing a U.S. nursing workforce capable of using EHRs to improve the delivery of healthcare. To meet the 2004 presidential mandate that all Americans use EHRs by the year 2014, it is clear that, as reported in *Building the Workforce for Health Information Transformation*,[4] "A work force capable of innovating, implementing, and using health communications and information technology will be critical to healthcare's success."

President Barack Obama continued this momentum when he took office in January 2009, proposing to "Let us be the generation that reshapes healthcare to compete in the digital age." Less than thirty days after taking office, President Obama signed the American Recovery and Reinvestment Act (ARRA), earmarking $19 billion to develop an electronic health IT infrastructure that will improve the efficiency and access of healthcare to all Americans. In addition to the substantial investment in capital, technology, and resources, the success of delivering an electronic healthcare platform will require an investment in people—to build an informatics-aware healthcare workforce.

This has accelerated the need for healthcare providers to obtain competencies needed to work with electronic records, including basic computer skills, information literacy, and an understanding of informatics and information management capabilities. A comprehensive approach to education reform is necessary to reach the current workforce of nearly three million practicing nurses, previously mentioned. The average age of a practicing nurse in the United States is 47 years. These individuals are "digital immigrants,"[5] as they grew up without digital technology and had to adopt it later or may not have had the opportunity to be educated on its use or be comfortable with technology. This is opposed to "digital natives:" younger individuals who have grown up with digital technology, such as computers, the Internet, mobile phones, and MP3 players. A number of digital immigrants are found in the nursing workforce, those who have not mastered basic computer competencies, let alone information literacy and how to use health IT effectively and efficiently to enhance nursing practice.

Five of the TIGER collaborative teams developed recommendations that focused on how to prepare nurses to practice in this digital era. The TIGER Informatics Competencies Collaborative (TICC) team was foundational to the workforce development effort. After an extensive collection of published and practice-based informatics competencies, they established a minimum set of informatics competencies that all nurses need to have to practice today. To help facilitate the transition to practice, they also identified training resources and educational curricula available for healthcare workers to address the minimum competencies. The TICC recommendations are available at www.tigersummit.com/Competencies_New_B949.html.

The TIGER Education and Faculty Development Collaborative Team focused on engaging stakeholders who influence and deliver nursing education and licensing, including academic institutions representing all levels of nursing education, educationally-focused professional organizations, federal organizations that fund nursing education, and state boards of nursing. There was widespread support of this effort from all of the key stakeholders. Most notably, both the American Association of Colleges of Nursing (AACN) and the National League for Nursing (NLN) have supported the inclusion of informatics competencies in all nursing curricula moving forward. The Health Resources and Services Administration (HRSA) has recognized the critical need for faculty development efforts related to informatics education and has made federal funds available for related projects under the Integrated Technology into Nursing Education and Practice Initiative (ITNEP). The TIGER Education and Faculty Development Collaborative recommendations are available at www.tigersummit.com/Education_New.html.

To address the educational needs of the existing nursing workforce, the TIGER Staff Development Collaborative team focused on practical approaches to professional development that meet the minimum informatics competencies defined by TICC. The TIGER Staff Development Collaborative recommendations are available at www.tigersummit.com/Staff_Development_New.html.

The TIGER Leadership Development Collaborative team expanded on the model developed by TICC to include additional competencies that nursing leaders need to accelerate successful adoption of EHRs. Professional organizations focused on nursing leaders, such as the American Nurses Association (ANA), American Organization of Nurse Executives (AONE), American Academy of Nursing (AAN), Sigma Theta Tau International (STTI), and American Nurses Credentialing Center (ANCC) Magnet™ Program, helped disseminate the TIGER agenda to their members and provided suggestions on how to integrate health IT into their practice. The TIGER Leadership Development Collaborative recommendations are available at www.tigersummit.com/Leadership_New.html.

Finally, limited access to the information systems and technology that could improve healthcare delivery remains one of the barriers to improving informatics education for the nursing workforce. Nursing schools frequently rely on the clinical practicum site to provide access to and education on EHRs. In any given practice environment, exposure to technology is limited to the systems that are currently deployed, a dynamic that often prevents nurses from adequately understanding the expanded capabilities that health IT can offer their profession. One TIGER collaborative team, the Virtual Demonstration Center, developed a virtual learning center supported by the Healthcare Information and Management Systems Society (HIMSS) to provide exposure and education to nurses on a variety of technologies and information systems available today and in the future. The TIGER Initiative recommends further exploration into virtual learning platforms to improve access to information technology education and has published its recommendations at www.tigersummit.com/Virtual_Demo_New.html.

Engagement of Nurses in National Health IT Policy. Nurses must have a unified and strong voice in the healthcare reform debate. This can only be achieved by engaging more nurses in the development of a national healthcare information technology (NHIT) infrastructure. The TIGER Initiative focused on engaging nursing stakeholders from various practice settings by working with nursing professional organizations. Nurses comprise more than 55% of the current healthcare workforce in the United States, and they can contribute to the redesign of the information flow of healthcare to be more efficient, equitable, accessible, patient-centered, and safe. Nurses are often at the center of care coordination for the patient and are well-versed on the workflow and information flow critical to minimizing shortfalls with communication handoffs in the delivery of healthcare.

Some practice specialty areas in nursing have been historically underrepresented in the development of use cases, technical infrastructure, and development of standards. This leaves a gap in creating interoperable EHRs that cover the continuum of healthcare delivery through different practice environments. Two TIGER collaborative teams focused on engaging more nurses in the development of the NHIT infrastructure—the Standards and Interoperability team and the National Health IT Agenda team. Both of these teams recruited nurses from various practice settings to participate in use case discussions and standards organizations and to provide their expertise with organizations representing the Office of the National Coordinator such as the Healthcare Information Technology Standards Panel (HITSP), American Health Information Community (AHIC), and Certification Commission for Healthcare Information Technology (CCHIT). Both teams also developed an inventory of standards and national health IT activities relevant to nurses, as well as tutorials to assist in educating nurses about the urgency of these activities. Much work remains as the national and regional effort to develop and demonstrate health IT infrastructure is just getting started, so the effort to engage nurses from all practice and educational settings needs to remain a high priority. The results of the TIGER Standards and Interoperability Collaborative can be found at www.tigersummit.com/Standards_New.html and the TIGER National Health IT Agenda Collaborative is published at www.tigersummit.com/HIT_Agenda_New.html.

Focus on Technology. Almost all TIGER Initiative participants agreed that nursing needs to *accelerate adoption of smart, standards-based, interoperable technology that will make healthcare delivery safer, more efficient, timely, accessible, and patient-centered.* Studies have demonstrated that the current information systems and technology in practice do not meet the workflow and information flow requirements of nurses. This fact has hampered adoption of EHRs. Nurses and their interdisciplinary colleagues need innovative technology to simplify their work and provide them clinical guidance for the safety of their patients. Additional nursing input into the design and implementation process can improve technology solutions to be more usable, accessible, timely, interoperable, patient-centered, and can improve the safety and efficiency of nursing care.

Three collaborative teams—Usability, Consumer Empowerment/Personal Health Records, and Standards and Interoperability—have developed an inventory of resources and guidelines to enable nurses to participate in the design process for both provider and patient-centered applications. The recommendations of these teams build on the efforts of organizations that are focused on the development and adoption of standards, usability, and PHRs, including the vendors that develop technology solutions. All teams advocate for broader participation of nurses in all of these interrelated efforts. These recommendations are published on the TIGER Web site at www.tigersummit.com/Standards_New.html, www.tigersummit.com/Usability_New.html, and www.tigersummit.com/PHR_New.html, respectively.

Summary and Next Steps for the TIGER Initiative

The TIGER Initiative is poised to enter the next phase of the road map put into place at the 2006 TIGER Summit. This move forward requires weaving technology and informatics into all aspects of nursing practice through educational and culture reform. The first phase was the summit meeting, to define the common vision and action plan. The summit brought together key stakeholders to create the agenda for the journey. The second phase was creation of the collaborative teams, a critical effort to flesh out the nine primary topics and report on their findings and recommendations. This task is reaching conclusion with the final summaries of each collaborative to be posted on the TIGER Web site at www.tigersummit.com. Finally, the fourth edition of a classic nursing informatics book, *Nursing Informatics: Where Caring and Technology Meet*, will detail the excellent achievements of the nine initiatives as a centerpiece, as well as bring the latest developments from well-known authors of nursing informatics to the table.

Although the TIGER Initiative has had a tremendous amount of visibility over the past few years, the Phase III, under the leadership of Dr. Patricia Hinton Walker, is targeted to move this agenda through the cultural reform that is necessary for all nursing to adopt this imperative. Phase III is currently underway and includes obtaining funding implementation for a larger outreach effort and convening an invitational working summit in early 2011. Building the Virtual Demonstration Center is in process, working in concert with HIMSS. The Virtual Demonstration Center will provide a resource for clinicians around the world to see what enabling technologies are available to practicing nurses and other clinicians.

Presentations on the findings and recommendations from the TIGER Collaboratives continue to be on the program of national and international informatics meetings. The Phase III executive team has communication as one of its strategic initiatives and will continue to work to ensure that TIGER's agenda and initiatives are embedded in the professional nursing and health policy organizations' meetings and programs throughout 2010 and 2011. Currently, the Phase III executive team is assembling the TIGER road map for the next seven years.

We are embarking on a journey and invite anyone who would like to join the TIGER Initiative to help us win the war on healthcare reform by signing up on the Web site at www.tigersummit.com. We have one common goal: *to strengthen the voice of the nursing profession in the transformation of healthcare for the 21ˢᵗ century.* This is the prime mission of the TIGER Initiative: Technology Informatics Guiding Education Reform.

References

1. Technology Informatics Guiding Education Reform. Evidence and Informatics Transforming Nursing: 3-Year Action Steps toward a 10-Year Vision. www.tigersummit.com. Accessed April 21, 2009.

2. Institute of Medicine. Health Professions Education: A Bridge to Quality. Washington, DC: The National Academies Press, 2003.

3. Technology Informatics Guiding Education Reform. Collaborating to Integrate Evidence and Informatics into Nursing Practice and Education: *An Executive Summary*. www.tigersummit.com. Accessed April 21, 2009.

4. AHIMA/FORE and AMIA, (2006). *Building the workforce.* www.ahima.org/emerging_issues/. Accessed April 21, 2009.

5. Prensky, M. (2001, October). Digital natives, digital immigrants. *On the Horizon.* www.marcprensky.com/writing/. Accessed April 21, 2009.

## CHAPTER 3

Informatics for Personal Health Management

By Melinda J. Jenkins, PhD, FNP; Pirkko Kouri, PhD, PHN, RN;
and Charlotte A. Weaver, PhD, MSPH, RN, FHIMSS

Introduction

Consumerism, the use of mobile and Internet technologies for health reasons, and personal involvement in healthcare decisions and self-management have grown exponentially over the past decade throughout the industrialized world.[1,2] These trends are not due solely to advances in technology but are also, just as importantly, a result in countries that have defined "self-management" and person-centered healthcare at the very core of their national health policy strategies.[3-6] Many nations are fostering this "personal health management" trend as a way to achieve better outcomes and more cost-effective care delivery through consumer-centered, health ICT initiatives.[7-9] This shift in health policy is based on solid research evidence that shows a strong correlation between patient engagement and participation in care decisions to improved health outcomes, quality, and costs.[10-12] Concurrently, nations are working to raise the health literacy levels of their citizens and use of the Internet and electronic records technologies to enable their citizens to be informed and engaged in their healthcare. This will allow citizens to be active participants in their care decisions, as well as in the management of their health and disease state.[13-16]

This chapter examines the literature on self-management and consumer-engaged care models and the current state of personal health management technology and the implication for consumer-centered eHealth systems. The chapter rounds out the discussion with reference studies in the United States and Finland to demonstrate advances in this field.

Self-care and Self-management

Self-management Defined

Self-care is essential to maintaining health and stabilizing chronic illness. Self-care in the presence of chronic disease is often referred to as *self-management* and is defined as "the individual's ability to manage the symptoms, treatment, physical and psychosocial consequences, and lifestyle changes inherent in living with a chronic condition."[16] Self-management is considered efficacious when individuals successfully monitor their conditions to "effect the cognitive, behavioral, and emotional responses necessary to maintain a satisfactory quality of life."[16] Achieving quality of life targets for chronic disease depends on the ability of people to manage one or more aspects of their care and is related to individual characteristics including, but not limited to, education, experience, and severity of illness. Typically, people with chronic disease are scheduled for quarterly primary care visits, spending, on average, one to two hours per year with their primary care provider. In the remaining thousands of hours each year, they care for themselves with varied levels of knowledge and skill. It is in this space that professional guidance, using interactive technologies and eHealth tools to support self-management, has the greatest potential.

Research in Self-management Support

"Self-management support is defined as the systematic provision of education and support-ive interventions by healthcare staff to increase patients' skills and confidence in managing their health problems, including regular assessment of progress and problems, goal-setting, and problem-solving support."[10] Online and in-person methods tested include group educa-tion and support, provider training, and individual interventions. Preliminary studies indicate that, when individuals are given periodic feedback and support, self-management improves.[17] For example, people at risk for coronary artery disease were most successful at changing their lifestyle and adhering to their medication regimen to lower their blood cholesterol when their blood test results, graphed on a coronary risk profile and compared with population norms, were shown to them at three-month intervals.[18]

One of the most studied methods of group education and support in self-management for people with chronic disease is Lorig's Stanford Model.[19] This approach is based on small group workshops held in community-based settings and facilitated by laymen who are pre-pared as licensed peer trainers.[19-21] Randomized controlled trials in both English and Spanish have demonstrated the efficacy of the Stanford Model for improving health and reducing costs. Lorig et al[22] are currently evaluating similar Internet-based groups to extend the Stan-ford Model to people who have arthritis, back pain, diabetes, and other chronic diseases and who are home bound or live in geographically dispersed locations (https://diabetes.stanford. edu/hl/hlMain).[23] The Expert Patients Program in Great Britain is based on Lorig's model of lay-supported, self-management and is being replicated in countries such as Australia, New Zealand, China, and the Netherlands with positive results.[24,25]

Two other models have shown promise in promoting self-management: the Flinders Model and the Chronic Care Model.[26-29] Both models use provider training and delivery system change to promote self-management. Both use "cue and response" interviews with patients to clarify patient-identified problems, self-management capacity, and goals, and to link closely with ter-tiary referrals using a shared care plan. Clinical decision support and electronic information systems that enable data sharing across care venues and with the patient are key components of these models. Studies applying the Chronic Care Model report a reduction in cardiac risk for patients with diabetes and significant improvements in processes of care for patients with congestive heart disease.[30,31]

Individual interventions shown to be effective include technological support and motiva-tional interviewing with case management. Total cholesterol level was lowered by an average of 14 points in people with heart disease who had support by telephone and mail and coaching from nurses and dieticians.[32] Mayo Health System-affiliated providers' performance in dia-betes care improved with the use of planned care enabled through the use of their Diabetes Electronic Management System (registry and medical records).[33] In the Mayo approach, a diabetes nurse educator and system super-user facilitate the care team's use of the electronic system at each site and provide self-management support to patients. At Partners Health Care System, technological support for collaborative diabetes care is included in a PHR linked to the electronic medical record.[34] At Palo Alto Medical Foundation, the PHR, linked to the EHR, displays to the individual the average expected lifespan based on a diagnosis by age and gender and compares it with the person's risk, based on actual parameters of laboratory results and physiologic measures in his or her medical record[35] (https://mychart.sutterhealth. org/pamf/).[36]

In the Primary Care Information Project of the Department of Health, New York City, proposed electronic self-management tools ("action kits") follow the design of paper goal-set-ting tools for patient support in chronic disease (see Figure 3-1).[37,38] The tools can be inserted into a patient portal (a PHR that is tethered to the provider's EHR), as well as into the EHR for use in patient assessment and follow-up. The tool steps a patient through the process of set-ting and documenting self-management goals and a specific plan to accomplish each goal in relation to the principles of behavioral change and motivational interviewing. Full integration

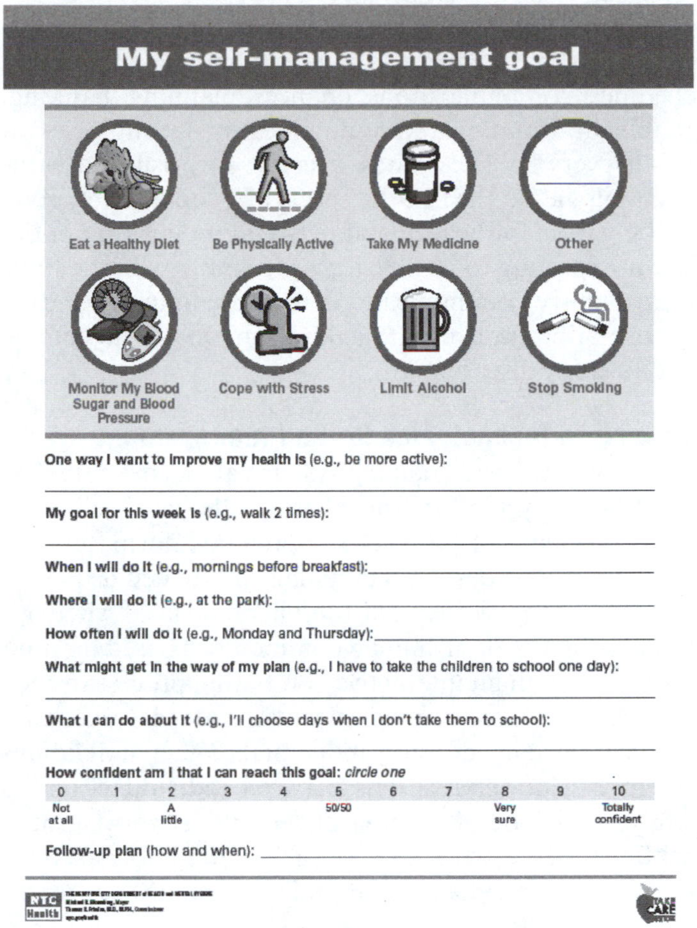

My self-management goal

Eat a Healthy Diet | Be Physically Active | Take My Medicine | Other

Monitor My Blood Sugar and Blood Pressure | Cope with Stress | Limit Alcohol | Stop Smoking

One way I want to improve my health is (e.g., be more active): ____________

My goal for this week is (e.g., walk 2 times): ____________

When I will do it (e.g., mornings before breakfast): ____________

Where I will do it (e.g., at the park): ____________

How often I will do it (e.g., Monday and Thursday): ____________

What might get in the way of my plan (e.g., I have to take the children to school one day): ____________

What I can do about it (e.g., I'll choose days when I don't take them to school): ____________

How confident am I that I can reach this goal: *circle one*

0	1	2	3	4	5	6	7	8	9	10
Not at all		A little			50/50			Very sure		Totally confident

Follow-up plan (how and when): ____________

Figure 3-1. *Department of Health, New York City, Self-Management Tool. Source: NYC Health.*

of the tool into the primary care encounter workflow will be required before self-management behaviors that support optimum chronic disease outcomes can be monitored over time. This integration implies that clinicians will focus on the patient's plan and goal progress in his or her assessment and care delivery decisions. It involves a change in clinical practice as well as workflow.

A meta-analysis of programs for hypertension, osteoarthritis, and diabetes suggests that "programs for older adults probably result in clinically and statistically significant improvements in blood glucose control and blood pressure control...[possibly achieving] some of their effect by increasing adherence to effective pharmaceutical agents."[39] However, no particular program component (tailoring, group setting, feedback, psychological emphasis, and interventions from medical providers) was found to be significantly more effective.[39] These findings on the efficacy of different care management approaches suggest by default the power of using a face-to-face, therapeutic relationship with a nurse in the home. Untried in these different approaches is the opportunity to bring "between visit" care into the home that integrates with self-management and educational strategies. This opportunity also extends to conducting the nursing research to capture the efficacy of nursing care in the home to do self-management teaching and support. In these scenarios, the nurse's role takes on a new dimension in "patient teaching," not so much as one imparting factual information, but as one facilitating and showing the patient how to use new tools and find information sources. Certainly, in terms of using online information sources, nurses will need to shift their educational skills to be able to show individuals how and where to find trusted information online.

Technology and Self-management

Throughout the industrialized world, people everywhere—in every occupation, age group, and socioeconomic class, have adopted the use of mobile technology and Internet tools to manage their schedules, communications, finances, planning, banking, and social communities.[1,4,40] Use of mobile information and communication technologies are ubiquitous with deep penetration into our everyday lives. Thus, it is not surprising to witness the growing use of these tools and technologies in the health aspects of people's lives. Today, we see online health communities, PHRs, games for health, and personal monitoring in the home.[1,40-42] People are increasingly using or expecting to be able to use technology in the following ways: as a means to access resources, manage communications and scheduling with care providers, gain expert knowledge and information for decision-making, and for social communities and networking around given conditions or diseases.[42-47]

The Finnish Approach to Technologies for Self-management

Patient-centered care delivery and enabling systems are a core value and information strategy of the Finnish healthcare system. All members of the care delivery team share respect for the knowledge and experience of patients and provide information for shared decision making and control. In patient-led design, individuals are treated as peer participants, not just as cases to be managed. Oesch[48] writes that the phenomena of virtual empowerment involves strengthening the social network of human communities based on human capabilities. Learning content is offered through an interactive computing process in the digital virtual environment. Social networking creates communities with added value, using creative informatics tools to combine the knowledge of many individuals. When individuals actively engage in the decision-making process, power relations between individuals and professionals are challenged. According to van Uden-Kraan et al,[46] online support groups enhance individuals' empowerment, with people reporting that they felt better informed and had an increased sense of social well-being. Malik and Coulson[47] found that unique features of online support groups positively impacted dimensions of social support, including improved relationship with someone close, better information and empowerment, and reduced sense of isolation. van Uden-Kraan et al[49] found that even online "spectators" who did not participate in social groups reported an increased sense of empowerment just reading others' conversations.

Self-management Technologies as a Defense Against Fragmentation

Regardless of the country, the engaged consumer is, in reality, the first line of defense against the fragmentation of our industrialized countries' medical systems. A recent survey that looked at care characteristics for chronically ill adults in eight countries found that all eight shared a pattern of chronically ill adults using multiple providers across different care settings and therefore, at being high risk of medical errors, having poorly coordinated care, and incurring disproportionate costs.[50] Major differences were reported in healthcare access, safety, and efficiency. While the Netherlands and the United Kingdom showed the best rankings, the United States ranked last. In the United States, people were found to be at the highest risk of foregoing care because of costs and experiencing errors and inefficient, poorly organized care, compared with the other seven countries. In another U.S. study, inefficiency and inadequate coordination of care were also cited as causes for the fact that 20% of elderly Medicare beneficiaries have to be readmitted to the hospital within 30 days of discharge, and 56% are readmitted within a year. Tellingly, more than half of those re-admitted within 30 days had no follow-up or ambulatory visit postdischarge.[51]

Finland is taking a multidimensional approach to addressing the needs of elderly patients with better continuity of care after discharge from an acute hospital stay. In the "Going Home" Demonstration Project, elderly patients are supported through a combination of technology services that involve aspects of the "medical home," telemonitoring, and assistance in self-management. The Going Home service includes interactive "CaringTV" programs delivered through three unique subprojects that were each created with user involvement (see http://kotiin.laurea.fi):[52] (1) Home Clinic for elderly patients supports seniors after hospital discharge with televised, interactive nurse visits, educational programs, and wireless transfer of home monitoring of blood pressure, weight, pain level, and blood glucose; (2) Digame, an interactive digital receiver application, supports peer interaction through study circles and face-to-face encounters; and (3) Going Home in Lappeenranta broadcasts programs to support social relations and the ability to cope independently after hospital discharge. These initiatives have all had the benefit of consumer participation in design and testing. The aim is to extend the program countrywide upon conclusion of the demonstration projects between 2009 and 2011.

This care-coordination risk may change with new technologies and tools, such as those in Finland's Going Home service and as people engage more fully in information-gathering, decision making, and care of themselves and their families.[53] Around the world, the reality of having engaged consumers is strongly supported by the new, mobile Internet technologies, such as iPhones and Blackberries with their minicomputer capabilities. Also important are the rich self-care resources provided by most governments' health Web sites today, such as the online health search portal, MedlinePlus.gov[54] and Finland's "Health Library" at www.terveyskirjasto.fi.[55] Just as people are accustomed to managing their own finances and schedules while moving through their daily lives, recent survey studies show that these behaviors are increasingly extending into taking responsibility for their own health behavior and schedules.[4,6,8,14] As the most important member of the healthcare team, individuals indicate that they want more access to their health data, such as medications, lab results, and treatment profiles, and the ability to interact with their providers and insurers, as well as guideline-based reminders and tools for self-care.[2,42,43,45]

Personal Health Record Technologies

Consolidating all the health information held by diverse provider entities across the healthcare system into one place that is accessible by consumers is key to consumer empowerment. Countries that reach this technological milestone will make it possible for their citizens to be informed, engaged, and active participants in their care and self-management. Countries are addressing this aim of consolidating health information using strategies that involve some sort of EHR repository with consumer access through health cards, Internet portals, and/or by electronic PHRs.[7-9,15,56-58] Finland's EHR strategy is an example of the central repository approach, health cards, and ePHR (see the Finland Case Study 16B in this book for a full description of National ICT strategy).

Finland's ICT strategy for providing PHR functions and technologies to support self-management—called "SAINI"—is currently under development and testing. The SAINI Project (interactive electronic services for citizens)[59] creates a framework for supporting the public in the independent promotion of their own health, as well as in flexible electronic transactions within the healthcare service system. As diagrammed in Figure 3-2, SAINI is a combination of centralized and decentralized electronic services that are connected to data systems and registers in a customer-focused, purposeful, and functional manner. These functions include appointment services, transmission of laboratory results, prescription renewals, payment and compensation services, and various types of information services. These consumer services are used to support a citizen's decision making in health-related matters, as well as interaction and information flow between professionals (see Figure 3-2).

SAINI aims to fulfil the requirements set for consumer user-friendly electronic services. The idea of a "one-stop-shop" was a strong guiding principle: one place at which all relevant services provided by the state and municipality, including healthcare, can be accessed. The SAINI PHR services will enable citizens to actively engage in self-management and participate in their healthcare. Just as SAINI is focused on building the infrastructure and services for engaging consumers and giving them access to their health information, the Oulu Self-

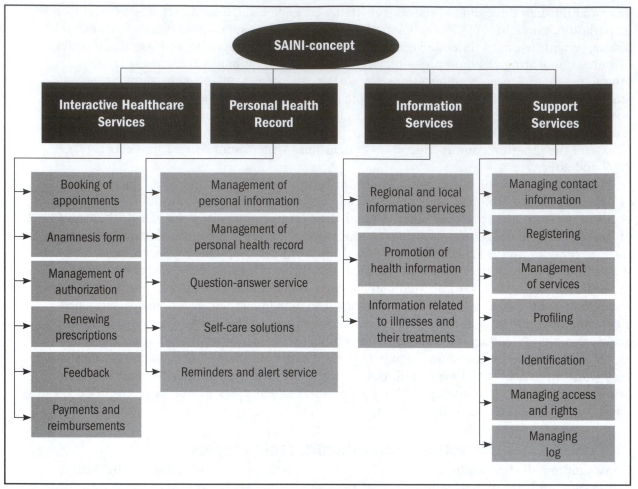

Figure 3-2. *The Saini-concept and National Strategy for Linking Health Services Data and Citizens Health Information Services.*[53] *Source: Sitra—The Finnish Innovation Fund.*

Care and Technology Healthcare Center Project is focused on testing the adoption and use of these new services in a community. The test site is a healthcare center working to: (1) activate the citizens' role and responsibility in healthcare processes, and (2) offer alternative, reliable tools to obtain information and communicate with healthcare services. The objective is to build a new service concept that offers citizens a self-controlled way to respond to their own health and diseases, to obtain guidance and information, and to communicate with their own health center, using a simple and reliable electronic service platform. The desired outcome is a national service model; this is shown in Figure 3-3.

Although in the United States there are more than 200 electronic PHR solutions available through healthcare organizations, providers, or insurance funds,[60] the entry of Microsoft and Google into the PHR solution market has fundamentally shifted the state-of-the-art to one that is consumer-controlled, standards-driven, Internet-based, and portable.[1,61] Technically, the hosting and integrated, standards-based Internet platform that Microsoft and Google have adopted for their PHR offerings represent a tool that can be used by any citizen in any country for his or her personal health information. Similarly, it can be adopted by a country as the technology strategy used to extend a consumer-controlled PHR to its citizens.[56,57]

Other notable PHR offerings in the United States are Revolution Health (www.revolutionhealth.com),[62] a consumer-controlled solution that links educational resources and tools to personal and provider health records; and "Patients Like Me" (www.patientslikeme.com),[63] a solution offering that allows people with common diagnoses to share data on symptoms, treatments, and response to treatments. Challenges unique to the United States are the wide

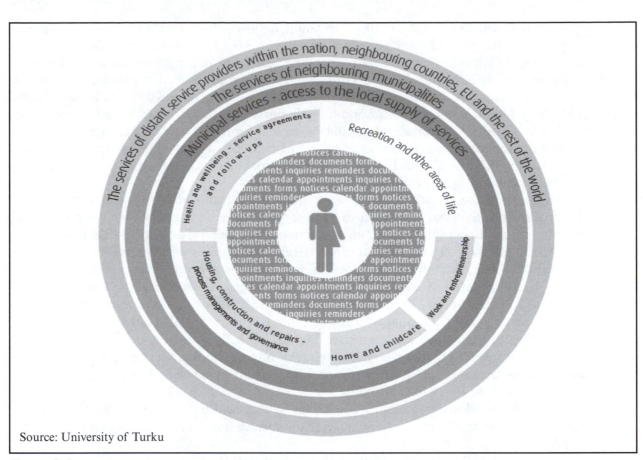

Source: University of Turku

Figure 3-3. *Finland's ICT Consumer-Based Strategy: Citizens at the Heart of Services*

range of payers in the health system and the lack of technology standards. The Office of the National Coordinator is charged with putting standards in place through bodies such as the Healthcare Information Technology Standards Panel (HITSP)[64] and Certification Commission for Healthcare Information Technology (CCHIT).[65] Also highly meaningful, the American Recovery and Reinvestment Act (ARRA) of 2009[66] has allocated $19.2 billion for the purpose of having EHRs extensively adopted and meaningfully used. The Government Accountability Office's newly appointed Health Information Technology Policy Committee[67] carries responsibility for the standards framework needed for a nationwide infrastructure. In the United States, these government initiatives, in conjunction with the entry of innovative companies such as Microsoft and Google, are causing profound changes in consumer engagement and care delivery options.

In contrast to the United States, most Finnish healthcare providers use electronic patient information systems; however, a consumer-based PHR and related technologies are just now being developed and tested and being made available to individuals. Initially, the mandated scope included electronic prescription systems and patient records, with providers having until 2010 to adopt and use the full functionality of the system. As mentioned earlier, the KanTa services consist of a patient data archive and citizen online access to personal health information and electronic prescriptions. With online access to personal health information, individuals have an enhanced ability to look up personal information and supervise its use. Individuals older than eighteen years have online access to personal information stored in the Prescription Center and the electronic archive of personal information. For example, individuals can use the system to check their own vaccination status, request a summary of their electronic prescriptions, or request the pharmacy or their physician to provide a summary of their electronic prescriptions.

Concurrently, Finland is building a common, national structure for Internet communication between people and their providers (see Figure 3-3.) In Finland, individuals complete information in advance of their healthcare-related visit. The information sent online becomes a valid part of the electronic health record after a health professional has read and accepted it. To improve clinicians' and patients' access to health information, in 2006, the Finnish Medical Society, Duodecim, built the second Internet portal, Terveyskirjasto (Health Library), for the public.[13] The portal contains thousands of patient-centric articles concerning diseases and treatments, and many municipalities and hospital districts have linked this portal to their own Web sites. In 2007, the Health Library received approximately 20 million requests for articles, and its growth in usage is continuing to accelerate.[9]

Augmenting the Health Library, is a national health information portal Tervesuomi.fi (HealthFinland) that was scheduled to open for public use in late 2009. This service would provide Finns with comprehensive, single-point access to reliable and up-to-date health information and eHealth services (see http://www.seco.tkk.fi/applications/tervesuomi/ui-presentation.html).[68] The health information portal aims to improve synergies between all actors in the field of health promotion and health services. The service also supports the Finnish government's Information Society Program, which aims to increase social and economic equality and improve the well-being and quality of life of Finns (see http://www.seco.tkk.fi/).[69]

The Health Center service has a user interface with rights to use patients' health cards. Service use is free for citizens who need their own Internet hook up and equipment. The new service concept enables electronic reciprocal interaction by consumers with healthcare services, including the following capabilities:

- Obtain information and guidance concerning health, health promotion and healthcare
- Follow-up the results of self-care and measure health outcomes by an asynchronous, reliable tool
- Create a personal electronic health card and control its use
- Message with health professionals
- Request appointments and view one's own official case records (including lab reports)

The citizen's self-care health card includes personal health information, electronic messaging and appointments, and laboratory results of thirteen of the most common samples. People can save measures, such as patient education forums (PEF), blood pressure, blood glucose, and weight, and can record health diaries. They can search for locations of healthcare organizations and apply online. The card provides access to medications, health data, and disease and nutrition information, with videos and simplified language to enhance health literacy. The new technology service is currently being piloted and the demonstration results were scheduled to be reported by the end of 2009.

PHRs in Microsoft's HealthVault and Google's Health Era

In 2007, both Microsoft and Google announced PHR-solution offerings that launched options for new PHR architectural approaches for use by entire countries on down to use by companies, healthcare organizations, and the individual.[70,71] Before these two technology giants' entry into the PHR world, solution offerings had largely been relegated to health providers, health insurance entities, or vendor offerings that were mostly not consumer-controlled nor portable.[60] Despite more than 200 PHR solution offerings available in the US marketplace in 2008, adoption and sustained use is estimated to have only been between 1–3% of the population.[72] Obstacles to wider adoption and active use by people with chronic conditions, who have the greatest need of self-management support, revolve around usability; value-delivery; and, most importantly, peoples' concern over privacy, security, and control over access.[43,72,73]

The approach used by Microsoft and Google, and their software platforms, is to act as the host of individuals' health information, with the ability to receive and exchange data from all sources.[1,70,71] The software and service platforms are based on Internet and health IT standards and built on a consumer-controlled model that allows access and data exchanges. This technologic approach allows individuals' health records to be portable, under their control, and enables them to compensate for the fragmented and disconnected nature of our healthcare systems. Both offerings essentially create a master record of an individual's health information by importing data from health-related institutions or by allowing the individual to add it himself or herself. Both Microsoft and Google built their solutions on Internet standards and, therefore, in the United States, they can communicate with most retail pharmacy systems to obtain the person's medication profile. This integration also holds with the major laboratories for obtaining lab results. Increasingly, EMR vendors are providing the capability to integrate with Microsoft and/or Google to enable the uploading of a person's EMR to HealthVault or Google Health's PHRs.

As more and more niche vendors, medical device companies, and home diagnostic products link their products to Microsoft's HealthVault and Google Health, the personal health applications will become increasingly useful to individuals and family members for self-health management. The list of companies and devices that are currently integrated with these two platforms can be found on their respective Web sites. But it is important to mention that in support of primary care extending into the home, several new devices and device categories—including weight scale, body composition scale, pulse oximeter, and pedometer—have been enabled to integrate with HealthVault's and Google Health's PHR solutions. Today, individuals using Microsoft's HealthVault and Google Health can monitor weight, blood pressure, blood glucose levels, peak flow, oxygen saturation of blood, body fat percentage, body mass index, aerobic steps, calories, and distance traveled, using device integration. While the number of EMR solutions able to exchange data with these types of medical devices today is limited to a handful, growth in this direction is inevitable because consumers demand it.[42,43]

Personal Health Information Management Design Considerations

Numerous reviews on PHR adoption and meaningful use by consumers indicate that products in the marketplace today lack sufficient user input in their design to be easy to use, deliver value, and to provide the functionality desired by consumers.[2,43,72]

As user-friendly and "state-of-the-art" as Microsoft's HealthVault and Google Health PHR solutions have been pronounced, they too have been judged as "lacking" in user-friendliness. The User Centric Survey Group recently conducted a user preference study that compared Microsoft's HealthVault with Google Health.[74] The 30 study participants preferred Google Health solution over HealthVault, rating it as more user-friendly, easier to understand, navigate, and use; most telling, these lay subject were most impressed with its drug interaction features (Health Vault did not have the drug-drug interaction checking feature). The study authors caution that the results found neither solution to be a "perfect application" and that both had flaws sufficient to block user adoption. Thus, we know that more study in PHR design needs to be done, and it is certain that the design, which involves actual end-users in its creation, will help us get to the end point more quickly.

Several PHR features that incorporate self-management tools for chronic disease, such as reminders to take medications and periodic assessment of signs and symptoms, are being tested in a Robert Wood Johnson Foundation (RWJF) funded initiative, "Project Health Design" (www.projecthealthdesign.org).[75] One of the RWJF-funded teams, Moen and Brennan,[76] report that people have been found to employ four strategies for health information management in the home: "Just-in-time," "Just-at-hand," "Just-in-case," and "Just-because." Just-in-time storage is that of important information kept on the person because it might be needed in an emergency, such as wearing a bracelet that identifies the person as having a particular condition. Just-at-hand storage is information readily accessible—the prototypic example is the family calendar on the refrigerator door showing provider appointments. Just-in-case is information kept on file that includes such items as when one was last vaccinated; and just-because is other information that may eventually be tossed out, such as information about an already-cured condition. This body of work suggests that people need at least three types of informatics tools for self-management support.

Just-in-time. The most frequent, possibly even daily, use of just-in-time storage may be that used by the home caregivers or the visiting nurses of a relatively small group of people with a severe illness. A very detailed PHR should be available—just-in-time—in case of emergency and to share information with a provider or with similar patients in health networking Web sites, such as http://www.patientslikeme.com.[63] For example, just-in-time detailed health information about meds and recent lab reports for a patient deemed a brittle diabetic can be kept in a mobile phone that will automatically dial an ambulance at the press of a button and make current information available to emergency personnel.

Just-in-time and just-at-hand information may best be kept in PHRs, such as Google Health and Microsoft's HealthVault, making the information accessible anywhere in the world and controlled by the individual, who can import and export information at will. These PHRs also have the capability to interface with a large array of monitoring devices and "gadgets," including personal calendars and diaries. As mobile computing spreads across national borders, it is likely that services such as these will become the standard for personally-controlled healthcare documentation and record maintenance. The more they can "talk" to data sources maintained by pharmacies, laboratories, providers, and payers, the more complete and useful the PHR will be. In this sense, "the term *personal health record* is inadequate because of its emphasis on "record" as past information. To make sense of their health and healthcare, people want useful tools and convenient services in addition to their records."[77,p2] Next generation PHRs under individual control will allow for more direct interaction with providers, self-scheduling, and the recording and analyzing of "observations of daily living" to facilitate self-management.[78]

Countries throughout the world are taking different approaches to achieve summarized EHRs that are accessible to qualified providers. And individuals are given the option to "opt in" or opt out" if they have concerns over the confidentiality and privacy of their health information. However, absolute consumer control over granting access to their health information is still a challenge, even in the most advanced countries' strategies. In the tethered EHR to PHR offerings, healthcare providers may retrieve data from a linked patient portal PHR to track use of the PHR and selected patient-entered data (e.g., goal, progress toward goal, blood pressure, blood glucose level). PHRs used in some large health systems, such as Group Health in Seattle, and Partners in Boston, have been very well-received.[35,79] A Continuity of Care Record (CCR), a summary of patient data in a standardized XML format that can be transferred to another provider to promote continuity of care, may be downloaded from the patient portal.[80-82] Once self-management has been established as a priority for the healthcare team, a PHR may be a useful tool for following up on goals.

Just-at-hand. Second, and even more numerous, are individuals and families actively managing a less severe chronic disease, pregnant women, or parents of young children—all of whom make visits to providers every two or three months. These groups may appreciate just-at-hand information on their medications, laboratory results, appointment schedule, and financial statements. Enabling people to quickly request medication refills, lab reports, appointments, referrals, and encounter records will enhance continuity of care and communication between primary care providers and any consultants or acute care providers. People actively managing a chronic health condition, such as hypertension or diabetes, would likely use self-management tools embedded in provider-held EHRs and linked to patient portals, or embedded in free-standing, usually online, PHRs, such as MiVia (www.mivia.org).[83] Individuals can keep track of their symptoms, exercise, weight, blood pressure, intake of medicine and food, etc., and send these data to their primary care providers, nurse-managed clinics, or other primary care/home healthcare teams.[84] For homebound elderly patients, this extension of primary care into the home setting can be greatly facilitated by coordinated programs, using home healthcare multidisciplinary clinical teams.[49,59,84-86]

In line with the just-at-hand type health needs, Finland is exploring different approaches for the most effective way—that is also appropriate, effective, and helpful—to put health information into the hands of individuals, other than in their health library and health information

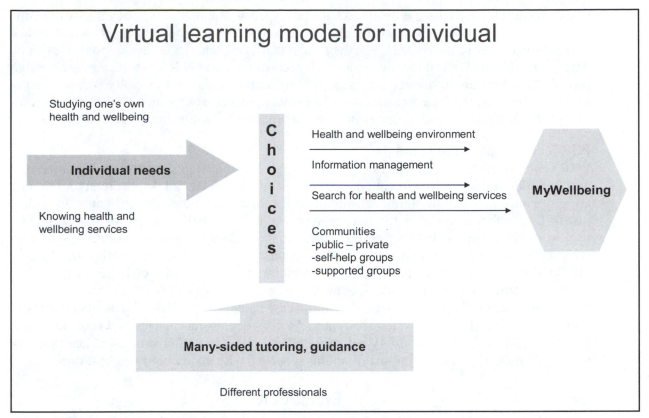

Figure 3-4. *Learning Model in Family-Coper*

portals. In the "MyWellbeing" research project, the notion of a citizen as an empowered and fully informed partner in various health and wellbeing services is being tested. This citizen learning model is depicted in Figure 3-4.

The main aims of the research project are to: (1) identify the needs of citizens and how they can become the foundation for different health and wellbeing services, and (2) identify how life changes, such as pregnancy or retirement, should be considered when different health and wellbeing service concepts are defined.[87] As a result of the project, the Coper, a digital support tool for personal health and wellbeing management, was built. Finland's MyWellbeing project aims to provide a solution by which citizens can better cope with life situations and concerns extending beyond healthcare and including such matters as insurance, taxation, and day care for children (see Figure 3-4). The Coper is tested in different technologies, i.e., personal computers, mobile phones, and partner company solutions, to gain platform independence and service provider interchangeability so the citizen can select the most suitable service options.[88]

Finland's MyWellbeing project exemplifies a just-at-hand PHR use for obstetric and well-baby care.[87] In this type of PHR application, pregnant women would be able to send their weight, blood pressure, and other health information, in addition to fetal movements, to their nurse midwife to review before their next scheduled visit and receive timely interventions as needed, as well as receive tailored educational materials. The prenatal and birth history data could be combined with newborn examinations and genetic testing records to begin a new child health record that includes ongoing immunization dates, growth charts, and well-child examination results.

Just-in-case. Third of all and the largest group consists of healthy people without frequent care needs who may once or twice a year appreciate e-mail reminders about preventive care guidelines and periodically may refer to their PHR for vetted self-care resources to maintain their own health. In addition, they may appreciate just-in-case easy access to records in order to print or submit required health forms for school or work. Public health alerts for food-borne illness, local infectious disease outbreaks, and emergency situations could be directly disseminated to patients by health departments or via providers. Healthy individuals and families may be most likely to use online file management platforms, such as Dossia, Google Health or Microsoft's HealthVault that will ensure their records are accessible when they move, change providers, or have an unforeseen emergency event. People may access specialty Web sites, such as the Family History Project (http://www.hhs.gov/familyhistory),[89] which guides entry of useful genetic data that providers can review and accept into the individual's medical record.

PHR Technologies in Demand

PHRs can integrate with providers' records through electronic interfaces to applications such as a calendar and home-monitoring devices. A calendar interface can display reminders about appointments, medications, home self-monitoring measures, progress toward goals, and other just-in-time information. Results that are stored in a linked PHR can be made available to professionals for review between or during encounters. Companies that have developed new self-monitoring equipment that can now communicate with EHRs and PHRs are: Microlife (http://www.microlife.com/),[90] Omron (www.omron.com/),[91] and HoMedics (http://www.homedics.com).[92] The development of standards and protocols will be important to increase the use of these machines. Home caregivers and case managers of disabled patients may desire a link to provider EHRs as well as to other services, such as pharmacies and transportation services. Testing of interoperability between PHRs, EHRs, and other sources of health information facilitated by export/import functions is needed with a variety of applications.

Evaluation

Measuring the effects of self-management tools is challenging. Short-term measures may be limited to counting the implementation of care processes by the care team and by patients (e.g., numbers of people with a goal, numbers of PHR contacts that replace live encounters). Long-term measures address improvements in health outcomes, which can be more difficult to capture. There is evidence that self-management increases the effect of provider actions to contribute to better chronic disease control and preventive care.[27,40,93] Investigation is needed to ascertain the relative contribution of electronic tools to changes in workflow and in the composition of the primary care team. Keeping in mind the potential of EHRs connected to PHRs for enhancing self-management for the most prevalent chronic diseases in developed countries, many challenges go beyond technology back to basic issues, such as financing, user characteristics, and practice traditions of data ownership and workflow. Opportunities, therefore, arise in each of these areas.

Practice Traditions

Data Ownership. Ownership and control of health data remain unresolved issues. Traditionally, providers have been legally responsible for recording and safely storing accurate records of patient care. Questions that have risen and continue unanswered over the acceptance, control, and storage of data are: How much of provider-generated information does the individual have a right to see? What if providers do not agree to share information? How will patient-generated information be incorporated into providers' records? For example, will blood pressure measurements from home and from the office populate the same slot in the database? How will the patient user be authenticated? Solutions are available and require agreement from the professional community; perhaps the existing EHR software certification process will create relevant standards.[65] When these questions are resolved and when PHRs and EHRs have more complete and accurate information, individuals will be able to share more fully in the ownership of their data and the knowledge, behavior, and health status that ownership represents.

Practice Workflow

EHR data models based on provider encounters may not necessarily accommodate practice changes to support self-management. For example, in the case of home self-monitoring, there are challenges associated with the incorporation of patient-entered data into: (1) an EHR that uses an encounter-based data model, and (2) a reimbursement-driven practice workflow. Some EHRs are designed to document only clinical data, such as blood pressure measurements or weight, into an EHR with a scheduled encounter. When blood pressure is monitored at home and received by the practice on a day when the individual is not present for an exam, the only way to pull the data into the clinical record is to create a "fake" encounter with no bill generated. Alternate visit documentation, such as a telephone encounter, may be used, but with some EHRs, such records may not be integrated into the individual's history. In addition, workflow issues arise with the receipt of home monitoring data, for example, how to respond quickly to troubling results, such as dangerous blood pressure measures, if no procedure has been created to address the problem. Expanding the channels of communication for remote nurse triage and advice may provide a viable solution and expand the capacity to intensify outpatient care and home healthcare for patients at high risk of decompensation. Currently, in primary care in the United States, most nurse visits are not billable and nursing job descriptions do not encourage the provision of self-management support. Emphasizing self-management support and informatics skills in nursing education will provide a foundation for more effective primary care teams for the future.

In the United States, it is conceivable that with changes in reimbursement that would allow payment for telephone visits and nurse self-management support, PHRs would become essential tools for telehealth encounters, allowing people to avoid the inconvenience and costs of a face-to-face visit for routine follow-up. More frequent communication among healthcare teams, including individuals and families, has been shown to improve outcomes and reduce acute care costs.

Addressing Health Literacy and Educational Material

Each individual's health knowledge depends on many factors, including language, culture, age, education level, reading level, and level of health literacy.[94] Health literacy assessment, including individuals' understanding of their illness, risk factors, and recommended treatments, is essential to effective self-management support. Users' health and computer literacy ranges from that of very limited users to that of sophisticated "power users." The health literacy challenge is not new, but it is taking on a new form with the addition of computer competency and access limitations; disparities in social class and language may be barriers to the universal use of PHRs. Despite such realistic fears, a number of Spanish-speaking migrant farm worker communities have embraced the free-standing online PHR MiVia because it provides helpful identification and background information as they move around.[83] This experience encourages the development of disease management applications in Spanish and other languages. On a related note, MedlinePlus has recently announced that many of their health education materials are available in more than 40 languages (see http://www.nlm.nih.gov/medlineplus/languages/languages.html).[95]

Educational Resources

Highly computer literate power users, impatient with old-fashioned, time-consuming methods to access and act on evidence-based and expert information, may drive changes in health communications. The evidence suggests that younger people are more active online and with mobile and multi-media technologies, such as educational and exercise games, avatar and simulation games, and cell-phone applications.[96-98] Resources will be needed to develop health uses of these promising new technologies. Health literacy is far more than learning the skills necessary to use hardware and software. To be digitally literate, a person must be able to navigate, locate, communicate online, and participate both in virtual and in physical communities.

Future definitions of literacy will include informatics abilities—a range of meaning-making/decision-making strategies required to assemble knowledge in the virtual world. Effective self-management will involve understanding the role IT plays in society, questioning the purposes for which IT is used, understanding how IT intervenes in our lives and our relations with others, and being able to choose when and which tools are appropriate for a task or problem at hand. IT literacy, therefore, involves developing a critical consciousness that enables us to make informed choices about the way we use and respond to novel technologies.

Tailored links to selected current literature are effective ways to enhance individuals' knowledge and encourage positive behavior change. Excellent sources that have been vetted by medical librarians and providers for accuracy and readability include www.medlineplus.gov[54] and www.healthwise.com.[99] There are also a growing number of high-quality multimedia Web resources with health content, such as www.videojug.com.[100] Patients with ongoing issues may be directed to online peer support networks, such as www.patientslikeme.org[63] and online courses, such as www.livinglifetothefull.com,[101] a course on cognitive behavioral therapy, sponsored by the British National Health Service.[102] Since so much misinformation is available on the Internet, having professionals recommend accurate materials through Web links on their own sites makes good sense.

Summary

Long-term, patient-centered relationships are mostly developed in the context of face-to-face interaction over time, and this most commonly is done through primary care delivered in the community and in the home. And as industrialized countries push self-management health strategies for their citizens' health and disease maintenance, this opens up great opportunity for nurses at all levels of practice. While advocacy, education, and support of the patient are core nursing functions that cross all care settings and national boundaries, 21ˢᵗ century practice also carries a requirement for nurses to know about an array of technologies and learning modalities. Nurses' efforts to assist individuals to fully engage in the self-management of their health and care decisions will require that they instruct individuals on how to use the technology resources available to them in their home, community, and country. Nurses will need to be able to teach their patients how to use health-enabling technologies, such as a PHR; how to access trusted health information sites; and how to use tools interactively to communicate with health resources and clinical providers. Having informatics competencies is rapidly changing from being an "option" to a necessity. As we close the first decade in the 21ˢᵗ century, nurses worldwide will need informatics competencies and skills for any role that they perform in any setting. Basic to our role as educators and advocates for our patients is the ability to use and demonstrate to others the use of health-enabling technologies and the knowledge of health information sites for e-mailing and document exchange, to show patients how to use appropriate social networks and to work with wireless monitoring patient data.

The examples presented in this chapter on the multidimensional ICT, consumer-focused work being done by Finland offers a marked contrast to the United States. Finland's rapid advancement (2002 to 2009) in transforming to an EHR and a PHR nationally, with adoption and use throughout their healthcare system, into communities and directly into the home, is striking. Technology advancement and new care delivery models, such as those being tested in Finland, will continue to enable more consumer engagement, better PHR tools, and national connectedness between EHRs and PHRs. This will result in more primary care delivered in the home involving multidiscipline teams, and will present new role opportunities for nurses. This, in turn, will increase the need to teach informatics competencies to all clinicians and information access skills to nursing students because patient education will be about acquiring information, rather than direct teaching or merely leaving patient education materials behind. There are many opportunities for nursing education, with simulation laboratories to develop informatics skills along with clinical skills and in venues using EHR technology and nursing research that link these skills and competencies to outcomes. The nursing workforce and nursing students will increasingly encounter this new emphasis on technology-assisted communication in care delivery approaches as an important technique to support continuity and care coordination. The PHR technologies as reviewed in this chapter will change the way clinicians work and interact with their patients and care team members. Informed and engaged consumers are an inevitability in our Internet-empowered societies. Nursing education and practice has the urgent challenge of embracing these new skills and knowledge within ICT health technologies. And if we can make this sea change in our nursing practice, the opportunity to expand nursing roles into new realms and to make significant contributions in primary care, consumer empowerment, and self-management will be our rewards.

Currently in the United States, there are no financial incentives to patients, providers, and payers to encourage self-management, with or without electronic support. Financial incentives can be a promising carrot to change behaviors. An example of a consumer incentive program currently being tested in New York City is cash transfers to low income families conditioned upon meeting criteria, such as having their children immunized and keeping them in school.[103] Financial incentives to providers and primary care teams for prevention and for meeting expected guidelines in "patient-centered medical homes"[75] may also encourage behavior change toward more active support of self-management. Furthermore, it is possible that a business model promoted by purchasers and insurers will drive cost savings through health information technology, in a way similar to banks reducing costs over the years by eliminating clerical positions and driving customers to ATMs (automatic teller machines).

Optimism for the future is based on the success of national ICT strategies, such as those of Finland, and on the rise of international commercial products for the general public, such as Google Health and Microsoft's HealthVault. As more applications are available, such as these Internet-based PHR solutions, people will have more tools to manage their health. In addition, communication channels are increasing with Internet connectivity from phones, PDAs, and home and go beyond the borders of industrial countries into Africa, the Amazon, and Antarctica. Access to health information found at reliable sites according to specialty, disease group, commercial venue, and government is evolving rapidly. More personal control of goal setting and monitoring will likely provide a significant breakthrough in disease management. Many people already recognize that individuals and communities share the responsibility for their own health with healthcare teams and hospitals. Incorporating self-management tools in EHRs may enhance the capacity for disease self-management and shared decision making among the healthcare team. In the United States, the development of national standards is improving interoperability among primary care practices, laboratories, pharmacies, and Internet PHRs. Remaining challenges to health informatics professionals include the need to: (1) match technology to skill/literacy; (2) agree on outcome success measures, both short- and long-term; and (3) keep pace with evolving technologies and the opportunities they create. Encouraging the use of new informatics self-management tools will potentially enhance the quality and continuity of care, will create opportunities for healthcare teams in primary care and home care, and will illuminate what works to improve public health.

Acknowledgment

Portions of this work on self-management support were presented at the AMIA Spring 2008 Conference and at the Nursing Informatics 2009 Conference. The contributions of Joslyn Levy, Ellen Cohen, Farzad Mostashari, and Sunmoo Yoon on a previous draft are appreciated.

References

1. Microsoft. *Working with Multiple Devices and Technologies with PHR. Microsoft Health Vault.* http://msdn.microsoft.com/en-us/healthvault/default.aspx. Accessed August 9, 2009.

2. Bishop L. *Are Personal Health Records Breaking Out?* Forrester Research. June 15, 2006. http://www.forrester.com/Research/Document/Excerpt/0,7211,39415,00.html. Accessed August 30, 2009.

3. Office of Disease Prevention and Health Promotion. US Department of Health and Human Resources. *Healthy People 2010*, Chapter 11, Health Communication 2000. http://www.healthypeople.gov/document/html/volume1/11healthcom.htm. Accessed July 11, 2009.

4. National Health Services. *NHS Choices: Your Health, Your Choices.* http://www.nhs.uk/choiceintheNHS/Yourchoices/Pages/Yourchoices.aspx. Accessed August 30, 2009.

5. Department of Health. *The NHS Constitution for England.* January 2009. http://www.dh.gov.uk/en/Publicationsandstatistics/Publications/PublicationsPolicyAndGuidance/DH_093419. Accessed August 30, 2009.

6. Canada Health Infoway. *Making Health Information Work Better for Canadians. Corporate Business Plan 2009/2010.* http://www2.infoway-inforoute.ca/Documents/bp/Business_Plan_2009-2010_en.pdf. Accessed August 30, 2009.

7. NHS Scotland. *Patient Focus and Public Involvement.* www.scotland.gov.uk/Resource/Doc/158744/0043087.pdf. Accessed June 22, 2009.

8. Department of Health and Ageing. Australian Government. 2009. *A HealthierFuture for all Australians–Final Report.* June 2009. http://www.health.gov.au/internet/main/publishing.nsf/Content/nhhrc-report. Accessed August 30, 2009.

9. *The Finnish Health Care System: A Value-Based Perspective.* 2009. http://www.sitra.fi/fi/Julkaisut/OhjelmienJulkaisut/teho/terveydenhuolto.htm. Accessed May 5, 2009.

10. Adams K, Greiner AC, Corrigan JM, eds. *First Annual Crossing the Quality Chasm Summit.* Washington, DC: The National Academies Press; 2004.

11. Lynn NB, Panzer AM, Kindig DA. eds. Committee on Health Literacy. Institute of Medicine. *Health Literacy: A Prescription to End Confusion.* Washington, DC: The National Academies Press; 2004.

12. Berkman ND, DeWalt DA, Pignone MP, et al. *Literacy and Health Outcomes.* Evidence Report/Technology Assessment #87. AHRQ Publication No04-E007-1. 2004. www.ahrq.gov/clinic/epcsums/litsum.pdf. Accessed July 3, 2009.

13. Duodecim. Finland's Health Library. 2009. www.terveyskirjasto.fi. Accessed May 5, 2009.

14. Office of Disease Prevention and Health Promotion. *Healthy People 2010. Progress Review.* Focus 11, April 19 2007. Department of Health and Human Services, 2007. www.healthypeople.gov/data/2010prog/focus11. Accessed July 11, 2009.

15. Department of Health and Ageing. Australian Government. Health Connect. *2009 e-Health: Overview of Health Connect.* http://www.health.gov.au/healthconnect. Accessed August 30, 2009.

16. Barlow J, Wright C, Sheasby J, Turner A, Hainsworth J. Self management approaches for people with chronic conditions: A review. *Patient Education and Counseling.* 2002;48:177-187.

17. Lorig K. Action planning: a call to action. *J Am Board Fam Med.* 2006;19(3):324-325.

18. Grover SA, Lowensteyn I, Joseph L, et al. Patient knowledge of coronary risk profile improves the effectiveness of dyslipidemia therapy: the CHECK-UP study: a randomized controlled trial. *Arch Intern Med.* 2007;167(21):2296-2303.

19. Lorig KR, Ritter P, Stewart AL, et al. Chronic disease self-management program: 2-year health status and health care utilization outcomes. *Med Care.* 2001;39(11):1217-1223.

20. Lorig KR, Ritter PL, Gonzalez VM. Hispanic chronic disease self-management: a randomized community-based outcome trial. *Nurs Res.* 2003;52(6):361-369.

21. Lorig KR, Ritter PL, Jacquez A. Outcomes of border health. Spanish/English chronic disease self-management programs. *Diabetes Educ.* 2005;31(3):401-409.

22. Lorig KR, Ritter PL, Laurent DD, Plant K. Internet-based chronic disease self-management: a randomized trial. *Med Care.* 2006;44(11):964-971.

23. https://www.diabetes.stanford.edu/hl/hlMain. Accessed October 23, 2009.

24. Kennedy A, Reeves D, Bower P, et al. The effectiveness and cost effectiveness of a national lay-led self-care support programme for patients with long-term conditions: a pragmatic randomised controlled trial. *J Epidemiol Community Health.* 2007;61:254-261.

25. Siu AM, Chan CC, Poon PK, Chui DY, Chan SC. Evaluation of the chronic disease self-management program in a Chinese population. *Patient Educ Couns.* 2007;65(1):42-50.

26. *Informed Partnerships for Effective Self-management of Chronic and Complex Lung Diseases.* Flinders Human Behaviour & Health Research Unit, 2005. http://som.flinders.edu.au/FUSA/CCTU/pdf/COPDfinal_report_22_07_05Malcolm_Battersb.pdf Accessed March 27, 2008.

27. Glasgow RE, Davis CL, Funnell MM, Beck A. Implementing practical interventions to support chronic illness self-management. *Jt Comm J Qual Saf.* 2003;29(11):563-574.

28. Glasgow RE, Funnell MM, Bonomi AE, Davis CL, Beckham V, Wagner EH. Self-management aspects of improving chronic illness care breakthrough series: Implementation with diabetes and heart failure teams. *Ann Behav Med.* 2002;24(2):80-87.

29. Wagner EH, Austin BT, Davis C, Hindmarsh M, Schaefer J, Bonomi A. Improving chronic illness care: translating evidence into action. *Health Aff.* (Millwood) 2001;20:64-78.

30. Vogt D, Bergeron A, Salgado D, Daley J, Ouimette P, Wolfe J. Can a chronic care model collaborative reduce heart disease risk in patients with diabetes? *J Gen Int Med.* 2007;22(2):215-222.

31. Asch SM, Baker D, Keesey J, et al. Docs the collaborative model improve care for chronic heart failure? *Med Care.* 2005;43(7):667-675.

32. Vale MJ, Jelinek MV, Best JD, et al. Coaching patients On Achieving Cardiovascular Health (COACH): A multicenter randomized trial in patients with coronary heart disease. *Arch Intern Med.* 2003;163:2775-2783.

33. Montori VM, Dinneen SM, Gorman CA, et al. The impact of planned care and a diabetes electronic management system on community-based diabetes care: the mayo health system diabetes translation project. *Diabetes Care.* 2003;25:1952-1957.

34. Grant RW, Wald JS, Poon EG, et al. Design and implementation of a web-based patient portal linked to an ambulatory care electronic health record: Patient gateway for diabetes collaborative care. *Diabetes Technol Ther.* 2006;8(5):576-586.

35. Halamka JD, Mandl KD, Tang PC. Early experiences with personal health records. *J Am Med Inform Assoc.* 2008;15(1):1-7.

36. https://mychart.sutterhealth.org/pamf/. Accessed October 23, 2009.

37. http://www.nyc.gov/html/doh/html/csi/csi-goalsht.pdf. Accessed October 23, 2009.

38. http://www.nyc.gov/html/doh/downloads/pdf/csi/hyperkit-clin-bp-goalsht.pdf. Accessed October 23, 2009.

39. Chodosh J, Morton SC, Mojica W, et al. Meta-analysis: chronic disease self-management programs for older adults. *Ann Intern Med.* 2005;143(6):427-438.

40. Pew Internet & American Life Project (2009). *Online Activities, 2000-2009.* http://www.pewinternet.org/Static-Pages/Trend-Data/Online-Activities-20002009.aspx. Accessed July 6, 2009.

41. Pew Internet Online (2008). Demographics of Internet Users. Fox S, Jones, S. *The Social Life of Health Information.* (2009) Pew Internet & American Life Project. http://www.pewinternet.org/~/media//Files/Reports/2009/PIP_Health_2009.pdf. Accessed July 6, 2009.

42. Deloitte. *Many Consumers Want Major Changes in Health Care Design, Delivery.* Deloitte LLP, 2008. http://www.deloitte.com/dtt/article/0,1002,cid%253D192717,00.html. Accessed July 16, 2009.

43. Seidman J, Eytan T. *Helping Patients Plug In: Lessons in the Adoption of Online Consumer Tools.* California Healthcare Foundation. 2008. www.chcf.org/documents/chronicdisease/HelpingPatientsPlugIn.pdf. Accessed July 3, 2009.

44. Wall Street Journal Online/Harris Interactive Health-Care Poll (2005). *New Poll Shows U.S. Adults Strongly Favor and Value New Medical Technologies in Their Doctor's Office.* http://www.harrisinteractive.com/news/newsletters/wsjhealthnews/WSJOnline_HI_Health-CarePoll-2005vol4_iss20.pdf. Accessed July 16, 2009.

45. Wall Street Journal Online /Harris Interactive Health-Care Poll (2006): *Few Patients Have Access to Online Services for Communicating With Their Doctors, but Most Would Like To.* Vol 5 No. 16. Sept 22. Harris Interactive Inc. All rights reserved. http://www.harrisinteractive.com/news/newsletters/wsjhealthnews/WSJOnline_HI_Health-CarePoll2006vol5_iss16.pdf. Accessed July 16, 2009.

46. van Uden-Kraan CF, Drossaert CH, Taal E, Seydel ER, van deLaar MA. Participation in online patient support groups endorses patients' empowerment. *Patient Educ Couns.* 2009;74(1):61-69.

47. Malik SH, Coulson NS. Computer-mediated infertility support groups: An exploratory study on online experiences. *Patient Educ Couns.* 2008;73(1):105-113.

48. Oesch K. Virtual empowerment: a case study based on the research and investment projects of Finnish Technology and Innovation Funding Organization's "TEKES" Fenix Technology Program "Innovative Computing" results during years 2002-2007. (Virtuaalinen voimaantuminen - Tapaustutkimus ammattikasvatuksen oppimisympäristön toimintaedellytysten ja tietokäytäntöjen kehitysmahdollisuuksista vuorovaikutteisen tieto- ja viestintäteknologian näkökulmasta). University of Tampere, Tampere. 2007.

49. van Uden-Kraan CF, Drossaert CH, Taal E, Seydel ER, van deLaar MA. Self-reported differences in empowerment between lurkers and posters in online patient support groups. *Journal of Medical Internet Research.* 2008;10(2):e18.

50. Schoen C, Osborn R, How SKH, Doty MM. In chronic condition: Experiences of patients with complex healthcare needs, in eight countries. 2008. *Health Aff.* 2009;28(1):w1-w16.

51. Jencks SF, Williams MV, EA C. Rehospitalizations among patients in the Medicare fee-for-service program. *N Engl J Med.* 2009;360:1418-1428.

52. http://www.kotiin.laurea.fi. Accessed October 23, 2009.

53. Pew Internet & American Life Project. *The Engaged e-Patient Population.* 2008. http://www.pewinternet.org/Reports/2008/The-Engaged-Epatient-Population.aspx. Accessed May 5, 2009.

54. MedlinePlus. 2008. http://medlineplus.gov/. Accessed May 5, 2009.

55. http://www.terveyskirjasto.fi. Accessed October 23, 2009.

56. Microsoft. TELUS licenses Microsoft HealthVault to launch TELUS Health Space, Canada's first consumer e-health platform. May 6, 2009. http://www.microsoft.com/presspass/events/healthvault/docs/HealthSpacePR.doc. Accessed August 6, 2009.

57. Donnelly L. *Patients to be Given Google Health Records Under Tories.* Telegraph.co.uk. August 9, 2009. http://www.telegraph.co.uk/news/newstopics/politics/conservative/5995382/Patients-to-be-given-Google-health-records-under-Tories.html. Accessed August 9, 2009.

58. In EK. Elektronische Fallakte. http://www.fallakte.de/index.html. Accessed August 30, 2009.

59. SAINI – Electronic Healthcare Services Concept Road Map for implementation in Finland. 2008. http://www.sitra.fi/fi/Julkaisut/OhjelmienJulkaisut/teho/terveydenhuolto.htm. Accessed Aug. 9, 2009.

60. Cronin C. *Personal Health Records: An Overview of What is Available to the Public.* AARP Public Policy Institute, April 2006. http://www.aarp.org/research/health/carequality/2006_11_phr.html. Accessed July 16, 2009.

61. Google. *Google Health Beta Test Begins.* http://news.cnet.com/8301-10784_3-9947389-7.html. Accessed August 9, 2009.

62. *Revolution Health.* www.revolutionhealth.com. Accessed May 5, 2009.

63. *Patients Like Me.* www.patientslikeme.com. Accessed May 5, 2009.

64. Healthcare Information Technology Standards Panel. 2009. http://www.ansi.org/standards_activities/standards_boards_panels/hisb/hitsp.aspx?menuid=3.

65. Certification Commission for Healthcare Information Technology. 2008. *Consumer's Guide to Certification of Personal Health Records.* http://www.cchit.org/sites/all/files/20080604IntroPHRAdvisoryTaskForce.pdf. Accessed August 2, 2009.

66. American Recovery and Reinvestment Act of 2009. 2009. http://www.recovery.gov/. Accessed May 6, 2009.

67. Health Information Technology Policy Committee, US Government Accountability Office. 2009. http://www.gao.gov/press/health_it_committee-2009apr03.pdf. Accessed May 5, 2009.

68. http://www.seco.tkk.fi/applications/tervesuomi/ui-presentation.html. Accessed October 23, 2009.

69. http://www.seco.tkk.fi. Accessed October 23, 2009.

70. Lohr S. Kaiser backs Microsoft patient-data plan. *NY Times,* June 10, 2008. http://www.nytimes.com/2008/06/10/business/10kaiser.html. Accessed July 6, 2009.

71. *New York Times.* About Google. http://topics.nytimes.com/top/news/business/companies/google_inc/index.html?inline=nyt-org. Accessed July 11, 2009.

72. Tang P, Ash J, Bates DW, Overhage JM, Sands DZ. Personal health records: definitions, benefits, and strategies for overcoming barriers to adoption. *JAMIA.* 2006;13(2):121-126.

73. Cain C, Clancy C. Commentary: Patient-centered health information technology. *Am J Med Qual.* 2005; 20(3):164-165.

74. User Centric. *Comparison of Google Health vs. Microsoft Health Vault. Consumers Compare Online Personal Health Record (PHR) Applications:* White Paper. 2009. http://www.usercentric.com/publications/2009/02/02/google-health-vs-microsoft-healthvault-consumers-compare-online-personal-hea. Accessed August 9, 2009.

75. http://www.projecthealthdesign.org. Accessed October 23, 2009.

76. Moen A, Brennan PF. Health@Home: The work of health information management in the household (HIMH): implications for consumer health informatics (CHI) innovations. *JAMIA.* 2005;12:648-656.

77. *Consumer Obtainment and Control of Information* (CP8). 2008. http://www.connectingforhealth.org/phti/#guide. Accessed June 26, 2008.

78. Health in Everyday Living. Robert Wood Johnson Foundation, 2008. http://www.projecthealthdesign.org/news/186281. Accessed June 26, 2008.

79. Ralston JD, Carrell D, Reid R, Anderson M, Moran M, Hereford J. Patient web services integrated with a shared medical record: patient use and satisfaction. *J Am Med Inform Assoc.* 2007;14(6):798-806.

80. *Continuity of Care Record Standard.* 2008. http://www.astm.org/cgi-bin/SoftCart.exe/DATABASE.CART/PAGES/E2369.htm?L+mystore+luuu5949+1167331453. Accessed February 15, 2008.

81. *Continuity of Care Record Tutorial.* 2008. http://www.youtube.com/watch?v=w4Yb9zpZBCo. Accessed February 15, 2008.

82. *Continuity of Care Record.* American Academy of Family Practice, 2008. http://www.centerforhit.org/x201.xml. Accessed February 15, 2008.

83. Stovall H. MiVia web demonstration. 2008. https://www.mivia.org/.

84. Nelson R. No place like a medical home? *Am J Nurs.* 2008;108(1):23-24.

85. Papasifakis B. *To Help Reduce Acute Care Hospitalizations – There's No Place Like Home Health.* Mod Hlt Care 2009; November 2. http://www.modernhealthcare.com/apps/pbcs.dll/article?AID=/20091102/REG/910309997#. Accessed November 8, 2009.

86. Avalere Health. *Medicare Spending and Rehospitalization for Chronically Ill Medicare Beneficiaries: Home health use compared to other post acute care settings.* Report. Avalere Health LLC, May 2009. http://www.avalerehealth.net/wm/show.php?c=1&id=815. Accessed August 30, 2009.

87. *MyWellbeing Project.* 2009. http://www.it.abo.fi/cofi/omahyvinvointi/index.php?id=70. Accessed May 5, 2009.

88. *Service Identification and Classification for Personal Wellbeing Management.* SOLEA 2009 Symposium. 2009. http://www.uku.fi/solea/symposium2009/keynotesabstracts.html. Accessed May 5, 2009.

89. http://www.hhs.gov/familyhistory.gov. Access October 23, 2009.

90. http://www.microlife.com. Accessed October 23, 2009.

91. http://www.omron.com. Accessed October 23, 2009.
92. http://www.homedics.com. Accessed October 23, 2009.
93. Glasgow RE. eHealth Evaluation and Dissemination Research. *Am J Prev Med.* 2007;32(5S): S119-126.
94. Kutner M. Greenberg E, Jin Y, et al. (2006) *The Health Literacy of America's Adults: Results from the 2003 National Assessment of Adult Literacy* (NCES2006-483). US Department of Education. Washington, DC: National Center for Education Statistics. http://nces.ed.gov/pubsearch/pubsinfo. asp?pubid=2006483. Accessed July 3, 2009.
95. http://www.nlm.gov/medlineplus/languages/ languages.html. Accessed October 23, 2009.
96. *Healthfinder.* 2008. http://www.healthfinder.gov/ kids/. Accessed February 15, 2008.
97. *The Game Closet.* 2008. http://www.kidshealth.org/ kid/closet/. Accessed February 15, 2008.
98. *Games for Health.* 2008. http://www.gamesforhealth. org/index3.html. Accessed February 15, 2008.
99. http://www.healthwise.com. Accessed October 23, 2009.
100. http://www.videojug.com. Accessed October 23, 2009.
101. http://www.livinglifetothefull.com. Accessed October 23, 2009.
102. *Creating a Patient-led NHS. Delivering the NHS Improvement Plan,* 2005. http://www.dh.gov. uk/prod_consum_dh/groups/dh_digitalassets/@ dh/@en/documents/digitalasset/dh_4106507.pdf. Accessed May 5, 2009.
103. *Opportunity NYC.* 2008. http://www.rockfound. org/efforts/nycof/opportunity_nyc.shtml. Accessed February 15, 2008.

CHAPTER 4

International Initiatives in Nursing Informatics

By Heimar De Fatima Marin, PhD, MS, RN, FACMI; and Nancy M. Lorenzi, PhD, MS, MA, AB, FACMI

Introduction

The advances in science and technology achieved during the last few decades addressed a number of problems in healthcare globally. Now, even more innovative solutions are needed to address complex problems, such as: (1) an aging population; (2) increased prevalence of chronic diseases; (3) high costs of care delivery; and (4) economic constraints to assure continuity, quality, safety, and cost benefits of treatments and care.

The healthcare reforms currently underway worldwide are closely related to the political and economic development of each country. However, the nature of changes within all healthcare systems requires that nurses everywhere be prepared for leading and managing, either on the redesign of nursing care delivery or to assume new roles and positions in the global health sector. Nurses must participate in this change process, providing expertise and knowledge to the planning, management, education, and care delivery.

Health systems in the global health sector face considerable challenges in providing healthcare services. These challenges extend into the broader need to improve the overall health situation by enhancing the operative capacity of national health programs, decreasing mortality and morbidity, and improving the quality of life through informatics-based systems.

Worldwide, more and more countries are using ICT as a means to improve quality of life and health conditions. Informatics-based systems are used as collaborative tools to create effective solutions in the current environment to enhance life conditions in all continents. These technological advances and information systems have not only transformed healthcare but also have an impact on revolutionizing the nursing profession generally, and in the daily practice of nursing.

Background

Several pioneers in nursing and health informatics predicted that nurses would become the primary users of many of the information systems. Given that technology can innovate, improve, and redesign the way nursing care is provided and because nurses depend on accurate and timely access to appropriate information for patient care, administration, education, and research, this prediction was highly plausible and, as is evident, already happening on a large scale. Decisions in the planning and delivery of nursing care are always based on the available information about what is needed to support patient care. The more that specific information is available to sustain clinical decisions, the better the care that is delivered to the patient/client. Since nurses use information very effectively, information systems are an important part of their working lives.[1,2,3]

Since the early stages of nursing informatics, technology resources have evolved considerably. Currently, it is virtually impossible to practice, or even communicate, without the support of an information-based system. Nurses across the world have incorporated information systems into their daily practice. According to Barnard, "One of the major reasons why nursing has increased its roles and responsibility this century originates from the introduction of various technology resources into nursing practice. Today, in acute care settings, nurses are responsible for increasingly machine-orientated healthcare dominated by administrative and bureaucratic structures. Nurses in all specialties are required to care for patients and develop the technical knowledge not only to manipulate machinery but interpret the world around them."[4]

In the nursing informatics community, a number of significant issues have been and still need to be addressed.[5] Several of the recurrent issues include terminology, data sets, interoperability and integration, usability, confidentiality, privacy, and the evaluation of IT's cost benefits. On the human side of technology implementation are issues related to the consumer and communities, training and education, humanization of care, and networks of collaborative environments. Many of these issues are highlighted in chapters from multiple countries within this book. The following discussion addresses a number of the universal issues that are of importance to nursing informatics.

Terminology

Terminology is an essential requirement to support the establishment of an EHR. Although advances have been made in the development of healthcare terminologies, a comprehensive nursing terminology to be used at the point of care is still a challenge for nurses and developers. There are nursing terminologies available, but they need to be updated, harmonized, and effectively used in informatics-based systems. The harmonization of terminologies for a variety of care contexts is very important and drives nursing documentation and decision making.[1]

For a terminology to be of value, it must meet the two criteria of being usable and useful. To be usable, a terminology must be appropriate to the cognitive skills and training of users and the infrastructure resources and must match the organizational context of its use. For instance, computer-based terminologies that depend on software tools for their management are only applicable when the required technology is available. There are instances of nurses adopting terminologies that were originally created for use in computer-based documentation systems for paper-based systems. Likewise, adoption of paper-based terminologies for electronic systems requires substantive attention to the technology implementation and potential invalidation of the terminiology. Implementors need to be aware that even the use of paper-based terminologies may not be possible if they are not accompanied by appropriate support to ensure adequate speed of use, accuracy, and comprehensiveness, and vice versa. Terminologies based on a particular culture (terminologies that support a particular nursing theory or model) may not be easy to translate into other cultures.

To be useful, a terminology must contain all of the features relevant to the targeted task, which may include populating standardized care plans, descriptions for referrals, and charting exceptions or any other nursing documentation to assure the communication and continuous care for patients.[6]

Data Sets

Nursing data are the primary level of nursing informatics and the basic tool used to elaborate and record patient information. If there are no data that adequately reflect nursing judgments about patient problems/needs, interventions, and outcomes of the nursing care, there will be no archival record of the significant contributions of nurses and the difference nursing care makes to both patient care and the healthcare system as a whole.[6]

The collected data are meant to provide an accurate description of nursing care and resources used when providing patient care. The data sets allow analysis and comparison of nursing data across populations, settings, geographic areas, and time.

Clustering needed information into prescribed data sets is a critical method to collect and provide the data needed. Clearer identification of what constitutes data sets or a minimum data set is a current topic of research in nursing informatics. Several countries are working to define the essential data for nursing care and to ensure inclusion of these data in the national health database. A great focus of interest is to determine nationally and internationally the types of nursing data that are essential to guarantee the highest quality of nursing care.

Interoperability and Integration

Interoperability refers to the ability of health information systems to work together within and across organizational boundaries. Interoperability is key to the ability to exchange data and speaks to the high degree of fragmentation that exits in our medical systems today. For these reasons, interoperability with full data exchange capabilities are critical to advancing effective and safe healthcare for individuals and communities.[7] Interoperability not only requires information sharing but also collaboration through connectivity between healthcare providers and systems.[8] System integration is the capacity to bring multiple components together into one system and ensure that they function as a system. It also includes the linking of different computer systems and software applications, physically or functionally.[9]

Interoperability has been recognized by many countries as one of the top priorities to ensure that information can be collected and shared. Interoperability not only includes the technical aspects of systems working together, such as standards-enabling connectivity, but also the semantic aspects, as well as the organizational issues that are involved. When conflicting technical standards exist, information systems are unable to share information. Because IT standards currently lack specificity, system developers can interpret the general "standards" in multiple ways. This behavior prevents information systems from "speaking" the same language, which would enable providers, patients, and institutions to exchange and access health information to provide, receive, and improve healthcare. Without specific standards, professions and organizations cannot effectively make improvements in patient safety, quality of care, and cost containment in healthcare.

System interoperability is necessary to ensure timely and secure access to relevant health data to improve quality and safety of care. At the same time, linguistic and semantic considerations must also be taken into account when exchanging data between different countries. Without standards, it becomes more difficult for consistent implementation of informatics-based systems.

Usability

Usability refers to how well the information system product was designed for users to learn as well as to use. It also refers to how the system allows users to carry out their tasks safely, effectively, and pleasantly. Without usability, the value of a system is lost to its users. In addition, usability is related to the human-centered design that is characterized by the active involvement of users and the clear understanding of user and task requirements. Since nurses are significant users of the ICT systems, they must be effectively integrated into the design and purchase of new systems and also in the usability testing of those systems.

The usability of a system, as defined by the ISO standard ISO 9241, can be measured only by taking into account the context of the system's use—i.e., who is using the system, what they are using it for, and the environment in which they are using it. Furthermore, measurements of usability have several aspects, such as effectiveness (can users successfully achieve their objectives?), efficiency (how much effort and resource are expended in achieving those objectives?), and satisfaction (was the experience considered satisfactory?).

In nursing and health informatics, issues of usability are important for the ultimate acceptance or rejection of ICT. To cope with the challenge of designing systems that provide desired functionality and that are easy to learn and use, a variety of techniques from the study of human-computer interaction have emerged and become important in the general software industry.[10]

Confidentiality and Privacy

Confidentiality and privacy are critical aspects in system development. Confidentiality is related to the privacy of information being disclosed and ethical usage of that information only for the original purpose. Privacy is the right of individuals and organizations to decide for themselves when, how, and to what extent information about them is transmitted to others.[11]

Nurses ask patients to share information related to their health conditions to create the most reliable plan of care. The quality of nursing care delivered is based on the knowledge and information from the patient that providers can access to underpin their clinical decision-making process. Informatics-based systems are a primary tool to support access to the information. It is important in healthcare that trust exists that healthcare providers will ensure the privacy and security of a person's health-related information. As health IT systems continue to be implemented at an ever-expanded rate, this issue becomes of more concern. Protecting access to health-related data must be balanced with ensuring that the data can easily be shared between professionals and patients. Nurses have a particularly important role in protecting the privacy and security of data in health information systems. Nurses are usually at the front line of data access, working and interacting not only with the technology but interfacing with the patient as well. Nurses use that interface to inform patients on what is about to happen, obtain their consent, and, at the same time, teach patients about information privacy and security.

Cost Benefits

Health information systems can provide multiple benefits in the clinical, organizational, and financial spheres. The benefits can be tangible, meaning that their measurement is simple to compute, or less tangible, meaning that, although obvious, they will not be easily quantified. All of these benefits are to be considered to determine the value of the system. Financial benefits generally fall into one of the following categories: cost reduction, productivity improvement (which translates into cost reduction), revenue generation, and competitive differentiation.[12]

A review of the evaluation of the cost benefits of IT shows that a high priority must be placed on establishing standards for the information that needs to be measured and reported in the health IT implementation studies. Reporting of developments and implementations must be improved by including more descriptions of the intervention, organization, and economic environment in which the resource was implemented. One study outlined several factors associated with successful implementation, including: (1) choose a system that is intuitive to use and that requires little training for users; (2) choose a system that can be easily modified and developed; (3) ensure that the decision-making process for developing and/or selecting a system is participatory; but once this decision has been made, (4) ensure that implementation is directed and driven.[13]

Implementation and Adoption

Change management in EHR implementations is a critical success factor to achieve organizational transformation in which the full potential for "meaningful use" is attained. Managing this transformative change that comes from introducing major information systems into complex healthcare organizations requires an effective blend of good technical and good organizational skills. The literature and two decades of industry experience are full of instances that demonstrate that a "technically best" system can be brought to its knees by people who have low psychological ownership in the system and who vigorously resist its implementation. We have found that the leader who knows how to manage the organizational impact of information systems can sharply reduce the behavioral resistance to change, including to new technology, to achieve a more rapid and productive introduction of information technology.[14]

Technology adoption is a process, not a product. If integration is not considered as a fundamental aspect of the initial design, the end product will be complicated and will not be completely adopted. In addition, integration among systems depends on the integration among healthcare professionals and between providers and patients.[3] IT changes clinical processes, and nurses have been at the forefront of implementing information systems within hospitals and clinical practices. Nurses must continue to be very active in implementation processes to ensure that the software programs are fully integrated into nursing workflows and/or workflows are re-examined.

A major issue facing nursing is that some information systems require complicated data entry processes, and these processes take away from direct patient care. Also, in some organizations, the nursing-based systems are not the first informatics-based systems to be implemented, thus adding to the daily workload of nurses without delivering counterbalancing value. In such instances, this is poor usability, as well as poor system integration design.

Doolan et al[15] identified five key factors for a successful implementation: (1) organizational leadership, clinicians committed to the vision; (2) improvement of existent clinical processes and patient care; (3) involvement of clinicians in the design or modifications made to the system; (4) maintenance or improvement of clinical productivity, and (5) enhancement of support among providers.

Education and Training

Themes related to education and training and nursing curriculum integration are frequently discussed by experts in the nursing informatics field. Technology is evolving, and the resulting change is occurring faster than the ability to incorporate available resources into nursing practice. Therefore, the nursing curriculum must frequently be reviewed to better educate people so that patients and information systems are smoothly integrated.

In the information era, it is mandatory to prepare students and professionals with the higher education needed to become independent learners prepared to solve problems. The methods available to achieve this include tutorials, simulations, virtual reality, eLearning, and computer-assisted instructions. Nurses must use these technologies to facilitate access to continuous education programs, to design patient education programs, and to prepare the next generation to face the current health challenges. The diffusion of IT resources provides the possibility of using these technologies to support healthcare professionals at all levels. ICT should be used to move toward high-quality care and excellent nursing. It is reasonable that nursing informatics programs seek to establish a basis for sustaining education programs through collaborations among countries and organizations.

Humanization

The ideal nursing care information system has the potential to give nurses more time to spend with patients. The hope is that the system will allow the nurse to focus more on the person, not only on the disease, protocols, and guidelines. Nurses need to have the time to actively listen to patients, thereby providing social and emotional support. Having this time will allow nurses to identify their patients' concerns, fears, and discomforts. Providing humanized care means to be connected, engaged, and integrated enough with the patient to establish real bonds that can foster the translation of patients' words into information.[3] Once again, nurses are at the forefront of effectively connecting patients, clinical providers, and the information that the patients need to better understand and integrate their health-related decisions. Computers can be used to empower and enlighten patients and can help forge a new partnership between patients and providers.[16,17] Nurses are significant in accomplishing this goal, as they can effectively translate the concept of healthcare to the patient. This humanization continues as the concept of patient empowerment continues to become more essential in virtually all aspects of healthcare delivery. Nurses the world over are working with this critical concept. They particularly understand the need for health behavior changes by patients and underlying theories to make patient empowerment a reality.

The Consumer

The concept of the patient as consumer has multiple aspects. Two aspects that are experienced throughout the world are that of consumers seeking information and taking care of their own healthcare needs. For example, people who have diabetes routinely administer their own insulin and make important decisions as when to see a practitioner and whom to see. Families commonly keep birth and death records and parents keep track of when their childrens' immunizations are due. Many people engage in exercise, diet, and other self-help activities as a deliberate commitment to their health and disease prevention. The capacity for partnership is already evident among patients and providers, and it is likely that with appropriate and targeted consumer health informatics tools, this partnership can be actualized further.[18]

One important tool is access to reliable health information. Patients have become active consumers of health information and, as a result, are finding abundant information about all aspects of their health. They are able to learn about illnesses, diseases, medications, prevention strategies, and so forth. These new health consumers want to learn as much as they can about their bodies and other health-related issues. The knowledge that consumers gain from the Internet and other sources of information, in turn, has an impact on nurses and other healthcare providers. A result of this is that nurses worldwide must be able to address issues of quality concerning the information patients encounter on the Internet.

A study by Eysenbach et al[19] that evaluated health-related information on the Internet concluded that "the criteria most frequently used to determine the quality of the information includes accuracy, completeness, readability, design, disclosures, and the number of references provided. Among other studies of the quality of health information on the Internet, 55 studies (70%) concluded that quality is a problem, 17 studies (22%) remained neutral [were inconclusive], and seven studies (9%) came to a positive conclusion. Given this situation, nurses become critical translators for consumers, and quality will continue to be addressed by nursing informatics professionals throughout the world.

The Grid

We are at the early stages of building an infrastructure to support worldwide collaboration. It is envisioned that this global network will create communities and support networked collaborative environments, so that nurses in Brazil can easily work with nurses in Mozambique, for example. Within this concept known as "The Grid," sharing of images, data, instant messaging, etc. are all possible. Grid technology can support multiple types of information and the output of this potential can be translated into publications and discovery operations. The Grid can and will be deployed throughout the world.

Information Systems that Impact Nurses

Healthcare experts, policy makers, payers, and consumers consider ICT critical to transforming healthcare services. Given the fragmented nature of healthcare, the large volume of transactions in the system and the need to integrate new scientific evidence into practice, computer-based healthcare systems are required to underpin the process of care delivery. Information systems are now a major component of healthcare, and this trend will continue at an exponential rate. The authors hold that nurses, more than any other health professionals, must blend this new technology into their care processes. This responsibility creates both problems and benefits for nurses and patients.

This book clearly demonstrates what is happening with nursing and information systems internationally. Our purpose in this chapter is to summarize what is happening from an impact standpoint and offer suggestions for the active involvement of nurses in this future.

Summary

Nurses as a group have the largest number of people involved in healthcare worldwide. They are at the forefront of connecting systems and patient-related issues. Nurses are critical to providing insight and information about the best process for system configuration and implementations. Since nursing is such a critical profession internationally, several suggestions follow that we think will be universally helpful:

- Nurses must be involved in the planning, design, selection or development, implementation, and evaluation of any healthcare application that will be in their environment.
- Only those systems that fit nurses' workflow should be selected. Information systems must not require nurses to adapt to the system rather than the system adapting/supporting their workflow.

- Only those systems that can be easily customized to the practice of nursing in your environment should be selected. Without this consideration, you will not be able to make changes that are needed for better patient care.
- Only those systems that have a behavioral component, that is, a system that presents information in an easy to understand manner, should be selected. For example, at Vanderbilt University in Nashville, Tennessee, the informatics department created a display board using evidence-based guidelines to better manage patients on ventilators. This display board gathered and presented information from nursing notes, point-of-care systems, and the EHR. When all care was current, the color green appeared in the guideline space; when care was needed, yellow appeared, and when care was past due, the color red appeared. The behavioral component was the color coding. No one needed to monitor the nurses, as they were more than capable of judging when care was needed.
- Nurses are the prime educators of patients worldwide. They are the translators of information and knowledge from the healthcare system and from the Internet directly to consumers. This role will only continue to grow in the future.

In this chapter, we have offered a summary of the multiple issues facing nurses and, in turn, nursing informatics worldwide. Other chapters offer details of these issues exclusive to their countries or geographic areas. Nursing informatics has made tremendous progress in the last several years, but other nursing informatics issues remain to be solved. We have great confidence in our colleagues worldwide to effectively address the multiple issues outlined in this chapter.

References

1. Marin HF. Nursing informatics: Advances and trends to improve health care quality. *Int J Med Inform.* 2007;76(2):267-269.
2. Weaver C, Delaney C, Carr R, Weber P, eds. *Nursing and informatics for the 21st century: An international look at practice, trends and the future.* Chicago: HIMSS; 2006.
3. Marin HF. The frontiers for nursing and health care informatics. *Int J Med Inform.* 2005;74:695-704.
4. Barnard A. A critical review of the belief that technology is a neutral object and nurses are its master. *J Adv Nurs.* 1997;26126–131.
5. Marin HF. Nursing Informatics: Current issues around the world. *Int J Med Inform.* 2005;74(11-12):857-860.
6. Marin HF, Rodrigues RJ, Delaney C, Nielsen GH, Yan J. *Building Standard-Based Nursing Information Systems.* Pan American Health Organization: Washington, DC; 2001.
7. Healthcare Information and Management Systems Society. *Interoperability: Definition and Background.* http://www.himss.org/content/files/interoperability_definition_background_060905.pdf. Accessed May 16. 2009.
8. Degoulet P, Van de Velde R. *Clinical Information Systems- a Component-based Approach.* Springer: New York; 2003.
9. http://en.wikipedia.org/wiki/System_integration#cite_note-0. Accessed May 16, 2009.
10. Rubin J. *Handbook of Usability Testing.* New York: John Wiley & Sons; 1994.
11. Hannah KJ, Ball MJ, Edwards MJA. *Introduction to Nursing Informatics,* 3rd ed. Springer: New York; 2006.
12. Meyer R. Degoulet P. Assessing the capital efficiency of healthcare information technologies investments: an econometric perspective. *IMIA Yearbook of Medical Informatics.* 2008:114-127.
13. Shekelle PG, Goldzweig CL. *Cost and Benefits of Health Information Technology: an Updated Systematic Review.* The Health Foundation London; 2009:43.
14. Lorenzi NM, Riley RT. Managing change: An overview. *JAMIA.* 2000;7:116–124.
15. Doolan DF, Bates DW, James BC. The use of computers for clinical care: a case series of advanced U.S. sites. *JAMIA.* 2003;10(1):94-107.
16. Brennan PF. The future of clinical communication in an electronic environment. *Hol Nurs Pract.* 1996;11(1):97–104.
17. Brennan PF. Harnessing innovative technologies: What can you do with a shoe? *Nurs Outlook.* 1999;47(3):128–132.
18. Kaplan B, Brennan PF. Consumer informatics supporting patients as co-producers of quality. *J Am Med Inform Assoc.* 2001;8:309-316.
19. Eysenbach G, Powell J, Kuss O, Sa ER. Empirical studies assessing the quality of health information for consumers on the World Wide Web A Systematic Review. *JAMA.* 2002;287:2691-2700.

Growth in Nursing Informatics Educational Programs to Meet Demands

By Diane J. Skiba, PhD, FAAN; Helen R. Connors, PhD, DrPS (Hon), RN, FAAN; and Michelle LL Honey, PhD, MPhil (Nursing), RN, FCNA (NZ)

Introduction

For the last thirty plus years, educational programs that target informatics have been scarce and not consistently part of the higher education venue. In the early 1970s, Anderson et al[1] wrote about the need to educate healthcare professionals about informatics. Since that time, numerous graduate degree programs were established in nursing, medical, and interdisciplinary healthcare professional schools, but demand still outweighs the ability of the programs to meet informatics educational needs. The route taken to meet the demand for nursing informatics educational programs has varied internationally. This chapter indicates some broad approaches and developments that have both driven and impacted the path of informatics education. A number of key developments have been led by nurses in North America; hence, there is a strong U.S. perspective within this chapter. This perspective is not meant to reduce or dismiss the growth in nursing informatics educational programs that has occurred and is occurring in Europe, South America, and Australasia, but rather reflects the dominance of North American initiatives within the last five years.

The purpose of this chapter is to describe the growing demand for the use of informatics tools in healthcare and the subsequent demand for informatics specialists in the workforce. The chapter also examines the growing need to prepare all healthcare professionals with informatics competencies in order to practice in an information-rich and consumer-centric healthcare environment. Lastly, the chapter concludes with a look to future global collaborations and the movement toward translational informatics.

Creating the Demand

Over the last decade, numerous forces have impacted and continue to impact the landscape of healthcare throughout the world. There are two forces that particularly influence the role of health IT and the increasing demand for informatics. First is the increased prominence of the issues of patient safety and quality improvement in the healthcare arena. Second is the increased importance of consumer-centric care and consumers' use of the Internet to access health information and healthcare experts across the globe. Underlying these forces is the growing demand for the use of health IT to mitigate error, promote safety, and support quality improvement to augment healthcare practitioners' clinical decision-making ability and empower consumers to be more active participants in their healthcare.

In the United States, a series of reports from IOM,[2-4] issued beginning in 2000, highlighted the number of medical errors in our healthcare delivery system and the chasm that exists between knowledge of good quality care and what actually exists in practice. These reports served as a catalyst to, as stated by IOM, "promote the use of health information technologies as one solution to mitigate error, facilitate patient safety, and improve the delivery of quality care." IOM also noted that, while widespread application of health IT is "not a panacea for all the complex and difficult problems in healthcare systems, it is a critical prerequisite to addressing many, if not most, of the key issues, such as higher quality care, increased access, more effective chronic care delivery, and the ability to empower active consumer participation in their own health."[5(p 3)]

As a result of these growing concerns, the Office of the National Coordinator for Health Information Technology was created in 2004. The strategic plan, *The Decade of Health Information Technology: Delivering Consumer-centric and Information-rich Care*,[6] was to increase the number of healthcare institutions (hospitals, clinics, physician practices, etc.) using EHRs, create a national health information network to facilitate access and sharing of health data, and deliver personalized healthcare. Numerous work groups were formed under the umbrella of the American Health Information Community (AHIC), a federal advisory body created to make recommendations to the secretary of the U.S. Department of Health and Human Services on how to accelerate the development and adoption of health IT. The AHIC work group's goal was to ensure that most Americans have access to secure EHRs by 2014 (http:// www.hhs.gov/healthit/community/background/).[7] Perhaps the most visible accomplishment of this federal initiative was the recognition that healthcare needs to move into the digital age and out of the paper-based systems inherent in most healthcare institutions.

A new five-year plan, posted in 2008, emphasized two major goals: patient-focused healthcare and population health. The first goal as stated was to "enable the transformation to higher quality, more cost-efficient, patient-focused healthcare through electronic health information access and use by care providers, by patients and their designees." The second goal was "to enable the appropriate, authorized, and timely access and use of electronic health information to benefit public health, biomedical research, quality improvement, and emergency preparedness."[8] The focus on these efforts has been heightened by the most recent federal stimulus monies made available to secure EHRs for all healthcare institutions, so that the goal set for 2014 can be reached.

Europe has followed a collaborative approach to electronic health developments, with clear advantages in increased capacity and funding.[9] Both Australia and New Zealand have government-led initiatives toward establishing EHRs.[10,11] In fact, the New Zealand health sector is ranked highly in terms of the penetration of computers and is second only to the UK in terms of primary healthcare use of EHRs (52% of New Zealand physicians versus 59%, respectively), which is double that in Australia (25%) and nearly triple that of the United States (17%).[12] However, the challenges remain of having EHRs, with the communication and connectivity required, for all partners in the health sector to use in order to share distributed information in a safe and timely manner that leads to better health and participation outcomes.

A second major force in the role of health IT and the increasing demand for informatics is consumers' use of the Internet for health information and their increasing demand to use technology to facilitate healthcare delivery. The growth of the Internet has significantly impacted access to health information, delivery of healthcare, patient-clinician interactions, and empowerment of the consumer to be actively engaged in their healthcare and in making healthcare decisions. The Pew Internet Project[13] estimates that between 75 to 80% of Internet users have looked online for health information. This estimate is similar to Harris Interactive's most recent data on health information seekers (81% of Internet users; 66% of all adults).[14] The Pew Internet data[13] confirmed that "information gathering has become a habit for many Americans, particularly those in the 55% of households with broadband connections." The use of the Internet by patients has spearheaded an industry that is quick to respond to market needs. As Kibbe and McLaughlin[15] stated:

> In a rush of Web-based health initiatives during the past two years, entrepreneurs, programmers, and some providers appear to have leapfrogged over issues of health IT adoption by doctors and hospitals to tackle much broader—and ultimately more important—issues such as how to use the Internet to track peo-

ple's health experiences, how to use the power of social networking to improve standards of treatment, and how to deliver medical advice over the Web.[15(p 197)]

Nurses need to be discerning users of information to meet the changing demands of patients and to work effectively in an increasingly complex healthcare system. The trend of healthcare consumers becoming more knowledgeable is international. This occurs in conjunction with an increased range of treatment options and a plethora of health-related information.[16-18] An illustration of the widespread consumer use of Internet-based health information is found at the Web site http://www.Discern.org, which states, "Despite a rapid growth in the provision of consumer health information, the quality of the information remains variable." The Disern site's purpose is to provide users "with a valid and reliable way of assessing the quality of written information on treatment choices for a health problem." As patients seek out information, become better informed, and request a range of options, nurses need to be able to assist patients in understanding their choices. Information literacy therefore becomes an important skill and competency for professional nursing practice and lifelong learning.

The rapid growth of the Internet is taking place not only in developed countries throughout the globe but in developing countries as well. As the World Health Organization (WHO) states, "Today the integration and assimilation of e-health into the everyday life of health-care workers is becoming a reality in developing as well as developed countries…a fact that the world is being digitalized. The rich world as well as the poor world."[19] This is especially true as one examines the use of e-health as it relates to chronic disease management.

Chronic conditions pose increasing problems for quality of life, with the burden of symptoms from chronic conditions internationally accounting for approximately 70 percent of all health expenditure.[20-21] WHO[22] identified chronic condition self-management as a significant factor for the future of healthcare delivery worldwide. Self-management is based on the consumer having knowledge of their condition, being informed enough to share in decision-making with health professionals, being able to monitor and manage symptoms and their impact, and adopting lifestyles that promote one's health.[23] Therefore, self-management is dependent on health information that meets consumers' needs. In New Zealand, the National Health Committee[24] identified that chronic health conditions accounted for nearly 80% of all deaths, and between 70 to 78% of healthcare expenditure. Patients with chronic conditions mostly live their lives in their own communities and gain support from health professionals and peers; therefore, an increased focus on effective self-management support is needed as this will aid consumers' independence and confidence.[24] Consumers having access to information that is appropriate and relevant for their situation underpins effective self-management. The need for this critical feature of self-management is found in reports from New Zealand that indicate consumers want better explanations about their conditions.[25,26]

According to a 2008 Pew Internet and American Life study,[27] engaged patients (e-patients) are more likely to connect to online resources if their health stakes are high. They report that "adults living with a disability or chronic disease are less likely than others to go online, but once online, are avid health consumers."[27] This is particularly true for patients with chronic diseases or disabilities where "Seventy-five percent of e-patients with a chronic condition say their last health search affected a decision about how to treat an illness or condition, compared with 55% of other e-patients."[27] They also noted that e-patients with chronic diseases reported that their engagement with the Internet affected their interactions with their physicians and helped with their ability to cope and manage their diet, exercise, and stress level.

Taken together, these catalysts have heightened the awareness of both the healthcare professional communities and the general public. Health IT has reached a tipping point, securing a critical mass of supporters. It is receiving the national and international recognition that healthcare informatics professionals have hoped for since the early 1970s. The time for healthcare informatics has arrived.

Meeting the Demand: Preparing Informatics Specialists

As a result of this international attention, several reports document the growing need for a workforce capable of meeting the demands for health IT throughout the world. Several studies have made projections about these future workforce needs. As early as 2000, Sable et al[28] surveyed eighteen U.S. health organizations to assess the role of medical informatics. They concluded there was an increasing role for personnel with combined expertise in healthcare and IT. It was no longer sufficient to only have IT personnel in the healthcare environment to lead and manage the health IT agenda. Hecker[29] reported that the U.S. Department of Labor projected a 49 percent growth in health information management personnel by 2010. Similar workforce studies surfaced in other countries. The British National Health Service and the Australian Health Service both released reports noting the need for health informaticians to meet the growing technology investments in healthcare facilities. The British NHS projected in 2006 the need for 25,000 full-time positions in their informatics workforce.[30]

In the United States, a nationwide Health Information Network Workforce Study[5] was conducted in 2007 to understand workforce issues and produce an initial estimate of the number of people needed in the field. This study gathered data from four focus groups, five site visits, and direct communications with health IT vendors. To assess the needed workforce, three specific types of health IT were addressed: electronic health records (EHRs) for physician offices; EHRs in hospitals and other healthcare institutions, and the health information infrastructure required in communities to link the various sources of records so that each patient's complete record could be available."[5(p 1)] Although they consider their estimates to be preliminary and possibly imprecise because of a small sample size, they projected the following workforce needs over the next five years: To install EHRs for more than 400,000 practicing physicians, there is a need for 7,600 (+/- 3,700) specialists. To install EHRs in approximately 4,000 hospitals and healthcare institutions, there is a need for 28,600 specialists.

Lastly, there is a need for 420 specialists to support the health information infrastructure for communities. As part of this study, numerous types of personnel were identified to help in the installation and maintenance of EHRs and the health information infrastructure for communities. Personnel types were either technical in nature (network engineer, database administrator, security officer, desktop specialist) or were aligned with roles and responsibilities identified by the ANA's *Scope and Standards of Nursing Informatics*[31] or by the HIMSS' 2009 Informatics Nurse Impact Survey.[32] Examples of these roles included trainer, project manager, implementation coordinator, change management specialist, help desk specialist, privacy officer, and chief nursing (medical) information officer. The HIMSS 2009 survey, in particular, found the following breakdown of informatics nursing roles that were similar: user education (99%), system implementation (89%), user support (percent), workflow analysis (84%), and getting buy in from end users (80%).[32] "These results emphasize the importance of the role of the informatics nurse with regard to change management and process improvement. At least 40% of respondents indicated that informatics nurses play a role in all of the other areas identified in this research, with the exception of pay for performance/reimbursement."[32]

The United States EHR Workgroup, part of the federal AHIC umbrella, heard testimony from several professional organizations and the author of the NHIN study. Based on their testimony, the group made several recommendations to the secretary of the U.S. Department of Health and Human Services related to the assessment of workforce needs, development of an action plan, and the need for monitoring of the progress of workforce development in the areas of clinical, research, public health, and translational bioinformatics.[33] Hersh and Wright[34] conducted a study to characterize the health IT workforce by examining a comprehensive health IT database to determine areas for future research related to workforce development. They categorized three broadly defined health IT workforce professionals: IT, health information management (HIM), and biomedical informatics. An interesting finding was biomedical informatics professionals "still have not been well-categorized but have been found situationally to be vital for HIT implementation success."[34(p 1)] These figures are solely based on U.S. estimates; with current developments in Europe and beyond there is a need for a significant number of informatics prepared nurses to meet the expected international demand.

Strategies to Educate Nursing Informatics Specialists

Numerous educational pathways are available to prepare informatics specialists. These specialists can be educated through formal educational programs at both the baccalaureate and graduate level in colleges and universities or through informal educational opportunities, such as conferences, workshops, professional development certificate courses, online courses or modules, on-the-job training, and self-study. For many years, the informal educational opportunities were by far the most prolific strategy, but in the last decade, there has been growth in more formal educational degree programs.

Informal learning may take many guises and include one-off and in-service or on-the-job training through to certificates and diplomas from a variety of providers. The mode of delivery for informal learning will vary, and this may depend on the situation and available resources, including the expertise of the educators and access to educational technology.[35] More recently online learning, ranging from formal educational courses to seminars has become more prevalent. Due to the low cost of running online seminars, some are offered at no charge, making them both accessible and affordable to many nurses.

National health informatics groups may also offer learning opportunities through seminars, workshops, and local and regional conferences. Numerous examples of these can be found, as most of the 54 countries that are affiliated with the International Medical Informatics Association (IMIA) hold national events, as well as promoting and supporting the larger regional and international conferences. More specifically for nurses, more than 30 countries have links with the Nursing Informatics Special Interest Group of IMIA (IMIA-NI). IMIA-NI was established in 1983 and as a non-profit organization, serves the specific needs of nurses in the field of nursing informatics (http://www.imiani.org). The focus of IMIA-NI is to foster collaboration among nurses, explore the scope of nursing informatics, support the development of nursing informatics, and provide informatics meetings and conferences (every three years) as opportunities to share knowledge and research, which will facilitate communication of developments in the field.

Nursing informatics learning opportunities that arise from the position of the nurse are often focused toward competencies required to work in a specific role. Unlike the United States, many countries do not have a credentialing process, which recognizes nursing informatics specialization, although they may offer postgraduate courses and higher degrees in health or nursing informatics. IMIA-NI is working toward a mechanism to certify nursing informatics expertise through a certification process. The Nursing Informatics Competency Recognition Certificate will be available to nurses who can demonstrate knowledge and skills in specified areas of nursing informatics based on a submitted portfolio. The portfolio will need to provide evidence of accomplishments in the field, which is assessed by an international panel and is expected to also be supported by a letter from the IMIA-NI representative of the applicant's country. Evidence within the portfolio may include a curriculum vitae or resume; continuing education certificates from workshops and other learning; performance assessments from informatics employment; system implementation plans, system analyses, project proposals, and reports; and academic publications and presentations.

Ozbolt[36] presented a variety of models being used to educate healthcare professionals in the Global South, which includes countries from the Americas, Africa, Middle East, Asia, and the Pacific. She highlighted a model program, The Réseau en Afrique Francophone pour la Télémédecine (Raft) Model, started by medical students in Mali. This project, through distance learning, connects numerous institutions from ten African countries with two European countries. Ozbolt notes, "The RAFT project is not about creating informatics training programs. Rather it is about meeting expressed needs of health professionals using informatics tools…Systematic efforts to create a health informatics workforce must take into account how those workers will be integrated into the healthcare workforce."[36(p 3)] She underscored that distance education will be vital to the continuing preparation of the healthcare informatics workforce throughout the world. "In North America, Australia, New Zealand and Europe, distance education in informatics is well-established.[36(p 3)] It is also expanding in Latin America through the work at the Federal University of San Paulo."[35]

There are also a growing number of formal educational programs to prepare informatics specialists. There are formal graduate degrees in the discipline of nursing informatics or healthcare informatics. The graduate program consists of master's, post-master's, and PhD degrees. Most recently there was the initiation of a Doctorate in Nursing Practice with a specialization in nursing informatics.[37] The largest growth in formal educational programs is occurring at the master's and post-master's degree levels. Although there is a demand for more PhD programs in the discipline, there is a lack of PhD prepared-faculty who have active research programs or can teach at the PhD level.

In the United States, the growth of educational programs in informatics has been mostly discipline-specific, such as medical, nursing, or public health. In 2004, the Nursing Informatics Work Group of the American Medical Informatics Association (NI-WG of AMIA) supported a think tank, called The NI-WG Think Tank Education Task Force, to examine the status of graduate education in nursing informatics. The taskforce examination included the body of knowledge and applications contained within the content of master's level informatics programs. At that time, 14 programs were included as part of the study. Now five years later, the number of programs in nursing informatics has increased to 17 programs in nursing along with a growing number of healthcare informatics interdisciplinary programs. The NI-WG Think Tank Education Task Force Report is available at http://www.amia. org/ni-wg/ni-wg-documents.[38]

The taskforce did not reach consensus on a single model to underlie an informatics curriculum. In fact, the step of choosing a model was deemed to be a premature step at this time. So a narrative organization of the concepts, themes, and content was selected to represent the taskforce's work. Four major constructs emerged: Data-Information-Knowledge, Decision Support, Knowledge Representation, and Human Computer Interaction. Context (including the cultural, economic, social, and physical aspects of internal and external environments) also surfaced as an important construct. Informatics practices (embodied knowledge or skills sets that are learned and perfected over time) also became apparent as a result of the review process. These practices included: information management, database management, systems management and project management. The results of these emerging themes are consistent with content areas generated by the American College of Medical Informatics' white paper on training future informaticists and the Education Working Group of the American Medical Informatics Association (AMIA).[39]

Recently, AMIA examined the subspecialty of clinical informatics and defined the core content for this medical subspecialty.[40] They acknowledged that "clinical informaticians use their knowledge of patient care combined with their understanding of informatics concepts, methods, and tools to: assess information and knowledge needs of healthcare professionals and patients; characterize, evaluate, and refine clinical processes; develop, implement, and refine clinical decision support systems and lead or participate in the procurement, customization, development, implementation, management, evaluation, and continuous improvement of clinical information systems (CIS)."[40(p 153)] The core content emphasized four major areas: Fundamentals, The Health System, Clinical Decision Making and Care Processes Improvements, and Health Information Systems. Many of these core content areas are readily found in some of the nursing informatics programs, but as the growth of programs increases, it is important for the nursing profession to revisit the core content necessary for graduate work in nursing informatics.

There is also a trend to offer more interdisciplinary educational opportunities in healthcare informatics. This is particularly true in areas for which a lack of qualified, discipline-specific, informatics faculties is found. Brittain and Norris[35] describe the slow response of higher education providers to offer health informatics courses leading to certificates, diplomas, and degrees. The authors cite the notable exception of the University of Wales, Aberystwyth, which offered a flexible and part-time master's degree in healthcare information, using a mix of distance education and a short residential period. North America was quicker to respond and courses in health informatics were in evidence in the early 1990s, although Europe and Australasia have taken longer.[35]

Health informatics education has evolved in a different manner in New Zealand, perhaps because of the numbers of nurses and the small population, which is such that separate post-graduate courses in nursing informatics have not been viable. A study that included an online survey and interviews with the major tertiary education providers offering postgraduate health informatics programs within New Zealand explored the potential for improving the health informatics workforce capability in New Zealand.[41] The study found that there is "clearly a role for graduates with a set of competencies that can provide a bridge between the IT specialist working in the health sector and the clinicians assisting with IT developments."[41(p5)] The nursing informatics specialist competencies are not in question, rather the educational approach to providing these has needed to be adjusted to suit the national environment. In New Zealand, four programs that provide postgraduate education in health informatics are slowly building enrollments and are well-regarded by students and graduates. A suggestion has been made that these health informatics programs need more extensive marketing to ensure that the subject domain of health informatics is better understood in the health IT sector, and the value of a formal qualification in the subject is recognized and rewarded. Additionally, national agreement on a postgraduate health informatics curriculum would improve the effectiveness and the marketability of programs.[41]

In the United States, many of the graduate programs are offered in an online format. The number of universities offering online degree programs has grown rapidly over the past decade as has the learner demand for online courses. More than two-thirds of all higher education institutions in the United States offered online courses and programs in 2007 and, in that year, more than 3.9 million students were enrolled in online courses.[42] This trend especially holds true for informatics courses and programs as most are taught in Web-based or Web-enhanced formats. More sophisticated, user-friendly technology tools have made the design of online courses easier for faculty.[43] Course management systems (CMS) coupled with the interactive tools now offered through Web 2.0 have further expanded the reach and quality of online courses. Web 2.0 technologies provides faculty with an array of powerful resources to be used in a pedagogically effective way. These technologies allow users to communicate, collaborate, and interact in both asynchronous and synchronous real and virtual environments. Web 2.0 does not refer to any Web technical specification update but rather to the new software designed to facilitate communication, information sharing, and collaboration on the Internet. It includes some of the most popular applications available online today, such as Facebook and MySpace, podcasting sites such as iTunes, video sharing sites such as YouTube and Flickr, synchronous voice tools such as Skype, wikis such as Wikipedia, social bookmarking sites such as Del.icio.us, and instant messaging/chat sites such as Twitter, to name just a few. These tools allow faculty to readily build interaction with others around the world and to share knowledge and experiences. Students from world-wide remote sites that are either bound by time or physical location can hook up with other students and an instructor in both real and virtual time. Whether in a plane cruising at 33,000 feet or at home, at any given moment a student can log into a virtual classroom. From desktop or laptop, assignments can be sent and received, and community learning environments can be cultivated.

Virtual worlds, such as Second Life, add a new dimension to Web-based education (http://secondlife.com/). A virtual world is a computer-based simulation environment in which individuals interact through a humanoid know as an avatar. Second Life, developed by Linden Labs, is a free online 3-D virtual world in which users can navigate through the environment, interact with objects, socialize, connect, and create using voice and text chat. This environment has grown dramatically with residents from all over the globe. Today, many colleges, universities, hospitals, and other businesses have a presence in Second Life. Second Life has also proven a valuable professional development medium for educators. Organizations such as the New Media Consortium (NMC) have fostered shared learning among educators and are networking, running seminars; conferences; and symposia on learning and creativity related to virtual worlds within the virtual world (http://secondlifegrid.net/slfe/education-use-virtual-world).[44] Virtual Worlds provide a vast range of opportunities for global collaboration in education, research, and clinical practice. The University of Kansas is using Second Life as a component of its online informatics program.[45]

Meeting the Demand: Preparing the Healthcare Workforce

The underlying factors driving the need for informatics specialization, described earlier, appear to be equally applicable to nursing, medicine, and allied health professionals. Several reports were issued highlighting the need to prepare all healthcare professionals with the necessary competency to use informatics tools. The International Council of Nurses (ICN) launched a new network in January 2009 to promote excellence in nursing education, recognizing the need to prepare a diverse 21ˢᵗ-century nursing workforce in the face of international shortages in the nursing workforce and in nursing faculty.[46] Many countries recognize that health information technologies may provide solutions to improving healthcare for ethnically diverse, geographically dispersed, and aging populations and in the growing burden of chronic diseases, epidemic disease outbreaks, and support health service delivery across the continuum of care in communities that may have been damaged by natural disasters and conflict.[47] In Australasia, concerns about the workforce being unskilled and not adequately prepared to harness the opportunities provided by new technology have been raised.[48-50]

There is an ongoing need to improve the integration of health informatics into undergraduate training for health professionals.[41,51] All nurses need to be prepared for increased use of technology in the health arena. The concept of a global village and the need for a global perspective in healthcare planning add credence to the necessity of considering trends in nursing education from an international perspective.[52] To gain a vision of the nurse for the future, an independent review of undergraduate nursing education was commissioned by the Nursing Council of New Zealand in 2000.[53] One of the key issues identified to impact on healthcare and nursing education in the future was technological advancements, similar to trends internationally.[54-59] A recent United States-based study using a standardized instrument found newly graduated nurses were most confident in their Internet, word processing, and systems operations skills, but the same students rated themselves lowest on valuing informatics knowledge, care documentation, skills development, and data entry competencies.[60]

In the United States, IOM issued a report in 2003, *Health Professions Education: A Bridge to Quality.* In this report, the IOM called for all health professionals, regardless of discipline, to be educated to possess five core competencies, described as goals: (1) provide patient-centered care; (2) work in interdisciplinary teams; (3) employ evidence-based practice; (4) apply quality improvement techniques; and (5) use informatics.[61(p 85)] This document provided the impetus for health professional education programs, accrediting agencies, professional organizations, and individual practitioners to examine their focus and commitment to meeting these specified requirements.

Forewarned about the educational challenge of the IOM report and the plea for widespread adoption of EHRs, as well as the concern about the lack of preparation of students, faculty, and practicing clinicians to use these informatics tools, a small group of nurse leaders from academia, practice, and industry convened to strategize a plan to advance nursing informatics for 21ˢᵗ-century practice. Two years later, the work of this group resulted in the 2006 TIGER Summit.

With funding from more than two dozen organizations, including the Agency for Health Research and Quality (AHRQ), the Alliance for Nursing Informatics, and the Robert Wood Johnson Foundation (RWJF), the summit brought together more than 100 nursing leaders representing 40 professional organizations or agencies to develop a 10-year vision and a 3-year strategic plan to better prepare nurses to practice in increasingly automated informatics-rich healthcare environments. Organizational leaders came armed with their own strategic plans to begin to align these plans to create synergy and momentum. The scope of this project extends beyond the EHR to include the impact of health IT on the broader community.

The defined action steps resulting from the TIGER Summit were themed and organized into nine key areas, and collaborative work teams were formed to promote various mechanisms to disseminate and augment the work of TIGER: (1) Standards & Interoperability, (2) National Health IT Agenda, (3) Informatics Competencies, (4) Education and Faculty Development, (5) Staff Development, (6) Usability and Clinical Application Design, (7) Virtual Demonstration Center, (8) Leadership Development, and (9) Consumer Empowerment and Personal Health Records. Each of the nine collaborative teams has developed a wiki that explains their goals, activities, and progress. For example, the education and faculty development team worked closely with the National League for Nursing in drafting their position statement on informatics.[62] The team provided input and support for the American Association of Colleges of Nursing's (AACN) revised Baccalaureate Essentials of Nursing Education, which includes "information management and application of patient care technologies."[63] In addition, the TIGER Web site has a wide range of press releases, journal articles, and seminars/conferences designed to disseminate the TIGER activities widely. Today more than 1,200 individuals are participating in this grass roots effort, and many are actively involved in disseminating the action plan.

Another effort that is advocating informatics competencies for nurses is the Quality and Safety Education for Nurses (QSEN) Project. RWJF funded the QSEN project at the University of North Carolina-Chapel Hill. Today, RWJF has funded three phases of this project, including a collaborative project with the AACN. The overall goal through all phases of QSEN is to address the challenge of preparing future nurses with the knowledge, skills, and attitudes (KSA) necessary to continuously improve the quality and safety of the healthcare systems in which they work. To accomplish this goal, six competencies were defined in phase one of the project. These competencies include (1) patient centered care, (2) teamwork and collaboration, (3) evidence-based practice, (4) quality improvement, (5) informatics, and (6) safety. For each of these defined competencies there is a list of subcompetencies that address the knowledge, skills, and attitudes required to improve the quality and safety of patient care.[64]

In the second phase of this project, 15 schools were selected to participate in a pilot project designed to integrate the six QSEN competencies into their nursing curriculum. The pilot schools have shared their work on the QSEN Web site (www.qsen.org),[64] contributing teaching and faculty development strategies, as well as other collaborative resources to assist other schools and educators to leverage the work of QSEN. Now, in phase three of the project, the work continues to promote the widespread sharing of these competencies to develop faculty expertise to teach to these competencies across all types of nursing programs. The work also extends to collaboration with professional agencies to help create mechanisms that sustain these quality and safety initiatives among all programs.

In the United States, the NLN and AACN are committed to working collaboratively with the education and healthcare communities to create a highly educated nursing workforce with the skill set to meet the expectations of today's e-health environments. These organizations strongly believe that encouraging all nurses to advance their education and faculty to teach to these new competencies is in the best interest of patients and an important step toward enhancing the quality, safety, efficiency, and effectiveness of healthcare. Their work is shared via the Web, so nurses internationally can utilize and build on their developments. Knowledge and skills in information and patient care technology are critical in the delivery of quality patient care throughout the world. In 2008, the NLN issued a position paper calling for educational reform.[62] The intent of this position paper is to support the reform of nursing education and to promote quality education that prepares a workforce capable of practicing in a healthcare environment for which technology continues to increase in amount and sophistication. The NLN, as a leader in the preparation of a diverse workforce, advocates for support of faculty development initiatives and innovative educational programs that address informatics preparation. This call for reform is relevant to all prelicensure and graduate nursing education programs, as the informatics revolution will impact all of nursing practice. Numerous forces are catalysts to incorporating information and communication technologies throughout the healthcare delivery system.

Specifically, the National League for Nursing as outlined in the position statement, recommends the following for faculty, administrators, and its own leaders and members:

For Nurse Faculty

- Participate in faculty development programs to achieve competency in informatics.
- Designate an informatics champion in every school of nursing to: (a) help faculty distinguish between using instructional technologies to teach versus using informatics to guide, document, analyze, and inform nursing practice, and (b) translate state-of-the-art practices in technology and informatics that need to be integrated into the curriculum.
- Incorporate informatics into the curriculum.
- Incorporate ANA-recognized standard nursing language and terminology into content.
- Identify clinical informatics exemplars, those drawn from clinical agencies and the community or from other nursing education programs, to serve as examples for the integration of informatics into the curriculum.
- Achieve competency through participation in faculty development programs.
- Partner with clinicians and informatics people at clinical agencies to help faculty and students develop competence in informatics.
- Collaborate with clinical agencies to ensure that students have hands-on experience with informatics tools.
- Collaborate with clinical agencies to demonstrate transformations in clinical practice produced by informatics.
- Establish criteria to evaluate informatics goals for faculty.

For Deans/Directors/Chairs

- Provide leadership in planning for necessary IT infrastructure that will ensure education that prepares graduates for 21st-century practice roles and responsibilities.
- Allocate sufficient resources to support IT initiatives.
- Ensure that all faculty members have competence in computer literacy, information literacy, and informatics.
- Provide opportunities for faculty development in informatics.
- Urge clinical agencies to provide hands-on informatics experiences for students.
- Encourage nurse-managed clinics to incorporate clinical informatics exemplars that have transformed nursing practice to provide safe quality care.
- Advocate that all students graduate with up-to-date knowledge and skills in each of the three critical areas: computer literacy, information literacy, and informatics.
- Establish criteria to evaluate outcomes related to achieving informatics goals.

For the National League for Nursing

- Disseminate this position statement widely.
- Seek external funding and allocate internal resources to convene a think tank to reach consensus on definitions of informatics, competencies for faculty and students, and program outcomes that include informatics.
- Participate actively in organizations that focus on education in nursing informatics to ensure that recommendations from those organizations are congruent with the NLN's positions on curriculum.
- Use Educational Technology and Information Management Advisory Council (ETI-MAC) and its task groups to (a) develop programs for faculty, showcasing exemplar programs, and (b) disseminate outcomes from the think tank.

- Encourage and facilitate accrediting bodies, regulatory agencies, and certifying bodies to reach consensus on definitions related to informatics and minimal informatics competencies for practice in the 21st century.[62]

In October 2008, AACN released the new *Essentials of Baccalaureate Education for Professional Nurses*.[63] Developed through a national consensus-building process, this new set of competency standards is designed to enhance the ability of baccalaureate-prepared nurses to use informatics and to provide safe, high-quality patient-centered care.

The nine *Essentials* delineated in the document underscore the importance of the following themes, which are fundamental to baccalaureate nursing education:

- A solid base in liberal education provides the cornerstone for the practice and education of nurses.
- Knowledge and skills in leadership, communication, quality improvement, and patient safety are necessary to provide high-quality healthcare.
- Professional nursing practice is grounded in the analysis and application of evidence for practice.
- Knowledge and skills in information and patient care technology are critical in the delivery of quality patient care.
- Healthcare policies, including financial and regulatory, directly and indirectly influence the nature and functioning of the healthcare system.
- Collaboration among healthcare professionals is critical to delivering high quality and safe patient care.
- Health promotion and disease prevention at the individual and population levels are necessary to improve population health.
- Professionalism is fundamental to the discipline of nursing.
- Integration of knowledge and skills is critical to practice. Practice occurs across the lifespan and in the continuum of healthcare environments. The baccalaureate graduate demonstrates clinical reasoning within the context of patient-centered care to form the basis for nursing practice that reflects ethical values.[63]

The TIGER and QSEN initiatives, as well as the position statements and revised competencies and standards related to integrating technology in the curriculum, have made many faculty, administrators, and accrediting bodies acutely aware of the need to change the education and practice of nursing. Professional organizations such as the American Nurses Association, the American Nurses Informatics Association, the American Association of Critical Care Nurses, and other specialty organizations under the leadership of the TIGER initiative, specifically the TIGER Education and Faculty Development Collaborative, have come together to identify faculty development resources available to help integrate informatics into the nursing curriculum. Activities of the various collaborative work groups are available on the work group wiki (www.tigereducation.pbwiki.com).[65] This Web presence and use of collaborative tools, such as wikis, make scarce resources available globally.

Faculty Development Needs

The nursing faculty shortage in the United States, as well as in other nations, is a critical problem that directly impacts informatics in the curriculum. If a substantial increase in informatics competencies is needed to meet the growing demands of the healthcare system, faculty must be prepared to teach to these competencies. They must have the skill set and resources available within the educational programs to do so.

Today, the average age of nursing faculty is 51.5 years, and the rate of projected retirements is expected to exceed the rate of replacements.[66] Even if the projected retirement changes slightly because of the economic downturn, most of the current faculty do not have the required knowledge and skills to teach informatics competencies. In addition, nursing programs do not have adequate access to the tools required. Even today, a relatively small proportion of nursing schools provides informatics training for generalist or specialist. Faculty informatics competencies have not been studied extensively; however, in 2005, the NLN Educational Technology and informatics management Advisory Council commissioned a survey of faculty and administrators to determine the extent of nursing informatics competencies in the curriculum of nursing schools.[67] Results indicated that few faculty had degrees, coursework, or certificates in informatics. Although faculty may possess adequate skills in computer literacy and information literacy, for the most part, they lack the informatics competencies. There is definitely work to be done in the area of faculty development.

To address these faculty development concerns, in 2006, the United States' organization, HRSA, in partnership with the Office of Health Information Technology, initiated a faculty development initiative to support the integration of IT into nursing education and practice. To date, six university-led collaboratives have been funded through this cooperative agreement. The grantees include Duke University, the University of Wisconsin-Madison, the University of Pittsburgh, the University of Kansas, Drexel University, and the University of Washington. The purpose of this initiative is to provide support to nursing collaboratives for faculty development in the use of information and other technologies to expand the capacity of collegiate schools of nursing to educate students for 21ˢᵗ-century healthcare practice. Nursing collaboratives use healthcare information systems to enhance nursing education and practice, optimize patient safety, and drive improvements in healthcare quality. More detail about these HRSA-funded faculty development programs and case exemplars can be found in Chapter 7.

Another program oriented toward faculty development is an online certificate in healthcare informatics for educators. This program, initiated as part of a HRSA training grant, allows educators in nursing schools or in staff development to enroll in three informatics courses offered by the University of Colorado, Denver College of Nursing.[68] The certificate program is built upon their online graduate program in healthcare informatics. The first course focuses on the basics of healthcare informatics and is foundational to the other two courses. The second course focuses on e-health applications and provides an overview of health information technologies—such as telehealth applications, smart homes, Web-based chronic disease management, PHRs, and a host of Health 2.0 tools being used by consumers. The third course can be selected from a variety of specialty courses that focus on knowledge management, decision support, databases and healthcare terminologies, or human computer interaction design.

On the Horizon

The advancement and adoption of health IT will continue to grow as we strive to attain the highest levels of quality and safety in healthcare. Current and emerging technologies, such as EHRs, computer-assisted clinical decision support, genomic data warehouses, and powerful data-mining capabilities promise efficiency, automation, effectiveness, transparency, personalization, portability, and consumer empowerment. This promise is accelerated by national efforts to increase adoption of health IT across all spectrums of healthcare, including PHRs, public health surveillance, and healthcare research. In the United States, there is a growing emphasis on translational informatics. The term has surfaced in relation to the National Institutes of Health's (NIH) focus on translational research. According to NIH, "Translational research includes two areas of translation. One is the process of applying discoveries generated during research in the laboratory, and in preclinical studies, to the development of trials and studies in humans. The second area of translation concerns research aimed at enhancing the adoption of best practices in the community."[69] At the current time there is not an unilaterally agreed definition, but one blog has offered the following definition, "Translational Research Informatics (TRI) is the sub-domain of Biomedical informatics or Medical Informatics concerned with the application of informatics theory and methods to translational research. It overlaps considerably with the related rapidly developing domain of Clinical Research Informatics."[70] This new emphasis on the use of TRI will ensure that informatics is threaded not only in clinical practice but is also an integral component of translating research from the bench to the bedside and, ultimately, diffused to the community.

With so much at stake, it is imperative that we understand what it will take to develop and implement diverse strategies that can lead to achieving the maximum potential for health informatics. During the last five years, important advances have been made, and valuable lessons have been learned. Now, we need to be sure that health professions are educated in environments that enhance the skill set to support widespread adoption of health IT.

Summary

Nursing Informatics as a specialty is in great demand. It is unique in that the rapid advances of technology are placing demands on a workforce that may or may not be qualified to meet those demands. It also raises questions of the availability of current informatics education programs and the availability of prepared informatics specialists with advanced knowledge of informatics models and theories. Clearly, the market, in many instances, is driving the practice. As a specialty, there is a need to refine and reflect on the specialist's preparation. It is important to ensure that further education in informatics, especially for the clinical arena, does not become co-mingled with the need to learn about teaching with technologies.

The challenge then is to forge collaborative coalitions among industry, clinical, and academic settings to support responsible, informed, and innovative models that promote the needs of all stakeholders. There are a number of global initiatives that involve nursing informatics. Of particular note is the long-standing ICN's work on classification in a project called International Classification for Nursing Practice (ICNP®). This project arose because of a common problem with naming the problems and situations nursing deals with and "to describe nursing's distinctive contributions to solving, alleviating, and preventing health problems or to promoting healthy living."[71] Collaborations of this nature can be used as a model to promote collaborative efforts in providing educational opportunities to prepare nursing informatics specialists. It is now time for new and innovative methods for collaborative learning opportunities. Nursing needs to take the lead in educating the next generation of nurses that can practice in an informatics-intensive and consumer-centric healthcare environment. It is also imperative that nursing prepares informatics specialists that can voice and represent nurses' needs in this emerging healthcare environment.

References

1. Anderson J, Gremy F, Page J. *Education in Informatics of Health Professionals.* New York: Elsevier Publishing, 1974.
2. Kohn LT, Corrigan JM, Donaldson MS, eds. *To Err is Human: Building a Safer Health System.* Washington, DC: The National Academies Press, 2000.
3. Committee on Quality Health Care in America, Institute of Medicine. *Crossing the Quality Chasm: A New Health System for the 21st Century.* Washington, DC: The National Academies Press; 2001.
4. Aspden P, Corrigan J, Wolcott J, Erickson S, eds. *Patient Safety: Achieving a New Standard of Care.* Committee on Data Standards for Patient Safety, Institute of Medicine. Washington, DC: National Academies Press; 2004.
5. Nationwide Health Information Network Workforce Study. Assistant Secretary for Planning and Evaluation. US Department of Health and Human Services. September 19, 2007. Washington, DC.
6. Brailer DJ. *Decade of Health Information Technology: Delivering Consumer-centric and Information-rich Health Care.* Washington, DC: US Department of Health and Human Services; 2004.
7. http://www.hhs.gov/healthit/community/background/. Accessed August 2, 2009.
8. The Office of the National Coordinator. *Coordinated Federal Health IT Strategic Plan: 2008-2012.* Office of the National Coordinator for Health Care Technologies. http://healthit.hhs.gov/portal/. Accessed May 1, 2009.
9. Kalra D. Medicine in Europe: Electronic health records: the European scene. *BMJ.* 1994; 309:1358-1361.
10. Health Information Strategy Steering Committee. *Health Information Strategy for New Zealand.* Wellington, New Zealand: Ministry of Health; 2005.
11. Heard S, Grivel T, Schloeffel P, Doust J. *Report to the Electronic Health Records Taskforce: The Benefits and Difficulties of Introducing a National Approach to Electronic Health Records in Australia.* Adelaide, Australia: Commonwealth Department of Health and Aged Care; 2000.
12. Kerr K. The electronic health record in New Zealand Health Care and Informatics. Review. *Online Journal.* 2004.
13. Fox S. *E-Patients: Chronically Ill Seek Health Information Online.* Pew Internet and American Life Project. August 28 2008. http://pewresearch. org/pubs/938/e-patients-chronically-ill-seek-health-information-online. Accessed May 1, 2009.

14. Harris Interactive Inc. *Four Out of Five Adults Now Use the Internet.* November 17, 2008. http://www.harrisinteractive.com/harris_poll/index.asp?PID=973. Accessed May 18, 2009.

15. Kibbe DC, McLaughlin CP. The Alternative route: Hanging out the unmentionables for better decision making in health information technology. *Health Aff.* 2008;27(5):396-398. http://content.healthaffairs.org/cgi/content/abstract/27/5/w396. Accessed May 1, 2009.

16. Honey M, Westbrooke L. Nursing informatics issues and progress in New Zealand. In: Hyeoun-Ae Park, Peter Murray, Connie Delaney, eds. *Consumer-centered Computer-supported Care for Healthy People.* Proceedings of The 9th International Congress on Nursing Informatics (NI2006). Seoul, South Korea. 9-14 June. Amsterdam: IOS Press; 2006:544-547.

17. Conrick M. *Health informatics: Transforming Healthcare with Technology.* Melbourne, Australia: Thomson Social Science Press; 2006.

18. Simpson RL. Coherent heterogeneity: Redefining nursing in a consumer-smart world. In: Hyeoun-Ae Park, Peter Murray, Connie Delaney, eds. *Consumer-centered Computer-supported Care for Healthy People.* Proceedings of The 9th International Congress on Nursing Informatics (NI2006). Seoul, South Korea. 9-14 June. Amsterdam: IOS Press; 2006:3-8.

19. World Health Organization. *eHealth for Health Care Delivery.* http://www.who.int/eht/eHealth-HCD/en/. Accessed May 18, 2009,

20. World Health Organization. *The World Health Report 2003.* Geneva: World Health Organization; 2003.

21. World Health Organization. *Why Are Chronic Conditions Increasing? The Demographic Tansition.* Geneva: World Health Organization; 2004.

22. World Health Organization. *Innovative Care for Chronic Conditions: Building Blocks for Action: Global report.* Geneva: World Health Organization; 2002.

23. Flinders Human Behaviour and Health Research Unit. *What is Self-management?* Adelaide, Australia: Flinders University; 2006. http://som.flinders.edu.au/FUSA/CCTU/Self-Management.htm, Accessed January 30, 2009.

24. National Health Committee. *People with Chronic Conditions: A discussion paper.* Wellington, New Zealand: National Advisory Committee on Health and Disability; 2005.

25. National Health Committee. *Meeting the Needs of People with Chronic Conditions.* Wellington, New Zealand: National Advisory Committee on Health and Disability; 2007.

26. Sheridan N, Parsons J, Afamasaga L, et al. Report to Counties Manukau District Health Board: *Chronic Conditions and Care: What Consumers Say.* Auckland: University of Auckland; 2009.

27. Fox S. *The Engaged E-Patient Population.* Pew Internet and American Life Project. August 26 2008. http://www.pewinternet.org/Reports/2008/The-Engaged-Epatient-Population.aspx. Accessed May 1, 2009.

28. Sable JH, Hales JW, Bopp KD. *Medical Information Healthcare Organizations: A Survey of Health Information Managers.* Proceedings of the American Medical Informatics Association. 2000:745-748. http://www.amia.org/pubs/proceedings/symposia/2000/D200327.pdf. Accessed May 1, 2009.

29. Hecker D. *Occupational Employment Projections to 2010, Monthly Labor Review.* 2001;124(11). http://www.bls.gov/opub/mlr/2001/11/art4exc.htm.

30. National Health Service. *NHS Informatics Workforce Survey.* Washington: NHS; 2006. http://www.bcs.org/upload/pdf/finalreport_20061120102537.pdf. Accessed May 1, 2009.

31. American Nurses Association. *Scope and Standards of Nursing Informatics.* Washington, DC; 2009.

32. *HIMSS 2009 Informatics Nurse Impact Survey Final Report. Healthcare Information Management Systems Society Analytics.* April 2, 2009. http://www.himss.org/ASP/topics_FocusDynamic.asp?faid=243. Accessed May 1, 2009.

33. Perlin JB, Gelinas LS. American Health Information Community; Washington, DC; 2008. *Electronic Health Records Workgroup Recommendations.* http://www.hhs.gov/healthit/documents/m20080115/09-ehr_recs_ltr.html. Accessed February 20, 2008.

34. Hersh W, Wright A. *Characterizing the Health Information Workforce: Analysis from the HIMSS Analytics™ Database.* http://medir.ohsu.edu/~hersh/hit-workforce-hersh.pdf. Accessed May 1, 2009.

35. Brittain JM, Norris AC. Delivery of health informatics education and training. *Health Libr Rev.* 2008;17:117-128.

36. Ozbolt J. *An Environmental Scan: Educating the Health Informatics Workforce in the Global South. Making the Health Connection.* Bellagio, Italy. July 13-August 8, 2008. http://ehealth-connection.org/content/health-informatics-and-ehealth-capacity-building-overview. Accessed May 1, 2009.

37. University of Minnesota School of Nursing Doctorate of Nursing Practice. http://www.nursing.umn.edu/DNP/. Accessed May 1, 2009.

38. http://www.amia.org/ni-wg/ni-wg-documents. Accessed June 4, 2009.

39. American College of Medical Informatics. Core content for the subspecialty of clinical informatics. Version 10.0 July 1, 2008. www.amia.org/reports. Accessed November 9, 2009.

40. Gardner RM, Overage JM, Steen EB, et al. Core content for the subspecialty of clinical informatics. *JAMIA.* 2009;16:153-157.

41. Kerr K, Cullen R, Duke J, et al. Health Informatics Capability Development in New Zealand: A report to the Tertiary Education Commission. Wellington, New Zealand: National Steering Committee for Health Informatics Education in New Zealand; 2006. http://homepages.mcs.vuw.ac.nz/~peterk/healthinformatics/tec-hi-report-06.pdf, Accessed April 25, 2009.

42. Allen IE, Seaman J. Staying the Course: Online Education in the United States. 2008. Needham MA: Sloan Consortium. http://www.sloan-c.org/publications/survey/pdf/staying_the_course.pdf. Accessed April 24, 2009.

43. Rodgerson-Revell P. Directions in e-learning tools and technologies and their relevance to online distance language education. *Open learning.* 2007;22(1):57-74.

44. http://secondlifegrid.net/slfe/education-use-virtual-world. Accessed August 7, 2009.

45. Brixey JJ, Warren JJ. (June 28 - July 1, 2009). Creating experiential learning activities using Web 2.0 tools and technologies: A case study. Paper to be presented at the 10th International Congress on Nursing Informatics.

46. International Council of Nurses. ICN Nursing Education Network. Geneva: ICN; 2009.

47. World Health Organization. Eleventh General Programme of Work, 2006-2015: A global health agenda. Geneva: World Health Organization; 2006.

48. Health Workforce Advisory Committee. *The New Zealand Health Workforce: A Stocktake of Issues and Capacity; 2001.* Wellington, New Zealand; 2002.

49. Productivity Commission. *The Health Workforce Productivity Commission Issues Paper.* Canberra, Australia: The Council of Australian Governments (COAG); 2005.

50. World Health Organization. *Strengthening Public Health Workforce in South East Asia Region Countries.* Geneva: World Health Organization; 2006.

51. Smedley A. The importance of informatics competencies in nursing: An Australian perspective. *CIN.* 2005;23:106-110.

52. Holloway K. The future for nursing education: UKCC review has relevance for New Zealand. *Nursing Praxis in New Zealand.* 2000;16:17-24.

53. KPMG Consulting, Nursing Council of New Zealand. KPMG *Strategic Review of Undergraduate Nursing Education: Final report to the Nursing Council of New Zealand.* Wellington, New Zealand: Nursing Council of New Zealand; 2001

54. Marin HF. International perspectives: Nursing informatics in South America. In: Saba VK, McCormick KA, eds. *Essentials of Nursing Informatics.* New York: McGraw-Hill; 2006:663-667.

55. Hovenga EJS, Carr R, Honey M, Westbrooke L. International perspectives: Pacific rim. In: Saba VK, McCormick KA, eds. *Essentials of Nursing Informatics.* New York: McGraw-Hill; 2006:629-645.

56. Hannah KJ, Hammell N, Nagle LM. International perspectives: Nursing informatics in Canada. In: Saba VK, McCormick KA, eds. *Essentials of Nursing Informatics.* New York: McGraw-Hill; 2006:607-619.

57. Ehnfors M, Ehrenberg A, Rolf N. International perspectives: Nursing informatics in Europe. In: Saba VK, McCormick KA, eds. *Essentials of Nursing Informatics.* New York: McGraw-Hill; 2006:621-628.

58. Park H. International perspectives: Nursing informatics in Asia. In: Saba VK, McCormick KA, eds. *Essentials of Nursing Informatics.* New York: McGraw-Hill; 2006:647-662.

59. Fetter MS. Curriculum strategies to Improve baccalaureate nursing information technology outcomes. *J Nurs Educ.* 2009;48:78-85.

60. Fetter MS. Graduating nurses' self-evaluation of information technology competencies. *J Nurs Educ.* 2009;48:86-90.

61. Greiner AC, Knebel E. eds. Institute of Medicine. *Health Professions Education: A Bridge to Quality.* Washington, DC: The National Academies Press; 2003.

62. *Preparing the Next Generation of Nurses to Practice in a Technology-rich Environment: An Informatics. NLN position statement.* 2008. http://www.nln.org/aboutnln/PositionStatements/informatics_052808.pdf. Accessed April 25, 2009.

63. *The Essentials of Baccalaureate Education for Professional Nursing Practice.* AACN. http://www.aacn.nche.edu/education/pdf/BaccEssentials08.pdf. Accessed April 25, 2009.

64. Cronenwett L, Sherwood G, Barnsteiner, et al. Quality and safety education for nurses. *Nurs Outlook.* 2007;55:122-131. www.qsen.org. Accessed April 30, 2009.

65. www.tigereducation.pbwiki.com. Accessed May 4, 2009.

66. Tanner A, Pierce S, Pravikoff D. Moving the nursing information agenda forward. *CIN.* 2004;22:300-302.

67. Thompson B, Skiba DJ. Informatics in the Nursing Curriculum: A National Survey of Nursing Informatics Requirements in Nursing Curricula. *Nurs Educ Perspect.* 2008;29(5):312-317.

68. University of Colorado Denver College of Nursing. Educator's certificate in healthcare informatics. http://www.nursing.ucdenver.edu/grad/off_prof_dev2.htm#5. Accessed May 18, 2009.

69. National Institutes of Health. Glossary. 2009. http://report.nih.gov/glossary.aspx?filter=T. Accessed May 18, 2009.

70. Payne P. *Defining Translational Research Informatics.* 2008. http://translationalresearchinformatics.blogspot.com/2008/01/defining-translational-research.html. Accessed May 18, 2009.

71. International Council of Nurses. *International Classification for Nursing Practice.* Geneva: ICN; 2009.

## CHAPTER 6

The Impact of Health Information Technology (I-HIT) Survey: Results from an International Research Collaborative

By Patricia C. Dykes, DNSc, MA, RN; Suzanne Brown, MSc Health Informatics, BNS; Rita W. Collins, PhD, MEd, BNS, RN, RM; Robyn Cook, MBA, BBus, RN; Charles Docherty, PhD, MN, MBCS, BN, RN, RNT; Anneli Ensio, PhD, RN; Joanne Foster, GradDipCIEdn, MEdTech, DipAppSc (NsgEd), BN, RN; Nicholas R. Hardiker, PhD, RN; Michelle LL Honey, PhD, MPhil (Nursing), RN, FCNA (NZ); Rosaleen Killalea, MSc Nursing, BNS, RN; and Kaija Saranto, PhD, RN

Introduction

The role of nurses as communicators and integrators of care is well-established.[1-3] Advances in technology generate new opportunities to enhance the role of nurses and to establish a linkage between nursing practice and patient safety outcomes. This is particularly true in acute care hospital settings at which nurses are at the hub of communication between professional and paraprofessional providers, patients, and family members. Nurses' access to technology improves communication and workflow and prevents information bottlenecks from occurring.[4] Information and communication tools such as messaging, tracking systems, hands-free paging, electronic medication administration, and components of clinical information systems are examples of technologies that hold potential to support effective and safe nursing care. However, poorly designed systems including systems that are not interoperable are frequently implemented.[5] Most end-users may reject these implemented systems as unhelpful and unsafe, but when used by others, these systems may present a danger to patients. To promote efficient and safe care, technology or devices must be implemented within a safe workflow process.[5] Recent studies suggest poorly designed or implemented technologies may be an impediment to effective communication and a contributor to adverse events.[6,7] The ability of bedside nurses to carry out integrating activities is dependent on ubiquitous access to information and tools to support effective communication. As is happening internationally, while hospitals are transitioning from paper-based to electronic systems, it is necessary to develop ways to explore the impact of health IT on nursing practice.

In 2005, HIMSS' nursing informatics community developed the Impact of Health Information Technology (I-HIT) Scale to measure the impact of health IT on the nursing role and on the interdisciplinary communication occurring in hospitals in the United States.[8] The development and testing of the I-HIT Scale in the United States has been described in detail elsewhere.[8,9] In 2007, nursing informatics colleagues from Australia, England, Finland, Ireland, New Zealand, Scotland, and the United States formed a research collaborative under the auspices of the International Medical Informatics Association – Nursing Informatics (IMIA-NI) Special Interest Group to validate the I-HIT in six additional countries. Each of the participating country leads was also the country representative into IMIA-NI, with the exception of England.

While the collaborative faced multiple barriers to full validation of the I-HIT Scale, key information was gained regarding content and face validity of the survey items. The survey responses to date provide a preliminary baseline for comparison of the current state of health IT in hospital settings. In addition, the resulting database from this effort may inform recommendations related to health IT design and implementation to better support nursing practice.

Objectives

This chapter provides an overview of the survey validation process, results to date of construct and face validation, and survey dissemination for reliability testing. In addition, a descriptive analysis of responses is outlined to provide an initial glimpse at the degree to which respondents believe that existing technologies support nurses and interdisciplinary communication in hospitals. In accordance with established procedures,[10] the international team originally agreed on five phases of survey validation and dissemination: (1) content and face validation (including translation/back translation in Finland), (2) dissemination of validated survey for reliability testing, (3) psychometric evaluation, (4) dissemination of validated survey, and (5) results reporting. The focus of this chapter is phases 1 and 2 and a descriptive evaluation of preliminary survey results across participating countries. Finally, case studies from members of the research collaborative are included to provide additional detail related to the validation process in several of the participating countries.

Methods

Materials and Methods: Content and Face Validation

Content and Face Validation. Content validation involved review of the I-HIT Scale by nursing informatics experts in participating countries to ensure that the language used was clear and culturally appropriate. Modifications were made so that each I-HIT item was conceptually equivalent with the same item in the U.S. version of the scale. International experts verified that each of the 29 survey items was clear, understandable, and culturally appropriate. Following established methods[10] of asking content judges to use a four-point scale to rate each item for content validity (CV), the 90% average congruency standard was used to retain items in each country's I-HIT. Each international colleague recruited four nurse experts in health IT to rate each item for relevance (the degree to which each item is relevant to the impact of health IT on the role of nurses and interdisciplinary communication in hospital settings) and interpretability (the degree to which each item can be interpreted and understood within the culture) using the following four-point scale: 1 = not relevant/not interpretable; 2 = unable to assess relevance or interpretability without item revision; 3 = relevant/interpretable but needs minor alterations; 4 = very relevant/easily interpretable. Experts also provided comments for improving relevance/interpretability for items rated ≤4. Scores and comments from experts were evaluated and used to modify items.

To establish face validity,[11] focus groups were held with hospital-based nurses to review I-HIT items. Nurses summarized the meaning of each item, made suggestions for language modifications, and provided feedback on administration instructions. Validated items were used to build a Web-based version of the I-HIT for each collaborating country and disseminated to initiate reliability testing.

Results: Content and Face Validation

All 29 items were scored as relevant and interpretable in Ireland; 28 in Scotland; 27 in Australia and New Zealand; and 23 in England. Two items related to the acknowledgment features of current health IT applications/tools were unable to be validated in three of the five participating countries. The following two items were initially rated poorly ("1" or "2") on relevance and interpretability (e.g., low relevance/ interpretability) by content reviewers in four of the five countries that completed this phase of testing:

- I find the acknowledgement features of current HIT applications/tools provide adequate assurance that my interdisciplinary colleagues have received the communications that I send.
- I find the acknowledgement features of current HIT applications/tools provide adequate assurance that my interdisciplinary colleagues have acted upon information that I send.

Modifications of language and the addition of examples brought the ratings up to "3" or "4" in Ireland and Scotland, so that the items were retained in the scale. These two items were not validated in Australia, England, and New Zealand. See Table 6-1 for content and face validation results. Modifications of survey items along with original I-HIT items are included in Table 6-2.

Materials and Methods: Survey Dissemination for Validation

Sample and Procedures. The I-HIT was modified to incorporate content and face validation results and a separate survey was posted to the Internet using the *Survey Monkey* software package for each participating country. The I-HIT Scale targets nurses practicing in acute care settings. Participants were recruited by each country's representative to the International Medical Informatics Association – Nursing Informatics Special Interest Group (IMIA/NI-SIG). Country representatives used their professional organization networks to invite participation via e-mail and healthcare-related listservs. Statistically, this approach would be described as a non-probability snowball sampling technique. Contacts were asked to pass the link on to others with contacts in acute care settings. An inherent disadvantage of using this sampling method is that we were unable to determine how many individuals received a request to complete the survey and therefore, we were unable to calculate a response rate.[12]

The I-HIT survey was formatted for the Web and organized under the four subscales identified from the psychometric analysis completed using U.S. responses[8]: (1) general advantages of health IT, (2) workflow implications of health IT, (3) information tools to support communication tasks, and (4) information tools to support information tasks. Respondents were asked to self-report their beliefs on scale items, reflecting their own experiences with health IT applications and tools currently available in their work setting. A 6-point Likert Rating Scale was used, with values ranging from "1" ("Strongly Disagree") to "6" ("Strongly Agree"). An additional item to explore overall satisfaction with health IT applications and tools currently available in hospital settings was added to the bottom of the Web survey, along with a demographic questionnaire.

Results and Descriptive Analysis

Responses to the reliability testing of the Web-based I-HIT ranged from 53 (England) to 1,135 (Australia). Responses by participating country are included in Table 6-3. While reliability testing of the I-HIT survey was conducted in the United States in 2005, U.S. results are included in the results tables here for comparison purposes.

A total of 2,822 respondents answered the Web survey across participating countries. Survey respondents were mostly female (89.8%), older than 40 years (69.3%), direct care providers (59.6%), employed in nursing more than 20 years (50.6%), and well-educated (73.2% held a bachelor's degree or higher). The Australian (1,144) and U.S. (1,079) sample sizes provide more than 10 respondents per item, which is adequate to undertake a principal component analysis to validate the survey items. The sample sizes in other participating countries, ranging from 53 to 173, are insufficient for this purpose.[13,14] A descriptive analysis of responses is outlined next and includes similarities and differences with the degree to which respondents believe that existing technologies support nurses and interdisciplinary communication in hospitals.

Survey results (in the aggregate across all countries) are included with each I-HIT item in Table 6-4. Most respondents (mean 60%) reported that they were satisfied with the health IT applications/tools currently available in their hospital (see Figure 6-1).

Table 6-1. I-HIT Scale Content/FaceValidation Results

	Australia	England	*Finland	Ireland	Scotland	New Zealand
General advantages of HIT						
1. HIT applications/tools have decreased the time I need for end of shift report.		E				
2. HIT applications have decreased the need for direct communication around writing patient orders.	E,L	E			L	E,L
3. HIT provides better information to prepare me for my assigned patients each day.		E,L		L		
4. HIT facilitates practice efficiency.		NV			L	
5. HIT allows for patient/family participation in care		L			L	L
6. The ability of interdisciplinary team members to access information electronically has reduced their need to communicate directly with each other face-to-face or via phone.		E				
7. The ability of nurses to access information electronically has improved their ability to independently make decisions.	L	E				
8. HIT applications available at my facility improve my ability to assume care for patients transferring into my unit.		E		L	L	
9. Work lists generated from HIT tools support efficient patient care.		L				
Workflow Implications of HIT						
1. The ways in which data/information are displayed using HIT improves access to data.	E,L	NV			NV	L
2. HIT depersonalizes care.		E				
3. The HIT applications available at my site help me to process data and therefore improve access to information necessary to provide safe patient care.		L		L	L	
4. The availability of electronic interdisciplinary documentation has improved the capacity of clinicians to work together.		L			L	
5. HIT applications/tools support the nursing process.						L
6. The ways in which data/information are displayed using HIT reduces redundancy of care.	E,L	E,L				L
7. The ways in which data/information are displayed using HIT facilitates interdisciplinary care planning.						L
8. HIT applications/tools facilitate interdisciplinary treatment planning.		L				
Information Tools to Support Communication Tasks						
1. My site is utilizing HIT strategies to optimize interdisciplinary communication (e.g. clinical messaging, Vocera or similar wireless voice communication system, text paging).	L	L		L		L
2. Available HIT applications/tools facilitate the process of patient tracking.		E				
3. I have access to HIT applications/tools that support interdisciplinary communication when I need them.						
4. Available HIT tools support both patient care and administrative processes.						
5. HIT facilitates ID communication that is patient centered.		L				
6. The availability of information afforded by HIT at my site helps nurses collaborate at a higher level with interdisciplinary colleagues than was possible with paper systems.	L	E,L		L	L	
7. I know how to access the HIT applications/tools available in the electronic medical record system.	L	NV			L	
Information Tools to Support Information Tasks						
1. I find the acknowledgement features of current HIT applications/tools provide adequate assurance that my interdisciplinary colleagues have received the communications that I send	NV	NV		E	E	NV
2. I find the acknowledgement features of current HIT applications/tools provide adequate assurance that interdisciplinary colleagues have acted upon information that I send.	NV	NV		E	E	NV
3. HIT promotes 2-way communication between clinicians about patient status.		E,L			L	L
4. Communication of critical events to interdisciplinary colleagues can be done effectively using HIT.		L			L	L
5. HIT applications/tools help me to be problem-focused in my communications.	E	NV		E	L	L

Key: Modifications required to establish content/face validity
L=Language modification   E=Example(s) added for clarification
NV=Content validity not established
*Translation/back translation required for validation

Table 6-1. *Continued*

	Australia	England	*Finland	Ireland	Scotland	New Zealand
General advantages of HIT						
1. HIT applications/tools have decreased the time I need for end of shift report.		E				
2. HIT applications have decreased the need for direct communication around writing patient orders.	E,L	E			L	E,L
3. HIT provides better information to prepare me for my assigned patients each day.		E,L		L		
4. HIT facilitates practice efficiency.		NV			L	
5. HIT allows for patient/family participation in care		L			L	L
6. The ability of interdisciplinary team members to access information electronically has reduced their need to communicate directly with each other face-to-face or via phone.		E				
7. The ability of nurses to access information electronically has improved their ability to independently make decisions.	L	E				
8. HIT applications available at my facility improve my ability to assume care for patients transferring into my unit.		E		L	L	
9. Work lists generated from HIT tools support efficient patient care.		L				
Workflow Implications of HIT						
1. The ways in which data/ information are displayed using HIT improves access to data.	E,L	NV			NV	L
2. HIT depersonalizes care.		E				
3. The HIT applications available at my site help me to process data and therefore improve access to information necessary to provide safe patient care.		L		L	L	
4. The availability of electronic interdisciplinary documentation has improved the capacity of clinicians to work together.		L			L	
5. HIT applications/tools support the nursing process.						L
6. The ways in which data/ information are displayed using HIT reduces redundancy of care.	E,L	E,L				L
7. The ways in which data/ information are displayed using HIT facilitates interdisciplinary care planning.						L
8. HIT applications/tools facilitate interdisciplinary treatment planning.		L				
Information Tools to Support Communication Tasks						
1. My site is utilizing HIT strategies to optimize interdisciplinary communication (e.g. clinical messaging, Vocera or similar wireless voice communication system, text paging).	L	L		L		L
2. Available HIT applications/tools facilitate the process of patient tracking.		E				
3. I have access to HIT applications/tools that support interdisciplinary communication when I need them.						
4. Available HIT tools support both patient care and administrative processes.						
5. HIT facilitates ID communication that is patient centered.		L				
6. The availability of information afforded by HIT at my site helps nurses collaborate at a higher level with interdisciplinary colleagues than was possible with paper systems.	L	E,L		L	L	
7. I know how to access the HIT applications/tools available in the electronic medical record system.	L	NV			L	
Information Tools to Support Information Tasks						
1. I find the acknowledgement features of current HIT applications/tools provide adequate assurance that my interdisciplinary colleagues have received the communications that I send	NV	NV		E	E	NV
2. I find the acknowledgement features of current HIT applications/tools provide adequate assurance that interdisciplinary colleagues have acted upon information that I send.	NV	NV		E	E	NV
3. HIT promotes 2-way communication between clinicians about patient status.		E,L			L	L
4. Communication of critical events to interdisciplinary colleagues can be done effectively using HIT.		L			L	L
5. HIT applications/tools help me to be problem-focused in my communications.	E	NV		E	L	L
Key: Modifications required to establish content/face validity L=Language modification E=Example(s) added for clarification NV=Content validity not established *Translation/back translation required for validation						

Table 6-2. Examples of I-HIT Scale Modified Items

Original Item	Modifications	Revised Item
HIT applications/tools have decreased the time I need for end of shift report.	• Example added • Language	Health Information Technology applications/tools have decreased the time I need for end of shift report (e.g., hand-over).
HIT applications have decreased the need for direct communication around writing patient orders.	• Example added • Language	Health Information Technology applications have decreased the need for direct communication around writing patient orders or requests (i.e., decreased the need to directly talk face-to-face or over phone with other providers about issues related to orders, requests, treatments, or lab orders).
HIT allows for patient/family participation in care.	• Language	Health Information Technology allows for (empowers) patient/family participation in care.
The ways in which data/ information are displayed using HIT reduces redundancy of care.	• Example added • Language	The ways in which data/information are displayed using Health Information Technology reduces duplication of recording care (i.e., record data once, but use the data many times).
HIT applications/tools support the nursing process.	• Example added • Language	Health Information Technology applications/tools support the nursing process (i.e., assess-plan-implement-evaluate).
Communication of critical events to interdisciplinary colleagues can be done effectively using HIT.	• Language	Communication of critical (i.e., emergency or high priority) events to interdisciplinary colleagues (multidisciplinary team) can be done effectively using Health Information Technology.

Table 6-3. Responses to Dissemination of Web-based Survey for Purpose of Reliability Testing

Country	Responses to Date
Australia	1144
England	53
Finland	129
Ireland	173
Scotland	112
New Zealand	132
*United States	1079

*I-HIT Reliability testing completed in the United States in 2005[8]

   I-HIT items for which most respondents reported disagreement related to the adequacy of existing HIT applications and tools are listed next under the corresponding subscale (see Table 6-5 for detail by country). For the purpose of the descriptive analysis, response options were collapsed into two categories: "Agree" and "Disagree." The "Not Applicable" (NA) responses were not included in the analysis.

General Advantages of Health IT
- Health IT applications/tools have decreased the time I need for end of shift report.
- Health IT applications have decreased the need for direct communication around writing patient orders.
- Health IT allows for patient/family participation in care.

Workflow Implications of Health IT
- Health IT depersonalizes care.

Table 6-4. I-HIT Subscales, Survey Items, and Mean Level of Agreement Across Participating Countries with Each Item

I-HIT Subscale	I-HIT Item	N	%
General Advantages of HIT	HIT applications/tools have decreased the time I need for end of shift report.	1829	48.6%
	HIT applications have decreased the need for direct communication around writing patient orders.	2090	50.8%
	HIT provides better information to prepare me for my assigned patients each day.	2033	68.9%
	HIT facilitates practice efficiency.	2172	74.9%
	HIT allows for patient/family participation in care.	2007	41.0%
	The ability of interdisciplinary team members to access information electronically has reduced their need to communicate directly with each other face-to-face or via phone.	2170	61.8%
	The ability of nurses to access information electronically has improved their ability to independently make decisions.	2174	70.7%
	HIT applications available at my facility improve my ability to assume care for patients transferring into my unit.	1987	59.7%
	Work lists generated from HIT tools support efficient patient care.	1861	68.4%
Workflow Implications of HIT	The ways in which data/ information are displayed using HIT improves access to data.	2021	81.4%
	HIT depersonalizes care.	2016	33.9%
	The HIT applications available at my site help me to process data and therefore improve access to information necessary to provide safe patient care.	2022	83.8%
	The availability of electronic interdisciplinary documentation has improved the capacity of clinicians to work together.	1837	74.4%
	HIT applications/tools support the nursing process.	1924	75.8%
	The ways in which data/ information are displayed using HIT reduces redundancy of care.	1926	65.6%
	The ways in which data/ information are displayed using HIT facilitates interdisciplinary care planning.	1917	72.2%
	HIT applications/tools facilitate interdisciplinary treatment planning.	1942	76.6%
Information Tools to Support Communication Tasks	My site is utilizing HIT strategies to optimize interdisciplinary communication (e.g., clinical messaging, Vocera, or similar wireless voice communication system, text paging).	1765	62.6%
	Available HIT applications/tools facilitate the process of patient tracking.	1856	85.8%
	I have access to HIT applications/tools that support interdisciplinary communication when I need them.	1862	68.3%
	Available HIT tools support both patient care and administrative processes.	1925	79.1%
	HIT facilitates ID communication that is patient centered.	1884	72.5%
	The availability of information afforded by HIT at my site helps nurses collaborate at a higher level with interdisciplinary colleagues than was possible with paper systems.	1836	62.7%
	I know how to access the HIT applications/tools available in the electronic medical record system.	1781	82.8%
Information Tools to Support Information Tasks	I find the acknowledgement features of current HIT applications/tools provide adequate assurance that my interdisciplinary colleagues have received the communications that I send.	1743	57.0%
	I find the acknowledgement features of current HIT applications/tools provide adequate assurance that interdisciplinary colleagues have acted upon information that I send.	1726	38.9%
	HIT promotes 2-way communication between clinicians about patient status.	1830	65.0%
	Communication of critical events to interdisciplinary colleagues can be done effectively using HIT.	1841	63.9%
	HIT applications/tools help me to be problem-focused in my communications.	1832	26.4%

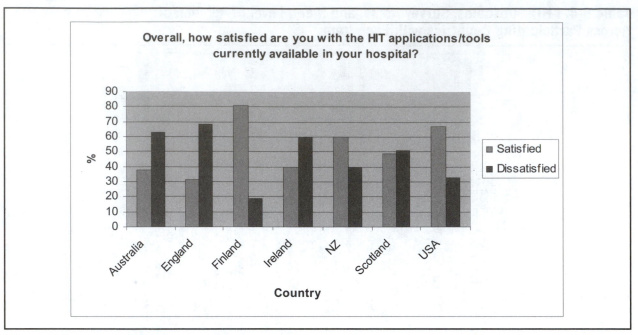

Figure 6-1. *Satisfaction with HIT Applications/Tools Currently Available*

Table 6-5. I-HIT Items with Mean Agreement <50%

	Subscale 1: General Advantages of HIT			Subscale 2: Workflow Implications of HIT	Subscale 4: Information Tools to Support Information Tasks
	HIT has decreased the time I need for end of shift report (e.g., hand-over)	HIT applications have decreased the need for direct communication around writing patient orders	HIT allows for patient/family participation in care	HIT depersonalizes care	I find the acknowledgement features of current HIT applications/tools provide adequate assurance that interdisciplinary colleagues have acted upon information that I send
Australia	41.2%	42.3%	27.2%	40.8%	26.0%
England	48.5%	54.5%	50.0%	38.5%	45.0%
Finland	68.2%	79.0%	33.3%	22.5%	24.9%
Ireland	45.6%	54.0%	42.2%	31.7%	46.9%
New Zealand	48.0%	42.5%	35.9%	36.0%	41.1%
Scotland	35.6%	35.7%	46.2%	42.0%	46.0%
United States	53.0%	47.4%	52.9%	31.0%	44.2%
Mean Agreement	**49.0%**	**47.5%**	**42.4%**	**33.9%**	**38.9%**

Information Tools to Support Information Tasks
- I find the acknowledgement features of current health IT applications/tools provide adequate assurance that interdisciplinary colleagues have acted upon information that I send.

Those I-HIT items with which most respondents reported significant agreement (e.g., ≥ 75%) were about the adequacy of existing health IT applications and tools and are listed next by country of origin under the corresponding subscale (see Table 6-6 for response detail by participating country).

Table 6-6. I-HIT Items with Mean Agreement >/=75%

	Subscale 1: General Advantages of HIT		Subscale 2: Workflow Implications of HIT			Subscale 3: Information Tools to Support Communication Tasks		
	HIT facilitates practice efficiency	The ways in which data/information are displayed using HIT improves access to data	The HIT applications available at my site help me to process data and therefore improve access to information necessary to provide safe patient care	HIT applications/tools support the nursing process	HIT applications/tools facilitate interdisciplinary treatment planning	Available HIT applications/tools facilitate the process of patient tracking	Available HIT applications/tools support both patient care and administrative processes	I know how to access the HIT applications/tools available in the electronic medical record system
Australia	64.9%	74.7%	76.3%	67.7%	67.5%	83%	74.6%	66.9%
England	83.7%	81.6%	78.8%	62.3%	67.6%	85.7%	70.6%	77.4%
Finland	80.0%	78.3%	90.7%	82.9%	83.0%	85.2%	82.2%	90.7%
Ireland	86.2%	90.1%	81.1%	84.5%	84.4%	87.7%	78.4%	73.3%
New Zealand	75.5%	89.8%	83.9%	69.1%	78.3%	90.9%	83.3%	92.2%
Scotland	75.2%	78.7%	80.5%	82.3%	69.7%	88.2%	78.1%	80.6%
United States	79.6%	83.9%	87.5%	78.4%	80%	86.5%	81%	88.8%
Mean Agreement	**74.9%**	**81.4%**	**83.8%**	**75.8%**	**76.6%**	**85.8%**	**79.1%**	**82.7%**

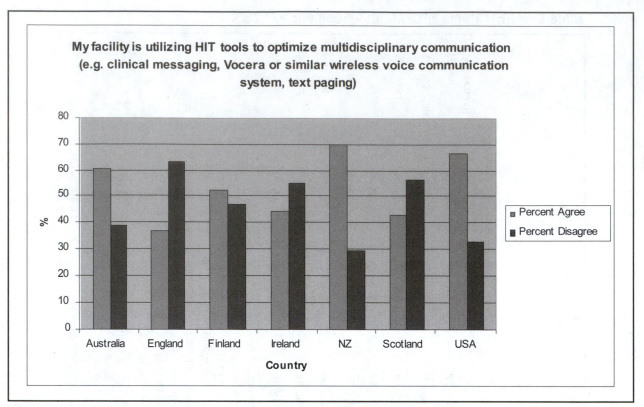

Figure 6-2. *I-HIT Item with Most Variable Response Across Participating Countries*

General Advantages of Health IT
- Health IT facilitates practice efficiency.

Workflow Implications of Health IT
- The ways in which data/information are displayed using health IT improves access to data.
- The health IT applications available at my site help me to process data and therefore improve access to information necessary to provide safe patient care.
- Health IT applications/tools support the nursing process.
- Health IT applications/tools facilitate interdisciplinary treatment planning.

Information Tools to Support Communication Tasks
- Available health IT applications/tools facilitate the process of patient-tracking.
- Available health IT tools support both patient care and administrative processes.
- I know how to access the health IT applications/tools available in the electronic medical record system.

The following I-HIT item had the most variability in responses across participating countries (see Figure 6-2):

- My facility is utilizing HIT tools to optimize multidisciplinary communication (e.g., clinical messaging, Vocera or similar wireless voice communication system, text paging).

Discussion

The I-HIT Scale was developed to provide a means to measure nurses' perceptions about the ways in which health IT influences interdisciplinary communication and workflow patterns, as well as nurses' satisfaction with health IT applications and tools currently available in hospitals. The I-HIT Scale was validated in the U.S. in 2007[8] and initial testing indicates that it has adequate psychometric properties for continued use in hospital settings. The validation work completed to date indicates that most I-HIT Scale items were rated as both relevant and interpretable by the international content experts. However, most items required minor modi-

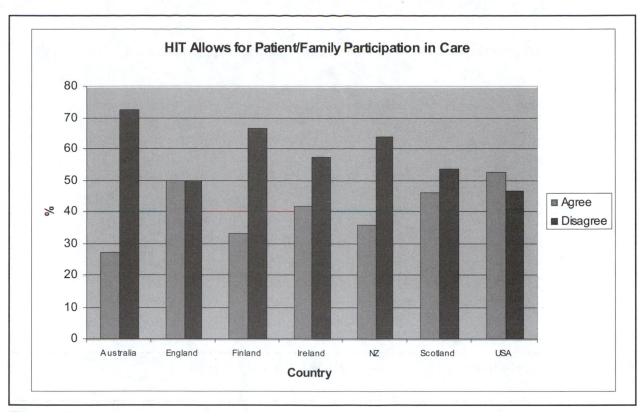

Figure 6-3. *HIT Allows for Patient/family Participation in Care*

fications in language or the addition of examples to improve relevance and interpretability (see Table 6-2 for examples). English was the official language in five of the six participating countries, but slight differences in the use of language and terminology exist. Content experts suggested wording changes to achieve consistency with a country's use of terminology and to improve item interpretability. Examples are included in the case studies included in this chapter.

The sample sizes for most participating countries reported in this chapter are small and were primarily gathered for the purpose of instrument validation. However, they are a first attempt at establishing a baseline measurement in this area of research. Measurement is an important step in achieving quality.[15] Many of the participating countries are committed to continuing to track the impact of health IT on the role of nurses in hospitals. Even with the small sample sizes, a few trends were noted across countries. For example, several areas in which improvement is needed in designing health IT applications and tools were consistently reported across participating countries. Respondents reported that better tools are needed to support patient-centered care and handoff processes (see Figures 6-3 and 6-4).

Respondents answered positively to many items related to the degree to which existing health IT applications and tools support efficiency in practice and access to the data and information needed to provide safe care. Moreover, respondents in all participating countries overwhelmingly reported that they know how to access applications available in the EMR system (see Figures 6-5, 6-6, and 6-7).

While much work has been accomplished though this international collaborative, we face several ongoing challenges. In Finland, content and face validity testing involves translation and back translation, adding significant complexity to the validation process. Survey dissemination for reliability testing proved to be difficult for the participating countries. To validate the survey items, ten responses per item are needed.[13,14] The main difficulty associated with dissemination (with the exception of Ireland) is securing ethics approval so that national list-servs can be used to contact potential participants. The process for national ethics approval is

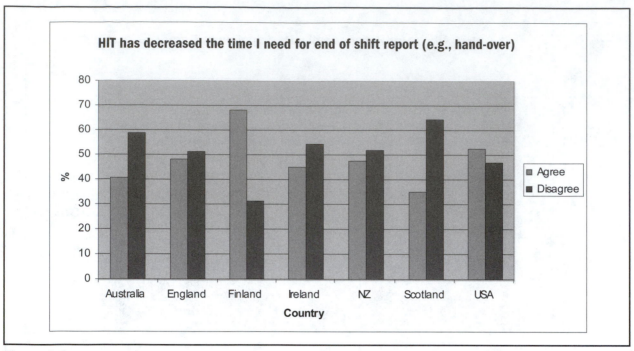

Figure 6-4. *HIT Has Decreased the Time I Need for End of Shift Report (e.g., Handoff)*

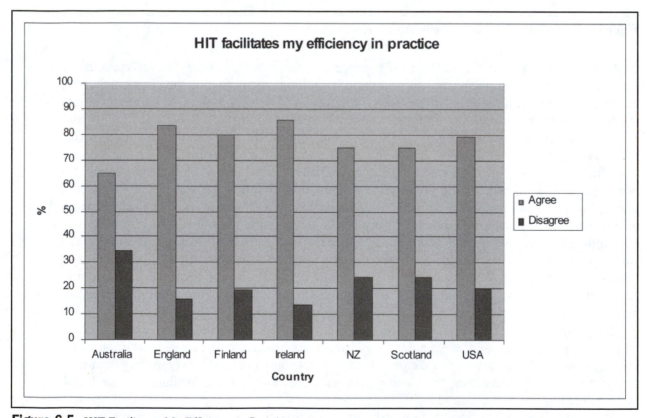

Figure 6-5. *HIT Facilitates My Efficiency in Practice*

labor intensive and adds additional burden on our all-volunteer team of nurse informatician researchers. However, based on response count to date, we believe national ethics approval is a prerequisite for securing an adequate response rate, so that we can move on to reliability testing. Recently, our Australian colleagues were able to secure national ethics approval and to gain access to national listservs. The result was that more than 1,100 Australian nurses

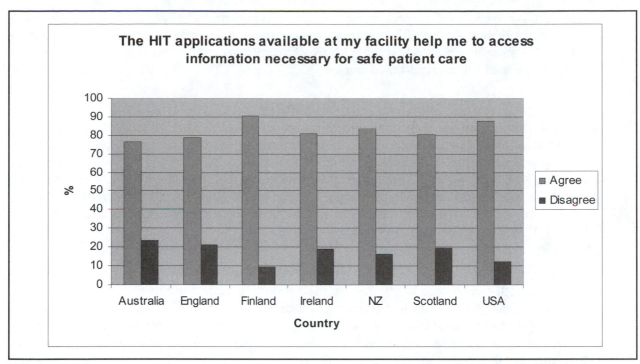

Figure 6-6. *The HIT Applications Available at My Facility Help Me to Access Information Necessary for Safe Patient Care*

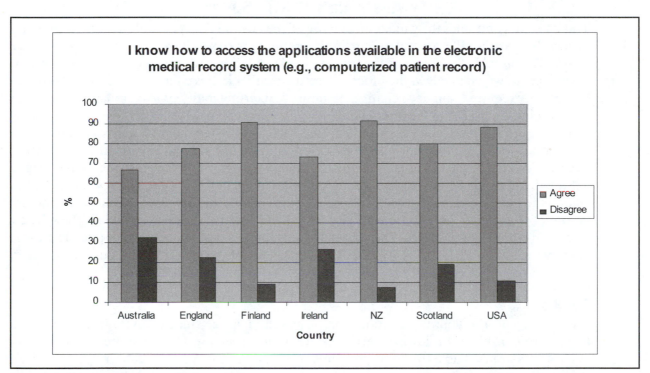

Figure 6-7. *I Know How to Access the Applications Available in the Electronic Medical Record System (e.g., Computerized Patient Record)*

responded to the Web-based survey in fewer than 30 days. In two of the other participating countries, Ireland and Scotland, lack of penetration of health IT in hospital settings proved to be an additional dissemination challenge.

Several limitations are associated with this work. The generality and validity of findings based on Web-based surveys are limited because respondents are restricted to those with access to the Internet, sufficient computer literacy skills, and time to complete an online survey.[12] In addition, the Web-based surveys are self-report, and non-probability sampling methods were used to recruit participants. The sample sizes are small in several of the countries. The non-probability sampling method, along with small sample sizes mean that responses may not be representative of all hospital-based nurses.

Summary

As hospitals around the globe transition from paper-based to electronic communication and documentation systems, it is necessary to develop ways to explore the impact of health IT on nursing practice. The I-HIT Scale is designed to measure the perception of nurses regarding the ways in which health IT influences interdisciplinary communication, workflow patterns, and the degree of satisfaction with health IT applications and tools. This international collaborative represents a first step toward devising a means to establish a baseline measure of the impact of health IT on nursing practice.

Case Studies

The authors for each case study discuss the validation work done in their country, including barriers and facilitators to validation and dissemination. Collectively these case studies provide a deeper understanding of local challenges, including socio-political factors that can impede a research agenda. Case studies are included from the following countries: Australia, England, Ireland, New Zealand, and Scotland.

Australia's (I-HIT) Survey

This case study outlines the validation and use of the health IT survey tool to assess the impact of health IT within the Australian nursing community and, specifically, within the acute care sector. The initial U.S. version of the tool required validation and conversion to the Australian environment, which involved the process described earlier in this chapter. Modifications to the tool mainly required language changes to improve interpretability by Australian nurses while maintaining alignment to the original intent of the survey tool. Most items were considered to be relevant to the Australian environment (see Table 6-1 for summary of modifications).

The health IT survey tool was constructed as an online survey. The Australian Nursing Federation (ANF), the key nursing industrial and professional body in Australia, was engaged for the distribution of the survey, through its state branches, to its members working in the acute care environment. Nurses self-selected participation in the survey. Due to the online nature of the survey, only those who had e-mail and Internet access were able to be advised of and to complete the survey. The completed surveys were automatically compiled in a database by the online survey tool. A total of 1443 participants responded to the survey; however, responses to any individual I-HIT item ranged from 485 (33.6%) to 738 (51.1%).

Results

The context of availability and utilization of health IT in the clinical environment has to be taken into consideration in the overall results from the survey. One or more of the following systems are available to the respondents (n=332): Patient Administration System (16%), Results Reporting (15%), Departmental Systems (12%), Order Entry (11%), Electronic Medical Record (10%), Text Paging (11%), Electronic Health Record (9%), and Messaging (9%). The mean agreement for I-HIT items for each of the four subscales ranged from 43 to 65%. Results are displayed in Table 6-7 and Figure 6-8.

Discussion

While nurses have access to a range of health IT applications, key nursing-related systems, such as clinical documentation and care planning tools, are still not readily available in the acute care sector. This impacts nurses' perceptions of the benefits of health IT, decreases satisfaction with health IT access, and reduces positive experiences related to using health IT in

Table 6-7. Australia Results; Mean Agreement by Subscale

Subscale	Mean Agreement Across Items
General Advantages of HIT	51%
Workflow Implications of HIT	63%
Information Tools to Support Communication Tasks	65%
Information Tools to Support Information Tasks	43%

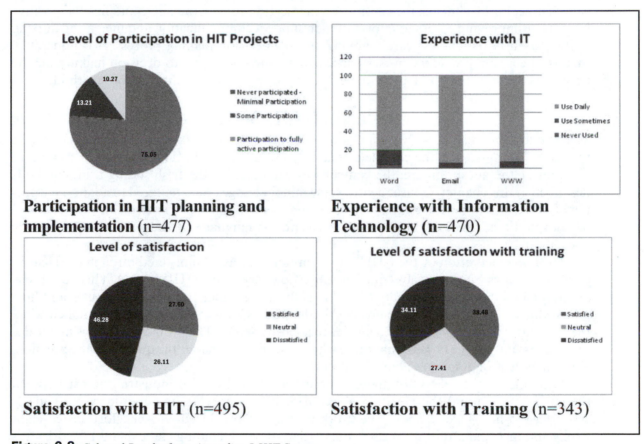

Figure 6-8. *Selected Results from Australian I-HIT Survey*

clinical practice. Nearly half (46.3%) of respondents reported that they were dissatisfied overall with health IT applications and tools available at their facility.

The nurse's role as a central communicator is impacted as health IT reduces the need for multidisciplinary face-to-face contact regarding patient care (58%); however, little impact in terms of safe care provision was identified by respondents to this survey. In contrast, health IT provides access to information that allows nurses to better prepare to deliver care (50.48%) and to support independent decision-making regarding care (63.56%). Positive aspects of health IT include the presence of information tools to support communication tasks including patient-tracking (75.52%), applications to support both patient care and administrative processes (69.73%). Other positive benefits of health IT include multiple access to information (76.52%), access to information for safe patient care (77.7%), support for the clinical decision-making process (58.26%), reduced duplication of care (51.66%), and facilitation of multidisciplinary care planning (53.85%).

The finding that more than 75% of respondents indicated they had not participated in implementing health IT at their facility is disturbing and highlights a potential impact on acceptance of and the integration of health IT into nursing practice. Most respondents are actively involved in direct patient care, thus requiring integration of health IT into their work practices. The lack of nurses' participation in health IT implementation at their facilities could have an impact on perceptions, as well as on the effective utilization of systems and tools.

Conclusion

Nurses can identify the positive aspects and benefits of health IT; however, many still do not have access to effective health IT tools to support effective nursing care. Survey results indicate that health IT changes the central communication role of the nurse and has the positive benefits of improving access to information to support communication and increasing nursing participation in the clinical care planning and the decision-making process. It is imperative that as direct care providers, nurses participate in and contribute to decision making for the implementation of health IT to ensure effective integration and utilization of health IT.

Ireland's (I-HIT) Survey

The Republic of Ireland, with a population of approximately 40,000 registered nurses, sought to recruit 300 nurses for the complete reliability testing of the I-HIT survey. Prior to administration of the questionnaire, the content was validated for the Irish setting using methods described in this chapter. Consequently, some minor changes were required to adapt the wording of some questions, for example, it was recommended that the word "facility" be changed to "hospital/organization" in an effort to ensure the language of the survey was culturally appropriate.

The implementation of the I-HIT survey in Ireland was administered through the Healthcare Informatics Society of Ireland Nursing-Midwifery Group (HISI-NM). This action circumvented the potential difficulty of seeking ethical clearance from numerous sites and hospitals which could potentially be involved in the study. Consent was taken to be implicit when the respondent accessed the site to answer the questionnaire. The problem with this method is that there is always the chance that those who are willing to answer the questionnaire are more apt to have a strong opinion about health IT.

The time of the release of the questionnaire coincided with industrial unrest between the nursing union and the Health Services Executive over working conditions, particularly a shorter (35-hour) work week. The 'work-to-rule,' an organized worker effort, lasted eight weeks and involved a refusal to carry out certain duties, including clerical and IT work. It is certain that this effort was instrumental in the relatively low response rate to participation in filling the questionnaire in Ireland. However, it is also possible that respondents did not see the questionnaire as relevant if their hospital did not have an information system in place. Across Ireland there are various levels of development/implementation of health IT adoption by hospitals, ranging from basic systems to fully integrated hospital information systems that include Computerized Physician Order Entry (CPOE) functionality. The survey sample in Ireland demonstrated a countrywide representation. This may have been helped by "word of mouth" (Network) and inclusion of the survey on an easily accessible Web site.

England's I-HIT Survey

Validation of the I-HIT Scale for England followed the agreed process to establish content and face validity before validation of the survey instrument itself. Ethical approval was granted by the University of Salford. The initial content validation activity resulted in substantial response to the original set of 29 items with revisions required for more than one third of items (see Table 6-8).

Many comments concerned writing style and confusion over key concepts. However, other comments alluded to the stage of health IT penetration within England's acute care sector (i.e.,

Table 6-8. Initial Content Validation Results from England

Content Validation (Initial)	Very Relevant (Range)	Not Relevant (Range)	Revisions Required
4 Participants; 75% Female	57% (17-86%)	10% (0-38%)	33%
	Very Interpretable (Range)	Not Interpretable (Range)	Revisions Required
	37% (10-62%)	28% (7-40%)	44%

many of the items were seen in terms of potential only). Following revision, a second round of content validation resulted in a far greater number of items being judged as very relevant and very interpretable, although one participant continued to judge items as less relevant and less interpretable than other participants (perhaps pointing to a need for methods for "smoothing out" anomalies, e.g., use of a larger number of participants). Face validation involved five practicing nurses (80% female), and 17 questionnaire items were considered valid. Suggestions for the remaining 12 items included the inclusion of examples, word substitutions, changes to ensure consistency across items, points for further clarification, and questions about the questionnaire layout.

The final questionnaire was released via existing links and e-mail lists (approximately 450 contacts), with an expectation that this would cascade further. As the uptake was far less than expected, the questionnaire was disseminated further, again via existing links with a total of 53 responses. Most respondents (n=41) skipped over a question on information of health IT use in the workplace. This may indicate that, at the time of the survey, IT had not been widely implemented at the participants' workplaces. For about one third of questionnaire items, the most frequent response was "not applicable." Most responses converged around the midpoint, with large agreement (>75%) found for only two items: Health IT facilitates my efficiency in practice (n=51; 80.4%) and the ways in which data/information are displayed using health IT improves access to data (n=40; 77.5%). See Table 6-9 for a summary of selected responses.

The lack of consensus across a small number of respondents would make it difficult to draw any clear conclusions from the English data. The following two main factors appear to have played a part:
1. The relatively small sample size. Wider ethical approval is needed before approaching National Heath Service (NHS) employees via NHS e-mail lists for the purposes of research. The NHS employs a great number of nurses in England. A larger sample would perhaps be more representative and might converge toward consensus.
2. Early stages of implementation. Although there is a large national program for IT in England, many organizations remain (particularly at the time of the survey) in the early stages of implementation. Hence it would be difficult, without speculating, for respondents to form and report well-founded opinions on the impact of health IT in their own workplaces.

Although validation of an instrument to assess the impact of health IT would appear possible, the problems associated with adapting a U.S.-oriented tool to an English context should not be underestimated, and investigators should not be seduced by any apparent commonality in language. More meaningful results and more definite conclusions might have been possible with a larger group of study participants who have more experience with information and communication technologies in a health context.

New Zealand's I-HIT Survey

The context of nursing in New Zealand is based on a predominantly, government-funded, public health system for a population of 4.3 million. In 2008, there were 44,571 registered nurses[16] with approximately 46% working in acute care. The study involved content and face

Table 6-9. Selected Demographic and HIT Satisfaction Results from England

Demographics	Number of Respondents	Percentage of Respondents
Gender: Female	32	97%
Age >40 years old	32	84%
Education: Bachelor's degree or higher	29	83%
Experience: >20 years in profession	32	81%
Position: Direct caregiver	32	41%
Daily use of word processing	32	72%
Daily use of E-mail	32	91%
Daily use of Internet	32	81%
Rated skill at obtaining patient care information from hospital computer system as good or excellent	32	78%
Completely satisfied with HIT applications/tools at hospital	31	0%
Completely dissatisfied with HIT applications/tools at hospital	31	16%

validation of the I-HIT Scale using the methods described earlier in this chapter. Overall few changes were needed to the I-HIT Scale; however, some terms were not known to the focus group participants. For example, one statement uses the term "redundancy of care," which was unknown among the focus group participants and instead they suggested "duplication and inefficiency." See Table 6-1 for a summary of the items modified.

The final step in phase one, survey validation, involved distributing information about the survey with the aim of recruiting 300 nurses to complete the online survey. With the total number of nurses in New Zealand being 44,571, and 46% of these working in acute care, there was a potential study population of about 20,500 nurses. Dissemination of information about the survey and the link to the Web site was sent by e-mail using a snowball sampling technique in which participants recruit other nurses from among their acquaintances. After an initial burst of responses in early January 2007, we sent follow-up e-mails and extended the deadline to the end of June 2007, to obtain 124 completed online surveys.

Table 6-10 presents a high-level overview of demographic and satisfaction findings to give an indication of the results, even though the sample size and distribution are insufficient for statistical purposes.

Most of the I-HIT survey items resulted in "middle of the road" responses. However, respondents placed strong importance on the need for nurses to know how to access their clinical systems. They also gave a high rating to "I have access to HIT that supports multidisciplinary communication" (91%) but indicated that health IT does not decrease the need for direct communication regarding patient orders (57.5%). The findings from this survey confirmed our assumptions about the state of health IT in New Zealand. The survey finding suggests that many hospital systems are not nursing-focused, and nurses use the systems mostly for accessing laboratory and radiology results. These findings indicate a growth potential for health IT that will provide nurses value and support more direct use. Comments added to surveys indicate that there remains both paper and e-communication in most organizations and that nurses consider face-to-face communication as still needed. The participants noted a variety of communication tools and included e-mail and mobile phones among these tools. The use of e-mail for such tasks as requesting maintenance was found to take longer, and e-mail was often used in addition to the traditional paper trail. The main benefits of health IT were seen to be in facilitating patient-tracking and administration.

Due to the poor response to the validation survey, reliability testing did not proceed. The low response rate from nurses working in acute care settings may be related to our methods of access, perception that the topic was not relevant, and lack of a national listserv distribution. We used our existing nursing networks that tend toward educators and informatics nurses and

Table 6-10. Selected Demographic and HIT Satisfaction Results from New Zealand

Demographics	Number of Respondents	Percentage of Respondents
Gender: Female	75	92%
Age >40 years old	75	75%
Education: Bachelor's degree or higher	76	72%
Experience: >20 years in profession	75	61%
Position: Direct caregiver	76	43%
Daily use of word processing	76	59%
Daily use of E-mail	76	88%
Daily use of Internet	76	67%
Rated skill at obtaining patient care information from hospital computer system as good or excellent	73	84%
Completely satisfied with HIT applications/tools at hospital	77	4%
Completely dissatisfied with HIT applications/tools at hospital	77	4%

also required personal or work e-mail access. Unfortunately, many nurses reported that Internet access was not permitted from their hospital systems, thus severely limiting survey access. Given these constraints, participants would have needed to have personal e-mail and broadband access to receive the invitation to participate and to access the Web survey. If we were to repeat this survey, a lesson learned would be to use more formal nursing networks, such as the New Zealand Nurses Organisation or the Nursing Council of New Zealand.

Currently health IT use has minimal adoption within acute care settings in New Zealand, and few of the information systems in use support nursing practice. Rather, in New Zealand the growth in health IT developments and use is within primary health care. With the status of health IT in acute care settings being unlikely to change significantly in the near future, it is unproductive to continue with I-HIT survey validation efforts at this time.

Scotland's (I-HIT) Survey

Scotland's Health IT program is small in scale but realistic in ambition for a country of five million people with tremendous geographic and demographic diversity and health challenges posed through chronicity and poverty. Tailoring IT provision to this context has been a difficult task, and the results reported here reflect varying degrees of adoption as our current state in 2007 at the time of this survey effort. Following the process established by our international colleagues, we established content and face validity of the I-HIT items (see Table 6-1 for a summary of results). Modification and clarification occurred in several items but was judged not to significantly alter the meaning, thus retaining a semantic association with the original questionnaire items.

Ethical approval for this research was gained through Glasgow Caledonian University, and it was anticipated that this approval would be sufficient. However this was not the case because reliability testing and psychometric analysis requires 300 participants. Access to the NHS staff networks would be needed for this level of recruitment. Unfortunately, the more rigorous NHS process designed for clinical research entailed a laborious process of form-filling that could have taken several of us far beyond the timescale of the validation project. Instead, personal contacts, informal networks, and those organizations, such as the British Computer Society and the Scottish Nurses eHealth Forum, were used to reasonable effect. The final number of respondents, following several attempts to widen participation, was 112. This was far short of our targeted 300 sample size and insufficient for statistical analyses. However, there was a wealth of information in free-text commentary that was potentially useful, providing insight into the nature of the changes occurring within the Scottish NHS. Comments painted the picture of a healthcare system in transition and one in which the experience of health IT cannot be easily generalized. For example, in the response to the item, "General Advantages of HIT at my site," comments ranged from "none" and "systems don't talk to each other" to "clear, concise accessible information."

A similar pattern of response was evident in other questions, such as, "Information Tools to support communication tasks at my site" where these were described as "not available," and "not linked to interdisciplinary colleagues." The statement, "works well in GP practices but not in secondary care," pointed to the contrast between community care, for which consistent investment has been made over time in a General Practice system, and secondary care, in which, for the most part, systems are currently underdeveloped. The range of comments within any one question, while seemingly contradictory, reflect the picture of the NHS IT developments as they were in Scotland in 2007. The health IT questionnaire is a tool potentially suited to longitudinal research design, capable of auditing and monitoring developments and providing feedback on progress, measuring the most important points of impact. For this reason, the finalized questionnaire will be a valuable aid to researchers and developers.

Acknowledgments

This chapter is based on the content of a paper and a workshop prepared by the authors and other collaborators from the HIMSS' Nursing Informatics Community for presentation and discussion at NI2009 in Helsinki, Finland. The authors wish to acknowledge the support of colleagues in all participating countries with dissemination efforts and for encouraging nurses to participate in the survey validation process.

References

1. Allen D. Re-reading nursing and re-writing practice: towards an empirically based reformulation of the nursing mandate. *Nurs Inq.* 2004;11(4):271-283.

2. Hockey L. *The Nurse's Contribution to Care.* Ciba Foundation symposium. 1976(43):59-74.

3. Page A. *Keeping Patients Safe: Transforming the Work Environment of Nurses.* Washington, DC: The National Academies Press; 2004.

4. Turisco F, Rhoads J. *Equipped for Efficiency: Improving Nursing Care Through Technology.* Oakland, CA: California HealthCare Foundation; 2008.

5. The Joint Commission. Sentinel event alert. Safely implementing health information and converging technologies. *JCAH Perspect.* 2009;29(1):10-13.

6. Ash JS, Berg M, Coiera E. Some unintended consequences of information technology in health care: the nature of patient care information system-related errors. *JAMIA.* 2004;11(2):104-112.

7. Koppel R, Metlay JP, Cohen A, et al. Role of computerized physician order entry systems in facilitating medication errors. *JAMA.* 2005;9;293(10):1197-1203.

8. Dykes PC, Hurley A, Cashen M, Bakken S, Duffy ME. Development and psychometric evaluation of the Impact of Health Information Technology (I-HIT) scale. *JAMIA.* 2007;14(4):507-514.

9. Dykes P, Cashen M, Foster M, et al. Surveying acute care providers in the US to explore the impact of health information technology on the role of nurses and interdisciplinary communication in acute care settings. *CIN.* 2006;24(6):353-354.

10. Waltz C, Strickland O, Lenz E. *Measurement in Nursing and Health Research.* Philadelphia: FA Davis Company, 2005.

11. Wyatt J, Altman D. Prognostic models: Clinically useful or quickly forgotten? *BMJ.* 1995;311(9):1539-1541.

12. Wyatt JC. When to use web-based surveys. *JAMIA.* 2000;7(4):426-429.

13. Nunnally J. *Psychometric Theory.* 2nd ed. New York: McGraw-Hill, 1998.

14. Tabachnick B, Fidell L. *Using Multivariate Statistics.* 3rd ed. New York: Harper Collins, 1996.

15. Pathways to Quality Health Care Committee. *Redesigning Health Insurance Performance Measures, Payment, and Performance Improvement Programs. Performance Measurement: Accelerating Improvement.* Washington, DC; AHRQ 2006.

16. Nursing Council of New Zealand. Report of the Nursing Council of New Zealand. March 31, 2008. http://www.nursingcouncil.org.nz/Annual%20repo rt%202007%202008%20for%20web.pdf. Accessed November 8, 2009.

SECTION II

Nursing Education and IT

Introduction

By Connie White Delaney, PhD, RN, FAAN, FACMI

Nursing education assumes the societal mandate to provide a nursing workforce with expertise to care for individuals, families, and communities around the globe. Moreover, this mandate calls for the education of our next generation of clinical nurse leaders, nursing faculty, nurse researchers, and corporate executives, across all care settings and business entities. It is clear throughout the profession that every nurse must possess a level of informatics competency to be effective in a global information society and transitioning healthcare systems anchored in the state-of-the-science information and communications technology.

Section II creatively provides an overview of state-of the-art initiatives and innovations that lead the way to empowering nursing in a technology intensive society. This section addresses three key innovations. First, in Chapter 7, Connors and colleagues provide case studies as examples of the development of faculty competency in informatics. Outstanding examples anchored in Duke University, University of Pittsburgh, University of Kansas, and Finland provide diverse approaches to defining competencies and implementing strategies to establish competency of students and faculty. In Chapter 8, Gugerty and Sensmeier outline a powerful national initiative to define informatics competencies for all nursing roles, from clinician to educator to administrator, etc. This initiative exemplifies partnerships across all professional and specialty organizations and particularly highlights how the expertise of sparsely available informaticians can be leveraged to address this challenge. And finally in Chapter 9, Warren and colleagues from the University of Kansas present their exemplar work in the use of an EHR and simulation to embed informatics competencies in a virtual clinical environment. The following case studies from Finland and St. Scholastica provide bold examples for transforming the education of our nursing and healthcare workforce to provide critical decision making within an electronically intensive healthcare delivery system. Case studies by Ora-Hyytiainen et al and Maki et al share three different strategies to address the challenge of educational innovation that leverages the e-health environment.

## CHAPTER 7

Faculty Competencies and Development

By Helen R. Connors, PhD, DrPS (Hon), RN, FAAN

Introduction

With the rapid integration of IT in the healthcare field, equipping faculty with the knowledge, skills, and attitudes to effectively teach others how to use the technology is imperative. As demand for the EHR and other supporting technologies considered essential tools in the delivery of healthcare continues to grow, nursing faculty need to become proficient at integrating these technologies into their teaching practices. Also, the advancement of informatics and other technologies in nursing education and practice is crucial to meeting the Institute of Medicine's (IOM's) recommendations for health professional education.[1] Nevertheless, of all the challenges facing health professional education today, perhaps the most difficult is the integration of the EHR technologies into academics. Today, for a variety of reasons presented in this chapter, relatively few nursing schools have incorporated these technologies in their curriculum.[2] This chapter describes the current state on levels of informatics in nursing curriculum and critiques faculty's and administrators' understanding of informatics differentiated from computer and information literacy skills. Against this critical review, this chapter describes a specific program that targets faculty development initiatives to increase informatics and other technology-related competencies that will transform nursing education.

Background

In 2000, IOM released its landmark report, *To Err is Human*. This document served as a catalyst for the transformation of healthcare and the use of IT to provide safe care.[3] The report became a driving force for changing the United States' healthcare system and precipitated a subsequent series of IOM reports on patient safety, quality, and health professions' education.[1,4] In 2003, the IOM issued its critical review of health professions' education with recommendations for embedding its five core aims for transforming healthcare delivery and for including information technology competencies.[1] Titled *Health Professions Education: A Bridge to Quality,* this report called for a major overhaul of the educational programs of all healthcare professionals. This health education report strongly recommended that all clinicians regardless of their discipline, possess five core competencies: (1) provide patient-centered care, (2) work in interdisciplinary teams, (3) employ evidence-based practice, (4) apply quality improvement techniques, and (5) utilize informatics. Accordingly, the report states, "Without a basic education in informatics, health professionals are limited in their ability to make effective use of communication and IT in their practice."[1,p85]

Although the nursing profession and nursing academic educational organizations have embraced the concept of nursing informatics, most nursing education programs still do not have access to information and communication technologies (ICT) within their academic programs. Furthermore, most nursing programs do not provide nursing informatics courses.[5] Echoing these same comments, Don Detmer, MD, MA, former chief executive officer (CEO) of AMIA, stated:

> If we are serious about transforming our system of healthcare to be safe, efficient, timely, patient-centered, equitable, and effective, then we need to not only

invest in technology, but also invest in the training of individuals to ensure our workforce is poised to meet this challenge. Virtually every hospital, clinic, physician office, or other healthcare provider organization will in some way utilize information technology solutions in the upcoming years and will need healthcare professionals versed in informatics to assist in the implementation, use and success of these systems.[6]

Detmer's vision, which acknowledged the need for an informatics-competent health workforce also inspired AMIA's *10 X 10 Program*, which aims for 10,000 health professionals educated in health informatics by the year 2010.

Faculty Informatics Competencies

A number of professional groups have studied the extent to which informatics competencies exist in today's nursing curriculum.[5,7-9] The findings from these different studies have made us all keenly aware of the need to strengthen the informatics component of nursing education, if we are going to provide the next generation of nurses with the skill set to become e-health practitioners. One example of such a study was conducted in March 2006, when the Informatics Competencies Task Force of ETIMAC5 at the NLN sent a Web-based survey to all NLN members, as well as non-member faculty and nursing education administrators in the NLN database. The purpose of this survey was to solicit input about how the nursing education community was preparing the next generation of nurses to practice in technology-rich environments. Responses were received from 1,557 faculty and 540 administrators. The results of this study are summarized in Table 7-1.

While the NLN survey was sent to all types of nursing programs, from practical to doctoral level, most of the administrators represented associate degree (47%) and baccalaureate and higher degree combined (64%). The largest majority of faculty responses were equally distributed between associate degree programs (42%) and baccalaureate or higher degree programs (42%). In this study, administrators and faculty were asked if students were required to own a computer or a PDA. Fifteen percent of faculty, but only 11% of administrators, responded that students were required to own a computer. Only 3% of faculty and 6% of administrators reported that their school required PDAs.

In response to a question about computer and information literacy requirements, more than half of the NLN survey respondents, 61% of administrators and 56% of faculty reported a computer literacy requirement and only 42% of administrators and 39% of faculty indicated that information literacy was required. When asked how their nursing program addressed informatics, 58% of administrators and 56% of faculty reported that informatics was integrated into their courses, and 65% of administrators and 51% of faculty said informatics was provided in their clinical experiences. Thirty-three percent of administrators and 40% of faculty reported that the library was responsible for informatics content. Relatively few administrators (13%) and faculty (11%) reported they provided a course in informatics within their curriculum. Yet, when the survey respondents provided the actual course names, it was evident that while many had the term *informatics* in the course title, some primarily addressed information or computer literacy knowledge and skills. Perhaps the most interesting finding was that only 17% of administrators and 18% of faculty reported that knowledge and skills related to informatics was included as a program outcome.

Nearly every question on the survey provided an option for respondents to submit an open-ended response. It is in these open-ended data that the most noticeable findings can be found. In multiple instances throughout both the administrator and faculty surveys, informatics is equated with online learning and the use of educational technologies. For example, in response to the question concerning how informatics is integrated into the curriculum, the following comments were not atypical: "We use Blackboard to supplement classroom experience"; and "All of our courses are Web-enhanced or online." Faculty also mentioned "Web searches" or "learning how to use online bibliographic resources" as their informatics inte-

Table 7-1. Faculty Competencies: NLN Survey Results 2006

Program Type	Administrators (N=540)	Faculty (N=1557)
Associate degree	47%	42%
Baccalaureate and higher degree	64%	42%
Informatics in the Curriculum	**Administrators**	**Faculty**
Students required to own computer	11%	15%
Students required to own PDA	6%	3%
Computer literacy required	61%	56%
Information literacy required	42%	39%
Informatics integrated	58%	56%
Provided in clinical experience	65%	51%
Library responsible for teaching informatics	33%	40%
Separate course in informatics	13%	11%
Informatics as a program outcome	17%	18%
Teach content related to informatics skills (privacy, security, confidentiality, etc)	NA	50%
Use informatics tools in clinical area	82%	71%
Faculty Proficiency in Informatics	**Faculty Self Report**	
Novice	13%	
Adv. Beginner	26%	
Competent	37%	
Proficient	20%	
Expert	4%	

Adapted from Informatics in the Nursing Curriculum: A National Survey of Nursing Informatics Requirements in Nursing Curricula. *Nursing Education Perspectives*. 2008,29(5):312-317.

gration. From these responses, it is apparent that faculty and administrators are confusing computer literacy and information literacy with informatics. On the positive side, half or more faculty reported teaching content related to informatics tools and issues, such as privacy, confidentiality, and security in their courses. While half reported that they taught how informatics tools can facilitate nurses' work, only 42% covered clinical decision support systems and informatics tools to promote patient safety.

While 82% of administrators and 71% of faculty reported that students use informatics tools in the clinical area, many added that students only *observe* the use of information systems, pointing to the fact that some hospitals would not allow students access to their CISs. In many instances, hospitals would only provide the instructor with a password. This reinforces the fact that most academic programs do not have access to the tools needed to teach students to develop informatics skills. It appears that faculty may be confusing the issue of "use of informatics tools" with "observation of the use of the tools." To fully integrate informatics competencies into professional behaviors, hands-on experience is essential.

At the conclusion of the NLN survey, administrators were asked to indicate the percent of faculty who fell on a continuum in terms of their knowledge of informatics. Most indicated that the majority of their faculty fell in the novice to competent range (see Table 7-1). A much smaller percent reported having faculty who were proficient or expert. Faculty self-reported their level of expertise as follows: novice, 13%; advanced beginner, 26%; competent, 37%; proficient, 20%; and expert, 4%. Eighty-one percent of faculty reported that their knowledge of informatics was self-taught. Again, open-ended responses confirmed the continuing confusion between informatics and educational technologies or online methodologies. Many faculty reported taking classes in Web-based teaching, such as WebCT training. Few faculty mentioned taking informatics courses or attending informatics conferences.

Although there has been progress over the last few years, the results of this survey are similar to previous faculty and administrator surveys. There appears to be relatively little informatics content in nursing curriculum. It is doubtful that many schools of nursing teach nursing practice within an informatics-intensive environment. The finding that faculty and administrators tend to co-mingle the ideas of informatics with the use of educational technologies or teaching online is disappointing and justifies the need for the continuing education of faculty and administrators in informatics. It is hoped that through these professional development initiatives, we will help faculty to reconceptualize how they will teach nurses to practice using clinical decision support and other informatics tools in the rapidly evolving, automated healthcare environments.[5]

In 1997, the National Advisory Council on Nurse Education and Practice reported that most informatics nurses had no formal preparation in informatics. So the 2006 NLN study findings in regard to faculty preparation in informatics should not be too surprising. Most had prepared for their informatics roles through on-job training, continuing education, and self-study. Unfortunately, a similar assessment of 776 informatics nurses conducted by HIMSS in 2007 indicated that not much had changed in ten years. In the HIMSS' study, 41% of the nurses surveyed indicated they had no formal education in informatics, 17% indicated they had a master's degree in informatics, and 2% had a PhD in informatics. Twenty-four percent indicated they either had a certificate in informatics or were enrolled in an informatics certificate program.[8] If nurses practicing in informatics roles do not have formal preparation in their chosen field, they can be ill prepared to implement systems or teach informatics in academic settings. Consequently, until there is sufficient faculty educated to teach informatics competencies, academic environments will not be able to keep up with the growing demand for graduates to have the information and communication technology competency and skill set required for 21ˢᵗ-century practice. Faculty development in informatics is crucial to transforming curriculum so that our health professional graduates possess the right skill set for the rapidly evolving technology-rich healthcare job market.

It also is important to note that until recently, most assessment of informatics in education focused on content and skills in the curriculum, with little attention to defining what informatics competencies faculty should possess. In addition, these studies used self-report survey instruments, which require the participants to "know what they don't know."[10(p320)] Therefore, little evidence-based literature exists that specifically addresses the knowledge and competency level of nursing faculty in teaching informatics skills. Hart[10] further postulates that although Staggers et al,[11] using a Delphi technique, produced a research-based list of informatics competencies and differentiated these competencies by level of nursing practice, a list of standardized, nursing-job specific competencies with associated valid and reliable evaluation tools remains to be created. Therefore, establishing a baseline of informatics competencies for the faculty workforce is vital to the design of faculty development and formal education programs intended to meet faculty needs. The questions to be addressed to best forecast and plan for growth in an ever expanding, technology-driven, health system are:

- What level of informatics competencies should faculty have?
- Should it be expected that all faculty need the same level of and proficiency in informatics as their students?
- Should faculty teaching informatics specialty courses be held to a higher competency standard than those teaching generalist courses?
- If so, what should that competency standard be?

Once these questions are answered and consensus is gained regarding the outcomes, we will be better able to develop and support faculty as they help students gain the necessary informatics skills.

Driving Forces for Nursing Informatics and Education Reform

Despite the lack of informatics competencies among practicing nurses and faculty, the nursing profession for some time now has provided continuous support for the field of nursing informatics. In 1992, ANA recognized nursing informatics as a clinical specialty and therefore established *Scope and Standards of Nursing Informatics Practice*. This document was last updated in 2008 to reflect rapid changes in nursing informatics roles and advances in the science of nursing informatics.[12] In 1997, HRSA's Division of Nursing convened a panel of informatics experts, National Nursing Informatics Work Group (NNIWG). NNIWG's mandate was to recommend a future direction for nursing informatics education and to identify initiatives designed to more adequately prepare the nation's workforce to use technology. The ensuing NNIWG report substantiated the need to clearly articulate the role of informatics in nursing education to prepare the next generations of nurses with needed competencies and skills, as well as to address the ongoing needs of the current nursing workforce.[7] Based on the gaps and needs identified, the NNIWG report made five recommendations: (1) educate nursing students and practicing nurses in core informatics content, (2) prepare nurses with specialized skills in informatics, (3) enhance nursing practice and education through informatics projects, (4) prepare nursing faculty in informatics, and (5) increase collaborative efforts in nursing informatics to gain efficiencies and economies of scale. Addressing the limited number of faculty with informatics competencies, the NNIWG report recommended increasing nursing faculty preparation in informatics through the use of innovative programs and collaboration across institutions. Through collaborative programs, nursing schools within a region could offer faculty development in either core or specialized informatics skills.[13] The Clinical Nursing and Health Informatics Consortium (CIC), launched in 1997, is an example of this type of collaboration. The CIC, with headquarters in Champaign, Illinois, is the academic consortium of the Big Ten Universities and the University of Chicago.[14]

From 2004 to 2010, health policy initiatives pushed adoption and "meaningful use" of EHR technologies, escalating the need for informatics competencies among nurses. This escalation began in April 2004, when then president George W. Bush issued the Executive Order "Incentives for the Use of Health Information Technology and Establishing the Position of the National Health Information Technology Coordinator."[15] The goal of this order was to provide leadership for the development and nationwide implementation of an interoperable health IT infrastructure to improve the quality and efficiency of healthcare and to ensure that the health records of most Americans are available in electronic format within ten years. On the heels of this order, then secretary of health and human services, Tommy Thompson, appointed David Brailer, MD, PhD, as the first National Coordinator of Health IT. Dr. Brailer was charged with implementing the strategic plan outlined in Secretary Thompson's report "The Decade of Health Information Technology."[16] This initial strategic plan (2004-2008) was released in July 2004. An updated four-year plan was released by the Office of National Coordinator (ONC) for Health IT in June 2008.

On February 17, 2009, President Barack Obama signed the Health Information Technology for Economic and Clinical Health (HITECH) Act (part of the stimulus package known as the ARRA).[17] This legislation codifies ONC within the Department of Health and Human Services, provides a budget of approximately $20 billion for health IT, and sets a goal for EHRs for all Americans by the year 2014.

ONC is responsible for creating a nationwide health IT infrastructure aimed at improving healthcare quality and care coordination. The HITECH Act provides immediate funding for health IT infrastructure, training, dissemination of best practices, telemedicine and provides for the inclusion of health IT in clinical education, and state grants that promote health IT. In addition, the legislation provides significant financial incentives through the Medicare and Medicaid programs to encourage doctors and hospitals to adopt and use certified EHRs. Incentive payments for both physicians and hospitals begin in 2011 and continue for several years but are phased out over time. Eventually, Medicare payments will be reduced for physicians and hospitals that do not use a certified EHR that allows for electronic communication with others. The legislation also provides additional funds to states for low-interest loans to help providers finance health IT and grants for regional health information exchanges to unite local providers. Grants are also offered for the development and adoption of EHRs for providers other than physicians. The HITECH Act is a powerful opportunity for physicians and other providers who use EHRs effectively to be rewarded, and it is intended to stimulate adoption for those who are not currently using EHRs.[17]

With these national forces as drivers of healthcare reform, it is clear that nurses need to take action and adopt IT faster than they have in the past or the action will be taken for them. Armed with these facts and incentives, leaders in the profession of nursing and, in particular, the healthcare IT sector joined forces to identify solutions to address the challenges and assist the profession in doing their part in reaching the national agenda.

Nurses Taking Action

The key to success in developing and deploying health IT is the adoption of new work roles and functions requiring new skill sets. To accomplish this, a new pedagogy is needed to prepare young health professionals so that they can use the vast amounts of new information that is constantly being produced within an increasingly complex practice and learning environment. The challenge the nursing profession faces in making this shift is to transition existing practitioners, educators, and researchers within current practice and training programs. The challenge although great is not impossible. We are currently beginning to see movement in this direction. Clearly, within the health professions and health professional organizations, considerable discussion is taking place concerning workforce requirements and the changing roles and skills required as we transition toward patient-centered, interdisciplinary team approaches for value-driven quality healthcare in technology enabled environments. The movement we now see toward establishing standards for education and practice that are organized around health IT competencies, teamwork, and more systematic decision making is not, as some might suggest, simply a fad.

Technology and Education Guiding Education Reform

In January 2005, a working group of nurse leaders from academics, practice, industry, and government met to discuss the challenges the profession faced to be able to cross the quality chasm through a reformation of nursing education and practice. This initiative, affectionately known as Technology Informatics Guiding Education Reform (TIGER), was a catalyst for change. The TIGER leadership group was not satisfied with discussion alone, they recognized that immediate action and big impact was critical. To this end, a two-day invitational summit was held in 2006 in Bethesda, Md. The summit brought together 120 leaders representing

70 nursing stakeholder groups to develop a shared vision, strategies, and specific actions for improving nursing practice, education, and the delivery of patient care through the use of health IT.[18] The outcome of the summit was a compelling ten-year vision and a three-year roadmap that was created and owned together by the stakeholders involved, thus establishing a shared commitment to action.

Initially, the TIGER Collaborative started out as a grass-roots effort to engage with all stakeholders committed to a common "vision" of an e-health-enabled nursing practice. Today, more than 120 diverse organizations have joined the TIGER effort. Also, while the original 70 organizations that attended the summit work toward completing their strategic action plan, more than 1,000 nursing professionals have joined the TIGER initiative to participate on nine important collaborative teams. The purpose of these teams is to operationalize the nine strategic imperatives that emerged from the 2006 summit. Two of these nine strategic imperatives teams are relevant to this chapter: the Education and Faculty Development team and the Staff Development/Continuing Education team. Both teams' work emphasizes the importance of developing informatics competencies in education and practice. Each collaborative team has developed a wiki (http://www.tigersummit.com/) that explains their goals, activities, and progress, and the work of these teams will be published in the forthcoming fourth edition of *Nursing Informatics: Where Caring and Technology Meet.*[19] The phase two TIGER report "Collaborating to Integrate Evidence and Informatics into Nursing Practice and Education" is available online.[20]

The TIGER initiative provided the thrust for some dramatic changes in nursing education in the United States. For example, the NLN[21] and the AACN[22] have since taken a stance on addressing informatics competencies in nursing curriculum. The TIGER initiative also is widely recognized by other countries. Its Web presence and innovative use of social networking tools makes the work of TIGER widely available around the world.

Quality and Safety Education for Nurses

As TIGER was beginning to get off the ground, in 2005, the RWJF funded a national study, named Quality and Safety Education for Nurses (QSEN). The QSEN initiative was formed in partnership with University of North Carolina-Chapel Hill School of Nursing, and targeted educating nursing students on patient safety and healthcare quality. In the first phase of the QSEN study, a panel of seventeen national nursing leaders outlined the essential knowledge, skills, and abilities (KSA) to be mastered by prelicensure nursing students to assure patient safety and healthcare quality. The critical competencies identified as core to nursing curriculum expanded upon the IOM recommendations for health professional education[1] and included patient-centered care, teamwork and collaboration, evidence-based practice, quality improvement, informatics, and safety. Each of the six core competencies are accompanied by sets of KSA created for use in nursing prelicensure programs.[23] The second phase of this project consisted of pilot schools that took on the work of integrating the QSEN six core competencies into their nursing programs and sharing their work on the QSEN Web site.[24]

In November 2008, phase three of the QSEN undertaking was funded. The purpose of this phase is to (1) promote continued innovation in the development and evaluation of methods to elicit and assess student learning of KSA of the six QSEN competencies and the widespread sharing of these competencies; (2) develop faculty expertise necessary to assist the learning and assessment of achievement of quality and safety competencies in all types of nursing programs; and (3) create mechanisms to sustain the will to change among all programs through the content of textbooks, accreditation, and certification standards, licensure exams and continued competence requirements.[25] In February 2009, AACN also received a grant from RWJF to partner with the QSEN project to extend their reach into faculty education. Through this partnership, the UNC School of Nursing and AACN will collaborate to develop the faculty expertise necessary for the nation's nursing schools to teach the competencies. The focus will be on instilling the competencies in textbooks and licensing, accreditation and certification standards and promoting continued innovation in teaching the competencies.[26]

HRSA Supported Faculty Development: Integrating Technology into Nursing Education and Practice Initiative

The Nurse Reinvestment Act of 2002 authorized Title VIII, Section 831 of the Public Health Service (PHS) Act to invest in projects to provide education in new technologies, including distance-learning methodologies. The purpose of this funding initiative is to solicit applications for nursing collaboratives that will partner with the government using a Cooperative Agreement mechanism for the Faculty Development: Integrated Technology into Nursing Education and Practice Initiative (ITNEP) Faculty Development. The Faculty Development: ITNEP Initiative provides support to nursing collaboratives for faculty development in the use of information and other technologies to expand the capacity of schools of nursing to educate students for 21st century healthcare practice. To date, seven institutions have been funded for these collaboratives—Duke University, Durham, N.C.; University of Wisconsin-Madison; University of Pittsburgh; University of Kansas; Drexel University, Philadelphia, Pa.; University of Washington; and Vanderbilt University, Nashville, Tenn.[27]

The goal of this federal initiative is to educate faculty to use healthcare information systems to enhance nursing education and practice, optimize patient safety, and drive improvements in healthcare quality. For this initiative, use of information and other technologies in nursing education and practice includes, but is not limited to, informatics, telehealth, mannequin-based and patient simulators, computer-based instructions, virtual simulation, interactive simulated case studies, advanced 3-D graphics, eLearning technology, and other simulated or virtual methods to enhance nursing education and practice. Based on the premise that no institution or organization alone currently offers the full spectrum of information and other technologies necessary to successfully carry out this initiative, the nursing collaboratives provide a mechanism to develop linkages and partnerships to undertake this massive faculty re-tooling.

The nursing collaboratives offer state-of-the-art training sites for immersing nursing faculty in information and other technologies. These cutting-edge training sites have the capability of providing virtual and real-time training to faculty members in the full range of relevant technologies necessary for transforming education. The nursing collaboratives promote the awareness of the latest simulated learning, informatics, and telehealth trends, advances, and issues. The nursing collaboratives utilize an innovative faculty development plan designed to provide "hands-on" learning opportunities that give faculty actual experiences using the technologies. This opportunity to use, observe, and see these technologies in actual live settings gives faculty the learning environments they require to gain the informatics knowledge and skills they will need to teach students. The focus is comprehensive so that faculty are solidly grounded in the use of simulated learning, informatics, and telehealth; consequently, at program completion they can begin to integrate information and other technologies into nursing education and practice at their respective institutions. Three case studies describing the ITNEP-funded, Faculty Development Initiatives accompany this chapter.

Designing Faculty Development Programs

The opportunity to transform nursing education through the use of technology has never been more apparent or more unified. As pointed out in this chapter, the government, regulatory boards, policy makers, healthcare delivery systems, healthcare technology vendors, and health professional schools—including nursing, medicine, and allied health—are all united on this front. Across all health professions, many faculty were educated prior to the emergence of informatics. If we want to insure that our current and future nurses are prepared to practice in the 21st-century clinical environments, we need to provide development opportunities for faculty. It is essential that we have innovative faculty development programs in nursing now. These programs should be designed to meet faculty's unique needs to enable them to respond to shifting expectations about the quality of education, as it relates to changing student populations, dwindling resources, and widespread use of technology in health environments.

Challenges facing new and senior faculty center on these changing demands. The dilemma of diminishing resources for faculty development must be balanced with the overwhelming need for faculty education in the changing environment. The next generation of nurses depends on strategic planning now that will allow us to build the pool of qualified faculty for the future. Effective faculty development for existing and future faculty is pivotal in this era of pervasive change in technology-enabled healthcare practice and education.

Despite the demand for technology-oriented faculty development and the funds spent to support these initiatives, there is a considerable lack of evidenced-based literature on the specific faculty needs or the effectiveness of existing programs.[28] The limited work published on faculty development programs does not focus on a comprehensive program evaluation, making it difficult to determine the value of such programs.[29] The design, dissemination, and evaluation of effective faculty development programs to assist faculty to integrate technology in the curriculum are of utmost importance.

Faculty development typically consists of newsletters, workshops, seminars, conferences, peer discussion groups, mentoring programs, classroom observations, career counseling, and sabbaticals. These approaches are often short-term and infrequent. In recent years, other models have developed that include expanded workshops across many sites, one- to four-week intensives and part-time or full-time fellowships.[30] Bakken et al,[31] recommend a three-prong approach to faculty development in informatics: (1) seminars and small workshops, (2) consultation with others on assignments for specific informatics competencies, and (3) guest lecturers or coteaching to assist inexperienced faculty to develop knowledge and skills. Today, with the plethora of Web 2.0 tools—blogs, wikis, podcasts, social networking, Skype, Twitter, Facebook, Second Life—readily available, we can think beyond these traditional faculty development methods. Augmenting the traditional faculty development with social networking technologies extends the life of the learning. It is no longer time-limited. It allows for expanded learning opportunities well after the face-to-face conference has ended because it creates a community of learners and supports opportunities to interact with others around the globe in an ongoing way. For example, using blogs, Really Simple Syndication (RSS) feeds, Second Life, or other similar tools can extend learning beyond the conference by providing new ways to interact before, during, and after the conference. This provides for an open dialogue between the experts and the conference attendees and creates a high-level of engagement in, and ownership of learning.[32] Surowieski,[33] in his book *The Wisdom of Crowds*, supports the idea of using collaborative technologies to capture this collective wisdom to help us better understand the most complex issues. These Web 2.0 tools enrich and expand faculty development programs.

Summary

To date, faculty's informatics needs have not been extensively studied.[30-32] Without this evidence–based scholarship, we can only draw on what we think we know is needed for faculty if they are to become proficient in teaching informatics at various levels in the curriculum. What we do know from survey studies of informatics in the curriculum[2,8,9] is that nursing faculty appear to be ill-prepared in terms of formal and/or informal preparation in informatics. Faculty competencies with computer and information literacy are generally better than their knowledge and use of clinical information system applications. Further study focusing on informatics specific needs for faculty is warranted.

We also have learned through these surveys of informatics competencies among nurses that few nurses in general have either the formal education in informatics or the necessary experience to teach informatics to others. The few that have this combination of knowledge and skills are working in the health IT industry or for provider organizations and not readily accessible to assist in the academic environment. This dearth of expertise makes it difficult to find well-qualified teachers and mentors who can be called on to help develop faculty. We are all well aware of the fact that the health IT train has left the station and is rapidly rolling down the track. Nursing educators need to quickly figure out how to get on board or they will not be able to prepare graduates with the knowledge and skill set and tools they need to provide safe, quality, and cost-effective healthcare. Graduates will not be able to meet the demands of the marketplace and will be placed at a serious disadvantage.

The literature on faculty development, although limited, points out that selecting a small cohort of faculty and developing a sense of community through ongoing work relationships are features that create sustained changes in targeted skills and behaviors.[29,30] A sustained change in the faculty's informatics knowledge and skills is essential to integrating these competencies in the curriculum across all program levels. Conferences and workshops are short-term, time-bound and often not specific enough to meet the needs of the faculty. The emergence of Web 2.0 collaborative technologies can add a new dimension to faculty development and support greater opportunities for interaction and socialization.[32] These new Web technologies enable us to design innovative faculty development programs that are more in line with faculty needs and pedagogical theory. The Internet makes it easier for us to bring together people with different backgrounds and expertise. Collectively, we can reach our goals for transforming the profession faster. In addition, this strategy immerses the learners in the very technology that they need to become comfortable using to meet the demands of the increasingly automated work environments.

The exemplar cases that follow this chapter demonstrate innovative faculty development initiatives that will help meet the acute needs for developing informatics competencies among faculty. These collaborative educational technology-enabled models are HRSA supported and each takes a slightly different approach to meeting HRSA's primary goal "to develop, implement, evaluate, disseminate, and sustain a faculty development collaborative (FDC) initiative to integrate information and other technologies in nursing curriculum to expand the capacity of collegiate schools of nursing to educate students for the 21st century."[27]

References

1. Greiner AC, Knebel E, eds. Institute of Medicine. *Health Professions Education: A Bridge to Quality.* Washington, DC: The National Academies Press; 2003.

2. Skiba DJ, Connors HR, Jeffries PR. Information technologies and the transformation of nursing education. *Nurs Outlook.* 2008;56(5):225-230.

3. Kohn LT, Corrigan JM, Donaldson MS, eds. Institute of Medicine. *To Err Is Human: Building a Safer Health System.* Washington, DC: The National Academies Press, 2000.

4. Committee on Quality of Health Care in America, Institute of Medicine. *Crossing the Quality Chasm: A New Health System for the 21st Century.* Washington, DC: The National Academies Press, 2001.

5. Informatics in the nursing curriculum: A national survey of nursing informatics requirements in nursing curricula. *Nurs Educ Perspect.* 2008;29(5):312-317.

6. AMIA. Detmer D. As cited in American Medical Informatics Association. 10x10 Brochure; 2005. https://www.amia.org/10x10. Accessed November 8, 2009.

7. National Advisory Council on Nursing Education and Practice. *A National Informatics Agenda for Nursing Education.* Washington, DC: Health Services Resources Administration, 1997.

8. Healthcare Information and Management Systems Society. *Nursing Informatics Survey 2007.* http://www.informaticsnurse.com/forums/nursing-nursing-informatics-news/18479-2007-himss-nursing-informatics-survey-results-released.html. Accessed May 18, 2009.

9. Booth RG. Educating the Future eHealth Professional Nurse. *Int J Nurs Educ Scholarsh.* 2006;3(1). http://www.ncbi.nlm.nih.gov/pubmed/16646940. Accessed January 15, 2010.

10. Hart M. Informatics competency and development within the US nursing population workforce: A systematic literature review. *CIN.* 2008;26(6):320-329.

11. Staggers N, Gassert C. Curran CA. Delphi study to determine informatics competencies for nurses at four levels of practice. *Nurs Res.* 2002;51(6):383-390.

12. American Nurses Association. *Scope and Standards of Nursing Informatics Practice.* Washington, DC: American Nurses Publishing, 2008.

13. McNeil BJ, Elfrink VL, Pierce ST. Preparing student nurses, faculty and clinicians for 21st century informatics practice: findings from a national survey of nursing education programs in the United States. *Medinfo.* 2004:903-907.

14. University of Iowa. Clinical Nursing and health Informatics Consortia. http://www.nursing.uiowa.edu/excellence/nursing_knowledge/nursing_informatics/CICClinicalNursingandHealthInformaticsConsortium.htm. Accessed July 9, 2009.

15. Executive Order No. 13335, 69. Federal Registry 24059, 2004.
16. Thompson TG, Brailer DJ. *The Decade of Health Information Technology: Delivering Consumer-centric and Information-rich Health Care.* Framework for Strategic Action. Washington, DC: Department of Health and Human Services, 2004.
17. American Recovery and Reinvestment Act of 2009. http://frwebgate.access.gpo.gov/cgi-bin/getdoc.cgi?dbname=111_cong_bills&docid=f:h1enr.pdf . Accessed July 9, 2009.
18. *Evidence and informatics transforming nursing: 3-year action steps toward a 10-year vision.* TIGER. http://www.tigersummit.com/uploads/TIGERInitiative_Report2007_Color.pdf. Accessed April 30, 2009.
19. Ball MJ, Hannah KJ, Newbold SK, Douglas JV, eds. *Nursing Informatics: Where Caring and Technology Meet.* 4th ed. Springer; In press.
20. Collaborating to integrate evidence and informatics into nursing practice and education. TIGER. http://www.tigersummit.com/uploads/TIGER_Collaborative_Exec_Summary_040509.pdf. Accessed April 30, 2009.
21. The National league for Nursing. *Preparing the Next Generation of Nurses to Practice in a Technology-rich Environment: An Informatics Agenda.* http://www.nln.org/aboutnln/PositionSTatements/index.htm. Accessed July 10, 2009.
22. American Association of Colleges of Nursing. *The Essentials of Baccalaureate Education for Professional Nursing Practice.* http://www.aacn.nche.edu/Education/bacessn.htm. Accessed July 10, 2009.
23. Cronenwett L, Sherwood G, Barnsteiner J, et al. Quality and safety education for nurses. *Nurs Outlook.* 2007;55:122-131.
24. *Quality and Safety Education for Nurses.* http://www.qsen.org. Accessed April 30, 2009.
25. *Quality and Safety Education for Nurses.* Press releases. http://www.qsen.org/overview.php. Accessed April 30, 2009.
26. American Association of Colleges of Nursing. *UNC School of Nursing Joins AACN in Helping Nursing Faculty Improve Quality and Safety Education.* http://www.aacn.nche.edu/media/NewsReleases/2009/qsen.html. Accessed April 25, 2009.
27. HRSA. *Faculty Development: Integrated Technologies in Nursing Education and Practice.* http://bhpr.hrsa.gov/nursing/grantprograms.htm. Accessed July 10, 2009.
28. Curran CR. Faculty Development initiatives for integration of informatics competencies and point-of-care technologies in undergraduate nursing education. *Nurs Clin North Am.* 2008;43:523-533.
29. Matthew-Maich N, Mines C, Brown B, et al. Evolving as nurse educators in problem-based learning through a community of faculty development. *J Prof Nurs.* 2007;23,(2):75-82.
30. Williams B, Weber V, Babbott SF, et al. Faculty development for the 21st century: lessons from the society of general internal medicine-Hartford Collaborative Centers for the care of the older adults. *Journal of the American Geriatric Society.* 2007;55(6):941-947.
31. Bakken S, Cook SS, Curtis L, et al. Promoting patient safety through informatics-based nursing education. *Int J Med Inform.* 2004;73:581-589.
32. Siemens G, Tittenberger P, Anderson T. Conference connections: Rewiring the circuit. *Educause Review.* 2008;43(2):15-28.
33. Surowieski J. *The Wisdom of Crowds.* New York: Random House, Inc, 2004.

Case Study 7A

University of Pittsburgh—Faculty Development Program: Emerging, Learning, and Integrated Technologies Education (ELITE)

By Helen K. Burns, PhD, MN, BSN, RN, FAAN; and Karen L. Courtney, PhD, RN

Introduction

One of the most comprehensive efforts to improve healthcare quality was launched by the IOM in 1996. In its subsequent crucial publication, *Crossing the Quality Chasm*, which outlines a plan for the complete redesign of the American healthcare system, the IOM notes that "information technology must play a central role in the redesign of the healthcare system if a substantial improvement in quality is to be achieved over the coming decade."[1] According to the IOM report, one of the biggest challenges to integrating IT technology into the current healthcare system is that "the workforce is highly variable in terms of IT-related knowledge and experience"[1] and this is the case, in large part, because nursing education has not begun to integrate informatics education in any significant way.[2-4] However, this type of education is critical for successful nursing practice because of the way IT has revolutionized the healthcare delivery system. It has provided immediate access to evidence-based practice standards, multimedia, Internet resources, and other technology-based applications.[5] Nurses, both newly graduated and experienced, assume the role of knowledge workers within an increasingly complex and information intensive healthcare arena. As a result, nurses at all levels need knowledge management skills and information system skills in their armamentarium. These competencies extend beyond familiarization with devices, desktop computers, and specific software and hardware and include an understanding of informatics concepts; the relationships between data, information, and knowledge; and the role of the nurse in creating knowledge.

Integration of such education into both undergraduate, graduate, and professional development nursing curricula is an ideal way to not only help promote change in the healthcare field but also to ensure that the new crop of technologically savvy students, those of the "Net Generation," will practice in an environment in which they are most comfortable—a fully wired, interactive, and customizable workplace.[6-7] Creating this technologically rich learning environment enables nursing education to align with the electronic workplace. This alignment adds to the "attractiveness" of nursing as a career option for the current and upcoming generations and can help stem the trend of nursing shortages.[8]

Even when educators have the needed knowledge base in informatics to teach undergraduate and graduate students, they face multiple barriers in trying to change educational curricula. Some of the major barriers include lack of access to technology, time constraints, lack of vertical support, and intolerance for change.[5] Therefore, any program that is going to address basic informatics knowledge among nursing faculty must also address these larger systemic barriers for adoption and meaningful integration to happen in a timely way. Over the past decade, the University of Pittsburgh, School of Nursing (Pitt-SON) has been creating an environment for technologic innovation and curriculum change. Concurrently, the school has offered the educational background that supports faculty in their efforts to integrate new educational content related to informatics into the undergraduate and graduate nursing curricula. The school has also worked with other universities on an individual basis to share its knowledge and experience in teaching informatics-related content to facilitate integration of the latest research into practice.

Therefore, in 2006, when HRSA's Division of Nursing announced the availability of federal funding to support faculty development programs related to technology, Pitt-SON took advantage of this opportunity to expand its partnership work in informatics and learning technology education. Drawing upon years of experience in embedding informatics and technologies into our nursing programs and faculty development, we designed the Emerging, Learning, and Integrated Technologies Education (ELITE) Faculty Development Program. The program, described next, provides strategies that faculty and their universities can use to incorporate learning technologies and informatics concepts into nursing curricula. We successfully obtained HRSA funding in 2007, and began Year 1 of the five-year program in July of that year. This chapter describes the first two years of the ELITE Program's activities, the five-year program design, and early results.

Organization of the ELITE Program

Based on the experience of Pitt-SON in teaching informatics and working with other institutions to increase their capacity, the school set the initial goals of the grant-funded program as follows:

- Develop an innovative Faculty Development Program to enhance the knowledge, skills, and abilities of nursing faculty in the application of simulated learning, informatics, and telehealth into nursing education and practice.
- Assist nursing faculty with initiating and integrating technology strategies into nursing education programs to address the learning needs of their student populations.
- Measure changes in nursing faculty knowledge, skills, abilities, and confidence in simulated learning, informatics and teleheath into their nursing curricula.

While these goals formed the basis for the ELITE Program, the school realized that to understand and eventually meet the diverse needs of institutions and faculty who have not been teaching informatics or teaching it on a very limited basis, they would have to conduct a needs assessment. The needs assessment encompassed multiple sources, including a survey of nursing school faculty and nurse educators; an online survey of nursing deans/chairpersons; an online survey of registered nurses including nurse educators; evaluations from Pitt's continuing education programs on learning technologies and simulation; and a review of pertinent literature.

Results from the survey validated that the respondents perceived a need for high-quality, cutting-edge education for learning technologies. The respondents indicated that they preferred on-site education at the School of Nursing over other options because they wanted direct access to our broad technologies, as well as to the expert faculty. They also indicated that earning continuing education credit was important to faculty. Most importantly, schools of nursing deans, faculty, and educators all expressed current and planned use of ICTs. There was also broad agreement among survey respondents on topics for education, including human simulation and informatics. Such consensus indicates that school administration will likely be supportive of faculty attending informatics educational offerings. The survey data also identified several barriers to faculty development, including lack of faculty resources to attend on-site training, challenges in reaching faculty in rural locations, and lack of ongoing support to translate knowledge into practice. The insights gained from the needs assessment survey influenced both the content and delivery mechanisms for the ELITE Program.

Based on the needs assessment data, Pitt-SON faculty designed the ELITE Program as continuing education workshops covering five thematic categories: Learning Technologies, Distance Education, Informatics, Telehealth Technologies, and High-Fidelity Simulation. These workshops were intended to educate both undergraduate and graduate nursing faculty on the implementation, evaluation, and dissemination of learning technologies while overcoming the barriers to faculty implementation. The current anticipated outcome of the program, which was in place from its inception, is to expand the capacity of schools of nursing to educate students for 21st century healthcare practice.

Collaborative Partnerships

The HRSA grant requested collaboration, and although the Pitt-SON has expertise in many aspects of technology-related education, the program faculty recognized that partnering with other institutions would be an ideal way to meet all of the wide and varied needs of potential learners. This multipartner collaborative, based on well-established relationships formed through previous work, included expert faculty and state-of-the-art training sites in simulated learning, informatics, and telehealth. Instructional partners contributed to course development and, when deemed appropriate, provided faculty and physical space for workshops. These partners included: the Center for Innovation in Clinical Learning (CICL) at the University of Pittsburgh, School of Nursing; the Winter Institute for Simulation Education and Research (WISER); West Virginia University, School of Nursing Distance Education Center; the Center for Excellence for Remote and Medically Under-served Areas (CERMUSA) at St. Francis University; and The University of Hawaii Telemedicine Research Institute (TRI). Additionally, through the ELITE Program, the Pitt-SON has established strong links with an array of committed collaborative learning partners who have supported faculty attendance at the ELITE workshops.

These partners include the University of Pittsburgh rural campuses, West Virginia University, University of Connecticut, University of Oklahoma, Kent State University, and the 43 member schools of the Pennsylvania Higher Education Nursing Schools Association (PHENSA) located throughout Pennsylvania. These instructional and learning partners also served on the Internal Executive Committee to establish and implement all ELITE Program activities.

ELITE Program Design

As noted previously, the ELITE Program was organized into workshops in five thematic areas. A difficulty in developing the program lay in considering the different levels of knowledge and skill that program participants would have, even within the same institution. Program partners developed workshops that would be appropriate to meet the needs of diverse learners and to build on their individual skills by designing a broad-based educational program with a variety of delivery formats. While workshops in each thematic area logically build from introductory to advanced level, participants do not have to take all workshops. Learners can choose individual workshops that fit within their experience level and comfort zone.

To create a program that could meet the learning needs of the target audience, Pitt-SON developed a number of workshops in each of the five thematic areas to be delivered initially face-to-face over five years and then converted to an online, self-paced format (with the exception of workshops related to simulation) so as to be available to a greater number of faculty, especially those in remote locations (see Table 7A-1). A Pitt-SON program coordinator led instructional partners in development of each workshop's content and presentation format. Each of the workshops was developed as an eight-hour educational offering. The simulation series consisted of two and a half days of content and was designed to stand-alone or be offered in conjunction with another workshop. All workshops were initially presented by Pitt-SON as on-site continuing education offerings. Feedback from the initial workshops and changes in technology and research guided development of subsequent workshops. On-site workshops were offered in pairs, so faculty that had to travel to attend the workshops could maximize their educational acquisition. In addition to the workshops themselves, a set amount of technical assistance is offered to each faculty learner to facilitate implementation of new technologies.

ELITE Workshop Content

As noted previously, workshops were developed in five thematic areas and ranged from introductory to advanced topics, which are detailed next. The year associated with each workshop indicates the year in the grant program that the workshop was or will be offered in a face-to-face format. All workshops, with the exception of simulation-related workshops, will be converted to online format and will be available every year following the face-to-face offering.

Learning Technologies

Introduction to Learning Technologies (Year 1). The purpose of this workshop is to introduce nursing faculty to a sampling of available learning technologies for use in the clinical and didactic education of nursing students. The workshop focuses on in-classroom learning technologies, such as electromagnetic panels, smart boards, and video copystand. Module topics in this workshop include: Learning Science and Teaching: Misconceptions and Realities About New Teaching Methods, Using Audience Response Systems to Measure Learning, Social/Educational Networking (wikis, blogs/voicethread, and screencast), Applying Today's Technology in Your Classroom, and Moving to a Distance Learning Environment.

Advances in Learning Technologies (Year 3). This workshop focuses on more advanced instructional hardware, including digital scanners, capture devices, and projectors. It also includes instruction on other advanced technologies, including podcasting, course management software, digital video, virtual simulation, digital integration, classroom response systems, advanced video and Web conferencing.

Distance Education

Introduction to Distance Education (Year 2). This workshop provides an overview of distance education methods and use models, demonstrates remote distance education methods, and outlines a conceptual framework for learning technology decision making.

Table 7A-1. Workshops for the ELITE Faculty Development Program

Year	Learning Technologies	Informatics	Distance Education	Telehealth	Simulation
2007-2008	Introduction to Learning Technologies (on-site)	Introduction to Nursing Informatics (on-site)			Basic Application in Simulation Education (on-site)
2008-2009	Introduction to Learning Technologies (online)	Introduction to Nursing Informatics (online)	Introduction to Distance Education (on-site)	Introduction to Telehealth (on-site)	Basic Application in Simulation Education (on-site)
					Advanced Application in Simulation Education (on-site)
2009-2010	Introduction to Learning Technologies (online)	Introduction to Nursing Informatics (online)	Introduction to Distance Education (online)	Introduction to Telehealth (online)	Basic Application in Simulation Education (on-site)
	Advances in Learning Technologies (on-site)	Advances in Nursing Informatics (on-site)			Advanced Application in Simulation Education (on-site)
2010-2011	Introduction to Learning Technologies (online)	Introduction to Nursing Informatics (online)	Introduction to Distance Education (online)	Introduction to Telehealth (online)	Basic Application in Simulation Education (on-site)
	Advances in Learning Technologies (online)	Advances in Nursing Informatics (online)	Advanced Distance Education Techniques (on-site)	Advances in Telehealth (on-site)	Advanced Application in Simulation Education (on-site)
2011-2012	Introduction to Learning Technologies (online)	Introduction to Nursing Informatics (online)	Introduction to Distance Education (online)	Introduction to Telehealth (online)	Basic Application in Simulation Education (on-site)
	Advances in Learning Technologies (online)	Advances in Nursing Informatics (online)	Advanced Distance Education Techniques (online)	Advances in Telehealth (online)	Advanced Application in Simulation Education (on-site)

Advanced Distance Education Techniques (Year 4). This workshop encompasses integrating interactive communication with static and dynamic Internet access for new learning experiences.

Informatics

Introduction to Nursing Informatics (Year 1). This workshop provides an overview of the field of nursing informatics, including nursing standardized languages, electronic health records/computerized provider order entry systems, clinical decision support systems, and privacy and information security (HIPAA).

Advances in Nursing Informatics: E-Health & Mobile Computing (Year 3). This workshop builds on the core concepts of the informatics introductory workshop. Participants review e-health applications and the role of the nurse and patient in e-health. This workshop also covers the current application of mobile computing devices, such as tablet PCs and PDAs in healthcare.

Telehealth Technologies

Introduction to Telehealth (Year 2). This workshop covers the basic principles and history of telemedicine/telehealth and insights into its future applications. It also describes the use of the various educational tools used in telehealth and reviews common impediments faculty encounter when using telehealth in education and practice. Issues related to remote patient assessment, intervention, and evaluation are discussed, as well as ethical concerns such as privacy, confidentiality, informed consent, and equity of access and autonomy. Participants work with basic telehealth equipment in a hands-on session using a variety of telehealth technologies.

Advances in Telehealth: Virtual Hospitals (Year 4). Participants will be given various problems facing nursing leaders for a 250-bed community hospital. Participants will be asked to generate appropriate solutions that meet specified criteria. The instructor will also provide teaching strategies and application examples for clinical faculty.

High Fidelity Simulation

Basic Application in Simulation Education (Year 1-5). Through this workshop, instructors introduce participants to the role of simulation in nursing education and the way simulation can be incorporated as a thread within undergraduate and graduate curricula. The workshop consists of lecture, demonstration, and hands-on experience with a focus on creating introductory scenarios and includes an introduction to simulation software programs. It also includes information related to teaching concepts for simulation-based education, provides access to curriculum tools and templates, and stresses the relevance of the debriefing process.

Advanced Application in Simulation Education (Year 2-5). This workshop is designed to sharpen and broaden nursing faculty knowledge, skill, and abilities in the application of high-fidelity simulation. Workshop modules included: Debriefing in Simulation-Using a Structured and Supported Model, Metrics for Nursing Simulation Education, Just-in-Time and Point-of-Care Simulations, Best Practices in Simulation Education, and Multidisciplinary Approaches in Instructor Development.

Technical Assistance

As mentioned earlier, technical assistance was an important aspect of the ELITE Program and helped address some of the new technology implementation barriers identified during the needs assessment. Pitt-SON faculty offered one hour of technical-assistance consultation to each individual who attended an ELITE Program workshop. In addition, as the program has progressed, partnering institutions have identified a need for on-site technical assistance for institution-specific issues. This has resulted in Pitt-SON faculty traveling to partner institutions to consult with faculty and conduct workshops that meet their institution's specific needs.

Special Workshop

During the first year of the ELITE Program, the Pitt-SON faculty also held a special one-day dissemination symposium in Pittsburgh entitled *Faculty Development in Innovative Learning Strategies*. This workshop provided a learning community forum for educators to discuss curriculum integration and implementation strategies using current and emerging learning technologies. Nationally-recognized experts shared their innovative practices with learning technologies in undergraduate education. Education theories underpinning teaching and learning strategies were offered.

Program Outcomes—Early Results

Response to the ELITE Faculty Development Program has been positive from the first two years of faculty participants. During these first two years of the program, Pitt-SON has provided seven on-site topical workshops, one dissemination workshop, and is in the final stages of converting the Learning Technologies and Informatics workshops into online formats. Pitt-SON has hosted participants from more than 40 institutions and both evaluation and anecdotal feedback has been very positive. The hands-on, interactive format included within each workshop is the biggest plus for faculty and is a main reason why workshops that rely on hands-on learning, such as those related to high-fidelity simulation, will be offered only in a face-to-face format. As one participant noted, "The interactive format was very helpful in facilitating learning—very adult learner friendly. Bringing faculty together like this facilitates using evidence-based practice and improving student education, which will eventually improve patient outcomes."

Overall, participating faculty indicated they had learned how to use the technologies presented in Year 1 and Year 2 workshops. The program participants left with clear plans for how they would integrate the skills they had learned into their curricula. Program faculty were also positive that they had imparted knowledge to their faculty students and that, subsequently, these faculty would be more successful in their technology use. As previously noted, the programs also encouraged consultations by faculty participants and their institutions, leading directly to increased integration of technology into nursing education. Feedback from custom-designed workshops for schools of nursing in Pennsylvania and other states have been very positive, with participants enjoying the hands-on format and leaving the programs energized and highly motivated. We are in the process of surveying past participants to ascertain the extent to which faculty are integrating technology into their curriculum on return to their own facilities. We are encouraged by these early results and see them as validating the learning content, methods, and approaches. However, at this point in the program, these early results are anecdotal. Once we have completed our formal surveys, from Year 3 through Year 5, we will be able to report quantitative results on the extent of the impact the ELITE Program is having on adoption of technologies and informatics in new nursing curricula.

Summary

Initial data and workshop feedback from the first two years of the program indicate that the ELITE Program is successful. Pitt-SON is currently in the process of completing the first round of online workshops (based on face-to-face workshops offered during the first year of the program) and believes that this method of information delivery will be as successful as the live format. Once posted online, workshops will be available to any faculty with Internet access. Pitt-SON will continue to offer consultations, provide cutting-edge information and hands-on learning opportunities through face-to-face workshops, and disseminate successful experiences from the ELITE Program as strategies in an ongoing effort to expand the capacity of schools of nursing to educate students for healthcare practice in the 21st century.

References

1. Institute of Medicine. *Crossing the Quality Chasm: A New Health System for the 21st Century.* Washington, DC: The National Academies Press; 2001.

2. Booth RG. Educating the future ehealth professional nurse. *Int J Nurs Educ Scholarsh.* 2006;3(1):1-10.

3. Curran CR. Faculty development initiatives for the integration of informatics competencies and point-of-care technologies in undergraduate nursing education. *Nurs Clin North Am.* 2008;43(4):523-533.

4. Oyri K, Newbold S, Park HA, et al. Technology developments applied to healthcare/nursing. *StudHealth Technol Inform.* 2007;128:21-37.

5. Baldwin RG. Technology's impact on faculty life and work. *New Directions for Teaching and Learning.* 1998;76;7-21.

6. Tapscott D. *Growing Up Digital.* New York: McGraw Hill, 1998.

7. Richards J. Nursing in a digital age. *Nurs Econ.* 2001; 19(1):6-11,34.

8. Kupperschmidt BR. Understanding net generation employees. *J Nurs Adm.* 2001;31(12):570-574.

Case Study 7B

University of Kansas School of Nursing—
Faculty Development Program:
Health Information Technology Scholars (HITS)

By Helen R. Connors, PhD, DrPS (Hon), RN, FAAN

Introduction

This case study reports on a multi-university collaboration targeting informatics competency development in nursing faculty. Funded in 2007 by the HRSA's Faculty Development Collaborative Initiative,[1] the University of Kansas Health Information Technology Scholars Program (KU HITS) has completed two cohort educational cycles. Although the results are still in early stages for impact evaluation, all indications show the HITS approach to be a highly effective model for rapid faculty development in informatics competencies. A specified vision of HRSA's Faculty Development Collaborative (FDC) Initiative is to expand the capacity of schools of nursing across the United States to educate students for 21ˢᵗ-century healthcare practice. Since at this time, no institution or organization currently offers the full spectrum of information and other technologies necessary to carry out this initiative, HRSA proposed that the nursing collaboratives must develop linkages and partnerships to successfully meet the vision. To date, seven collaboratives have been awarded HRSA funding. This case study presents one collaboarative's approach.

HITS: Overview

The KU HITS Program works in collaboration with the schools of nursing at the University of Colorado, Denver, and Indiana University, Bloomington, and in partnership with NLN. Johns Hopkins University School of Nursing was added as a partner to the HITS Program in 2009. The HITS Program brings together thought leaders in informatics (Diane J. Skiba, University of Colorado, Denver), eLearning (Diane M. Billings, Indiana University), simulation (Pamela Jeffries, Indiana University), and telehealth (Helen R. Connors, University of Kansas), along with the leadership and professional development expertise of a national professional organization such as the NLN (Mary Anne Rizzolo). Using the knowledge, expertise, resources, and social capital of these thought leaders, the HITS Program has developed linkages with other institutions and organizations that offer a full assortment of leading-edge technologies for the advancement of nursing education and practice.

The HITS Partners

The success of the HITS Program is due in large part to the strength of the partners. Each collaborating institution provides resources and expertise that are well-recognized, nationally and internationally. This case study only briefly discusses the partnering institutions, since the major focus is on the HITS Program and its outcomes. For more complete information about the collaborating institutions, the reader is referred to their respective Web sites.[2-5]

The University of Kansas School of Nursing (KU-SON). KU-SON offers baccalaureate, master's, and doctoral degrees, as well as statewide continuing education programs. The school enrolls approximately 700 undergraduate and graduate students annually. The state-of-the-art school of nursing building includes a multidisciplinary clinical learning laboratory with low-, medium-, and high-fidelity simulators and classrooms equipped for distance learning and multimedia presentations. A major contribution that KU brings to the FDC is the Simulated E-health Delivery System (SEEDS). In 2001, KU-SON and Cerner Corporation, also in Kansas City, created a first-of-its-kind partnership to educate future nurses using a live-production clinical information system (CIS) designed to support and document the development of informatics competencies.[6-8] Also, the KU Center for Telemedicine and Telehealth (KUCTT) is a leader in the telehealth field and one of the most active programs in the world, with literally thousands of clinical consults including telehome health,[9,10] school-based telehealth, and mental health services.[11]

The University of Colorado Denver School of Nursing (UCD-SON). UCD-SON offers baccalaureate, master's, and doctoral education, as well as certificate programs and continuing education. The school enrolls nearly 700 undergraduate and graduate students annually. Of particular note is the I-Collaboratory Project: Partnerships in Learning,[12] an HRSA-funded project designed to create a learner-centered environment to support, socialize, mentor, and connect students who are engaged in computer-mediated learning. Also, UCD-SON is the home of the Center for Human Simulation (CHS)[13] and the Work Education and Lifelong Learning Simulation (WELLS) Center of the Center for Nursing Excellence.

Indiana University School of Nursing (IU-SON). With baccalaureate, master's, and doctoral programs on eight campuses throughout the state, IU is the largest school of nursing in the United States. IU-SON is internationally recognized for its many years of leadership in Web design/development. Additionally, the school is recognized for its leadership in simulation and simulation research. The SON's Learning Resource Center and the new Interdisciplinary Simulation Center create high-fidelity learning environments with cutting-edge technologies for educating future health professionals.[14,15] The school's Center for Teaching and Lifelong Learning[16] offers a variety of services including faculty development. The center advances the scholarship of teaching by disseminating knowledge and best practices in nursing education and healthcare worldwide.[17]

The National League for Nursing. NLN's mission is to "advance excellence in nursing education that prepares the nursing workforce to meet the needs of diverse populations in an ever-changing healthcare environment."[5] NLN is committed to helping faculty learn about informatics and helping them to develop proficiency in technology use.[17] Through NLN's access to more than 28,000 nurse educators, 1,200 institutional members, as well as 20 regional constituent leagues, NLN is in a strong position to assist the HITS Program to widely disseminate project findings to the greater nursing education community and ensure the sustainability of the project.

HITS Program Leaders

The executive leadership team for the HITS Program consists of leaders from each of the partnering institutions—Dr. Connors, Dr. Skiba, Dr. Jeffries, Dr. Rizzolo, and Dr. Billings in collaboration with the HRSA Project Officer for the FDC Initiative. With the exception of the HRSA Project Officer, these individuals have a history of working collaboratively. As a result, the team has a clear understanding of strengths, limitations, and work styles. They know how to work together as a team, with an understanding of what each brings to the table in terms of resources and responsibilities. Through past experience, they have built ongoing trust and respect for each other.

Purpose and Goals

The HITS Program is designed to develop, implement, disseminate, and sustain a faculty development collaborative (FDC) initiative to integrate IT into nursing curriculum and expand the capacity of collegiate schools of nursing to educate students for the 21st century. The goals of the project are: (1) merge informatics, telehealth, simulation, and eLearning to create powerful learning environments; (2) develop faculty to integrate IT in curricula to educate future practitioners; (3) educate a cadre of well-informed faculty who focus on real-world applications of technologies in their education practices; and (4) better educate future workforce with competencies to provide safe, quality, and efficient healthcare through technologies.

Target Audience

The target audience is faculty from diverse academic settings who are enthusiastic about integrating health information and other technologies into their curriculum. The participating faculty will advance their leadership skills within and beyond their own institutions. They will acquire the KSA to educate practitioners to meet the competencies required for improving quality, safety, and efficiencies in healthcare. In addition, HIT Scholars will develop a support network for innovative education, receive a HITS certificate of recognition, and be awarded continuing education credit for their participation.

The call for HITS Program applications is posted through NLN's listserv in early fall. All applications are reviewed using the following criteria: diversity of the faculty applicant, diversity and size of the student population, variety across levels of nursing program (2-year, 4-year, graduate, etc.), geographic distribution of the schools, range and quality of projects to be undertaken (simulation, informatics, eLearning, telehealth), and perceived commitment from the dean or program director in terms of resources, time, and match with institutional goals. The plan is to accept 30 to 50 HIT Scholars per year. Applicants are encouraged to apply as a team of two, but single applicants are acceptable. Figure 7B-1 displays the 2008 HIT Scholars.

Figure 7B-1. *2008 HIT Scholars. Photo courtesy of University of Kansas.*

Program Format

The program is designed for one calendar year and consists of four distinct phases: online learning modules, immersion workshop, project planning and eMentoring, and implementation and evaluation. While there is no fee for these program activities, the HIT Scholars or their institution must pay for expenses related to workshop travel, meals, and expenses related to the implementation of their technology projects at their respective institutions.

Phase 1: Online Learning Modules. The program year starts in January with the HIT Scholars completing six online modules from NLN's *Living Book on Technology*.[18] These modules are interactive and request that the faculty and HIT Scholars participate in eCommunity discussions and complete assignments.

Chapter 1: Getting Started. Here the framework for the Faculty Development: HITS Program is delineated. The framework is based on the work of the QSEN initiative.[19] The HITS Program is designed to help faculty develop the KSA competencies defined in the QSEN work. QSEN expands on the five core competencies required for all health professionals, as listed in the IOM's 2003 report, *Health Professions Education: A Bridge to Quality*,[20] and also addressed by the TIGER Collaborative.[21] Informatics, eLearning, simulation, and telehealth are mentioned as the core technologies of the FDC initiative and HITS Program. Work products from this module include a Goal Attainment Scale (GAS) for scholars' proposed projects and personal goals. This information helps the leadership team mentor HIT Scholars through their projects and helps scholars develop professionally.

Chapter 2: eLearning. Scholars learn a variety of eLearning technologies, including Web 2.0 tools, and explore how to fully use these tools for teaching/learning. HITS leadership mentors scholars to apply these technologies, while focusing on the IOM core aims: to prepare students to provide patient-centered care; to collaborate and work in teams; to gather, analyze, and synthesize evidence for practice; to continuously improve patient care; to ensure patient safety; and to use principles of informatics to retrieve, synthesize, and document information from client records and databases.[20] In this module and throughout each module, HIT Scholars are asked to consider how their identified project can incorporate some of the principles learned.

Chapter 3: Simulation. A beginning foundation is presented to get started with the design and development of simulation; the foundation is based on a theoretical framework that will help guide the design and implementation of simulations in nursing education. HIT Scholars first learn about the design and how to develop the case scenarios before moving into the implementation and evaluation phase of incorporating simulations into teaching-learning practices. Scholars work with a simulation template as they learn to design a simulation for their specific needs.

Chapter 4: Nursing Informatics and Health Information Technology Initiatives. Basic trends and current state of nursing informatics are presented. The healthcare delivery environment is dramatically changing as emerging HICTs impact how healthcare professionals practice. HIT Scholars use this information to ensure that these new technologies are integrated into curriculum to meet workforce demands and quality and safety competencies.

Chapter 5: Building Telehealth in Nursing Curriculum. Basic information about telehealth/telemedicine and its role in healthcare delivery is included. The role of the nurse in telehealth is emphasized. Although telehealth services are on the rise, few faculty have thought about incorporating this practice in nursing education. The intent is to help HIT Scholars explore opportunities for engaging students in telehealth practices.

Chapter 6: Integrating Health IT into Nursing Courses and Programs. Here HIT Scholars clarify and finalize their project goals and develop a plan for integrating health IT into their teaching. At this point, HIT Scholars review/revise their project, based on the new learning, and develop an implementation plan. They are reminded of the thoughtful planning that is essential to successfully transform nursing programs. They are provided a framework to help plan for the adoption of innovation in the curriculum and to assist with the process of managing change. Final products for this module are a comprehensive implementation plan and a set of slides for presentation of their project at the HITS Workshop. The plan and slides help the leadership team prepare for providing feedback and eMentoring.

Phase 2: HITS Immersion Workshop. A three-day workshop is held each spring to immerse HIT Scholars in learning with and about technology. The workshop has a common core curriculum that builds on the online modules. Sessions present leading-edge, technology-enhanced education and practice models and includes demonstrations and applications, mentoring/consultation sessions, networking opportunities, and field trips to technology-rich environments. During the workshop, HIT Scholars present their project to their assigned group and receive feedback from both the group and designated mentor. Scholars are also introduced to a social network site on "ning" that provides a mechanism for interacting during and after the conference. This social network site augments the workshop and helps HIT Scholars learn the richness of social networking.

Phase 3: Technology Project Planning and eMentoring. In this phase, HIT Scholars continue planning and developing their institution-specific projects. They continue studying using the online modules, and they participate in mentor led eCommunities. Webinars also are conducted during this time to share experiences, advance learning, and provide support for HIT Scholars to implement projects. The outcome of this phase is an approved technology-enabled project to be implemented in the fall (or summer) semester. Figure 7B-2 shows a HIT Scholar introducing simulation and the EHR in the curriculum.

Phase 4: Project Implementation and Evaluation. In this phase, the HIT Scholars implement and evaluate the integrated technology project at their respective institutions and continue participation in the eCommunities discussions with mentors. They use the goal attainment evaluation strategies presented in their GAS and implementation plan to evaluate the progress. Also, it is in this phase that HIT Scholars participate in the summative evaluation of the HITS Program. During this time, they reflect on their GAS (project and personal), complete their QSEN competencies assessment as a posttest measure, submit a diffusion of innovations index, and finalize a "shovel ready" abstract of their project.

HITS Program Outcomes

The HITS Program evaluation plan includes both formative and summative evaluation techniques. The Internal Executive Committee and the External Advisory Committee serve as the Quality Improvement (QI) team. To date, the HITS Program has been highly successful at meetings its goals. In terms of outcome evaluation of the HITS Program, one of the most telling indicators is the increasing demand for this program. In Year one

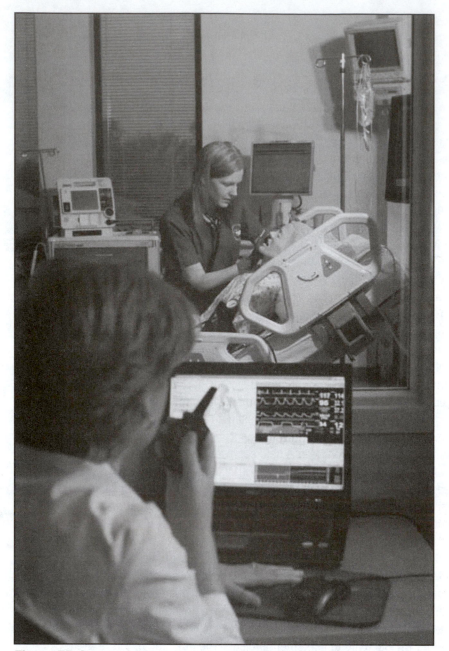

Figure 7B-2. *HIT Scholar Introducing Simulation and the EHR in the Curriculum. Photo courtesy of University of Kansas.*

of the project, we received 513 applications for the 30 positions we had allocated. Due to the tremendous response, we accepted 50 applicants, and these applicants represented 27 diverse schools across twenty-two states. Forty-eight of these 50 applicants completed the HITS Program in December 2008. In Year 2, we received 403 applications and accepted 53 faculty representing 27 diverse schools and 20 states.

Formal outcome evaluation includes a number of measures.

Online Module Evaluations

Participants reported that the objectives of the six online modules were met, module content was new and was presented clearly, and the presentation format was appropriate and adequately covered the topic. Participants indicated they planned to incorporate what they learned in the modules into their teaching. There were limited suggestions for improvement of the modules.

On-site Workshop

Thirty-nine of the 48 participants completed the workshop evaluation. All but one objective was above the 85% benchmark for strongly agree/agree that the objective was met. The one workshop objective that did not meet the benchmark was "Use various metrics for evaluating outcomes of innovation in education." HITS project leaders agree that this objective was not adequately covered because of time. The plan is to add a new online module that will more adequately address this content area.

Goal Attainment Scale

Goal Attainment Scale (GAS) is used to assess the HIT Scholars' project goals. For this first cohort, 19 of 27 project teams submitted the GAS for their projects. At the one-year mark (2009), five (26%) schools were able to complete all their goals. Eight (42%) of the schools were able to complete 70% of their goals. For the latter group, most met all goals but had one that was partially completed. The remaining six schools completed half or fewer of their goals. For the second cohort of HITS, we are doing a better job of assisting scholars to establish realistic goals, and we are monitoring their progress more closely.

Diffusion Index

Each project team is asked to complete a spreadsheet of items related to the diffusion of the work completed as a part of the HITS Program. There are three major categories of diffusion: (1) impact on students, courses and curriculum, (2) impact on faculty and colleagues, and (3) dissemination mechanisms, such as meetings, presentations, and publications. Twelve of 27 teams were represented in the diffusion index. Ten schools reported an impact on a number of their courses, ranging from 1 course to 12 and affecting between 24 and 360 students and between 1 and 60 members of the faculty. Two projects focused on faculty development and reported having an impact on between 500 and 800 faculty members. Eight schools reported an impact on their curriculum. All schools reported an influence on their faculty colleagues, ranging from one member to an entire faculty. Five schools reported they had influenced colleagues outside of their school/department of nursing, ranging from a handful of faculty to hundreds attending a consortium meeting. Only one school had a press release about the faculty being selected as a HIT Scholar. Eight schools had articles announcing their selection in their alumni or college/university newspapers. Nine presented information at a faculty meeting, and seven presented at a curriculum committee meeting. Two schools gave campuswide presentations. Two schools gave one to two local presentations. Three schools gave presentations at national conferences, and one presented at an international conference. One person wrote an article for their school publication and one had submitted an article to the *Journal of Nursing Education*. Several schools had plans for presentations and publications in the near future. A summary table of the impact on curriculum, courses, students, and faculty, as well as the overall number of presentations and publications is presented in Table 7B-1.

QSEN Competencies

Participants were asked to rate the importance of (Importance Scale) and their perceived preparation to teach to (Performance Scale) three specific QSEN areas of competency: Evidence Based Practice (EBP), Safety, and Informatics. Importance, assessed through a Likert Scale, ranged from unimportant (1) to extremely important (5). Performance, also assessed on a Likert Scale, ranged from poor (1) to excellent (5). Results of the pre-HITS program assessment demonstrate that participants consistently perceived the importance of the competency to be significantly higher that their ability to teach to the competency. Comparison of the pre– and post-HITS Program assessment of these same competencies is currently being analyzed.

Summary

The advancement and adoption of HICT is seen as central to achieving the highest level of quality and safety in healthcare. This promise has been captured in a variety of national reports and initiatives, including the HRSA-sponsored Faculty Development Collaborative: Integrating Technology into the FDC: ITNEP Project.[1] It is evident by the overwhelming response to the HITS Program that this type of faculty development is crucial and welcomed. In addition, the collaborative creates a robust approach to meeting the demand for faculty development.

Table 7B-1. *HITS Program Outcomes: Summary Table*

Goal Attainment Scale 19 of 27 Schools Reported	All Goals Met (100%)	Goals Partially Met (70%)	Goals Minimally Met (50% or less)
	5 projects (26%)	8 projects (42%)	6 projects (32%)

Diffusion of Innovation Index 12 of 27 Schools Reported	Impact on Students, Courses, Curriculum	Impact on Faculty	Presentations, Publications
# of school's curriculum	8		
# of courses/range	69 (1-12)		
# of students/range	2432 (24- 360)		
# of faculty/range		1727 (1-800)	
# of presentations			21
# of publications			10

Individually, the academic partners for this project, the University of Kansas, University of Colorado, and Indiana University, have a strong history of technology-enabled education and innovations in academics and scholarship. All three project directors have demonstrated outstanding leadership in academic innovations. Joining with NLN and its vast networks and information/communication technologies has created an infrastructure that not only supports the HIT Scholars Program but paves the way to develop and expand this program into a world-class faculty development initiative that could not be accomplished individually.

The outcomes of the HITS program are promising based upon the early results from the first cohort. We expect the true impact of this faculty development effort within a given institution to unfold over a five-year period as curriculum changes reach a critical inflection point and publication/presentation are forthcoming from this body of HITS faculty. We will continue to monitor the progress of this first cohort as we build and strengthen the future cohorts over the next four years. For complete and up to date information about HITS, visit www.hits-colab.org.

References

1. Health Resources and Services Administration. *Faculty Development: Integrated Technologies in Nursing Education and Practice.* http://www.hrsa.gov. Accessed July 10, 2009.
2. University of Kansas School of Nursing. http://www2.kumc.edu/son/. Accessed July 17, 2009.
3. University of Colorado, Denver. http://www.nursing.ucdenver.edu/. Accessed July 17, 2009.
4. University of Indiana, Indianapolis. http://nursing.iupui.edu. Accessed July 17, 2009.
5. National League for Nursing. http://www.nln.org. Accessed July 17, 2009.
6. Simulated E-hEalth Delivery System (SEEDS). http://www2.kumc.edu/healthinformatics/video.html. Accessed July 17, 2009.
7. Connors HR. Transforming the nursing curriculum: Going paperless. In Weaver C, Delaney C, Carr R, Weber P, eds, *Nursing and Informatics for the 21st century: An International Look at Practice, Trends and the Future.* Chicago: HIMSS; 2006:183-194.
8. Warren JJ, Fletcher KA, Connors HR, Ground A, Weaver C. The SEEDS Project: From healthcare information system to innovative educational strategy. In P Whitten, D Cook. eds. *Understanding Health Communication Technologies.* San Francisco, CA: Jossey-Bass, 2004:225-231.
9. Popkess-Vawter SA hybrid view of weight management. *Kans Nurse.* 2005;80(10):6-8.
10. Smith CE, Dauz ER, Clements F, et al. Telehealth services to improve non-adherence: A placebo-controlled study. *Telemed J E Health.* 2006;12(3):289-96.
11. Connors HR. Telehealth technologies enhance children's health care. *J Prof Nurs.* 2006;18(6):311-2.
12. University of Colorado Health Science Center. *Center for Human Simulation.* Available at: http://www.uchsc.edu/sm/chs/. Accessed July 17, 2009.
13. University of Colorado School of Nursing. *I-Collaboratory: Partnership for Learning.* http://www.nursing.ucdenver.edu/grad/healthinformatics.htm. Accessed July 17, 2009.
14. Indiana University School of Nursing. *Learning Resource Center.* http://nursing.iupui.edu. Accessed July 17, 2009.

15. Indiana University. *Interdisciplinary Simulation Center.* http://medicine.iu.edu/body.cfm?id=7080&fr=true. Accessed July 17, 2009.

16. Indiana University School of Nursing. *Center for Teaching and Lifelong Learning.* http://www.iupui.edu/~solctr/research/details.php?id=230. Accessed July 17, 2009.

17. NLN. Educational Technology and Informatics Advisory Council. http://www.nln.org/getinvolved/AdvisoryCouncils_TaskGroups/etimac.htm. Accessed July 17, 2009.

18. National League for Nursing Living Books. http://www.nln.org/facultydevelopment/onlinecourses/livingbooks.htm. Accessed November 25, 2009.

19. Cronenwett L., Sherwood G., Barnsteiner J, et al. Quality and safety education for nurses. *Nurs Outlook.* 2007;55:122-131.

20. Greiner AC, Knebel E, eds. Institute of Medicine. *Health Professions Education: A Bridge to Quality.* Washington, DC: The National Academies Press, 2003.

21. Evidence and Informatics Transforming Nursing: 3-year action steps toward a 10-year vision. TIGER. http://www.tigersummit.com/uploads/TIGERInitiative_Report2007_Color.pdf. Accessed April 30, 2009.

Case Study 7C

Technology Integration Program for Nursing Education and Practice (TIP-NEP)

By Barbara S. Turner, DNSc, RN, FAAN; and Mary E. Paden, MSN, RN, CPNP

Introduction

Schools of nursing across the nation face a similar dilemma—an aging faculty workforce and insufficient numbers of nursing faculty to meet the demand of those seeking admission to nursing programs. The situation is complicated by the projection of a continuing faculty shortage for the next 15 years.[1] How are schools handling the shortage? One answer is to hire faculty who are clinical experts in the practice arena and/or those who are new graduates of doctoral programs. The problem then becomes that many of these new faculty have inadequate expertise or foundations in teaching. As one junior faculty member told us during a focus group on teaching nursing students in a community college "I am teaching by the seat of my pants and my pants are on fire!" Thus, we have a cadre of faculty who tend to teach the way they were taught because they have no foundation in pedagogy. Most of us were taught using passive techniques, with a focus on facts. The faculty who taught us recognized that we had a learning curve but often neglected to recognize that there was a "forgetting curve"—that is, when information is not applied, it is forgotten.[2,3]

If it were as easy as teaching faculty how to teach using traditional methods, the problem could be solved, but there is the added complexity that today's students learn and expect to be taught very differently from students of even five years ago. Present day students want and expect "just-in-time" information; thus, they do not want to learn pharmacology one semester and apply it the next; they want to learn the information as it is needed for application. Therefore, the challenge is that while faculty continue with their old ways of teaching, students are learning in new ways and expect innovative technologies and teaching strategies in the classroom. These new learners yearn for inductive reasoning opportunities over a daily outpouring of facts. Besides having immediate feedback and answers to questions using just-in-time-learning, new learners are also looking for learning interaction with their peers. An important difference is the use of communication, Internet, and IT. Today's students are technology savvy and use technology in almost every aspect of their lives, a descriptor Prensky has termed as being *digital native*.[4,5] All of us who teach have experienced the student who says, "Another lecture; another slow death by PowerPoint"; or the students with their laptops who pipe up in class and say, "You just cited the incidence of breast cancer as X, but this Web site indicates that the incidence is Y. Can you comment on this?"

We recognize that advances in educational technologies are increasing at an extremely rapid pace; however, their inclusion in the classroom occurs at a much slower rate. Since this explosion has implications for the way students learn and the way faculty need to tailor their teaching in nursing programs, it is difficult for nursing faculty to stay current on existing and emerging technological developments available for the classroom or at clinical practice sites. Currently, a wide variety of technologies are used by students and faculty in schools of nursing across the country. Wikis and blogs assist students and faculty in the sharing of information, as well as with various collaborative ventures. Texting, instant messaging, and PDAs have, for most students, become second-nature at this juncture. Many faculty, however, do not use these tools and consider them technologies of the young. Newer technology most commonly used in nursing programs includes interactive modules with decision matrices and online textbooks. The interactive modules require students to be engaged in the course content and to explore various Web sites to reach a decision and then to document why they support the decision that they made.

Simulation has long been used in nursing programs, but the type of simulation used was most often static rather than interactive. The newer interactive simulators engage the students in patient scenarios. Simulation allows students to repeatedly practice scenarios without chance of harm, until done correctly. Students' performances can then be reviewed and discussed with immediate feedback given. Simulation also allows students to learn by trying new things and making different choices, choices they may not have made if working with real patients. The ability to digitally record the student's performance and review it with an instructor allows students to step back from the scenario and self-assess their decision-making choices.

Simulation is not "the" answer for teaching and learning. There are barriers to simulation: the staff and space that are required and the high cost of purchasing and maintaining simulation equipment and infrastructure Thus many schools cannot afford the equipment. Students using simulation must be onsite, which presents obstacles for distance-based or online learners. Performance anxiety may interfere with some students' progress and their ability to learn.

The TIP-NEP Program

A significant barrier in integrating technology into nursing programs is promoting nursing faculty buy-in. Nursing faculty may be intimidated by technology and retreat to teaching in old familiar ways. Our team's challenge was to address how best to bring nursing faculty up to speed on current and emerging technologies. We recognized a need for an innovative technology education program for nursing faculty members from across the country. And importantly, we wanted to create a safe and supportive environment in which they could learn how to incorporate educational technology into nursing curricula. Thus, we developed a five-year, three-part educational program for faculty in schools of nursing across the nation. We responded to a call for applications from U.S. Department of Health and Human Services (HHS). Duke University School of Nursing, Durham, N.C., in collaboration with two other North Carolina schools of nursing, Western Carolina University and Fayetteville State University, were selected by HRSA to develop the program (HRSA U1KHP07713). We entitled the program, Technology Integration Program for Nursing Education and Practice or TIP-NEP (http://www.tip-nep.org),[6] as it is commonly known.

The goal of the program is to provide new information and skills related to educational and clinical technologies to nursing faculty teams in the United States. This is accomplished through a three-phase program, which we describe next.

Phase I

The first phase of TIP-NEP consists of online technology modules. The goal of Phase I is for participants to become familiar with, and advance their knowledge of, various types of educational technology that are being used to enhance nursing education and practice. The modules are open to anyone in the United States who teaches nursing students. Learners can customize their experience by enrolling only in the modules that are of interest to them. There is no cost to the learner to access and complete these modules, and CEUs are awarded upon successful completion.

TIP-NEP modules have included the following topics: recording audio to PowerPoint presentations; using Adobe Captivate to develop multimedia enhanced presentations, scenarios, and application demonstrations; using Camtasia for classroom capture and developing lecture material; intellectual property and copyright issues; and academic use of Web 2.0 tools. Each year, at least three online modules are added to the module listing. What we have found is that within 24 months of posting the modules, the content becomes obsolete or common knowledge. Thus, the grant has a technology committee that works with eLearning experts and instructional technologists locally and nationally to determine what technologies are becoming available that have application to the classroom. These topics are evaluated, and content experts are contracted to prepare the modules for presentation using the assumption that the learner has no knowledge in that area.

The modules can be completed at the users' convenience. For those modules that address computer programs, the narrator of the module uses screen shots of the computer program and directional arrows so that the learner is guided through the learning experience. At the completion of the module, there is a post-test; successful completion of the post-test generates a CEU certificate. Feedback on the modules has been uniformly positive.

Phase II

Unlike the first phase of TIP-NEP, which is open to anyone who teaches nursing students, the second phase is a competitive selection for a four-day symposium at Duke University. The goal of Phase II is for nursing faculty to overcome the barriers and gain tips on the use of current and emerging technologies. To be eligible, faculty from a nursing program in the United States form a team (consisting of three faculty members) and submit an abstract of an innovative use of technology in their educational programs. Because the goal of the grant is to enhance the integration of technology into nursing programs, part of the application consists of each team member indicating the influence they have in their nursing program (community colleges, four-year colleges, or universities) for technology adoption. Team members do not have to be nurses but must teach in associate's, bachelor's, master's, DNP, or PhD nursing programs. Applications are reviewed by the executive leadership group of the grant and assessed using a weighted scale. Selection for the program is highly competitive; approximately 25% of the applicants are selected for attendance. Once selected, team members must complete the online educational modules (Phase I) before attending the four-day, on-campus symposium (Phase II). This requirement ensures a current knowledge on technologies used in education.

Each year, we accept approximately 11 TIP-NEP teams. The teams are housed at an executive conference center on the Duke University campus. This setting allows informal and formal education to take place both in and outside the classroom. During the day, there are formal presentations by experts in technology. We have cutting-edge presentations that stretch the mind of the learner to envision how this technology, now or in the future, can be applied to their educational programs. The real excitement of the conference takes place when the teams present what they have done with technology in education, the barriers they encountered, and their tips for success. These presentations spark the evening conversations in the common areas of the executive conference center as participants discuss in detail with the other teams what they did and how it could be used at another institution. The small number of attendees (~33) allows them to get to know each other over the course of the four days.

The Phase II conference includes lectures, team presentations, hands-on demonstrations, a technology fair with invited vendors, and facility tours of the Duke Simulation Labs, the Duke immersive Virtual Environment (DiVE) Center (www.duke.edu)[7], and the Duke Telepresence Room (www.fuqua.duke.edu/admin/extaff/news/global_conf_2002).[8] For the second phase of the TIP-NEP, the cost of travel to the conference (up to $400 per person), hotel, meals, and conference materials are paid for by the grant. Additionally, the selected teams are awarded a $3,000 stipend that they can use to further integration of technology into their curricula. CEUs are awarded to team members. Phase II lectures have included topics such as:

- Incorporating Informatics Competencies
- Creating a Sense of Community in the Online Classroom
- Advances in Electronic Medical Records
- The Use of High-Fidelity Scenarios in Simulated Cultural Encounters
- Competency Assessment of Clinical Skills Through Technology
- Integration of Technology in the Simulation Hospital
- Simulation: Improving Patient Safety and Quality of Care
- Serious (Educational) Gaming
- Personal Health Records
- Structuring a Tech Team for Your Nursing School
- The Evolution of Integrating Technology
- Tablet PC in the Wireless Classroom
- Developing a Simulation Center for Your Nursing School
- iTeaching and iLearning: Presenting Content on iPods

Examples of Faculty Team Presentations

- Vance-Granville Community College in North Carolina developed a simulation hospital unit. The unit includes seven patient rooms, multiple simulation mannequins, a computer room with eight computers, a storage room, a clean/sterile room, a debriefing room, and a contaminated ("dirty") room. They also use podcasts and Blackboard in their simulation scenarios.
- California State University, Fresno, is using PDAs to teach diagnostic skills, with instruction that has a strong visual component. The faculty videotape clinical skills, such as examination techniques, maneuvers, and finding anatomical landmarks. Students then load the videos onto PDAs. This way, students can watch and study the clinical skills at any time and as often as needed.
- In Miami Beach, Florida, Barry University's nursing program is using high-fidelity simulation scenarios that incorporate cultural encounters to develop cultural awareness, knowledge, and competence. While interpreting and assessing symptoms, students tailor their communication to the level of comprehension of Spanish-speaking patients and develop the ability to handle multicultural requests. The scenarios are videotaped and then discussed.

- Binghamton University's nursing program (New York) added a media arts expert to its simulation team. Their video scenarios are now of a higher quality due to the added technology, theater, and scene development skills of the media expert.
- Montana State University, Bozeman, created a realistic community health clinic using simulation technology, which challenges students to manage all clinic operations. High-fidelity simulation manikins and culturally diverse live actors are used in the simulation clinic. Students manage telephone triage, follow epidemiologic trends, make budget amendments, and carry out many other clinical responsibilities.
- Georgia Perimeter College's (Atlanta) nursing faculty noted that since students' time in the skills laboratory was limited, they decided to videotape segments on clinical nursing skills and convert them to podcasts. Students can download the podcasts and watch them over and over anywhere, anytime, until the skills are mastered.
- University of Detroit Mercy created an avatar-guided, online orientation for nursing adjunct faculty. This online orientation accommodates the many diverse schedules of adjunct faculty, and they have reported that it has helped them feel more engaged in the orientation process. The online orientation includes topics such as faculty development, future teaching opportunities, and FAQs (frequently asked questions).
- San Diego State University, California, opened the Human Patient Simulation Center in 2006. The center includes seven simulators, a nurse's station, hospital rooms, computers, and a debriefing station. Each patient space has a camera and a microphone so that simulations can be recorded, discussed, and reviewed with students at a post-session conference or class.

To demonstrate for conference attendees what future learning environments might be, a tour of the DiVE and the Telepresence Room are provided. The Duke immersive Virtual Environment (DiVE) Center was opened in November 2005, and is only the fourth such system in the United States. The DiVE is a 3m x 3m x 3m room with all six surfaces—the four walls, the ceiling and the floor—used as screens onto which computer graphics are displayed. The virtual features include head- and hand-tracking and real-time computer graphics. The DiVE room is a fully immersive room in which the individual (researcher, educator, etc.) literally walks into the world, is surrounded by the display, and is capable of interacting with virtual objects in the world. Stereo glasses provide depth perception, and a handheld "wand" controls navigation and input into the world for manipulating virtual objects. Once in the room and experiencing the virtual environment, participants in the program are able to envision how the room might be used for teaching. A virtual brain can be disassembled, examined, and reassembled; a virtual room in a virtual house can be used to experience the difficulty in completing tasks of daily living as one ages.

The Duke Telepresence Room, located in the Fuqua School of Business, provides an immersive collaboration experience. Those participating in the conference sit on one side of a long table and on the other side are eight-foot, high-definition cinematic views that show another room in life-like proportions. Participants in the second room can be across the world or across the street. The use of high-definition sound results in natural sounding conversation and the "EyeConnect" technology puts the camera at eye level for what seems to the participants as natural face-to-face interaction. Those participating in the conference often forget that those on the other side of the table are not actually in the room. During one session, a participant reached across the table to shake the hand of the person who was actually several miles away.

Phase III

We know that after a stimulating and thought-provoking conference, the hardest part is returning home. Participants have learned new information and are filled with ideas about what can be done, at what cost, and what barriers to expect. For that reason, our project requires that teams be made up of three faculty members who have an influence on technology use at their institutions. Having a cadre of three creates a critical mass for initiating changes or trying new projects. It is very difficult for one faculty member to do this alone but having partners who have been through the same experience enables the team to institute changes. The goal of TIP-NEP Phase III is to not let the momentum from the on-campus session fade. Thus, we provide online resources that are useful for participants as they educate colleagues, as well as develop and integrate technology content into their curricula. All presentations are video-recorded and posted to a password-protected Web site. The presentations are not open to the general nursing community, as our participants have indicated that they would like to have their projects published. However, we have an "Ask the Expert" forum and a participant discussion forum that are featured on the Web site. Project faculty mentors are available to answer participant questions once they return to their home institutions. Faculty teams also have $3,000 to spend on integrating technology into the classroom.

Summary and Outcomes

Our primary outcome is to determine if there is a change in the integration of technology into the nursing curricula and to determine the impact of the conference on faculty and, ultimately, on students. What follows is a short summary of the outcome from the 2007 TIP-NEP teams and how they used their stipend funds to integrate technology into their nursing programs. We present only a few for illustrative purposes.

The California State University, Fresno, team held PowerPoint and Impatica workshops for their faculty members and purchased Impatica software. They also hired a student actress and re-filmed one of their diagnostic examination skills videos and formatted the video for use on a PDA.

The University of Alabama, Birmingham, team built a partnership between the school of nursing and other professions by developing a mock trial of a civil case that was enacted in the mock trial courtroom of the law school. Law students enacted all the aspects of courtroom attorney roles. The nursing students were jury members and witnesses for the defense. The major nursing part was played by a theatre major to elevate the level of performance. The nursing and legal aspects included in the mock trial script were standard of care, reasonable prudent nursing behavior, best safety practice in medication administration, negligence, and personal accountability. The case was based on an actual case that occurred when a Digoxin (lanoxin) decimal error led to a patient death.

The Oregon Health and Science University, Portland, team created three faculty development resources, including a Web-based tutorial on using online technologies, an online resource indexing all faculty development offerings, and a Web space that allows a partner school to access and share curricula outlines.

The Binghamton University team purchased Camtasia and Captiva software, as well as "clickers" for more interaction in the classroom. They also held their First Annual Faculty Development Workshop, to which they invited ten nursing schools. They had a total of 52 participants.

The benefits of TIP-NEP are reaching far beyond the TIP-NEP participants themselves. Faculty teams are enabled to return to their home institutions with the skill set and didactic tools necessary to integrate into their curricula the knowledge they have gained, as well as the ability to train other faculty members and students. From the 2007 cohort alone, there are more than 4,500 undergraduate students, graduate students, and nursing faculty from across the country who are benefitting from the ongoing technology integration projects funded by TIP-NEP.

References

1. American Association of Colleges of Nursing. *Faculty Shortages in Baccalaureate and Graduate Nursing Programs: Scope of the Problem and Strategies for Expanding the Supply.* Washington, DC: AACN; 2005.
2. *Forgetting Curve.* (2009) http://encarta.msn.com/encnet/refpages/search.aspx?q=forgetting+curve. Accessed September 28, 2009.
3. Ebbinghaus. *Human Memory.* http://users.ipfw.edu/abbott/120/Ebbinghaus.html. Accessed June 5, 2009.
4. Prensky M. Learning in the digital age. *Educational Leadership.* 2006:63;(4):8-13.
5. Prensky M. Digital natives, digital immigrants. *On the Horizon.* 2001:9;(5):1-2.
6. http://www.tip-nep.org. Accessed February 8, 2009.
7. www.duke.edu. Accessed June 1, 2009.
8. www.fuqua.duke.edu/admin/extaff/news/global_conf_2002. Accessed May 18, 2009.

Case Study 7D

Health Informatics and Continuing Education: The Italian Case

By Julita Sansoni, PhD, MScN, RN; Anna Rita Marucci, MsNs, BaNsc, RN;
Francesco Tarantini, MSN, BSN, RN; and Walter De Caro, MNs, DAI

Introduction

Different health reform processes have brought with them new regulations and laws. Information and Communication Technology (ICT), as a useful strategy, has become part of ordinary practice in the economic sector and also for the management of all healthcare trusts and institutions. This reorganization process shifted to a management system in which hospitals, as business trusts, have the decision-making capacity to fulfil the objectives of efficacy, efficiency, and economic robustness. In this process, it has been necessary for the senior management of healthcare systems and hospital trusts to utilize analytical tools to keep data readily available in order to permit prompt and timely decision making.

Obviously these analytical tools might be ICT-supported systems able to handle a massive amount of data sourced in real time from healthcare and administrative activities.

This new movement also impacts the nursing profession, which has faced a revolution in administrative organization and career advancement promotion, with many becoming senior managers of their departments and sectors. In order to have competent, skilled, up-to-date professionals who are able to respond to the needs of the population, an efficient system of continuing education was needed.

Telemedicine in Italy

In 1990, the European Commission created the European Health Telematics Observatory. Italy had begun utilizing telemedicine in 1976, with the first electrocardiogram (EKG) sent from a distance, with subsequent acts of data-sharing. This prefaced several plans initiated in Italy that are being used to enhance the transmission of data between health institutions. For instance, St. Rafaele Hospital in Milan and Sarajevo Hospital are involved in a program called "Shared" in which they have a joint agreement for transmission and receipt of data. This makes the telemedicine between Naples and the islands of Ischia and Procida possible. Also, the Pediatric Hospital Bambino Jesus in Rome is currently experimenting with telemedicine for monitoring cardiac patients. This experiment started in Milan with equipped ambulances capable of connections with the 118 emergency telephone number and cardiac units of the hospitals, thus opening up electronic links that embrace both distance and mobility.

The AIR-TEM (Home care COPD Monitoring Patients Project) monitors patients at home. The team is composed of general medicine, nursing staff, and the added support of a pneumologist. Milan hospitals are also responsible for making this organizational plan happen with the intention of shortening the waiting time for the patient, while at the same time making possible an early diagnosis to avoid further complications. The majority of the professionals involved in this program become part of an interdisciplinary team in which each individual's professional input is seen as integral to the team's success. There are more than 600 patients enrolled in this plan of care. The aim is to create a virtual hospital, from which patients with chronic conditions may obtain care from home.

Another project named "Simply...to be born" (*Semplicemente...nascere*), created by the University Hospitals Company: Vittorio Emanuele, Ferrarotto, Saint Bambino of Catania (Sicily), aims to guarantee prompt advanced assistance to premature infants by utilizing telemedicine tools. Infants will be monitored and controlled from their houses with a series of medical devices, such as pulsometers, balances, and glucometers. Daily monitoring of premature patients is possible by sharing updated data from the head office to family members, physicians, and nurses in the neonatology unit at the hospitals. The end goal is to reduce hospital visits and support parents in the management of premature infants at home. Initially, 20 infants from Catania and nearby provinces were enrolled in the program.

Telemonitoring technology allows notification of an individual's status change by activating a series of alarms at hospitals near the patient's house, so that immediate advanced intervention, as well as parents' participation in the care, can be achieved. The hospital has created a multidisciplinary team to assist premature babies and their families, embracing neonatologists, nurses, psychologists, home care assistants, drivers, and social workers. Competent experience in telemedicine values both medical and nursing documentation in hospitals in Italy. To achieve competency in telemedicine, both medical details and nursing documentation are needed. Some ongoing studies are exploring development of common documentation elements, but we are still far from any sort of generalization of these technological services.

Continuing Education in Medicine: The Italian Development

Thus far, the necessity of staff trained in the new technologic environment has been established. In fact, the rapid development of health sciences and technological innovations obligate organizations to not just keep the elevated standard in terms of acquaintances and clinical, technical and managerial, and behavioral abilities, but also to grow on par with technological advances as they emerge.

Continuing education:

- Represents a moral obligation and deontological duty specially previewed from the Deontological Codes.
- Represents a citizen's right to be treated with new facets of health technology as they emerge and are proven.
- Is the first objective of the Healthcare Service.

In light of the information previously discussed, in numerous countries, Continuous Education programs in Medicine (ECM) are required after degree completion at a university. In fact, the only way of operating adequately is doing so early and in an organized manner, then effectiveness, appropriateness, promptness and efficiency can also be assured. In Italy, this system has been implemented by law (Decree Legislative of December 30th, 1992, N. 502 in combination with the decree legislative of July 19th 1999, N. 229). This law monitors the continuing education interests of all healthcare professionals in Italy. This is directed at a draft of approximately 850,000 practitioners (of which 354,000 are physicians, 340,000 nurses, and 52,000 dentists, citing the numbers of the more representative healthcare professions). Between 2002 and 2007, Italy has provided for more than 360,000 ECM events for a total of approximately 12 million participants. These numbers make evident the size of this phenomenon. Of these participants, 72,149 were from health trusts, with a total participation of 1,850,000 professionals.

There are differences between the events offered by hospitals and those offered by other providers. The ECM system involves organizing and controlling every educational activity, theoretical and practical, that is promoted by accredited organizations (scientific or professional organizations, hospitals, specific healthcare structures and specific educational professional companies), with the aim of keeping the level of education high and serving the needs of healthcare professionals. This means hours of education for which ECM credits are given. For example, one educational day dedicated to the ECM—at maximum level for the national commission—corresponds to ten ECM educational credits.

Acquisition of educational credits is not free, but is regulated by a progressive system that foresees in the first 5 years of experimentation that started in 2002, the acquisition of 150 credits, distributed as follows:

- 2002: 10 credits (minimum 5, maximum 20)
- 2003: 20 credits (minimum 10, maximum 40)
- 2004: 30 credits (minimum 15, maximum 60)
- 2005: 30 credits (minimum 15, maximum 60)
- 2006: 30 credits (minimum 15, maximum 60)
- 2007: 30 credits (minimum 15, maximum 60)

In 2007, the experimental phase was completed, and the revision established the structure and the roles of who would be entitled to ECM education.

As the experimental phase had left some "gaps" in education with the national healthcare service and with the regional healthcare services, the state-regions conference in August 2008 established the new organization and the new rules for the continuing education system for the period 2008-2010. The conference promoted the document "Riordino del Sistema di Formazione Continua" (Reorganization of the Continuing Education Systems) that lists the new rules for governance of the ECM Program in 2008-2010.

The fundamental function for continued formation in the ECM system governance is initiated by the national commission, then promoted by the state and the region. It was recognized in the role promoted by healthcare professionals who took responsibility for participating in the ECM system and utilizing the number of choices available.

National ECM Commission

The president of the commission is the health minister and is supported by two vice-presidents. The commission will establish the national formative objectives, such as rules for obtaining formative credits, and minimal requirements and universal policies in all national territories for provider accrediting and control.

Professional Orders

The institutions of higher education have recognized the role that certification providers play in the efficacy of the training. In particular, they will be entrusted with overseeing the programming and evaluating the professional training and resuming preparation, certification, and attestation of educational credits. Through the design of the rules, a net of regional and provincial observatories have been activated which will produce the verification and control of the education activities and provider requirements. In virtue of such tasks and with the aid of the registrar's office of the formative credits, the Orders can monitor the appropriateness of the national, regional and professional formative objectives, advise professionals on how to enroll, and through representatives within the national Commission ECM, develop a way to address the aim of matching individual needs with study opportunities.

Recipients

An agreement between the state and the regions confirms the obligatory nature of the ECM formation for all healthcare professionals that directly operate within individual and collective health, as well as freelance practitioners. The same Conference supported the idea that it is necessary to expand this requirement to all health-related professions.

Formative Objectives and Dossier Format

Healthcare professionals have to obtain ECM credits specific to their own profession; therefore, they must specify the objectives to be met, and these must be congruent with the national, regional, and business objectives. The objectives, selected and characterized on such bases from every professional, will go to compose the dossier (portfolio) format which will constitute, for each professional, the plan for scheduling their own distance education. For the professional Order, the document for the appraisal and the verification of the continued education is carried out by the assessors trained in certification of ECM credits.

Educational Credits

Every ECM credit corresponds approximately to an hour of updated education for the health professional. The Conference State-Regions recognize, between the various healthcare professions, differing normative levels of modernization gained from respective working contracts and invite the new ECM Commission to recognize the specificities of the health professions in attributing value to the formative credits. Starting in 2008, every professional has to obtain 50 educational credits annually (minimum 30, maximum 70) until they catch up to the 150 credits required within the years 2008-2010. When they have accumulated 150 credits, the professional will be able to use maximum of 60 valid acquired formative credits gained between 2004-2007; also in such cases, it remains the professionals' obligation to acquire "at least" 90 new credits.

Didactic Formats

Beside the traditional residential-base education, the Commission recognized some didactic modalities in order to do more training, while looking at the possibilities and the attitudes of the individual professional. Between the didactic types they introduced, a process of education, embracing both distance study and self-learning, was used. Moreover, the following are recognized as ECM credits; research, teaching, and overseas courses. However, it will be up to the national Commission to determine the quota percentages of credits required with reference to the didactic types (in the agreement it was suggested to limit up to 20% of the credits from deontological, legislation, managing, computer science, and foreign languages matters) and to the thematic ones of the course (it is suggested in this case to distribute the debits as 20% from national objectives, 50% from regional and business, and 30% from individual interest).

Provider

The agreement foresees the passage from the accreditation of the single event (arrangements covering 2002-2007) to the accreditation of the provider (for 2008-2010), which could be either national or regional. The minimum requirement in order to obtain accreditation, created by the ECM National Commission, will be national equivalents and the credits distributed from the provider will have national recognition.

Recording and Certification of the Credits

Recording educational credits through the registrar's office of the ECM is performed by the Cogeaps (Consortium that re-unites the professional Federations of the Orders and the Colleges and other associations). The certification of the same qualifying credits, that conclusively represent professionals' distance learning, is entrusted to the professional Order, which will have to verify the dossier of the student (the distribution of the formative credits, the objectives, thematic and other various types of education implemented; and the assessment of the eventual exemptions from the education obligation). The Order, assessing exceptions that prevented the professional from fulfilling the total education required, will be able to concur with the other interested parties on satisfying the formative debit within the next year after the deadline (2008-2010, meaning in this case 2011).

Dismissals and Transitory Norms

The State-Regions Conference, knowing the difficulties faced in the five years of experimentation, and considering the complexity of some matters, has changed the definition of some arguments. Consequently, the new national Commission for continuous education was invited to provide comparisons and define the purposes of education program incentives and endorsements, promoting a comparison of the professionals and the associations they are representing.

Sponsors

Careful attention is given to the declaration of the Sponsors online guidelines: the Organizations declare all Sponsors. Some Organizations omit the Sponsors trade candidature; however, Sponsors ask to indicate them to the validation; others are invited by the Secrétariat to specify them as a result of verification of the requests for accreditation. It has been prohibited, among other things, to credit ECM events carried out on cruise ships and sponsored from pharmaceutical companies.

The Role of the Referee

The accreditation takes place through the www.ministerosalute.it/ecm Web site and the documents are validated through a digital signature as an instrument. In this phase, the referees come into the scene. They are experts chosen from every profession whose task is to estimate and validate the events. They give the score based from a colleague-made checklist found at the Ministry of Health Web site. The system is formatted so that the reading of the files is obligatory. The appraisal process can be concluded with the validation and the identification of incongruence to be corrected within 60 days from the notification. In this case, other referees are involved for greater accreditation control. In some events, it is necessary to involve referees from every profession so the interest of every formative event can be estimated. When the event is different and the objectives are not appropriate, it cannot be credited. The referee is not qualified to appraise the events in which he or she participates as faculty. It is accepted that the referees must refuse the appraisal of the event noting "conflict of interest."

In order to access the site ID, a password and authentication of the digital signature are required at the ECM Web site (http://www.ministerosalute.it/ecm/ecm.jsp).

Digital Signature Necessary for the ECM Operations

The electronic signature has the same legal value as the conventional one. It is associated with the document and enriches the authenticity.

- **Authenticity:** A digitally signed document guarantees the identity of the underwriter.
- **Integrity:** Guarantees that the document had not been modified after its subscription.
- **Do not repudiate:** The signed electronic document is legally valid and cannot be repudiated from the underwriter.

The digital signature is the final result of a complex mathematical algorithm that allows an electronic document to gain the same validity as an autograph. The process of electronic signatures is based on asymmetric cryptography: every holder has two keys, a private one—secret and guarded on a Smart Card and protected by an access code (PIN); and a public one—guarded and published by the certificating agency that is used for the verification of the electronic signature. The two keys are correlated in an univocal way; however, after activation of the public key, it is impossible to go back to the private one. The electronic signature is generated with the aid of a Smart Card and application software on a personal computer (PC) equipped with the corresponding operating system. It is indispensable to adopt some minimal measures of security in order to get the maximum reliability of the operating atmosphere.

In order to generate the digital signature, a digital signature kit is necessary which contains:

- A generation device for the signature (Smart Card)
- A Smart Card reader
- Software that supports the device

The digital signature eliminates the necessity to produce the documents in the original paper form (as of article 65 of D. Lgs 7 March 2006, n. 82 from the Code of the Digital Administration). In order to use the function, users must complete the ECM credits and this requirement is checked by a computer function. Health professionals can use the Smart Card for the signature to underwrite relative documents and to be able to use the function for the following documents:

- The organizer recording sheet
- The absence of conflict of interest (according to Article 48, code 25, of the d.l. 269/2003, converted in law 24 November 2003, n. 326.)
- The message of validation of events and the business formative plans
- The record of the relationship of the event

For the referee, the appraisal process is completed by affixing the Company signatures of the appraising organization. All these procedures occur online, according to the policy of the Code of the Digital Administration.

Summary

The slow and progressive construction of the continuing education system in Italy, which aims to maintain an optimum of healthcare quality, will have to have all members of the healthcare system working towards common objectives. They must be committed to the progressive standardization of the processes as a sole instrument to guarantee real appropriateness and effectiveness of educational action. The objective is to convince health professionals that:

- Continuous education does not have to be identified exclusively with participation in formal conferences, but also can be tied to initiatives in the field or through FAD technologies that allow for a controlled learning process.
- ECM should become a continuous process instead of an accidental activity that is sporadic or opportunistic.
- The goal should be to identify important problems, to search for and interpret the new processes and to incorporate them into practice.
- They should develop an intense practical activity in order to audit the professional practice.

These priorities can be applied through a powerful development of the systems and of the homogeneity of "informative" language between the interested members. The system must accommodate a variety of nursing roles and consider the diversity of the professionals. From an information system point of view, numerous problems related to poor communication have been found, due to the implementations of different technologies, with consequent problems of inconsistent data across systems.

The challenges faced in the health IT field are relative to:

- Definition and information standardization of files between regional and national registrars offices to enable system integration and data exchanges and data bank standardization.
- Re-balancing of educational methods with potential distance and on-site education, through interactive methodologies.
- Procedures of accreditation, with improvement of the interaction in the sequential processes.
- Control of the conflict of interest (pre and post event).

The ECM System must be engaged to guarantee quality, transparency, and reproducibility of the accreditation of the educational events. This can only be guaranteed through rigorous control and coordination of activities. In the initial phase of experimentation, the impression is that the educational focus has not been on the healthcare staff's needs, but rather has served to slow down system adoption and to put its credibility at risk. However, it is imperative to improve the system itself so healthcare professionals view education as a continuous and evolving process.

Acknowledgement

A special thanks to Florida International University student, Camilla Avendano. Without her help, efforts, and commitment, this case study would have not have come to fruition.

Bibliography

Agenzia sanitaria regionale dell'Emilia-Romagna. *Educazione continua in medicina in Emilia-Romagna.* www.ecm.regione.emilia-romagna.it. Accessed January 20, 2009.

Bertazzi P. Continuing medical education and advanced professional qualification in occupational health, *G Ital Med Lav Ergon.* 2007;30(3):249-251.

Bonetti M, Vesprini A, Concetti M, et al. New guidelines on the use of iodinated contrast media: a report on an implementation project. *Radiol Med.* 2009;114(3):496-508.

Comodo N, Tarsitani G. The academic education of the district medical officer. *Ann Ig.* 2004:14(2 Suppl 2):55-60.

Garrison GR. Three generation of technological innovation, *Distance Education.* 1998;6(4):235-241.

Marchionni B, Bacchielli, M. Continuing education in medicine: CME. *Assist Inferm Ric.* 2007;28(2):96-105.

Ministero della Salute. *Progetto ECM.* www.ministerosalute.it/ecm. Accessed January 21, 2009.

Moja L, Moschetti I, Liberati A, et al. Using Clinical Evidence in a national continuing medical education program in Italy. *PLoS Med.* 2007;4(5):106-113.

Osservatorio ANEE sull'eLearning. L'E-Learning nelle aziende sanitarie. *Panorama della salute* 2003; 20(5):18-22.

Peters P, Plötz W. Mountain medicine education in Europe. *Wilderness Environ Med.* 1998;9(1):19-27.

Pinto A, Selvaggi S. Sicignano G, et al. E-learning tools for education: regulatory aspects, current applications in radiology and future prospects. *Radiol Med.* 2008;113(1):144-157.

Pressato L. The Italian way to Continuing Education in Medicine. *Clin Chim Acta.* 2002;319(2):155-159.

Putoto G. (2006). Teaching and continuing professional development: an Italian experience. *Clin Chem Lab Med.* 2002:44(6): 704-707.

Quintaliani G, Zoccali C. Continuous medical education. *G Ital Nefrol.* 2006;21(4):355-361.

E-learning in sanità. Collana Dossier dell'Agenzia sanitaria regionale dell'Emilia-Romagna. 149, 2007.

Regione Lombardia. Linee di indirizzo del sistema ECM (Educazione Continua in Medicina). www.regione.lombardia.it. Accessed December 11, 2008.

Senato della Repubblica. *Atti della Commissione Paramentare di inchiesta sull'efficacia e l'efficienza del Servizio sanitario nazionale.* www.senato.it. Accessed November 11, 2008.

Villani G. (2009). Sponsorship and conflicts of interests in CME: the Italian experience. *Med Law.* 2009;28(2):197-209.

## CHAPTER 8

Informatics Competencies for Nurses Across Roles and International Boundaries

By Brian Gugerty, DNS, MS, RN; and Joyce Sensmeier, MS, RN-BC, CPHIMS, FHIMSS

Introduction and Background

For several decades, interest in the competencies nurses need to effectively "use computers" in clinical, administrative, research, and educational settings has increased. In 1988, NLN published a document titled *Nursing Informatics Competencies for Nurse Educators and Researchers.*[1] It included computer, informatics, and information literacy competencies, most of which was relevant to all nurses. Looking back on that work in light of recent interest and efforts around informatics competencies, it was quite prescient and is, in many ways, still relevant to the dialog taking place on this topic today. Our assessment is that the concept of informatics competencies for nurses has evolved through four phases: (1) Attitudes toward computers (1980-1990), (2) Basic computer skills (1985-1995), (3) Nurse informatician competencies (1989-2000), and (4) Informatics competencies for all practicing nurses and graduating nursing students (2001-present, and beyond). You will note that our estimates of the years associated with these phases sometimes overlap. This is because of the considerable variability among organizations, institutions, and individuals in the evolution through these phases.

During the 1980s, in the "attitudes toward computers" phase, there was an expectation that computers and information systems in healthcare would change nursing practice, but in actuality, very few implementations of computers and CISs occurred at that time. Healthcare organizations were focused on "automating" billing and other back office functions, as well as ancillary department applications, such as laboratory, radiology, and pharmacy. The outcome of those implementations demonstrated the potential value of computers and information systems for nurses and thus helped nurses overcome their fear and mistrust of this new technology. Further discussion ensued that focused on concerns about computers creating a barrier between nurses and patients. Attitude scales were soon developed and extensively studied.[2,3,4]

The "basic computer skills" phase began when nursing faculty, informaticians, and staff educators in healthcare delivery organizations transitioned their focus from simply convincing nurses to use computers, and helping them get over their fear, to focusing on providing key skills for nursing practice. By the mid 1990s and the end of this era, computers had become ubiquitous in many parts of society, and the revolution that would bring computers into every household was well underway. Many nurse informaticians argued that computer use in practice was inevitable, whether or not nurses were anxious about such use. The transformation from mainframe and DOS-based operating system environments to graphic-user interfaces and client-server approaches also unfolded during this era. This technology transition had significant implications for the input, output, and throughput devices used in all areas of nursing practice. Profound changes in software were realized as computers became more accessible and usable for the average professional, not just for the technology specialist, with the advent of word processing, spreadsheet, and database applications for the PC and Macintosh computing environments. Thus educators and practice managers who wanted to engage nurses in this rapidly progressing environment focused on basic computer hardware and software knowledge and skill development.

In the very late 1980s and throughout the 1990s, nursing informatics pioneers turned their attention to training the next generation of nurse informaticians. They realized the need to not only replace themselves, but that they must do so in large numbers to meet the growing demand for and potential of nursing informatics for supporting all domains of nursing practice. In 1989, the first graduate program in nursing informatics was founded at the University of Maryland in College Park. Over the past 20 years, the Maryland program has graduated more than 600 master's degree and doctoral-trained nurse informaticians. The focus during this third phase was on nurse informatician computer and informatics competencies.[5,6]

There are now more than 20 nursing informatics or healthcare informatics undergraduate and graduate education programs hosted by schools of nursing in the United States. AMIA NI-WG maintains a list of and information about such programs on its Web site.[7] There are also increasing numbers of nursing informatics graduate education programs outside the United States. Even with this progress, Barton[8] notes that there are still not enough formally trained nurse informaticians to meet the demand. Hart affirms our assessment of the first two phases of informatics competencies for nurses and points to justification for the fourth phase when she writes:

> A review of the literature relevant to informatics competency and education in U.S. clinical settings indicated that not only were computer and information nursing competencies not effectively defined until 2002 but also clinical assessment regarding informatics components was predominantly limited between 1999 and 2006 to attitudes and use of online resources. Establishing a baseline of informatics competencies in the existing workforce is vital to forecasting and planning for growth in an expanding electronic healthcare delivery era.[9]

We are presently in the fourth phase, which focuses on informatics competencies for all practicing nurses and graduating nursing students. Computers, business productivity/communication applications, and CISs/EHRs are no longer optional; they are necessary for all nursing practice environments. Because of this reality, at a minimum, basic computer and informatics competencies are needed by all nurses. Yet, many nurses do not presently meet this minimum level of competency. It is also important at this point to recall that nurses are not all alike. In 2001, Prensky[10] coined the phrase *digital native* to describe young students and workers who have experienced information and communication technology as part of their lives from the very beginning. Digital natives have learned computer and informatics competencies more organically than many of their older colleagues, who are often referred to as *digital immigrants*. Since the average age of U.S. nurses in 2008 was 48, there are many digital immigrants in practice today. Many of these so-called digital immigrants do not have the computer and informatics competencies needed to excel and evolve in their practice. Although clearly not as challenged as digital immigrants, an important reality to note is that a significant number of digital natives may also have gaps in their computer and informatics competencies. Therefore computer and informatics competencies are relevant for all practicing nurses and graduating nursing students.

Why Is This Important? Why Do We Care?

With nearly three million nurses in practice today, nurses constitute the largest single group of healthcare professionals and serve as providers and coordinators of care in every healthcare setting. In their front-line roles, nurses have a profound impact on the quality and effectiveness of healthcare. Nurses are also key leaders in the effective use of IT to impact the quality and efficiency of healthcare services and act on behalf of patients, families, and other care providers to promote health and advocate for an environment of patient-centric care.

As coordinators of care, nurses are often the focal point for connecting acute, ambulatory, long-term, community-based, home care, and public health settings, ensuring that data necessary for managing specific patients and populations are not only shared but translated into action. Further, nurses are active in education, implementation, research, and optimization of IS throughout the healthcare system. Even though a cadre of nurses has obtained informatics competencies expertise and has been performing informatics roles for decades, a recent review of the literature in the United States discovered that computer and informatics competencies were not effectively defined until 2002 by Staggers and colleagues.[11]

While many nursing education programs have focused on computer literacy skills, there are relatively few that have incorporated informatics competencies into their curricula. In order to engage all nurses in the unfolding digital era, the TIGER Initiative was founded in 2004.[12] TIGER is a grass roots volunteer initiative whose mission is to bring together nursing informatics organizations and nursing professional organizations to promote education and practice reform, thus enabling nurses' fuller participation in the digital revolution which is transforming healthcare. Today, in the United States, more than seventy professional nursing organizations, associations, vendors, and government entities have come together in collaborative teams to implement the following recommendations:

- Develop a U.S. nursing workforce capable of using EHRs to improve the delivery of healthcare.
- Engage more nurses in the development of a nationwide health IT infrastructure.
- Accelerate the adoption of smart, standards-based, interoperable, patient-centered technology that will make healthcare delivery safer and more efficient, timely, and accessible.

As a result of the TIGER effort to bring numerous organizations together to craft an informatics agenda, NLN and AACN have responded with a renewed emphasis on requiring informatics competencies in the nursing curriculum. Progress is being made to further define and develop informatics competencies for nurses both nationally and globally. Regardless of region or country, there is a need for nurses to apply their ability to understand all sides of the IT process by acting as translators between the language of technology and the needs of clinicians and patients.

At the highest level of competency, informatics nurses represent a discipline of nursing practice that focuses on the integration of data, information, knowledge, and wisdom to support patients, nurses, and other providers in their decision making in all roles and settings. In a recent study of the value and impact of informatics nurses, results suggest that while nurse informaticians play a crucial role across a wide variety of IT areas, those areas of greatest impact are patient safety, workflow, and end-user acceptance.[13] These findings suggest the nurse informatician is a driver of quality care and acts as an enabler of clinician adoption within their practice settings. It is essential that informatics competencies be consistently defined and adopted across the nursing profession for all citizens to realize the desired outcomes in our healthcare systems.

Recommended Informatics Competencies for All Practicing Nurses and Graduating Nursing Students

This decade is characterized by many independent efforts in colleges, universities, and healthcare delivery organizations to enumerate computer and informatics competencies and insure that nurses obtain them. TIGER, among other initiatives, has recently addressed computer and informatics competencies for nurses in the United States.[12] TIGER has established nine collaborative teams:

1. Standards and Interoperability
2. Healthcare IT National Agenda/Health IT Policy
3. Informatics Competencies
4. Education and Faculty Development
5. Staff Development/Continuing Education

6. Usability/Clinical Application Design
7. Virtual Demonstration Center
8. Leadership Development
9. Consumer Empowerment/PHR[14]

The TIGER Informatics Competencies Collaborative (TICC) formed and was tasked with addressing informatics competencies. Dozens of volunteers participated in its activities. Those activities consisted of (a) literature review; (b) collecting, organizing, categorizing, and synthesizing academic and "real world" lists of computer and informatics competencies for nurses; (c) aligning categorized competencies to existing standards; and (d) producing a final report which includes recommendations.[14] Many articles, books, and other documents were included as part of the TICC literature review. Summaries of that work can be found on the TICC wiki site.[15]

Seminal publications written by Staggers et al[11,16] that are focused on informatics competencies are found in the literature. These articles describe the development and validation of a framework of informatics competencies for nurses at four levels of practice. This rigorous work expanded the predominate focus at the time which was on basic computer and informatics competencies for nurses to include knowledge and skills in using computers and CISs for nursing practice. It also emphasized the importance of CISs and informatics competencies for nursing practice. This work greatly informed the work of the TICC; the influence of the framework can be discerned in the final recommendations. Another very important influence on TICC was the updated 2008 ANA *Nursing Informatics: Scope and Standards of Practice*,[17] which focused on newly expanded competencies relative to the previous edition.

After analyzing the literature, TICC collected many lists of academic and "real world" computer and informatics competencies for nurses from educational and healthcare delivery organizations. Many of these organizations and institutions of higher learning had adapted the Staggers et al[11,16] framework and created more specific competencies with which to evaluate their nurses. Based on TICC's review of the academic and real-world competencies and the excellent framework, direction, and competencies asserted by Staggers et al, TICC determined that the competencies published in the literature remained too general. During deliberations, TICC identified existing competencies that included recommendations or syllabi of informatics competencies, which were de facto standards in healthcare and other industries.

TICC then compared its lists of academic and real-world competencies with candidate informatics competency standards and found excellent matches (see Table 8-1). TICC chose the European Computer Drivers Licence Foundation's European Computer Drivers License (ECDL) syllabus to cover basic computer competencies.[18] TICC chose the American Library Association's Information Literacy Competency Standards to cover Information Literacy Competencies.[19] Finally, for the largest category of informatics competencies for nurses—information management, TICC choose both Health Level Seven's (HL7) Electronic Health Record Functional Model—Clinical Care Components[20] and the European Computer Driving Licence Foundation's International Computer Driving Licence—Health (ICDL-Health) syllabus.[18]

Choosing de facto industry standards to be the recommended fulfillment of each of the TICC competency categories has significant strengths. The standards were developed through years of work by experts in the field. The standards are represented by organizations that will evolve them into the future, thus giving needed sustainability to TICC Informatics competency recommendations. Finally, these standards, for the most part, have companies and institutions that provide educational resources to assist with their implementation. We will now describe each category of standard in more detail.

Table 8-1. TIGER Informatics Competencies Collaborative Selected Standards and Standard-setting Bodies

Components of the TIGER Informatics Competencies Model	Standard	Standard-setting Body
Basic Computer Competencies	European Computer Driving Licence	European Computer Driving Licence Foundation
Information Literacy	Information Literacy Competency Standards	American Library Association
Information Management	Electronic Health Record Functional Model - Clinical Care Components	Health Level Seven (HL7)
	European Computer Driving Licence - Health	European Computer Driving Licence Foundation

Adapted from: Gugerty B, Delaney C: *TIGER Informatics Competencies Collaborative Final.* Available at http://tigercompetencies.pbworks.com/ 2009.

Basic Computer Competencies

To demonstrate the relevance of basic computer competencies to nurses, the TICC report states:

> There are a substantial number of digital immigrants in the nursing workforce who have not mastered basic computer competencies. Many digital natives have gaps in their basic computer competency skill set. Europeans realized this shortcoming in the workforce across many industries and acted on it. The European Computer Driving Licence (ECDL) Foundation set basic computer competencies in the late 1990s and again in this decade. About seven million Europeans have now taken the ECDL exam and become certified in basic computer competencies.[15]

Basic computer competencies are fundamental to the other two sets of TICC competencies. The TICC recommends the ECDL syllabus to address needed basic computer competencies for all U.S. practicing nurses and graduating nursing students. The modules of ECDL are:

- Module 1: Concepts of Information and Communication Technology (ICT)
- Module 2: Using the Computer and Managing Files
- Module 3: Word Processing
- Module 4: Spreadsheets
- Module 5: Using Databases
- Module 6: Presentation
- Module 7: Web Browsing and Communication[18]

However, ECDL-certification requires 30-plus hours of study and costs more than some institutions may be able to afford. Therefore, TICC has ranked the relative importance of ECDL syllabus items and recommends the following as a first step to basic computer proficiency for all practicing nurses and graduating nursing students. These are considered feasible and affordable and will provide basic computer competencies for nurses and allow them to go on to obtain other TICC competencies.[15]

Module 1: Concepts of Information and Communication Technology (ICT)
Module 2: Using the Computer and Managing Files
Module 3, Section 3.1: Word Processing: "Using the application"

Module 7: Web Browsing and Communication

TICC basic computer competencies recommendations are listed in Table 8-2.

Table 8-2. TICC Basic Computer Competencies Recommendations

TIGER Basic Computer Competencies Recommendations	Timeline for Adoption
All practicing nurses and graduating nursing students gain or demonstrate proficiency in ECDL modules 1, 2, and 7, as well as ECDL Section 3.1	By January 2011
All practicing nurses and graduating nursing students become ECDL-certified or hold a substantially equivalent certification.	By January 2013

Adapted from: Gugerty B, Delaney C: *TIGER Informatics Competencies Collaborative Final.* Available at http://tigercompetencies.pbworks.com/ 2009.

Information Literacy

Information literacy builds on TICC Basic Computer Competencies. The TICC report states that:

> Information literacy is the ability to
> - Identify information needed for a specific purpose
> - Locate pertinent information
> - Evaluate the information
> - Apply it correctly[15]

Information literacy is critical to incorporating evidence-based practice into nursing practice. The nurse/provider must be able to determine what information is needed. This involves critical thinking and assessment skills. Finding the information is based on available resources, which can include colleagues, policies, and literature in various formats. Evaluating or appraising the information also involves critical thinking and the ability to determine the validity of the source. The actual implementation of the information results in putting the information into practice, or applying the information. The evaluation process is necessary to determine whether the information and its application resulted in improvements. Thus, information literacy competencies are fundamental to nursing and evidence-based practice.

As shown in Table 8-3, the American Library Association's report "Information Literacy Competency Standards for Higher Education" identifies the five numbered competencies. The TICC is recommending these for all practicing nurses and graduating nursing students.

Information Management

Information management can be usefully conceptualized as a process consisting of (1) collecting data, (2) processing the data, and (3) presenting and communicating the processed data as information or knowledge. A critically important component to nurses' work is knowledge work, such as critically assessing individuals and communities. In the digital age in which we live, information management is a core competency for knowledge workers.[21]

Increasingly, clinical information is managed by nurses through information systems. Today, the most important information management competencies for nurses are those that relate to the EHR system.

The TICC report states that:

> Using an EHR will be the way nurses manage clinical information for the fore-
> seeable future. However, nursing responsibilities are not changing in the shift to
> increased use of EHRs. For example, nurses are still required to exercise due care
> in protecting patient privacy. But the manner in which these responsibilities to

patients and communities are upheld may be different. Therefore, all practicing nurses and graduating nursing students are strongly encouraged to learn, demonstrate, and use information management competencies to carry out their fundamental clinical responsibilities in an increasingly safe, effective, and efficient manner.[15]

Table 8-3. Five Competencies Identified in American Library Association's Report "Information Literacy Competency Standards for Higher Education"[19]

TIGER Information Literacy Recommendations	Timeline for Adoption
1. Determine the nature and extent of the information needed 2. Access needed information effectively and efficiently 3. Evaluate information and its sources critically and incorporate selected information into his or her knowledge base and value system 4. Individually or as a member of a group use information effectively to accomplish a specific purpose 5. Evaluate outcomes of the use of information	By January 2011

Adapted from: Gugerty B, Delaney C: *TIGER Informatics Competencies Collaborative Final.* Available at http://tigercompetencies.pbworks.com/ 2009.

A rigorous as well as practical work on identifying the parts of the EHR for clinicians was done by the HL7 EHR Technical Committee. It was published in February 2007 as an approved American National Standard Institute (ANSI) publication titled "The HL7 EHR System Functional Model, Release 1."[20]

The direct care component of the HL7 EHR System Functional Model serves as a basis of information management competencies for practicing nurses and graduating nursing students. Although these clinical information management competencies are numerous, they merely make explicit the competencies for proficient use of EHRs that practicing nurses and graduating nursing students are responsible for today in a paper information management environment or a mixed paper- and electronic-environment.

Regarding the EHR System Functional Model, the TICC report states that:

> The direct care component of the HL7 EHR System Functional Model is not quite sufficient by itself to cover the information management responsibilities of nurses in the digital era. What is needed in addition is a set of competencies that address the importance of electronic health record systems to nurses and the "due care" that nurses need to take in managing information via these systems. Again, the European Computer Driving Licence Foundation has developed a set of items that address these concerns, with International Computer Drivers Licence (ICDL) -Health.[18]

Here are the ECDL-Health syllabus items transformed into TICC competencies:

The Nurse Will:
Concepts
- Verbalize the importance of health information systems to clinical practice.
- Have knowledge of various types of health information systems and their clinical and administrative uses.

Due Care
- Assure confidentiality of protected patient health information when using health information systems under his or her control.

- Assure access control in the use of health information systems under his or her control.
- Assure the security of health information systems under his or her control.
- Have the user skills as outlined in the HL7 EHRS model, which includes all of the ECDL-Health user skills of navigation, decision support, output reports and more.

Policy and Procedure

- Understand the principles upon which organizational and professional health information systems use by healthcare professionals and consumers are based.

TICC recommendations for information management competencies are listed in Table 8-4.

Table 8-4. TICC Recommendations for Information Management Competencies

TIGER Information Management Recommendations	Timeline for Adoption
Schools of nursing and healthcare delivery organizations will implement the information competencies listed in Appendix A.	By January 2012
Schools of nursing and healthcare delivery organizations will implement the transformed ICDL-Health syllabus items previously listed.	By January 2012

Adapted from: Gugerty B, Delaney C: *TIGER Informatics Competencies Collaborative Final.* Available at http://tigercompetencies.pbworks.com/ 2009.

Current Activities

To demonstrate informatics competency, nurses must be able to see relationships among data elements, make judgments based on trends, and use informatics solutions.[16] In addition to the recommendations previously discussed, a number of activities are currently underway to equip nurses with these skills. The Healthcare Leadership Alliance (HLA)—a consortium of six major professional membership organizations representing more than 100,000 management professionals—is leveraging the research and experience of their individual credentialing and certification processes to define five competency domains among all practicing managers. These areas are (1) communication and relationship management, (2) professionalism, (3) leadership, (4) knowledge of the healthcare systems, and (5) business skills and knowledge, which include information management. This process resulted in the development of the HLA Competency Directory, which is an interactive tool that allows a user to sort competencies by skills, knowledge, core and specialty areas, key words, and professional association. As a partner in development of the HLA competency framework, AONE uses the tool to allow their members to rate their performance in each competency area and develop a plan for areas in which improvement is needed.[22]

In collaboration with the American Health Information Management Association (AHIMA), AMIA has created core competencies for all healthcare workers who use EHRs. The core competencies in the free tool include five domains: health information literacy, informatics skills, privacy and confidentiality of health information, data technical security, and basic computer literacy skills.[23] The matrix tool captures the core competencies and sorts those thought to be applicable to varied roles and settings of healthcare delivery and their workflow needs. One of the aims of this effort is for healthcare professions and related organizations to adopt and incorporate applicable basic competencies in professional development and training activities for the current work force, as well as including them in academic curricula.

Call for Reform

In response to forces within the United States emphasizing the need to reform nursing education and prepare a workforce that is capable of applying informatics skills and competencies, the board of governors of the NLN approved a position statement calling for reform in the development of faculty and informatics content in nursing programs.[24] The need for reform was emphasized by the results of a survey of faculty and nursing education administrators that revealed approximately 60% of programs had a computer literacy requirement and 40% had an information literacy requirement. Only half of the respondents indicated that informatics was integrated into the curriculum and that clinical experience with information systems was provided during clinical experiences. Additionally, many respondents could not differentiate computer and information literacy from informatics.

Skiba and colleagues detail the NLN's recommendations to advance the informatics agenda, for faculty, administrators, and its members in Chapter 5. In addition to these recommendations for faculty, deans and administrators, the NLN has made the following recommendations to guide faculty, administrators, and its members.[24]

For Nurse Faculty
- Participate in faculty development programs to achieve competency in informatics.
- Designate an informatics champion in every school of nursing to: (a) help faculty distinguish between using instructional technologies to teach versus using informatics to guide, document, analyze, and inform nursing practice; and (b) translate state-of-the-art practices in technology and informatics that need to be integrated into the curriculum.
- Incorporate informatics into the curriculum.
- Incorporate ANA-recognized standard nursing language and terminology into content.
- Identify clinical informatics exemplars—those drawn from clinical agencies and the community or from other nursing education programs—to serve as examples for the integration of informatics into the curriculum.
- Achieve competency through participation in faculty development programs.
- Partner with clinicians and informatics people at clinical agencies to help faculty and students develop competence in informatics.
- Collaborate with clinical agencies to ensure that students have hands-on experience with informatics tools.
- Collaborate with clinical agencies to demonstrate transformations in clinical practice produced by informatics.
- Establish criteria to evaluate informatics goals for faculty.

For Deans/Directors/Chairs
- Provide leadership in planning for necessary IT infrastructure that will ensure education that prepares graduates for 21st-century practice roles and responsibilities.
- Allocate sufficient resources to support IT initiatives.
- Ensure that all faculty members have competence in computer literacy, information literacy, and informatics.
- Provide opportunities for faculty development in informatics.
- Urge clinical agencies to provide hands-on informatics experiences for students.
- Encourage nurse-managed clinics to incorporate clinical informatics exemplars that have transformed nursing practice to provide safe, quality care.
- Advocate that all students graduate with up-to-date knowledge and skills in each of the three critical areas: computer literacy, information literacy, and informatics.
- Establish criteria to evaluate outcomes related to achieving informatics goals.

The NLN is also reaching out to other accrediting bodies, regulatory agencies, and certifying bodies to further build consensus on the informatics competencies needed to advance nursing practice in the 21st century.

Global Perspectives

Canada Health Infoway has developed an end-user EHR engagement strategy after identifying key issues of concern among clinicians.[25] This strategy intends to advance the adoption of IT solutions by nurses, physicians, and pharmacists. Specific applications of the strategy to the nursing profession include efforts to increase the involvement and collaboration of nurses in EHR initiatives, address the educational needs of future graduates and practicing nurses, and demonstrate the value of EHR solutions. To this end, a National Nursing Advisory Group was formed to provide a forum for bringing together representatives from key nursing organizations around the country to advance the dialogue while further developing and implementing the end-user strategy. Additionally, a Learning-Academic Advisory Panel was formed to advise Infoway as to what is needed to support the integration of EHR content into the core curricula of health disciplines and address the training needs of practicing clinicians. This advisory group includes academics, students, and practitioners from health informatics, nursing, medicine, and pharmacy who will inform Infoway's future efforts to integrate informatics into practice environments, education, and basic training programs.[26]

Many European countries are making significant, sometimes nationally mandated efforts toward ensuring their nurses have the informatics competencies they need to practice in the 21ˢᵗ century. Finland is making ECDL certification available to all nurses, and Finland, Norway, Italy, and Great Britain have localized the content of ICDL-Health. All have ICDL-Health programs available to nurses. For example, to improve basic IT skills of staff members, the National Health Service (NHS) of the United Kingdom has implemented a Basic IT Skills Programme (ECDL). The primary goal of this widespread training is to prepare staff for IT advancements of the national EHR program. Comprehensive surveys of the benefits of this training have been conducted. Results show an increase in confidence of the respondents in terms of computer tasks, and for those with clinical contact, there was a perceived increase both in the time available with patients as well as in the quality of care provided.[27] The greatest impact was seen in nurses whose negative feelings about the new systems dropped from 31% to 3%. On the other hand, Scotland, part of the now decentralized United Kingdom, is creating its own content both for basic computer competencies and for competencies similar to those in the ICDL-Health syllabus. Norway too, as they enter their next phase of experience with nurse informatics competencies, is exploring options other than those promulgated by the ECDL Foundation. It is a complex picture and there is no one grand solution, but progress is being made by the Europeans who have led in this area.

A similar program to the Basic IT Skills Programme, the Health Informatics Training System (HITS),[28] is an electronic self-learning tool for use by healthcare workers as they seek to learn basic concepts and terminology in the use of computers in healthcare. The program is also designed for frontline healthcare workers who have little or no knowledge of IT. Objectives of the program are to:

- Improve knowledge level of health informatics.
- Improve efficiency of service and quality of care.
- Clarify the link between technology and clinical practice.
- Provide a consistent and objective training and certificate program for IT in health informatics.

The original program was developed by the Health Informatics Society of Ireland (HISI) and ICS SKILLS, the certification body of the Irish Computer Society; it has recently been updated by the Healthcare Information and Management Systems Society (HIMSS) for use in its eLearning Academy. The course modules are divided into three units focused on IT Basics, Information Management, and Information Systems in Healthcare. A certificate of completion is awarded to those successfully passing the program.

The AMIA-endorsed Digital Patient Record Certification (DPRC) Program also covers many of the TICC recommended information management competencies. The DPRC is a certification test to validate understanding of key, basic concepts for safe and effective use of digital patient records. Although many concepts covered in the DPRC are relevant in non-U.S. countries, it was designed to cover concepts and practices specific to U.S. healthcare practice. An example of this is its significant coverage of HIPAA. AMIA members chaired subject matter expert panels that developed the test questions, provided informatics expertise to the program, and coordinated the DPRC study guide development. The DPRC examination has been validated and demonstrated strong content and criterion validity. In addition to the study guide text, the DPRC Program provides a Web-based training course to prepare for the exam.[29]

Implications for Advanced Practice

A recent survey of nurse practitioners was performed to understand the extent of IT usage in their practice.[30] Study results showed that while more than 90% of respondents utilize computers at work, slightly less than half felt that their academic preparation equipped them to use and leverage technology in their practice. These results carry a number of implications for healthcare organizations and nursing practice, including a concern for how graduate programs can ensure that advanced practice nurses are equipped to deliver 21st century healthcare.

The Doctor of Nursing Practice (DNP) is an emerging doctoral degree for clinical nurse leaders that was approved in 2006 by the AACN. It is essential that nurse leaders who have achieved this advanced degree can demonstrate mastery of informatics competencies in their practice.[31] To this end, informatics leaders recommend inclusion of a course within the DNP program that integrates informatics knowledge, skills, and attitudes to support evidence-based practice at a leadership level.

According to Jenkins et al,[31] selected informatics topics that should be included are (1) the development, use, and evaluation of computer systems for clinical practice, education, decision support, and shared clinical and educational decision-making; (2) standards in terminology, data storage, and transmission; (3) data capture, analysis, and application for quality improvement; (4) informatics as a fundamental tool for the creation of evidence; and (5) computer-aided instruction. DNP programs that apply these recommendations will ensure their graduates are equipped to apply informatics competencies in their practice. These competencies include the ability to (1) understand the design, use, and evaluation of CISs; (2) use informatics tools to record, retrieve, and analyze data, information, knowledge and wisdom; (3) evaluate cultural, ethical, and legal implications of IT in healthcare; (4) evaluate electronic resources for nurses and consumers; (5) apply informatics tools in nursing and consumer education; and (6) understand, articulate, and demonstrate leadership in relevant current issues.

Summary

Informatics competencies are essential for novice to expert levels of nursing practice and graduating nursing students. Numerous mechanisms, endorsed and supported by multiple industry organizations, professional societies, and national bodies exist to enable nurses to achieve and maintain these competencies. As clinical information systems and EHRs are incorporated into nursing practice and workflow, adoption of these competencies will be realized and nurses will be equipped to deliver high-tech, high-quality patient-centric care.

References

1. Ronald, J, Skiba D. *Guidelines for Basic Computer Education in Nursing.* New York: National League for Nursing. 1987.

2. Brodt A, Stronge JH. Nurses' attitudes toward computerization in a mid-western community hospital. *Comput Nurs.* 1986;4:82-86.

3. Bongartz C. Computer-oriented patient care: A comparison of nurses' attitudes and perceptions. *Comput Nurs.* 1988;6:204-210.

4. Burkes M. Identifying and relating nurses' attitudes toward computer use. *Comput Nurs.* 1991;9:190-201.

5. American Nurses Association. *Scope of Practice for Nursing Informatics.* Washington, DC: American Nurses Publishing, 1994.

6. American Nurses Association. *Standards of Practice for Nursing Informatics.* Washington, DC: American Nurses Publishing, 1995.

7. American Medical Informatics Association. *Nursing Informatics Academic Sites.* http://www.amia. org/mbrcenter/wg/ni/resources/academic.asp. Accessed July 25, 2009.

8. Barton AJ. Cultivating informatics competencies in a community of practice. *Nurs Adm Q.* 2005;29(4):323-328.

9. Hart MD. Informatics competency and development within the US nursing population workforce: A systematic literature review. *CIN.* 2008;26(6):320-329.

10. Prensky M. Digital natives, digital immigrants. *On the Horizon.* 2001;9:5.

11. Staggers N, Gassert CA, Curran CA. Delphi study to determine informatics competencies for nurses at four levels of practice. *Nurs Res.* 2002;51(6):383-390.

12. *Technology Informatics Guiding Education Reform. Collaborating to Integrate Evidence and Informatics into Nursing Practice and Education: An Executive Summary.* 2009. http://www.tigersummit. com/uploads/TIGER_Collaborative_Exec_ Summary_040509. Accessed July12, 2009.

13. Healthcare Information and Management Systems Society. *2009 HIMSS Informatics Nurse Impact Study.* http://www.himss.org/content/ files/HIMSS2009NursingInformaticsImpact SurveyFullResults.pdf. Accessed June 30, 2009.

14. *Technology Informatics Guiding Education Reform. TIGER Collaborative.* 2009. http://www. tigersummit.com/ Accessed June 6, 2009.

15. *TIGER Informatics Competencies Collaborative. Literature Review.* http://tigercompetencies. pbworks.com/ Accessed June 6. 2009.

16. Staggers N, Gassert C, Curran C. Informatics competencies for nurses at four levels of practice. *J Nurs Educ.* 2001;40:303-316.

17. American Nurses Association. *Nursing Informatics: Scope and Standards of Practice.* Silver Spring, Maryland: American Nurses Association; 2008.

18. European Computer Driving Licence Foundation (2008). *ECDL/ICDL Health Syllabus.* http://www.ecdl.com//products/index.jsp?b= 0-102&pID=764&nID=766 Accessed December 15, 2008.

19. American Library Association. *Information Literacy Competency Standards for Higher Education.* http://www.ala.org/ala/mgrps/divs/acrl/standards/ informationliteracycompetency.cfm.   Accessed April 17, 2009.

20. HL7 EHR Technical Committee (2007) *Electronic Health Record - System Functional Model, Release 1 Chapter Three: Direct Care Functions.* http:// www.hl7.org/EHR/. Accessed December 15, 2008.

21. Porter-O'Grady T. *Nurses as knowledge workers.* Interview by Kathy Malloch. Creative Nursing. 2003;9(2):6-9.

22. Stefl M. Common competencies for all healthcare managers: The healthcare leadership alliance model. *J Healthc Manag.* 2008;53(6):360-373.

23. American Medical Informatics Association. *Health Information Management and Informatics Core Competencies for Individuals Working with Electronic Health Records.* http://amia.vmtllc.com/ files/shared/Workforce_2008.pdf Accessed July 15, 2009.

24. National League for Nursing. *Preparing the Next Generation of Nurses to Practice in a Technology-rich Environment: An Informatics Agenda.* http:// www.nln.org/aboutnln/PositionStatements/infor-matics_052808.pdf. Accessed July 19, 2009.

25. Nagle LM. Infoway's EHR user engagement strategy. *Can J Nurs Leadersh.* 2007;20(2):31-33.

26. Nagle LM. Everything I know about informatics, I didn't learn in nursing school. *Can J Nurs Leadersh.* 2007;20(3):22-25.

27. Warm DL, Thomas SE, Heard VR, Jones VJ, Hawkins-Brown TM. Benefits of information technology training to National Health Service staff in Wales. Learning in Health and Social Care. 2009;8(1):70-80.

28. Healthcare Information and Management Systems Society. HITS: Health Informatics Training System.   https://himss.learn.com/learncenter.asp?id= 178411&DCT=1&sessionid=3-F602E8F9-BE88-4437-9708-991176633BB2&mode=preview&page =55. Accessed August 1, 2009.

29. Digital Patient Record Certification Program. The DPRC. http://www.dprcertification.com/. Accessed June 15, 2009.

30. Gaumer GL, Koeniger-Donohue R, Friel C, Sudbay M. Use of information technology by advanced practice nurses. CIN. 2007;25(6):344-352.

31. Jenkins M, Wilson M, Ozbolt J. Informatics in the Doctor of Nursing Practice Curriculum. American Medical Informatics Association Annual Symposium Proceedings. 2007;364-368.

APPENDIX

TIGER Clinical Information Management Competencies

This Appendix is reprinted with permission from the TIGER Informatics Competencies Collaborative (TICC). It is a list of recommended TIGER Information Management Competencies for all practicing nurses and graduating nursing students. (Note that ICDL-Health or similar competencies are also recommended Information Management competencies for nurses. They are provided in the body of the text of this chapter.)

TICC has transformed the Direct Care components of the HL7 EHR System Functional Model into these recommended Clinical Information Management Competencies for nurses:

Using an EHRS, the nurse can:
- Identify and Maintain a Patient Record
- Manage Patient Demographics
- Capture Data and Documentation from External Clinical Sources
- Capture Patient-Originated Data
- Capture Patient Health Data Derived from Administrative and Interact with Financial Data and Documentation
- Produce a Summary Record of Care
- Present Ad Hoc Views of the Health Record
- Manage Patient History
- Manage Patient and Family Preferences
- Manage Patient Advance Directives
- Manage Consents and Authorizations
- Manage Allergy, Intolerance, and Adverse Reaction Lists
- Manage Medication Lists
- Manage Problem Lists
- Manage Immunization Lists
- Interact with Guidelines and Protocols for Planning Care
- Manage Patient-Specific Care and Treatment Plans
- Manage Medication Orders as Appropriate for her Scope of Practice
- Manage Non-Medication Patient Care Orders
- Manage Orders for Diagnostic Tests
- Manage Orders for Blood Products and Other Biologics
- Manage Referrals
- Manage Order Sets
- Manage Medication Administration
- Manage Immunization Administration
- Manage Results
- Manage Patient Clinical Measurements
- Manage Clinical Documents and Notes
- Manage Documentation of Clinician Response to Decision Support Prompts
- Generate and Record Patient-Specific Instructions

- Manage Health Information to Provide Decision Support for Standard Assessments
- Manage Health Information to Provide Decision Support for Patient Context-Driven Assessments
- Manage Health Information to Provide Decision Support for Identification of Potential Problems and Trends
- Manage Health Information to Provide Decision Support for Patient and Family Preferences
- Interact with Decision Support for Standard Care Plans, Guidelines, and Protocols
- Interact with Decision Support for Context-Sensitive Care Plans, Guidelines, and Protocols
- Manage Health Information to Provide Decision Support Consistent Healthcare Management of Patient Groups or Populations
- Manage Health Information to Provide Decision Support for Research Protocols Relative to Individual Patient Care
- Manage Health Information to Provide Decision Support for Self-Care
- Interact with Decision Support for Medication and Immunization Ordering as Appropriate for Her Scope of Practice
- Interact with Decision Support for Drug Interaction Checking
- Interact with Decision Support for Patient Specific Dosing and Warnings
- Interact with Decision Support for Medication Recommendations
- Interact with Decision Support for Medication and Immunization Administration
- Interact with Decision Support for Non-Medication Ordering
- Interact with Decision Support for Result Interpretation
- Interact with Decision Support for Referral Process
- Interact with Decision Support for Referral Recommendations
- Interact with Decision Support for Safe Blood Administration
- Interact with Decision Support for Accurate Specimen Collection
- Interact with Decision Support that Presents Alerts for Preventive Services and Wellness
- Interact with Decision Support for Notifications and Reminders for Preventive Services and Wellness
- Manage Health Information to Provide Decision Support for Epidemiological Investigations of Clinical Health Within a Population
- Manage Health Information to Provide Decision Support for Notification and Response Regarding Population Health Issues
- Manage Health Information to Provide Decision Support for Monitoring Response Notifications Regarding a Specific Patient's Health
- Access Healthcare Guidance
- Interact with Clinical Workflow Tasking
- Interact with Clinical Task Assignment and Routing
- Interact with Clinical Task Linking
- Interact with Clinical Task Tracking
- Facilitate Inter-Provider Communication
- Facilitate Provider-Pharmacy Communication
- Facilitate Communications Between Provider and Patient and/or the Patient Representative
- Facilitate Patient, Family and Care Giver Education
- Facilitate Communication with Medical Devices

This list of competencies came from the Direct Care components of the HL7 EHR System Functional Model. In some cases functional statements were not changed as they can also serve as competencies. For example, the HL7 EHR System Functional Model statement of "Access Healthcare Guidance" was unchanged, except for the preamble that applies to all Clinical Information Management Competencies, as "Using an EHR, the nurse can: Access Healthcare Guidance." The HL7 EHR System Functional Model statement of Communication with Medical Devices was changed from "Communication with Medical Devices" to "Facilitate Communication with Medical Devices" to make it a Clinical Information Management Competency.

## CHAPTER 9

Transforming Nursing Education: Integrating Informatics and Simulations

By Judith J. Warren, PhD, RN-BC, FAAN, FACMI; Mary N. Meyer, MSN, RN; Teri L. Thompson, PhD(c), RN, CPNP; and April J. Roche, MBA, CPEHR

In 2000, the University of Kansas School of Nursing (KU-SON), in partnership with an EHR software supplier, adapted their EHR solution to fit the learning and teaching workflows of baccalaureate nursing students and faculty. Over the ensuing decade, this innovative program, titled Simulated E-Health Delivery System (SEEDS), has been rigorously developed and extended into all facets of undergraduate and graduate nursing, nursing informatics, medical school, and health information management. While we have long reported on our work at numerous national and international conferences and have published widely,[1-8] this chapter, an update to our chapter in the first edition,[1] focuses on our work to merge this EHR technology with laboratory simulations to provide students with virtual clinical experiences that closely mimic the electronic clinical environments of today's practice workplaces We also provide a detailed outline of techniques for designing and implementing case studies in the system and discuss the curriculum implications and technology challenges of using a solution designed for clinical care delivery as an educational application.

Introduction

Health professionals will need a new skill set and language to function competently in the electronic information age. At the most fundamental level, they must at least have knowledge of the way data are structured, and recorded and communicated changes in the digital medium. Teaching nursing students to think critically and in a data-driven mode lays the foundation for evidence-based practice and reduces the risk of treatment errors.[9] All nursing students are required to master basic informatics concepts and IT competencies, as these are now required to function in increasingly automated clinical environments. Educational programs can emphasize the importance of IT in clinical care, but unless there is an opportunity for students to use EHR technologies as they learn their clinical skills, these competencies cannot be taught nor learned as concepts. For instances in which training happens in academic arenas that are not equipped with real EHR or faculty lacks informatics skills, this important set of competencies is missed.[10] In our present health policy climate, the expectation for clinicians and organizations alike is to deliver care that is based on best practices. Teaching our next generations the basic skills in practice based on evidence means that they learn to use data to create information that generates new knowledge to inform our practice. These informatics competency skills must be an integral component of the curriculum, and to get there, our health professional schools need to provide EHR-like environments with access to clinical data that enables enhanced critical thinking and clinical decision making. The impetus for the teaching/learning strategy we have developed in our SEEDS initiative originally was in response to IOM reports that addressed the quality, error, and waste in the United States' healthcare system.[9,10] The IOM's recommendations clearly mandate these curriculum changes and integration of IT for core clinical competencies of all health professionals.[11]

SEEDS is an exciting innovative program. First, it challenges students to develop information management and critical thinking skills. Second, it challenges faculty to develop teaching strategies that take advantage of this unique technology. SEEDS provides the structure to implement an evidence-based, academic EHR that fully supports nursing practice. Furthermore, SEEDS provides the platform for realizing the informatics competencies identified by the QSEN project[12] and by TIGER.[13] Both QSEN and TIGER have acknowledged the SEEDS program and endorsed our approach of using the EHR in the classroom to provide experience, well as to deliver patient care content to the student. Nursing education accrediting organizations are also very interested in having student experiences with the EHR. AACN has added competency in using EHRs and IT in their accreditation requirements.[14] In 2008, NLN published a white paper calling for more informatics development and use of the EHR in the curriculum. This white paper, "Preparing the Next Generation of Nurses to Practice in a Technology-rich Environment: An Informatics Agenda," refers to the SEEDS program on the first page and acknowledges SEEDS' contribution as an exemplar for preparing the next generation of nurses.[15]

Designing SEEDS for Educational Use

The KU SEEDS program and software solution developed from a close business partnership between KU and Cerner Corporation, Kansas City, Missouri, that started in 2000.[1,6-8] SEEDS as a software solution is the result of adapting Cerner's EHR software so that it could be used in the classroom and learning laboratories. In many instances, the functionality, screen designs, and content of the base EHR was repurposed to serve educational needs.

Learning Theories and SEEDS

The design of SEEDS is based on three major learning theories: Gestalt theory, cognitive theory, and constructivism.[16] Gestalt theory guided the design of documentation forms by ensuring a distinct difference between background and interactive elements on the screen. Students need to have space around these elements so that they are not distracted by too many elements crowded together. They are still learning what information goes together and how to understand it—one basis for engaging in critical thinking. By organizing elements on the screen, the student's understanding and comprehension is focused on grouped elements and their importance to the task at hand (see Figure 9-1). In contrast, the practicing nurse knows these basic clinical relationships of elements and consequently does not need this grouping and separation of elements. In practice, clinicians prefer their screens to be packed with elements crowded together to ease their speed of documentation. Finally, Gestalt theory specifies that one must ensure the completeness of the learning task. As forms and order sets are designed, it is critical that attention be paid to where they support the curriculum. The forms and orders must reflect the content in lecture, textbooks, and evidence-based practice approaches; therefore the forms should contain both normal and abnormal signs and symptoms, thereby assisting the student to learn the pattern of patient responses (or the gestalt of the response).

Cognitive theory focuses on cognitive mapping, concept attainment, activation of previous knowledge, and motivational aides. This is evident in the structure of the documentation forms, which guide learning by using organizers, such as labels and placement on the form, to assist the student in understanding the concepts and how things are related. Students comment that the placement of elements on the forms helps them "see a picture" of what is important and "helps me in my clinical experience to know what to assess." Forms have multiple sections that are deliberately organized to clue the student in knowing "what goes together." For example, the respiratory assessment form has the following sections:

- Physical examination, subjective symptoms
- Laboratory data related to pulmonary function
- Incentive spirometry readings
- Peak expiratory flow assessment
- Pain on respiration assessment

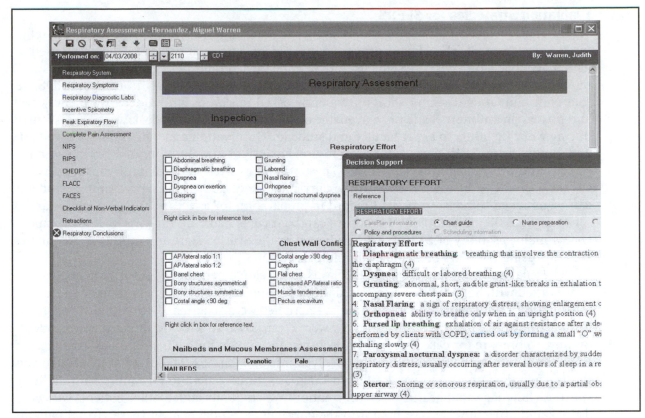

Figure 9-1. *Application of Gestalt, Cognitive, and Constructivism Learning Theories in the Design of SEEDS.*

This physical construction assists the student in learning and remembering. Next, we took advantage of the reference text functionality to embed terminology definitions, guidelines, literature evidence, and links to Web sites and resources throughout SEEDS. Today, our reference text content includes definitions of healthcare terminology, links to the Internet for supplemental material, guides for gathering assessment data, information on calculations (BMI, BSA, etc,), and medication information. Having this information at the point of learning, only a right click away, motivates the student to learn and explore (see Figure 9-1).

Constructivism is based on the student constructing meaning, engaging in social interactions, and problem solving real world situations. SEEDS is a tool designed to help the student construct meaning from all the information and knowledge they must master in nursing school. It also shows the application of knowledge and how it provides communication of patient information to the healthcare team at the point of care. Learning through social interactions is accomplished through a variety of learning exercises—"scavengers hunts"—to learn EHR navigation, case studies for a team of students to resolve, nursing care plan documentation for real patients; documentation of skills performance; and EHR use in conjunction with human patient simulators. Basic clinical decision support is also introduced in skills lab exercises and case studies, as well as in nursing care plan documentation of actual patients. Alerts for allergies and drug-drug interaction checking are activated so that students experience clinical decision support and learn to evaluate this information and use it in their care delivery. Conditional forms are designed to be activated only when certain information is documented. This helps the student learn how to respond to clinical decision support in the real world and to expect that support. Constructivism also provided the guidance to add a last section to each of the assessment forms—the "Conclusion." The conclusion section is where the student interprets the meaning of the information documented in previous sections (see Figure 9-1). SEEDS becomes the vehicle for the students to construct meaning and engage in problem solving in simulated and clinical settings.

Evaluation Strategies for SEEDS

Traditional evaluation strategies were employed to evaluate and to provide input for refining the design of SEEDS. Focus groups, both students and faculty, were extensively used to gather feedback on screen design, use of SEEDS for learning, and orienting students and faculty in the use of SEEDS. Most of the feedback was about support in using SEEDS. To that end, numerous teaching sheets, frequently asked questions, and videos were developed and posted on an Internet site to be available on all days/times. A help desk was also instituted during working hours to assist faculty and students. Observation and videotaping of students and faculty using SEEDS was also used to provide insight into usability of working with the screens and other functions of SEEDS. These studies assisted in developing innovative ways for the SEEDS to be integrated into the curriculum (not added on). For example, students can be assigned to review a patient record in preparation for a lecture or a simulation, and a series of SEEDS and simulation exercises can be used as make-up for missed clinical experience. Finally, usability of SEEDS was evaluated by the SEEDS staff and graduate informatics students using Nielsen's heuristic evaluation criteria.[17]

The final innovation in using SEEDS was to develop a neighborhood of patients. As faculty worked with SEEDS they discovered they could incorporate culture and other contextual information about patients. Traditional case studies were redesigned to be delivered in the format of patient records. Clinical notes were repurposed to provide directions to students on how to prepare for case study work, lectures, and simulations. Then families were created to be the actors in the case studies that evolved into simulations. The first family created was the Hernandez family, and we developed them as a three-generational family with cultural, spiritual, language, and health-risks information. We gradually added other patients with conditions and attributes that we taught in the curriculum. Students meet these virtual patients throughout their program. They see them age and observe as their conditions evolve. They learn to manage these virtual patients, taking into consideration their attributes, as the students perform skills check offs and engage in high-fidelity simulations. We even use these patients as examples in lectures. The students begin to understand the wholeness of the patients instead of focusing on the performance of tasks. The use of the neighborhood of patients has dramatically influenced the way SEEDS is used. The next sections will describe the application of SEEDS in the undergraduate and graduate curriculum.

EHR Bridges the Gap Between Nursing Education and Practice

Three basic principles of the constructivist learning theory propose that in order to construct learning, the environment should be structured with opportunities for learners to:
1) Actively test their knowledge,
2) Experience cognitive challenges or puzzlement, and
3) Evolve comprehension through testing in social contexts.[18]

What learning environment is more easily adapted to meet these criteria than today's high-fidelity simulated clinical environments? Traditionally, simulated learning environments have offered students opportunities to practice and validate new skills in a nonthreatening arena. With the addition of highly technical simulated healthcare environments, including human patient simulators, researchers have identified a positive relationship between fidelity (realism) and student learning. Since EHRs are prevalent in today's practice environments, students experience an added level of realism when the simulated EHR is integrated into the simulation process. In this section, you will learn how the EHR is being used as a pedagogical strategy to enhance simulated learning environments for students in a Nursing Techniques course.[19-21]

The KU Baccalaureate program admits 120 students each year. All 120 students are enrolled in Nursing Techniques for both fall and spring semesters of their junior years. The course has both a didactic and a lab component. The lab experiences are conducted in these complex simulated environments: a seven-bed acute care unit, a critical care room, a seven-room clinic, a birthing room, and a home care setting. Students are actively engaged with the

EHR in all learning activities in all settings. By deeply embedding the electronic patient record in the course activities, this technology has become another transparent pedagogy within the constructivist learning environment. The course is structured to include weekly content modules with faculty-driven documentation requirements and periodic skill set assessments that use the EHR to present a case study and evaluate their documentation skills. The following is a detailed description of both teaching strategies, including how the EHR supplements the constructivist learning environments:

Strategy 1: Students Document Activities of Weekly Lab Sessions in the EHR

Each week students learn and demonstrate nursing techniques and assessment skills. Upon completion of each skill, students document their activities in the EHR. Since several courses utilize the simulated EHR as a teaching strategy, the charts are identified by the student's name and a middle initial that represents the course. For example, the chart for "Nursing Techniques" is identified by the student's first and last name with the middle initial of "T" for Techniques. Students and faculty refer to this as "documenting in your 'T' chart."

When students open the EHR, they enter a non-linear learning environment that is student-centered with unlimited opportunities for enrichment. Using the system twice a week, this technically savvy group of students quickly becomes adept at using the EHR for documentation. As the students record their assessment findings each week, they learn to differentiate normal from abnormal very quickly. Independent and self-directed learning is enabled in this approach as learners explore the abnormal parameters either on their own or with faculty. In these weekly encounters, the documentation requirements are implicit in the assignments, and students are required to document at the point of care. Since both the students and faculty have Web-based access to the record, the feedback process is user-friendly, timely, and paperless. Faculty use "sticky notes" (these look much like the yellow sticky note used on paper documents) technology in the EMR to offer feedback (see Figures 9-2 and 9-3).

Strategy 2: Skill Set Competency Validation within the Context of a Simulated Case

In the Advanced Nursing Techniques course, there are four weeks in which student competency is validated during simulated patient encounters. One week prior to testing, students are instructed to review three or four patient cases that are presented in the EHR and to come to the lab prepared to care for any of the patients. Students are scheduled in teams of two, with each team caring for two patients. Every student will be the primary caregiver for one case and the team member for the second case. The assignments are based on faculty convenience and manikin availability. Students are evaluated according to their ability to identify and perform the nursing care that the simulated patient requires. During each simulation, a faculty member can play the part of patient and physician as needed, as well as evaluator. Each student is expected to document his or her encounter without cues from faculty as part of the workflow of providing care, which is pictured in Figure 9-4. During the course of the simulation, faculty may play the role of physician by entering new treatment orders into the EHR for the student to respond to and carry out. Faculty may also take on being the "voice" of the patient in the simulation to require the student to respond in an appropriate way and teach relationship interaction under pressure of decision making and care delivery.

Each patient simulation is scheduled to allow 30 minutes for the patient encounter and 30 minutes for the debriefing. The EHR provides an added level of fidelity for the students as they begin to collect and analyze data. In addition to allowing faculty to realistically assume the role of a physician by sending orders in the EHR in real-time during the simulation, the student's documentation in the EHR allows faculty to validate all aspects of their performance.

The electronic record supports a learning environment in which students formulate and test hypotheses. Each scenario presents a "puzzle" for the students to solve. As they construct learning in the simulated setting, the EMR offers detailed and trended patient data, i.e., daily weights, past vital signs, intake and output, labs, and radiology reports. Additionally students use the reference materials embedded in the EHR as they provide care. During the encounter,

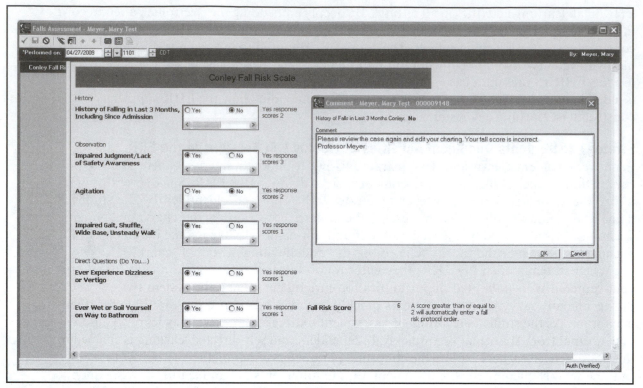

Figure 9-2. *Faculty Use "Comments" Feature of the EMR to Offer Formative Feedback to Students.*
© *Cerner Corporation. All rights reserved.*

successful students supplement the data from the record and other electronic resources with other subjective and objective data they obtain by asking appropriate history questions and assessing the patient and the environment. After validating the hypothesis, students perform the appropriate nursing interventions in the low-risk simulated environment. Basic patient safety principles are enforced with each patient encounter. These include active patient identification, falls prevention, medication safety principles, including the seven rights, and employing patient teaching opportunities as appropriate.

This pedagogic approach to teaching nursing techniques offers many benefits to the learner. As a basic, students must learn the skill well enough to repeat it more than once during the semester. Additionally, students have the opportunity to demonstrate psychomotor skills while developing communication and clinical judgment skills. The debriefing session allows students time to reflect on their practice by exploring the case with faculty and peers, validating their learning and identifying future learning goals. Providing patient-centered care is the "way we do business" in our lab. When students use the EHR to prepare for simulation, they begin to look for cues in the chart and formulate a plan of care that allows them to anticipate the nursing care that they will need to perform. Although the student's goal is to do well on the exam, reinforcing the knowledge, skills, and attitudes necessary to anticipate patient's needs becomes a "win-win" for students, faculty, and patients.

EHR Bridges the Gap for Nurse Practitioner Students

Nurse practitioner practice has evolved over the past 20 years. Some of the challenges in practice include patients that present with increasing complexities, new technologies, and development of evidence-based practices.[22] Nurse practitioners are advanced practice nurses who are considered advanced not only in skills and knowledge but also in experience.[22] Nurse practitioner students gain advanced experience through the use of interactive case-studies, simulated learning experiences, and clinical preceptorships. As experienced nurses, they are expected to be "highly skilled in using information management and computer technology skills to sup-

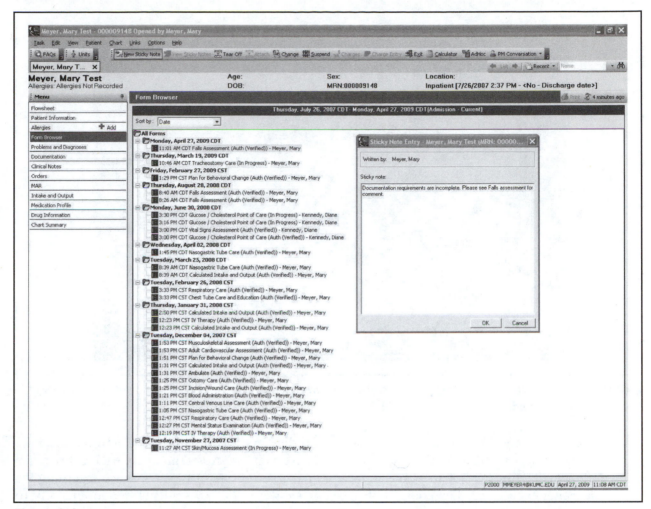

Figure 9-3. *Faculty Use "Sticky Notes" Feature of EMR to Offer Summative Feedback. © Cerner Corporation. All rights reserved.*

port their major area of practice."[23] Nurse practitioners should be able to use information systems, such as EHRs to do their assessments, develop their treatment plans, and evaluate their outcomes.[23]

Advanced practice education is challenged to prepare nurse practitioners for the evolving practice. To keep pace with changes in practice and education, educators must develop new educational methodologies for nurse practitioners. The SEEDS system can be developed as an educational methodology to meet educational objectives for nurse practitioner students. SEEDS can be used to educate nurse practitioner students to progressively make complex clinical decisions while learning valuable informatics skills. This can be done as nurse practitioner students interact with case-based studies; document SOAP notes; and practice electronic prescribing, coding, and billing.

When incorporating and developing a new teaching methodology, educational objectives must be developed. The following educational objectives guided the development of SEEDS: (1) demonstrate advanced critical thinking skills, (2) advance clinical decision-making skills through the use of standardized patient data, (3) evaluate patient care through aggregation of data, and (4) develop informatics infrastructure for an evidence-based practice.

Simulation Plus EHR: Virtual Clinical Teaching

Faculty, with the help of the SEEDS development staff, created a simulated learning experience within an advanced clinical nurse practitioner chronic care course. An interactive case-based study was created and students took turns progressively interacting with a case and evaluating

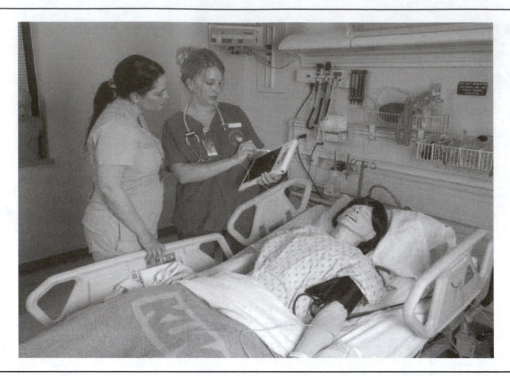

Figure 9-4. *Student Documenting Simulation Information in SEEDS on a Tablet PC. Photo courtesy of the University of Kansas School of Nursing.*

the care given. The faculty also developed a discussion board within an electronic teaching platform in which students could discuss the case as it progressed and help each other make clinical decisions. Students wrote a reflection paper at the end of the experience regarding the learning experience. The goals of this experience were to allow students the opportunity to (1) interact progressively with the same patient, (2) make complex clinical decisions, (3) evaluate patient care by different providers, and (4) document clinical notes including treatments, placing orders, coding patient interactions, and billing.

Jessie's chart was developed using actual clinical experiences and included the necessary background information to allow for interactions with the virtual patient (see Figure 9-5). His chart included allergies, immunizations, and social history (see Figure 9-6). Figures 9-5 through 9-8 show screen views into Jessie's chart and the student workflow as the nurse practitioner students do their assessment, place orders, and document their clinical notes.

Students then evaluated not only their visits but all the visits for continuity of care, quality of care, and the clinical decision making. They were instructed to interact with each other, sharing their thoughts and insights regarding care of Jessie. At the end of the course, they were asked to reflect on the experience in the form of a reflective paper. Students interacted easily within SEEDS and reacted favorably to the experience. Students reported that the "experience broadened my clinical experiences. The evaluation of the documentation allowed me to understand the case and make better clinical judgments." The students also felt that the documentation skills they gained would benefit them in the future as many of their future employers were in the process of implementing an EHR.

Students found they developed evidence-based practice skills as they interacted within the SEEDS. Students had to look at all of the previous and current evidence to make clinical decisions. They used current sources of evidence located in the SEEDS. The Multum© medication reference provided current information on prescribed medications (this reference is updated monthly in the SEEDS). The documentation forms helped students focus their assessment, diagnosis. and plan. Students reported that this focus helped them "understand the documentation process, while giving [them] experience with electronic records."

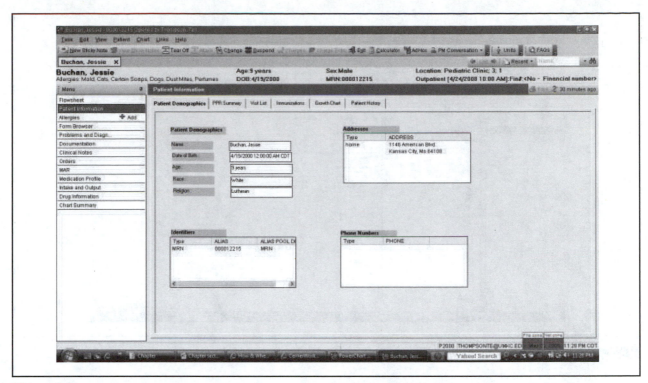

Figure 9-5. *Jessie's Demographic and Background Information Provides Context for the Case Study.*
© *Cerner Corporation. All rights reserved.*

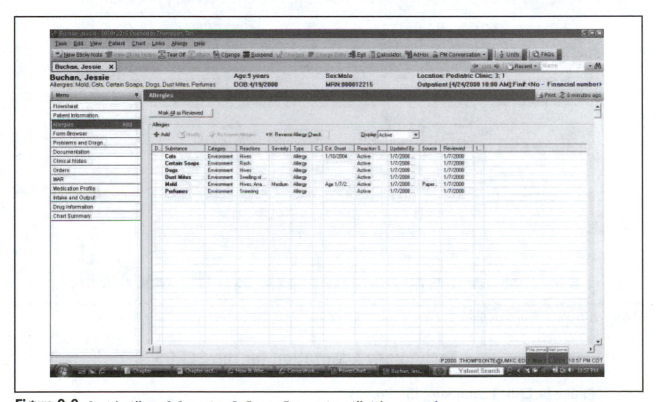

Figure 9-6. *Jessie's Allergy Information.* © *Cerner Corporation. All rights reserved.*

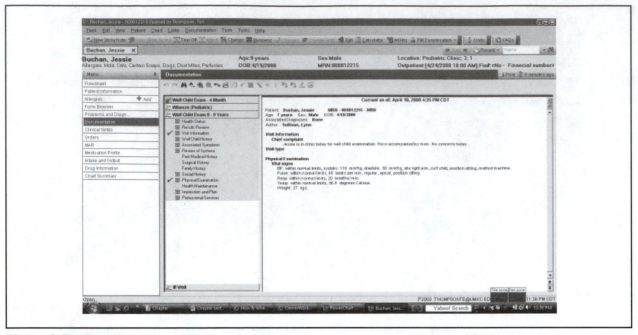

Figure 9-7. *Clinical Note Documentation of the Visit.* © *Cerner Corporation. All rights reserved.*

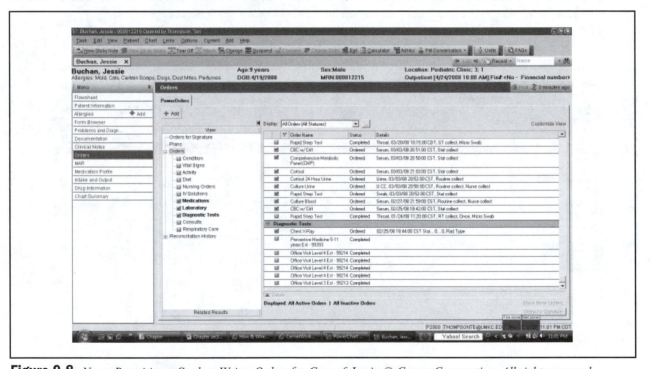

Figure 9-8. *Nurse Practitioner Student Writes Orders for Care of Jessie.* © *Cerner Corporation. All rights reserved.*

Technology Adaptation for the SEEDS

Paper to EHR: Rethinking the Process

The process of transitioning case studies from paper to an EHR is not quick and simple. Evolving a paper-based case into an EHR format requires various steps performed iteratively and must consider inherent differences in presenting the material. Additionally, the constraints of using a live CIS need to be addressed. These requirements present many challenges both for the instructors and developers. Though the process may initially appear overwhelming, with appropriate planning, preparing, and creating, the integration of EHR case studies into the curriculum of health professional students can be successfully accomplished.

Traditional paper-based case studies can be delivered in many formats through various types of media. Common characteristics can be found in each variety and include small amounts of content, events occurring linearly, and information that is well-defined based upon the desired outcomes of the case. A prevalent method uses cases written in a narrative, with descriptive paragraphs illustrating appropriate facts that are aligned with what students need to know at that point in time. This type of exposure to cases is centered on the knowledge and ability each individual student possesses.[1]

Cases presented within an EHR are delivered in an electronic format with data and information accessible through different areas of the patient record. Additional data elements are included as students tend to need more electronic information to process these cases than in their paper counterparts. Paper-based case studies are usually stories with statements such as: elevated blood pressure; or hypokalemia; or the chest x-ray shows infiltrates; or an IV (intravenous fluids) is hanging with normal saline; or that the patient is taught about his treatment. None of these statements is the type of data needed in an EHR. So we must add specific blood pressure values and potassium value or find an image of a chest x-ray showing infiltrates that is gender correct, or document the status of the IV according to evidence-based practice. It is also important to document the patient education encounter as required by hospital accrediting bodies to simulate a real patient record. When the students interact with rich data, they learn to interpret and manage the data. Students also learn that the documentation of patient data is driven by both evidence and regulatory requirements and to not make the same assumptions they saw in a paper-based case study in a story format. The richness of the data in SEEDS improves their critical thinking as evidenced by higher-level questions and insights as to problem identification. Students know that they are improving in their thinking and report doing better on national licensing examinations. SEEDS becomes the framework utilized for "delivering the data, information, and knowledge to students at the point of learning" and the activity focus transforms into a "learner-centric" one.[1]

Using our SEEDS' EHR system to deliver clinical content information to students required faculty to rethink and redesign their original cases, as most paper-based cases did not have sufficient data (quality and quantity) to translate directly into an EHR. In converting our paper-based case studies into SEEDS, the assessment documentation data elements in the screens quickly exposed our deficiencies. Therefore, adequate planning of the case's transition from paper to EHR is required before the actual build of the patient record should begin. Many items need to be considered during the planning for conversion. Included in these steps is the need to identify additional data elements to help complete the chart and tell the patient's story. Also, it is helpful to consider the timeline of all data elements and coursework, potential reuse of the case and or patient record and history, and how students will be required to interact with the chart (expectations and outcomes).

All EHRs have multiple sections or pieces and include many categories of information. The records can contain, but are not limited to, patient history such as allergies and immunizations, focused assessments, clinical notes with diagrams or pictures depicting relevant reports, many types of orders, lab results, and identified problems and diagnoses. One must decide how detailed the patient record needs to be for the current case study and identify the appropriate information to include in the chart. Written narratives, pictures, slide presentations, and faculty notes from the current paper-based case can serve as a starting point.

The goal is to tell the patient's story based upon the information displayed in their electronic record. The record can be as simple as a few clinical notes and assessments or can grow to be as complex as needed for the level of difficulty required by the course. Enough data elements need to be included to deliver the content and story as intended. Students should be able to access the record and assimilate the information with limited facilitator intervention.

Timelines within the EHR

As with any case, the time line of events is important to communicate to the students. With an EHR, the time line should take into consideration all aspects of a patient record that will be seen and include the patient's admission and relevant discharge dates and times. Faculty will also need to determine if the dates displayed within the EHR should coincide with the actual schedule of the course it is being used in. For example, if the case is to be reviewed during week 3 of the semester, do the dates on the patient record need to correlate to week 3 of the current semester? If the case is to be reused every semester and the dates need to correlate to each use, then the chart will have to be rebuilt for each instance. After the time line and course schedule are determined and all required data elements are identified, every individual component of the chart needs to be mapped to a specific date and time appropriate for the case study.

Within the EHR, most of the dates and times can be manipulated when building charts to exemplify important learning objectives (see Figure 9-9). This has many benefits for illustrating the appropriate time line of the case. Dates can be dated in the future, allowing for the ability to prebuild charts for cases to be delivered months in advance. Dates can also be set in the past to provide trending of results and documentation over time. When accessing the different sections of a patient's chart to view the patient data, users have the ability to change the date range of results that are currently viewable. By being able to change the date range of available data, users can limit results and disclose information in a timely manner. Changing the dates of data elements within a chart to past, present, or future allows for the time line to be controlled and revealed as appropriate for each case.

Another factor to consider when planning the transition from paper to EHR is how often the patient record will be used. Questions to consider, as previously mentioned, are: Will the single patient record be used repetitively each semester with a new group of students? Will the patient history be developed to be used across multiple courses throughout the curriculum, giving students the ability to interact with the same patient in different scenarios? Will the patient age over time as encountered by students? All of these questions directly impact how the charts need to be built. It may be that one chart is sufficient for all or it may be that a separate chart needs to be created for each interaction, with careful consideration given to how and when the students have access to the charts.

One of the constraints of using an EHR specifically applies to the number of charts a single patient needs. If the patient needs more than one chart built, doing so in an EHR will allow the students access to both charts, no restrictions. This could interfere with the intended case study if the other record occurs afterwards in time or if the history for one scenario is not included in the history of another. For example, if James Robinson requires a chart to be built for students in a first semester course and also for students the following semester, then two charts are required. If both charts are built at the same time, students could potentially see both patient records when performing a patient search and inadvertently open the incorrect chart for the assignment (see Figure 9-10).

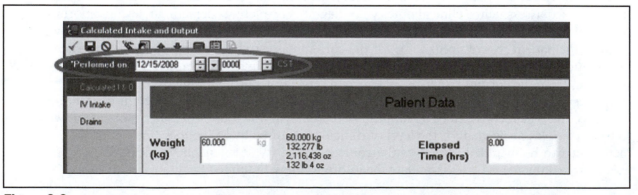

Figure 9-9: *Ability to Change the Date and Time of an Assessment Form.* © *Cerner Corporation. All rights reserved.*

Name	MRN	Gender	Age
Robinson, James 301 Prep	000011690	Male	76 Years
Robinson, James 366 Prep	000015503	Male	76 Years

Figure 9-10. *Multiple Records for Same Patient Returned During Patient Search.* © *Cerner Corporation. All rights reserved.*

Name	MRN	Gender	Age
Ruiz, Maria Theresa Prep09	000016876	Female	40 Years
Ruiz, Maria Theresa Prep08	000012982	Female	41 Years
Ruiz, Maria Theresa Prep07	000008763	Female	42 Years

Figure 9-11. *Chronological Aging of Patients as Real-time Time Passes.* © *Cerner Corporation. All rights reserved.*

EHRs also possess another constraint for building case studies, chronologic passing of time. If a patient's record is to be reused each year but not rebuilt, the age of the patient will increase chronologically in the database, which demonstrates the chronological aging of patient records in the EHR (see Figure 9-11). This can be overcome by manually changing the date of birth for that patient record or rebuilding the patient record each time it is to be used.

Both scenarios described illustrate creation of multiple records for the same patient accessible to users of the system. If records need to be hidden from users until appropriate times to reveal them, they can be renamed to another name not relevant to the case, and thus remove the record from appearing during a patient search. Another method to address this would be to have a knowledgeable database analyst manually update the record to 'hide' it from the search results. However, with either method, faculty must manually keep track of when to update the records to either hide or reveal them to students.

Rebuilding the Chart

A final item to consider when transitioning paper cases to the EHR is how the students are anticipated to interact with the chart, specifically the expectations and outcomes faculty has for the assignment. A case study might be used once a year during lecture. In this instance, it would not need to be rebuilt each semester to update the dates/times. Rather, the original case could be used repetitively. However, if each student or groups of students are expected to interact directly with the case study's chart, then a separate chart for each student must be built in the EHR. The ability to copy an entire record and paste all contents into a new patient record is not supported in the EHR. Therefore, each chart has to be manually populated. Figure 9-12 shows how multiple copies of a single patient record were created to allow multiple groups of students to interact with their own chart. Each copy of the record was completed with identical information as the original case study and required each element to be entered on each chart. This can be time consuming but allows a historic record of each group's interaction with the case study.

Though the required planning to prepare a case study for migration into an EHR may seem daunting, it is a necessary step that cannot be overlooked. Students are quick to find items in a chart that do not flow with the story being told and have an eye for noticing even minor mistakes. The success of this process lies in the details and the overall goal of planning each item of the patient record such that the case study's chart mirrors reality as much as possible. The closer the chart is to reality, the more the students feel they are getting real-life experience and benefit from the assignment.

Name	MRN	Gender	Age
Ruiz, Maria 2008-21-Apr-1030	000012961	Female	41 Years
Ruiz, Maria 2008-21-Apr-1300	000012962	Female	41 Years
Ruiz, Maria 2008-21-Apr-1430	000012963	Female	41 Years
Ruiz, Maria 2008-22-Apr-0730	000012986	Female	41 Years
Ruiz, Maria 2008-22-Apr-0900	000012987	Female	41 Years
Ruiz, Maria 2008-22-Apr-1030	000012988	Female	41 Years

Figure 9-12. *Identical Copies of Case Study for Each Group Interaction.*

After proper planning is completed, developers can proceed in building the different elements of the chart(s). This might seem like a fairly simple step in the development of an EHR case study, but careful attention must be paid to every item documented on a chart. If a data element is documented, but the date and time were not appropriately updated when doing so, the chart would have a mistake on it. If this occurs, developers have the option to retire (or delete) the patient record and create a new chart for the next exercise. However, this can be cumbersome and time consuming, as each data element has to be rebuilt on the new patient record. Another alternative is to have a knowledgeable database analyst correct the specific data element through updating records at the table level of the database. These records can be updated to reflect the correction, be permanently deleted from the database, or their association to the case study patient record updated to point elsewhere. It is also good practice to routinely monitor the case study records for "cleanliness" of the data, or rather, any additional charting completed by users that is not meant to be on the chart. Often students erroneously chart on the case study record and these activities need to be "cleaned" off the chart in the same manner discussed earlier to present the case as intended for future use.

As with any project, gaining buy-in from end-users is vital. Faculty need to be convinced the process of transitioning paper-based case studies into an EHR is advantageous and worth their time and effort. Values for faculty utilizing this technology to deliver case studies lie in many places within the system. One valuable aspect of using an EHR is the powerful database behind the end-user application. The EHR database holds data regarding how the system is built, but more importantly for faculty, it holds all the activities their students (or any user) engage in when interacting with patient records. If a student opens a patient record, it is stored in the database. If a student charts an assessment form, the form and the information documented are stored in the database. If a student adds an allergy to the chart, it is stored in the database. Any action taken to a patient record is written to the database tracking the specific action, who took it, and when it was taken. This level of activity of data allows many opportunities for faculty to engage in research projects, track the progress of their students, and monitor potential cheating.

Reports have been created, based on requirements identified by faculty and their evaluation needs, to mine data from the database and turn it into information and knowledge. Faculty can essentially identify any piece of data that is stored in the database and include all actions taken on a patient record or by a specific student. Depending on the information returned, faculty can evaluate their students' work for a specific assignment, monitor case-study interaction by course, and evaluate the current curriculum goals and guidelines based on students' work. Most reports can be configured to allow for individual faculty to run them on their own time with their own parameters. Figure 9-13 illustrates a sample report asking for parameters to be entered before it is run. Figure 9-14 shows the report output based upon the entered parameters. Specifically, the report generated details about what users (by position) entered the application on specific dates and gives a total for the university.

One value for using an EHR to deliver case study content can easily be found by mining the data generated by end-users. Courses and curriculums can also be evaluated based on this

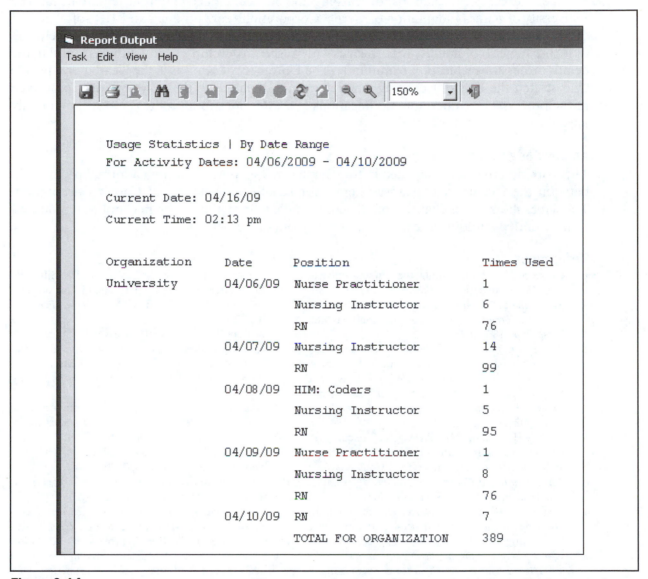

Figure 9-13. *End-user Prompts to be Completed Prior to Running a Report.* © *Cerner Corporation. All rights reserved.*

Figure 9-14. *Output from the Report Run with the Prompts in Figure 9-13.* © *Cerner Corporation. All rights reserved.*

same data. When proper planning and implementation is taken for transitioning paper-based cases to an EHR, additional value can also be found.

Summary

The designers and developers of SEEDS created a simulated healthcare delivery system so that students and faculty could interact with an EHR in a virtual environment. The EHR software was adapted to support educational activities—sometimes this meant thinking outside the box or looking at the software "sideways" to see how it could be repurposed. Forms and orders were designed for an educational workflow, using learning theories, as opposed to the clinical workflow for which the EHR software was designed. Next strategies for using SEEDS in the classroom, learning laboratories, and simulation laboratories were designed, including the development of a neighborhood of patients. Technical strategies for building realistic patient records for use in simulations were developed. Finally, usage reports were created to reveal student performance and usage—very necessary when evaluating a curriculum or teaching strategy and not readily possible in a paper-based world. The journey to developing a simulated health record as a teaching/learning platform has been a challenge and success.

SEEDS is an innovation created by IT developers, designers, and users. As such, SEEDS meets and exceeds expectations for learning and curriculum accreditation requirements. The University of Kansas adaptation of Cerner Corporation's core product, an EHR software and database, creates a fringe market for Cerner. The faculty and students have become members of a "prosumer" community that engages with Cerner to develop a product that is useful to the health professions education community. The University of Kansas is the "lead user—people who stretch the limits of existing technology and often create their own product prototype in the process—often develop modifications and extensions to a product that will eventually appeal to mainstream market."[24]

Acknowledgments

The work described and depicted in this chapter was supported through a formal partnership between the University of Kansas Center for Health Informatics and Cerner Corporation. The screenshots in this chapter contain confidential information which may not be reproduced or transmitted without the express written consent of Cerner.

References

1. Connors HR Transforming the nursing curriculum: Going paperless. In: *Nursing and Informatics for the 21st Century: An International Look at Practices, Trends and the Future.* Chicago: HIMSS Press; 2006:183-194.

2. Warren J, Connors HR, Weaver C. Academic-business partnership: An innovative curriculum model for applied informatics. In: *Proceedings of The State of the Science Congress: Advancing Nursing Practice Excellence.* Indianapolis, IN: Sigma Theta Tau; 2002.

3. Warren JJ, Connors HR, Weaver C. Clinical information systems and critical thinking: Outcomes of an innovative educational strategy. In: *Proceedings 8th International Congress in Nursing Informatics.* Rio de Janerio, Brazil: ISO Press, 2003.

4. Weaver C, Delaney C, Warren JJ, Strachan H. Strategies to generate evidence-based knowledge for nursing practice. In *Proceedings of the 11th World Congress on Medical Informatics: Building High Performance Healthcare Organizations.* Bethesda, MD: American Medical Informatics Association, 2004.

5. Weaver CA, Warren JJ, Delaney C. Bedside, classroom and bench: Collaborative strategies to generate evidence-based knowledge for nursing practice. *Int J Med Inform.* 2005;74:989-999.

6. Warren JJ, Connors HR. Health information technology can and will transform nursing education. *Nurs Outlook.* 2007;55(1):58-60.

7. Connors HR, Weaver C, Warren JJ, Miller K. An academic-business partnership for advancing clinical informatics. *Nurs Edu Perspect.* 2002;23(5):228-233.

8. Warren JJ, Connors HR, Weaver C, Simpson R. Teaching undergraduate nursing students critical thinking: An innovative information strategy. In: *Proceedings 9th International Congress in Nursing Informatics;* 2006.

9. Committee on Quality Health Care in America, Institute of Medicine. *To Err Is Human: Building a Safer Health System.* Kohn LT, Corrigan JM, Donaldson MS, eds. Washington, DC: The National Academies Press, 2000.

10. Committee on Quality Health Care in American, Institute of Medicine. *Crossing the Quality Chasm: A New Health System for the 21st Century.* Washington DC: The National Academies Press, 2001.

11. Committee on the Health Professions Education Summit, Institute of Medicine. *Health Professions Education: A Bridge to Quality.* Washington, DC: The National Academies Press, 2003.

12. Cronenwett L, Sherwood G, Barnsteiner J, et al. Quality and safety education for nurses. *Nurs Outlook.* 2007;55(3):122-131.

13. TIGER Summit. Evidence and Informatics Transforming Nursing: 3-Year Action Steps toward a 10-Year Vision. http://www.tigersummit.com/. Accessed May 15, 2009.

14. *Standards for the Accreditation of Baccalaureate and Graduate Programs.* http://www.aacn.nche.edu/Accreditation/pdf/standards.pdf). Accessed May 15, 2009.

15. National League for Nursing. *Preparing the Next Generation of Nurses to Practice in a Technology-rich Environment: An Informatics Agenda.* (http://www.nln.org/aboutnln/PositionStatements/informatics_052808.pdf. Accessed May 15, 2009.

16. *Can Learning Inform Screen Design in E-Learning Settings?* http://www98.griffith.edu.au/dspace/bitstream/10072/1989/1/28732_1.pdf. Accessed May 15, 2009.

17. *Nielsen's Heuristics for Interface Design and Evaluation.* http://www.useit.com/papers/heuristic. Accessed May 15, 2009.

18. *Aligning Teaching for Constructing Learning.* The Higher Education Academy. http://www.heacademy.ac.uk/assets/York/documents/resources/resourcedatabase/id477_aligning_teaching_for_constructing_learning.pdf. Accessed April 10, 2009.

19. Hawkins K, Todd M, Manz J. A unique simulation teaching method. *J Nurs Educ.* 2008;47:524-527.

20. *Problem Based Learning: An Instructional Model and its Constructivist Framework.* http://crlt.indiana.edu/publications/duffy_publ6.pdf. Accessed April 10, 2009.

21. Wong F, Cheun S, Chung L, et al. Framework for adopting a problem-based learning approach in a simulated clinical setting. *J Nurs Educ.* 2008;47:508-514.

22. McLaren P. The evolution of the nurse practitioner. *Evidence-Based Healthcare & Public Health.* 2005;9:265-266.

23. Staggers N, Gassert CA, Curran C. Informatics competencies for nurses at four levels of practice. *J Nurs Educ.* 2001;40:303-316.

24. Tapscott D, Williams AD. *Wikinomics: How Mass Collaboration Changes Everything (expanded edition).* New York: Portfolio. 2008:128.

Case Study 9A

The ATHENS Project: Advancing Technology in Healthcare Education Now at St. Scholastica

By Shirley Eichenwald Maki, MBA, RHIA, FAHIMA; Marty Witrak, PhD, RN, FAAN; Sally K. Fauchald, PhD, RN; Beth A. Donahue, MA, BAN, RN-BC; Susan I. Hyndman, EdD, RN; and Janelle Wapola, MA, RHIA

Introduction

The education of competent, cutting-edge healthcare professionals has been a key mission for nearly 100 years at The College of St. Scholastica in Duluth, Minnesota. In 1998, the college's Department of Health Information Management and the academic leadership within the Division of Health Sciences saw that the future infrastructure of the healthcare system would be based on emerging technologies. This realization resulted in the development of a shared vision: "to educate students in our health professions programs to assure that they enter the work world prepared to competently and confidently practice their professions using electronic health information systems (aka the Electronic Health Record) as a practice enhancing tool."

In fall 2001, the college conducted a survey of employers to validate the perceived need for graduates with multiple competencies in effectively using an EHR system. Most respondents reported that their organization would be implementing health IT and that graduates able to demonstrate appropriate competence would be critical in the next five to ten years (by 2006-2011). With a compelling vision and supporting data, staffing and funding were obtained through the U.S. Department of Education in a five-year, $1.8 million grant to support a new model for health professions' education. We named this undertaking "The ATHENS Project" (Advancing Technology in Healthcare Education Now at St. Scholastica).

The EHR Goes To College

In 2002, the ATHENS Project began with the goal to increase the decision making and practice competence of health professions' graduates by the use of a state-of-the-art EHR that provides access to clinical data and best practices' guidelines at the point-of-care. Each of the six health professions' programs modified their curriculum to integrate the teaching approaches into classroom and clinical lab experiences with the ATHENS academic EHR (A-EHR). For nursing, we focused heavily on increasing use of the A-EHR and computer-based, clinical simulation experiences to develop and assess student decision-making and problem–solving skills. These identified goals and objectives also addressed core competencies needed for 21st century healthcare professionals, as identified in the 2003 IOM report.[1] Specifically, these goals are to educate the future healthcare workforce to function in interdisciplinary teams, use evidence-based practice, and utilize informatics.

The ATHENS Project was staffed by a project manager, a technology lead, and faculty leads from each of the health professions' programs: exercise physiology, health information management, nursing, occupational therapy, physical therapy, and social work. They actively participated in the planning and development of the A-EHR content and supporting hardware to assure that the A-EHR would effectively support the use of this specialized electronic CIS by faculty and students. This included students in the classroom, skills labs, and educational clinics, all of the primary settings for academic programming on campus. An external advisory board was established to keep project members informed from the practice environment.

In 1998, we engaged three EHR vendors in discussions to determine their interest in partnering with us to advance the use of a state-of-the-art EHR as a teaching/learning tool in health professionals' education. The Cerner Corporation in Kansas City, Missouri, responded positively, and a successful longstanding partnership was born. The ATHENS Academic EHR (A-EHR) is remote hosted by CernerWorks. It is accessible to faculty and students at all days/times via a secured Internet connection from any computer lab on campus and at home. Wireless PC notebooks—some located in mobile wireless carts—also make it possible for students to use the A-EHR in every educational setting used by their program faculty: classroom, skills labs, simulation labs, and educational clinics.

A unique feature of the A-EHR is the bank of real-world clinical cases that we refer to as our "Pristine" cases. The Pristine cases are actual patient medical records with each focused on a given diagnosed problem or type of acute care episode. These cases provide students with opportunities to evaluate and interpret physiologic and diagnostic findings, define care protocols based on evidence-based practice knowledge resources, and initiate interventions. Initially the Pristine cases were obtained from alumni who authorized their medical records to be secured from a cooperating local hospital. From these cases, those included in the A-EHR were selected by faculty because they met learning objectives in key courses. One of the benefits of utilizing real (Pristine) cases for study is that the scope is beyond that which faculty could produce via data compilation. Thus, faculty does not inadvertently provide students with cues related to the area of concern. The student must sort through realistic clinical data and engage in a higher level of critical thinking and clinical reasoning as they must do in the real clinical setting. In addition, a comprehensive array of reference resources, including evidence-based practice guidelines, standards of practice, multidisciplinary practice codes, cultural references, laboratory values/diagnostic procedure descriptions and norms, and medication resources are updated monthly. These resources are especially effective as students access them at the point-of-care and serve to inform the student and thus enhance patient care.

Phasing It In

The first year of the project was devoted to vendor contracting and in-depth application training for the project director and the technology lead to prepare for the application build required to bring the EHR "live" as a teaching/learning tool. Faculty leads were first oriented to the Cerner *PowerChart*© through online demonstrations and direct training sessions. In year two, additional faculty were identified and trained. Program-specific documentation tools (e-forms and templates) were designed by faculty to emphasize important concepts and skills and to increase students' familiarity with those documentation requirements before they had an active clinical experience. Reference content to support point-of-care knowledge was identified by faculty and project staff. The second and third years were also devoted to the acquisition of real clinical cases through solicitation. Faculty evaluated and selected cases that had potential; project staff acquired the cases and embedded each de-identified case in the A-EHR.

The A-EHR began to be actively used in the third year of the project. The project targeted one course per program per semester (e.g., six courses per semester, twelve courses in total). In the initial academic year, the A-EHR was incorporated into 19 courses, with a total of 26 faculty members involved with its use. In the fourth and fifth years of the project, additional faculty were trained in using the A-EHR, with all faculty having received at least a basic orientation to the A-EHR at the conclusion of the grant-funded project. Over the years, specific forms and reference content continued to be developed and added to the system. Annual upgrades were taken to ensure availability of the most current functionality in the A-EHR. In the final year of the grant, adoption in curriculum had grown to 62 courses, involving 77 faculty from all six of the health professions' programs.

Integrating the A-EHR Into Nursing Education

The school of nursing offers traditional, postbaccalaureate and RN to BSN undergraduate programs. Graduate programs include advance practice master's and postmaster's degrees and doctor of nursing practice degrees. In the early 2000s, the school of nursing began experiencing rapid change on many fronts: a restructuring of the college from divisions to schools; an increasing volume of applicants, which stressed clinical and laboratory resources; and limitations of locally-based clinical experiences for students. These changes led faculty to consider ways to increase levels of problem-based learning. The result was faculty development of the extensive use of hands-on laboratory experiences threaded throughout the curriculum with the integration of simulation and the A-EHR technology, which was embedded into the curriculum. Nursing faculty envisioned the use of simulation and virtual clinical experiences as viable strategies to address many of these emerging curricular challenges. These changes provided the nursing faculty then and now with the opportunity to increase their cooperative work between academic levels and programs.

Undergraduate Nursing Program

Integration of the A-EHR into nursing education intentionally began within the undergraduate nursing program. In the newly revised curriculum, concepts are presented in an integrated fashion, utilizing a stepped curriculum that moves the student from simple to complex theory. Problem-based prototypes are included based on data contained in the Centers for Disease Control and Prevention's Top Ten Disease lists (http://www.cdc.gov/nchs/FASTATS/lcod.htm) and from the goals outlined in Healthy People 2010,[2] among other resources. Every week throughout the two-and-a-half year nursing program, students have the opportunity to transition current theory into practice by participating in simulation and active-learning laboratory experiences within the safe clinical laboratory environment.

The introduction of the A-EHR into the nursing curriculum was carefully planned to occur in phases to allow for regular adaptations based on lessons learned. For example, during the first year of implementation, a student's ability to quickly adapt from paper-based clinical charting to working within an electronic patient chart was overestimated. We mistakenly believed students were sufficiently computer-savvy, thus they would be able to navigate the A-EHR following a basic two-hour, structured orientation. We discovered that students were uncomfortable using the A-EHR, and the discomfort brought on stress followed by overt resistance. Faculty were bewildered by the students' response. However, after some contemplation, the faculty realized that students were experiencing the same resistance patterns seen in healthcare organizations trying to implement EHRs into the practice environment. Faculty decided to change the approach with students to increase their appreciation of the relevance of the A-EHR experience to nursing practice. As a result, the introduction of the A-EHR to the second and third cohorts of 112 nursing undergraduates was adapted to start with simple tasks and build to more complex functions. Students were introduced to the A-EHR through a guided exploration of the created orientation clinical case—"Jacob Flynn."

Jacob Flynn was chosen for the orientation case because his hospitalization plays out like a tragic medical television drama, and students seem to easily identify with him. Jacob is a 22-year-old highway worker who suffered a seemingly minor head injury while at work. He is hospitalized for observation after his coworkers report short periods of altered consciousness. On admission, Jacob is charming and jovial; he is a favorite of the nursing staff. But within eight hours, his vitals go from robustly normal to critical. Students are guided through the orientation by a series of clinically-based questions that lead the student through the content of the clinical chart embedded in the A-EHR. Seeking to discover the answer to these questions, the student is required to visit each component of the A-EHR, including the embedded point-of-care references. The student is asked to research the meaning of Jacob's falling Glasgow Coma scores, view his CT (computed tomography) scan, and read the radiologist's report detailing a cranial bleed. Students need to use the point-of-care references to look up one of Jacob's drugs, mannitol, and to determine the expected outcomes when he is placed on a ventilator. In this manner, the student becomes comfortable using an EHR as an educational resource and as a practice tool while completing an interesting in-class activity.

Following the case-based orientation, students regularly experience the A-EHR as an integrated teaching/learning tool within the curriculum. Each student creates his or her own case record in the A-EHR. This allows students to document and retain work done with the A-EHR in a single location that the student and faculty can access at any time. The student uses this case record location to practice charting health assessment data obtained when assessing a partner in the skills lab and to write health histories and nursing progress notes associated with clinically related assignments, including simulation experiences. The creation of this personal chart within the A-EHR allows for the existence of a meaningful electronic portfolio of students' work through which the student and faculty can monitor individual or program progress over time. Clinical faculty can review each student's portfolio to assess strengths and weaknesses prior to clinical rotations.

Integrating the A-EHR into Simulation

An exciting way the ATHENS A-EHR has strengthened the nursing curriculum is how it complements clinical simulations. Faculty select Pristine cases to use as the basis for their clinical simulations in each semester of the program. Each Pristine case can be adapted for use at various levels of the curriculum, based on the specific learning objectives associated with each occasion the case is used and also by altering the simulation itself. One example of how a specific case can be adapted for use at various curriculum levels based on specific learning objectives involves a 48-year-old man who undergoes a gastric bypass procedure. His hospitalization is unremarkable, and he is discharged on post-op (postoperation) day three. This case is used on the sophomore level with students who have not yet had any medical surgical content. (Sophomore students focus on communication, assessment skills, learning to analyze clinical data, and documenting effectively.) Sophomore faculty introduce students to the case by providing clear objectives and allowing students one week of access to the EHR chart for preplanning prior to class use. The same case is utilized with senior students. Senior students arrive for the simulation session without prior access to the patient's chart. They receive a verbal report of the 48-year-old gastric bypass patient they are to care for during the day shift of second day post-op. However, during the report they learn that "Mr. Pristine" has had a rough night and is experiencing significant pain.

Unlike the sophomores, the seniors have only 10 minutes to analyze the record and plan their care. Both of these simulations last less than 10 minutes. During each simulation session, students use a notebook-style laptop computer and gain access to the Pristine case, along with trusted point-of-care reference resources through a wireless Internet connection. Following the simulation, students are expected to document their assessment, diagnosis, and interventions within their own chart in the A-EHR. Faculty can then review the student's documentation and provide feedback at a convenient time. Faculty report improved clinical readiness in students since implementing the integrated, weekly simulation sessions using the A-EHR and the Pristine cases. Faculty use the simulation lab to teach sophomores clinical skills and, midway through their first semester, bring students into a subacute setting for their very first clinical experiences.

Integration of the A-EHR in the Classroom
Another example of how integrating the EHR into the nursing curriculum affords students opportunity to transition theory into practice was evidenced with the seniors as they used a Pristine case to learn about care of a patient with cancer. As students learn key theoretical components, they are asked to explore the clinical case of a young woman with acute lymphocytic leukemia, which is posted in the A-EHR. While learning about the impact of chemotherapy on lab values, nutrition, and particular body systems, students view the data in the patient's record in the EHR system that shows these anticipated responses and trends over time. In reading the multidisciplinary notes, students are able to assess the complex needs this client has related to financial burdens, role changes, fear of death, bodily changes, and communication with her young children. The students explore online resources and evidence-based interventions accessible through the references as they develop their plan of care for the patient. The case becomes intensely real to students, and they grieve when the patient succumbs to her illness. This sense of realism not only makes learning more meaningful, but students also report that they will never forget this "real patient."

Early Evaluation of Student and Faculty Experience
During the early phase of A-EHR implementation, student and faculty versions of a user evaluation survey were developed. The evaluations focused on obtaining perceptions in the following educational dimensions, extent to which the A-EHR positively enhanced student competence, enhanced the transfer of knowledge, positively affected performance of clinical tasks, positively affected communication with the patient, positively affected interprofessional interactions, engendered positive attitudes toward EHRs, and improved the students' professional marketability. In addition, the evaluation assessed the users' general comfort with technology and the users' satisfaction with the customer service of ATHENS Project staff. The results of the annual survey were shared with each program with recommendations for addressing those areas specifically identified for improvement. For example, the evaluation done in year four of the project revealed key findings in all areas for both faculty and students surveyed. There was satisfaction with the availability and responsiveness of project staff in support of both students and faculty. Also, there was satisfaction with the length of the initial training and orientation to the A-EHR among both students and faculty. Nearly one third of the student respondents agreed or strongly agreed that "Technology stresses me out." While students generally claim to be savvy in technology, the survey results indicated that this was not the case for the nursing students. This was a key finding, and it led to the restructuring mentioned previously.

Generally, students felt their experience with the A-EHR was positive and beneficial. However, for nursing students, in particular, some resistance was evident in the evaluation results. It was also noted that nursing faculty's confidence in using the A-EHR and their general attitude about the value of having the A-EHR as a teaching/learning tool directly impacted student perceptions of its value in their education. Only 27% of nursing student respondents were convinced that having this experience in their academic portfolio would make them more marketable. Anecdotally, program graduates have indicated that they have gotten summer internships or job interviews *because* they had worked with an EHR during their college years. One student wrote that using ATHENS A-EHR was a good experience and gave her the confidence to believe that no matter which EHR she used, she would be able to catch on quickly and be able to work at a high-level rapidly. In response to these findings, faculty increased their efforts to affirm with students the importance of having this experience as part of their professional education so they enter their clinical settings competent and confident in their abilities to use the EHR.

While integration of the A-EHR was initially focused within the traditional undergraduate program, usage continues to evolve within the school of nursing. St. Scholastica's School of Nursing RN/BS Program, the Master's Degree Program and the Doctor of Nursing Practice Program have each initiated steps toward integration of the A-EHR into their respective online course offerings. At each academic level, students employ the knowledge resources and clinical data accessible through the A-EHR to meet identified student outcomes of application, critical thinking, and collaboration appropriate to their level of nursing practice.

Future Directions

The School of Nursing has articulated a vision for the curricula in all programs that provides an integration of innovative technology to promote competent professional nursing practice and critical thinking through application and multidimensional collaboration. The curriculum plan associated with that vision is being developed to address student learning in the key areas of collaboration, critical thinking, and application. Student outcomes have been developed for each level of the nursing curriculum, based on these three key areas. Table 9A-1 details the learning objectives for each of the outcome areas.

With the recent addition of the ambulatory EHR application to the A-EHR system, interest has increased among faculty in utilizing the A-EHR within the primary care, nurse practitioner tracks. Faculty at the doctoral level also envision a future in which the volume of clinical cases available in the A-EHR will provide opportunities for data mining to examine patient and care trends.

Two years following the conclusion of the ATHENS Project, faculty in all nursing programs continue to add new strategies for integrating the A-EHR into courses. Students currently use the system in Web-based classes, on ground classes, and in the simulation lab. Many faculty have proposals for novel A-EHR system expansion. The nature and scope of the multiple levels of nursing education and practice at The College of St. Scholastica will require additional and multifaceted Pristine cases. Adding specialty and outpatient clinical types of cases to the existing case bank and continuing to push the envelope on learning within the context of the A-EHR will create greater opportunities for learning at all academic levels throughout the school of nursing.

Major Lessons Learned

The nearly simultaneous initiation of a new curriculum with integrated high-fidelity simulations and a state-of-the-art EHR system was an awesome undertaking. Critical decisions were made along the way that contributed to the project's success:

1. Developing a variety of key partnerships was vital to project success. The EHR vendor partner was willing to engage in pioneering educational efforts. Their product met industry benchmarks and had a solid reputation. An area clinical facility was willing to give permission to use their common forms and pathways as models for creating new documentation tools within the A-EHR. Finally, the Pristine cases could not have been created without strong alumni partners.

2. After the plan was drafted and partners identified, the faculty were drawn in. The project coordinators recruited lead faculty based on research related to successful idea adoption. Key faculty members were chosen from complementary levels of the nursing curriculum. One faculty member was an established "early adopter," who was enthusiastic about change and new ideas. The other faculty member was a well-respected "steady presence," intended to bring credibility to the project. The lead faculty was given support from administrators and, most importantly, time within their semester credit load for project implementation.

3. The project elements were first implemented within courses taught by the lead faculty. This allowed other faculty to slowly become comfortable with the project and new way of teaching. Then, one by one, other faculty were trained and supported to implement the project within their courses. This allowed for a low-

Table 9A-1. Outcomes and Learning Objectives by Program Level

The student will	Sophomore	Junior	Senior	Graduate
Collaboration	Identify various professionals, caregivers, and family and their potential roles that impact patient care	Initiate collaborative relationships in developing a plan of care	Participate in (or contribute to) and implement interdisciplinary plan of care	Facilitate interdisciplinary team meetings and family conferences (shared decisions)
Critical Thinking	Examine pertinent patient data in the A-EHR	Interpret patient data to develop a prioritized plan of care	Anticipate and plan for actual and potential problems based on relationships and trends in A-EHR	Analyze and synthesize the A-EHR and resources when designing and modifying care management
Application	Navigate A-EHR and its linked resources	Use A-EHR and its resources to develop a plan of care that focuses on a single health issue	Integrate A-EHR and resources to develop a comprehensive plan of care for clients with complex healthcare needs	Utilize A-EHR to design and appraise an evidence-based plan of care

stress start to the ATHENS Project and gave time to develop the complete integration of the AEHR, simulation, and the new curriculum.

4. This A-EHR type of project is transformational in nature. As a result, it was led and managed in ways that promoted transformation change. We adopted a change management methodology to effect an organization wide, change vision. The steps involved communicating the vision and the driving forces behind the need for change, actively engaging change champions, directly addressing the needs of end-users at their unique levels of readiness for the change, and motivating end-users to step into their zone of discomfort. And most importantly, throughout our transformation journey, we took every opportunity to recognize and celebrate the achievement of incremental successes through the change process.

Summary/The Journey Continues

The U.S. Department of Education grant funding for the ATHENS Project ended in 2008. The project's success has been validated by faculty, students, and employers. The ATHENS EHR is integrated into all health professions curricula. The faculty continues the evolution of the A-EHR. The true nature of technology implementations are, in reality, more about change in culture, attitudes, behavior, and workflows than they are about new hardware and software. The College of St. Scholastica continues its journey through this transformational change so that "All health professionals [will] be educated to deliver patient-centered care as members of an interdisciplinary team, emphasizing evidence-based practice, quality improvement approaches, and informatics."[1(p.3)]

References

1. Institute of Medicine. The core competencies needed for health care professionals. In: AC Greiner, E Knebel, eds. *Health Professions Education: A Bridge to Quality.* Washington, DC: The National Academies Press; 2003:45-74.

2. Healthy People 2010. http://healthypeople.gov/LHI/lhiwhat.htm. Accessed July 20, 2006.

Case Study 9B

Learning By Developing

By Elina Ora-Hyytiäinen, PhD, MNSc, RN; Helena Ikonen, MSc;
Outi Ahonen, MNSc; Elina Rajalahti, MNSc; and Kaija Saranto, PhD, RN

Introduction

In 2001, the Finnish government initiated the National Health Project to address the future viability of the Finnish healthcare system. One part of the National Health Project was the development of a national electronic patient record (EPR). Implementing a national electronic health record (EHR) was a key component in this effort to reform and restructure healthcare to be more effective, efficient, and of the highest quality. An EHR is necessary to enable better multidisciplinary team communication, resulting in continuity and coordinated healthcare across all sectors. Ideally the EHR could also tie together data from public, private, social, and volunteer sectors.

In 2003, the definition of core data items for the EHR was completed. The nursing care plan data components were included in this EHR data definition standard. And by 2005, we completed developing, testing, and validating the Finnish Classification of Nursing Interventions (FiCNI) to support electronic nursing documentation within the EHR.[1-3] A national nursing documentation project (2005-2008), funded by the Ministry of Social Affairs and Health, allowed for development of a nationally unified standard for nursing documentation. Based on these development activities, a coherent model for electronic nursing documentation with FiNCC will be used in Finland. The structured nursing documentation has demonstrated the following advantages: effectiveness, continuity, real-time information, and safety of nursing care.[4] This case study describes the efforts that we adopted to transform nursing competencies for standardized, electronic nursing documentation and the education model used to strengthen the knowledge and skills of nurses, nurse educators, and nurse students.

Nursing Education and Informatics in Finland

In Finland, baccalaureate nursing education is conducted in 23 universities of applied sciences (UAS). Advanced master degrees are offered to nurses at scientific universities in nursing science, health management, or health informatics. However, the nursing curricula at any of the UAS institutions lacks any unified national norms or guidelines concerning studies in nursing informatics. At the time of this writing, although there is still no nationally accepted definition on nursing informatics and its contents, many universities of applied sciences are arranging courses on nursing documentation, decision making, and knowledge management.

For the last few years in Finland, nursing education has been confronting the major challenge of how to best transform a nursing workforce of approximately 80,000 nurses, 15,000 nurse students, and 2,500 nursing faculty, all of whom lack competence in nursing informatics. Time is also a great challenge in this scenario because the national EPR is mandated to be in use in all healthcare organizations by 2011. Another large challenge is the fact that the nursing informatics competence of nurse educators is dependent on their individual interest in the subject, which of course can vary.

The technology and hardware equipment for teaching and learning electronic structured nursing documentation are not available in all of the 23 UAS locations. In fact, there are only about 11 electronic patient care documentation systems in use today; thus, it is not possible to supply access to each of these systems in the UAS facilities. Also, learning situations and environments vary from learning in a classroom and planning the nursing care of a "patient" manually, as guided by a nurse teacher, to learning in an authentic situation and planning the care of a real patient in an EPR, as guided by a qualified nurse. Traditional belief in learning style is still based on transmission of knowledge from one individual to another.

The use of structured documentation in nursing care means making a change in daily practice. The change is not individual; it is a change in work processes, division of multiprofessional labor, delivery of care, and the role of patients. There is a strong need to manage change in work communities. Therefore creation of nursing informatics competence also includes creation of development competence. The definitions of nursing informatics competence are often presented in several levels. Competence at a basic level can be that required of a nurse. The content of nursing informatics on the basic level should include national legislation on electronic documentation, decision-making processes, nursing documentation with FiNCC, knowledge management, and systematic development of nursing care. The future curriculum of nurse education at every UAS will be one that integrates studies of nursing informatics and its basic elements to a part of all education courses and degree programs of professional studies.

The eNNI Project – 2008-2012

The eNNI Project was launched in May 2008, as the research and development initiative for creating and developing the informatics skills and competencies needed in our nursing curriculum. eNNI is financed by the Ministry of Education and their partners, including 19 UAS, their nurse educators, and their students. The name, eNNI is a Finnish acronym from the English name, electronic-Documentation of Nursing Care—the Research and Development Project for the Creation of Nursing Information Competence in cooperation with those in education and nursing practice.[5] The nursing informatics competencies defined in the eNNI Project were constructed on basic elements: national legislation, decision-making processes, nursing documentation with our EHR, and the systematic development of nursing care.

The method of the project is based on deepening the partnership between healthcare organizations and the UAS. Partnership between organizations has a long tradition, but joint development work is new for them. There are three levels in partnership: between organizations, between guidance and leadership, and between developers. The developers are the nurses and the nursing students. In this project, it is essential to create new competencies for all participants: nurses, nurse managers, nurse educators, and nurse students.

The following are the goals of eNNI:

- Dissemination of knowledge concerning the joint model and usage of FiNCC
- Development of the competence needed, both individual and communal competence
- Promotion of the change required in working processes of nursing care
- Development of the competencies needed in constant improvement of nursing action

Methods

Knowing the problems the project was going to confront, it was easy to choose the method. The method of the project is called Learning by Developing (LbD), and it is a process that is described in phases, with partners from the nursing profession and education learning together in order to develop the practice.[6] LbD combines the processes of learning and of developing. Figure 9B-1 illustrates the project's aims, participating partners, and the approach used. The national project group of eNNI comprises five members; these are experts in: FiNCC and nursing documentation, teaching with LbD, managing change, eLearning, and knowledge management. The national group has coached approximately 30 regional groups all over Finland to use the LbD-method. Regional groups consist of nurses and nurse teachers from the particular region. The learning environments in which coaching takes place are workshops and eEnvironments. Regional groups have planned the development of nursing informatics competence using the LbD-model for each region.

The theoretical assumptions of the model concern perceptions of reality,[7] knowledge,[8] human,[9] learning,[10] change,[11] and partnerships.[12] Reality is assumed to have been interpreted within a sociocultural framework, meaning that people create their cultural norms and models of behavior in interaction. Members of a practice community negotiate their cultural norms and models together.[7] Negotiation is seen broadly as interaction that includes words, gestures, and body language. Negotiation is not always conscious and targeted. Although negotiation takes place in official, arranged situations, it also takes place in unofficial situations, for instance, as discussions during lunch break.

Knowledge is seen as being of two kinds: tacit and explicit. Tacit knowledge is the type used in nursing practice. In many ways, tacit knowledge is based on theoretical and research knowledge, but it especially formed through an individual's reflection on his or her experiences. It is also procedural knowledge and depends on context. Explicit knowledge is that which you encounter when reading papers, books, reports, or statistics, and when using databases. Explicit knowledge used in this project is theoretical and is knowledge from research and experts. Legislative and formal norms issued from ministry that concern nursing documentation are also important forms of knowledge.[8]

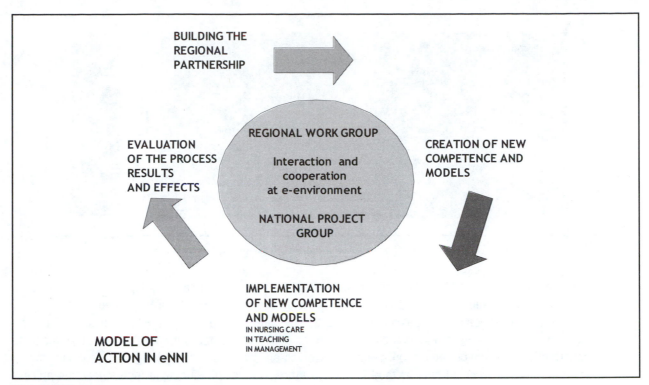

Figure 9B-1. *The model of the eNNI-Project 5. Adapted from www.enni.fi.*

Participants taking part in this project are willing to learn and grow professionally. Nurses, nurse managers, nurse students, and nurse educators are all actively working together and learning from each other. Adopting new ways to learn and develop together is emotionally demanding on everybody. It is important to understand and accept this demand and to support each other in this new cooperation between practice and education. Traditional roles and expectations of behavior can cause distress for partners; however, awareness and open discussion can relieve this distress.[9]

Building a partnership between organizations does not automatically translate to partnerships between the individuals in regional project groups or between nurses and nurse students. However, the interaction that occurs between these learners and developers is the most important tool for the creation of new competence and models for the practice of documentation. Mutual language and concepts are often said to be different for practice and education. Building mutual understanding of these tools is essential for the interaction in the project.[7] Learning in LbD means creating new knowledge and competence using processes of knowledge-creation.[9] Tacit and explicit knowledge are compared, combined, and integrated by nurses and nurse students in this process. Mutual understanding of the use of both kinds of knowledge in nursing documentation is creating a new type of knowledge for the practice. Knowledge-creation is directed to action and its results.

Argyris and Schön[10] defined "single-loop learning" as learning that allows the possibility to change one's habits at work. The aim of the eNNI Project is to change the community's habits or models to better carry out nursing documentation. However, double-loop learning is needed in achieving this if the aim is to develop mutual work habits.[11] Double-loop learning refers to learning that is targeted to support interprofessional clinical care and documentation (justifications of joint habits) and to models used in documentation. Combining tacit and explicit knowledge for the rationale for actions (of the justifications of action) in the community of practice allows for mutual understanding of the habits used in nursing documentation in that specific context. Conception of change is always affecting the process of development. The practice community is changing its way of carrying out nursing documentation; therefore, learning has to be mutual if this goal is to be achieved. Each community (healthcare providers, educators, and students) must be willing to learn from the other participants, and new knowledge and skills must be put into practice and program curriculums in a way that is appropriate and adoptable.

Kim[13] provides a theoretical description of nursing action in which the concept of nursing action is divided into two parts: nursing deliberation and nursing enactment. Figure 9B-2 depicts this conceptual

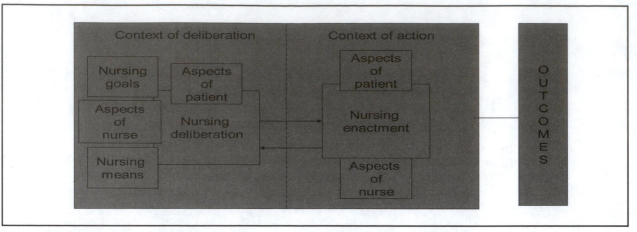

Figure 9B-2. *Adaptation of Analytic Representation of the Concept of Nursing Action*[13,14,15]

framework and shows the components that fall into each nursing action category. Figure 9B-2 is based on models created by Kim,[13] Salanterä and Walta,[14] and adapted by Astala and Ora-Hyytiäinen.[15]

The eNNI Project aims to create change in nursing deliberation (creation of new knowledge) and in nursing enactment (creation of new competence). From the educator's point of view, the method integrates three important tasks of higher education: teaching, research and development, and regional development.[16,17] From the nurse's viewpoint, the method introduces a new strategy of learning, a mutual learning process for members of the practice community.[18,19] From the nursing student's perspective, the method provides a new strategy for learning: learning in a real practice environment, creating new knowledge together with those already in the profession, and learning to understand and use the nursing documentation in a national model.[20,21]

Following creation of the LbD-model, we identified the following project phases:

1. Dialog between partners to clarify learning needs and what constitutes development on both sides.
2. Description of the present state of nursing documentation to identify and specify the targets to develop in each community of practice (unit of care).
3. Creation of new knowledge concerning the justifications of the practice of documentation.
4. Creation of a new evidence-based model for the specific area in practice of documentation.
5. Evaluation of the new model and its suitability to the multiprofessional processes of care in this unit.
6. Dissemination of the new model into daily practice.

The method used in the evaluation of eNNI is realistic evaluation.[22] The evaluation process is in its first year and is focusing on the competencies of the members of regional groups (nurse educators, nurse directors, and nurses). The quantitative data was gathered using a questionnaire at the beginning of the project. The questionnaire was built and transformed into an eQuestionnaire with the following elements: background variables, ICT-skills and knowledge, and development and transition to systematic documentation in nursing practice.[23] The second data collection will be completed in fall 2009. Data analysis will use the methods of correspondence analysis, regression analysis, and content analysis. We have chosen these different analyses methods to understand the statistical relationships, as well as qualitative contexts, such as the mechanisms that impact the process creating the competencies. Factors that promote and that also prevent the competence-creation have to be recognized and understood.

Current Project Status

The national project group for eNNI has coached approximately 30 regional groups to use the LbD-method to create nursing informatics competence throughout Finland. Regional groups consist of nurses and nursing faculty/educators from the region. Coaching has had to also include knowledge of the national, structured model of nursing documentation and competency when performing documentation within this framework. Regional groups have planned the creation of nursing informatics competence using the LbD-model in each region, thereby, effectively distributing this national documentation model. However, knowledge about the documentation model does not lead to its daily use; implementation needs support from the LbD-model.

As of April 2009, with the completion of the first project year, we have accomplished the creation of nursing informatics competence initiatives generated as a result of the work of 1,200 nurses and 72 nurse managers within 59 units or wards from 30 social and healthcare organizations and 30 nurse teachers and 120 nurse students within 30 units of UAS. The students are reporting on this creation of competence and this development process in 59 units as their bachelor's theses.

Project Experiences

The experiences encountered by eNNI participants in different regions are collected using several methods, in particular, questionnaires and focus group interviews. It is planned that data will be collected between 2008 and 2012. The participating educational and healthcare organizations have involved many nurses and teachers who have presented eNNI-model. Participants in regional workshops share knowledge, experiences, and understanding concerning the meaning of the project to the region and the profession. Discussions that take place at the workshops are important to participants because the talks allow them to get to know each other and to use the network as supportive elements in the project. The Web-based online meetings have been found to be the best communicative tool. The creation and sharing of knowledge requires e-tools that enable information-sharing, meeting planning, and discussion, and supports the work of data analysis and writing up study findings and subsequent publications.

The activity of the teacher was an important factor affecting the creation of partnership. Organizational cultures should also support the activities that are needed to create partnership; however, we found that in many organizations, the leaders did not commit to developing and learning together. This model of partnership and working together has been shown to be a good method of disseminating the national nursing documentation model and creating nursing informatics competence within a place of cooperation between practice and education.

Summary

The primary aim of the eNNI Project is to introduce informatics competencies as a standard in university-based nursing. At the time of this writing, we have completed our first project year. We are beginning the second year of data collection and LbD activities, which we use to teach participants the knowledge and skills that the nursing workforce will need to use the standard national nursing documentation model. The results and the experiences reported so far show that the three-year timeframe in which we have committed to complete the project will be sufficient. Both educators and practitioners have been enthusiastic and active. The passage of time will show the power of this solution.

References

1. www.sabacare.net. Accessed June 12, 2009.
2. Ensio A, Ikonen H, Iivari A. The national evaluation of standardized terminology. In: H-A Park el al, eds. *Proceedings of the 9th International Congress of Nursing Informatics.* Seoul: Adis International Limited, 2006:47.
3. Jokinen T. 2005. *Using Standardized Terminology for Documentation of Nursing Interventions. Master's Thesis in Social and Health Informatics.* University of Kuopio. Department of Health Policy and Management.
4. Ikonen H, Tanttu K, Hoffren P, Mäkilä M. Implementing nursing diagnosis, interventions and outcomes in multidisciplinary practice; Experiences in Finland. Proceedings of the 6th Biennial European Conference of the Association for Common European Nursing Diagnoses, Interventions and Outcomes. Amsterdam. Oud Consultancy: 2007:183-187.
5. www.enni.fi. Accessed June 12, 2009.
6. Raij K. Learning by developing. Laurea Publications, 2007: A58.
7. Wenger E. Communities of Practice. *Learning, Meaning and Identity. Learning in Doing: Social, Cognitive and Computational Perspectives.* USA: Cambridge University Press, 1998.
8. Nonaka I, Takeuchi H. The Knowledge-Creating Company. *How Japanese Companies Create the Dynamics of Innovation.* New York: Oxford University Press, 1995.
9. Ahonen O, Karhu J, Kinnunen R, Ora-Hyytiäinen E, Soikkeli T. Kirjaamisen kehittäminen sairaanhoitajan ja opiskelijan yhteistyönä. *Sairaanhoitaja.* 2007;80(1):27-30.
10. Argyris C, Schön D. 1978. Organizational learning: A theory of action perspective. In Leskelä J. 2005. Mentorointi aikuisopiskelijan ammatillisen kehittymisen tukena. Tampereen yliopisto, kasvatustieteen laitos. Acta Universitatis Tamperensis. Tampere: Tampereen Yliopistopaino-Juvenes Print 2005.
11. Rogers PJ, Williams B. Evaluation for practice improvement and organizational learning. In: IF Shaw, JG Greene, MM Mark, eds. *The Sage Handbook of Evaluation.* London: Sage Publications; 2006.
12. Goddard J. Supporting the Contribution of Higher Education to Regional Development. Luento. The Role of Higher Education Institutions in Regional Development. University of Karlstad, Sweden, Oct. 4-5, 2005.
13. Kim HS. *The Nature of Theoretical Thinking in Nursing.* NY: Springer Publishing, 2000.

14. Lauri S, Salanterä S, Chalmers K, et al. An exploratory study of clinical decision-making in five countries. *J Nurs Schol.* 2001;33(1):83-90.

15. Astala L, Ora-Hyytiäinen E. *The Model of Participating Development of Nursing Care. Quality in Services.* Conference Proceedings of the 8th Toulon-Verona Conference. University of Palermo. 8-9. 2005;9:155-162.

16. Ora-Hyytiäinen E, Rajalahti E. 2006. *The Role of a Teacher in a Knowledge-creation Process.* The Annual Conference of European Education Research Association. ECER in Geneva 13-16 September 2006. http://www.leeds.ac.uk/educol/documents/157519.htm. Accessed June 12, 2009.

17. Vyakarnam S, Illes K, Kolmos A, Madritsch T. 2008. *Making a difference. A Report on Learning by Developing* – Innovation in Higher Education at Laurea University of Applied Sciences. B 26. www.markkinointi.laurea.fi/b/b26.pdf. Accessed June 12, 2009.

18. Ahonen O, Ora-Hyytiäinen E, Silvennoinen P. 2005. Juurruttamalla hoitotyön kehittämiseen. *ProTerveys.* 2005;6:4-11.

19. Ahonen O, Ora-Hyytiäinen E, Silvennoinen P. Juurruttaminen hoitotyön kehittämistoiminnassa. *ProTerveys.* 2006;2:16-19.

20. Hautala R, Ora-Hyytiäinen E. *Learning in a Research and Development Project. Changes in Nurse Students Developmental Competence During the Project.* The Annual Conference of European Research Association. ECER in Ghent 19-21.9.2007, University of Ghent. www.leeds.ac.uk/educol.

21. Ahonen O, Ora-Hyytiäinen E, Partamies S. Juurruttaminen kehittämismenetelmänä. Ammatillisen ja ammattikorkeakoulututkimuksen päivät 10.–11.10.2007 Diakonia-ammattikorkeakoulu.

22. Pawson R, Tilley N. *Realistic Evaluation.* London: Sage Publications, 1997.

23. Rajalahti E, Saranto K. Standardized nursing documentation – developing together in Project eNNI. In: K Saranto, PF Brennan, H-A Park, M Tallberg, A Ensio. eds. 2009. *Connecting Health and Human.* Proceedings of NI2009. Technology and Informatics 146. Amsterdam: IOS Press, 2009.

SECTION III

Innovation Through Applied Informatics

SECTION III

Introduction

By Patrick Weber, MA, RN

Innovations permeate our daily work in health informatics. The explosion of new technical possibilities is a great potential for health and health informatics. This section gives you an overview of projects that help nurses through applied innovations, targeting quality of care, management of complex information, and data standardization. We invite you to review these innovative works and find value from the different approaches nurse leaders are taking to push new milestones in ICT adoption and standards in their countries.

Nurses are the largest group of contributors to patient care in all sectors across the health system, yet their practice is essentially invisible in databases. Nurses and nursing are critical to measuring and improving the quality of healthcare delivery, one of the critical challenges facing clinicians, researchers, decision makers and policy makers. This theme can be found in each of the chapters and case studies in Section III. Hannah and White, in Case Study 12B, make the point that while many kinds of data are collected, the healthcare environment has a scarcity of the right type of information upon which to base decisions.

There is an emphasis on greater accountability of hospitals and physicians to produce the best clinical outcome for the least costs. This value-based approach to healthcare payment is subsumed within the notion of shared accountability; that is, each physician has a duty to work collectively with other physicians to find the best treatment options (see Chapter 10, Welton and Sermeus) Where is nursing in this paradigm?

In Case Study 10A, Hübner and co-authors present examples of nursing-driven collaborations in Germany to obtain a discharge summary standard that will support their efforts to provide optimal care transitioning. The eNursing Summary is an ICT communication instrument which supports integrated care delivery scenarios. While "integrated care" addresses the political and financial dimensions of continuity of care, "eHealth"—as a technical counterpart to integrated care—seeks to close information and communication gaps in the system.

In Chapter 11, Coenen and Bartz present the accomplishments achieved over the last two decades with ICNP's® maturation into an international standard reference terminology. As program directors, Coenen and Bartz have provided vision, continuity, and long-term commitment to realizing ICN's vision for ICNP. The consistency of their leadership presence to the international standards bodies (e.g., ISO) and health organizations (e.g, WHO) made these doors open and without which, the ICNP milestones would not have been achieved. These milestones include recognition within ISO and WHO classifications, release of Version 2 (representing five versions total), collaborations for software development tools, translations into multiple languages, and harmonization work with SNOMED-CT. We are extremely proud to have this chapter included in our 2nd edition and invite you to read this seminal work.

In Case Study 11A, Kim and co-authors describe the work they are doing to develop standardized, structured nursing documentation across a four-hospital, healthcare system. One of the key aspects of the work under development at the Partner Health System located in the Boston/New England area of the United States, is attaining that balance between useable documentation tools for frontline nurses, while at the same time developing structured data using terminology standards. Kim and colleagues address how they use knowledge management principles to represent data in unambiguous and consistent ways that support data reuse and interoperability in an electronic documentation system. They carefully describe the methods they developed and used to harmonize across different terminologies and to map to a standard, so that we can all follow the critical steps employed in their content modelling efforts.

In Chapter 12, Kerfoot and co-authors detail the progress they have made in developing a methodology for generating and embedding evidence-based nursing knowledge into a clinical information system. The business partnership undertaken to achieve this groundbreaking milestone in our industry is a three-way collaboration between a large healthcare system (Aurora in Wisconsin), a university-based school of nursing (University of Wisconsin, Milwaukee), and a major international EHR software provider (Cerner Corporation). The chapter describes the critical contribution that each entity in the collaboration brings to the project and to its remarkable success in a six-year undertaking to date. The Kerfoot chapter includes updates to their journey to implement their clinical documentation system at two hospital sites, complete with decision supports embedded in all phases of the nursing process and care plans.

Kraft describes data management strategies for the Veterans Health Administration (VHA) in Case Study 12A. The VHA is the home of America's largest integrated healthcare system by its sheer size and mandate to provide healthcare to veterans in every state, with multiple sites in some states. The use of IT to support electronic collection, storage, retrieval, and transfer of clinical and administrative data has the potential to greatly improve the quality and efficiency of healthcare. The success of IT implementation in the VHA healthcare system has been recognized as significantly enhancing the quality of patient care.

Terminology coding systems assure the standardized assessment, recording, and encoding of clinical data for use in electronic record systems. These coded data are central to the efficient exchange of information in messages sent across documents, systems, and applications. For example, see Hannah and White's work on developing national nursing outcome standards for all care venues, again referring to Case Study 12B).

Hardiker and a team of renowned researchers known for their work in standards, terminology, system development, and data structures for research collaborate in Chapter 13 to present a state-of-the-art overview on international standards as an underpinning for better information management. There have been significant efforts to date and movement forward from the development of international standard terminologies to other standards that seek to support semantic interoperability. It is important that nursing continues to inform wider standards development and continues to be informed by standards, so that we do not revert to silo-based information management.

In Case Studies 13A and 13B, Westra and co-authors provide updates on the work being done with the U.S.A. Nursing Management Minimum Data Set (NMMDS) and Delaney and co-authors present the numerous collaborations in process using the International Nursing Minimum Data Set (iNMDS). The NMMDS serves as a foundational dataset for the collection of core essential nursing management data, at the unit or service level, to describe the context of nursing care. Similarly, the iNMDS is focused on describing nursing care around the world. The work described in the Westra case study illustrates how these data can provide information to describe, compare, and examine nursing practice. Finally, in Case Study 13C, Dunton describes the rich database of nursing quality indicators data generated over the past decade by hospital organizations and used in the Magnate hospital certification program.

## CHAPTER 10

Use of Data by Nursing to Make Nursing Visible: Business and Efficiency of Healthcare System and Clinical Outcomes

By John M. Welton, PhD, RN; and Walter Sermeus, PhD, RN

Introduction

What does the "registered" part of registered nurse (RN) mean? In the late part of the 19th and early 20th century, nurses primarily provided care in the home after receiving their initial training in hospitals. Patients and families hired nurses directly and often relied on lists or registries of nurses found in schools, libraries, physicians' offices, and pharmacies. Nurses were paid either directly by the patient or families or through the registries, engendering a direct economic relationship between nurses and patients during this time. Acute care moved from home to hospital during the 1920s and 1930s. Nurses followed their patients and actually billed for private duty in hospitals during this time.[1] Realizing the value of nursing employment, hospitals quickly absorbed nurses as workers and struggled with the question of how to charge for nursing care. Ultimately, administrators adopted the billing model used by hotels, and nursing became part of the cost of room and board, right alongside brooms and bedpans.[2] Nurses not only lost the direct economic relationship with their patients, they became invisible within the hospital billing and payment system.

The salient point to this fascinating historical perspective is the lack of nursing data reflecting the core product of hospitals and other healthcare institutions. The business of healthcare involves drugs, devices, procedures, and skilled professionals—especially nurses—to carry out this work. What are the data we can use to determine the efficiency, effectiveness, and overall performance of nursing care? What is the economic value of nursing care? How can we improve nursing quality and safety, while decreasing the overall cost of nursing care?

In this chapter, we will address these concerns and identify problem areas in which nursing data are missing from widely used administrative and billing databases and provide potential remedies to overcome these limitations and help make nursing more visible to payers and policy makers.

Making the Case for Better Nursing Data

What is the optimum assignment of patients to nurses that produces the best outcomes of care? How much additional money should we spend to improve the quality of nursing care? These are pressing questions often included in news reports or other media events. For example, nearly half of all states in the U.S. have either enacted or are contemplating enacting laws to address hospital nurse staffing ratios[3] and, pending congressional legislation, will create mandatory hospital nurse-to-patient ratios (see http://www.thomas.gov/ for the latest information regarding Congressional legislation). The impetus for this legislation is a core set of studies that found significant associations between a nurse's workload and patient safety and quality of care.[4] In a widely reported and quoted study, Aiken and colleagues[5,6] found higher hospital risk-adjusted mortality levels with higher nursing workloads and lower mortality in hospitals that have a higher percentage of bachelor's degree (BSN)-prepared nurses. Another element in improved nursing care being considered is level of nurse education versus outcomes. An optimum staffing level remains elusive because there are no data collected at the nurse-patient level of care that are part of the important claims and discharge databases used by policymakers to craft regulations.[7] There is also the related problem of inconsistent or missing nursing workforce data.

International Perspective

The most referenced nursing workforce data are those given by the Organization for Economic Cooperation and Development (OECD). Established in 1961, OECD brings together the governments of countries around the world that are committed to democracy and the market economy with the intention to support sustainable economic growth, boost employment, raise living standards, maintain financial stability, assist other countries' economic development, and contribute to growth in world trade. The density per 1000 population (head counts) of practicing nurses and practicing physicians is available for 32 OECD member countries (see Figure 10-1). As of June 2009, the most recent available data are those of 2007, although data for 2007 are not available for all countries, e.g., the most recent data for Australia is from 2006, data for Belgium is 2005, and for the Slovak Republic is 2004. The highest nurse density is found in Norway (32 RNs per 1000 population). The lowest nurse density is found in Turkey (2 RNs per 1000 population), which is a ratio of 16 between the highest and lowest densities in these European countries. The highest physician density is found in Greece (5.3 MDs per 1000 population). The lowest physician density is also found in Turkey (1.5 MDs per 1000 population), which is a ratio of 16 between the highest and lowest densities. The ratio between all highest and lowest densities is less than 4. The variation in nurse density among European Union countries is four times higher than that of physician density. A striking observation is that physician and nurse density is not closely related (r=0.29). In fact, Greece has even more doctors than nurses.

It is obvious that these differences in densities are realized but are usually not well-documented and understood. A recent study funded by the European Union called *RN4CAST* (nurse forecasting) is documenting nursing workforce, work environment, and patient outcomes in 11 European countries to evaluate whether these differences in density do indeed lead to differences in patient outcomes. If so, the study will investigate if recommendations about nurse staffing levels and the number of nurses per population can be made. OECD data are only available on a global scale, and, unfortunately, most countries do not have data available on a more detailed level of providences, states, or particular hospitals that could help identify important patterns and trends that link nurse staffing with patient cost, quality, and safety.[8]

The business case for nursing, as Needleman et al[9] have argued, is based on the assumption that nursing care hours and the skill mix of nurses caring for patients are directly related to outcomes of care. Significant improvements in quality and decreases in costs related to lower adverse events can be realized.[10] However, little, if any, available nursing data exist to confirm or monitor the efficacy of nursing care on a per patient basis. Nursing data are fragmented and are inconsistently collected in aggregate state level abstracts. National hospital care databases tend to use summary annual aggregate data about nurse staffing patterns across inpatient and outpatient settings, leading to potential bias in using these data for studies addressing nursing care and patient safety, quality, outcomes, and costs of care.[11]

Weaknesses in current data regarding nursing care affect the ability to study the number of nurses and the associated distribution, costs, and skill mix of the nursing workforce. Multiple, disparate data sources are sometimes used to provide rudimentary information about changes in the nursing workforce. For example, data compiled from the American Hospital Association Annual Hospital Survey[12] and the National Sample Survey of Registered Nurses (NSSRN) administered by HRSA every four years[13] provide a means to compare aggregate hospital length of stay with nursing hours per patient day. In 1980, patients stayed in hospitals on average 7.6 days and received 4.7 hours of nursing care per day; in 2004, hospital length of

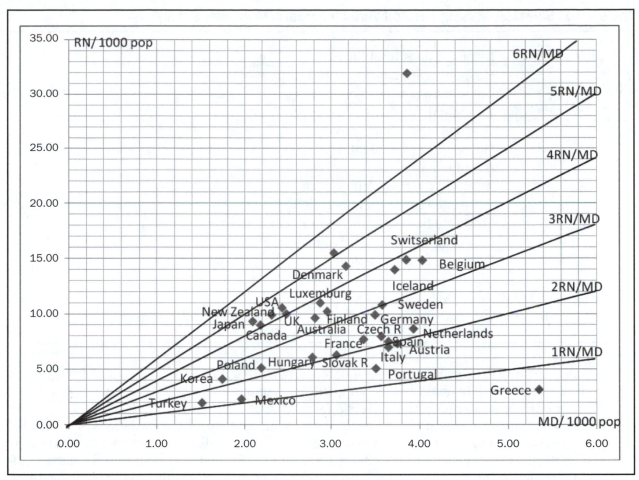

Figure 10-1. *Comparing Nurse Density and Physician Density per 1000 Population (in head counts) for 2007. Source: OECD Health Data 2009 - Version: June 09, www.oecd.org*

stay decreased to 5.6 days, but daily nursing hours increased to 10.7.[14] Such types of analyses can contribute to changes in healthcare policy, such as creation of a policy that addresses nurse-to-patient ratios or adjusting hospital reimbursement for differences in nursing intensity.[15] Having provided an example of how data influence policy, the next section discusses weaknesses in data collection that may skew these policy efforts.

Hospital Nursing Skill Mix and Intensity Data

One issue to address regarding nursing care is the distribution and the skill mix of registered nurses (RNs) and licensed practical nurses (LPNs). There are known associations between the skill mix, complexity and severity of patient care, and these various effects on patients.[16,17,18] The American Hospital Association Annual Survey[12] (mentioned earlier), provides aggregate nurse staffing and skill mix data that have been used in a number of nurse staffing and outcomes studies. Several nursing-related variables are noted in Table 10-1. These annualized summary data provide a general measure of how hospitals use different mixes of nurses, for example the ratio of RNs to LPNs or the estimated nursing hours per patient day from total days and total nursing hours using the assumptions that a full-time nurse works 2080 hours per year and a part-time nurse works 1040 hours per year.

The AHA Annual Survey[12] only provides information about hospitals in the United States that respond to the survey, and the data can be erroneous or parts of the data may be missing and therefore, may lead to inaccurate or misleading interpretations, such as over- or underestimating the number of nursing care hours. Also, the AHA Annual Survey includes data from both inpatient and outpatient settings, potentially problematic for researchers interested in

Table 10-1. Selected Nursing Related Variables from AHA Annual Survey[12]

•   Licensed beds total facility
•   Hospital unit beds set up and staffed
•   Total facility admissions
•   Total facility inpatient days
•   Hospital unit admissions
•   Hospital unit inpatient days
•   Average daily census
•   Adjusted average daily census
•   Full-time registered nurses (RN)
•   Full-time licensed practical or vocational nurses (LPN)
•   Full-time nursing assistive personnel
•   Full-time total personnel

Adapted from AHA Annual Survey:
http://www.ahadata.com/ahadata/PDFs/2008/SurveyFileLayout.xls

only studying the inpatient population, for instance. Another weakness of this survey is the lack of nursing data about individual units, for example, data for just the medical or surgical floor or for just intermediate care versus intensive care.

There are examples of databases that have overcome some of the limitations of the annual AHA survey. One example is ANA's National Database for Nursing Quality Indicators (NDNQI). Hospitals collect data every three months for each inpatient unit for nurse staffing, turnover, satisfaction, and selected quality indicators.[19,20] Analysis is possible based on changes or variability at the unit level. For example Dunton et al.[21] found higher falls rates in units with lower nursing hours per day and lower RN skill mix; however, this rate was partially influenced by unit type. The primary detractor of the NDNQI is the amount of time and effort needed to collect quarterly data for each unit at participating hospitals, upload information into the central data repository, and the associated costs for annual membership. Each hospital receives quarterly summary reports and benchmark data that are useful to nurse managers and executives in comparing their units with a nationally representative sample of like-sized hospitals.

A second example of collecting nursing data at the unit level is the Patients First database developed collaboratively by the Massachusetts Hospital Association[22] and the Massachusetts Organization of Nurse Executives. Patients First is a publicly reported annual summary of nurse staffing, census, and quality variables available on the Internet. This database differs from the NDNQI by including essentially all hospitals in the state. Anyone can view the data online, which provides a means to compare nurse staffing and quality across hospitals. However, the average layperson would find the raw display of nurse staffing patterns difficult to interpret. There is also no information about the case mix of patients on these units or the acuity or severity of illness. The Patients First data allow researchers to analyze patterns and trends that could be helpful to clinicians, mangers, and policymakers. For example, Welton et al.[23] examined the distribution of mean unit level nurse staffing hours for each medical/surgical unit in Massachusetts. Such analysis can help describe and show differences in nurse staffing patterns that can explain differences in nursing resource use and quality.

A third example of data collection is the Belgian Nursing Minimum Dataset in which nursing intervention data and nurse staffing per nursing ward data are systematically collected in all Belgian hospitals several times each year. Using these databases, Van den et al.[24] were able to analyze nurse staffing for all Belgian cardiac centers (n=28) in 2003, which included data from 58 intensive care and 75 general nursing units comprising 9,054 patients. They were able to show that increased nurse staffing in postoperative general nursing units was significantly associated with decreased mortality. Nurse staffing in postoperative intensive care units, however, was not significantly associated with in-hospital mortality, possibly because of the lack of variation in ICU staffing across hospitals. The authors also showed that the cost of increasing the number of nursing hours per patient day up to the level of the 75th percentile would lead to 5.9 fewer deaths per 1000 admissions. The cost to do this would be less than $2,000 per life-years gained.

All three of these examples provide a greater level of data specificity than the nursing care variables in the AHA Annual Survey[12] and allow study of nursing sensitive variables at individual inpatient units compared with the entire hospital. There is still no direct linkage between individual nurses and patients with any of these databases. The important distinction is between overall staffing patterns—how many nurses are available at each hospital or unit over a period of time—versus who were the nurses actually assigned to care for each patient. Each patient has unique care needs, different severity of illness, and multiple levels of complex therapies that vary each day and possibly within a shift. Nursing care is adjusted for these different needs within the unit, but the number and skill mix of the nurses is not allocated to each patient within the billing and administrative databases used to summarize and bill for hospital services.

Unfortunately, nursing care is subsumed within room and board charges. This makes nursing invisible at the payment and policymaking levels of the healthcare system. The lack of payment adjustment for different levels of nursing care distorts the payment system.[25,26] CMS has acknowledged this flaw in the reimbursement system and has asked both the nursing and hospital community to propose solutions to better reflect the variability in nursing care hours and costs within the prospective payment system.[27] The crucial question is: What nursing data can be defined to make nursing visible in the billing and discharge abstracts used to set state and national healthcare policy?

Implementing the NMDS to Make Nursing Visible

The essential solution to making nursing visible and having the necessary data to adequately measure the direct effects and associated costs of nursing care is to link individual nurses with each patient. The Nursing Minimum Data Set (NMDS) provides a potential data source that can identify the problems (nursing diagnoses), interventions, outcomes, and intensity of nursing care. It has now been over two decades since the groundbreaking consensus conference met to establish the NMDS.[28] In the ensuing years, a wide variety of codes and vocabularies have been developed. However, the primary, if not overarching objective of the NMDS has not been met, which was to add nursing specific data to the administrative, discharge, and claims data.

Placing the NMDS and other data about nurse-patient interactions into existing databases would have several favorable results:
- Information about the direct relationship between nurses and patients independent of the medical data would become available.
- Nursing care could be compared across similar patients (e.g., by the Diagnosis Related Group or DRG) or across hospitals.
- A direct nursing cost per patient could be calculated and allocated to each patient and billed separately from the daily room charge.
- The aggregate nursing intensity could be used as a basis for an inpatient pay for performance metric, e.g., hospitals that provide higher quality of care at lower costs might receive financial or other rewards for high performance.

With independent nursing data collected in the billing data, nursing intensity could be linked to the discharge diagnoses and associated with adverse events, such as pressure ulcers, infections, injuries to investigate relationships between nursing care and quality and safety outcomes, and an evidenced-based staffing method could emerge.

The key question is which data can be used and how could these NMDS data be added to existing data without substantial increases in costs and administrative burden needed to collect, store, and process the new nursing data. Nursing diagnoses have been collected and used to examine patterns of nursing care. An early effort at the University Hospitals of Cleveland to capture daily patient assessment used a bar code to indicate the presence up to 61 nursing diagnosis.[29,30] These data were used to analyze changes in patient condition and nurse staffing patterns. The classification data were used to explain differences in severity of illness, mortality, and hospital charges.[31,32] Another study found that the nursing diagnosis was an independent predictor of hospital and intensive care length of stay, charges, mortality, and discharge to a nursing home.[33,34,35]

Although ample evidence exists that nursing diagnosis can be used in a variety of settings and provide important clinical and administrative information about patient care, no comprehensive effort to disseminate this use within U.S. hospitals has occurred. Moreover, the documentation of nursing diagnoses has not consistently been integrated with documentation of other clinical data, such as vital signs, assessments, intake, and output. As noted previously, there is still no direct link between the nursing diagnoses and the billing system.

Costing and Billing for Nursing Care Using the NMDS

Nursing diagnosis, nursing interventions, or nursing outcomes can be used to cost and bill for nursing care. Belgium has used a minimum data set since the late 1980s to allocate payment to hospitals based on differences in nurse staffing patterns.[36] The Belgian Nursing Minimum Dataset (B-NMDS) tool was originally based on 23 nursing interventions, and these data are collected four times a year for 15-day periods. The instrument explains 70.1% of the variability in nurse staffing.[37,38] Since 2008, a new version of the B-NMDS has been introduced, based on the Nursing Intervention Classification (NIC) and incorporating 78 nursing interventions.[39] Moreover, the B-NMDS is no longer a stand-alone system. It is integrated in the hospital discharge dataset, which makes it possible to link the data with DRGs, financial data, etc.

Could a system similar to B-NMDS be used in other countries? The first detractor to this idea is the difference in how hospitals cost, bill, and pay for services. Belgium has a national health service in contrast to other countries, which may have multiple and various payers for healthcare, including private third-party insurance companies and payers.[40] In a budgeted healthcare finance system such as Belgium's, a wide range of criteria such as differences in case mix, severity mix, volume, and even variation of nursing intensity based on the quarterly B-NMDS can be used to calculate the target budget.[41] Most countries, such as the United States, use payment systems to hospitals that are based on medical diagnosis or procedure for each patient. The approach used in Belgium could be adapted for use in other countries and congruent with the payment mechanisms in place. The B-NMDS version 2, introduced in 2008, has an explicit link with DRGs and patient data and could be an appealing method to link nursing data with existing diagnosis data used for payment.

A similar approach has been used in New York for the past two decades. Each state Medicaid hospital discharge is adjusted for nursing intensity based on the DRG. Hospital charges for routine (medical/surgical floor) and intensive care are adjusted based on nursing intensity weights (NIW) for each DRG established by an expert panel.[42] The system works well for the purpose of adjusting hospital charges for differences in nursing intensity with the assumption that similar patients will have similar hours of nursing care within a particular DRG.[43] The NIW is assigned after the patient is discharged, so there is no additional burden for nurses to collect new data. The NIW cannot be used to predict nurse staffing on a day-to-day basis because the DRG is based on information in the discharge abstract that may not be available during a shift. Also, the NIW data are not patient-specific but an estimate of the average nursing intensity for all patients within a DRG. Therefore, the NIW cannot be used to analyze differences in nursing care for individual patients.

The NIW does have potential in adjusting payment to hospitals and improving payment accuracy. In a study funded by the American Organization of Nurse Executives, the NIW was applied to data obtained from the AHRQ State Inpatient Database for four states during 2004, encompassing 1.8 million patients. The NIW weight was applied to each routine or intensive care day of stay during hospitalization and compared with the unadjusted days.[44] The findings show that when hospital billing is adjusted for nursing intensity using NIW, the explained cost variance improves by 8.5% for all patients and 9.4% for Medicare patients. This study bolsters the argument for including nursing intensity data in the normal hospital billing mechanism because they improve payment accuracy.

Nursing and the DRG

In the United States, CMS is fiscally responsible for healthcare and hospitalization for elderly patients. To achieve this function, the payment mechanism reflects a balance between both accuracy and burden. Each DRG has an assigned payment weight based on average costs derived from hospital charges submitted for each discharged patient. The weight reflects the relative costliness of each DRG compared with another, so that a DRG with a weight of 2.0 is twice as costly, on average, than a DRG with a weight of 1.0.[45] Hospital charges are grouped into ancillary services, such as labs, x-rays, drugs, etc., or daily room charges. The ancillary charges are allocated to each patient based on actual services provided; however, the daily room rate is usually billed as a single rate, for example, as a private or semi-private room. Most of the variable nursing costs are subsumed within the daily room charge and do not reflect the variability of nursing intensity and patient acuity that determines the amount of nursing care a patient receives.

Making the case for a separate nursing adjustment has been difficult because there are no readily available nursing data in the billing or discharge datasets used to establish payment. It is interesting to note the original model of the DRG published in the late 1970s included a separate nursing cost center and a unique nursing intensity adjustment to each DRG.[46,47] A study conducted in the early 1980s in New Jersey could not validate the use of nursing classification data to adjust the DRG, and the final implementation did not have any nursing adjustment.[48,49,50]

In the past few years, there has been growing interest at CMS to improve DRG-based hospital payment. This is, in part, a result of bias in how ancillary charges are collected on a per patient basis, whereas daily room charges reflect the same charge for all patients. These accounting and billing practices affect hospital behavior by favoring high-technology diagnoses, such as cardiac care.[51] The lack of nursing data in the DRG is likely also skewing the payment system in favor of ancillary services.[25,26] Because the daily room charge reflects average care for all patients, there is no variability by patient; therefore the DRG does not reflect differences in nursing intensity; and therefore, the ancillary charges dominate the weight applied to the DRG to determine payment.

CMS is interested in incorporating nursing data into the DRG calculation but has set a number of boundaries for any data instrument used to establish an NMDS for payment purposes.[27] CMS was not favorable toward fixed weights, such as those used in New York for their Nursing Intensity Weight, ostensibly due to the labor intensive method of forming expert panels to establish static weights. Also, the NIW would not be reflective of the actual nursing care delivered. CMS was also "very skeptical" of using acuity-based patient classification instruments. The interpretation of this nonsupportive view is possibly related to the questionable validity and reliability of past nursing or patient classification instruments. In one Canadian study, four classification instruments were applied to the same patient; each produced a widely different nursing intensity estimate by several hours per patient day.[52] The use of different classification instruments could lead to payment inequities and lack of confidence in the actual reported values of nursing intensity.[53] Classification systems are also subject to classification creep, which if used for billing purposes, could escalate payment based on gaming the instrument rather than changes in actual patient acuity.

The other boundary CMS imposed was to avoid adding additional administrative burden on hospitals to collect new data. This may be problematic because nursing data would have to be collected in a similar manner throughout the country, have high-reliability and validity, not be subject to classification creep, and accurately reflect the actual nursing care delivered to patients. Such a system must be administratively feasible and not add additional data collection burdens on the nursing staff or hospitals.

Nurse-Patient Assignment

Interestingly, there is one source of data that is collected by every hospital and could be used to derive direct nursing care hours and costs—the shift-by-shift assignment of nurses to patients. This contemporaneous document, traditionally collected as the charge nurse or shift report, is omnipresent, has essentially the same data structure wherever it is collected, reflects the actual care delivered to each patient, identifies the individual nurses caring for each patient sequentially throughout the course of hospitalization, and can be used as a reasonable proxy of the actual nursing care hours delivered (see Table 10-2). For example, if an RN is assigned four patients in a 12-hour shift, on average, each patient is receiving three hours of care or six hours in a 24-hour period. Direct nursing care hours can be prorated for patient admission and discharge using a simple algorithm, e.g., if two of the patients in the 12-hour shift were discharged home, the actual hours could be recalculated.[54] The added hours for unlicensed assistive personnel (nurse aide) could also be included in the total nursing hours per day. Because the data model is not proprietary; that is, it is widely used in essentially the same way in hospitals, any electronic database developed to capture the nurse-patient assignment and calculation of nursing intensity would be vendor neutral.

With little effort, the nursing hours and cost data could be automated for use within the billing system, using a preexisting UB04 revenue code specific for nursing.[55] This 023X code captures nursing incremental charges and can be used to separate nursing hours and costs from the daily room rate based on individual patient differences linked to the assignment. If such a system were implemented at U.S. hospitals, each patient day would have an estimate of the hours and costs of nursing care within the billing system used for hospital payment for each day of stay within the hospital and have a separate itemization of nursing care hours and charges on the hospital bill.

A study of the nurse-patient assignment data was conducted at an academic medical center, which has used a classification system in which nurses allocate and record their time during the shift for each patient in their assignment.[56] A second measure of estimated nursing hours for each shift was calculated from the nurse-patient assignment and compared with the actual nursing intensity for each shift from the classification system. Two other measures of nursing intensity were calculated; an average for each nursing unit, and the average for all units across the hospital. These last two measures are equivalent to summary nursing data used in the NDNQI and AHA Annual Hospital Survey[12] mentioned previously. All three nursing intensity measures were placed into regression models; the results are shown in Table 10-3.[54]

The results clearly show that the nursing intensity estimate derived from the nurse-patient assignment explains 76.0% of the variability of actual nursing intensity for each patient on the day shift and 81.5% for the night shift. Using the aggregate unit mean only explains 55.6 and 60.9% for the two shifts, and the hospital aggregate mean 42.4 and 54.5%. The findings support the use of the nurse-patient assignment as a potential source of nursing intensity information. Since the assignment data are readily available in any setting in which nurses are assigned to patients for care, this could be a feasible and non-burdensome method to capture nursing intensity in the billing system.

Table 10-2. Estimate of Nursing Intensity Based on Assignment and Wage per Hour

Assignment	8h Shift	12h Shift	Daily Hrs	$25/h	$30/h	$40/h	$50/h
1	8.0	12.0	24.0	600	720	960	1200
2	4.0	6.0	12.0	300	360	480	600
3	2.7	4.0	8.0	200	240	320	400
4	2.0	3.0	6.0	150	180	240	300
5	1.6	2.4	4.8	120	144	192	240
6	1.3	2.0	4.0	100	120	160	200
7	1.1	1.7	3.4	86	103	137	171
8	1.0	1.5	3.0	75	90	120	150

Note: The assignment is based on the number of patients each nurse is assigned during a shift

Source: Welton JM, Zone-Smith L, Bandyopadhyay D. *J Nurs Adm.* 2009 Jun;39(6):276-84

Table 10-3. Comparison of Nursing Intensity Measures[54]

Measure	Day R^2	F	P	Night R^2	F	P
Patient NPA	.760	20225.4	<.001	.815	27649.8	<.001
Unit NPA	.556	7997.1	<.001	.609	9769.5	<.001
Hospital NPA	.424	4696.3	<.001	.545	7515.9	<.001

Patient NPA: measures from actual nurse-patient assignment

Unit NPA: measured as mean nursing hours per patient day for unit

Hospital NPA: measures as mean NHPPD for all similar units (e.g. med/surg)

Source: Welton JM, Zone-Smith L, Bandyopadhyay D. *J Nurs Adm.* 2009 Jun;39(6):276-84

The weakness of the nurse-patient assignment method for calculating nursing hours and costs is the oversimplification of nursing care. Within any assignment, a nurse may give more or less care to any of his or her patients. The lack of any acuity adjustment decreases precision of the nursing intensity mechanism. For example, a patient may become confused or have a change in vital signs that warrants increased attention from the assigned nurse or a very obese patient may need multiple nurses for moving, bathing, etc.

What about the other NMDS elements, such as nursing diagnosis, interventions, or outcomes? The expedient approach to implementing the NMDS in the billing data is to use the revenue code to capture nursing intensity. The potential to insert additional data, for example, separate nursing diagnoses or interventions, is appealing and could better explain the variability in nursing intensity for different patients.[35] Modification of the hospital discharge abstract might be possible in the future to capture both nursing diagnoses and/or interventions. The new ICD-10 code set includes both nursing codes. The data model to capture the additional NMDS data adds complexity to existing data sets. For example, if nursing diagnoses were collected on a daily basis, how could these be summarized for inclusion in the hospital discharge abstract? Should there be a new section for nursing data in the discharge abstract?

Measuring Nursing Performance

One of the underlying concepts of the NMDS is to make nursing visible and comparable across multiple settings and patients. This is even more relevant as the payers for healthcare in the United States have embarked on restructuring hospital reimbursement to decrease payment for the added costs of hospital-acquired adverse events. There has been ample study of the relationship between nursing workload and nursing intensity (often referred to as nurse-to-patient ratios) and clinical outcomes of care. A recent summary of this literature by Kane and colleagues[57] identifies the unique contribution of nurses to care outcomes and the potential for higher levels of adverse events (AE) with lower nursing intensity than needed or through changes in the nursing skill mix, for example, use of licensed practical nurses.[58]

One potential problem with the change in reimbursement is the lack of existing instruments to measure nursing care and nurse characteristics in relationship to AEs. A potential solution to real-time monitoring of these is to use the data from billing for nursing intensity as a metric of staffing levels. In this instance, the ability to link individual nurses with each patient is desirable to better understand and respond to changes in the nursing workforce in acute care hospitals.[59]

The ultimate goal of the NMDS is to create a "…uniform standardized data base that will allow for the grouping and comparison of nursing data collected across various populations, settings, geographic locations, and time would be a boon to both assessing and comparing nursing care provided and resources used, as well as to research."[60] The comparability of nursing care is related to the type, consistency, and availability of data specific to the nurse-patient interaction. The sheer volume of clinical data collected in the normal course of care would not be practical to analyze across several thousand hospitals, not to mention many other healthcare settings in which nursing care is delivered.

The use of nursing intensity as a summary of the amount of nursing care and the associated costs could be reasonably collected and compared across multiple settings to meet the overall intent of the NMDS. For example, the intensity and cost of nursing care could be examined for each patient within a DRG to find the optimum cost/quality tradeoff. Hospitals in the lower percentile of nursing intensity for a particular DRG would be as risk for higher AEs.[61] This would be useful to hospitals, as CMS is reducing payment to hospitals when AEs occur and were preventable such as pressure ulcers, injuries, and certain types of infections.[62] Having the same nursing intensity data collected in the same way and in the same data source would allow comparison of inpatient nursing performance and could possibly become the basis for a nursing pay for performance program.

One last consideration is the difference between nurse staffing and nurse-patient assignment. The major emphasis of research and policy has been on staffing, often measured as the nurse-to-patient (NTP) ratios. Mean nursing intensity can be derived from the average NTP ratios similar to Table 10-2. As noted earlier, using mean unit or hospital-level ratios do not explain as much variability in actual nursing intensity compared with the nurse-patient assignment. The assignment data offers another opportunity to capture the relationships between individual nurses and the patients they care for during a shift and across the entire hospital experience.[54] If the actual assignment data were collected, in addition to nurse demographic data such as license (RN, LPN), years' experience, academic preparation, credentials, they could provide a rich source of information about the effects of nurse characteristics on patient outcomes (see Table 10-4).

If actual nurse wage data were available, the actual or "true" nursing costs based on nurse characteristics could be calculated and evaluated. For example, a new graduate could make $25 per hour and an experienced nurse $50 per hour. If a patient received 10 hours of nursing care, the difference in cost between the new graduate and experienced nurse would be $250 for a particular patient day. These costs are currently hidden in the hospital accounting and billing system. These cost differences will become increasingly relevant in future years as healthcare reform focuses on reducing costs and increasing value of delivered healthcare services. One can also ask whether the added cost of an experienced nurse has tangible returns in improved quality and overall decreased hospital costs. This level of analysis is possible by capturing the existing nursing assignment data in an electronic database and linking to the patient clinical, administrative, billing, and discharge databases.

Table 10-4. Nurse Assignment Analysis Example

Hospital Day	1	1	2	3	3	4	4	5	5	6
Shift	7p-7a	7a-7p	7p-7a	7a-7p	7p-7a	7a-7p	7p-7a	7a-7p	7p-7a	7a-7p
Location	ICU	Rout	Rout	Rout	Rout	Rout	Rout	Rout	Rout	Rout
Assigned Nurse:	A	B	C	B	D	E	D	C	D	E
Patients assigned	2.0	5.0	7.0	5.0	7.0	4.0	6.0	4.0	8.0	6.0
Hours of care	6.0	2.4	1.7	2.4	1.7	3.0	2.0	3.0	1.5	2.0
Experience level	3.0	12.0	6.0	12.0	5.5	15.0	5.5	6.0	5.5	15.0
License	RN	LPN	RN	LPN	RN	RN	RN	RN	RN	RN
Academic prep	BSN	LPN	AD	LPN	BSN	BSN	BSN	AD	BSN	BSN
Traveler/Agency					Y		Y		Y	

Total hours in hosp		60.0			
Total nursing intensity hours	[NI_TOT]	5.1	5.0	Days	[DAYS_HOSP]
Mean ICU nursing intensity	[NI_ICU]	12.0	0.5	Days	[DAYS_ICU]
Routine nursing intensity	[NI_ROUT]	4.4	4.5	Days	[DAYS_ROUT]
Routine nurse experience level	[EXP_ROUT]	9.2			
Routine % RN	[pctRN_ROUT]	77.8			
Routine % BSN	[pctBSN_ROUT]	55.6			
Routine % Traveler/Agency	[pctTRAV_ROUT]	33.3			

Source: Welton JM, Zone-Smith L, Bandyopadhyay D. *J Nurs Adm.* 2009 Jun;39(6):276-84

The assignment data allow more detailed analysis of patterns and trends that are not noticeable with staffing data alone. For example, a particular unit could be well-staffed, but the assignment is not optimum because there are mismatches between patient need, complexity of care, the nurses' experience or credentials, and ability to care for complex patients. In one study, researchers found that nurses with associate degrees were more likely to care for a chronically ill patient and bachelor-degree-prepared nurses tended to care for short-term acute patients.[63] Since longer stay patients are more likely to be at a higher risk for many nursing-sensitive AEs, it may be worthwhile to investigate nurse characteristics within the assignment pattern that produces the best outcome of care.

Two final questions are posed:

1. Should hospital or other healthcare related payment mechanisms reflect differences in levels of nursing care? For example, should patients who receive more nursing care time and resources than other patients be billed at a higher rate?

2. Should there be incentives or additional payment for high-quality nursing care? For example, should nurse managers and executives, nursing units, or individual nurses receive a bonus payment for superior nursing care outcomes?

The questions are relevant within the emerging healthcare reforms being considered in the United States and other countries. There is an emphasis on greater accountability of hospitals and physicians to produce the best clinical outcome for the least cost. This value-based approach to healthcare payment is subsumed within the notion of shared accountability, that is, each physician had a duty to work collectively with other physicians to find the best treatment options.[64,65] These ideas will likely lead to payment bundling as a way to increase shared accountability between physicians and hospitals, coordinating their efforts within the single payment. Where is nursing in these formative ideas? If the nurse-patient assignment data were used to identify all nurses caring for a particular patient, should there be a shared accountability among the nurses to produce the best outcomes of care?

The question is rhetorical for the moment; yet with increasing scrutiny on healthcare costs and quality, and nursing being one of the largest expenditures within the healthcare system, there will be mounting pressure to reform inpatient and outpatient care. Could nurses take the lead and use the new data discussed in this chapter to support the efficacy of nursing care and seek payment adjustments for higher quality outcomes? Should such data about care given by individual nurses be used in job appraisal or salary considerations within an institution? Should a nurse's performance be considered within all nurses caring for patients and individually compared by the types of cases; complexity; and outcomes of care, such as length of stay, occurrence of AEs, or patient satisfaction? These are provocative questions that are necessary to address within the rubric of healthcare reform. The data we collect are inherently valuable and can be used to examine patterns and trends related to nursing care that has not been possible.

Summary

Nursing intensity, estimated as the direct nursing care hours for each patient derived from the nurse-patient assignment and allocated as a separate and distinct daily charge, provides the most expedient way of including nursing specific information in the claims and administrative databases than can subsequently be used to examine the clinical and cost outcomes of inpatient care. These data can be used by policymakers to craft legislation that will lead to important and profound changes in how we deliver healthcare in the United States and in other countries. The use of the universal nurse-patient assignment data allows a reasonable calculation of actual direct nursing care hours and would be a vendor neutral solution that could be used in many, if not most, healthcare settings. There is a UB04 revenue code specific to nursing which allows input of the actual hours of care a patient received and the nursing charge that is an approximation of the actual intensity and cost of nursing care. Collection of these new data would raise the visibility of nursing care and allow for calculation of the economic value of that care. Additional nursing data would be desirable to better explain why patients are getting different levels of nursing care, such as nursing diagnoses, interventions, or outcomes.

Collection of nursing intensity data would allow comparison of nursing care at the individual nurse-patient level of analysis and lead to new analysis and comparisons of nursing care across healthcare settings. These data could be used in new nursing pay-for-performance measures. They could also be used in evidence-based staffing analysis to find the optimum level of nursing staffing.

Lastly, plans are in process to reconvene a new Nursing Minimum Data Set conference at the earliest possible time to focus on implementation of the NMDS with a specific priority to investigate ways to add all NMDS elements into existing billing and administrative data and to recommend additional changes to existing databases to allow incorporation of other nursing specific and relevant data.

References

1. Reverby SM. *Ordered to Care: The Dilemma of American Nursing, 1850-1945.* Cambridge University Press, Michigan 1987.

2. Thompson JD, Diers D. Nursing resources. In: Fetter RB, Brand DF, Gamache eds. *DRGs. Their Design and Development.* Ann Arbor: Health Administration Press; 1991, pp. 121-183

3. Conway PH, Tamara KR, Zhu J, Volpp KG, Sochalski J. Nurse staffing ratios: trends and policy implications for hospitalists and the safety net. *J Hosp Med.* 2008;3:193-199.

4. Kane RL, Shamliyan TA, Mueller C, Duval S, Wilt TJ. (2007b). The Association of Registered Nurse Staffing Levels and Patient Outcomes: Systematic Review and Meta-Analysis. *Med Care.* 2007;45:1195-1204.

5. Aiken LH, Clarke SP, Sloane DM, Sochalski J, Silber JH. Hospital nurse staffing and patient mortality, nurse burnout, and job dissatisfaction. *JAMA.* 2002;288:1987-1993.

6. Aiken LH, Clarke SP, Cheung RB, Sloane DM, Silber JH. Educational levels of hospital nurses and surgical patient mortality. *JAMA.* 2003;290:1617-1623.

7. Unruh L. Nurse staffing and patient, nurse, and financial outcomes. *Am J Nurs.* 2008;108:62-71.

8. Unruh L, Russo CA, Jiang, HJ, Stocks C. Can state databases be used to develop a national, standardized hospital nurse staffing database? *West J Nurs Res.* 2009;31:66-88.

9. Needleman J, Buerhaus PI, Stewart M, Zelevinsky K, Mattke S. Nurse staffing in hospitals: is there a business case for quality? *Health Aff.* 2006;25:204-211.

10. Pappas SH. The cost of nurse-sensitive adverse events. *J Nurs Adm.* 2008;38:230-236.

11. Harless DW. Mark BA. Addressing measurement error bias in nurse staffing research. *Health Services Research.* 2006;41:2006-2024.

12. American Hospital Association. *Annual Survey: American Hospital Association.* http://www.ahadata.com/ahadata/html/AHASurvey.html. Accessed September 7, 2009.

13. U.S. Department of Health and Human Services (2004). *The Registered Nurse Population: Findings from the March 2004 National Sample Survey of Registered Nurses.* Health Resources and Services Administration. http://bhpr.hrsa/gov/healthworkforce/rnsurvey04. Accessed September 7, 2009.

14. Welton JM. (2007) Mandatory Hospital Nurse to Patient Staffing Ratios: Time to Take a Different Approach. *Online J Issues in Nurs, 12,* www.nursingworld.org/MainMenuCategories/ANAMarketplace/ANAPeriodicals/OJIN/TableofContents/Volume122007/No3Sept07/MandatoryNursetoPatientRatios.aspx.

15. Thompson JD, Diers D. DRGs and nursing intensity. *Nurs Health Care.* 1985;6:434-439.

16. Spetz J, Rickles J, Chapman S, Ong PM. Job and industry turnover for registered and licensed vocational nurses. *J Nurs Adm.* 2008;38:372-378.

17. Kash BA, Castle NG, Naufal GS. Hawes C. Effect of staff turnover on staffing: A closer look at registered nurses, licensed vocational nurses, and certified nursing assistants. *Gerontologist.* 2006;46:609-619.

18. Seago JA, Spetz J, Chapman S, Dyer W. Can the use of LPNs alleviate the nursing shortage? Yes, the authors say, but the issues—involving recruitment, education, and scope of practice—are complex. *Am J Nurs* 2006;106:40-49.

19. American Nurses Association (2009). NDNQI: Transforming Data into Quality Care. American Nurses Association, file://C:\Documents and Settings\Administrator\My Documents\ArticlesAndResearch\References\ANA2009.pdf. Accessed September 7, 2009.

20. Montalvo I. The National Database of Nursing Quality Indicators (NDNQI). *Online J Issues Nurs.* 2007;12.

21. Dunton N, Gajewski B, Taunton RL, Moore J. Nurse staffing and patient falls on acute care hospital units. *Nurs Outlook.* 2004;52:53-59.

22. Massachusetts Hospital Association (2006). Patients First. Massachusetts Hospital Association. http://www.patientsfirstma.org/. Accessed September 23, 2008.

23. Welton JM, Unruh L, Halloran EJ. Nurse staffing, nursing intensity, staff mix, and direct nursing care costs across Massachusetts hospitals. *J Nurs Adm.* 2006;36:416-425.

24. Van den HK, Lesaffre E, Diya L, et al. The relationship between inpatient cardiac surgery mortality and nurse numbers and educational level: analysis of administrative data. *Int J Nurs Stud.* 2009;46:796-803.

25. Dalton K, Freeman S, Bragg A. (2008) *Refining Cost to Charge Ratios for Calculating APC and MS-DRG Relative Payment Weights.* RTI Project Number 0209853.008. Prepared for Centers for Medicare & Medicaid Services, Office of Research, Development, and Information, http://www.rti.org/reports/cms/HHSM-500-2005-0029I/PDF/Refining_Cost_to_Charge_Ratios_200807_Final.pdf. Accessed September 7, 2009.

26. Dalton K. (2007). *A Study of Charge Compression in Calculating DRG Relative Weights.* RTI Project Number 0207964.012.008. Prepared for Centers for Medicare & Medicaid Services, Office of Research, Development, and Information, http://www.cms.hhs.gov/reports/downloads/Dalton.pdf. Accessed September 7, 2009.

27. Centers for Medicare & Medicaid Services Medicare Program; Changes to the Hospital Inpatient Prospective Payment Systems and Fiscal Year 2009 Rates. *Fed Regist.* 2008;73:48464-48465.

28. Werley HH, Lang NM, Westlake SK. The nursing minimum data set conference: Executive summary. *J Prof Nurs.* 1986;2:217-222.

29. Kiley M, Halloran EJ, Weston JL, et al. Computerized nursing information system (NIS). *Nurs Manage.* 1983;14:26-29.

30. Halloran EJ, Kiley M. Case mix management. *Nurs Manage.* 1984;15:39-41,44-45.

31. Rosenthal GE, Halloran EJ, Kiley M, Pinkley C, Landefeld CS. Development and validation of the Nursing Severity Index. A new method for measuring severity of illness using nursing diagnoses. *Med Care.* 1992;30;1127-1141.

32. Rosenthal GE, Halloran EJ, Kiley M, Landefeld CS. Predictive validity of the Nursing Severity Index in patients with musculoskeletal disease. *J Clin Epidemiol.* 1995;48:179-188.

33. Welton JM, Halloran EJ. A comparison of nursing and medical diagnoses in predicting hospital outcomes. In NM Lorenzi, ed. *The Annual Symposium of the American Medical Informatics Association Proceedings* (pp. 171-175). Washington, DC: Hanley & Belfus, 1999.

34. Welton JM, Halloran EJ. A comparison of nursing diagnosis to the DRG and APR-DRG in predicting hospital death and discharge to a nursing home. In V Saba, R Carr, W Sermeus, P Rocha, eds. *Proceedings of the Seventh IMIA International Conference on Nursing Use of Computers and Information Science, Auckland, New Zealand, April 28 - May 3, 2000* (pp. 156-160). Auckland, New Zealand: Adis, 2000.

35. Welton JM, Halloran EJ. Nursing diagnoses, diagnosis related group, and hospital outcomes. *J Nurs Adm.* 2005;35:541-549.

36. Sermeus W. Hospital care financing and DRGs: how Belgium takes nursing care into account. *Inforum.* 1991;12:31-37.

37. Sermeus W, Delesie L, Van den Heede K, Diya L, Lesaffre E. Measuring the intensity of nursing care: Making use of the Belgian Nursing Minimum Data Set. *Int J Nurs Stud.* 2008;45:1011-1021.

38. Van den Heede K, Diya L, Lesaffre E, Vleugels A, Sermeus W. Benchmarking nurse staffing levels: the development of a nationwide feedback tool. *J Adv Nurs.* 2008;63:607-618.

39. Van den, HK, Michiels D, Thonon O, Sermeus W. Using nursing interventions classification as a framework to revise the Belgian nursing minimum data set. *Int J Nurs Terminol Classif.* 2009;20:122-131.

40. Laport N, Sermeus W, Vanden BG, Van HP. Adjusting for nursing care case mix in hospital reimbursement: a review of international practice. *Policy Polit Nurs Prac.* 2008;9:94-102.

41. Sermeus W, Gillet P, Tambeur W, Gillain D, Grietens J, Laport N. (2007) *Financing of Hospital Nursing Care.* KCE reports 53 Suppl.(D2007/10.273/08), http://kce.fgov.be/index_nl.aspx?ID=0&SGREF=5260&CREF=9071. Accessed September 7, 2009.

42. Ballard KA, Gray RF, Knauf RA, Uppal P. Measuring variations in nursing care per DRG. *Nurs Manage.* 1993;24:33-36.

43. Knauf RA, Ballard K, Mossman PN, Lichtig LK. Nursing cost by DRG: nursing intensity weights. *Policy PolitNurs Pract.* 2006;7:281-289.

44. Welton JM. Dismuke CE. Testing an inpatient nursing intensity billing model. *Policy Polit Nurs Pract.* 2008;9:103-111.

45. Centers for Medicare & Medicaid Services (2007). *Acute Inpatient Prospective Payment System.* US Department of Health and Human Services, http://www.cms.hhs.gov/MLNProducts/downloads/AcutePaymtSysfctsht.pdf. Accessed September 7, 2009.

46. Thompson JD, Averill RF, Fetter RB. Planning, budgeting, and controlling—one look at the future: case-mix cost accounting. *Health Serv Res.* 1979;14:111-125.

47. Thompson JD. The measurement of nursing intensity. *Health Care Financ Rev, Suppl.* 1984;47-55.

48. Grimaldi PL, Micheletti JA. DRG reimbursement: RIMs & the cost of nursing care. *Nurs Manage.* 1982;13:12-22.

49. Grimaldi PL, Micheletti JA. A debate: RIMs and the cost of nursing care: a defense of the RIMs reliability and value? *Nurs Manage.* 1983;14:40-41.

50. Caterinicchio RP, Grimaldi PL, Micheletti JA. A debate: RIMs & the cost of nursing care. *Nurs Manage.* 1983;14:36-41.

51. Medicare Payment Advisory Commission (2005). Report to the Congress: *Physician Owned Specialty Hospitals.* MedPAC. Accessed: November 5, 2006.

52. O'Brien-Pallas L, Leatt P, Deber R, Till J. A comparison of workload estimates using three methods of patient classification. *Can J Nurs Adm.* 1989;2:16-23.

53. Shaha SH, Bush C. Fixing acuity: a professional approach to patient classification and staffing. *Nurs Econ.* 1996;14:346-356.

54. Welton JM, Zone-Smith L, Bandyopadhyay D. Estimating nursing intensity and direct cost using the nurse-patient assignment. *J Nurs Adm.* 2009;39:276-284.

55. Welton JM, Zone-Smith L, Fischer MH. Adjustment of inpatient care reimbursement for nursing intensity. *Policy Polit Nurs Pract.* 2006;7:270-280.

56. Zone-Smith L. Predicting real-time nurse staffing needs in hospitals: A new tool to measure nursing intensity. *J Nurs Adm.* 2004;34:210.

57. Kane RL, Shamliyan T, Mueller C, Duval S, Wilt T. (2007a) *Nursing Staffing and Quality of Patient Care. Evidence Report/Technology.* Assessment No. 151 (Prepared by the Minnesota Evidence based Practice Center under Contract No. 290-02-0009.) AHRQ Publication No. 07-E005. Agency for Healthcare Quality and Research, http://www.ahrq.gov/downloads/pub/evidence/pdf/nursestaff/nursestaff.pdf. Accessed September 7, 2009a.

58. Stone PW, Mooney-Kane C, Larson EL, et al. Nurse working conditions and patient safety outcomes. *Med Care.* 2007;45:571-578.

59. Welton JM. (2008b) Implications of Medicare reimbursement changes related to inpatient nursing care quality. *J Nurs Adm.* 2008;38:325-330.

60. Werley HH, Devine EC, Zorn CR, Ryan P, Westra BL. The nursing minimum data set: abstraction tool for standardized, comparable, essential data. *Am J Pub Health.* 1991;81:421-426.

61. Welton JM. (2008a) Implications of Medicare reimbursement changes related to inpatient nursing care quality. *J Nurs Adm.* 2008;38:325-330.

62. Kurtzman ET. Buerhaus PI. New Medicare payment rules: danger or opportunity for nursing? *Am J Nurs.* 2008;108:30-35.

63. Bastin HL, Halloran EJ. Nurse education and patient data to assess hospital nursing care quality. In: Marin HF, Marques EP, Hovenga EJS, Goossen WT, eds. *Proceedings, 8th International Congress in Nursing Informatics, Rio de Janeiro, June 20-25, 2003.* Rio de Janeiro, Brazil: E-papers Servicos Editoriais Ltd.

64. Fisher ES, Staiger DO, Bynum JP, Gottlieb DJ. Creating accountable care organizations: the extended hospital medical staff. *Health Aff.* 2007;26:w44-w57.

65. Shortell SM, Casalino LP. Health care reform requires accountable care systems. *JAMA.* 2008;300:95-97.

Case Study 10A

Standardizing the Electronic Nursing Summary: Motivation, Methods, and Results

By Ursula Hübner, PhD; and Daniel Flemming, Dipl. Kaufmann, RN

Introduction

Continuity of Care and Discharge Management

Decreased values for length of stay in hospitals, early discharges from hospitals, and the proliferation of fragmented healthcare services have contributed to a renewed interest in continuity of care as a concept for ensuring quality of care. The continuity of care concept aims at bridging gaps between settings, institutions, shifts, and healthcare professions. According to the current literature it is a multidimensional concept that comprises informational, management, relational, and contact issues.[1,2] Informational issues typically address the need for consistent, complete, up-to-date, and timely patient information to be transferred between healthcare institutions or healthcare professionals in charge of providing follow-up. New studies provide insight into these issues and also into how technology and EHRs, in particular, can support a seamless flow of information within[3,4] and across institutions[5] without compromising information privacy.[6] Within continuity of care, discharge management is one method that allows continuity of care to be translated into practical work.[7]

Information and Communication Gaps and Patient Safety

Despite growing awareness of discharge planning among healthcare professionals, information and communication gaps still exist that eventually may lead to clinical errors and may compromise patient safety. For example, it was found that because of missing information, adverse drug events occurred when patients were transferred from acute- to long-term care facilities.[8] Poor communication was reported to be one of the common themes of official inquiries in the British National Health Service (NHS), which were made as a result of severe problems and mistakes in patient care.[9] In a literature review, discontinuities and a breakdown in communication between the hospital team and the patient or the general practitioner were found to be responsible for AEs after discharge. The review authors, therefore, recommended that we develop the means to improve information transfer to make discharge a less vulnerable care transition phase.[10] These accounts reflect the urgent need for improvements in the way healthcare professionals communicate and exchange information. In this chapter we focus on asynchronous, interorganizational communication at the end of a care episode in a given organization or department.

Need for Interoperable EHR Tools

Traditionally, paper-based discharge or transfer summaries are sent to the organization, department, or individual healthcare professional that provides follow-up care. However, there are intrinsic flaws in paper-based information exchange (e.g. lack of completeness, no standardized terminology). Electronic procedures promise to be better suited for transmitting complete and timely information of a patient, and therefore promise better results in nursing.[11] EHRs and any other electronic document used for communication must be interoperable, meaning that they must be capable of exchanging information between the electronic systems involved that meets the requirements of those who need to inform each other about a clinical case.

Interoperability is not an absolute feature that either exists or does not exist. Rather, it can be achieved at different levels of integration, reflecting varying hierarchical degrees of automation and service levels. The different stages at which interoperability is manifested are: the technical, structural, syntactical, semantic, and organizational/service levels. *Technical* interoperability embraces simple plug mechanisms, as well as compatibility of signals and protocols; *structural* interoperability is given if data can be exchanged in a simple way, e.g., via electronic data interchange (EDI); *syntactical* interoperability requires vocabularies to be agreed upon to exchange messages and documents; *semantic* interoperability is achieved when common information models are used to be able to interpret the information correctly. And finally, *organizational* and *service* interoperability builds upon common business process models and service chains.[12]

While syntactical interoperability describes grammatical features of the exchange process, semantic interoperability aims at an unambiguous interpretation of the message or document content.[13] In the ideal case, an electronic nursing summary is a document that provides interoperability at the semantic level. User and information driven approaches, however, stress the necessary co-existence of structured and unstructured information within the electronic nursing summary.[14] Caution must be taken to find the right balance between structured and unstructured parts of the nursing summary, because the extensive use of unstructured information inevitably leads to a lower level of machine interoperability.

Information and Communication Standards in Nursing

Overview and ISO Reference Terminology Model for Nursing

Nursing informatics and nursing science have paid much attention to terminology standards in the last decades, and there is a plethora of such standards available. Although terminologies play an important role in enabling all levels of interoperability, from the syntactical level onwards, we will refrain from enumerating the various vocabularies and refer the reader to the literature.[15] Co-existence of different nursing terminologies is accepted because none of these terminologies has gained the status of a worldwide accepted and politically enforced classification system, such as the ICD (International Classification of Diseases) in medicine. Thus, efforts were undertaken to develop an overarching model, which allows, among other allowances, the representation of nursing diagnoses and actions in a manner that supports its use in computerized systems. These efforts resulted in the ISO standard "Health Informatics—Integration of a Reference Terminology Model for Nursing."[16] The model is important for structuring nursing documents to be processed electronically, such as an electronic nursing summary. The Reference Terminology Model for Nursing is a common model in nursing that describes the structure and content of nursing information irrespective of the classification system preferred and independent of a particular nursing theory. It consists of two separate models: one for nursing diagnoses, the other for nursing actions.[16]

Messaging and Document Standards

Health Level Seven's (HL7) messaging (V2 and V3) and documentation standards—Clinical Document Architecture[17] (CDA)—are one of the world's most renowned global standards in healthcare. HL7's Reference Information Model (RIM) permits healthcare and system analysts to model specific application areas, including nursing.[18] The HL7 framework of standards is therefore a powerful concept for standardizing the eNursing Summary that provides the necessary building blocks in the modelling phase and generally during the different stages of development. It had been used to standardize other clinical documents, such as the German eMedical Summary.[19]

The Electronic Nursing Summary

What is a Nursing Summary?

The nursing summary is part of the nursing record (see Figure 10A-1). It summarizes the nursing process, in particular the patient's status, and provides information on the treatment and care given to the patient. It may also contain further recommendations. Used as a document for discharge and transfer of a patient, it also comprises administrative and social information necessary for the recipient to provide follow-up care. The nursing summary makes use of the wealth of information from the maximum data set (nursing record). It is distinct from the nursing minimum data set with regard to a lower degree of aggregation (see Figure 10A-1). For example, the information contained in the nursing summary is related to an individual patient and has impact on the care given to that patient. In contrast, the nursing minimum data set is meant to have an impact on health policy.

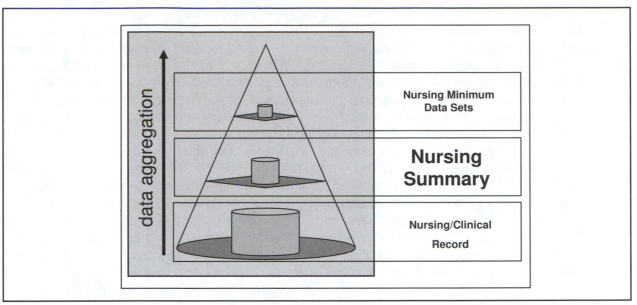

Figure 10A-1. *The Nursing Summary in the Context of Other Data Sets (modified – after NURSINGData[20])*

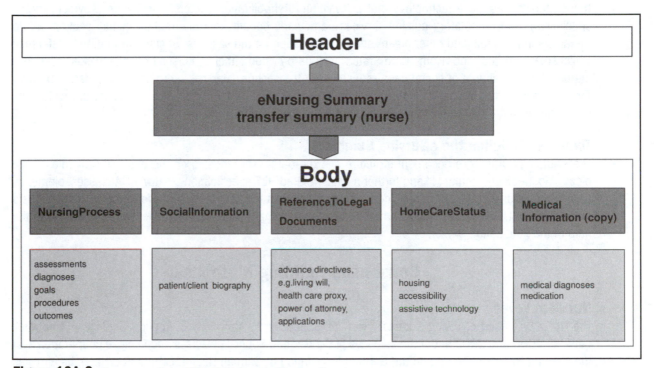

Figure 10A-2. *Structure of the HL7 CDA-based eNursing Summary*

The HL7 CDA-based eNursing Summary

CDA documents are divided into a document header and the document body (see Figure 10A-2). The header contains administrative data; primarily about the patient, the sender, and the destination. The body of a CDA document can be configured in principle according to needs, in that it can embrace unstructured as well as structured data. The HL7 CDA-based, eNursing Summary is a highly structured clinical document. The structure and content of the header was adopted from the German CDA-based medical summary,[19] with only minor modifications made to it. By contrast the document body is specific to nursing and was developed separately in a project which had started in 2006.

Major experience was drawn from previous work, mainly an analysis of discharge summaries in use[11] and the participatory development of an electronic nursing discharge form.[21] Based on these results, the document body was organized into the following sections: a) Nursing Process, b) Social Information, c) Reference to Legal Documents, d) Home Care Status, and e) Medical Information. The "Nursing Process" section is the central part of the HL7 CDA-based eNursing Summary. It is subdivided into the classes "nursingScore," "nursingDiagnosis," "nursingGoal," "nursingProcedure," and "nursingOutcome." The category "nursingDiagnosis" is further specified by the classes "Etiology, "Symptoms," and "Resources." Also, "nursingProcedure" is always triggered by other nursing classes, such as "nursingDiagnosis," and can be followed by a "nursingOutcome." Groups of scores, nursing diagnoses, nursing goals, nursing procedures, and nursing outcomes may be clustered by themes, such as the activities of daily living (ADL) or by user-defined themes. ADLs are not mandatory, neither is any other taxonomy because any predefined scheme would imply a specific nursing theory as default. Also at the level of entries, the "Nursing Process" section does not propose any particular nursing terminology but is open for different controlled vocabularies. The standard, however, recommends regional or local specifications of the standard terminologies preferred by the healthcare providers in that network.

The "Social Information" section covers a short, non-structured note on the patient's or client's biography. The "ReferenceToLegal Documents" section allows legal and official documents to be referenced, i.e., metadata of these documents to be communicated, such as date of issue, the depository, and contact persons. These two sections were added pursuant to special requests from institutions that are in charge of the care of elderly patients, in particular of patients with dementia, e.g., nursing homes, geriatric clinics, geriatric hospital departments, and ambulatory care services, and from psychiatric care institutions. The "Home Care Status" section describes the private and social environment in which the patient lives, constructional issues of the home, and the assistive technology that is available. Rehabilitation centers, home care providers (nurse specialists), and ambulatory nursing services particularly benefit from information in this section, as do therapists in hospitals and other organizations. Information for the sections "Social Information," "Reference To Legal Documents" and "Home Care Status" may be provided either by nurses or social workers, depending on who is in charge of social care issues. Finally the section "Medical Information" is a data container for medication data and medical diagnoses. It is typically copied from the medical summary or provided by physicians who are the authors and the signatories of this section.

Tools for Modeling the eNursing Summary

The eNursing Summary's document structure and the data were modeled on the basis of CDA rules,[17] the electronic medical summary,[19] and further nursing-related HL7 specifications.[22] HL7 CDA classes, elements, data types, and attributes were specified and modelled with the help of HL7-RIMDesigner in Microsoft Visio and RoseTree. LOINC-codes were used for coding the document sections. XML code was generated with the help of the XML editor, Oxygen.

Consensus Building Methods

National Level

The HL7 CDA-based eNursing Summary was developed by the University of Applied Sciences, Osnabrück between 2006 and 2009 under the auspices of the German Council of Nurses and in close cooperation with the German HL7 User Group and the German Association of German Health IT Vendors (VHitG). Its aim was to provide a standard which would be accepted by nurses providing care in different settings and for different types of patients and clients. In a first step, relevant data and their interrelationships were collected in interviews and workshops together with nursing experts from the Network of Continuity of Care (see Figure 10A-3). This network is an alliance of healthcare providers from various settings (hospitals, nursing homes, ambulatory nursing services, home care providers, pharmacies) in the Osnabrück region, situated in northwest Germany. The data were then cross-validated on the basis of existing clinical datasets, such as the Continuity of Care Record[23] and the NURSING data maximum dataset.[24] The overall structure was synchronized with the ISO Reference Terminology Model for Nursing.[15] In contrast to this model, which contains two separate models for nursing diagnoses and nursing interventions, we are working on a newly proposed structure that will link diagnoses and interventions.

In a second step, the header and the five data clusters of the body were presented to nursing experts in workshops at three different nursing and healthcare conferences in 2007 and 2008 and underwent minor

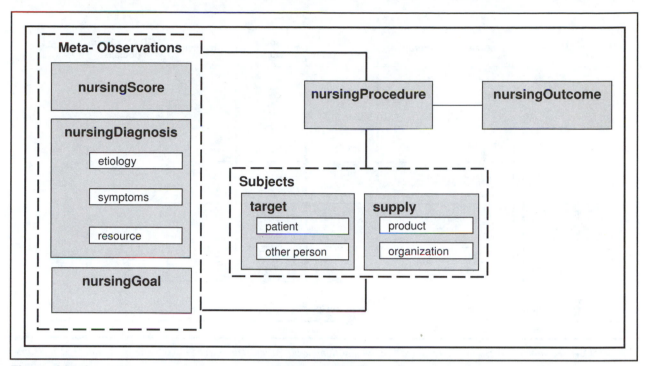

Figure 10A-3. *Classes and Interclass Relationship of the Section "Nursing Process"*

modifications. Mid-2009, the data set was evaluated by the regional Nursing Network of Heilbronn in southwest Germany that comprises 100 providers of nursing care in the region, including hospitals, ambulatory care services, and nursing homes. These institutions presently use a common paper-based nursing summary form, which had been developed in a joint effort to accommodate various demands for information. This form was used as a reference document for validating the eNursing Summary. The results show that all data fields of the Heilbronn form could be translated into the standard. Furthermore the users of the Heilbronn form emphasized the importance of subtitles denoting different sections or areas of nursing care. They did not insist on utilizing the ADL but rather stressed the point of using flexible subtitles that are defined at regional level to suit the special needs of that network. Also the Continuity of Care Network in the Osnabrück Region had expressed the demand of subtitles and subsections that could be adapted to the local needs.

The discharge form used in Heilbronn differed from the standard with regard to the relations between diagnoses and interventions. Whereas the standard requires interventions to be linked to the cause of the intervention, typically the nursing diagnosis, the Heilbronn form consists of a loose enumeration of unrelated problems and interventions. The Nursing Network Heilbronn indicated interest for changing their approach when switching from paper to electronic nursing summaries. Continuous monitoring of the information demands at discharge is planned and will include regular evaluations of samples of paper-based discharge forms, which are currently in use by various types of institutions across the country.

International Level

In order to coordinate the German activities with international developments, contact was established with the International Council of Nurses (ICN) to define a collaboration project that would bring together interested parties from different countries. The project would allow for us to build a platform for discussing the various approaches that have been developed, e.g., in Finland where the CDA has been adopted as the Finnish national standard for the electronic patient record,[25] in the Netherlands where HL7 V3 based nursing discharge messages have been defined[26] and in Austria, where a first concept has been proposed.[27]

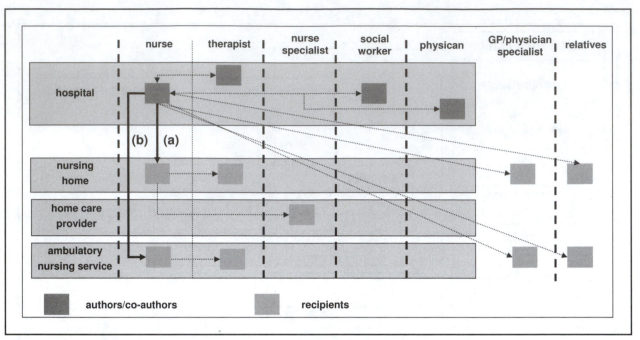

Figure 10A-4. *Information Flow Enabled by the eNursing Summary: Patient Discharged to (a) Nursing Home, (b) to Home*

Summary and Outlook

Application of the eNursing Summary in the eHealth Context

The eNursing Summary is a communication instrument in ICT-supported, integrated care delivery scenarios (see Figure 10A-4). We contend that these regional networks will become the preferred way of providing care not only in Germany but in many countries as a result of efforts to combat fragmentation undertaken by national healthcare systems and their stakeholders.[28] While "integrated care" addresses the political and financial dimension of continuity of care, "eHealth," as technical counterpart to integrated care, seeks to close information and communication gaps in the system. Many nations have adopted eHealth plans to foster interoperable, countrywide information exchange among healthcare providers, e.g., in the European Union[29] and in the United States.[30] Besides practical applications such as electronic prescriptions and EHRs, eHealth initiatives aim at the promotion and enforcement of standards. Electronic nursing records and nursing summaries are integral components of advanced electronic health records[31] and need to be designed according to a standardized structure to support the overarching goal of EHRs, i.e., providing information across the care continuum.

Not only may multi-morbid patients,[32] who frequently see different healthcare professionals during an acute episode of their illness, benefit from a higher degree of informational continuity, but so do many other types of patients, such as mentally ill patients[33] and patients at the end of life.[34] Robust eHealth tools could positively influence the perception of continuity of care by those patients who experienced informational discontinuity,[32] in particular, at the primary-secondary care interface[35] and allow relatives to be better informed and involved.[7]

Eventually, it is not only the eNursing Summary that accompanies a patient at discharge or transfer, but a series of summaries—first and foremost the medical summary. These different summaries will have to be coordinated both in terms of contents and recipients. The German eNursing Summary already integrates with different professions (see Figure 10A-4), such as nurses, physicians, therapists, and social workers. However, this document focuses primarily on nursing related issues. Therefore, it is not truly a multi-professional summary in its very meaning. Instead, it reflects the nurses' role in healthcare, as generalists who are in charge of coordinating and conciliating the different care processes for a patient, and who need to amalgamate different pieces of information originating from these many strands.

References

1. Wierdsma A, Mulder C, de Vries S, Sytema S. Reconstructing continuity of care in mental health services: a multilevel conceptual framework. *J Health Serv Res Policy.* 2009;14:52-57.

2. Hadjistavropoulos H, Biem H, Sharpe D, Bourgault-Fagnou M, Janzen J. Patient perceptions of hospital discharge: reliability and validity of a Patient Continuity of Care Questionnaire. *Int J Qual Health Care.* 2008;20:314-323.

3. Patel VP, Raptis D, Christofi T, et al. Development of electronic software for the management of trauma patients on the orthopaedic unit. *Injury.* 2009;40:388-396.

4. Crooks VA, Agarwal G. What are the roles involved in establishing and maintaining informational continuity of care within family practice? A systematic review. *BMC Fam Pract.* 2008;9:65.

5. Mostashari F, Tripathi M, Kendall M. A tale of two large community electronic health record extension projects. *Health Aff.* 2009;28:345-356.

6. Heimly V, Berntsen KE. Consent-based access to core EHR information. *Methods Inf Med.* 2009;48:144-148.

7. Damiani G, Federico B, Venditti A, et al. Hospital discharge planning and continuity of care for aged people in an Italian local health unit: does the care-home model reduce hospital readmission and mortality rates? *BMC Health Serv Res.* 2009;9:22.

8. Boockvar K, Fishman E, Kyriacou CK, Monia A, Gavi S, Cortes T. Adverse events due to discontinuations on drug use and dose changes in patients transferred between acute and long-term care facilities. *Arch Int Med.* 2004;164:545-550.

9. Walshe K, Higgins J. The use and impact of inquiries in the NHS. *BMJ.* 2002; 325:895-900.

10. Kripalani S, Jacksom AT, Schnipper JL, Coleman AE. Promoting effective transitions of care at hospital discharge: a review of key issues for hospitalists. *J Hosp Med.* 2007;2:314-323.

11. Hübner U, Giehoff C. Why continuity of care needs computing: results of a quantitative document analysis. *Stud Health Technol Inform.* 2002;90:483-487.

12. Lopez D, Blobel B. A development framework for semantic interoperable health information systems. *Int J Med Inform.* 2009;78:83-103.

13. Blobel B, Pharow P. Analysis and evaluation of EHR approaches. *Methods Inf Med.* 2009;48:162-169.

14. Hellesø R, Lorensen M, Sorensen L. Challenging the information gap – the patients transfer from hospital to home health care. *Int J Med Inf.* 2004;73:569-580.

15. Westra BL, Delaney CW, Konicek D, Keenan G. Nursing standards to support the electronic health record. *Nurs Outlook.* 2008;56:258-266.

16. International Standards Organization. *Integration of a Reference Terminology Model for Nursing.* ISO 18104:2003. www.iso.org. Accessed March 1, 2008.

17. Health Level Seven Inc. *Clinical Document Architecture.* Ann Arbor. www.hl7.org. Accessed February 20, 2009.

18. Health Level Seven Inc. *Reference Information Model.* Ann Arbor. www.hl7.org. Accessed February 20, 2009.

19. VHitG. Arztbrief auf Basis der HL7 *Clinical Document Architecture Release 2* für das Deutsche Gesundheitswesen. Berlin; 2006.

20. NURSING data. Modell eines Informationssystems für die Gesundheitsund Krankenpflege. ISE Lausanne 1999. www.isesuisse.ch/nursingdata/de/dokumente/modele_systeme_information_d.pdf. Accessed June 21, 2009.

21. Giehoff C, Hübner U. Der elektronische Pflegebericht des „Netzwerks Versorgungskontinuität in der Region Osnabrück" – Evaluationsergebnisse und ihre Konsequenzen. Pflegewissenschaft – www.printernet.info. 2006/06, 371-377. Accessed November 8, 2009.

22. Goossen W, Ozbolt J, Coenen A, et al. Development of a provisional domain model for the nursing process for use within the Health Level 7 Reference Information Model. *JAMIA.* 2004;11:186–194.

23. ASTM International. Continuity of Care Record. Available at: www.astm.org/Standards/E2369.htm. Accessed June 18, 2009.

24. Berthou A, Junger A. NURSING data Modell eines Informationssystems für die Gesundheits- und Krankenpflege. Available at: www.isesuisse.ch/nursingdata/en/index.htm. Accessed June 18, 2009.

25. Health Level Seven (HL7). *The Brochure of HL7 Finland.* 2009. www.hl7.fi. Accessed June 19, 2009.

26. Goossen W. *Sending Electronic Nursing Discharge Messages using the HL7 v3 Care Provision Standard.* Conference Proceedings of NI 2009 Helsinki, forthcoming.

27. B Stangl. Entwicklung eines normierten Pflegeentlassungsberichtes auf Basis der Clinical Document Architecture. Vienna, Technical University of Vienna, 2007. www.meduni-wien.ac.at/msi/mias/studarbeiten/2007-DA-Stangl.pdf. Accessed June 19, 2009.

28. Mur-Veeman I, van Raak A, Paulus A. Comparing integrated care policy in Europe: Does policy matter? *Health Policy.* 2008;85:172–183.

29. European Communities – *EC. eHealth Priorities and Strategies in European Countries. Luxembourg 2007.* ec.europa.eu/information_society/newsroom/cf/itemdetail.cfm?item_id=3346. Accessed May 23, 2009.

30. US Department of Health and Human Services. *The ONC coordinated Federal Health IT Strategic Plan: 2008-2012.* healthit.hhs.gov. Accessed June 19, 2009.

31. Häyrinen K, Saranto K, Nykännen P. Definition, structure, content, use and impacts of electronic health records: A review of the research literature. *Int J Med Inf.* 2007;77:291-307.

32. Cowie L, Morgan M, White P, Gulliford M. Experience of continuity of care of patients with multiple long-term conditions in England. *J Health Serv Res Policy.* 2009;14:82-87.

33. Knowles P. Collaborative communication between psychologists and primary care providers. *J Clin Psychol Med Settings.* 2009;16:72-76.

34. Michiels E, Deschepper R, Van Der Kelen G, et al. The role of general practitioners in continuity of care at the end of life: a qualitative study of terminally ill patients and their next of kin. *Palliat Med.* 2007;21:409-415.

35. Nazareth I, Jones L, Irving A, et al. Perceived concepts of continuity of care in people with colorectal and breast cancer—a qualitative case study analysis. *Eur J Cancer Care.* 2008;17:569-577.

Case Study 10B

Improving Patient Safety, Increasing Nursing Efficiency, and Reducing Cost through Technology-Supported Pull Systems

By Thomas R. Clancy, PhD, MBA, RN; and Susan C. Hull, MSN, BSN, RN

Introduction

A quotation often recited by general system theorists is, "Over time, systems become increasingly complex."[1] This statement certainly rings true in the healthcare environment of today. Numerous providers, multiple service lines, an aging population, increased regulation, competition, and the exponential growth of new technology all fuel increased complexity in the work place. Unfortunately, the more complex a work environment becomes, the greater the potential for human error and serious harm to patients. In its landmark reports, *To Err is Human*[2] and *Crossing the Quality Chasm*,[3] the Institute of Medicine (IOM) estimates that 98,000 deaths occur annually in United State's hospitals as a result of medical errors. Studies have shown that medical errors frequently take place when nurses are under time pressure, fatigued, and distracted.[4] This often occurs at the end of the shift when numerous tasks need to be completed within a compressed time frame in an effort to prevent overtime. In fact, a name has been coined for this growing phenomenon: complexity compression.

Complexity compression (CC) is defined by Kritchbaum[5] as the accommodation of additional, unplanned events, while simultaneously conducting multiple responsibilities in a condensed time frame. The emergence of CC, especially at shift end, is a likely cause for medical errors, inefficiency, and waste. The purpose of this case study is to discuss the impact of CC on patient safety, nursing efficiency, and cost and then provide recommendations to reduce it. Specifically, this chapter will demonstrate, through a case study, how a community hospital reduced CC through intentionally designed automation (IDA), clinical practice guidelines (CPG), and positive deviance (PD).

Complexity Compression

The underlying cause of CC is the discontinuous flow of events interspersed with hard constraints in a nurse's typical daily workflow. Discontinuous flow of events refers to events, such as unplanned admissions or emergencies that interrupt *scheduled* events, such as medication administration, vital signs, and clinical documentation. Because scheduled events must occur at certain times, they are considered "hard constraints." Unless less urgent tasks can be reprioritized, a discontinuous flow of events imposed on hard constraints can cause delays or queues (backups) to develop. Complexity compression leads to stacking, which is characterized by multiple tasks "stacked" in an imaginary "to do" pile.[6] As the hard constraint imposed by the shift's end approaches, reprioritized activities, such as charting and care planning are rushed, which results in errors and causes overtime to occur.

The solution to CC, in part, is leveling the workload through "pull" systems. Leveling the workload means redistributing work into small batches throughout the shift, rather than in one large batch at the end of the shift. For example, implementing computerized clinical documentation systems that enable nurses to chart hourly can prevent the cascading effect of CC. Pull systems allow users to access the right information at the right time by facilitating the flow of information from clinical practice guidelines (CPGs) stored in a central data repository. To achieve this continuous flow of information throughout the shift, a number of process variables must be aligned. The following case study highlights how this can be achieved through enabling technology.

Background and Historical Perspectives

In 2006 the nursing leadership in a seven-hospital integrated delivery system (IDS) embarked on a journey to reduce end-of-shift CC. The desire to reduce CC emerged after it was noted that intershift report (professional exchange report) varied considerably among nursing units: anywhere from 40 minutes to more than an hour. A characteristic of CC is a prolonged professional exchange report (PER), coupled with frequent end-

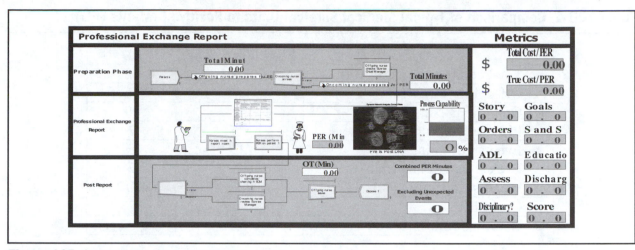

Figure 10B-1. *Simulation Model of PER*

of-shift overtime. To better understand the impact of CC on nursing processes such as PER, a collaborative project between the University of Minnesota School of Nursing, the Clinical Practice Model Resource Center, Elsevier,[7] and the Eclipsys Corporation[8] was conducted.

The collaboration investigated the following question: "What PER practice within the IDS best meets organizational performance metrics for efficiency, effectiveness, and expense?" A PER was defined as the inter-shift exchange of information between two nurses on one patient. Effectiveness represented the information exchange between the off-going and on-coming nurse during PER and how well they understood the patient's story and progress with respect to the entire interdisciplinary team's plan of care. Efficiency represented how long PER actually took to complete, while expenses measured the labor costs associated with PER.

Building a Computational Model

A key component in understanding the effect of CC was building a computational model of the current PER process. Computational modeling takes a set of assumptions regarding a system and translates them into mathematical or logical relationships that can be represented on a computer.[9] These models accept real systems inputs and act as a simulation for the process under investigation. Outputs from the model are statistically validated against outputs from the actual health system. Typically, models are built visually, using standard flow-chart symbols. Computational modeling and simulation allow unpredictable and predictable processes with multiple variables to be analyzed. The benefits of modeling include low-cost scenario analysis, which can also uncover unexpected system behavior. It also allows simulated parameters to be exercised beyond capacity on a computer without harm or expense to patients.

The model was built using commercially available simulation software. PER between an in-coming and off-going nurse was modeled (see Figure 10B-1). Three primary nursing activities were represented in the model for both in- and out-going nurses: information gathering from paper records and the hospitals computer system prior to PER, verbal exchange and documentation during PER, and completion of documentation post PER. The total number and duration of interruptions during PER were also built into the model.

The Current State Model

Results of the simulation model revealed that the combined average time for preparation, communication, and post PER for the on-coming and off-going nurse was 120 minutes. The average total labor and benefits expense per PER (including off-going and on-coming nurse) was $65.16. In addition, there was an average of 7 minutes of overtime per off-going nurse or approximately 1,572 total overtime hours per year for the entire unit. Table 10B-1 presents the efficiency outputs from the computational model. Observations by team members noted that both the on-coming and off-going nurses spent 85% of their preparation time searching for PER information in multiple areas (paper and electronic), waiting for computers to become available and responding to interruptions (phone calls, call lights, and communication with other providers). During change of shift, multiple providers converged on computers located in the nursing station and created queues waiting for computers to become available. Potential report information was contained on six different paper forms,

Table 10B-1. Comparison of Typical Medical Surgical Units to Positive Deviants (PD)

Metric	Med./Surg. Unit	PD
Total combined time/PER (min)	120	45
Off-going Nurse (min)	67	16
On-coming Nurse (min)	44	19
PER verbal (min)	9.7	2
Events Off-going (min)	22	5
Events On-coming (min)	2	2
Process Capability (%)	28%	100%
Cost/PER	$65	$23
Overtime (min)	7.0	0

as well as in the computerized clinical information system. On average, only 28% (process capability) of the available fields on the paper forms were actually used for documentation of information. Combining many of these factors contributed to the average overtime of seven minutes per off-going nurse.

Team members also noted that as the end of the shift approached, the number of unplanned events increased, as well as the duration of events. For example, the average duration of unplanned events within the last hour of shift change was 22 minutes. As one nurse stated, "It is not only the end of shift for our nursing unit, it is for many of the other departments in the entire hospital as well. As the shift comes to a close, patients are transferred from other units, lab and radiology tests are phoned up, physicians call back (responding to) phone messages left earlier in the shift, and pharmacists clarify medication orders. It is as though a wave of activity sweeps through the hospital just before shift end. If you haven't been documenting your care and updating care plans every hour, you are going to be swamped."

A survey of nurses involved in the PER process revealed a combined average score of 3.4 on a Likert Scale (with 5 representing high satisfaction). It was noted that the primary focus of PER was on patient assessment, significant signs and symptoms, and impending orders (see Table 10B-2). There was limited discussion regarding progress toward goals or outcomes, discharge needs, integration of the interdisciplinary team, and nursing orders. To complete charting by end of shift, nurses simply omitted doing these tasks. These observations aligned well with low scores regarding the effectiveness of PER in the survey.

A benefit of computational modeling and simulation is the ability to develop predictive scenarios. Multiple scenarios were developed to optimize both the effectiveness and efficiency of PER. Results of the scenario analysis indicated that if access to computers improved, interruptions to nurses would decrease; PER information would be centralized in an electronic repository, and nurses would not have to wait until the end of the shift to chart, resulting in significant improvements in PER. Results of the predictive modeling indicated that PER could be decreased from a combined 120 minutes (on-coming plus off-going nurse) to as low as 40 minutes if delays in the process were removed.

Positive Deviance

It was beyond the scope of the project to investigate all nursing units within the seven hospitals of the IDS. Consensus among chief nursing officers (CNO) indicated that project results represented the typical PER process on most nursing units. To improve the overall performance of PER within the IDS, the concept of positive deviance (PD) was used.[10] PD is a method that searches for the highest performing individuals within an organization to learn and replicate their practices. A positive deviant is an individual located in the top 1% of specific performance metrics (e.g., patient satisfaction, productivity, clinical expertise). By engaging positive deviants in teaching other nurses their best practices, cycle time for performance improvement projects can be significantly reduced.

In reviewing various hospitals and nursing units within the IDS, one hospital's nursing units consistently completed PER, on average, for both on-coming and off-going nurses in 40 minutes or less (20 minutes per nurse). Team members studied this nursing unit and discovered the existence of a highly effective PER pro-

Table 10B-2. Likert Scale for PER Effectiveness (1 – 5 scale with 5 being highly effective)

Measure (0 – 5 scale)	Med/Surg Score	PD Score
Patient's story	3.5	4.5
Assessments	3.8	4.6
Orders and significant results	3.2	4.0
Integration of team goals	3.2	4.7
Patient progress toward goals	3.0	4.5
Activity, diet and nursing orders	3.3	4.0
Significant signs & symptoms	3.6	4.8
Interdisciplinary education	3.8	4.6
Discharge needs	3.0	4.0
Average Score	3.4	4.41

cess that integrated technology into workflow and pulled information to the user for clinical documentation when needed.

Knowledge Based Charting™ and Intentionally Designed Automation™

The unit utilized The Clinical Practice Model Resource Center Elsevier processes for PER, including use of Knowledge Based Charting™ (KBC) developed with Eclipsys Corporation. KBC is an integrated, interdisciplinary clinical practice and documentation system that incorporates Intentionally Designed Automation™ (IDA) that pulls data from electronically stored clinical practice guidelines used by the nurse for daily documentation.[7,8] The integration of KBC and IDA allows nurses to pull CPG content into electronic medical record fields when needed. The PER utilizes KBC to chart continuously (hourly), establish care prioritization, reduce the risk of incomplete information exchange, assure continuity of care, clarify and track progress toward outcomes, minimize the need for data retrieval, and provide time for consultative interchange between caregivers.

The manager on the orthopedic/neurosurgery unit suggested that two high-performing nurses (positive deviants) be selected for observation of the unit's PER process. One nurse had more than twenty years of nursing experience, while the other was a recent graduate with two years' experience. Observations of the two nurses were conducted in the same manner as the original project. A computational model was then created to compare the two positive deviant's best practice.

The Positive Deviance Model

The PER process for the positive deviants was actually the culmination of numerous iterations and improvements conducted on the unit over a five-year-period. The result was a highly refined process that viewed PER as one step in the progression of clinical documentation and care planning during a patient's acute length of stay. The process started when the on-coming nurse arrived at the beginning of a shift. The nurse would first print a one-page paper template to write down key information regarding the patient assignment. This paper form acted as a reminder for scheduled events (next tests, medications, procedures, and so forth). It was interesting to note that an automated report could be electronically generated that included much of the same information as the paper form. However, after numerous experiments with electronically generated forms, the nurses found that paper was still the most convenient, informative, and efficient method to remind them of upcoming events. It is important to remember that at one time, paper was even considered "new technology" and still has its benefits today.

The on-coming nurse would then enter Eclipsys Sunrise Clinical Manager™ on a computer located in the centralized nursing station and review each patient's Clinical Summary™.[8] The Clinical Summary tab represented a centralized location for key information, such as patient health issues, trended vital signs, discipline-specific progress notes, lab and test results, the KBC profile, the plan of care, and so forth. The nurse then transcribed information from the Clinical Summary tab to his or her assignment form in a standardized format. A key insight by the observers was that all the information in the Clinical Summary tab was complete, up-to-date, standardized, and located in one centralized location. This allowed the on-coming nurse to gather relevant data within a matter of minutes.

Once the on-coming nurse had completed the assignment form, he or she dialed into VoiceCare™, an automated system for recording PER, and listened to a brief report on each of the assigned patients from the off-going nurse.[11] It was noted that the automated report for each patient was conducted in a standardized sequence of steps and only described exceptions to the patient's critical pathway. Reporting exceptions only shortened the duration of phone reports significantly. Once the automated PER was completed, the on-coming nurse used the Vocera™ mobile communication device to contact the off-going nurse. The use of a mobile communication device alleviated the on-coming nurse from having to find the off-going nurse. The off-going nurse and on-coming nurse would meet briefly in the nursing station and collectively review the Clinical Summary tab and update the care plan at that time. The entire PER process for the out-going and on-coming nurses took an average of 45 minutes, assuming an average assignment of four to five patients.

The positive deviants were observed throughout the day to understand how they conducted their charting and care planning. At the conclusion of PER, the on-coming nurse would briefly meet (called "huddles") with his or her care partner, a nursing aide. Patients were assigned to care teams by geographic location to minimize travel time between rooms. The purpose of the huddle was to clarify the roles and responsibilities of each partner in the team for the upcoming shift. This allowed the nurse to distribute nursing interventions in a way that buffered periodic spikes in workload and allowed the nurse to chart in small batches throughout the shift. In addition, a relief nurse was available to the unit to assist with large increases in nursing workload, which would help maintain a consistent level of work among the nurses.

The positive deviants consistently charted in the electronic record for short periods of time every hour. Charting was also expedited because computers were located at the bedside and prompts from the KBC application pulled information regarding CPGs to the nurse, rather than the nurse having to be vigilant and search for the needed information. This allowed the continuous flow of information even in the face of unplanned events on the unit. By the end of the shift, the positive deviants were able to prepare for PER, provide an automated report, and briefly meet with the on-coming nurse in 16 minutes or less on average. The average combined total PER for both in-coming and out-going PD nurses was 45 minutes, with no overtime noted during the observations (see Table 10B-1).

Discussion

Results of the observations made on the medical/surgical unit suggest that the frequent occurrence of long PERs, coupled with end-of-shift overtime were indicative of CC. Effectiveness survey scores indicated that although nurses were not dissatisfied with PER, they were not necessarily satisfied. The results indicated that nurses were satisfied, which is defined as an outcome that is good enough but by no means the best. In recent decades, doubts have arisen regarding the view that in all rational decision making, individuals seek the best result. Often individuals do not or cannot search for the optimal solution.

In contrast, observations made on the PDs were characterized by the infrequent occurrence of long PERs and no end-of-shift overtime. The findings suggest that the PD's practice moderated the effects of CC. The average cycle time of PER was 62% shorter in duration, while the average PER effectiveness score was nearly 30% higher. How did the PDs achieve this order of magnitude change?

A principle of lean manufacturing used to improve process cycle time is balancing the workload.[12] This can be accomplished by leveling the inputs to a process. Inputs include the inter-arrival rates of admissions to the nursing unit, medication orders, and unexpected events such as emergencies. Strategies to control inputs include distributing the workload through bed management systems, standardizing medication administration times, and charting in small batches every hour. These strategies moderate the queuing effect of a discontinuous flow on hard constraints by decreasing the variation in inputs. The result is a leveling of workload and a more efficient process. By charting every hour, the PD nurses were actually following the lean principle of balancing the workload.

The act of charting every hour appears to be a simple concept in theory. However, to successfully implement such a program in practice requires the complex integration of technology, protocols, and consistent coaching of staff. This implementation was achieved through a culture of continuous experimentation over a five-year-period. As the CNO stated, "We kept asking the nurses what was working and what was not. If it didn't work, we studied it and then quickly revised it. The best word to describe this process is "messy." But that is how you implement change in complex systems; frequent experimentation with full engagement of the staff."

The implementation of continuous charting starts with building a pull system through the integration of KBC with IDA. To do so, the Clinical Practice Module Resource Center (CPMRC), Elsevier, and Eclipsys worked closely with the hospital to design a system that efficiently pulled relevant information to the Clinical Summary page in Eclipsys Sunrise Manager. This change provided one access point for all the information nurses needed to update charting and care planning. By utilizing various information buttons and mouse "hovering" applications, nurses could quickly find test results, care planning guidelines, and historic data. Prompts associated with the evidence-based CPGs relieved nurses from having to rely on vigilance to remember key data inputs. In this way, not only was hourly charting updated, care plans were reviewed and outcomes documented throughout the shift and not at the end of it.

To enable the nurse's ability to continuously chart, computers were placed in patient rooms, allowing nurses to input data as they completed interventions. Computers were also placed in the hallways and at the nursing station to further reduce nurses having to wait for use. In addition, Vocera mobile communication devices allowed nurses to communicate with their partners without having to physically look for them. Patient assignments were also localized to one area of the unit to decrease travel time. Finally, the use of huddles improved communication between partners and clarified responsibilities when unexpected events occurred. Collectively, the incorporation of these improvements to support continuous charting created a highly efficient and effective PER.

A key strategy in the success of PER was the unit's commitment to coaching nurses on best practices. Once a protocol was established, the nurse manager, charge nurses, and clinical specialists regularly analyzed staff nurses adherence to it. For example, a best practice was established for the sequence of steps used in VoiceCare. Today, charge nurses regularly listen to off-going nurse reports prior to the start of a shift to insure the protocol is being followed; if not, the nurse is coached on effective communication skills and use of the protocol. This strategy of coaching is used in all aspects of PER, including the use of KBC, IDA, and Vocera to enable continuous charting and reduce CC.

Of note is the importance of balancing the need for standardization of best practices with an understanding of human nature. We all process and respond to environmental stimuli in our own unique way. It is not unusual for nurses to resist the use of protocols because they may appear counterintuitive. Clearly, many different ways to design a process such as the PER exist. However, in the space of all alternatives, there are some that best meet the collective needs of the patient, nurses, and unit. The development of protocols should be an iterative process that hones down this enormous space of solutions through frequent experimentation and engagement of the staff. This is the creative period during which each individual staff member can defend the merits of his or her method. At some point, however, consensus on a best practice should occur, and a commitment by all staff to use it must be gained. Once staff agree on a best practice, coaching the sequence of steps, no matter how small, becomes extremely important.

The rationale for the use of positive deviants in this study is also worth discussing. In part, the objective of this study was to discover who within the IDS was consistently demonstrating best practices for PER. This is a departure from the usual controlled study in which significant differences in selected performance metrics are compared across all nursing units in the IDS. PD is a form of rapid prototyping in which "diamonds in the rough" are discovered and their practices studied. Managers and peers within the IDS typically know who these individuals are, and this expedites the search process. Rather than measuring the performance of the entire unit, which can be time-consuming and expensive, we compared a typical unit in the IDS with the PDs. A simulation model of both the typical medical/surgical and PD PER process was then built and compared. The simulation model allowed us to see the subtle differences between practices, understand the theory behind them, and quantify the order of magnitude change that could be realized if all the units utilized the PD's practice. This has significant implications for expediting performance improvement initiatives in health systems, given the focus on implementation cycle times and cost.

Summary

This case study discussed various methods to reduce CC through the use of pull systems enabled by KBC, IDA, VoiceCare, and coaching. Through the use of positive deviance methods, key nurses exhibiting the most effective, efficient, and least expensive PER were rapidly identified and then modeled using simulation software. The use of simulation software to show how pull systems can reduce CC is an essential tool in implementing performance improvement strategies that address patient safety, staff efficiency, and cost.

Acknowledgments

The authors would like to thank the following individuals for their assistance in writing this manuscript; Priyarajan Tokachichu, MD; Bonnie Wesorick, RN, MSN; Catherine Swartz, MS, RN; Becky Jo Lekander, PhD, RN; Mary J. Vickers, MS, RN; and Steven Shaha, PhD, and the staff at Fairview Southdale Hospital and the University of Minnesota Medical Center.

References

1. Skyttner L. *General Systems Theory: Ideas and Applications,* Singapore: World Scientific Press; 2001.

2. Institute of Medicine. *To Err is Human: Building a Safer Health System.* Washington, DC: The National Academies Press, 2000.

3. Institute of Medicine. *Crossing the Quality Chasm: A New Health System for the 21ˢᵗ Century.* Washington, DC: The National Academies Press, 2001.

4. Institute of Medicine. *Keeping Patients Safe: Transforming the Work Environment of Nurses.* Washington, DC: The National Academies Press, 2004.

5. Kritchbaum K. *Complexity Compression: The Tipping Point for Nurses in the Practice Environment.* The Minnesota Nurses Association. http://nursesrev.advocateoffice.com/index.asp?Type=B_BASIC&SEC=%7B624EE994-85CD-4854-87EB-7956EF397988%7D. Accessed April 27, 2009.

6. Ebright P. *Developing a Knowledge Base for RN Stacking: A Critical Patient Safety Strategy for Nursing Care Delivery.* National Patient Safety Foundation Grant. http://nursing.iupui.edu/research/documents/EbrightDevelopingNPSF.pdf. Accessed April 27, 2009.

7. *The Clinical Practice Model Resource Center,* Elsevier. http://www.cpmrc.com/. Accessed April 27, 2009.

8. The Eclipsys Corporation. http://www.eclipsys.com/. Accessed April 27, 2009.

9. Law AM, Kelton DW. *Simulation Modeling and Analysis.* 3rd ed. Boston: McGraw-Hill International Press, 2000.

10. Wikipedia. *Positive Deviance.* http://en.wikipedia.org/wiki/Positive_Deviance. Accessed April 27, 2009.

11. VoiceCare. http://www.voicecare.com/index.asp?mid=77. Accessed April 27, 2009.

12. El-Haik B, Al-Aomar R. *Simulation Based Lean Six Sigma and Design for Six Sigma.* Hoboken, NJ: John Wiley and Sons, Inc., 2006.

## CHAPTER 11

ICNP®: Nursing Terminology to Improve Healthcare Worldwide

By Amy Coenen, PhD, RN, FAAN; and Claudia Bartz, PhD, RN, FAAN

Introduction

As we come to the close of the first decade of the 21st century, the world continues to experience political, social, and economic challenges that influence healthcare delivery, from the most advanced system to the least resourced point of care. In many areas of the world, accurate data and information about nursing care practice and resources are not adequate to support decision making. Nurse leaders since Florence Nightingale have emphasized that a clear articulation of nursing practice is essential to support decision making for nursing.[1,2] The International Classification for Nursing Practice (ICNP®) is a terminology that can facilitate the description of the broad, diverse, and constantly changing domain of nursing practice.

With the release of ICNP Version 2 in June 2009, major advances were achieved in the areas of technical development, partnerships, and program support for future work. The purpose of this chapter is to describe ICNP in terms of the state of the science, international partnerships, and future directions. A brief description of Version 2 is followed by specific examples of partnerships that facilitate ICNP harmonization with other healthcare terminologies. The ICNP terminology life cycle, consisting of three phases: research and development, maintenance and operations, and dissemination and education is presented. Finally, program infrastructure to support the future of ICNP is discussed, taking into consideration ongoing advances in electronic health information systems and international health informatics standards development.

ICNP Version 2

The vision of ICNP is to become an integral part of the global information infrastructure, thereby informing healthcare practice and policy to improve patient care worldwide. Strategic goals to meet this mission include that ICNP and the ICNP Programme:

- Serve as a major force to articulate nursing's contribution to health and healthcare globally.
- Promote harmonization with other widely used classifications and the work of standardization groups in health and nursing.[3]

The release of ICNP Version 2 was a landmark event for the ICN and the ICNP Programme. The International Council of Nurses is a nonpartisan, nongovernmental federation of national nursing organizations that was organized in 1899. ICN began the work of developing a nursing terminology in 1989; five versions (alpha, beta 1, beta 2, Version 1.0, and Version 1.1) preceded the 2009 release of ICNP Version 2.

Over nearly 20 years of development and testing, ICNP has evolved to become a reference terminology for nursing. As a reference terminology, ICNP exploits advances in computer science, information science, artificial intelligence, and linguistics to represent and maintain the domain content for nursing. In addition, a reference terminology has greater synergy with the processes and products of other standards, such as HL7, for the enhancement of interoperability within the EHR.

More specifically, ICNP Version 2 is an ontology of nursing practice concepts. An ontology, in health informatics, is a hierarchical organization of concepts created for a specific purpose.[4] Version 2 added more than 400 new concepts to the terminology and expanded formal models through testing various approaches to representing nursing assessment, diagnosis, intervention, and outcome concepts. ICNP includes primitive concepts and precoordinated nursing diagnosis, outcome, and intervention concepts. The primitive concepts are organized using the ICNP 7-Axis Model.[5] Concepts are combined according to predetermined rules into nursing diagnosis, outcome, and intervention statements. The rules for the combinations are consistent with the logic and structure of the ICNP ontology.

As ICNP continues to increase in size and complexity, existing tools are extended and new tools are added to meet the requirements for development and management. Version 2 was developed using a representation language with formal modeling rules (Web Ontology Language or OWL) in Protégé software. With Version 2, all of the representations and delivery formats for ICNP are derived from the single formal OWL representation. The use of the formal modeling language allowed automated reasoning to be applied to the terminology to ensure consistency and accuracy of concepts. Development and maintenance are sustained in the Version 2 environment as well. Although a formal terminology is the foundation of Version 2, two representations, the 7-Axis Model and ICNP catalogues, were maintained for users. ICNP catalogues are discussed next.

ICN understands and supports the importance of current, international standards for terminology. ICNP Version 2 conforms to the International Organization for Standardization (ISO) Technical Specification 17117, which stipulates structural attributes for terminologies.[4,6] The structural attributes of ICNP include concept-orientation, non-redundancy, non-ambiguity, non-vagueness, and internal consistency. The terminology also has context-free and unique identifiers, concept descriptions, and established processes for version control.[7,8] In addition, ICNP Version 2 tested the ISO Standard 18104:2003 that defined reference terminology models for nursing diagnoses and nursing interventions.[9,10] As a reference terminology, ICNP Version 2 can work with and complement other nursing classifications. In the effort to support harmonization among nursing and other health terminologies, ICNP is often described as a unified nursing language system.[3,5]

ICNP Harmonization and Partnerships

ICN is uniquely positioned to be the international representative for nursing domain content in healthcare terminology. The ICN infrastructure of national nursing organizations across 132 countries provides a global network by which to convey information and collaborate with nurses in many communities internationally. ICN partners with a wide variety of organizations to continue advancement of ICNP, as well as other terminology-related standards and products. Because of the diversity of health specialties and providers across the world, it is important to assure partnerships in all phases of the ICNP life cycle. Active partnerships facilitate, encourage, and value the exchange of ideas and contributions from all participants.

ICNP partners include professional nursing organizations, specialty nursing organizations, health ministries and governments, academic institutions, terminology developers, standards development organizations, vendors, and United Nations organizations, such as the World Health Organization (WHO). Through these partnerships, ICN seeks to be informed and involved in the development, testing, implementation, and evaluation of standards and products related to terminology in healthcare. As multiple terminologies continue to be developed and implemented, it is imperative to examine the complementary characteristics and contributions of each in relation to others. In 1989, when ICN began to explore development of ICNP, a number of nursing and healthcare classifications were already in existence. Technology was advancing rapidly, and classifications and terminologies were developing as their usefulness began to be recognized. There will likely continue to be a need for multiple healthcare classifications and terminologies because of the diversity of users and nursing practice settings, as well as the need for accurate and accessible electronic health data and information. At the same time, as the tools and technologies for development, maintenance, and implementation of healthcare terminologies continue to increase in sophistication and capability, interoperability and harmonization among terminologies is not only increasingly feasible, but necessary.

Three examples of formal partnerships between ICN and international organizations are discussed next. The partnerships are with WHO, the International Health Terminology Standards Development Organisation (IHTSDO), and the International Organization for Standardization (ISO).

ICN and the World Health Organization's Family of International Classifications

The proposal to ICN in 1989 for development of the ICNP set out a number of specific criteria.[11] One criterion was that ICNP must be usable in a complementary or integrated way with the WHO Family of International Classifications (WHO-FIC), the core of which is the International Classification of Diseases (ICD). This criterion stimulated collaborative work toward the formation of a partnership with WHO-FIC. In 2008, ICNP was approved for inclusion in the WHO-FIC as a related classification.

The WHO-FIC is a suite of classification products that may be used in an integrated fashion to compare health information internationally, as well as nationally. The purpose of WHO-FIC is to assist the development of reliable health statistical systems at local, national, and international levels, with the aim of improving health status and healthcare.[12] As a related classification and member of the WHO-FIC, ICNP represents the domain of nursing practice, an essential and complementary part of professional health services, necessary for decision making and policy development aimed at improving health status and healthcare worldwide. ICNP will extend WHO-FIC to the nursing domain, with the opportunity to improve communication, data collection, and statistical reporting practices at WHO and ICN.

In 2008, we started the work to harmonize ICNP with other family members of WHO-FIC. As part of ICN's participation in WHO-FIC, a project is underway to map ICNP and the International Classification of Functioning, Disability and Health (ICF). This project will describe shared and unique concepts across ICNP and ICF. In addition, the ability to model health status and nursing diagnosis concepts using shared or similar models will be explored during the project.

ICN and IHTSDO

IHTSDO is a not-for-profit association that develops and supports the use of Systematized Nomenclature of Medicine Clinical Terms (SNOMED CT®).[13] In 2009, ICN and IHTSDO entered into a mutual Agreement on Harmonization Principles. With this agreement, each organization seeks to work together to ensure that the organizations' roles with respect to terminologies shall be complementary, not duplicative and will emphasize interdisciplinary collaboration. The 2009 agreement sets the stage for the harmonization of ICNP and SNOMED CT.

Preliminary work on mapping ICNP Version 1 and SNOMED CT (2007 July Release) was reported by Park et al.[14] This study found that SNOMED CT could potentially represent most (92.5%) of the ICNP nursing diagnosis and intervention catalogue concepts that constituted the study data set. In a study that modeled collaborative effort toward development of tools necessary for interoperability, Hardiker and colleagues[15] mapped the North American Nursing Diagnosis Association – International (NANDA-I) nursing diagnoses to ICNP Version 1 and then compared the resulting representations and relationships with those in SNOMED CT. Results identified differences in how SNOMED CT and ICNP classified the NANDA-I diagnostic tables. The findings of this study described potential benefits for NANDA-I, SNOMED CT, and ICNP.

With the new ICN-IHTSDO harmonization agreement, it is anticipated that work proposals will be designed to develop maps for ICNP and SNOMED CT that will be useful for researchers, vendors, and nurses in multiple care settings. Early projects may include the mapping of ICNP catalogues with representations of precoordinated nursing diagnoses, outcomes, and interventions statements. The IHTSDO Nursing Special Interest Group has recommended a project to map the ICNP catalogue for Canadian Health Outcomes for Better Information and Care (C-HOBIC) to SNOMED CT and to evaluate shared and unique content coverage.

ICN and ISO

In 2008, ISO granted Liaison A status to ICN. With this status, ICN can participate at the ISO Technical Committee level in addition to the Working Group level and can propose that existing standards be considered through the ISO "fast track" procedure. ICN participates regularly with ISO Technical Committee 215: Health Informatics. ICNP Program staff periodically report to IMIA-NI on TC 215 issues of relevance to nursing.

Through formal, productive partnerships with international organizations, ICNP can be integrated with healthcare standards and terminologies worldwide. As a reference terminology compliant with international standards, ICNP can contribute to improvements in quality and continuity of healthcare through sharing of information that can be used to enhance communication and decision making across and among healthcare providers and settings.

ICNP Terminology Life Cycle

ICNP development is an ongoing process, always targeted at improving the terminology for worldwide use. Concepts used to describe nursing in practice environments are constantly tested as ICNP concept modelers aim to represent the domain of nursing through the terminology. Concepts describing nursing in all practice environments are examined for consistency, accuracy, and fitness for use. Along with terminology principles and standards guiding development, the life cycle model was developed to direct the program and support the identification of quality improvement benchmarks to assure continuous attention to all aspects of the program (see Figure 11-1). The life cycle approach helps to identify the wide array of simultaneous activities necessary for a successful terminology. It further organizes multifaceted review and analysis of the terminology's processes and products for their contribution to the program vision and for continuous quality improvement in all phases of the life cycle.

To ensure that ICNP reflects the dynamic state of the science of terminology development and nursing, three major phases of the life cycle were identified: (a) research and development, (b) maintenance and operations, and (c) dissemination and education. These components are not mutually exclusive but serve to inform and support each other. Work is continuous and simultaneous in all three phases of the life cycle. Intentional and constant integration of processes and products serve to strengthen and expand the terminology. To assist the reader in understanding how the life cycle model is applied to ICNP, examples of processes and outcomes for each phase of the cycle are provided next.

Research and Development

Research and development projects are initiated by ICN and independently, by nurses and other experts worldwide. An example of a research and development effort coordinated by ICN is the establishment of ICN-Accredited ICNP Research and Development Centres. An ICNP Centre is an institution, faculty, department, national association, or other group that meets ICN criteria and has been designated by ICN as a Centre.[3] Nurses around the world are actively scrutinizing ICNP with the objective of making it dynamic and relevant, today and in the future. The aim of ICNP Centres is to acknowledge and work with groups of nurses and other experts to both concentrate and disseminate new thinking and to promote new discussion to advance ICNP.[3] Each Centre identifies specific aspects of their work (e.g., translation, concept validation, or ICNP applications in the practice setting) in a work plan of goals and

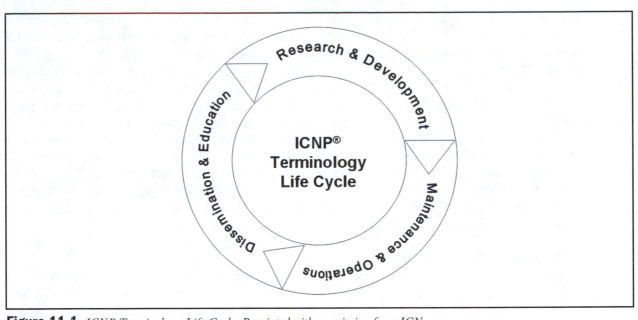

Figure 11-1. *ICNP Terminology Life Cycle. Reprinted with permission from ICN.*

objectives that is reviewed by the centre and ICN on a three-year schedule. Currently, there are five ICNP Research and Development Centres.

The first accredited centre, the ICNP German-speaking User Group, includes participants from national nurses associations, universities, and healthcare industries in Germany, Austria, and Switzerland. The centre members translated early versions of ICNP from English to German. A team lead by Schrader developed the ICNP Browser and Translation (BaT) tool.[16] The BaT software tool supports Web-based distributive work by translation teams and has been used by nurses in China, Poland, and Norway to translate ICNP for their respective languages.

Terminology Maintenance and Operations

Terminology maintenance and operations are, for the most part, processes internal to the ICNP Programme. Continuous maintenance and regular distribution of ICNP are essential to ensure that the terminology represents the nursing domain reliably, accurately, and in a timely manner. Terminology development is a dynamic process, always requiring attention to best practices for content analysis and process improvement. Maintenance policies, quality improvement methods, and conformance with related international standards are necessary to support successful terminology implementation worldwide.[3]

With the release of ICNP Version 2, maintenance and distribution policies and procedures were updated and codified. This important step ensures that the terminology has predictability and longevity, independent of the makeup of the development team. ICNP maintenance and development procedures are used to guide version management of the terminology. Two important principles influence both the way that changes are made in the terminology and the pace and extent of change from version to version.[8] The first principle is that the meaning of an ICNP entity should never change; that is, there should be concept permanence to ensure the integrity of data over time. Second, ICNP should change incrementally, that is, with so-called graceful evolution to limit the impact of updates on users.

Consistent with these maintenance principles, a concept and its unique identifier are inactivated whenever there is any change in the meaning of a concept. A release cycle of every two years was established for new versions to assist users to plan their own updates of the terminology. With a predictable release schedule, ICNP users can build version management into their own work programs. Maintenance also includes updating mappings and translations. Version 1 was the first ICNP version to be mapped with the U.S. National Library of Medicine Unified

Medical Language System (UMLS) Metathesaurus. ICNP, followed by Version 1.1, Version 2, and future versions will also be mapped with UMLS as they are released. The UMLS Metathesaurus is a data set of many vocabularies in the biomedical and health sciences.[17] The ICNP-UMLS mapping process provides another resource for examining ICNP in relation to other terminologies. It also contributes to the constant quality improvement aim held by ICN. Scrutiny of ICNP in the context of the UMLS serves to clarify concepts and relationships in the terminology and to identify any redundancy and ambiguity among the concepts.

An ICN study (Tae Youn Kim, personal communication, June 22, 2009) is underway to examine the mappings between SNOMED-CT and a subset of ICNP nursing diagnosis and intervention concepts in the UMLS Metathesaurus. The discovery of gaps and difficult or problem mappings could be important in mutual development and improvement of ICNP and other terminologies. ICN plans to continue to work with UMLS to explore future opportunities with use of the Metathesaurus.

Dissemination and Education

Dissemination of ICNP-related material online and in print, as well as education about ICNP in a variety of settings, makes up an essential component of the ICNP life cycle. ICN is committed to facilitating the use of ICNP across all healthcare settings and specialties in which nurses practice. Because ICN is a federation of national nurses associations, the ICNP Programme emphatically pursues opportunities to facilitate nurses' worldwide understanding, participation, and implementation of ICNP. Dissemination and education strategies and processes have accelerated with each version update as ICNP continues to gain recognition as a terminology suitable for worldwide application.

Integrating Research, Maintenance, and Dissemination with ICNP Catalogues

One criterion identified by the original ICNP Development Team was that the terminology be "simple enough to be seen by the ordinary practitioner of nursing as a meaningful description of practice and a useful means of structuring practice."[11] ICNP developers recognized that nurses using the terminology at the point of care needed more user-friendly resources. Catalogues, one representation of ICNP, were developed to meet this need (see Figure 11-2). ICNP catalogues are subsets of clinically relevant precoordinated nursing diagnoses, interventions, and client outcomes for a select health priority.[18] Catalogues are organized by specialty, setting, client health condition (e.g., diabetes), or client care phenomena sensitive to nursing interventions.

ICNP catalogues are designed to fill a practical need in building nursing content to support clinical documentation in electronic health record systems. The catalogues are organized so as to describe the nursing diagnoses, outcomes, and interventions appropriate particularly for a specific health priority or area of care.[18] The development of ICNP catalogues was further explored and initiated during development of Version 2. There was a considerable expansion of ICNP concepts in the new version, as concepts were added from new catalogues. The first two catalogues published by ICN were "Partnering with Individuals and Families to Promote Adherence to Treatment" and "Palliative Care for Dignified Dying."[19,20] To complete the two catalogues, 230 concepts were added to ICNP Version 2. Of the 230, 50 were primitive or elemental concepts and 170 were precoordinated nursing diagnoses, outcomes, and interventions.[21]

A number of exciting projects in ICNP catalogue development are currently underway. One project is a collaboration between ICN and the Scotland National Health Service to develop a Community Nursing Catalogue comprising a subset of community nursing diagnoses and interventions. In another project, ICN is collaborating with the Canadian Nurses Association in the C-HOBIC project, to apply standard terminology concepts to assessment measures and health outcomes using ICNP.

With clinically relevant content developed by nurse experts, catalogues are key instruments in the development and expansion of ICNP structure and content. Consistent with the

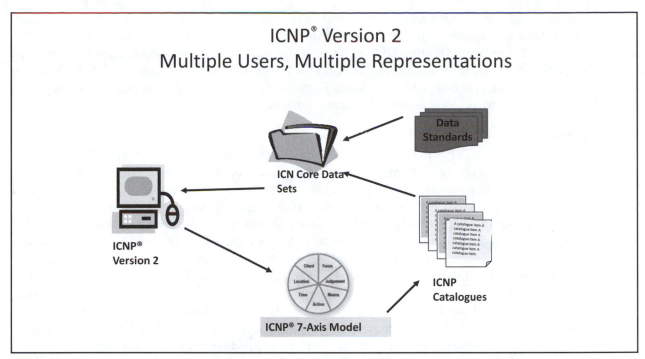

Figure 11-2. *ICNP Representations. Reprinted with permission from ICN.*

life cycle model, further development and testing of catalogues in health information system applications will generate more content by which the nursing domain can be represented in ICNP. New diagnoses, outcomes, and interventions for selected health priorities will be generated from practice and included in future versions of ICNP.

Future Directions For ICNP

The future of ICNP is guided and challenged by the vision and strategic goals as set forth by ICN. The ICNP Strategic Advisory Group provides leadership and recommendations to ICN for the advancement of ICNP. Three major initiatives that will move ICNP forward in the next years include translation support, the ICNP C-Space, and ICN Core Data Sets.

Translation Support

C-Space will be enhanced to provide access to the current English version of ICNP and additional language translations. Work is in progress to integrate the ICNP BaT tool with the ICNP C-Space. BaT is a software tool that assists distributive work by translation teams using Web-based processes. A hierarchy of users can be established for the work of translation, allowing and encouraging wide participation and support, while also ensuring a clear mechanism for decision making.[16]

ICNP is developed in English. Current translations of the English version of ICNP are needed to support best use of the terminology in practice worldwide. ICN has published translation guidelines that addressed translation methods, cross-cultural equivalence, and general procedures for translations.[22] To assure version control, anyone considering translation is asked to sign an agreement with ICN and also to inform the ICN National Member Association(s) about his or her intent.

As of March 2009, current translations of ICNP were completed in Arabic, German, Japanese, Korean, Mandarin, Norwegian, Polish, Portuguese, Spanish, and Taiwanese. Updated or initial translations in Farsi (Persian), French, Greek, Indonesian, Italian, Swedish, and Thai are in-process.[3] Translation of ICNP is a considerable undertaking. The BaT tool has proven effective when translations involve nurses and other experts from multiple countries or across a country. The BaT tool facilitates the reuse of translations when updating becomes necessary as new ICNP versions are released on the two-year schedule. In addition to facilitating implementation of ICNP in more countries worldwide, the work of translation stimulates ICNP concept validation. For example, a recent French translation project that involved French-speaking countries and regions provided considerable insight and feedback regarding ICNP concepts, especially gerunds. Some English words, such as *alleviating* and *relieving*, need further review to assure standard use across languages

ICNP C-Space

Upon the release of ICNP Version 2, ICN launched a Web-based workspace called the *ICNP C-Space* (http://icnp.clinicaltemplates.org/). C-Space was developed to encourage and allow nurse experts and other experts to participate and collaborate in the continuous development and improvement of ICNP. As noted earlier, ICNP development and concomitant improvement uses the life cycle model to encompass research and development, maintenance and operations, and dissemination and education. The workspace is envisioned to support the processes of the life cycle model. C-Space represents ICN's continuing commitment to use state of the science technology and to involve as many experts as possible in the ICNP Programme to support development, rigorous testing, and systematic evaluation of ICNP. For example, the workspace will use interactive strategies to facilitate participation of nurses in ICNP Catalogue development. C-Space will eventually be expanded to support the ICNP review process, allowing easy submission of new concepts and expert review of existing concepts.

ICNP C-Space provides a tool set for ICNP development and dissemination. Initially, C-Space will be used for ICNP catalogue and mapping projects. Project leaders will be able to form teams, control access levels to their work, specify the rules for their projects, and support free flow of information among the team. A pilot test of C-Space use for catalogue development is underway in a partnership between ICN and the Scotland National Health Service, using the 2008 Scottish Community Nursing Census (www.isdscotland.org/isd/5373.html) as the source data set. This project supports and encourages the participation of domain experts in community health nursing to validate ICNP representations of the concepts they use to represent and describe their domain.

Ongoing development of the ICNP C-Space will mean that more tools will be added to support continued development of the ICNP terminology. C-Space will be expanded for worldwide expert review of concept addition, modification, or inactivation recommendations, as well as for recommendations for improvement of concept descriptions. As C-Space gains users, cross-cultural validation studies of ICNP concepts or subsets of the terminology found in catalogues can be pursued. These studies have the potential to foster and advance collaboration with other nursing terminologies and classifications and to facilitate harmonization at the international level.

ICN Core Data Sets

ICN has, for several years, considered various use cases for core data sets that would advance its vision and mission and integrate the standardized nursing data documentation capability inherent in ICNP. This work included consideration of the iNMDS as well, which has data points for care environment, nursing resources, ICNP data, and care intensity.[23,24] The release of ICNP Version 2 and the simultaneous launch of the ICNP C-Space gave new impetus to the question of what core data sets could accomplish for ICN. Version 2 includes hundreds of pre-coordinated, coded statements for nursing diagnoses, interventions, and client outcomes. C-Space is a Web-based platform that can support ICNP as a nurses' initiative with worldwide involvement. The data elements in ICNP and other data sets could be used with the new platform to support ICN core data sets. These purpose-focused data sets would be the instruments with which data would be collected from and about nurses and nursing worldwide in a nimble and timely way. The goal of this process would be to generate meaningful and useful knowledge for nursing.

The label, core data set, is used in a variety of ways in the healthcare literature.[25,26,27,28] Much like the label "fruit market" or "coffee shop" can mean anything the purveyors want it to mean, core data sets can be any arrangement of data points that accomplish the desired aims. Ahmadian et al,[28] for example, have developed a national core dataset for preoperative assessment. ICN core data sets, then, are sets of data points joined to answer specific questions using targeted, focused data collection methods with nearly simultaneous aggregation, analysis, and display. ICN core data sets can be formulated and critiqued collaboratively using the C-Space. They might also be developed internally by ICN. Most important is that the core data sets be useful to ICN projects, programmes, and membership worldwide. ICN member National Nurses Associations and interdisciplinary partners are seen as prime users of core data set-generated knowledge.

The H1N1 flu pandemic with its substantial impact on nursing provides a number of use cases for ICN core data sets. Questions could address self-care management, social support, adherence, family care providers, infection control, or screening of close contacts. On the topic of self-care management, questions generating useful information for nurses might address nursing diagnoses (e.g., patients' level of knowledge), interventions (e.g., education strategies), patient outcomes related to interventions, or lessons learned in dealing with patients with flu. Surveys would be designed to be user-friendly and brief. With data about successful or unsuccessful outcomes related to interventions, nurses can be informed about their own interventions, revising and changing them on the basis of input from nurses in other parts of the world.

ICN core data sets provide a new way to use ICNP, other minimum data sets, and additional data points that will help to answer questions and address issues for nursing. The use of the C-Space platform for the implementation of core data sets will generate information that is more timely, accessible, and relevant for nurses worldwide.

Summary

In this chapter, the authors presented a brief description of the ICNP followed by discussion of international partnerships, the terminology life cycle model, and new directions for the terminology. The necessity for nursing and interdisciplinary collaboration, and for healthcare terminology harmonization, is a basic theme throughout the chapter.

As healthcare technology continues to advance in capability and application, the nursing domain must be consistently and accurately represented in information systems and resulting data sets. Nursing terminologies must therefore conform to the state of the science for continued development that reflects nursing globally. Since its inception in 1989, ICNP has advanced to become a complex ontology maintained with state-of-the-science tools and processes. As terminologies are always dynamic, a need exists to continue to press for developmental opportunities and to respond positively to the possibilities and challenges engendered by new knowledge and technology. A major catalyst for advancing terminology is through partnerships with other standards development organizations. Involving both informatics and clinical experts in all phases of the ICNP life cycle can help cultivate growth and breakthrough toward new discovery. Finally, it is through using the ICNP in applications that we will learn more about what is needed for the future. ICN is committed to advancing nursing and health worldwide. ICNP, as an ICN Programme, aims to contribute to the mission of ICN as an international standard for nursing terminology.

References

1. Clark J, Lang N. Nursing's next advance: An international classification for nursing practice. *Int Nurs Rev.* 1992;39(4):109-112.
2. Nightingale F. *Notes on Nursing: What It is and What It Is Not.* London: Harrison, 59, Pall Mall. (Reprinted in Commemorative Edition, 1992, Philadelphia, PA: J.B. Lippincott Company; 1859.
3. International Council of Nurses. *ICNP® Version 2.* Geneva Switzerland: International Council of Nurses; 2009.
4. International Organization for Standardization. *Health Informatics – Controlled Health Terminology – Structure and High-level Indicators* (ISO/TS 17117). Geneva Switzerland: International Organization for Standardization; 2002.
5. International Council of Nurses. *International Classification for Nursing Practice Version 1.0.* Geneva Switzerland: International Council of Nurses; 2005.
6. Hardiker NR, Coenen A. Standards to support the ongoing development and maintenance of nursing terminologies. In Oud N, Sheerin F, Ehnfors M, Sermeus W, eds. *ACENDIO 2007 6th European Conference of Acendio.* Amsterdam: Oud Consultancy. 2007;39-43.
7. Chute CG, Cohn SP, Campbell JR. A framework for comprehensive health terminology systems in the United States. *JAMIA.* 1998;5(6):503-510.
8. Cimino JJ. Desiderata for controlled medical vocabularies in the twenty-first century. *Methods Inf Med.* 1998;37:135-139.
9. International Organization for Standardization. *Health Informatics – Integration of a Reference Terminology Model for Nursing* (ISO 18104:2003). Geneva Switzerland: International Organization for Standardization; 2003.
10. Hardiker NR, Coenen A. Interpretation of an international terminology standard in the development of a logic-based compositional terminology. *Int J Med Inform.* 76S, 2007;S274-S280.
11. International Council of Nurses. *The International Classification for Nursing Practice A Unifying Framework The Alpha Version.* Geneva Switzerland: International Council of Nurses; 1996.
12. World Health Organization. (2009). http://www.who.int/classifications/en/. Accessed June 2, 2009.
13. International Health Terminology Standards Development Organisation. (2009) http://www.ihtsdo.org/. Accessed June 2, 2009.
14. Park H, Lundberg C, Coenen A. Making connections: SNOMED-CT and ICNP. Unpublished presentation, Summer Institute in Nursing Informatics, Baltimore, MD; 2008.
15. Hardiker N, Casey A, Coenen A, Konicek D. Mutual Enhancement of Diverse Terminologies. In D Bates, JH Holmes, G Kuperman G, eds. *Biomedical and Health Informatics: From Foundations to Applications to Policy.* Proceedings of American Medical Informatics Association (AMIA) Symposium 2006. (pp. 319-323). Washington, DC; 2006.
16. Schrader U, Tackenberg P, Widmer R, Portenier L, König P. The ICNP-BaT – A multilingual Web-based tool to support the collaborative translation of the ICNP®. In K Kuhn et al. eds. *MEDINFO 2007.* IOS Press, 2007;751-754.
17. Unified Medical Language System. www.nlm.nih.gov/pubs/factsheets/unlsmeta.html. Accessed June 2, 2009.
18. International Council of Nurses. *Guidelines for ICNP® Catalogue Development.* Geneva Switzerland: International Council of Nurses; 2008.
19. International Council of Nurses. *Partnering with Patients and Families to Promote Adherence to Treatment.* Geneva Switzerland: International Council of Nurses; 2008.
20. International Council of Nurses. *ICNP® Catalogue: Palliative Care for Dignified Dying.* Geneva Switzerland: International Council of Nurses; 2009.
21. Coenen A, Kim T. (In Review) Development of terminology subsets using ICNP. *Int J Med Inform.*
22. International Council of Nurses. *Guidelines for ICNP® Translation.* Geneva Switzerland: International Council of Nurses; 2008.
23. Goossen WTF, Delaney CW, Coenen A, et al. The International Nursing Minimum Data Set (i-NMDS). In: Weaver CA, Delaney CW, Weber P, Carr RL, eds., *Nursing and Informatics for the 21st Century,* Chicago: HIMSS, 2006;305-320.
24. MacNeela P, Scott PA, Treacy MP, Hyde A. Nursing minimum data sets: A conceptual analysis and review. *Nursing Inq.* 2006;13(1):44-51.
25. Bull R. (2009) *NDTMS Data Set F Guidance for Adult Alcohol Treatment Providers Version 6.0.0.* National Treatment Agency for Substance Misuse, National Health Service. http://www.nta.nhs.uk/areas/ndtms/core_data_set_page.aspx. Accessed April 22, 2009.
26. *Core Data Sets – Natural Disaster Hotspots – A Global Risk Analysis.* (2005) Center for Hazards & Risk Research at Columbia University. http://www.1deo.columbia.edu/chrr/research/hotspots/coredata.html. Accessed April 22, 2009.
27. Shaw V. Health information system reform in South Africa: Developing an essential data set. *Bull World Health Organ.* 2005;83(8):632-636.
28. Ahmadian L, Cornet R, Kalkman C, de Keizer NF. Development of a national core dataset for preoperative assessment. *Methods Inf Med.* 2009;2:155-161.

Case Study 11A

A Process for Standardizing Documentation Contents for Electronic Documentation Systems

By Hyeoneui Kim, PhD, MPH, BSN, RN; Patricia C. Dykes, DNSc, MA, RN;
and Roberto A. Rocha, PhD, MD

Introduction

In most of the teaching hospitals affiliated with Partners HealthCare System (PHS), inpatient bedside care documentation relies on locally developed, paper-based documentation systems. To mitigate many problems of paper-based documentation systems in supporting data interoperability, consistency, and completeness of documentation,[1-3] PHS is working toward implementing an enterprisewide electronic inpatient documentation system. We are currently in the early stage of this initiative, and our initial efforts focus on the two pillar hospitals of the PHS, the Brigham and Women's Hospital (BWH) and Massachusetts General Hospital (MGH).

The importance of the "whats" and "hows" of the bedside documentation templates cannot be overstated. If documentation templates are not properly prepared, redundant documentation may result and, therefore, reusing and sharing data may be a challenge. Many commercial computerized documentation products come with predesigned documentation templates. However, we have several concerns that adopting a complete package of vendor-proposed solutions might lead to: (1) unnecessary alterations in the nursing workflows already established in each hospital of PHS, and (2) the vendor lock-in situation that will adversely affect the flexibility of changing the product when inevitable needs arise. Therefore, PHS decided to take on the responsibility of developing the templates to be used in the new computerized documentation system. This effort will not only ensure a smoother transition to the new system but will also provide full flexibility in modifying the documentation system in the future, when necessary.

This case study describes the process of preparing standardized templates for the computerized documentation system in PHS. The process consists of three major steps. As the first step, we conducted a baseline content analysis of the existing paper documentation forms. The purposes of this analysis were to better understand the barriers to an effective and complete documentation process using a computerized system, and to identify existing documentation templates that could potentially be reused in the computerized documentation system. As the second step, we modeled draft sets of standardized documentation templates by combining content from the existing paper forms in use by the two hospitals and by adding content identified from external reference standards. Finally, subject matter experts from each hospital were invited to review and validate by consensus the draft sets as the acceptable standardized documentation templates to be adopted by both hospitals. The methods and procedures we adopted in each step are further detailed in the following sections.

Content Analysis

Collecting Existing Documentation Paper Forms

We have collected various paper forms used by nurses for bedside care documentation at the two hospitals. Examples of these forms include: assessment and intervention flowsheets, admission assessment templates, transfer reports, clinical event records, daily treatment sheets, procedure checklists, and special intervention records. We manually transcribed the data items (i.e., labels of the entry fields) contained in the paper forms into a Microsoft Access database built to support this analysis. The response format of a documentation item was captured using the categories of "free text," "pick-list," and "Boolean." When a data item was associated with a pick-list, we transcribed the pick-list values into the database as well.

Analyzing Documentation Templates

Assigning "Normalized" Expressions. We observed that many data items sharing the same meaning were expressed using different terms. Therefore, an informatics-trained nurse assigned a "normalized" expression to each item to identify redundant items. The normalized expressions were created to capture the intended meaning at a fine-grained level and in a nominal form. For example, three normalized expressions, "presence of dietary restriction;" "presence of dietary requirements;" and "presence of dietary learning need," were created from the original data item: "Do you have any dietary restriction, requirements, learning needs?" We did not conduct terminology mapping at this stage because many data items were referencing two or more discrete concepts and would have required complicated concept decomposition.

Validating the Normalized Expressions and Assigning Metadata. Four nurses reviewed and validated the normalized expressions. After collaboratively reviewing 100 sets of normalized expressions and their original terms(s), the reviewers divided the remaining sets and performed independent review. Normalized expressions considered inadequate by any of the reviewers were flagged and later reviewed collaboratively by all four reviewers, who then provided more appropriate expressions by reaching consensus. There were a number of items whose intended meaning was not easily identifiable, thus neither a normalized expression nor metadata could be assigned. Most of those items were presented in locally developed "short-hand" expressions. For example, a locally developed abbreviation "BG" was later clarified as "bedside glucose" and the item expressed without clear indication of "what aspect is to be documented about the given item such as "(cardiac) alarm history" was later clarified as "whether the (cardiac) alarm history was reviewed or not." Such challenging cases were flagged separately and later reviewed by the site review teams that consisted of three or four practicing nurses for each hospital.

The reviewers also assigned additional metadata to the normalized expressions. The assigned metadata included three descriptor categories. The first category was the "Clinical Care Classifications" (CCC) care component category. The CCC is a standardized nursing terminology designed to encode the discrete elements of nursing practice. Its 21 care components cover four nursing care patterns, such as health behavioral, functional, physiological, and psychological, along with guides for encoding nursing diagnoses, interventions, and evaluation data with the CCC.[1] The second descriptor category is a flag indicating if the item was from a standardized assessment scale, such as the Morse fall scale. In the third descriptor category, the nursing action type is documented (e.g., assessment, diagnosis, and intervention).

The screenshot of the content review user interface is presented in Figure 11A-1. In the upper portion of the screen (marked A), "NDI id" (normalized data item id) and "Normalized Data Item Name" are prepopulated. The reviewers determined whether the normalized data item name was correctly assigned to the original data items displayed in the lower portion of the screen (marked B). The reviewers checked the "Accept" check box when the normalized name was accurately assigned. Otherwise, the reviewers left the "Accept" box empty and explained in the "Reviewer's Comments" check box why the normalized name was not acceptable.

The reviewers also assigned the additional meta-data using this screen. The care component categories are provided in the list box at the right portion of the screen. When the reviewers wanted to see the source forms to complete the review, they checked the "form" check box at the bottom of the screen. These items were collected separately and reviewed later with the source forms. For the items that were difficult to identify the intended meaning, the "tricky?" check box at the bottom of the screen was checked. These tricky items were collected separately and forwarded to the site review teams.

Findings from Analyzing the Collected Documentation Templates Redundancy in the Documentation Templates

A total of 4,043 documentation items were collected from the 92 forms. The number of items was reduced to 2,587 after redundant items were identified and excluded. Table 11A-1 shows detailed frequency distributions of the documentation items collected from the two hospitals. In this analysis, data items expressed with different levels of abstractions (e.g., allergy type vs. medication allergy, food allergy, and latex allergy) or with different concept granularity are treated as distinct items (e.g., pain severity, pain scale vs. pain severity measured with numeric scale). More accurately defined relationships among these items will be established when we conduct standardized terminology mapping. We anticipate that this process will identify more redundant documentation data items.

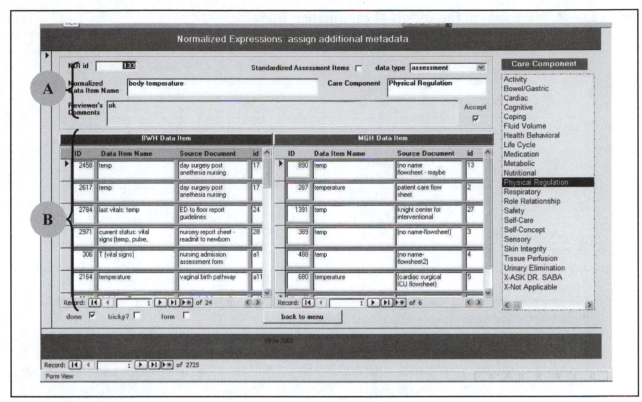

Figure 11A-1. *Content Review Screen*

Table 11A-1. Documentation Data Items Counts

Number of Data Items Collected	BWH	MGH	ALL
Raw count	1,909	2,134	--
Normalized (unique) count	1,458	1,558	2,587
Percent duplicates	31%*	37%*	17%**

** duplicates within the site across various forms; ** duplicates between the sites across various forms*

Source: Nursing Content Manager V0.42

Frequent Use of Free-text Format. The most common mode of data entry was free-text at 59%. Approximately 30% of the documentation items required Boolean responses and the remaining 11% were documented using predefined pick-lists. Consistent and unambiguous capture of clinical data for subsequent computerized processing (e.g., quality reporting, decision support) makes the transformation of relevant free-text data items into coded value sets (i.e., pick-lists) a high-priority task in designing the new documentation system.

Majority of the Documentation Templates are "Assessment" Data. We produced the distributions of various metadata assigned to the normalized items to understand the nature of the information that nurses document in the paper forms. The frequency distributions of the four information types are presented in Table 11A-2. We found that nursing documentation in both hospitals focused mostly on capturing assessment data. Paucity of diagnosis items was expected, as they are usually documented as free-text; thus, entry field labels of the forms are unlikely to reflect specific diagnosis concepts. However, we found the low fraction of interven-

Table 11A-2. Frequency of the Different Information Types

Information Type	BWH	MGH	Overlaps	Row Total
Assessment	704 (48.29%)	928 (59.56%)	247 (57.58%)	1,385 (53.54%)
Diagnosis	8 (0.55%)	11 (0.71%)	6 (1.40%)	13 (0.50%)
Intervention	246 (16.87%)	340 (21.82%)	70 (16.32%)	516 (19.95%)
Other	500 (34.29%)	279 (17.91%)	106 (24.71%)	673 (26.01%)
Column Total	1,458	1,558	429	2,587

Source: Nursing Content Manager V0.42

tion items potentially problematic. To accurately define and evaluate "nursing sensitive" outcomes, adequate documentation of nursing interventions is required.[2-3]

Approximately one-fourth of the items did not fit into any care process categories and were thus grouped as "other." Many of these items were directly related to patient care. A few examples of such items are "arranging diagnostic tests," "handling patient belongings," and "obtaining contact information from the long-term care facility," among others. However, the "other" items also included a few nonclinical ("housekeeping") data, such as patient belongings.

Comprehensive Domain Coverage, Focused on Physiologic Assessment

The distribution of the care component categories is presented in Table 11A-3, in which the five largest categories are shaded. Although the coverage is somewhat unbalanced, the distribution of the care component categories shows that the current documentation covers complete aspects of nursing care. However, current documentation seems less focused on psychological aspects of nursing care. This indicates that the psychological documentation items need to be enhanced in the computerized documentation system. The "health behavioral" category is broadly defined as nursing activities related to maintaining and regaining the health status of the patient.[1] Therefore, various content items could be related to it, from care coordination to patient education.

Content Modeling

Structuring a Data Item into Template Components

The prototype documentation template design team was formed with one physician informatician, four nurse informaticians, and one application analyst. The content design team generated a draft model of documentation templates by nursing domains based on the analysis previously described. By combining the paper forms from the two hospitals, the team compiled a comprehensive set of existing documentation templates. The compiled templates were modeled as three major components: "data elements," "coded value sets," and "concepts."

The "data element" component represents each discrete piece of information that is documented. The content team specified various properties of the "data element" such as response format, alternative designations, value domain, and presentation (display formatting) constraints. When the data element is documented using a pick-list, the allowed values of the pick-list are specified as a "coded value set" component. A designation to the entire "coded value set" was specified in the value domain. The third component, "concept," was identified in the terminology mapping step, which is described in the following section.

Table 11A-3. Distributions of the Care Component Category

CCC Care Component Categories	Assessment	Diagnosis	Intervention	Other	Row Total & Percent	
Activity	151	3	10	10	174	6.73%
Bowel/Gastric	57	0	13	5	75	2.90%
Cardiac	81	0	26	29	136	5.26%
Cognitive	74	0	5	3	82	3.17%
Coping	11	0	0	1	12	0.46%
Fluid Volume	97	0	25	32	154	5.95%
Health Behavioral	105	3	55	312	474	18.32%
Life Cycle	11	0	0	0	11	0.43%
Medication	60	1	133	18	212	8.19%
Metabolic	24	2	7	8	41	1.58%
Nutritional	37	0	7	10	54	2.09%
Physical Regulation	166	3	40	121	330	12.76%
Respiratory	117	0	88	30	235	9.09%
Role Relationship	41	0	0	15	56	2.16%
Safety	57	0	40	29	126	4.87%
Self-Care	30	0	1	3	34	1.31%
Self-Concept	5	1	1	1	8	0.31%
Sensory	52	0	4	5	61	2.36%
Skin Integrity	115	0	34	9	158	6.11%
Tissue Perfusion	33	0	8	4	45	1.74%
Urinary Elimination	57	0	16	6	79	3.05%
Not Applicable	4	0	3	23	30	1.16%
column total &	1,385	13	516	673	2,587	
percent	53.54%	0.50%	19.95%	26.01%		

Source: Nursing Content Manager V0.42
© Copyright 2009 Par

Referencing the External Concept Sources

Standardized Terminology Mapping. The data elements and the coded values were then mapped to selected standard (reference) terminology systems such as the "Logical Observation Identifiers, Names, and Codes" (LOINC), the "Systematic Nomenclature of Medicine, Clinical Terms" (SNOMED-CT), and the "International Classification of Nursing Practice" (ICNP).

Through terminology mapping, the "concept" component, i.e., the unique concepts that formed the data elements and/or the values within a value set, were identified. In addition, any relevant concepts that existed in the standardized terminology systems but were not used in the current paper-based documentation system were obtained and added to the content table as illustrated in Figure 11A-2.

Referencing Policies and Best Practice Guidelines

The team also reviewed policies and best practice guidelines put forth by regulatory bodies[2-3] to supplement the existing documentation templates. For example, The Joint Commission specifies detailed data require-

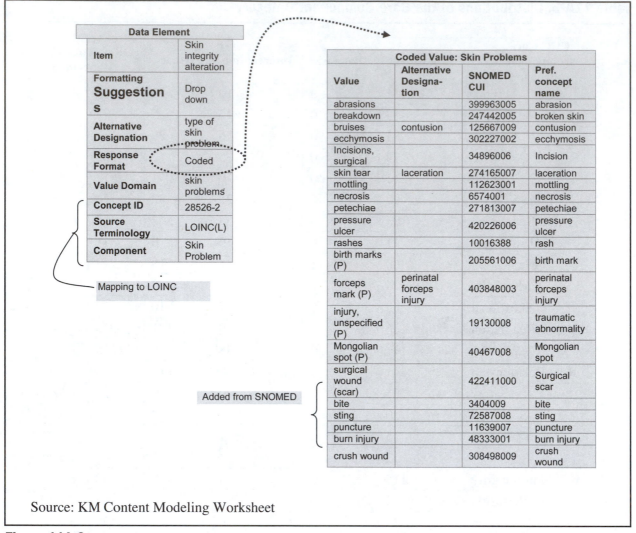

Source: KM Content Modeling Worksheet

Figure 11A-2. *Content Modeling Example*

ments that need to be captured when assessing pain. The team collaboratively reviewed applicable policies and guidelines and added the applicable items to finalize the candidate templates.

Creating Mock-up Screens for Template Display

To present the templates in a user-friendly manner, the candidate templates were expressed as Web-based forms, mimicking data entry screens of an electronic documentation system. These mock-up screens were kept simple in design to avoid pulling away the reviewers' attention from the content being presented. Each data element was linked to its source, such as the original paper forms or the policy/practice guidelines, so that the reviewers could reference them whenever necessary. A portion of the mock-up screen created for the "Skin and Wound Assessment" template is presented in Figure 11A-3. The source paper form that opens via the hyperlink (circled) is shown in the dotted square. The annotations that show how the "Data Element," "Value Set," and "Value" were defined in our modeling process are added in Figure 11A-3.

Content Validation

Content Review by the Subject Matter Experts

The modeled templates are currently under review by six subject matter experts invited from each hospital. These reviewers will evaluate the templates based on standard review criteria developed by PHS' Knowledge Management team.

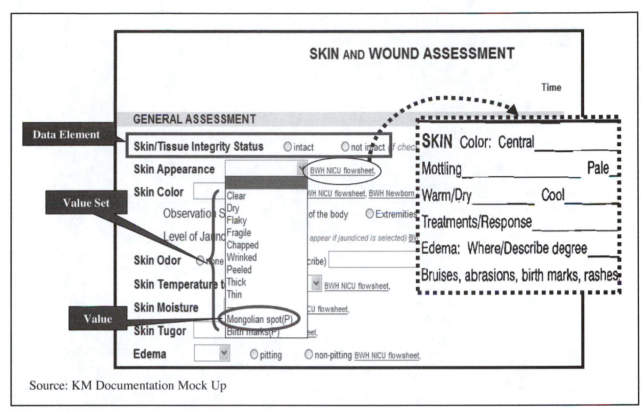

Figure 11A-3. *Screen-shot of the Skin Assessment Template Screen*

The application analyst and one nurse informatician from the content modeling team are serving as facilitators, providing instructions to the review process, guidance to the discussion, and resolutions to any problems that reviewers experience in the review process. The facilitators had a face-to-face meeting with the reviewers to provide instructions on the review process. Since the introduction meeting, the actual review has been taking place using a virtual collaboration environment in an effort to accommodate the busy and irregular schedules of the reviewers who are practicing clinicians. The virtual collaboration, known as "eRoom," is a Web-based environment where clinicians can review and exchange opinions on various artifacts produced in PHS, from documents to clinical applications (see Figure 11A-4).[4] The facilitators are also responsible for aggregating and analyzing the exchanged information within the eRoom. Once a cycle of review is completed, the feedback from the reviewer is collated and the mocked-up templates are revised accordingly. The process continues until no further revisions are necessary, indicating that consensus has been achieved.

Summary

One of the key aspects of the PHS knowledge management principles is representing data in unambiguous and consistent ways to support data reuse and interoperability in an electronic documentation system. Therefore, mapping to standardized terminology systems is considered a critical step of the content modeling efforts. Because the content modeling process presented in this case study is an ongoing effort we have not completed terminology mapping of the existing documentation contents in its entirety. However, based on the terminology mapping that we have done with the limited domains of "Skin and Wound Assessment" and "Pain Assessment," we found that no one single terminology system satisfied the representational needs of the nursing documentation content of the two domains. For example, while ICNP provided a comprehensive and nursing-oriented framework to represent nursing domains, the framework lacked many detailed concepts.

On the other hand, although SNOMED-CT provided many detailed descriptive concepts, it lacked nursing-specific judgment concepts (e.g., compromised) and many other bedside observation concepts (e.g., wound tunneling, wound undermining). LOINC provided broad concept coverage to the data items (i.e., the question part of a data element), especially around standardized scales. However, it lacked many descriptive concepts (i.e., the response part of a data element). This finding was consistent with the lessons we had

Skin Assessment

a database entry created by Linda Winfield on 20 Jan 09

| next | previous | summary |

Content Name	Skin Assessment
Status	Ready for Clinical Review
KM Engineer Owner	Drew Novack
Clinician Participants	Virginia Capasso (MGH) Ilene Fleischer (BWH), Jackie Collins (MGH)
Comments Due By	2 Mar 2009
Instructions	Steps for vetting content: 1. Review the mock-up assessment by clicking the link below 2. Add new comments (using the number next to each element on the mock-up) to suggest edits or additions 3. Reply to other's comments to agree/disagree with their suggestions 4. KM Engineer owner will make agreed upon changes 5. Review mock-up after changes for final approval
Attachment	Skin/Wound Assessment Mockup Skin_Assessment.mht ▷ mark read commands ▭ ▤ ▤
Comment Area	**Skin Appearance - Additions** (Andrew Novack, 27 Jan 09 11:08am) ⬇ Per Ilene Fleischer: add the following to skin appearance: Cracked, scars, atrophy, hemosiderin staining, purpura, gangrene, lipodermatosclerosis, hyperpigmented, scaly, moist, dry **Level of Jaundice** (Diane Bryant, 2 Mar 09 4:14pm) ⬇ How is this measure? it seems subjective. **Level of Jaundice: Reply** (Andrew Novack, 9 Mar 09 3:18pm) ⬇ I am not sure I understand your question? If you do not believe it should be measured in the way we have provided, can you provide alternate suggestions? Or do you suggest we remove the question? **Skin odor** (Diane Bryant, 2 Mar 09 4:18pm) ⬇

Source: PHS KM eRoom.

© Copyright 2009 EMC Corporation. All rights reserved.

Figure 11A-4. *Screenshot of the eRoom Review and Discussion. Reprinted with permission from EMC².*

learned through the earlier work related to modeling of nursing assessment data.[5] This finding signifies the importance of supporting the use of multiple terminology systems in encoding nursing data in an electronic documentation system.

Our approach includes a complete baseline assessment and modeling of contents (inpatient clinical documentation system) and review and validation of content by subject matter experts. This approach will support ongoing content management and reuse across PHS systems and will avoid key challenges associated with existing vendor solutions. We believe that this approach will ensure a smooth transition to the new electronic documentation system but will also provide full flexibility in maintaining and modifying the documentation system in the future.

Acknowledgment

We thank Deborah Thomas, RN; Linda Winfield, RN; and Andrew Novack, who are the members of the template design team but who had not co-authored this manuscript, for their invaluable contributions to this effort. We also wish to thank the subject matter experts from MGH and BWH for reviewing and validating the documentation templates.

References

1. Saba VK. *The Clinical Care Classification*. http://www.sabacare.com. Accessed Oct. 26, 2009.

2. The Joint Commission. http://www.jointcommission.org/. Accessed Oct. 26, 2009.

3. National Quality Forum. http://www.qualityforum.org/. Accessed Oct. 26, 2009

4. Hongsermeier T, Kashyap V, Sordo M. Knowledge management infrastructure: evolution at Partners Heathcare System. In: Greenes RA, ed. *Clinical Decision Support: The Road Ahead.* Academic Press. 2006:447-468.

5. Dykes PC, Kim HE, Goldsmith DM, Choi J, Esumi K, Goldberg HS. The adequacy of ICNP version 1.0 as a representational model for electronic nursing assessment documentation. *J Am Med Inform Assoc.* 2009;16(2):238-246.

## CHAPTER 12

Building an Intelligent Clinical Information System for Nursing: The Aurora, Cerner, and University of Wisconsin, Milwaukee, Knowledge-based Nursing Initiative - Part II

By Karlene M. Kerfoot, PhD, RN, NEA-BC, FAAN; Sally P. Lundeen, PhD, MSN, BSN, RN, FAAN; Ellen Harper, MBA, RN; Norma M. Lang, PhD, RN, FAAN, FRCN; Laura J. Burke, PhD, RN, FAAN; Mary L. Hook, PhD, RN, PHCNS-BC; Judy Murphy, BSN, RN; Elizabeth C. Devine, PhD, MSN, RN; Tae Youn Kim, PhD; Andrew F. Carlson, BS Systems Analysis; Jennifer Conner, BA; and Tera J. Watkins, MS, RN

Introduction—It Began With a Vision

For years, nurses have complained that clinical information systems (CIS) for nurses have merely been an upload of a paper and pencil system into a digital record. Nurses spend their scarce and valued time entering data into EHRs but receive back very little information in return. Furthermore, although some progress has been made in recent years to provide nurses with evidence to guide their practice, most CISs remain awkward to use and are not easily accessed at the point of care, at which nurses most need clinical decision support. In the opinion of many nurses, CISs merely provide electronic patient records with little ability to provide intelligent clinical information to inform and guide nurses through the assessment, diagnosis, and intervention phases of the nurse-patient encounter.

It was with these issues in mind that, in 2004, two nurse leaders, executive vice-president, Sue Ela, of Aurora Health Care, and dean and professor, Sally Lundeen, of the University of Wisconsin-Milwaukee (UW-Milwaukee), College of Nursing, aimed to create a vision that would leverage an existing Cerner Corporation EHR in place at Aurora Health Care into an intelligent nursing information system.[1] They initially sought and received the support needed from chief executive officers G. Edwin Howe, Aurora Health Care, and Neil Patterson, Cerner Corporation, to explore their vision further. Early in this journey, two other visionaries were added to the leadership team. Chief of Innovation Paul Gorup of Cerner Corporation and Norma M. Lang were recruited by Aurora and UW-Milwaukee as a Wisconsin Regents Distinguished Professor and the Aurora Distinguished Professor for Health Care Quality and Informatics, respectively. Dr. Lang assumed responsibility as project leader. All embarked on a unique partnership that sought to create a legacy for nursing practice and research.[1] Although these pioneers understood they would be "building the tracks as they went" toward a destination that had yet to be explored, they proceeded. All agreed that the new nursing information system design would provide each staff nurse with actionable, evidence-based knowledge and decision-making tools to assess, diagnose, and intervene to provide individualized and effective patient care. This new system would integrate evidence-based practice into nursing workflow by introducing knowledge in an actionable format—including triggers and alerts—to every nurse at the point of care.

To accomplish this vision, these leaders recognized that it was necessary to forge a very uncommon partnership between a health informatics vendor, a college of nursing, and an integrated healthcare system.[2] Although across the nation, partnerships between any two of these three types of organizations exist, there are few that include all three. The challenges of bringing together three such disparate organizational cultures were daunting, but the outcomes that were envisioned for the project necessitated just such collaboration. The partnership between Aurora Health Care, a large integrated healthcare system; Cerner Corporation, a global leader in healthcare IT; and the University of Wisconsin-Milwaukee College of Nursing, a research intensive academic setting was forged to achieve that vision. After a period of planning, the ACW Knowledge-Based Nursing Initiative (KBNI) became a reality in July 2004. The story of the initial phase of this project was documented by Lang and other members of the ACW team (2006) in the first edition of *Nursing and Informatics for the 21st Century: An International Look at Trends, Practice and the Future.*[3] The ACW knowledge development and IT tools and processes were tested in a small Aurora hospital in 2006, and the lessons learned were applied to the implementation of a highly successful "go-live" on two pilot units in a large tertiary, urban hospital in Milwaukee, Wisconsin, in July 2008. This chapter describes the second phase of this project and the lessons learned from its launch and implementation.

A Journey of Innovation

The KBNI vision has remained consistent since discussions began in 2003. The vision encompasses a belief that nursing evidence could be translated into referential, actionable, and executable knowledge™ in a real-time and intelligent CIS. A robust research agenda was also part of the original vision of KBNI, offering the promise of simultaneous transformation of nursing practice and nursing research through the use of CISs. For the past five years, a team representing Aurora, Cerner, and UW-Milwaukee has developed a conceptual framework, designed methodologies to identify and synthesize evidence, built evidence electronically into the workflow of nursing at the point of care, and developed a plan for the extraction of data for operational reports, quality improvement, and research.

An initial major challenge was to build a common, workable understanding of KBNI across a complex network of stakeholders: administrators, IT vendors, researchers, clinicians, and even consumers/patients. A clear conceptual framework has been critical to success and continues to guide all aspects of the KBNI process from knowledge development to clinical reporting and research (see Figure 12-1). The KBNI conceptual framework was vetted repeatedly and modified to reflect this common understanding.[3,4] This analysis of the framework required significant time and energy in the early phases of development, but as a result, all executive, operational, and research partners now refer to the framework as the "roadmap" for KBNI. There is an ongoing struggle to maintain a clear vision and conceptual clarity in the face of significant pressures from both the marketplace and the practice environment. During the past five-year-period of intense collaboration among all partners, we have encountered and negotiated a number of challenges and have learned lessons that continue to strengthen both the processes and the products that we are developing.

Early in the KBNI process, two nursing phenomena of concern (PoC) were chosen to test the entire KBNI process model: medication adherence and activity tolerance. A research librarian identified and a team of researchers synthesized the published evidence for each of these phenomena. The intention was to link recommendations for patient care across assessments, interventions, and outcomes and to make them actionable, so as to inform nurses through content, alerts, and triggers at the point of care. Recommendations were to be represented in the form of coded data elements that informed the design and build of the electronic decision support and documentation system. All recommendations were also to be linked to the original evidence and research publications, so that those who chose to review the primary knowledge sources could do so.

These two pilot PoC sites were embedded in the design and build of the nursing components within an electronic record at a small community hospital in the Aurora system. Nurses were oriented to the design and trained to use the system. Several months after implementa-

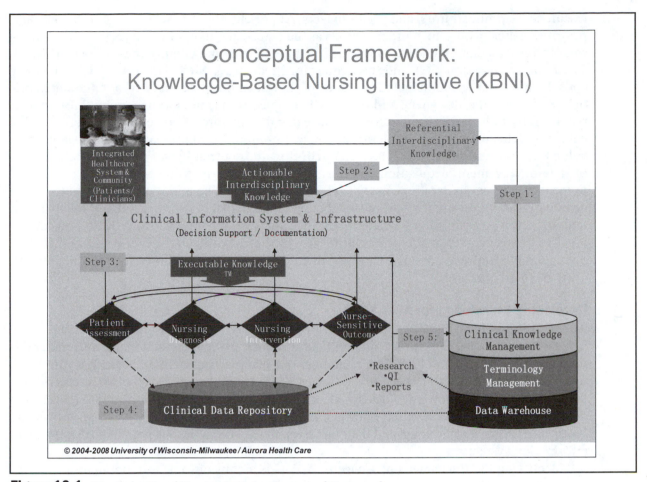

Figure 12-1. *Knowledge Based Nursing Initiative Conceptual Framework*

tion, operational data were acquired, analyzed, and shared with stakeholders for evaluation and recommendations. The pilot work resulted in lessons learned that have been critical in moving the ACW-KBNI project forward. Major lessons learned during this pilot implementation and evaluation included (1) the importance of concise, standardized and defined terminology and coding to represent nursing concepts; (2) the importance of adding more decision supports to link the assessments with the diagnoses and interventions; (3) the need to develop a process for efficient data extraction from the clinical data repository and the data warehouse for operations, quality improvement, and research; (4) the need to develop both clinical operational data reports and a research data repository; (5) the need to educate clinicians about evidenced-based practice and the clinical implications of decision support of the recommendations; and (6) the importance of involving clinicians, as well as informaticians, in the EHR system validation, design, and build. Most importantly, we learned that providing clinicians, managers, designers, builders, and other stakeholders with data about practice was and is a strong source of motivation for involvement in change activities. Nurses participating in the pilot were strong advocates for moving the KBNI project forward.

The great complexity of nursing practice also presented a significant and on-going challenge to the KBNI because it required an understanding of medical and psychosocial knowledge, as well as expertise in nursing knowledge. Unlike clinical support for physician practice that utilizes a fairly linear approach to link diagnosis and treatment of medical conditions, nursing PoCs apply across medical diagnostic categories and frequently must be dealt with in clusters or groups. Therefore, the KBNI team has spent considerable energy delineating the PoCs to be researched, synthesized, and embedded in the Cerner and Aurora electronic system.[5-7] The current and future nursing PoCs are selected as topics meaningful to clinicians, researchers, administrators, and policy makers. At present, they are selected based on national priorities delineated by such organizations as the National Quality Forum (NQF), the American Nurses Association (ANA) National Database of Nursing Quality Indicators (NDNQI), The Joint Commission (JC), and the Centers for Medicare & Medicaid Service (CMS). Other considerations for selection include the state of the science for potential PoC and the stated priorities of clinicians, designers, and builders. Examples of current and upcoming PoC include: risk for falls, falls, medication non-adherence, risk for pressure ulcers, pressure ulcers, risk for delirium, delirium, activity intolerance, physical immobility, acute pain, chronic pain, fluid volume excess, and infections. The ACW-KBNI team is currently working on the challenges of data management, acquisition, analysis, and timely reporting of operational data. Development of a research data repository is also a top priority. The initial data retrieved from the demonstration pilots are very promising, but our shared goal is to have valid and reliable data that are easily accessible to clinicians, managers, and researchers. The ACW-KBNI has developed robust processes to identify, synthesize, embed, acquire, analyze, and use knowledge-driven data to improve nursing care and patient outcomes. The remainder of this chapter will describe these processes.

Developing Knowledge for ACW-KBNI

ACW-KBNI knowledge development involves five major steps: (1) identifying the PoCs, (2) searching for and (3) synthesizing relevant evidence, (4) making actionable recommendations for nursing care, and (5) understanding and using operational and research outcomes to improve patient care. The recommendations address assessments, diagnoses, interventions, and outcomes. The knowledge development team includes nurses with graduate (preferably doctoral) preparation; a research librarian; doctorally prepared nursing experts in knowledge synthesis, coding terminology, and data mining; and experts in the development of healthcare information systems.

Identifying the Phenomena of Concern. A PoC is a clinical topic in a population (i.e., an age group in a venue of care). An example of a PoC would be risk for falls in hospitalized adults. PoCs are selected through a collaborative process of the three-partner organizations. Priority is given to nursing topics that are (1) related to quality indicators, and/or (2) likely to have high impact (e.g., in terms of the number of patients affected). The selection process is informed by the results of a preliminary evidence search and data extraction from the clinical partner's clinical data repository. Topics are not selected if sufficient evidence to warrant synthesis is unlikely or if the topic occurs infrequently in practice. A topic focusing meeting is held and all three partners participate in this discussion. It is very challenging to isolate the nursing concepts for the specified patient population within the care venue of interest.

Searching for the Evidence. Members of the knowledge development team then collaborate to identify relevant search terms and search strategies for each PoC. The research librarian is responsible for conducting the evidence search and documenting the search strategies used. Relevant evidence is sought from research reports, reviews of literature, and clinical articles, as well as from clinical practice guidelines, professional or governmental organizational standards and guidelines, and books. Quantitative, qualitative, and methodologic (e.g., psychometric) research is used. However, when there is no research to support an aspect of nursing care (e.g., an assessment), it is necessary to seek other sources of evidence to support that care aspect (e.g., evidence on the defining characteristics of rapid weight gain in adults at risk for fluid volume excess or the cut point for moribund obesity). The primary sources searched include databases of journals such as PubMed® and CINAHL®; electronic databases for topic-specific journals, when available; databases of systematic reviews (e.g., Cochrane); databases of guidelines (e.g., guideline.gov); Google searches; and ancestry searches of the reference lists of relevant sources. The evidence is provided to the individual(s) assuming primary responsibility for synthesizing it and making recommendations for that PoC (hereafter called the knowledge developer).

The knowledge developer reviews identified sources to determine which are relevant to the nursing care (i.e., assessment, diagnosis, interventions, or outcomes) for that PoC. Relevant sources are critiqued, using type-of-evidence specific criteria. Relevant sources of acceptable quality are entered into an evidence table, using the ACW- KBNI© format. All relevant findings are included on the evidence table, whether or not they are statistically significant.

Synthesizing the Evidence. When synthesizing the evidence into recommendations, the quantity, quality, and consistency of evidence are considered. Each recommendation is rated according to the strength of evidence supporting the recommendation, using a rating system modified from the evidence rating system proposed by Melnyk and Fineout-Overholt.[8] Modifications were done to account for types of evidence not specified in the original rating system (e.g., meta-analyses based on research other than randomized clinical trials, qualitative research, and psychometric research).

Making the Recommendations Actionable. It is extremely challenging to make actionable, evidence-based recommendations so as to best support clinical decision making of nurses at the point of care. To accomplish this, several strategies are used. A one-page PoC focus statement is used to define the topic and the population and to summarize the background/significance of the topic. The Aurora and Cerner teams conduct a current state analysis of the system policy, utilizing paper documents, electronic documents, electronic alerts (if any), staff education materials, and patient education materials. These were compared to the synthesis document; any gaps were identified and solutions to close the gap were discussed as a team until consensus was reached. To facilitate the development of decision support, notes for embedding (e.g., alerts and referential text) are provided with the recommendations.

To facilitate decisions related to adoption, each recommendation is rated according to the strength of supporting evidence, and a detailed rationale is provided that summarizes the evidence. Standardized terminology is used to facilitate the documentation of care provided and the subsequent retrieval of data for quality assurance or research. To ensure efficiency and to avoid recommending assessments that do not support clinical decision making, the flow of recommended care is examined. Embedding the recommendations within the clinical workflow as executable knowledge™ has been vital to the broad acceptance of nurses. A swim lane process modeling tool is used to visually display the clinical process and at which point the system should provide decision support to the clinician to depict the "for whom do what" instructions. This ensures that the appropriate patients are identified and that the nursing actions are clearly specified. Based on the learning from the earlier work, the broad clinical expertise of the development team was used to validate the balance, and resulted in adding "doing the right thing at the right time." The solution design recommendations are reviewed for accuracy, clarity, and usability on several occasions by members of the knowledge development team that is clinical partner-based, research scientists, and clinical nurse specialists before being discussed with the clinical transformers for workflow integration recommendations.

Operational and Research Outcomes. Standard terminology has long been recognized as a central building block that is essential for evidence-based practice implementations in health IT.[9,10] Currently, the ACW-KBNI team is focusing a considerable investment of time and expertise on (1) developing clinical reporting to improve practice; (2) defining the empirical outcomes for each PoC, that is, assuring that they can be designed into the workflow and data capture; (3) coding the key concepts to standard terminology SNOMED CT; and (4) creating a research data repository. Each of these activities was part of the initial vision and conceptual framework. The maturity of the KBNI project allows that to be the focus of our work in 2009 and beyond.

The ACW-KBNI Implementation: Success Factors

The failure to execute is unfortunately all too common a cause for the loss of innovative projects.[11] What appears brilliant in the plan too often cannot be translated into reality because of a myriad of operational breakdowns.[12] Execution is particularly difficult with a consortium of partners with very different backgrounds. However, the ACW project not only achieved the goal of a go-live in 2008 but met all milestones for an on-time implementation. Factors contributing to the success of this project will be described in the remainder of this chapter.

Creating a Shared Vision

The KBNI vision was and is clear: embed best evidence into the EHR to support nursing practice. Although clear, this vision is not simple to implement. It involves using executable knowledge™ to create an intelligent information system to guide nurses at the right time to make the right decision for the patient's unique needs—every time. The system must also provide staff and nurse leaders with feedback and outcomes in a timely manner. This vision is embraced by the leadership of all three partners and has been shared repeatedly with staff nurses and staff in all partnership organizations in a variety of venues over the past five years.

Aligning the Vision as a Strategic Healthcare System Initiative

Each year, a team of clinical and IT leaders at Aurora creates a business case for improving the EHR. The chief clinical officer (CCO) was the champion for the KBNI business case in 2007; it was selected for implementation from among a number of potential initiatives during the annual strategic planning process.

Creating a Clinical Practice Partner-based Implementation Team

A unique feature of the design and implementation of the KBNI content at Aurora is the clinical leadership of the project. In February 2008, the Aurora KBNI Implementation Team was formed. The clinical leadership team included the organization's CCO, two nurse Research Scientists, and six staff nurses who were appointed to new roles as "Transformers." An experienced team was needed for this challenge, and this team was well-qualified for the implementation. The CCO and the research scientists were doctorally prepared nurses who collectively represented nearly 70 years of experience as nurse administrators, clinical nurse specialists, and/or community-based nurse case managers. They were trained in human factors, engineering, and workflow analysis and had experience leading major research and clinical projects. The Transformer Team included a balance of novice-to-expert staff nurses. They shared a systems-thinking approach to problem solving and were technically competent with the EHR. This team was also capable of creating educational modules, testing staff on practice competencies, conducting practice and documentation audits, and giving constructive feedback to peers. Each of the Transformers maintained 50% active practices in ICU and medical-surgical units. Two Transformers worked on the pilot units, and the others were selected from other Aurora sites that were users of the electronic care planning feature of the EHR. All were provided with a thorough orientation to the KBNI process and immersed in the best evidence synthesis for each PoC.

The Aurora IT team was also an integral part of the implementation process, including the vice president of Information Services, project managers, and clinical analysts; many of whom were nurses. These experts had worked collaboratively with clinicians over the previous 12 years to create the current Aurora EHR and were intimately familiar with the functional capabilities of the Cerner software. The successful implementation of the KBNI vision is in no small measure the result of the ACW project to forge an unusually strong partnership between our clinical and IT teams.

Conducting a Pilot-unit Content and Workflow Gap Analysis

In March 2008, the Aurora Clinical Implementation Team spent time on each of the pilot units, observing nursing workflow by shadowing nurses. It was important to see how the nursing practices and workflows differed between the current and the ACW-KBNI "evidence based-practice workflow." In addition, the research scientists attended staff meetings and had dialogues with staff about what worked and what did not work, related to clinical practice workflow and software and hardware resources. After the observation period was completed, the team debriefed and summarized their observations of the current-state gaps related to nursing practices and workflow and resolved them with training and or policy changes.

Measuring Baseline Nurse Satisfaction with Clinical Documentation and Quality Outcomes

To evaluate Aurora nurses' baseline satisfaction with clinical documentation and use of the EHR before implementation of the new ACW application, the team created a short online survey. The survey was included in the electronic newsletter, *Aurora Nurse,* which was directly circulated to 4,400 nurses. The survey was online from April 1 through April 15, 2008. Six hundred and thirty-seven responses, for a 14% response rate, were returned during the two-week period. Only 64% of the nurses responding agreed with the statement, "I have everything I need in the electronic record that I need to plan my patient's care." In addition, baseline measures of each outcome are now standardly collected prior to implementation in order to do a comparative analysis pre- and post-go live for each PoC.

Building the Localized Content

The nursing process is highly iterative and touches all aspects of the care delivered to patients. Not unexpectantly, the Aurora gap analysis defined a number of current state physical assessment parameters that were, at times, inadequate. For example, as the current documentation tools were evaluated for the risk factors associated to risk for falls, the physical assessment questions evaluated by nurses on admission were found to be inadequate to define nursing diagnoses and to direct appropriate interventions. Therefore, the intake tool was supplemented with additional questions and responses. These improvements to the documentation tools were implemented across the Aurora system and not limited to the pilot.

The Clinical Analysts modified/created the forms, care plans, interactive data entry screens, scoring algorithms, rules, alerts, and reports that would enable streamlined data entry, diagnosis, patient risk factor-specific intervention planning and outcome planning and data entry. The design team collaborates on any customization for the Aurora system and ensures that changes do not cause deviations from the best evidence to drive practice decisions. This collaborative decision making ensures the integrity of the content.

Revising Policies and Developing Educational Materials

ACW-KBNI project has provided the impetus for the review and updating of system policies at Aurora. One of the research scientists led the pairs of Transformers to critically analyze the gaps between the system policies, staff education materials, patient education materials, and the "best-evidence" content generated from the knowledge synthesis per PoC. The Aurora Clinical Implementation Team members and other Aurora stakeholders (e.g., interdisciplinary team members) reviewed all drafts. Final drafts were sent to specific councils of the Aurora Shared Governance structure for approval: the System Nursing Practice Council, the System Nursing Management Council, the System Nursing Leadership Council, and/or the System Patient Education Council for approval. Once revised and approved, staff education materials were added to the online course catalogue available to all Aurora nurses.

One of the research scientists drafted extensive communication to staff that summarized the significant practice changes to be implemented and the process for completing training modules. The Aurora System Clinical Education Council, made up of educators and clinical nurse specialists, made certain that all staff affected by the foundational changes were knowledgeable about the changes and competent to use the new content. This systematic and extensive clinical staff input has resulted in policies and education materials that are aligned with an intelligent CIS that can boast a meaningful design, high utility, and excellent alignment with clinical practice.

Validating the Cerner and Aurora Builds

Once both the Cerner and Aurora builds were completed, a review day was scheduled for all members of the ACW team (the UWM knowledge developer, synthesis expert, Aurora research scientists, Aurora transformers, Aurora IT clinical analysts, and Cerner design solution experts). Every form, care plan, data entry screen, outcome evaluation screen, rule, algorithm, and alert developed for the Cerner solution and the Aurora localization were compared and contrasted. All differences were discussed and debated and the designs were realigned, so that the Cerner and Aurora builds both met the minimum agreed upon content of the knowledge synthesis but optimized the nurses' workflow through the use of the system.

Finally, the staff nurse transformers presented several robust PoC-specific clinical case scenarios that they had developed in teams to test all of the algorithms, rules, and alerts in the new build. Simultaneous mock charting was conducted on the Aurora EHR by a transformer and the Cerner EHR by a Cerner design solutions specialist. The KBNI Design Team validated that the Cerner and Aurora builds functioned as designed and leaders from each partner organization formally signed-off on the final build. Cerner then packaged the solution for general release, and Aurora moved the code into the training and production environments for training and go-live.

The Actual Go-Live

Planning for the Pilot Deployment

In March 2008, the two pilot units at Aurora St. Luke's Medical Center in Milwaukee were chosen for implementation. The Aurora Health Care strategic planning process dedicated operational resources to fund implementation in the two pilot units. To be considered eligible as a pilot unit, the units had to primarily provide care for medical patients, and have strong managerial leadership, a clinical nurse specialist, shared governance staff nurse leadership, and nursing staff that embraced change. The two units at Aurora St. Luke's Medical Center met those criteria, and the units' leaders welcomed the opportunity to be the pilot units for ACW-KBNI. Weekly or biweekly meetings were held between the Clinical Implementation Team leader, the IT Build Team leader, and pilot site administrators, executives, and unit leaders. Target dates were selected for training and go-live that each group agreed would be achievable. Risks were identified and risk minimization strategies were planned. Staff was informed of upcoming changes, classes, materials, and support staff that would be available during go-lives.

Training the Pilot Unit Staff

Findings from a workflow analysis conducted in March 2008 identified variability between nurses in the use of the EHR and the need to educate staff on core fundamentals. The Aurora Implementation Team designed and delivered computer laboratory sessions in May 2008 on "Documentation Competence – Managing Your Orders" and "Documentation Competence – Finding Information in the Electronic Health Record." These classes were held two months before providing KBNI content, so the staff could become competent on using the EHR as designed. Transformers taught the classes with a 1:10 mentor:nurse ratio. The staff worked through scenarios and reported that they found the hands-on coaching to be extremely helpful.

In June 2008, staff completed four online education modules through a Web-based learning management system (Learning Connection). The "New Era in Electronic Care Planning" module described the KBNI vision and how use of KBNI executable knowledge™ would transform nurses' clinical practice. These educational modules provided staff with a summary of the best evidence related to assessments, diagnoses, interventions, and outcomes related to the three PoC. All learning modules ended with cognitive test questions, using multiple choice or true/false questions to assess competency.[13] In July 2008, staff participated in two additional three-and-a-half-hour-computer laboratory sessions to learn about the evidence behind activity intolerance and medication non-adherence and to practice using the clinical decision supports for all of the PoC included in the first bundle of KBNI content. Staff worked through the nursing process components of scenarios of patients who experienced all of the PoC. By the end of each session, all participants were able to demonstrate competency in using the new evidence-based nursing content in our CIS system.

Implementing the Pilot

At the end of July 2008, the new KBNI content was put into live use. On-site support for the two pilot units was maintained on all days at all times (24/7) for two weeks. The go-live team worked in the background on a shift-by-shift basis to triage and resolve system and training issues in a timely way. The research scientists and Transformers also provided a second period of go-live coverage the following weekend to assure that weekend staff had adequate live coverage during the conversion to KBNI. Newly admitted patients were started on the new system upon admission. After four days, patients who were still on the pilot units had their care plans "converted" to the KBNI content. Midpoint through the first week, half of the patients were on the prior method of care planning and half were on the new KBNI method. A spot-check comparative audit on one of the pilot units showed that the average time from admission to initiation of a care plan decreased from 6.8 hours to 3.1 hours within four days of implementing KBNI. Qualitative discussions with staff nurses indicated that this decrease occurred because the embedded decision supports increased nurses' confidence in care plan initiation. They felt confident that, based on their assessment of the patients' risk factors, the system-generated diagnoses were the appropriate ones to initiate for each patient. The ACW-KBNI is clearly transforming practice at the bedside.

Extracting Valid and Reliable Data

The ACW-KBNI Outcomes Team comprises scientists from both UW-Milwaukee College of Nursing and Aurora Health Care, as well as health informatics operations specialists and nurse leaders from the ACW partnership. As each PoC was developed, the team established meaningful process indicators and outcome metrics. The population inclusion criteria created the denominator, and the components of the process or outcomes that were to be measured created the relevant numerators. The Aurora Implementation Team compared the results of chart audits and direct observations with electronically extracted data on the pilot PoCs to determine the extent to which data pulled from the EHR clinical data repository are valid and reliable. Feedback was provided to unit leaders to improve the accuracy of the use of the decision-support and data entry tools. This clinical data validation is the first step in a strategic plan that includes the development of a research data repository at Aurora Health Care that will facilitate ACW researchers from UW-Milwaukee College of Nursing, Aurora Health Care, and others to advance knowledge discovery in the area of nursing's impact on patient/client health outcomes. Research on clinical outcomes and the challenges of conducting outcomes research using clinical data will be the subject of future publications.

Measuring System Outcomes

The success of Bundle 1 implementation for the Aurora System was based on measurement of changes in nurse satisfaction with using the EHR for clinical documentation. In November 2008, an online survey was e-mailed to all 90 nurses who worked regularly on one of the two pilot units. Seventy-eight (86%) responses were received. Overall, compared with nurses' responses from this site in the prelaunch survey in March 2008 survey, we found:

- A 33% improvement in nurses agreeing that the EHR improves their organization of nursing care with 97% agreeing, compared to 64% on the first questionnaire.

- A 24% improvement in nurses agreeing that they used some component of the EHR to guide their patient care delivery.
- An 11% improvement in nurses agreeing that they "chart-as-they-go" and no change in nurses indicating that they spend any less time in direct patient care.

These results were amazing, considering that the nursing staff had just started working with new evidence-based nursing content, the addition of new assessments, diagnoses, interventions, and outcomes and were initiating almost twice as many nursing care plans per patient as they had preimplementation. It is rare for clinicians to find that EHRs improve their workflow. The pilot unit nurses report that the new clinical intelligence system improved their workload, introduced an improved ability to identify patients at risk for serious problems, and has begun to reduce negative outcomes and improve positive patient outcomes.

The Aurora Clinical Implementation Team's next steps are to continue work on developing, embedding, and testing Bundle 2 PoC and go-live with this new content in May 2009 and Bundle 3 PoC and go-live with additional new content in November 2009. The KBNI Outcomes Team continues to extract outcomes and improve the validity and reliability of the data. They are also working on gathering long-term outcomes in a research data mart related to length of stay and 30-day hospital readmission rates, so that a rich, researchable database is available for researchers to use. The KBNI Outcomes Team recently applied for and received funding from AHRQ to study processes to improve the utility of the KBNI data. The KBNI Executive Team continues to define the list of PoC to be newly developed and maintained for 2010 and 2011.

Evaluating Our Success: Why Is it Working?

By all very early initial measures, the ACW KBNI is a success. As a group, the leadership team has thoughtfully considered factors that are contributing to this success. Three key factors have been identified that will be reviewed here: an uncommon tripartite partnership; innovative and accelerated project management; and extensive collaboration between clinical and IT teams in the design, build, and implementation of the ACW KBNI. Each will be discussed briefly.

An Uncommon Tripartite Partnership

The strongest partnerships are those that bring a wide variety of needed skills and specific knowledge to the endeavor to accomplish the necessary work. While a wide divergence of talent is optimal, it is also very difficult to create partnerships made from organizations with highly diverse agendas. This project is testimony to the significant outcomes that can be accomplished when a common vision is truly shared by all entities, and individual differences are viewed as strengths to accomplish a very significant project. It is clear that the ACW KBNI project would not have been successful without the full participation of three successful organizations: Aurora Health Care, Cerner Corporation, and the UW-Milwaukee College of Nursing. Each of our organizations brings a unique and vital perspective to this collaboration, as well as an existing culture related to problem solving and solutions.

The ACW collaborators provide the strengths of the organizations they represent. UW-Milwaukee team members identify and monitor the rigor of evidence and synthesize to actionable recommendations integrated into clinical decision support and take the lead of the research agenda. The nurses and research scientists at Aurora bring real-world perspectives and scientific rigor to the complexity of patient quality and safety issues related to clinical practice at the bedside and train staff nurses to adopt the new solutions as they go-live on the units. The nurse informaticians and engineers from Cerner work with the other partners to appropriately code data elements to standard terminology and leverage the technology of the CIS to deliver evidenced-based practice at the point of care. A joint research team works to validate and extract data for analysis, both for operations and outcomes research. Collectively, the partners are leveraging the technology of a CIS to fill the gaps between practice and knowledge.[2]

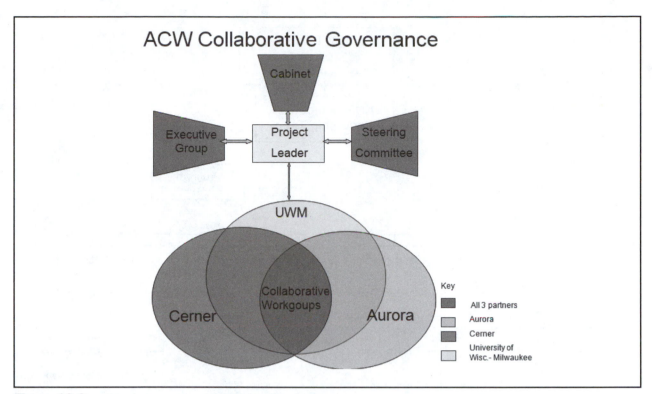

Figure 12-2. *ACW Collaborative Governance. Used with permission: © ACW Knowledge-Based Nursing Initiative (September 1, 2009).*

Shared Governance Structure

It has been critical to establish a viable structure for shared governance that is consistent with standards within each of the organizations that would cultivate the professional practice environment for all involved with the project. The structure and governance of the project has made it possible to facilitate innovation, while minimizing the disruptions that transformative change brings. The structure has also served to improve communication and decision making, within and across the three organizational partners (see Figure 12-2). The structure was built on the four primary principles of shared governance: partnership, equity, accountability, and ownership. The organizational structure is shown and described in Figures 12-2 and 12-3.

A cabinet comprised of one executive from each partner organization is responsible for the vision, resources allocation, contractual arrangements, and the policies and procedures of each of the partners. The Cabinet appoints the project leader and Executive Group members.

The project leader is an academic research scientist, who serves as the key liaison to multiple stakeholders and the greater health, research, and IT communities. This position has the overall responsibility for organizing the research, the dissemination of knowledge, securing of research grants, and future directions for the project. The Executive Group comprises one person from each partner, who is responsible for the scope, prioritization, timeline, operations, and oversight of the budget and resources, as well as arbitration of disputes. This group has authority and responsibility to meet the objectives outlined by the cabinet.

As shown in Figure 12-3, Collaborative Work Teams include multiple members from each partner. They act as tightly integrated units guided by a commitment to the synergy of team science and implementation to best meet the goals of the project. Each partner contributes their own unique expertise with resources that fully understand and respect one another's domains of knowledge. The Collaborative Work Teams own the development process, from knowledge synthesis to implementation.

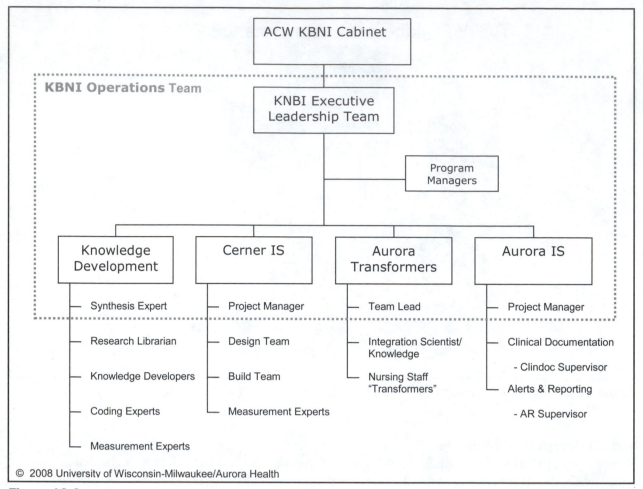

Figure 12-3. *Organizational Structure of Collaborative Work Teams. Used with permission: © ACW Knowledge-Based Nursing Initiative (September 1, 2009).*

Excellence in Project Management

The role of KBNI project management is to establish and support the governance structure described earlier and monitor consistency of project processes and methodologies to enable the team to effectively and efficiently execute the goals of the project. To manage the scope of work envisioned for this project, we needed defined team processes and methodologies in place to produce consistent, replicable results. We first developed key integrated work groups to deliver on the specific objectives outlined by the governance groups. The membership of the work groups spans research scientists, clinicians, nursing informaticists, IT developers, and project management. This cross-functional group approach has been particularly effective in the design process, in which the adoption of Joint Application Design (JAD) principles has significantly reduced the time spent in design, as well as reducing rework and improving overall quality. Throughout the project, the collaborative approach has helped facilitate consensus across the partners and has avoided silos that typically appear in clinical IT projects. By having all parties represented, we have smoothed the transition from old practice to new standard, as well as improved communication to broader peer groups and stakeholders.

Specific tools were used to document roles and responsibilities within the project as well as in the overall flow of the development cycle. A RACI document was used to document for each activity or deliverable who is **R**esponsible, **A**ccountable (gives approval), **C**onsults, or needs to be **I**nformed. We also developed a role-based process map or "swim lane" diagram to illustrate the PoC development cycle across the project roles. Our approach is illustrated in Figure 12-4. To streamline a repeatable process, we established a comprehensive work plan that outlines work group objectives, tasks associated, and milestones throughout develop-

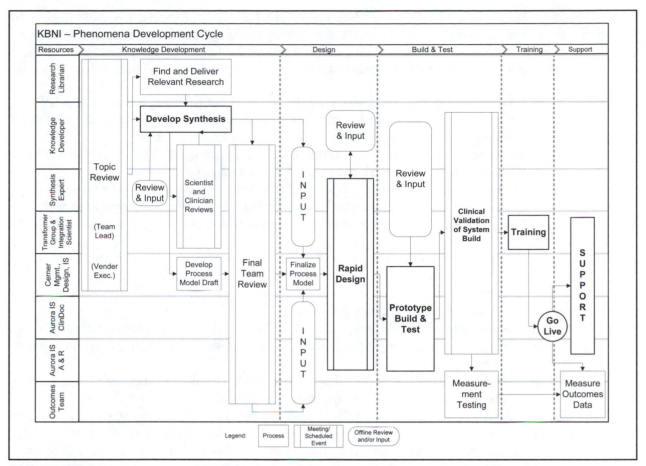

Figure 12-4. *Phenomena Development Cycle. Used with permission: © ACW Knowledge-Based Nursing Initiative (September 1, 2009).*

ment, regardless of topic. The work plan supports a full circle approach, from collecting the evidence for synthesis development to outcome measurement postconversion and incorporating findings into topic maintenance and research. This model supports the end-to-end collaboration of the best minds.

First, an assembly-line approach was put in place to support concurrent development activities and leverage appropriate resources in line with expertise. Then, guiding principles were developed to ensure standards and gain efficiencies during the design and build process. An escalation process was put in place to provide structure and direction to build consensus when difficult to reach. A validation sign-off step also was added to ensure that what was built in the prototype domain supported the evidence and the validation of the design using the patient scenario developed by the Transformers. To keep the outcomes of the content consistent between the Cerner release and the Aurora domain, we established guidelines for acceptable "localizations" to the agreed upon design to accommodate specific needs of the Aurora environment. An analysis is done postconversion to ensure that learning and process improvements are incorporated into the topic's yearly maintenance cycle. This pipeline is managed to allow us to continue perfecting our content based on real data. Analysis is also done from a research perspective to develop new evidence consistent with the project findings. Finally, a topic roadmap was developed to guide strategic decision making about the selection and ordering of the PoCs to be delivered each of the next five years.

Essential Skill Set for Clinical Information Technology Project Managers

The initial tendency when organizing teams for a clinical project such as this one is to want to bring in project managers with deep clinical knowledge who can fully grasp the complex clinical concepts involved. However, when assembling a team of experts, it is more important for the project manager(s) to be experts in the discipline of project management than to have expertise in the clinical content of the project. Given the following list of essential skills, a project manager will not be hindered by a lack of clinical expertise (and may in fact find it an asset).

Project Management Expertise. The baseline requirement for a project such as ACW is a strong working knowledge of project management techniques, tools, and methodologies demonstrated through experience successfully managing complex projects.

- **Communication:** Effective communication skills are paramount. The ability to facilitate common understanding across all team members is invaluable.
- **Quick Learner:** While expertise is not required, the ability to understand the basic needs of the project and identify its unique challenges is required. An effective project manager can use the lack of detailed knowledge as an opportunity to ask challenging questions that others may be unwilling to ask.
- **Conflict Resolution:** Working on very important nurse-sensitive topics with passionate clinical people mean differences of opinion and conflicts will inevitably arise. Focusing on the patient and knowing how to channel those conflicts into constructive discussions helps smooth tensions and increases overall quality.
- **Virtual Collaboration:** With the geographic distribution of the team members, much of the work is done virtually, utilizing conference calls and online collaboration tools, in order to be time- and cost-effective.

Creating synergy across the partnership is what makes this project successful. It is both its greatest strength and its greatest challenge. We established that synergy by aligning efforts via project planning that reflects and tracks on tasks, timeframes, resources, gaps, barriers, and key milestones for the lifecycle of each topic. Checkpoints along the course of the project have allowed us to incorporate lessons learned from prior releases and ensure we continue to meet the goals for scope, timing, and budget. These checkpoints help us confirm that we are meeting the needs and requirements from all aspects of the project-science, IT, and most importantly, at the bedside.

A Clinical Project, Not an IT Project

In our implementation of this intelligent information system for nursing, the importance of planning and executing this initiative as a *practice* change *supported* by a technology implementation cannot be overemphasized. The IT took a supportive role to the people/process/practice change being enabled by the technology. We worked hard to ensure that IT was seen as the *means to an end*, and not as *an end unto itself*.[14] Four factors ensured that the KBNI project was driven as a clinical practice change and added to its successful adoption by nursing. First, the project was initiated by nursing as a professional practice change, recognizing that for evidence-based practice to become a reality, nursing would need to change its practice model, as well as all the corresponding job expectations; processes; and workflows. Second, the project was owned, sponsored, and championed by a clinical nursing team. The project was clearly seen as the most important thing the team was doing; they were empowered and knew they were creating the future of nursing at Aurora. Third, the clinical nursing project team was integrally involved in the design of the solution, as well as the training, go-live support, and postimplementation support. The IT team supported them with detailed design specifications, system build, and testing, and provided invaluable input regarding the capabilities of the system's features and functions. Fourth, the training was done by focusing first on the practice changes, then correlating how the practice changes were "hard-wired" into the information system, and lastly determining how to navigate through the software application itself. There is no question that most successful implementations are owned and sponsored by the leaders and staff that will be making the practice change and will be benefiting by the innovations being introduced. In this project, nurses sponsored, championed, and created the practice transformation required to design and implement an innovative intelligent CIS to support nursing practice.

Next Steps

With the success of the project on the pilot units, the "proof of concept" has been achieved, and we have demonstrated the value and usability of this CIS application for nursing. There is great interest in the application by other Aurora nurses and the application will be rolled out to other units and hospitals within the Aurora system as quickly as resources allow. The two Aurora hospitals that will be opened in the next two years will have the ACW-KBNI system in place for the nursing staff to use from the first day. The other hospitals in the system have continually benefited from the project because we have rolled out aspects of the project as new information has been acquired. For example, the new neurologic assessment that was a part of the CIS has been deployed to all appropriate sites. Consequently, nurses have access to additional selected evidence-based information throughout the Aurora system, even before the full implementation of KBNI at their sites.

Best evidence must stay current; therefore, we are committed to review each nursing PoC in use annually with a thorough search of recent evidence. If new evidence is found that meets the criteria for valid research, this new knowledge will be incorporated into the design; thus, nurses at the bedside will have the advantage of being able to practice with evidence that has been published within the last year, rather than the previously noted reported 17-year-lag from research to implementation in practice. Finally, the research components of the ACW projects are being honed as the next step in the project. A key component of the original conceptual model, the work of validating data and extracting data from the data warehouse into a clinical data repository has begun. Our ability to capture the appropriate data elements for analysis will be key to our success in this next phase of the project. We seek to develop both operational reports and research protocols that use clinical data to both improve practice and advance knowledge generation. These exciting next steps will be reported in future publications.

The Future of Intelligent Clinical Information Systems for Nursing

While there are challenges that still need to be overcome to make the best evidence available at the clinician's fingertip, ACW-KBNI demonstrates the potential of a strong partnership among a large healthcare system, a major software vendor, and a research-intensive college of nursing to improve the delivery of nursing care. The lessons learned to date through the ACW-KBNI partnership further informs us about the future of intelligent CIS for nursing. In particular, nursing's contribution to patient outcomes, still largely invisible decades after the treatise of Fagin,[15] is unlikely to become visible without designing and integrating robust evidence-based clinical nursing decision support and documentation within an EHR system. Future plans include expansion to an interdisciplinary application with information automatically sent from the nursing assessment to other disciplines to be integrated into the patient's plan of care.

An interoperable specification for nursing CIS will include clinical documentation templates and decisional logics, as well as quality measurement, feedback, and reporting requirements in accordance with the nursing care process model (i.e., nursing assessment, diagnosis, intervention, and outcome evaluation). A clinical documentation template with data elements and value sets, derived from the best evidence for a given PoC, will assist clinicians and researchers to gather evidence-based patient care data regardless of the software platforms adopted. In addition, designing decisional logics with a set of rules will further ensure that the best knowledge is delivered to clinicians at the point of care in a timely manner. Both timeliness and at point of care are key to supporting clinicians decision-making and documentation practice in their respective workflows. Another key component of future interoperable specification will require the identification of quality measurement, feedback, and reporting in order to facilitate automated data collection, aggregation, and comparison of nursing care provided across settings.

Developing specifications for the nursing components within EHR systems, however, will not be an easy task. It will require input from various stakeholders to achieve true interoperability, while addressing and minimizing the complexity of integrating those specifications into an EHR system. Interoperable specifications developed for nursing will need to be consensus-driven and documented using recommended standards so both humans and machines can interpret and maintain the specification in a systematic way. For example, encoding and storing each specification in XML (Extensive Markup Language) format will allow clinicians and researchers to examine the current best standards of care identified. This approach also makes it easier for software vendors to incorporate such standards into their systems. Also, conforming to existing technical standards (e.g., HL7 messaging standards and Clinical Documentation Architecture) along with the adoption of recommended healthcare terminologies will ensure data exchange and sharing across settings.

Summary

It should be kept in mind that implementing an EHR system with decision-support functionalities is not a replacement of human judgment. Further research on clinicians' information needs and decision-making processes at the point of care is needed to develop a better EHR system for nursing. It is apparent that nursing care is not easily quantifiable because nursing practice is influenced by multiple care providers. Nonetheless, clearly defined interoperable specifications will contribute to developing the next generation of EHR systems that will facilitate closing the gap between nursing research and practice. The transformation of intelligent EHR systems to enable "evidence-based practice" for nurses will ultimately lead to a transformation of the knowledge discovery process as well. In addition to our evidence-based practice focus, the ACW-KBNI team is working to ensure that that the future of intelligent clinical information systems for nursing will also generate "practice-based evidence" generated from care documentation at the bedside.[16,17] The ACW project also is structured to be repeatable at other Cerner clients to capture and analyze clinical data using KBNI protocols to generate new knowledge regarding nursing practice and its impact on client outcomes.

The ability to implement and sustain this complex project is testimony to the partners' belief in the importance of creating a new level of nursing care for patients based on immediate access to evidence-based information. Many challenges continue to make the work of the Aurora-Cerner-UW-Milwaukee initiative a dynamic and evolving process with many challenges still facing the team. We believe that we are ready to meet these challenges and are proud of the part we are playing to usher in a new era of clinically intelligent systems that supports our collective vision of a new reality for nursing.

References

1. Ela SE, Lang NM, Lundeen SP. (2006) Time for a nursing legacy: Ensuring excellence through actionable knowledge. *Nurse Leader.* 2002;4(6):42-44, 55.

2. Lundeen S, Harper E, Kerfoot K. Translating nursing knowledge into practice: An uncommon partnership. *Nurs Outlook.* 2009;57(3):173-175.

3. Lang NM, Hook ML, Akre ME, et al. Translating knowledge-based nursing into referential and executable application in an intelligent clinical information system. In: Weaver C, Delaney C, Weber P, Carr R, eds. *Nursing and informatics for the 21st century: An international look at practice, trends and the future.* Chicago: Healthcare Information and Management Systems Society (HIMSS), 2006.

4. Lang NM. The promise of simultaneous transformation of practice and research with the use of clinical information systems. *Nurs Outlook.* 2008;56(5): 232-236.

5. Hook ML, Devine EC, Lang NM. Using a computerized fall risk assessment process to tailor interventions in acute care. In: Henriksen K, Battles JB, Keyes MA, Lewin DI, eds. *Advances in Patient Safety: New directions and alternative approaches* (Vol. 1, pp. 387-405). Washington, DC: Agency for Healthcare Research and Quality, 2008.

6. Agency for Healthcare Research and Quality, (2002) Systems to rate the strength of scientific evidence. Summary, evidence report/technology assessment number 47. AHRQpublicationno02-E015 http://www.ahrq.gov/clinic/epcsums/strengthsum.htm. Accessed August 10, 2007.

7. Devine EC. Knowledge-Based Nursing Initiative system for rating the strength of evidence supporting recommendations. In: Devine EC, Kim TY, Johnson B, Hook M, Lang N, eds. ACW *Knowledge-Based Nursing Initiative Evidence Table Protocol.* Milwaukee, WI: University of Wisconsin-Milwaukee, College of Nursing. 2007;8.

8. Melnyk BM, Fineout-Overholt E. *Evidence-based Practice in Nursing and Healthcare.* Philadelphia: Lippincott Williams & Wilkins, 2005.

9. Bakken S. An informatics infrastructure is essential for evidence-based practice. *J Am Med Inform Assoc.* 2001;8,3:199-201.

10. Bakken S, Mead N. Nursing Classification Systems: Necessary but not sufficient for representing "What Nurses Do" for inclusion in computer-based patient record systems. *J Am Med Inform Assoc.* 1997;4:222–232.

11. Finkelstein S. *Why Smart Executives Fail.* New York: Portfolio, 2003.

12. Inouye S, van Dyck C, Alessi C, Balkin S, Siegal A, Horwitz R. Clarifying confusion: The confusion assessment method. *Ann Int Med.* 1990;113(12):941-948.

13. Hook M, Burke L, Murphy J. *An IT Innovation for Individualizing Care: Success with Clinicians Leading the Way.* The 10th International Congress on Nursing Informatics (NI2009) 2009.

14. Murphy J. The best IT project is not an IT project. *J Healthcare Inf Manage.* 2009;23,1:6-8.

15. Fagin C. On the dangers of invisibility. *Image.* 1992;24(4): 326.

16. Aurora Health Care Top Quality System in Nation in Medicare, Premier Healthcare Alliance Pay-For-Performance Project, *Bio-Medicine.* PRNewswire, http://www.bio-medicine.org/medicine-news-1/Aurora-Health-Care-Top-Quality-System-in-Nation-in-Medicare—Premier-Healthcare-Alliance-Pay-For-Performance-Project-22123-1/. Accessed June 17, 2008.

17. Kim TY, Lang NM, Berg K, Weaver C, Murphy J, Ela S. Clinician adoption patterns and patient outcome results in use of evidence-based nursing plans of care, pp. 423-427. AMIA Symposium Proceedings, 2007.

Case Study 12A

The USA National Veterans Administration Clinical Information System

By Margaret Ross Kraft, PhD, RN

Introduction

The Veterans Health Administration (VHA) is the home of America's largest integrated healthcare system. This system provides care for all persons who have served in the United States Military system and received an honorable discharge. VHA consists of 153 medical centers, 135 community living centers (CLC) (formerly known as nursing home care units), 108 comprehensive home-care programs, more than 800 community-based outpatient clinics (CBOC), 232 community-based Vet Centers, and 48 domiciliaries. In addition to providing acute care and home care services, CLCs are skilled nursing facilities for veterans with chronic stable conditions, such as dementia, those requiring rehabilitation, or those who need comfort and care at the end of life. "The CBOCs offer outpatient services, including health and wellness visits, and are geographically located to provide care closer to the veteran's home. Domiciliaries provide care to veterans with a wide range of medical, psychiatric, vocational, educational, or social problems and illnesses in a safe, secure homelike environment. Vet Centers are community-based and provide readjustment counseling and outreach services to all U.S. Veterans who served in any combat zone and their families. Annually, this integrated healthcare system provides comprehensive care to over 5.5 million veterans."[1]

VHA Information Technology

IT systems within the VHA are designed to support both administrative and clinical functions. Administrative systems support activities such as patient registration, scheduling, purchasing, payroll, and timekeeping, including employee leave requests. The VHA e-mail system has become a major communication link within and between VHA facilities. The use of IT provides nursing service administration with readily available staffing data, including demographics such as age, role, education, certification, and retirement eligibility. Financial data, such as hours worked and dollars paid, paid days off, and leave without pay, are available per pay period. Hours per patient day and the percent of each level of skill mix can be electronically extracted from the timekeeping application. Turnover rates and reasons for turnover are tracked, and data about the incidence and types of staff injuries are also available.

Decision Support System

The VHA decision support system (DSS) is one of the organization's management systems. It integrates data from clinical and financial systems from both inpatient and outpatient care settings. At each VHA facility, a DSS database combines cost data; selected clinical data, such as resource utilization, patterns of care, patient outcomes; and workload captured at the production level, i.e., by case (encounter), day, utilization, and laboratory results levels. The DSS software includes a set of tools for reporting, analysis, budgeting, and modeling. Reporting capabilities allow for the production of a variety of reports, such as follow-up to a cohort of patients over time, analyses of patterns of care by day of inpatient stay, association of laboratory tests ordered with particular diagnoses, etc. The DSS is commercially available software that has been interfaced to VHA systems to allow the use of locally generated data, but it lies outside the scope of VistA (www.va.gov_VistA_monograph).[2]

Clinical Information System

The VHA clinical information system (CIS) was developed internally in the early 1980s; it was initially known as DHCP (Decentralized Hospital Computer Program). Over time, DHCP matured and evolved into the current system known as VistA (Veteran's Health Information Systems and Technology Architecture). Plans are already underway for the next generation of the VHA CIS VistA, which will be known as "HealtheVet." HealtheVet will be an evolution of VistA from what is currently a facility-centric system to a patient-centric system.[3] VistA includes the clinical applications of pharmacy, laboratory, inpatient, and outpatient care.

VA patient data are retrievable from anywhere in the national VA healthcare system. This system is totally interoperable, since every institution in the VHA system uses the same software. In addition, the VA shares electronic health information with the Department of Defense (DOD),[4] which is responsible for the healthcare of all United States active duty military personal. After stabilization in military hospitals, many wounded active duty military persons are transferred to VHA facilities for extended episodes of acute care and rehabilitation care. Sharing of electronic health information between these two agencies ensures the availability of all vital health information and supports continuity of care.

Three award winning features of VistA include the VA electronic medical record called the Computerized Patient Record System (CPRS), VistA Imaging, and Bar Code Medication Administration (BCMA).[5] A fourth widely recognized VHA IT application is the patient portal, MyHealtheVet.

Electronic Medical Records—Computerized Patient Record System

Since 1999, the facilities within the VHA healthcare system have been linked by a universal medical record network that allows authorized persons access to any patient's record, including, for example, nurses' notes, results of blood tests drawn at a clinic visit, or moving-picture film of a coronary angiogram performed in a cardiology lab. The CPRS is an "integrated, comprehensive, sophisticated suite of clinical applications that work together to create a longitudinal view of a veteran's EHR" (www.innovations.va.gov). The CPRS system is seen as having largely eliminated errors stemming from lost or incomplete records. Additionally, the system is attributed with having created a substantial increase in the quality of patient care delivered and the reform of the VA healthcare system with improved safety and efficiency.[6] CPRS supports entry of notes and orders, rules-based order checking, and results reporting. Allergies and/or adverse reactions are displayed on the cover sheet of a patient's computerized record. Another function of CPRS, which is not stored as an element in the clinical record, is the clinical reminder system, a clinical decision support tool offering evidence-based recommendations to providers.[7]

VistA Imaging

A second VistA feature integrated into CPRS is VistA Imaging, a system that communicates with radiology imaging systems, electrocardiograph (ECG) tracings, and other image-based information from other sources, such as pathology slides. VistA Imaging also includes the scanning of documents into the electronic medical record system.

Bar Code Medication Administration

VistA also includes BCMA, a wireless point-of-care technology with an integrated bar code scanner designed to address the potentially serious issue of inpatient medication errors through an electronic validation and documentation medication process. Each time a nurse scans the barcode on an ordered medication, BCMA validates whether the patient received the correct medication, in the correct dose, at the correct scheduled time, and electronically documents the medication as given. When correct parameters are not met or the patient has the potential for an adverse reaction to a medication, the BCMA system visually alerts the staff. A system of reports reminds the nurse when medications need to be administered or when clinicians need to assess the effectiveness of doses already administered. "New features include an IVP/IVPB tab (intravenous push and intravenous piggyback) and an IV admixture tab that incorporates additional check-and-balance mechanisms needed to further enhance patient safety. A link is provided to the CPRS order entry system for documenting the administration of verbal or phone-type STAT or NOW orders to streamline the workflow in busy ICU settings."[8] Evidence exists that the BCMA medication administration process reduces medication errors, improves the medication administration process and procedures, and enhances documentation of medication administration data.[9]

Patient Portal

My HealtheVet (MHV)[10] is the gateway to Veteran health benefits and services. It provides access to trusted health information, links to federal and VA benefits and resources, the Personal Health Journal, and the online VA prescription refill service. In the future, MHV registrants will be able to view appointments, co-payments due for prescriptions, and key portions of their VA medical records online. Registrants will be able to record and track personal health information, such as non-prescription medications, blood pressure, blood glucose, temperature, weight, or pain levels. My HealtheVet is a powerful tool to help veterans better understand and manage their health, improve access to services, enhance health literacy, and improve patient/provider communication.[11] My HealtheVet has been recognized as a tool of consumer empowerment.[12]

The VistA system is public domain "open source" software, available directly from the VA through the Freedom of Information Act. The act is a federal law that mandates that with few exceptions, all the records created and kept by federal agencies in the executive branch of government must be open for public inspection and copying. A demonstration of the CPRS software can be freely downloaded and supports trial use of CPRS from the perspective of a provider by entering orders, entering documentation, retrieving reports (and graphs), and viewing alerts and notifications that help with decision support.[13] VistA has been implemented internationally in a number of healthcare organizations in Finland, Germany, Egypt, and Nigeria.[14] Most recently, the state of West Virginia has selected VistA for implementation in all seven of the state-owned and operated hospitals.[15] Moreover, the Community Health Network of West Virginia has deployed a version of VistA in 80 clinics.[16]

Veterans Information Resource Center

As clinical data collected through VistA applications have been more and more recognized as valuable to health care and health systems research, the VA has developed a resource center to support database researchers. The VA Information Resource Center (VIReC),[17] established in 1998, is a resource center of the Department of Veterans Affairs Health Services Research and Development Service. The mission of VIReC is to improve the quality of research using VA databases and information systems. Numerous national, geographic, and local facility data sources within the VA system allow researchers to address many areas of inquiry. VIReC staff includes experts on databases, database content, and informatics who provide knowledge to VA researchers about VA databases and data resources specific to research areas (www.virec.research. va.gov).[17]

The National Resource Directory

The National Resource Directory (NRD) resides outside the VHA IT systems but is a valuable resource for both active duty military and veterans. The NRD is an online resource for wounded, ill, and injured military service members, veterans, and their families. The NRD provides access to more than 11,000 services and resources at the national, state, and local levels that support recovery, rehabilitation, and community reintegration. The NRD is maintained by the Departments of Defense, Labor, and Veterans Affairs and links to federal and state government agencies, veterans service and benefit organizations, non-profit and community-based organizations; academic institutions, and professional associations that provide assistance to wounded warriors and their families."[18]

VHA Nursing Service

Leadership, guidance, and strategic direction on issues related to nursing practice and the VHA nursing workforce are provided by the centralized VHA Office of Nursing Services (ONS).[19] VHA nurses are recognized as dynamic, diverse, respected, and compassionate professionals. VA Nursing Service encompasses clinical practice, education, research, and administration. VHA nurses provide a continuum of care across primary, ambulatory, acute, geriatrics, and extended care settings for medical/surgical, psychiatric, intensive care, rehabilitation, spinal cord injury, geriatric, blind rehabilitation, and hospice patients. Excellence is valued as essential for quality healthcare for veterans.

In the current strategic plan of VA nursing service, data management to promote data-driven decision making is a key goal. Informatics and IT are also identified along with the need for state-of-the-art electronic tools that can contribute to improved quality of care.

Nursing service within the VHA has more than 66,000 employees, with a staffing mix of registered nurses, licensed practical and vocational nurses, and nursing assistants (see Table 12A-1). All nursing service employees use some applications of the VHA information.

Table 12A-1. VA Nursing Staff Mix Technology (IT) Systems

Registered Nurses	33,052
Certified Registered Nurse Anesthetists (CRNAs)	494
Nurse Practitioners (NPs)	4317
Clinical Nurse Specialists	672
Licensed Practical/Vocational Nurses	10,894
Nursing Assistants (NAs)	12,484

(Adapted from DVA Fact Sheet, April 2008)

VA Nursing Outcomes Database

The VA nursing service has a vision of being "recognized as a valued, essential producer of reliable and usable information for both clinical and administrative decision making."[20] This has led to the creation of the VA Nursing Outcomes Database (VANOD), which is a national database of "clinically relevant, nursing-sensitive quality indicators to identify trends and areas for improvement."[20] The goals of VANOD are to improve the quality and safety of veterans' care, support the strategic decision process, provide data for clinical and staffing decisions, and research the relationship between the nursing-sensitive indicators and patient and staff outcomes. Development of the VANOD database with totally electronic extraction of data elements has meant a process of transitioning from "free-text notes" to nationally standardized electronic documentation and a national standardized assessment tool with embedded clinical terms.

The VANOD database currently includes administrative indicators, annual nurse satisfaction survey information, an annual RN Practice Environment Survey, and information on nursing-sensitive indicators (the first identified is the prevalence of pressure ulcers). National standardized assessment templates for pressure ulcer risk and presence were released in October 2007. The templates examine 15 indicators that address nursing process and patient outcomes. Data are now collected from 100% of discharges since the release date of the templates. In 2008, 23% of patients admitted to VHA hospitals were identified as at risk for skin breakdown.[21] Available patient data related to pressure ulcers include the Braden Scale score, the patient's risk, the actual presence of a pressure ulcer, and the clinical observations as documented in progress notes.

Additional clinical issues to be addressed within VANOD include: fall risk assessment and falls, the use of restraints and strategies to avoid restraint use, dysphagia screening, heart failure education, counseling regarding the use of tobacco, pain management, and failure to rescue. As VANOD matures, it is seen as providing support for the strategic goals of VA Nursing Service.

Standardized reports are developed from the VANOD data automatically extracted from VistA. Nurse executives have a dashboard, with a desktop icon for report access that can give both local and national data views. The VANOD database updates automatically as new data are entered. Further software development is projected for VANOD to achieve a greater level of granularity and precision for this database.[21]

The VANOD project is closely related to ANA's NDNQI program. Established in 1998 as part of ANA's Safety and Quality Initiative, the NDNQI is part of the National Center for Nursing Quality (NCNQ). The NDNQI program collects nursing-sensitive data affecting patient outcomes with the goals of providing comparative information to healthcare facilities and developing national data on the relationship between nurse staffing and patient outcomes. NDNQI reports on indicators, such as staff mix, patient falls, pain management, and nurse satisfaction on a unit-by-unit basis. VA facilities around the country contribute data to the NDNQI.

Summary

The use of IT to support electronic collection, storage, retrieval, and transfer of clinical and administrative data has the potential to greatly improve the quality and efficiency of healthcare. The success of IT implementation in the VHA healthcare system has been recognized as significantly enhancing the quality of patient care.[22]

Fortune recognized technology as the reason for transformation of VA hospitals to national leaders in efficiency and quality.[23] VistA has been identified as a building block for e-health networks nationwide.[16]

References

1. Department of Veterans Affairs Fact Sheet (2009). *Facts about the Department of Veterans Affairs.* Office of Public Affairs. www.va.gov. Accessed July 6, 2009.

2. *Decision Support* (2009). www.va.gov/VISTA_MONOGRAPH. Accessed July 16, 2009.

3. Center for Health Transformation (2009). www.healthtransformation.net/cs/veterans_administration_healthcare_system. Accessed July 7, 2009.

4. Government Accountability Office. *Electronic Health Records: DOD's and VA's Sharing of Information Could benefit from Improved Management.* January 2009. GAO-09-268.

5. Harvard University. *Innovations in Government Award* (2006). www.innovations.va.gov. Accessed July 10, 2009.

6. Kussman M. Medical Journal Praises VA Electronic Health Record. *Medical News Today.* www.medicalnewstoday.com. Accessed July 6, 2009.

7. Department of Veterans Affairs (August 25, 2006.) *VHA HANDBOOK 1907.01.* Washington, DC. Accessed July 8, 2009.

8. Johnson C, Carlson R, Tucker C, Willett C. (2007) *J Healthc Inform Manage.* 2007;16(1):46-51.

9. Bates D, Leape L, Shabot M. Reducing the frequency of errors in medicine using information technology. *J Am Med Inform Assoc.* 2001;8(4):299-308.

10. MyHeantheVet. (2009). www.myhealth.va.gov. Accessed July 7, 2009.

11. Nazi K. My HealtheVet: Personal Health Record. *20th National Conference on Chronic Care Disease Prevention and Control.* February 2009.

12. VA's My HealtheVet Honored for "Consumer Empowerment" (2007). www.reuters.com. Accessed July 7, 2009.

13. CPRS Demo. www1. va.gov/cprsdemo/. Accessed July 6, 2009.

14. Department of Veterans Affairs. (2004) News Release. *Use of VA's Electronic Health Records Expanding.* Office of Public Affairs. www.va.gov/opa/pressrel. Accessed July 10, 2009.

15. Groen P. (2007) *West Virginia 'Open for Business' to VistA.* www. linexmednews.com. Accessed July 15, 2009.

16. Brewin B. (2009) *VA's Health Record System Cited as Model for a National Network.* NEXTGOV. www.nextgov.com. Accessed July 6, 2009.

17. VIReC. (2009). www.virec.research.va.gov. Downloaded on 7/16/2009. www.innovations.va.gov/innovations/page.cfm?pg=11. Accessed July 6, 2009.

18. National Resource Directory (2009). www.nationalresourcedirectory.gov. Accessed July 7, 2009.

19. Department of Veterans Affairs Fact Sheet (April, 2008) *Facts about VA Nursing Service.* Office of Public Affairs. vaww1.va.gov/nursing/ Accessed July 6, 2009.

20. Presley J, Bedecarre B. (2007) Navigating the VA Nursing Outcomes Database (VANOD) Indicators. www.vehu.med.va.gov/vehu/vehu2007. Accessed July 10, 2009.

21. Rick C. (2009) *Nursing Quality Databases* (VANOD). April 13, 2009. www.ingri/uploads/INQR/VANOD. Accesssed July 12, 2009.

22. Department of Veterans Affairs Press Release (2009). *Medical Journal Praises VA Electronic Health Record.* April. www1.va.gov/opa/pressrel. Accessed July 6, 2009.

23. Stires D. (2006) Technology has Transformed the VA. *Fortune.* May 11. www.cnnmoney.printthis.clickabilitiy.com. Accessed July 6, 2009.

Case Study 12B

Canadian Health Outcomes for
Better Information and Care (C-HOBIC)

By Kathryn J. Hannah, PhD, RN; and Peggy White, MN, BA, RN

Introduction

C-HOBIC

The Canadian Health Outcomes for Better Information and Care project (C-HOBIC) is introducing the collection of standardized clinical outcomes reflective of nursing practice in four sectors of the healthcare systems of participating provinces, with investment from Canada Health Infoway (CHI) Innovation and Adoption Program. CHI is a federally-funded, independent, not-for-profit organization and is the Canadian catalyst for collaborative change to accelerate the use of electronic health information systems and EHRs in Canada. CHI invests in a common, pan-Canadian framework of EHR systems in which best practices and successful projects in one region can be shared or replicated in another region.[1] C-HOBIC is the first nursing project to be funded by CHI.

The Canadian Nurses Association (CNA) is the sponsor of the C-HOBIC project. CNA is a federation of 11 provincial and territorial registered nurses associations, representing more than 133,714 Canadian registered nurses.[2] As the national professional voice for registered nurses in Canada, CNA supports nurses in their practice by advocating for healthy public policy and a high quality, publicly funded, not-for-profit health system. In Canada, as in many other countries, most clinical care information is not structured, collected, or aggregated; it is available only in the individual written record. CNA's position is that it is essential to good health system administration and evaluation that the clinical care information of all members of the multidisciplinary team be collected in an integrated standardized terminology.[3] Project deliverables of C-HOBIC are to:

- Standardize assessment and documentation of patient-centered outcomes by nurses in the participating provinces.
- Capture nurse-sensitive, patient-centered, clinical outcomes data across four sectors (acute care, complex continuing care, long-term care, and home care) of the health system.
- Standardize the language concepts used by C-HOBIC to the standardized clinical reference terminology of nursing—International Classification for Nursing Practice (ICNP®).
- Store the captured and standardized data in relevant secure jurisdictional data repositories/databases in preparation for entry into provincial EHRs.
- Foster EHR adoption by nurses in participating provinces by providing content in the EHR that is of use in nursing practice.

C-HOBIC is working with three provincial partners to implement the electronic collection of evidence-based, nursing-sensitive, patient-centered outcomes, as well as ensuring that nurses have access to this information to inform their practice. The provinces participating in C-HOBIC are Ontario, Manitoba, and Saskatchewan. An additional province, Prince Edward Island, is participating in the education and preparation of nurses regarding C-HOBIC, its measurement instruments, standardized clinical terminology, and documentation.

The C-HOBIC outcome measures can be referred to as "indicator outcomes." As people move through the healthcare system, it is important for them to know that their symptoms are being managed, their function is being maintained/improved, and that they are being adequately prepared for discharge. The use of standardized measurement instruments to collect this information allows for improved communication among the healthcare team regarding patients' clinical status. Standardized measurement instruments allow for the same information to be collected longitudinally, and collection of health outcomes supports the continuity of information across the healthcare system. This is essential within an integrated healthcare system.

C-HOBIC Methodology

There are valid and reliable measures that provide the rationale for the collection of the C-HOBIC concepts. In Canada, many sectors of the healthcare system have or are implementing the collection of the interRAI series of measures (see Table 12B-1).[4] With the focus of introducing standardization and in the spirit of not adding burden to nurses' workload, components of the interRAI instruments were utilized to collect information about functional status, continence, symptoms (pain, fatigue, dypnea), falls, and pressure ulcers. A numeric rating scale of 1-10 was used to collect information about the frequency and intensity of pain for acute care settings. A scale was developed by the Ontario team for collecting information on nausea. Therapeutic self-care was assessed with an instrument developed by Doran and Sidani.[5] Therapeutic self-care addresses patients' ability to manage their care, either on their own or with supports, once they transition from the hospital to home and once home care services are no longer provided.

The concepts are assessed by nurses on admission and discharge in acute care and quarterly, and if condition changes in other sectors of the healthcare system.

C-HOBIC introduces standardized questions that are embedded into existing assessments. This allows for coding of the information. Through the collection of the same quantitative information at different points in time, nurses can begin to see the outcomes of their practice. Is a patient's pain improving? Has his or her function improved during the stay? This approach to the collection of standardized information allows for the outcomes information to be aggregated to support benchmarking related to nursing practice and provides valuable information for research to advance nursing practice regarding practices that lead to improved outcomes.

Rationale

A significant portion of nursing documentation is in a narrative form, with descriptions of patients presented a qualitative rather than numeric approach.[6] The introduction of a standardized assessment instrument with a quantitative format that allows for coding is a shift for a profession that tends to use a qualitative narrative format to describe patients' conditions. Narrative documentation limits our ability to see improvements in patients' conditions over time. Standardized information allows nurses to monitor trends in patient outcomes over time and allows for reflective practice through access to standardized clinical information that is outcomes-focused.

In many cases, nurses complete voluminous assessments of patients on admission to healthcare organizations, which is then filed away in the paper health record and often never utilized again. The introduction of standardized evidence-based assessments to produce standardized clinical information requires a refocus on the value of the admission assessments and how this information should inform practice. Additionally, a standardized discharge assessment is new for many sectors of the healthcare system. By assessing the same standardized information on admission and then again on discharge, nurses are able to see whether patients improve as a result of care.

Background

C-HOBIC builds and expands on work that was conducted in the province of Ontario as part of the Nursing and Health Outcomes Project (now know as Health Outcomes for Better Information and Care). This project, funded by the Ministry of Health and Long-Term Care, was developed to fill a critical information gap and make the contribution of nurses visible through the provincewide, standardized collection of evidence-based nursing-sensitive outcomes. Nursing-sensitive outcomes were defined as those that are relevant to nursing, based on nurses' domain and scope of practice and for which there is empirical evidence linking nursing inputs and/or interventions to the health outcome.[7] The evidence-based outcomes for collection are organized into five categories:

- Functional status
- Continence
- Therapeutic self-care (readiness for discharge)
- Symptom management: pain, nausea, fatigue, dyspnea
- Safety outcomes: falls, pressure ulcers[8]

Table 12B-1. InterRAI Series of Measures

Concept	Measurement Instrument
Functional status	interRAI
Continence	interRAI
Therapeutic self-care	Doran & Sidani tool
Pain - Frequency	interRAI
Pain – Intensity	0-10 numeric
Fatigue	interRAI
Dyspena	interRAI
Nausea	MOH scale
Falls	interRAI
Pressure ulcers	interRAI

Each component of this suite of clinical outcomes has a concept definition, a valid and reliable measurement instrument, and empirical evidence linking to some aspect of nursing (inputs and/or interventions).[9] Furthermore, they can be collected using a standardized tool across all sectors of the healthcare system.

In Ontario, as part of background work, demonstration projects were conducted to assess the feasibility, utility, quality, and costs associated with the collection of this standardized suite. This work supported the value of collecting this information.[10] Nurses reported that the measures made sense clinically (construct validity) and that the measures were reflective of the quality of care (content validity). They commented on the "value added" component of having this information available to them. Furthermore, these measures are dimensions of patients' health status that nurses assess every day in their practice. The difference is that the information is now being assessed in a standardized way and therefore supports comparison at selected points in time across settings and allows for abstraction onto databases. While these measures are not comprehensive of all nursing care, they are robust and sensitive to change and provide nurses with valuable information about the health status of people for whom they provide care.

Changing Clinical Practice

Engaging Nurses in the Use of Standardized Information – Impact on Workflow

The collection of standardized information at different points in time provides valuable information for nurses to examine aspects of their practice. The concept of therapeutic self-care is a new way of thinking for nurses. C-HOBIC introduces a 12-item instrument for assessment of therapeutic self-care that requires nurses to assess a patient's knowledge regarding his or her illness, symptoms, and their treatments.[5] Therapeutic self-care is not routinely assessed in healthcare organizations. With shorter lengths of stay, there is an increased focus on preparing patients for discharge. A standardized assessment on admission allows nurses to determine the areas on which to focus in preparation for discharge. There is an opportunity to improve nurses' understanding of their role and the role of the healthcare team in preparing patients for discharge through the introduction of a standardized assessment that is available to all clinicians.

C-HOBIC is presenting a change in practice standards for nursing with the introduction of standardized clinical terminology into nursing assessments that generate clinical outcomes information. It provides information for clinical practice that supports decision support at the point of care to compel a new way of thinking from work that is task-focused to practice that is outcomes-focused. Nurses will embrace change but only when they see the benefit to people for whom they provide care. To date, nurses have not had information available to them in a format that allows them to see whether a patient's status is changing as a result of the care that is provided. As part of C-HOBIC, nurses are provided with the standardized assessment instrument and also education about how to use this information in evaluating the effect of their interventions on patient outcomes. C-HOBIC makes information available to nurse managers and executives to use in examining the quality of care in their unit or organization. This information will allow them to benchmark their unit's or organization's outcomes to similar units and develop best practices based on information related to nursing practice, for example, management of fatigue and preparing patients for discharge.

In addition to collecting standardized information, the C-HOBIC team is working with the provincial partners to make this information available to nurses to use in clinical care. The original objective was to make sure the information was available in real time; however, through the implementation process, it became apparent that this was not achievable in all sectors in all provinces. While this still remains the ultimate objective, in the short-term, the goal is to provide the information to nurses as a paper-based report to use in comparing changes in the outcomes throughout the course of stay. As provincial EHRs are developed, these measures will be included, and the information will then be available to nurses in real time across the healthcare continuum.

Mapping to ICNP®

CNA recognizes the need for a single clinical terminology with the capacity to represent patient health data and the clinical practice of nursing. To support this, CNA endorsed the adoption of the International Classification of Nursing Practice.® The goals of ICNP are to:

a) Serve as a major force to articulate nursing's contribution to health and healthcare globally; and
b) Promote harmonization with other widely used classifications and the work of standardization groups in health and nursing.[11]

ICNP is a compositional terminology for nursing practice that facilitates the development and use of cross-mapping among local terms and existing terminologies. It consists of the following elements: nursing phenomena, nursing actions, and nursing outcomes. Essentially, the components of the ICNP are the elements of nursing practice: what nurses do relative to certain human needs to produce certain results. As such, it provides the critical data management capability for documenting nursing practice and developing a knowledge-based understanding of the work of nursing in the context of global healthcare. ICNP offers an approach for coding nursing information that will support interoperability, consistency, and comparability of clinical information that is reflective of nursing practice across the healthcare system.

One component of the Infoway investment funding for C-HOBIC supported mapping the C-HOBIC concepts to ICNP. A consultant with expertise in ICNP was recruited to achieve the mapping. This involved an analysis of the C-HOBIC concepts with a review of the definition, conceptual meaning, and measurement scales.[12] Subsequent to this work, a national forum was held to solicit feedback and foster consensus among the C-HOBIC partners, nurse educators, nursing informatics experts, and nurse researchers from across Canada. ICNP representatives also participated in this forum. Fifty-eight HOBIC concepts were matched and validated as C-HOBIC terms at the forum, while 13 HOBIC concepts were partially mapped and required a new term for completion as C-HOBIC terms. We identified 24 new C-HOBIC concepts and submitted these for inclusion in ICNP. One HOBIC concept could not be mapped to ICNP ("activity did not occur").[13] The outcome of this work resulted in 96 terms being mapped to ICNP and is the basis of the standardized nursing data used in the C-HOBIC project.[13] In addition, we developed a Canadian-specific ICNP catalogue in support of the C-HOBIC project.

This effort enables information to be abstracted into relevant secure jurisdictional EHRs, data repositories, or databases and made available to nurses for use in patient care across the healthcare system.

SNOMED Clinical Terms

In Canada, Canada Health Infoway has adopted the Systematized Nomenclature of Medicine-Clinical Terms (SNOMED CT) as the terminology of choice for the pan-Canadian EHR. The adoption of SNOMED CT is being recommended for the interoperable EHR (iEHR) in Canada. SNOMED CT is a comprehensive clinical terminology that provides a common language that enables a consistent way of indexing, storing, retrieving, and aggregating clinical data within the healthcare system. A recent memorandum of understanding has been created between the International Health Terminologies Standards Development Organization (IHTSDO) (the holders of the intellectual property of SNOMED CT) and the International Council of Nurses (ICN) to review and design cross-referencing and mapping opportunities. The SNOMED CT structure allows for the convergence of nursing content from standardized nursing language sources. Nursing concepts with similar meaning can be placed within the same hierarchies. Frequently, nursing concepts become synonyms of existing

SNOMED CT concepts. Efforts to cross-map terminologies will support clinical decision making, data mining, benchmarking, and comparisons of nursing data across organizations; various healthcare sectors; and even countries. The report, "Mapping Canadian Clinical Outcomes in ICNP,"[13] allows for future mapping of the C-HOBIC concepts to SNOMED CT to provide for inclusion of standardized clinical outcomes information in provincial EHRs in Canada for nurses to use in practice across the continuum of care.

Educating Academic Leaders

One of the key activities of C-HOBIC has been to connect with faculty in colleges and universities in the participating provinces regarding incorporating aspects of this initiative into nursing curricula. While academic leaders have recognized the benefit of C-HOBIC to the nursing workforce and our profession, the incorporation into nursing curricula has been challenging, as assessment of patients is taught in many different ways in nursing programs. The C-HOBIC team continues to work with faculty to develop a strategy and toolkit that will meet the needs of nursing faculty and advance the agenda of "outcomes-focused care." The future goal is for graduating nurses to enter the practice setting with knowledge about standardized clinical assessments, standardized clinical terminology, the benefits of standardized information in EHRs and its use in outcomes-focused care.

Creating a Database to Support Nursing's Research Agenda

As healthcare costs continue to rise, decision makers need to know whether investments in human resources and implementation of best practices translate into improved health for people in the system. There is a need for comprehensive, comparable, longitudinal, health system-wide information that focuses on the people who are receiving care.[14] As standardized clinical outcomes become available through the C-HOBIC jurisdictional databases or EHRs or from within individual healthcare organizations, the amount and range of research undertaken could accelerate because of the accessibility of the data and its reduced cost. The availability of the C-HOBIC outcomes data should increase the efficiency and reduce the cost of conducting research that requires clinical patient outcomes data to answer research questions related to the role of nursing in health outcomes.

Lessons Learned

Creating the "value link" of this information for nurses is essential. The C-HOBIC concepts are not new to nursing as this is information that nurses assess in their practice; however, the concept of standardization is new. It is important that as standardized information is introduced into practice settings, it is integrated into existing assessments and that nursing practice is focused on using standardized information that is available at different points in time across the continuum of care to evaluate whether nursing interventions are making a difference in patient outcomes.

Nursing leadership is essential. While the focus of C-HOBIC is on providing nurses with standardized information to use in care, the buy-in and support of the provincial nursing leadership has been key to the success of this project. Provincial leadership has played a key role in designing the approach for introducing the concept of standardized information and access to this information in each participating province. Nursing leadership will continue to play a role in developing a practice model to sustain this in the longer-term.

Summary—Toward a New Approach for Practice

Measuring and improving the quality of healthcare delivery is one of the critical challenges facing clinicians, researchers, decision-makers, and policy-makers. While many kinds of data are collected, the healthcare environment has a scarcity of the right type of information upon which to base decisions. Terminology coding systems assure the standardized assessment, recording, and encoding of clinical data for use in electronic record systems. These coded data are central to the efficient exchange of information in messages sent across documents, systems, and applications. While ICNP had been endorsed by the CNA, C-HOBIC is the first cross-jurisdictional use of ICNP in Canada. This initiative has provided the mapping to support the classification of specific nursing concepts in EHRs in Canada. This collection of standardized clinical outcomes provides a foundational piece for the EHR. The opportunity exists to link clinical documentation to practice guidelines, so that we can build knowledge for nurses and for other clinicians around which practices lead to improved outcomes. The C-HOBIC work is essential and will support the sharing of best practices across organizations and across sectors to improve the quality of care for people within the healthcare system.

Nurses are the largest group of contributors to patient care in all sectors across the health system, yet their practice is essentially invisible in databases. The consequences of this invisibility are that nursing practice may be attributed to the practice of other disciplines; and therefore, it is difficult to demonstrate nursing's professional accountability. C-HOBIC introduces standardized outcomes information reflective of nursing practice for inclusion in EHRs and databases. This information will begin to demonstrate the role of nursing in quality care. C-HOBIC is a foundational step in making nursing practice visible in databases and EHRs.

References

1. Canada Health Infoway. http://www.infoway-inforoute.ca/en/home/home.aspx. Accessed March 29, 2009.

2. Canadian Nurses Association. http://cna-aiic.ca/CNA/about/who/default_e.aspx. Accessed March 29, 2009.

3. Canadian Nurses Association. *Collecting Data to Reflect Nursing Impact: A Discussion Paper.* http://www.cna-aiic.ca/CNA/documents/pdf/publications/collct_data_e.pdf. Accessed March 28, 2009.

4. www.interRAI.org. Accessed April 3, 2009.

5. Doran D, Sidani S, Keatings M, Doidge D. An empirical test of the nursing role effectiveness model. *J Adv Nurs.* 2002;38(1):29-39.

6. Pringle DM, Nagle L. From the editor-in-chief: Leadership for the information age: The time for action is now. *Nurs Leadersh.* 2009;22(1):1-6.

7. Doran D, ed. Nursing-sensitive Outcomes: *The State of the Science.* Sudbury, MA: Jones & Bartlett Inc., 2003.

8. *Health Outcomes for Better Information and Care: HOBIC Measures.* http://www.health.gov.on.ca/english/providers/project/hobic/measures/measures_acute_care.html. Accessed April 10, 2009.

9. Doran D, Harrison M, Hirdes J, et al. *An Evaluation of the Feasibility of Instituting Data Collection on Nursing Sensitive Outcomes in Acute Care, Long-term Care, Complex Continuing Care and Home Care.* Final report submitted to the Ontario Ministry of Health and Long-Term Care. Toronto, Ontario; 2004.

10. *Health Outcomes for Better Information and Care.* Report to the Nursing and Health Outcomes Project. http://www.health.gov.on.ca/english/providers/project/nursing/phase_two/phase_two.html. Accessed March 28, 2009.

11. International Council of Nurses. *About ICNP®.* http://www.icn.ch/icnp_about.htm. Accessed March 29, 2009.

12. Hannah KJ, White PA, Nagle LM, Pringle DM. Standardizing nursing information in Canada for inclusion in electronic health records. *J Am Med Inform Assoc.* 2009;M2974v1. http://www.jamia.org/cgi/reprint/M2974v1. Accessed April 21, 2009.

13. Canadian Nurses Association. *Mapping Canadian Clinical Outcomes in ICNP.* http://www.cna-aiic.ca/c-hobic/documents/pdf/ICNP_Mapping_2008_e.pdf. Accessed April 8, 2009.

14. Hannah KJ. Transforming information: data management support of health care reorganization. *J Am Med Inform Assoc.* 1995;2(3):147-155.

## CHAPTER 13

International Standards to Support Better Information Management

By Nicholas R. Hardiker, PhD, RN; Suzanne Bakken, DNSc, RN, FAAN, FACMI; William T. F. Goossen, PhD, RN; Derek Hoy, MSc, BSc, and Anne Casey, MSc, RN, FRCN

Introduction

Several types of international standards are essential to support better information management—a key prerequisite of care that is safe, timely, effective, patient-centered, efficient, and equitable. Historically, much of standards work within nursing has focused on terminology development. Over recent years, substantial progress has been made in regards to other types of standards that ensure that nursing practice is both represented and supported.

Semantic interoperability is the goal:

- To exchange clinical information between different information systems, while preserving the meaning of the information.
- To interface accurately with decision support and other knowledge resources.[1,2]

A number of different standards are required to achieve semantic interoperability:

- Clinical standards, supporting evidence-based care from which required data elements can be derived
- Terminology standards, giving defined meanings to data
- Standardized information modeling, allowing the data to be used in electronic patient record systems and electronic messages
- Process and communication modeling, allowing exchange of information at the right time
- Technical standards, allowing the safe use of information and communication technology in healthcare.[3]

In this chapter, we focus on a subset of standards, which are international in scope and address both the terminology models and information models that are particularly relevant to nursing.

International Standards Development Organizations

International Organization for Standardization

International Organization for Standardization (ISO) is the largest developer and publisher of international standards. Its work is supported through an international network of 161 national standards institutes and a coordinating secretariat in Geneva, Switzerland. One ISO standard has been developed specifically for the domain of nursing, ISO18104 Integration of a Reference Terminology Model for Nursing. Other ISO standards that relate to concept representation, electronic record structure, and privacy and security are also of relevance to nursing.

European Committee for Standardization

European Committee for Standardization (CEN) provides a platform for the development of European Standards (ENs) and other technical specifications, including those for use in healthcare. ENs are also national standards in each of the member countries. The CEN network includes a large number of technical experts, as well as business federations, consumer and other societal interest organizations. CEN and ISO collaborate for standards harmonization in certain areas through a formal arrangement commonly known as the Vienna agreement.

Health Level 7 International

Health Level 7 International (HL7 International) is a standards development organization accredited by the American National Standards Institute, a constituent organization of ISO. HL7 International has as its mission to provide standards for the exchange, management, and integration of data that support clinical patient care and the management, delivery, and evaluation of healthcare services.[4] HL7 International has international affiliate members, and its focus increasingly is on the development of international standards.

International Health Terminology Standards Development Organisation

The International Health Terminology Standards Development Organisation (IHTSDO) is an international not-for-profit organization based in Denmark whose purpose is to develop, maintain, promote, and enable adoption and correct use of its terminology products. Its primary product is SNOMED CT, a large concept-oriented terminology, which integrates concepts from many nursing terminologies and classification systems.

International Council of Nurses

Founded more than a century ago, the International Council of Nurses (ICN) is a federation of national nurses' associations (NNAs) that represents nurses in more than 128 countries. The International Classification for Nursing Practice, a compositional terminology for nursing practice, is one of ICN's work programmes and was developed in the context of ICN's efforts to ensure quality nursing care for all, sound health policies globally, the advancement of nursing knowledge and the presence worldwide of a respected nursing profession with a competent and satisfied nursing workforce.

Logical Observation Identifiers, Names, and Codes

Logical Observation Identifiers, Names, and Codes (LOINC) was initiated in 1994 by the Regenstrief Institute and developed by Regenstrief and the LOINC committee. LOINC efforts initially focused on laboratory data but have broadened to other types of clinical observations including nursing goals, assessments, measurements, and document structures such as document names and sections.

International Medical Informatics Association Nursing Informatics Working Group

Although not a standards development organization itself, the International Medical Informatics Association Nursing Informatics Working Group (IMIA-NI) has a committee focused specifically on healthcare standards whose goals are to:

- Promulgate standards that enable:
  - Nursing knowledge use and development in the EHRs representation of nursing-related measurements
  - Development and communication of nursing knowledge and comparisons of nursing interventions and outcomes
  - Optimization of the communication of data, so coordination of the work processes of the care delivery team (nursing) is maximized for the delivery of quality care
  - Nursing decision support and evidence-based practice
- Establish, build, and participate in an international nursing informatics standards community.
- Provide a platform for international, asynchronous, collaborative working.
- Collaborate with IMIA Working Groups of relevance to health informatics standards to present a nursing perspective.

- Increase the number of nurses with expertise in health informatics standards.
- Encourage collaborative multi-professional working.
- Encourage the publication and dissemination of research and development materials related to healthcare informatics standards of relevance to nursing.
- Ensure that standards meet the needs and reflect reality for patients, families, communities, and societies.
- Establish a useful standards-related resource on the IMIA-NI Web site that is linked to relevant standards organizations.

Standard Terminologies

The International Classification for Nursing Practice

The International Classification for Nursing Practice (ICNP®) is a unified nursing language system. It is a compositional terminology for nursing practice that facilitates the development of and the cross-mapping among local terms and existing terminologies. ICNP Version 2.0 was released in July 2009. Further information on ICNP is presented in Section III Chapter 11 of this edition.

SNOMED® Clinical Terms

Systematized Nomenclature of Medicine-Clinical Terms (SNOMED CT) is considered the most comprehensive, multilingual clinical healthcare terminology in the world and integrates concepts from multiple nursing terminologies and classification systems. These include Clinical Care Classification, International Classification of Nursing Practice, North American Nursing Diagnosis Association Taxonomy, Nursing Interventions Classification, Nursing Outcomes Classification, Omaha System, and Perioperative Nursing Data Set. SNOMED CT and its related products are distributed through the IHTDSO.

Logical Observation Identifiers, Names, and Codes

Designed to support HL7 messaging, Logical Observation Identifiers, Names, and Codes (LOINC) initially focused on standardization of names of laboratory tests. It was subsequently expanded to include creation of universal identifiers for other types of clinical observation. The laboratory portion of the LOINC database contains identifiers, names, and codes for chemistry, haematology, serology, microbiology (including parasitology and virology), toxicology observations; as well as categories for drugs, cell counts, and antibiotic susceptibilities. Of particular relevance to this chapter, LOINC now includes assessment measures such as those related to vital signs, obstetric measurements, clinical assessment scales (e.g., Braden Scale), assessments from standardized nursing terminologies (e.g., Clinical Care Classification goal status), and research instruments.[5]

Terminology Models

Clinical terminologies are used to help structure information about the healthcare of individuals, groups, and communities and to support the analysis of data about health and healthcare. When implemented in electronic systems, standardised terminologies support data entry, display, messaging, retrieval for analysis, and links to decision support. They provide a means to represent patient states, behaviours, and concerns; clinical judgments and decisions; treatments, interventions, and outcomes in a standardised, structured format. In nursing, multiple terminologies exist. This is not unique to nursing; there are terminologies to cover every aspect of care provision, from intensive care to social services.

National and international standardisation efforts aim to ensure that the terminologies used in healthcare are well-formed, facilitate comparison, and most importantly, contribute to semantic interoperability. Both ISO and CEN have Technical Committees that are concerned with health informatics and that share the goal of semantic interoperability. Each Technical Committee has a working group that is specifically concerned with terminology and knowledge representation. As discussed previously, the activity of the two Technical Committees is harmonised through a mechanism known as the Vienna agreement.

International standardisation efforts by CEN and ISO related to semantic interoperability in healthcare have resulted in the publication of a number of standards that take the form of categorial structures. These are conceptual frameworks that support the development of terminologies according to shared models—models that help to determine relationships between terminologies, thus supporting maps or "cross-walks" between terminologies.

Several categorial structures have been published as standards (or are in development). These are applicable to a number of healthcare domains: anatomy, surgical procedures, laboratory measurements, medical devices, continuity of care, nursing, traditional medicine, and clinical findings. It is important to note that this work is not concerned with the content of terminologies *per se* but rather with their underlying structure (i.e., concept models). For example, the categorial structure for clinical findings allows an anatomical site to be associated with a finding or problem but does not include specific anatomical sites.[6]

In addition to categorial structures, a number of reports and specifications have been produced (or are in development). These cover a range of topics, such as methods for mapping between terminologies and classifications and criteria for evaluation of terminologies. One such document, originally produced by CEN and now being considered by ISO, considers the metadata required to describe clinical knowledge resources, such as clinical guidelines. The standards development organisations recognised the importance of providing this information in a standardised form to assist in judgments about the nature, status, and scientific credibility of such documents.

Two international terminology standards are of particular relevance to nursing: ISO 18104 Integration of a Reference Terminology Model for Nursing[7] and EN 13940 System of Concepts to Support Continuity of Care.[8]

Work on ISO 18104 was initiated by ICN and IMIA NI, building upon a European pre-standard (ENV 14032 Health Informatics—System of Concepts to Support Nursing). The aim of ISO 18104 was to establish a nursing reference terminology model that was consistent with other health terminology models to provide a more unified health reference model. ISO 18104 defines the concepts that are required to represent nursing diagnoses and nursing actions in terminologies and specifies the relationships among those concepts. It has several potential purposes including supporting the development, refinement, and maintenance of particular terminologies; facilitating comparisons among different terminology systems; and allowing system developers to specify the system of concepts required for internal organization of the system, for data warehouse management or middleware services. Evidence collated by ICN for a review of the standard five years after its publication indicated that it had been used to inform terminology development[9-11] and mapping among terminologies.[12,13] There was anecdotal evidence that the standard had been used in the implementation of nursing terminology in an electronic record system.

EN 13940 recognises that continuity of care depends on the effective transfer of information about the healthcare provided to an individual (i.e., "Subject of Care") between the different parties involved in the process and within a framework of ethical, professional, and legal rules. The standard defines concepts related to continuity to help ensure a common understanding across national, cultural, and professional boundaries. Part 2 of the standard covers the terminology for planning, delivery, and follow-up of those activities that form the healthcare process. Nursing has long been concerned with the process of care; in many healthcare systems nurses are key to continuity of care. Nurses have much to offer to this kind of standards development work, helping to ensure that standards reflect reality and address the problems of informatics in practice.

Information Models

To be useful, information standards must realise three benefits for those developing and implementing information systems: save effort through re-use; improve the quality of system con-

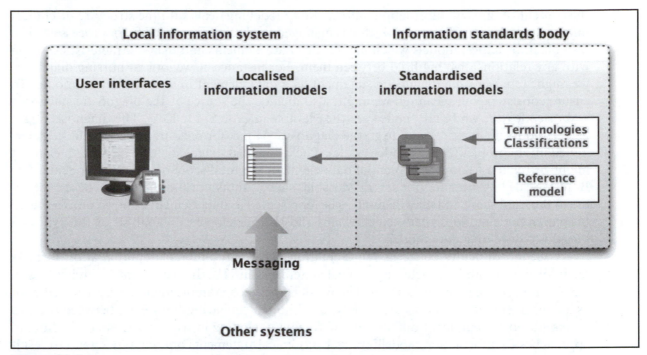

Figure 13-1. *Information Models and Other Information Standards*

tent; and enable interoperability between systems. Against these benefits are the risks that standardised models will not be flexible enough for local needs, or be too difficult or expensive to develop to a sufficient scale to cover the complex domain of healthcare.

Various groups have developed standardised information models, and we describe the key international projects next. The general intent can be summarised in Figure 13-1. Information standards bodies exist as government agencies in many countries, while other countries have nongovernmental bodies, or even large commercial providers offering de facto standards. The standardised models offered by these bodies can have 'terminology bindings' included in the model, which will offer selected terms from a standardised source, for example, SNOMED CT. These models should be developed based on expert input, ensuring they are of a sufficient quality.

This raises a key issue for the nursing professions—the development of high-quality, evidence-based, standardised clinical content is clearly not a technical issue. For this reason, these models are likely to be developed in collaboration with professional groups of expert practitioners, researchers, and educators, and they may even be owned, maintained, and distributed by professional bodies. The content would then be aligned with technical standards by information standards bodies, working in a partnership role. These standardised models must then be customisable to local needs, while carrying over the underlying standardised components to ensure consistency within the local system and interoperability across other systems, for example, by messaging.

The remainder of the chapter looks at work that aims to develop generic standardised clinical information models, i.e., detailed clinical models, and a range of technical standards that might implement those models.

Detailed Clinical Models

In applying technical standards in nursing, developers of health IT, including EHRs, face major difficulties. One difficulty concerns knowledge. Clinicians have knowledge of healthcare but may lack knowledge of health IT; conversely health IT developers have knowledge of IT but may lack knowledge of healthcare. It is widely believed that information modelling might help to bridge this gap. In contrast to terminology modelling, which as we have seen deals with the content of clinical information, information modelling deals with the structure of clinical information and the context in which it is managed (including associated work processes). The result is information models which include key data elements and their characteristics, along with any relationships that hold between them. For instance, if we look at nursing diagnosis, we might represent the diagnostic statement as a data element in an information model. To ensure consistency in meaning, we might also include the source of the diagnostic statement and its code (e.g., an ICNP® code - see the example in Case Study 13A). The diagnosis might be derived from an assessment (e.g., the diagnosis "At risk for pressure ulcer" might be determined after completing the Braden Scale). The associated diagnostic statement data element might be related to another potential data element, the total score of the Braden Scale. The Braden Scale has measures for several variables such as moisture and shearing. These contribute to the total score and may themselves be represented as data elements, and so on. To bridge the gap in understanding between clinicians and HIT developers, an analysis of this type can be used to develop a data model.

A second difficulty concerns representation. There are different representation formats for information models, including clinical statements in HL7 International or archetypes in CEN and ISO—see the next section. The Braden Scale, for example might be represented both as a clinical statement and as an archetype. Although similarities may exist between the two representations, significant differences will remain, including in style and format. Traditional approaches to information modelling, such as clinical statements or archetypes, tend to result in complex schemata comprising hundreds of components. However use of a simpler generic schema, as in a relatively recent initiative called Detailed Clinical Models (DCM), can result in greater efficiency in use and greater flexibility in adapting to the changing information needs of healthcare.[14] Just as the information models previously described seek to bridge a gap in understanding, DCMs seek to bridge the technology gap arising from the use of different information models.[15,16]

Within the HL7 community, several DCMs have been developed and are awaiting approval, including vital signs and assessment scales, such as the Braden Scale, Glasgow Coma Scale, Barthel Index, and Apgar Score.[17] An emerging work item within ISO seeks to focus development methodologies and quality criteria for DCM. Quality criteria fall into four main areas:

- Involving stakeholders, including clinicians, in DCM development and endorsement
- Modelling, including transformation rules (e.g., from clinical statement to archetype)
- Meta-data, including authorship, purpose, evidence, interpretation, etc.
- Storage, maintenance, and retrieval[18]

HL7

At the heart of HL7 International development is the Reference Information Model (HL7 RIM). HL7 RIM is a generic, non-discipline specific, object-oriented information model of patient care (including the providers, institutions, and activities involved).[4] In common with other information models, HL7 RIM represents data classes relevant to healthcare and the relationships that might hold between such classes.

At the top level, HL7 RIM distinguishes between six main classes: entity, role, participation, act, act-relationship, and role-link as shown in Figure 13-2. These classes may be interpreted as:

An *entity* (e.g., person) plays a *role* (e.g., patient, employee) in which he/she *participates* in an act (e.g., observation).

An act may be part of a complex of acts, for example systolic blood pressure observation and diastolic blood pressure observation might be part of blood pressure observation. Likewise, a role can be related to another role. Therefore, the HL7 RIM backbone also contains two relational classes: act_relationship and role_link.

Figure 13-2 is a simplified representation drawn from the HL7 Version 3 Standard: Reference Information Model, Version 2.26 (2009). The complete HL7 RIM extends this backbone with domain-independent subclasses. Each class has specific characteristics or attributes.

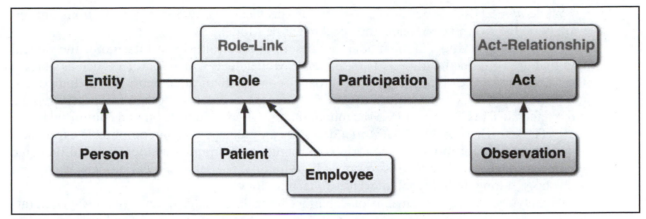

Figure 13-2. *Major Classes in the HL7 RIM. Source: HL7 International Version 3 Standard.*

Attributes are inherited from superclass to subclass. Subclasses refine superclasses with at least one additional attribute. Classes are related via relationships.

The HL7 RIM can be used to derive domain-specific models. From these, specific message information models can be derived, for instance to transfer patient information from one institution to the other. This can be achieved using Care Provision messages for referral and discharge. The core of these Care Provision messages is the Care Record message, which contains a structure in which any kind of clinical information; including nursing assessments, diagnoses, goals, interventions, and outcomes, can be included. For instance, a 20 question assessment may require 20 HL7 Observation classes (one per finding), with perhaps an additional Observation for a conclusion. HL7 International calls the resulting structure a Clinical Statement Pattern. One structure of particular interest is the Care Plan. There are currently many different messages for many different purposes. This is not always the best way to exchange information because the data within the messages may need to be stored in different areas (fields) of the EHR system. An alternative is to use the HL7 v3 Clinical Document Architecture (CDA).

The CDA builds upon the same HL7 Reference Information Model and includes the same Clinical Statement structure.[4] The CDA consists of three levels:
1. Sender, receiver, and patient identification
2. Structure of a document, e.g., different sections
3. Clinical information

The CDA presents a more complete (and human readable) picture, along with contextual information.

The HL7/LOINC Clinical Document Ontology[19] was developed to support the naming of clinical documents in a manner that facilitates the sharing of documents across institutions and the organization of documents within a particular institution. Document names are represented using the axes of the Clinical LOINC semantic model and include a specification of subject matter domain (e.g., cardiology), type of service (e.g., evaluation and management), setting (e.g., inpatient), and role (e.g., nurse). A recent evaluation of the document ontology that uses a sample of document names inclusive of nursing documents from Columbia University Medical Center indicated that 98.5% of the document names could be fully represented (the proportion of unique representations was 39.4%,[20] indicating that several document names in the sample mapped to the same standard representation).

openEHR

The entity, *open*EHR is an international not-for-profit foundation that develops open specifications, open-source software, and knowledge resources; engages in clinical implementation projects; participates in international standards development; and supports health informatics education.[21]

While *open*EHR has developed a range of specifications, two key specifications are relevant here: the Reference Model, and the Archetype Model.

The Reference Model is the model that describes the health record itself, not the clinical data that are contained within it. The Reference Model deals with containers such as Folders and Compositions. Compositions are a broader concept than documents but include documents. Examples of Compositions are an ECG report, a progress note, a laboratory report, and a referral. The Composition is the minimum unit of communication and committal to the EHR. The *open*EHR Archetype Model describes an archetype as "a computable expression of a domain content model in the form of structured constraint statements, based on some reference model."[22,23] The goal is to create high-quality, re-usable clinical models of content and process, along with formal interfaces to terminology.

Archetypes are seen as a means of defining clinical knowledge in an explicit way, separating it out from the system software that uses it. This has dual benefits of enhancing clinical ownership and making system development and maintenance easier.

An *open*EHR template is "a directly, locally usable definition which composes archetypes into a larger structure logically corresponding to a screen form." Templates have an important role in grouping and refining archetypes for specific local applications.

*open*EHR archetypes are sometimes described as "maximal datasets," meaning that, for example, a blood pressure archetype will have a formal description of anything that might reasonably be required to describe a blood pressure recording across many clinical or laboratory settings. This means that the archetype will be too large for most uses. The *open*EHR template is used to constrain or "switch off" detail that is not required for a particular application. Templates can therefore be developed based on the same archetypes but be different in the data items they contain (while being consistent in the items they share). This means that clinical consensus at the implementation level (template level) will be required if interoperability is to be ensured, for example, in messaging.

The *open*EHR framework forms the basis of ISO's EHR communication standard, ISO 13606.[24]

Summary

As we have shown in this chapter, there have been significant efforts to date and movement forward from the development of international standard terminologies to other standards that seek to support semantic interoperability. It is important that nursing continues to inform wider standards development and continues to be informed by standards so that we do not revert to silo-based information management.

ISO has recognised that clinical stakeholder participation "helps ensure the quality of clinical aspects of international health informatics standards."[25] The ISO Health Informatics Committee is encouraging national member bodies to consider how they can facilitate engagement of clinical stakeholders in standards activity—not an easy task when many of the standards are highly technical. Clinical professional organizations, such as nursing associations may lack awareness of health informatics standards and their relevance. Or they may lack the capacity to participate or be unsure about routes by which they can contribute.[25] However, the International Council of Nurses (ICN) and the Nursing Informatics Special Interest Group of the International Medical Informatics Association (IMIA NI) have taken a leadership role by actively participating in a number of international health informatics standards initiatives.

Review of the utility of a standard is an essential part of the standards development life cycle. If a standard is no longer needed, it should be withdrawn; if it does not meet the requirements of the target groups for which it was developed, it should be revised. A major goal of the 2009 eHealth interoperability framework published by the European Union is to satisfy the real requirements of stakeholders in a timely manner.[26] This framework, along with the strategies developed by international standards development organisations, recognises the challenges associated with producing standards that remain responsive in rapidly changing environments. More emphasis is being placed on adopting or adapting at the international level those standards that have been developed to address real world problems at national or regional levels. However, there will always be a role for international standards activity if the basic goal of healthcare content standardisation—being able to communicate about patients across boundaries in a way that preserves meaning and supports safe and effective healthcare—is to be met.

References

1. Gibbons P, et al. *Coming to Terms: Scoping Interoperability for Health Care.* 2007, Health Level Seven: Ann Arbor.

2. Garde S, Knaup P, Hovenga E, Heard S. Towards semantic interoperability for electronic health records. *Methods Inf Med.* 2007;46(3):332-343.

3. Goossen WTF. Representing clinical information in EHR and message standards: analyzing, modelling, implementing. In: Peck C, Warren J, eds. *Health Informatics New Zealand (HINZ). Primary Care and Beyond: Building the e-Bridge to Integrated Care.* Health Informatics New Zealand (HINZ)/Health Informatics Society of Australia Ltd (HISA): Auckland/Brunswick East, 2006.

4. HL7. *Health Level 7.* http://www.hl7.org. Accessed April 15, 2009.

5. Matney S, Bakken S, Huff SM. Representing nursing assessments in clinical information systems using the logical observation identifiers, names, and codes database. *J Biomed Inform.* 2003;36(4-5):287-293.

6. ISO/DTS 22789. *Health Informatics—Conceptual framework for patient findings and problems in terminologies.* 2007. International Organization for Standardization: Geneva; 2007.

7. ISO 18104. *Health informatics—Integration of a reference terminology model for nursing.* 2003, International Organization for Standardization: Geneva.

8. EN 13940. *Health Informatics—System of concepts to support continuity of care.* 2006, European Committee for Standardisation (CEN): Brussels.

9. Bakken S, Warren JJ, Lundberg C, et al. An evaluation of the usefulness of two terminology models for integrating nursing diagnosis concepts into SNOMED clinical terms. *Int J Med Inform.* 2002;68(1-3):71-77.

10. Hardiker NR, Coenen A. Interpretation of an international terminology standard in the development of a logic-based compositional terminology. *Int J Med Inform.* 2007;76S2:S274-S280.

11. International Council of Nurses. *ICNP® Catalogue Guidelines.* http://www.icn.ch/icnp_catalogues.htm. Accessed April 21, 2009.

12. Goossen WTF. Cross-mapping between three terminologies with the international standard nursing reference terminology model. *Int J Nurs Terminol Classif.* 2006;17(4):153-164.

13. Matney S, DaDamio R, Couderc C, et al. Translation and integration of CCC nursing diagnoses into ICNP®. *J Am Med Inform Assoc.* 2008;15(6):791-793.

14. Johnson SB. Generic data modeling for clinical repositories. *J Am Med Inform Assoc.* 1996; 3:328-339.

15. Parker CG, Rocha RA, Campbell JR, et al. *Detailed Clinical Models for Sharable, Executable Guidelines.* In: Fieschi M, Coiera E, Yu-Chan J, eds. MEDINFO 2004: Proceedings of the 11th World Congress on Medical Informatics 2004, San Francisco: IOS Press, 2004,145-148.

16. Huff S, Rocha RA, Coyle JF, et al. *Integrating Detailed Clinical Models into Application Development Tools.* In: Fieschi M, Coiera E, Yu-Chan J, eds. MEDINFO 2004: Proceedings of the 11th World Congress on Medical Informatics 2004, San Francisco: IOS Press, 2004,1058-1062.

17. de Bel E. Ontwikkeling van een Elektronisch Patiëntendossier op basis van HL7 V3. *HL7 Magazine.* 2005.

18. Goossen WTF. Using detailed clinical models to bridge the gap between clinicians and HIT. In: de Clercq E et al, eds. *Collaborative Patient Centred eHealth. HIT@Healthcare 2008.* Brussels: IOS Press, 2008, 3-10.

19. LOINC Manual. http://loinc.org/downloads/files/LOINCManual.pdf. Accessed May 1, 2009.

20. Hyun S, Shapiro JS, Melton G, et al. Iterative evaluation of the Health Level 7—Logical observation identifiers names and codes clinical document ontology for representing clinical document names: a case report. *J Am Med Inform Assoc.* 2009;16(3):395-399.

21. OpenEHR. *OpenEHR.* 2008. http://www.openehr.org. Accessed July 8, 2008.

22. Beale T. *Archetypes: Constraint-based Domain Models for Futureproof Information Systems.* 2000. http://www.openehr.org/publications/archetypes/archetypes_beale_web_2000.pdf. Accessed January 13, 2008.

23. Beale T. Archetypes and the EHR. *Stud Health Technol Inform.* 2003;96: 238-244.

24. ISO 13606. *Health Informatics—Electronic health record communication, Part 2: Archetype Interchange Specification.* 2008, International Organization for Standardization: Geneva.

25. ISO/TR 11487. *Health Informatics—Clinical stakeholder participation in the work of ISO TC 215.* 2008, International Organization for Standardization: Geneva.

26. SA/CEN/ENTR/000/2007-20, *eHealth Mandate M/403 – Phase 1 Report.* 2009, NEN: Delft.

Case Study 13A

Application of iNMDS using ICNP®

By Bonnie L. Westra, PhD, RN, FAAN; William T.F. Goossen, PhD, RN;
Lynn M. Choromanski, MS, RN; Beverly J. Collins, MS, RN; Colleen M. Hart, MS, RN;
and Connie White Delaney, PhD, RN, FAAN, FACMI

Introduction—Overview of iNMDS

Core essential minimum data sets were conceived to be tools used by nursing to honor nursing's long-standing social contract with society worldwide. Keeping this social contract is dependent upon our ability to collect, analyze, and share data that empower nursing to meet the strong demands for adequate nursing staff and expertise for a rapidly growing, multicultural population, with many in need of chronic care. This social contract is dependent upon our ability to collect, analyze, and share data that empower nursing to be accountable for knowledge-based, safe, and cost-effective patient-centric nursing care. This ability related to data also empowers nursing to maximize the use of information and communication technologies, understand variations in practice, decrease duplication of effort, and increase access and safety of care.

Core essential minimum data sets were conceived to support contemporary nursing research leveraging formal and computerizable depictions of health-related phenomena, and defining data structures and standards to insure that nursing captures important clinical phenomena and the linkage of clinical observations and research findings across many care environments. Minimum data sets support knowledge management. Core essential minimum data sets are knowledge representations relevant to nursing that enumerate elements to describe patients, patient and family experiences in a nursing care system, and care resources.

The vision for the International Nursing Minimum Data Set (iNMDS) grew out of several national level core essential nursing data sets. One of the first contributions to core essential minimum data sets was the development of a Nursing Minimum Data Set (NMDS) for clinical care in the United States,[1] The USA NMDS is a description of the data that are essential for every healthcare event that involves nurses. These data include the problems of care, and the interventions used by nurses to address these problems, outcomes, and intensity of nursing care. The USA Nursing Management Minimum Data Set (NMMDS) complements the USA NMDS patient focus with the specific contextual covariates of patient outcomes derived from the setting in which the nursing care is delivered.

The iNMDS, cosponsored by the International Council of Nurses (ICN)[2] and the International Medical Informatics Association Nursing Informatics Special Interest Group (IMIA NI SIG),[3] is focused on describing nursing care around the world. These data can provide information to describe, compare, and examine nursing practice. Development of the iNMDS built on several national efforts, including the USA, Switzerland, Belgium, The Netherlands, Iceland, Canada, Australia, Portugal, and Thailand. It includes the core, essential, minimum data elements to be collected in the course for providing nursing care. The iNMDS (International Council of Nurses, 2004)[4] as a key data set will support:

- Describing the human phenomena, nursing interventions, care outcomes, and resource consumption related to nursing services.
- Improving the performance of healthcare systems and the nurses working within these systems worldwide.
- Enhancing the capacity of nursing and midwifery services.
- Addressing the nursing shortage, inadequate working conditions, poor distribution and inappropriate utilization of nursing personnel, and the challenges as well as opportunities of global technological innovations.
- Testing evidence-based practice improvements.
- Empowering the public internationally.

Meeting the objectives of the iNMDS builds on the work of the International Classification for Nursing Practice® (ICNP). The ICNP provides the terms for operationalizing the data elements of the iNMDS. ICNP catalogues describe subsets of terms focused on a particular patient problem, care need, etc.

ICNP Catalogue Development

An ICNP catalogue is the selection of a subset of ICNP terms useful for describing the care of a specified population with a particular health priority. A catalogue narrows the terms for documenting nursing care and can support consistency of documentation across settings and geographical locations. At the time we began creating a catalogue for nursing care of children with HIV/AIDS in developing countries, no formal process for catalogue development had been defined by the ICNP Programme. A nine-step process was used for catalogue development. Natural language or local terms for nursing diagnoses, outcomes and interventions (ND/O&Is) were identified and then mapped to the ICNP. These ND/O&I concepts were validated using international, national, and local standard nursing or medical care plans.

Since this work was completed, the ICNP Programme published a 10-step process (ICN, 2008).[5] The ICNP Programme suggests that catalogues be developed directly from the ICNP browser or book; however, as noted, we used natural language or local terms. Whereas the ICNP process focuses on a broader method of developing applications and tools for the identified population and health priority, our process included specificity for how to identify and select terms for a catalogue. This case study outlines the process for creating a catalogue for the care of children with HIV/AIDS.

A catalogue for the care of children with HIV/AIDS was developed using the process identified in the left column of Table 13A-1. The team selected HIV/AIDs care of pediatric patients (ages 1 – 12) in developing countries because this is one of the World Health Organization priorities. The focus of the catalogue was narrow enough to make it useful to nurses. A catalogue with a very broad focus may be too cumbersome to be useful. For example, the care for adults and adolescents is quite different in some aspects than care needed by children, and the care needed by children may be very different than that of infants. The health priority in this catalogue of HIV/AIDS care is narrow, as compared with the problem of immune deficiencies, which would encompass a large number of diseases with different nursing needs.

The process started with the selection of a conceptual framework which influenced the order in which ND/O&Is were chosen and coded. A conceptual model by Bindler and Ball[6] was selected and adapted to address the unique needs of the population of children in developing countries, shown in Figure 13A-1.

The conceptual framework guided selection of ND/O&Is by levels of care across the health spectrum, from health promotion to end-of-life care for a child with HIV/AIDS. In this framework, there are three recipients of nursing care identified (see outer perimeter of the pyramid): (1) the individual (the child), (2) the families or caregivers of the individual, and (3) the communities in which these individuals, families, and caregivers reside.

The nursing diagnoses, outcomes, and interventions identified for each level of care were the result of applying expert nursing knowledge in the care of the child with HIV/ AIDS. Natural language terms that might be found in a nursing care plan were assigned to one of the levels of the framework. Once terms were identified, the first iteration of the catalogue was compared with the literature on best practice in the care of this specific health priority. Multiple sources of best practices were used, including international, national, and local resources. Terms identified through this process were added to the catalogue. Some terms were not confirmed in the literature but were retained in the catalogue, as it was likely that the framework guiding the catalogue development was broader in focus than the resources used for confirmation of the items.

Next, the local or natural language terms were mapped to ICNP terms. Tools, which were available from the ICNP Programme at the time of this catalogue development, included an online browser of versions 1.0 and 1.1, a book with version 1.0, and an Excel version of ICNP 1.1 and 1.0. An example of the natural language terms, along with the mapped terms to ICNP for end-of-life care, is illustrated in Table 13A-2.

The first column represents the type of statement indicating whether the term is a diagnosis, outcome, or intervention. The second column includes the natural language we identified. The ICNP term includes the judgment and focus for the nursing diagnoses and outcomes and the action and target terms for the interventions. Corresponding columns contain the code for the terms. Comments were recorded including the lack of or incomplete representation of the term when there was no equivalent term in ICNP.

Next, mapping of natural language terms to the ICNP terms was a time-consuming and detailed process. The problems encountered in this step of the process related to semantics, absence of equivalent terms, and spelling differences.

Table 13A-1. Comparison of Two Processes for ICNP Catalogue Development

Our Process	ICNP Process
1. Select a target population and problem focus.	1. Identify the client category and health priority for the catalogue.
2. Review knowledge sources that focus on the population and problem area selected.	2. Document the significance for nursing of the selected health priority and client group.
3. Select, develop, or adapt a nursing conceptual framework to serve as a foundation for catalogue development.	3. Contact ICN to determine if other groups are already working with this health priority in order to establish networking with others and direction for your work.
4. Identify nursing diagnoses/outcomes and interventions (ND/O&Is) that address the problem focus.	4. Use the ICNP 7-Axis model browser, book, along with the guidelines for composing ICNP® statements to develop diagnosis, outcome, and intervention statements.
5. Validate the above identified ND/O&Is with knowledge sources (e.g., literature) that represent best nursing practice.	5. Identify evidence and literature that can help you find relevant nursing diagnosis, outcome, and intervention statements.
6. Map the natural language terms for ND/O&Is to the ICNP® language terms.	6. Develop supportive applications or documentation tools for the catalogue's client population and health condition.
7. Validate the ND/O&Is terms by nurse experts.	7. Test or validate the ICNP catalogue statements with specified client population and with nurse experts in the selected health priority.
8. Integrate the catalogue into nursing practice.	8. Add, delete, or revise the ICNP catalogue statements as necessary.
9. Establish quality control measures for evaluation of the catalogue and maintenance of the catalogue as needs change.	9. Work with ICN to develop a final copy of the ICNP catalogue after the draft catalogue has been submitted for evaluation and coding in ICNP.
	10. Assist ICN as appropriate in the dissemination of the ICNP catalogue.

Following the mapping process, validation of the catalogue by expert nurses as described in step seven (see Table 13A-1) of the process occurred. This step included inviting nurses who have expertise in caring for children, caring for HIV/AIDS patients, and nurses with experience in working in developing countries to comment on the catalogue. Next steps include development tools or applications to include in a catalogue to help nurses visualize how to incorporate the ICNP terms into practice. The final step is submission of the catalogue to the ICNP Programme and work with ICN to create the final copy that is maintained and disseminated through the ICNP Programme.

Evaluation of iNMDS

This section focuses on the establishment of quality control measures for evaluation of the ICNP catalogue and maintenance of the catalogue in the perspective of actual application of it for iNMDS data collection on nursing care for children with HIV/AIDS. As described in the first part of this case study, the iNMDS includes

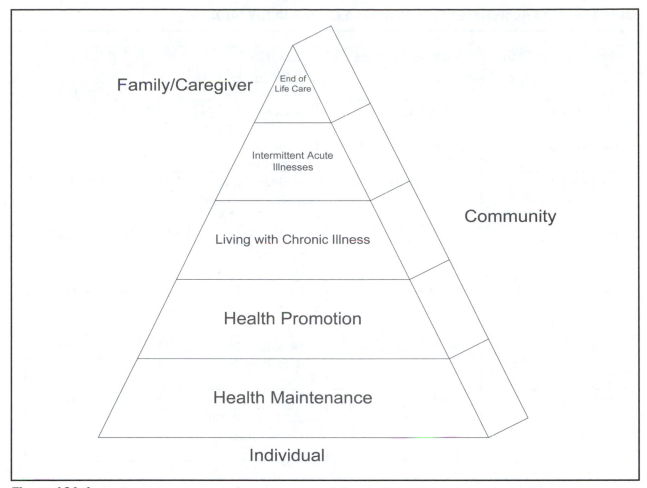

Figure 13A-1. *A Conceptual Framework for the Care of the Child with HIV/AIDS in Developing Countries*

data elements that pertain to the specific nature of nursing care on behalf of the diversity of patients and variation of nursing practice. The specific nursing data elements include the nursing diagnoses, interventions, and outcomes. Relevant data elements for children with HIV/AIDS have been described and mapped to ICNP. The next step is evaluation in order to establish the validity of the data elements and accuracy of the mapping. Further, we can evaluate the catalogue against the criteria for an iNMDS—whether it facilitates data collection and analysis of nursing care for children with HIV/AIDS.

Quality of the Catalogue

The catalogue for HIV/AIDS for children was selected for its clinical relevance, feasibility to map it to the ICNP, and the evidence to support the selection of terms. The next step suggested is to have the content validated by practice experts. A further step is to test the mapping against the nursing reference terminology model.[7] This approach is based on dissection along the different components of nursing diagnoses and interventions and is considered the gold standard for cross-mapping between terminologies.[8] However, the EN ISO 18104 standard currently does not have a similar reference terminology model for outcomes, which is one recommendation for the ongoing review. This approach can establish the quality of the semantic content.

Completeness of the Data Set

In addition to the specific nursing care data, additional data elements are included in the iNMDS, pertaining to the patient and his or her need for healthcare, along with data about location, service, and nursing workforce.[8] Other data suggested by Sermeus et al.[9] would include the intensity of nursing care, which is considered the fourth nursing variable (in addition to diagnoses, interventions, and outcomes).

In order to allow appropriate comparison of data across time, location, and settings, additional data about the data collection method are required.[10,11] Further, the iNMDS should always include the following

Table 13A-2. An Abbreviated Care Plan for a Child with HIV/AIDS

Statement Type	Natural Language	ICNP Terminology	ICNP Code
Problem	Pain	Actual pain	10000420_10013950
Outcome (Goal)	Reduce pain	Decreasing level of pain	10005616_10013950
Intervention	Provide pain relief	Provide pain management	10015935_10024799
Intervention	Provide palliative care	Provide palliating complex treatment regime	10015935_10013984_10022350
Problem	Fear of dying	Actual anxiety before death	10000420_10000483
Outcome (Goal)	Coping with fear of dying	Enhanced coping with anxiety before death	10014844_10000483
Intervention	Assess fear of dying	Assessing coping with anxiety before death	10002723_10000483
Intervention	Provide opportunity for child to express fears	Enhance communication of anxiety before death	10014828_10000483

characteristics about the data set: the start and stop dates of the iNMDS collection and the unit of measurement (type of client): e.g. individual patient/client, family, group, community. In particular the HIV/AIDS catalogue includes multiple types of clients; therefore, it is crucial to distinguish them. Practical details of the data set include the ISO country code, the responsible person and agency for iNMDS collection, contact information, and the medium of collection. Modern technology could allow Web-based collection in locations where this technology is available.

Criteria for Study Design and Methodology

Previously, appropriate data collection elements were described based on iNMDS.[8] The principles for catalogue development are similar to the principles for development of a study design:

1. Identify the specific study purpose(s).
2. Assure of the linkage between nursing diagnoses, interventions, and patient outcomes, which is established via the catalogue, but needs an equivalent in a database.
3. Develop a prospective design, which is timely to establish at this stage.
4. Assure that the ICNP-based dataset contains all iNMDS data items/variables, including codes, data types, values, etc. Currently, the Detailed Clinical Modeling (DCM) approach[12] can be recommended for this. (DCM is described elsewhere in this chapter.)
5. Allow for the local terminology to be the guide for mapping to ICNP; this was the core of the previous section and has been developed.
6. Use terminology from ICNP; this was described.
7. Select prioritized topics by ICN and/or WHO for nursing and midwifery; HIV/AIDS is selected because it is one of the priorities for international health and nursing care.

8. Show contribution of evidence-based nursing practice; the catalogue was developed employing evidence when available. The integration of iNMDS and ICNP will deliver data which can further be analyzed to develop new evidence.

9. Disseminate the results to the global community. This is a core procedure after completion of a project.

iNMDS Collection and Analysis for Nursing Care for Children with HIV/AIDS

If we are to evaluate the usefulness and effectiveness of nursing care for children with HIV/AIDS, using the iNMDS and ICNP the following approach is recommended:

1. Identify the purpose(s) of the nursing data collection. An initial purpose would be to determine frequencies of the identified nursing variables, i.e., the nursing diagnoses, interventions and outcomes. Future purposes might include the comparison of the effectiveness of different intervention approaches.

2. Specify each data element in such a way that evidence, data-item, terminology and coding, data type, and unit are represented and modeled. In the current catalogue development, the focus was on identification of relevant data and the mapping to ICNP® concepts and codes. However, a data model is necessary to achieve functionality. In particular, it is necessary for the linkage between diagnoses, interventions, and outcomes.[13] The DCM approach allows information modeling, which is useful for data entry design, e.g., via electronic patient records or Web forms, database design, and for application of different standards such as Health Level 7, version 3, archetypes and others.

3. Develop a plan for matching the purpose of the catalogue, method of data collection, and plan for evaluation. A number of statistical analyses can be performed on the data collected from the catalogue, e.g., intensity of nursing care or principal component maps,[9] patient outcomes,[14] or others such as described by Goossen.[15] It is important that the purpose of the data collection and the methods for analysis are developed in a consistent manner. In earlier discussions about the iNMDS design, the recommendation was made to principally employ prospective designs, which represent the best option for and is feasible for the iNMDS for children with HIV/AIDS.

4. Formalize the data collection, analysis, and dissemination methods. This includes record formatting; identifying the sample, collection period and data collection method, along with the aggregation of data into a workable data set by data cleaning; and then applying analytic techniques. Finally feedback and results of the analysis need to be disseminated in an effort to improve patient outcomes.

Summary

Since 1989, considerable work has gone into the development of the ICNP to provide a unified nursing language system. The granular level concepts of nursing diagnoses and interventions provide useful language for nurses to communicate patient needs, care provided, and outcomes achieved in working with populations on a global basis. The iNMDS framework provides a method for aggregating data to compare nursing care and the context of care for populations such as HIV/AIDS pediatric clients in developing countries. The example of catalogue development demonstrates a method for selecting a limited set of terms that are useful for documentation and improve the consistency in selection of terms. Catalogue development by itself, however, is not sufficient without validation and evaluation. In this case study, we provided an example of moving from catalogue development to validation of the catalogue, data collection, and then evaluation to demonstrate the effectiveness of nursing care for select populations.

References

1. Werley HH, Lang NM. *Identification of the Nursing Minimum Data Set.* New York: Springer publishing comp. Inc. 1988.

2. http://www.icn.ch. Accessed September 20, 2009.

3. http://www.imiani.org. Accessed September 20, 2009.

4. http://www.icn.ch/icnpbulletin.htm. Accessed September 20, 2009.

5. International Council of Nurses (ICN). (2008) Guidelines for INCP® Catalogue Development. http://www.icn.ch/icnp_Catalogue_Develp.pdf. Accessed March 31, 2009.

6. Bindler RC, Ball JW. The Bindler Ball Healthcare Model: A New Paradigm for Health Promotion. *Pediatrics.* 2007:33,121-126.

7. EN ISO 18104, 2003 – Health informatics: Integration of a reference terminology model for nursing. Under review.

8. Goossen W. Cross-mapping between three terminologies with the International Standard Nursing Reference Terminology Model. *Int J Nurs Terminol Classif.* 2006;17 (3-4): 139-150.

9. Sermeus W, Delesie L, Van den Heede K, Diya L, Lesaffre E. (2008) Measuring the intensity of nursing care: making use of the Belgian Nursing Minimum Data Set. *Int J Nurs Stud.* 2008;45(7):1011-1021.

10. Goossen W, Delaney C, Coenen A. (2005). International Nursing Minimum Data Set (iNMDS). [Paper] 5th European Conference of ACENDIO Slovenia, pp.31-34.

11. Goossen W, Delaney C, Coenen A, Saba V, Park H, Casey A, Oyri K. Towards the International Nursing Minimum Data Set. In *Nursing and Informatics for the 21ˢᵗ Century: An International Look at Practice, Trends and the Future, First Edition.* Weaver C, Delaney C, Weber P, Carr R (eds). Chicago: Healthcare Information and Management Systems Society, 2006.

12. Goossen WTF (2008). Using Detailed Clinical Models to Bridge the Gap Between Clinicians and HIT. In: De Clercq E, De Moor G, Bellon J, Foulon M, van der Lei J, (eds). Collaborative Patient Centered eHealth. Proceedings of the HIT@ Healthcare 2008 conference, Brussels, 10 October 2008. Amsterdam: IOS press, 3-10.

13. Junger A, Berthou A, Delaney C. Modeling, the essential step to consolidate and integrate a national NMDS. *Stud Health Technol Inform.* 2004;107(Pt 1):521-524.

14. Van den Heede K, et al. Nurse staffing and patient outcomes in Belgian acute hospitals: Cross-sectional analysis of administrative data; *Int J Nurs Stud.* (2008). doi:10.1016/j.ijnurstu.2008.05.007.

15. Goossen WT. Statistical analysis of the nursing minimum data set for the Netherlands. *Int J Med Inf.* 2002;68(1-3):205-218.

Case Study 13B

Update of the NMMDS and Mapping to LOINC

By Bonnie L. Westra, PhD, RN, FAAN; Susan Matney, MSN, RN;
Amarnath Subramanian, MD, MS; Colleen M. Hart, MS, RN;
and Connie White Delaney, PhD, RN, FAAN, FACMI

Introduction

The Nursing Management Minimum Data Set (NMMDS) is a research-derived data set that was developed to capture useful, accurate, and reliable data for nurse managers and administrators.[1] It is specifically designed to contain the minimum essential data needed by nurse managers and administrators for decision making, resource management, and to improve patient care and outcomes.[2,3] The NMMDS v2005 is comprised of 18 data elements grouped into three higher order categories (environment, nurse resources, and financial resources). Each data element includes sub-elements as shown in Table 13B-1.

The NMMDS captures data representative of the context of patient/client care delivery at the unit level and in all types of healthcare settings.

Purpose of Minimum Data Sets

Minimum data sets in general are created to meet information needs and designed to meet the needs of multiple users for diverse and many purposes. To address specificity, minimum data sets are thus dependent upon the conceptualization and information needs as agreed on by their developers (C. M. Hart, unpublished manuscript, January 2008). In the 1980s, Huber, Delaney, and colleagues[1-4] identified a lack of uniform and comprehensive data elements needed by nurse managers. The researchers also recognized that the provision and effectiveness of nursing care are not only determined by specific nurse-patient interactions but are also influenced by organizational structures and provider characteristics, that is, contextual factors.[4] For example, management structure and style and staff mix can enhance or challenge patient care quality and delivery.[4] Therefore, to better understand and manage nursing care and resources, nursing care provided by nurses must be understood in the context of care delivery.[2,4]

Need for NMMDS Revision, Standardization, and Availability

Prior to development of the NMMDS, nursing management relevant data elements, if collected, were documented on paper or in information systems used for human resources, scheduling, or billing. Information systems were proprietary, and nursing management data were not uniformly named, defined, coded, or otherwise structured. This lack of data standardization and availability to the care managers and administrators has limited our ability to understand the provision of nursing services in the context of the care environment. Moreover, health information system developers, researchers, managers, and administrators have sought to reinvent sets of data to meet their information needs.

Development of the NMMDS

The development of the NMMDS began in 1989 with the intent of identifying and defining core essential nurse-management variables at the unit level.[1,4] NMMDS was created using a variety of research methods: grounded theory, focus groups, validation by domain experts, cross-sectional descriptive surveys, national Delphi surveys, and a national consensus working conference.[1,3-5] Early work resulted in a list of 18 management variables agreed on by a focus group of nurse executives.[3] A state-wide pilot followed by a national Delphi study supported the development of an acute care version of the NMMDS.[3,5] To expand the applicability of the data set to one that was valid for diverse healthcare settings, the acute care version of the data set was sent to experts in home care, occupational health, long-term care, and ambulatory care for their input.[4] This was followed by an invitation consensus conference co-sponsored by AONE.[4,5] The workshop produced a final list of 17 elements with measures and standardized definitions.[4,5] In 2005, the NMMDS was updated and made available to anyone requesting the definitions and survey instrument. Revisions began in 2008.

Table 13B-1. The Nursing Management Minimum Data Set Data Elements and Definitions

NMMDS: Environment	
Variable	**Definition**
1. Facility unique identifier (Unique facility identifier, Place of service, Geographical location, Postal code, Reporting period, Facility name)*	Facility defined as the highest level of an organization for data aggregation for which unit level data are reported. In some cases, a facility is the same as a unit if there is only one unit.
2. Nursing delivery unit/service (Unique unit identifier, Unique name, Type of nursing unit/service) *	Identify the unique name, identifier, and type of nursing unit or service for each component of the facility.
3. Patient/client population (Chronologic age, Population type)*	Characteristics of the population served by nursing delivery unit or service. Identify all categories that best describe the actual patient/client population served by the nursing delivery unit/service.
4. Volume of nursing delivery unit/service (Type of encounter, Type of client, Hours per encounter/client)*	Number of nursing encounters with related hours for direct and indirect activities that can be associated with the provision of care to a client for a unit or service during a reporting period. The volume of nursing care is determined by combining a type of encounter with a type of client and then either the designated number of hours per encounter, estimated number of encounters, or actual number of encounters on a unit for a reporting period
5. Method of care delivery*	The ways in which nursing work is organized on a unit. Methods differ and are delineated by nursing responsibilities and accountability for how work is planned and delivered, resources allocated, and care coordinated
6. Patient/client accessibility	Time and distance factors associated with the point of care
7. Clinical decision-making complexity (Patient/client care, Computerization)	Extent of routineness, uniformity, predictability, knowledge, and information system support associated with care delivery
8. Environmental complexity	Perceived extent of impact of environmental factors on the nursing delivery unit/service
9. Autonomy	Extent of participation in and distribution of organizational decision making
10. Nursing delivery unit/service accreditation	Recognition of nursing delivery unit/service by relevant accrediting or certifying agency

Table 13B-1. *Continued*

NMMDS: Nursing Care Resources	
Variable	**Definition**
11. Management demographic profile	Demographics of the leadership of the nursing delivery unit/service; demographics of the person, by whatever title, designated as the nurse manager with 24-hour administrative accountability for a nursing delivery unit/service
12 Staff demographic profile (Direct Care Staff; Management, Administrative, Support staff)	Demographics of the personnel of a nursing unit/service including quantity, educational profile, certification, professional affiliation, age, and family responsibilities for direct care and management, administrative, and support staff
13. Staffing (Quantity, Turnover, Retention)	Quantity, turnover and retention of direct care and management, administrative, and support staff of the nursing delivery unit/service
14. Satisfaction Position (specific job), Context (environment)	Percentage of direct care staff and management, administration and support staff having a positive or negative attitude toward their position and environment

NMMDS: Financial Resources	
Variable	**Definition**
15. Payer type	Quantity of claims for care associated with each reimbursement source assessed at the health system, organization, nursing department, and nursing delivery unit/service levels
16. Reimbursement	Distribution formula or payment for services source assessed at the health system, organization, nursing department, and nursing delivery unit/service levels
17. Nursing delivery unit/service budget	Percentage of the nursing delivery unit/service's planned and actual costs and revenues compared at the health system, organization, nursing department, and nursing delivery unit/service levels
18. Expenses	Percentage of the nursing delivery unit/service's direct, direct material, and indirect expenses compared at the health system, organization, nursing department and nursing delivery unit/service levels

© DHuber, CDelaney, 2005

*These data elements have been updated in the 2008-2009 revisions

Foundational Elements of the NMMDS

The conceptual frameworks that were foundational for the creation of the NMMDS are Donabedian's[6] quality of care, the Nursing Minimum Data Set,[7] and the Iowa Model of Nursing Administration.[1] Development requirements included that the NMMDS be minimal, pertinent to the healthcare business environment (i.e., managed care), representative of nursing care provided across the life span and in all delivery systems, and include the broad spectrum of nursing care from health promotion to illness care delivery.[8] The data set also needed to facilitate ease of use, quick data capture, and consistency, as well as to enable internal benchmarking and benchmarking with external agencies.[1] The variable criteria included necessity, clarity, and collectability.[8] An iterative consensual approach was ultimately used to create a data set of essential data elements that were valid for use across healthcare delivery settings and that represented the context of care delivery.

American Nurses Association Recognition

ANA, noting the importance of available standardized research-based nurse relevant data sets, has recognized two nursing datasets: Nursing Minimum Data Set (NMDS) and NMMDS. In addition to nurse management data represented by the NMMDS, clinical nursing data are represented by the NMDS. The data sets are complimentary, and together they support data capture of the care provided by nurses and the context of that care. This more complete representation of nursing care can support measurements of patient care and management outcomes, safety, quality, and the efficiency of care delivery. Furthermore, since both datasets are standardized they can also enable aggregation and analyses of nursing data across populations, systems, and geographical settings.

NMMDS Use

NMMDS Integral to National Quality Initiatives

The NMMDS has been integral to several national quality initiatives. These efforts include development of the National Database of Nursing Quality Indicators (NDNQI®), Magnet Status recognition, and the management quality indicators in the National Quality Forum (NQF) nurse-sensitive quality indicators.[9-11] The NDNQI is a national database that collects and reports some data elements that are comparable with the NMMDS along with selected clinical data. Data elements that are comparable between the NDNQI and NMMDS are Nursing Hours per Patient Day, RN Education/Certification, RN Satisfaction, Skill Mix, and Turnover. NDNQI-participating hospitals use the NDNQI to benchmark structure, process, and outcome indicators.

Use of NDNQI also provides evidence that it is possible to collect reliable and valid quality indicators that are sensitive to nursing practice on a large scale.

Magnet Status is a formal recognition program that is granted by the American Nurses' Credentialing Center to hospitals that demonstrate excellence in nursing. As part of the recognition process, hospitals share data to support high-quality standards. Some of the data shared for Magnet Status recognition are closely related to NMMDS data elements. The Magnet Status and NDNQI share similar elements and Magnet Status hospitals can choose to use the NDNQI for the required benchmarking with other hospitals. In addition, the ANA has collaborated with these and other organizations, such as The Joint Commission, to include 15 nurse-sensitive quality indicators as NQF-endorsed quality indicators. The NMMDS contributed to the conceptual foundation for this work.

Adoption of the NMMDS beyond the U.S. is occurring. Nurses in Iceland have taken the lead in translating and testing the NMMDS for an entire nation. G.A. Hardardottir's dissertation research focuses on translation and validation of the NMMDS in Iceland (e-mail communication, March 26, 2009). M. Ólafsdóttir Thorlacius' thesis work focuses on validating the NMMDS-ICE (Icelandic version) across pediatric units in Icelandic hospitals and tests whether the NMMDS-ICE survey includes information needed to support daily nurse decision making in these settings (e-mail communication, March 15, 2009).

Current NMMDS Revision Work

Integration with Data Standards

Since initial development of the NMMDS, many advances have occurred in data standards, modeling methods, and computer technology. The NMMDS, while originally designed for computerization, has largely been collected using a paper-based data collection tool. To be useful in computerized healthcare systems, the ANA requires that datasets and other recognized terminologies be structured in a format that can support electronic exchange of data.[12] In an effort to support interoperable use and to meet ANA recommendations, the NMMDS is currently undergoing a major revision to align the data elements, definitions, and codes with other national standards. The revision process requires harmonization of the NMMDS data elements with comparable research, national requirements for nursing management data, and other national terminology standards.

The Federal Consolidated Health Informatics (CHI) Initiative, now subsumed by the public-private HITSP organization, recommends terminology standards for use in EHRs within the United States.[13] The Logical Observations Identifiers Names and Codes (LOINC) is one of the federally recognized terminologies. Additionally, LOINC has been officially designated by the ANA as an ANA-recognized nomenclature because it represents and captures observations or assessments important for nursing.[14] Given this background, in 2007, the NMMDS research team approached the LOINC committee with a proposal for a collaborative effort to include the revised version of the NMMDS in the LOINC database. The goals of this combined work were to ensure that the NMMDS codes are harmonized with an existing federally recognized standard and to provide a mechanism for NMMDS public distribution through LOINC.

LOINC Basics

LOINC is a publicly available database that provides a set of universal names and codes for laboratory results, clinical measurements, and attachments (names of documents or sections of documents). For example, clinical measurements or observations include assessments such as the Braden Pressure Ulcer Scale, vital signs, and wound assessments. The goal of the LOINC has been to create codes that are universally used by all healthcare systems to facilitate clinical data exchange and use across healthcare organizations.[15,16] An objective in the development of LOINC was to structure the names in a format that could facilitate rapid matching, either automated or manual, between local vocabularies and the universal LOINC codes.

Mapping the NMMDS to LOINC requires an understanding of the LOINC semantic structure and codes. The LOINC semantic structure is modeled using a multiaxial approach. The LOINC name is a combination of six different axes or attributes that are combined to create a precoordinated expression.[17] The LOINC axes include component, kind of property, time aspect, system, precision, and type of method as shown in Table 13B-2. A LOINC code is similar to a question such as "What is the level of pain?" followed by a response, which is the actual value recorded, for example, on a scale of 1–10.

The LOINC database includes fields for each of the six axes represented in the name. In addition, it also contains short names, related words, comments for all observations, and additional information about the person or organization submitting the terms. Related words ("synonyms") are included to facilitate searches for individual laboratory test and clinical observation results.

The LOINC database is hierarchically grouped by "common sense" categories or "classes" to make it easier to find information. The high level classes are "Laboratory," "Clinical," and "Attachments." Each high-level class contains multiple subclasses. The Laboratory category contains subclasses, such as chemistry, coagulation tests, blood bank tests, etc. The Clinical category contains subclasses that are pertinent for nursing, such as body measurement, intake and output, nursing survey instruments, vaccination records, and vital signs. The Attachments class contains names of documents and document sections, such as "Operation Report," "History and Physical," and "Initial Assessment." The NMMDS LOINC codes are located in the "Nursing Survey Instruments" subclass under the "Clinical" class.

Process, Challenges, and Successes in Mapping the NMMDS to LOINC

Mapping NMMDS elements to LOINC requires that NMMDS data elements are semantically consistent with the LOINC structure (see Table 13B-2 for an example). An additional underlying decision rule for the mapping

Table 13B-2. Sample Mapping of an NMMDS Mapping to LOINC

NMMDS Variable: 01.01 Environment - Facility Unique Identifier
NMMDS Question Text: The National Provider Identifier (NPI) is a unique identification number for healthcare providers specified by HIPAA. For the NMMDS, the NPI for organizations will be used to indicate the place that sends the bill.
LOINC Code: 45399-3 Federal Provider Number:ID:PT:Facility:Nom
Value Set: The National Plan and Provider Enumeration System (NPPES) found at https://nppes.cms.hhs.gov/NPPES/Welcome.do

LOINC Axis	Description	NMMDS to LOINC Mapping
Component	The thing that is measured, evaluated, or observed (e.g., systolic blood pressure, pain onset, and nursing unit).	Facility Unique Identifier
Property	The characteristic or attribute of the item being measured, evaluated, or observed (e.g., length, volume, time stamp, ratio, number, temperature).	Identifier
Timing	The interval of time over which the observation or measurement was made (e.g., point in time, 24 hour).	Point in Time
System	The system within which the observation was made (e.g. patient, family, nursing unit).	Facility
Type of Scale	The scale of the measure (e.g., quantitative (a true measurement), ordinal (a ranked set of options), nominal (e.g., zip code, facility), or narrative.	Nominal
Type of Method	The procedure used to make the measurement or observation. Method is the only axis that is optional.	None

included harmonization of the conceptual and operational definitions of the NMMDS elements with existing standards when possible. Priority was given to establishing clear, precise measures that can be used to record data in ways that are reliable and valid for the variety of settings in which nurses work. For example, the NMMDS Data Element 1: Facility Unique Identifier includes the geographic location for a facility. The recent revision included a standard for states (in the United States)[18] and the standardized list of zip codes for postal locations.[19] The NDNQI and Magnet Status data elements were also evaluated to harmonize with the NMMDS conceptual and operational definitions for similar concepts. For instance, when working on NMMDS Data Element 2: Nursing delivery unit/service, the type of nursing unit is now defined in a manner consistent with NDNQI standards.[20]

Challenges arise when there are no nationally recognized or universally agreed upon standards matching NMMDS data elements. For instance, describing the population served by age was originally captured as the developmental stage. The review of the literature produced no single standard for developmental stages or a best method for categorizing a population of care for a nursing unit or service. Recognizing that it is difficult, if not impossible at times, to develop one standard that meets all user needs, multiple use cases for age in reporting on a unit population were discussed. Categorizing age as the percent of the population represented by five-year increments was chosen as the measurement. The newly proposed standard for age was submitted to the LOINC Committee and was accepted without modification. Additionally, in adopting this age range, a new LOINC code was developed for each age interval.

At the time of this writing, the collaborative work between the NMMDS workgroup and the LOINC has succeeded in revising and mapping the first five NMMDS data elements into LOINC. These data elements were included in the January 2008 release of the LOINC database. The remaining NMMDS elements will be mapped and submitted 2009-2010.

Summary

The NMMDS serves as a foundational dataset for the collection of core essential nursing management data, at the unit or service level, to describe the context of nursing care. Inclusion of this research-derived dataset in national, routinely collected discharge and other data sets has the potential to greatly enhance understanding of variables that contribute to differences in patient care, including those needed for a better understanding of patient safety and patient outcomes. At this time, although the NMMDS has not been fully implemented as a data collection tool, it has influenced major quality initiatives in the United States, including the NDNQI, Magnet Status, and NQF quality indicators. While the NDNQI, Magnet Status, and NQF have raised the visibility for the importance of collecting contextual data influencing nursing care, these efforts have been limited to hospital settings. The understanding and provision of quality care across the healthcare delivery spectrum now requires the use of datasets that are relevant to care in the wide array of today's healthcare delivery settings. The NMMDS has been validated in inpatient and outpatient care settings, and it is presently being updated to support harmonization with various recognized standards. At this time, NMMDS is being mapped into LOINC to enable its use by inclusion into a freely available federally and ANA-recognized dataset.

References

1. Huber D, Schumacher L, Delaney C. Nursing Management Minimum Data Set. *J Nurs Adm.* 1997;27(4):42-48.
2. Delaney C. Nursing minimum data set systems. In: Saba VK, McCormick KA. *Essentials of Nursing Informatics.* 4th ed. New York: McGraw-Hill Companies, Inc. 2006:249-261.
3. Huber DG, Delaney C, Crossley J, Mehmert M. A nursing management minimum data set significance and development. *J Nurs Adm.* 1992;22(7/8):35-40.
4. Mass ML, Delaney C, Huber D. Contextual variables and assessment of the outcome effects of nursing interventions. *Outcomes Manag Nurs Pract.* 1999:3(1):4-6.
5. Huber D, Delaney C. The Nursing Management Minimum Data Set. *Appl Nurs Res.* 1997;10(3):64-165.
6. Donabedian A. *Explorations in Quality Assessment and Monitoring: The definition of quality and approaches to its assessment.* Vol. 1. Ann Arbor, MI: Health Administration Press, 1980.
7. Werley H, Lang N, eds. *Identification of the Nursing Minimum Data Set.* New York: Springer;1988.
8. Delaney C, Huber D. The University of Iowa Nursing Management Minimum Data Set Research Team. *Report of an Invitational Conference Nursing Management Minimum Data Set (NMMDS)* Monograph. Chicago: The American Organization of Nurse Executives-A Subsidiary of the American Hospital Association; 1996.
9. Montalvo I. The national database of nursing quality indicators (NDNQI). *Online J Issues Nurs.* 2007;12-13.
10. American Nurses Credentialing Center (ANCC). *Application Manual: Magnet Recognition Program.* Silver Spring, MD: American Nurses Credentialing Center, 2008.
11. Kurtzman ET, Kizer KW. Evaluating the performance and contribution of nurses to achieve an environment of safety. *Nurs Adm Q.* 2005;29:14-23.
12. American Nurses Association. Public comment: Draft nursing terminologies recognition criteria. http://www.nursingworld.org/HomepageCategory/NursingInsider/Archive_1/2007/Sept07Insider/DraftNursingTerminologiesRecognitionCriteriaforPublicComment.aspx. Accessed April 25, 2009.
13. Healthcare Information Technology Standards Panel. http://www.hitsp.org/. Accessed April 25, 2009.
14. Matney S, Bakken S, Huff SM. Representing nursing assessments in clinical information systems using the logical observation identifiers, names, and codes database. *J Biomed Inform.* 2003;36(4-5):287-293.
15. Payne TH, Sengupta S, Sittig DF. Electronic Exchange of Patient Information: The Infrastructure for Electronic Health Records. In: Murphy GF, Hanken MA, Water KA, eds. *Electronic Health Records: Changing the Vision.* Philadelphia: WB Saunders, 1999:129-130.
16. Forrey AW, McDonald CJ, DeMoor G, et al. Logical observation identifier names and codes (LOINC) database: a public use set of codes and names for electronic reporting of clinical laboratory test results. *Clinical Chemistry.* 1996;42(1):81-90.
17. McDonald CJ, Huff SM, Vreeman DJ, Mercer K. *Logical Observation Identifier Names and Codes (LOINC®) Users' Guide vs. 1.0 - Release 1.0j.* Indianapolis, IN: Regenstrief Institute; 2006.
18. Federal Information Processing Standards Publications. http://www.itl.nist.gov/fipspubs. Accessed April 25, 2009.
19. United States Postal Service. ZIP Code Lookup. http://zip4.usps.com/zip4/citytown_zip.jsp. Accessed April 25, 2009.
20. NDNQI®. Appendix D NDNQI® Unit Structure. https://www.nursingquality.org/Documents/Public/APPENDIX%20D.pdf. Accessed April 25, 2009.

Case Study 13C

Nursing Quality Measures: National Database of Nursing Quality Indicators®

By Nancy E. Dunton, PhD

Introduction

With the publication of *To Err Is Human* by IOM[1] in 2000, the incidence of medical errors in the nation's hospitals became evident and healthcare providers, consumers, and policy makers were stirred to action. Underscored by the high and continually rising costs of healthcare, the policy response was to increase the safety of healthcare by holding providers accountable with mandated reporting of healthcare quality or patient safety indicators to The Joint Commission and other federal and state regulatory bodies. In the ensuing years, the policy response moved from reporting on healthcare indicators to regulatory bodies, to public reporting of indicators[2] and value-based purchasing, based on indicators of healthcare quality and efficiency.[3] Most recently, CMS implemented a rule designed to promote high-quality healthcare by eliminating payment to healthcare providers for a number of serious, largely preventable, and costly hospital-acquired conditions.[4]

ANA had anticipated the movement toward measuring patient outcomes by several years. With the expansion of prospective payment systems in the late 1980s and early 1990s, nursing positions were being eliminated as hospitals attempted to contain costs. Concerned about the loss of nurses' jobs and the resulting risk to patient safety, ANA launched the Patient Safety and Quality Initiative in 1994 to demonstrate the value of nursing in hospitals.[5,6] As part of this initiative, ANA established the National Database of Nursing Quality Indicators® (NDNQI). NDNQI collects data on unit-level nursing indicators for acute care settings and issues performance reports to hospitals. With more than 1,400 participating hospitals and 19 nursing-sensitive indicators, NDNQI is the largest nursing indicator database worldwide.

Uses for Nursing Indicators Reports

Hospitals use nursing quality indicator reports for a variety of purposes. Quality improvement (QI) professionals and nurse managers use the reports to identify patient outcomes for QI initiatives and also to track progress. NDNQI nursing indicator reports contain eight-quarter trend data on each unit for each indicator, as well as a wide variety of comparisons data, including unit type averages for the hospital and unit-type data for hospitals of specific types (e.g., academic medical centers, Magnet hospitals, hospitals with under 100 staffed beds, and hospitals in a specific state or region of the country). Hospitals may select the comparison data most like the characteristics of their own hospital. Nurse administrators use the reports to report to hospitals administrators and boards of directors on the quality of nursing care. Nursing administrators and managers use the measures of nurse job satisfaction and nurse turnover to improve the nursing work environment and nurse retention. Hospitals also use information in the reports to identify staff education needs, recruit patients and nursing staff, and support clinical research projects. ANA has published two monographs of quality improvement case studies written by hospital nurses.[6,7,8]

Hospitals that are applying for Magnet Recognition® from ANCC or that are recognized as Magnet facilities are required to monitor nurse satisfaction and nursing-sensitive indicators.[9] Approximately 90% of Magnet hospitals meet these requirements by participating in NDNQI.

Nursing Quality Indicators

The first set of nursing quality indicators was established by an expert panel established by ANA from a literature review that identified patient outcomes that varied in relationship to the characteristics of the nursing workforce.[5] The measures were organized according to Donabedian's[10,11] conceptual framework in which the structure of nursing care affects the process of nursing care, both of which in turn affect patient care outcomes. Five of the original ten measures were pilot-tested for feasibility of data collection. The pilot studies and the definitions developed by the ANA task force provided the foundation for the design and development of NDNQI.

Measure Alignment

A great proliferation of healthcare performance measures followed publication of the 2000 IOM report. In 1999, NQF, a not-for-profit membership organization, was created to develop a national consensus regarding alignment, or standardization, of healthcare quality measures among databases. The NQF identified 15 national quality consensus standards to measure nurses' contributions to patient safety and quality outcomes.[12] ANA was the original developer of four of the NQF measures and has implemented an additional seven. In addition to the 11 NQF measures, NDNQI has developed and implemented six additional measures for a total of seventeen indicators.

NDNQI Indicators, Data Sources, and Data Quality

All NDNQI data are collected and reported at the patient-care unit level, not at the hospital-level or the individual patient-level. Data come from a variety of sources, including payroll systems, staffing systems, patient censuses, human resource records, incident reports, infection control reports, medical records, special one-day prevalence studies conducted by hospitals, and an annual survey conducted by NDNQI (see Table 13C-1).

The quality of nursing indicator data and the value of indicator reports to hospitals rest on data collection practices that reinforce standardized definitions. NDNQI provides hospital-site coordinators with detailed data collection guidelines, including indicator definitions, data collection procedures, and recommended data sources. The guidelines are available on the members-only portion of the NDNQI Web site in a .pdf format for quick reference (www.nursingquality.org).[18] Additionally, hospital data collectors and data entry staff must complete the relevant portions of the NDNQI Web-based site coordinator tutorial and pass quizzes on the key points with 100% accuracy before they are granted access to the Web-based data entry site. The NDNQI site coordinator must complete all 15 sections of the tutorial. Hospitals are provided with standardized Excel-spreadsheets for special data collection activities, when data are not routinely available from electronic sources. NDNQI staff provides individual site coordinators with technical assistance via telephone or e-mail. Staff respond to approximately 1,000 phone or e-mail contacts per month. Finally, NDNQI staff conduct quarterly teleconferences and produce quarterly electronic newsletters focused on improving data standardization.

Nursing indicator data are submitted to NDNQI within 45 days of the end of a calendar quarter. Data are submitted to NDNQI through a secure Web site, either by data entry in standardized Web-screens or by XML up-load. The Web site is programmed to provide immediate feedback to data entry staff when obvious out-of-range values or blanks are encountered. Three times before a data submission deadline closes, error reports are pushed out automatically to hospitals. Data analysts examine the data for additional outliers, a change in trend, or for illogical values. They contact hospitals by telephone and e-mail to make corrections. On average, one-third of the hospitals are contacted each quarter regarding a potential error. Analysts spend approximately five weeks in data cleaning.

The RN survey data are collected from individual RNs through a secure Web site. There are no open-ended questions. Data analysts spend two weeks cleaning data before reports are issued.

The level of effort in collecting standardized, accurate data is significant, both for hospital and NDNQI staff. The time spent for data collection by hospitals varies according to the number of indicators the hospital participates in, the size of the hospital, and the ability to access information in electronic systems. Approximately 16-60 hours per quarter are required for data entry. NDNQI staff spend approximately ten hours per hospital annually providing technical assistance to hospitals or cleaning data.

Timeliness of Reports

Hospitals receive quarterly nursing indicator reports within four weeks of the close of data submission. Since data submission closes 45 days after the end of the quarter, there is a three-month lag between the period of performance and the ability to use the report. According to NDNQI's customer satisfaction surveys, nurse administrators and managers would like more timely performance feedback. Yet, most hospitals are unable to report the data to NDNQI in fewer than 45 days, and based on the amount of error in the raw data, NDNQI is unable to provide reports in under a month.

Table 13C-1. Nursing Quality Indicators Included in NDNQI

No.	Measure	Developer	Data Source
	Nursing Structure Indicators		
1	Nursing Care Hours per Patient Day	ANA, NQF-endorsed	Nursing care hours: payroll system or staffing system Patient days: Patient census
2	Skill Mix (Percent of total nursing care hours supplied by RNs, LPNs, and unlicensed nursing assistants. Also percent of nursing care hours supplied by agency or contract staff.)	ANA, NQF-endorsed	Nursing care hours: payroll system or staffing system

3	Nurse Turnover
	  1. Total
	  2. Voluntary
	
	  3. Controllable
		1. NDNQI
		2. Voluntary Hospital Association, NQF-endorsed
		3. Magnet Commission
			Human resources records

4	RN Education	ANA	Human resources or unit managers
5	RN Certification	ANA	Human resources or unit managers
6	Practice Environment Scale	E. Lake (2002), NQF-endorsed	Annual RN Survey
7	Eleven RN Job Satisfaction Scales	ANA adaptations of existing instruments (Aiken & Patrician, 2000[13]; Aiken et al., 2003[14]; Brayfield & Rothe, 1951[15]; Stamps, 1997[16]; Taunton et al., 2004[17])	Annual RN Survey

Summary: Informatics and the Future of NDNQI Data Collection

Informatics, in general, and EHRs in particular, hold the promise of reducing the level of effort required by hospitals to collect nursing indicator data, while improving the accuracy of the data. Electronic information systems may contain errors; however, an XML upload of electronic data from the various hospital systems will eliminate data entry errors. Programmers at NDNQI hospitals typically spend one or two quarters creating

Table 13C-1. *Continued*

	Nursing Process Measures		
8	Physical Restraint Prevalence	CalNOC, NQF-endorsed	One-day prevalence study per quarter
9	Assessment of the Completeness of the Pain Assessment, Intervention, Reassessment (AIR) Cycle for Pediatric units	ANA	One-day prevalence study (medical record review), conducted quarterly
	Nursing-Sensitive Outcome Measures		
10	Patient Fall Rate (Total falls per 1,000 patient days)	ANA, NQF-endorsed	Falls data: Incident or variance reports Patient days: Patient census
11	Patient Injury Fall Rate (Total falls with injury per 1,000 patient days)	ANA, NQF-endorsed	Patient Fall Rate (Total falls per 1,000 patient days)
12	Hospital-Acquired Pressure Ulcer Rate	ANA, NQF-endorsed	One-day prevalence study per quarter
13	Catheter-Associated Urinary Tract Infections ((Infections/ devise days)*1000)	Centers for Disease Control, NQF-endorsed	Infection control reports, collected daily
14	Central Line-Associated Blood Stream Infections ((Infections/ devise days)*1000)	Centers for Disease Control, NQF-endorsed	Infection control reports, collected daily
15	Ventilator Associated Pneumonias ((Infections/ devise days)*1000)	Centers for Disease Control, NQF-endorsed	Infection control reports, collected daily
16	Pediatric Peripheral IV Infiltration (PIV rate)	ANA	One-day prevalence study, conducted monthly
17	Physical/Sexual Assault Rate, Psychiatric Patients	ANA	Medical records, incident reports, special data collection forms, collected continuously

XML data files that meet NDNQI validation rules. This includes the time obtaining data from various sources, compiling it into an integrated database, developing and testing validation rules, as well as the actual XML programming time. Pressure ulcer data, the most complicated, have more than 90 validation rules. A small minority of hospitals currently submit data to NDNQI using XML, although this may become more common with the growth of informatics and increasing requirements to report on healthcare indicators to federal and state agencies.

The feasibility of extracting reliable performance indicator data from electronic sources is dependent on the maintenance of standardized definitions for nursing quality indicators and incorporating the definitions into EHRs and other electronic data sources, as well as designing user-interfaces that promote high-quality data collection at the bedside. ANA has approved the Nursing Minimum Data Set and the Nursing Minimum Management Data Set as supporting nursing practice. These are essential, foundational elements for advancing nursing informatics. As NDNQI progresses toward the collection of nursing-sensitive indicators from EHRs, we will see guidance from ANA's Information and Infrastructure Committee to implement state-of-the-science standards for EHR data collection, extraction, and reporting (www.nursingworld.org/npii/nmmds/htm).[19] The challenges are great, but the benefits are substantial with less time devoted to data collection and more timely feedback on performance levels.

References

1. Kohn LT, Corrigan JM, Donaldson MS, eds. *To Err is Human: Building a Safer Health System.* Washington, DC: The National Academies Press, 2000.

2. US Department of Health and Human Services. *Hospital Compare, a quality tool provided by Medicare.* http://hospitalcompare.hhs.gov. 2009. Accessed September 3, 2009.

3. Leapfrog Group. www.leapfroggroup.org. 2009. Accessed October 20, 2009.

4. Centers for Medicare and Medicaid Services. *Changes to the Hospital Inpatient Prospective Payment Systems and Fiscal Year 2009 Rates.* http://www.cms.hhs.gov/AcuteinpatientPPS/downloads/CMS-1390-F.pdf. 2008.

5. American Nurses Association. *Nursing Report Card for Acute Care.* Washington, DC: American Nurses Publishing, 1995.

6. Montalvo I. The National Database of Nursing Quality Indicators® (NDNQI). *OJIN: Online J Issues in Nurs.* 2007;12(3), Manuscript 2. www.nursingworld.org/MainMenuCategories/ANAMarketplace/ANAPeriodicals/OJIN/TableofContents/Volume122007/No3Sept07/NursingQualityIndicators.aspx.

7. Dunton N, Montalvo I, eds. *Sustained Improvement in Nursing Quality: Hospital Performance on NDNQI Indicators, 2007-2008.* American Nurses, Association, Silver Spring, MD, 2009.

8. Montalvo I, Dunton N, eds. *Transforming Nursing Data into Quality Care: Profiles of Quality Improvement in US Healthcare Facilities.* American Nurses Association, Washington, DC: 2009.

9. American Nurses Credentialing Center. *Application Manual, Magnet Recognition Program®.* Washington, DC: American Nurses Credentialing Center, 2008.

10. Donabedian A. The quality of care: How can it be assessed? *JAMA.* 1988;(260):1743-1748.

11. Donabedian A. The role of outcomes in quality assessment and assurance. *Qual Rev Bull.* 1993;(11):356-360.

12. National Quality Forum. *National Voluntary Consensus Standards for Nursing-Sensitive Care. An Initial Performance Measure Set—A Consensus Report.* Washington, DC: National Quality Forum, 2004.

13. Aiken L, Patrician PA. Measuring organizational traits of hospitals: The revised Nursing Work Index. *Nurs Res.* 2000; (49):146-153

14. Aiken LH, Clark SP, Sloan DM. Hospital staffing, organization, and quality of care: cross-national findings. *Int J Qual Health Care.* 2002;(14):5-13.

15. Brayfield A, Rothe H. An index of job satisfaction. *J Appl Psychol.* 1951(35):307-311.

16. Stamps P. *Nurses and Work Satisfaction: An Index for Measurement.* Chicago: Health Administration Press, 1997.

17. Taunton RL, Bott MJ, Koehn ML, et al. The NDNQI-Adapted Index of Work Satisfaction. *J Nurs Meas.* 2004;(12):101-122.

18. www.nursingquality.org. Accessed June 4, 2009.

19. www.nursingworld,org/npii/nmmds/htm. Accessed September 3, 2009.

SECTION IV

EHR Initiatives
Across the Globe

SECTION IV

Introduction

By Robyn L. Carr, RGON

E-Health

E-health is the adoption and effective use of electronic health record (EHR) systems and other health information technology (IT) to improve healthcare quality, increase patient safety, reduce healthcare costs, and enable individuals and communities to make the best possible health decisions. Around the world, e-health is emerging as a powerful strategy to transform ailing healthcare systems. Strong e-health policies are required to accelerate the adoption of EHRs and related health IT globally. Section IV gives an around-the-world look at the current state for uses of information and communication technologies (ICT) in healthcare and, specifically, the status of nursing within these EHR initiatives. The move toward EHRs is rapidly becoming a world-wide phenomenon, driven by governments' search for more effective and efficient mechanisms to manage the health of their populations and to curb the escalating costs associated with care delivery.

Over the past decade, the consumer public has been shocked by publications documenting the high level of error, quality deficits, waste, and inefficiencies in Western medical systems generally. Governments have been spurred to invest in EHR technologies in the face of growing evidence that healthcare systems around the world are marked by extensive variances in treatment approaches, surgical procedure rates, outcomes, and costs. As of 2010, most governments are implementing health policies that mandate or actively push for the adoption and meaningful use of IT as a means for more cost-effective and efficient coordination of care based on best practices. The difference over these past four years between the first edition and the second edition of this book is the extent to which governments are willing to invest and fund their EHR initiatives to achieve these cost containment goals.

The transition to using IT in all aspects of care delivery work processes is happening at an explosive rate of change. And as a result, nurses are increasingly being recruited to work as part of the project groups, in leading teams, for strategic planning, and to lead major health organizational or government level initiatives. Even more importantly, however, is the dependence on nursing for transformation in our healthcare systems to happen.

As healthcare systems struggle to achieve transformation, at some point along the journey, it is discovered that the need for significant and lasting change requires full engagement by the nursing profession. Thus, this demand translates in two ways. Nurses are engaged to help make change happen, and nurses are asked to amend their own culture and work practices to support transformational change—and in the process bring along the other disciplines. These EHR initiatives present both challenges and great opportunity for nursing as a profession, for the discipline of nursing informatics, together with the career path options created for nurses.

Section IV aims to capture a look at the impacts on nursing that are occurring now as a result of EHR initiatives, in all their variations and similarities. It is important that we do not miss this snapshot in nursing's evolution and that we pause to document these developments for our own understanding and for our history. This section is organized by geographic areas into six chapters: The Americas, U.K. and Ireland, Europe, Middle East, South Africa, and Asia Pacific. Grouped under these major geographic sections are 35 case studies that provide rich descriptions of the role and status of nursing, level of development of nursing informatics, and the impact of EHR initiatives on nursing within their given countries. Even in countries where health informatics has been active for over three decades and national EHR strategies are in process, these case studies show extensive variation in nursing's involvement, inclusion, and integration. In the United States, the Minnesota e-Health case study represents the extensive involvement of nursing in four domains: consumers and personal health records; clinicians and their engagement in electronic health records; policy/research and their need for supporting scientific information systems; and in the realm of population health, the systems needed in public health.

Additionally, the breadth of countries covered in this second edition speaks to the commitment of nursing leaders from nations in the early stages of health information technology who stepped forward to ensure that their countries are represented in this overview. These countries include: Cuba, Chile, Taiwan, Thailand, India, Pakistan and countries within Africa and the Middle East. Despite the economies, political structures, and geographic differences across these 35 case studies, there are many similarities and common themes to be found in their stories. However, the contrasts provide remarkable insights into the correlation between nursing education and professional status to the extent to which nursing is included in EHR initiatives within a given country.

## CHAPTER 14

The Americas: Overview of EHR National Strategies and Significance for Nursing

By Lynn M. Nagle, PhD, MScN, BN, RN; Heimar De Fatima Marin, PhD, MS, RN, FACMI; and Connie White Delaney, PhD, RN, FAAN, FACMI

Introduction

The global impact of national electronic health record (EHR) initiatives has yet to be realized. However, there is growing evidence that the world economy, populations' access to technology, and the worldwide call for reform of healthcare systems demand the expedited adoption of EHRs. These EHRs must focus on enabling increased access to care, supporting people-centric service, and facilitating the delivery of state-of-the-science evidence-based care. National and international standards and informatics organizations, e.g., Healthcare Information and Management Systems Society (HIMSS), American Medical Informatics Association (AMIA), and International Medical Informatics Association (IMIA), are crucial for leveraging informatics knowledge and supporting informatics competencies for the population in general, and particularly, educators, researchers, and administrators, and healthcare providers. This chapter is an overview of the state of the science for nursing and EHR initiatives across the Americas. Capturing the succinct synopsis of the state of EHR adoption is a daunting task, given the diversity and variation across this massive geographic area. This overview highlights a sampling from Canada, the United States, Latin America, and South America, rather than attempting an in-depth description of the status of EHRs in all countries in this geography. Eight case studies follow this overview. Significant exemplars represent North America (Canada, US); Latin America (Cuba); and South America (Argentina, Brazil, and Chile).

Overview of the Americas

Geographically, the Americas consist of 35 sovereign states and 23 dependencies[1] that span four major areas. The geographic expanse of the Americas is enormous. North and South America alone include more than 42 million square kilometers, 29.5% of all land in the world. Adding the land mass of the Caribbean and Central America extends this total by more than 20 million kilometers,[2] giving an approximate total land mass of more than 60 million kilometers.[2] Canada is ranked by land as the second largest country in the world when volume and area are measured (which includes water); Brazil ranks eighth in total land. The Americas contain 858 million people or 13.5% of the human population.[1] This population is very diverse, descending from eight large ethnic groups.[1] The most prevalent faith is Christianity.[1] While many languages are spoken, the most dominant are Spanish, English, and Portuguese.[1] To provide a more detailed health context for examination of EHR initiatives, each component of the Americas, including geographical composition and health-related statistics, follows.

North America includes Canada, the United States, Mexico, and Greenland. Table 14-1 summarizes health-related statistics for the four countries comprising North America.[2,3] Although English is the predominant language spoken, French is spoken in parts of Canada, Spanish in Mexico, and Greenlandic in Greenland. A review of their health statistics indicates wide variation in most dimensions, including population, GDP, and both infant and adult mortality. Across the gradient of developing, developed, and industrialized countries, health

Table 14-1. Health Statistics of Countries in North America, 2006

Country	Total population (2006)	Life expectancy at birth years (2006)	Child mortality per 1000 (2006)	Adult mortality per 1000 (2006)	Total health expenditure as % of GDP (2006)
Canada[2]	32,577,000	81	6	72	10.0
US[2]	302,841,000	78	8	109	15.3
Mexico[2]	105,342,000	74	35	122	6.2
Greenland[3] (2008)	57,564	70	--	--	--

expenditures are used as a key indictor to reflect a population's health status and healthcare quality. However, the United States is an exception to this statistical correlation, having the highest healthcare expenditures per GDP in the world but ranking far below other industrial countries on most quality indicators.

Latin America encompasses eight countries, and the Caribbean includes 23 nation states and islands. The socio-economic status across these nations ranges from considerable affluence throughout many of the Caribbean countries (e.g., Aruba) to the most dire (e.g., Haiti). This marked variation in economics, health expenditures, and health status indicators across the countries within this geography is outlined in Table 14-2.

Finally, the South American continent encompasses Argentina, Bolivia, Brazil, Chile, Colombia, Ecuador, Guyana, Paraguay, Peru, Suriname, Uruguay, and Venezuela. Culturally, in land mass and through language, Brazil stands apart from its Spanish-speaking neighboring countries, and its uniqueness is addressed in Case Study 14G. Table 14-3 outlines key health statistics for the larger countries comprising South America.[2] Many variances in statistical reporting occur, making even simple comparisons, such as land mass, population, and economic indicators difficult. In other circumstances, particularly in emerging countries, statistics simply do not exist. The Pan American Health Organization provides an excellent two-volume analysis and comparison of health systems, population health statistics, and healthcare access across this diverse geopolitical aggregate in the 2007 edition of *Health in the Americas*.[4]

Electronic Health Record Progress

The complexity of developing EHRs within countries, as well as the challenges of interoperability across countries and continents, is massive. The following section describes EHR initiatives in Canada and the United States in North America, and the current situation in Latin America and South America. Significant exemplars represented in the case studies that follow this chapter include North America (Canada, United States); Latin America (Cuba); and South America (Argentina, Brazil, Chile).

Canada

Canada is in the midst of delivering the functional components of an interoperable EHR for all Canadians. Established in 2001, Canada Health Infoway[5] is an independent, not-for-profit organization whose members are Canada's 14 federal, provincial, and territorial deputy ministers of health. Infoway jointly invests with every province and territory to accelerate the development and adoption of EHR projects in Canada. The Infoway vision is to achieve interoperable EHRs for 50% of all Canadians by 2010. Significant progress has been made in achieving this vision with federal investments of more than $2.1 billion to date.[5] More specifically, most jurisdictions have the beginnings of the basic infrastructure in place to support an interoper-

Table 14-2. Central America Selected Country Health Statistics[2]

Country	Total population (2007)	Life expectancy at birth years (2006)	Child mortality per 1000 (2006)	Adult mortality per 1000 (2006)	Total health expenditure as % of GDP (2006)
Guatamala[2]	13,354,000	69	39	229	5.3
Honduras[2]	7,106,000	71	24	169	6.4
Nicaragua[2]	5,603,000	73	35	164	9.6
Costa Rica[2]	4,468,000	79	11	86	7.7
Panama[2]	3,343,000	76	23	111	7.3
Cuba[2]	11,268,000	78	6	102	7.7
Jamaica[2]	2,714,000	72	31	170	4.7
Dominican Republic[2]	9,760,000	72	38	159	5.6

Table 14-3. South America Selected Country Health Statistics

Country	Total population (2007)	Life expectancy at birth years (2006)	Child mortality per 1000 (2006)	Adult mortality per 1000 (2006)	Total health expenditure as % of GDP (2006)
Brazil[2]	191,791,000	73	22	159	7.5
Argentina[2]	39,531,000	75	16	126	10.1
Chile[2]	16,635,000	78	9	86	5.3
Venezuela[2]	27,657,000	75	19	142	4.9
Columbia[2]	45,156,000	75	20	120	7.3
Peru[2]	27,903,000	76	20	111	4.4
Bolivia[2]	9,525,000	66	57	204	6.4

able EHR including client registries, provider registries, and drug, laboratory, and diagnostic imaging information systems. In addition, as a result of the 2003 SARS outbreak, a national public health surveillance system has been adopted nationwide. Beyond these foundational systems, several other areas, such as telehealth, infostructure, and standards development, have been the focus of targeted investments.[6]

The Infoway Standards Collaborative was launched in 2006 as a Canada-wide coordination function to support and sustain health information standards in Canada. It is responsible for the implementation support, education, conformance, and maintenance for EHR standards currently being developed by Infoway. Infoway was also a charter member of the International Health Terminology Standards Development Organization (IHTSDO) in 2007.[7] The development and deployment of health data and technical standards are germane to the evolution of an interoperable EHR, and Infoway recognizes the centrality of this work in the achievement of their mission.

While Canadian nurses are involved in health informatics work across Canada, the most remarkable nursing initiative is the Health Outcomes for Better Information and Care (HOBIC) effort. In addition, to further identify a suite of outcome measures proven to be impacted by nursing practice, efforts are underway to have them consistently embedded in the electronic documentation tools used by nurses in acute care, long-term care, complex continuing care, and home care. Originating in the province of Ontario in 1999, HOBIC has been expanded to several other jurisdictions through the support of CHI. Sponsored by the Canadian Nurses Association (CNA), the C(anadian)-HOBIC initiative has also provided a demonstration and documentation of mapping the HOBIC measures to the International Classification of Nursing Practice (ICNP). This mapping exercise resulted in the provision of feedback to ICN for further revision and expansion of ICNP. The CNA is presently seeking additional funding to extend the implementation of these standardized outcome measures by nurses within other Canadian jurisdictions. The HOBIC initiative has the hallmark of being the first Canadian demonstration of nursing terminology and practice standardization.[8,9]

The Canadian Institute for Health Information (CIHI)[10] is an independent, not-for-profit organization that provides essential data and analysis on Canada's health system and the health of Canadians. Founded in 1992, the Canadian Institute for Health Information remains the central health data repository for all standardized health data collections. These data provide the primary basis for national health and health human resource statistical reporting. It is the hope of the nursing community that the HOBIC documentation by nurses will someday find a place of importance among the CIHI holdings and analyses.

The Canadian Nursing Informatics Association (CNIA)[11] continues to provide the networking and communication vehicle for nurses working and interested in the area of informatics. With more than 200 members, CNIA is the voice of Canadian nurses on informatics issues related to nursing. Biannual conferences have been extremely popular and successful and demonstrate the need for a Canadian venue for nurses to share their work, experiences, and expertise. In 2012, Canada will host the 11th International Nursing Informatics conference in Montreal, Quebec. Case Study 14A describes details related to Canadian initiatives to advance a national EHR.

United States

The United States is among several countries, such as Australia, Canada, England, New Zealand, Malaysia, Hong Kong, and Singapore, which have established a comprehensive national vision for health information infrastructure. The National Health Information Infrastructure (NHII)[12] is an initiative to improve the effectiveness, efficiency, and overall quality of health and healthcare in the United States through a comprehensive knowledge-based network of interoperable systems of clinical (provider notes, clinical orders, decision-support programs, digital prescribing programs, and practice guidelines); public health (sharing of information to improve the clinical management of populations of patients, such as vital statistics, population health risks and disease registries); and personal health information (personal health record that is created and controlled by the individual or family, plus non-clinical information, such as self-care trackers and directories of healthcare providers) that would improve decision making by making health information available when and where it is needed.

The NHII is the set of technologies, standards, applications, systems, values, and laws that support all facets of individual health, healthcare and public health; it is not a centralized database of medical records or a government regulation. There is consensus in the United States that the purpose of the NHII is to improve patient safety (alert for medication errors, drug allergies, etc.); improve healthcare quality (includes having the availability of complete medical records, test results, and x-rays at the point of care; integrating health information from multiple sources and providers, incorporating the use of decision support tools with guidelines and research results, etc.); enable real-time aggregation of health data to detect patterns; and better inform and empower healthcare consumers regarding their own personal health information. It is expected that the mandate to address skyrocketing costs of healthcare will be supported by an effective NHII.

Establishing the NHII and EHR are not without challenges. The very nature of healthcare is complex. It involves multiple provider associations, health systems, payer organizations, consumers, and local, state, and federal agencies. It is highly fragmented and largely delivered by the private sector. Medical and health information is complex, and there are few incentives in place for information sharing. Organizational and change management issues are also difficult to manage in a clinical environment. Establishing the NHII is further challenged by the costs of health technology and fragmented connectivity with minimal interoperability. Although extensive accomplishments have occurred in developing standards to support the EHR including the messaging standards contributions of HL7, X12N, DICOM, NCPDP, IEEE—and the terminology standards of LOINC, Drugs, Billing, and Clinical[13]—little to no consensus has occurred supporting actual adoption of these standards. Further, there are privacy and security issues which continue to garner widespread attention.

The engagement of many major HHS agencies in the NHII Initiative is clear evidence of the importance of the initiative. Examples of the agencies involved in the NHII effort include the Agency for Healthcare Research and Quality,[14] assistant secretary for planning and evaluation,[15] Centers for Disease Control and Prevention,[16] Centers for Medicare & Medicaid Services,[17] Data Council (interagency),[18] Food and Drug Administration,[19] Health Resources and Services Administration,[20] National Center for Health Statistics,[21] National Institutes of Health,[22] National Library of Medicine,[23] Office of Civil Rights,[24] Deputy Assistant Secretary for information resources management,[25] and the Office of Public Health and Science.[26]

Despite these major advances in the United States, focused leadership has been necessary to bring about collaboration between stakeholders in the private and public sectors and among all levels of government. At Health and Human Services, the National Committee on Vital and Health Statistics (NCVHS)[27] serves as a public advisory committee to the Secretary of Health and Human Services on national health information policy. Their report "Information for Health: A Strategy for Building the National Health Information" outlined a three-stage process over ten years for achieving the vision.[27] The first stage (within two years) included developing leadership within the Department of Health and Human Services (HHS)[28] and other agencies and clarifying the vision for implementation and policy. The second stage (within five years) focused on building collaboration among stakeholders. The third stage (within ten years) involved carrying out the plan in all relevant public and private sectors.

The EHR initiative in the United States gained a national commitment and focused leadership in 2004 when the Office of the National Coordinator for Health Information Technology (ONC) was created under the Secretary of Health and Human Services.[29] The national health IT initiative 2004-2013 identified the U.S. national priority—and consequently ONC's primary goal—as ensuring that most Americans have an EHR by 2014.

ONC provides leadership for the development and the nationwide implementation of an interoperable health IT infrastructure to improve the quality and efficiency of healthcare and the ability of consumers to manage their care and safety. Despite the work of ONC, minimal adoption of the EHR and continued use of paper systems (outside the Veterans Administration System) has persisted. However, the American Recovery and Reinvestment Act (ARRA)[30] of 2009 is expected to be an added impetus to the advancement for the adoption of health IT and the EHR. This $19 billion investment is expected to improve healthcare quality, prevent medical errors, reduce healthcare costs, increase administrative efficiencies, decrease paperwork, and expand access to affordable care. It is clear that the goals remain the same across the several initiatives that have moved the development and adoption of the EHR in the United States. The commitment to interoperable health IT is reaffirmed; the resultant expectations of this investment continue to be not only improved individual patient care but also enhanced early detection of infectious disease outbreaks around the country; improved tracking of chronic disease management; and evaluation of healthcare based on value enabled by the collection of de-identified price and quality information that can be compared. Nursing is integral to the deliberations of the two ARRA Committees: the HIT Policy Committee[31] includes Connie White Delaney, and the HIT Standards Committee[32] includes Judy Murphy and Linda Fischetti as members. Numerous nurses populate the working groups of these entities as well.

Additional nursing-centric initiatives contribute to developing and advancing the EHR in the United States. The Alliance for Nursing Informatics (ANI),[33] supported by HIMSS and AMIA, is a collaboration of organizations representing a unified voice for nursing informatics. ANI represents thousands of nurses and brings together more than 25 nursing informatics groups in the United States that function separately at local, regional, national and international levels. ANI provides a single point of connection between nursing informatics individuals and groups and the broader nursing and healthcare community; and provides a mechanism for transforming care, developing resources, guidelines, and standards for nursing informatics practice, education, scope of practice, research, certification, public policy, terminology, best practice guidelines, mentoring, advocacy, networking, and career services. ANI efforts support nursing leadership and expertise in the advancement of the EHR in the United States.[33]

Another example of a national nursing effort to support the adoption of EHRs in the United States is the Technology and Informatics Guiding Educational Reform (TIGER) Initiative.[34] TIGER aims to enable practicing nurses and nursing students to fully engage in the unfolding digital electronic era in healthcare. The purpose of the initiative is to identify information/knowledge management best practices and effective technology capabilities for nurses. TIGER's goal is to create and disseminate action plans that can be duplicated within nursing and other multidisciplinary healthcare training and workplace settings. In 2007, the TIGER Initiative catalyzed a dynamic, sustainable, and productive relationship between ANI, with its 25 nursing informatics professional societies, and the major nursing organizations, including the American Nurses Association (ANA),[35] the Association of Nurse Executives (AONE),[36] the American Association of Colleges of Nursing (AACN)[37] and others, which collectively represent more than 2 million nurses. In Phase 1, TIGER engaged stakeholders to create a common vision of ideal EHR-enabled nursing practice. Phase 2 facilitated collaboration among participating organizations to achieve the vision. Phase 3 is a call to action in the following crucial areas: Standards & Interoperability, National Health IT Agenda, Informatics Competencies, Education and Faculty Development, Staff Development, Usability & Clinical Application Design, Virtual Demonstration Center, Leadership Development, and Consumer Empowerment & Personal Health Records.

Moreover, both national organizations representing schools of nursing have provided major leadership in advancing a nursing workforce that possesses competencies to support the development, adoption, and implementation of the EHR. The American Association of Colleges of Nursing[37] has required informatics competencies in all curricula for baccalaureate and doctorate of nursing practice programs. The National League for Nursing has included such criteria as well.[38]

Three US case studies exemplify the critical role of nursing and nurses in the development and adoption of EHRs and the transformation of healthcare. Case Study 14B and Case Study 14C describe the EHR developments within the Mayo Health System and Intermountain Health Care, respectively. Case Study 14D describes the e-Health Statewide Initiative in Minnesota,[39] one of the most progressive of its type and exemplifying state-wide collaborations in the United States.

Latin American/Caribbean and South America

Several national initiatives are underway in Latin America/Caribbean and South America to advance the EHR. Latin America/Caribbean is a heterogeneous region with diverse social, economical, and political structures. In those countries with political and economic stability, purchase and implementation of clinical information systems is occurring, but this is not always linked to an EHR national strategy. There may also be healthcare organizations within developing countries that have the economic resources to purchase and implement electronic medical record systems, but these tend to be organization-specific rather than part of countrywide strategy. Nationwide health IT strategies across this region can be found in varying developmental stages. And importantly, there is a shared vision among healthcare leaders of the function of EHR systems and a commitment for their adoption to transform healthcare systems.[40] Targeted goals include improving health system accessibility, reducing inequity, providing high quality and integrated services, and orienting healthcare delivery toward primary care centered on people. Structurally, change is being promoted in the areas of healthcare systems roles, new insurance and payment methods, and human resources' needs with new workforce competencies, legal framework, and organization of work processes with an emphasis on teamwork.

Within Latin America and the Caribbean, there is movement toward becoming more involved in global healthcare initiatives. The Internet supports these new trends of using information internationally. Companies that operate internationally have introduced technology and related standards, which are consistent with international strategies and activities supported by the International Medical Informatics Association,[41] International Standards Organization (ISO),[42] and the European Community.[40] Advancements in Cuba are profiled in Case Study 14E. Cuba is advancing in the use of the Internet to support advanced education; the development of minimum nursing data collection; implementation of nursing terminologies including NANDA, NIC, NOC, and the ICNP; and coordinating countries developments with regional and national initiatives and standards.

South America

In South America, 40 notable national EHR initiatives include Argentina (Bases para un Plan Estratgico de Mediano Plazo en Ciencia, Tecnologa e Innovacin (Ministerio De Educacin, Ciencia Y Tecnologa), 2005-2015); Columbia (Red de Telemedicina - Telemedicine network); Brazil;[43] Ecuador (2007 "La Agenda Nacional de Conectividad"; 2008 national electronic patient record system Historia Clinica Digital; Estrategia Nacional para la Sociedad de la Información y el Conocimiento: Plan de Acción 2005-2010); and Peru (Plan Nacional de Telesalud - National Telehealth Plan).[40]

Challenges to advance the EHR agenda in Argentina continue while noting the early work in this country in the 1990s to advance computer documentation.[40] In Case Study 14F, the marked advancement of the EHR work in Argentina is highlighted, as well as the progress made in nursing and nursing informatics. EHR adoption in ICYCC (University Hospital), the evolution of medical informatics, the establishment of the Association of Nursing Informatics of the Argentina Republic,[41] the 2007 Latin-American Symposium of Nursing and 2008 Argentine Symposium of Nursing Informatics, and the emergence of informatics major area of study at the School of Nursing of Federal Police University of Argentina are remarkable advancements.

Development of the EHR and leadership in nursing informatics in Brazil[43] is highlighted in Case Study 14G. The development and organization of nursing informatics have a clear relationship to nursing's role in participating in Brazil's EHR design and deployment. Brazil continues to make great strides in addressing the NI specialty capacity. For example, under Marin's leadership, standards for building the nursing information component within EHR systems have been defined and placed in the context of strategies for increasing the EHR capacity across Central and South America.[40]

Building on the pioneering work at the Nursing Informatics Research Group at the Federal University of Sao Paulo, more than 16 research groups now foster informatics knowledge discovery and dissemination in the country. Brazil's progress[43] in advancing the RUTE network, now connecting approximately 57 healthcare organizations in the country, is exemplary. EHR deployment in the country has expanded to include telehealth applications for monitoring and consulting. Implementation of the ICNP and augmentation of the ICNP in community health terms, as well as implementation of other classifications, including NANDA and

NIC are occurring. Critical informatics advancements in the last few years support nursing practice, education, management, and research.

Another example of considerable growth in EHR work and leadership is the country of Chile. Case Study 14I captures the adoption of information technologies in Chile in the last few years. Building upon the 2003 Digital Agenda initiative, investments are being made in the health information infrastructure to support the National System of Health. In addition to many EHR applications, telemedicine advances are also included.

Conclusion

This chapter has summarized some of the most progressive initiatives within the Americas. It readily acknowledges that further progress, or at the least, fast adoption in all countries, is dependent upon increasing the availability of informatics specialists. It also is clear that independent of country, there is a critical training need for all clinicians in IT, the EHR, and in all of the transformative potential of these technologies.

There are examples of the integral role of nursing in leading standards, EHR, and educational initiatives. The elevated status of nursing creates the foundation for the emergence of nursing informatics. Increasingly the healthcare world is being positioned for interoperability across national boundaries.

References

1. Wikipedia. http://en.wikipedia.org/wiki/Americas. Accessed October 10, 2009.
2. World Health Organization. http://apps.who.int/whosis/database/. Accessed October 20, 2009.
3. MUNDI Index. http://www.theodora.com/wfbcurrent/greenland/greenland_people.html. Accessed October 20, 2009.
4. Pan American Health Organization (PAHO). *Health in the Americas,* 2007. Washington, DC: PAHO, 2007; 425-744.
5. Canada Health Infoway (2009). Canada boosts electronic health record system spending by $500 million. http://www.infoway-inforoute.ca/lang-en/about-infoway/news/news-releases/390-le-canada-hausse-les-depenses-pour-les-systemes-de-dossiers-de-sante-electroniques-de-500-millions. Accessed April 25, 2009.
6. http://www.infoway-inforoute.ca/lang-en/about-infoway/approach/investment-programs. Accessed October 10, 2009.
7. International Health Terminology Standards Development Organization. Members of IHTSDO. http://www.ihtsdo.org/members/. Accessed April 26, 2009.
8. http://www.health.gov.on.ca/hobic. Accessed October 10, 2009.
9. www.cna-aiic.ca/c-hobic. Accessed October 10, 2009.
10. Canadian Institute of Health Information (2009). CIHI – Taking Health Information Further. http://secure.cihi.ca/cihiweb/dispPage.jsp?cw_page=profile. Accessed April 25, 2009.
11. www.cnia.ca. Accessed October 20, 2009.
12. National Health Information Infrastructure. http://aspe.hhs.gov/sp/NHII/. Accessed October 19, 2009.
13. National Health Information Infrastructure Standards. http://aspe.hhs.gov/sp/NHII/standards.html. Accessed October 15, 2009.
14. http://www.ahrq.gov. Accessed October 1, 2009.
15. http://aspe.hhs.gov. Accessed October 10, 2009.
16. http://www.cdc.gov. Accessed October 10, 2009.
17. http://www.cms.gov. Accessed October 1, 2009.
18. http://aspe.hhs.gov/datacncl/index.htm. Accessed October 10, 2009.
19. http://www.fda.gov. Accessed October 1, 2009.
20. http://www.hrsa.gov. Accessed October 1, 2009.
21. http://www.cdc.gov/nchs. Accessed October 5, 2009.
22. http://www.nih.gov. Accessed October 5, 2009.
23. http://www.nlm.hih.gov. Accessed October 10, 2009.
24. http://www.hhs.gov/ocr. Accessed October 20, 2009.
25. http://www.hhs.gov/oirm. Accessed October 5, 2009.
26. http://www.osophs.dhhs.gov/ophs. Accessed October 20, 2009.
27. National Committee on Vital and Health Statistics (NCVHS). 2001. Information for Health: A Strategy for Building the National Health Information. http://aspe.hhs.gov/sp/NHII/Documents/NHIIReport2001/default.htm. Accessed October 10, 2009.
28. HHS Agencies. http://aspe.hhs.gov/sp/NHII/hhsrole.html, Accessed October 5, 2009.
29. Office of the National Coordinator. http://healthit.hhs.gov/portal/server.pt?open=512&mode=2&cached=true&objID=1200. Accessed September 28, 2009.
30. American Recovery & Reinvestment Act of 2009. http://www.whitehouse.gov/the_press_office/arra_public_review/. Accessed August 26, 2009.

31. Health IT Policy Committee (Federal Advisory Committee). http://healthit.hhs.gov/portal/server.pt?open=512&objID=1269&parentname=CommunityPage&parentid=1&mode=2&in_hi_userid=10741&cached=true. Accessed October 15, 2009.

32. Health IT Standards Committee. http://healthit.hhs.gov/portal/server.pt?open=512&objID=1271&parentname=CommunityPage&parentid=2&mode=2&in_hi_userid=10741&cached=true. Accessed October 15, 2009.

33. Alliance for Nursing Informatics. http://www.allianceni.org/default.asp. Accessed September 2009.

34. TIGER Initiative. http://www.tigersummit.com/. Accessed September 26, 2009.

35. www.ana.net. Accessed October 10, 2009.

36. www.aone.org. Accessed October 10, 2009.

37. American Association of Colleges of Nursing.

38. National League for Nursing. http://www.nln.org/index.cfm, Accessed October 20, 2009.

39. Minnesota e-Health Initiative. http://www.health.state.mn.us/e-health/. Accessed October 2, 2009.

40. Open Clinical HIT in South America. http://www.openclinical.com/hitGlobalAmericaSouth.html. Accessed October 20, 2009.

41. www.imia.org. Accessed October 10, 2009.

42. www.iso.org. Accessed October 10, 2009.

43. National Information & Communication Infrastructure in Brazil. http://www.who.int/goe/data/country_report/bra.pdf. Accessed October 15, 2009.

Case Study 14A

Canada's Journey Toward an Electronic Health Record: Nursing's Role

By Lynn M. Nagle, PhD, MScN, BN, RN; and Peggy White, MN, BA, RN

Introduction

Canada's Healthcare System

Canada is the second largest country in the world. It encompasses 3.9 million square miles and has approximately 33 million residents.[1] The principles governing the Canadian healthcare system are symbols of the underlying Canadian values of equity and solidarity. The national health insurance program is designed to ensure that all residents have reasonable access to medically necessary hospital and physician services.[2] Instead of a single national plan, Canada has a national program that is composed of thirteen interlocking provincial and territorial health insurance plans, all of which share common features and basic standards of coverage. Canadian health services are delivered by more than 400,000 healthcare professionals within more than 700 hospitals, primary and community care settings, and long-term care facilities.[3]

While health service delivery is supported by a combination of public and private funding, the public-sector share of healthcare spending has remained relatively constant at approximately 70%,[4] since 1997. Nonetheless, as is occurring in other nations around the world, Canada's healthcare spending continues to rise every year. Expenditures were projected to reached $171.9 billion in 2008, and since 1998 have grown faster than the gross domestic product (GDP) in Canada. As a result, the total health expenditure-to-GDP was forecasted to approximate 10.7% in 2008, with an estimated $5,170 per capita. In 2008, hospitals consumed the largest share of health dollars at 28%, drugs accounted the second largest share at 17.4%, and physician costs were third at 13.4% of the total health expenditure.[4]

Health informatics or e-health—the application of information and communication technologies (ICT) in the healthcare sector—is viewed as an essential element of cost containment and healthcare renewal in Canada. Current investments in ICT to support healthcare delivery, public health surveillance, and chronic disease management are viewed as a means to derive benefits for Canadians through improvements in system accessibility, quality, and efficiency.[5]

Electronic Health Records in Canada

In 2001, with the support of federal funding, Canada Health Infoway (*Infoway*) was established as an independent, not-for-profit corporation and given a mandate to deploy the infrastructure and system components to support the concept of a "pan-Canadian" EHR. *Infoway* purports that investments in key aspects of "infostructure" will have direct benefits to Canadians by improving the quality, accessibility, portability, and efficiency of health services delivery across the continuum of care.[5] *Infoway's* mandate includes (1) strengthening and integrating health services through EHRs, (2) empowering the public by increasing health information access, (3) addressing issues of privacy, (4) developing and implementing standards, and (5) assuring the adoption of emerging technologies through private and public sector collaboration.[5] Strategic investments have been directed to each of the provinces and territories in support of initiatives that provide the foundation for an interoperable pan-Canadian EHR.

In 2008-2009, the *Infoway* business plan outlined investment strategies to complete the implementation of the following elements within every jurisdiction across Canada: (1) infostructure (e.g., standards, interoperability), (2) registries (e.g., patient, provider, and location, (3) interoperable drug information systems, (4) regional diagnostic imaging systems, (5) laboratory information systems, and (6) telehealth[5] (see http://www.infoway-inforoute.ca/lang-en/about-infoway/approach/investment-programs for additional information[6]). In addition, several demonstration projects focused on specific clinical populations (e.g., mental health, cancer care, chronic disease management) and targeted innovations (e.g., caregiver portal, emergency triage kiosks) are also being funded. To date, *Infoway* has received approximately $2.1 billion in investment capital for the development, replication, and deployment of reusable interoperable EHR solutions across Canada.[7]

In Canada's healthcare system, business and operations systems account for the highest number of ICT installations, followed by admission-discharge-transfer (ADT) and core departmental systems such as pharmacy, laboratory, and diagnostic imaging information systems. However, much work remains to achieve the degree of interoperability and health information exchange needed throughout the healthcare system. Clinical applications such as online documentation and computerized provider order entry (CPOE) still need to be embraced by many health service organizations in Canada. These are likely the most difficult and disruptive of all clinical applications, yet have the most to offer in terms of safety, continuity of care, and continuity of information. "In many instances, we are still some way from having basic information digitized within hospitals, let alone having the ability to transmit data among groups of hospitals and across the country. There is still a need to boost IT budgets in hospitals and health regions."[8]

Nursing in Canada

The Canadian Nurses Association (CNA) is a federation of 11 provincial and territorial registered nurses associations representing more than 136,200 Canadian registered nurses.[9] CNA has taken a leadership role in the development of an e-health strategy for nursing in Canada. CNA supports that as knowledge workers in the technologic age, nurses need access to up-to-date information about their patients and that ICT initiatives are integral to nursing practice. The *E-Nursing Strategy* was designed to guide the development of ICT initiatives to improve nursing practice and patient outcomes.[10] The aims of the e-Nursing strategy is to ensure that nurses have access to ICT technologies, that nurses are competent in their use of ICT technologies, and that nurses play an increased role in the development of ICT solutions.

CNA has developed a nursing portal—NurseONE—to support the ongoing competence and professional development of nursing in Canada.[11] This portal is a personalized interactive Web-based resource developed to provide nurses and nursing students with a reliable one-stop information source for all their professional needs. NurseONE supports nursing practice through enhancing their evidence-based decision-making process, managing their careers, and connecting with colleagues and healthcare experts. NurseONE allows nurses and nursing students across Canada access to up-to-date, accurate information relevant to their practice.

Nursing Informatics in Canada

The term *informatics* is now consistently applied to the work of Canadian nurses engaged in the use of ICT in all settings and sectors. Historically, Canadian nurses have had limited education and involvement in the area of informatics. However, a recognition of the significance of ICT to support the work of nurses and the advancement of nursing knowledge is emerging. There are increasing efforts to engage nurses in activities such as system selection, design, implementation, and evaluation, but the majority of practicing nurses still lack core informatics competencies. Based on the findings of a national study conducted in 2003,[12] few Canadian schools of nursing have integrated core concepts of informatics within their basic nursing curricula. As of mid-2009, the significant lack of faculty capacity and expertise to facilitate this integration continues to exacerbate this situation. Yet it is clear that the heightened focus on and profile of clinical information systems in Canada necessitate attention to the informatics education of nurses. In anticipation of this emerging focus, the CNA has begun work to integrate informatics competencies into the national registered nurse examinations.

Many nurses have embraced informatics as a new area of nursing specialization, and the number of nurses in informatics roles has been gradually increasing over the years. This increase can be attributed to the recognition of the need to converge nursing expertise with knowledge of informatics to better inform systems design, implementation, education, and evaluation. Nevertheless, much work still remains to be done to initiate all nurses into the world of informatics as it relates to their practice and in order to educate them appropriately. We face a growing demand for nurse informaticians, as well as an entire nursing workforce that needs to be far more knowledgeable about the capacity and use of information and IT.

Canadian Nursing Informatics Association

The Canadian Nursing Informatics Association (CNIA) was established in 2002 and is an affiliate group of the CNA. CNIA's mission is to provide a voice for Canadian nurses on issues of health and nursing informatics. The intent of the CNIA is to engage nurses in all sectors and in all roles related to informatics practice, administration, education, and research. CNIA membership is primarily registered nurses but is also open to vendor and non-nurse participation. The board of directors comprises nursing informatics leaders that represent each provincial and territorial region. The CNIA has leveraged its position and formalized linkages with regional nursing informatics interest groups previously in existence and is working to support the emergence of new regional groups. The CNIA seeks to:

- Provide nursing leadership for the development of nursing and health informatics in Canada
- Establish national networking opportunities for nurse informaticians
- Facilitate informatics educational opportunities for all nurses in Canada
- Engage in international nursing informatics initiatives
- Act as a nursing advisory group in matters of nursing and health informatics
- Expand awareness of nursing informatics to all nurses and the healthcare community[13]

The CNIA has enjoyed a very positive working relationship with the Canadian Organization for the Advancement of Computers in Health (COACH), Canada's health informatics organization. The two organizations established a formal strategic alliance at the outset, which facilitated the appointment of a Canadian country representative to the International Medical Informatics Association–Nursing Informatics Special Interest Group (IMIA-NI SIG). IMIA-NI SIG provides an opportunity to collaborate and network with international nursing informatics colleagues. The CNIA works collaboratively with many other organizations, participating in pivotal Canadian health informatics discussions and planning in relation to national ICT strategies.

Informatics in Nursing Practice

Over the past decade, the extension of nursing services and expertise beyond urban centers has been made possible through the use of ICT. Given Canada's vast geography and numerous remote communities, applications of telehealth and telenursing are among the earliest and most significant success stories of informatics in Canadian nursing practice. At this juncture, numerous efforts are underway to weave informatics into the fabric of every nurse's daily practice. Nurses are increasingly engaged in the design, implementation, and evaluation of CISs. Yet to date, Canada's national health data repository includes no specific data and information related to nursing clinical services. National and provincial nursing organizations are beginning to take action to advance the adoption of a consistent nursing data set and a reporting structure that will reflect nurses' contributions to the healthcare services provided to Canadians. Unequivocally the most exciting and potentially the most important nursing informatics projects currently underway are those connected to the nursing and health outcomes initiatives that will be discussed further in this chapter.[14,15]

Nursing Data. Increasingly, in the healthcare environment, databases are being used for decision making regarding funding and health human resources planning; however, nursing is essentially invisible in these databases.[14] Furthermore, nursing executives are accountable for sustaining quality care in a financially constrained environment; therefore any investments in nursing resources need to be cost-justified. While nursing workload measurement data are used for planning, budgeting, and research purposes, numerous concerns have been raised with respect to the validity and reliability of these types of data. Many efforts are underway to develop new methodologies that more accurately reflect the intensity of nursing resources being brought to bear on patient care; without adequate measures of the work of nursing, nurse leaders will continue to face difficulties justifying nursing resource requirements.[16,17]

Since the early 1990s, CNA as been engaged in discussions regarding a nursing minimum data set (NMDS). Originally formulated as health information: nursing components (HI:NC), this data set includes information on patient status, nursing interventions, nursing resource use, and patient outcomes. The intent of capturing the HI:NC dataset is to assist and support clinical, administrative, educational, research, and policy development decisions.[18] In addition, linking these data elements to measures of nursing intensity and unique nurse identifiers has been proposed as a means to represent nursing contributions in the broader context of patient-centered health information.[19]

In 2000, a CNA discussion paper provided an overview and comparison of major nursing classification systems and promoted testing of the International Classification of Nursing Practice (ICNP)®.[20] The following year, a position statement was developed endorsing the adoption of nursing data in a manner consistent with the approach of the ICNP.[21] CNA supports the position that registered nurses should be advancing and leading efforts to collect, store, and retrieve nursing data at the national level. Since the late 1990s, the Canadian Institute of Health Information (CIHI) has managed centralized national health data reporting; however, while data are available on the numbers and location of nurses, limited information is available about the nursing care delivered, the use of nursing resources, and related health outcomes. The existence of this national reporting repository provides Canadian nurses with an opportunity to influence future directions of clinical data reporting.

During the late 1990s in the province of Ontario, the Ministry of Health and Long-term Care was interested in developing a methodology to capture the costs associated with nursing care. The Nursing and Health Outcomes project was established to drive this work. Early in the process of reviewing potential methods, it became apparent that a focus on outcomes of nursing practice would conceivably provide more meaningful information to understand nurses' contributions to clinical care. Subsequent to a comprehensive literature review and testing, a standardized data set reflective of nursing care was recommended for collection in Ontario.[22] The data set includes measures of functional status, symptoms (pain, nausea, dyspnea, and fatigue), therapeutic self-care, falls, and pressure ulcers. Strong evidence exists that nursing makes a difference in these clinical outcomes.[23]

The scope includes four sectors: acute care, chronic care, long-term care, and home care. The standardized clinical information is collected electronically at the point of care by nurses on admission and discharge for acute care; and on admission, quarterly and at discharge for chronic care, long-term care, and home care. Nurses are provided with access to real time information to use in planning for and evaluating care. Nurse managers and executives have access to real time reports at the unit level to use in examining the quality of care for patients on their unit.

In the province of Ontario, as part of the Nursing and Health Outcomes initiative, eight acute care organizations worked together to develop a common standardized admission and discharge assessment.[24] These standardized documents are now available to small, acute care organizations through a Web-based application to support introducing nurses to the electronic collection and use of standardized information. Recommendations for system-wide implementation of health outcomes data collection have been given high priority on Ontario's provincial health ministry's agenda. In 2005, the scope was expanded to other disciplines and other sectors of healthcare, and the name was changed to Health Outcomes for Better Information and Care (HOBIC) to reflect this expanded role.

In fall 2006, CNA partnered with the ministries of health in three provinces to develop a proposal to Infoway for funding to support the inclusion of nursing-related information in EHRs. Funding for this project—Canadian Health Outcomes for Better Information and Care (C-HOBIC) was approved in May 2007. This was the first nursing initiative funded by *Infoway*. C-HOBIC builds on and expands on the work of HOBIC to two other provinces in Canada. Similar to the work in Ontario, the standardized suite of evidence-based clinical outcomes are embedded into nursing assessments and the information provided back to clinicians to use in planning for care. A major deliverable of this project is to have nursing content documented in a standardized clinical terminology and coded in a format suitable for inclusion in the EHRs that are being implemented across Canada. The C-HOBIC concepts have been mapped to ICNP®.[25] This work provides an opportunity for nurses in Canada to contribute to the ongoing development of the standardized clinical terminology for nursing—ICNP.

Standardized clinical information on health outcomes will assist health planners and policy makers in evaluating whether investments in full-time nursing positions are resulting in better patient outcomes. In the long-term, information about specific clinical outcomes from all care settings will guide decisions about the appropriate care setting and caregiver mix for specific patient populations.

Informatics and Nursing Education

Over the past decade, there have been a couple of key national initiatives focused on the need for nurses to develop informatics competencies. Specifically, in 1999, several nursing groups submitted a collaborative report to the CNA on the National Nursing Informatics Project.[26] This report addressed (1) informatics competencies for entry-level nurses and specialists, managers, educators, and researchers; (2) curriculum implications and strategies for both basic and continuing nursing education; and (3) priorities for implementing national nursing informatics education strategies. The nursing groups, which developed this report by building on previous related works, set the foundation for national discussions of nurses and informatics.

In May 2002, the CNIA secured funding from the federal OHIH to undertake a national study of Canadian schools of nursing. This study sought to better understand the informatics curricula provided in basic nursing education programs across the country. In particular, the study focused on the availability of informatics expertise among nursing faculty, informatics content within core curricula, and the state of the technology infrastructure to support informatics in schools of nursing. Completed in 2003, the study findings highlighted the significant gaps in the informatics knowledge of nursing faculty, the lack of informatics integration into core curricula, and the need for ICT investment in Canadian schools of nursing.[13,27] Recommendations have been directed to a number of professional nursing organizations but particularly to the Canadian Association of Schools of Nursing (CASN), the Association of Canadian Executive Nurses (ACEN), the Office of Nursing Policy (ONP), the CNIA, and the CNA.[27]

The CNIA is currently focused on addressing the need for education and communication on issues of nursing informatics using a variety of media, including workshops, e-rounds, and national nursing informatics conferences. In total, each of these initiatives has and will contribute to the advancement of the national nursing informatics agenda in Canada. Like other countries, significant opportunity exists to advance the basic and expert levels of understanding within Canada's nursing community. The rapid evolution of Canada's e-Health agenda underscores the criticality of addressing this need immediately.

Summary

This case study has provided a brief overview of the Canadian healthcare system and highlighted nursing's role in our journey toward a pan-Canadian EHR. As with many countries, we have a long way to go. However, we hope to have demonstrated that Canadian nursing is part of this process and that Canadian nurses are taking a highly active role in helping to shape and direct the course we take. Our focus on the capture of clinical outcomes related to nursing care has begun to shift the culture of practice from one of data collection to one based upon the use of information to support clinical decision making. The recognition that nurses are truly knowledge workers is finally beginning to emerge as a central and important dimension of clinical care delivery in Canada. Nurses and the evolution of the EHR are clearly focused on optimizing the benefits to be derived for all Canadians, including ourselves!

References

1. Statistics Canada. http://www.statcan.ca/Daily/English/071219/d071219b.htm. Accessed March 20, 2009.

2. Department of Canadian Justice. http://laws.justice.gc.ca/en/showtdm/cs/C-6. Accessed March 20, 2009.

3. Canada Health Infoway (2007). Vision 2015: *Advancing Canada's Next Generation of Healthcare*. http://www.infoway-inforoute.ca/lang-en/working-with-ehr/health-care-providers/nurses. Accessed April 27, 2009.

4. Canadian Institute of Health Information (2008). *National Health Expenditure Trends, 1975 to 2008*. http://secure.cihi.ca/cihiweb/dispPage.jsp?cw_page=AR_31_E&cw_topic=31. Accessed April 24, 2009.

5. Canada Health Infoway (2008). *Corporate Business Plan 2008-09: Paving the way to collaborative care*. http://www.infoway-inforoute.ca/lang-en/about-infoway. Accessed April 22, 2009.

6. Canada Health Infoway (2008). *Infoway's Investment Programs*. http://www.infoway-inforoute.ca/lang-en/about-infoway/approach/investment-programs. Accessed June 9, 2009.

7. Canada Health Infoway (2009). *Canada Boosts Electronic Health Record System Spending By $500 Million*. http://www.infoway-inforoute.ca/lang-en/about-infoway/news/news-releases/390-le-canada-hausse-les-depenses-pour-les-systemes-de-dossiers-de-sante-electroniques-de-500-millions. Accessed April 25, 2009.

8. Irving R. *2005-2006 Report on IT in Canadian Hospitals: Current capabilities and upcoming acquisitions*. Thornhill, ON: Canadian Healthcare Technology: 2005.

9. Canadian Nurses Association. http://www.cna-aiic.ca/CNA/about/who/default_e.aspx. Accessed March 21, 2009.

10. Canadian Nurses Association. http://www.cna-nurses.ca/CNA/practice/informatics/default_e.aspx. Accessed March 21, 2009.

11. Canadian Nurses Association. http://www.cna-aiic.ca/CNA/documents/pdf/publications/2008_Fact_Sheets_e.pdf. Accessed March 21, 2009.

12. Clarke H. (2005). *Assessing the Informatics Education Needs of Canadian Nurses*. Project G3-6B-DP1-0054 report to the Office of Health Information Highway. http://www.cnia.ca/research.htm. Accessed April 24, 2009.

13. Canadian Nursing Informatics Association. *Goals of the CNIA.* http://cnia.ca/about.htm. Accessed April 26, 2009.

14. White P, Pringle D. Collecting patient outcomes for real: The Nursing and Health Outcomes Project. *Can J Nurs Leadership.* 2005;18(1):26-33.

15. *Health Outcomes for Better Information and Care* (2009). http//:health.gov.on.ca/hobic. Accessed June 9, 2009.

16. Hernandez C. O'Brien-Pallas L. Validity and reliability of nursing workload measurement systems: review of validity and reliability theory. *Can J Nurs Leadership.* 1996;13(2):32-50.

17. O'Brien-Pallas L, Irvine D, Peerebroom E, Murray M. Measuring nursing workload: understanding the variability. *Nurs Econ.* 1997;15(4):171-182.

18. Canadian Nurses Association (2003). International classification for nursing practice: Documenting nursing care and patient outcomes. *Nursing Now: Issues and trends in Canadian Nursing,* 14. http://www.cna-aiic.ca/CNA/documents/pdf/publications/NN_IntlClassNrgPract_e.pdf. Accessed March 20, 2009.

19. Canadian Nurses Association (2008). *Position Statement: Nursing Information and Knowledge Management.* Ottawa: Author. http://www.cna-aiic.ca/CNA/documents/pdf/publications/PS87-Nursing-info-knowledge-e.pdf. Accessed March 29, 2009.

20. Canadian Nurses Association (2000). *Collecting Data to Reflect Nursing Impact: A discussion paper.* Ottawa: Author. http://cna-aiic.ca/CNA/documents/pdf/publications/collct_data_e.pdf. Accessed March 20, 2009.

21. Canadian Nurses Association. Position statement: *Collecting Data to Reflect the Impact of Nursing Practice.* Ottawa: Canadian Nurses Association; 2001. http://www.cna-aiic.ca/CNA/documents/pdf/publications/PS54_Collecting_Data_Nov_2001_e.pdf. Accessed March 20, 2009.

22. *Health Outcomes for Better Information and Care.* http://www.health.gov.on.ca/english/providers/project/nursing/nursing_mn.html. Accessed March 20, 2009.

23. Doran D. ed. *Nursing-sensitive outcomes: the state of the science.* Sudbury, MA: Jones & Bartlett Inc., 2003.

24. Tracey P. Integrating a standardized assessment into acute care settings: One LHINs Approach. *Can Nurse.* 2008;104(5):25-26.

25. Canadian Nurses Association. *Mapping Canadian clinical outcomes in ICNP®.* Ottawa: Author: Kennedy. http://www.cna-aiic.ca/c-hobic/documents/pdf/ICNP_Mapping_2008_e.pdf. Accessed March 21, 2009.

26. Hebert M. A national education strategy to develop nursing informatics competencies. *Can J Nursing Leadership.* 2000;13(2):11-14.

27. Nagle LM, Clarke HF. (2004). Assessing Informatics in Canadian Schools of Nursing. In: Fieschi M, Coiera E, Yu-Chuan JL, eds. *Proceedings 11th World Congress on Medical Informatics.* San Francisco, CA: published on CD.

Case Study 14B

Mayo Clinic

By Marceline R. Harris, PhD, RN; David N. Mohr, MD, FACP; Jane A. Timm, MS, RN;
Catherine E. Vanderboom, PhD, RN; and Scott W. Eising, BS

Introduction

Since its founding over a century ago, Mayo Clinic has been committed to the organization and stewardship of clinical data. These data are an essential component of the infrastructure that enables Mayo Clinic to meet its tripartite mission of excellence in patient care, clinical research, and the education of health professionals. The development and deployment of the electronic medical record (EMR) at Mayo Clinic and its use by nurses as members of the care team are firmly grounded in the history and culture of the Mayo Clinic mission. Therefore this case study is necessarily an intertwined story of Mayo Clinic, nursing at Mayo Clinic, Mayo Clinic's legacy medical record system, and the digital technologies that support the use of clinical data today and into the future.

The Legacy

Mayo Clinic's history begins with a devastating tornado in Rochester, Minnesota, in 1883. After collaborating to attend to the immediate needs of tornado victims, the founder of the Sister of St. Francis, Mother Alfred Moes, approached William Worrall Mayo, MD, and proposed they collaborate to build and staff a hospital. As a result, St. Marys Hospital opened in 1889, the first hospital in southeastern Minnesota. The physician sons of Dr. William W. Mayo, William J. "Will" Mayo and Charles H. "Charlie" Mayo, both MDs, invited other doctors to join them and together, these physicians pioneered the idea of a multispecialty group practice clinic. This concept of collaborative and integrated care delivery continues to be identified as one of the most capable methods of delivering high-quality, cost-effective care. Donald Berwick, president and CEO of the Institute for Healthcare Improvement (IHI) recently noted: "That same integrated approach, which puts the needs of the patient first, is still in place at the Mayo Clinic today. As we look at national healthcare reform efforts, the Mayo model of care also provides a real-life example of the best forms of teamwork to deliver high-value care."[1]

From the beginning, nurses have been integral members of the Mayo Clinic team. When St. Marys Hospital opened in 1889, Edith Graham, then office nurse of the Mayo brothers, was appointed head nurse and taught the basics of nursing to the Sisters of Saint Francis. By 1906, a school of nursing was founded at St Marys Hospital, and by 1919, the Methodist Kahler School of Nursing was launched. Rochester Methodist Hospital was another hospital in Rochester used by Mayo physicians for inpatient care. Until 1970, these two schools prepared nurses at the hospitals that supported the Mayo Clinic. Although Mayo Clinic no longer offers academic degrees in nursing, each year more than 800 nursing students from across the U.S. and other countries complete clinical and research experiences at Mayo Clinic.

It was not until 1986 that Mayo Clinic, St. Marys Hospital and Rochester Methodist Hospital began functioning as one business entity; the previously separate departments of nursing across the hospitals were integrated shortly after that. The integration of staff working across inpatient, surgical services, and ambulatory nursing was accomplished in 2004, establishing for the first time a department of nursing infrastructure to direct and manage nursing practices across the practice, research, and education mission of Mayo Clinic. Today, the department of nursing comprises more than 7,000 employees who work across 20 nursing divisions, 56 inpatient units, 72 outpatient areas, surgical services, an emergency department, and social services. Mayo Clinic received its first Magnet Recognition in 1997, an important benchmark of the excellence, professionalism, leadership, and quality of the department of nursing.

Early Mayo Clinic leaders recognized that the ability of geographically dispersed individuals to work as a collaborative team required a medical record that organized clinical data in an integrated manner. In 1907, Henry Plummer, MD, and his assistant, Mabel Root, created a dossier medical record that contained each patient's entire medical history at Mayo Clinic, which was indexed by a numeric registration number (the Plummer Root System) that identified each patient's record and documents related to each episode of care. The concept of a "unit record" covering an episode of care was thus realized, with all of a patient's information tied to episodes residing in a single packet of documents that was stored in a central repository. A medical record transportation system was subsequently built on an infrastructure of lifts, conveyors, and pneumatic tubes so that records could be moved swiftly throughout the clinic and hospitals.

These technologies, developed to support the Mayo Clinic model of care, were truly innovations at the time they were developed and became the standard for medical record keeping around the world. In addition to making clinical data available whenever and wherever patients received their care (at least across the physical spaces in Rochester, Minnesota), the concept of a unit medical record also made longitudinal clinical data available to researchers. This research was greatly facilitated by the comprehensive medical and surgical diagnostic and procedural indexing systems introduced by Joseph Berkson, MD, in 1935. Later, building on the unit medical record and Berkson codes, Leonard Kurland, MD, led an effort to develop a population-based data resource that combined the clinical records of Mayo Clinic with the clinical data obtained by other community providers, most notably the Olmsted Medical Center. The Rochester Epidemiology Project (REP) emerged as a unique medical records-linkage system that continues to encompass the care delivered to residents of Rochester and Olmsted County, Minnesota. By organizing and indexing the clinical data for an entire population area, the REP is used by researchers from around the globe for population-based analytic studies of disease causes, trends, and long-term outcomes. The REP database of diagnoses was computerized in 1975, although the remaining clinical data continued to be abstracted from paper medical records. In 1987, a local Mayo modification to Hospital International Classification of Diseases (ICD-8) Adaptation (HICDA) codes was introduced and further expanded the detail or "granularity" of the indexing system.

Two key themes emerged from this legacy and guided the EMR development and the methods for making clinical data available electronically; first, the theme of integrated clinical data as core infrastructure for delivering the Mayo Clinic model of care across an episode of care, and second, the theme of standardized and coded indexes to organize clinical data for practice, research, and education. These underlying requirements for all systems that contain clinical data have driven many of the decisions that informed Mayo Clinic's EMR development.

The Electronic Medical Record

As Mayo Clinic patient volumes continued to increase, so did the content within the paper medical records of each patient. Furthermore, as new medical and surgical specialties emerged, the categorization systems used to organize the content in the paper record became inadequate. Regulatory and accrediting agency expectations of the additional detail of clinical data within the medical record also expanded, requiring additional burdens of documentation that needed new electronic processes. Within nursing, two influences on decisions about nursing documentation were (1) the concept of completeness of charting ("if it's not charted it's not done"), and (2) the goal of clearly documenting all aspects of the nursing process. Related to completeness of documentation, nurses were taught to document detailed information on essentially everything that occurred around the patient interaction. The expectation was that data needed for future retrospective reviews with unknown purposes, ranging from legal discovery to accreditation to research, would benefit from the detailed information nurses recorded in the medical record.

Related to documenting the nursing process, the major nursing terminologies (NANDA: North American Nursing Diagnosis Association; NIC: Nursing Intervention Classification; NOC: Nursing Outcomes Classification) were both used as organizing constructs and recorded as data in both the paper documentation environment and the EMR environment.

Jointly, these changes greatly expanded the content in the medical record; and chart volumes became unmanageable. Because of both space limitations and weight load restrictions for multi-floored buildings, Mayo Clinic records were for the first time separated into component parts with some components stored off-site. Finally, the geographic growth of the campus made the once-famous chart availability challenging to maintain.

In 1993, the Mayo Clinic Board of Governors appointed a committee to lead the envisioning, development, and implementation of an EMR and the associated reengineered inpatient and outpatient clinical processes. The reciprocal focus on an EMR-enabling processes of care and also on an EMR offering opportunities for improvements in processes of care again reflect the influence of the Mayo culture. This contemporary commitment to an electronic system that makes clinical data available to support today's Mayo model of care and care delivery processes is not different than the legacy commitment of the early Mayo leaders who developed the paper record system and manual transport system.

This EMR decision was made in the context of a 1991 IOM report on computer-based patient records that highlighted the problems with paper records.[2] By 2004, an integrated EMR system was fully operational across the clinics and hospitals in Rochester, becoming one of the most comprehensive EMRs in the United States. As in the days of Henry Plummer, at the time of the EMR roll-out the system supported the integration of clinical data, so that more than 16,000 physicians, nurses, pharmacists and others who required access to the system could coordinate the care delivered across 1.5 million outpatient visits and 60,000 hospital admissions per year. In 2009, documentation, ordering, decision support, results reporting, messaging, billing, pharmacy functions, medication management technologies (for example, bar coded medication administration) and administrative process support were implemented across the practice.

The first Informatics Nurse Specialist (INS) was actually hired in 1987, shortly after the integration of nursing staff across the two hospitals, to facilitate the development of a common documentation system for nurses who were newly integrated into one organizational unit, and in light of plans for an EMR. A nursing system model was defined to provide a framework for analyzing and communicating the information needs for nursing, examining the use of standard nursing classification systems, and organizing the clinical data provided by nurses.[3]

Throughout this 10-year effort to move from a paper-based medical record to an EMR, the mission of the Mayo Integrated Clinical System (MICS) teams paralleled the mission of Mayo Clinic and the Mayo model of care. Next, we provide a number of examples of decisions that were guided by the heritage of integrated clinical data and robust indexing.

The core clinical modules that were initially developed included a documentation entry system, a complex form entry system, a patient-provided information system, an ordering system, a viewer, and an electronic result inquiry system. All but the latter were designed and built by Mayo teams. The result inquiry (or viewing) system was purchased from a vendor, and it has gradually subsumed more and more of the integrated core functions of the core modules and added additional functions. This system was initially built by PHAMIS and is now supported by General Electric (GE). Mayo's use of a best-of-breed approach, as well as substantial in-house development efforts, were very purposefully undertaken within the paradigm of the needs to support one of the largest, complex clinical practices in the country. It was undertaken, as well, to address the need for an integrated clinical environment to support collaborative care. The name given to Mayo's CIS is an indication of the decision to focus on integration, i.e., the name is the Mayo Integrated Clinical System (MICS). Prior to determining whether to select a single vendor for the entire clinical suite or make use of several highly customized existing legacy systems (e.g., scheduling, registration, and the pharmacy system), a careful analysis was undertaken to consider these two alternative approaches to achieving an integrated environment. After review, a decision was made to only build or purchase new modules and interface them with the legacy applications.[4] This decision required a long-term commitment to developing an IT team focused on maintaining interfaces across multiple source systems and managing semantic interoperability; today the MICS application integrates data from more than 40 source systems.

A prerequisite to integration was the need for a way to move data from source systems into an integrated EMR. The (at that time emerging) HL7 message specifications offered a way to accomplish this in a standards-based manner. Because the value of rapid access to integrated clinical data was so embedded in the culture of medical record decision making, clinical proponents and IT staff were able to readily translate the construct of moving data to achieve an integrated view of an episode of care into technical specifications for EMRs. They jointly understood that the data generated by the care team needed to be available at the point of care, as well as stored in the ancillary systems such as lab, microbiology, etc.[5] Of note, members of the Mayo Clinic staff continue to be highly involved in the development of new generations of standard message specifications, document structures, information models, computational terminologies, and ways to "bind" terminologies to models.

The requirement of robust systems for indexing clinical data is another legacy strategy for enabling the Mayo Clinic mission and, similar to the integration of clinical data, has persisted into the EMR development and implementation. Mayo Clinic's research and development efforts on techniques for building terminology systems, including their application to the indexing of electronic clinical data, have long been recognized in the literature (e.g., see Chute and Yang, 1995).[6]

An example of the application of these newer technologies to indexing MICS data is evident in the development of a lexicon based on clinical data grouped within the unit of a clinically meaningful episode of care. A Master Sheet Index was developed in MICS, an implementation that transferred the concept of episode of care, defined as non-overlapping periods of clinical care that begins with first service or test and end with the dismissal of care. This definition of episode of care is not equivalent to other concepts of episode, such as episodes of service associated with, for example a hospital stay or a clinic visit interaction.[7]

At Mayo Clinic, a specific provider assumes responsibility for problem management across the episode of care, including managing the problem list that accrues as multiple providers enter problems and as the patient has multiple interactions with providers over the course of the time required to resolve an episode of care. Detailed and managed problem lists are then applied as an organizing construct for indexing the EMR across an episode of care. By merging the Master Sheet Index list of problems with the problems identified in the Clinical Notes system, a clinically derived lexicon was created; this lexicon was then used to write retrieval queries with far more precision than the HICDA codes described earlier.[8]

This definition of episode of care had significant implications for the department of nursing, however, because of its interest in identifying nursing-sensitive patient outcomes aggregated by both inpatient and ambulatory geographic areas of care. Subsequently the department of nursing built a system that links clinical data in the EMR to its electronic nursing workload system (i.e., patient classification data), in which each nursing unit of service to a patient is tied to a geographic area of care delivery. This has become a valuable resource for the institution as attention has focused on safety, quality, and the specific work environments in which patient care is delivered. While there are clearly important reasons to focus on time and geographically constrained intervals of care delivery (for example, a clinic visit or a hospital admission), it is a core pillar in Mayo's mission that the more fundamental concept of care coordination over a longitudinal episode of health or illness is maintained.

Nursing data are not yet indexed by a standard terminology or indexing system; electronic retrievals in the EMR are accomplished by familiarity with the "metadata" that is known about unique data elements stored within specific documents (e.g., flowsheet rows). A granular, clinically detailed terminology system that is organized to accurately represent and electronically process nursing knowledge constructs has been an ongoing focus of discussion among Mayo Clinic nurses. For example, are the three terminologies of NANDA, NIC, and NOC sufficient for providing the detailed level of data needed to, for example, launch decision-support systems, support retrieval of quality metrics, and overall capture at a sufficient level of detail the scope of information needed to fully represent the contributions of nurses to patient care? We have not been successful in implementing a system that can link nursing observations to the coded labels in those three systems.[9] Furthermore, the EMR has highlighted the need for nurses to engage in discussions, such as when standardized and controlled terminologies are required and when unstructured text is preferable. When controlled terminologies are required, which of the terminology systems will enable the EMR and clinical data analytic repositories to provide enhanced functionality, such as decision support, more efficient retrievals and analytics, and of increasing importance, assistance in reducing the complexity of nursing work? We are actively evaluating the extent to which the International Classification of Nursing Practice (ICNP®), SNOMED CT and other computational terminologies will meet these needs and also support the goal of referencing nursing classification systems.

Building on the long-standing institutional knowledge of clinical indexing system, Mayo Clinic is currently working on the development of a formal Mayo Clinic terminology. With a close eye turned to international standards-based terminology groups, the goal is to have terminology systems and detailed clinical models that will enable knowledge-based strategies within the EMR and the data repositories that support the practice, research, and education mission of the organization. We are living in a time of rapid knowledge development. Meeting the mission requires that individual patients receive personalized care and the context of that personalization may be a patient's genome, the course of an individual's condition within an integrated and indexed Mayo knowledge base, or within the context of external knowledge bases.

The focus of this discussion has been on Mayo Clinic in Rochester, Minnesota; at the time of writing this chapter Mayo Clinic Rochester has 15 years of experience with an EMR system. Other Mayo Clinic practice sites, including Jacksonville, Florida; Scottsdale, Arizona; and the Mayo Health System (a family of community-based clinics, hospitals, and other healthcare facilities in 70 communities in Minnesota, Iowa, and Wisconsin) also have had experience with electronic clinical systems. Mayo Clinic Arizona and Mayo Clinic Florida are in the midst of converging to a single EMR platform by 2010. Although clinical system convergence is a central theme, the need to converge on practices as well as the EMR is a central objective of this major initiative. Similarly, the Mayo Health System (MHS) is in the process of converging to a single EMR platform and the highly focused practice convergence that is necessarily part of an EMR implementation. The MHS effort is entitled "A Clinical Information Systems Transformation Strategy" (ASYST), and the goal is to create a single EMR across their hospitals and outpatient practices. These large-scale implementations required that many difficult decisions were made, some involving discussions of whether the Mayo Clinic Rochester constructs of episodes of care, clinical problem lists, and indexing tools were transportable to other Mayo Clinic practices and other EMR vendors.

Across sites however, the Mayo Clinic mission is consistent. Councils that span the "enterprise" have been developed to address this next stage of Mayo Clinic organization and stewardship of clinical data. Key committees at the enterprise level include a clinical practice committee, a practice convergence council, information technology (with oversight of the clinical data warehouse and data governance activities), a joint health information coordinating council, and a clinical decision support workgroup. Nursing across the entire Mayo Clinic enterprise has formed nursing councils that similarly focus on clinical practice, quality, evidence-based practice, and informatics across Mayo Clinic.

New Directions

Mayo Clinic, like other healthcare organizations, faces challenges tied to the national economy, the role of healthcare expenses within the national economy, and as yet unknown, healthcare reforms. There are however enormous opportunities to support the Mayo model of care by applying new technologies.

Fundamental concepts are being revisited. For example, the concept of "patient" does not fit in environments where people are not only being asked to become much more engaged in their health and healthcare but also demanding to become more involved. Similarly, the concept of "clinical data" must be augmented by the concept of "health data." The Web has become a primary resource for consumers to find health information and research their symptoms and diagnosis. Mayo does and will continue to play a leading role in providing trusted information, reviewed by experts and published on the Web, so people can access information whenever they need it most (see http://www.mayoclinic.com). Consumers are also becoming far more involved in generating and sharing health information with each other. Mayo is participating in this social networking activity by actively facilitating and engaging in the discussion and providing an expert voice.

To support consumers in managing their clinical data and their personal health data, it is necessary to provide access to personal health data. Mayo is an early thought leader in this area with the launch of Mayo Clinic Health Manager, a personal health application that is integrated with Microsoft's secure and private HealthVault platform. Health Manager is considered to be a next generation personal health record that moves beyond simple data repositories and actually offers personalized guidance to users based on their health data. Obviously, consumers need to use devices to access their electronically stored health data, and Mayo Clinic is closely watching the evolution of "smartphones" that provide mobile access to the Web and applications designed to specifically run on mobile devices. This will dramatically change how consumers access information and both manage and monitor their health in the future (see https://healthmanager. mayoclinic.com/default.aspx).[10]

If the consumer is also a "patient," Mayo is committed to providing a robust online patient portal to access information and complete transactions related to their care at Mayo (see http://www.mayoclinic.org/ news2008-mchi/4780.html). On the administrative side, this may include the ability to view and pay a bill, refill a prescription, or complete registration online. In the near future, patients will also be able to securely view parts of their EMR, securely message a member of their care team, and, when appropriate, complete an eVisit with their primary care provider. In addition, the systems will help Mayo to stay better connected with patients between visits by delivering reminders and alerts related to upcoming appointments or preventative services. Longer term, interoperability between Mayo systems and platforms such as Microsoft HealthVault would allow patients to share pre-visit information and personal data collected from remote monitoring devices for chronic conditions, such as hypertension, diabetes, obesity, fibromyalgia, or any number of other conditions.

Many healthcare professionals external to Mayo Clinic also need to have relationships with Mayo Clinic to help provide coordinated care. Through a provider portal, external professionals have the ability to request a referral, then follow the progress and outcome of that patient visit all online through a secure Web interface. Additional features include the capability to request a specialty eConsult, avoiding the need for the patient to come to one of our campuses but still benefit from the Mayo model of care. Mayo Clinic nursing is an active collaborator in developing these systems, and in defining what collaboration means when consumers are active participants of the care team.

Summary

Over the past 100 years, Mayo Clinic has retained a focus on the central role of organized clinical data for meeting the mission of excellence in patient care, clinical research, and the education of health professionals. The concept of a "medical record" has evolved from ledgers and coded index cards, to paper medical records, EMRs, and most recently, to electronic and personal *health* records. New technologies will continue to emerge and present new opportunities for organizing, accessing and using clinical data; the technologies will also require that we remain open to redefining the concept of a medical record and the role of clinical data in enabling the health of individuals and populations.

References

1. Mayo Clinic (2009). *Mayo Brothers to be Inducted into Healthcare Hall of Fame.* http://www.mayoclinic.org/news2009-rst/5186.html. Accessed May 5, 2009.

2. Dick RS, Steen EB, eds. (1991). *The Computer-Based Patient Record.* Washington, DC: The National Academies Press, 1991.

3. Behrenbeck JG, Davitt P, Ironside P, Mangan DB, O'Shaughnessy D, Steele S. Computers in Nursing. Strategic planning for a Nursing Information System (NIS) in the hospital setting. Development of a Nursing System Model. *Comput Nurs.* 1990;8(6):236-242.

4. Mohr DN, Sandberg SD. Approaches to Integrating Data Within Enterprise Healthcare Information Systems. *Proceedings /AMIA Annual Symposium.* 1999;883-886.

5. Cahill BP, Holmen JR, Bartleson PL. (1997). Mayo Foundation electronic results inquiry., the HL7 connection. *Proc Annu Symp Comput Appl Med Care.* 1991;516-520.

6. Chute CG, Yang Y. An Overview of Statistical Methods for the Classification and Retrieval of Patient Events. *Methods Inf Med.* 1995;34(1/2):104-110.

7. Claus PL, Carpenter PC, Chute CG, Mohr DN, Gibbons PS. (1997). Clinical care management and workflow by episodes. *Proceedings /AMIA Annual Symposium.* 91-95.

8. Elkin PL, Mohr DN, Tuttle MS, et al. Standardized problem list generation, utilizing the Mayo canonical vocabulary embedded with the Unified Medical Language System. *Proceedings/AMIA Annual Fall Symposium.* 1997;500-504.

9. Timm JA. Implementing the Nursing Outcomes Classification in a clinical information system in a tertiary care setting. *J Nurs Care Qual.* 1998;12(5):64-72.

10. https://healthmanager.mayoclinic.com/default.aspx. Accessed October 23, 2009.

Case Study 14C

Intermountain Healthcare

By Laura Heermann Langford, PhD, RN; and Nancy C. Nelson, MS, BSN, RN

Introduction

This case study focuses on the evolution, current use, and future of clinical information systems used at Intermountain Healthcare. The use of computers by nurses is given special attention. Also covered is the use of Clinical Programs, an organizational structure supporting efficient care for optimal outcomes and the critical role clinicians and clinical user groups play in the development of Healthcare Information Systems.

History of Intermountain Healthcare

Intermountain Healthcare is a non-profit integrated delivery network consisting of 22 hospitals and more than 100 general and specialty clinics that provide care throughout the state of Utah and southeastern Idaho. It is also the major referral center for western Wyoming, eastern Nevada, and northern Arizona. With more than 30,000 employees, including 12,000 registered nurses, 600 physicians, and specialty providers, Intermountain Healthcare is nationally recognized as providing excellent clinical care at affordable prices. *Modern Healthcare* has consistently ranked Intermountain Healthcare in the top three integrated health systems since 2000. Intermountain Healthcare was founded in 1975, after the Church of Jesus Christ of Latter Days Saints divested itself of several hospitals it owned and operated in the region, donating them to the community as a system. A stipulation of the donation was that the healthcare organization be not-for-profit and serve the healthcare needs of the community. The original system consisted of 15 hospitals, with four more hospitals joining the healthcare system during the 1980s. The system organized into hospitals, physicians, and a health plan in the early 1990s. The hospitals are also organized and managed by six geographic regions, Urban North, Urban Central, Urban South, Urban Southwest, Rurals, and Primary Children's Hospital.[1]

History of Clinical Information Systems at Intermountain Healthcare

HELP™

Informatics has long been an integral part of Intermountain Healthcare, contributing to the organization receiving the Hospital & Health Network's "Most Wired" award for the last nine years (since 2000). Latter Day Saint (LDS) Hospital, the initial flagship hospital of Intermountain Healthcare, was at the forefront in the use of computers in the clinical setting. The development of a comprehensive computer system called *HELP™* (Health Evaluation through Logical Processing) had its beginnings in the late 1960s, thanks to the pioneering work of Homer R. Warner, PhD; T. Allan Pryor, PhD; and Reed M. Gardner, PhD, as part of the LDS Department of Medical Biophysics and Computing. The system, as it exists today, is the result of a long evolution of incremental growth and development in parallel with the emerging discipline of medical informatics. It is interesting to note that early efforts of the system were geared toward exploring the use of computers to aid in the diagnosis of congenital heart disease. The most distinctive feature of the system is the integrated database, which allows the collection of clinical data from multiple sources. The value of a coded terminology to store and retrieve clinical data collected in the system to realize desired decision-making support from the computer quickly became apparent, and work began on creating a centralized coding scheme for medical terminology.[2] This integrated database allows quick access to comprehensive patient data. The research and development that unfolded at LDS Hospital in physiologic monitoring, systems integration, database development, medical equipment interface, and clinical decision support made LDS Hospital a pioneer in the field of computerized hospital information systems, both nationally and internationally.[3]

Following are some of the *HELP* clinical implementations that most significantly impacted nurses at LDS Hospital. The years of development and implementation have brought challenges, successes, and a few failures for the nurses who have been on the user end of the computer. Highlights of a few of these experiences follow:[3]

- Medications, vital signs, intake and output, and cardiac output data entered by technicians from nursing flow sheets
- Computerized nursing care plans
- ICU (intensive care unit) acuity via automated questionnaire
- Bedside data entry in ICU by nurses
- Bedside data entry on first acute care unit
- Automated ICU acuity from documentation
- Computerized Laboratory Alerting System (CLAS) experiment
- Blood order entry for physicians
- Medical information bus (MIB) in ICU
- New joint venture charting product installed on acute care pilot unit
- Original Computer Care plan program de-installed
- Implementation of acute care units on bedside charting
- Nursing diagnosis-based care plan installed
- New ICU charting program installed
- New medication charting program installed
- New order communications program installed
- ER (emergency room, emergency department) nurse documentation installed

Clinical Workstation

In the early 1990s, with the formalization of the physician group now called Intermountain Medical Group, it was necessary to provide computerized decision support and documentation tools for Intermountain's ambulatory clinics served by the Medical Group. The *Clinical Workstation* consisted of a graphical user interface (GUI) written in Visual Basic connected to an object-oriented central data repository (CDR) housed in a commercial relational database. This CDR model differed from the regional, hierarchical database of the *HELP* system in that it allowed more complex modeling, indexing, and retrieval of patient data. The CDR has also proven to be an essential tool throughout the enterprise, as it provides longitudinal records that are easily accessed at any care setting as patients move throughout the system. The lessons learned from the *HELP* system regarding coded terminology and decision support were brought forward into the *Clinical Workstation*, enabling the implementation of several care practice models and other decision-support tools at the point-of-care in the outpatient setting. The GUI was easy to use and allowed flexibility in template creation for specialty areas based on their unique needs and workflow. Coordination and development of the various specialized templates, while maintaining the centralized terminology and data repository, could be challenging, but the benefits of enterprise deployment were immediate.

A benefit realized by *Clinical Workstation* was more customization at the user level, by users, for documentation and reports. Features such as macro-driven text entry and common lists for data entry, in areas such as allergies and during prescription writing, were huge satisfiers for users. Users had complete control over content used in these features and could update them in real time. Features such as these were a significant step forward from similar activities in the *HELP* system, in which programmer support is required.

As an ambulatory-based tool and in its use in nursing, *Clinical Workstation* has had the greatest value to the advanced practice nurses. Several tools have been developed within the *Clinical Workstation* environment to assist advanced practice nurses with management of chronic conditions, such as anticoagulation management, diabetes management, organ transplant, cardiovascular care reporting, and NICU (neonatal intensive care unit) care.

HELP2 Clinical Desktop

Within a few years after initial implementation of the *Clinical Workstation*, Web-based tools came into vogue. The lightweight "thin client" or server based Web-tools promised to be much simpler than the "thick client" *Clinical Workstation* tools that had to be installed and updated on each terminal. The Citrix environment tools were used to support the deployment, maintenance, and support of *Clinical Workstation*, but these tools did not allow ubiquitous access outside the Intermountain Healthcare network.

Results Review was Intermountain Healthcare's first foray into Web-based tools. *Results Review* was a Web-based lab reporting and clinical document review tool built on top of the same relational CDR used by

Clinical Workstation. Results Review was a successful tool and quickly grew to include data entry tools for problem list management, allergy management, and outpatient medication list management with prescription writing functionality.[4] Other popular tools include the info button, physician documentation, user templates for structured narrative text and coded data elements, decision-support tools, and ED patient-tracking. As *Results Review* grew in functionality and was no longer just a review tool, it was rebranded by Intermountain Healthcare as *HELP2 Clinical Desktop.*

Systems in Use Today at Intermountain Healthcare

Each of the tools created at Intermountain Healthcare have been embraced and used extensively by the clinicians. Intermountain Healthcare's application of CISs to improve patient care is well-established.[5] *HELP* continues to be the primary tool used for inpatient nursing documentation, order communication, and results reporting. In the outpatient setting, the *Clinical Workstation* Visual Basic user interface has been almost entirely replaced by *HELP2 Clinical Desktop* functionality and is slowly being removed from care settings. Using *HELP2 Clinical Desktop*, outpatient providers and other caregivers document allergies, medications prescribed, problems, or other visit information into the CDR.

Data from the three main clinical information systems and a few niche systems are interfaced to and stored in the CDR, providing a single longitudinal patient record. An authorized provider is allowed a comprehensive view of patient health information via the combination of data from acute hospital encounters within the longitudinal clinical data repository.[5] *HELP2 Clinical Desktop* provides access to information in the CDR, independent of where the information is being requested or where the care was actually provided—inpatient, Intermountain outpatient facilities, or affiliated clinics. Caregivers appreciate the flexibility of the highly secured Web-accessible tools, enabling them access from home or other Internet-connected sites, such as airports and hotels.

In addition to the integrated record, advanced decision-support capabilities for alerting, as well as privacy safeguards to protect the electronic medical record are available in all CISs used by Intermountain Healthcare.[5] Intermountain Healthcare's integrated CISs provide versatile access to patient data, individually targeted decision support designed to provide best practice for patients with a wide variety of diseases, and convenient inter-provider collaboration.[6]

Applying Computerized Tools to Nursing Practice at Intermountain Healthcare Care Plans

The first application designed exclusively for the use of nursing was the nursing care plan. The pioneers for this early work, begun around 1981, were nurses Marjorie Cengiz, Jane Ranzenberger, Dickey Johnson, and Ann Killpack, in conjunction with Dr. T Allan Pryor and the LDS Department of Medical Biophysics and Computing. The ultimate goal of the project was to develop a dynamic nursing care plan that could be expeditiously written, easily updated, and serve the nurse as a valuable tool for delivering patient care.[7] The computerized care plan program was developed at the grass roots level with input from nursing staff from each nursing unit in the hospital. This group of nursing unit representatives became the first nursing user group.

The design of the care plan was based on body systems and patient problem format, including standard actions automatically generated based on the problem. The program offered the ability for optional actions to be selected based on specific patient needs. The nursing user group members were closely involved with testing the program by using it on patients in their respective units. The program, refined after several iterations of testing and feedback from the user group, was easy to use and more efficient than handwriting a care plan. It also included a care plan report, which allowed the head nurse to monitor care plan compliance, with the result that care plan compliance increased with the introduction of this new program. Computerized nursing care plans were almost unheard of in 1981, and therefore, many articles were written and published about the program at LDS Hospital.[7,8,9]

The nursing staff used the care plan program until 1990. While the novelty of the care plan program eventually wore off, the program was still used as the official care plan. It was felt by some that the program did not allow for enough individualization of care and was a traditional model based on medical practice, not on nursing practice.

In 1991, the era of Nursing Diagnosis lead to the development of a new version of the care plan based on the use of Nursing Diagnosis and was linked to the development of the patient history based on Functional Health Patterns. This new program development was done off-site and did not have the close collaboration with nurses from the nursing user group. The program was implemented in 1992, but never enjoyed the success of the original care plan program. The fact that Nursing Diagnosis was not widely embraced might have been part of the reason for the lack of success, but most likely the lack of involvement of the end users and the nurses in the design and development of the program was a factor. An important lesson about collaboration can be learned from this effort.

Inpatient Bedside Computer Documentation

While much of the patient data collected by nursing have been electronic since 1972, the actual data entry was not performed by nurses until the mid-1980s. Nurses first began documenting with the computers in 1985 in the ICU.[10] Bedside computers had been placed in the rooms of all the ICUs when the new wing was added in 1984. At first, nurses were reluctant to do their own data entry, a task that had previously been done by computer techs. The nurses soon found, however, that they could incorporate documentation at the bedside into their workflow, and thereafter, techs no longer entered data for the nurses.

In 1986, computer documentation moved from the ICUs to the first acute-care nursing unit, West 8, a 48-bed medical unit. At the time of implementation, it was not known whether bedside terminals would be needed, or if the placement of a terminal outside each four-bed pod would meet the needs of the nurses. An experiment was performed: bedside terminals were placed on one half of the unit, pod terminals on the other half of the unit. It became obvious quite soon after implementation of charting that bedside terminals would be needed if the charting were to be incorporated into the workflow of the nurses.[11,12] The pod end of the hall quickly became the least favorite assignment for nurses because of the queuing up that occurred in order to get their documentation into the computer. Nurses preferred working on the hall with the bedside terminal and even came to work early to make sure they got an assignment on that end of the hall.

Terminal placement aside, the introduction of computerized charting required individualized training strategies for each unit; in addition, adaptation to the workflow and culture of each nursing unit was required. The nursing information systems coordinators (NIS), also known as "computer nurses," had a huge task implementing computerized nursing and medication documentation throughout LDS Hospital. At one time, this team comprised five full-time nurses. The NIS Coordinators noted that the installation of the same charting program provided five completely different implementation experiences in the different units! One mechanism the NIS coordinators promoted to ensure adoption on various units was the development of user groups on each unit. Some of the tasks of the unit-based user groups included reviewing the database, serving as unit resource, identifying unit-specific requirements, assisting with testing, assisting with unit staff training, and providing nursing unit support during installations. An active and involved user group was critical to a successful implementation. A new role, "computer helper," was developed during the installations in 1991. Computer helpers were staff nurses who were very committed to the installation of the charting system. They were experienced users familiar with the program who knew the problems and could anticipate the needs of the staff on the unit. Computer helpers were used from various units to help with the implementation on other units. Their experience and expertise, as both clinicians and computer-user, were invaluable and greatly contributed to the success of the implementations. The use of front line clinicians is a hallmark of success for implementation at Intermountain Healthcare.[3]

Engagement of Clinicians with Clinical Information Systems

Engagement of clinicians as key members of the CISs development teams is heartily endorsed at Intermountain Healthcare. Clinicians of all disciplines are involved through strategic and operational leadership with development team members, user groups, as well as implementation training and support.

Clinical Programs

Intermountain Healthcare has developed clinical programs, an organizational structure which helps physicians, nurses, and other clinical professionals develop best practice care process models, set goals, measure results, and systematically apply best practices with the ultimate goal of providing higher quality care and improving patient outcomes.

To achieve this, the clinical program identifies key clinical processes. These processes are discussed among groups of clinical providers who are directly involved in the key processes. These clinical providers (nurses, physicians, pharmacists, etc.) comprise the development team for their specialty areas. The development team works together to develop guidelines based on evidence-based practice research. These guidelines are called Care Process Models (CPM). Intermountain also uses the evidence-based intervention bundles, which are a collection of interventions that, when performed together rather than individually, lead to improved outcomes. Using CPM and intervention bundles, the development team sets clinical goals and determines quality and outcome measures. The Clinical Program structure is particularly important to CIS development, as they are a point of clinically based collegial standards development for the entire enterprise. This allows the CIS developers to focus on enterprise solutions, as opposed to multiple facilities-based solutions.

With the help of the Clinical Program development team members, data collection processes and tools are developed. These tools are designed to fit into the clinician workflow and electronically capture the data whenever possible. Data are then imported into the data warehouse and reported and communicated electronically throughout Intermountain Healthcare via the reporting applications on the clinical program's Web site.

The Enterprise Data Warehouse (EDW) is a large database that combines medical records from the CDR with other relevant records, including administrative data. The EDW is unique from the CDR because it supports analytical studies of populations, whereas the CDR is meant for patient-specific queries needed to support patient care. The EDW is an important resource for quality initiatives and outcomes research. Data Managers, who are often clinicians, continually monitor the data being collected by bedside caregivers in the routine course of care and report back to the clinical programs in order to track progress toward clinical outcome goals. These data help drive the clinical programs that are recognized for helping clinicians provide the best outcomes for patients in hospital and clinic settings. Nursing plays a critical role in quality improvement initiatives, and informatics plays an important role in providing data that can be transformed into powerful information and knowledge in support of these initiatives.

Other Clinical Roles

Clinical Collaboration Lead (CCL) is another important role in the development of CISs at Intermountain Healthcare. CCLs are each associated with one of the clinical programs and are the direct day-to-day representatives of the clinical program to the development teams. The CCL is integral in organizing clinical user groups and for arranging site visits or focus groups when needed by the development teams. The CCL is also an important member of the implementation teams, ensuring consistency from development through implementation. This allows development team members to continue focusing on new development projects and enhancements to existing projects, while still supporting the implementation teams and new product users.

The success of the *HELP* system can be attributed to the collaborative relationship between the nurses, physicians, and informaticists. Clinicians play an active role in the analysis, design, and development of all CISs created at Intermountain Healthcare. They work closely with the system architects and software developers to perfect the systems. This successful relationship started with the *HELP* system, in which the proximity of system designers and clinicians that was afforded at LDS Hospital made it possible.[13]

Clinicians Embedded in Information Systems

In recent years when development has had a more enterprise focus and IS teams are too large to house at individual hospitals, clinical engagement has continued through the roles of clinical analysts and various user groups. The Information Systems Department at Intermountain Healthcare employs clinicians in dedicated roles as clinical experts, clinical analysts, and informaticists. Clinical experts are clinicians whose primary working responsibility is as bedside caregivers but who also work dedicated hours (or shifts) with information system development teams. They spend anywhere from eight to twenty-four hours per week embedded on specific development teams, creating requirements or providing input to designs and prototypes. Clinical analysts are clinicians who are full-time employees to development teams. They are responsible for defining and documenting workflow and requirements pertinent to the project assigned. They are also responsible for maintaining and soliciting feedback from user groups as needed. Informaticists at Intermountain Healthcare are specialists in CIS architecture and design and have a strong understanding of clinical environments, workflow, and clinical decision making. They are also knowledgeable in how to apply computerized tools to clinical information management.

User Groups

Several different types of user groups are applied to CIS' development at Intermountain Healthcare. Some groups, called the *expert design teams*, are small groups of eight to twelve people who meet on a regular basis (one to two hours every week or every two weeks) contributing to and following the development of specific products. Expert design team members are selected by CCLs when requested by development teams. They consist of domain experts of intended-use audiences for the product under development.

The challenge of getting input from clinicians across a geographically diverse organization has been addressed by holding distributed product review meetings every month using Web-based meeting tools. Product review teams consist of six to ten clinicians from each region, participating in an overview and feedback discussion from a conference room in their local area. Products are presented on a rotating basis throughout their development to get input from a broad audience of future users. Product review teams help the development teams ensure that they do not build a product too specific to one facility or region.

Other user groups that have been important to CIS development at Intermountain Healthcare are ad hoc groups formed specifically for needs unmet by the other user groups in place or to allow other stakeholders to view and provide input into the development process and, ultimately, the end product. These ad hoc groups could consist of bedside clinicians not already represented in other user groups or of clinical leadership.

Summary

Intermountain Healthcare has been a major force in clinical informatics research and development over the years. It has led the way in the formation and use of IS in healthcare and offers key insights into some of the processes and procedures required to implement these systems successfully.

References

1. Intermountain Healthcare. http://en.wikipedia.org/wiki/Intermountain_Health_Care. Accessed April 14, 2009.

2. Kuperman GJ, Garner RM, Pryor TA *HELP: A Dynamic Hospital Information System.* New York, NY: Springer Verlag; 1991

3. *First Annual Nicholas E. Davies Computerized Patient Record (CPR) Recognition Symposium Proceedings,* Steen EB, ed. Pp. 19 to 55. April 4-6, 1995. ISBN: 007-1349650 McGraw-Hill.

4. Del Fiol G, Haug PJ, Cimino JJ, Narus SP, Norlin C, Mitchell JA. Effectiveness of topic-specific infobuttons: a randomized controlled trial. *J Am Medical Inf Assoc.* 2008;15(6):752-759.

5. Wilcox A, Kuperman G, Dorr DA, et al. Architectural Strategies and Issues with Health Information Exchange. *AMIA Annual Symposium Proceedings.* 2006:814-818.

6. Dorr DA, Wilcox A, Burns L, Brunker CP, Narus SP, Clayton PD. Implementing a multidisease chronic care model in primary care using people and technology. *Dis Manag.* 2006;9(1):1-15.

7. Cengiz M, Ranzenberger J, Johnson DS, Killpack AK, Lumpkin RW, Pryor TA. Design and Implementation of Computerized Nursing Care Plans. *Symposium on computer applications in medical care (SCAMC).* 1983;7:561-564.

8. Chapman R, Ranzenberger J, Killpack AK, Pryor TA. Computerized Charting at the Bedside: Promoting the Nursing Process. *Symposium on computer applications in medical care (SCAMC).* 1984;8:700-702.

9. Johnson DS, Ranzenberger J, Pryor TA. Nursing Applications on the HELP System. *Symposium on computer applications in medical care (SCAMC).* 1984;8:703-708

10. Bradshaw KE, Sittig DF, Gardner RM, Pryor TA, Budd M. Computer-based data entry for nurses in the ICU. *MD Comput.* 1989;6(5):274-280.

11. Halford G, Burkes M, Pryor TA. Measuring the impact of bedside terminals. *Nurs Manage.* 1989;20(7):41-42, 44-45.

12. Willson D. Survey of Nurse Perceptions Regarding the Utilization of Bedside Computers. *Proc Annu Symp Comput Appl Med Care.* 1994:553-557.

13. Gardner RM. Observations and Opinions: Collaborations in Clinical Computing at LDS Hospital. *MD Computing* 1994;11(1):10-13, 63.

Case Study 14D

Minnesota Statewide e-Health Initiative

By Bonnie L. Westra, PhD, RN, FAAN; Martin LaVenture, PhD, MPH; Barbara J. Wills;
and Sripriya Rajamani, PhD, MBBS, MPH

Introduction

Minnesota is a national leader in successfully moving toward interoperable EHRs across the entire state. This is a case study about the state's collaborative process, which is based on health data that support credible recommendations for actions. This is also about balancing the "stick" of policy requirements with the "carrot" of policy incentives and recommendations for achieving success. The process includes broad stakeholder involvement through the Minnesota e-Health Initiative, adding Minnesota-focused value for providers and consumers, as well as supporting the objective of advancing the adoption and effective use of interoperable EHRs statewide. The Minnesota e-Health Initiative[1] is an open public process that welcomes everyone to participate. The ongoing collaborative spirit and the continuous interplay between the carrot (policy incentives and recommendations) and the stick (legislative policy mandates) has resulted in sustaining five years of steady success in Minnesota.

e-Health

E-health is the adoption and effective use of EHR systems and other health IT to improve healthcare quality, increase patient safety, reduce healthcare costs, and enable individuals and communities to make the best possible health decisions. Across the nation, e-health is emerging as a powerful strategy to transform our ailing healthcare system. Minnesota is a leader in pursuing bold e-health policies to accelerate the adoption of EHRs and related health IT statewide.

Minnesota e-Health Initiative

The Minnesota e-Health Initiative is a private-public collaborative authorized in 2005 by the Minnesota state legislature with a vision to accelerate the adoption and use of health IT to improve healthcare quality, increase patient safety, reduce healthcare costs, and improve public health (http://www.health.state.mn.us/e-health).[1] While many states have begun planning for interoperability of EHRs, Minnesota is recognized as one of the top five states with the longest histories of engaging multiple stakeholders and examining barriers and developing action plans to support the entire state in the electronic exchange of health information. The initiative is guided by a 25-member advisory committee to advance a statewide implementation plan for interoperable EHRs. The committee has multiple stakeholders representing hospitals, health plans, physicians, nurses, other healthcare providers, academic institutions, state government purchasers, local and state public health agencies, citizens, and others with knowledge of health IT and EHRs systems. The committee meetings are open to the public and materials and updates are available to interested stakeholders via the Web site or e-mail delivery service.

Vision and Roadmap for Strategic Action. The vision of the Minnesota e-Health Initiative[1] is to:

> ... accelerate the adoption and effective use of health information technology to improve health care quality, increase patient safety, reduce health care costs and enable individuals and communities to make the best possible health decisions.

The model[2] in Figure 14D-1 reflects the comprehensive focus of the vision with inclusion of key domains:

- **Consumers** (e.g., personal health records)
- **Clinicians** (e.g., electronic health records)
- **Policy/Research** (e.g., scientific information systems)
- **Public Health** (e.g., population health needs for individuals and systems)

Figure 14D-1. *Minnesota e-Health's Vision*

The areas of overlap rely on exchange of information, a major contribution of e-health. This vision is closely aligned with the goals of healthcare reform and transformation in that they both focus on increasing quality, safety, and access for the benefit of purchasers and consumers of healthcare.

Model for Statewide Focus: Building Consensus for Common Action. Goals established by the commissioner of health with recommendations from the Minnesota e-Health Advisory Committee and legislative priorities guide the Minnesota e-Health Initiative's work to achieve this vision. Goals are based on several factors including:

- Trends and needs that are spotlighted at the annual June statewide Minnesota e-Health Summit, which brings statewide health community leadership together.
- Feedback and priorities from the e-health work groups and advisory committee meetings.
- Laws passed from preceding legislative sessions.
- An assessment of what statewide needs and topics fit within the priorities and are appropriate to work on together for the following year.

The advisory committee holds a strategic planning retreat during the summer to assess the status of all of these factors and determine the committee's action plan and work groups for the coming work year, which culminates at the summit at the end of June each year.

Work Group Process - Charter Driven. The advisory committee meets quarterly and charter-driven work groups are the vehicle for investigating specific e-health topics through discussion and consensus-building. Each work group has a charter containing the purpose, schedule, deliverables, and co-chairs that guide the process. Minnesota Department of Health (MDH) staff members are assigned to support the research, logistics, drafting of materials, and preparation of meeting agendas. The co-chairs and the work group participants contribute subject matter expertise in discussions, research and analyses through hundreds of hours of volunteer time. The staff analyzes and interprets data and summarizes findings that will contribute to e-health policy development. Workgroup participants are recruited statewide, and dozens of volunteers contribute thousands of hours each year through participating in work groups staffed by the MDH Center for Health Informatics. Meetings are in-person and options are available to participate via telephone conference calls. Each work group focuses on different aspects for implementing interoperable EHRs. Overall coordination and identifying cross-cutting issues across work groups occurs through the MDH staff and the advisory committee.

The focus and composition of work groups adjusts annually to flexibly focus on new goals from the Commissioner of Health, legislative priorities, and advice from the Advisory Committee. For instance, the work groups in 2007 – 2008 were the Statewide EHR Plan; Standards' Privacy and Security; Population Health and Public Health Systems; and, Communications, Education, and Collaboration. In 2008 – 2009, one of the major priorities became implementing e-Prescribing as a result of legislation that all providers and payers would use e-Prescribing by 2011. The workgroups changed to accommodate the new goal and included e-Prescribing, Standards, and Effective Use of EHRs. Each of these work groups produced a "guide" to augment and update the statewide plan so that it continues to be a significant resource with relevant information about meeting the health IT challenges facing the health community in Minnesota.

Minnesota e-Health Summit – Building Statewide Consensus, Sharing Lessons Learned. Since June 2004, the Minnesota e-Health Initiative has co-sponsored an annual statewide e-health summit. The meeting objectives are to disseminate the results of the advisory committee's work and hear reports from community exemplars on progress toward achieving the initiative's vision. The summits have been at room capacity, drawing more than 400 attendees in 2008; attendees have included statewide leaders of health systems, consumers, providers, software vendors, research, public health departments, long-term care, clinics, and others interested in EHRs and health IT.

Accomplishments and Highlights

For a list of accomplishments of the Minnesota e-Health Initiative[3] year by year, please refer to Tables 14D-1, 14D-2, and 14D-3.

Statewide Plan for Implementing the 2015 Interoperable EHR Mandate

Minnesota Statutes, section 62J.495, required the commissioner of health to develop a plan for the state to achieve the statutory mandate that all providers and hospitals have in place "an interoperable electronic health records system within their hospital system or clinical practice setting." The plan, *A Prescription for Meeting Minnesota's 2015 Interoperable Electronic Health Record Mandate—A Statewide Implementation Plan, 2008 Edition,* was developed through the Minnesota e-Health Initiative and released in June 2008.

An industry as complex and competitive as healthcare does not naturally collaborate for the greater good without a neutral venue in which to make policy for the collective good. The creation of this plan, and especially its policy recommendations and calls to action, demonstrate the value that the e-Health Initiative brings to these transformative discussions as a neutral convener and one that can bring together the collective wisdom of many for the greater good of all.

The plan introduces the "Minnesota Model for Adopting Interoperable Electronic Health Records" in the form of a continuum that graphically communicates the seven steps toward effective use and interoperability that are required to achieve the 2015 mandate (see Figure 14D-2). The stages and activities in the continuum do not always occur in a linear fashion, since some can occur concurrently.

The model includes three main stages:

- **Adoption** includes the sub-steps of Assess, Plan, and Select: all the critical steps that lead up to picking the right EHR product for the job.
- **Utilization** includes implementing the system, then working to get the most value out of it.
- **Exchange** includes the two steps of being ready to exchange (in terms of your systems and your interorganizational agreements), and interoperability, which is the ability to electronically exchange health information from point to point securely and in a timely manner.

The model reflects:

- The process from needs assessment to true interoperability.
- Steps that help focus collective efforts toward achieving statewide interoperability.
- Applicability across various settings covered by the EHR mandate.

This model and the complete statewide plan are available online at: www.health.state.mn.us/ehealth/ehrplan2008.pdf.[2] The plan was released at the Minnesota e-Health Summit in June 2008, in hard copy and electronically to more than 400 thought leaders from Minnesota's health industry.

Standards for Minnesota e-Health

MDH coordinates the Minnesota e-Health Initiative Standards Work Group,[4] which is charged with identifying, monitoring, and recommending specific standards for sharing and synchronizing patient data across interoperable EHR systems and across the continuum of care (http://health.state.mn.us/e-health/standards/index.html).[4] The work group consists of industry experts who follow a detailed process for recommending statewide adoption and use of specific types and versions of standards, based on Minnesota needs and industry readiness (see Figure 14D-3).

This process is a constant cycle as standards are continually improved and new versions are released to meet user needs. Even as standards are recommended and adopted, their successor versions are already

Table 14D-1. Minnesota e-Health Initiative Accomplishments September 2004 – June 2006

Minnesota e-Health Advisory Committee and Work Groups Actions	Legislative Accomplishments
e-Health Initiative Established - Convened the Minnesota e-Health Advisory Committee, and work groups - Developed e-Health vision and roadmap w/ 4 strategic goals - Provided input and oversight of the creation of MN-PHIN **Grant and Loan Program** - Expanded eligibility for Rural Health HIT grants - Awarded $246,000 for 3 Rural Health HIT grants - Secured Robert Wood Johnson Foundation InfoLinks grant - Awarded $173,000 for 7 Rural Health HIT grants - Awarded $1.3 million for 12 Interconnected EHR grants **Communication** - Established e-Health Web site with more than 650 resource links - Issued e-Health Progress Report to Minnesota Legislature; Published e-Health Information Technology Adoption Status Report - Minnesota e-Health Pre-Summit Workshop held: 50+ Participants - Minnesota e-Health Summit held: 350+ Participants - Published Minnesota e-Health Recommendations Report	**e-Health Initiative Established** - Minnesota e-Health Initiative established - Legislature authorizes formation of the e-Health Steering Committee (M.S. s 62J.495) **Grant and Loan Program** - Gov. Pawlenty proposed $12 million in matching grants for interconnected EHR grants Legislature funds $1.3 million in matching EHR grants for state fiscal yr. 2007 (M.S. s 144.3345)

under development. This does not preclude adoption of standards. Rather, it reflects the reality that standards need to be monitored constantly for revisions and appropriate versions recommended for statewide use.

Through the Standards Work Group, Minnesota's health industry representatives actively review relevant standards materials and offer suggested improvements based on Minnesota's experience and needs. In 2008, Minnesota was the only state to submit coordinated, statewide, industrywide responses to federal requests for comments on standards for certifying EHRs. In 2008, work group members and MDH staff reviewed more than 1,400 criteria in six areas (ambulatory, inpatient, emergency department, cardiovascular, child health, and network), providing specific feedback on 77 criteria and proposing an additional 40 new ones. Many of Minnesota's suggestions were adopted nationally in the final set of EHR certification criteria.

This is of particular significance since only nationally certified EHRs may be acquired in Minnesota since passage of Minnesota Statutes, section 62J.495. This ensures that EHRs have adopted national standards for information exchange and for functionality, two critical components for achieving interoperability and

Table 14D-2. Minnesota e-Health Initiative Accomplishments September 2006 – June 2007

Minnesota e-Health Advisory Committee and Work Groups Actions	Legislative Accomplishments
MN e-Health Advisory Committee - Convened the MN e-Health Advisory Committee and work groups **Grants and Loans** - Awarded $3.5 million for 16 Interconnected EHR Grants - Secured RWJF Common Ground Grant Funding - Issued e-Health Progress Report to MN Legislature **Privacy and Security** - Secured federal funds and completed Minnesota Privacy and Security Project/Analysis (MPSP) - Published Framework of Security Principles - Published Privacy and Security Barriers/Solutions Report **Communication** - Published first directory of Minnesota HIT Projects - Minnesota e-Health Pre-Summit Workshop held: 50+ Participants - Minnesota e-Health Summit held: 350+ Participants - Published e-Health Progress Report - Published e-Health Personal Health Records Fact Sheet, June 28, 2007 - Published e-Health Information Technology Adoption Status Report Updated the MN e-Health Web site, resources and links	**Grants and Loans** - Gov. Pawlenty proposed $29.5 million in grants - Legislature funds $14.5 million for grants & interest-free loans (M.S. s 144.3345 & 62J.496) **Mandate for Interoperable EHRs** - Minnesota enacts a mandate that all healthcare providers must have an interoperable EHR system by Jan. 1, 2015 (M.S. s 62J.495) - Commissioner of health is required to develop a statewide implementation plan to meet the 2015 mandate **Standards** - Commissioner of health is required to establish uniform standards for exchange (M.S. s 62J.495) **Privacy and Security** Minnesota Health Records Act is revised and recodified to ensure that all privacy requirements are updated for the exchange of data (M.S. s 144.291-.298)

improvements in quality. It also helps to ensure that the considerable financial investment in an EHR system will bring both value and longevity to the provider.

Ongoing and Upcoming Activity

Standards setting and adoption is an iterative, ongoing process. Existing standards are continually refined and updated, and new standards will continue to emerge. In short, the work of standards setting, adoption, and use will never be done.

In 2008-2009, the Standards Work Group is focusing on defining the key elements that determine "interoperability" for Minnesota and on creating a Roadmap for Standards and Interoperability. The former is needed to understand the various concepts that are part of healthcare interoperability and for assessing progress toward the 2015 mandate for interoperable EHRs. The roadmap is essential to guide, focus, and coordinate Minnesota's efforts in a complex and rapidly-evolving arena.

Table 14D-3. Minnesota e-Health Initiative Accomplishments September 2007 – June 2009

Minnesota e-Health Advisory Committee and Work Groups Actions	Legislative Accomplishments

Minnesota e-Health Advisory Committee & Work Groups
- Convened the Minnesota e-Health Advisory Committee, and 8 work groups
- Identified priority areas/recommendations for exchange of electronic health information for MDH, LPH, and DHS
- Assessed MDH Informatics Exchange Capability and Created Sage Use Cases
Grants and Loans
- Awarded $2.386 million for three Interconnected EHR Loans
- Awarded $3.5 Million for 11 Planning Grants and 10 Implementation Grants
- Awarded $6.3 Million for 8 Interconnected EHR Loans (08-09)
Privacy and Security
- Secured federal funding for MPSP Project
Standards
- Published MN e-Health Standards for eRx Management, Lab Results Reporting, and Immunization Exchange
Communication
- Issued 2 e-Health Progress Report to MN Legislature
- Published Statewide EHR Implementation Plan
- Developed a MN e-Health Communications Plan
- Published Framework for Population Health in MN
- Published MN e-Health Resource Guide
- Published MN e-Health Information Technology Adoption Status Report
- Published Health Informatics Education and Training Resource Guide
- Published Guide on Effective Use of EHRs
Annual MN e-Health Pre-Summit Workshops held: 100 to 400+ Participants
	E-Prescribing Mandate
	- Minnesota enacts that all healthcare providers and payers must establish and use an e-Prescribing system by Jan 1, 2011 (M.S. s 62J497)
	Standards
	- Minnesota enacts first standards requirements, specifically:
	  – By 2015, EHRs must be certified by the CCHIT, or its successor
	  – The standards for e-Prescribing systems set out in (M.S. s 62J.497)
	- Minnesota publishes the uniform standards for Administrative Transactions for eligibility verification and healthcare claims;
	Minnesota enacts compliance mechanism to ensure all healthcare providers and payers implement the administrative transaction requirements

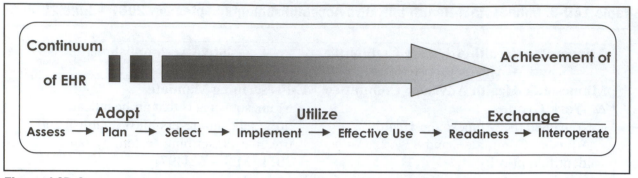

Figure 14D-2. *Minnesota Model. Source: www.health.state.mn.us/ehealth/ehrplan2008.pdf*

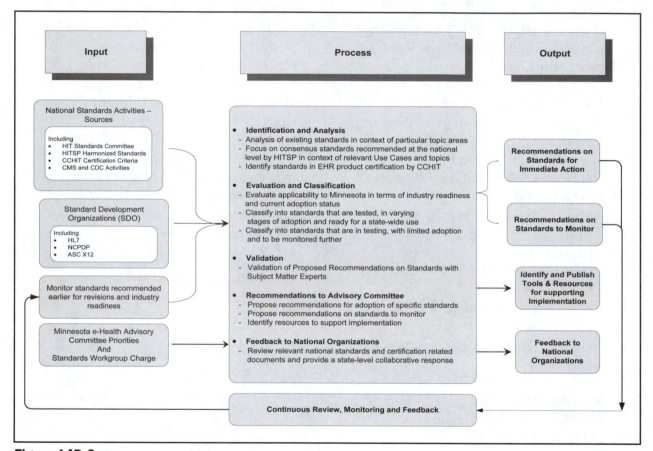

Figure 14D-3. *Minnesota e-Health Standards Process. Source: http://health.state.mn.us/ehealth/standards/index.html*

e-Prescribing. Another rapidly emerging metric of e-health success is the adoption and use of e-Prescribing. Minnesota is the only state to have an e-Prescribing mandate (Minnesota Statutes, section 62J.497). The mandate exists to improve medication safety, reduce costs, and improve health outcomes. The mandate should also dramatically improve Minnesota's ranking, in terms of the percentage of prescriptions routed electronically (see Table 14D-4).

E-Health Grants and EHR Loans. The e-health grant and EHR loan programs have been very popular and highly successful for each year offered. Beginning in 2006, the state of Minnesota appropriated funding to support the planning or implementation of interoperable EHRs, related applications, and health information exchange (see Figure 14D-4). The considerable need for these grants is demonstrated by the Request for Proposals from years 2007 - 2008 as shown in Table 14D-5. In 2008 alone, MDH received $25 million in requests for the $7 million available to be awarded (http://health.state.mn.us/e-health/funding.html).[5]

In addition to the e-Health grant program, MDH administers a six-year no-interest EHR revolving loan program to assist in financing the installation or support of interoperable EHR systems. Total funding of $6.3 mil-

Table 14D-4. Electronic Prescriptions in Minnesota and Rank Compared to Other States

History	Current	Target
2005	**2007**	**2011**
0.02%	1.20%	80%
Rank 42	Rank 26	Rank in Top 10 States

Source: SureScripts/RXHub and MDH

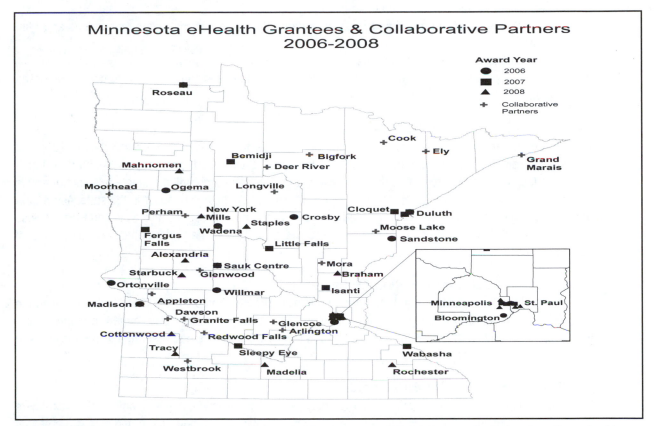

Figure 14D-4. *Minnesota e-Health Grantees and Collaborative Partners 2006-2008 Awards. Source: http://www.health. state.mn.us/ehealth/summit/s2009cundbladcooney.pdf*

Table 14D-5. Minnesota e-Health Grants, 2007-2009

	Requests	Requested Amount	Awards	Awarded Amount
Planning	29	$1,276,411	25	$821,000
Implementation	64	$25,946,031	24	$7,479,000
Totals	93	$27,222,442	49	$8,300,000

Source: http://health.state.mn.us/ehealth/funding.html

lion for fiscal years 2008-2009 was made available on a first-come, first-serve basis to eligible applicants. As with grants, loan applicants must clearly state plans for achieving interoperability with other providers.

2008-2009 e-Health Initiative Priorities

Priorities for the Minnesota e-Health Initiative[1] are:

- Advancing adoption and use of e-Prescribing technologies and standards.
- Supporting the effective use of EHRs to improve quality of care and population health, especially for those with chronic conditions.
- Defining interoperability between EHR systems to enable community eHIE (defined in next section) to improve continuity and coordination of care.
- Supporting widespread adoption and use of standards based on national recommendations and Minnesota law.
- Supporting community clinics and rural provider collaboratives.
- Assessing the progress on adoption and use of EHRs, identifying gaps and barriers to success, and developing pragmatic guidance and resources for organizations.

e-Health and Healthcare Reform

When used effectively, EHRs and health IT are powerful tools to increase quality and safety of care and enhance coordination and continuity of care. In a January 2008 report, the Minnesota Health Care Transformation Task Force estimated the potential net long-term savings from implementing a fully interoperable EHRs system in Minnesota at $2.467 billion (or 4.3%) of total healthcare spending in the state. About one-third of the projected savings are from reduced medical costs (e.g., fewer duplicative tests and fewer adverse drug interactions), and two-thirds from increased productivity of healthcare professionals and lower costs of administrative functions.

e-Health and Health Information Exchange

The growth of the Minnesota Health Information Exchange (MN HIE) has been significant since its inception in 2007. This partnership of payers, provider systems, and state government was formed to connect doctors, hospitals, and clinics across the state. MN HIE will enable physicians and other healthcare providers to quickly and securely access electronic medical information with patient consent.

The State of Personal Health Records

E-health is also consumer-focused, seeking to engage individuals in their health and in the healthcare choices they make. An increasingly popular tool to support individuals in their health and care is a personal health record (PHR). National efforts are underway to address PHR standards and product certification in 2009. MDH and the Minnesota e-Health Initiative continue to monitor the evolution of PHRs.

Key Lessons Learned:
Effectively Moving a State Forward for Effective Implementation of Interoperable EHRs

- Encourage broad participation of multiple stakeholders in the process. All meetings are open to the public. Anyone can ask to be included on e-mails to receive notification and handouts for meetings of working groups and the advisory committee.
- Keep everyone informed of activities and progress in a timely manner. The Web site for the initiative is regularly updated to include materials from all meetings. Gov-delivery services push e-mails out to more than 2,500 people who self-subscribed to receive regular updates.
- Talk to a diverse group of providers in the trenches about what works and what does not work; do not just read the literature.
- Use real-life stories as exemplars to effectively communicate information.
- Focus on the benefits to various stakeholders, particularly consumers.
- Use a data driven approach to identify gaps. Collect assessment data from various settings to keep track of progress made. The latest adoption metrics are available from http://health.state.mn.us/e-health/hitassessmentsummary2008.pdf.[6]

- Create an interactive working relationship between stakeholder and staff to provide complementary skills for capturing insights and framing them into an effective work plan and strategies to move the effort forward.
- Plan for effective meetings. Prior to each Advisory Committee and work group meeting, a conference call with the co-chairs is held to discuss the agenda and supporting materials. While it seems to "double" the number of meetings for the co-chairs and staff, in fact, it dramatically improved the effectiveness of meetings and motivated stakeholders to continue engagement in the work.
- Focus on inclusivity. While the Web site does acknowledge credentials of providers and their affiliations, at meetings, everyone is on a first-name basis. Use of words is critical to support inclusivity. Members practice respectful listening and staff incorporates the ideas of all. Membership represents small and large healthcare providers, as well as rural and urban, public and private, clinical and research.
- Identify actions and resources for successful implementation of EHRs, not just barriers.

Nursing Involvement and Implications

- Nursing involvement on the Advisory Committee was assured through a legislative mandate to include at least one nursing representative. Membership on the work groups is open to all stakeholders and include many nurses.
- Nurses have been very active participants in the Minnesota e-Health Initiative as co-chairs or members of the Advisory Committee and as co-chairs and participants in work groups. Often they represent diverse perspectives in addition to their nursing expertise, including chief information officer, public health, or long-term care.
- One strategy that assures that all consumers, nurses, and stakeholders feel welcome and represented has been consistent clarification of broad terminology. For instance, through constant reminders, the terms "provider" or "clinician" are used rather than "physician," and "diverse healthcare settings" in place of "hospitals."
- The work of the e-Health Initiative has been incorporated into the informatics course at the University of Minnesota School of Nursing to prepare all graduate nurses as active participants in e-health policy. Student assignments in the informatics course include selecting a use case important for interoperability of patient data across healthcare settings and demonstrating knowledge of workflow analysis, optimizing workflows, mapping local terms to standardized terminologies and functional requirements, and developing a business case for the Minnesota e-Health Standards work group to consider prioritizing their work for interoperability.

What Remains to be Done

- Develop metrics and benchmarks for regularly assessing progress toward achieving the adoption, effective use, and interoperability of EHR systems and other health IT.
- Continue to identify priority data exchange scenarios that require uniform adoption of standards; evaluate any national recommendations; recommend standards for adoption in Minnesota.
- Support current exchange and interoperability priorities by supporting implementation of the recommended standards for e-Prescribing, laboratory reporting, and immunizations.
- Identify and address the unique challenges to health IT adoption in special settings, such as long-term care, public health, and alternative care providers.
- Apply research and evaluation of e-health activities to measure the value of EHR systems and other health IT in improving quality and population health.

Summary

Health IT and HIE offer transformative opportunities to improve the health and care of citizens. Minnesota has been a leader in pursuing bold e-health policies to accelerate the adoption of EHRs and other health IT, including the use of statutory mandates and governmental funding to accelerate adoption of EHRs and health data standards. It has also provided a model for effective public-private collaboration to advance e-health goals. While much of the foundation has been laid through the Minnesota e-Health Initiative, considerable work remains to ensure all providers and all Minnesotans can share in the benefits of e-health.

The State e-Health Alliance noted that "...the high costs, avoidable deaths, poor quality, and inefficiency of the current system drive urgency for transformation. But ... if not smartly coordinated, it may only result in an electronic version of the 'siloed,' inefficient system we have today."[7] Ensuring the smart and coordinated implementation of health IT and electronic HIE to improve the health and care of Minnesotans will continue to be the vision and focus of the Minnesota e-Health Initiative and the MDH.

References

1. http://www.health.state.mn.us/e-health. Accessed October 23, 2009.
2. www.health.state.mn.us/ehealth/ehrplan2008.pdf. Accessed October 23, 2009.
3. http://www.health.state.mn.us/e-health/reports.html. Accessed October 23, 2009.
4. http://health.state.mn.us/e-health/standards/index.html. Accessed September 21, 2009.
5. http://health.state.mn.us/e-health/funding.html. Accessed September 20, 2009.
6. http://health.state.mn.us/e-health/hitassessmentsummary2008.pdf. Accessed August 2, 2009.
7. Accelerating Progress: Using Health Information Technology and Electronic Health Information Exchange to Improve Care, State Alliance for e-Health, September 2008.

Case Study 14E

Redirecting the Development of the Electronic Registry for Nursing in Cuba

By Yoadis Cuesta García, MS Health Informatics, Teacher in Health Informatics, BSN, BCN

Introduction

With a comparative and reflective focus, this case study presents some of the initiatives developed in Cuba directed toward improving the nursing registry by integrating computing tools in the care process. The case study identifies the benefits of two systems currently in use in different health departments and describes and reconsiders the initial stage of the TelePAE project as an example of the clear necessity to redirect the conceptual model of design for the Electronic Nursing Registry (ENR), with the conception of the systematic approach to care. While neither of these systems is purported to be ideal, both provide valuable aspects to consider in the redesign of a national system, in light of the use of international classifications for the treatment and representation of care as a scientific foundation for the profession of nursing.

The use of IT as a tool to improve quality of care is the perspective from which we examine strategies to implement informatics in different levels of nursing that need attention in Cuba. Despite the shortage of resources, since the inception of nursing informatics, we have been developing projects oriented to this purpose in some of our services.

In the late 1990s, interest developed in decreasing the time required in traditional clinical documentation and dedicating more time to patient care, as well as developing a repository of data that support evidenced-based decision making in the nursing profession. This motivated a group of nurses from the Neurological Restoration International Center (CIREN) to develop an Informational System (IS). The aim of this system was to support the definition and documentation of the nursing diagnosis without consideration of other elements of care, except nursing outcomes, interventions, and evaluation of each treatment plan. This continued to be defined and elaborated for each patient in text form, without considering the possibility of accumulating this information in a computerized database. The primitive system helped, however, and replaced manual records. Printouts from this primitive system helped support the diagnostic definition.[1]

In 2005, the Computer System for Nursing Care (CSNC) was created for use in the Intermediate Unit Care (IUC) at the Clinical Surgical Hospital of Guantánamo. This application also focused on the management of care through the systematic storage, retrieval, and update of nursing interventions in an Access Data Base (DB), administered by Delphi. Its structure considered some of the categories of the Minimum Data Collection for Nursing (MCBD-N) (see Figure 14E-1). Although the definition of nursing input is derived from the medical diagnosis, the database defines all of the nursing treatments for each of the medical diagnoses. This was compiled as a result of a previous work in standardization that utilized literature and experiences in clinical practice (see Figure 14E-2).

The system relates back to the reference for feedback regarding the medical diagnosis and to support decision making. In this way, it draws together data related to diagnostic causes and complications[2] (see Figure 14E-3). CSNC completes its task of facilitating legible documentation quickly, standardizing treatment, and providing simulation as a tool for learning in each intermediate care unit in which it was implemented. It also supports gathering a uniform and standardized form of nursing inputs (data) for comparison when conducting similar studies. Although the system is limited in its abilities, it aids in decision making and offers information for critical reasoning. However, the system is not able to electronically discern every patient case; therefore, it still requires various nurses to revise the record of every patient. In addition the printing of a care report is still necessary to store in the traditional paper clinical registry (see Figure 14E-4). The system eradicates problems that have been identified following actual incidents of patient care in the following ways:

- Defining standards in the methodology of the record for treatment plans that, although not aligned with the national or international requirements, do establish guidelines that permit improvement of the management process and nursing research.

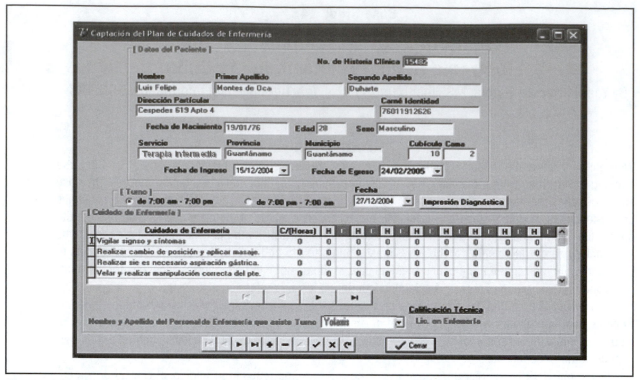

Figure 14E-1. *Demographic Elements that ISCN Registers, Not Considering Race. Plan of Nursing Actions. Adapted from Sanchez G.* SICENF, in front the traditional methods of registry. *Havana: Health Informatics, 2007.*

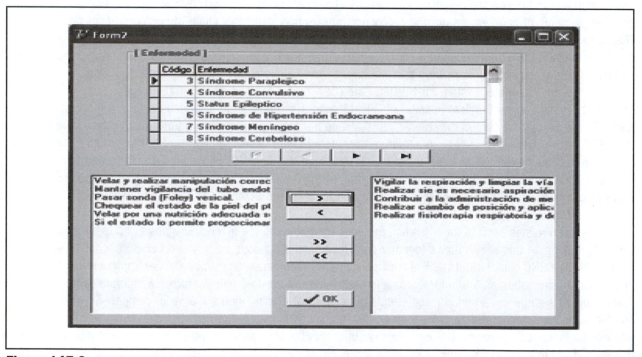

Figure 14E-2. *Relation Between Medical Diagnosis and Nursing Care. Final Selection of Care. Adapted from Sanchez G.* SICENF, in front the traditional methods of registry. *Havana: Health Informatics, 2007.*

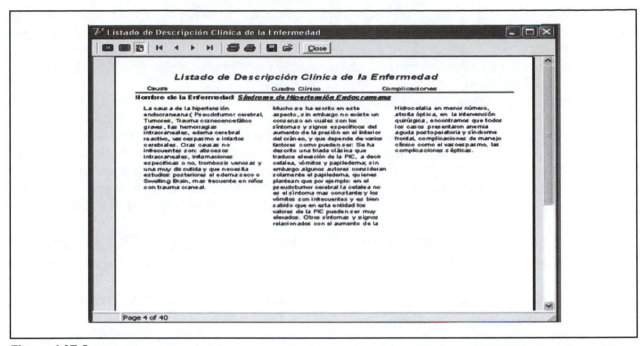

Figure 14E-3. *Clinical Description of the Diagnosed Syndrome. Adapted from Sanchez G. SICENF, in front the traditional methods of registry. Havana: Health Informatics, 2007.*

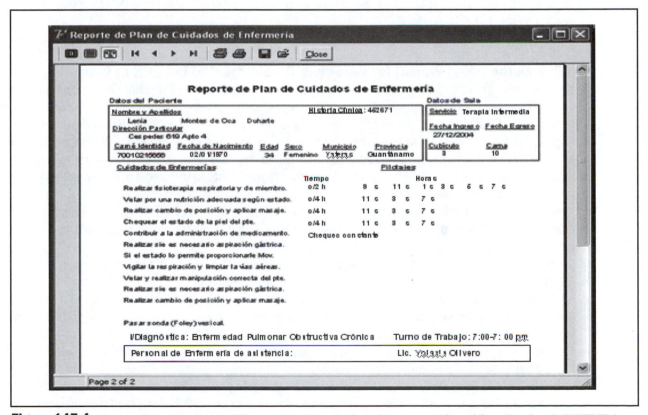

Figure 14E-4. *Report of Nursing Care to File in the Traditional Clinical Registry. Adapted from Sanchez G. SICENF, in front the traditional methods of registry. Havana: Health Informatics, 2007.*

- Establishing rules for interventions aligned to problems identified that can also apply to similar cases and providing references and information about treatment plans of patients previously treated with the same diagnosis.
- Guaranteeing the maximum collection of nursing actions in a form that is organized, is legible, and has a common vocabulary.
- Permitting the control of individual nursing interventions.

The two described variants of the record respond to needs that are diagnosed and focus-driven for each unit in which they were developed. One focuses solely on the diagnosis, while the other on nursing inputs, ignoring remaining stages of the processes of action. These systems do not permit communication, exchange, or research any further than the borders of health service for which they were developed and do not focus on the systematic process of nursing. However, they do achieve the objectives for which they were created and also redirect development of the projects to create an electronic record for nursing (ERN) in Cuba.

Considerations for Redirecting the Development of ERN in Cuba

The assessment of the systems described in the previous paragraph causes us to reflect on the necessity of:

- Validating the interventions against definitions of affected human responses, later identifying actual or potential problems of the patient.
- Algorithmically defining a system that simulates the method of nursing action and shows a clear organization of its stages.
- Identifying the elements of nursing for ERN.
- Developing a system with levels of communication that are understandable by any nursing personnel, local or international, that consider the classification for the practice of nursing, its standards, and its taxonomies.
- Bringing together, out of necessity, national ideas and experiences to develop the ERN.

TelePAE as the Initial Project for the Future Development of the ERN in Cuba

TelePAE is the name of a project still in development for the presentation of nursing cases using Internet services. The project was created with the objective of developing a system directed toward recording the care process in order to initiate online discussion and group support for the nursing intervention. Because of the lack of portable computers in care units, the system only searches for a universally acceptable system (within the health network). Also, it has emerged as a call to dedicate an identifiable space for the nursing profession in the virtual health clinic. It invites the nurses to participate in the discussions, regardless of the model of medical record presented.[3]

The cases that are modeled in the clinic are actual cases, selected according to professional interest and the method of intervention. Because of this, we propose that TelePAE redirect the criteria by which it develops the ERN by:

- Identifying the elements of interest and importance for documentation and debate in nursing.
- Defining the methodology that also embraces the identified elements.
- Defining and designing an understood and familiar structure for users (nursing interface).
- Defining and programming a structure for the management and processing of the nursing data, in conjunction with the algorithm developed by its professionals during the clinical activity.
- Choosing and developing the computerized tools that facilitate meeting the proposed objective.

The documented revision and analysis of content has allowed us to assess the ability of the International Classification for Nursing Practice® (ICNP) to describe the nursing elements and to provide data that can represent the practice of nursing and make visible the process of care.[4] It is suggested that the elements tested in the ICNP should be those capable of being modeled in any ERN, as exemplified in TelePAE. These elements are the:[5]

- Phenomenon of nursing
- Nursing actions to meet the patient's needs
- Results of the nursing actions

The rest of the elements defined for the design of the CMBD-E should also be considered in order to design a model for the presentation of cases within nursing or ERN, according to system criteria, and should include all that is known about the patient and all input from caregivers. This Minimum Data Collection (MCDB-N) considers these elements of nursing:

- Four elements of nursing attention: the three covered by ICNP and the addition of the intensity of nursing service.
- Demographic elements corresponding to the patients.
- Six elements of service. In Cuba, the element related to "the payer of the greater part of the total bill" is not applied, as this is a free service of a government-financed health service.

The elements of the ICNP should be treated in the ERN according to the classification and taxonomic structure used in the North American Nursing Diagnosis (NANDA), the Nursing Outcomes Classification (NOC) and the Nursing Interventions Classification (NIC). The support of the model by elements of ICNP facilitates the understanding of every nursing decision as a result of the controlled vocabulary and standardization of its components.[6,7]

The Nursing Process, Assessment, Nursing Diagnosis, Planning, Intervention, and Evaluation, is the chosen method to develop the presentation of cases for the electronic record of care. This guarantees a holistic vision of the developed process and organization to structure the information. Using this structure facilitates understanding, study, discussion, and communication.

The user interface for the record supports the stages of the process of care. Each screen represents an entity or related entities that accumulate information about its classes. In the case of a model such as TelePAE, the entities defined were—Nurses, Assessment, Nursing Diagnoses, Planning, Evaluation of Care, Presentation of Cases, Opinion of User, and Cases Presented.[3]

In the 'nurse entity,' TelePAE records the standard attributes: first name, surname, country, function (teaching, welfare, administration, and research), specialty, scientific degree, focus of work and applicable department, years of work, and e-mail, (see Figure 14E-5). For the ERN, we also consider data that are reported to us with information to evaluate the quality of care at any given moment, such as how it is done in CNSC and should include the shift that was worked, date, and clinical unit of attention (see Figure 14E-1).

The "patient entity" should be viewed in an independent manner as happens in SICENF (see Figure 14E-1) and not as part of the assessment entity, as is demonstrated in TelePAE (see Figure 14E-6). This guarantees reuse of each initial patient record for each patient that is seen with health problems; the same happens with the independent record of the nursing entity for the number of patients that are seen, whether repeated or not. In this way the database is optimized.

The ERN should overcome the deficiencies of TelePAE through ensuring the typed documentation of information in the fields, current history of illness, previous family history, personal pathologies, toxic habits, and summary of objective and subjective data compiled during the physical examination. Each one of these fields should be further subdivided into fields of data. These units of information should pre-populate from forms previously validated, preventing the nurse from typing and making a mistake in the record (see Figure 14E-7).

The link between the phase of assessment and the nursing diagnosis for the ERN would have been able to be tested to the same extent as in TelePAE. In the nursing diagnosis entity, the data gathered in the assessment phase for its classification, interpretation, and validation are reused in the function of deriving the diagnoses related to the health problems. The classification of data spans two levels. In the first level of 13 domains of nursing diagnoses following the taxonomy of the NANDA II,[6] data are taken as a nomination; also added to the classification are data such as previous personal pathology, history of personal illness, and family history.[8] These last four classifications are for data that cannot be sorted in some domains of NANDA diagnoses and are additional data to the required focus. Each domain is coded alphabetically, and its continuation in the other four classifications is determined for the summarized data.

The second level of classification is dependent on the first; in conjunction with the selected domain in the classification. The specific classes are derived from the same domain for their selection. The classes are coded in an alphanumeric form, conserving the alphabetic code of the domain and acquiring a numeric code following the order given in the taxonomy (see Table 14E-1). In the ERN, the declaration of the nursing diagnoses can be achieved by respecting the international codes assigned to each diagnosis and establishing their relation between these and the codes of the classes, such as in TelePAE (see Table 14E-2).

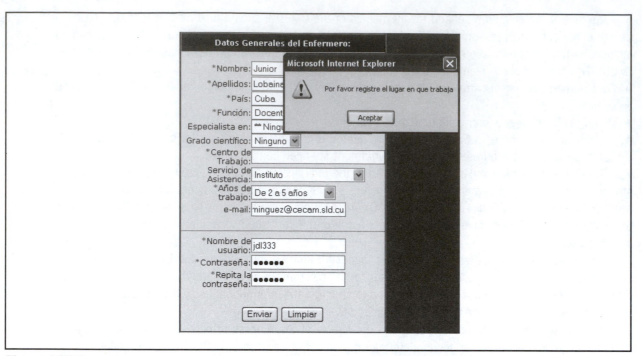

Figure 14E-5. *Compiled Fields in the "Nursing" Entity in the TelePAE Project. Adapted from Cuesta Y.* Project TelePAE to support the nursing care on line. *Havana: CECAM, 2006.*

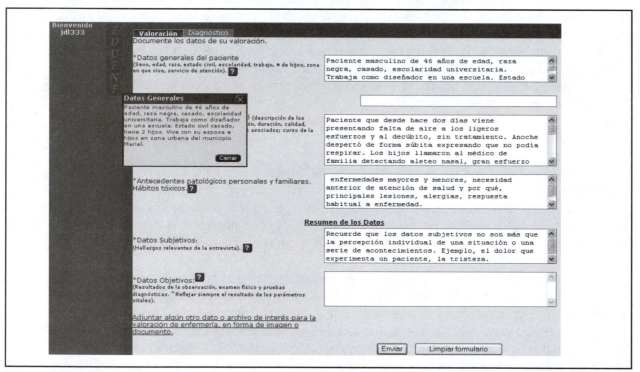

Figure 14E-6. *Screen Assessment of the TelePAE Project. Fields Compiled in this Entity. Adapted from Cuesta Y.* Project TelePAE to support the nursing care on line. *Havana: CECAM, 2006.*

The relationship proposes to identify the elements that conform to the taxonomy II of the NANDA through the assignment of codes to the domains, classes, and use of the international codes for the diagnoses. This supports the diagnostic definition of nursing in any record developed. But the ERN should give an integral focus of care like the TelePAE project does. It should derive the nursing care from the outcomes from which we can develop the database that relates the domains of those diagnoses and those of the Nursing Outcomes Classification (NOC), including relationship to its classes. This relationship permits showing options of pos-

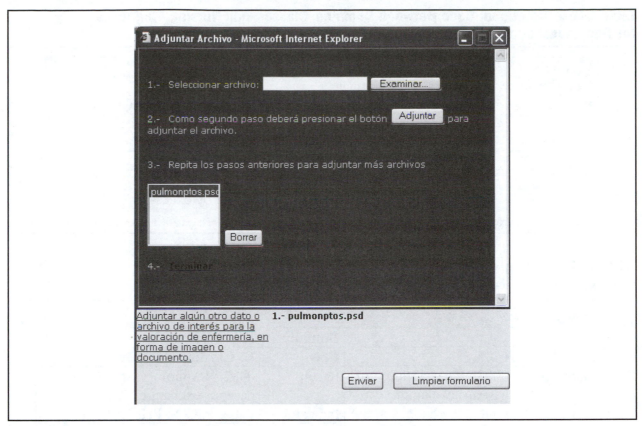

Figure 14E-7. *Assessment Screen of the TelePAE Project. Field of Enclosing Files for this Entity. Adapted from Cuesta Y.* Project TelePAE to support the nursing care on line. *Havana: CECAM, 2006.*

Table 14E-1. Relational Code Between Domains and Classes of the Nursing Diagnoses for Selection

Domain		Classes	
Code	Name	Code	Name
B	Nutrition	B1	Ingestion
		B2	Digestion
		B3	Absorption
		B4	Metabolism
		B5	Hydration

Adapted from Cuesta Y. *Project TelePAE to support the nursing care on line.* Havana: CECAM, 2006.

sible proposed outcomes for the patient for the defined human response. Later the correlation between the four entities: domain of outcomes, classes of outcomes, outcomes, and indicators with the associated scale of measuring the result, should support decision making and documentation of this part of the process. For this, we use the codes of the NOC. Currently this part of the project has not been modeled further in the database. With the nursing interventions, we will continue in similar form, using the items of the Nursing Interventions Classification (NIC), validating this previously in the core of the investigation and defining later a related model of integration (see Table 14E-3).

Table 14E-2. Relational Code Between Domains, Classes, and Nursing Diagnoses for Documentation

Classes		Nursing Diagnosis	
Code	Name	Code	Diagnosis
B1	Ingestion	00107	Ineffective standard of nutrition of the unweaned infant
		00103	Deterioration of swallowing
		00002	Nutritional imbalance by defect
		00001	Nutritional imbalance by excess
		00003	Risk of nutritional imbalance by excess

Adapted from Cuesta Y. *Project TelePAE to support the nursing care on line.* Havana: CECAM, 2006.

Table 14E-3. Example of a Relational Integration Model of NANDA and NOC, Proposed by the Development Group in the TelePAE Project

NANDA		NOC	
Domain	C	Domain	II
Class	C4	Class	E: Cardiopulmonary
Diagnosis	00030: Deterioration of gaseous exchange related to changes in the capillary alveolar membrane.	Result	0402, Respiratory Status: gaseous exchange.
		Indicator	PaO₂, PaCO₂, PH, HBO₂, etc.....
		Scales (maintained by being the same problem)	1: Extremely compromised. 2: Substantially compromised. 3: Moderately compromised. 4: Slightly compromised. 5: Not compromised.

Adapted from Cuesta Y. *Project TelePAE to support the nursing care on line.* Havana: CECAM, 2006.

Summary

The systems described in this case study show the possibility of reaching results qualitatively superior for the ERN3. These individual efforts would benefit from being combined. It is necessary to incorporate terminological guidelines, taxonomies, and nursing standards to develop the electronic nursing record in Cuba. We can incorporate the international classification for the practice of nursing, validating for our system the contents of NANDA, NOC, and NIC. We hope to exceed the scientific quality of the applications designed for the registry, giving a systematic and holistic nursing focus, in addition to developing a data base for scientific evidence. The international experience of developing the ERN3 must be integrated into our national project. It is important to validate those in our context and contribute to their improvement.

References

1. Sánchez G. *Sistema Informático de Enfermería, SICENF, frente al Método Tradicional.* http://www.informatica2007.sld.cu/Members/gustavo/sistema-informatico-en-enfermeria-sicenf-frente-al-metodo-tradicional/2006-11-15.4095926211. Accessed May 11, 2009.
2. CIREN. *Proceso de Atención de Enfermería computarizado.* http://www.ciren.cu/paginas/SERVMED_COMPONENTES/servicios_medicos_neuroenfermeria.htm. Accessed May 21, 2007.
3. Cuesta Y. *Bases Metodológicas y de Gestión para la Presentación Virtual de Casos en Enfermería.* Versión 1.0, fases 1-4. http://www.nursite.com.ar/phpBB2/viewtopic.php?p=2914&sid=968ee0ff05eaaad84cba083c03d736e6. Accessed May 21, 2009.
4. CIE. *Clasificación internacional para la práctica de enfermería (ICNP).* http://www.icn.ch/matters_ICNPsp.htm. Accessed May 15, 2009.

5. Marín HF, Rodrigues R, Delaney C. Desarrollo de Sistemas normalizados de información de enfermería. OPS. Washington, DC; 2001.

6. Sparks C, Craft-Rosenberg M, Herdman TH, at el. NANDA: Diagnósticos Enfermeros, Definiciones y Clasificación 2003-2004. España: Elsevier; 2003.

7. Jonson M, Maas M, Morread S. *Clasificación de Resultados de Enfermería (CRE).* Harcourt, España; 2001.

8. Iyer PW, Taptich BJ, Bernocchi-Losey D. *Proceso y Diagnósticos de Enfermería.* USA. McGraw-Hill Interamericana, 1995.

Case Study 14F

A Historical Account and Current Status of Nursing Informatics in Argentina

By Carlos Hugo Leonzio, PhD(c), BSN; and Cristina Barrios, BSN

Introduction

The Encounter

In Argentina, massive use of the personal computer began in the early 1990s. "Nursing informatics" was unknown among nurses. The computers in use at that time were XT and 286. Only a few individuals had a PC in their homes.

Most health institutions had computerized, but not centralized their computer systems. Most of these systems processed administrative and quantifiable information. Some of these computer systems were commercial and had been purchased by the health industry, while other systems were generic and were designed in individual institutions of health for informatics personnel. Nurses did not use these systems because the systems were limited in use for administrative support.

Within this period, a medical movement began, which included other members of the health team, but excluded nurses at first. Work in health informatics began and some linking with other professionals abroad regarding informatics occurred. However, the time was not yet propitious for the consolidation of nursing informatics as a specialty. It is probable that in Argentina, at this time, some nurses were using the computer and probably tried to use informatics in nursing, but no formal arrangement for this was in place. In addition, a few physicians were developing and implementing computer systems; one such physician was Dr. Mandirola who developed the system BIOCOM in the Adventist Belgrano Clinic and Municipal Hospital of Villa Gesell in 1993. It is worth mentioning that during this time, no laws or regulations for the development or regulation of healthcare computer systems existed in Argentina. There were only discussions about the topic and the recognition of the need for its implementation.

It is estimated that the very beginning of the formal organization of the nursing informatics movement began in 1991. At this time, Hugo Leonzio (one of the authors) was working as chief of nursing in Banfield Clinic in Buenos Aires. The institution had several computers set up for general use, and Leonzio began to take an interest regarding the application of informatics in nursing. One of the supervisors in the same clinic was Jorge Castro, who had training in development of computer systems in Clipper and was constructing some particular systems, which were not related to health. The two health leaders met to talk about informatics and nursing; they were joined by Andrea Besozzi (supervisor of Banfield Clinic) and her husband Marcelo Sanchez (also a nurse). They developed ideas, made attempts, fortified their friendship, and got involved in informatics.

The Beginning

In January 1993, Leonzio left Banfield Clinic and joined the staff at the Institute of Cardiology and Cardiovascular Surgery (ICYCC) of Favaloro Foundation (now known as University Hospital of Favaloro Foundation) as chief of "Teaching and Research" in the Department of Nursing. He immediately asked to incorporate nursing informatics into his area, which resulted in renaming the area as "Area of Teaching, Research, and Informatics."

The chief of the nursing department, Juana Bustingorry, realized the potential of the idea and personally financed the purchase of the first computer (a late-generation 386 PC), so that Leonzio could work in nursing informatics. Within a short time, institutional leaders adopted the idea and provided the necessary support, and Leonzio requested to incorporate Marcelo Sanchez into the area. Leonzio and Sanchez created (using Clipper) the first designs for a system that processes both administrative information for the nursing department, as well as patient information so as to replace the traditional paper records of individual patients. The new system was named Computer System for Activities of Nursing (SIPADE); it had one module for administrative details and another for patient-specific details.

The administrative module handled nurses' absenteeism, personnel data files, and, with the nurses present in each service, SIPADE also included patient data. The module for patient information contained the elements found in traditional records: Vital Signs, Water Balance, Records of Nursing, Treatments, and Medical Indications, etc. This information was used for documentation and reporting of nursing using the Nursing Module and allowed pharmaceutical orders to be issued, depending on the patient information and medication used.

The patient module was tested in the Services of the Coronary Unit and Intensive Therapy with very good results; unfortunately, this use could not continue because the system was not compatible with the institutional network system. However, developing this module was useful to learn about the designing, testing, and improving of the functionality of the system.

The administrative module of the SIPADE worked very well, and therefore, creators progressively added modules. This was then converted into Visual Basic with SQL. Tests were performed to measure work load and a "basic" system was created to handle different instances in the nursing care process. These two systems, the patient module and the administrative module, can be considered Argentina's first nursing computer systems, and also one of the first in all of Latin America.

When Sanchez retired from ICYCC, Jorge Castro took his place. It is important to mention that during the first months of development in this area, a doctor from ICYCC travelled to the United States, and Leonzio arranged for him to return with books on nursing informatics. This then is how the first scientific information about nursing informatics arrived in Argentina.

ICYCC, now known as University Hospital, was very important in the development of nursing informatics because it was one of the first institutions in Argentina that began the systematic application of nursing informatics performed "for nurses" in a specific area, and also because it is where the idea of ADIERA (Association of Nursing Informatics of the Argentina Republic) was proposed.

Contacts Critical To Medical Informatics In Argentina

In 1993, contact was made through the Bulletin Board System with Dr. Fernando Humberto Mandirola, one of the precursors of medical informatics in Argentina. This was a very important link for nursing informatics. This led to a number of other very useful contacts who were all predecessors of medical informatics and health informatics in Argentina. This further brought the nursing informatics enthusiasts in contact with the representative for Argentina in IMIA. From this point, an introduction to the SIG NI of IMIA occurred and linked the fledgling nursing informatics group in Argentina to the international community.

In 1993, the First Symposium of Biomedical Informatics of Buenos Aires convened the meetings on "Problems of Informatics in Clinics and Hospitals" at the GESELLINFO 93' conference. Those present at this event founded the Society of Biomedical Informatics (SIB), which gathered together enthusiasts of health informatics. It is important to mention that a relationship was established during this event with Dr. Nora Oliveri, president of the Medical Informatics Foundation (FIM), another pioneer of health Informatics in Argentina. Dr. Oliveri was a leading participant in the organization and in the establishment of nursing informatics in our country because of her constant invaluable and interested support.

The Organization—ADIERA

Following the GESELLINFO conference, a small number of nurse informatics leaders organized to promote the idea for a nursing association. These colleagues advanced the idea and in February 1994, a group of nurses met for the first time in an office of the French Hospital of Federal Capital, Republic Argentina. They understood that nursing informatics could be an indispensable tool in nursing and concluded the meeting with the intention of creating an Association of Nursing Informatics (ADIERA) to gather together nurses interested in informatics.

In 1996, a conference was held to which nurses from eleven institutions of Federal, Capital and Buenos Aires suburbs attended. The meetings created a sizable response, to the point that a bigger venue to contain the increasing number of interested attendees was needed. The founders of ADIERA did not hesitate to advance the cause. They immediately obtained the donation of a computer, their first, from laboratory representatives and the offer of a physical place where ADIERA could be housed for more than four years. This was located in Callao in the Federal Capital. Later, ADIERA moved to premises donated by the Nursing School of the University of Buenos Aires and worked there up to the crisis of 2001, a general economic recession. Nurses in ADIERA organized working groups to satisfy the needs that were quickly arising. In this way, ADIERA was born as an entity, constituted of fact (1994) by direct vote of its founding associates, and achieved juridical legal status.

ADIERA's activities in the beginning consisted of providing training in basic informatics to transform colleagues into computer users. These courses were offered very cheaply to serve as many people as possible. More computers were purchased (purchasing one PC per month). The courses lasted four months and consisted of the following topics: hardware assembly, disarmament and functioning of PC one, DOS and Windows, Word, Excel, graphics, and introductory topics on nursing informatics. Hundreds of colleagues took the courses, and some of them continued working in the association.

Other activities were added that covered:

- Participation in any nursing event (congresses, symposiums, sessions, etc.) and seeking permission to introduce nursing informatics.
- Visits to schools of nursing to talk about nursing informatics to students.
- Organizing areas of nursing across institutions to include nursing informatics.
- Producing nursing informatics' workshops in ADIERA.
- Publishing articles about nursing informatics and informatics in health in nursing and speciality magazines.

Nursing informatics was "the innovation." At first, this was met by both ignorance and resistance, but ultimately, doubts were addressed and clarified and interested colleagues moved closer to using PCs and adopting nursing informatics. The initial resistance, however, prevented the association from receiving needed support. All the work done by members of ADIERA would not have been possible without the enthusiasm and will of associates who initiated the way for nursing informatics in Argentina.

The following topics were developed as a result of the foundational work of ADIERA:

1. Study of Working Group's project of nursing informatics, possibilities for organization and functions.
2. Philosophical organization of the organization.
3. Study of the need for development of nursing informatics. Diverse opinions were gathered and projects identified for future study. It was decided that each participant must try to bring guests to add to the group of work.

Overseas Contact

In 1993, e-mail contact with Pat Jeselon from Canada, Evelyn Hovenga from Australia, Robyn Carr from New Zealand, and Heimar Marin from Brazil, among other professionals specializing in nursing informatics, permitted access to reports of progress being made overseas. The nursing model in Argentina was strongly centered on organic pathology, and nurses had a great dependence on the medical model (this is changing very slowly, but in some places remains this way) and, further, very few nurses could travel to other countries. This inability to travel was highly significant because the possibility of contact with overseas nurses was very difficult due to distance, expenses, and time. The use of e-mail changed that reality and made possible communication between Argentinean nurses and other nurses around the world.

In June 1994, Hugo Leonzio and Gabriel Schmit traveled to the United States to attend the "Fifth International Conference on Nursing Use of Computers and Information Science" in San Antonio, Texas, which allowed contact with the International Medical Informatics Association—Nursing Informatics (IMIA-NI) Special Interest Group. Schmit and Leonzio were invited to a meeting of the Managerial Commission of IMIA-NI to represent Argentina. Argentine nurses are grateful for the important support offered by Ulla Gerdin, Susan Grobe, Robyn Carr, Susan Bakken, Patricia Abbott, Evelyn Hovenga, and Hans Peterson, with a special mention of Heimar Marin. These individuals provided support and information and the possibility of continuing contact with the SIG NI of IMIA. At one point, Ulla Gerdin and Robyn Carr, members of the SIG NI of IMIA, visited Argentina so they could view and appreciate the association's activities being developed.

National Participation In Use Of Health Informatics In Argentina

Since its foundation in 1994, ADIERA members formed a part of the Association Argentina of Medical Informatics (AAIM), the organization with which ADIERA was associated, to gain its country membership in IMIA-NI. Members of ADIERA became a permanent presence, with important participation in meetings and events, and forming a part of the Managerial Commission. Also, they participated in and/or were present in other groups, such as the SIB, FIM, Group of Biomedical Informatics of Buenos Aires (GIBBA), and Society Argentina of Operative Research (SADIO).

Nursing Informatics Events in Argentina

A great number of presentations and participations were undertaken, but there have been three outstanding events held in Argentina concerning nursing informatics:

First Argentine Symposium on Nursing Informatics. The 1st Symposium of Nursing Informatics in Argentina "IE '96" was organized by ADIERA, through collaboration with the Buenos Aires University (UBA) School of Nursing. It was held December 4-6, 1996, in the hall of the Faculty of Medicine of UBA, and more than 400 persons attended.

4th Latin-American Symposium of Nursing, "Nursing and the Challenge of Informatics." Held in June 2007 and organized by ADIERA, this event introduced the experiences of the development of informatics systems in Hospital Italiano, Swiss Medical Group, Hospital Austral Clinica del Sol y el Hospital Albert Einstein de San Pablo, Brazil.

II Argentine Symposium of Nursing Informatics. Within the "III Latin-American Congress of Medical Informatics," the Nursing Informatics Group of the Argentina Association of Medical Informatics organized the "II Symposium Argentine of Nursing Informatics - Calling to Nursing Informatics, which was held November 1, 2008 at the school of Biomedical Sciences of the Austral University, Pilar, Buenos Aires, Argentina.

Nursing Informatics Education in Argentina

The School of Nursing of Federal Police, University of Argentina was the first school of nursing in Argentina that formally introduced the subject "Nursing Informatics" and "Informatics." Since 1999, the subject and study of Informatics have been used to turn the students into computer users. The subject of Nursing Informatics was used to further introduce them to nursing informatics as a speciality.

Other schools of nursing also incorporated the informatics subject area to introduce students to using computers. It is important to emphasize also that a "Residence in Biomedical Informatics," a two-year program, was developed and promoted through Velez Sarsfield, Hospital of the Government of the City of Buenos Aires, initially coordinated for Dr. Antonio Lago, creator and counsellor of this residence. His task was continued by nurses Alejandro Sanchez and Rosa Bessa in collaboration with other professionals who graduated in the same residence.

Lists in Nursing, A Special Mention

The "Lists of Nursing by e-mail" in Argentina turned into a phenomenon of outstanding importance because thousands of colleagues of all strata levels became heavily involved. These lists allowed direct contact between widely dispersed colleagues, effectively shortening the distance between them. The email lists served as "think tanks" for analysis and discussion of diverse topics, contribution of ideas, exchange of information, and diverse searches, as well as for arranging places for meetings. A virtual phenomenon, "Lists of Nursing" with hundreds of daily messages, mobilized more people and more topics, bringing together all the associations and other organized groups. The two more important lists are Enfermeria de las Americas and Sinenfra.

The NurSite

The NurSite (http://www.nursite.com.ar) was the first formal site for nursing informatics in Argentina and one of the first ones in Latin America. Since 2000, when we created the Web site, it has passed diverse stages, while continually online and transmitting information and knowledge, offering services, and making friends.

Current State and Developments

Most health computer systems in use in Argentina were acquired from the health software industry and the rest belong to local developments. In both cases, there are only a small number of those that have modules for nursing activities. Most of these systems do not allow recording of medical indications that are needed for fulfilment of the electronic records of nursing. For example, the administration of a medicine is missing. The lack of this linkage causes certain services that are not yet automated to be performed separately from the modules, wasting personnel and time and further complicating other actions, such as invoicing and restocking of materials. A few health computer systems, which have nursing modules linked, were developed by colleagues of ADIERA (Hugo Leonzio's group), for the company MEDIBase. They are being used in some institutions: Hospital San Juan de Dios (from 2000), Clinica de la Ciudad (from 2002), Sanatorio Quintana (from 2004), and FUNDALEU (from 2009).

The regulative laws that provide a framework and support to the development and implementation of the Systems Computerized in Health and Health Electronics' Records are slow to develop and implement, and to this, add the resistance that arises from those who hold the power, make the decisions, and who do not value correctly the need and importance of the development of the these systems. There are consequently delays in making correct decisions.

From the current works of Nursing Informatics' Working Group of Argentine, we highlight the following projects:

- Plan of development, promotion, and support of the Nursing Informatics for Argentinean Nursing across a project of work with AECAF (Association of Nursing of Capital Federal) and AEUERA (Association of University Schools of Nursing of Argentina Republic)
- Project TAXO e-research to support multicentral research online
- Project ELNI e-learning platform in Moodle for Nursing Informatics' education across Internet

Summary

The path for implementation of nursing informatics in Argentina is already identified and recognized, and though there are few systems compatible with the Hospital Information System's (HIS) concept. There are people trained in the area and there are discussions occurring about the laws that will eventually provide a framework for the implementation and regulation of these systems. In nursing, due to the hegemony of a care model centered on organic pathology, there was always scanty or low-key support of companies or entities toward nursing projects. That is why work in the development of nursing informatics in Argentina was achieved by the personal effort of the interested parties and the help of the predecessors of the use of informatics in healthcare in Argentina. In summary, without looking for it, without wanting it, without thinking it, Argentinean nurses are incorporating the computer as a tool in their labor, education, and personnel areas. We are satisfied and believe we have constructed this change, practically and effectively, with minimal resources.

Case Study 14G

Brazil

By Grace T.M. Dal Sasso, Nursing Informatics PhD, RN; Denise Tolfo Silveira, PhD, MS, RN; Heloisa Helena Ciqueto Peres; and Heimar De Fatima Marin, PhD, MS, RN, FACMI

Introduction

Healthcare has been growing in complexity all over the world. Most recent research has been focused on new approaches regarding diagnosis, treatment and care, yet few efforts are being dedicated to the integration of operational systems to support the needs of professionals and the issue of patient safety. However, this exponential growth generates possibilities and challenges in the work performed by nurses, researchers, and faculty in the development of teaching, research, management, and nursing care.[1]

In Brazil, for more than a decade, informatics has been helping to increase efficiency, organization, speed, and versatility in the nursing profession. The utilization of informatics in teaching and research has made it easy to view and review literature and to collect data for the development of research in nursing and healthcare.[1,2]

The ICT resources have become a part of the daily life of healthcare providers and organizations. Over the last ten years, nursing informatics and telenursing have advanced considerably in the Brazilian healthcare scene, following this tendency throughout the world. In this chapter, challenges, difficulties, outcomes, and possibilities are described, demonstrating what has been achieved up to the present and what needs pursuing. Strategies are also discussed, so that professionals, who work with ICT, can continue to make contributions to the health of the Brazilian population, developing a safer healthcare environment, promoting the culture of security, and stimulating research to redesign the professional practice, according to new trends and tendencies.

Brazil is the largest country in South America and the fifth largest in the world, with its 8,514,876 square kilometers covering nearly half (47.3%) of the South American continent. There is enormous diversity experienced by the population, which is around 200 million, in cultural, social, economic, meteorological, and geographical areas. These characteristics stimulate development and utilization of the ICT in the most diversified scenarios and contexts.

On the other hand, problems that result from these characteristics continually challenge healthcare professionals, particularly nurses, and in regards to management of a large volume of information, development of their professional practice with countless methods of documentation, and advancement of knowledge in nursing informatics and telenursing.[3,4]

These advances have made it possible for nursing care to be supported on the basis of organized data by means of accurate and specific documentation available to the providers. However, factors such as the difficulty of adopting a standardized nursing terminology and the lack of systematization in nursing care have been causing constraints when analyzing or utilizing the information systems in professional practice to support decision making and to produce new knowledge.[1,3,4]

A retrospective search was performed in the electronic directory of the National Research Council for Science and Technology (CNPq) of Brazil, for the period between 1922 and 2008. It was found that among the 323 research groups included in this directory, approximately 28 groups (42%) performed some type of study and research in ICT. Specifically, there are 16 research groups in nursing informatics in Brazil; the pioneering group is the Nursing Informatics Research Group at the Federal University of São Paulo (NIEn-UNIFESP). However, a growing research movement in this field is seen, with several groups across the country being established in the last seven years, such as the Research Group in Technology, Information, Health and Nursing Informatics (Federal University of Santa Catarina) and the Research Group in Information Technology and Nursing Work Process (GEPETE - Nursing School at São Paulo University).

Nursing work is complex, and it is a great challenge to perform this work in a variety of clinical settings. The priorities of each sector are also very different, particularly as a result of oversight and lack of integration that are inherent in healthcare systems. Considering this situation, in 2002, the Interest Group on Nursing Informatics was created at the Brazilian Society of Health Care Informatics (SBIS-NI) and, in the same year, the Telenursing Department, integrated into the Brazilian Council of Telemedicine and Telehealth Care, was also established. This structure was specifically created for the purpose of pushing for the advancement of developments regarding nursing informatics and telenursing in Brazil and, above all, to improve healthcare in Brazil, based on the utilization of these technologies.[1]

Since 2006, an important project in ICT is being deployed in Brazil named RUTE Network.[5] The infrastructure was developed by the University Network of Telemedicine and Telehealth Care of the Science and Technology Ministry (MCT), which is coordinated by the National Network of Teaching and Research (RNP)[6] and the National Program of Telehealth Care for primary healthcare. The RUTE project integrates teaching hospitals and basic healthcare networks.[5,7] Currently, this infrastructure integrates approximately 57 healthcare institutions throughout the country and hundreds of basic healthcare units in their respective states. In addition, it handles multi-professional integration in the healthcare of the community. Above all, the structure has made possible better accessibility for the populations of remote and difficult access regions to obtain care and health information.[5,6]

In the following sections, we describe the experiences, challenges, and achievements resulting from the development of the Brazilian Nursing Informatics and Telenursing, and will also share our plans for the upcoming years.

Brazilian Experiences With Nursing Informatics and Telenursing

Nursing Healthcare

The nursing process is the elementary methodology that is applied in the development of information systems for nursing care. However, in general, these systems are not yet either standardized or structured in accordance with the needs of the respective facilities. Since 2002, an important initiative to assure interoperability is a project to certify systems, conducted by the Brazilian Society of Health Informatics, in which software used in healthcare can be certified according to defined requirements for national standardization.[1]

Several reasons force this change and investment in the development of an electronic register system for Nursing Health Care, and include (a) the need to improve the quality of nursing documentation, which requires not just new or modified tools but new ways of thinking; (b) the need to reduce time spent by nurses recording patient information order to bring the nurse closer to the point of care; (c) the need to limit the costs required to analyze the recorded documentation and also to make it more efficient to optimize available resources; (d) the need to improve data collection and information for delivering care to ensure, for example, that patients are not asked the same questions multiple times by various professionals; (e) the need to increase the emphasis on the results of nursing care, which requires modifications in the contents of the nursing documentation, including, standardized terminology to document the nursing process; (f) the need for better planning for healthcare and improved focus on the customized clinical evidence and on the healthcare plans that address the needs of the patients; (g) the need to define a set of essential data for documentation and analysis with national coverage, and (h) the need to increase emphasis on patients' outcomes, which requires modifications in nursing documentation to attend to the requirements of nursing process implementation.[1,4]

In some hospitals and local healthcare units, nurses are directly involved with the development of systems. However, this does not happen in the majority of institutions. Consequently, not all healthcare institutes have developed either a written nursing process or even an electronic one. On the other hand, at the healthcare institute in which the nursing process is a priority, the process has been structured according to a nursing reference terminology. This aspect has also been considered a priority in regards to patient safety, including the utilization of the ICT in healthcare, the integration of alert systems for the prevention of errors, and early detection of adverse events.[8,9]

In a very specific way, hospital units and other private healthcare institutes were the first to develop the EHR. However, the nursing process or nursing needs for documentation were not considered as fundamental. Nevertheless, during the last five years, public teaching hospitals have intensified development of the EHR, and nurses have participated more actively in this process. In addition, telenursing activities are being performed at basic healthcare units and in public and private teaching hospitals, such as Tele-Consult and Telemonitoring, and clinical immersion for collaborative discussion of actual clinical cases.[5] These units are gradually being structured as they are considered as isolated cases in some regions of Brazil and, consequently, their performance needs to be evaluated.

Several computerized systems based on the nursing process are being developed and deployed. Examples include: the system of the Porto Alegre Clinics Hospital (HCPA),[10] the nursing system of the University Hospital of the University of Sao Paulo (HU-USP),[11] the nursing Web-system on intensive and emergency care of the Federal University of Santa Catarina (UFSC),[12] and the system developed by the Brazilian Nursing Association in Paraná State for the area of public health using the CIPESC Classification (a project to add community healthcare terms to the ICNP).

Since 1997, the HCPA has been implementing a corporate computerized system for hospital management to perform the main health assistance processes. It makes available data collected from the identification records of patients in ambulatory care, diagnosis and therapeutic support services, patient admission, medical and nursing orders, medical summaries of discharges and deaths, appointment schedules, and the performance of surgeries.[10]

Since 2000, the HU-USP and the Nursing School of Sao Paulo University (EEUSP) have been conducting development of an information system for clinical care documentation in nursing. The main objective is implementation of the nursing diagnosis. The system provides integration of the nursing classifications as proposed by the alliance of NANDA-I and the Center of Classification and Nursing Effectiveness, called NNN (NANDA, NIC – Classification of the Nursing Interventions, NOC – Classification of Nursing Results), including the diagnoses of the NANDA-I Classification of 2007. The nursing documentation computerized system, called *PROCENF*, is composed of two environments: education and assistance, covering rules of safety and ethics regarding the patient. It allows the nurse to choose a set of diagnoses that best explains the patient's status at admission.[11,13]

The Nursing System for Critical Care and Emergency of the UFSC, based on the nursing process, uses the ICNP 1.0®[14] as a standardized terminology for documentation. It was developed from the practice experiences of intensive care and emergency care nurses, using the data collection in accordance with the Human Systems as a guide, stimulus, and support for decisions about clinical processes made by nurses related to the collection of patient data and information. Based on this data collection, a set of patient problems or diagnoses is identified using ICNP terms. The result is that for each problem/diagnosis shown on the screen, the nurse decides which nursing interventions would be the best option, according to the identified problems.[9,12,14]

Nursing Education

The nursing education focus has been at undergraduate and graduate level. At the undergraduate level, most schools of nursing (629 in the country) have a discipline of nursing informatics that is integrated into the regular curriculum. There are also several graduate programs, both at the specialization level, and in master's and doctorate programs focused on training nurses as users, developers, educators, and researchers of the ICT.

These courses aim to train professionals to increase the quality of patient care and outcomes through the development, implementation, and evaluation of information and telecommunication tools at different levels of education. Investment is also made by research groups in nursing schools and universities, to train nurses to analyze information requirements, plan and develop low-cost systems to manage IT, and identify and implement training strategies for professionals, users, and communities. In addition, the training programs provide resources to evaluate the effectiveness of the EHR in clinical information and management and safety of patient care.

Related to the graduate programs in Brazil, the focus has also been on training leaders in the conceptualization, design, and research of computer-based systems in healthcare organizations, including applications for learning based on evidence. These programs also support online Learning Management Systems (LMS).

Examples of universities and nursing schools that have devoted increased effort to nursing education for development and implementation of the ICT include: The Federal University of Sao Paulo/UNIFESP (the pioneer in the country since 1990), Nursing School of the State University of Sao Paulo (EEUSP), Nursing School of Ribeirão Preto (EERP-USP), Nursing School at Federal University of Santa Catarina (UFSC) and the Nursing School of the Federal University of Rio Grande do Sul (UFRGS). It is important to point out the Open

University of Brazil, a program for distance learning provided by UNIFESP that offers a specialization degree in Health Care Informatics for 500 professionals with 10 centers spread all over Brazil.

Other examples of education and training can be added. The Telenursing Center of the School of Nursing in USP (CETEnf/EEUSP) is developing learning objects in three-dimension with the Telemedicine discipline of Sao Paulo University School of Medicine (FMUSP) aggregated to the virtual man project (http://www.projeto-homemvirtual.com.br/), covering themes such as arterial pressure, vital signals, application of intramuscular medications, and lactation. In addition, nurses, researchers, undergraduate and graduate students, members of the Research Group in Information Technology and Nursing Work Process (GEPETE), have developed learning units in virtual learning environments about decision making in nursing care, cardio-respiratory problems in neonatology, nursing management, pressure ulcers, vesicle catheters, digital photography in nursing, conceptual maps, and IT in nursing and healthcare.[15,16]

The Virtual Learning Laboratory (LEVI) at the Federal University of Rio Grande do Sul (UFRGS) has developed digital learning objects. The importance of this as a pedagogic reference, not just at the time of its conception but also during its use with students, was demonstrated by the experience of learning objects in the field of nursing fundamentals.[17,18] The conception of learning objects was based on problem-based learning—PBL, and on the constructivist paradigm, when considering the contents that would be developed and reflection about the practice. This becomes a constant during the pathway performed by the user in the exploration of the educational objectives.

Up to the present time, twenty digital learning objects for vital signals have been developed, consisting of eight hypertexts, eight educational games, and four simulations, covering the themes of semi-techniques in nursing and following the stages of conceptual modeling, implementation, and evaluation of its use. Digital learning objects for clinical assessment were also developed in order to learn the problems faced by students in their daily activities, transposing that information through formulation of hypotheses for integration phases of the clinical assessment in nursing content. In this manner, analysis about the practice becomes a constant during the journey performed by the user in the exploration of digital learning objects.[19] The learning objects are also being developed in the field of women's health in themes such as nursing clinical assessment in pregnant women.[20]

At the Nursing Department and the Nursing Graduate Program of the Federal University of Santa Catarina (UFSC), among the educational highlights are developments of learning environments via the Web, such as: the environment in support of the decision for physical examination of the pregnant woman and the virtual learning environment for HIV/AIDS and arterial hypertension prevention in children (http://www.giateinfo.ufsc.br).

The learning objects being developed are: problem-based learning in RCP—Basic Life Support; problem-based learning for evaluation of pain, and as the mobile learning object in RCP—ACLS (Advanced Cardiac Life Support) in a multimodal structure for Web and mobile devices denominated Guideview.®[21,22] Other activities conducted by the group include training of 180 nurses at Santa Catarina State, the development of the Electronic Nursing Process, and integrating the universities of UFSC, UNIFESP, USP, and UFRGS. The project is also linked to the Telenursing–Santa Catarina Project in a distance course on Moodle®—Learning Management System using a streaming environment for synchronic and asynchronic learning (http:///giateinfo.ufsc.br/videoconferencia).[23]

In February 2009, the first social Web network was created on Nursing Informatics and Telenursing, with the purpose of creating an ongoing space for nurses and other professionals for sharing information, innovation, and knowledge as well as to gather specialists for the development of the Brazilian nursing profession.[24]

Nursing Research

Research on nursing informatics and telenursing has been a priority in Brazil. Studies have been focused on the development and the appraisals of technologies that can meet the needs of professional practice and nursing education. For this purpose, the research on nursing informatics is configured within the contexts of the research groups linked to the universities. Each research group develops its studies in accordance with the needs of its region as well as those of the nation, and in accordance with guidelines of the graduate programs. As mentioned earlier, 16 research groups are registered in the database regarding the Brazilian Council of Research (CNPq).[25] These groups show that nursing has an important place in the national scene that is related to the production of knowledge in nursing and healthcare informatics. This visibility and production have been growing throughout the1990s but have shown an exponential growth in various regions of the country since 2000. Among all of the groups undertaking nursing research and work with technology of information and communication (approximately twenty-eight groups), 16 have research in nursing and healthcare informatics as their main focus. And within these, five groups, 31.2%, list Nursing Informatics Terminology in their registration/identification in the directory.

It is important to point out that these groups are integrated into the Brazilian Universities that have regular courses in the area of Nursing Informatics at the undergraduate and graduate levels. Consequently, they pay particular concern and willingness to the education of nurses and the development of studies in this area. However, this fact also demonstrates a tendency of the nursing informatics and telenursing applicability being more centered on education and research. There is still a lack of incentive for integration and translation of the ICT in professional practice by nurses in hospital environments and in public healthcare facilities.

Nursing Management

The adoption of informatics resources in nursing management in Brazil intends to cover the institutional policies and the individual commitment for the technological development of human resources in nursing, based on the ethical-political consideration, the needs of the profession, and the human dimension of nursing.

The computer-related program Dimensioning, Based on Informatics, of the Nursing Personnel (DIPE)[26] stands out in nursing management, having as its aim the forecasting of quantitative and qualitative dimensioning of professional dimensions for inpatient units of healthcare institutions. This application, which utilizes a Web interface, is available to the whole community with free access at (http://www.ee.usp.br/dipe).[27]

Related to the management of materials, the use of IT can also help in sharing data among buyers, suppliers, and users, allowing it to create a virtual supply chain based on information and not just on physical inventory. For this purpose, a Management Material System was developed and implemented at the (HU-USP).[26] A study was conducted to compare the effectiveness of the system based on informatics with the traditional one in the use of the materials inventory at the unit of the HU-USP Surgery Center.[28]

Therefore, the challenges of nursing in Brazil are related to the strong need to develop systems that can measure nursing care outcomes according to patients' needs. An additional requirement is to implement automated systems to prevent errors in patient care. For this reason, a national strategy in nursing informatics education, practice, research, and administration should address methods to evaluate the effectiveness of nursing care according to regional demands. The strategy should also review nursing competency and educational methods to make them more effective and efficient.

Summary and Future Perspectives

Various questions emerged when we considered perspectives on the future of Brazilian nursing and, based on these questions and achievements, a plan of action was developed to measure the results obtained, what needs to be modified, and what should be kept.

The Brazilian Interest Group on Nursing Informatics (SBIS-NI) is building a national architecture designed for continuous integration to stimulate the development and the applications in nursing informatics and telenursing in Brazil for the next five years. Within this architecture, ANIET's (National Architecture of Nursing Informatics and Telenursing) central focus and the common purpose is safety of the user. Also, due to the RUTE project that integrates teaching hospitals and universities, all interest groups in informatics and telenursing, regulating bodies of the nursing profession, public and private agencies for research and education, and scientific societies will be working to improve health care efficiency and effectiveness.

This process is being made effective in the long-term, considering that the high-quality, safety, and efficiency of healthcare are always increasing. It is a process that involves various levels and instances of management regarding health, education, and technology. Consequently, it has become necessary to develop a safety culture in the country and, at the same time, it is possible to commit consumers to improve the population's health and to transform the delivery of healthcare.

Despite the progress that has been made, we realize that the globalization of information technologies is in dynamic and continuous development. Therefore, the challenge is not a mission just for the federal, state, or municipal governments, but also for the organized civil society. The successful initiatives in this area require a collective effort and creative solutions being adapted to the Brazilian reality and aiming at a more effective inclusion of all citizens into the information and knowledge society.

References

1. Marin H, Sasso GTM. Brazil Study Case: The Americas, Case Study 14H – Brazil. In: Weaver C , Delaney C, Weber P, Carr R. *Nursing and Informatics for the 21ˢᵗ Century: An International Look at Practice, Trends and the Future.* First edition. Chicago: HIMSS; 2006, 350-353.

2. Marin HF. Informática em enfermagem. São Paulo, SP: EPU; 1995:100.

3. Silveira DT, Marin HF. Conjunto de Dados Mínimos em Enfermagem: identificação de categorias e itens para a prática de enfermagem em saúde ambulatorial. Revista Brasileira de Enfermagem. 2006;59(2):142-147.

4. Marin HF. Os componentes de enfermagem do prontuário eletrônico do paciente. In: Massad E, Marin HF, Azevedo Neto RS, eds. *O Prontuário Eletrônico do Paciente na Assistência, informação e conhecimento médico.* São Paulo (SP): OPAS/OMS; 2003:73-83.

5. Rede Universitária de Telemedicina e Telesaúde. RUTE. http://www.rute.br. Accessed March 2, 2009.

6. Rede Nacional de Ensino e Pesquisa. RNP. htttp://www.rnp.br/index.php. Accessed March 2, 2009.

7. Brasil. Ministério da Saúde. Programa Nacional de Telesaúde. Portaria, 35 de 4 de Janeiro de 2007. Brasília;2007.http://portal.saude.gov.br/portal/arquivos/pdf/portaria35jan07telessaude.pdf and http://www.telessaudebrasil.org.br/php/index.php. Accessed April 10, 2009.

8. World Health Organization. World alliance for patient safety. Summary of the evidence on patient safety: implications for research. The Research Priority Setting Work Group of the World Alliance for Patient Safety. 2008, 1-136.

9. Sasso GTM, Barbosa SF, Souza ML. Patient safety in the intensive care unit: automatic alerts generated by computer. In: Seguridad del Paciente, ética y atención primaria de salud en el cuidado holístico de enfermería. XI Coloquio Panamericano de Investigación en Enfermeria. Quito 2008.

10. Revista Clínicas. Porto Alegre, RS: Hospital de Clínicas de Porto Alegre; 2003:1:20-22.

11. Peres HHC, Ortiz DCF. Sistemas eletrônicos de informação em saúde e o processo de enfermagem. In: Gaidzinski RR et al., eds. *Diagnóstico de Enfermagem na prática.* Porto Alegre: Artmed, 2008:339-53

12. Barra D, Sasso GTM. Avaliação do processo de enfermagem informatizado em UTI em ambiente PDA a partir da CIPE® versão 1.0. In: Anais XI Congresso Brasileiro de Informática em Saúde, SBIS: Ribeirão Preto; 2008. http://www.sbis.org.br/cbis11/arquivos/707.pdf. Accessed March 2, 2009.

13. North American Nursing Diagnosis Intervention I. Nursing diagnoses: classification and definitions 2007-2009. Philadelphia: NANDA-I, 2007.

14. International Council of Nurses - ICN. Classificação Internacional para a Prática de Enfermagem – CIPE versão 1.0. Translation, Heimar de Fátima Marin. Sao Paulo (SP): Algol, 2007.

15. Peres HHC, Leite MMJ. Inovação e interação tecnológica na Escola de Enfermagem da USP. Rev. Esc. Enferm. USP [online]. 2008:42 (4):614-615.

16. Peres HHC, Kurcgant P. O ser docente de enfermagem frente a informática. Rev. Latino-Am. Enfermagem, 2004;12(1):101-108.

17. Cogo ANP, Silveira DT, Catalan VM. Objetos de aprendizagem digitais como ferramenta de apoio na educação em enfermagem In: Anais X Congresso Brasileiro de Informática em Saúde; 2006: Florianópolis:368-9.2006.

18. Cogo ANP, Pedro EM, Schatkoski AM, Alves RHK, Catalan VM. Objetos educacionais digitais sobre oxigenoterapia: avaliação de docentes de um curso de graduação em enfermagem. Revista HCPA. 2006;26(1):4-5.

19. Catalan VM, Neutzling AL, Martinato LHM, Treumann MF, Silveira DT. Consulta de enfermagem: criação e desenvolvimento de objetos de aprendizagem. In: Anais X Congresso Brasileiro de Informática em Saúde. Florianópolis. 2006:368-9.

20. Neutzling AL, Catalan VM, Martinato LHM, Silveira DT. Saúde da mulher: objetos de aprendizagem na consulta de enfermagem. CBIS2008.

21. Sardo PG, Sasso GTM. Aprendizagem baseada em problemas em ressuscitação cardiopulmonar: suporte básico de vida. Rev. Esc. Enf. USP. 2008;42(4):784-792.

22. Sasso GTM, Phelps C. Mobile Learning Object on Cardiopulmonary Resuscitation (CPR): a collaborative, simulated and constructive proposal on Health and Nursing. In: Advances in Teaching & Learning. Houston. 2008;5:12-13.

23. http:///giateinfo.ufsc.br/videoconferencia. Accessed July 20, 2009.

24. INFOTELEN. Brazil's Nursing and Telenursing Network. http://www.infotelen.ning.com. Accessed June 3, 2009.

25. CNPq. http://dgp.cnpq.br/buscaoperacional/. Accessed March 3, 2009.

26. Gaidzinski RR, Fugulin FMT, Peres HHC, Castilho V. Software Dimensionamento Informatizado de Pessoal de Enfermagem (DIPE). Universidade de São Paulo. 2009.

27. http://www.ee.usp.br/dipe. Accessed June 2, 2009.

28. Paschoal MLH. Estudo do consumo de materiais de um Centro Cirúrgico após a implementação de um sistema de Gestão Informatizado. Tese (doutorado) Escola de Enfermagem da Universidade de São Paulo. São Paulo, 2009. 190p.

Case Study 14H

The Electronic Health Record in Chile

By Erika Mayela Caballero Muñoz, MEd Instructional Design, RN-BC

Introduction

This case study presents an overview of the current state for the use of electronic health records (EHR) in Chile and will discuss this in the context of other EHR initiatives together with the need for clinical data that support nurses and other health professionals in best-practice care delivery.

The term *electronic health record* is used to describe the concept of a longitudinal record of health conditions and healthcare of patients.[1] The record contains detailed information about health events that a person receives in conjunction with facts that are derived directly from the model of care that is used for the client or patient.[2] In Chile, we are moving toward a national strategy to provide an EHR that assists health professionals to make evidence-based decisions. To better understand the concept of the EHR in Chile, clinical information needs to be defined. Whatever its form, class, or type, clinical information in electronic records is that set of data that permit acquisition or expansion of knowledge about the health condition of a person. This clinical initiative is independent of the technology and software that health providers use for the transmission of patient demographic information and clinical knowledge.

National Statistics, Information Technology and Communication, and the Need for an EHR

According to the census of 2006, Chile contains 15 regions, 16.5 million inhabitants, a per capita income of US \$4,591, and a human development index of 0.85437 in global ranking. Some health indications that graph the change of the socio-demographic profile of Chile are the life expectancy from birth, 77.9; literacy rate, 95.7%; percent of the population below the poverty line, 13.7%; inequity of income, (Gini) 57.1; and the increase of the population over 65 years of age. It is worth noting that in recent years infant mortality has decreased by 15%, and life expectancy has increased to 78 years, though chronic problems continue to appear and are becoming more complicated to treat. These changes have made the implementation of health reform a necessity.

In Chile, current health reform has involved a process of transforming structural, legal, and administrative order toward an effective performance of the principles of equal and dependable health services. Its objective is to generate conditions for the development of healthy individuals, communities, and environments, causing a change from the culture of illness toward a culture of health—balancing the promotional (long-term effect) with the healing (short- and medium-term effect). This permits achievement of strategic national health objectives, such as decreasing inequalities in health, confronting the challenges of aging of the population and resulting societal changes, providing services appropriate to the expectations of the population, and improving previously achieved health objectives.

This Chilean health reform proposes implementing a model of comprehensive care, supported in a human bio-psychosocial perspective in relationship with its situation, characterized by a familiar community focus that integrates a holistic vision of high-quality technical and human care. Within health reform a system of explicit guarantees in health (GES) is being considered, a system that guarantees the access, opportunity, quality, and financial protection of health activity; prioritizing the main problems of the population by considering the most frequent, serious, expensive factors, and those most damaging to the quality of life. This system of GES proposes effective interventions in relation to the promotion, prevention, treatment, and rehabilitation of health and incorporates criteria of practicality, such as the ability of a country to fulfill needs in balance with available resources. It is worth noting that this GES system, in effect from July 2005 through 2008, served more than 5 million individuals, 86.4% of the people seen in primary care.[3]

The introduction of information and communication technology (ICT) into health was established by the Ministry of Health in 2003 by an initiative called Digital Agenda. This agenda considered a series of initiatives whose objectives are to contribute to healthcare development in Chile—through the use of the ICT—to increase the competitiveness, equality of opportunities, quality of life, efficiency, and openness of the public sector, while at the same time enriching the cultural identity of the nation and its native people. The Digital Agenda of the health sector is a master plan that looks to guarantee the alignment and coordination of technologic supports with the strategies of the national system of health, and incorporating all of the advantages.

Chile is investing in ICT in health, specifically in the update and improvement of technological equipment in the Health System and implementation of a platform of integration that simplifies the creation and management of the interfaces between applications and systems. A system of online procedure has been created which has aided the development of an architectural model that strengthens the system of surveillance of illnesses of obligatory notification for the monitoring of infections within hospitals. Chile has also invested in training for professionals in this sector aimed at improving the use of IT, communication, and applied computer science.

Many hospitals and centers of healthcare are using the evidence-based systems in conjunction with monitoring of vital signs, traceability of medicine, bar code systems, EHRs, ambulatory information systems, and systems of telephone communication by users and files of integrated images among many other applications for the management of health problems.

With EHRs incorporating ICTs, the following initiatives are noted:

- The electronic clinical record for primary healthcare (APS) has improved the quality of welfare processes and the distribution of resources, using online information to measure the status of the health of the population.
- The ICARO System (Sistema de Información de Atención Pre-hospitalaria) involves information about ambulatory care, known as SAMU 133, which integrates the different technological components of telephone, radio, global positioning system, and observed facts. It collects the principal processes that are applied in the activity of regulation and intervention of the pre-hospital care.
- The System of Information for the Health Network (SIRA) is an ecosystem of applications of national scope, that are flexible and adaptable to the operation of health networks and their processes of care that have previously defined standards of information and technology. It is structured under inclusive criteria, which are able to complement and differentiate interoperable technological solutions, therefore being applicable to the entire network and explained with a case model for use of reference and counter reference. This is an initiative emanating at a ministerial level, propelled by the Division of the Management of Health Network (DIGERA), the Department of Statistics and Health Information (DEIS), and the Department of Digital Agenda in Health (DADES).
- System of Indicators of Quality of Attention and Health Results (SICARS) corresponds to an application in development that will contribute to improving the quality of present systems for study of intra-hospital infections, initially including infections, adverse reactions, indicators of results, and quality of information, with details of the study and personal health systems.
- SinetSure corresponds to a basic solution, developed by professionals of the South Araucanian Health System, in a Web environment. Currently, it is used in applications for planning, pharmacy, emergency, supplies, cardiovascular, register III, and the interface with the management systems of explicit guarantees of health.
- A telemedicine system was implemented at a national level for the diagnosis of early stage acute myocardial infarction for places in which there are no medical specialists; it aims to reduce the number of deaths.

In Chile and elsewhere in Latin America, the construction of systems in the EHR have also been explored where clinics actively participate in the update and determination of the best clinical evidence for the care and security of the user/patient, with the use of systems such as openMRS or OpenEHR. It should be noted that in Chile, a standardized system of national information still does not exist, resulting in a lack of overall communication in networks and shared knowledge. The desired health information is found distributed between heterogeneous and autonomous systems whose interconnection and integration are difficult to achieve, though this differs between public and private centers.

It would be beneficial to health professionals if clinical work processes were the initial starting point for transforming the work environment and data capture from a paper-based system to an electronic system. As health organizations in Chile move into the implementation phases of EHR systems, we are encountering the challenges of the lack of health professionals with informatics training and the presence of technical barriers, such as the lack of standardization and the use of systems that permit interoperability.

Benefits of an Electronic Health Record

EHRs are a computerized solution for clinical and administrative processes, based within a specific model of care supporting caregivers of health services, at all levels. EHRs are a concept that spans the community referring to a computerized solution that unites and integrates the distinct caregivers in the health system and participants that make decisions in the distribution of services for the citizen, for example, financial entities and the system's own users. It allows the management of a unique record of longitudinal health along the life of an individual, integrating computerized clinical histories of multiple caregivers.[4]

The response as to why we need an electronic record in healthcare, as stated by Garde[5] is because of the ease of mobility it provides within and between countries of their current population and because of the large number of healthcare providers needing access, a product of globalization. Other factors include the critical problems and treatments that continue to become more complex, the increased cost of healthcare, the increased life span which calls for more inclusive records, the need to prevent damage and risk to individuals' health and the necessity to increase knowledge and manage the security and privacy of data. In this context, currently, a large quantity of information exists in distinct places and in a distinct form, which do not support a centralized vision of the patient and leads to the fragmentation of information. Additionally, the necessity of exchange of information between health professionals or between computerized systems is currently a critical process for the health sector. To our knowledge, no unified computerized system exists that responds to reforms in the region that involve multidisciplinary work and a network between the distinct levels of healthcare, incorporating a familiar self-care model of health. Thus there remains a lack of communication in the network, in which a shared understanding and continuity of care is desired, as well as health information being distributed between heterogeneous and autonomous systems in regions where interconnection and integration are difficult to achieve.

As a consequence of this fragmentation indicated by Garde,[5] examinations and questions are repeated, care is repeated and also omitted, and the administration of resources and the flow of work are difficult. There is also a larger probability of clinical errors due to the inability to see relevant information in a timely manner. Thus the support of decision-making is limited to local incidents, which collectively causes the cost to be higher and the quality of care much lower than desired.

The primary purpose of an EHR is to provide a documented health record that supports present and future healthcare in all clinics. This documentation provides a method of communication between clinics that contributes to the care of the patient. The principle beneficiaries are the patient(s) and the clinic(s).[6]

Capturing nursing care information constitutes a challenge, and the clinical modeling of information for advanced nursing practice for an EHR should integrate knowledge in such a way that reflects its application in the practice of care management based on standards, the optimum evidence, and the known preferences of the user with professional experience.

Having clinical information at the patient's point of care permits the improvement of health services and saving lives. It thus becomes necessary, in the age of information management, to use EHRs that permit the collection of high-quality clinical information to guide clinical decision-making in a secure and effective manner. EHRs represent the key, sensitive, and critical processes of nursing work. An EHR permits the acquisition of information in a faster and more efficient method, introducing the possibility of sharing with other services, facilitating the transmission of information and the daily work dynamic in the health network, causing the process to be more agile, saving time, and avoiding errors. Standard documentation facilitates the communication between health professionals, the continuity of care, and the management of department costs. However, if standardized records are not used, EHRs facilitate the appearance of risks related to the integrity, security, and confidentiality of healthcare information and potential resultant legal problems.[7]

Summary

There is no doubt that electronic health records are becoming essential in the integration of administrative and clinical processes in healthcare organizations. At the same time, they constitute a basis for inquiries in health and the discovery of the educative necessities of the users. Nursing, as noted by Cuesta,[8] has favored the integration of ICT, though it should not just be recognized for the benefits that any inclusion of computers contributes to profiles, but also for the process of reorganization of the information that is provided by nursing. The volume of facts that can be captured, processed, stored, and consulted is vast, and this assists with a collection of information that extends and enhances the base of decision making, representing an invaluable help.

References

1. Reche D, García-Linares A. La Arquitectura de Documento Clínico XML-CDA. VII Congreso Nacional de Informática de la Salud. http://www.Seis.Es/Seis/Inforsalud04/Reched1.htm. Accessed September 20, 2009.

2. Hobbs FDR, Hawker A. Computerised data collection: practicability and quality in selected general practices. *Fam Pract.* 1995;12:221-226. http://fampra.oxfordjournals.org/cgi/content/abstract/12/2/221?ijkey=2b6cd4908356dce69b1bcc9ae0c4629f684ec590&keytype2=tf_ipsecsha Kleinbeckj. Accessed September 20, 2009.

3. Espiñeira Francés AJ, López Cabañas JA, Díaz Berenguer JA, Cabeza Mora A. Informatización de la Atención Primaria de la salud. Historia de salud Electrónica. Information & communication technologies in healthcare development-3rd virtual congress in Internet: March 1-30, 2004. http://www.informaticamedica.org/I04/papers/espineira_26.pdf. Accessed February 1, 2009.

4. Bonelli Pablo. 2006. Desarrollo de Registros Electrónicos de salud objetivos, desafíos y tácticas. Senior Manager Health & Life Sciences Argentina & Chile. http://www.accenture.com/NR/rdonlyres/FD661A0E-2273-485D-90D4-4F303F67DBB2/0/Newsletter_de_salud_Accenture_0307.pdf. Accessed September 2, 2009.

5. Garde S. Registros clínicos electronicos en salud. Presentación interna realizada en Escuela de Enfermería de la Universidad Mayor; 2006.

6. Barroso S. Tecnologías de servicios de registro electrónico de salud (EHR) 2001. http://neutron.ing.ucv.ve/comunicaciones/Asignaturas/DifusionMultimedia/Tareas%202004-3/Sistemas%20EHR.doc. Accessed October 5, 2009.

7. Ziel ES. Managing the risk of electronic health records. *Rev. AORN Journal.* 1998;68(2):281-283.

8. Cuesta Y. Enfermería desde un Enfoque Informático. Revista Habanera de Ciencias Médicas. 2006;5(2). http://www.ucmh.sld.cu/rhab/vol5_num2/rhcm01206.htm. Accessed October 2, 2009.

## CHAPTER 15

Information Technology Strategies in the United Kingdom and Ireland

By Anne Casey, MSc, RN, FRCN

Introduction

Widespread uptake of interoperable EHRs is seen in the United Kingdom (U.K.), Ireland, and Europe as the most important advance that health services can make "towards the provision of faster, better integrated and more patient centered care."[1-3] Personal health records, owned and managed by the health consumer are increasingly seen as part of that advance.[4] However, there is some way to go before systems are able to support "the cognitive tasks of clinicians or the workflow of the people who must actually use the system."[5] Despite developments in technology and increased investment in healthcare systems, a systematic review in 2009 found no strong evidence that nursing record systems provide benefits for nurses and patients.[6]

One advance that is supporting improvements in workflow, communication, and patient safety is mobile technology. Wherever robust, portable, and cleanable devices are deployed, nurses are reporting benefits.[7,8] As costs of hardware come down and national infrastructures improve, access to IT is becoming less of a challenge for nurses. Now, attention is focused on other challenges, such as the nursing content of healthcare systems. The nursing profession's contribution to informatics developments in the U.K. and Ireland today focuses heavily on nursing content and the clinical safety of systems. Practice standards and patient safety are core to nursing and, as a result, nurses who are not informatics experts have been able to engage more confidently with system suppliers and developers of information standards. Specification of evidence-based content standards for electronic records and communications not only supports best practice but also benefits the system provider who can assure nursing staff of the professional acceptability of the content. Application of clinical risk management to the manufacture and use of health software provides assurance to clinicians, patients, and payers/managers that patient safety hazards have been identified and mitigated as far as possible.

The "bridging" role of nursing informatics specialists remains essential to support effective links between practice and technology, so that we achieve systems that support nursing work, rather than merely supporting data capture. However, there are few such specialists in the U.K. and Ireland, and it is still common for nurses with little or no informatics expertise to find themselves advising system designers on requirements and participating in signing-off systems for deployment. This gap has at last been recognized: three of the four U.K. countries now have full-time nursing leads at senior levels in their national health service (NHS) information programs. These new national level leadership roles are already having a significant impact on nurses' engagement with the ICT programs and on the prioritization of nursing issues within multidisciplinary e-health projects.

This chapter and the case studies that follow provide updates on the current state for nurses' engagement with health informatics in the United Kingdom and Ireland and summarizes progress made in national ICT programs in England and Wales. In addition, this chapter reviews the five goals for nursing informatics introduced in the first edition[9] and concludes with a discussion of emerging standards for the content of systems and standards to minimize risks to patient safety of ICT.

Health Policy Developments in England and Wales

The U.K.'s Royal College of Nursing (RCN) has identified seven policy challenges that face the nursing profession in the next few years:

1. Increased efficiency and effectiveness in health and social care.
2. Changes in population demography, including a decline in the birth rate and predicted rise in the numbers of older people.
3. Changes in patterns of disease, especially non-communicable disease and chronic and long-term illness.
4. Changes in lifestyle patterns, for example, diet, exercise, and sexual activity.
5. Changes in public expectation and demand for quality and personalized care.
6. Inequalities in health status and healthcare outcomes.
7. Reconciliations in demand, need, and access to healthcare with safety and quality.[10]

As a way of trying to reduce demand, governments are encouraging self-help and self-care, which in turn is having a significant impact on the direction of e-health developments. Use of assistive technology is increasing as health and social care services move to provide people with more independence, choice, and control, particularly those with long-term conditions. Governments no longer see patients as mere recipients of care but now recognize that many people are key decision-makers in their care and treatment process.[11,12]

The seven challenges just listed are being addressed in similar ways by the Irish and the four U.K. governments, although there are differences in areas, such as funding models and organization of services. For example, Northern Ireland combines provision of health and social care in its publicly funded service. Patients along the borders of the countries and those traveling between them may receive healthcare in any of the countries, making interoperability between health systems essential. Reducing inequalities and improving effectiveness have top priority, and standards are defined centrally for both service delivery and clinical practice. For example, a growing number of national service frameworks in England and Wales define the level of service that patients can expect for conditions such as cancer, heart disease, diabetes and other long-term conditions.[13,14] The National Institute for Health and Clinical Excellence[15] publishes evidence-based guidelines that healthcare professionals are expected to follow and which are made available through national e-health libraries.[16,17] Cross-boundary work between health and social care is encouraged, as are patient choice and public empowerment to participate in service planning. Quality improvement is supported by formal inspection processes,[18,19] and all healthcare professionals are expected to participate in clinical governance activities, such as audit and performance review. In England, there is now a strong policy focus on outcome measurement, and this is driving decisions on data collection at local levels.[20]

Effective service delivery requires well-trained staff. Some countries have developed or adopted standard descriptions of the competencies required by all healthcare professionals and ancillary staff, including information and knowledge management competencies.[21] The future envisaged in national IT strategies requires that staff at all levels "are prepared not only for the technological challenges, but also for the changing social relationships and ethical challenges that IT-supported access to clinical information will bring about."[22]

National Strategies for Information Technology

Although specific plans and levels of investment vary across the U.K. and Ireland, the IT strategies have common themes. First, the single, shared patient record is accepted as the best way to ensure communication across organizational and professional boundaries in health and social care; unidisciplinary, stand-alone systems, such as nursing care planning systems, have no place in this integrated future. Unique patient identifiers and other standards for interoperability are a basic requirement irrespective of whether the country has adopted a centralist approach or is enabling local innovation, or both. The case studies that follow this chapter provide more detail of developments in Ireland, Northern Ireland, and Scotland; progress with national strategies for England and Wales is summarized here.

England: The National Program for IT

The intention of the English strategy is to introduce new systems and services to improve the way information is stored and shared, so that the NHS can "deliver better, safer care for patients."[23] Several regional programs have been established to supply and integrate systems for primary, community, and acute services. Local systems are beginning to link with new national systems and services, such as the personal demographics service and the NHS care record service, which allows authorized staff to access a summary record for the patient.

Nurses and other healthcare professionals are already seeing some of the benefits of the national approach. Community nurses have been using the demographics service to obtain or confirm patient details, including the patient's unique NHS number, to ensure, for example, accurate labelling of blood samples. National rollout of picture archiving and communications systems across all hospitals was completed at the end of 2007. Nurses in assessment units, emergency departments, and elsewhere are reporting fewer delays or wasted appointments with immediate availability of the digital images. As in Wales and Scotland, the availability of a summary patient record is improving safety and continuity in walk-in centers, emergency departments, and places in which telephone triage is used. One example of the potential of these summary records is a trial of content related to end-of-life care. This project has shown how the patients' preferences can be communicated more effectively to their professional caregivers.[24] Patients opting into the system can be reassured that their wishes and medical history will be known if they need care from out-of-hours or emergency services, rather than from their regular provider. Other work streams in the English national program include: a national electronic prescription service; "choose and book" service for electronic referrals and appointments; and a directory service which allows a user to find contact details for all organizations, the services they provide, and their staff.

One of the successes of the IT program in England has been the rollout of an NHS e-mail facility to all clinicians. Wherever they work, clinicians take their e-mail address with them. Case study reports illustrate benefits to staff and patients of NHS mail and the service directories.[25] For example, nurses report using this latter service to find the address or phone number of the patient's general practitioner when the patient has been unable to provide this information. Other organizations are using the system for SMS text appointment reminders and to speed up referral communications. Although guidance is provided for using NHS mail to exchange sensitive patient information, concerns have been raised about the security of identifiable clinical information, such as that included in referral and discharge communications. Information is encrypted while in transit, but staff at either end of the communication need to adhere to the "acceptable use" policy.[26] Any exchange of sensitive information has to be part of an agreed process with those sending and receiving the information. Both parties must know what is to be sent, what it is for, and have agreed how that information will be treated. Another requirement is that those sending patient information should request an acknowledgement of "receipt" and of "by the recipient." These acknowledgement requirements are especially important for time-sensitive information, such as referrals or test results.

The long history of general practice computing in the U.K. and the more recent localized innovation in acute hospitals meant that there was a good foundation for the national ICT program to build upon. However, although some parts of the program have been implemented successfully, key elements such as the care records system could be delivered up to five years late.[27] Staff in some hospitals have been frustrated and disappointed when local systems that were working well were replaced with new systems that did not, at first, have the same level of functionality. In these situations, the longer-term benefits of a national approach are difficult to appreciate, and there have been calls for local organizations to be allowed to purchase systems outside the program, if sufficient progress is not being made to meet their requirements. In its 2008 report, the English government's National Audit Office that monitors public spending said: "the original timescales proved to be unachievable, raised unrealistic expectations and put confidence in the Programme at risk."[27] The NHS in England continues to invest heavily in the national IT infrastructure and to drive projects forward at a rapid pace, but there are questions about the value of this kind of "big bang" approach versus the more gradual rollout that is underway in other countries such as Wales.

Wales: Informing Healthcare

The Welsh Assembly Government's program for NHS IT aims to improve health services in Wales by "introducing new ways of accessing, using and storing information."[28] As in England, there are plans for a health record that can be accessed by clinicians in emergency departments and other out-of-hours services. Essential information provided from the record held by the general practitioner, such as current medication, major health conditions, allergies, and test results, will be available to be viewed with the permission of the patient. This requirement for explicit consent can be overruled by a clinician in an emergency. Achievements to date of the Informing Healthcare program include replacement of all hospital pharmacy systems and new radiology systems. A new national e-mail and directory service is in place, and progress has been made on the two other strategic projects: My Health Online and the Welsh Clinical Portal.[28] Through My Health Online patients are beginning to use the Internet to order repeat prescriptions and book appointments with their general practitioner. The intention is that they will eventually be able to view their own medical records. The Clinical Portal is establishing secure access for healthcare staff to the varied systems that are used to support patient care in hospitals.[28]

In contrast to the rapid national approach that was initially taken in England, the Welsh government is focusing on "incremental change," working with clinicians and other NHS staff to create prototypes, learn lessons, and build on experience. An example of this approach is the new service for cancer data-sharing, which involved the national rollout of an information system developed in 1991 and used successfully in one organization since that time.[29] *Telecare* is another area in which NHS Wales is investing. A 2004 review of telemedicine activity in the U.K. indicated that Wales could make more of the opportunities that telehealth technology afforded, particularly given the geographic spread of its citizens.[30] There are now a number of telecare demonstration projects that are testing ways to use technology to support the independence of individuals living with chronic conditions in communities across Wales, as part of Informing Healthcare's service improvement projects.[31]

Progress Toward National Goals for Nursing Informatics

The requirement for nurses to have *information and knowledge management skills appropriate to their roles* was one of five national goals for nursing informatics identified by the U.K. nursing professions in 2002 (see Table 15-1).[9] In 2007, more than 40% of the 2,600 U.K. nurses who responded to an online survey by the RCN[32] did not feel ready for the introduction of electronic records. More than half had not received any IT training in the previous six months, although, since this was an online survey, the results are likely to be biased in favor of those with existing skills and perhaps an interest in health IT. In 2009, there is still some way to go before topics such as structured recordkeeping, principles for use of decision support, seeking consent for information-sharing from patients, and using data for auditing practice are integrated into nursing curricula. In Ireland as in the U.K., there are efforts to supplement the widespread uptake of the basic European Computer Driving License with content specific to healthcare workers.[33]

Aside from basic IT skills, the NHS recognizes seven areas in which clinical staff must be competent:

1. E-health: the future direction of clinical care
2. Protection of individuals and organizations
3. Data, information, and knowledge
4. Health and care records
5. Communication and information transfer

6. The language of health: clinical coding and terminology
7. Clinical systems and applications.[22]

Table 15-1. Goals for Nursing Informatics

Access to appropriate tools and resources to support patient care
Education in information and knowledge management
Career pathways for nurses in informatics
Nursing perspectives will be integrated in local and national developments
Data about nurses and nursing will be available to decision-makers

National guidance makes it clear that health informatics should not be taught as a separate subject but should be "woven and integrated into the wider clinical curriculum."[22] However, although guidance, teaching materials, and other resources are widely available, teaching staff and those responsible for nursing educational policy have yet to recognize the critical importance of information and knowledge management and IT to the nursing role. Information competencies for qualified nursing staff are generally linked to the use of specific systems, rather than being seen as core aspects of professional development that are required because the nature of practice is changing with the deployment of more advanced clinical systems.

There has been some progress toward the other four goals for nursing informatics, *including improved access to relevant information tools and resources in support of nurses' roles.* Since 2002, access to computers at work has improved considerably, when a third of nurses in a U.K.-wide survey reported they could not access the Internet at work.[34] In 2007, all nurses responding to the RCN survey reported that they had Internet access, although most share the computer that they use and only two thirds felt the level of access was adequate for their current needs. The extent to which the available information tools actually support nurses in their roles is difficult to assess, as only a minority of nurses in the U.K. and Ireland currently use electronic records, prescribing systems, telecare, or other technologies. Nurses' attitudes reflect limited or poor experience of healthcare computerization to date: 42% of respondents to the RCN survey do not agree that electronic records will save nursing time. A third feel that electronic records threaten patient confidentiality, and fewer than half (42%) believe they will improve clinical care compared with 70% in a similar survey conducted in 2004.[32]

The view of the United States' National Research Council that systems do not yet support decision making or workflow is supported by what little research evidence exists about the value of nursing information systems.[5] Urquhart et al.'s most recent systematic review identified studies that compared a) different formats for nursing records, b) paper records with computer records, and c) patient-held with centrally held records.[6] The reviewers concluded that it was unclear whether changing an entire system of recording nursing care (for example, from paper to computer) had any effect on care. A significant issue raised by the review was the relationship between practice and the record, and it was concluded that, as a precursor to further development of information systems for nurses, there needed to be further qualitative studies to explore the relationship between practice and information use by nurses.[6]

Progress toward the goal of *an informatics career pathway for nurses* was assisted by the formation in 2002 of the U.K. Council for Health Informatics Professions.[35] This organization operates a voluntary register of health informatics professionals who meet defined standards and agree to work according to a code of conduct. Another factor supporting career pathways has been the employment opportunities that have arisen in the national IT programs for nurses with an informatics background. Also, new career paths have opened up for other nurses who perform a number of roles from terminology management to deployment training, as secondment assignments. This means there is a growing number of nurses who understand informatics roles and help bridge the gap between practice and technology. Nursing and multidisciplinary networks that have been set up as part of local and national projects provide forums for support and learning where previously there were few opportunities for such exchanges. Professional networking for nurses in informatics roles is supported by the Healthcare Informatics Society of Ireland, the British Computer Society, and the Royal College of Nursing. However, informatics is still not regarded as a specialty by the nursing profession in the U.K. and Ireland. Consequently, those nurses who wish to move into the informatics field may limit their career opportunities in nursing.

In the past two years, there has been a marked improvement in the way *nursing perspectives are integrated in national and local information developments*. In Wales, for example, a strategic framework for engaging the nursing profession in national developments has been published and regional reference groups set up.[36] Wales' strategic framework aims to identify, develop, test, and evaluate the benefits of potential electronic solutions. They deliberately seek to capture the views of nurses and provide them with opportunities to influence the design and testing of new technologies. Professional organizations are taking a more active role in engaging practitioners in national developments, such as record content and e-health practice standards. This change is reflected in the full participation of nurses in a recent U.K.-wide consultation that addressed the governance, medico-legal, and patient safety consequences of shared electronic records in primary care.[37] The guidance principles developed by this project have been endorsed by nursing, medical, and other health professionals' organizations and will inform practice in hospital and community settings as single, shared patient records become more common.

The picture is perhaps less clear in relation to how nurses are consulted and included in local developments. Two-thirds of the nurses who responded to the RCN's 2007 survey said they had not been consulted about electronic records being introduced into their organizations. However, 11% of nurses surveyed reported having had "a great deal" or "quite a lot" of consultation, suggesting that the perspectives of many nurses are being included in local design and deployment.[32] Many organizations could learn lessons from the national approach being taken in Wales, which focuses on change management and the engagement of nurses as part of that process, rather than simply on implementation of systems.[36]

Perhaps the most challenging of the five goals relates to data and information: *meaningful, good-quality information about patient care and nursing practice is available to decision makers (including patients and the public)*. The nursing professions in the UK and Ireland have been working to identify data and indicators that reflect the cost, quality, and outcomes of nursing as the case studies that follow this chapter demonstrate. Scotland and Ireland have had more success than the other three countries in development of nursing-specific data standards at the national level. In England and Wales, the national strategies have driven development of patient group or condition-based national datasets. Although these provide opportunities for making visible the nursing contribution to care, there is still a lack of consensus on definitions for valid and reliable data elements for this purpose. In response to government proposals for national quality measures for England, the RCN has proposed three themes to underpin person-centered quality measurement:

1. **Person-Centered Care** (represents needs, values, patient-reported outcomes, priorities, patient experience)
2. **Effective Care** (interventions, evidence-based, evaluation of care/intervention)
3. **The System Adapting to Ever-changing Healthcare Needs** (context, environment, skill mix, work force, decision making).[38]

Translation of these themes into measurable indicators is the next challenge facing nursing, but the RCN is clear that professionally defined standards must be the basis for quality measurement, that is, the measures must be made against statements of good practice developed in collaboration with healthcare consumers and across disciplines. Such standards are also part of the solution to the two major challenges still to be overcome to achieve health IT that is interoperable and safe and supports evidence-based practice. These are the development and maintenance of content standards and clinical safety standards, discussed next.

Standards for Nursing Content of Electronic Records

Designing the content of electronic records and messages is frequently undertaken by panels of clinical staff based in the organizations for which the systems are to be deployed. A typical approach has been to take existing paper records and design screens and forms that reflect existing recordkeeping practices. However, there are multiple versions for every type of chart and record even within organizations, let alone across a national health service. For most areas of nursing practice in the U.K. and Ireland, there are no standards for what should be recorded and communicated or for how that information should be structured. For example, there is no minimum standard for the information to be communicated between the hospital nursing team and the community team when a person is discharged from hospital. Initial work in the United States toward defining an ontology for nursing document sections[39] was not adopted in the U.K., although nurses did contribute to multidisciplinary efforts to agree to the names and definitions of record section headings.[40] This lack of standards means that system designers must either impose a single approach or support multiple variations. Neither of these solutions is acceptable. The quality and content of nursing records is a professional issue, not one to be left to systems designers or local decision. Unlimited variation in the structure and content of electronic records makes data exchange and comparison impossible. Standardization is therefore essential to minimize duplication of effort, maintain quality, and support interoperability.

Standards for the content of records and communications aim to ensure consistent meaning across care settings and within information systems. Both professional and technical aspects of content standards need to be addressed, that is:

- Best practice for record and message content, as decided by regulatory and professional organizations.
- Formal representation standards, including data structures and terminology codes.

A joint effort between the professional organizations and the informatics community is required to ensure that nursing content of electronic patient records: "supports effective clinical judgements, decisions, care and communication; accurately represents the work of nursing and identifies the nursing contribution to patient outcomes; and reflects core nursing values, such as patient focus, partnership working, respect and choice."[41] Legal or regulatory requirements and general best practice for record content can be found in professional recordkeeping standards, such as those produced by the U.K. Nursing and Midwifery Council.[42] However, detailed and specialist content requirements are rarely specified at the national level. Having recognized this gap, the RCN is moving to a position in which all its practice standards will include the minimum record content requirement along with definitions of the data needed to support audit and quality improvement in relation to the practice standard. For example, an evidence-based guideline for assessment of acute pain in children should specify the validated assessment tools to be used to assess pain in different age groups. The standard should also specify what needs be recorded to support decisions about pain management and the data requirements for auditing outcomes of pain assessment and management. Terminology and data definitions used in these publications should align as far as possible with NHS information standards, such as SNOMED Clinical Terms[43] and national data dictionaries. This standards alignment will assist in the task of integrating professional standards into national content standards, incorporating them in electronic records and messages and making links to decision-support tools.

Technical aspects of record and message content such as terminologies, archetypes, message specifications, and clinical models are being addressed nationally and internationally (see Hardiker et al.'s Chapter 13 in this book). To date, there has not been a close relationship between those undertaking this technical work and the wider nursing community. Nurses involved in terminology development and content design may refer to evidence-based practice standards, but there has been little progress in the development of professionally supported record content specifications. This situation is set to change in England where a program has been established to develop and maintain precise definitions of information structures based on professional recordkeeping standards. The Logical Record Architecture program[44] is addressing three categories of content standards and the relationships between them: recording and presentation; communication; and interpretation and aggregation. A major objective of this national care records data standards framework is to produce content specifications that can be easily incorporated into the lifecycles of all software developments.[45] Among the challenges to be overcome is the interrelationship between different standards, so that there is alignment between the content standards and component standards, such as the national standard terminology, SNOMED Clinical Terms.

Clinical Safety and Health Information Systems

There is a growing body of evidence demonstrating that information systems can significantly improve patient safety through more effective communication, better decision making, and increased access to information when and where it is needed. However, systems and the way they are designed and used can also increase the potential for harm to patients. For example, the U.S. National Research Council noted that, in 2009, many healthcare applications "do not take advantage of human-computer interaction principles, leading to poor designs that can increase the chance of error."[5] Other common system hazards relate to patient identification, data migration, mapping, and corruption. IT in healthcare should be seen in the same light as any other healthcare innovation, that is, its introduction should be evidence-based and risk-managed. Rather than simply accepting a new or changed system, nurses should be asking to see evidence of safety testing and fitness for purpose. Nurses should report safety concerns and incidents related to their use of health IT in the same way that they would for other kinds of clinical incidents.

These principles are being applied throughout England with the introduction of two new NHS information standards: application of risk management to the manufacture of health software and application of risk management to the deployment and use of health software.[46] NHS Connecting for Health, the organization responsible for the English national program for IT, has put in place a national safety support infrastructure and provides training for staff in organizations that are designated to take responsibility for system safety.[46] Guidance on the *Nine Steps for Safer Implementation* summarizes the activities that need to be considered when implementing systems in a clinical environment and recommends that health organizations integrate their approach to health software risks with their overall approach to clinical governance.

At the core of the risk management process is clinical hazard and risk evaluation which should be undertaken for any changes made to systems, as well as prior to the deployment of new systems. Nurses and other clinical staff play a lead role throughout the risk management process, from "clinical authority to release" a new product at the manufacturing end of the system lifecycle, to incident reviews and clinical safety audits throughout the period that the system is in use.[46] The Connecting for Health clinical safety management system has been in place for four years during which time approximately 430 incidents have been reported centrally. These are assessed by clinicians and safety engineers and made safe within 24 hours. Lessons learned through this central safety system are now being incorporated into a more proactive safety strategy which focuses on the design stage of systems and on human factors, so that safety incidents are prevented as much as possible.

Summary

Significant progress is being made in the U.K. and Ireland through national approaches to information and communication technologies in healthcare. Strategic goals established in the 1990s are being realized. There are:
- Lifelong EHRs for every person

- Round-the-clock online access to patient records and information about best clinical practice, for all NHS clinicians
- Seamless care for patients through general practitioners, hospitals, and community services sharing information
- Fast and convenient public access to information and care through online information services and telemedicine
- Effective use of NHS resources by providing health planners and managers with the information they need[47]

Standards have always been a core element of national IT strategies. The recent emphasis on standards for content of records and messages and standards for risk management throughout the system lifecycle is to be welcomed. However, if these new types of standards are to be maintained and managed appropriately, they will require significant investment and infrastructure. For example, long-term funding that is safe from budget cuts is needed to maintain Connecting for Health's national safety help desk, its investigators and auditors, and the network of individuals responsible for system safety in every organization. In addition, repositories in which terminologies, record content standards, and message specifications are maintained are not static data dictionaries. These databases demand significant expert resources to ensure timely updates are done to keep up with the constant and rapid pace of developments in healthcare.

We are also much closer to achieving strategic goals for nursing in relation to informatics, but there are several challenges still to be overcome. Nurses need to begin thinking in new ways if they are to support effective use of electronic records and knowledge resources by patients and healthcare consumers. Strong nursing leadership is still required to continue to merge the technical and professional agendas and drive the changes that must take place in nursing education in support of competent practitioners of the future. Systems designers need to better understand clinical practice to develop products that truly support "the cognitive tasks" and workflow of nurses in the many settings in which patients and citizens receive care. To help with this task, nursing needs to investigate the relationship between the ways we use information, the decisions and judgments we make, and the care we provide. As the NRC noted, only when IT can be shown to enable them to do their jobs more effectively will clinicians be drawn to using IT to achieve the goals of better and less costly health care.[5]

References

1. HM Government. *House of Commons Health Committee Sixth Report.* 2007 www.publications.parliament.uk/pa/cm200607/cmselect/cmhealth/422/42202.htm. Accessed May 12, 2009.

2. Department of Health, Social Services and Public Safety. *HPSS ICT Programme: From Vision to Reality.* 2005. www.dhsspsni.gov.uk/hpss-ict-programme-summary.pdf. Accessed May 12, 2009.

3. European Commission. Recommendation on Cross-border Interoperability of Electronic Health Record Systems. 2008. http://ec.europa.eu/information_society/activities/health/policy/interoperability/index_en.htm. Accessed May 12, 2009.

4. Kaelber DC, Jha AK, Johnston D, Middleton B, Bates DW. A research agenda for personal health records (PHRs). *J Am Med Inform Assoc.* 2008;15(6):729-736.

5. National Research Council. *Computational Technology for Effective Health Care: Immediate Steps and Strategic Directions.* 2009. www.nap.edu/catalog.php?record_id=12572#toc. Accessed May 12, 2009.

6. Urquhart C, Currell R, Grant MJ, Hardiker NR. Nursing record systems: Effects on nursing practice and healthcare outcomes. *Cochrane Database of Systematic Reviews.* 2009, Issue 1. Art. No: CD002099.

7. Garrett B, Klein G. Value of wireless personal digital assistants for practice: perceptions of advanced practice nurses. *J Clin Nurs.* 2008;17(16):2146-2154.

8. Forbat L, Maguire R, McCann L, Illingworth N, Kearney N. The use of technology in cancer care: applying Foucault's ideas to explore the changing dynamics of power in health care. *J Adv Nurs.* 2009;65(2):306-315.

9. Casey A. The United Kingdom: Progress towards national goals for nursing informatics In: Weaver C, Delaney C, Carr R, Weber P, eds. *Nursing and Informatics for the 21st Century.* Chicago: HIMSS, 2006.

10. Royal College of Nursing. *The future nurse: the RCN vision.* London: Royal College of Nursing; 2004.

11. NHS Scotland. *Patient Focus and Public Involvement.* www.scotland.gov.uk/Resource/Doc/158744/0043087.pdf. Accessed June 22, 2009.

12. NHS Choices. *Your Health, Your Choices.* www.nhs.uk/Pages/HomePage.aspx. Accessed June 22, 2009.

13. Department of Health. *National Service Frameworks.* www.dh.gov.uk/en/Healthcare/NationalServiceFrameworks/index.htm. Accessed May 12, 2009.

14. Welsh Assembly Government. *National Service Frameworks for Wales.* www.wales.nhs.uk/sites3/home.cfm?OrgID=334. Accessed May 12, 2009.

15. National Institute for Health and Clinical Excellence. *Our Guidance.* www.nice.org.uk/guidance/index.jsp. Accessed May 12, 2009.

16. NHS Evidence. *Health Information Resources.* www.library.nhs.uk/. Accessed May 12, 2009.

17. Welsh Assembly Government Informing Healthcare. *NHS e-Library for Wales.* www.wales.nhs.uk/sites3/home.cfm?orgid=520. Accessed May 12, 2009.

18. Care Quality Commission. CQC: *What We Do.* www.cqc.org.uk/aboutcqc/whatwedo.cfm. Accessed May 12, 2009.

19. Healthcare Inspectorate Wales. *Welcome to Healthcare Inspectorate Wales.* www.hiw.org.uk/. Accessed May 12, 2009.

20. Care Quality Commission. *Measuring Clinical Performance Better.* www.cqc.org.uk/guidanceforprofessionals/healthcare/allhealthcarestaff/improvingclinicalquality.cfm. Accessed May 12, 2009.

21. Skills for Health. *Competence Application Tools: Health Informatics.* https://tools.skillsforhealth.org.uk/suite/show/id/54. Accessed May 12, 2009.

22. NHS Connecting for Health. *Learning to Manage Health Information: a theme for clinical education.* www.connectingforhealth.nhs.uk/systemsandservices/capability/health/hidcurriculum/brochure.pdf. Accessed May 18, 2009.

23. NHS Connecting for Health. *Supporting transformation: A practical guide to NHS Connecting for Health.* http://information.connectingforhealth.nhs.uk/prod_images/pdfs/31556.pdf. Accessed May 18, 2009.

24. Tait C, Braunold G, Jeeves R, Hopwood L, Thick M. Summary Care Record–the Bury experience. *European Journal of Palliative Care.* 2009;16(3):124-126.

25. NHS Connecting for Health. Case studies www.connectingforhealth.nhs.uk/systemsandservices/nhsmail/about/studies. Accessed May 18, 2009.

26. NHS Connecting for Health. *About NHSmail.* www.connectingforhealth.nhs.uk/systemsandservices/nhsmail/about. Accessed May 18, 2009.

27. House of Commons Public Accounts Committee. *The National Programme for IT in the NHS: Progress since 2006.* 2009. www.publications.parliament.uk/pa/cm200809/cmselect/cmpubacc/153/153.pdf. Accessed May 18, 2009.

28. Welsh Assembly Government. *Informing healthcare.* www.wales.nhs.uk/ihc/home.cfm. Accessed May 18, 2009.

29. NHS Wales Informing Healthcare. *Cancer Network Information System Cymru.* www.wales.nhs.uk/sites3/page.cfm?pid=33503&orgid=770. Accessed May 18, 2009.

30. Debnath D. Activity analysis of telemedicine in the UK. *Postgraduate Medical Journal.* 2004;80:335-338.

31. NHS Wales Informing Healthcare. *Telehealth.* www.wales.nhs.uk/sites3/page.cfm?orgid=770&pid=33644. Accessed May 18, 2009.

32. Royal College of Nursing. *Health Select Committee Inquiry into the Electronic Patient Record and its use: Findings of the RCN E-Health Survey 2007.* www.rcn.org.uk/newsevents/government/briefings/electronic_patient_record_and_its_use. Accessed May 18, 2009.

33. Healthcare Informatics Society of Ireland. *Health Informatics Training System.* www.hisi.ie/html/hits.htm. Accessed May 18, 2009.

34. Lipley N. Net gains fail to meet targets. *Nurs Stand.* 2002;16(39):4.

35. UK Council for Health Informatics Professions. *Welcome to UKCHIP.* www.ukchip.org/. Accessed May 18, 2009.

36. NHS Wales Informing Healthcare. *Strategic framework for engaging nurses, midwives and health visitors in the Informing Healthcare change management agenda.* www.wales.nhs.uk/sites3/Documents/770/Strategy_270607.pdf2. Accessed May 18, 2009.

37. Royal College of General Practitioners and NHS Connecting for Health. *Shared Record Professional Guidance Project.* London: Royal College of General Practitioners, 2009.

38. Royal College of Nursing. *Measuring for quality in health and social care: An RCN position statement.* 2009. www.rcn.org.uk/__data/assets/pdf_file/0004/248872/003535.pdf. Accessed May 18, 2009.

39. Hyun S, Bakken S. Toward the Creation of an Ontology for Nursing Document Sections: Mapping Section Headings to the LOINC Semantic Model. *AMIA Annual Symposium Proceedings.* 2006; 364-368.

40. NHS Information Authority. *Headings for Communicating Clinical Information.* 2000. http://userweb.port.ac.uk/~mxw/headings/pdf/standard.pdf. Accessed May 18, 2009.

41. Royal College of Nursing. *Nursing content of electronic patient/client records.* London: RCN, 2008.

42. Nursing and Midwifery Council. *NMC Record Keeping Guidance.* www.nmc-uk.org/aDisplayDocument.aspx?documentID=3795. Accessed May 18, 2009.

43. International Health Terminology Standards Organisation. *About SNOMED CT.* www.ihtsdo.org/snomed-ct/snomed-ct0/. Accessed June 22, 2009.

44. NHS Connecting for Health. *Logical Record Architecture for Health and Social Care.* www.connectingforhealth.nhs.uk/systemsandservices/data/lra. Accessed May 18, 2009.

45. Leach J. Logical Record Architecture. *Assist News and Views.* April 2009. www.assist.org.uk. Accessed May 18, 2009.

46. Baker M. *Safer Systems for a Safer NHS.* etdevents.connectingforhealth.nhs.uk/events/uploads/1155_1215_dr_maureen_baker.ppt. Accessed May 18, 2009.

47. NHS Executive. *Information for Health: An Information Strategy for the modern NHS.* 1998. www.dh.gov.uk/prod_consum_dh/groups/dh_digitalassets/@dh/@en/documents/digitalasset/dh_4014469.pdf. Accessed May 18, 2009.

Case Study 15A

Ireland

By Rita W. Collins, PhD, MEd, BNS, RN, RM; and Rosaleen Killalea, MSc Nursing, BNS, RN

Introduction

The integration of ICT in healthcare has had a profound impact on the patient journey through the healthcare system. From the initial contact with primary care personnel, through hospitalization, and community care, including palliative services, there is a constant presence of technology that tracks, monitors, and shares information about the status of the patient. It is this ability to monitor and share information that has had the single greatest impact on patient care, as a result of employing ICT within healthcare.

As part of the National Development Plan (NDP) 2007-2013, the Irish Government plans to invest 490 million Euros in e-health over the next seven years.[1] The government indicated that

> ...developments in the health service will be targeted at improving patient-centred systems in our hospitals and community settings. Developments will be directed at implementing systems that improve the operational processes in our services by supporting healthcare professionals, while capturing the information necessary to ensure proper planning for the future (2007).

Within Ireland, healthcare informatics interests are represented by the Healthcare Informatics Society of Ireland (HISI). Nursing is represented within this group by the two authors of this chapter and a nursing/midwifery subgroup of HISI that is especially involved with issues of particular concern to these professions and offer educational sessions specifically targeted at nurses and midwives. One of the chief outputs of HISI in conjunction with the Irish Computer Society (ICS) is the development of an online training program called Healthcare Informatics Training System (HITS). This program is aimed at enhancing healthcare professionals' knowledge of ICT and at assisting them in using the technologies that support the delivery of optimal patient-centred care within clinical and administrative services. This program has been integrated into hospital training and development programs, academic courses, and has found an audience both nationally and internationally. It is approved by the Irish nursing regulatory body, An Bord Altranais, as well as the Irish Institute of Radiology and Radiation Therapy (IIRRT).

In 2008, the Irish Council for Health Informatics Professions (I-CHIP) was launched. It is a voluntary register of health informatics professionals compiled and maintained by the ICS and HISI to promote professionalism in health informatics in Ireland. I-CHIP was launched to address the concern about standards and efficiency in the development and maintenance of ICT within healthcare in Ireland. It also aims to advance the use of healthcare informatics in the promotion of health and well-being of individuals and communities. This register is voluntary and verifies the level of expertise of those registered against the standards of the Skills Framework for the Information Age (SFIA). Together HITS and I-CHIP provide a baseline for the validation of personnel working with ICT in a healthcare environment.

ICT and Irish Nursing

From a clinical perspective, nurses at all levels are involved at some level with the use of ICT, and this has an impact on the delivery of nursing practice. In 2007, nursing unions united in their quest for a 35-hour working week for nurses on par with other members of the multidisciplinary team (MDT). The actual implementation of a 37.5-hour week in 2008 has had a huge impact on how nursing work is organized, as no provision was made for the employment of extra staff. As a result, the nursing profession has to take into account what it is that nurses do and consequently what they need to hold onto and what they may need to hand over to, and share with, other members of the MDT. Nurses are frequently referred to as the "glue" that holds patient care together.[2,3] This idea places nurses in a position of power when decisions are being made on what to give away, as they hold the total picture of the patient journey from admission to discharge over a 24 hour period while in the hospital. Information-sharing is the key to this notion of the patient journey. However, this information needs to be coordinated and managed in a manner that will benefit the patient. To this end, there needs to be that one person who takes on this responsibility to ensure that information is gathered, shared, and acted upon in a timely and efficient manner. Information systems provide the "nuts and bolts" to enable this to happen.

The Hospital Experience

The development of information systems within nursing has been led in Ireland by the Mater Misericordiae University Hospital, (MMUH) in Dublin. The hospital is an acute tertiary referral university teaching hospital established in 1861 under the auspices of Catherine McAuley and the Sisters of Mercy. The hospital has more than 600 beds, including day beds, and approximately 3,000 employees. As well as a range of specialist in-patient, daycare, and outpatient services, and a busy emergency department (ED), the hospital is the national centre for cardio-thoracic surgery.

Information and Communication Technology

As part of the hospital's overall strategy, information has been viewed with the associated computer technology within the Information Management Services (IMS) department as a fundamental element in enabling it to deliver optimum patient care in the most efficient and quality manner. This approach is based on an integration of information systems centered on the patient. It is recognized that the healthcare environment today is probably the most complex in terms of information processing, as it includes data that are computer-generated, manually transcribed and voice-generated, as well as radiologic images, video, scanned documentation, data from clinical instrumentation, etc. Among the goals and objectives of the IMS department are the following:

- To provide a technology and systems environment to support all staff in their use of technology and systems consistent with their individual needs and in accordance with the hospital's mission statement and strategic objectives.
- To support the objectives of the National Health Strategy, ICT Strategy, National Health Information Strategy, and e-Government initiatives.
- To ensure technology and systems development, acquisition, implementation, and utilization processes that reflect best professional practices.

The IMS department's current ICT implementation schedule is focused on using the potential of technology to accommodate the complexity of information sources and collect, integrate, and distribute electronically all these sources to support staff in undertaking tasks associated with their responsibilities, optimizing cost-effectiveness and quality in support of the hospital's objectives. The current clinical systems in place include the following:

- Hospital Information System (HIS)
- Integrated Order Communications/Results Reporting within the following departments:
  - Departmental Clinical, Audit, Operational, and Research systems.
  - General Practitioner Access – HealthLink.
  - Management Information Systems (Statistical/Reporting).
  - Integrated Nursing Information System including Nursing Discharge Summaries.
  - ICT and Nursing.

In the context of ICT developments in the hospital and nurses' enthusiastic day-to-day usage of the order communications/results reporting system, a high-level Nursing Project Group was established in the late 1990s. The group recognized that nursing information systems were going to be key to helping nurses and nurse managers in managing data, information, and knowledge into the future.

Information and Nursing Workflow

The initial task of the project group was to investigate the workflow of nurses and managers in the administration of patient-centered care and the associated information required to provide that care. It was established that nurses collect patient-specific data from the patient during assessment, planning of care, and implementation of that care, interventions, evaluation, and outcomes. This information, once collected and in particular from care implementation data, forms the essential building blocks from which nursing workload measurement could be determined on a day-to-day basis and provides the data to assist with the day-to-day duty roster/schedule by the ward/unit manager. The nursing workload information, in turn, assists senior

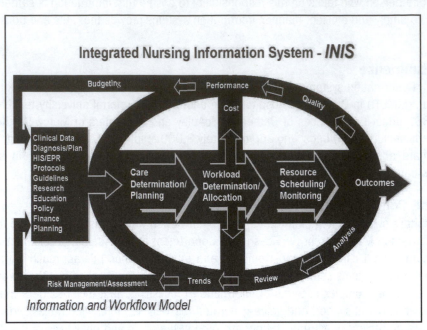

Note: This figure is an original figure from the department of Nursing MMUH.

Figure 15A-1. *INIS – Information and Workflow Model, MMUH*

nurse managers with strategic planning in relation to staffing requirements to provide the necessary patient-centered care. It was recognized by the group that real-time data, once collected at the bedside, could support nurse participation in the development of interdisciplinary integrated care pathways, patient research and outcomes monitoring, and the generation of reports for future planning of nursing services. From the organization/hospital perspective, the data and information generated would assist in terms of risk management, quality improvement, reviewing guidelines, protocols, and estimating cost. As a result of combining the workflow of the nurses with the information, the project group developed an "Information and Workflow" (see Figure 15A-1) model for the MMUH. This is the model that underpinned the proposal by the nursing project team to introduce an integrated nursing information system (INIS) hospitalwide with the objective of introducing and implementing structured information and communications processes, and decision-support mechanism, using appropriate methodologies and technologies, to support the development of an optimum work environment. The INIS therefore was to provide for the integration of information needs of nursing and, at the same time, support the workflow and decision-making processes, which enable nurses to deliver optimum patient care. With this objective in mind, the decision was made by both the hospital and nursing management to fully support the introduction of INIS.

INIS consists of three integrated modules designed and developed within an open standards framework to provide connectivity with all appropriate information systems (such as Clinical Decision Support, Patient Administration and Hospital Information Systems, Finance, and Human Resources) utilized in supporting optimum healthcare delivery. The three modules, which can also be implemented on an individual basis, are care planning, workload determination/allocation, and resource scheduling monitoring.

The Three INIS Projects

Three individual projects were set up, each in accordance with the project methodology used for the introduction of ICT in the hospital. Each project was led by a clinical nurse manager (CNM) who oversaw the individual project group, team, and the user groups undertaking the work associated with the project. The INIS modules will be described in order of the development, rather than their place within the Information and Workflow Model.

Workload Determination System. The workload determination system, based on a classification/dependency model, was previously introduced into the hospital in the 1990s, as part of the HIS. It has since been upgraded to a new user-friendly "Windows Version" and is integrated with the HIS. Nurses at the patient care level record patient workload (up to four times a day, if required) and the information that is generated permits clinical nurse managers and senior nurse managers (on a day-to-day basis) to assess workload and to allocate staff to the different care areas, based on their professional judgement. The information generated can also be used for strategic and long-term planning of resources, as well as a baseline for future workforce analysis and planning projects and quality improvement work.

The ward and the nurses have control over the entries and have entered the rules into the background. Once the function is selected, the ward/unit patient list automatically appears on screen. Nurses on duty can record their own workload on their own patients and can attach comments, if necessary. This can be done currently and prospectively. The information generated can also be used for strategic and long-term planning of resources, as well as for a baseline for future workforce analysis, planning for projects, and quality improvement work. The Workload Determination system is simple and easy to use, and has the benefit that patient dependency can be recorded real-time and prospectively to support decision making. As a result of integration with the rostering system, real-time information is available, rather than the more limited availability of information that is dependent on a ward/unit level relative to actual staff availability.

Resource Scheduling System. Following a tendering process, the hospital purchased the automated resource scheduling system, which is used to produce nurse schedules/rosters automatically. It consists of four components: Intragale, ShiftMaker, Credential Manager, and CentralStaffer. It is implemented in all wards/units, operating theatres, and the emergency department. Nurses request off-duty/shifts via Intragale on the hospital's Web site. ShiftMaker permits the resource schedules/rosters to be produced automatically by the manager. Staff can be booked by the ward/unit manager into hospital training sessions/classes within the Credential Manager module, and attendance at those training sessions/classes can be also verified. CentralStaffer, available to senior nursing management, demonstrates real-time information regarding the actual staff on duty at any particular time, in any part of the organization.

The resource scheduling and workload determination systems are integrated. The workload determination system, in turn is integrated with the HIS. This integration facilitates managers to view nurses' workload and the different skills of the staff on duty coping with that workload. The resource scheduling system has the potential to be used in all departments hospitalwide as a result of its excellent flexibility.

The main features of this system are the automated roster generation and its ability to configure real-time and prospective schedule totals to show exact staffing levels and to quickly identify problem days, as it facilitates real-time viewing of actual staff on duty hospitalwide. It can track absenteeism and sick calls with stated reasons in staff records. It also manages classes, meetings, holidays, and other indirect activity and can be utilized by the centralized "Nurse Bank" that has recently been set up as part of a "Health Services Executive (HSE) value for money" initiative. All these activities interface with other systems to proactively adjust staffing levels, e.g., Workload Determination/Allocation system and can be utilised for budgeting and reporting purposes.

This system provides senior managers and employees in complex scheduling environments (e.g., nursing) with the tools they need to efficiently and fairly assign staff across multiple disciplines. Both the Workload Determination/Allocation and Resource Scheduling systems provide the basis for the undertaking of a Workforce Analysis and Planning (WAPP) study on six wards in the MMUH, late 2005-2006. All training, support, and follow-up at ward/unit level in the use of these systems is undertaken by the Nursing Informatics Project Team (NIPT) in the IMS department.

Care Planning. The team has conducted an in-depth investigation, review, and analysis of all the manual documentation, including the data recorded by nurses in the documentation of the day-to-day care of patients in the hospital. The team has drawn up a specification of requirements for the automated system, which will include decision-support and alerts.

Conclusion

Overall the MMUH has acknowledged that by developing INIS and involving nurses in the process from the early stages on, appropriate information will be available to nurses to empower them to continually improve the delivery of overall care to patients. This fits in with the government's plans to use ICT to help staff deliver patient-centered care and to promote greater time efficiency and expertise within health services. The expected gains would include the availability of quality information for planning, management and decision making.

Summary

Clearly, the implementation of a nursing information system, INIS as outlined in this chapter, demonstrates the value to nurses of the integration of nursing work and patient services that complement each other and facilitate the emergence of quality information for sharing in education, administration, and care delivery with the ultimate aim of improving the patient journey through the hospital system. The system also provides sound information for estimating the cost of nursing care, thereby promoting the visibility of nursing work. As well as organizing and developing integrated hospital records, the development of nursing modules allows for the construct of professional documentation that has the capacity to demonstrate the role of the nurse/midwife within healthcare. Throughout the process of developing electronic systems, the partnership of healthcare professionals, institutions, and computer technologists is key to good quality information for use in patient care.

From a wider perspective, electronic clinical systems are instruments of accountability as they provide information for audit and are held as legal records of institutional performance. Consequently, it behooves the nursing profession to be actively involved in the implementation of records and systems that collect nursing information and in the communication of this information to others.

References

1. Eurohealth Newsletter. http://www.ehealtheurope.net/News/2935/Ireland. Accessed May 25, 2009.
2. Corner J, Halliday D, Haviland J, et al. Exploring nursing outcomes for patients with advanced cancer following intervention by Macmillan specialist palliative care nurses. 2003: *J Adv Nursing.* 2003;41(6):561-574.
3. Goorman E, Berg M. Modelling nursing activities: electronic patient records and their discontents. *Nurs Inq.* 2000;7:3-9.

Case Study 15B

Northern Ireland's Information and Communications Technology Strategy: A Case Study of Nursing Activity

By Mary Chambers, PhD, BED(Hons); and Claire Buchner,
MSc Health Informatics, BSc(Hons) Nursing Studies

Introduction

The need for nursing to keep pace with the rapid changes in society is paramount if the profession is going to continue to make a difference in health and social care. The advances taking place in the development and application of IT in today's society are unparalleled. Carty[1] states that preparing nurses for the challenges of technologies which include electronic communications, electronic patient records, decision support, and information management systems is a daunting task.

As a result of the ever-improving accessibility and availability of healthcare information from sources such as the Internet, the role of healthcare professionals is about to change. As well as needing to have specific healthcare knowledge and expertise, they will also have to become managers of information, thus enabling patients and their caregivers to use the accessed information effectively to make informed decisions about their care. This change from a care practitioner/provider who traditionally took the lead in decision making for patients will now require a more collaborative, consultative approach and requisite knowledge, skills, and aptitude to seek out and manage information using available technology.

In Northern Ireland, the Department of Health and Social Services and Public Safety (DHSSPS) recognized that the application of new technology in the health and social care field would have a significant role to play in the modernization of services. Benefits which the DHSSPS envisaged that technological solutions could provide included improved patient and client experience through remote monitoring of vital signs, improved service responses, better communication across and between multidisciplinary care teams, improved patient and client access to the information that they require to manage their conditions, and better use of resources. Also recognized was the role of technology in improving diagnostics and treatment in secondary care, as well as in facilitating getting the right information to the right people at the right time, therefore making a significant contribution to patient safety and the patient caregiver, and to enhance one's professional satisfaction. It was this realization that led the DHSSPS to embark on a new IT strategy for Northern Ireland.

This chapter will outline the context of healthcare delivery in the United Kingdom (U.K.), the background that lead to the information and communications technology (ICT) strategy for Northern Ireland, its key features and the process for implementation. Attention will also be given to a number of nursing projects that have formed part of the ICT strategy in Northern Ireland. The chapter will conclude with consideration of lessons learned from the achievements to date.

Healthcare in the United Kingdom

The delivery of healthcare in the U.K. is available through a mixed economy but delivered mainly within the National Health Service (NHS). This is the collective term used to describe health services in the four countries of the U.K.; England, Scotland, Wales, and Northern Ireland.

The NHS came into being in 1948, following presentation of the Beveridge Report, which was published in 1942. This was the report of an Inter-Departmental Committee on Social Insurance and Allied Services, which was chaired by economist, William Beveridge. The report recommended that all citizens of the U.K. have access to healthcare that was not based on ability to pay, but rather would be free at the point-of-delivery and funded in part through national taxation.

The NHS in each of the four countries of the U.K. was established independently by different legislation; for example, the department of health had responsibility for England and Wales, the Scottish office for Scotland, and the government of Northern Ireland had responsibility for NHS developments in the province. However, in Northern Ireland, it was referred to as public health, and although Northern Ireland does not use the term *National Health Service*, the healthcare system is often referred to locally as NHS. There is another fundamental difference between Northern Ireland and the other countries of the U.K. in that Northern Ireland has an integrated Health and Personal Social Services (HPSS).

Re-organization of Health and Social Care in Northern Ireland

The organization and delivery of health and social care in Northern Ireland, as in other areas of the U.K., are influenced by politics and differing political ideologies, such as devolution, with power devolved to local administrations. For Wales and Scotland, this change in power took place 10 years ago. However, for Northern Ireland, the change occurred somewhat differently due to nearly 40 years of political unrest.

Following changes in the political climate in the 1990s, a Northern Ireland Assembly was formed in 1998 but only served as a shadow administration until 1999, when it first became fully functioning. However, as a result of political differences, the assembly has been non-functioning for long periods on four occasions.

Since the assembly has taken over, despite the periods of suspension, it has been responsible for bringing about reforms within the health and social care system. The first major reform took place in 2007 when five integrated health and social care trusts were formed to replace the 18 existing trusts. In April 2009, the second reform took place when a Health and Social Care Board, a Public Health Agency, the Patient and Client Council and the Business Services Organization were established.

The assembly was very conscious that for the reforms to be fully realized, an effective ICT infrastructure needed to be in place. It would require this ICT base to make a difference in the quality of health and social care services, and achieve more effective communication at all levels of services and access to evidence-based, clinical information.

IT Strategy and its Key Points

In 2000, the assembly set about introducing an ICT strategy, using a staged, consultative approach aimed at creating dialog between DHSSPS, HPSS, and the public. The five-stage process included:
- Stage 1 - Preliminary consultation paper
- Stage 2 - Business context document
- Stage 3 - Draft consultation document – ICT strategy vision statement[2]
- Stage 4 - Outline of a program of work
- Stage 5 - Strategy document

The Stage 3 document reflected a realistic position, acknowledging the potential that an effective ICT infrastructure could offer. It also emphasized that the vision statement, which presented a wide range of requirements and potential ICT developments, probably would be impossible to deliver within the proposed timeframe. Made clear was that this consultation should focus on any omissions in the proposals and gain broad consensus on priority areas for investment. Contained within the document were questions for which responses were particularly welcome.

The work program outlined at Stage 4, entitled *From Vision to Reality*,[3] made it clear that central to all aspects of work of DHSSPS and to effective ICT was an ICT infrastructure, education and training, and organizational development.[4] These key areas would support:
- Delivery of direct care
- Support for direct care
- Support for staff
- Business administration
- Planning and commissioning
- Performance management
- Health and Personal Social Services for the citizen[4]

In addition to these key features, the strategy highlights the importance of information governance; implementation principles; and education, training, and development.

Strategy Work Program

The work program identifies, initiates, and monitors initiatives and individual projects aimed at achieving the vision set out in the strategy. Key projects currently underway include:
- Health and Care Number (HCN)

- Electronic Prescribing and Eligibility System (EPES)
- Person-centered Community Information System (PCIS)
- ICT training for all healthcare professionals
- Server consolidation—toward the electronic care record (ECR)
- Regional laboratory ICT modernisation
- Public sector broadband aggregation
- Secure remote access
- Infrastructure strategy
- Health and personal social services (HPSS) data warehouse

Infrastructure Programs to Support Implementation of ICT

Work is well underway regionally to select specific systems that will support clinical services across Northern Ireland, including Picture Archive and Communication System (PACS), theatre services, pharmacy/prescribing, and laboratory services. Some projects have a local solution focus; however, these do not interfere with the overall regional objectives, such as best value for money and affordability through procurement processes.

Other program activities have included:

- All general practitioner practices in Northern Ireland connected to the secure general practitioner network, with most practices having access to a managed e-mail and Internet service and the new electronic pathology results service.
- General practitioner systems populated with the new Health + Care Number and connected to the Electronic Registration system. This enables all new general practitioner registrations and all changes to patient demographic information to be transferred electronically between the Central Services Agency and general practitioner practices.
- The new personal identifier across the HPSS speeds the referral process and helps reduce administration costs. This is a necessary prerequisite for building a service-wide electronic patient records system.
- An Electronic Prescribing and Eligibility System (EPES) will be province-wide within two years. Paper prescriptions will be printed at the general practitioner's surgery, with a two-dimensional barcode that encodes all of the prescription information. At the Community Pharmacy, the 2D-barcode will be scanned, with all "prescribing" information (including physician, surgery, and patient details) captured by the pharmacist's system. When the pharmacist confirms what they will and have dispensed, any changes are recorded as "dispensed" information. The full record of the transaction (prescribed information, patient details, and method of payment or claim for free prescriptions) will be sent by the community pharmacist to the central EPES database and used to support their claim for payment of services rendered and to check the validity of the patient's claim.
- Electronic Care Record (ECR): The ECR will contain structured data, text, and images generated from a variety of sources and accessible wherever and whenever there is a legitimate need to access them. Access will be managed under a strict "need-to-know" regime that complies with agreed rules and procedures for confidentiality and consent. To create an ECR, it is necessary for the data to be read in an electronic format, typically through the use of ICT at an operational level. The development of the ECR is well underway; however, it will be some time before rollout will be completed.

Common Systems

The scale of HPSS and the use of common systems offer opportunities for an innovative approach to ECRs. In effect, the combination of developing care records within all organizations, increasing use of HPSS-wide specialist systems; consolidation of ICT; a single Health and Care Number; and the use of common systems, creates a virtual ECR.

Electronic care communication across all sections of the HPSS is vital for a high-performing, effective, and efficient service. Almost every contact with the HPSS involves communication between healthcare professionals, between HPSS organizations, or with other public, and private, sector bodies. Examples of such contact include appointments, referrals between care professionals, requests for services and communication of the service outcome, discharge letters and other follow-up communications, and prescribing. Current ICT systems manage some aspects of these processes, but in most cases only within individual organizations.

As a result, communication of care information in the HPSS today heavily relies on paper. For there to be a shift from paper to electronic communication, more widespread access to ICT is required, and capabilities—that in some cases already exist—need to be made simpler to use and seamless for the user.

Education and Training

In the future, professional training will provide more emphasis on supporting the redesigned care system and working with information and applying IT. There will be a need to learn new skills, to agree on best practice standards, collect and analyse data; and procure, develop, and apply high-quality information systems to support person-centered care. Much remains to be done in preparing and equipping those who work in health and social care, not only with the technology but especially with the skills to confidently exploit ICT routinely. The enormity of this task should not be underestimated.

To address this need, the Basic ICT for Care Professionals project has been set up by introducing a step increase in the number of care professionals who have access to basic ICT services—a PC with desktop services and Internet access. There is a large PC population in the HPSS (approximately 20,000), but these are often located where access to existing ICT systems is required or in administrative areas. To date, £1.8m has been allocated to trusts under this heading. Although it is recognized that this is not sufficient to bring ICT to all care professionals, Trusts report significant numbers of new users having access to basic ICT services and receiving ICT training as a consequence.

Nursing Projects

With respect to the development and implementation to date of the ICT strategy, nursing as a profession has been represented in a number of ways. For example, there is a nurse representative on the Connected for Health Board and also a nursing officer at the DHSSPS with responsibility for developing better services, changing the culture, connected health and social care. All "nursing projects" were initiated, developed, implemented, and evaluated by nurses.

Within the IT strategy itself, a number of projects relevant to the nursing profession and health and social care delivery have been identified. Over the last two years, a number of these have been designed, tested, implemented, and developed by nurses.

The projects can be subdivided into five categories, namely, those for service users, delivery of care, business administration, planning and commissioning, and performance management. Those most pertinent to the nursing profession are those involving users and service delivery.

Several of these projects have fallen into the "telemonitoring" category of healthcare delivery and have included the home care of clients with chronic obstructive pulmonary disease and heart failure. From 2001 to 2004, the Northern Ireland Housing Executive funded a project to offer support to older people within a specific Trust area in Northern Ireland.

The objective was achieved by supplying a range of assistive technology/telecare services and community telemedicine services. A house was fully adapted with assistive technology, ranging from heat and floor sensors to fall sensors and video/television door entry systems. Approximately 25 older people each year received assistive technology/telecare packages in their own homes linked to Fold's existing community alarms service, while a bungalow facilitated earlier discharge of two people from the hospital on a bi-weekly cycle, as part of a reablement strand. In addition, appropriate technology with a GP practice for each year of the project was set up to support primary care.

Overall clients' acceptance of the technology was good, and the active self-participation in care and the ability to be involved in decision-making were cited as positive outcomes. In some cases, the telemonitoring also facilitated earlier and more appropriate admission to the hospital and decreased hospital stays, while in some instances, home visits and reviews by nursing staff were decreased.

In December 2008, a teledermatology project was set up to address the Department of Health targets in the treatment of clients with suspected cancer. The service has met its aim and has allowed more efficient referral of clients to appropriate clinicians.

The use of technology has also developed services within tissue viability through the use of an e-Pen. This device allows practitioners to load and store data regarding patient care. The data can then be transmitted through a docking station directly to a PC via a compatible Bluetooth Blackberry or mobile phone to a central server for storage, further processing/manipulation and analysis/reporting or transmission to colleagues. Nurses working in this field have evaluated the e-Pen favorably, and its use has led to improved data capture, analysis, and audit of patient care and delivery.

e-CAT Electronic Tool for Caseload Analysis

To support caseload management practice within the community sector, a regional project commenced in 2004. Traditionally, within this sector a labor-intensive data-gathering process would be completed by staff and statistical packages then used to generate statistics regarding patient caseloads. However, use of this system required technical data management skills, and feedback to nurses in the field was limited.

The aim of the project was to assist caseload management practice for the caseload holder (nurses and health visitors) to improve effective and equitable resource allocation at team, local, and regional levels. In addition, it would change nursing practice and service delivery through providing operational nurse managers in the community having a statistical tool to measure clinical need and nursing performance, thereby allowing them to analyze need in relation to the skill and distribution of the workforce. The Web-based electronic tool has been tested in three community Trusts in Northern Ireland. An independent evaluation was carried out in 2008.

The e-CAT tool has the potential to be used by other disciplines, and because it is a "modular" system, it is dynamic and allows adaptation to meet local requirement. The tool allows direct input of data with resulting graphical reports on a range of caseload measures. It can also provide links to assist with analysis and provides templates for reporting. In 2009, e-CAT has been commercialized and will be utilized regionally within community practice.

Over the next three years, £44 million will be available to move forward the development of proactive case management arrangements and specialist nursing and treatment services. This should ensure that patients with long-term conditions are not admitted to the hospital unnecessarily.

These resources will also enable the implementation of a "remote vital signs monitoring" service for 5,000 patients, which will enable more efficient response to sudden deterioration in a patient's condition and help patients to manage their own condition.

The government's support for people living with long-term conditions in Northern Ireland, particularly recognition of the importance of self-management and patient involvement is welcomed. People with long-term conditions have a real contribution to make in shaping the services that support them. Their input can help the health service to target resources more effectively.

Service User Category

Within the service user category, these initiatives are focused on clients being able to access lifestyle information to improve health prevention. Additionally, accessing their own health records and having the ability to book appointments online has the aim of streamlining the patient's experience with primary, secondary, and tertiary care. The use of electronic community prescribing and telecare can only serve to improve services for those clients with chronic and long-term illness.

In delivering health and social care, professionals will have access to reliable individual client records, ensuring improvements in the management of information between the sectors. Evidence-based practice, electronic protocols, and care pathways available at the point of access will aim to guarantee quality care. Developments in telemedicine and telecare are also happening. To date, these projects have been sporadic in their development and implementation. Those currently active include:

The Regional Infection Prevention and Control Manual was commissioned by the Department of Health Social Services and Public Safety, Northern Ireland, as recommended in "Changing the Culture Action Plan." It is intended that this manual will help achieve standardization in infection prevention and control across all healthcare facilities and may be adapted as required to reflect specific local needs. The manual provides an evidenced-based resource for healthcare workers of all grades and professional groups and is available for use in all healthcare settings, including hospital, community, primary care, private, or voluntary sectors.

Many of these projects are interdependent and could not be taken forward as separate, individual initiatives. Successful implementation involves integrating information right across the HPSS in a streamlined system centered around the service user, meeting the needs of the care professional, and as a consequence, meeting more general management information, monitoring, and planning requirements. A practical, coherent work program that recognizes and manages the relationships and interdependencies between projects is essential.

Challenges

Throughout the development process of these ICT strategies, a number of major political and organizational changes took place. It could be suggested that these led in part to a delay in getting the strategy off the ground. As the DHSSPS wanted to be as inclusive as possible and engage in wide consultation, this too presented challenges with the timeframe; however, it was an essential activity.

Despite the inclusivity and consultation, there remain key issues yet to be overcome. For example, some of the nursing projects undertaken so far have been conducted as pilot projects and have not been integrated into core service delivery. A major reason for the non-integration is lack of funding. The implications are far reaching; it could be argued that the original monies devoted to the project have been wasted, given that the outcomes were, on the whole, very successful. Secondly, those patients, nurses, and other healthcare staff involved in the projects and familiar with the outcomes had expectations raised and now dashed. This presents moral if not ethical dilemmas that should be taken into consideration in the planning of future projects.

Culture change is also a major challenge. Attempts are being made to address this through the wide engagement of staff at all levels in the strategy development, the ICT for Care Professionals project, and the curriculum for all health and social care professionals. The delay in getting the strategy off the ground has meant that the technologies have "moved on" with financial implications for all levels of the health system. Despite these challenges, there is considerable energy and achievement to date and an air of optimizm that this will continue.

Summary

This chapter has given a broad overview of the ICT strategy for health and social care in Northern Ireland. It has highlighted aspects of the strategy development and plans for implementation. Emphasis was given to the range of projects currently underway, planned, or completed that form part of the strategy implementation. Particular mention was given to the role of nursing with some key nursing-led projects outlined. Finally the chapter ended with consideration of some key challenges yet to be overcome.

References

1. Carty B ed. *Nursing Informatics: Education for Practice*, New York, Springer, 2000.
2. Department of Health and Social Services and Public Safety. (2001) *Information and Communications Technology Strategy Vision Statement.* DHSSPSNI www.dhsspsni.gov.uk/hpss-ict-programme-summary.pdf. Accessed September 2, 2009.
3. Department of Health and Social Services and Public Safety (2005) *HPSS ICT Programme: From Vision to Reality–Implementing the Strategy.* DHSSPSNI. www.dhsspsni.gov.uk/hpss-ict-programme-summary.pdf. Accessed August 23, 2009.
4. Department of Health and Social Services and Public Safety (2006) *HPSS ICT Programme Plan.* DHSSPSNI. www.dhsspsni.gov.uk/hpss-ict-programme-summary.pdf. Accessed August 23, 2009.

Case Study 15C
Clinical eHealth Lead (NMAHPs), Scotland
By Heather Strachan, MSc, MBCS, Dip.N, RGN

Introduction

The Scottish government's eHealth programme aims to improve the safety, effectiveness, and efficiency of patient care by enabling appropriate access to information in an efficient and timely fashion. Information is added to patient records at every stage in a patient's journey, from initial assessment through to hospital discharge and transfer of care back to the community. Some of this information is on paper, while some is electronic and held in either local or national systems. Electronic information within NHS Scotland is largely held in information "silos," and dynamic sharing of this information between different groups of clinicians or organizations is usually limited. However, if the electronic record is to support the delivery of integrated, patient-centered care, then this needs to be addressed. Scotland's approach is to provide clinicians with access to a "clinical portal." A clinical portal will allow nurses, with their clinical colleagues, to access a range of information about an individual patient from several source systems, through a "virtual" electronic patient record.

NHS Scotland's eHealth Strategy

Scotland's population of just over 5 million receives healthcare from fourteen territorial health boards, which provide primary and community care and acute services. There are another six "special" health boards, which provide specialist services direct to the public or to other NHS boards.

Scotland's vision for eHealth is to support the overall NHS Scotland goals, those of health improvement, reducing health inequalities, and improving the quality of healthcare.[1] This will be accomplished by exploiting the power of electronic information to help ensure that patients get the right care, involving the right clinicians, at the right time, to deliver the right outcomes. The eHealth Strategy 2008-2011 is working towards electronic patient records and electronic communication and is becoming the primary means to manage healthcare information within our healthcare system.[2]

Nationally and within each health board, we have invested in modern eHealth systems that have already delivered benefits to patients and staff. Because of this, starting from scratch is not considered a realistic or appropriate option. Instead, an incremental approach will be taken, which involves making best use of clinical systems that already exist and filling the gaps with new clinical systems. Implementation of clinical portal and integration technology will allow data held in these existing and new systems to be shared more easily, thereby delivering a virtual electronic patient record. This reduces the complexity and potential risks associated with trying to develop a large single clinical database. This approach will also enable us to derive better value from our investments in eHealth by focusing on gaining benefits from current and new systems, as they are introduced and supported by change management. eHealth is not about technology for its own sake but about improving patient care supported by technology.

Current eHealth Progress

Across the NHS in Scotland, there are currently a number of clinical systems available to all health boards. Some of these systems are managed on a national basis, while others are managed locally but are using the same software nationally.

National applications and information repositories include:

- Picture Archiving and Communication System (PACS) provides access to digital radiology images and results
- Accident & Emergency system
- Diabetes management
- ePharmacy allows electronic transmission of prescriptions between general practitioners and community pharmacists

- Scottish Care Information (SCI) clinical information repositories (SCI Store) and messaging (SCI Gateway) support electronic referrals and discharges between primary and secondary care and storage of test results and clinical letters.
- Emergency Care Summary (ECS) provides access to patients' demographics, prescribing data, and allergies during out-of-hours and emergency situations.

A number of national projects are in progress that will support the delivery of new clinical applications, or replace legacy systems:

- A Patient Management System (PMS) that provides a suite of modules that include order entry and laboratories reporting, patient administration, outpatients management, clinical notes, and maternity services
- General Practice management systems for primary care records and services
- A theatre system
- A sexual health system
- A national shared services dental program
- Chemotherapy prescribing
- eCardiology

Nurses use many of these national systems to input and access patient information. In addition a number of health boards have implemented local systems for nurses, covering such areas as mental health, community, and acute services, which will contribute to the virtual electronic patient record. However it is recognized that more could to be done to support the delivery of electronic nursing records and other clinical notes across Scotland. A number of projects within the national eHealth programme are addressing this issue. Importantly, they involve a collaborative approach with health boards, suppliers, and the government to draw on good practice, ensure clinical engagement, and support a benefits-led approach. This approach aims to support shared learning in the design, implementation, and delivery of new systems. One example is a Multidisciplinary Information System that is being developed by a consortium of three health boards. Its users will include community and public health nurses, allied health professionals, mental health practitioners, social care professionals, and other partners in care. This application's components include:

- Form building for clinical assessments and care plans
- Letter generation
- Referrals management
- Messaging
- Consent management
- Caseload management
- Clinicians' diary
- Reporting and audit tools

Once completed, this system will be available for use by other health boards in Scotland should they wish to adopt it. It is also anticipated that the PMS could be used to support electronic nursing records in the acute sector.

Approach to Developing a Virtual Patient Record

The eHealth strategy makes a commitment to give NHS Scotland's clinicians access to a clinical portal. A clinical portal is an electronic window that displays a range of information that is essential for clinicians to deliver patient care, even if the information is actually held in a number of different places.

The aim of the portal is to provide:

- A summary view of patient information from multiple applications and information repositories.
- Seamless access to these applications and repositories for viewing or data entry, as appropriate.
- The ability to query data from a range of sources.

Figure 15C-1 shows the architecture vision for the clinical portal described below.[3]

- **Information Access:** The portal provides a personalized view for clinicians. It includes features such as electronic forms and is integrated with an Identity and Access Management service for authentication, authorization, and single-sign-on.

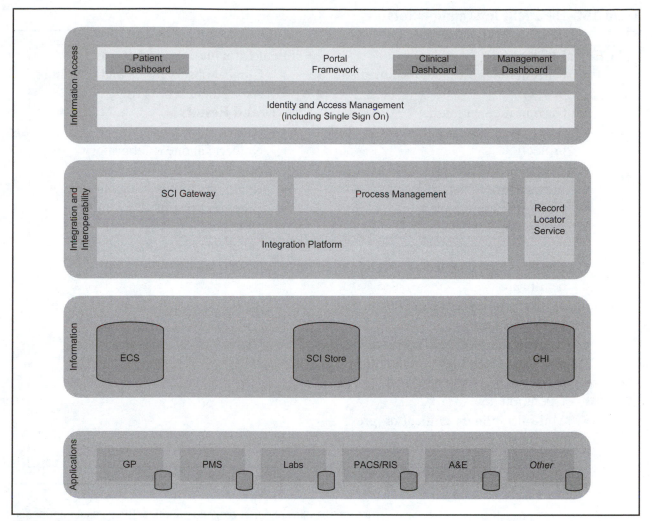

Figure 15C-1. *Architecture Vision for the Clinical Portal*

- **Integration and Interoperability:** The Record Locator Service will identify the location of individual pieces of the Virtual Electronic Patient Record, distributed across various applications and information repositories. The integration platform will provide reliable transfer of data (messages) between healthcare locations and systems.
- **Information:** Various information repositories will provide information to the clinical portal.
- **Applications:** Applications will provide information to the clinical portal and where integrated with Identity and Access Management, support the single-sign-on to those applications.

The clinical portal program will provide a "toolbox" of technology and services that can be used by health boards to create their own local clinical portal. Health boards will develop local delivery plans to deploy a clinical portal for clinicians in the locations that are most appropriate to them. This approach will allow health boards that are already forging ahead to continue to develop their approach, while supporting other health boards to reach at least a minimum clinical portal baseline.

Current examples include one health board that has a clinical portal for patient-centric information in their new Ambulatory Care Hospitals. It supports the whole patient pathway by removing information silos and provides easier access to information and applications. It supports a "paper-light" facility, and the portal will be combined with a scanning and electronic document management solution. A second health board has a clinical portal that provides patient-centric information for the wider primary care team, from information originating from a significant subset of the patient's health record held by their general practitioner.

To identify what electronic information clinicians currently have access to and what they need to access via the clinical portal for clinical decision making, nurses and other clinicians across Scotland have been surveyed to identify their information needs and priorities.[4] The results of the survey will be compared with

Table 15C-1. Patient Information Sets

Clinical History	Clinical Information
• Current diagnoses and past medical history • Current medication list • Alerts, e.g., advanced directive, child protection • Allergies • Immunization history • Current treatment plan • Procedures • List of future appointments • List of other agencies involved in healthcare **Clinical Correspondence and Notes** • Referral letters • Clinical letters (Inpatient final discharge letters, Accident and Emergency, etc.) • Operation notes • Multidisciplinary clinical progress and meeting notes • Therapy assessments	• Clinical observations and diagrams • Assessment scores (e.g., pain) **Orders and Results** • Orders placed • Numeric and text laboratory results • Radiology text results and images • Other text results (e.g., endoscopic procedures) • Other image results (e.g., electrocardiogram [ECG])

what is technically possible and used to inform the clinical portal program priorities. The clinical information needs identified in the survey included patient information sets (see Table 15C-1) and clinical information sets (see Table 15C-2). Table 15C-1 shows a brief description of the types of patient information that might be considered for delivery through the clinical portal. Table 15C-2 shows some of the types of information available to support clinicians in their professional role.

Benefits of the Clinical Portal and Its Management

The eHealth strategy sets out a strategic principle for eHealth to have a "focus on benefits, supported by technology and change."[2] To achieve this, the Scottish Government is working with NHS Health Boards to improve the focus on gaining benefits from current and new applications and information repositories and from the clinical portal program.

Benefits realization involves the following steps:
- Identifying and prioritizing the benefits of proposed eHealth technology
- Identifying who will receive these benefits
- Quantifying and evaluating the benefits, if possible
- Identifying the process and cultural changes required to achieve the benefits, including possible barriers
- Detailing the information system/information technology changes needed to support business changes that realize the intended benefits
- Measuring progress in benefits realization during and after implementation of eHealth technology

The benefits of the clinical portal will be dependent on what information and functionality is available to nurses and their clinical colleagues to support their clinical decision-making process. In the early stages of the clinical portal implementation, there may be only a limited amount of data available; however, this will be used as a foundation for continued incremental improvement. It is anticipated that benefits for nurses will include:

Table 15C-2. Clinical Information Sets

Clinical Lists	**Knowledge support,** e.g.,
• Patient lists	• Local and national clinical guidelines
• Procedure or work list	• Local and national referral protocols
Forms and Templates	**Clinical Performance Indicators,** e.g.,
• Admission form	• Achievement towards\ national targets (e.g., 4 hour unscheduled care waits, 18-week referral to treatment)
• Clinical handover template	
• Integrated care pathways	**Information to Support Professional Activities,** e.g.
• Assessment scores (e.g., waterlow)	• Appraisal documents
• Early warning score charts	• Links to continued professional development and knowledge skills framework Web sites

- Improved communication and teamwork between nurses, other members of the clinical team and patients.
- The ability to search with a patient "in context," allowing quick and easy retrieval of information held in different silos, and reducing nursing time spent searching for information
- Support nurses to deliver safer, faster patient care, based on better access to patient, clinical, and service information, for example medications and laboratory results
- Access to a library of electronic forms to support improved nursing record creation
- Improved information governance by regulating access to a patient's record, based on a role-based access model of authentication.
- Improved access to information due to ability to personalize the portal for nurses.
- Support for evidence-based nursing care by providing links to clinical guidelines and sources of knowledge management.
- Support to analyze anonomysed clinical data for quality assurance and performance management purposes.
- Less need for numerous logins or passwords to different systems.
  Patients too will benefit from:
- Less need to answer the same questions repeatedly, since all authorized clinicians involved in care will be able to access the information they need.
- Reassurance that staff have the necessary information to be able to manage their care safely.
- Improved patient confidence in the ability to detect inappropriate access to their information.

Summary: The Future

The clinical portal is aimed at delivering benefits to nurses, their clinical colleagues, and ultimately, to patients. It is also recognized that the infrastructure on which it is built could be reused by other communities, such as managers and patients. It will be able to support a "patient portal" to enable the people of Scotland to securely access health information, services, and alternative communication channels to help them manage their health. In the future, a patient portal could allow people access to their own health records, as well as enabling them to record their own health data, such as personal preference, health assessments, or signs and symptoms. This could support better communication between the nurse and the patient, and therefore result in improved patient-centered care. It could also provide patients with better access to health services, for example, ordering medication or making appointments. Like the clinical portal, a patient portal has potential to have a significant impact on how nurses deliver care to patients in the future, promoting shared decision making based on sharing access and shared control of the patient's health record. The clinical portal and the patient portal are two sides of the same coin. This innovation could provide the nurse with tools to support patient care, and patients with the opportunity to better manage their own health.

Scotland's eHealth strategy is patient-focused, clinically-led, and benefits-driven. The delivery of the Virtual Electronic Patient Record will be a significant step toward exploiting the power of electronic information. This will ultimately help nurses, alongside their clinical colleagues, improve the safety, effectiveness, and efficiency of patient care.

Acknowledgments
I would like to acknowledge the contribution to this case study of my eHealth Directorate Colleagues in the Scottish government, particularly Dr. Cathy Kelly, Alastair Bishop, Alan Hyslop, Jonathan Meddes, Gareth Adkins, Thomas Buchendorfer, Gerald McLafferty, and Tony McLaughlin.

References
1. The Scottish Government Better Health Better Care. *An Action Plan.* http://www.scotland.gov.uk/Publications/2008/01/29152311/0. Accessed July 12, 2009.

2. The Scottish Government. *eHealth Strategy* 2008-2011. http://www.scotland.gov.uk/Publications/2008/08/27103130/0. Accessed July 12, 2009.

3. The Scottish Government. *eHealth Architectural Vision*, Version 1.0 August 2008. http://www.ehealth.scot.nhs.uk/wp-content/documents/ehealth-architecture-vision-august-08.pdf. Accessed July 12, 2009.

4. The Scottish Government. The Clinical Portal; Information for Clinicians. May 2009. http://www.ehealth.scot.nhs.uk/?page_id=224. Accessed July 12, 2009.

CHAPTER 16

Electronic Health Initiatives: European View

By Patrick Weber, MA, RN; and John Mantas, PhD, MSc, BSc(Hons)

Introduction

"Spending on health is not just a cost, it is an investment. Health expenditure can be seen as an economic burden,[1] but the real costs to society are the direct and indirect costs linked to ill-health as well as a lack of sufficient investment in relevant health areas."[2]

European Goals

The European Commission has supported research and development in the field of e-health since 1988. Since 1998, about 650 million Euros in European Union (EU) contributions have been granted to approximately 450 research and development (R&D) European e-health projects. Over the years, funded programs have included research topics such as regional health networks and security, home care and telemedicine, decision-support systems, systems and services for increased efficiency in the delivery of healthcare, and electronic health records (EHR) systems for continuity of care. More recently, R&D has focused on prevention, prediction, and personalized health systems. High on the current R&D agenda is interoperability (technical and semantic) between different EHR systems, other health information systems, and work on terminologies and ontologies. Patient safety is another top priority in the upcoming new EU R&D Framework Program 2007-2013.[3]

The strategic approach for the EU 2008-2013 reinforces the importance of health policy that recognizes people's right to be empowered in relation to their health and healthcare. Action plans within these national strategies represent work across all health sectors.

Electronic Health Record

Ideally, EHRs in today's world are based on interoperable standards that are shared across multiple healthcare sectors, as well as at the national and international levels. Toward attaining this level of interoperability, the EU is taking the lead for e-health projects. Fulfilling this goal requires a trustworthy EHR that provides all necessary clinical information to support a good quality for continuity of care. The EuroRec Institute, a non-profit organization, promotes the development and the use of high-quality EHR systems. EuroRec has expressed its ambition to become a European agency responsible for the certification of EHR systems and for semantic interoperability for related e-health applications.[4]

Population

The "graying of Europe" also means that the prevalence of chronic diseases within our populations is on the increase, as are related management costs. All these factors are starting to place additional strain on European healthcare systems. By 2050, average public spending for health and long-term care in countries of the Organization for Economic Co-operation and Development (OECD) may rise to between 10% and 13% of the gross domestic product (GDP). The emerging situation will not be sustainable unless action is taken at all levels to change the way healthcare is delivered. To promote this transformation of the European healthcare landscape, continuity of care will need to be assured at all points of care delivery, whether in hospital settings or ordinary living environments. This care continuity will be facilitated by the deployment of interoperable e-health services within and across European countries in a way that enables access to a patient's medical history and data from any location. Moreover, the new healthcare landscape will be characterized by enhanced patient safety and personalized care, based on the following:

- Management of health risks.
- Disease prediction, prevention, early diagnosis, and management.
- Individualized medications and treatment.[5]

A Point about EHRs

At the EU level, the e-health project aims at exploring how public authorities could use EHRs for public health purposes by collecting data on the health status of the population.[6] In the first version of this book, the introduction noted that every European country was in the process of implementing and integrating their national EHRs into their healthcare systems.[6]

EHR implementations are done more for medical purposes and less for nursing purposes. Nurses still have to find their place into this process and take the lead for the nursing parts. Nevertheless, to build a successful EHR system, nursing is one of the key elements that must be included in the process. This means that the nursing part of the EHR has to be developed in close collaboration with the nurses. That is why the nursing informatics competencies are needed and are recognized in Europe, as well as globally.

Nursing Informatics

Nursing informatics was restated in 2009 by the Nursing Informatics Special Interest Group of the International Medical Informatics Association (IMIA-NI) as follows: "Nursing informatics science and practice integrates nursing, its information and knowledge and their management with information and communication technologies to promote the health of people, families and communities world wide" (adopted by the General Assembly IMIA-NI July 2009, Helsinki, Finland).[7] The nursing practice in this definition is taken in the broad sense and is in alignment with WHO's definition.[8] In both definitions, the emphasis is not on the technology but in using the technology to better focus on the people and, specifically, elements in the environment particular to individuals. The ethics dimension is also a part of this definition. In nursing curricula, ethics is a major component and could also be applied to informatics. In IT, the ethical aspect should be considered as follows: "Ethical issues are not founded on whether technology is acceptable for humankind, but rather on whether people have the humanity with which to make technology a true instrument of man's will"[9]—the point being that technology itself does not have any value but rather value is derived from the users and designers.[9] In the future, nurses will face new roles in assisting patients to update their own medical data. The role of being an advocate for patients will be very important and should be taken into account in nursing and nursing informatics studies.

Education

Schools at all levels—from the most basic to the most advanced—need to include the new technologies and the new roles of nurses and nursing informatics. These new care delivery models and informatics skills also contribute to nurses being the most competent resource in their organization to guide other professionals engaged in the IT development processes. Nurse competencies are at the service of persons needing to be advised and supported in the use of IT related to healthcare. New Web tools are coming into the market for example, Web 2.0, that can be combined to Virtual Worlds, such as Second Life, for virtual simulations and demonstrations that will be commonly used in the future to facilitate the dissemination of knowledge and distance teaching.[10] These Web 2.0 tools allow creation of a virtual environment with virtual patients, so as to facilitate interaction with the student. Currently, we are just in the early stage of using these new tools in nursing education, but the Web 2.0 tools show great promise as learning tools for health professionals. We should also be considering application of these tools for non-professionals, patients, and family caregivers.

Aside from these new technologies, the competencies and skills that our nursing faculty and educators need going forward are very important, and, thus, they will be required to master these new tools and apply them in their own domain to be able to inform others about possibilities in the virtual domains. Continuing education delivered in a way that makes these new technologies easy to learn for nursing faculty and educators is crucial for nursing education to keep pace with the emerging technologies. Nurses IT education in Europe is very different from one country to another. Nordic countries have better integrated IT at both the graduate and post-graduate levels in nursing studies than other European countries.

Nursing and Patients at Hospitals

During the past decade, most European countries introduced clinical information systems into their hospitals, including the ward level, to manage their clinical data. Most of the time, the clinical data capture is related to administration and is linked to billing systems. We are still a ways away from realizing the goal of having a real and complete EHR that fully supports work processes and the capture of clinical data as a byproduct of care delivery; however, most European countries are in the process of implementing EHR systems, and visitors to major hospitals can see these systems in various stages of completion.

In a complete EHR, the nursing care activities have to be recorded and the nursing science and practice should be implemented. For change to take place in the hospital sector, it will be necessary to move from an institution to a patient-centered focus and from cost to value.[11] Nurses are at the hub of communication in hospitals, and the nursing role of coordinator of care is fundamental to effective and safe patient care.[12] As such, nursing data are becoming more important now than ever before and this is related to financing the hospital sector. Many countries have adopted the DRG, or DRG-like systems, as the basis for budgeting and financial reimbursement. The financial analyses are more precise and are downsized to the analysis of each patient stay; therefore, nursing activities need to be included in the services and the cost data recorded in the EHR in support of DRG reporting. This need for nursing service data helps the nursing department to claim a partnership with the decision team responsible for EHR development and implementation. A good clinical system that delivers value for the clinicians as well as the hospital system can only be built with the involvement of the professionals who will be using the system, and that includes nursing.

For health systems to be able to contribute to better care delivery, their EHR systems must ensure that they can support continuity of care and the ability to follow the patient over time.[3] The challenge is to have a data collection that fulfills two goals:

- The first goal is to gain better and more accurate data for managing the quality of care. In terms of quality of care, this means that the care given is accurate, safe, and utilizes the best procedure, at the best cost, at the right time.
- The second goal is to prove that the investment brings the best results. Most of the time, nursing care is taken into account as a global cost and not as an investment. Now is the time to begin considering nursing care as an investment. An investment is related to high value, and high value in nursing is a synonym for quality of care and fulfilling patients' and institutions' needs.

To reach good quality of care, EHR systems should allow for the management and measurement of the care delivered, as well as the comparison of the practice with Evidence-Based Practice (EBP) data. This should be the case, not only for nurses but for any health professional. In Switzerland, some of the French-speaking areas of the country are using "focus charting documentation" that is a part of a clinical pathway, but this content should be linked to an evidence-based, best practice database to optimally support clinicians' use of best practices.

Implementing an EHR system is the best opportunity to redesign the nursing process in adopting standards, monitoring clinical outcomes, and enhancing clinical decisions. This is a shift of culture and should begin in nursing.[13] Because the introduction of EHR technologies drives transformative change in clinical thinking, practices, and the way that nurses document,

EHR implementations carry an enormous need for reeducating the nursing workforce in all these dimensions within their clinical skills and work practices. It is very difficult to persuade nurses to change their work habits, so this must be done through nursing leadership with a clear message on the benefits to them as well as to patient care.

Personal Health Records Adoption in Europe

Under the influence of the EU's e-health initiatives, many European countries are focusing on the personal health record (PHR) as a means to enable self-management, better care continuity, and an informed, health literate society. E-health initiatives that extend health information, access to health libraries, and e-communication with primary care resources are becoming a strategic priority in most European countries' national health policies. The PHR, along with broader complement of tools and resources, is considered a major tool to improve care efficiency, care safety, and to empower patients. To fulfill these goals, the availability of data from hospitals are mandatory as the base of the EHR. Hospitals are under pressure to ensure that good, reliable data are collected from the clinical field and to be able to share these data with other authorized healthcare institutions. The EHR is not only important for the acute care organization in a community; it also needs to extend to rehabilitation sectors for geriatrics and elderly patient care. Each care facility, from the hospital to the community, physician to home, needs access to the individual's medical and health information for effective and efficient quality of care to happen.

The link between the EHR and the PHR is important and offers individuals a way to easily access their medical record. This encourages patients to be proactive and will help them manage their own health record. For the patient, it is a way to be sure that what was recorded is correct. Mistakes in recording medical files are not so rare.[14] Nurses will provide help for patients in accessing their health records, in accompanying patients, and in offering help in facilitating the link with health professionals.

Nursing and Patients at Home

The EHR and its supporting information and communication technologies are playing a strong role for enabling improvements in continuity of care for at-risk populations, such as elderly patients, chronic disease populations, and maternity/new baby groups. E-health perspectives bring together information needed to provide appropriate and better care, as well as to help individuals become active participants in their own health and disease management. In the e-health concept, a link with every healthcare sector is proposed. With budget restrictions at the hospital level, length of stay was dramatically reduced in past years. This decrease in acute care length of stay has had consequences for the care provided at home, with more complex patient treatments being performed in the home. Additionally, people are living longer. Across European countries, the proportion of the population who exceed 80 years is increasing markedly, and this proportional growth in our geriatric aged population is projected to continue. These demographic changes also correspond to an increasing prevalence of the numbers in our populations with chronic diseases. On the other hand, the proportion of the young and very young in our populations is decreasing decade over decade. This will have an impact on the financing of the healthcare sectors because our solidarity model is based on the incomes of the working people. "The cost of providing pensions, and long-term health and social care will increase and is estimated to rise by 4 percent to 8 percent of GDP by 2050."[15]

Overcoming the distance between healthcare professionals and the person at home is stimulating new development in the domain of tele-surveillance. Getting the right information at the right time is crucial for preventing major health problems at home. Development of smart home and telenursing and telemedicine is very active. Within the e-health initiatives, it is also of utmost importance to collect accurate health-related data from patients at home. This data collection is a part of the EHR for home care. This EHR has to be fully compatible with the one in use at the hospital level. Therefore, nurses have a new role to play in patient education. New technology cannot be installed in the patient's home without the nurse teaching the patient or family member how to use these new tools. Nurses will need to add to their teaching skills, those of being a coach and facilitator to empower patients to manage these new technologies, interact directly with the health system, and to seek out information to manage their own health. A full education component will be needed in these initiatives to have the technologies adopted by individuals and used in a meaningful way; otherwise, there will be few or no benefits. Good practice analyses should be performed for home care evaluation. The availability of EBP documentation, as well as medication adverse event prevention and all the elements needed to ensure safe care, have to be available at the point of care or at the point of encounter.

Home Hospitalization

A day at home for a sick person is less expensive, less stressful, and safer than at the hospital. The degree of satisfaction in this situation is very high for the patient and family. The number of home hospitalizations is increasing throughout European countries, as a means to more effective and cost-efficient care. In France, the latest statistics showed an availability of 6,700 places for home hospitalization in 2006, but the forecast for 2010 is to have 15,000 places available. Home hospitalizations are being used for many conditions, treatments, and diseases. The most common are oncology treatments, cardiopulmonary diseases, conditions in young children and in those in the perinatal period, and self-management reeducation.[16] In home hospitalization, risk for nosocomial infections is reduced and kept at a minimum. For elderly patients, the home environment is less disruptive and risky than the hospital, and in terms of costs, the infrastructure is less expensive. Even when nurses have to visit the patient several times a day, the costs of home care compared with hospital care for the same treatment is markedly less. In this context, the need for a good follow-up of the data is crucial.

Need for Common Reference on Classification

Nursing classification used for home care and interventions is not the same as the one used at the hospital level, but it should have cross-references to a general nursing classification available for both, which could be the International Classification of Nursing Practice (ICNP®).

Communication

New technologies, such as the smart phone, are an ideal platform for home care documentation. With full Internet connectivity, these new technologies could be used alone or in conjunction with a personal computer. This is especially suitable for remote areas where there is no other way to reach people and the infrastructure is low. Given their Internet connectivity, smart phone-like devices can offer the option of a direct link with the database and provide up-to-date information at the point of care at which an Internet connection might not otherwise exist.

Nursing and Persons

By definition a person is not a patient until he or she becomes sick and seeks advice from healthcare professionals.

Historic Role of Health Professionals

Until the 18th century, Hippocratic medicine rules were applied: illnesses were observed and the formulation of prognoses were essential. Patients had little help to alleviate pain or discomfort. The physician helped the patient with his knowledge, dedication, his sense of dialogue, and his sympathy. There was a close relation between the patient and the physician.

In the 19th century, scientific medicine enabled the study of diseases. As medical science advanced its knowledge base, a physician became a scientific person with expert knowledge and the power to cure, and the patient's role was to follow the physician's advice. There was no close relation between patient and physician. The patients did not have to understand their disease pathophysiology or the prescribed treatment; they only had to follow the physician's directions and suffer whatever treatments were thought best. The term *patient* is really appropriate in this regard and for that time. With the Internet technologies that emerged in the late 20th century, including widespread adoption of the personal computer across the world, laymen were suddenly empowered by having access to the latest science and evidenced-based best practices for disease-specific conditions. And the patient-physician relationship was dramatically transformed in a matter of just a few years. As a result, as we close on this first decade of the 21st century, the patient is no longer waiting "patiently" in a passive role; he or she is now an actor with expectation of being fully integrated in decision making about his or her care. The 21st century patient is literate about health-related problems. Increasingly we see the expectation for a therapeutic, contractual relationship to be built between the physician and the patient. The person is taken as a whole with his or her history, relations, and knowledge and has to be part of the therapeutic contract.[17]

Person Empowerment

Nurses have a key role to play with the empowerment of the person in health-related problems or needs. New roles include, for example, providing guidance to the patient to find the right information at the right place; helping the patient complete his or her personal health record; being an advocate for the patient in a health-related action; instructing patients in the use of the Internet, smart phones, or other smart devices, and obtaining or maintaining basic care items such as clothing. All these new roles should be learned at nursing school, which also means that schools have to develop new domains of teaching.

Personal Health Record

With the promotion of the PHR, individuals will have the responsibility to maintain their own health record online. The development of the PHR belongs to the European Health project. The implementation of the PHR has started slowly at the governmental level. Some companies have begun development and implementation, among them are Microsoft with Health-Vault and Google with Google Health. These initiatives are not yet compatible with actions taken by governments concerning e-health. Most of the professionals are afraid of the private initiative and would prefer that governments or official bodies take the lead for implementing PHRs compatible with standards applied to e-health development. Nurses will have to guide the individual in the use of the PHR system—helping them to understand the fundamentals and also guiding them in completing the data. To summarize, EHR systems with linked PHR solutions offer promising opportunities to bridge the gap between patient self-care needs and provider resources. Self-management tools in EHRs and PHRs have the potential to improve patient outcomes by facilitating patient and provider education and communication around goal-setting; prompting consistent, evidence-based treatment; and providing reminders and feedback. Nurses are well-positioned to respond to the demand for development, implementation, and evaluation of new informatics tools for self-management support.[18]

Summary

Throughout Europe in the coming years, major changes in the way health providers document patient data and share these data with the individual will take place. Changes will also occur in how to exchange and share data between the EHR/PHR continuum. E-health is a major initiative that joins the countries in Europe in fulfilling a common goal. Efforts are made at the governmental and political levels, and while the implication for physicians is good, the implication for nurses and nursing is poor. It is not too late for nursing to join the group and promote the science and practice of nursing to be fully integrated into the e-health vision. Many good examples across Europe are available and should be mentioned to support nursing actions in the eHealth strategy.[19] The case studies that are included in this section are good examples of the leading efforts by the nursing leadership and profession within the European countries represented here. The case studies for Chapter 16 show an unevenness in the extent to which nursing is included in national EHR initiatives, in the form of automation of nursing work processes, nursing documentation with decision support, capture of structured nursing data, and the storage and retrieval of those data to support nursing research. At the speed national EHR initiatives are moving, it is imperative that nursing leadership, universities, and nurse informatics professionals work together to make certain that nursing is not left behind in this transformative inflection point in our healthcare systems.

References

1. *Snapshots: Health Care Spending in the United States and OECD Countries.* January 2007. http://www.kff.org/insurance/snapshot/chcm010307oth.cfm. Accessed June 2009.

2. EU Commission White Paper. *Together for Health: A Strategic Approach for the EU.* 2008-2013. COM 2007.

3. Comyn G. Electronic Health Record Systems-A Main Pillar in European e-Health Developments for Better Delivery of Care. September 22, 2007. http://www.aarpinternational.org/gra_sub/gra_sub_show.htm?doc_id=531144. Accessed September 2009

4. De Moor G, Kalra D, Devlies J. Certification of Electronic Health Record systems and the importance of the validation of clinical archetypes. In: De Clercq E, De Moor G, Bellon J, Foulon M, Van der Lei J, eds. *Collaborative Patient-Centred eHealth,* IOS Press. 2008; pp 82-91.

5. European Commission. *ICT for Health: 2010 Transforming the European Healthcare landscape.* European Communities 2006.

6. Weber P. Electronic Health Initiatives: European View. In: Weaver CA. Delaney CW. Weber P. Carr RL, eds. *Nursing and Informatics for the 21st Century.* Chicago: HIMSS Publishing, 2006:371-376.

7. General Assembly IMIA NI. *Nursing Informatics Definition.* www.imiani.org. Accessed September 10, 2009.

8. Expert Committee, *Nursing Practice.* Report of WHO, Technical Report Series, No 860 1996.

9. Leino-Kilpi H. Ethics and Nursing Informatics. Keynote Address: Presentation Slides. *11th International Congress of Nursing Informatics – Connecting Health and Humans.* NI2009 Helsinki, Finland, June 25, 2009.

10. Hansen MM, Murray PJ, Erdley WS. The potential of 3D virtual worlds in professional nursing education. In: Saranto K, Brennan PF, Park HA, Talberg M, Ensio A, eds. *Connecting Health and Human.* Proceeding of NI2009. IOS Press 2009.

11. Hofdijk J. *The Health Care Delivery Revolution is About to Start: Take your chance.* Keynote Address: NI2009 Helsinki 2009.

12. Dykes PC, Hurley AC, Brown S, et al. Validation of the Impact of Health Information Technology (IHIT) Scale: An International Collaborative. In: Saranto K, Brennan PF, Park HA, Talberg M, Ensio A, eds. *Connecting Health and Human.* Proceeding of NI2009. IOS Press, 2009.

13. Nagle LM, Yetman L. Moving to a Culture of Nurse as Knowledge Worker and a New Way of Knowing in Nursing. In: Saranto K, Brennan PF, Park HA, Talberg M, Ensio A, eds. *Connecting Health and Human.* Proceedings of NI2009. IOS Press, 2009.

14. Wibe Slaughter L, Patients Reading Their Health Records: What Emotional Factors Are Involved? In: Saranto K, Brennan PF, Park HA, Talberg M, Ensio A, eds. *Connecting Health and Human,* Proceedings of NI2009. IOS Press, 2009.

15. Layzell B, Manning B, Benton S. The Elderly Demographic Time Bomb: Sharing the Load with the Active Ageing: Can eHealth Technologies Help Defuse it? In: Saranto K, Brennan PF, Park HA, Talberg M, Ensio A, eds. *Connecting Health and Human,* Proceedings of NI2009. IOS Press, 2009.

16. Afrite A, Chaleix M, Com-Ruelle L, Valdelièvre H, L'hospitalisation à domicile, une prise en charge qui s'adresse à tous les patients. Questions d'économie de la santé No 140 Mars 2009.

17. Fragu P. La relation médecin-patient, Histoire d'une transformation. Elsevier Masson. Ethique&Santé Vol 1. No 1. Janvier 2004 : pp 26-31.

18. Jenkins M, Levy J, Cohen E, Yoon S, Singer J, Mostashari F. Integration of Self Management Tools in Personal and Provider eHealth Records. In: Saranto K, Brennan PF, Park HA, Talberg M, Ensio A. eds. *Connecting Health and Human,* Proceedings of NI2009. IOS Press, 2009.

19. Mantas J. Future trends in health informatics – theoretical and practical. *Stud Health Technol Inform.* 2004;109:114-27.

Case Study 16A

The Development and Implementation of the EHR in Iceland

By Asta Thoroddsen, PhD(c), MSc, RN; Herdís Gunnarsdóttir, MSc, MBA, BSc, RN;
and María Heimisdóttir, PhD, MD, MBA

Introduction

Midway between Greenland and Norway lies Iceland, one of the five Nordic countries and home to 310.000 people. The country has long taken pride in its healthcare system, which is based on a national health insurance system. It boasts the lowest infant mortality rate of all OECD (Organisation for Economic Co-operation and Development) nations (2.3 per 1.000) and life expectancy at birth is high at 81.2 years, lagging only behind Japan and Switzerland.[1] Iceland also has a good track record in the treatment of chronic illnesses, as reflected in the low mortality rates from cancer and ischemic heart disease.[1] Healthcare comes at a price, however, and in 2008, the national total expenditure (public and private) on healthcare was 9.4% of the Gross Domestic Production (GDP). Public expenditure on healthcare was 7.8% of GDP, and approximately one third of that amount (2.48% of GDP) was allotted to Landspitali University Hospital.

Government Policy on the Information Society 2008-2012

The Icelandic government formulated its 2008 to 2012 policy on the information society, following the motto: "Iceland, the e-nation."[2] This policy builds on three pillars: service, efficiency, and progress, which entails all governmental authorities working together as one whole. In terms of healthcare, the main objectives of service are that e-citizens can serve themselves online without delay, anywhere at any time and that they can access any information stored on themselves in official data systems. One example of such a service is the health portal, on which users may book appointments at health centers with general practitioners, as well as with specialists, and gain access to their personal health history including vaccinations, hospitalizations, and medications. Citizens can also access their service information, such as their entitlement to discounts for health service.

To enhance efficiency and quality, the Ministry of Health has issued a policy regarding the development of an EHR. The goal is to provide healthcare providers with access to necessary healthcare data for their patients, irrespective of the data origin. This goal will be accomplished by linking all healthcare establishments by a health net. Thus, a comprehensive health record from "cradle to the grave" will be created for each citizen. The project is based on a new law on patient records that was passed in 2009.[3] Further specifications on the health net and its use are in the process of being developed, and these will address definitions of data to be shared, interoperability, reuse of data, access and logging, data security, and formal coordination and cooperation among the healthcare providers sharing the data. Such specifications are of paramount importance to ensure patient privacy and confidentiality, while still obtaining the desired efficiency in services. Given the small size of Iceland, this country case study will focus on a single site initiative for full EHR development and deployment, with a detailed description of the components that pertain to nursing within Iceland.

Landspitali University Hospital

Landspitali University Hospital (LUH) is the only tertiary care hospital in Iceland and is situated in the capital, Reykjavik. A midsize hospital, it provides services in all major medical specialties and serves as the country's only university hospital and referral center. In 2008, LUH had 28.600 discharges, 530.000 ambulatory visits, 14.600 surgical procedures, and 3.400 deliveries. Employees number approximately 5.100 (3.870 full-time equivalents). An interdisciplinary EHR committee, appointed by the executive board of LUH, is the governing body of development and implementation of all EHR projects at LUH.

EHR Project at LUH

The EHR system, SAGA, has been in use at LUH for 20 years and is now a central part of the hospital's modular EHR. The contract between the hospital and the vendor was renegotiated in 2007, aiming to strengthen the relationship and to cooperate on developing SAGA into a more efficient software solution that LUH could use as the backbone for its modular EHR. A three-year roadmap was drawn up to create a common view on the developments planned and to define milestones (see next section) by which progress could be measured. By agreeing on the roadmap, both LUH and the vendor committed themselves to cooperating on designing, developing, testing, and implementing specific new functionalities or modules of SAGA.

Content of the Roadmap

To start filling in the content of the roadmap, the EHR committee and key people from the IT department held a brainstorming session during which the most important alterations, as well as new functionalities needed, were listed. The list was arranged according to clinical urgency and divided into three phases, one for each year of the contract. Milestones were defined for each item on the list so that both LUH and the vendor could objectively follow the progress of the work and thus minimize the risk of conflict. Term payments of the contract were linked to the milestones to create an incentive for both parties to maintain the schedule and reach each milestone at the time defined in the roadmap.

Although many projects needed urgent attention, the group was fairly unanimous regarding the tasks for Phase 1. First, the access control and logging functions in SAGA were long outdated, and since a new law on privacy protection in patient records was in preparation, it was deemed absolutely necessary to include a rewrite of these functions in the first phase. Second, a new patient administrative system (admission, discharge and transfer or ADT) for inpatient wards was added. The third project in Phase 1 was an integration of SAGA and Theriak Therapy Management (TTM), LUH's medication management software, to create a comprehensive medication record for both inpatient and outpatient care. Last but not least, the fourth project in Phase 1 was to develop new modules for care delivery documentation.

Documentation of care within SAGA was defined as all documentation within inpatient units, outpatient clinics at LUH, and hospital-affiliated home care. Some aspects are interdisciplinary, such as data on vital signs, fluid balance, results from bedside measurements and scales, use of invasive devices (e.g., tubes, drains), and discharge planning. Other aspects are mostly related to planning of nursing care, i.e., nursing assessment, nursing diagnoses (with signs, symptoms, and etiologies), nursing interventions, and nursing outcomes. Since family nursing had been implemented at LUH, functionality to provide a genogram for family and significant others was also needed.

The main functional requirements with respect to documentation of nursing care were the following: (1) nurses should be able to document all data relevant to the planning of nursing care; (2) all patient data should be available in one place and be reusable and accessible to all healthcare professionals involved in the care of the patient; (3) overview of patients' status and treatment should be easy and complete; and (4) patient data should be accessible for retrieval and analysis for the purpose of quality improvement and administration. With the end of Phase 1, it became clear that certain projects, namely the documentation of nursing care, had been underestimated and would have to be completed in Phase 2. Physician documentation was kept in Phase 1 (admission and discharge notes, progress and ambulatory notes, consultation reports), as well as order entry for selected services, such as clinical tests or examinations for which the results of the test are documented in SAGA. The final component in Phase 1 is, to create a patient overview that is a comprehensive summary of the most pertinent patient data. As of this writing, Phase 2 is currently in progress and Phase 3 is being planned. What seem to be the logical next steps are essentially variations on the themes already in progress as parts of Phase 1 and 2, making use of the enhanced clinical coding already in place. Among those are flow sheets, templates for questionnaires, clinical calculators, and various features to provide users with more control over the user interface.

Documentation Modules in the EHR System SAGA

Vital Signs and Bedside Use of Scales and Measurements. Pulse, blood pressure, temperature, and respiration can be documented and are presented both in a table and graphically. The user can choose which vitals signs are presented graphically. By moving the cursor over the graph, the relevant values for each measurement are displayed. Qualifiers for each measurement, such as dyspnea or nasal flaring for respiration or the mode of blood pressure measurement (patient standing, lying, or sitting) can be documented. Bedside measurements, e.g., oxygen saturation and liters of oxygen given, are grouped together in one screen for convenience in documentation and view of data. Other examples for scales and measurements are the Visual Analog Scale for pain, patient scoring on the Glasgow Coma Scale, Mini Mental Status Exam (MMSE), and the Barthel Index. An easy overview of results from bedside tests, such as blood glucose, urine, or feces, is also available.

Invasive Devices. Patients with tubes, drains, catheters, or other invasive devices require frequent observations and various types of bedside care most frequently provided by nurses. To ensure safety and quality of care, access to a quick overview of the extensive and complicated care provided to each patient is essential. This can be obtained in a single screen on which, by placing the cursor over the name of each device, information is displayed on the type of device inserted, the site and time of insertion, and the care provider responsible. The scheduled time for removal or replacement of the device can be set. In the current version this is done manually, but in later versions, this functionality will be programmed to suggest appropriate timing of removal or replacement based on clinical evidence.

Nursing Assessment. The nursing assessment is a structured format that follows the 13 domains of NANDA-International (NANDA-I).[4] The framework of the NANDA-I taxonomy is based on Marjorie Gordon's Functional Health Patterns[5] that are familiar to nurses in Iceland. The structured format is a combination of predefined pop-up lists, check boxes, and free text.

Discharge Planning. On admission, an interdisciplinary discharge plan is set up with an estimated discharge date. Data from the nursing assessment, like home services prior to admission, are pulled forward to prevent re-entering of data. Needs for services at home following discharge are assessed and documented as part of the discharge planning to ensure patient safety and to prevent re-admissions. Colors and check boxes are used to remind staff and give a quick overview on items to be completed, as well as items that are already completed.

Nursing Care Plans. The most time-consuming and resource requiring task within the overall project was the development of the nursing care plans. In order to improve quality of care, it was considered important to provide clinical decision support. This was done by loading the EHR with nursing knowledge, such as nursing terms and phrases to document nursing diagnoses, nursing interventions, and nursing outcomes. To accomplish this, nurses in all clinical wards updated nursing content according to the nursing process in all standardized nursing care plans and unified their structure throughout the hospital. The nursing knowledge content in each care plan was provided by nurses within each specialty; for example, nurses working with cardiac patients developed the care plans for that patient group. Nurses were encouraged to base the care plans on up-to-date evidence to the extent possible.

Standardized nursing care plans are defined as predefined order sets for nursing care to be provided for a group of patients with a specific (medical) condition or undergoing a specific procedure (e.g., surgery). Most care plans are labeled according to a medical indication, such as surgical procedure (e.g., mastectomy) or medical diagnosis (e.g., pneumonia, dementia, depression). Generally, the care plans contain a set of nursing diagnoses and collaborative problems, signs and symptoms, related factors, goals, nursing interventions, and related nursing activities. Collaborative problems denote problems or potential complications, most often resulting from medical treatments that nurses monitor to detect the onset of symptoms or changes in patient status.[6] The care plans had to comply with the relevant nursing terminologies of NANDA-I[4] and Nursing Interventions Classification (NIC)[7] and information structures. End users participated in the development of the care plans, and heavy emphasis was put on using nursing terminologies for nursing data. Both NANDA-I and NIC terminologies have been translated into Icelandic. Nursing Outcomes Classification (NOC)[8] is being piloted on paper, and results are pending.

To compose a care plan in the new EHR modules, nurses can use two main clinical decision-making methods: (1) Select a standardized care plan that best fits the patient's status and condition. Appropriate items on the standardized nursing care plan are then chosen, changed, or added based on the patient's condition; or (2) Tailor a nursing care plan specifically to the patient. For each nursing diagnosis, a shortlist (sub-selection) of relevant signs and symptoms and related factors appear based on NANDA-I. If appropriate, a selection can also be made from a complete list of signs and symptoms and related factors. A shortlist of relevant nursing interventions (NIC) appears for each nursing diagnosis. A selection can also be made from the complete list of nursing interventions. To be able to individualize the care plans, nurses can add relevant activities in free text under each intervention that the system saves and makes accessible in a shortlist for the next user.

Family Tree to Support Family Nursing. The genogram and ecomap are part of nurses' documentation. These tools can be used together or independently and are designed to provide a graphic display of a family tree of four generations and interrelation between the patient and his/her family members. The names and ages of relatives and significant others are documented, the relationship between individuals is defined by different symbols and lines, and, optionally, a written note can be added.

Planning and Management of Nursing Within the EHR

Since the first two phases of the SAGA roadmap involved large nursing components, the Chief Nursing Executive (CNE) established a Nursing Documentation Steering Committee in early 2008. The committee's role was to manage the development of electronic nursing documentation within the EHR, and a project manager was hired to coordinate the development and implementation of the new documentation modules. The committee was chaired by a nursing director and included the project manager and representatives from all clinical divisions. Each representative was responsible for the nursing documentation within their division. Other stakeholders and collaborators on the project were the academic chair for nursing informatics, a project manager from the IT department, nursing directors and managers, contact persons in the wards, and a representative from the vendor, TM Software.

Nursing managers are professionally accountable for maintaining nursing documentation in their wards. In this project, they delegate a part of that function to a ward representative who assumes responsibility for quality control of the documentation and plays a role in the implementation. The steering committee can call on nurses, in collaboration with nursing managers, to work on defined, smaller projects related to the delvelopment or implementation of the EHR. The main tasks of the steering committee during preparation and development of nursing within the EHR were:

- Needs analysis and collaboration with the vendor in developing the EHR
- Revisions and development of standardized nursing care plans using NANDA nursing diagnoses and NIC nursing interventions to be included in the EHR
- Needs analysis and appraisal of available hardware at the hospital wards
- Development of new work procedure guidelines for electronic documentation
- Mapping of nursing interventions' codes to the Nordic Classification of Surgical Procedures (NCSP) for DRGs
- Budget plans for the project
- Activation of all stakeholders, managers, and ward representatives
- Research on nursing documentation and other project-related issues

The nursing steering committee established three subgroups on: (1) coding and classification of patient data; (2) development of modules for documentation of care for the EHR; and (3) needs analysis for hardware and the development of guidelines on electronic documentation to prepare nurses for new and different work procedures. Concurrently, the EHR committee appointed an implementation taskforce to ensure safe, effective, and efficient implementation of electronic nursing documentation within inpatient wards. This was an extensive project as implementation of electronic documentation was seen as one of the key factors to enhance patients' safety at LUH and to improve quality of care. The roles of the implementation taskforce were to plan, execute, and follow up on all aspects of the implementation (teaching and training, gathering user feedback, monitoring progress of implementation, reviewing implementation plans, performing risk analysis and defining necessary resources, including hardware, staff and overall budget), as well as serving as a communication forum for all managing parties involved. The implementation taskforce was comprised of three members from the steering committee and a project manager from the IT department, who manages the technical aspect of the implementation. The chair of the steering committee was the professional leader of the implementation and was responsible for leading change management.

Risk Assessment of Implementation

The purpose of a risk assessment is to identify harmful events that may come up during the preparation and process of an implementation, to assess the potential impact of each event on the project, to estimate the

Table 16A-1. Risk Events during Preparation and Implementation of the Project

Risk Event	Likelihood (L) (1-5)	Impact (I) (1-5)	Total Risk (L x I)
Staffing of the project	5	5	25
Delays in system refinement	5	5	25
Hardware in wards not sufficient	5	5	25
Scope of the project underestimated	4	5	20
Resistance to change of work procedures in documenting nursing	4	5	20
Clinical staff do not prioritize the project well enough	4	5	20

likelihood of each event, and to identify measures to prevent these events from occurring. The risk analysis for this implementation covered six major events that were analyzed to estimate their consequences and the risk of occurrence. The total risk associated with each event was assessed by multiplying the score for likelihood and the score for impact as shown in Table 16A-1.

The risk of insufficient staffing of the project was addressed by working with top managers to ensure the support of nursing managers to prioritize the project, respect deadlines, and adjust staff schedules to accommodate the needs of the project within working hours. Those involved in the project had to dedicate a specific proportion of their time to the project, keep track of the hours put into the project, and follow the implementation work schedules. The risk of delays in system refinement (i.e., modifications to respond to user complaints during the implementation itself) were addressed by timely recording and reporting necessary alterations, careful follow-up, and prompt implementation of patches including the modifications. The risk of insufficient hardware in the wards was addressed by a comprehensive review of hardware needs and perceived benefits, followed by careful planning of acquisition, set-up, and costs. Necessary hardware had to be up and running prior to implementation kick-off. To address the risk of underestimation of project scope, all tasks were parsed into manageable pieces, strict deadlines defined, and emphasis placed on allocating sufficient resources to each task. Several measures were taken to reduce the risk of resistance to change in work procedures in nursing documentation. Care was taken to collaborate with nursing staff on changing daily work procedures and to get them involved in making work procedure guidelines. Champions or spokesmen of the change were identified in each ward, and benefits of the new work procedures were emphasized. Emphasis was placed on positive publicity of the project and to create and maintain active dialogue with all parties involved. The risk of insufficient prioritization of the project by clinical staff was addressed by providing extensive information on the project, its benefits, and the negative effect of delays. The information was relayed to staff in meetings and via newsletters and Web postings. Nursing managers and executives received the same information plus additional data on follow-up and progress.

The Implementation Plan

The process of implementing new modules into SAGA were based on Kotter's[9] most important change management processes, the compass methodology by Speculand,[10] project management processes, respective laws, and regulations. A crucial part of the implementation was to change healthcare professionals' behavior in order to create even better results in documentation. The parties of interest who together made the coalition around the implementation of the EHR are shown in Figure 16A-1. Their collaboration and communication of the urgency and vision for the EHR documentation was also critical for a success.

Implementation of the new modules in SAGA was started in pilot wards. The objectives of selecting pilot wards were to: (a) receive feedback from prospective users; (b) reduce the likelihood of resistance from staff; (c) minimize change fatigue of staff during implementation; (d) do necessary revisions on the system; (e) increase the flow of information between staff during the change; (f) review the policy and the plan of

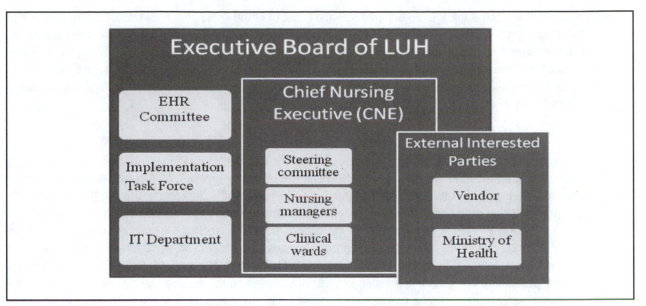

Figure 16A-1. *Organization of the Development and Implementation of the EHR at LUH*

implementation; (g) gather feedback from staff on how the implementation plan might be improved. A longer timeframe was given for the implementation in the pilot wards than when the actual implementation started in the fall of 2009.

A key strategic project milestone was to introduce the comprehensive implementation plan to the hospital management and prospective users. The objectives of that were to: (a) provide clinicians and managers with information on the importance and benefits of implementing new modules in SAGA and that the implementation is in accordance with the hospital policy on making LUH one of the best university hospitals in the Nordic countries; (b) create a group of managers and contact persons in the wards who are likely to be successful and are spokesmen of change in SAGA implementation; (c) introduce to nursing staff the organization of the implementation, reduce the resistance of nursing staff during the implementation, increase nursing staff's understanding of the role they have in the implementation, and to speed up the implementation.

Preparing for Success

The work environment at LUH needed careful preparation before the implementation of the new modules in SAGA. New work procedure guidelines were in place that addressed electronic documentation instead of paper documentation. Emphasis was on systematic real-time documentation at the point of care. The goal was to promote further safety in handling medical and nursing records and treatment of patients, promote better accessibility and communication of information regarding treatment of patients, and to minimize disruption in nursing care. Actual place of documentation was not limited to a desk but could be mobile. To accomplish that, appropriate hardware, such as wireless network and computers with acceptable memory and screen size, had to be available.

At this writing, the implementation is not completed. The key elements to success are considered to be the training and teaching of the new modules of SAGA to staff. Courses are offered and also training of staff on site. Discussions on active participation of staff in the implementation of the system, what use of it can bring to clinical practice, patient safety, flow of information, and efficiency in use of time are important. Project managers as well as representatives from all clinical divisions, nursing managers, and superusers at each ward play key roles in the implementation among nursing staff, along with support from the IT department. Support and understanding from directors and executives are also crucial for success.

The aim of the implementation is to ensure the adoption of new work procedures by all healthcare providers, improved quality of documented data, and better management of healthcare data within the patient record. As professional leaders, the nurse managers in each ward are key players in the implementation. They define the expectations of the staff and set the ground rules for what will be required of the care providers. Other key parties are those responsible for the project in each clinical division, the contact persons or champions in each ward, the project manager and the staff of the implementation taskforce. The progress of the implementation will be actively followed, and some aspects of it will need to be reevaluated and modified based on the lessons learned on the way. Changes need to be ongoing and contingency plans must be in place for unexpected events. Active participation by all parties is essential to success; positive attitude needs to be maintained as well as tolerance to constant change. Intensive support to the nursing staff is thus imperative at all steps of the implementation.

Summary

Currently, one of the largest health IT projects in Iceland is the implementation of electronic documentation of patient care processes as part of the EHR within the university hospital. As a result, electronic data on patients' needs and nursing care of hospitalized patients in Iceland will become available for the first time. This project is one of the most important stepping stones toward the government's health policy strategy to improve service, efficiency, and progress of the citizens by use of electronic healthcare data. Nurses have played a pivotal role in this project, while important lessons regarding the interdisciplinary documentation of care have been learned. The commitment to the SAGA EHR system at a government health policy level has made it possible to bring nursing practice to a standard based on the nursing process, evidence, and standard care plans supported by a terminology standards and structured data. At the submission of this case study, we are still in process of the new SAGA rollout, and thus, it is not possible to address the anticipated benefits to nursing and patient outcomes. That will be a future report.

References

1. *OECD. Health at a Glance,* 2007. http://www.oecd.org/document/health/healthataglance. Accessed June 5, 2009.
2. Prime Minister's Office. *Iceland the e-Nation. Icelandic Government Policy on the Information Society 2008-2012;* 2008. http://eng.forsaetisraduneyti.is/information-society. Accessed July 1, 2009.
3. Law on patient records [In Icelandic], No 55/2009. http://www.althingi.is. Accessed July 1, 2009.
4. NANDA International (NANDA-I). Nursing diagnoses: *Definitions & classifications 2003-2004.* Philadelphia, PA: NANDA International; 2003.
5. Gordon M. *Nursing diagnosis: Process and application.* 3rd ed. St. Louis: Mosby Yearbook, 1994.
6. Carpenito LJ. *Nursing diagnosis: Application to clinical practice.* 8th ed. Philadelphia, PA: Lippincott, 2000.
7. Dochterman JM, Bulechek G. *Nursing Interventions Classification (NIC).* 4th ed. St. Louis: Mosby, 2004.
8. Moorhead S, Johnson, M, Maas, ML. *Nursing Outcomes Classification (NOC).* 3rd ed. St. Louis: Mosby, 2003.
9. Kotter J. *Leading Change.* Boston, Massachusetts: HRB, 1996.
10. Speculand R. *Bricks to bridges. Make your strategy come alive.* Singapore: Starlite Printers, 2006.

Case Study 16B

Finland's National EHR

By Kristiina Häyrinen, MSc; Pirkko Kouri, PhD, PHN, RN; and Kaija Saranto, PhD, RN

The Finnish Strategy Toward a Modern EHR

The Structure of the Finnish Healthcare Service System

The population of Finland is 5.3 million. Its welfare state is extensive and provides a wide range of social and healthcare services mainly funded by tax revenues. Integration between the fields of social and healthcare needs to be strengthened, however, to clarify the division of labor and to avoid duplicating of services. The responsibility for organizing healthcare services rests with the local authorities, i.e., municipalities across the country. These can either provide primary healthcare services independently or form joint municipal boards with neighboring municipalities and then set up joint health centers. They may also purchase healthcare services from other municipalities or from the private sector. Municipalities also are responsible for organizing specialist medical care for their residents. The municipalities must be members of hospital districts, which organize and provide specialist medical services for the populations in their areas. Public healthcare is supplemented by private healthcare services, which are primarily concentrated in the larger municipalities. Further, there are some private hospitals in Finland.[1,2]

The public (first) sector forms the main basis for healthcare, and the private (second) sector supplements it. The role of the third sector, volunteerism, is to complement public and private healthcare services. The voluntary contribution in Finland comprises activities, e.g., unpaid voluntary work; visiting friends; voluntary rescue services; support person services; providing first aid; hosting youth, cultural, and sports events; and common neighborly help. Voluntary work is widely accepted locally, regionally, nationally, and even internationally. Moreover, businesses are increasingly taking the third sector into account by providing financial support or use of facilities, e.g., hosting health education seminars. Some researchers have started to speak about societal responsibility of businesses, so-called corporate citizenship. In the future, as the costs of healthcare services grow, it will be crucial to take into account the meaning of volunteerism and citizen empowerment.[3,4]

National Strategies

For more than 30 years, the main strategic goals of the Ministry of Social Affairs and Health (MSAH) have been promoting health and functional capacity, making work more attractive, preventing and alleviating social exclusion, and guaranteeing functional services and reasonable income security. The strategic steering tool for MSAH to manage national social and health policy in 2008-2011 is the "Kaste Programme." The key goals of the Kaste Programme are improving the quality and effectiveness of services, as well as increasing the inclusion of the population and reducing social exclusion. These goals are to be achieved by ensuring the availability and competence of personnel, as well as by creating consistent service entities and effective operational models in social welfare and healthcare. One aim in creating effective operational models is to develop indicators that can be utilized in nursing human resources management. These indicators include data (nursing minimum data set) which nurses record in EHRs in daily practice and some other jointly defined indicators, which describe outcomes of patient care (patient safety, length of stay, and patient satisfaction) and also indicators which describe human resources well-being (days of absence due to illness, job satisfaction) and turnover of personnel. The aim is to achieve these indicators as part of a national nursing benchmarking system.[5]

The latest strategy concerning IT in health services is Finland's e-health Roadmap. The strategy is a continuation of the work with national strategies started in the middle of the 1990s. The strategy is moreover a continuation of the work accomplished during the past decade; an interest in building up an operational network for health services in Finland emerged as a part of national health project 2003-2007. Finland's national objective is to ensure access to information for those involved in care independent of time or place, in both public and private sectors. The means used to achieve this objective have included a comprehensive digitalization of patient data, development of the semantic and technical compatibility of the EHR systems with regard to the entire content of records, development of the national healthcare infrastructure and information network solutions, identification and authentication solutions and electronic signature, and also maintaining information supporting decision making on the net.[6]

Another major objective is to enable the involvement of citizens and patients to increase citizens' access to information and to ensure high-quality health information (see also Chapter 3). The aim is to set up electronic services which could be used throughout the public sector, such as an identification service or electronic services, which would help promote the well-being and health of the population or electronic services, taking advantage of social and health services such as TerveSuomi-portal or for access to their own patient/health records, as well as to information about who has accessed their patient/health records from the national eArchive. The first national electronic services will include booking of appointments, e-discussion, e-document transfer, and online consultation.[5,6] These electronic services are intended to enable the citizens to do for themselves things previously done by nurses, but they also pose challenges in making nursing documentation comprehensible to citizens. In the development work on these electronic services in healthcare, account must also be taken of development plans and the action plan for eServices and eAdministration.[7] Ideally, the EHR should also tie together data from the social and volunteer sectors. This goal has been acknowledged at the national level. Because the social sector has its own national project, i.e., the Development Project for ICT in Social Welfare,[8] cooperation between the health and social sector should increase in the future.

The Basis of Secure Healthcare Services in the Information Society

Today, healthcare is strictly regulated in Finland, both externally through legislation and internally by the practitioners themselves via ethical guidelines and professional codes of conduct. Equality as a part of patients' rights has been considered a central objective in the Finnish health policy in recent decades. The Constitution of Finland (Act 731/1999) is the legislation under which provision is made for important issues related to basic human rights in the information society. The legislation follows the international development in these issues and adapts them to national legislation. One of the most important norms is the EU Directive 95/46/EC, also known as the "The Data Protection Directive." Its objectives are to protect individual healthcare data and to ensure the free movement of such data.[9]

As the healthcare sector enters the era of knowledge management, it must have security as the foundation of the transition. With secure practices based on the law and seeking to avoid or mitigate the effects of these risks, e.g., patient data misuse, healthcare organizations can ensure that health-related knowledge is attained, stored, distributed, used, destroyed, and restored securely. The challenge in creating ethical guidelines for systems of health informatics is connected to the multiprofessional teams involved. The ethical principles relevant in the context of health informatics are the following: human dignity, autonomy, justice, beneficence and non-maleficence, and solidarity. Human dignity serves as a basis for the requirements of privacy, confidentiality, and medical confidentiality. The right to privacy means that everyone's privacy is respected. In Finland, the Personal Data File Act came into force in 1988 as the first national law concerning data protection and best data processing practices. In 1999, the Personal Data Act was introduced. This act accommodates the constitutional reform and the EU Data Protection Directive (1995) and Data Protection Act (2003), both of which aim to protect personal data and the free movement of such data. All those using personal health data must be able to show a legitimate purpose for collecting and processing such data. Access to personal health data by legitimate users requires the explicit informed consent of the data subject. Furthermore, the patient/client should have the right to participate in the design of the information and communication technology systems in healthcare, and appropriate procedures for achieving this must be developed.[10]

Implementation of a national e-health strategy has necessitated the formulation of new legislation. In 2007, a new act has passed in Finland on the electronic processing of healthcare and social welfare client data (9.2.2007/159),[11] and likewise the Act on ePrescriptions (2.2.2007/61).[12] The legislation requires healthcare organizations to join the national information system architecture. This architecture's essential services include archiving and distribution of EHRs, a national prescription database, an electronic certification service for healthcare professionals, and a maintenance service for classifications, codes, and terminology. Under the legislation, the Social Insurance Institution will maintain the following national healthcare information services: patient record registering and directory services, archive, consent management services, logging and monitoring services, and prescription database. The National Supervisory Authority for Welfare and Health (Valvira) will provide certification services for healthcare professionals and organizations, and the authority responsible for the maintenance, development, and coordination of classifications is the National Institute for Health and Welfare (THL). All public healthcare providers are required to adopt these systems and to achieve full functionality by 2011, after a four-year transition period. Private healthcare providers are only required to join the system if they want to archive EHRs electronically. The new Decree of the Ministry of Social Affairs and Health on Patient Documents was passed in 2009.[13] The decree contains mandatory provisions concerning the drawing up of patient documents and their retention and other material produced in the context of care and treatment. The new decree takes account of the legislation governing on the electronic processing of healthcare and social welfare client data.

Evolution of Patient Records

In Finland, the paper-based patient record has evolved in the form of longitudinal (cumulative) content. Documentation has evolved from physicians' notes into a multidisciplinary paper record following the changes made in the health service system. As more healthcare practitioners took part in patient care, the need for collecting data from these different healthcare professionals grew. In response, the different professional groups developed their own forms for documenting care. The lack of unified documentation led to proposals for a unified national manual patient record (MPR). Both the specialized medical care[14] and primary healthcare[15] sectors formed their own MPRs and used them for more than 30 years. The unified MPR formed a basis for the unified EHR.

The first EHR system, Finstar, was introduced in 1982 and is still in use today. In primary care, 99.1% of health centers, all hospitals, and the biggest private sector organizations used EHRs in 2007.[16] However, over the years, a number of different software applications have been built which have developed in heterogeneous ways. Moreover, there are different versions of the same software application in use in various organizations. Most of the current EHR applications are only for storing the paper form in the computer system. Additionally, they are passive, inflexible, and do not automatically support education, statistics, quality assessment, healthcare management, or continuity of care. Furthermore, the development of the EHR systems has taken place under the control of commercial software producers and has been directed only toward immediate practical solutions.[17]

The nursing care plan is usually a part of the EHR systems. In the 1990s, nurses were active in developing electronic nursing documentation. The application was separate from the EHR system and was used only by nurses. The nursing care plan, using an application named Florence, followed the nursing process model as a structure, and the Swedish VIPS (this acronym stands for, in Swedish, Well-being Integrity Prevention Safety) model[18] was used as a standard. Despite the positive attitude of the nursing facilities toward the adoption of this software, it was used in only a few organizations. Thus, the vendor ceased to maintain the software after 2000. However, the experiences of the use of structured documentation with VIPS terms was seen as a great advantage when new EHR systems were implemented.

In 2003, the core data elements of the EHR (see Figure 16B-1) were introduced as part of the national EHR project.[19] The information required for data exchange between information systems uses a standardized format. The core data are defined as the data that can be standardized. Documentation of the core data requires the use of vocabularies, nomenclatures, and classifications. The core information is the most significant information in the patient care process in different healthcare sectors, describing the patient's state of health or disease. The core information accumulates chronologically during patient care by different professionals. The aim of the core information is to provide a holistic description of the patient's health and disease history and of the care and guidance provided.

The structure of the EHR has also been developed on the basis of the well-established and widely used MPR format (see Figure 16B-2). Structure refers to the unified views (documents), main headings, and subheadings of the EHR. These headings provide the context for the core data elements. The main headings identify the part of the care process in which the core data element is documented; the core data element and unstructured text are documented under the subheading.

Now, EHR systems must be developed to achieve semantic and technical compatibility before healthcare organizations can join to the national eArchive or the national prescription database. In the national eArchive,

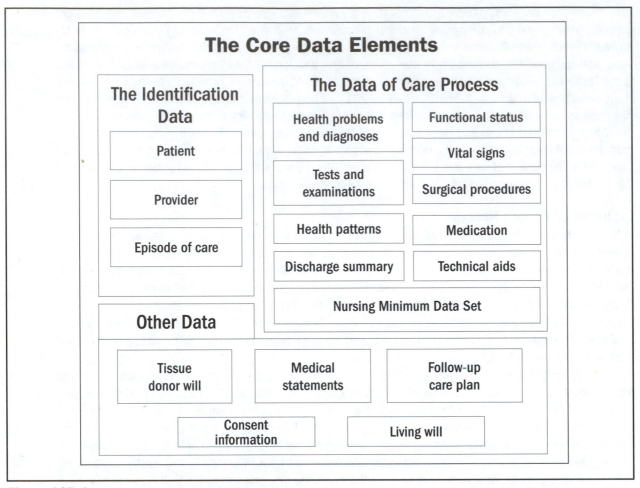

Figure 16B-1. *Core Data of EHR¹⁹. © Kristiina Hayrinen*

every healthcare organization will have its own EHR archive maintained by the Social Insurance Institution. However, the structure of all healthcare organizations' archives will be uniform, and they will be stored in a single system. Every healthcare provider will be able to access all patient archives in the system through an index service. However, patient consent will be needed to access another healthcare provider's records. In the electronic prescription system, prescriptions are sent electronically from healthcare organizations to the national database, to which pharmacies have electronic access. All providers will be obliged to write prescriptions electronically. Patients will have the option of refusing an electronic prescription and receiving a conventional paper prescription instead.

In addition, through the unified EHR system, information will be available at the national level to monitor healthcare services and the health of the population. This will enable earlier anticipation of the steering and healthcare policy measures required.

The Model of Finnish Nursing Documentation

As a part of the national EHR project, nursing documentation was developed on the National Nursing Project (2005-2008).[20] The aims of the project were (1) to harmonize and standardize nursing documentation, (2) to integrate the nursing documentation into the multiprofessional EHR, and (3) to define the Nursing Management Minimum Data Set (NMMDS).

As shown in Figure 16B-3, the model of Finnish Nursing Documentation is based on a nursing process model and the use of standardized terminology. The nursing documentation model consists of four phases of the nursing process: needs assessment, determining of nursing needs and nursing care aims, planning and delivering nursing interventions, and the evaluation of outcomes. Terminologies are used for nursing diagnosis and interventions to facilitate retrieval of data. The Finnish Classification of Nursing Diagnosis (FiCND 2.0.1) and the Finnish Classification of Nursing Interventions (FiCNI 2.0.1) are validated translations of the

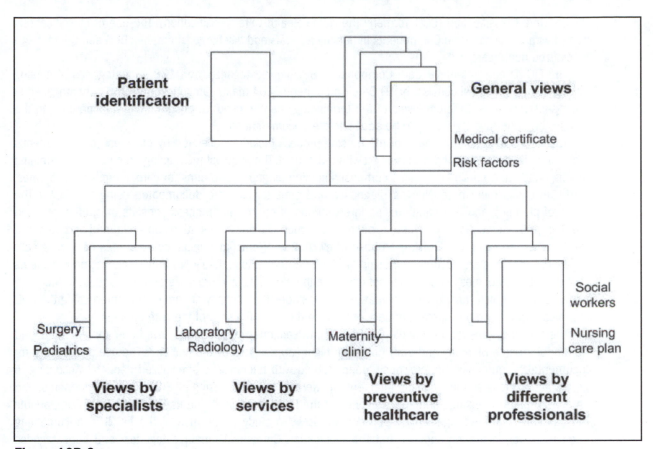

Figure 16B-2. *Structure of EHR[19]. © Kristiina Hayrinen*

STANDARDIZED NURSING DOCUMENTATION

NURSING CARE PLAN

Nursing process model	Data collection and nursing needs assessment*	Determining nursing diagnoses and nursing care aims	Planning and delivering nursing interventions	Evaluation of outcomes	Nursing discharge summary	
Classifications	-	FiCND, expected outcome	FiCNI	FiCND Care Component, outcome improved, stabilized or deteriorated	Summary of the nursing process data exploiting the structured documentation and the patient care intensity grade.	
Nursing minimum data set	Core data set*	Nursing Diagnoses	Nursing Interventions	Outcomes of care	Nursing discharge summary	Patient Care Intensity **

*Core data set include patient identification data, risk factors, reason for care, medication, medical diagnoses, laboratory tests, radiology examination, surgical prodedures, functional status and technical aids

** Patient care intensity measures in nursing process model phase: evaluation of outcomes and used: **OPC** (Oulu Patient Classification) or **OPCq** (Rafaela)

Figure 16B-3. *Standardized Nursing Documentation. Adapted from National Nursing Documentation Project in Finland 5/2005-5/2008. Available at http://www.vsshp.fi/fi/4519.*

Clinical Care Classification (CCC, formerly the Home Health Care Classification). The use of classifications started with the use of Care Components in nursing referrals and discharge summaries between primary and specialized healthcare.[21]

The FiCND consists of 19 Care Components, 88 major categories, and 178 subcategories of nursing diagnosis, and the FiCNI consists of 19 Care Components, 164 major categories; and 266 subcategories of nursing interventions. Different levels of the terminology can be used for documenting nursing care. In the EHR system, narrative text can also be added to the documentation.

The needs assessment phase of the nursing process includes collection by the nurse of the patient's health data by examining and discussing it with the patient. The phase of the nursing process for determining nursing needs and nursing care aims comprises nursing diagnosis and aims for care, along with outcomes, based on assessment data. Nursing diagnoses and aims for care are documented using the FiCND. The phase of planning and delivering nursing interventions of the nursing process consists of optimal planned and delivered interventions to achieve expected outcomes. Nursing interventions both planned and delivered are documented using the FiCNI. The phase of evaluation of outcomes includes outcomes of nursing care achieved. Outcomes are documented using the Care Components of the FiCND and an assessment made as to whether the outcomes of care were met using the three qualifiers: improved, stabilized, or deteriorated. The model for the Finnish Nursing Documentation also includes the intensity of care documented using the OPC classification and the discharge summary combining the essential data of the care episode.

The classifications for nursing diagnoses and interventions and outcomes have been implemented, and the model for care planning and daily notes are highly appreciated by the nurses.[22] The use of the FiCNI for documentation purposes has previously been studied with reference to specialized care.[23-28] According to the results of these studies, nursing interventions were documented using all FiCNI Care Components, and almost all major categories and subcategories of the FiCNI were used. The use of FiCNI Care Components and categories differed significantly between wards[23,28] A study on the use of the FiCNI in documenting medication administration showed that the Medication Component, main categories, and subcategories had indeed been used. The most frequently used intervention was "Medication Administration per os" and in almost all cases, the intervention was complemented with narrative text concerning dosage and route.[25] Nursing discharge summaries included nursing diagnoses, nursing interventions and outcomes of care, and all the Care Components of FiCNI were used.[24] The FiCNI has moreover been found suitable for the documentation of wound care.[26] In a recent study, nursing documentation was shown to be based on the nursing process. All phases of the nursing process were used, although the use of the nursing process varied between patients. Furthermore, lack of notes relating to needs assessment, the identification of nursing problems and nursing care aims, and the nursing interventions planned were noted in the documentation. The standardized terminology was used in the documentation, but inconsistencies emerged in the use of the different classifications.[27,28] Studies have also shown a need for the further development of FiCNI[23,26] and FiCND.[27,28] In educating nurses in the use of standardized nursing documentation, attention must be paid to how the nursing process model is to be followed.[27,28]

During the National Nursing Project, nurses were educated in documenting according to the nursing process model and in the use of standardized terminology. Since 2008, the eNNI Project has also been ongoing. The aim of the project is to educate nurses in healthcare organizations, as well as teachers from universities of applied science, and to root the standardized nursing documentation model in nursing practice.

Summary

Development of a national EHR system is a very demanding undertaking, entailing various challenges. According to the MSAH's national strategies, a comprehensive digitalization of patient data and development of semantic interoperability between EHR systems will be achieved by a nationally defined structure and content for the EHR. For purposes of achiving national objectives, the commitment of various stakeholders is needed. At national level the legislation has only just been amended to cover the needs of electronic data processing. Political commitment is also significant for the development of e-health. At the organizational level, the commitment of leaders is prerequisite for diffusing the standardized nursing documentation model in practice.

Nurses, like all other healthcare professionals, have been involved in the development work for the standardized nursing documentation on all levels. At the national level, nurses have networked especially under the auspices of the MSAH and the Finnish Nurses' Association. Seminars and workshops and education have been arranged. At the organizational level, expert nurses educated other nurses on the subject of the nursing process model and the use of standardized terminologies in documentation.

The nationally unified model of Finnish Nursing Documentation has been defined. The software vendors, experts, authorities, and end users are working in networks toward implementing national specifications, including the standardized nursing documentation model in EHR systems. This work has been in progress since spring 2005. Furthermore, all approved terminologies, classifications, nomenclatures and codes, including nursing classifications, have been located in a national code server and delivered through a national code server. Although the national model of Finnish nursing documentation has been implemented in EHR systems and nurses have documented according to the model, the use of nursing classifications is not yet consistent, and therefore training and continuous support are needed.

The semantic and technical compatibility enhance the transfer of data between healthcare providers to manage resources and to maintain the quality of care. For health authorities and professionals, this standardization also yields advanced opportunities to collect comparable data at the national and international level. The use of a unified national nursing documentation model and also other core data in EHRs enables the reuse of data in effective operational models, e.g., human resource management, according to national strategies. The quality of data in EHRs must be good before being reused, e.g., for health management purposes. The quality of data must be evaluated systematically.

References

1. The Ministry of Social Affairs and Health 2009. *Social and Health Services.* http://www.stm.fi/en/social_and_health_services. Accessed July 16, 2009.

2. Vuorenkoski L, Mladovsky P, Mossialos E. Finland: Health system review. *Health Systems in Transition.* 2008;10(4):1–168. http://www.euro.who.int/Document/E91937.pdf. Accessed July 8, 2009

3. Kaunismaa P. Transformations in associational life in the rural Finnish localities in 1990s. Paper presented at: ISTR Fourth International Conference; July 5-8, 2000; Dublin, Ireland. http://www.istr.org/conferences/dublin/abstracts/kaunismaa.html. Accessed July 16, 2009.

4. Zadek S. The Civil Corporation. *The New Economy of Corporate Citizenship.* London: Earthscan, 2001.

5. The Ministry of Social Affairs and Health 2008. *National Development Plan for Social and Health Care Services.* Kaste Programme 2008–2011. [in Finnish].

6. Annakaisa I, Pekka R. 2007: *eHealth Roadmap – Finland.* Ministry of Social Affairs and Health's Reports 2007:15. http://www.stm.fi/en/publications/publication/_julkaisu/1056833. Accessed July 16, 2009.

7. Ministry of Finance 2009. *Development Plans and Action Plan for eServices and eAdministration between 2009 - 2012.* Ministry of Finance publications, 6/2009.

8. *Development Project for ICT in Social Welfare 2009* [in Finnish]. http://www.sosiaaliportti.fi/tikesos. Accessed July 16, 2009.

9. Ylipartanen A. *Tietosuoja terveydenhuollossa: potilaan asema ja oikeudet henkilötietojen käsittelyssä* [in Finnish]. Helsinki: Tietosanoma; 2004:34.

10. The European Group on Ethics 1999. *Ethical Issues Of Healthcare in the Information Society.* Opinion of the European Group on Ethics in Science and New Technologies to the European Commission. http://ec.europa.eu/european_group_ethics/docs/avis13_en.pdf. Accessed June 16, 2009.

11. Act on ePrescriptions, 2.2.2007/61.

12. Act on the electronic processing of health care and social welfare client data, 9.2.2007/159.

13. Decree of the Ministry of Social Affairs and Health on Patient Documents, 30.3.2009/298.

14. Sairaalaliitto. *Terveys ja Sairauskertomus Erikoissairaanhoidossa* [in Finnish]. Printel Oy; 1991.

15. Suomen Kuntaliitto. Terveyskertomusjärjestelmä: Ohjekirja [in Finnish]. Suomen Kunnallisliitto: Helsinki ; 1982.

16. Hämäläinen P, Reponen J, Winblad I. 2009. eHealth of Finland. Check point 2008. National Institute for Health and Welfare Report 1/2009. http://www.thl.fi/thl-client/pdfs/f5ca5a36-f2c6-4e94-ae95-a7b439b1169b. Accessed June 16, 2009.

17. Hartikainen K, Kuusisto-Niemi S, Lehtonen E. *Survey of Social and Health Care Information Systems 2001* [in Finnish]. Publications of the Network of Excellence Centers; January 2002.

18. Ehrenberg A, Ehnfors M, Thorell-Ekstrand I. Nursing documentation in patient records: experience of the use of the VIPS-model. *J Ad Nurs.* 1996;24:853-867.12.

19. Häyrinen K, Saranto K. Nursing minimum data set in the multidisciplinary electronic health record. *Stud Health Technol Inform.* 2006;122:325-328.

20. *National Nursing Documentation Project in Finland.* 5/2005- 5/2008. http://www.vsshp.fi/fi/4519. Accessed June 24, 2009.

21. Ikonen H, Ensio A, Saranto K, Keskisärkkä P. The development of an electronic nursing referral system. In: Marin H, Marques E, Hovenga E, Goossen W, eds. *eHealth for all: Designing a Nursing Agenda for the Future.* Proceedings of the 8th International Congress on Nursing Informatics. Rio de Janeiro: Adis International Limited; 2003:716.

22. Ensio A, Saranto K. The Finnish classification of nursing interventions (FiCNi) – development and use in nursing. In: Clark J, ed. *Naming Nursing. Proceedings of the First ACENDIO Ireland /UK Conference.* Bern: Verlag Hans Huber; 2003:191-195.

23. Jokinen T, Ensio A, Saranto K. Using standardized terminology for nursing documentation. *Stud Health Technol Inform.* 2006;122:995.

24. Remes K. *Structured Documentation in Nursing Discharge Summaries.* Master's thesis. University of Kuopio 2006 [in Finnish].

25. Saranto K, Ensio A, Jokinen T. Patient medication— how is it documented? *Stud Health Technol Inform.* 2006;122:738-741.

26. Kinnunen UM. *Structured Data in the Wound Care Documentation.* Master's thesis, University of Kuopio; 2007. http://www.uku.fi/tht/opinnaytteet/UMKinnunengradu. pdf [in Finnish].

27. Häyrinen K, Saranto K. *The Use of Nursing Terminology in Electronic Documentation.* Connecting Health and Humans. Proceedings of NI 2009.

28. Häyrinen K, Lammintakanen J, Saranto K. *Evaluation of Electronic Nursing Documentation - Nursing Process Model and Standardized Terminologies Keys to Visible and Transparent Nursing* (submitted 2009).

Case Study 16C

National Leadership in eHealth: The Norwegian Case

By Kathryn Møelstad, RN; and Merete Lyngstad, MSN, RN

Introduction

Following the report concerning documentation from one of the university hospitals presented in the first edition of *Nursing and Informatics for the 21st Century*, a Norwegian research project, we present findings from national projects that have facilitated changes in nursing practice through informatics. This is a national effort under the leadership of the Norwegian Nurses Organisation (NNO) and includes an e-health strategy for nursing, recommendations for a nursing terminology, and a project to enable interoperability and information-sharing across levels of care (Elin-K). Norway has 4.7 million citizens with a well-developed welfare state system that is publicly financed that operates the social and healthcare system which provides every citizen the right to services. The political vision and goal is to provide the best healthcare in the world. There are two levels of care, which are governed by different aims, roles, and responsibilities, as well as differences in reimbursement structures and legislation.

Compared with other sectors in Norway, prioritization of ICT in healthcare services is not extensive. The percentage share of ICT cost is only 2 to 5%, compared with 10 to 20% in other sectors.[1] To meet the future challenges of an aging population, persons in need of long-term and coordinated services, shorter hospitalization, and increased specialization, there is a need for larger investments in ICT and e-health. The Department of Health has developed a National Strategy for ICT in the health sector.[2] Electronic systems must be developed, applied, and evaluated, while serious attention needs to be given to issues such as ethics, information security, competence and knowledge building, and contributions to patient outcomes.

This case study presents a short version of the e-health strategy and two specific initiatives; a recommendation for terminologies and a project that will make interoperability possible.

e-Health—Everyone's Responsibility and in Everyone's Interest

The Norwegian Nurses Organization's eHealth Strategy is written as a collaborative effort between the NNO and the special interest group in nursing informatics.

Nurses are the largest group of health personnel in healthcare services; they work in all areas of the sector, deliver services close to the patient 24 hours a day, and have an essential coordinating function. There are approximately 110,000 RNs in Norway, of which 89,000 are members of the NNO. This gives the organization a unique position as a political and professional force. The overall goal is that the e-health strategy will support patient safety, communication, and continuity in patient care, integrated nursing practice, leadership, through competency, and knowledge building.[2] e-Health is therefore particularly important, as nurses produce, collect, treat, and communicate large amounts of information about patients.[3]

There are many stakeholders responsible for e-health and its integration into nursing practice. Figure 16C-1 indicates the different responsible stakeholders.

Education and research institutions are responsible for building knowledge and competence about e-health through education, research, and professional development. Employers/leaders are responsible for processes of providing, implementing, and organizing application and development of e-health. The authorities should provide sufficient resources, ensure sustainable development and implementation of e-health, and prepare laws and regulations that comply with development. In addition, nurses have an individual responsibility for acquiring knowledge and staying current professionally. The strategy's overall goal is for e-health to support continuity in patient care and its integration in nursing practice, leadership, competency, and knowledge building. Several strategic goals are highlighted in Table 16C-1 as areas of concern.

The quality and results of healthcare depend on the available interactions of resources, accessibility, reliable information, and knowledge. Employers/leaders, educational and research institutions are responsible for contributing to the development and opportunities implied in e-health. Nurses must become involved and ensure that modern technology is effectively developed in the best interests of patients and family members and in nursing practice. Therefore, an updated strategy is instrumental. The increasing number of elderly

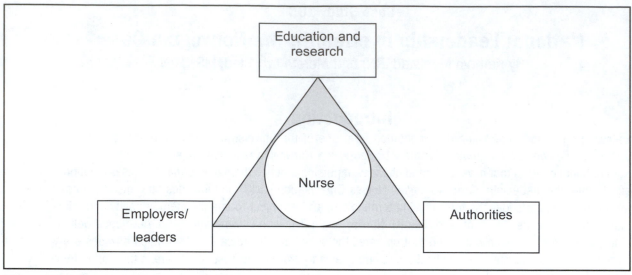

Figure 16C-1. *e-Health Stakeholders*

people and others who need long-term and complex services will create priorities in healthcare. E-health will be an important means to streamline and improve the quality of healthcare services. The NNO will be a driving force that will contribute to work for good electronic solutions to be integrated, implemented, and developed in all areas of the healthcare service. The overall goal is to ensure continuity and the provision of the best patient care.

Two areas that are described in the e-health strategy will be focused on here: terminologies and electronic interaction/interoperability.

Use of a Specific Terminology/Classification System

The NNO has for many years participated in efforts to structure and contribute to standards that ultimately contribute to patient safety and quality of care. However, in the debate, various ideological perspectives about what nursing is have surfaced. In Norway, there is limited use of classification systems or terminologies in EPR systems. It has been a significant problem that terminology systems have required translations from English. Additionally, available classification systems do not cover all aspects of nursing and problems have occurred in accommodating the need for adjustments to existing concepts so that they will fit the individual patient. Consequently, free text is widely used for all documentation as part of templates and standard texts, or to complement classification systems. The following nursing classifications and terminologies are translated and available: NANDA,[4] NIC,[5] NOC,[6] ICNP,[7] and CCC.[8] The Norwegian government is not participating in the use of SNOMED CT, and it has not been translated into Norwegian but is included in this evaluation. In addition, ICF (World Health Organisation 2001)[9] is included in this evaluation, since several rehabilitation facilities are using this as a model for care. A major EPR hospital vendor has integrated NANDA and parts of NIC in their software for the Norwegian market. One municipality (there are 30 municipalities in Norway) has integrated CCC.

When vendors implement terminologies in their EPR systems, important decisions about nursing are also being made, but without nursing's participation or a broad discussion within the nursing society. This may lead nursing leaders and educators to pay attention to the content of terminologies so they can stay in control of nursing practice. Decisions about terminologies can be made by other stakeholders, and we may end up having to use a terminology that does not include vocabulary feasible for documenting nursing.

Therefore, in accordance with the e-health strategy, a task force with 10 nurses was established in March 2008 to review and recommend terminologies. To move the work further along, the mandate was to advise the NNO on the following: *What (or which) nursing terminology(ies) is/are most appropriate in the documentation of healthcare?* Experts in many fields were recruited as task force members: researchers, leaders, health informatics experts, representing clinical practice, nursing colleges, hospitals, and community care. Their knowledge of terminologies varied and represented different perspectives in the healthcare services.

Table 16C-1. Overview of Priorities in the eHealth Strategy[2]

Priority Area	Description of Strategic Goal – Expected Achievements
Information Security	Required levels of information security, privacy and confidentiality are maintained, and development of reflected and ethically-accountable attitudes to e-health is part of the nursing service.
Terminologies	Provide relevant and reliable data about nursing processes and outcomes that contribute to knowledge development and competence-building for clinical practice.
Electronic Patient Record (EPR)	Next generation of EPR supports work processes of nurses in more timely manner, healthcare documented according to professional standards and legal requirement. Sufficient access to ICT equipment, and nurses contribute premises for design and development of EPR.
Electronic Interaction - interoperability	Electronic information exchange and interaction are formalized within the health service and levels of care. User-friendly electronic interaction solutions are developed and available in all healthcare services.
Quality and Staffing Education, Professional Development and Research	Knowledge-based clinical practice through application of e-health. Access to electronic professional support and further developed sources of knowledge applied as tools and measures in knowledge and competence-building and clinical practice. Knowledge and professional development plans in e-health for clinical nurses, faculty, and researchers are developed and implemented. Bachelor and master degree programs have a framework and professional study programs contain descriptions of expected knowledge and competence in e-health after completed education
Telemedicine Solutions and Patient Participation	Telemedicine solutions are developed and implemented in nursing service. Electronic tools for interaction with patient and family members are available to gather patient's experiences and reactions regarding symptoms and illness experiences for participation and directly, as systematic feedback to health personnel by means of e-health.

The goal was to provide a future-oriented recommendation of a terminology or classification system that contributes to high-quality nursing documentation and continuity in patient care. To this daunting challenge, an important condition was that the recommendation(s) involve the whole healthcare system, and thus, required the task force to consider the appropriateness that goes beyond hospitals to community care. The task force was given one year to complete the work.

The reviewed terminologies and classifications systems may be labeled as interface terminologies or combinatorial.[3] The interface terminologies are enumerated terminologies with prepared concepts, optimized for use by the clinicians in their documentation efforts.[10] Combinatorial terminologies are more flexible, combine words from different axes, and require computer support.[7]

A literature review led to a list of the 10 most important criteria for reviewing the available terminologies. The criteria are based on international research[3,11-15] and national policy documents.[16,17]

The task force focused on the process of reviewing literature, taking a close look at the criteria described in Table 16C-2. The mandate had to be discussed thoroughly several times during the process and was

Table 16C-2. Criteria and Common Interpretation

Criteria	Explanation, Interpretation
Comprehensiveness and completeness	Sufficient depth and level of detail, and sufficient coverage/amount of concepts to provide a detailed description of nursing practice and all episodes of care, including hospitalization, home healthcare, etc.
Further development of the terminology, ownership and participation	Influencing further development of the system, planned maintenance and version control. Ownership has an influence on participation and further development.
Patient perspective and participation	In the future, the patient will control information in the patient journal; it is therefore imperative that systems allow this and terminologies contribute to this perspective.
Synonyms	Alternative terms and words are absolutely necessary to provide cultural differences, both local and national. It also makes it possible to use patient-friendly terms.
Cross-reference	This provides the possibility of mapping one terminology to another.
Compositionality	The possibility of combining different terms to make a complex statement.
Unique codes	There should be a unique coding system in which no other concept has the same code.
Attributes	Modifiers and qualifiers provide flexibility.
Definitions	Concise explanation of meaning.
Hierarchy	Multiple parents or children as clinically appropriate.

somewhat redefined in the beginning. The NNO's mandate was strict, requiring a conclusion about a specific terminology and not just a list of criteria. Deciding which criteria were important and coming to a consensus was a major achievement for all involved. In line with Norwegian debate, flexibility and usability are important factors, and the criterion embeds these as well. In addition, patient perspective and influence are very strong; although this was not described in any of the reviewed international articles, we added this element to the criteria. To support the recommendation to the NNO, the task force scored the different terminologies and classification systems against the criteria.

The terminologies were scored to the 10 criteria, with each criterion on a scale from 0 to 3, for a maximum of 40 points. The scale describes the number that was deemed appropriate to the criterion: 0 – none, 1 – little, 2 – middle, 3 – large. Each terminology was judged by two of the task force members, then discussed in a task force meeting, and adjusted according to the other terminologies. For example, none of the terminologies were judged as being complete. The terminologies that the task force evaluated appear below, numbered by rank:

1. International Classification in Nursing Practice
2. Systematized Nomenclature of Medicine – clinical terminology
3. Nursing Outcome Classification
4. Nursing Interventions Classification
5. Clinical Care Classification
6. International Classification for Functioning, Disability, and Health
7. North American Nursing Diagnosis Association

The evaluation shows that the reference terminologies ICNP and SNOMED CT have an advantage over the other terminologies when using the criteria we proposed. ICNP can provide the flexibility needed in future EPR systems.[7]

The investment in terminologies is long-term. Important next steps are to convince the national health authorities that terminologies are important, that ICNP is a good investment that will reap benefits in the future, and make sure the vendors build ICNP into their systems. Nursing leaders and politicians need to know the patient problems nurses are addressing, what interventions they perform, and patient outcomes that are the result of nursing care. We believe that ICNP will be an important tool for documenting nursing and achieving knowledge about patient care. ICNP will build a nursing vocabulary that will contribute to interoperability. The use of terminologies in a certain care setting will only have a limited amount of value if interoperability is not achieved. Different levels of healthcare must include the possibility of electronic communication. Fast-track patient information to healthcare personnel and facilities represents a major change in work processes and patient safety.

In the Elin-K project, nursing vocabulary requirements are defined and will again contribute to continuity and cooperation in healthcare services.

Interoperability: Improvement of Information Flow Through ELIN-K

There is a growing elderly population in Norway, which accounts for more than one-third of all hospital admissions. As mentioned earlier, there are two different levels of healthcare—hospitals and community care. The community care system is made up of home care, nursing homes, public health nurses, and GPs, among others. Patient hospitalization has an average length of stay of 4 to 5 days. Over the years, there have been fewer hospital beds and increased treatment from the community healthcare system in earlier stages of illness. Studies show that nurses in community care do not receive accurate written information when needed, and when they do receive information, it may be wrong or deficient.[18,19] Oral tradition prevails, which can create a source of misunderstanding, and the lack of formalization and standards for content and structure contributes to a risk that the information exchanged is not complete.[20,21] Health professionals need the necessary information to ensure that patients receive proper healthcare.

To meet the national e-health strategy goal[2] for interoperability between healthcare levels, the project Elin-K was established.[22] The acronym "ELIN-K" can be translated as electronic interchange of health information in community care. This project focuses on collaboration internally, as well as across levels of care in the healthcare system. The project develops systems for interoperability that enable electronic communication and seamless transmission of health information between community care, hospitals, and GPs. The vision for the Elin-K project is this: correct health information, to the right person, at the right time. ELIN-K is a joint venture, owned by NNO and KS (the Norwegian Association of Local and Regional Authorities which is the organization for all the municipalities in Norway), and financed by the NNO, KS, National ICT, Innovation Norway and The Directorate of Health. The vendors must contribute 50% of the development costs, but they own the IT-solutions and can sell them and thereby gain profit.

The Elin-K project has focused so far on the communications needs between nurses in the community care system and general practitioners and hospitals, but nurses also collaborate with pharmacies, centers for assistive devices, laboratories, and others (see Figure 16C-2). In the future, the project may be expanded to deal with these issues.

The goal is to develop, implement, test, and achieve widespread use. To reach these goals the electronic healthcare communication solutions must be based on common standards, common professional content, and structure.

The progress in ICT systems has often been driven by technology development and vendors. This Elin-K project transforms this process, since health professionals lead the development and implementation of ICT-systems (see Figure 16C-3). Elin-K is focused and designed on the premise that community healthcare professionals describe the requirements for the electronic interchange of healthcare information according to structure, content, workflow and presentation. This has been done in user groups and an editorial group together with technology professionals from KITH, the Norwegian Center for Informatics in Health and Social Care. KITH is a limited company owned by the Ministry of Health and Care Services (70%), Ministry of Labour

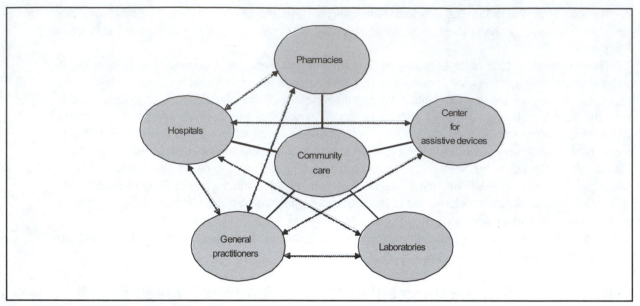

Figure 16C-2. *Cooperation from the Community Care Point of View*

and Inclusion (10.5%), and the Association for Municipalities (19.5%). The company has responsibility for activities related to standardization and coordination of ICT in healthcare.

The vendors then develop the EPR systems in collaboration with health professionals. The systems are tested, piloted, and finally approved. The process is never completed, the needs change, and technology changes with new possibilities. This method called *user steered ICT-projects* is developed by Innovation Norway.

The pre-project has focused on development of functional requirements and standards. The following questions had to be answered:

- **Content** – what information do the recipients need to provide good healthcare?
- **Structure** – what information should come first and last, in which format?
- **Presentation** – in which way can the information be presented so that it is highly readable and easy to understand?
- **Workflow** – how can the functionality be designed to support the workflow and be user friendly?

This work has resulted in common requirements and standards that have been presented to the vendors. In the main project, the vendors have developed and implemented the solutions in the EPR systems. The solutions have then been tested and piloted in seven municipalities, four hospitals, and twelve GP offices, and will soon be ready for widespread use. ELIN-K contributes to qualities, such as secure and precise health information, many-to-many communication, better workflow, and reuse of structured information from and to the EPR, highly readable presentation, and the reduction of paper use. The NNO is now in the process of expanding the project to public health and follow up of newborns after hospitalization.

Conclusion

This case study illustrates examples of e-health important to nurses. The NNO's e-health strategy helps steer and influence policymaking, internally and externally. The NNO has made major contributions to development and innovation with these projects. This has been necessary to achieve progress for nursing services in this area. There is reason to believe that healthcare quality is improved according to content of documentation, more written documentation and available information, and reduced risk of mistakes. Efficiency is also improved by better work flow. There is a lot of work remaining to implement this into the entire healthcare system. And it will take time, patience, and extreme optimism, but these projects contribute to continuity of care and better healthcare for our citizens.

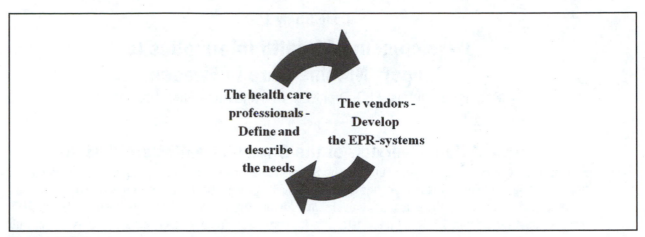

Figure 16C-3. *Process of Development of the Electronic Patient Records-systems in This Project*

Acknowledgments

We would like to thank Dr. Anne Moen for initiating this paper and Mette Ramstad Dønåsen, director of Department of Professional Policy Issues at the Norwegian Nurses Organisation, for making our contribution possible.

References

1. Norwegian Nurses Organisation. *Ethical Guidelines* (2007). (see http://www.icn.ch/global/) Accessed November 18, 2009.
2. Norwegian Nurses Organisation, *eHealth Strategy: Everyone's Responsibility and in Everyone's Interest,* 2008. http://www.epsu.org/r/23. Accessed November 18, 2009.
3. Moen A, Henry SB, Warren JJ. Representing nursing judgements in the electronic health record. *J Adv Nurs.* 1999;30(4):990-997.
4. North American Nursing Diagnosis Association. (2002) (Norwegian Version 2003) Sykepleiediagnoser: Definisjoner & klassifikasjon 2001–2002.
5. McCloskey J, Bulechek G. Nursing Intervention Classification, 2004, Norwegian version; 2006 Klassifikasjon av sykeleieintervensjoner (NIC) Akribe.
6. Moorhead Johnson og Maas. *Nursing Intervention Classification,* 2005 (Norwegian version 2007) Klassifikasjon av sykepleieresultater (NOC) Akribe.
7. *International Classification for Nursing Practice.* Version 1, 2005. Norwegian Version 2008: www.icn.ch/icnp. Translations. Accessed September 28, 2005.
8. Saba V. Clinical Care Classification System. Version 2.0. 2003. www.sabacare.com. Accessed November 2, 2008.
9. World Health Organization. International Classification of Functioning Disability and Health, 2001, Geneva.
10. von Krogh G, Nåden D. Nursing-specific model of EPR documentation: organizational and professional requirements. *J Nurs Scholarsh.* 2008;First Quarter;40,1.
11. Bishop CW. A name Is not enough. *MD Comput.* 1990,7:210-215.
12. Computer-based Patient Record Institute. *Computer-based Patient Record System. Description of Functionality.* CPRI; 1996. www.cpri.org/resources/docs/functions.html. Accessed October 1, 2009.
13. Chute C, Cohn S, Campebell J. A framework for comprehensive health terminology systems in the United States: Development Guidelines, Criteria for Selection, and Public Policy Implications. *JAMIA.* 1998;4:6.
14. Hardiker N, Hoy D, Casey A. Standards for Nursing Terminology. *JAMIA,* 2000:7(6):523-528.
15. Goossen WT. Cross-mapping between three terminologies with the international standard nursing reference terminology model. *Int J Nurs Terminol Classif.* 2006;ct-Dec;17(4):153-64.
16. National ICT Strategy, Te@mwork 2007 Electronic Interaction in Health and Social Sectohelse-og sosialsektoren Statlig strategi 2004-2007.
17. Norwegian Parliament, Health Personnel Act 1999. www.lovdata.no/. Accessed October 2, 2009.
18. Hellesø R. Ord over skigard – informasjonsutveksling og samhandling mellom sykepleiere i spesialist- og kommunehelsetjenesten før og etter innføring av elektronisk pasientjournal. Det medisinske fakultet, 2005 Universitetet i Oslo.
19. Paulsen B, Grimsmo A. God vilje - dårlig verktøy. Om samhandling mellom sykehus og kommunale omsorgstjenester ved utskriving av omsorgstrengende eldre. Trondheim: SINTEF; 2008.
20. Jensen SA, Øien T, Jacobsen G, Johnsen R. Feil i medikamentkortene - en helserisiko? Tidsskrift for Norsk Lægeforening. 2003;123(24):3598-3599.
21. Bakken K, Larsen E, Lindberg PC, Rygh E, Hjortdahl P. Mangelfull kommunikasjon om legemiddelbruk i primærhelsetjenesten. Tidsskrift for Den Norske Lægeforening. 2007;127(13-14):1766-1769.
22. Christensen T, Grimsmo A; Development of functional requirements for electronic health communications: preliminary results from the ELIN project, Informatics in Primary Care, 2005; 13:203-208.

Case Study 16D

Development of Health Informatics to Support Nursing Care in Sweden

By Margareta Ehnfors, PhD, Dipl NEd, RN; and Anna Ehrenberg, PhD, RN

Introduction—Overview of the Swedish HealthCare System

Similar to that of other developed countries, the Swedish healthcare system is facing increasing demands from an aging population. These demands are especially challenging because Sweden is one of the top ten countries in the world with the oldest population.[1] In addition, Sweden has reduced its hospital staff by 20% over the past decade. In 1992, all responsibilities for care of elderly and disabled individuals, along with 55,000 healthcare employees, were transferred from county councils to local municipalities. To cope with this dramatic change, improved efficiency in hospital care has resulted in a 25% decrease in the average length of stay in the hospital. Thus, a greater extent of patient care is now provided in primary and home care. Hospitals have been enabled to increase specific procedures, e.g., cataract outpatient surgery, a treatment available in Sweden to more people than in any other European Union country. Swedish healthcare costs are approximately 50% per person of the costs of the same healthcare in the United States and lower than in most other EU countries. Sweden also has the lowest proportion of hospital beds per inhabitant in the EU.

Nevertheless, the increase in healthcare costs has been considerable during the past few years, having increased approximately 45% (a figure similar to that of many other countries). Cost constraints have a substantial impact on the working environment and staff conditions, as well as on reduced accessibility to healthcare services.[2]

Despite their vital importance to keep up with quality of care in a changing healthcare environment, EHR systems that actually facilitate care processes and communication of information between healthcare providers are still not in place. Systems for continuous measurement and evaluation of healthcare productivity, efficiency, and quality are also largely lacking. There are increasing amounts of information in healthcare: for instance, in 1971, a four-week Swedish hospital stay for hip surgery generated three sheets of paper; in 1984, this same surgery generated 18 sheets, and in 1999, a shorter stay of 10 days generated 34 sheets of record information.[3] Although the amount of clinical data is continuously increasing, the resources or routines to make proper use of this information are limited. An efficient use of a well-functioning EHR system has the potential to solve many of these problems.

The Swedish healthcare system is mainly tax-financed. Thus, the potential for expansion of standardized ICT solutions in healthcare is relatively favorable, and Sweden has one of the most developed ICT support systems for healthcare in the world. Although the state has the responsibility for healthcare policy, responsibility for healthcare delivery falls to the regions and local county councils (N=21), and municipalities (N=290). The extensive decentralized healthcare system and the division of the management of healthcare between regions, county councils (hospitals and primary healthcare centers), and municipalities (care of elderly and of mentally and physically disabled individuals) have resulted in innumerable ICT solutions that are not interoperable or compatible for data exchange. This lack of standards contributes to fragmented patient information, loss of patient data, non-accessible data, and high risk of errors in healthcare. However, a national ICT strategy has been implemented and is on its way to being operational.

Current Situation of EHR in Swedish Healthcare

The development of the EHR was first initiated in the 1980s in some Swedish counties. The estimated occurrence of EHR is close to 100% in primary healthcare, 92% in psychiatric care, 88% in hospital care, and somewhat less in municipality care. Although collaboration in patient care is taking place daily between primary healthcare, hospitals, and psychiatric care, to date only four counties have an integrated seamless system that operates across institutions. The transfer of information between county councils (e.g., hospital care) and municipality care is problematic as there are no uniform solutions at local level. To overcome this barrier, most counties have implemented electronic transfer systems for coordinated care-planning.[4]

Despite expected improvements in efficiency in electronic information management, in a consumer survey of 2,000 healthcare units, it was found that users reported serious problems with the EHR.[5] The major criticisms are summarized in the following key points:

- Users are not satisfied with the systems but appreciate the shift from paper-based records.
- Some systems focus on the hospital organization, rather than on the patient.
- Disruption in healthcare is caused by many incompatible systems, leading to inefficient use of resources; staff has to log in to different systems to complete tasks.
- Integrity of the patient/individual obstructs transfer between caregivers.
- Security log-ins are complicated.
- Systems are not very flexible.
- Implementation of systems is often flawed, marked by low end-user involvement.
- Evaluations of user satisfaction are not conducted.

Accessibility and security issues are crucial factors in the development of the EHR. There are, however, conflicts between the need for security and easy access for professionals and patients. Swedish law allows the transfer of individual health data between caregivers only with the consent of the patient, which is now emphasized in the new Patient Data Act. This strict requirement for patient consent leads to risks of omissions and errors, particularly in the care of elderly and cognitively impaired patients. A few projects to make patient records accessible to patients over the Internet have been initiated to promote patient participation in care.

Multiprofessional Work toward Integrated EHR

Currently, there is no multidisciplinary professional Swedish classification system for healthcare. Such a classification system is needed to support quality assurance efforts and to capture all types of healthcare data to ensure appropriate resource allocation. The work of professional groups, e.g., nurses, physiotherapists, and occupational therapists, is still partly invisible in patient records. Therefore, the National Board of Health and Welfare initiated a project to describe a multidisciplinary professional collaborative work on classification development and to provide suggestions for an organizing structure that would capture interventions made by different healthcare services. Under this umbrella, the professional groups have reached a common understanding about the use of the International Classification of Functioning, Disability, and Health (ICF) as a unifying framework. This approach was seen as fruitful in overcoming professional differences and supporting consensus about the use of a common language. Nursing interventions have also been developed based on the ICF and are included in the classification and are available for use in healthcare.

Development and Research in Nursing to Facilitate EHR Progress

To achieve optimal value from the implementation of EHR, it is imperative to outline the process of care, to document outcomes of care, and to ensure that records contain valid and reliable information. Because Swedish law mandates nurses as responsible for recording health data, the quality of nursing documentation has been the focus of several research projects. Nurses are compelled to record essential information about the reasons for care, the patient's diagnosis, planned and implemented interventions, and outcomes of care, all of which correspond to the five phases of the nursing process.

Development of ICT in healthcare is currently one of five prioritized areas of research, according to the Swedish Society of Nursing. On a national level, expert nurses and researchers have worked together in professional organizations for almost two decades—first to promote the training of the diagnostic reasoning process and, more recently, for the development of the entire nursing informatics (NI) knowledge base. There is a national professional interest organization closely linked to the national nurses' organization, with members throughout the country. Areas of shared interest include networking, decision support, terminology, nursing diagnoses and interventions, education, and the strategic influence of decisions in the health informatics field. Swedish nurses and nurse researchers have contributed considerably to EHR progress by developing terminology and models for documentation and by studying how nursing data are represented in health records.

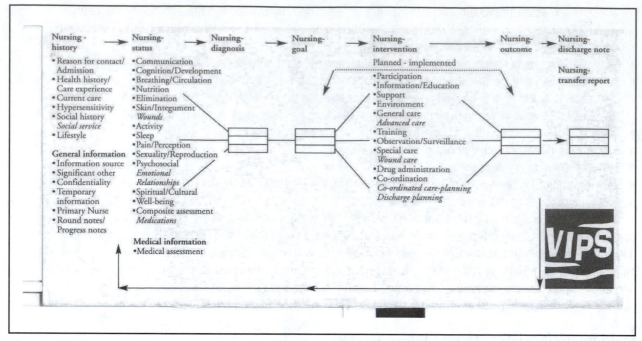

Figure 16D-1. *VIPS Model for Nursing Documentation Showing Terminology and Nursing Process*

Terminology

The VIPS Model

For more than 20 years, it has been mandatory for registered nurses to keep patient records, and this requirement has sparked efforts to apply the nursing process for recording.[6] A research-based model for nursing documentation, called the VIPS model (an acronym for the Swedish spelling of Well-being, Integrity, Prevention, and Safety), was developed to conceptualize essential elements of nursing care, to clarify and facilitate systematic thinking, and to capture nursing recording.[7,8] The VIPS model is based on the structure of the nursing process and focuses on patients' functioning in daily life activities, rather than on patho-physiological problems or organ systems, and it facilitates a process-oriented, patient-centered approach. Experience from its use has shown that the model has good content validity in many areas of nursing care, including stroke, dementia, geriatric, pediatric, peri-operative, and psychiatric care.[8] The VIPS model is used for recording everyday nursing and individual care planning throughout Sweden, as well as in Denmark, Norway, Estonia, and Latvia. Several software applications for computerized patient records have included this nursing documentation model. Also, the VIPS model is taught in most nursing undergraduate programs in Sweden, and nursing textbooks are organized according to the VIPS model.

The documentation model consists of key words on two levels (see Figure 16D-1). As shown in Figure 16D-1, the first level corresponds to the nursing process model with the following key words: Nursing History, Nursing Status, Nursing Diagnosis, Nursing Goal, Nursing Intervention, Nursing Outcome, Nursing Report, and Nursing Discharge Note. The second level of key words consists of subdivisions comprising three categories: Nursing History, Nursing Status, and Nursing Intervention. For every key word, explanatory text and prototypes are given.

The terms used in the model are a synthesis between clinically oriented everyday nursing language and internationally recognized, professional terms. Well-known terms with distinct meanings in health services were chosen, including Nursing Status and Nursing Diagnosis. The term *Nursing Status* signifies the patient status from a nursing perspective; the term was chosen for practical reasons in that it could be more easily identified when appearing together with medical notes in the EHR. Implementation of the VIPS model has resulted in significant improvements in nurses' use of the nursing process as their documentation framework in nursing home care in municipalities[9] and in hospital care.[10]

Quality of Nursing Documentation

Several Swedish studies have described the quality and comprehensiveness of data in nursing documentation in patient records. There are a number of studies on nursing documentation in a variety of areas, such as hospital care,[10] nursing home care,[9] pressure ulcer care,[11] pain management,[12] primary healthcare,[13] leg ulcer care,[14] and care of patients with chronic heart failure.[15,16] The findings from these studies reveal several important flaws in the recording of specific assessment and interventions, as well as poor adherence to current clinical guidelines. However, knowledge about the accuracy and reliability of nursing data in the records is limited, and is also the case from an international perspective. Nevertheless, there are considerable expectations for data from EHRs to be readily available to support healthcare decisions, such as quality improvements, budgeting, and staffing. One Swedish study explored the accuracy of pressure ulcer recording in a large university hospital before and after implementation of an EHR. With paper-based health records, the overall prevalence of pressure ulcers obtained by record auditing was 14.3% compared with 33.3% when two nurses examined the patients' skin.[17] Four years later, after implementing EHR with templates for pressure ulcer care, improvements were found in the coherence in patients' condition and record content. There were 21.6% recorded pressure ulcers and 30.0% found by physical examination of patients.[18] Additional studies are needed in specific areas of nursing care to develop the use of EHRs for decision support and to ensure reliable data for evaluation of care quality.

Evidence-based Decision Support Integrated in the EHR

To base their practice on evidence and to generate evidence from the data captured through clinical practice, nurses need easy access to high-quality patient data, as well as to expert knowledge databases, e.g., research-based clinical guidelines in usable formats. The overwhelming amount of healthcare information, increasing time constraints on providers, and the exponentially growing scientific knowledge are obviously too immense for a single nurse to manage. EHR opens new possibilities for integrating knowledge and decision support, so they are readily available to clinicians when needed.

With the purpose to support clinical decisions, facilitate documentation, and, ultimately, to ensure quality in nursing care, Swedish nurses have been involved in developing standard care plans. Considerable effort has been invested in many parts of healthcare to develop standard care plans from clinical guidelines for specific patient groups and common care procedures. The intention with the standard care plans is to provide a readily available evidence-based support based on research and clinical experience. The National Board of Health and Welfare initiated a national survey with the objective to give an overview of the prevalence, design, and quality of existing care plans.[19] The findings showed that few standard care plans were based on reviews of the current knowledge within the area. This finding demonstrates the difficulties in producing sound guidance for clinical decision making. As such, compilation of knowledge is labor intensive, and national and international collaboration is needed in the development of decision support for large groups of patients and prevalent nursing care needs. Also, standard care plans or clinical guidelines need to be integrated in clinical information systems. Effects of implementing medical computerized decision-support systems in patient records were assessed in a systematic review of randomized controlled trials.[20] Enhanced performance of physicians was shown in most studies. A systematic review of trials that tested the results of computerized decision-support systems for physicians showed significant correlation on improved practice and decision support with the following characteristics: automatic access to support in the work process, availability at the point of care, and electronic applications.[21] Although research in this area is beginning to happen within nursing, there are only a few studies available on the impact of clinical decision-support systems on nursing performance. However, early indications show improvements in nursing performance and clinical judgment with the use of computerized decision-support systems.[22]

Informatics in Nursing Education

Today, almost all undergraduate nursing programs in Sweden include NI competencies in the curricula, covering terminology and documentation. In many healthcare organizations, nurses participate in shorter NI programs as part of their continuing education. One important aim for the near future is basic informatics training for all healthcare personnel. To achieve this, there is a crucial need for faculty and healthcare managers trained in informatics competencies.[23]

A National Strategy for E-health in Sweden

Today, the use of ICT within the healthcare sector in Sweden varies greatly and is neither developed nor used to its full potential in activities such as tailoring personalized healthcare to meet the patient's needs, enhancing the efficiency of healthcare, or optimal cooperation and planning between stakeholders. Although the access to technology is high in Swedish healthcare—there is a mean of 1.22 employees per computer—the main problem is that many of the systems cannot communicate with each other. The Swedish government has set goals for establishing a high-speed information infrastructure for all regions of the country within a few years.[24]

A National Strategy for e-health with the ultimate purpose to provide safe, accessible health and social care of high quality, based on public need, has been established in Sweden.[25] The strategy has three main objectives: to develop confidence in IT, to increase levels of competence in using the technology, and to make information about various social services available to all citizens. The government also supports private enterprises to reach these objectives, as well as other ICT-related goals. Since 2005 in Sweden, there has been a National Steering Committee for ICT in the Health Care and Social Services.

Six Action Areas within the National Strategy for e-Health

1) Laws and Regulations

- **Bringing laws and regulations into line with extended use of ICT** is highly important. To help meet this goal, a new Patient Data Act went into effect in July 2008. This act allows health and social care professionals to digitally access a person's record from different care providers in the medical and social care system. It also allows the patient/citizen to determine, upon mutual consent, who is to be given access to their medical record. Citizens will also have digital access to their own information and the rights to view a log showing what personnel have had access to their record. Confidence in ICT also implies that individuals must trust that when information is retrieved, it is done in a secure manner, and the data are not available for others to use. The use of electronic signatures will facilitate information security and integrity of the individual's data.

2) Information Structure

- **Creating a common national information structure** because uniform, consistent descriptions of activities to be supported by ICT are crucial to the development of supportive, interoperable ICT solutions. An overall activity analysis is being undertaken as part of the National Information Structure project.
- **An architecture steering group** on applied information structure has been established that, in collaboration with the National Board of Health and Welfare, will design an applied information structure for care documentation based on a National Information Structure.
- **A national interdisciplinary terminology** includes recommendations and standards setting for concepts and terms, using national and international classifications, and the international nomenclature system SNOMED CT. The system adapts terminology for use in a digital environment. Translated into Swedish and adapted to Swedish conditions, it will help generate less ambiguous and more measurable information.
- **Care information in the population register** will improve the quality and service level of information exchange between the care system and the Swedish register of its population. It will lead to greater patient safety and better service, as well as boost the efficiency of patient administration and reduce resource consumption.
- **National format for e-prescriptions** will develop, establish, and support a national e-Prescription format adapted to the basic requirements and regulations currently being established for care information management.

3) A Common Technical Infrastructure

Creation of a common and overarching technical infrastructure will facilitate communication, access, and the sharing of sensitive information between involved and authorized healthcare providers. Citizens' contacts with health and social care will also be simplified. Personnel and managers in healthcare and social services will have better access to national registers and databases to facilitate reporting and communication.

- **SJUNET** is a national network for all digital communication in the care sector, building a platform for secure communication over organizational boundaries and geographical distances.

- **The Health Services Address Registry**—the information on personnel duties and tasks supplied by the catalogue services is a basis for individual authorization to register and to read confidential information.

- **Secure ICT in health services** provides the framework needed for secure communication of sensitive information as a national service responsible for issuing e-certificates. These enable care professionals to confirm their identity and authorization.

- **Basic services in information maintenance** is responsible for supplying the role and authorization management services for secure information handling across organizational boundaries in the care sector, as required under the Patient Data Act.

- **Standards for electronic interoperability in healthcare and social services** provide a regulatory framework for the creation and interpretation of information so it can be exchanged and used jointly by the health and social services without risk of misunderstanding. More reliable, clear, and useful information will help improve patient safety and reduce resource consumption.

- **Video/distance meeting service** for up to 12 people/workplaces taking part in a video conference at the same time will mean time and cost savings for personnel and more effective and efficient health services to our elderly population.

4-5) Supportive and Interoperable ICT Systems

The objective is to facilitate ICT systems with good interoperability that allow the exchange or sharing of information, that are user-friendly for personnel and do not disturb the dialogue with patients, that provide information and knowledge support to safe and secure medical treatment, and that can communicate with surrounding ICT systems.

- **National patient summary** will provide access to safer and more comprehensive support data for the care of patients, facilitate follow-up of care measures, and reduce the cost of locating and reading important patient information. The service is intended to facilitate access to important information about patients who have received care from other care providers, including other county councils, private providers, and municipalities. In the long-term, authorized care providers using these services will be able to locate and read relevant patient information, regardless of where in the country or in which part of the care sector it is located. The service will provide information about current care contacts, chronic diseases, warnings about hypersensitivity to drugs, etc., and current medication regimens.

6) Accessibility for Citizens and Personnel

This covers many initiatives, some of which have been in service for years and some which are currently under development.

- **Care Online** is a gate for citizens who want information and help in choosing the right care solution. The service will boost care accessibility, extend better service to patients and the general public, improve public health, enable care to be compared in different parts of the country, and contribute to more efficient use of collective care resources. The objective here is the development of a highly useful, accessible, and easy-to-use service for citizens and care personnel.

- **Care Online – Personal Services.** A part of Care Online, My Care Contacts will, in due course, be incorporated into the base platform produced. It will enable citizens to reschedule appointments online, apply to renew a prescription, ask questions, and obtain advice. It will also reduce the workload on healthcare staff.

- **Web-based Youth Family Planning Clinic** is a national clearing house and a development and support service for young people aged 13–25 years that provides reliable, easy-to-read information and improved accessibility and advisory services on issues that may be perceived as sensitive.

- **The Handbook – online information, primarily for nurses** is designed to help improve patient safety and care quality; this service provides scientifically- and professionally-based information on overall guidelines for care work and descriptions of practical application in different areas and situations.

- **The <1177.se web Site>** provides up-to-date, easy-to-read, fact-checked texts on frequently asked questions by patients and members of the public. The service promotes health and advances knowledge of health and medical care among patients and the general public. It is part of the health services and provides information ahead of, during, and after care. It also strengthens the patient's position and involvement. Images and animations are available for children of pre-school and primary school age. It has existed for 10 years. The site had one million visitors per month in 2008. THE 1177 – TELEPHONE ADVISORY SERVICE is another national health helpline (1177) that gives citizens around-the-clock access to advice by nurses supported by expert advisory services. The aim of the service is to increase accessibility to care information and guide members of the public to the right care provider.

Summary: Future Needs

In conclusion, Sweden is moving rapidly toward better informatics support for improved efficiencies and effective healthcare. However, we still need to optimize development of the EHR, including the following prerequisites:

- Software support for healthcare processes.
- Multidisciplinary professional integration in EHRs without compromising the unique contributions of each healthcare profession.
- Development and implementation of computerized decision-support systems for bedside use, including the integration of research-based knowledge in patient records.
- Decisions on and development of recommendations for a national curriculum for ICT in all healthcare education programs.

Nurses have a key role to play in this development, as they have a major responsibility for healthcare support to individuals and families in all phases of the lifespan. Swedish nurses' knowledge in health informatics is still limited and needs to be a priority for nursing educational programs to make the best use of informatics in the care of patients.

References

1. http://www.mapsofworld.com/world-top-ten/world-top-ten-countries-with-oldest-population-map.html. Accessed October 25, 2009.
2. Landstingsförbundet, Kommunförbundet. *Swedish Health Care in Transition: resources and results with international comparisons* [in Swedish]. http://uno.svekom.se/brsbibl/kata_documents/doc35570_1.pdf. Accessed February 3, 2005.
3. National Board of Health and Welfare. Omfattningen av administration i vården [The extent of administration in health care] [in Swedish]. http://sos.se/FULLTEXT/0077-001/0077-001.htm. Accessed February 2005.
4. Jerlvall L, Pehrsson T. IT-stöd i landstingen – December 2008 (*IT support in the county councils – December 2008*). Unpublished report. In Swedish.
5. Users Award 2004. Användare och IT-system inom svensk vård och omsorg [Users and IT-system in Swedish health care and social services] [in Swedish]. http://www.usersaward.com. Accessed February 10, 2005.
6. Svensk Författningssamling. Patientjournallagen [The Patient Record Act] [in Swedish]. SFS 1985;562. http//www.notisum.se. Accessed February 10, 2005.
7. Ehnfors M, Thorell-Ekstrand I, Ehrenberg A. Towards basic nursing information in patient records [Vard Nord Utveckl Forsk] [in Swedish]. *Nurs Sci Res Nordic Countries,* 1991;21(3/4):12-31.
8. Ehrenberg A, Ehnfors M, Thorell-Ekstrand I. Nursing documentation in patient records: experience of the use of the VIPS model. *J Adv Nurs.* 1996;24,853-867.
9. Ehrenberg A, Ehnfors M. Patient records in nursing homes: effects of training on content and comprehensiveness. *Scand J Caring Sci,* 1999;13:72-82.
10. Björvell C, Wredling R, Thorell-Ekstrand I. Long-term increase in quality of nursing documentation: effects of a comprehensive intervention. *Scand J Caring Sci.* 2002;16(1):34-42.
11. Gunningberg L, Lindholm C, Carlsson M, Sjoden PO. The development of pressure ulcers in patients with hip fractures: inadequate nursing documentation is still a problem. *J Adv Nurs.* 2000:31(5):1155-1164.
12. Idvall E, Ehrenberg A. Nursing documentation of postoperative pain management. *J Clin Nurs.* 2002;11(6):734-742.
13. Törnkvist L, Gardulf A, Strender LE. Effects of pain-adviser: district nurses' opinions regarding their own knowledge, management and documentation of patients in chronic pain. *Scand J Caring Sci.* 2003;17(4)332-338.
14. Ehrenberg A, Birgersson C. Nursing documentation of leg ulcers: adherence to clinical guidelines in a Swedish primary health care district. *Scand J Caring Sci.* 2003;17:278-284.
15. Ehrenberg A, Ehnfors M, Ekman I. Older patients with chronic heart failure in home care. A record review of nurses' assessments and interventions. *J Clin Nurs.* 2003;13:90-96.
16. Ekman I, Ehrenberg A. Fatigued elderly patients with chronic heart failure: Do patient reports and nursing documentation correspond? *Int J Nurs Term Class.* 2002;13(4):127-136.
17. Gunningberg L, Ehrenberg A. Accuracy and quality in the nursing documentation of pressure ulcers: a comparison of record content and patient examination. *J Wound Ostomy Continence Nurs.* 2004;31(6):328-325.
18. Gunningberg L, Fogelberg DM, Ehrenberg A. Accuracy in the recording of pressure ulcers and prevention after implementing an electronic health record in hospital care. *Qual Safe Health Care.* 2008;17(4):281-285.
19. Socialstyrelsen. Standardvårdplaner (SVP). En Kartläggning av förekomsten av SVP i akutsjukvården (*Standard care plans. A survey of the prevalence in hospital care*). Socialstyrelsen, Stockholm, 2006. In Swedish.
20. Hunt DL, Haynes RB, Hanna SE, Smith K. Effects of computer-based clinical decision support systems on physician performance and patient outcomes. A systematic review. *JAMA.* 1998;280(15):1339-1346.

21. Kawamoto K, Houlihan CA, Balas EA, Lobach DF. Improving clinical practice using clinical decision support systems: a systematic review of trials to identify features critical to success. *BMJ.* 2005;330(7494):765.

22. Jirapaet V. A computer expert system prototype for mechanically ventilated neonates development and impact on clinical judgment and information access capability of nurses. *Comput Nurs.* 2001;19:194-203.

23. Ehnfors M, Grobe SJ. Nursing curriculum and continuing education: future directions. *Int J Med Inform.* 2004;73:7-8,591-598.

24. Socialdepartementet. An information society for all [in Swedish]. Prop.1999/2000;86.

25. Swedish Strategy for eHealth. Safe and accessible information in health and social care. Status Report 2009. http://www.regeringen.se/content/1/c6/12/48/00/680cf61e.pdf. Accessed October 20, 2009.

Case Study 16E

The Netherlands: Virtual Electronic Health Records Based on Safe Data Exchange

By William T.F. Goossen, PhD, RN; A.T.M. Goossen-Baremans, MSN, RN; and Lejo Bouma, RN

Introduction

The Netherlands has a long history of development and use of IT in healthcare. Beginning in the 1960s with the implementation of some national projects, the dissemination of systems grew explosively. However, despite these IT developments, the realization of the EHR throughout the healthcare system is still problematic today. From the perspective of the nursing profession, we have seen few improvements over the past 20 years, although recent developments seem more promising. Since 2000, agreement among healthcare institutions, professionals, patients, insurers, government, and industry has led to the realization of a safe national IT infrastructure, based on standards for semantic interoperability. Today, after nearly 10 years of development, we are seeing the first implementations being ready but still at a slower pace than anticipated.

This case study on the use of IT in Dutch healthcare describes a brief history, the problems encountered at the end of the last century, current implementations, and results. Nursing as a profession in the Netherlands is challenged to participate in these developments to contribute and gain benefits to improve nursing care. The reader should not expect a complete historic analysis or coverage of everything that is going on in Dutch nursing care. Rather, this case study is a status report that only highlights specific examples.

A Brief History on the Use of IT in Dutch Healthcare

During the 1960s and 1970s, healthcare in the Netherlands began applying computer systems for administrative tasks from which hospital information systems later evolved. General practitioners (GP) in the Netherlands were among the first to use EHRs in their practices, and now more than 90% use such a system.[1]

The first nursing information system ever developed was called, in Dutch, the Verpleegkundig Informatie Systeem VISY (Nursing Information System).[2] It was developed as part of a larger hospital information system. This was the first Dutch system that included nursing components—a nursing assessment module, a care-planning module, and sections for recording vital signs and body weight.[2]

Today, various health information systems are available on the Dutch market. The use of health information systems is almost 100%, with only a few areas not using the systems. However, from a clinical and nursing perspective, several areas are still only using more administrative and financially driven systems. However, all sectors including psychiatry, nursing homes and home care are adopting the EHR for clinical and care-planning purposes. In general, nursing's complete use of the EHR has been estimated some years ago at only 1 or 2%.[3] There are studies underway to determine current use.

By the end of the 1990s, the major problems standing in the way of further advancement of EHR were identified, and final plans to establish a national EHR were created. All challenges that were (and are) encountered require intelligent information management and safe exchange of patient-related information. Mid-2001, the National IT Institute for Healthcare (NICTIZ) was established; projects were started and are currently underway.[4]

Exchanging Patient Information in a Safe Infrastructure for Healthcare

NICTIZ created several standards, set up an infrastructure and carried out projects to establish a safe infrastructure for healthcare information exchange. It is already—on a small scale—improving the flow of information about the patient/client, with a view to raising the quality and effectiveness of healthcare.[4]

At the beginning, NICTIZ had three areas of concern: (1) building the national IT infrastructure for healthcare; (2) standardizing data for both EHR and electronic messages; and (3) ensuring the security of patient data for broader use. The national IT infrastructure for exchange of patient data—called AORTA, as its use for information in healthcare is similar to the aorta vessel's use for the blood in the human body—is based on linkages between EHR systems that will allow authorized healthcare professionals to access patient data from any location at any time via the use of Health Level 7 version 3 (HL7 v3) messages. One part of the AORTA provides a shared data service center, in which healthcare professionals can query information about their patients in other providers' information systems.

At the same time, the Ministry of Health established the legal framework to support this, which is in the final stage of handling by Parliament.[4] The most important responsibility of the Ministry of Health in this change was to legally facilitate the use of the social security number for healthcare purposes. This is now required by law and is called the Burger Service Number or BSN (Civilian Service Number). This number is important to use as a unique patient identifier, among other uses. Care professionals and care insurers have also received unique numbers by which they can be uniquely identified.

Standards that Support Information Exchange for Projects

The uniform exchange of information demands health sector-wide use of standards. NICTIZ takes into account several of the international standards (e.g., CEN and ISO) and in particular, the HL7 v3 standard.[5] Currently, HL7 version 2x are used in almost all Dutch hospitals, and harmonization is taking place between standards organizations; therefore the HL7 v3 standard was chosen for NICTIZ projects.[4] In particular, the HL7 v3 Reference Information Model (RIM), domain and message models, and associated modeling tools are being used.

In the first project, NICTIZ established a domain message information model (D-MIM) for perinatology.[6] An electronic message derived from this model was tested with success.[6] This project served as a national pilot to test the applicability of HL7 v3, in particular the RIM.[4,5] The perinatology D-MIM eventually became the base of what is now the Care Provision Domain Message Information Model in the HL7 v3 standard.[5] Another NICTIZ project focuses on an EHR system for stroke services and has led to a D-MIM for stroke patients and one use case from cardiology.[7]

Today, three additional projects are using the HL7 v3 Care Provision models and messages as core for their project. These include the national Perinatology Masterplan, the e-Diabetes National Project, and the Juvenile Care Record (JCR) systems.

It has become clear that the D-MIM approach suits many clinical domains, its reusability is high, and, even if information is not 100% similar, the same methodology can be used to add specialized content. Thus, the focus is now moving from specific clinical models to mapping the clinical data sets to the generic HL7 Care Provision D-MIM, which reduces the time, effort, and costs for projects and improves the reuse and semantic interoperability of clinical information.

These three 2009 projects do include nursing to some extent. In particular, diabetes nursing care and nursing care for juvenile preventive care are included. The current approach is that findings of the modeling work can be used for many different patient categories and that they are so powerful, they facilitate information management and exchange for all health professionals.[5,7] This in particular has led to the Detailed Clinical Modeling approach which is described in Chapter 13.[8]

Two example projects will be discussed from here: the first is a practical case for Juvenile Care Records. The second example will discuss the national program for e-Diabetes, which is still under development.

Example Project One: Juvenile Care Records (JCR) to Solve Problems

This case describes how 10 healthcare organizations in the northeast part of the Netherlands are about to implement a modern, standards-based JCR for preventive care for children and adolescents. The JCR is seen as the solution for the problems occurring in information exchange in preventive care. This section describes the project according to the system development cycle. However, implementation and maintenance will not be addressed, since that will take place later in the year.

In the present situation, the information exchange does not run optimally. The problems are as follows:[9]

- Obtaining recent data of children and youth is done only with considerable effort. Thus, sufficient insight is lacking into the correlation between the data about preventive care.
- Monitoring of the health of children is not possible to the fullest extent because it is hard to access data or because data are lacking.

- Indicating what added value the sector delivers to the health of children and the prevention of the risks for health is difficult.
- The aims of the national guideline for healthcare for 0–19 year-old children are impossible to reach without ICT support. Because uniformity in information and in healthcare cannot be realized, the quality of care is not guaranteed.
- An integral JCR will support youth healthcare and early risk detection.

Optimization of the information exchange is inevitable in two areas. First, ICT is required for the availability of data about childbirth, early risk detection, administrations of immunizations, and growth and development in all areas of childhood and adolescence. Second, information exchange is necessary at population level for the purpose of quality measures and epidemiologic research.

Goals for the JCR

The implementation of a JCR should optimize the information exchange whereby existing problems will be solved.[9] The JCR will result in the following changes for the youth healthcare institutions involved.[10]

- Optimal care will be provided to 0–19 year-old children.
- Care professionals can have current and other relevant data about the child at their disposal at all times.
- Data for the city council administration, as well as administration of immunization and birth information can be obtained automatically by electronic messages.
- Records can be transferred to other institutions easily, safely, and completely by the use of standards for data and messages. For this function, the Dutch Aorta national infrastructure and HL7 v3 messages would be used.
- Improvement of workflow and thus more efficient preventive care.
- Research can be carried out much easier and for more purposes.

To accomplish the objectives, a project for child healthcare is underway in 10 institutions. This project follows the system lifecycle. The purpose has been described earlier. Although this was established by national organizations, most child healthcare institutions also agreed to this implementation and started new projects. The second phase includes the functional and technical requirements that serve as a basis for the JCR.

To determine the requirements of the care providers, a consensus method, the Delphi method, was used by the 10 organizations. The method is used to systematically reach consensus for certain topics in different rounds by means of questionnaires sent to a panel of experts.[11] One of the benefits of the Delphi technique is that there is no social pressure exerted on the participants. This makes it easier to give deviant opinions.[12] After each round, the answers submitted by the panel are analyzed, summarized, and reported back. For the JCR project, two rounds have been carried out: one anonymous round with an electronic questionnaire and one panel meeting. The anonymity in this second round was maintained by using voting devices with numbers, so the individual responses could not be retrieved. The expert panel for this study comprised 66 experts in the field of preventive healthcare for children and youth. All relevant health professions from the 10 organizations were represented in the expert panel.

Functional Requirements that Gained Consensus

First, the Basis Data Set for JCR, as developed by NICTIZ in collaboration with national organizations for juvenile care, was put to the test for usability by experts. The Basis Data Set JCR consists of 53 concepts. For every concept, attributes (observations or variables) and value sets (answering possibilities) are formulated. For every concept in the Basis Data Set for JCR, all relevant data elements that are needed for the monitoring of preventive care from age 0 to 19 are made explicit, a total of approximately 1,000. This set has been defined, in particular, to facilitate the exchange of data between organizations in youth healthcare with use of HL7 v3 messaging. With the Basis Data Set JCR, it is also possible to perform epidemiologic studies. These 53 concepts of the Basis Data Set YHC have been added to the questionnaire. The Basis Data Set JCR gained a high level of consensus among the health professionals. However, they wanted several additions and corrections. This meant additional specification of data elements in attributes, preferably with value sets.

As an example, for the concept of congenital heart defect: in the questionnaire, the following statement was presented to the expert panel: "The specifications 'congenital heart defect' are complete." Only 60% of the required 75% of the panel agreed with this statement. This meant no consensus was reached on this

Table 16E-1. Basis Data Set Item for the Concept of 'Congenital Heart Defect'

Attribute	Value Set
Examined	0=Not examined 1= Examined, no special circumstances 2= Examined, special circumstances
Intervention	0=None 1=Education/advice 2= Additional encounter 3=Referral
Follow up	Free text
Overall impression professional	1=Fatigued 2=Passive 3=Undernourished impression, thin 4= Dysmorphism
Overall impression parents	Free text
Effort tolerance	*First year during feeding of effort (for example, crying):* 1=Easily fatigued 2=Perspire 3=Rapid breathing 4=Hungry, but cannot empty bottle 5=Stops drinking from the mother's breast 6=Blue or grey skin color *Toddler age:* 7= Rapid fatigue with effort, such as walking (stairs), cycling 8= Interruption of play by crouch *School age and Adolescent age:* 9= Fainting (in particular with effort) 10=Easily fatigued 11=Heart palpitation 12=Chest pain

statement. In the second round, it was decided that a focus group would come up with an appropriate representation of the concept (see Table 16E-1).

Second, a cluster of unique personal details is discussed. NICTIZ has made arrangements for these frequently-occurring data groups, called HL7 v3 Common Message Element Types (CMET),[5] for connection to the national infrastructure arrangements. For patient details, the CMET's Patient and Person can be used. Similar arrangements have been made for health professionals in the CMET Provider. All messages from and to the JCR use the same data. These consist of common patient data such as name, date of birth, gender, address and insurance, adapted to the Dutch situation.

Third, to gain insight in the workflow of the preventive care for youth ages 0–19 and to improve these, a flow chart has been developed (see Figure 16E-1).[10] The chart gives an overview of the workflows that are part of the Basic Tasks Package for preventive care for the 0–19 year old.[13] By means of a timeline, the phases of life that a child goes through from 0–19 years are shown. On this timeline, the processes and encounters are defined—for instance, for immunization administrations. This makes the flow chart an important description of the functionality of the JCR to support the workflow.

The fourth part of the questionnaire dealt with additional functional specifications. These include a use case-driven summary of functions and the mandatory, required, or optional requirements for the JCR.

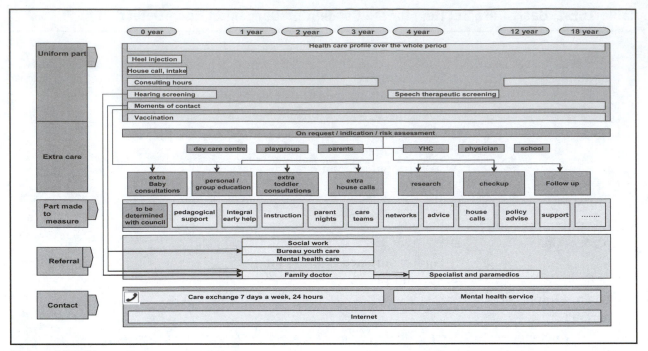

Figure 16E-1. *Workflow Chart for Youth Health Care*

Examples include secure log in, manual record maintenance, record search, data entry (according the 1,000 plus data elements listed previously, in logically accessible screens), handling of incoming and outgoing electronic messages, selections on records, data and reporting, handling of planning requests for follow-up encounters, work lists, alert list, correspondence management, entry lists (e.g., for epidemiologic or administrative surveys) report generation. The JCR eventually will have safe electronic data interfaces for birth records, immunization records, regional and national indexes for risk assessment, and of course, to exchange full records between health organizations via the Aorta infrastructure. In this section, requirements for the technical realization are included such as the data security measures, Web-based access, offline options, configuration of encounters (which of the 1,000 data will be entered during which encounter).

Examples of concrete requirements that gained consensus are:

- In one glance, it should be immediately apparent what risk factors exist for a child. For this, there was 100% consensus.

- The system provides an alert when certain time limits are about to be exceeded. For this requirement, 97.8% consensus was determined.

- It should be possible to register in the system how many times parents/caretakers call to consulting hours by telephone and with what questions. For this requirement, 90.5% of the care professionals agreed.

- On requirements for usability for 25 statements, consensus was reached (86.2% or more). In the second consensus meeting, three new statements were presented to the expert panel. For these, 100% agreement was reached.

- More than one record for children of the same family can be edited at the same time. For this 96% agreed, and it was added to the specifications.

As a result of organizational issues in the development of the national JCR, several changes occurred. Therefore, the set of functional requirements and the BDS have changed accordingly. In principle, the requirements of the care professionals that were part of the requirements gathering phase are still relevant, but within 2 years additional requirements and changes based on testing of some of the functions have led to some changes. But finally after 2 rounds of procurement, the 10 health organizations were ready to sign a contract with a vendor that makes it reality.

Development and Testing the JCR

By December 2008, the contracts were signed, and the vendor started the development work for the JCR. The Functional Requirements document is the basis for development. However, the vendor is also using this

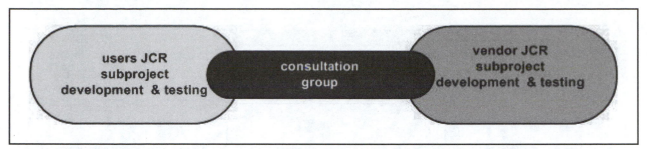

Figure 16E-2. *Consultation Group as Intermediary Between Users and Vendor. Source: Topicus Jeugdzorg.*

document for the full Functional and Technical Designs, for rapid prototyping, and for the final development and delivery of the JCR for the 10 healthcare institutions. A project teams leads the development.

All steps are carried out only after heavy consultation with the users. This is done via a user consultation group that is responsible for optimal system development (does it represent the optimal care support) (see Figure 16E-2).[10] In the consultation group, two professionals from each of the 10 members represents their institution and colleagues.

The consultation group is reviewing the Functional Design of the vendor. The Functional Design is the translation of the requirements into the actual JCR. It documents how the different use cases and requirements are translated into the system, as illustrated by screens. Members of the project team check whether all requirements are met in the Functional Design description. The consultation group checks further whether all requirements are workable and will support effective and efficient care.

A test group developed actual patient cases, against which the rapid prototyped JCR is tested under the leadership of a test manager. In particular, the log in, selection of record, data entry, flow of screens, system speed, and logical screen layout are tested in simulated real-world data entry. In some instances, consultation group members have to go back to their respective organizations to tackle issues that come up and were not yet defined.

Testing itself consisted of both system tests that revealed whether the function itself is available and does what was agreed and user acceptance test that determined the practicality of the system to support the workflow and data entry in practice situations in youth healthcare.

Realization of the JCR is based on an incremental process, each increment consisting of a specified functionality. Figure 16E-3 illustrates this overall process. Each increment consists of the following steps or components: First the functional design is completed including the details of screens, content and dynamics of the system, including test cases and guidelines for use. Then the functional design is checked against specifications.

Second, the software is developed as a prototype based on UML 2.0 methodology, and the prototype version is discussed with the consultation group. After the comments from the consultation group have been handled, the technical designs are specified and built. During the development of the increment, demos are presented.

Finally, the test team carries out the different system tests, and finally, depending on the test results, the increment is approved or will be further improved until the test shows it is capable of supporting the work in practice. The final product will be documented in the functional and technical design, and approval of the system tests and acceptation tests will be carefully documented. During testing, errors will be found and entered in an issue log. The essential factor here is the successful completion of the test activities and error management using a "bug tracker."

This incremental approach has advantages, such as continuous visibility of the development status and errors and the way these are handled (how and when). Thus the project can be broken into smaller components, leading to better project management. Also, user involvement is guaranteed and does support the overall system acceptance. Further, it allows making well-informed decisions about changes in the design due to unexpected events.

The development is done with standard system components that have been tested in practice in other systems and that are combinable and configurable to a very high extent. The quality of the final system, and timely and full approval are crucial for the implementation strategy for the 10 organizations. It also has con-

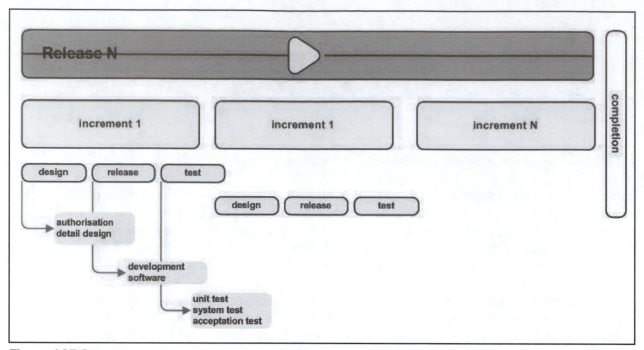

Figure 16E-3. *Depiction of an Incremental System Development, Test and Approval. Source: Topicus Jeugdzorg.*

tractual implications, such as simple payment and moving to the service organization. The implementation will start at the sites of two project partners, each with two pilots, a total of four pilot sites. One task for each organization is to work out what the contact moments are for encounters and which of the many data elements will be available on the screen for that visit. A step-by-step approach will be taken to roll configuration and implementation out over the other eight partners and within each partner a location-by-location implementation strategy. The whole implementation strategy, including long-term planning in the 10 organizations, has been developed simultaneously with the JCR system.

Example Project Two: The e-Diabetes Program on National Level

At the national level, the Netherlands is trying to realize a national program for ICT in healthcare: the national EHR. It is based on the assumption that there will be a "virtual integration of data from existing systems," not one large information system. This is more or less following the principles of the ISO 18308 standard for the EHR.[14]

NICTIZ has created the ICT-basis infrastructure (AORTA), which is a central infrastructure for safe data exchange, consisting of the unique patient identifier BSN, the UZI (Unique Care professional Identification), and the LSP (National Switchboard). In addition, there are many rules and standards developed for its use, and national legislation has been adapted to facilitate all of this.

The first two targets include the e-medication record and the e-GP to GP record. These function as chapters in the national EHR.

Like many Western countries, the Netherlands face a growth in the prevalence of diabetes. Thus, a National Action Program for Diabetes was established as an initiative of the Netherlands Diabetes Federation (NDF) and the Ministry of Volksgezondheid, Welzijn en Sport (healthcare).[15] The purpose of this national program is to limit the growth of the number of persons with diabetes (increase 2005–2025 less than 15%) and to reduce diabetes-related complications (65% no complications). The program has five themes, including education and lifestyle intervention, patient empowerment, improved organization of diabetes care, better regulations and cost models, and the e-Diabetes program.

e-Diabetes Program

As an addition to the other chapters for the national EHR, e-Diabetes is carried out as a development plan and full-scale implementation in the coming years.[4] The Business Case for e-Diabetes is found in improvements in information management, support of care delivery, and reporting from EHRs. According to an inventory carried out by NICTIZ, the following results support a business case to work on this topic. It revealed that for 93% of the care groups, ICT is an issue:

- Different GP EHRs (62%)
- Connecting to ICT-chain partners (40%)
- No appropriate ICT-tools (38%)
- Information collection (36%)
- Desired ICT-functions and requirements
- Data exchange outside the care group (79%)
- Patient access (63%)
- Internal data exchange (58%)

Thus, the plan was developed with the following purpose for the e-Diabetes Action Program: within some years, standards will be available for the exchange of information between different EHR systems, patient access and collaboration and automated reporting, using secondary data use from EHR.

The actual standards that are developed include a set of professional standards including the Diabetes Professional Care Guideline, including business and processes (2007), the e-Diabetes dataset and Inventory and data description that professionals want to exchange among themselves and with the patient (April 2008), multidisciplinary indicators, and harmonization of the different sets and development of an uniform set of indicators (2009).[4]

The information standards include: Architectural design e-Diabetes (Phase 1), which is a description of architecture for electronic data exchange in diabetes care as part of national infrastructure for EHR (2008), the HL7 implementation Guide for use of Care Provision in e-Diabetes.[4] Further the e-Diabetes Dataset is mapped to relevant code systems, including LOINC and SNOMED CT and to the relevant classes of the HL7 v3 Care Provision messages. In addition, a set of Detailed Clinical Models will be ready by June 2009.[8]

The Functional Requirements for EHR will be developed and technical and functional tests are under preparation for the end of 2009. Supporting measures include a communication plan and the ICT-monitor diabetes care, an investigation towards current ICT-use and ICT requirements of cooperative groups in diabetes care (2008). Finally, an e-Diabetes quarterly is issued every quarter.[4]

Summary

The Netherlands was an early adopter of ICT use in healthcare. However many developments can be seen as silo approaches. The need to have data readily available for continuity of care, both internal and external of healthcare organizations and their respective EHR systems, has led to the development of a national infrastructure for the safe and semantically interoperable health data exchange. The use of standards is a core enabler in these endeavors. Thus, national use of HL7 v3 and SNOMED CT are long-term goals for standard adoption. The data security activities are now almost complete and a large scale rollout is being prepared.

The JCR is presented as an example of how clinicians can express their needs for data capture, process support and reporting. The e-Diabetes program illustrates how under the national infrastructure, a full program approach leads to the development of several standards—clinical, informational, and technical—to support a national action plan. The ultimate goal is to limit the number of patients with diabetes and to reduce the number of complications in existing patients. Joint efforts on population education, organization of healthcare, changes in cost and funding structures, use of quality indicators and, finally, ICT developments are being carried out side by side.

References

1. Van der Lei J, Duisterhof JS, Westerhof HP, et al. The intro-duction of computer-based patient records in the Nether-lands. *Ann Intern Med.* 1993;119:1036-1046.

2. Pluyter-Wenting ESP, Nieman HBJ. Ontwikkelingen in de verpleegkundige verslaglegging. Tijdschrijft voor Medische Informatica. 1987;16(4):13-17.

3. Hilderink HGM, Epping PJMM, Goossen WTF. ICT in nursing in Dutch hospitals. In: France FH. Roger De Clerq E, De Moor G, eds. E-Health in Belgium and in the Netherlands. *Stud Health Technol Inform.* 2002;93:83-88.

4. Nationaal ICT instituut in de Zorg. Nictiz Web site. www.nictiz.nl. Accessed May 5, 2009.

5. Health Level Seven. Health Level 7, the Netherlands. www.HL7.org and www.HL7.nl. Accessed May 5, 2009.

6. Goossen WT, Jonker MJ, Heitmann KU, et al. Electronic patient records: Domain message information model peri-natology. *Int J Med Inf.* 2003;70(2-3):265-276.

7. Goossen WTF. *Model Once, Use Multiple Times: reusing HL7 domain models from one domain to the other.* In: Fieschi M, Coiera E, Jack Li YC, eds. Proceedings of the 11th World Congress on Medical Informatics, Medinfo 2004. Amster-dam: IOS Press, 2004:366-370.

8. Goossen WTF (2008). *Using Detailed Clinical Models to Bridge the Gap Between Clinicians and HIT.* In: De Clercq E, De Moor G, Bellon, J, Foulon M, van der Lei J, eds. Collab-orative Patient Centred eHealth. Proceedings of the HIT@ Healthcare 2008 conference, Brussels, 10 October 2008. Amsterdam: IOS Press, 3-10.

9. Nationaal Instituut voor ICT in de Zorg (NICTIZ). Plan van Aanpak Programma Informatisering Jeugdgezondheidszorg versie 1.2. Leidschendam, 2004 [in Dutch].

10. Bouma L. Projectplan and project documents EKD JGZ. Meppel, ICARE, 2005/2009 [in Dutch].

11. Murphy MK, Black NA, Lamping DL, et al. Consensus devel-opment methods, and their use in clinical guideline devel-opment. *Health Technol Assess.* 1998;2(3):i-iv,1-88.

12. Klop R, Wijmen van FCB. Delphi-Methode bij onderzoek naar voorwaarden voor overdracht van zorg. In: Francke AL, ed. Kwalitatief onderzoek in de verpleegkunde. Amster-dam/Lisse: Swets & Zeitlinger; 1990; 43-57 [in Dutch].

13. Ministerie van Volksgezondheid, Welzijn en Sport. Basis-takenpakket Jeugdgezondheidszorg 0-19 jaar. Den Haag; 2002 [in Dutch].

14. ISO (2009). *Health Informatics - Requirements for an Elec-tronic Health Record Architecture.* ISO/DIS 18308. ISO, Geneva.

15. Ministry of Health. Web documents. http://www.minvws.nl/nieuwsberichten/pg/2009/tien-miljoen-voor-diabetes.asp. Accessed May 15, 2009.

Case Study 16F

Toward Integrating Nursing Data into the Electronic Patient Record: Current Developments in Germany

By Ursula Hübner, PhD; Bjöern Sellemann, Dipl. Pflegewirt, RN;
and Daniel Flemming, Dipl. Kaufmann, RN

Introduction—The German Healthcare System

The German healthcare system is based on social health insurance and is controlled by the Federal Ministry of Health, which proposes health acts to Parliament and delegates tasks to the health self-governance sector, which consists of nongovernmental corporate bodies. Approximately 87% of the population are covered by statutory health insurance. According to income, membership is mandatory for approximately 77% and voluntary for 10%—the remaining 13% are insured by a private health insurance company or by governmental plans.[1] The insurance covers outpatient and hospital healthcare services (Social Code, Book V). Since 1995, long-term care insurance (Social Code Book XI) has been mandatory for nearly the entire population. It is operated by long-term care funds or private insurance companies. Entitlement to long-term care benefits depends on need, which is expressed in three stages. A specific "care benefit" is allocated to each of the stages.

Like all other industrialized countries, Germany is confronted with steadily increasing healthcare expenditures (see Table 16F-1) and, therefore, the government has enacted a series of cost-containment measures, among them reductions in the salaries of general practitioners (GP), limited budgets for prescription drug coverage, decreases in the administrative costs of sickness funds, and increases in beneficiary co-payments for certain services.

Since the early 1990s, government regulations have been aimed at reinforcing outpatient and home healthcare, because outpatient care is less costly than inpatient care. With the advent of the long-term care insurance in the mid-1990s, hundreds of private home healthcare services were established. There are now approximately 10,000 such services, providing either treatment ordered by a physician or nursing interventions within the framework of long-term care insurance.

During the 1990s, inpatient and outpatient services in Germany were only loosely linked, if at all. Since 2004, hospitals interested in building a network of healthcare providers (integrated care delivery networks) can do so more easily. Under the Statutory Health Insurance Modernization Act, hospitals can negotiate contracts on behalf of their network with the administrators of the sickness funds. Such networks comprise general practitioners, medical specialists, home healthcare services, rehabilitation institutions, clinics, pharmacies and other self-employed healthcare professionals.

Compared with other countries, Germany is known for its high rate of hospital beds per inhabitant and an average length of stay that is higher than that of other European Union countries (see Table 16F-1). However, over the last few years, there has been a decline in the average length of stay. This trend has been reinforced by the German DRG system (G-DRG) that took effect as the mandatory budgeting system for hospitals at the beginning of 2004.[6] The G-DRG system is an all-patient classification system developed on the basis of the Australian DRG system.[6] Patients are grouped into homogeneous categories according to their ICD-10 medical diagnosis and their OPS procedure (Operationen- und Prozedurenschlüssel). The OPS is a German development originating from the International Classification of Procedures in Medicine (ICPM).[7] Neither nursing diagnoses nor interventions are used for grouping. However, nursing documentation is employed for revealing patient co-morbidities and complexities. These data do not contain nursing-specific information but rather represent medical problems that are mainly dealt with by nurses. As shown by Fischer,[8] nursing diagnoses cannot be coded into ICD-10, and only a small percentage of the NANDA diagnoses can be expressed in ICD-10 terms.

The DRG topic has entailed several new developments. Among clinicians and hospital managers, the adoption of the DRG system has led to an increased awareness of the importance of strategies that help to decrease the length of stay and thus contribute to keeping costs at bay. This focus has led to an emphasis on using clinical pathways because they are seen as a proven means for standardizing processes, control-

Table 16F-1. German Healthcare System in Numbers[2,3,4,5]

Population of Germany[2]		
	2007	82,217,800
Healthcare Expenditures[3] (% of Gross Domestic Product)		
	1993	10,2 %
	2007	10.4 %
Number of Hospitals[4]		
	1993	2,354
	2007	2,087
Number of Hospital Beds[4]		
	1993	628,258
	2007	506,954
Average Length of Stay in Hospitals in Days[4]		
	1993	12.5
	2007	8.3
Total Number of Physicians[5]		
	2007	315,000
Total Number of Nurses[5]		
	2007	1,079,000

ling length of stay and other cost and quality critical parameters, such as number of tests.[9] Importantly, the role of IT in healthcare, as an instrument for providing visibility and easy communication, has finally been acknowledged by the government. Pursuant to the Statutory Health Insurance Modernization Act, the health insurance card containing administrative data is being replaced by a health card containing administrative and clinical data.

The new health card is integrated into a nationwide, health telematics infrastructure that provides security, administrative services, data management, and application services. In principle, all clinically relevant data will be kept on the card or will be stored elsewhere and will be referred to by the card. The clinical data to be stored include electronic prescriptions, emergency data sets, and medical summaries. In addition to government-led activities for establishing a health telematics infrastructure, there are several new initiatives founded by hospital groups and other consortia for implementing EHRs in their institutions.[10]

In summary, the major elements of the German healthcare framework are health and long-term care insurance; focus on outpatient and home health care, integrated care delivery networks, the G-DRG-system, the German Health Telematics Infrastructure and other related initiatives. These forces drive the activities that are integral to the formation of a multidisciplinary patient/health record.

Electronic Patient Records in German Hospitals

New and more complex hospital financing methods based on the G-DRG system fostered an increased investment in hospital information systems (HIS), including clinical systems and the implementation of electronic patient record (EPR) systems. Nationwide surveys conducted in 2002, 2005/2006, and 2007 confirm a recognizable increase in the prevalence of clinical systems in hospitals (see Figure 16F-1).[11-13]

This positive trend also affected electronic nursing documentation and other nursing-related systems, such as rostering/staff scheduling and ordering systems (for examinations and supplies) as Figure 16F-1 shows. Although installation figures for nursing documentation systems (approximately 27%) were still not as high as other clinical systems, e.g., ordering examinations and supplies, they increased by nearly fourfold

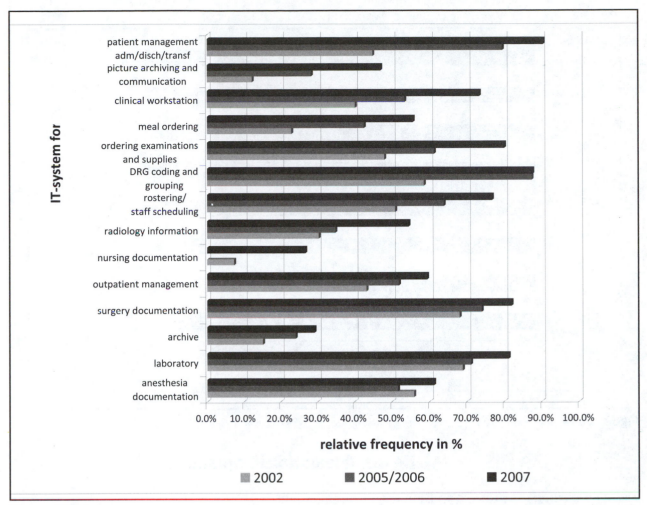

Figure 16F-1. *Development of the Prevalence of Clinical Systems in German Hospitals Over a Five-Year Period – Sorted by Magnitude of Growth[11-13]*

over a 5-year period (see Figure 16F-1). This underlines the increasing importance of systems supporting the nursing process.

While the number of clinical IT-systems installed can be seen as an indicator for the implementation status of EPRs,[14] there is not a direct relationship between the two. Hospitals that have many different clinical systems need not automatically have a fully operational EPR. In 2007, approximately 7–10% of German hospitals reported having a complete EPR.[13] Compared with the prevalence of clinical HIS modules (see Figure 16F-1), these values are rather small. When hospitals that are currently implementing an EPR are included,[13] the number rises to approximately 45%, which shows that about half of all German hospitals are involved in building or using an EPR or parts of it.[1]

Nursing managers in German hospitals tend to highly value the benefit of EPR systems.[13] This also holds true for nursing managers in hospitals which neither had a fully operational EPR nor were implementing one. The criteria that received the highest marks were availability of the data, improved data quality, quality assurance and reporting (see Figure 16F-2). It appears that nurse managers perceive that EPRs can assist in many different ways when it comes to data management and using the data for statistics (reporting), as well as in quality assurance, e.g., quality reports. Also, nearly 70% of the nursing managers said that the EPR positively affected treatment quality (see Figure 16F-2).

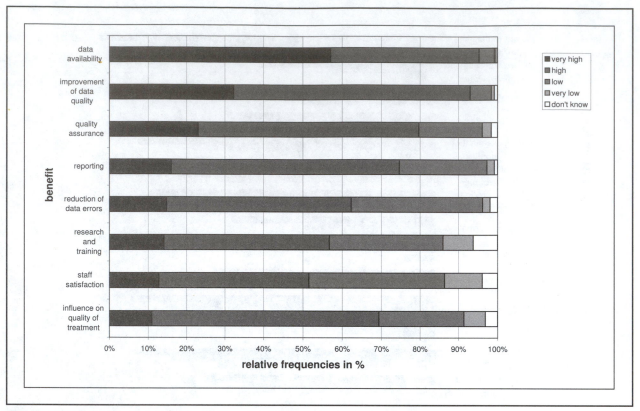

Figure 16F-2. *Benefit of the EPR – Valued by Nursing Managers in German Hospitals[13]*

Health Telematics in Nursing

Continuity of Care and Discharge Management

Financial and technical driving forces are important; however, the need to improve quality of care should be the strongest impetus for sharing patient data, not only within a single institution (EPR) but also among different healthcare providers (EHR). The need for continuity of care, established by informational continuity, is a strong motivation for implementing health telematics applications. One of the classical cases of use for health telematics is discharge management. It is a process often overseen by nurses who are in charge of coordinating the various activities. There is a great interest among nurses in optimizing this process, as the success of the German expert standard for discharge management developed by the DNQP (Deutsches Netzwerk für Qualitätsentwicklung in der Pflege) shows.[15]

The deficiencies in providing patients with an uninterrupted level of care when they are moved between institutions or when they are discharged to their homes has spurred nursing leaders from northwest Germany to establish a network named "Continuity of Care Network in the Region Osnabrück." Its goal is to foster the idea and culture of providing care across the entire continuum by strengthening the electronic communication between the healthcare providers. Founded in 2001 as an informal group of hospitals, nursing homes, home care services, a healthcare center, and ambulatory nursing services; it became a registered association in 2006. The network receives scientific, strategic, and technical assistance from the University of Applied Sciences Osnabrück. It has organized workshops on different issues of health telematics, such as systems and platforms for electronic communication in regional networks, data protection, wound management and continuity of care, the HL7 CDA-based standard for the eNursing Summary (see Case Study 10A in this book), and the Health Professional Card for nurses in Germany. Furthermore, the Continuity of Care network tested and evaluated a technical pilot system for an electronic nursing summary,[16] investigated the usability of different coding systems for nursing diagnoses,[17,18] and developed a list of criteria for evaluating wound documentation software.[19]

Similar networks also exist in other regions of Germany (for example, in the southwest region). Typically, these networks start by defining a paper-based version of a transfer summary that is then promoted in the region. More networks, such as the one in Heilbronn,[20] are seeking to implement electronic solutions for transferring the summary and closing the information gap at discharge or transfer.

The Use of Nursing Terminologies

In Germany, both German as well as international terminologies co-exist. Among the international terminologies, ICNP (International Classification of Nursing Practice) and the NANDA (North American Nursing Diagnoses Association) taxonomy are the ones best known. Both ICNP and NANDA have been translated into German and are available for all to use.[21,22] Other classification systems have also been translated into German. These include: the Clinical Care Classification (CCC),[23] the Nursing Intervention Classification (NIC),[24] and Nursing Outcome Classification (NOC).[25] Similar to other countries, the International Classification of Functioning, Disability and Health (ICF) is used in Germany for describing and coding nursing-related information, such as the patient's status. Among the terminologies originating from the German language, there are LEP (Leistungserfassung in der Pflege)[26] for nursing interventions, apenio® (Assessment based Planning and Evaluation of Nursing Interventions and Outcome)[27], and ENP (European Nursing Pathways).[28] Both apenio® and ENP link nursing diagnoses/problems with nursing interventions and therefore, are not classifications in a narrow sense but rather knowledge bases.

With the advent of electronic nursing record systems, more and more nurses realized the importance of structured data and controlled vocabularies (see Table 16F-2). This development is reflected by the plans for coding diagnoses, resources, and interventions expressed by nursing managers in 2002 compared with 2007.[29] In 2002, hospital-specific catalogues and free text still took the first and second place for coding diagnoses and resources. By 2007, however, free text was consistently replaced by ICNP coding as the second most frequent descriptor used. Use of NANDA diagnosis codes moved up to the third rank frequency for coding diagnoses/problems. LEP alone and in combination with hospital-specific catalogues were ranked second and third for interventions in 2007. Over the period 2002-2007, hospital-specific catalogues remained stable as the method of choice for coding diagnoses, resources, and interventions.

To support the collaborative process of translating ICNP from English into other languages, Schrader et al[30] built a Web-based tool that allows the user to suggest translations and to make comments. It has been used by Austrian, Swiss, and German translators of ICNP and subsequently, by experts evaluating the translated terms.[30] With the constant growth and vocabulary changes as found in ICNP, this tool becomes very useful for keeping the translations up-to-date.

The German Health Telematics Infrastructure and the Health Professional Card

Standardized vocabularies are a major component of ensuring interoperability in IT landscapes with heterogeneous systems, such as the German Health Telematics Infrastructure. The term *telematics infrastructure* refers to all hardware and software components at the level of basic services and applications. The term *telematics* is a neologism composed of *tele* from telecommunications and *matics* from informatics. It is a synonym for Information and Communication Technology (ICT) that is frequently used in Europe in various notations, e.g. as *Telematik* (German), *télématique* (French) and *telematics* (English).

In telematics infrastructure, the goal is to connect all actors in the German healthcare system by providing a nationwide IT infrastructure, including telematics applications and services. Within this infrastructure, the electronic Health Card plays a major role.[31] Proposed as a solution for the electronic prescription and medication record, the concept for the electronic Health Card has broadened to include these data sets: emergency data; medical discharge letters; the electronic patient record; data provided by the patients themselves; and, finally electronic receipts given to the patients by physicians after each treatment or diagnostic procedure. On the basis of extensive experience in the use of smart cards for administrative purposes in Germany (Krankenversichertenkarte), the decision to implement a card solution for health data was intuitive.[31] However, cards are insufficient as the sole media for keeping all health data because of their low storage capacity. Thus from the beginning, the strategy has included the complementary concept of data residing on servers that could be accessed from the card. Access to all health data is strictly controlled and generally requires an electronic Health Professional Card (HPC) with a digital signature function.

According to the original plans, the electronic Health Card was to have been used Germany-wide by 2006. But the process was severely delayed by political discussions and criticism from the physicians' associations. The resulting new plans comprise more concise and focused applications than originally planned.

Table 16F-2. Plans of Nursing Managers in German Hospitals for Using Nursing Terminologies

Rank	Diagnoses		Resources		Interventions	
	2002	2007	2002	2007	2002	2007
1	Hospital catalogue	Hospital Catalogue	Hospital Catalogue	Hospital Catalogue	Hospital Catalogue	Hospital Catalogue
2	Free Text	ICNP	Free Text	ICNP	Free Text	LEP
3	ICNP	NANDA	ICNP	Free Text	LEP	ICNP or LEP with Hospital Catalogue
4	NANDA	Free Ttext	Others	Others	ICNP	Free Text
5	-	-	-	-	Others	Others

Regrettably, lost in these discussions and new plans were the original concepts for establishing an EHR within the German Health Telematics Infrastructure.

The German nurse associations also expressed their concerns about the electronic Health Card because the design and its legal basis do not provide for use of the data on the card by nurses. This omission of nurses from using the electronic Health Card may have serious implications leading to information gaps that compromise patient safety.[32]

Despite the problems associated with the German electronic Health Card, the Health Professional Card was never debated, and it is an accepted element of the Health Telematics Infrastructure. HPCs are issued to physicians and pharmacists with the help of their professional associations in which they are registered on a mandatory basis. Nurses and other healthcare professionals who are not officially registered in Germany will receive their HPC through the eGBR (electronisches Gesundheitsberuferegister). The eGBR organization has just recently been established and acts as a national register and a trust center for issuing the HPC, including its digital signature function. The HPC is important beyond its use within the German Health Telematics Infrastructure. It is also a means for generating legally accepted, qualified digital signatures. This function enables healthcare professionals to actually sign their electronic documents, such as the medical discharge letter or the nursing summary that are sent electronically to their recipients. The HPC with digital signature is a quantum leap in terms of moving from the paper-based world into a truly digital era because it makes the printing out of documents and signing the paper versions superfluous.

EHR Initiative of Healthcare Providers

There was a considerable amount of disappointment among healthcare provider organizations because of the slow progress made in implementing the electronic Health Card, and particularly because initial plans for a German-wide EHR had been discarded. To overcome this vacuum, a consortium consisting of all major private hospital groups in Germany and large teaching hospitals decided to develop specifications for an electronic "case record" and to realize these specifications in the short term. These pilot projects focused on improving the communication between the acute care and the ambulatory sectors by making results of examinations and medical summaries electronically available to general practitioners and medical specialists outside the hospitals.[10]

Summary

The implementation of the G-DRG-based hospital financing system in 2004 made it imperative for healthcare systems to use IT-based methods for processing clinical data including EPRs and EHRs. The introduction of the G-DRG-based hospital financing system contributed to a decrease of the average length of stay, the establishment of integrated care delivery networks, and an increased need for cooperation among health-care providers, all factors that promote the use of IT-systems in healthcare. These factors exerted pressure on all segments of the healthcare system and made the need for EHR technologies clear to all. The results of these pressures within the German healthcare system are evident in survey data that reveal a steady trend for increased adoption of clinical IT-based applications, including electronic nursing documentation systems. The survey data show that nearly half of all German hospitals are involved in implementing EPR systems or are already using a fully operational EPR system.[13] Availability of data and improved data quality are regarded as the main benefits of EPR systems. The results also show that the potential benefits are well-known to a large majority of nurse leaders.

Implementing the German Health Telematics Infrastructure as an all-embracing means for sharing health data is a challenge not only for nurses but for all health care professionals. The nurses' role in this undertaking is to make sure that all patient data are represented in the system so that the risk of injury to patients can be minimized and decisions can be made on the basis of an optimal level of information. The Health Professional Card for all health professionals including nurses is a big leap forward toward a fully digital world in healthcare that includes nursing.

References

1. World Health Organization. *Country Highlights on Health, Health Systems,* Germany 2004. http://www.euro.who.int/document/e88527.pdf. Accessed May 2, 2009.
2. Statistisches Bundesamt. Bevölkerungsstand. http://www.destatis.de/jetspeed/portal/cms/Sites/destatis/Internet/DE/Navigation/Statistiken/Bevoelkerung/Bevoelkerungsstand/Bevoelkerungsstand.psml. Accessed May 1, 2009.
3. Statistisches Bundesamt. Gesundheitsausgaben. http://www.destatis.de/jetspeed/portal/cms/Sites/destatis/Internet/DE/Navigation/Statistiken/Gesundheit/Gesundheitsausgaben/Gesundheitsausgaben.psml. Accessed: May 2, 2009.
4. Statistisches Bundesamt. Gesundheit. Grunddaten der Krankenhäuser. Fachserie 12 Reihe 6.1.1 https://www-ec.destatis.de/csp/shop/sfg/bpm.html.cms.cBroker.cls?cmspath=struktur,vollanzeige.csp&ID=1023231. Accessed May 1, 2009.
5. Statistisches Bundesamt. Gesundheitspersonal. http://www.destatis.de/jetspeed/portal/cms/Sites/destatis/Internet/DE/Content/Statistiken/Gesundheit/Gesundheitspersonal/Tabellen/Content75/Berufe,templateId=renderPrint.psml. Accessed May 1, 2009.
6. *German Diagnoses-Related Groups.* http://www.g-drg.de. Accessed May 10, 2009.
7. Deutsches Institut für Medizinische Dokumentation und Information. Operationen und Prozedurenschlüsse. www.dimdi.de. Accessed May 14, 2009.
8. Fischer W. *Diagnosis Related Groups (DRGs) und Pflege.* Bern: Springer-Verlag: 2002.
9. Graeber S, Richter S, Folz J, Pham PT, Jacob P, Schilling MK. Clinical pathways in general surgery. Development, implementation, and evaluation. *Methods Inf Med.* 2007;46:574-579.
10. Elektronische Fallakte. http://www.fallakte.de/index.html. Accessed May 10, 2009.
11. Hübner U, Sellemann B. Current and future use of ICT for patient care and management in German acute hospitals – a Comparison between the Nursing and the Hospital Managers' Perspectives. *Methods Inf Med.* 2005:44:528-536.
12. Hübner U, Sellemann B, Frey A. *IT-Report Gesundheitswesen – Schwerpunkt Integrierte Versorgung.* Hannover: Schriftenreihe des Ministeriums für Wirtschaft, Arbeit und Verkehr Hannover, 2007. www.it-report-gesundheitswesen.de. Accessed May 2, 2009.
13. Hübner U, Sellemann B, Flemming D, Genz M, Frey A. *IT-Report Gesundheitswesen – Schwerpunkte Pflegeinformationssysteme und eBusiness.* Hannover: Schriftenreihe des Ministeriums für Wirtschaft, Arbeit und Verkehr Hannover; 2008. www.it-report-gesundheitswesen.de. Accessed May 2, 2009.
14. Frey A, Sellemann B, Hübner U. Was zeichnet Innovatoren im Bereich EPA aus? In: Wichmann HE, Nowak D, Zapf A (eds) Kongress Medizin und Gesellschaft 2007 – Programm- und Abstractband, Augsburg, 2007;146-147. www.egms.de//en/meetings/gmds2007/07gmds093.shtml. Accessed May 2, 2009.
15. Deutsches Netzwerk für Qualitätsentwicklung in der Pflege. Expertenstandard Entlassungsmanagement in der Pflege, Entwicklung - Konsentierung – Implementierung. Osnabrück, 2009. http://www.dnqp.de. Accessed October 20, 2009.
16. Giehoff C, Hübner U. Der elektronische Pflegebericht des Netzwerks Versorgungskontinuität in der Region Osnabrück" – Evaluationsergebnisse und ihre Konsequenzen. Pflegewissenschaft - www.printernet.com. 2006/06, 371-377. Accessed October 20, 2009.
17. Kuntze A, Hübner U. Vergleich von. NANDA, ICNP und HHCC Pflegediagnosen. Pflegewissenschaft - www.printernet.com. 2006/02, 34-37. Accessed October 20, 2009.
18. Giehoff C, Hübner U, Berekoven B, et al. The Interaction of NANDA and ICNP Coded Nursing Diagnoses: an Application Driven Perspective. *Medinfo. 2004;* (CD):1615.
19. Hübner U, Flemming D, Schulz-Gödker A, Strotmann U. Software zur digitalen Wunddokumentation: Kriterien zur Bewertung von marktgängiger Software. Wundmanagement. In press.
20. Pflegenetz-Heilbronn. www.pflegenetz-heilbronn.de. Accessed May 14, 2009.

21. NANDA International (NANDA-I). NANDA Pflegediagnosen. Aus dem Amerikanischen von Michael Herrmann und Jürgen Georg. Deutschsprachige Ausgabe herausgegeben von Jürgen Georg. Bern: Verlag Hans Huber, 2005.

22. International Council of Nurses. ICNP V1.0 German. http://www.icn.ch/icnp_translations.htm. Accessed May 10, 2009.

23. Saba VK. Pflegepraxisklassifikation (CCC). Deutschsprachige Ausgabe übersetzt und herausgegeben von Karl-Heinz Grimm. Bern: Verlag Hans Huber, 2009.

24. McCloskey-Dochterman J, Bulechek GM. Pflegeinterventionsklassifikation (NIC). Aus dem Amerikanischen von Ute Villwock, Michael Herrmann, Rudolf Widmer und Jürgen Georg. Deutschsprachige Ausgabe herausgegeben von Rudolf Widmer. Bern: Verlag Hans Huber, 2009.

25. Johnson M, Maas ML, Moorhead S (eds.) Pflegeergebnisklassifikation (NOC). Übersetzt, bearbeitet und herausgegeben von Peter Tackenberg und Andreas Büscher. Bern: Verlag Hans Huber, 2005.

26. What is LEP? http://www.lep.ch/index.php?lang=en. Accessed. May 10, 2009.

27. Güttler K. [Knowledge based software solution for nursing care planning and documentation: uniform and reproducible recording with apenio.] Article in German. *Pflege Z.* 2006;59(9):541-544.

28. Wieteck P. [Documentation using ENP standardized nursing nomenclature: recording detailed and current nursing process] Article in German. *Pflege Z.* 2007;60(5):257-259.

29. Sellemann B, Flemming D, Frey A, Hübner U. Informationssysteme in der Pflege: Fortschritt oder Stagnation in den letzten 5 Jahren? In: I. Zöllner und R. Klar (Hrsg.) Tagungsband 53. Jahrestagung der Gesellschaft für Medizinische Informatik, Biometrie und Epidemiologie. 2008. 576-578. http://www.egms.de/en/meetings/gmds2008/08gmds171.shtml. Accessed May 10, 2009.

30. Schrader U, Tackenberg P, Widmer R, Portenier L, König P. The ICNP-BaT - a multilingual web-based tool to support the collaborative translation of the International Classification for Nursing Practice (ICNP). *Stud Health Technol Inform.* 2007;129(Pt 1):751-754.

31. Elektronische Gesundheitskarte. www.gematik.de. Accessed May 14, 2009.

32. Hübner U. Telematik und Pflege: gewährleistet die elektronische Gesundheitskarte (eGK) eine verbesserte Versorgung für pflegebedürftige Bürgerinnen und Bürger? *GMS Med Inform Biom Epidemiol.* 2006;2(1):Doc01.

Case Study 16G

Spain: The Growth and Development of Nursing and Information Systems—An Update from 2006 to 2009

By Myriam Martin Fernández, PhD, MSN, RN; and Luis Cibanal Juan, PhD, BPsy, RN

Introduction

The Path toward Technological Innovation in the Use of Nursing Records—Changes Since 2006

Since writing the case study in the first edition of this book in 2006, rapid change has occurred in the adoption and use of EHR technology within Spain's healthcare systems, nursing, and society, in general. The standardization initiatives in interoperability and terminology being driven by the EU continue to influence Spain's EHR strategies and, specifically, nursing's thinking. One of the most critical benefits of the EU standardization initiatives has been the support it has given to nursing education in Spain. In order to have a standard level of education across professions, the EU defined standards for university-based degree programs and advanced graduate degrees. The Declaration of Bologna defined the strategy for European higher education programs and set 2010 as the date for having the changes in place. The significance of these educational initiatives for nursing in Spain is that the Declaration of Bologna made it possible to establish the first nursing graduate programs at the master's and doctoral levels in schools of nursing with nursing faculty. Unfortunately, as of mid-2009, no additional nursing degree programs have been developed in Spain. Currently, nursing education is offered as a three-year university degree. There is very restricted access to master's or doctoral programs as a result of the very limited number of graduate programs that have been created in response to the Bologna Declaration. Only a few university programs exist today that offer a master's program and also provide access to a doctoral program. Although there are a number of programs in early development, no defined curriculum structures for graduate studies have been applied nor are new areas, such as informatics, being offered as a class, degree, or competencies in our nursing curricula. Even in our few graduate programs, the nursing faculty have their advance degrees in other subjects; importantly though, the first generation of doctorally-prepared nurses in Spain is beginning now.

In the intervening four years since our previous case study was written, developments within the nursing realm of ICT have revolved around questioning "nursing records" as a single discipline view, compared with a "team" view, and the need to interchange patient information across disciplines. Terminology standards and nursing models continue to be core initiatives that nursing leadership in Spain use to drive professional advancement and system requirements for nursing within EHRs.

Nursing in Spain: Background

Nursing in Spain evolved over the past century as a religious-vocational calling. As scientific knowledge expanded over the late nineteenth and twentieth centuries, Spanish nursing shifted from being in religious domains to being in secular vocational schools. Similar to England and the United States, by the 1950s, nursing was clearly defined as an auxiliary to medicine, with education focused on carrying out tasks under the direction of physicians. Spain's professional nursing leaders succeeded in elevating nursing education to a university degree level in the late 1970s as part of the effort to raise nursing to a full professional status.[1] These efforts drew heavily upon the nursing theory and nursing process models emerging from the United States during the 1960s and 1970s.[2] Spain's nursing leaders moved the base for nursing education and practice to holistic concepts derived from a theoretical scientific base of nursing science independent from medical science. In Spain, this newly achieved professional autonomy is still playing out in our workforce and educational programs and is most vividly captured in our dialogues around the building and use of nursing electronic record systems.

The current state of the nursing knowledge framework reflects the fact that "care" has been an activity that for centuries has lacked conceptual systematization, as well as interest in the research of phenomena, and even lacks a solid historiography tradition that would allow us to rebuild our past from primary sources. Joined to the conceptualization and the religious philosophy imposed was also the fact that the people in charge of care were traditionally women, who were denied access to formal education.[1]

In the last few decades, nursing has undergone an important transformation that has followed the changes in how we view the concept of health-illness. At the beginning, nurses were identified with the technical aspects of care, exams, and medical treatment that all focused on "curing." Later, the evolution of nursing theories and models saw the incorporation of the caring concept and explained health maintenance as "helping the person that requires care, or providing a substitute for aspects where the person is not independent, and understanding health in a dynamic way, with the intervention of biological and psychological aspects, including those related to culture, social services, and the person's beliefs."[3] This view of healthcare, thus, requires a multi-sector intervention.

In the same way that the concept of care has evolved, the environment for professional practice has also undergone important changes. With time, nursing has been developing into a science and profession, and it has modified the way it tends to people's needs and the way care is applied, together with the evolution of the understanding of health-illness processes. This is why nursing is continually being defined and adapted to change, as mentioned before, from technical and intuitive nursing to nursing supported by its own body of knowledge and by a nurse role that focuses in the human aspects.[3]

Nursing in Spain understands that to think critically is to think with a purpose, toward the attainment of a well-defined outcome. This is why critical thinking is based on scientific principles and the scientific method and requires strategies that maximize human potential and compensate for problems caused by human nature. In other words, critical thinking, strives for generating decisions based on evidence (facts) instead of conjectures (assumptions).

By 2006, nursing in Spain had many ongoing initiatives in which nursing found itself "learning to learn." In the area of electronic records, nursing leaders very clearly defined that ICT systems had to be a helping tool because conclusions and decisions made by nurses affect the lives of people. Electronic records were to be designed to help critical thinking as guided by solid reasoning, a precise and disciplined way of thinking that promotes exactitude and depth in the gathering of data, and a looking toward a clear identification of nursing problems.

It is because of this historic context that the efforts to implement electronic nursing records in Spain over the past fifteen years have always been done hand-in-hand with standardization of care plans under diagnostic taxonomies that are guided by nursing models.[4,5] Most nursing organizations in Spain decided to guide their care following the Virginia Henderson model[6] for organizing and structuring their nursing documentation. However, a small number have also implemented other models, such as those from Dorothea Orem, Callista Roy, or Madeleine Lenninger.[2] Regardless of nursing model adopted, there is general consensus across all nursing organizations in Spain in carrying out efforts to incorporate a nursing terminology based on the three "N's": NANDA (North American Nursing Diagnosis Association), NIC (Nursing Interventions Classification), and NOC (Nursing Outcomes Classification).[5] The first information systems in Spain began from administrative systems and slowly extended into covering clinical processes. For nursing, the approach was to implement unique electronic documentation records as a separate system that would become part of the everyday nursing practice. Because of the requirements to include a nursing model framework and NANDA, NIC, and NOC terminology, the development of nursing systems in Spain has commonly shared base requirements. This is the current state of nursing electronic record systems today in Spain.

Nursing Professionalism and Technology

Nursing, understood as the science and the art of caring for the health and well-being of people, revolves around care based on human needs and responses of the individual. Nursing care refers to professional care for health recovery and maintenance and provides the highest degree of well-being.[1] From this perspective, no other profession currently offers these services and has led nursing to become a solid, society-entrenched profession and an important part of the healthcare system. Nursing is the most numerous health professional group, and its contribution in terms of assistance is fundamental within the healthcare system.

The following elements are those that have been adopted to raise nursing to a professional level within Spain, facilitate change, and serve as the basic requirements for nursing electronic record systems:[7]

- The utilization of a nursing model that conceptualizes the person and the role of nursing.
- The use of the nursing process, as a method for providing care that forces the establishment of criteria for outcomes.
- The utilization of standardized systems of nursing language for clinical information referring to care.

Adopting a Conceptual Model

In the 2006 case study,[4] we referenced that nursing thought leaders in Spain recognized a need for a scientific model to structure the practice of nursing, as well as to support research. Pragmatically, a nursing model was also needed as a reference marker that allows nurses to state the nature of their profession and to differentiate it from others in the field of health services. A professional nurse can explain the nature of her/his job to co-workers and users, as well as the underlying nursing management and administration responsibilities in a model that reflects care provisions. Moreover, a model guides activities, helps with professional obligations, and sets a unified goal to which the nurse can refer. Therefore, a model serves as a practical and theoretical instrument that clarifies and helps nurses to communicate in a more significant manner, as well as acting as a guide for caring, teaching, and investigating.[7]

The development of the first computerized nursing solution in Spain had a huge impact around 1996. It was implemented in eighty hospitals in Spain due to winning a public bid for all the Spanish healthcare at that time, before regional government decisions could be made by each autonomous region. It was the first solution created by nurses for nurses, and, in the beginning, it used the Virginia Henderson model[6] as the basis for its development. Assessments were made using the fourteen requirements of the model, provided decision support for the diagnostics in the assessment process, suggested objectives, and pushed guidelines for planned activities.

Still today, the main nursing model used in Spain as a reference marker for hospital practice is based on the Henderson model. The Henderson model's straightforwardness and relative simplicity has made it easy for Spanish nurses to apply in practice and to comprehend as a framework for their critical thinking. For these reasons, it is judged to be the best nursing model and is the basis for its widespread adoption in Spain. Virginia Henderson originally published her model in 1956,[6] and subsequent theorists have challenged, refined, and built upon her work.[1,2]

There has been a comparative analysis about the relation between the Henderson model and Donabedian's model that helped to extend the justification for using these models to improve care quality. Donabedian explains in his total quality model[8] that one has to determine the needs of the patient after evaluating the necessities and establishing the objectives that are to be attained from caring for the person. Donabedian's schematic presentation about which components come into play in the healthcare process, also makes the point that needs are the cause behind determining the behavior of both the client and the care provider.[8]

Conceptual Model and Standardized Terminologies

Clinical practice and nursing models in Spain today have not changed much since 2006. At this point in delimiting what nursing used to do and the rationale behind it, we saw the emergence of a way of recording care based on an electronic format supported on the following:

1. **Assessment:** it is based on a nursing model, mostly on Virginia Henderson's model,[5] which assesses the 14 basic needs of the individual. For each need, there is a series of signs and symptoms (defining characteristics) and their causes (related or risk factors).
2. **Diagnosis:** it is based on the normalized NANDA language and offered because the system provided assistance regarding the different weights assigned to the components of the assessment, what used to be named a "diagnosis assistant." This assessment used label diagnosis characteristics "per se" from NANDA.
3. **Planning:** when selecting diagnoses, electronic records provided associated goals to the nurse. First efforts had objectives that were to be accomplished in terms of the presented problem; the most current efforts on electronic records include result criteria (NOC) and indicators to be evaluated. And, based on the objectives mentioned previously, a series of actions (care) to carry out, currently known as interventions (NIC).

4. **Execution:** these actions or interventions create a care agenda that the nurse would print at the beginning of her/his shift, containing the care to be carried out for her/his patients and which provided an estimation of the workload regarding each patient.

5. **Evaluation:** the objectives and/or results were measured to evaluate the status of the patient.

Many systems for nursing electronic records could also include predefined standard plans with this same format: plan selection, selection of diagnoses, objectives and/or results, and of actions and/or interventions. In many cases, the nursing organization and system developers added the concept of "potential complications" or "collaboration problems" based on Carpenito's work (1995).[9] Thus, aside from nursing problems, there was an addition of potential complications that the patient could sustain, together with their corresponding actions and/or interventions.

As we referenced in 2006, any information system intended for use in Spanish hospitals must fulfil these requirements for a nursing model and terminology. It would not be accepted otherwise, as it would be equivalent to taking a step backwards in all the efforts taking place in Spain. All the nursing managers in all the hospitals in Spain are in agreement on these requirements as basic to professional nursing practice. Although certain critics believe that NANDA diagnostics should adopt a cultural change in order to be applied to the clinical Spanish community, nursing leaders all agree that it should be used in spite of its cultural lack of fit. The need to adapt NANDA applies to hospitals primary care, emergent and intensive care unit. This has not changed—no progress has been made on developing a culturally appropriate Spanish version of NANDA.

But since 2006, other questions related to this situation have arisen. There has been a general agreement on the necessity of including the concepts of complication and collaboration problems from Carpenito's model.[9] Also, given the many projects in process for implementing nursing documentation, the focus on how nursing has to electronically document work started critical review discussions. From these discussions emerged questions around the need of documenting the interdisciplinary work and not just centralizing in the nursing methodology. Even though Spain is divided into 17 autonomous governmental communities, the development and maturity of this recognition to move to a more interdisciplinary approach in care delivery and in nursing electronic record systems is variable, depending upon community. Some communities are moving in this direction and others have not yet done so.

One of the points beginning to provide evidence about what these electronic recording systems are missing and what they need to include is the ability to share documentation with the other health team members on collaboration of a patient's problems. It is evident that these systems have not stopped being isolated when the nurse needs to record points of collaboration with physicians and, at the same time, physicians are not part of an electronically integrated process. Certain nursing communities have started to ask themselves: "Are we charting interdisciplinary work twice?" or "Would physicians have to chart their problems when collaborating with nurses?" and, even more broadly, "Why only chart collaboration with physicians and not with therapists?"

Since the beginning, there have been multiple efforts in healthcare organizations to adapt to the previously discussed schemes that defined nursing records. And, leveraging the capabilities of the electronic record, these organizations have joined the effort of incorporating in their everyday activities, a nursing process that required a lot of dedication and effort. Many times these efforts have even served as training for nurses regarding their own terminology, something that they may never have been exposed to previously in their education or practice. The introduction of nursing terminology with the implementation of electronic record systems in many cases proved to be extremely difficult for nurses. As a matter of fact, the utilization of electronic records has even been viewed as an opportunity to help define the field of action for nursing.

A satisfaction survey carried out by the Colegio de Enfermería de Málaga (Nursing College of Málaga) in 2008 about nursing information systems on more than three nursing record systems, provided the following conclusions:

- Utilization of total or partial nursing methodology, or the use of help systems, when present, is widespread.
- The incorporation of nursing terminology may be a reflection of the change in culture that is occurring in this profession regarding the use of the methodology.
- It is worth noticing that there are key improvements that are revealed from the results, such as structural–time and computers–and training–NOC, NIC, and time management–improvements.

- Qualitative analysis reinforces all findings from quantitative analysis and adds contextual matters, such as the importance given to information systems and their relationship with the quality of care and professional development.[10]

Since 2006, other key developments are that many discussions have started about the plan for all nursing documentation in nursing record systems to follow the nursing process. Documenting one-by-one the steps in the nursing process is found by nurses to be highly complex in its use and application, both in language and the way it works. But aside from this, the fact that this nursing process scheme was not incorporated into workflow processes made it much more difficult to manage. Thus, nursing begins to realize that something is missing.

The discipline of nursing works in collaboration with other professionals, but it is also the axis of everything that happens to the client, it manages the patient's care. The nurse is "in the patient's front line of defense;" she/he knows when the patient is stable, when something is not right and she/he is the first one to perceive this and to manage the necessary resources to control any urgent situation. The nurse is in the patient's care core venue.[11] In Spain, the first efforts to ensure that integrated processes and coordination of care were actually happening started with the generation of nursing discharge reports. Patients would take these reports home to ensure continuity with primary care, or they would be sent electronically to different care centers for the patient to go and continue with his or her care. These reports (it could not be any other way) incorporated at the least the diagnoses from NANDA that were resolved during the patient's stay plus those diagnoses that remained active at discharge. Obviously the discussion is still maintained among the nursing leaders, but this is not enough. More continuum of care is needed. Exchange of information cannot only be based on sending a discharge report. The need to continue in primary care those care plans that were started, for example, in the hospital, is one of the next goals.

Requirements for Electronic Nursing Records in 2010

In 2006, we explained how the experience with computerized solutions was the first approach to standardized nursing language use, but there was a lot left to do. Spanish nurses found huge difficulties in the practical integration of information systems into the work setting, due to two major reasons. The first challenge was that many nurses had not used computers and had poor computer skills. Over these past four years, however, personal computers and Internet use has become widely adopted by the Spanish population. Also, health organizations began to implement information systems, and therefore, nurses' computer literacy skills increased. The second factor that has presented major challenges is that the nursing workforce was not familiar with the practical use of the nursing care process and scientific method, model use, or the NANDA, NIC and NOC nursing terminologies. Consequently, when nursing record systems were implemented, nursing had to learn these new professional dimensions of nursing, as well as the new technology. This implies that the workload in the nursing units was increased by this learning process and especially with the implementation of nursing record systems that carried all these changes.

As we examine the current state of electronic nursing record systems, it is clear that this first generation has fallen short of expectations. Some stand-alone nursing solutions were not flexible enough and did not allow purely computer-driven care, not to mention the fact that this electronic chart needed to coexist with others on paper. For many hospitals, these deficiencies have resulted in a partial use of the computerized solutions only for graphs, intake/output, and progress comments—much to the disappointment of system users and administrators. Now, nurses have become increasingly more familiar with these nursing languages and way of working using the nursing record system. There is absolutely no document generated by a Congress or Symposium in Spain related to nursing work that does not mention the issues of nursing system's methodology and analysis.

In 2000, the Institute of Medicine in the United States published its report "*To Err is Human*"[12] in which it demonstrated that between 44,000 to 98,000 people died every year due to errors in the medical system. Since then, other developed countries have carried out like studies with similar findings. The most recent study has been ENEAS[13] (National Study of Adverse Events Linked to Hospitalization, acronym from Spanish). Published in March 2006 in Spain, the ENEAS study reported an incidence of 8.4% of patients with adverse events directly related to hospital care, which is a higher rate than that observed in the United States (3.7%).

Spain's adverse events rate is similar to the rates reported from studies from Australia, the United Kingdom, and New Zealand.[12]

Knowing that nursing surveillance is one of the key factors to reducing adverse events, nursing leaders in Spain have started to be conscious of the need for integrated electronic systems. Professionals assisting the patient on his/her health need to have at hand tools that are not fragmented, that start from a unique architecture to ensure integrated processes, and that make sure that patients are being cared for under total quality criteria. This constant patient evaluation establishes nurses in a role described as a "front line of defense" for patient safety, according to The Joint Commission (formerly known as the Joint Commission on Accreditation of Healthcare Organizations) in 2001.[11]

In the 2006 case study, we presented some of the early thinking in which the patient chart was starting to be determined as unique and use of a nursing model (mostly Henderson) and normalized nursing language began. Since then, widespread attention and discussions have focused on these aspects of professional nursing in Spain. And this shift in nursing's thinking and focus is the main difference in the past four years. In 2006, all discussions were focused on nursing methodology, models, and care planning with NANDA, NIC, and NOC. Four years later and benefiting from the first generation of nursing systems implementations, the theme now is the imperative that nursing professionals cannot continue to be overloaded with partial systems because by doing this, we are inducing another factor altering patient safety and adding to nurses' workload.

Summary

In a multidisciplinary healthcare environment, it is essential to integrate healthcare data into multiple systems for the provision of care. With the increasing relevance of globalization, we should promote the development of information systems that facilitate communication and data exchange among different professionals, healthcare-providing environments, geographical regions, and languages. Likewise, systems should favor efficient communication with clients and families. Our initial efforts to integrate the information started with fragmented systems that did not originate from a common database; we reached a partial integration, but not a functional one. A concept change is needed that considers process implementation, and not the implementation of isolated systems, when establishing an IT system in a hospital. We are talking about communication, and communication is indispensable to meet the efforts to coordinate care for optimum safety and care quality—the goals pursued by all healthcare organizations.[14]

References

1. Hernandez Conesa J, Esteban Albert M. Fundamentos de la Enfermería. Teoría y Método. McGraw Hill: Madrid, 1999.

2. Marriner. Teorías y Modelos en enfermería. Elsevier: Madrid, 2003

3. Alberdi-Castells RM. (2000) Nosotros cuidamos: la práctica en el ámbito comunitario. Palma. www.enfermeriacomunitaria.org/actividades/IIICongreso/alberdi.html. Accessed October 20, 2009.

4. Fernández Martín M, Siles González J. Spain: The growth and development of nursing and information systems. In: Weaver C, et al, eds. *Nursing and Informatics for the 21ˢᵗ Century. An international look at practice, trends and the future*. Chicago: HIMSS, 2006, pp. 422-426.

5. Leonor Rodriguez, S (2004). El lenguaje común enfermero y la normalización de la práctica: un camino hacia la excelencia enfermera. Revista Excelencia Enfermera. Num 1.

6. Henderson V. La naturaleza de la Enfermería. Reflexiones 25 años después. Madrid: McGraw-Hill Interamericana, 1995.

7. Morales Asensio, J. M. (2000). Ponencia. http://www.asanec.org/Congreso/Evaluacion_Morales.htm. Accessed October 1, 2009.

8. Esteban Albert M. (1992). La construcción de una disciplina. Sevilla: AEED.

9. Carpenito L. Planes de cuidados y Documentación en Enfermería. Madrid: McGraw-Hill Interamericana, 1993.

10. Duarte Climents G, Sánchez GómezB. (2008). Sistemas de información y enfermería: encuesta de opinión. Colegio de Enfermería de Málaga. http://www.colegioenfermeriamalaga.com/Web/Publicaciones/SSII%20y%20Enfermeria_v4.pdf. Accessed October 1, 2009.

11. Fernández Martín M. (2007). La disciplina enfermera: epicentro de los errores clínicos. Cultura de los Cuidados, 1er semestre, año XI, n.21. Alicante: CECOVA.

12. IOM. Kohn L, Corrigan G, Molla S. *To Err is Human: Building a Safer Health System*. Washington, DC: The National Academies Press, 2000.

13. ENEAS (Estudio Nacional sobre los Efectos Adversos ligados a la hospitalización). (2005). Ministerio de Sanidad y Consumo.

14. Cibanal Juan L, Siles González J. In: Pacheco M (2001). La comunicación, niveles y las relaciones humanas. http://www.monografias.com/trabajos25/comunicacion/comunicacion.shtml?monosearch. Accessed May 2009.

Case Study 16H

Information Technologies and Nursing Practice: The Portuguese Case

By Filipe Suares Pereira, ND (PhD), MNSc, BN, RN;
and Abel Paiva e Silva, ND (PhD), MNSc, BN, RN

Introduction

This case study abstracts key aspects of the Portuguese experience on the introduction of information technologies in nursing practice documentation. Three main action-research projects are chronologically summarized here to promote a comprehensive understanding of the national case.

The first project, started in 1996 by Silva,[1,2] develops a study with two cycles of change on nursing documentation in three hospital units. The first cycle of change was focused on data structure and content and the second one focused on Nursing Information System (NIS) support. Adopting a constructivist research paradigm, this process began with the following aims: (a) build a data model for the NIS by adapting the NIS currently used; (b) develop the core concepts that describe nurses' practice and; (c) integrate nursing terminologies—International Classification for Nursing Practice (ICNP®)[3] in Portuguese into the EHR.

In 1998, a second research effort, coordinated by Sousa et al.[4] and based on the same methodology and objectives was carried out in three primary health centers. These two studies were sponsored by the Information Technologies' Department of the Portuguese Ministry of Health and represent the first substantive contribution of nurses to the Portuguese EHR.

Between 2003 and 2006, the global research program evolved to the third study[5] of a data aggregation model that would allow a consistent production of indicators about nursing care.

The Initial NIS

As the work developed, a model of NIS emerged. The characteristic aspects of the data model were acquired to account for the observed care, and the data presented allow us to determine the consistency between the characteristics of the model and the needs for organization, management, and treatment of information in nursing. There are seven characteristics associated with the content and with the structure of the developed NIS model:

1. The inclusion of the ICNP as the reference terminology used
2. The pre-combination of terms for nursing diagnoses, interventions, and outcomes documentation
3. The articulation between the natural language and the classified language
4. Efficient documentation with minimal data duplication
5. Referential integrity between the elements of nursing documentation
6. Inclusion of unit-specific common aspects of care
7. Data collection for dynamic and meaningful care planning

It is believed that the language used to describe nursing is an important aspect for describing the specific knowledge of nursing and its development. The language used by the theorists in description of theories, conceptual models, and nursing ideologies is also considered important, as well as the language used by nurses in their practice to describe the provided nursing care.[6]

Nursing Documentation

The content analysis of the nursing documentation—not only for the ones involved in these studies, but also for previous studies—clearly demonstrates that there are nursing classifications in use, but these are usually related to local customs, which are often not usable to develop nursing knowledge that supports nurses' involvement on an international level.

The parameterization of the contents per care unit refers to the process of suitability of the items of information determined by frequency of use in the unit. At that stage, there was a reflection on practice with the purpose of developing consistent parameters on the nursing content. Achieving this consistency would support structured nursing documentation and promote the adoption of the NIS model.

Nursing Practice

The identification of the main focuses of nursing practice in each care unit included diagnostic judgments, nursing interventions and the need for the guidelines for implementing these interventions, and the gathering of data to monitor the patient's progress. All of these topics serve as points for starting discussions among the nurses about nursing practice, and for promoting the self-identification of the nurse's professional needs.

Using the natural language proved to be indispensable to the adequate description of the nursing care. The natural language in free text documentation must be used, even in the phase of precombination of terms, to avoid syntactic constructions (based in ICNP® terms) that make no sense.

Evolution of NIS

Another characteristic of the NIS model, which emerged from these works, was the evolution from a side-by-side positioning of the entities to the vertical positioning of these entities. For example: first noted was the description of the need for nursing care through the documentation of the active nursing diagnosis, and second were the prescribed interventions. This characteristic of the model is more coherent with the critical thinking involved in the nurses' conception of care: each intervention is prescribed according to the global situation defined by the set of active nursing diagnoses and not according to a particular diagnosis independently of the other active nursing diagnoses. In addition, it prevents the duplication of nursing interventions, which have a connection with more than one of the active diagnoses.

This characteristic of the model is also aligned with another aspect related to decision making. There are situations in which the nursing diagnosis documentation is important because it conveys the experience of the patient's process of transition,[7] independent of receiving or not receiving prescribed interventions (nurse's behaviors). This arrangement of the information simplifies the nurse's identification of the nursing diagnosis without feeling necessarily compelled to prescribe interventions which could inhibit his/her documentation of these phenomena, which are very important for the continuity and quality of the care.

The Change's Impact

The change in the structure and in the content of the NIS generated modifications on a set of aspects, including:

- **Production of the Data** – duplication of data, time spent producing the documentation, standardization of the documentation and referential integrity between the data;
- **Access to the Data** – making the information guided by the temporal criterion available (visualization of all of the information relative to a specific moment – visualization criterion: moment);
- **Making the Information Guided by the Type of Documented Information Available** (e.g., visualization of all the information relative to the nursing diagnosis – visualization criterion: type of information);
- **Care Description** – documentation of the common aspects of the nursing care in the unit, specific data referring to the documentation of the patient's progress related to the nursing diagnosis, complete care description;
- **Usefulness of the Data for the Management/Investigation** – possibility of producing process and outcomes (results) indicators and potential to change information into knowledge.

Figure 16H-1 illustrates the impact produced by the change in the NIS structure and ICNP implementation in the four referred aspects. The implementation of the revised NIS—from a narrative logic based on the moment of production, to a logic of production based on the type of information—had a positive impact on the attributes/qualities of the data produced, the description of the common aspects of care, as well as a systematic documentation of the nursing diagnosis status.

The NIS model that includes ICNP improved the aspects referring to the production of data, comparative to the NIS previously in use. The NIS used in the initial phase, before the change produced by Silva and by Sousa and collaborators, generated the need to duplicate information between shifts and increased the amount of documented information, since they valued the documentation of what had occurred in a specific period of time in a narrative style (usually in the shift). Therefore, the production of indicators was impracti-

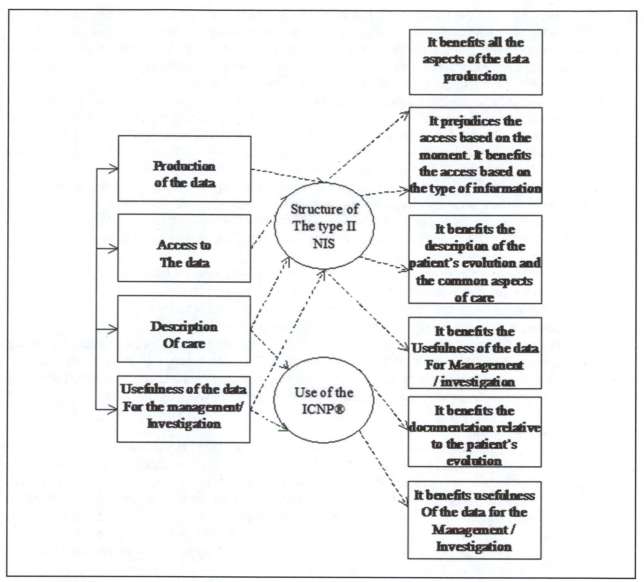

Figure 16H-1. *Illustration of the Relations between the Concepts Referring to the NIS*

cable, and the use of the nursing documentation data for research purposes was difficult. The exclusive use of the natural language emphasized the previous difficulties.

ICNP into NIS

The implementation of the new NIS incorporating the ICNP improved all the aspects associated with the production of the data. The complexity of the use of multi-axial classifications—which are more interesting from the point of view of the flexibility of use, the creation of almost infinite possibilities, and culturally much more adjustable and suitable—demand terminology services working behind (back end) the NIS, since the possibility of using the ICNP regularly in real time for documentation is complex. Consequently, the use of free text and natural language are essential to correctly describe the provided care. It is important to stress that the use of the free text together with texts which are precombined with terms of the ICNP is perfectly possible (and desirable).

The care descriptions benefited from the structure and content change of the NIS. The description of the common aspects of care was assumed and the standardized documentation relative to the nursing diagnosis status became a fact, which benefited the continuity of the care and the production of outcomes (results) indicators. Although the description of individualization of care was influenced by the nature of the NIS, it strongly depended on aspects related to the care models and, maybe above all, on the nurse's intention.

Bearing in mind that the introduction of uniform language does not itself change the care conception, we decided to use a nursing diagnosis documentation model which allowed all nurses to describe the identified care needs according to the way they interpreted them (in the light of the care conception that they hold). Nevertheless, it is important to emphasize that the data showed a higher number of nursing diagnoses, status of diagnosis and interventions per patient, after this implemented change.

In relation to the nursing diagnosis status, the area of the patient's *knowledge and abilities* about how to deal with health transitions took a great deal of importance in the documentation. This change observed in the analysis shows a considerable qualitative difference. The fact that more importance was given to the patient's knowledge and abilities about how to deal with the situation was not present in the initial phase. This is a direct influence of the change process based on the reflection on the action.

A considerable increase in the documentation of the nursing diagnoses status took place. In comparison with the initial evaluation, there was a more systematic documentation with verification of more than one record relative to the diagnosis status in several situations. This very important change affects the evaluation of the patient's evolution and also evaluation of the possibility of the nursing-sensitive outcomes inference and resulting outcomes (results) indicators.

From the nursing interventions documentation, it is possible to verify the following:
- Rise in the number of documented nursing interventions in the care plan
- Fall in the number of documented nursing interventions in the nursing notes
- Increase in the use of interventions from all types of action, in ICNP

However, it is important to emphasize that the difficulties with the granularity of the description of nursing interventions may disturb the reliability of the comparison. This problem occurs because the same nursing behavior can be named with different levels of description, even after the standardization work is done. This aspect raises several questions and challenges when we discuss a data aggregation model.

Impact for Nurses

In spite of the problems, nurses' opinion about the changes operated in NIS was very positive. Evaluation of nurses' opinions about the changes with the NIS included 26 questions using a five-point Likert type scale. The focused questions refer to topics related to: continuity of care; care planning; systematization of the documentation; duplication of the data; accessibility of the data; language used; and suitability of the NIS. The questionnaire also included two open-ended questions asking nurses' opinions about the positive aspects/advantages and the negative aspects/disadvantages of the change that had taken place in the NIS. The 26 structured questions of the questionnaire were repeated (52 questions), 26 of them referring to the initial NIS and the other 26 to the implemented NIS.

After the data analysis, significant differences became evident in three of the produced scales. The incorporated language in the nursing documentation, the quality of the NIS, the improvements related to the care planning and continuity of care are the main advantages in the structure and content change of the NIS.

From 1996 to now, a great number of public hospitals and primary health centers adhered to the utilization of the informatics tools that resulted from the projects described above. In this national context, Sousa[8] developed (2001/2005) a tool to allow the real-time sharing of information between hospitals and primary health centers. With this tool, the "family-nurse" can look at the care plan of a patient who was discharged from the hospital when the patient still is physically inside the hospital building. Similarly, nurses from the hospital can see "patient's care plans" defined in primary health centers by their family-nurses. Of course, this represents an enormous advantage for ensuring continuity of care and its benefit to the patient.

Toward a Portuguese Nursing Minimum Data Set

The potential use of data documented in the NIS is an aspect strongly valued by nurses. So, the use of the electronic NIS can create new tools to describe, evaluate, and research nursing care. All the work completed prior to 2003 represents the starting point to a Nursing Minimum Data Set (NMDS) in Portugal. We have a significant number of hospitals and health centers that share the same Nursing Data Model in their NIS and use the same nursing language—International Classification for Nursing Practice (ICNP).[3]

The use of the same nursing language to document nursing diagnoses, interventions, and outcomes is a central question in any data aggregation strategy since the ability to compare nursing care rests on data and information based on "... definitions and uniform categories..."[9(p422)] In the actual Nursing Data Model in use at Portuguese hospitals and health centers, nursing diagnoses, interventions, and outcomes are predetermined combinations of ICNP terms. The incorporation of nursing diagnoses, interventions, and outcomes in the content of the NIS made possible a paradigm change in terms of "nursing visibility." We now can "turn visible what nurses do," and "make visible what clients reach with nursing care."

Recognizing the potential associated with the NMDS definition and implementation, different organizations have been endeavoring to do NMDS development and consolidation, around the world.[10,11] In Portugal, after the studies of Sousa et al.[4] and Silva,[1,2] the Portuguese Nurses Association (OE – Ordem dos Enfermeiros) recognized the "need of a Nursing Minimum Data Set..."[12(p157)] based in a common nursing language (ICNP) as strategic to promote the continuous improvement of nursing care quality.

The benefits that result from the existence of the NMDS have been explored by several authors. We can talk about two great "force lines." First is the nursing care quality promotion and improvement, based on information concerning the outcomes (results) obtained from nursing care activities.[13-17] Second is the identification and description of patterns of nursing "problems" and interventions, starting from the analysis of significant samples of data obtained with the NMDS.[18-23]

In this context, we developed the NMDS in partnership with the Portuguese Nurses Association (OE) and the Ministry of Health. Development is based on the idea that the NMDS is a part of NIS content, collected at the point-of-care, and analyzed and interpreted systematically and regularly to answer to the specific needs for nursing information from multiple users. The NMDS clinical elements represent a subset of the totality of the nursing data, that does not demand additional tasks of documentation by nurses, with the same definitions and codes around the Portuguese Health Network. The Portuguese Health System is almost entirely public and funded by the government.

The methodology used to determine the NMDS definition was based in an Action – Research approach that took place between January 2003 and October 2006. The effort involved seven hospitals and ten health centers from the Portuguese Northern Regional Health Administration. The purpose of this research was to define and implement a nursing data aggregation model, that allows the production of information—indicators—with the capacity to translate the nursing contribution to clients health.[5]

The different care contexts involved in the study are health centers and medical and surgical wards, pediatric and obstetrics wards, emergency departments, operating theaters, and intensive care units.

The data aggregation model addresses two purposes: describing client needs and nursing sensitive outcomes; as well as providing nursing indicators useful as a resource for the different levels of decision making. The nursing professionals are committed to continuous quality improvement activities. The nursing outcomes (indicators) serve these two purposes.

Nursing Indicators

Three types of nursing indicators were drafted in the study's first stage: nursing diagnoses frequencies; health gains sensitive to nursing care; and risk prevention indicators. Nursing diagnoses frequencies represent the relative frequency over a period of time of specific nursing diagnoses experienced by patients (for instance, pressure ulcer frequency; or frequency of dependency in self transferring).

Health gains sensitive to nursing care represent the positive evolution or resolution of a previous (negative) nursing diagnosis. For example, when the nursing diagnosis "Dependency in Self Transferring, to a very high degree" was documented, and afterwards, at the end of the period of time in analysis, "Dependency in Self Transferring, to a lesser degree" was documented illustrates this change. Effectiveness of risk prevention represents the accuracy of nurses in preventing the development of a negative impact that was previously identified by a nursing diagnosis of risk. Here are included indicators, such as Pressure Ulcer or Fall Prevention. As defined and tested, the NMDS aggregation model incorporates requirements of availability, reliability, protection and data comparability. It also allows the automatic production of defined indicators from the registered data "at patient bedside," as well on health centers nursing contacts.

Each nursing diagnosis, intervention, and outcome included in this NMDS has the same identification code in patients' records, even if some free text is added to the original sentences built with ICNP terms.[4] All of the extraction, organization, and data aggregation procedures are automatic, taking place at the Health Network and are shared by all of the hospitals and health centers.

The NMDS clinical content focuses around a core of areas of attention. We highlight: self care and adherence; learning (cognitive and of abilities); adaptation and caretaking, concepts associated with parenting and family caregiver roles.[3] The nature of the nursing interventions included in the NMDS content is characterized by a great emphasis in providing cognitive contents and informational resources to clients. Approximately, 85% of the defined interventions are related to "Informing" and "Assisting" the client.[3] The elements incorporated in NMDS content, beyond nursing clinical data, include patients' socio-demographic characteristics, care setting elements, and time elements (e.g., care episode beginning and end date), according to iNMDS recommendations.[24]

Based on findings from the first phase of the research, we consolidated characteristic care dimensions in the different contexts of attendance. In the second research phase, we were able to find the nursing care dimensions represented in the defined NMDS clinical data (these dimensions already existed in the patient documentation), as well as those nursing care dimensions that still remain in "exposed intentions."[2,25]

Evaluation for NMDS

Based on a sample of approximately 90,000 cases (15,363 from hospitals and 73,265 from health centers), we see that the NMDS clinical content related to the dimensions of self care and adherence constitute the aspects that appear in the documentation with larger frequency. In the same way, elements referring to pressure ulcers prevention also assume a major importance. Preparing family for the caretaking activities, as well as the clients' independence promotion in self care, represent aspects that still remain absent from nursing documentation.

We grouped some factors that can explain the gap between the nursing care dimensions that the documentation translates and those still "invisible" in what nurses write into two categories: one related to aspects that are behind the documentation, such as nurses' care conception or nurses' work organization models; another related to the documentation itself, meaning the structural requirements of NIS. When we look at the nursing indicators results, calculated from nursing data collected with this NMDS, in the hospital context, the best results were verified at the level of "complications prevention." In health centers, "knowledge acquisition" deserves prominence. The comparison of results between different contexts of care discloses the potential that local initiatives may lead to health gains, admitting that the quality of nurse professionals contributes to health quality.[5,26]

Summary

The use of nursing quality approaches centered on results can be explained by the difficulties related to the systematic collection and data analysis based in standardized criteria.[25] The existence of mechanisms of regular nursing data analysis can represent a central element for the improvement of the quality of nurses' professional practice.

This NMDS development path allows us to rethink the value associated with the information that results from nursing care. Nursing documentation isn't only a mere "product" of nurses' everyday activities, or to satisfy the promotion of continuity of care or for legal questions. Nursing data documented and stored in the NIS must be conceptualized as an "information substratum" which has potential to be transformed in new products—Outcomes (Indicators) / Knowledge.

At this moment, the debate about political strategies related to the utilization of information technologies in the health sector is emphasizing improving quality of care and clinical governance. It is possible to anticipate that Portugal will soon have a Health Minimum Data Set nationally defined and an established Master Patient Index. With the national harmonization of some structural aspects of the information system and of the taxonomies to be used, at the institutional level; should support attainment of having different levels of consistent information aggregated to the different levels of decision making in the health sector.

In this context, we hope that the work done since 1995 supports the visibility of nursing's contribution to people's health in information systems of the future.

References

1. Silva A. *Registos de Enfermagem - da tradição Scripto ao discurso Informo*. Porto: Dissertação de mestrado em Ciências de Enfermagem, Universidade do Porto, Instituto de Ciências Biomédicas Abel Salazar (ICBAS), 1995.

2. Silva A. *Sistemas de Informação em Enfermagem - uma teoria explicativa da mudança*. Porto: Tese de Doutoramento, Universidade do Porto, Instituto de Ciências Biomédicas Abel Salazar (ICBAS), 2001.

3. International Council of Nurses (ICN). Classificação Internacional para a Prática de Enfermagem: Versão 1.0 (ICNP version 1- Tradução oficial Portuguesa). Lisboa: Ordem dos Enfermeiros Portugueses, 2005.

4. Sousa P, Gonçalves P, Silva A, et al. *Projecto Enfinco*. Porto: Administração Regional de Saúde do Norte, Sub-região de Saúde de Vila Real e Escola Superior de Enfermagem de São João, 1999.

5. Pereira FS. *Informação e Qualidade do exercício profissional dos Enfermeiros: Estudo empírico para um Resumo Mínimo de Dados de Enfermagem*. Porto: Tese de Doutoramento, Universidade do Porto, Instituto de Ciências Biomédicas Abel Salazar (ICBAS), 2007.

6. Blegen M; Tripp-Reimer T. Implications of nursing taxonomies for middle–range theory development. *Advances in Nursing Science*. 1997;(3):37.

7. Meleis AI. *Theoretical Nursing: Development and Progress*. 3rd ed. Philadelphia: Lippincott Williams & Wilkins; 2005.

8. Sousa P. Sistemas de Partilha de Informação de Enfermagem Entre Contextos de Cuidados de Saúde. Coimbra, Formasau, 2006.

9. Werley H, Devine E, Zorn C, Ryan P, Westra B. The Nursing Minimum Data Set: Abstraction Tool for Standardized, Comparable, Essential Data. *AJPH*. 1991;81(4):421-426.

10. Goossen W. *Towards strategic use of nursing information in the Netherlands*. Groningen: Gegevens Koninklijke Bibliotheek Den Haag, 2000.

11. Volrathongchai K, Delaney C, Phuphaibul R. Nursing Minimum Data Set development and implementation in Thailand. *J Adv Nurs*. 2003;43(6):588-594.

12. Ordem dos enfermeiros (OE), Conselho de Enfermagem. Conselho de Enfermagem: Do Caminho Percorrido e das Propostas (análise do primeiro mandato - 1999/2003). Lisboa: Ordem dos Enfermeiros Portugueses, 2003.

13. Anderson BJ, Hannah KJ. A Canadian nursing minimum data set: A major priority. *Can J Nurs Adm*. 1993;6:7-13.

14. Coenen A, Schoneman D. The Nursing Minimum Data Set: use in the quality process. *J Nurs Care Qual*. 1995;10(1):9-15.

15. Delaney C, Moorhead S. The Nursing Minimum Data Set, standardized language, and health care quality. *J Nurs Care Qual*. 1995;10(1):16-30

16. Blewitt DK, Jones KR. Using elements of nursing minimum data set for determining outcomes. *J Nurs Admin*. 1996;26(6):48-56.

17. Bostick J, Riggs CJ, Rantz M. Quality Measurement in Nursing: an update of where we are now. *J Nurs Care Qual*. 2003;18(2):94-104.

18. Delaney C, Reed D, Clarke M. Describing Patient Problems & Nursing Treatments Patterns Using Nursing Minimum Data Sets (NMDS & NMMDS) & UHDDS Repositories. In: *AMIA 2000 Converging Information, Technology, & Health Care*. Los Angeles: Ed. AMIA; 2000.

19. Coenen A, Weis DM, Schank MJ, Matheus R. Describing parish children's nurse practice using the minimum Nursing Data Set. *Publ Health Nurs*. 1999;16(6):412-416.

20. Bernaerts K, Evers G, Sermeus W. Frequency of intravenous medication administration to hospitalised patients: secondary data-analysis of the Belgian Nursing Minimum Data Set. *Int J Nurs Stud*. 2000;37(2):101-110.

21. Evers G, Viane A, Sermeus W, Simoens-de smet A, Deslesie L. Frequency of and indications for wholly compensatory nursing care related to enteral food intake: a secondary analysis of the Belgium National Nursing Minimum Data Set. *J Adv Nurs*. 2000;32(1):194-201.

22. Goossen W, Epping P, Feuth T, Van Denheuvel W, Hasman A, Dassen T. Using the Nursing minimum Data Set for Netherlands (NMDSN) to illustrate differences in patient populations and variations in nursing activities. *Int J Nurs Stud*. 2001;38(3):243-257.

23. Park M, Delaney C, Maas M, Reed D. Using a Nursing Minimum Data Set with older patients with dementia in an acute care setting. *J Adv Nurs*. 2004;47(3):329-339.

24. Delaney C, Hovenga E, Coenen A, Park H. The International Nursing Minimum Data Set (i-NMDS) & The International Classification for Nursing Practice (ICNP): Next Steps. In: *MEDINFO 2001 Proceedings of the 10th World Congress on Medical Informatics*. Amsterdam: IOS Press, 2001: 1537.

25. Argyris C, Shön D. *Theory in Practice: Increasing Professional Effectiveness*. San Francisco: Jossey-Bass Publishers, 1982.

26. Donabedian A. *An Introduction to Quality Assurance in Health Care*. New York: Ed. by Bashshur R., Oxford University Press, 2003.

Case Study 16I

Nursing and Informatics Past, Present, and Future in Switzerland

By Alain Junger, MPA, RN

Introduction—Who Are We?

With four national languages—Suisse, Schweiz, Svizzera, and Svizra—Switzerland is an alpine country of roughly 7.7 million people with an area of 41,285 km². Switzerland is a federal republic consisting of twenty-six states called *cantons*. This political structure considerably influences aspects of the overall health organization. Each canton defines their heath policy locally. The effect of this is a parceling process, which occurs even in medical informatics. In Switzerland, there are 321 specialized clinics and hospitals, which represent 5.4 beds per 1,000 habitants. A total of 48,706 caregivers and 19,371 doctors work in these institutions. Hospital accommodation can be summarized as follows: 12,989,475 a day with an 88% bed rate and a length of stay of 10.9 days. (Source Federal Office of statistics: OFS-BFS).[1]

This case study will describe the strength and weaknesses of nursing informatics in the context of Switzerland. The exploration of several aspects, such as research, education, and new developments, will show a sliced reality in a changing context.

Nursing Education and Information Science

Following the adoption of the Bologna Declaration for the universities, the organization of the nursing studies program and all other caregivers were completely changed to the model: bachelor, master, and PhD.[2]

If each canton has one or more University of Applied Sciences (HES) faculty teaching nursing at the bachelor level, only two universities propose a master and a PhD in Nursing Science. The oldest one is German-speaking and is located in Basel, and the second is French-speaking and is in Lausanne.

This major reform of the study programs was followed by a redefinition of the professor's role. To add to their historically teaching-only role, they must now also be part time researchers. It is the first step in building professional know-how. These changes are focused on Nursing Science. In this changing process, information and informatics are, at all study stages, poorly presented within the curricula.

The computer is essentially perceived as a tool used for office purposes and to communicate and retrieve information on the Internet (chat and e-mail). It will be a challenge to overcome these notions about computers and forward the role of information in nursing decision making.

Informatics Competencies: Example of the CHUV

In 2006, the CHUV Nursing Head Office was reorganized into four pillars: communication, information, organization, and education. The Information Pillar has a role in all of the dimensions of nursing practice[3] as a support of clinical intelligence and as a resource for decision making. This model creates the link between clinical information, management, and finance at all levels of the organization to support caregivers and managers in their daily work.

In particular, the members of this pillar are deeply involved in the deployment of the hospital information system and the EPR. This organization creates a network and a culture in order to share information about the field and to share technical knowledge. The creation of an interface between nurses and computer scientists, economists, etc. was a critical point in managing the needed changes. In particular, it was critical to think through the reengineering processes following the introduction of an EPR.

Nursing Summary: NURSINGdata

Between 1999 and 2006, Anne Berthou[4] managed a national project on a Nursing Minimum Data Set (NMDS), called NURSINGdata.

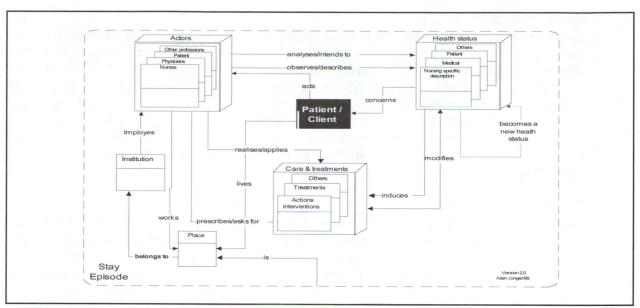

Figure 16I-1. *Object Model as It Was in 1999*

The general concept of NURSINGdata was developed between 1998 and 2000,[4] with the final report published in 2006. For the people involved at this early stage, the priority was to not only find potential financial partners but others willing to participate in its realization.

The Swiss NMDS worked on the two following preconditions: the nursing information system had to be unified at the Swiss level and compatible at an international level; as far as possible, it had to be built from what exists and is used. It had to be extended to all the domains of care and had to apply to all parts of the country. Moreover, it had to be flexible and as complete as possible, in order to avoid duplicate data collections.

The first conceptual step was to define the information system in place using four complementary models: from data to languages, the clinical process, the data object model (see Figure 16I-1), and the pyramid of aggregation.[5] The terminological system conceptualization is based on current international work (ISO/CEN/ICF/ICNP).

NURSINGdata developed a Swiss Nursing Minimum Data Set and two reference classifications: one for nursing phenomena and one for nursing interventions. Within the framework of a NMDS, it is indispensable to use classifications with a restricted list of terms. On the other hand, to insure the quality of the information, the classification has to be structured and exhaustive. The semantic structure for the Swiss reference classifications builds on the ISO model (ISO/TC215WG3, 2002) and the hierarchy is the structure of the International Classification of Functioning, Disability and Health (ICF-WHO).[6] A *nursing phenomenon* has been defined by NURSINGdata as a "health aspect of one or of several persons, which justifies the nursing interventions." Fifty-six items (focus) can be combined with three qualifiers (judgement): risk, resource, and problem. A *nursing intervention* is defined as "a set of nursing actions which are organized with the intention to achieve a nursing goal." Fifty-one items (target) have to be completed by four verbs or actions (observe/ evaluating, teaching/counseling, guiding/supporting, executing/acting).

NURSINGdata was initially focused on caregivers, entitling them to make visible their substantial contribution to the Swiss health system by developing a recognized professional language. This is why the project integrates as largely as possible the primary caregivers. The information system recommended by NURSINGdata is meant to be used for a wide range of applications: nursing management and work planning, contracting for healthcare services, pricing for health and accident insurance, research into nursing practice, and nursing science. It is further meant to complete the existing health information system, with a view to anchor essential nursing data in a future decree or revision of the federal law on statistics. One of the major challenges for the success of such a project must be the quality of the data analysis process. If it ends up as just another "data graveyard," then it will not have fulfilled its promise to the nursing profession, and the interest and motivation that individual nurses have for the project will be seriously compromised.

Use of Terminologies

Most of the publications are about projects on terminology[7] usage and workload measurement. Few are related to informatics. To name nursing problems or interventions, most of the institutions use local terminologies or none. Rare hospitals have adopted NANDA© or NIC. One of the rare studies[8] showed in 2007 that the implementation of NANDA, NIC, and NOC (NNN) in a regional hospital led to higher quality of nursing diagnosis documentation, etiology, specific nursing interventions, and nursing-sensitive patient outcomes.

Due to the law on health insurance, LAMaL (Loi sur l'assurance maladie), and Article 49 or tools to measure the workload, such as the Swiss: Leistung in des Pflege (LEP,)[9] the Canadians from EROSINFO[10] Company: Process Research Nursing (PRN©) and Planification informatisée des soins infirmier requis (PLAISIR©) are in use.

Current State of ICNP

Practically, ICNP is not used in Swiss hospitals, even though some projects were done in Geneva in 1996.[11] The problem stems from the absence of a concrete implementation in an EPR. Actually few commercial products propose a solution. But at the same time, the Swiss Nurse Association is deeply involved in the translation of ICNP to German and French in collaboration with the other National Nursing Associations (Germany, Austria, France, Belgium, Luxembourg, Canada). The German translation was finished some time ago. The French one was expected to be finished by the summer 2009. It is managed by the CHUV in Lausanne with the participation of the HUG in Geneva.

As soon as possible, studies must be conducted on the use of ICNP for nursing electronic documentation and for the NMDS. In the French part of the country, a model of paper nursing documentation is dominant. It is a combination of focus charting and charting by exception, generally without using Nursing Diagnosis. The concept of focus is extended to signs and symptoms and even to medical diagnosis. Future developments are based on the hypothesis that ICNP used as a reference terminology could be the reference to code the local terminologies, which are included in local catalogs of focuses and interventions.

Use of Data to Make Nursing Visible

AP-DRG and PRN. Having gathered data since 1998 from hospitals to calculate yearly versions of cost-weights, we witnessed the impressive improvement in data quality in most cost components of DRGs. Nevertheless, one of the most difficult cost elements to gather was nursing care, since either the nursing data were not collected by case or the hospitals' accounting systems could not produce its cost per case. Things have changed with the improvement of hospital information systems: more hospitals have acquired the capacity to do case-based costing, which includes case-based nursing data.

A first study described the proportion of nursing care in each APDRG Cost weight. It was carried out in an 800-bed teaching hospital with more than 30,000 cases. This case study will show the result of a second study based on data collected daily with PRN©[12] tool (Projet de Recherche en Nursing) and linked to the APDRG. It describes factors that influenced the nursing cost and the length of stay. A third work built a regression model to identify outliers from the nursing point-of-view in a clinical perspective.

A recent study analysed the question: What is the contribution of nursing in the analysis of hospital stays? Based on all the patient stay in the same teaching hospital during 2005 and 2006, a model with medico-administrative data and a model with nursing data were compared. For this study a logistic regression model was applied to the probability of the patient exit. The pseudo R2 of the reference model is equal to 0.0957. With nursing, it improves with a pseudo R2 of 0.152. The power of discrimination of the model is assessed by the area under the ROC curve is 0.7852.

This approach provides the first evidence regarding the feasibility of the using standards of care pathways, allowing managers to analyze the organization of patient care, and have better estimations of the hospital funding. The next step is to enlarge the research on DRGs and care costs to the Nursing Diagnoses. After having found an answer to the *what,* is it time to explore the *why*.

Swiss DRG.[13] In 2010, a new hospital payment system based on the German DRG must be set up. In 2007, the canton and all the partners of the health insurance tariff created a limited company of public utility, SwissDRG S.A.,[13] with an operational team grouped in the "Case mix office" (CMO).

For different reasons, the Nursing National association (ASI-SBK) could not participate in this process. But the ASI supports or participates in complementary research or studies. The first one was recently published; "Reporting der Pflege in SwissDRG."[14] This case study will be added to the overall SwissDRG report, which will be edited before the start of the new system. The result of this investigation confirms that the use of nursing workload data is a good distribution key for accountability to define the nursing cost by DRG. Like the study done with PRN five years earlier, the average nursing cost ration is 30% of the overall cost.

Evidence-based Practice

Several experiences are now carried out in Switzerland. Clinically oriented, these projects are generally not linked to nursing informatics.

There are similarities across the German Swiss Hospital and the University Hospitals of Inselspital in Bern or USZ in Zurich. In Bern,[15] a pilot project was conducted based on experiences in British Nursing Development Units. The care concept was specifically developed and based on a definition of professional nursing, an evidence-based practice approach; resource oriented self-management, and caring; the project is focused in a pediatric hospital.

In the French Swiss part of the country, after many reflections and discussions, a project emerged between hospitals and the HES. Named BEST, the Office of Exchanges of the Knowledge for practices specimens of care (BEST) was officially opened January 1, 2009. Anchored in the movement of Evidence-Based Practice (EBP), BEST wants to support the development of competencies of information retrieval, analysis of scientific publications, and changes in the clinical practices. Intended for the occupational therapists, physiotherapists, nurses, midwives and technicians in medical radiology, BEST is also addressed to the teacher (E) S and students. The systematic use of EBP is a goal for all, but the requested changes are important and will take time. The two university centers in Basel and Lausanne are a chance to reach this qualitative change in research and teaching.

EHR Initiatives Across the Country

The Swiss government voted to support an important process in June 2007: the cyber-health strategy called eHealth. It started concretely in April 2008 with six sub-projects. The two main objectives of the Swiss eHealth strategy are to achieve by 2015 the introduction of an electronic patient record, as well as the development of a health portal, providing information and offering everyone access to his or her own data. The sub-projects "Standards and Architecture" and "Pilot Testing and PPP" will define the technical and organizational basis for the implementation of eHealth solutions. The sub-projects "Legal Basis" and "Financing and Systems of Incentives" are preparing a legal basis for the Confederation and the cantons. The sub-project "Online Health and Skills" highlights the culture of the people. "Education" examines the needs for basic, postgraduate and continuing education in all health professions.[16] The absence of representatives of nurses in this phase reflects an important political weakness of the nursing organizations on this topic. But it is also due to a major difficulty having long-term involvement from people within the nurse associations (national, managers, research, etc.).

A recent meeting showed a change; the five CNOs of all the university hospitals presented "Nursing: Part of the Electronic Patient Documentation: Myth or Reality?" during a central point in the agenda. It appears that two hospitals, Geneva and Zurich, developed their own solutions, Lausanne and Bern are at the beginning of the deployment of a commercial tool and Basel is looking for a simple and efficient tool after having looked for an ideal software. In some other regional hospitals, nurses are in leadership within electronic documentation initiatives.

These examples show the lack of standards and the absence of a real collaboration between experts. The analysis of these projects reveals a similar need in which each hospital "reinvents the wheel."

Summary

In this small country, each canton or health institution defines their own needs, resources, and plans on all aspects of health policy and related issues, such as medical informatics. The eHealth project is an opportunity for major improvements. The National Nursing Associations have to defend the presence of nurses in each subgroup. The future of nursing informatics will pass through the integration of this subject in all nursing curricula. It is not only a question of computer integration, but a matter of science integration. Nursing informatics gives us the opportunity to put another focus on nursing practice, to conceptualize it as an information process.

Today the focus is always on nursing workload evaluation for economic goals; an increasing knowledge of nursing informatics should open broader fields of research by improving the use of terminologies, the modeling of nursing documentation, or the implementation of tools supporting the clinical intelligence of all the caregivers and managers.

References

1. Statistique des hôpitaux 2007 – Tableaux standard - Résultats définitifs; http://www.bfs.admin.ch/bfs/portal/fr/index/themen/14/22/publ.Document.119065.pdf. Accessed October 20, 2009.
2. 414.712 – 2 septembre 2005 - Ordonnance du DFE concernant les filières d'études, les études postgrades et les titres dans les hautes écoles spécialisées.
3. WHO. *Nursing Practice.* Geneva: WHO; 1996.
4. Berthou A, Junger A. *NURSING data Final report 1998-2000 period.* Lausanne: NURSING data; 2000.
5. Junger A, Delaney C, Berthou A. Modeling, the Essential Step to Consolidate and Integrate a National NMDS. *Medinfo04.* San Francisco: Medinfo; 2004.
6. http://www3.who.ch/icf. Accessed October 20, 2009.
7. Swiss Association of Nursing Science: http://www.pflegeforschung.vfp.ch/index.php?language=fr&page=forschungsberichte. Accessed October 20, 2009.
8. Müller-Staub M, Needham I, Odenbreit M, Lavin MA, van Achterberg T. Improved quality of nursing documentation: Results of a nursing diagnoses, interventions and outcomes implementation study. *Int J Nurs Terminol and Classif.* 2007;18(1):5-17.
9. LEP-AG- http://www.lep.ch/index.php/en. Accessed October 20, 2009.
10. EROSINFO - http://www.erosinfo.com/main_en.htm. Accessed October 20, 2009.
11. Assimacopoulos A, De Roulet A-M. *Classification internationale de la pratique des soins infirmiers ICNP:* Telenurse - Hug Belle-Idée; Traduction française, décembre 96 1996. Projet européen no. HC 1113.
12. Neyrolles C. Indicateurs d'activités: La méthode P.R.N. *CEE-IEC-Rip infirmière enseignante.* 1991;21(5):4-9.
13. SwissDRG S.A. : www.swissdrg.ch. Accessed October 20, 2009.
14. B.Kuster DB, Beirat P. *Reporting der Pflege in SwissDRG.* St Gallen 2009.
15. Geiser BB, Geschwindner H, Stauffer Y, E. S. Nursing unit: nurses co-ordinating hospital care - an answer to new challenges in acute medicine. *Pflege.* 2007(20):7.
16. eHealth - federal office for public health: http://www.bag.admin.ch/themen/krankenversicherung/04108/index.html?lang=fr. Accessed October 20, 2009.

Case Study 16J

Reengineering of Nursing Process: e-Documentation Case

By Vesna Prijatelj, MSc, RN; Uroš Rajkovič, MSc; Olga Šušteršič, PhD, RN;
and Vladislav Rajkovič, PhD

Introduction—Facts About Slovenia

Slovenia lies at the heart of Europe where the Alps and the Mediterranean meet. Covering an area of 20,273 km^2 and having a population of approximately two million, Slovenia shares borders with Italy, Austria, Croatia, and Hungary. Slovenia became an independent state in 1991 and a member of the EU on May 1, 2004. The euro has been Slovenia's chosen monetary unit since 2007. Slovenia has a democratic political system with a parliamentary form of state power.

Healthcare in Slovenia Health is a constitutional right and is declared to be egalitarian. The healthcare delivery system is defined by the Law on Medical Services. Apart from public healthcare institutions (63 healthcare centers and 26 hospitals), three private healthcare institutions are also part of the public health network.

Moving Toward a National Electronic Health Record

Intense ICT adoption in healthcare services began in Slovenia in the 1990s. Within the framework of the Health Sector Management Project (HSMP), activities were planned with a view to transforming health policy in the areas of funding, management, and formulation of professional guidelines. Two major objectives were the development and introduction of an electronic health insurance card and an electronic patient record.

The development of the electronic health insurance card (eHIC) began in 1996. In 2000, the card became the exclusive health insurance document in Slovenia. It is an electronic tool for communication between the insured person, physician, health center, hospital, health insurance provider, and pharmacy. Slovenia was one of the first European countries to implement such a system at the national level.

The HSMP has also yielded the implementation of a Diagnoses Related Group (DRG) scheme, for categorization of acute inpatient episodes, and implementation of a new reimbursement model for hospitals. All hospitals have been connected to the government health information network by means of secure ID cards and digital certificates. The development of reimbursement models for other levels of healthcare (primary care, rehabilitation, specialist treatment) and formulation of Slovene Clinical Guidelines and Clinical Pathways are still in progress.[1]

In December 2005, the Slovenian Ministry of Health launched its strategy for automating the healthcare system in Slovenia (eHealth 2010). With eHealth 2010 strategy, we are building a state-of-the-art infrastructure for secure information exchange, capable of supporting the previously mentioned eHealth services. eHealth strategy and Operational plan 2007-2010, which is based on the strategy, have three main focuses:[2,3]

- Upgrade the basic information infrastructure for the safe and transparent exchange of information between patients, healthcare service providers, and payers: establish a private network of the healthcare sector; introduce public key infrastructure; and define the most important health informatics standards and classifications.
- Define and introduce interoperable healthcare records and integrate the records into the daily work of medical and allied professionals with patients.
- Introduce and sustain the national healthcare portal and implement data exchange between patients, various healthcare providers, payers, and others.

Seven Picture Archiving and Communication Systems (PACS) systems have been implemented since 2005. The next stage includes teleradiology connection between these hospitals and the radiologist-at-home. The implementation of the Teleradiology Network is only the first step in digitalization of Slovenian Healthcare and in implementation of available Telemedicine Solution.

Automation of the Register of Births, Deaths, and Marriages (eBirth) has created an environment that allows for allocation of personal ID numbers to infants immediately after birth in the maternity hospital and electronic entry of births and deaths into the register. It enables data interchange between hospitals and Ministry of the Interior. Authorized users from hospitals access registers with digital certificates and security schema at eCentral Register of Population (eCRP). eBirth registration implementation brings about achievements in several fields:[2]

- For administrative services: Data for birth registration is received by the registrar more quickly, in electronic form, with National Patient Identifier Number that shortens the administrative procedure of birth registration; data in administrative registers are up-to-date.
- For parents: Shorter and easier procedures at social welfare canters; shorter procedure for birth certificate acquisition; shorter procedure for eHIC acquisition.
- For healthcare: Reduced volume of manual work and potential number of errors at data input; supplemented healthcare documentation on hospitalization of newborns and checked and fulfilled data of mother; improved data quality and integrity for health statistics and analytics and planning.

In 2006, renovation of the eHIC system was started. Despite constant modernization and development of additional functionalities, there is a growing number of business and technical reasons for the gradual renovation of the card system. The final goal of the renovation is the transition from the current system, in the context of which data are exchanged between users in the healthcare system using the card as a data carrier, into a comprehensive online system in which the card will merely serve as a key to access data stored on data servers. The renewal of the system establishes the following solutions:[4]

- A new professional card for healthcare workers, which will contain a digital certificate for secure access to personal medical data and for the electronic signatures on documents (electronic prescriptions, orders, medical referrals, etc.).
- A new health insurance card with digital certificates for secure access by the user to his/her personal data and acting as a key whereby the holder permits the healthcare worker to access his/her personal medical data.
- Establishment of an online system for direct, instant, secure, and reliable exchanges of data via the network. The exchange of data between healthcare providers and health insurance providers will be set-up in the first phase.
- The system provides an open infrastructure for the development of solutions to also enable the exchange of data within the healthcare organizations.

The renewed card with digital certificates and an online system also opens up possibilities for the healthcare sector's cooperation with other sectors in the country. The system will be introduced gradually from region to region until the end of year 2009.

In recent years, Slovenia has successfully completed the first steps of implementing ICT technologies in the healthcare system, following the document e-Health 2010, by introducing basic computer technology and computer exchange of information, defining standards, and establishing basic data bases. Several research and applicative projects are underway to create a common supportive ICT environment for support of integrated care processes.

Evolution of Nursing Informatics and Nursing Data Standards

Efforts to have nursing included in health informatics go back to the 1990s when Slovenia participated in two international projects designed to develop an internationally comparable minimum data set for nursing care: Telenursing (1992-1994), and Telenurse (1996-1998). A national project aimed at developing a computer information system for home nursing was conducted in the years 1996-1999. The alpha version of ICNP was used in this project and was also translated to Slovene.[5]

In 1998-2000, Slovenia participated in a European project entitled "Informatics and Diagnoses – European Nursing Terminology as a Basis for Information Technology" (Telenurse ID-ENTITY). Slovenia's main tasks in this project were to translate the beta version of ICNP; verify the translation and test the vocabulary; devise a strategy for the development of an information system for nursing in Slovenia and its integration into the National Health Information System; establish a national database for nursing care; integrate the beta version of ICNP into the nursing education curriculum; and develop a browser based on the beta version of ICNP.[6]

In 1999, Slovenia joined the Workflow Information Systems for European Nursing Care (WISECARE) research initiative, a European project started in 1997. The goal of WISECARE is to systematically exploit clinical nursing data for clinical management, resource management, and knowledge sharing. Clinical management focuses from a nursing point of view on determining patient outcomes. Resource management focuses on the right use of staff competencies. Knowledge-sharing focuses on the creation of a learning environment. The overall result is that by using ICT, nursing practice is felt to be more benchmarked, evaluated, and is increasingly based on principles of evidence-based care.[7]

Nursing Data Standards: Current Status

According to the Slovenian Health Care Databases Act passed in 2000, databases may be maintained on paper or in electronic format. Currently, most databases for healthcare in Slovenia provide practically no information on nursing. There are only two health data sets that focus on nursing data: the Home Nursing Data Set and the Nursing Data Set. Both contain data on nursing diagnoses, nursing plan, nursing interventions and procedures, patient categorization according to nursing intensity, and adverse events. However, they provide no information on nursing outcome.

At present, uniform terminology is used in Slovenia in the field of patient categorization according to nursing intensity. For nursing diagnoses, both ICNP and NANDA (North American Nursing Diagnosis Association) are employed, and a national consensus has not been reached. The DRG coding system is used for nursing procedures. There is no uniform standard for nursing plan, nursing intervention, and adverse events in institutionalized or home care. Uniform terminology and standards for nursing care should be adopted at the national level to make comparison among healthcare institutions possible.[5]

Documentation-Based Quality Assurance in Nursing

This case study is based on findings and models developed within the framework of a Project Documentation-Based Quality Assurance in Nursing at the Ministry of Health of the Republic of Slovenia.

Discussed next are the elaboration and implementation of the proposed model, as well as testing of the prototype software for community nursing. Analyses of the current state of nursing documentation consisted of interviewing nurses in field, survey research, studying literature, and existing documentation. Process modelling was conducted by defining business rules, maximum data set, and by designing a relational database. Prototyping method was used for software development. Functionality of the proposed model was tested with input/output data analysis and interviews.

Analysis of Nursing Documentation

Using the survey research, we first analyzed the current state of documentation in nursing in selected primary, secondary, and tertiary health organizations in Slovenia. The sample included three residential homes for elderly people, the Ljubljana Health Centre with five units and the University Medical Centres in Ljubljana and Maribor. We distributed 386 questionnaires, of which 286 (response rate of 74.1%) were returned.

From the results of the survey on the use and suitability of nursing documentation, we can conclude both the actual state of the documentation itself and the process of documenting and also the perception (opinions, considerations) of existing problems and possible solutions on the part of those surveyed.

The majority of documents (86%) are prescribed on the level of the institution. The only exceptions are community nursing and residential homes for elderly people. Documentation for community nursing is prescribed and unified throughout the country, while residential homes for elderly people have a uniform computer-supported information system. Rather less than 13% of documents are computer-supported. Among different types of documents, the following were most frequently listed: nursing care plan, referral/discharge document, continuation notes and variance report, admission document and report on an undesired event.

It can be concluded that these five most frequently used documents should be unified first, taking into account the specificities of individual services. Given that, with contemporary ICT, we can generally provide effective support to documentation and increase the use of computers in healthcare.

From the perspective of content, a process method of work is only used in 32% of nursing documentation. Over 52% use only a fragmented process approach. It appears that existing documentation is, to a large extent, at fault here, since the majority uses only those elements that the documentation enables. It is therefore sensible to reengineer the documentation in a way that will enable documenting all phases of the nursing process.

Minimal datasets on patients are recorded by three quarters of the survey participants. One of the reasons that the percentage is not higher is unsuitability of the existing documentation.

Discussions with a patient, observation of a patient, and measurements are used as a source of data for completing documentation in more than half of the cases. Slightly less than half have also stated nursing documentation as a regularly used source of data. It is sensible, then, to consider links between other health documentation and nursing documentation.

In their opinion, surveyed nurses see the purpose of documentation as being mainly to capture the continuity of nursing, security for members of the nursing team and patients, and an account of the work of individual members of the nursing team. The content thus supports the work, with emphasis on the legal security of members of the nursing team and the patient.

Among reasons given for the non-use of nursing documentation, according to a quarter of nurses, are understaffing and insufficient knowledge of the nursing process. In the unspecified reasons in the questionnaire, nurses cited most often the reason that "existing documentation is unsuitable."

In terms of the influence of nursing documentation, the following are highlighted: the quality of nursing, standardization of work, and reducing the possibilities of mistakes. With improved documentation, we expect most changes in the quality of collaboration inside the health team and in the distribution of work and responsibilities among nurses and other health team members.

The results have shown that reengineering of documentation using ICT can and should positively influence the quality of nursing care. Because of unified documentation in the community of nursing, we have decided to begin the reengineering of documentation in this area.

Reengineering of Nursing Workflow

The basis for developing e-documentation is the nursing process. Figure 16J-1 shows a schematic presentation of the process method of work in the IDEFO standard (Integration DEFinition for function modelling is a part of IDEF family model languages in the field of software engineering). The division in the figure differs from the literature.[8,9] A major difference is in the stage of evaluation due to standardization restriction. There is also a difference in the feedback loops, which are of crucial importance for system management; in this case, nursing.

The user interface of the prototype supports this process method in the nurse's job sequence. Only a few elements must be added, which are specific to community nursing.[10] These are elements such as entering referrals for community care visits to patients or families and for planning dates of home visits. Home visits can only be planned on the basis of referrals received from a general practitioner or on the basis of instructions for implementing community nursing. Later on, the same steps apply for each home visit as in the previously mentioned process scheme.

Computer Aided Process

It is worth highlighting some particularities in the database which supports the e-documenting process. The nursing diagnosis is directly bound to the subject of nursing. In the nursing diagnosis, we record to which basic living activity it is bound, and we are aware that after the evaluation of the nursing care plan, it may remain in the care plan throughout one or more of the following visits. The subject of nursing can be a patient or a family.

The steps that comprise the desired course of work of the community nurse (CN) required for each home visit are in accordance with the process method of work in nursing. When the CN selects a patient or a family and one of the planned home visits, a screen image is shown for the individual home visit. In the upper part, data on the selected patient or family are shown, and below, the individual steps of the nursing process supported through four tabs: nursing history, assessment of patient's/family's need, planning and implementation. We will describe later how the evaluation phase is supported.

We have grouped criteria for an overall assessment of a patient's needs in a tree structure based on the fourteen basic living activities.[11-13] It is a professionally accepted and well-known division as it has been confirmed in our survey. A list of parameters opens for each basic living activity of which we wish to remind

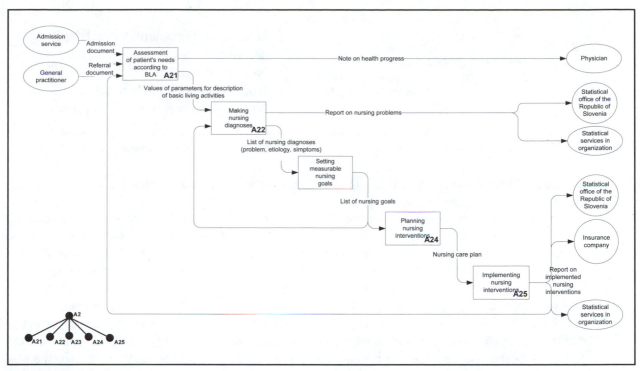

Figure 16J-1. *Schematic Presentation of the Process Method of Work in Nursing According to the IDEF0 Standard*

the CN for gathering relevant data. These parameters are taken from the profession, and in nomenclature, we followed the Slovene translation of the ICNP.[14]

With each parameter, there is a field with free text for the entry of values, e.g., with the parameter of excessive body weight, we can insert the body mass index. In addition, with each parameter, we can also determine the degree of a problem according to a five-point scale (no problem, minor problem, medium problem, major problem, very severe problem).

The CN chooses the values in relation to the assessed state with individual nursing subjects. From the values describing degrees of problems for parameters under the same basic living activity, the degree of a problem for that individual basic living activity is calculated. These calculated values are then shown in the phase of planning. We will later show how we have used these grades in supporting the evaluation phase.

Thus, for example, the value of the parameter "appetite" has an impact on a "diet," this impacts the basic living activity of "diet and drinking," which affects the "physical basic living activities" and, consequently, the "overall assessment" of a patient. Values of the higher-level parameters in the tree structure of parameters are calculated. The CN records values only for final parameters in the tree structure, that is, parameters on the tree leaves. After a simple calculation, we then obtain the grade of a nursing problem for an individual basic living activity, or a total overall assessment.

Under the tab planning, we compose a nursing care plan in a tree structure. At the first level we see a list of basic living activities and with each activity, we see a calculated degree of a problem. On the second level, we can add to each basic living activity an arbitrary number of nursing diagnoses. To each nursing diagnosis, we must further add at least one nursing goal, and to each nursing goal at least one nursing intervention (see Figure 16J-2).

The nursing diagnosis is made according to the Problem, Etiology, and Symptoms system (PES). In denoting a problem, the nurse can get help from the ICNP (version beta 2) or from the NANDA classification.[6,15-17] Nursing interventions are described by name and the frequency of performing them. Nurses denote interventions with the aid of the Slovene classification of nursing interventions and the ICNP beta 2.

The nurse can store the most often used nursing diagnoses and interventions in her personal directory. In the prototype, this is a planned solution, which can simply be supplemented with the catalogues that International Council of Nurses propagates as lists of the most often used nursing diagnoses and interventions for

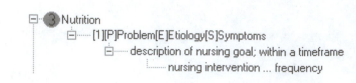

	Degree of a problem, basic living activity
	Nursing diagnosis
	Nursing goal; with timeframe
	Nursing intervention … frequency

Figure 16J-2. *Schematic Presentation of a Nursing Care Plan in a Tree Structure with Explanation of Individual Levels*

an individual field of nursing. Under the implementation tab, we see all planned nursing interventions, and the nurse only has to select those carried out.

For the needs of evaluation, we can record comments on individual nursing interventions, e.g., ongoing evaluation or values of measurements, materials and time used. After carrying out nursing interventions, it is necessary to reassess the condition at the end of the visits. The evaluation phase is supported with the following visualization elements: comparison of overall assessments that shows progress for every parameter, a progress graph for a selected parameter throughout all previous visits. CN uses these measurements of changes in patient's needs to evaluate nursing goals and other elements of the nursing care plan.

The result of the evaluation phase is reflected in the changed nursing care plan. This means in practice that the nurse can do the following: seek inappropriate elements in the nursing care plan, supplement and add to the existing plan, exchange or remove items, and plan a new part of the nursing care plan for a new problem focus. The tabs are similar for home visits to the family, differing only in the parameters by which we describe the overall assessment. Instead of basic living activities, we divided the parameters of families into the following groups: socio-economic state, health histories, relations within the family and with the wider environment and functions of the family. Computer support is provided by a client-server prototype software solution.

Testing the Model in Practice

Testing of the software took place in the community nursing units of the Ajdovscina Health Centre and the Ljubljana-Bezigrad Health Centre. Data inserted at locations were gathered on the server. Our plan for testing consisted of:

- More than 80 entries in the period of one month provide the framework for testing various subjects with various needs and difficulty of work, and
- Documenting all home visits in a period for two months.

At meetings, we then discussed possible difficulties and proposals of improvements and examined the entered records.[18] A SWOT analysis was carried out, which we performed with the help of the participants of testing at a final meeting.

Strengths:

- Provides users with integral nursing of high quality;
- Timely recognition of some dangers that threaten the patient;
- Systemically arranged data of a relatively large quantity, which provide an easily viewed information picture;
- Encouragement for the CNs' own professional development.

Weaknesses:

- Insufficient ICT equipment;
- In dealing with patients with existing solutions, we do not cover some administrative needs (e.g., reading health insurance cards);
- Too many patients per day prevent concurrent insertion of data into the computer (work norms are frequently exceeded);
- Lack of professional knowledge;
- The question of whether we know and can suitably use the available data.

Opportunities:

- More attuned to the user by means of the available data and therefore able to offer a higher quality of nursing;
- Users can become better informed and educated;
- Timely recognition of conditions;
- Production of guidelines for professional treatment and higher quality services for users;
- Includes family and others in the nursing process;
- Motivation of staff.

Threats:

- Insufficient ICT equipment of community nursing services could hold back the use of the system;
- Lack of permanent professional training and the willingness of nurses to change could negatively affect the use of such a system;
- Changes in existing methods of work often trigger resistance in staff;
- Commitment to the computer rather than to the patient.

Although the model and its prototype are already suitable for use in practice, we will continue to take certain comments into account and make the necessary changes. Extended testing will follow, which means monitoring use of the model in practice in a larger number of community nursing institutions throughout a longer period of time.

Discussion

The presented model of e-documentation covers the treatment of patients and families, both from the aspects of processes and data. On this basis, a prototype organizational and informational solution of nursing documentation for the community-nursing segment has been developed, tested in practice, and critically evaluated.

The added value that contemporary ICT can contribute to nursing has been presented, derived primarily from a structured information picture, which monitors the patient and the nurse in the nursing process.[19,20] It is worth highlighting in particular the use of hierarchical models in the treatment of basic living activities. The model of calculating the grade of a nursing problem, which the computer carries out concurrently in relation to the condition of the patient, thus enables an integral overview of the patient and, systemically links apparently separate problems. It is thus a direct contribution to reducing the possibility of overlooking something important. E-documentation relies on the nursing record of the patient as a part of the overall health record of the patient.[21,22] This way, we avoid duplication of data and the associated excessive work and obtain an overall information picture, which significantly contributes to a greater security for the patient and members of the nursing team. A similar solution was developed for hospitals and is ready for testing.

Summary

In recent years, Slovenia has successfully implemented the first steps of information technology in the healthcare system following the document e-Health 2010 by introducing the basic computer technology and computer exchange of information, defining some standards, and establishing basic data bases. Several research and applicative projects are underway to create a common supportive ICT environment for support of integrated care processes.

The 'Project Documentation Based Quality Assurance in Nursing' focuses on nursing information needs and includes opportunities offered by modern IT. Documentation is viewed as an information model for organizing and managing processes. It is thus considered to be a basis for the successful work of the health team and a way of ensuring quality. A prototype software model for e-documentation in nursing was developed.

References

1. Prijatelj, V. (2008). Integrated care: theory and practice. *Pr-Internet* (Online-Ausg.), vol. 10: 565-568. http://www.printernet.info. Accessed December 20, 2008.

2. Ministry of Health (2009). *eHealth activities in Slovenia.* http://www.eu2008.si/en/News_and_Documents/download_docs/May/0505_eZdravje/040_activities.pdf. Accessed March 25, 2009.

3. Fact sheet Slovenia. Available (2009). http://www.ehealth-era.org/database/documents/factsheets/Slovenia.pdf. Accessed March 25, 2009.

4. Health Insurance Institute of Slovenia (2009). *Development in Progress—Renovation of the Health Insurance Card System.* www.zzzs.si. Accessed March 25, 2009.

5. Prijatelj V (2006). Opportunities and obstacles in electronic data collection in nursing. *Consumer-centered computer-supported care for healthy people: proceedings of NI2006: the 9th International Congress on Nursing Informatics.* Park H, ed. Amsterdam: IOS, pp. 329-332.

6. Rajkovič, V, Šušteršič O, Rajkovič U, Porenta A, Zupančič MJ. (2003). *How E-Representation brings International Classification of Nursing Practice Closer to User.* ACENDIO 2003. 4th European Conference of ACENDIO. Making nursing visible. Oud N, Bern, ed. Verlag Hans Huber; pp. 166-170.

7. Sermeus W, Kearney N, Kinnunen J, Goossense L, Miller M. *Wisecare: Work Flow Information Systems for European Nursing Care.* Amsterdam: IOS Press Incorporated, 2000.

8. Taylor C, Lillis C, LeMone P. *Fundamentals of Nursing, The Art and Science of Nursing Care,* 4th ed. Philadelphia: Lippincott, 2001.

9. Potter PA, Griffin Perry A. *Basic Nursing,* 5th ed. St. Louis: Mosby, 2003.

10. Rajkovič V, Šušteršič O, eds. *Information System for Community Nursing (in Slovene language:* Informacijski sistem patronažne zdravstvene nege), Založba Moderna organizacija, Kranj, 2000.

11. Henderson V. *Basic Principles of Nursing Care.* International Council of Nurses, Geneve, 1997.

12. Bohanec M, Zupan B, Rajkovič V. Applications of qualitative multi-attribute decision models in health care. *Int J Med Inf.* 2000;58-59:191-205.

13. Šušteršič O, Rajkovič V, Kljajič M, Rajkovič U. (2003). *Improving Nursing Care Documentation by Computerised Hierarchical Structures.* Proceedings of the 8th International Congress in Nursing Informatics. Eds.: de Fatima Marin HM, Marques EP, Hovenga E, Goossen W. Rio de Janeiro: International Council of Nurses; pp. 212-216.

14. Cibic D, Dogša I, Filej B, Šlajmer-Japelj M, Šušteršič O. (2000). *International Classification of Nursing Practice* (in Slovene language: Mednarodna klasifikacija prakse zdravstvene nege), Kolaborativni center SZO za primarno zdravstveno nego, Maribor.

15. Gordon M. *Nursing Diagnosis. Process and Application.* 3rd ed. St. Louis: Mosby, 1994.

16. ICN - International Council of Nurses. (1999) *International Classification of Nursing Practice* Beta Version. International Council of Nurses, Geneve.

17. Šušteršič O, Rajkovič V, Kljajič M. *An Evaluation of Community Nursing Process in the Frame of the International Classification for Nursing Practice.* ICNP and Telematic Applications for Nurses in Europe, The Telenurse Experience. Ed.: Mortensen RA, Amsterdam: IOS Press Ohmska, 1999;243-249.

18. Šušteršič O, Rajkovič U, Prijatelj V, Rajkovič V. *Evaluating patient's health by a hierarchical decision model.* V: CONLEY, Edward C. (ur.), DOARN, Charles (ur.), EL-HASSANI, Amir Hajjam-. International Confrence on eHealth, Telemedicine, and Social Medicine eTelemed 2009, 1-7 February 2009, Cancun, Mexico. eTelemed 2009 : proceedings. Los Alamitos: IEEE Computer Society: CPS, 2009, str. 136-139.

19. Hammond WE, Cimino JJ. *Standards in Biomedical Informatics. Biomedical Informatics, Computer Applications in Health Care and Biomedicine.* 3rd ed. Eds.: Shortliffe, EH, Cimino JJ. New York: Springer, 2006;265-311.

20. Abdelhak M, Grostick S, Hanken MA, Jacobs E. *Health Information: Management of a Strategic Resource.* 3rd ed. Philadelphia: Saunders Elsevier, 2007.

21. Hammer SV, Moen A, Børmark SR, Husby EH. *A Hospital-Wide Approach to Integration of Nursing Documentation in the Electronic Patient Record.* Proceedings of the 8th International Congress in Nursing Informatics. de Fatima Marin HM, Marques EP, Hovenga E, Goossen W, eds. Rio de Janeiro: International Council of Nurses, 2003;212-216.

22. Leskovar R, Baggia A, Vukovič G. *Building and Scheduling Teams in Hospitals.* ECON '03, Research works proceedings, Vol. 10. Ed.: Jaškova M. Ostrava: Technical University of Ostrava, Faculty of Economics, 2003;259-269.

## CHAPTER 17

Healthcare Information Technology and Electronic Health Records: A View from the Middle East

By Roy L. Simpson, RN,C, DPNAP, FAAN; and Deirdre M. Stewart, Dip HCI, RGN, RPN

Defining the state of healthcare information technology for all of the Middle East resembles the folly of attempting to place all European countries into the "Pan-European" category. Each European country is unique, with its own set of economic, political, and social issues. Just as there is no "one size fits all" conclusion that can be made about the European continent, generalities cannot be made about the region known as the Middle East. This region of the world operates as a loosely held collection of independently functioning countries, each with its own set of opportunities and challenges. Broad brush assumptions and generalities do not do justice to the Middle East and its adoption of healthcare technology. The case studies that appear in this chapter illustrate that point.

One of the most visible new technologies to come into healthcare is the electronic health record (EHR), which is sometimes called an electronic patient record or computerized patient record.[1] This digital record, which reflects an aggregated, longitudinal collection of electronic health information, is made available to all the healthcare professionals involved in patient care—regardless of setting or affiliation. In hospitals and integrated health delivery systems, EHRs reside on an enterprise information system and include such data as patient demographics, a full medical history, medication and allergies, immunization updates, laboratory test results, radiology images, and billing information.[1] While EHR adoption remains in its infancy, a discussion of healthcare technology must address this evolving concept.

For the purposes of this discussion, the term *Middle East* will refer to Syria, Lebanon, Israel, Palestine, Jordan, Cyprus, Turkey, Iraq, Egypt, Iran, Kuwait, Saudi Arabia, Bahrain, Qatar, United Arab Emirates, Oman, and Yemen. It is important to make this distinction because economic and political alliances often set apart subsets of the region's countries, creating confusion. One such example is the Gulf Cooperation Council, which includes Bahrain, Kuwait, Oman, Qatar, Saudi Arabia, and the United Arab Emirates. Often referred to as *The GCC States* or, more simply as *GCC*, these countries have operated under a unified economic agreement since 1981. As widespread as is the use of the term GCC, it actually only refers to a handful of the countries that call the Middle East home.

Despite the fact that GCC represents only a portion of the Middle East, this council of countries provides insight into the trends impacting the region, including exponential population growth and heightened demand for healthcare professionals in areas already struggling to fill open positions, especially in nursing. In the next 20 years, GCC expects its population to double, rising to approximately 80 million.[2] After decades of underinvestment in the area's healthcare infrastructure, more than $10 billion of health-related projects are underway to provide healthcare on par with this explosive growth.[2] Kuwait, for example, plans to build nine hospitals in as many years. If those facilities come to be, Kuwait will need 4,000 doctors and 10,000 nurses by the year 2016.[2]

As multiple positive trends converge in the Middle East, one conclusion is clear—the region's readiness to reap the benefits of advanced healthcare technology in general and EHR specifically may be approaching an all-time high. Specifically, three trends advance this line of thinking:

1. As new hospitals come "online," they feature the latest healthcare IT infrastructure.
2. Ubiquitous mobile phone usage may be creating a "ready made channel" for SMS-delivered services.[3] (Note: SMS, which stands for Short Message Service or Silent Message Service, refers to sending text messages from one mobile device to another.)
3. An increasingly mobile population could accelerate the use of personal health records.[3]

In addition, the Middle East's overarching patient profile makes the region ripe for accelerated expansion of healthcare services. Today, the regional population's sedentary lifestyle has created a legion of people suffering from chronic and pervasive health conditions in need of medical intervention, including those having diabetes, cancer, and cardiovascular- and obesity-related disease.[2]

Staffing Depends on Foreign Nationals

Building and expansion plans aside, the real constraint on healthcare in the Middle East comes not from facilities and technology but from an ongoing and severe shortage of healthcare professionals. Today, staffing the Middle East's existing healthcare delivery system depends heavily on foreign nationals. Approximately 80% of the doctors now practicing in Saudi Arabia and United Arab Emirates hail from outside the region, as do 93% of Qatar's nurses.[3]

Unable to meet that staffing demand from inside the region, some countries in the Middle East have decided to recruit nurses from other regions of the world. For example, Filipino nurses who would have migrated to the United States are increasingly making their way to the Middle East. Earlier this year, recruiters from Saudi Arabia and other countries in the region traveled to the Philippines in an effort to fill 20,000 open nursing positions. Timing of the recruitment effort capitalized on the United States' slow processing of nurse visas. Hiring of Filipino nurses has been on the decline in the United States (U.S.) since 2004, despite the U.S. Citizenship Immigration Service's estimate that 1.2 million new registered nurses would be needed by 2014.[4]

Urban Areas' Internet Usage Rivals Rest of the World's

A popular misconception is that the Middle East is somehow disadvantaged in the use of cellular phones and the Internet. Nothing could be further from the truth. While the region accounts for only 2.7% of the world's Internet users, the percentage of Internet penetration in the Middle East population tracks with the rest of the world (ROW). Approximately 24.7%, or 1,668,870,408 people, of the Earth's global population of 6,767,805,208 have access to the Internet. In the Middle East, Internet penetration rates are similar—23.7%, or 47,964,146 people. What is even more astounding than the penetration rate for the Middle East, however, is the region's exponential growth in Internet usage. From 2000 to 2009, worldwide growth in Internet usage totaled 362.3%. During this same 9-year period, Internet usage in the Middle East increasing an amazing 1,360.2%.[5]

Despite a respectable rate of Internet penetration and exponential growth in Internet usage, the "Digital Divide" in the Middle East tightly maps to users' locations. Urban dwellers experience a "more wired" life than their rurally located peers. For example, cellular phones are fairly ubiquitous in the Middle East/Northern Africa region, according to recent research conducted by Muslim West Facts Project,[6] a non-profit partnership between Gallup and the Coexist Foundation. However, residential access to the Internet dominates only in the Persian Gulf area. While Internet cafes located in urban areas give residents access to the Web, there is no comparable experience for those who live in rural areas.

Looking at wired patterns in Iran, for example, one sees that the highest concentration of digirati (those skilled in digital technology) live in urban areas. As one's focus moves from cities and urban hubs to smaller towns and finally to the rural areas, cell and Internet use trails significantly. For example, 75% of Iranians living in urban areas have cell phones, while only 66% of those living in small towns and fewer than 45% of Iranians living in rural areas can make that claim. Fewer than half of Iranians living in urban locales (48%) said they had residential access to the Internet, while 36% of those living in small towns and only 9% of rural dwellers can surf the Web from home. Several other countries in the region recognized similar urban/rural divides when it came to cell phone use and Internet access.[6]

Just as the so-called Digital Divide signals the split between the "haves" and "have nots" when it comes to cell phones and residential Internet access, a similar division can be seen when it comes to the availability of healthcare services in the Middle East. Highly educated, wealthy residents have access to a wide range of quality medical care in the region, while the impoverished, especially those living in rural areas, find access challenging and, in many cases, non-existent.

Consider the world class healthcare services that are available in Jordan. There, the majority of Jordanian hospitals carry international accreditation from the Joint Commission International as well as through the Health Care Accreditation Council, a national accreditation system.[7] In 2008, 210,000 patients traveled from 48 countries to seek medical treatment in Jordan.[7] As a result, the country expects to gain US $650 million of medical tourism revenue by the end of 2009 and has set an aggressive target of US $1 billion by 2012.[8]

No discussion of healthcare technology in the Middle East would be complete without addressing the cultural mindset that complicates patient care. Make no mistake about it— healthcare providers, especially those involved in what patients and their families view as "bad outcomes" find no immunity from the retaliatory "eye for an eye" thinking that persists in the region. EHRs will give patients and their families more visibility into the members and responsibilities of the healthcare team. This access could produce an escalated level of potential physical harm to healthcare professionals.

However, the Middle East operates with a disadvantage relevant to healthcare technology adoption: indecisiveness due to a lack of understanding. This disadvantage has slowed the adoption of IT[6] and points up the need for education specific to technology's benefits and advantages, a requirement especially pertinent to adoptions of EHR technologies.

Summary

Explosive population growth, an unprecedented surge in healthcare-related building and expansion, and proliferation of chronic conditions linked to the region's sedentary lifestyle make the Middle East ripe for an infusion of advanced technologies, such as EHR. However, the region's already constrained supply of healthcare professionals, which is heavily dependent on foreign nationals, is likely to be further stressed as new facilities come online.

EHR systems will give patients and their families more information about their care and their caregivers' responsibilities than before. Given the region's long-held advocacy for "eye for an eye" retaliation, this knowledge could likely increase the risk of physical harm to healthcare professionals. Healthcare professionals have reported being accosted, sometimes at gunpoint, by members of their patients' families.[9]

Technology offers the Middle East, a region whose residents already possess familiarity with cell phones and the Internet, a platform for creating a portable medical record that reflects the totality of a patient's care. While the comprehensive technology infrastructure needed to support an EHR does not exist today, the Middle East can be expected to leverage its booming medical tourism market to unite providers, facilities, and organizations across the region. Adopting advanced technology-based healthcare solutions, such as an EHR, will require that decisions makers in the Middle East fully understand the benefits associated with these advances.

References

1. *HIMSS Dictionary of Healthcare Information Technology Terms, Acronyms and Organizations.* Chicago: HIMSS, 2006:123-131.

2. *Special Report: Healthcare and Pharmaceuticals,* MEED. http://www.meed.com. Accessed March 20, 2009.

3. Research and Markets. *Future IT Trends and Projects: Healthcare Technology in the Middle East (Industry Focus),* Research and Markets, 2009, http://www.researchandmarkets.com/research/da2493/future_it_trends. Accessed October 29, 2009.

4. Jaymalin M. 20,000 jobs await Filipino nurses in Middle East. *The Philippine Star,* 2009. http://www.philstar.com/Article.aspx?articleid=428817. Accessed October 30, 2009.

5. Miniwatts Marketing Group. *Internet Users in the Middle East and Around the World.* Miniwatts Marketing Group, 2009, www.internetworldstats.com. Accessed October 30, 2009.

6. Crabtree S. *Cell Phones Outpace Internet Access In Middle East: Home Internet access common only in oil-rich Gulf countries.* Muslim West Facts Project, 2009. http://www.muslimwestfacts.com/MWF-HOMEPAGE/home.aspx. Accessed October 30, 2009.

7. *Achievements,* Private Hospital Association. http://pha-jo.com/achieve.html. Accessed October 30, 2009.

8. Vicuna G. Jordan – Rising Medical Hub of Middle East. *Medical Tourism Magazine,* October 2009. www.medicaltourismmag.com. Accessed October 30, 2009.

9. Simpson R. Personal Communication. 2009.

Case Study 17A

Israeli Healthcare

By Ayala Gonen, PhD, RN

Introduction: Israeli Health Services Structure

Israeli health services are considered to be among the most technically advanced and publicly accessible services in the world. They evolved from a health system that had been established during the British Mandate (1920-1948). The current Israeli healthcare system is largely dependent upon the activities of the four major health funds ("Kupot Holim"- the equivalent of HMOs), which were created by the workers' unions even before Israel became an independent state in 1948.

The Ministry of Health is the owner and the operator of the largest hospitals in Israel and receives the third largest allocation in the fiscal government budget after defense and education, sports and culture. The general manager of the office of the Minister of Health is the only technocrat head of ministry, and he/she is usually appointed from among the governmental hospital managers or former chief officers of the Israeli Medical Corps of the military services.

In 1995, national health insurance became obligatory, and currently, every citizen in the country is insured under one of the four HMOs of his or her choice. The four HMOs are member-associate organizations for the purpose of medical insurance on the basis of mutual guarantees between its associates. Table 17A-1 lists Israeli Health Services statistics for 2006.

Hospitals in Israel

In Israel, there are eleven government-owned general hospitals, seven general hospitals that are owned by one of the HMOs—Clalit Health Service, and six other general hospitals that belong to private owners or foundations, such as Hadassa in Jerusalem.

Computerized Technologies

Up to the mid-1990s, the focus of computerized technologies in the Israeli health systems was largely on those whose main objective was clinical-administrative use (such as admitting and discharging patients – ATD) or auxiliary systems such as computerized labs. From the late 1990s, following an organizational development, there was a trend to concentrate on healthcare in the non-hospital setting. This trend focused on the patient's information and clinical needs. Some of the hospital information systems switched from being administrative-oriented to systems that store and manage all the individual patient's medical records and clinical data. As of early 2000, there has been a trend to use the stored clinical data to produce performance assessments, for research, for marketing and for other purposes. To that end, information systems were and still are being developed that rely on the clinical information systems that process the data, analyze them, and translate them into knowledge for various applications.

The Israeli health system is currently undergoing extensive revamping of its clinical records systems. Each of the HMOs now invests money and resources into developing advanced systems to record and manage clinical information on its patients. Interaction between those systems, however, is not yet regulated. From a patient's point of view, accessing critical medical information in the course of medical treatment is crucial. Also, maintaining continuity of treatment while controlling the spread and use of the medical information are key elements to providing vital and quality medical care. The goal of these efforts is to integrate clinical information from multiple sources and to make it available to the caregiver as required. Some steps toward reaching this goal have already been achieved and will be discussed later.

Nursing Informatics in Israel

The rapid growth of information technologies is stimulating the advancement and development of the nursing sector worldwide, giving it a more structured and professional approach to the process of patient management. It is also affecting the decision-making processes, the conducting of research, and the provision of

Table 17A-1. Israeli Health Services- Basic Statistics for 2006

1	**7.8%** = of the National government expenditure used for health
2	**7,116,000** = Israeli population
3	**14,582** = General hospital beds
4	**2.09** = Hospital beds per 1,000 people

ongoing evidence-based control and care. Using IT, high-standard professional nursing and continuing quality control are more accessible, as is research that includes the development of new nursing care modules.

During the last decade, Israeli health services have begun incorporating clinical information systems in its hospitals. There are differences between these systems according to the ownership of the hospitals (government or HMO). One difference is the variety of systems that had been purchased by the various owners. A recent trend is to develop a unified computerized policy for clinical information systems among the hospitals nationwide to support optimal efficiency on the part of the nurses who use the system.

Nurses Training in Israel

There are two formal training programs for registered nurses in Israel, academic and generic. The academic program involves a combination of a bachelor's degree in nursing and certification as a registered nurse. In both programs, the nursing student is required to attend a semester-long introductory computer course (including Excel and SPSS studies).

Formal training for nursing informatics is not currently available in Israel. One of the reasons is the lack of awareness of the importance of this kind of training for professional nurses. In 1997, a group of nurses working in nursing informatics established the "Israeli forum for nursing informatics." This group became active in promoting the subject nationwide, and as a result, more and more hospitals have recognized their valuable contribution and have begun to assign personnel to become competent in the field.

Developing a Unified Terminology in Nursing

The enormous advances in technology have enabled the gathering, filtering, sharing, distributing, and clarifying of information on single patients, groups of patients, and even on entire populations by several users simultaneously. Information technology supports knowledge management on three main levels: executive, operational, and clinical. Developing a terminology affects the nature and the level of professionalism in which care is given to a patient in the following ways:

- It makes the contribution of nursing more "visible."
- It allows measurement tools for nurse researchers.
- It creates a common language among nurses.
- It improves communication between nursing and other therapeutic disciplines.
- It provides data on nursing activities and, by doing so, influences health education and policy.
- It reflects trends in patient care, use of resources, and treatment results.

Presented next are two examples of steps taken by Israeli nurses to unify terminology.

Interventions by Nurse Coordinators Using "Nurses Intervention Classification" (NIC)

The new millennium has witnessed vast expansion of nursing functions. Nurse coordinators are specialists in their fields who work independently and are directly accountable to the nursing management unit. Due to the lack of standards in documenting interventions performed by nurse coordinators and the process of implementing clinical information, it became apparent that there was a need to establish a standard documentation that would reflect the nature, character, and professionalism of the nurse coordinator's interventions and to be later integrated into the nurse's computerized documentation. Eighteen nurse coordinators received a standardized list of 514 NIC interventions and were asked to mark the ones they considered as being most relevant. Their responses were analyzed statistically and 57 interventions were identified and implemented into the EHR. At the beginning of 2008, the implementation of the project was started.

After five months of operation, there were 3,380 recorded interventions per month. Five of the fifty-seven interventions were identified as the most common: documentation, case management, healthcare information exchange, referrals, and consultation. This new standardized language provided a tool for uniform measurement and comparison of treatment for communication and for educational opportunities.

Developing a Nationwide Database in Nursing Based on the Nursing Minimal Data Set (MNDS). The nursing management of one of the HMOs—Clalit Health Service—understood that the clarity of information helps make the nursing contribution more "visible" and decided to develop a professional nursing terminology according to the taxonomy of international classification methods and based on rules and regulations, professional guidelines, and organizational policy. After the implementation, they found that the unified language came with a logical structure that is compatible with a multidisciplinary contribution and allows the translation of this professional contribution into terms of cost and benefit.

A Unified Computerized Electronic Health Record System in Israel

In 2004, the Ministry of Health decided to create a national medical health record system in Israel. The purpose of that project was to improve medical care and the quality of medical service by employing a computerized system that allows the selection and presentation of data and clinical information from the patient's medical file without having to retrieve that information from wherever treatment was being administered (hospitals, HMOs, community clinics, military clinics, etc).

The expected results of this project were:
- Shortening the diagnostic and treatment process
- Reducing duplications resulting from verification of identity by difference sources
- Implementing availability of patients' medical histories when they are unable to communicate
- Improving patient's safety (see next discussion)

The advantages of the national health record system are:
- Accessing and sharing of medical information between institutes in a way that enables the doctor to save time while researching a patient's medical history
- Alerting to a patient's sensitivity to certain medications
- Creating a digital medical file that is accessible to patients and healthcare providers

This ambitious project has been indefinitely halted because the four HMOs which had earlier invested considerably in their own internal computerized system are now reluctant to cooperate and because the medical staff appears to be reluctant to share the responsibility of learning and updating the new systems.

The four HMOs are already partially connected to certain hospitals using the "Ofek" system (dbMotion solution). There is a computerized system that documents domestic violence cases (in recognition of the fact that domestic abuse victims often self-refer to different hospitals to prevent the identification of a pattern).

In spite of the clear-cut potential benefits of this project in terms of improving the quality of care and service, it has been necessary for special committee reviews of the many associated ethical, legal, and technical issues before launching it. There is some concern that the availability of medical information will impinge upon patient confidentiality and privacy and that the information obtained might be used in illegal ways. There is also concern about malpractice suits against the treating staff based on the comprehensive documentation of the treatment process. The availability of the information can also have an effect on patient's willingness to undergo certain treatments or to opt for treatments. These concerns led the committees to decide that there is a need for some legislative changes to deal with these issues, and the Ministry of Health is not acting until such legislation is passed.

EHR in Israel—An Introduction

Professor Stephan Simon of Harvard University, Cambridge, Mass., who participated in the annual convention of the Israeli Society for Health Care Quality[1] (Tel Aviv, 2008) claimed that Israel is a pioneer in using computerized medical records, along with countries such as Sweden, Holland, and Denmark. He maintains that the implementation and education of these systems must be increased and intensified in order to encourage doctors to use these systems to provide better quality medical care and to lower the risk of errors.

In opening remarks, Philip Libman from Gartner Institute (which provides consultation to companies as a non-biased party on the use of healthcare information systems by employing a group of analysts worldwide) noted that Israel holds a very respectable position in terms of its use of computerized information systems, placing fifth in using IT technologies in healthcare, after Denmark, Holland, Sweden, and Finland.

Libman describes five generations of computer-based patient recording (CPR), based on functionality and availability: the collector, the documenter, the helper, the colleague, and the mentor. Israel reached the third generation in 2009.

There are several factors that contributed to this position:

- The four HMOs, which represent the health insurance, as well as the service provider. These organizations have a vested interest in saving money, but not at the cost of providing better service, and so they are highly motivated to incorporate modern efficacious technology into their systems.
- Israeli healthcare is provided by public and private health systems. This is an advantage over having only one public health system, such as that in Canada.
- Each citizen has an ID number, which provides a unique and convenient key for identifying the patient and sharing the information about him or her.

Electronic Health Record Leading Information Systems in Israel

NAMER - ISH–MED–SAP. This project is a wide-horizontal information management system connecting the 11 governmental hospitals. It was acquired by the Ministry of Health with the intent of jump-starting the hospital computerization process and allowing safe and quick access to information that can save lives. The main goal of the NAMER project is to handle the administrative-medical aspect: admission to hospital, documentation of medical treatment and follow-up, discharge from the hospital, and billing.

The NAMER project is run by a committee headed by the general manager of the Ministry of Health, and the committee members are representatives of the health staff and hospital managers. The application manager is an IT specialist from the Ministry of Health. The committee chose an EHR system developed by SAP.

After four years of intense work with HP representatives who implemented the NAMER project and its advisors, three of the eleven government-owned hospitals activated the system in 2003, and it was fully implemented by 2005.

The new information system contains a vast amount of information. It can trace lateral information, beginning with the identification and admission process of a patient and his or her movement through the different hospital departments and units and outpatient clinics. It can retrieve medical history and follow the course of previous treatments as well as billing. The NAMER system is also linked to the National Insurance Institute and to the Ministry of the Interior.

The NAMER system is an integrated system (ERP), which controls processes and the flow of information from start to finish, enabling clarity of organizational processes, as well as the potential production of unlimited reports. The NAMER system can provide a nurse with information about each patient's location, information about a given ward (capacity, admissions, discharges, etc.), patient information (age, gender, diagnosis, etc.), review of current as well as previous conditions, and patient status (ventilation, infection drug sensitivity, etc.).

There are also some modules that have already been implemented:

- **Medical History & Discharge.** Each patient's history (as recorded by nurses and doctors), lab and radiology results, as well as discharge summary are now carried out through the NAMER project.
- **Medical Follow-up.** Medical and nursing staff complete follow-up forms in the NAMER system.
- **Consultation.** Modules for various consultations (cardiology, surgical, etc.) are ready for implementation in a number of medical centers nationwide.

The NAMER project has proven to be a great success in sharing the knowledge between all disciplines, clinicians, and departments involved in providing services and patient care, and for laying a foundation to integrate future systems.

dbMotion Solutions. The dbMotion Solutions was implemented in Israel in 2001 and currently serves close to five million patients in a population of around seven million. The network successfully provides caregivers with an EHR representing integrated clinical data from a large variety of disparate clinical systems within and between three major acute and ambulatory care providers—all within fewer than eight seconds from time of request. The network's ability to meet the complex challenges of organizational growth and clinical system development has been key to its success. It currently supports more than 10,000 users nationwide and holds more than two billion data records.

In 1999, one of the HMOs, Clalit Health Services, faced the problem of collecting medical data in an automatic, online manner from all its data sources. At that time, approximately twenty-five health information systems were used in different areas and departments within Clalit and operated as isolated information repositories. The data from these systems required collection and compilation in a reliable form that was available to all caregivers in the organization. The solution needed to use existing infrastructures for communication and data transfer and a Web-based viewer, without impacting Clalit's existing health information systems and the way they were used. It was also required that different hospitals retain their independence in managing their information infrastructure. Besides these requirements, complex privacy and security needs arose because of the inherent sensitivity of medical information.

The dbMotion has contributed to the efficiency of processes as well as the improvement in quality and availability of medical information for a majority of Israel's population. dbMotion has reduced general concern about medical negligence as a result of the lack of available information. It has also proven to provide major cost savings by preventing duplication of tests due to the lack of cross-site real-time information. Adoption of the system has been extremely easy with consequent rapid growth in the number of users.

MetaVision by *iMDsoft*. *iMDsoft*'s MetaVision Suite of integrated critical care solutions delivers comprehensive patient information throughout the critical care and preoperative continuum. MetaVision streamlines routine tasks and delivers clinical decision support tools that enable nurses to spend less time on paperwork and more on providing direct care to patients.

The MetaVision system automates routine, manual documentation tasks by collecting data from medical devices, such as monitors, respirators, and intravenous pumps and presenting patient information in online, interactive flow sheets. It integrates these data with hospital information systems' laboratory and demographic data, as well as imaging and pharmacy information. The system also collects multidisciplinary clinical and administrative data to create a comprehensive, patient-centric information repository.

MetaVision is adaptable to the specific workflow of the individual clinical care team, covering patient flow sheets, medication and fluid management, diagnosis, problem lists, care plans, charting, reporting, assessments, and more. The MetaVision Event Manager constantly scans the patient-centric information repository to flag problems and issue smart notifications that help expedite effective clinical interventions. Clinicians can immediately access critical information in emergencies, or can proactively monitor patient status against care plans, hospital protocols, regulatory requirements, and best practice standards. MetaVision provides solutions that support and streamline the existing workflow. The system can remind nurses of outstanding tasks and saves time documenting observations, while complementing nursing shift changes. It generates a to-do list based on the patient treatment plan and issues reminders for on-time delivery. Integrated order management modules capture orders, calculate doses, and help schedule administration. Fluid balances and clinical scores are automatically calculated, and discharge and handoff reports are automatically generated, saving time and improving communications.

Major medical centers across the U.S., Europe, and Asia use *iMDsoft* solutions. MetaVision is installed broadly throughout Israel.

Elad IT Solutions – Chameleon. Elad Solutions Ltd. was established in 2003 to provide software solutions to the medical market, especially focusing on hospitals. The company has been providing its flagship solution "Chameleon" as of 2004, and it is currently installed in more than 20 medical institutions in Israel. Chameleon covers total patient electronic management, from registration, scheduling, and check-in, through clinical visits and the entire course of medical treatment. The Chameleon solution is designed to manage both inpatient and outpatient treatment processes.

The Chameleon Inpatient clinical system spans across hospital wards and specialties, giving the tools needed to deliver safe, high-quality care. Chameleon is also highly configurable, allowing the optimizing of displays, features, and information access for physicians, nurses, therapists, dietitians, and any other health provider in the hospital setting.

Chameleon Ambulatory EHR is an intuitive, flexible system with special features, such as Best Practice Alerts to help physicians improve care and save lives.

EHR in the Community

The community health system was designed to provide routine medical services to the population: preventive health services; day-to-day issues in their clinics and institutes; community rehabilitation; and various activities to promote health, such as family planning, exercise, and healthy lifestyles. A community health system is designed to bring medical care in close proximity of the client and to prevent hospitalization as much as possible.

HMO Clinics. The community health system in Israel is based mainly on public clinics owned by the four HMOs. In the past, most nurses and doctors worked with manual filing systems and management software that did little to help their clinics reach their full potential. The challenge facing clinic managers was to provide their medical staff with tools to accelerate case treatment, while being appropriately attentive to the patients. The various HMOs computerized their community clinics to reach these objectives and there are now a number of computerized information systems that answer these needs, affording nurses and doctors more time to relate to the patient rather than spend valuable time searching through files and other records. In addition, it became possible for a medical staff to monitor administrative matters, as well as the individual patient's requirements, appointment schedule, billing information, and medical records.

Summary

Future plans include expanding the system in order to provide health providers with more information for better patient management. The goal is to reach the next generation, colleagues, and settings in which we will integrate the following modules into the EHR:

- Clinical decision support
- Computerized order entry
- Knowledge management
- Evidence-based nursing and medical care

We believe that achieving these goals will result in improved outcomes, fewer medical errors, and evidence-based practices that will lead to provision of optimal healthcare.

Reference

1.   Annual convention of the Israeli Society for Health Care Quality. Tel Aviv, 2008.

Case Study 17B

Lebanon/Beirut Healthcare

By Sana Daya Marini, PhD(c), BSN, BS, RN, HCC

Introduction

Consistency and accuracy of medical health records in healthcare organizations are crucial for the evaluation of hospital services, administrative planning, accurate billing, legal protection, research purposes, and to demonstrate that clinical pathways and policies are operational and ensured at the healthcare enterprise. Leading up to this mandate is the acquisition of leadership and implementation of EHRs.

This case study depicts the current state of EHR in Lebanon—the progress, success stories, human factors, and outcomes. In Lebanon, every hospital is responsible for the design of its own medical record forms. The size and construction of these forms are required to be consistent, with accurate documentation of diagnosis, laboratory results, and treatments. It is also required that medical record documentation by all care providers meets strict criteria. Every page of the patient medical record file must have the allocated medical record number, ideally, typed, stamped, or generated by a computer. The *master index register* would be computerized with a back-up system that is operational, so that any future visits to the hospital by a patient would result in the patient's file *being retrieved using the medical record number.*[1]

The admission department must generate the demographic data sheet, which becomes the first page of the patient's medical record to provide a comprehensive overview of the patient's general and medical details. It is vital to maintain the medical record files and secure their storage in the hospital according to a predetermined sequence. Every hospital must have policies and procedures that govern the process of admitting a patient to the hospital.[1]

Moreover, the medical record should contain all results of any tests performed; it is prudent that a system be developed so that results are affixed in chronologic order. File storage should be in a secure place protected from any potential damage, a location which also allows easy retrieval within a maximum of 30 minutes from the request time.[1]

Although full automation of medical records is not yet mandatory by the Lebanese government, the Accreditation Standards and Guidelines for Acute Hospitals (ASGAH) requires computerization of certain entries as listed under the section of standards for the Medical Records standard MC 11.1 "Data has been collected and computerized for the medical record department."[1]

Practice Overview

American University of Beirut Medical Center (AUB-MC), Beirut-Lebanon, has always been, and continues to be, a leader in the healthcare field in the region. AUB-MC (http://www.aubmc.org/users/index.asp) is accredited by the Joint Commission International (JCIA) and the Lebanese Ministry of Public Health.

The Department of Pathology and Laboratory Medicine at AUB-MC has been accredited by the Commission on Laboratory Accreditation of the College of American Pathologists (CAP), based on the results of a site inspection in February 2004.[2]

The Nursing Services Department at AUB-MC, established in 1993, was awarded an aspiring Magnet designation by the American Nurses Credentialing Center (ANCC). Achieving Magnet status means that AUB-MC provides the highest quality with lowest cost healthcare possible to the patients in the community.[3]

Problem Driving Change to EMR Solution

Rapidly accumulating paper charts became less manageable and made documentation slow and difficult to store because of space, acquisition of reports laborious, and the execution of administrative tasks increasingly time-consuming, all of which was inhibiting the delivery of high-quality care. In response to the problems, AUB-MC developed and implemented the enterprise practice management (EPM) and the electronic medical record (EMR) solution to streamline office administration, enhance documentation, empower professional growth, qualify for many quality-based incentives, and improve the quality of patient care.

Benefits
- Improved clinical documentation and coding
- Improved patient data storage/less storage space
- Efficient chart access
- Improved communication/fewer illegible handwriting problems
- Comprehensive interfacing
- Enhanced overall quality of care
- Improved chronic disease management and health maintenance
- Superior coordination of care
- Expanded efficiencies/increased time savings
- Reduced risk and improved safety
- Improved patient-provider satisfaction
- Compliancy with ASGAH standards

Initiation of EPM/EMR Technology at AUB-MC

AUB-MC is a leading, contemporary, and technologically advanced medical center, which was constructed and inaugurated in 1970. It includes 420 beds for inpatient care, an elaborate outpatient facility, an emergency department, classrooms, offices, and research laboratories for academic staff. It offers an extensive range of specialist medical and surgical services. The hospital includes 10 general theatres and a day surgery unit together servicing between 70 and 120 inpatients a day and approximately 400 outpatients per day.

Today, AUB-MC is proud of its advanced diagnostic and treatment facilities that are the product of consistent and thorough research work. Its recent history continues to be a story of steady growth, periodic expansion, and renovation as it strives to meet the healthcare needs and services required by the patients and community. The AUB-MC is among the most prominent and respected medical institutions in the Middle East. The hospital is a major teaching and research healthcare center that constitutes the healthcare "safety net" for Lebanon and the region.

In an effort to enhance quality care, attain consistent and complete clinical documentation, and secure patient chart storage, the administrator of the medical record, Leila Haidar, began exploring how technology solutions helped improve the center's overall efficiencies and reporting capabilities. Haidar says, "We needed to develop a centralized database at AUB-MC for entailing the patients' health records components collectively and electronically to ease the flow of work, save time, aid in clinicians' decision making, facilitate the acquisition of reports, and improve the execution of administrative tasks. To achieve this, we envisioned transformation to the EHR, in which information would be readily available to clinical and non-clinical staff, such as insurance companies, and easily accessed and browsed with a few clicks of the mouse." Haidar clarifies, "We are not going totally paperless but rather adding e-records—because Lebanese law did not approve the electronic signature yet, we still need to have hard copies signed for official purposes."

In considering potential solutions, AUB-MC had to pay attention to some key considerations. Haidar explains, "We conducted an intensive financial analysis at the executive level before deciding to proceed with a combined EPM and EMR solution. After keen evaluation of technology providers, we chose to develop all the software in-house, which met the organization's needs, community needs, and is in line with our culture, rather than purchasing ready-made software from vendors that might be expensive and needing a large amount of modifications to meet our community and organization's needs."

To help ensure successful implementation, AUB-MC was meticulous in assigning the required internal resources to the project. Haidar clarifies, "I correlate the success to several critical factors. Most important among these was to tap into our goal, which is to be a competent leader in the healthcare field in the region, in addition to the experience and knowledge of the project team regarding training and appropriate timelines. Also critical was to acquire the complete buy-in of the project—unfortunately, so far not all of the physicians value the benefits of the EMR. Finally, because AUB-MC established a core group to head up the project, we met weekly to move it forward and devoted the necessary on-site space and time for training. As a result of this effort, the implementation went relatively smooth, although we had some hitches."

AUB-MC implemented EPM in 2005, followed by EMR in 2007.

The Challenge: EHR at AUB-MC

Haidar illuminates, "Electronic health records are promoted by advocates within the healthcare industry as a means to both improve quality and reduce cost through a combination of reduced errors and improved communication. To digitize every patient medical history, test results, medications, clinical notes and other healthcare data and convert them into electronic medical records with a low cost, we started to scan the previous medical records of patients that are currently being readmitted post-implementation and added the old record to the newly created electronic record to make it accessible from anywhere."

Haidar continues, "The use of master patient index number (MPI) allowed us to capture the patient's various records under one umbrella, and the use of the personal vCards (PvC) helped us to streamline the patient's visits to the various outpatient specialty clinics, emergency units, and admissions. The use of PvC helped us manage patients' heath information quickly and reliably to communicate when needed." (see Figure 17B-1.)

Some of the challenges experienced in conceptualizing and developing the e-records for outpatients centered around the different assessment templates requested by physicians of different specialties. Each specialty department wanted its own assessment template and this added to the work required to get the system built. Currently, we are working on a master template that can meet the needs of all physicians.

In the emergency unit (EU) at AUB-MC, a dashboard was developed that serves as the clinicians' desktop. The "Dashboard" allows clinicians to access their schedule, patient files, pending results, and other clinical data. Staff in the EU unit are very well-trained to use Dashboard, and it has been adopted well. Unfortunately, not all of the Dashboard capabilities are currently operable, specifically the nursing assessments and notes. The nursing documentation is still paper-based. The main barrier to implementing e-nursing documentation in our emergency unit is the limit on the number of computer devices. Going forward, the plan is to equip each registered nurse with a PDA, put a PC in each room, and have more than eight PCs on each nursing station to support workflow.

Dani Badreddine, MSN, RN, in the EU, describes, "The Dashboard was developed in-house by Dr. Nicholas Batley in collaboration with IT personnel. For sure, the system has positively impacted the flow of work in the EU; it links clinician and staff and is updated as tasks are assigned and completed throughout the day. The clinician can assign tasks, such as scheduling a follow-up visit, requesting laboratory and radiology tests, accessing test results, etc. Dashboard also provides configurable 'inboxes' for normal vital signs, abnormal results, and other work items." Badreddine adds, "The dashboard eased the flow of work in EU, eliminated potential errors resulting from illegible handwriting, allowed timely documentation and will be complete with the application of e-nursing documentation."

Nurse managers, registered nurses, and clerks from various inpatient units achieved consensus about the system being user-friendly and simple to use in terms of data entry and retrieval. One nurse manager emphasizes, "We are very happy with the system and satisfied with the change it has introduced in terms of quality of care and ease of workflow. We have easy access to patients' laboratory results and recently, radiology results; also we can request medications from the pharmacy with just a click." (see Figure 17B-2).[4]

Another nurse adds, "The system ensures patient safety and delivery of precise, timely nursing care to patients. Moreover, the system requires standardization in documentation."

Finally, Joe-Max Wakim, assistant director for medical applications, in recognizing the usefulness of the current EHR at AUB-MC, says, "The EHR has improved the quality of care at AUB-MC by presenting clinical information and comprehensive patient data to the clinician at the point of care. This allowed more informed decisions in a shorter timeframe. Additionally, the cost of care has been decreased by streamlining data collection, decreasing the likelihood of medical errors and associated costs, as well as eliminating the cost of duplicative capture of information."

AUB-MC is not using all the EHR capabilities. Modules currently being used are:

- **Billing:** The system handles the billing practice internally.
- **Practice management system:** A practice management system is in place at the facility.
- **E-prescribing:** The organization uses e-prescribing technology for medications and refills only. Future plans are to use e-prescribing for physician order entry with clinical decision support.

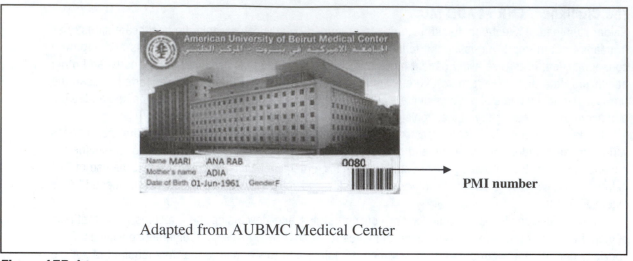

Adapted from AUBMC Medical Center

Figure 17B-1. *PvCard Issued by AUB-MC*

- **Imaging connectivity:** For diagnostic studies, results and Picture Archiving and Communication System viewing.
- **Patient self-reporting and messaging** (not in use yet).

Reaping the Benefits of EHR Implementation

AUB-MC achieved the following key capabilities as a result of EHR adoption:

- Index documents by MPI number: documents of all care episodes (emergency, outpatient clinics, preadmission, etc.), location of episode, beginning or end of episode, discharge date, document date, document type (physician note, request, examination report, laboratory and radiology results, etc.)
- View scanned documents
- Annotate scanned documents
- Create or import documents in various formats (Word, Excel, photo, etc.), and incorporate them in the patient file
- Print or send documents
- Consult documents linked to a care episode or a list of problems
- Generate an official electronic signature and manage the multiple versions of the same document

Future Plans

The future plan for complete EHR use at AUB-MC includes automating all assessment forms, and complete scanning of all physicians' and nurses' notes. Notes will be e-filed into patients' e-medical record, which is step one toward a complete EHR. AUB-MC still has to address the major challenge of maintaining privacy and confidentiality of health data, standards, and the ability to communicate and collaborate with other hospitals. And lastly, we will need to find contemporary solutions with the Ministry of Health to legalize issues, such as approval of electronic signature."

As the stages of our EHR development progress, we will look to provide an adequate number of PCs and other pertinent hardware to all clinical units. The future plan entails that the PC on wheels be used to access patients' medical history/records, treatments, x-ray and lab results, and reports right at the point-of-care. Table 17B-1 lists the adopted functionality at AUB-MC with the future plan for complete adoption.[4]

Future plans also include service to our patients. The intent is to construct and implement a system in which patients will be able to access their own records for the continuity of care with their own family physician and to enhance compliance of the patient. However, this plan requires Internet access for both the family physician as well as the patient.

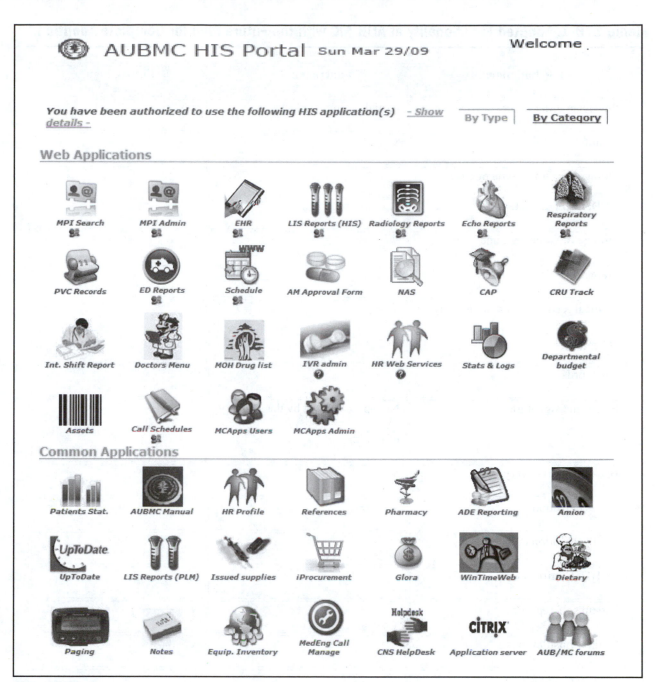

Figure 17B-2. *Snap Shot of AUB-MC EHR System (Still Under Construction)*[4]

Summary

Undeniably, the testimonies of these clinicians at AUB-MC authenticate the benefits behind the EHR adoption at their enterprise. EHR provided immediate access to patient health record information, which improved quality of care. The automated patient health information helped clinicians and nurses at AUB-MC in streamlining their workflow and closed the loops in communications and responses that could result in delays or gaps in care. In addition, the EHR supported the collection of data for uses other than direct clinical care, such as billing, quality management, outcomes reporting, resource planning, and public health disease surveillance and reporting. Furthermore, the EHR enhanced patient safety by improving the quality and timeliness of clinicians' decision making, by providing comprehensive and up-to-date information at the point of care, and by being a source of data for error reporting and analysis.

AUB-MC is one of those healthcare institutions that initiated the implementation of EHR with a strong drive to attain consistent and complete documentation. AUB-MC is still in the EHR implementation process

Table 17B-1. Adopted Functionality at AUB-MC with the Future Plan for Complete Adoption.[4]

EHR Functionality	Function in Use	Future Plan
Physician order entry	Partial on some units	√
Results reporting	√	
Storage of reimbursement codes (ICD, CPT), data, text		
Storage of voice or sound	√	
Storage of clinical images	√	
Medical record document imaging systems	√	
Passwords	√	
Electronic signatures	Not approved yet by the Ministry of Health	√
Backup and recovery	√	
Virus detection	√	
Data encryption (SSL)	√	
CCHIT Certification		√
Patient self-reporting		√
Online consultations		√
Decision support		√
Evidence-based medicine/nursing		√

Adapted from AUB-MC-HIS Portal owned by AUB-MC and is available at
https://his.aub.edu.lb/portal/default.asp

and is very cautious of the required operational changes in the clinical processes, which are the most difficult aspect of the adoption process and which are creating barriers. Some of these are technical barriers, such as the scarce resources in terms of money for the purchase of hardware and maintenance, spaces to host this hardware, lack of standardized terminology, and legalization of electronic signature. Others are human factors, such as the need for staff training and obtaining and analyzing their feedback on system use. There are separate concerns about the growing adoption of EHRs. However, making a clear case for how interoperability positively changes the daily work of physicians, nurses, patients, and others in healthcare would be a catalyst to EHR adoption.

The lessons learned by AUB-MC— recipient of JCI certification and aiming for Magnet certification—will help other hospitals thinking of adopting EHR. This case study which describes the development and implementation phases of the EHR at AUB-MC and identifies certain barriers faced and the strategies used to overcome the barriers, may help others in the same circumstances.

References

1. Accreditation Standards and Guidelines for Acute Hospitals, in Lebanon. 2004

2. http://www.aubmc.org/users/index.asp. Accessed September 15, 2009.

3. http://nursingservicelb.aub.edu.lb/users/subpage.asp?id=116. Accessed October 20, 2009.

4. https://his.aub.edu.lb/portal/default.asp. Accessed October 20, 2009.

Case Study 17C

United Arab Emirates (UAE) Healthcare

By David Printy, MS; Philipp Vetter, PhD; and Kelly Marie Damon, MAL, BSN, RN

Introduction/Background

The influx of capital from the West to the Arab Gulf Region for oil has created a race to improve the lives of Gulf residents, including the availability and quality of healthcare. In addition, the UAE Political Leadership understands that healthcare is a key foundational element, along with education for sustainable economic growth that relies heavily on an expatriate workforce. These facts have led to a revolution in the healthcare delivery environment. The Emirate of Abu Dhabi, capital of the United Arab Emirates (UAE), representing over 80% of the land of the UAE and the wealthiest of the seven Emirates, has taken a leadership role in health-care system reform and regulation.

In 2005, the Emirate of Abu Dhabi passed a law which provides the framework for financing its vision for an improved healthcare delivery system. The cornerstone of the framework is mandatory private health insurance for all residents, paid by employers. It is complemented by a subsidized program for low wage earners and a fully funded program for UAE Nationals. Preparation for the effective date of insurance in January 2007 required a revolution in regulatory and provider processes to cope with processing claims and an increase in patient volumes.

No data standards were in place, including international codes for diagnoses or procedures. In addition to data and administrative process decisions, the UAE was faced with a severe nursing shortage (see Figure 17C-1), as well as large variations in education, experience, and standards. The nursing resource challenge also includes diverse cultural norms and language barriers.

The newly created regulator Health Authority Abu Dhabi (HAAD) sought to create standards that would strongly encourage streamlining care processes, while using the new insurance mechanism to capture and then monitor data on the health status of residents, their patterns of clinical care, the quality of that care, and patient satisfaction (see Figure 17C-1). The data were also used to monitor the substantial financial risk created when the government guaranteed increased benefits for large parts of the population without having access to accurate relevant historic data. This was an undertaking of enormous proportions.

The data standards and procedures were developed in 2007 through two consecutive formal consultation processes that actively sought public and private healthcare providers, payers, and influential groups with technical expertise, such as the Clinical Coding Steering Committee or the Abu Dhabi Dental Association, in various meetings and workshops. The standards officially launched in January 2008, and created a commonly shared language and incentives for compliance, as well as an e-health platform. For example, HAAD supported a commonly shared language by mandating and licensing ICD-9-CM codes for diagnoses and CPT4 codes for procedures across the Emirate—for payer and providers, clinicians and administrators, public and private sector. A key element of the compliance framework was the requirement that all claims for UAE Nationals be submitted and paid electronically commencing June 2008. Finally, all the clinical and financial data coded according to internationally recognized standards helped populate a "Knowledge Engine for Health" (KEH, pronounced "key") used to monitor health activity and support the exchange of e-claims. KEH holds the potential for further e-health applications, such as an EHR or clinical research.

The timing of these changes coincided with a "sea shift" in the delivery of care. Prior to the new insurance law, 80% of care was provided by government-funded facilities. Abu Dhabi transferred all government-owned facilities to a new public joint stock company called SEHA that relied on contracts with US and European academic health systems for management.

The lack of qualified coders required nursing leadership from the United States, Australia, South Africa, and Europe to become a driving force for the education and mentoring of physicians and administrative staff. This core mentoring leadership group became a driving force for meeting HAAD Data Standards and e-claims processing readiness. HIMSS online programs were utilized to train staff to play a central role in the new profession of medical coders in the UAE. HAAD adopted a scorecard to share in the public domain (see Figure 17C-2) the status of healthcare providers' compliance with new data standards that would allow for

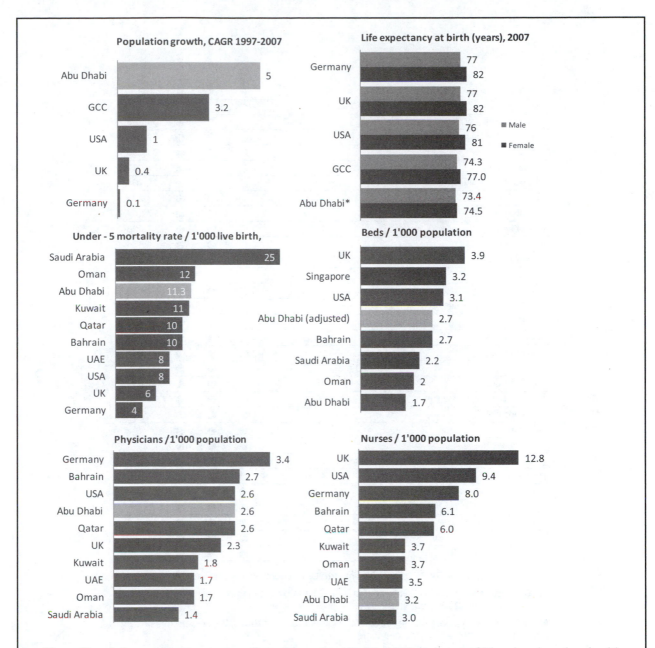

Population growth, CAGR 1997-2007

Abu Dhabi	5
GCC	3.2
USA	1
UK	0.4
Germany	0.1

Life expectancy at birth (years), 2007

Legend: ■ Male ■ Female

	Male	Female
Germany	77	82
UK	77	82
USA	76	81
GCC	74.3	77.0
Abu Dhabi*	73.4	74.5

Under - 5 mortality rate / 1'000 live birth,

Saudi Arabia	25
Oman	12
Abu Dhabi	11.3
Kuwait	11
Qatar	10
Bahrain	10
UAE	8
USA	8
UK	6
Germany	4

Beds / 1'000 population

UK	3.9
Singapore	3.2
USA	3.1
Abu Dhabi (adjusted)	2.7
Bahrain	2.7
Saudi Arabia	2.2
Oman	2
Abu Dhabi	1.7

Physicians /1'000 population

Germany	3.4
Bahrain	2.7
USA	2.6
Abu Dhabi	2.6
Qatar	2.6
UK	2.3
Kuwait	1.8
UAE	1.7
Oman	1.7
Saudi Arabia	1.4

Nurses / 1'000 population

UK	12.8
USA	9.4
Germany	8.0
Bahrain	6.1
Qatar	6.0
Kuwait	3.7
Oman	3.7
UAE	3.5
Abu Dhabi	3.2
Saudi Arabia	3.0

Notes: Population assumptions were adjusted from the Abu Dhabi Department of Planning, based on health insurance data; Physicians, nurses and beds statistics in WHO and other reports are reported for different years; Bed ratio calculations were adjusted, as the population in Abu Dhabi is young and is not expected to need to go to hospital as frequently as other, older population. To enable a fair comparison, the bed ratio was adjusted by mapping the population age structure of Abu Dhabi to that of Germany, using German resource consumption profiles

Sources: WHO Statistical Information System/World Health Statistics 2009, Public health department, and health facility submissions.

Figure 17C-1. *HAAD Health Statistics*

Hospitals	Timely	All Encounters	All Fields	Encounters
Oasis Hospital	○	○	○	18,633
Al Ahli Hospital	○	○	●	64,308
Sheikh Khalifa Medical City	○	○	◐	52,934
Al Mafraq Hospital	○	○	●	35,536
Al Noor Hospital	○	○	●	31,622
Madinat Zayed Hospital	○	○	◐	11,704
Specialized Medical Care Hospital	○	○	●	9,228
Al Rahba Hospital	○	○	●	7,247
Al Noor Al Ain	○	○	●	7,028
Al Noor Airport Road	○	○	●	4,484
Ghiathy Hospital	○	◐	◐	3,567
Delma Hospital	○	◐	◐	2,013
Tawam Hospital	○	●	○	6
N M C Specialty Hospital - Llc	○	●	●	9,001
Liwa Hospital	○	●	◐	2,289
Al Salama Hospital	○	●	●	1,991
Marfa Hospital	○	●	◐	1,281
Sila Hospital	○	●	◐	835
Corniche Hospital	◐	◐	●	11,649
Al Reef International Hospital	◐	◐	●	1,660
Al Ain Hospital	◐	●	◐	617
Al Wagan	●	●	●	
Dar Al Shifaa Hospital	●	●	●	
Cosmesurge Emarites Hospital One Day Surgery	●	●	●	
Lifeline Hospital	●	●	●	
Emirates International Hospital	●	●	●	
General Medical Centre	●	●	●	
Gulf Diagnostic Center	●	●	●	
Magrabi Specialized Hospital	●	●	●	
Emirates French Hospital	●	●	●	

Timely White: submission by 15th of the month; Gray: submission late; Black: no submission

All Encounters White: >= 85% of encounters in July 2007 submitted; Gray >= 60% of encounters in July 2007 submitted; Black: < 60% submitted

All Fields White: All elements required for e-claims available; Gray 1-2 elements missing for e-claims; Black: more than two elements missing

Figure 17C-2. *Scorecard Adopted by HAAD*

electronic claims submission and the development of reliable health statistics. This public scorecard became a major factor in hospital leaders' commitment to investing in staff and IT system improvements.

The next strategic step was to adopt an EMR/EHR system to capture opportunities to streamline and improve care processes created by standardization. The former government facilities (SEHA) established a central data center utilizing a common U.S.-sourced EMR and HIS system. Private hospitals have chosen a variety of systems from internally developed to various worldwide providers.

Preliminary Case Study

Oasis Hospital, a private non-profit facility of CURE International has partnered with the UAE Military health system to install a French EMR, which is integrated with Oracle Business Suite software for a comprehensive hospital information system. This approach appears to be favorably accepted by clinical staff, while other solutions in various UAE hospitals have been met with strong resistance. The ability to have a "greenfield" approach regarding hospital e-systems has proven to be an advantage over legacy system "ownership" by hospital leadership in both clinical and business functions. The additional advantage of a green-field approach has provided a process for a diverse medical and nursing staff to research and adopt best practices guidelines, which will be integrated in the new EMR protocol library.

Oasis Hospital's patient care is challenged with a multilingual staff from 33 nations caring for patients from 102 countries. The staff's varied training, culture approach to clinical team work, language, varied knowledge of best practices and temporary vision of their work in UAE has driven leadership to develop a program of clinical standards in cooperation with University of Minnesota School of Nursing (UMSN) and Harvard School of Public Health. This approach addresses the need for all clinical staff to apply approved researched best practice guidelines (BPG) of care. In addition, a nursing leadership curriculum has been developed in cooperation with UMSN as a foundation for BPG application across clinical enterprise. The UMSN/Oasis educational intervention will be lead by UMC faculty through e-courses and in-person presentations. The following is outline of the course.

Nursing Leadership and Healthcare Systems

Course Objectives

- Discuss the origin and characteristics of contemporary health systems
  - In relation to global health conditions.
  - In terms of social, political, technologic, and economic factors with regard to financial mechanisms that affect access, safety, and quality.
  - In light of current legal and regulatory requirements.
- Assess a healthcare unit/agency/organization in terms of structure; governance; distribution of power, authority and responsibility; decision-making processes; and the roles and functions of nursing.
- Analyze models of nursing and healthcare delivery in terms of:
  - Effectiveness and acceptability with diverse populations.
  - Future nursing roles and functions.
  - Improvements in providing client and community-focused services.
  - Preventing illness and injury, improving health outcomes, and maintaining health.
- Explore the role of contemporary nursing leadership and management in promoting innovation in healthcare systems, including applications of technology, information management, and human development.
- Develop a personal philosophy of leadership based on knowledge of situational and contemporary leadership theory and practice.
- Demonstrate leadership skills in planning, organizing, implementing, and evaluating nursing care in collaboration with nurse colleagues, other licensed and unlicensed caregivers, and members of the interprofessional health team.
- Apply evidence-based strategies to improving the quality of health services and client outcomes.
- Apply theories of planned change, mindful of organizational culture and behavior, in nursing and healthcare.
- Develop core skills in staffing and scheduling, resource management (creating and managing a nursing budget), critical thinking and decision making, assessing nursing competency, performance improvement methodologies, recruitment and retention strategies, and communication strategies.

An additional advantage of the new EMR installation is the review of Joint Commission International Standards (JCI) regarding documentation. The JCI review process is guiding forms development around specialty teams. Medical staff is also reviewing all clinical protocols and guidelines that are evidence-based and specialty-board approved.

Once the full implementation of EMR is complete, Oasis Hospital will have automated KPI report monitoring of all clinical care, including compliance with best practice guidelines and JCI documentation standards. The KPI monitoring includes real-time "flagging" of any deviation from best practices and will require input of reason for adjustment in approved protocols.

Summary

The United Arab Emirates' rapid implementation of national data standards including e-claims processing in an unimaginably short timeline, as compared with a worldwide approach to healthcare improvement and EMR installation is truly remarkable. It is the goal of Abu Dhabi to use its health data warehouse KEH to monitor public health, cost of care, and compliance with best practice.

Case Study 17D

The EHR Initiatives in Turkey

By Firdevs Erdemir, PhD, RN

Turkey

Geographically, Turkey is like a bridge that connects Asia and Europe. Neighboring countries to Turkey include Greece, Bulgaria, Georgia, Armenia, Azerbaijan, Iran, Iraq, and Syria. The Republic of Turkey was founded in 1923 on 814,578 km^2 that remained within the Ottoman Empire following World War I. Divided into seven regions based on geography and climate, Turkey consists of a central government and 81 provinces. The three big cities, which have the most dense populations, are Istanbul, Ankara, and Izmir, respectively. In 2006, the Turkish population was 74.5 million, 65.8% of whom resided in urban areas and 34% in rural areas. The total fertility rate (births per woman) is 2.2, and the life expectancy at birth is 68 years for men and 73 years for women.

In Turkey, studies on the Information Society Strategy are in progress, mainly in the framework of the e-Transformation Turkey Project and of the e-Europe Action Plan 2005. Important steps have been taken in the area of education in order to produce the workforce necessary for implementing and using the technologies of an information society. The core of this project is e-government. In this context, an e-government portal focused on citizens and business requirements is foreseen. Laws on electronic signature, the right of access to information and a draft law on protection of personal data have been approved.

There is no doubt that developments in information technologies and EHR systems provide many opportunities to organize and maintain healthcare services for the country with its large population and exceedingly large land mass. Over the last few years, Turkey has made remarkable progress in the field of healthcare information and management systems, such as the e-Health Project, but there is still a very long way to go. Although this reality is now recognized by many decision makers, it has mostly remained a rhetorical concern; and therefore, progress in the field of healthcare information and management systems is still limited, even with the efforts of various disciplines and/or units.

Turkey's Health System

Health services in Turkey are provided by a multitude of public and private providers. The Ministry of Health (MoH) is the major provider of primary and secondary healthcare and essentially the only provider of preventive health services. The public sector accounts for 92% of hospital capacity in Turkey. There are 7,676 village health stations, 6,066 health centers, and 1,215 hospitals and approximately 82,246 nurses and 97,763 doctors in Turkey, one nurse per 836 people. In 2003, the ratio of physicians to nurses was 1.2:1.

Social security and health systems in Turkey are experiencing various structural problems as low funds and unsatisfactory accessibility remain as barriers. In 2006, the Social Security system in Turkey was radically transformed with the enactment of the Social Security and General Health Insurance Law and the Social Security Institution Law to make the system fiscally affordable and to extend the system (particularly for health insurance) to the uncovered.

EHR in Healthcare Units

Although hospital computerized automation systems are limited in terms of meeting financial and administrative goals, electronic health records and information systems have taken their place in the healthcare agenda of Turkey since the early 1990s. For example, a standard information system project began development with a plan to be completed by MoH in 2005 within the framework of development of a World Bank project in 1992-1993.

Turkey's e-Health Project, in the context of the Health Transformation Project, was developed and was expected to be implemented by the Ministry of Health and the Ministry of Labor and Social Security in 2002, by the 58th Government of the Republic. The project takes into consideration harmonization with the EU Acquits.

The vision of the e-Health Project in Turkey as a part of the Health Transformation Program is explained as *"improvement of healthcare services in Turkey by developing a Secure Health Information Platform that enables healthcare providers, health professionals and citizens, easy and safe access to health related information by using latest Information and Communication Technologies."*

The existing network of the MoH, which is largely used for e-mail and access to the Internet, was enriched and transformed into a National Health Information Platform. This platform includes networking and communications links between all the health sector institutions, enabling the flow, exchange, and use of information, for and by the different levels of the healthcare services (e.g., hospitals, clinics, laboratories) and became the respected health information network of Turkey, referred to as Saglik-Net (Health-Net).

Whereas a few hospitals in Turkey appear to have good management information systems (MIS), there is a strongly expressed need for a nationwide information system for direct support of the day-to-day delivery of healthcare services.

In terms of coding standards, the following have been studied by a working group (WG) and selected for adoption for nationwide uses: disease and clinical procedures coding (ICD-10 Australian Modification), drugs coding (anatomic, therapeutic and chemical coding), and medical devices (Global Medical Devices Nomenclature). There are ten such working groups established within the context of National Health Information Studies, namely: Action Plan WG, Health Information Standards WG, Minimum Health Data Set WG, Security and Confidentiality of Health-Related Data WG, Early Warning Systems for Health Threats WG, Virtual Private Network for Healthcare WG, Training WG, Telemedicine WG, Coordination and Monitoring WG. Working groups are directed by and/or collaborate with the Ministry of Health, universities and the Higher Education Committee, the Scientific and Technical Research Council of Turkey, the State Planning Organization, and the Turkish Medical Informatics Association.

Most of the hospitals have implemented EHRs compatible with international technical and terminology standards, such as ICD-10 and ISO. Internet and other new digital technologies are also targeted in the action plan. The policy document recommends reorganizing health delivery along the lines of general practitioners, capitation as the way of paying physicians for health services, hospital autonomy, and decentralization for decision making. There are no clear statements concerning quality and needs evaluation systems, such as DRGs. Supporting legislation and health information systems are suggested as the necessary anchors for the overall health system. Nurses and the nursing profession are not involved in the development of the EHR systems.

Nursing Education

Nurses constitute the largest group of healthcare professionals in Turkey. Unfortunately, nurses and the Turkish National Nursing Association could not be a part of e-Health Projects due to various reasons (heterogeneous educational levels, lack of IT competencies and of a common nursing language and old nursing regulations on nursing professional autonomy and accountability).

Turkey has two different categories of basic nursing education and all graduates from these programs are employed as nurses. The four-year (based on eleven years elementary school) high school level diploma programs are run and accredited by MoH. The second type is based on BSc degree programs. The nursing curricula are mostly organized in a manner similar to nursing curricula in the United States and include computer skills at a beginning level. In Turkey, Master of Science (MS) degree programs were started in 1968. Master's programs in Turkey include eight departments but do not include nursing informatics (YOK: Higher Education Board, 2007). Since the 1970s, there are in place associate degree programs, and these are standardized by the Council of Higher Education.

Turkey is a candidate country for membership in the European Union (EU). Potential membership in the EU has been the driving force behind Turkey making major political and social reforms, including those that have to do with regulations in nursing education. In 2002, the National Nursing Core Curriculum Council was established to prepare a National Nursing Core Educational Program to present to the Turkish Higher Education Council. The purpose of the program is to standardize nursing curriculum on a national level according to the standards in the European Union criteria, including a holistic approach to patient care with the protection of human rights, professional ethics, teamwork, critical thinking, and a dedication to the profession through the ability to make changes and through lifelong learning. Although nursing informatics concepts were not mentioned clearly in the core curriculum, it is known that all nursing schools in Turkey have a computer course in their curriculum, which is a mandatory course. Computer and IT skills have been taught by nursing faculty at schools of nursing since the 1995. The baccalaureate nursing programs focused more on computer literacy skills than on information literacy skills.

Regulation of Nursing Practice in Turkey

The first legislation regulating professional nursing in Turkey passed in 1954. The law outlined educational requirements for those desiring to become professional nurses. However, for some time, this law has not been comprehensive enough to meet societal needs. After many efforts to propose a new bill regarding nursing since early 1990s, a revision of the 1954 nursing law passed in April 2007. This revised law provides the following:

- A description of nursing
- Criteria for entrance to a nursing school
- Criteria for nursing educational program content
- Criteria for graduate specialist education
- Clarification of nursing roles and responsibilities

According to the new regulations, nurses are authorized to (a) determine the health-related needs of the individual, family, and community that can be met through nursing; and (b) plan, implement, supervise, and evaluate nursing care within the framework of needs identified by the nursing diagnostic process.

Nurses can work as "specialist nurses" after they complete graduate education and specialize in a given clinical area. Following graduation from a baccalaureate program, nurses receive an authorization document. This allows them to practice within a given framework of standards that is determined at the unit level, based on the care required by patients in a specific unit such as occupational health, emergency care, stoma care, and diabetes care as determined by the Ministry of Health. This updated law of 2007 will strengthen nursing care in Turkey in several ways. The fact that roles and responsibilities of nurses who graduated from schools with differing levels of educational preparation had never been completely described had caused serious problems in achieving the professional goals of nursing in Turkey. With the introduction of the 2007 law, the specific responsibility and authority of nurses will be determined according to their educational level. Additionally, the authorization document for specific clinical areas and the acknowledgment of the specialization of nurses with graduate education in a given nursing specialty, such as nursing informatics, will make important contributions to the development of the nursing profession in Turkey and to the health of the country.

Nursing Informatics in Turkey

Efforts and progress are being made for creating and increasing the awareness and competencies of nurses, such as teaching nursing informatics, existing nursing classification systems (such as NANDA diagnoses, ICNP, NIC and NOC) as a prerequisite for the electronic nursing record. NANDA diagnoses were translated to the Turkish language in 1997. A symposium on nursing classifications systems was conducted in 2003 and another one specifically for ICNP was held in 2005. Although there is a common demand from healthcare and information sectors for translation of ICNP to the Turkish language, the translation of ICNP has not yet been done, although ICN has given permission for translation of ICNP to the Turkish Nurses Association (TNA).

A workshop on nursing informatics education and informatics in the nursing curriculum was held in collaboration with the Turkish Medical Informatics Association and TNA. Turkish nurses are gradually becoming active members of the Turkish Medical Informatics Association (MIA), and key notes and panels on nursing informatics are now taking place at annual meetings of Turkish MIA.

Some research and surveys have been carried out to determine the nurses' readiness, opinions, and attitudes on information technology and the effectiveness and content of informatics education in the nursing curriculum in BS programs. Results of the studies show that most of the nurses and nursing students have positive attitudes and approaches to using IT and use computing and Internet technologies extensively. Although there are electronic nursing records systems at only a few private and university hospitals, information competencies are not yet taught in nursing curriculum. Some master and doctorial thesis studies are still being conducted on utility and use of various classification systems, electronic nursing care plans and documentation, and decision-support systems. Although there is a considerable interest and strong belief about the need to have national nursing documentation systems and a nursing minimum dataset that is compatible with international technical and terminology standards, nursing informatics is in a beginning stage, and there is a long way to go for nurses in Turkey.

Summary

It is well-known that governmental policies on nursing training at the high school level and outside the control of the nursing professional bodies has created a formidable obstacles for professional nursing. With the standardization of nursing's definition and educational programs supported by the EU, Turkey has made great strides in the past five years. In regards to the development of nursing informatics, there is a small but growing group of nurses engaging in this specialty. We are only at the early stages in efforts to develop standardized nursing documentation using a common language and terminologies and look to our new nurse graduates from our degree programs to provide leadership in this area. Inconsistent policies about nursing education have created new problems in spite of the progress made in differentiating between types of educational programs. Additionally, the organizational structures in hospitals do not have uniformity, and nursing services as a whole lack organizational structure.

As previously discussed, new regulations (nursing law passed in April 2007) acknowledge that, nurses are authorized to:

- Determine the health-related needs of the individual, family, and community that can be met through nursing.
- Plan, implement, supervise, and evaluate nursing care within the framework of needs identified by the nursing diagnostic process. Regarding all these roles and responsibilities, daily nursing practices and nursing management of patient care are based on data and intensive information as the fundamental elements of nursing.
- Practice problem solving, decision making, data collection and recording, and information processing.

It is a targeted goal in Turkey that nurses should use an evidence-based approach to care in order to improve nursing practice and client outcomes. It is our view that EHRs can help support this goal because nurses need a variety of information at the point of care that they can retrieve quickly and in a format they can use for better decision making about client needs. To take full advantage of the current electronic environment, nurses need up-to-date equipment, access to information technologies and competencies to use the technologies. There must be sufficient equipment to provide adequate access to all nurses in care settings.

The importance of preparing nursing students to apply information technologies to their work as professionals has been emphasized in many publications. The ability to use information and technology effectively is an increasingly important skill for nursing students. It is essential to support the learning experiences of students on the basics of informatics skills that they will need in practice once they are qualified nurses. In this consideration, a nursing curricula that incorporates nursing informatics competencies in basic, graduate, and continuing education programs should be developed and implemented. In addition to this, recognition of nursing informatics competencies among the nursing's professional competencies could be a driving force for nursing informatics education and programs.

Nurses are expected to provide safe, competent, and compassionate care in an increasingly technical and digital environment. A major theme in this new healthcare environment is the use of information systems and technologies to improve the quality and safety of patient care. Nurses are directly engaged with information systems and technologies as the foundation for evidence-based practice, clinical decision-support tools, and the electronic health record. Therefore, nurses should be involved in decision making about IT and IS.

Nurses constantly handle enormous volumes of data and patient care information. In fact, nurses constantly process information mentally, manually, and electronically. Like nurses in other countries, Turkish nurses integrate information from various sources throughout the organization to provide patient care and to coordinate the patient's contact with healthcare services and facilities. In addition, they manage patient care information for purposes of providing nursing care to patients. It has been widely recognized that nurses spend enormous amounts of time engaged in information handling. Nurses must be able to manage and process nursing data, information, and knowledge to support patient care delivery in diverse care delivery settings. There is an essential linkage between access to information and client outcomes and patient safety.

Another major issue is that nursing is frequently underrepresented in the decision making related to health information systems and EHRs in Turkey. Nurses were considered as data recorders rather than data owners. Turkish policymakers and executives must recognize the importance of the nursing profession in the strategic planning process and policymaking for information systems and EHRs in their organizations and national organizations. Health information systems initiatives must also recognize the importance of nursing input into the strategic planning process and decision/policy making related to such initiatives. Nurses and related professional bodies should be involved in decision making about information technology and information systems.

The definition of nursing components of health information is essential to influence health policy decision making. Historically, health policy in Turkey has been created in the absence of nursing data. Nurse clinicians need to know what nursing elements are essential for archiving purposes so that nursing documentation is inclusive of these elements. In the absence of data that reflects nursing activities, there is no archival record of what nurses do, what difference nursing care makes, or why nurses are required. At times of fiscal restraint, objective nursing data are required to substantiate the contribution of nurses to patient care, the role of nurses, and the nurse patient ratios required in the clinical setting.

Bibliography

Aksayan S, Cimete G. Nursing education and practice in Turkey. *J Nurs Scholarsh.* 2000;32(2):211-2.

Dal U, Kiris Y. The Historical Development and Current Status of Nursing in Turkey. *OJIN—The Online Journal of Issues in Nursing.* 2008. www.nursingworld.org/MainMenuCategories/ANAMarketplace/. Accessed April 5, 2009.

Erdemir F, Akman A, et al. *The Opinions of Senior Nursing Students about Informatics Education and Their Attitudes towards Using Technology* (in Turkish). TurkMIA Medical Informatics '08 Conference, 2008: Antalya, Turkey.

Erdemir F. *Nursing Informatics Education.* Keynotes at the workshop of Nursing Informatics Education and Nursing Curriculum in Turkey. 22 Mart 2008, Ankara (in Turkish). Available at: http://www.turkmia.org/dokumanlar.php.

Erdemir F, Akman A. Evaluation of nurses' approaches and readiness towards using computerized care plans in pediatrics services at Baskent University, Ankara Research and Practice Hospital, in Turkey, Proc. 5th *ACENDIO—Association for Common European Nursing Diagnoses, Interventions and Outcomes—European Conference, Documenting Nursing Care* (Eds: Nico Oud, Walter Sermeus, Margareta Ehnfors), 2005: 424-430, Verlag Hans Huber, Bern.

Ministry of Health: The Progress So Far Health Transformation Program in Turkey, November 2002-June 2007. www.health.gov.tr. Accessed April 28, 2009.

Official Journal of Republic of Turkey. (2007, May 2). Bill about revision on nursing law. Wednesday Number: 2651.

Ozsoy SA. The struggle to develop nursing research in Turkey. *International Nursing Review.* 2007:54;243-248.

The Republic of Turkey Prime Ministry State Planning Organization. *The ninth development plan 2007-2013.* State Planning Organization Directorate of Publication and Presentation Ankara 2006.

TUIK (TURKSTAD): *The Republic of Turkey Prime Ministry Turkish Statistical Institution.* (2007) www.tuik.gov.tr/VeriBilgi.doc.

TUIK (TURKSTAD): *The Republic of Turkey Prime Ministry Turkish Statistical Institution.* (2005) www.tuik.gov.tr/.

Turkiye Nüfus ve Sağlık Arastırması (TNSA) Turkey Demographic and Health Survey 2003. Ministry of Health, Hacettepe University, Institute of Population Studies, Ankara.

World Bank. Turkey Reforming the Health Sector for Improved Access and Efficiency. (In Two Volumes) Volume II: Background Papers. World Bank Report No. 24358-TU., Human Development Sector Unit Europe and Central Asia Region Document of the World Bank, 2003.

World Bank. Turkey eHealth Strategy—review & recommended improvements, Oct 2004 by Dr Salah Mandil, Senior Expert Consultant to the ITU, Geneva Page II of iteresources.worldbank.org/TURKEYEXTN/Resources/ - 2008-03-24.

Yavuz M. Computer Courses in the Undergraduate Nursing Curriculum in Turkey. *CIN: Computers, Informatics, Nursing,* 2006: 24(3);159-168.

Yavuz M. International communication via the Internet: Turkish nursing students' experiences. *Comput Inform Nurs.* 2005;23(5): 207-213.

Case Study 17E

Challenge, Change, Hope, Excellence-Oriented: Children's Cancer Hospital Egypt 57357—Icon of Change
By Patricia Pruden, RN

Introduction

Twenty percent of children with cancer diagnosed annually worldwide have an 80% chance of cure if they happen to live in the developed world, while the other 80% who live in developing countries have less than a 40% chance of cure.[1] Egypt is the most populous country in the Middle East and the second-most populous on the African continent (after Nigeria). Nearly 100% of the country's 83,082,869 (2009 est.) people live in three major regions of the country: Cairo and Alexandria and elsewhere along the banks of the Nile; throughout the Nile delta, which fans out north of Cairo; and along the Suez Canal. These regions are among the world's most densely populated, containing an average of over 3,820 persons per square mile (1,540 per square kilometer), as compared to 181 persons per square mile for the country as a whole.[2]

Children comprise 29 million of Egypt's population, according to UNICEF's (United Nations Children's Fund) 2007 statistics.[3] The incidence of childhood cancer in Egypt is estimated to be at 8,400 cases per year, and although no reliable statistics have been kept, the overall survival rate for children with cancer is estimated to be at 40% or lower. Cancer Research UK reports that Africa has 20% of the world's cancer cases and 25% of the deaths, with Northern and Eastern Africa having the highest numbers.[4]

Lack of adequate facilities, lack of expertise of healthcare workers, lack of equipment and medications, and lack of an adequately funded healthcare system are all reasons that so much of the developing world is far behind in the survival rates.

This problem was identified by a group of committed Egyptian physicians from the National Cancer Institute Egypt and businessmen who, in 1997, realized that to achieve survival rates equaling those of the West, change had to occur. This change came in the form of the creation of the Children's Cancer Hospital Egypt 57357 (CCHE 57357) in Cairo.

CCHE is an incredible project that is a true example of the goodness of mankind and what can be achieved when people work together for a common goal.

CCHE 57357

Egyptians and people from all over the world, and most particularly in the Arab world, have contributed generously to the hospital in their wish to support change and improvement and also in their desire to contribute in any way to the future of our countries and our children, both sick and healthy. Egyptians have demonstrated their love for children through the building of CCHE 57357, which was built completely through generous donation (see Figure 17E-1).

Since the inception of the idea in 1995, many have worked together to build a state-of-the-art children's cancer hospital to achieve the dream of a better tomorrow for our children. For not only is this project attempting to increase the childhood cancer survival rate in Egypt, it is also attempting to create a new system of healthcare, in which management and treatment utilize the most scientific approaches practiced today. As shown in Table 17E-1, the hospital vision and mission state that quality care will be provided to children with cancer, regardless of creed, race, or ability to pay.

The hospital began the most important phase of start-up and operation on July 7, 2007, making the hospital free of charge for all patients and accepting patients with the following criteria:
- The patients are newly diagnosed or are suspected cases of cancer.
- The patients must be referred by a physician.
- The age of patients is from newborn to 18 years.

The need for CCHE's services is great. Since opening in July 2007 through to March 2009, CCHE 57357 has received 1,657 confirmed cases of children with cancers. The hospital opening was phased in over a

Figure 17E-1. *Children's Cancer Hospital Egypt (CCHE). Photo courtesy of Children's Cancer Hospital Foundation.*

ten-month period to ensure that all aspects of hospital operation were running smoothly and that the system was mature before proceeding.

Currently there are 179 beds open, and all departments are operational and are working to establish a good foundation of processes, policies, and procedures in alignment with the hospital mission, vision, and core values. The dedicated staff, from all levels of healthcare professionals, have been oriented to the new standard of healthcare, believe in the mission and vision of the hospital, and are committed to the CCHE slogan, "Justice in Quality."

Inpatient Units

As shown in Figure 17E-2, the inpatient units are in the circular bed tower. The circular design promotes better observation of patients and more efficient access for staff. There are 30 rooms that are semi-private and 119 rooms that are fully private. All rooms have bathrooms, televisions, and wall-to-wall windows for children and family to view the outside world during the long days they are confined to their room. Studies have shown that the use of windows and outside light is extremely important for healing and emotional well-being. Physicians and nurses have been assigned to specific wards and are caring for specialized groups of patients, such as those with leukemia, brain tumors, and other malignancies. Each ward has a play room, library, and large outside waiting area for visitors, as well as a staff lounge and locker space.

CCHE 57357 is a Learning Organization

One of the mission statements of CCHE is: "Recognizing that achieving the goal of providing superior services depends upon a dedicated and highly trained staff; we place the highest priority on supporting personal and professional growth, and fostering a team environment." The Department of Academic Affairs, which includes training of all staff from physicians to maintenance workers, developed a comprehensive education plan for all staff. From the start of operation, 547 professional clinicians and 1500 staff have received intensive training in a variety of areas: computer literacy, English, equipment training, cardio-pulmonary resuscitation, infection control, quality management, disease and treatment management, and leadership. In addition, 61

Table 17E-1. Children's Cancer Hospital Egypt 57357 Vision and Mission

Children's Cancer Hospital Egypt 57357 Vision
The Children's Cancer Hospital Egypt 57357 will continuously strive to be one of the leading comprehensive pediatric oncology hospitals worldwide, an international magnet of care, and a model of a philanthropic financially viable organization.

Children's Cancer Hospital Egypt 57357 Mission
The mission of the Children's Cancer Hospital Egypt 57357 is to achieve cure and to improve the quality of life for all children with cancer regardless of race, creed, or ability to pay. We will achieve this by:

- Caring for children with cancer and their families with compassion, innovation, and passion for service by providing outstanding cost-effective patient care and by setting the national standards (scientific, educational, technological, and clinical) for pediatric cancer care.

- Serving as an international magnet of care by providing effective clinical and management systems in treatment, education and research for all levels of healthcare professionals and CCHE will share this knowledge gain with other healthcare centers internationally and nationally.

- Being committed to research that will seek to understand the epidemiology of pediatric cancer, improve prevention, early diagnosis and treatment effectiveness for the ultimate objective of cure without long term physical and psychological adverse effects.

- Recognizing that achieving the goal of providing superior services depends upon a dedicated and highly trained staff; we place the highest priority on supporting personal and professional growth, and fostering a team environment. We regard our staff as the essence of our humanitarian effort.

- Utilizing information and communication technology as an integral component of our patient care, research, and outreach programs.

- Ensuring that the administration and Board of Directors of the Children's Cancer Hospital Egypt and the Children's Cancer Hospital Foundation Board of Governors work in alliance to develop a financially responsible strategy for the sustainability of the hospital and fostering accountability to the hospital stakeholders and our generous donors, ensuring the best use of their contributions.

- Recognizing our roots stem from the National Cancer Institute we will continue a strong alliance and affiliation with the National Cancer Institute by sharing services, clinical expertise, research, knowledge and a vision of quality cancer care for all patients.

- Integrating the concepts and best practices of quality through all parts of the CCHE operation and services ensuring justice in quality.

- Serving our community by being a good employer, leading in public health education and environmental issues, and caring for our neighborhood.

Figure 17E-2. *Inpatient Unit at CCHE. Photo courtesy of Children's Cancer Hospital Foundation.*

are taking degree courses, such as healthcare business administration, health information systems, clinical research associate certification, epidemiology, inventory control, financial management, pharmaco-economics, as well as clinical training abroad. These courses are being provided free of charge through generous education grants from the Egyptian Social Fund for Development, Industrial Modernization Centre, Pepsi Cola, and US AID. To ensure that staff are retained once they receive their education, they must sign a contract committing to two years of service. Although professional development is encouraged in the West in healthcare, it is unique in Egypt to have such an active comprehensive program. Peter Drucker, management guru, said, "The basic economic resource—the means of production—is no longer capital, nor natural resources, nor labor. It is and will be knowledge." The CCHE administration believes firmly that to achieve the level of excellence that is required today in pediatric oncology healthcare and to be recognized as a leader, the most crucial component is to have an expert staff in all areas. It is this philosophy that framed the objectives and the need for a digitized hospital.

Information Technology Department

From the beginning of the planning in 1999, the vision for the information system was to have a hospital that would be competitive with the leading systems in the West but that might not necessarily be at the leading edge of technology. Thinking has evolved since then with the recognition that it is important to achieve a fully automated hospital with the best programs and technologies available. CCHE 57357 administration believes that timely and easy access to information is critical to the pursuit of excellence in all clinical, academic, research, and administrative matters and that (according to Peter Drucker) "you cannot manage what you cannot measure." The required tender was divided into six distinct packages: Health Information Systems (HIS), Enterprise Resource Planning (ERP), Security, Picture and Archiving Communication System (PACS), Voice Over Internet Protocol (VoIP), and Hardware.

The Mission statement of the CCHE IT Department is:

1. To maintain all department quality standards in action
2. Keep the learning curve of users up through learning systems
3. Act as a resource center to facilitate IT knowledge transfer to the rest of the region
4. Assist in keeping the hospital and the foundation financially sustainable
5. Enable the education of patients, families, and public about cancer
6. Research, analyze, and store epidemiologic data in a cancer registry to be accessible to health authorities for better cancer control
7. Communicate with other healthcare entities, gaining and sharing through different innovative and modern up-to-date technologies

As described, it is crucial for the hospital to be able to capture all the data about the patients and treatments. The vision also extended to research projects data collection, cancer registry, expenditures, and all hospital work to be able to develop long-term planning and policies that will affect future expansion or program development. Becoming an automated hospital will not only manage data better but will also improve the work of the hospital to become more efficient, reduce errors, and be more cost efficient. Our software, infrastructure and hardware vendors (Cerner, Cisco, Oracle, Fujitsu-Siemens, Healthy, and SEE) began the complicated process of installing and implementing systems with our HIS staff in 2008. The first end-user project brought live was the telephone VoIP and security systems. It was the first time that most staff had ever used telephones that were multi-functional, and training classes were provided to all staff and employees to learn their functions. Physicians in the Radiology Departments are able to record their reports, while other physicians could access these reports by phone (see Figure 17E-3).

The CCHE 57357 IT team also developed a PACS system for diagnostic imaging, which negates the need for hard copies. Physicians can view images anywhere and make quick and accurate evaluations. By May 2009, most of the systems were installed and implemented with the final go-live for the HIS system in August 2009. Working from the framework of the CCHE 57357 IT Tender Agreement, the HIS supplier worked with all specialty teams and departments to define user requirements, not just looking at current functions but also at what future needs would be required. Super-users were selected from each department to begin the process of training, so that they would be able to train the majority of the staff. Up to this point, this process also identifies the basic process followed in Western hospitals involved with digitizing.

Figure 17E-3. *Digitized Data Sharing at CCHE. Photo courtesy of Children's Cancer Hospital Foundation.*

But imagine that 80% of the 1,500 CCHE staff has never operated a computer before, never spent time in an Internet café, and are not aware of the multiple uses of computers and the limitless capability of the Internet (never mind the need for it in the workplace). The Egyptian government has made it easy for people to access the Internet through their telephone since 2000. Also since 2004, the government has conducted an aggressive campaign to have a computer in every house. This initiative was supported with financial incentives through the Ministry of Communication and Information Technology (MCIT). Despite these efforts, many people do not recognize the need or benefits of having a computer and many others view it with suspicion. The MCIT states, "It is envisaged that the PCs for the Community initiative, through the Egypt PC 2010 – Nation Online program, will cover 3 million families by the end of 2010, with greater focus on citizens in the C and D economic brackets. This would represent coverage of at least 25% of Egyptian families. Currently, only 7% of Egyptian families own PCs, the majority from the A and B economic brackets."[5] It must be stated that the majority of CCHE 57357 staff fall in the C and D economic brackets, which accounts for their lack of computer knowledge.

Hiring computer specialists also proved a challenge because although they were proficient in using the computer and the technical aspects, their English was very limited which made it difficult to communicate with the suppliers and consultants. The majority of the staff has taken intensive English courses over the last eighteen months and now has a working knowledge of English. English proficiency is critical since the major language of all programs is English. As well, none of our physicians, nurses, or administrators had participated in such a project before. The scope of the CCHE automation project represents a first in Egypt. Only a few Egyptian hospitals have basic systems for lab results and possibly patient admissions, while most are using paper records with no automation.

The IT department started with four dedicated young men who had worked with the fundraising arm of the project since its establishment in 1997. They began by developing the Web site and working with IT fundraising software program using e-payment. Next in the process was the IT tender development for the hospital, which included the previously mentioned components. The IT department rapidly expanded to include more than 40 people whose responsibilities include those of a help desk, security, and call center, as well as the VoIP, the implementation of the ERP, and now the implementation of the hospital information system.

As happens in the West, most CCHE physicians have some working knowledge of the computer but initially have had reservations for entering all their notes, orders, and other communications on the system, believing it will be more labor intensive. One of the other issues for our medical staff is that participating in the entirely new system of healthcare that is being practiced at CCHE 57357 has put extra demands on them in regards to time management. This is due to increased involvement in hospital committees, such as the infection control committee, quality assurance, scientific medical advisory committee, pharmacy and therapeutics, and combined clinics. The number of physicians is few (90) with many of them participating in several committees. Resistance to participating in the health information system development was at first high because they saw it as an added demand on their time. As stated by one of the HIS implementers, however, "The system is only as good as the people who use it....it can be the best system in the world but it must be used." Although it has taken some time for acceptance, there have been two major motivators: the first being the numerous scientific presentations by visiting professors from international centers, such as Harvard who have demonstrated repeatedly the necessity of data management to evaluate treatment and conduct research to reach excellence. The second has been the establishment of the research program—the first of its kind in Egypt—and physicians realizing the importance of conducting research and the vast potential that CCHE has to become a leader in pediatric cancer care, being the largest pediatric oncology facility in the world.

A group of clinical research associates (CRA) was formed and recruitment deliberately pulled from a variety of backgrounds, e.g., medicine, pharmacy and nursing. This group was tasked with establishing care protocols standards, data collection, and to become "super users" for the HIS system. The super user role was an expanded aspect to what CRAs usually have in other hospitals, but it was quickly recognized that the HIS implementation process needed people who were computer proficient and who could assist the various hospital departments and programs in planning the HIS system. In addition the CRAs will be some of the major users of the system in terms of data management and collection. CRAs traditionally act as the quality control for protocols regarding medication dosage, timings, and diagnostics, and so this was a logical extension of their roles. In a brief period of seven months, the group of 15 individuals has helped significantly to develop the HIS department programs and have been taking intensive training to begin the important role of training the staff.

The 55 pharmacists working at the CCHE Department of Pharmaceutical Services are a dynamic group of individuals who are computer aware. From the onset of hospital operation, they were anxious to utilize electronic ordering and the concept of pharmaceutical care, capturing the medication history of all patients from the initial admission and individualizing patient medication care plans, as well as acting as a resource for physician and nursing regarding the individual patient's medication plan. Pharmacists are present on all wards to interact with all members of the care team, including families, ensuring that the percentage of errors is significantly reduced and the maximum therapeutic effect is reached. Clinical pharmacy is also a major specialty in the hospital, with pharmacists specializing in various areas from oncology and intensive care to nuclear medicine. A small automated pharmacy system was developed in-house until the major system was implemented because this incredibly busy department is processing more than 30,000 prescriptions monthly! This is a major achievement in an Egyptian hospital pharmacy system, in which, as a general rule, medications did not include proper patient identification, dosage, method of administration, or expiration labeling. From the onset, unit dosing was initiated and now Pyxis, the automated drug delivery system, is being initiated.

Nursing in Egypt

So far, we have described the situation and challenges for other CCHE 57357 staff, of which nurses are a huge component; after all they will be the largest number of users of the system. Nurses have two levels of educational preparation—the diploma and the degree program. Nursing is not a highly regarded profession in Egypt due to one significant factor: Youth who are not performing well in school are channeled by the age of fourteen into technical professions, such as plumbing, electrician work, and nursing. They are then enrolled into hospital schools, which usually are using outdated nursing books and have little in the way of educational resources—with instructors who may or may not have a degree. Their learning occurs usually by passing information from one person to the other and modeling more senior nurses, who may or may not be following accepted standards of care. They typically graduate by the age of 16 or 17 and must work in a government institution, which is chosen by the federal department of nursing, for three years. Often after the first few months of training has begun, they are already working in private hospitals because hospitals are so understaffed. These young women and men have limited knowledge of aseptic technique, basic nursing care, medication administration, and emergency care. In fact, Egyptian physicians prescribe medications by writing the number of cc's of medication or drops of intravenous fluid per minute as the majority of Egyptian nurses do not know how to do drug calculations.

The degree-qualified nurses are better prepared, receiving a four-year program, but the numbers are fewer and after graduation, they are immediately placed in supervisory positions, even though they have had little in the way of training both clinically and administratively.

As a result, there are many horror stories about nursing care in Egypt. There is no countywide final examination to ensure a standardized level of knowledge, and it is believed that the diploma nurses lack the intelligence, discipline, and ethics to be competent nurses. While all sectors of society complain about nursing competency, families of middle class backgrounds would never allow their children to enter nursing, viewing it as a degrading career.

Recognizing that this too must change, the CCHE accepted its first group of 29 nurses in December 2005, in anticipation that the hospital would open in spring 2006. The group comprised 25 diploma-trained nurses and four baccalaureate-prepared nurses. The average age of the diploma nurses was 17 years, while the baccalaureate nurses were 21 or 22 years. When addressed by the VP of Academic Affairs, Research and Outreach on their first day, they looked at him in total confusion when he said in English, 'We have to be patient-focused." He then repeated word by word in English, translating each word into Arabic. We knew then, that we had a long road ahead of us! A pre-test was given of 20 basic nursing questions and five simple drug calculations. Examples of the questions were: (1) If a patient is short of breath, what position would you put her in? and (2) A two-year-old is hospitalized and is crying all the time, what would you tell the mother: stay at the hospital at all times, come at visiting hours, stay home until he is ready for discharge? The lowest grade was 19%, the highest was 55%, with an average of 35%. Being newly graduated, this was devastating for them, but showed them that their learning was only just beginning. The VP of Academic Affairs, Research and Outreach challenged them on that day by forming them into teams and giving them two weeks to develop presentations on Hepatitis B and C, chemotherapy, the difference between adult and pediatric nursing, and HIV. They had no idea where to start. This was their introduction to computers, the Internet, and Internet cafes. However, within three weeks and having received significant help, each group had developed wonderful reports that were presented to the CCHE executive board who were amazed at the progress and potential of this young group.

A comprehensive training program developed with the Cairo University Faculty of Nursing focused on a wide range of subjects. Some of the topics covered include: leadership, managing change, team building, physical assessment, communication skills, anatomy and physiology, CPR, pediatric malignancies, symptom management, palliative care, chemotherapy, drug calculations, nursing process, care plans, patient education, computer training, English, and etiquette. The second exam given six weeks after starting the training program was three hours long and consisted of multiple-choice, long answers, and drug calculations. The average grade for this exam was 65%, and although it was not easy, the students continued to excel; learning about evidence-based practice, giving many presentations, for example, and therefore anxious to begin work. A full eighteen months later, the hospital was opened, and the nursing department expanded considerably to 400 nurses over the following year.

Under the direction of a Canadian director of nursing who was hired by the hospital's foreign management company to train an Egyptian director of nursing and develop the department, a comprehensive educational program was developed, and nurses were selected to be nurse educators. Since then, they have developed a standardized orientation, as well as teaching other courses on pediatric oncology. All nurses have received basic computer training, and many are taking English courses to ensure competency once training begins for the HIS. Nurse super-users have been identified, and they have begun the rigorous training by Cerner, with more being added. What might normally take a fewer number of nurses in other countries will require more in Egypt to ensure rapid system implementation.

CCHE 57357 nurses are considered to be an integral part of the healthcare team and are encouraged to attend all meetings given by visiting professors and experts on a variety of subjects. They have developed a sense of pride in the role they play and are proud of the hospital and its achievements. Egyptians are now beginning to view nurses with a new respect because of the 57357 nurses. On May 12, the first International Nurses Day was celebrated at CCHE 57357, and several nurses were given certificates for completing their course in computers. CCHE nurses have come to realize that learning is a lifelong process and that there are many achievements to be made professionally. While many of the nurses are apprehensive about the next phase of the HIS implementation, they are also proud to be part of the first completely automated hospital in Egypt and are anxious to maintain their role as leaders in nursing in Egypt and the region.

Summary

In conclusion, the CCHE 57357 is an inspiring example of cooperation, collaboration, and change and what can be achieved with visionary leadership and belief in the potential of human beings.

References

1. *Global Action against Cancer,* Updated 2005, World Health Organization. http://www.who.int/cancer/publications/en/index.html. ISBN 92 4 159314 8 (English). Accessed June 5, 2009.

2. http://www.all-about-egypt.com/egypt-facts-population.html. Accessed November 22, 2009.

3. Egypt Stats. http://www.unicef.org/infobycountry/egypt_statistics.html. Accessed June 5, 2009.

4. *Children in the Developing World Bear the Burden of Cancer,* 2003. Cancer Research UK http://www.cancerresearchuk.org/. Accessed June 5, 2009.

5. Access For All, Egypt PC 2010-Nation Online. http://www.mcit.gov.eg/ict_access.aspx. Accessed June 5, 2009.

CHAPTER 18

Nursing Informatics in South Africa: From a Historical Overview to the Emergence of EHRs, Telehealth and m-Health

By Peter J. Murray, PhD, MSc, RN; Irene van Middelkoop, Hons. BA (Cur); Elmarie Venter, Mcom (Informatics), Bcur; and Susan Meyer, B.Soc.Sci. (Nursing) Dipl. Paediatrics

Introduction

While South Africa may be the most economically developed country in Africa, ranked approximately 25th in the world by the World Bank and International Monetary Fund (IMF), with a Gross Domestic Product (GDP–purchasing power parity) of more than US $490 billion (2008 estimate),[1] some of its provinces are as underdeveloped as its poorer neighbors. This creates unique challenges, and the country experiences a range of problems that directly and indirectly affect the organization and delivery of health services, including nursing care and the use of informatics and technologies to support healthcare.[2]

South Africa has a population of 48 million, 46% of whom live in rural areas, has 11 official languages; and administratively is divided into nine provinces. While South Africa devotes 10% of its total expenditure to health, and most of its citizens access healthcare through the public sector, this accounts for only 39% of total health spending, with the rest covered by the private sector.[3] Many of the factors contributing to South Africa's health problems are similar to those of other African countries, although perhaps on a different scale; there is an official unemployment rate of 23% (unofficially more than 42%), and 50% of people live below the poverty line (with 11% living on less than $US1. per day). South Africa also has a significant burden of direct health issues; AIDS is the leading cause of death, and HIV prevalence in people 15 years or older is 17%, while for children under 5-years-old, child mortality is 58 per 1000 births and average life expectancy is 42 years.[2]

Since 1994, the government has identified the need for development of health information as a priority and has committed itself to working toward "a comprehensive health information system" for the country.[4,5] The transformation agenda for South Africa has been addressed in the African National Congress's (ANC) Reconstruction and Development Programme (RDP),[6] the National Health Plan,[7] and successor policies. The United Nations (UN) Millennium Development Goals (MDGs) also emphasize the need for proper health information systems to measure, monitor, and manage the targets toward achieving these goals.[8] However, South Africa's ability to deal with its health needs, in common with many other African countries, has been exacerbated by the "African medical brain drain" whereby doctors and nurses from Africa have migrated to developed countries. The absence of a properly trained and motivated workforce is a key constraint to achieving the MDGs. Current figures are difficult to obtain, and it is suggested that the situation may have worsened in recent years, but an estimate from the year 2000 is that 65,000 African-born physicians and 70,000 African-born professional nurses were working overseas in developed countries.[9] Such loss of clinical staff from low- and middle-income countries is causing significant problems for many already fragile healthcare systems, and health worker retention is critical for health system performance.[10]

A lack of reliable health information is another major obstacle to the effective planning of health services in South Africa; the health system faces challenges in collecting broad data sets and in summarizing the information appropriately to monitor progress in attaining the central goals of equity, access, effectiveness, efficiency, and quality in healthcare. In June 2007, South Africa launched its national electronic health record (EHR) strategy, which has considerable implications for the education and training of health professionals.[2] Any increase in the use of health information systems (HIS) and IT projects requires the government to increase both the quality and the quantity of education, training, and research.[11] The technology skills demand in the healthcare sector, especially in countries such as South Africa, exceeds the supply, although it is well-recognized that the effective use of information systems can be achieved if technology advances in healthcare are matched to the skills of the health professionals,[12] as well as to the development of leadership support, including skills in the management of change.[13,14] At present, many health workers do not have any computer training, and those from rural schools may have never used a computer.[2] These professionals need training that will equip them to deal with the challenges that come with the implementation of health IT projects, both locally and nationally.[11]

Within this chapter, we outline a history of the development of nursing informatics in South Africa and the contribution it has made, and might in the future make to the broader health information goals. Education is a critical element in ensuring the provision of a workforce able to meet the new challenges, and we therefore also address education issues in health and nursing informatics. We provide an overview of hospital information systems and the moves to develop EHRs, and conclude with discussion of leading edge uses of technology, through telehealth and telecare systems, as well as the emerging importance of mHealth.

The History of Nursing Informatics in South Africa

Despite South Africa being regarded as a cross between developed and developing countries (it is technically described as a "newly industrialized country [NIC]", i.e. a nation with an economy more advanced and developed than those in the developing world but not yet having the full signs of a developed country), it still has to fully embrace the speciality of nursing informatics. The need to recognize and develop nursing informatics expertise has been discussed since the mid-1990s,[15] when the necessity for readily accessible and reliable information to support cost-effective decision making and forward planning in an efficient and effective manner was addressed. Hospital nursing divisions, usually comprising at least one-third of the hospital establishment, with very specific and often complex needs, were seen as critical. The development of nursing informatics sections with specially trained nurses were seen as necessary and an integral part of nursing, to enable the profession to keep abreast of the increasing demand for accurate and timely information for effective decision making.[15]

A number of attempts have been made to develop nursing informatics as a discipline and foster its adoption by the nursing profession, including a nursing informatics workshop in 2002, funded by the Medical Research Council of South Africa, which attracted nurses from several other African countries.[16] As long ago as 1978, Marion Ball (IMIA past president, and seen by many as "the mother of nursing informatics") chaired IMIA's first working conference on hospital information systems held in Cape Town, South Africa.[17] Although the term *nursing informatics* has been in existence for some time, it is yet to gain wide recognition and momentum in South Africa. Nurses who work in informatics departments are not recognized as specialists, even though they may have the requisite IT and information management skills.

There are relatively few references in the literature to nursing informatics in South Africa, many references being linked to medical informatics. There is little nursing informatics activity at university level in South Africa, with only one university documenting a basic course in computers in its basic nursing course. Even the recently published nursing strategy for South Africa does not mention the word 'informatics.'[18] A number of universities offer a master's degree in medical/health informatics, which encompasses some of the nursing informatics requirements.[14] Where nursing informatics, or nurses' use of computer and information technologies to support their work, has been explored and discussed, results have not been encouraging for wider adoption of systems. A study comparing manual and computerized systems in primary care clinics in the late 1990s, for example, found "computerising the nurse's consulting room does not enhance the ratio between the time devoted to administrative tasks and the time devoted to patient care."[19]

With the number of hospital information systems increasing, as well as the intention to extend the clinic information systems, the need is even greater to develop expertise in the field of information management with the technological tools available. In the province of Kwa-Zulu-Natal, there is a project in progress to roll out hospital information systems to five of the public hospitals in the province, both urban and rural.

What are the obstacles to developing nursing informatics in South Africa? Finances are always a constraint, especially in the current economic climate. The immediate priority for funders is the care of the patients, particularly with the prevalence of AIDS and tuberculosis. The issue of whether nursing informatics belongs to the realm of the academics or the nursing fraternity is another. The inclusion of informatics in basic nursing training would be an ideal way to engender a feel for the speciality, as nurses in general do not see computers as a tool in their work but more of a burden and something extra which needs to be done. This of course also arises from the fact that a large percentage of nurses are computer illiterate and do not have the facilities or the opportunity to develop their skills. At the South African Health Informatics Association's (SAHIA) HISA 2008 conference, held in Durban, South Africa, it was noted that there were computers available for nurses at only two of five campuses. In 2004, there were 88 personal computers per 1,000 persons in South Africa, with 81 per 1,000 Internet users (up from 66 and 55, respectively, in 2000) which shows a slow increase but does also indicate the lack of resources existing at that stage.[20]

The shortage of nurses, both due to the nursing "brain drain" as well as the AIDS epidemic, leads to additional pressures at work, with fewer resources available to specialize, and in specializing, educate others in the field. In 2007, Médecins Sans Frontières reported that even though South Africa met the World Health Organization's target of 20 doctors, 100 nurses and 228 health providers per 10,000 people, it still lacked sufficient staff to provide essential services such as the provision of anti-retroviral drugs for the people living with HIV/AIDS.[21]

Currently, a master's program in medical or health informatics is offered at four universities in the country, but at the same panel discussion at the HISA 2008 conference, it was pointed out that the master's program takes too long and that there are too few qualified staff at the ground level. Those who are currently involved with nursing informatics are mainly self-taught and recognize the need to develop courses to ensure that information systems which are put into place are beneficial to the nursing staff in their line of work, rather than something which is seen as being additional and work-intensive.

Health and Nursing Informatics Education in South Africa

Nursing professionals carry the responsibility of bringing health services to all levels of care, from primary healthcare to tertiary level. With an increased drive to move healthcare delivery to lower cost levels, a heavier burden is placed on the healthcare provider in primary healthcare, particularly the nurse. Primary healthcare is the first point of contact in medical services for patients. In developing countries, the percentage of the population that depends on these services is enormous and still growing with increased numbers of patients suffering from chronic health conditions.

A shortage of these professionals can impact very negatively on the quality of and access to healthcare provided to communities. Retention of health professionals in under-resourced areas is a worldwide challenge and increasing attempts to attract and retain skilled workers to these areas are ongoing.[22] The attraction of higher salaries and better opportunities in urban areas contribute to the problem. Unsatisfactory working conditions, such as unmanageable workloads, poor infrastructure, and insufficient resources (medicines and other supplies) in rural areas force healthcare professionals to look for better employment opportunities elsewhere.

Skills and Responsibilities of Nurses

Responsibilities of a nurse include carrying out general nursing care (assessment, planning, implementation, monitoring, and evaluation), prescribing and administering treatment, and appropriate reporting and referral as required by the condition of healthcare user. Competencies required in primary healthcare range from general clinical care competencies (assessment, diagnosing, and prescribing medicine and other treatment) to clinic management. The latter requires a nurse to be familiar with the catchment area population profile and its health problems and needs, and to use data collected at clinic level to formulate specific and achievable PHC objectives, while using district, national, and provincial goals and objectives as a framework.[23]

Changing environments require responsive action from the healthcare delivery system to be able to support changing health needs. The competencies and skills required from nursing professionals in all categories of nurses on all levels of healthcare delivery are determined by the healthcare delivery system. Changes to these environments and the subsequent changes to required skills and competencies inform the education and training of nurses.[24]

The introduction of IT to manage the growing amounts of data in healthcare affects the work practices of those involved. Nurses have to change the ways they have done things before; their workload has increased with the additional responsibility of mastering computer skills. Further, although the promised benefits of IT are well-reported and probably known to them, the reality still holds that initially, IT places enormous burdens on the inexperienced users until they finally manage to master the skill to utilize the technology in their normal daily activities. When new applications are implemented in health facilities, basic computer literacy training is provided together with training on system use. High staff turnover, however, makes it hard to maintain the required skills among the healthcare workers.

Nursing Curriculum in South Africa

In South Africa, all training institutions develop their nursing curricula on regulations prescribed by the South African Nursing Council (SANC). The current education and training regulations include:

- 1969: Regulations for Colleges
- 1985: Regulations for the Course for the Diploma in Nursing Administration
- 1987: Regulations for the Diploma in Unit Management for Registered Nurses, Regulations
- Concerning the Minimum Requirements for Registration of the Additional Qualification in Nursing Education
- 1988: Regulations Relating to the Approval of and the Minimum Requirements for the Education and Training of a Nurse (General, Psychiatric and Community) and Midwife leading to Registration)
- 1997: Regulations Relating to the Course Leading to Enrollment as a Nurse, Regulations Relating to the Course Leading to Enrolment as a Nursing Auxiliary, Regulations for the Course for the Diploma in Psychiatric Nursing for Registration as a Psychiatric Nurse, Regulations Relating to the Minimum Requirements for a Bridging Course for Enrolled Nurses Leading to Registration as a General Nurse or a Psychiatric Nurse, Regulations for the Diploma in Clinical Nursing Science, Health Assessment, Treatment and Care, Regulations Relating to the Course in Clinical Nursing Science Leading to Registration of an Additional Qualification, Regulations for the Diploma in Community Nursing Science, Regulations for the Course for the Diploma in Midwifery for Registration as a Midwife

- 2004: Regulations Relating to Examinations of the South African Nursing Council) (SANC, 2004

A search through all these regulations for the words *computer, electronic, digital, information* and *technology* delivered no results.

The undergraduate curriculum for nurses in the Department of Nursing Science at the University of Pretoria dates back to 2000. Information technology-related subjects, mainly focused on computer literacy skills, are prescribed during the first year of study of all undergraduate students, and include:

- **Computer literacy 1:** Keyboard and mouse skills, e-mail, basic Internet and Web skills, basic theoretical introduction to hardware and software. Windows as an operating system.
- **Computer literacy 2:** Word processing programs: creation, editing and formatting of documents, outline editing, automatic numbering and footnotes, tables and columns, insertion of multimedia, data exchange, etc. Presentation programs: creation of presentations, incorporating figures, text, animation, and the insertion of multi-media.
- **Computer literacy 3:** Spreadsheet programs: basic skills, including formulas and diagrams. Database programs: basic skills, including searches, compilation of reports, etc.
- **Information literacy 4:** Search strategy formulation: the use of Boolean operators, natural language, and controlled language. Searches on CD-ROM and the Internet. The evaluation of Internet search engines. Analyzing, organizing, and synthesizing information. Studying sources.

However, the question has to be raised as to whether this computer education is enough for nurses today to perform their duties in the growing digital information environment. Even if computer literacy is mastered sufficiently during nurses' initial training, if not used and refreshed on a regular basis through clinical use after the studies have ended, the skill levels tend to deteriorate quickly.

Hospital Information Systems in South Africa

South Africa has an increasing demand for quality healthcare. Delivering healthcare that is safe, efficient and effective is the challenge that everyone working in the dynamic environment of a hospital or clinic setting faces. Whether they are dealing with patients with HIV and AIDS, or the recently re-emerging problems of tuberculosis (TB), or less high-profile diseases such as cancer, arthritis, and diabetes, having these skills is no less an important element in addressing the changing nature of health. However, it is often difficult for busy nurses, engaged in saving lives, to think about the strategy of the institution or organization for which they are working and to consider the possible benefits of new ways of working, including new ways of information management, to help them work more efficiently and have more effective outcomes.

As in many other countries, decisions are often made for clinical staff by non-clinical participants in healthcare. It is imperative for success that, when an institution or an organization embarks on a strategic planning initiative, healthcare matters include decision makers who are familiar with working in the clinical environment. To have effective information management, there is a need for an effective IT department, which includes staff who have clinical experience as well as a better than average grasp of technology and systems, manual or electronic, so as to play a major role in this decision-making process.

A study published in the *British Medical Journal*[25] found that three-quarters of implemented systems fail and that no evidence exists to show there has been improved productivity of health professionals. Evaluation of the effectiveness of a computerized HIS as an entity is crucial, but such evaluations need to acknowledge that the patient is the primary focus, not the health professionals per se.

HIS are tools that help to make nursing and medical documentation easier and holistic, with the primary intent to care for the patient and enhance patient safety. In addition, any useful system must not only simplify management of information, meet the demands of accreditation and legal documentation, and always provide confidentiality of that information, but should help its users learn and understand by providing appropriate auditing facilities.

There are five "pillars" in the successful implementation of a computerized HIS that need to be checked and balanced through corporate strategies, appropriate leadership styles, and change management:

1. **Preparation and Participation:** It is essential that the right people be involved from all levels of the institution. This stage cannot and must not be rushed, as poor decisions made at this stage will have far-reaching consequences later.

2. **Training and Translation:** This involves training of those involved in set-up of the system, who are then responsible for the translation of the software into reality, or the reality defined in that institution.

3. **Communication and Information Management:** If there is not an appropriate plan, then failure is essentially planned-in.

4. **Users:** Consultation with end-users is vital to reducing the risk of failure in using the system post-implementation. If users do not understand, they will never inculcate the system into their work processes. As a result, the patient will not derive the benefit of a highly sophisticated computerized HIS.

5. **Patients:** It is always about the patient. In one author's experience, patients who are treated at a hospital with a computerized HIS in place loathe being referred to other institutions that do not have the same or similar processes.

The key factor linking the five pillars is information. If these issues are not addressed, then implementation of any system—electronic or manual—will fail, with losses that are not just financial. From this general theory of HIS implementation, it is possible to see some of the South African experience. In the provincial hospital environment of KwaZulu-Natal, for example, there are only two hospitals that have electronic processes in place, and each uses a different system. In both institutions, it has been found that when users do not understand what the system is and what it can do for them, they resist using it; moreover, when the users do not understand how to use the system, the system will usually be blamed for any failings in the system.

Of the many computerized HIS available on the market, in resource-constrained environments such as South Africa, where both public and private health sectors suffer financial and personnel shortages, it is often difficult to fully test or evaluate systems. As has been found in many other countries and in studies of implementation success and failure,[14] the South African experience is that only through properly managed strategic planning, with alignment of goals and actions between management and staff, and the influence of champions, will systems be effectively implemented.

IT is an applied science, and it always involves people. Through an understanding of people—their language, their culture, their wishes, and their dreams—and including how patients feel about the benefits of using computers to safeguard their information, comes the greater chances of success. The multilingual, multicultural diversity of a country such as South Africa demonstrates the truisms of applying strategic planning theory into practice.

Electronic Health Records in South Africa

Introduction

If decision-makers have access to relevant, valid, and timely quality information they will be empowered to make better decisions and devise better implementation plans for these decisions. Some health data related to an individual are captured at the source (point of care), but more data can exist in different location-points at which they were captured at different intervals. The progress of an acute illness into a chronic condition increases the information requirements. To enable caregivers to effectively manage a patient's health over time, some form of longitudinal record must be available, whether in paper or electronic format. The vastness of the task of integrating large amounts of generated information from various sources has lead to the view that automation of systems has become essential.

The objectives of the national policy in EHR are to integrate individual records of different episodes, track patients for continuing healthcare, reduce medical errors, increase easy access to records, monitor healthcare behaviors, improve referral systems, and promote transparency and efficiency. Notably, however, clinicians' support for patient care is not one of the main objectives.[11] There is also no clear policy on how the private sector will be incorporated into the national EHR program. Currently, the National Department of Health is working with the Council for Medical Schemes in some aspects of health informatics.[26]

In its EHR, the National Health Information System of South Africa (NHISSA) has decided to adopt ICD-10, and OPCS coding standards as part of the health information strategy of the Department of Health. They decided to use HL7 as a standard structure. It is one of the several American National Standards Institute (ANSI)-accredited standard developing organizations operating in the healthcare arena. The ICD-10 currently serves as the diagnosis coding standard of choice in both the public and private sector.[11]

In the South African setting, ICD-10 coding is important in that it lends itself well to the improvement of efficiency of healthcare through appropriate and standardized recording of diagnosis, analysis of information for patient care, research, performance improvement, healthcare planning, and facility management. It also enables fair reimbursement for healthcare services provided and communicates health data in a predictable, consistent, and reproducible manner.

Standardization

Electronic Health Record. An electronic health record (EHR) consists of integrated data from multiple sources. Health data collected and stored securely in an electronic format to support decision making can be accessed by both the patient and the caregiver with the consent of the patient.[27] The identity of a patient can be verified through the use of biometric technologies, and his or her health status can be monitored more effectively, while laboratory results and prescriptions to streamline drug supplies are added. Data contained in an EHR should be structured and the following elements should be included: patient demographic details, history of complaints, previous treatment, and drugs prescribed; with associated adverse drug events, findings of physical examinations, laboratory investigations results, socio-economic circumstances (including housing and occupation), as well as a complete description of the clinical history and assessment and subsequent treatment prescribed.[28]

HL7. Information exchange between disparate systems requires standardization of electronic data collected in those systems, as well as a standardized data interchange mechanism. In South Africa, HL7 was adopted as the preferred mechanism of communication with the EHR.[27] "HL7 is a standard, approved by the American National Standards Institute, for the exchange of healthcare information between computer applications."[29]

Security, Privacy, and Confidentiality. Due to the nature of health data and information, the issues of security, privacy, and confidentiality need particular attention. Patients and caregivers need to trust that technologies support data being stored and exchanged securely, that patients' privacy is respected throughout the handling of the data and that information is kept confidential.

Patient Consent. A patient has the right to allow or deny individuals access to his or her health data. The general belief is that through the voluntary use of fingerprint biometric identification technologies, the patient provides consent to a certain service provider to access his or her health data. The exchange of data for use by external parties has to be authorized by the patient involved. This would mean that EHRs can be accessed by healthcare providers at the physical point in which the patient is located, but for integration to other systems and sharing of that information to another location, the patient must provide consent. If the patient would be unable to provide such consent, the care provider would only gain access to the most critical information, such as allergies and existing heart conditions.[27]

Access Rights. User access should also be regulated within one facility. Staff members' job descriptions would determine the necessity of access to information; thus information is shared on a need-to-know basis. An administrative clerk, for example, needs to know the demographic details of a patient, while the professional nurse or the doctor who is responsible for the treatment of the patient's condition needs access to clinical information as well. These access rights need to be assigned to each staff member by an authorized system administrator.[27]

Encryption Mechanisms. Utilization of encryption methods in databases can ensure that patient demographic information and related clinical encounter information cannot easily be used to identify a single individual linked to a specific condition and/or treatment.[28]

Modifications to and Deletions of Records. It is important to track changes and deletions made to any health record, as these records can be used in a court of law when necessary. Every action on a health record must therefore be logged, and a history of all actions must be available for auditing through an audit trail.[27]

Confidentiality. A service provider that treats a patient stores information about the encounter in an EHR, and has the right to make changes to documentation about the encounter. If the encounter was marked as "confidential," any authorized user must also get expressed consent (not only via fingerprint) from the patient, to view details of the encounter.[27]

Personal Health Record. Patients are increasingly becoming health information consumers and are enabled through ICTs to add to the data in their own EHRs. A personal health record can thus be defined as "the patient view of the data that resides in the EHR repository and additionally allows the patient to supplement the data from providers."[27]

The long-term goal of the National Department of Health, when it issued a request for information for an electronic health record for SA in 2005, was that every SA citizen should have an EHR. As the majority of the existing health information systems in use are not patient-centered information systems and contain the minimum (if any) clinical information, this goal will not easily be achieved in the near future.[27]

The Emergence of Telehealth, Telecare, and m-Health in South Africa

Telehealth and Telecare

With the high prevalence of HIV and TB, South Africa, together with much of sub-Saharan Africa, faces a substantial burden of disease. The additional shortage of medical and nursing staff reinforces the need for considering innovative ways of providing healthcare to the population. Telecare, a term often used interchangeably with telehealth and telemedicine, which encompasses the use of electronics, information systems, and telecommunications within the healthcare environment[30] has had some success. There has been a drive to implement programs in telehealth, one particular success being the use of video-conferencing facilities at universities. At the University of KwaZulu-Natal, regular training sessions are held by video-conferencing between a number of hospitals and staff at the medical school. This facility is also utilized for meetings between various parties, nationally or internationally. The Internet also provides a source of information for educational purposes, with many journals available through sources, including the Medline database with the PubMed search engine.[31] These facilities are especially important in sparsely populated rural areas, where valuable time is often spent travelling to urban areas for training or education; online facilities obviate the need for travel, thus allowing more time in the community with patients.

The cost-effectiveness of properly implemented telehealth systems has been proven, especially with respect to reducing the burden of disease among the poor population, yet telehealth applications are not yet widely recognized and utilized.[31] In South Africa, there are several telemedicine projects across the country, one of the most recent being that of the Botshabelo community, which in March 2009, became one of the first recipients of a primary healthcare telemedicine workstation.[32] This will provide support to this rural community and also strengthen the referral systems. Many of the rural clinics are nurse-led, with a medical doctor attending only once a week or less frequently. Hence these support systems should improve medical care for the patients, with the nurse having the facility to liaise with members of the medical discipline.

However, there is still a need to provide better infrastructure which will allow communication between areas, both urban and rural. This includes the provision of adequate bandwidth. The training of nurses and other staff in the usage of the technology will have to increase and educating in basic computer skills is also essential. The allocation of funding from government or grants would be required to build the infrastructure with support and maintenance. There is also a need for evaluation and research to assess whether applications would be suitable and applicable in the various areas, and buy-in of the staff who would be utilizing the facilities would also be needed. The equation is made more complex by aspects of the ethical debate, as to whether it is ethical to put so much money into these projects when there is such a desperate need for ARV (antiretroviral) treatment for HIV/AIDS, as well as treatment for TB among others, and to improve the plight of the poor. The positive point is that projects have been proven to be successful and beneficial to the patient, improving their health status. The challenges facing the provision of quality healthcare in under-resourced areas are experienced worldwide. A growing demand for continued healthcare caused by HIV and chronic lifestyle diseases, such as diabetes mellitus and hypertension, emphasize the need for solutions that can easily be accessed by millions of patients in need. Mobile health technologies that are at the same time available, affordable, effective, and accessible can empower healthcare workers to provide quality healthcare services to the developing communities.

mHealth in South Africa

mHealth (mobile health; also written as m-health) has been defined as the "emerging mobile communications and network technologies for healthcare systems."[33] It is a recent term used to encompass the use of mobile devices, such as mobile phones, patient-monitoring devices, PDAs, and other wireless devices, to support medical and public health practice. mHealth applications include the use of mobile devices in collecting community and clinical health data, delivery of healthcare information to practitioners, researchers, and patients; real-time monitoring of patient vital signs; and direct provision of care (via mobile telemedicine). The proponents of mHealth see it as revolutionizing healthcare delivery in much of the developing world.[34]

The development of mHealth has been made possible by the rapid rise in ownership and availability of mobile phones (cell phones) in many countries. There were more than 4 billion mobile devices in use around the world in 2009, with 64% of them in the hands of people living in developing and emerging economies.[34,35] Eighty percent of the world's population lives in areas with mobile phone coverage, making mobile technology probably the most viable type of technology to reach the largest part of the world's population.[36] The highest growth rate in mobile phone availability is in Africa, where nearly 30% of the population now has a mobile phone,[35] and Africa now has more mobile phone users than North America.[37] Mobile phones have become a very popular method of communication in South Africa despite the relative high cost,[38] and coverage is fairly extensive in the populated urban areas and slowly increasing in the rural areas, allowing this technology to be utilized for telecare.

However, the level of Internet access is currently far lower in most developing countries than in developed; in Africa, just 5% of the population now uses the Internet,[39] generally through slow and expensive fixed line connections. Broadband Internet availability is limited and the software may not be available in the language in the area.[31] Eighteen percent of clinics in South Africa have Internet-connected computers, while 96% have a least one cell phone.[40] The lack of general computer expertise is another barrier to their use in healthcare and nursing. While more people are being exposed to computers through school and work, there are still many areas in which computers are unavailable due to lack of electricity, lack of funds, or other reasons.

Seen as a "leapfrog technology," the growing availability of mobile phones and other mobile devices offers opportunities for developing countries, even those with poor infrastructure, to bypass 20th century fixed-line technology and jump straight to 21st century mobile technology.[41] Mobile phones have the ability to dramatically change the lives of those who use them significantly, including healthcare providers.[34] This allows the possibility of using phone messages, texts/SMS, and increasingly mobile and high-speed broadband access to support a wide variety of mobile health applications, as the next stage of evolution of telehealth.

South Africa stands out among other countries in a recent United Nations Foundation report because of its adoption of mHealth projects.[36] Project Masiluleke, for example, uses SMS message campaigns to provide HIV/AIDS education, taking advantage of the 120 spare characters on free "please call me" SMS (short messaging system) messages to provide HIV/AIDS education and awareness.[36,42,43] The project sent 365 million text messages (one million per day) in 2008 to encourage people to be tested and treated for HIV/AIDS and TB; it represents the largest use of mobile devices for the delivery of HIV/AIDS and TB information and treatment in South Africa, with the potential for future expansion to other countries. Messages are written in local languages, and are used to direct recipients to the national AIDS help line.

Within Africa, mobile (cellular) phones are used increasingly for communication between health provider and patient, as well as for triggering reminders for certain events such as pill-taking.[44] As adherence to the ARV regime, as well as for TB treatment has been a problem leading to drug resistance, the use of SMS via mobile phones has been proven to be successful in reminding patients to take their drugs.[45] The AfriAfya (African Network for Health Knowledge Management and Communication) study concludes that the use of mobile phones and SMS is the number one ICT strategy in the fight against HIV/AIDS.[46]

The Millennium Villages Project[47] provides several examples of exploring the use of wireless and Internet infrastructure to promote the achievement of MDGs for global health and development in a number of African countries. Projects have aimed at improving access to emergency and general health services, enhancing collection of vital statistics on births and deaths to refine public health interventions, reducing child and maternal mortality and morbidity, improving efficiency of health service delivery, and improving monitoring and evaluation of health system activities for enhanced planning and decision making. The use of mobile phones and Internet access provides the opportunity for health workers to consult specialists and so overcome some of the restrictions of the shortages of specialized nurses and doctors in many rural areas.

The Dokoza system is another South African example of using mobile technology to share information between health professionals and institutions so as to improve the delivery of healthcare services. The system was initially developed for use in HIV/AIDS (specifically in respect of the roll-out of ARV therapy) and TB treatment with a view to including other diseases. The system involves the use of SMS and mobile phone technology for information management, transactional exchange, and personal communication.[48,49] A 2007 pilot in South Africa showed that with SIMpill, 90% of patients complied with their medication regime, compared with the typical 22% to 60% compliance rate without the system.[36] Cell-Life provides health information management and monitoring tools through the use of ICT innovation to support ARV treatment in the public health sector of South Africa.[50,51]

As mHealth develops, it will be increasingly important for supporting nurses in their work and delivering nursing care as well as health and medical care, and nurses in all countries will need to be increasingly aware of the possibilities for impacting their everyday practice.

Summary

While South Africa and many other developing and newly industrialized countries face many challenges, in terms of particular burdens of health and disease problems, the mixed economy of healthcare between public and private sectors,[52] the provision of nursing healthcare, the education and retention of the healthcare workforce, and education and training in many areas, including nursing and health informatics, there is emerging evidence of the use of innovative solutions to address the problems. In the period between 1995 and 2002, South Africa had no national formalized, coordinated, and standardized health informatics training and education program, although some universities offered informatics as a module in the Masters in Public Health course.[11] At both strategic and operational levels in South Africa, there is still a great need for experts in the areas of theories of health information and the social perspective of health information and informatics, health information systems development and principles, health computing science, and electronic patient records.

In September 2010, the 13th World Congress on Health and Medical Informatics, MedInfo2010, will be held in Cape Town, South Africa.[53] This will bring the opportunity for African and South African health professionals, including nurse informaticians, to interact with colleagues from around the world, sharing issues, experiences and problems, and exploring solutions. It will build on the long-established experience of SAHIA[54] and other emerging health informatics associations within Africa[55] and could provide the opportunity for a renaissance of health informatics and nursing informatics in the region.

References

1. CIA. *The World Factbook: South Africa.* https://www.cia.gov/library/publications/the-world-factbook/geos/SF.html. Accessed July 8, 2009.

2. Mars M, Seebregts C. *Country Case Study for e-Health: South Africa.* http://ehealth-connection.org/files/resources/County Case Study for eHealth South Africa.pdf. Accessed July 8, 2009.

3. World Health Organization. *World Health Statistics 2006.* http://www.who.int/whosis/whostat2006/en/index.html. Accessed July 8, 2009.

4. Department of Health, Republic of South Africa. *White Paper for the Transformation of the Health System in South Africa.* April 1997. http://www.info.gov.za/whitepapers/1997/health.htm. Accessed July 8, 2009.

5. Department of Health, Republic of South Africa. *Strategic Priorities for the National Health System 2004-2009.* http://www.doh.gov.za/docs/policy/stratpriorities.pdf. Accessed July 8, 2009.

6. African National Congress. *The Reconstruction and Development Programme: a Policy Framework.* Johannesburg; 1994. http://www.anc.org.za/show.php?doc=rdp/rdp.html. Accessed July 8, 2009.

7. African National Congress. *The National Health Plan for South Africa.* Johannesburg; 1994. http://www.anc.org.za/show.php?doc=ancdocs/policy/health.htm. Accessed July 8, 2009.

8. United Nations Department of Economic and Social Affairs. *The Millennium Development Goals Report,* 2006. http://mdgs.un.org/unsd/mdg/Resources/Static/Products/Progress2006/MDG Report2006.pdf. Accessed July 8, 2009.

9. Clemens MA, Pettersson G. New data on African health professionals abroad. *Human Resources for Health.* 2008;6:1doi:10.1186/1478-4491-6-1. http://www.human-resources-health.com/content/6/1/1. Accessed July 8, 2009.

10. Willis-Shattuck M, Bidwell P, Thomas S, Wyness L, Blaauw D, Ditlopo P. Motivation and retention of health workers in developing countries: a systematic review. *BMC Health Services Research.* 2008;8:247 doi:10.1186/1472-6963-8-247. http://www.biomedcentral.com/1472-6963/8/247. Accessed July 8, 2009.

11. Mbananga N. *Introduction to Health Informatics.* Pretoria: Notoro Publishers, 2006.

12. Berg M. Implementing information systems in healthcare organizations: myths and challenges. *Int J Med Inform.* 2001;64:143-156.

13. Lorenzi NM, Ash JS, Einbinder J, McPhee W, Einbinder L. *Transforming Health Care Through Information.* New York: Springer, 2005.

14. Murray PJ, Betts HJ, Wright G, Mashiya NV. Health Informatics Education and Capacity Building in Eastern Cape Province, South Africa. In: Geissbuhler A, Kulikowski C, eds. *IMIA Yearbook of Medical Informatics 2009.* Methods of Information in Medicine. 2009;48 Suppl 1. In press.

15. Babst TA, Isaacs S. Recognizing nursing informatics. In: Greenes RA, Peterson H, Protti DJ, eds. *MEDINFO '95—Proceedings of the Eighth World Congress on Medical Informatics.* Edmonton, Canada: IMIA/HC&CC Inc., 1995, part 2:1313-15.

16. Mbaganga N. Nursing Informatics in the African Continent. In: Weaver CA, Delaney CW, Weber P, Carr RL, eds. *Nursing Informatics for the 21st Century: An International Look at Practice, Trends and the Future, First Edition.* Chicago: HIMSS, 2006:435-441.

17. Safran C. Presentation of Morris F. Collen Award to Dr Marion J. Ball. *J Am Med Inform Assoc.* 2003;10(3):287-288.

18. Department of Health, Republic of South Africa. *Nursing Strategy for South Africa* 2008. http://www.doh.gov.za/docs/misc/nursing-strategy.pdf. Accessed July 8, 2009.

19. McDonald T, Blignaut PJ. A comparison of a manual and a computer system in a primary health care clinic. *Curationis.* 1998;Sep;21(3):8-13.

20. The World Bank. 2006. *Information & Communications for Development (IC4D)—Global Trends and Policies.* http:// www.worldbank.org/ic4d. Accessed July 8, 2009.

21. Médecins Sans Frontières. Help wanted. *Confronting the healthcare worker crisis to expand access to HIV/AIDS treatment: MSF experience in Southern Africa.* http://www.msf.org/source/countries/africa/southafrica/2007/Help_wanted.pdf. Accessed July 8, 2009.

22. Yumkella F. (2009) *Worker Retention in Human Resources for Health: Catalyzing and Tracking Change.* Technical brief 15, The Capacity Project. http://www.capacityproject.org/images/stories/files/techbrief_15.pdf. Accessed July 8, 2009.

23. Department of Health, Republic of South Africa. *The Primary Health Care Package for South Africa: a Set of Norms and Standards.* 2000. http:// www.doh.gov.za/docs/policy/norms/contents.html. Accessed July 8, 2009.

24. The South African Nursing Council (SANC). *Charter of Nursing Practice.* Pretoria, South Africa: SANC. http://www.sanc.co.za. Accessed July 8, 2009.

25. Littlejohns P, Wyatt JC, Garvican L. Evaluating computerised health information systems: hard lessons still to be learnt. *BMJ.* 2003;326;860-863. doi:10.1136/bmj.326.7394.860.

26. Council for Medical Schemes. *ICD-10 Implementation Review,* January 2004–October2006. Pretoria, South Africa: National Task Team on ICD-10 implementation. http://www.medical schemes.com/Publications/ZipPublications/PMB%20Coded%20List/ICD10_Implementation_Review_October2006.pdf. Accessed July 8, 2009.

27. Alger R, Klopper L. *An Electronic Health Record (EHR) and a Personal Health Record (PHR).* Hout Bay, South Africa: Electronic Patient Records (Pty) Ltd. (unpublished).

28. Fraser HSF, Jazayeri D, Nevil P, et al. An information system and medical record to support HIV treatment in rural Haiti. *BMJ.* 2004;329;1142-1146. doi:10.1136/bmj.329.7475.1142.

29. World Health Organization. *HL7/ART Technical Meeting. Meeting Report;* 2005. Geneva, Switzerland. http://www.who.int/kms/initiatives/HL7_ART_meeting_report_FINAL.pdf. Accessed July 8, 2009.

30. Doughty K, et al. Telecare, telehealth and assistive technologies—do we know what we're talking about? *Journal of Assistive Technologies.* 2007;1(2):6-10.

31. Wootton R. The future use of telehealth in the developing world. In: Wootton R, Patil N, Ho K, eds. *Telehealth in the Developing World.* IDRC, 2009:299-308.

32. Department of Science and Technology, South Africa. Press release. *Telemedicine to Benefit Rural Community.* http://www.dst.gov.za/media-room/press-releases/partnership-enables-launch-of-telemedicine-workstations/. Accessed April 3, 2009.

33. Istepanian RSH, Laxminarayan S, Pattichis CS. *M-Health: Emerging Mobile Health Systems.* Heidelberg, Germany: Birkhäuser, 2005.

34. United Nations Foundation. M-health alliance. http://www.unfoundation.org/global-issues/technology/mhealth-alliance.html. Accessed July 10, 2009.

35. International Telecommunication Union (ITU). *Measuring the Information Society—The ICT Development Index.* Switzerland: Geneva. http://www.itu.int/ITU-D/ict/publications/idi/2009/material/IDI2009_w5.pdf. Accessed July 8, 2009.

36. Vital Wave Consulting. *mHealth for Development: The Opportunity of Mobile Technology for Healthcare in the Developing World.* Washington, DC and Berkshire, UK: UN Foundation-Vodafone Foundation Partnership, 2009. http://www.globalproblems-globalsolutions-files.org/pdf/UNF_tech/UNF_mHealth_for_Development_Brochure.pdf. Accessed July 8, 2009.

37. Turrettini E. African mobile subscribers surpass North America. http://www.textually.org/textually/archives/2008/05/019983.htm. Accessed July 8, 2009.

38. Mars M. Telemedicine in South Africa. In: Wootton R, Patil N, Ho K, eds. *Telehealth in the developing world.* IDRC, 2009:222-231.

39. MacInnis L. *Mobile Phone Growth Helps Poorer States:* UN. http://www.reuters.com/article/technologyNews/idUSTRE5211GJ20090302. Accessed July 8, 2009.

40. Bristol N. *Are Cell Phones Leading the mHealth Revolution? Global Health.* http://www.globalhealthmagazine.com/top_stories/are_cell_phones_leading_the_mhealth_revolution/. Accessed July 8, 2009.

41. Next Billion. *The Limits of Leapfrogging.* http://www.nextbillion.net/news/the-limits-of-leapfrogging. Accessed July 8, 2009.

42. PopTech Institute. *Project Masiluleke.* http://www.poptech.com/project_m/. Accessed July 10, 2009.

43. Johnson B. Text messages could help turn the tide of HIV and AIDS in South Africa. *The Guardian.* http://www.guardian.co.uk/technology/2008/oct/24/hiv-aids-text-message-project-masiluleke. Accessed July 10, 2009.

44. Lester R, Karanja S. Mobile phones: exceptional tools for HIV/AIDS, health and crisis management. *Lancet Infect Dis.* 2008;8(12):738-739.

45. Hüsler J. *Evaluation of the On Cue Compliance Service Pilot:* testing the use of SMS reminders in the treatment of tuberculosis in Cape Town, South Africa. 2005. www.Bridges.org. Accessed July 10, 2009.

46. Elder L, Clarke M. Past, present and future: experiences and lessons from telehealth projects. *Open Medicine.* 2007;1(3):E166-170.

47. Mechael P. *mHealth in the Millennium Villages Project.* Earth Institute at Columbia University. http://mobileactive.org/directory/practitioners/millennium-village-project-mhealth-program. Accessed July 13, 2009.

48. Mishra S, Singh IP. *mHealth: A Developing Country Perspective.* http://ehealth-connection.org/files/conf-materials/mHealth_%20A%20Developing%20Country%20Perspective_0.pdf. Accessed July 13, 2009.

49. Dias-Alf J. *Mobile Technology To Improve Health Service Delivery Within Government.* http://www.changemakers.com/en-us/node/1014. Accessed July 13, 2009.

50. Stockholm Challenge Award. *Cell-life.* http://www.stockholmchallenge.se/data/cell_life. Accessed July 13, 2009.

51. Sørensen T, Rivett U, Fortuin J. A review of ICT systems for HIV/AIDS and anti-retroviral treatment management. In South Africa. *J Telemed Telecare.* 2008;14:37-41 doi:10.1258/jtt.2007.070502. http://jtt.rsmjournals.com/cgi/content/abstract/14/1/37. Accessed July 13, 2009.

52. Matshidze P, Hanmer L. *Health Information Systems in the Private Sector.* http://www.healthlink.org.za/uploads/files/chap6_07.pdf. Accessed July 13, 2009.

53. MedInfo2010, *13th World Congress on Health and Medical Informatics.* http://www.medinfo2010.org. Accessed July 10, 2009.

54. SAHIA. *South African Health Informatics Association (SAHIA).* http://www.sahia.org.za/. Accessed July 10, 2009.

55. IMIA. International Medical Informatics Association (IMIA): National Member Societies. http://www.imia.org/members/national_list.lasso. Accessed July 10, 2009.

## CHAPTER 19

Nursing and the Electronic Health Record in Asia, Australasia, and the South Pacific

By Karolyn Kerr, PhD Information Systems, MHSc, RN; and Polun Chang, PhD

Introduction

Nurses provide holistic care to patients with diverse healthcare and social requirements, within many different types of organizations and geographical locations. This can mean nurses are delivering care in isolation from their colleagues and sometimes in isolation from medical staff support. Access to information, including the patient's previous health encounters, and to intelligent decision support are becoming essential for all healthcare providers in the modern healthcare environment. However, recent extensive research undertaken in Australia[1] highlights that nurses continue to lack confidence in the use of IT. Also, nurses in this study recognized the benefits of adopting more IT in the workplace but were frustrated by the limitations of access to technology. Significantly, training in how to use various applications was very limited. These issues have also been noted in a New Zealand study.[2]

All of the countries outlined in this chapter are experiencing nursing shortages. These shortages are congruent with international trends of an aging nursing workforce and the struggle to attract new recruits. By necessity, this is leading to innovative ways to improve the efficiency of care delivery. Economic constraints vie with increased expectations from the educated consumer for better healthcare and more response to individual's needs and wants. Nursing and medicine need to work together with e-health specialists to meet these expectations. The developments worldwide toward implementation of effective electronic health record (EHR) systems to record care delivery and assist with decision making appear to provide improvements in information management in healthcare.

The economies of each country in this region are varied. New Zealand and Australia enjoy considerable affluence, with resultant extended life expectancies and excellent quality of life. Some countries in the South Pacific, however, have to provide basic healthcare services to geographically diverse populations with only minimal funding and infrastructure available to do so. The current economic crisis has impacted all countries in the region. There is at least one positive implication for the health sector, however, with some nurses returning to the profession after having left for higher paid positions outside of health.

While the cultures within the region are also very diverse, they are actively merging. For example, New Zealand's Asian population has increased by 5% over the past five years through relaxed immigration policies seeking to attract people to meet employment opportunities where local skills are lacking. There is considerable emigration out of the Pacific Island countries into Australia and New Zealand, leaving ever-decreasing populations to support local infrastructure. Further, nurses in this region, including those from the Pacific Islands, are being recruited to work in other countries, such as the United Kingdom, United States, Canada, and Ireland, where nursing shortages are having considerable impact.

The countries in this region rely heavily on a professional nursing workforce to provide the bulk of hospital-based and primary care services. Those in Australasia and the South Pacific structure and train their nursing workforce in a similar manner, initially closely aligned to traditional hospital based three-year courses provided by the United Kingdom. Most have now moved to a degree program offered in polytechnics or universities.

Nurses today have increased expectations and are demanding improved working conditions and pay increases to reflect the degree status and specialization of nursing services. Nurses are often heavily relied on to overlap with the duties of the junior house officer, and several countries have now introduced a Nurse Specialist/ Nurse Practitioner qualification that allows nurses to prescribe.

Knowledge of what nurses do is required. But this is often not explicit and is hard to define, making it difficult for nurses to "prove their worth." The EHR has the potential to provide nurses with a medium for recording the effectiveness of the care they deliver that is transparent and available in a format understood by those outside of nursing. At present, nursing in this region:

- Cannot compare nursing practices across locations.
- Have no means to validate nursing by measuring what it entails.
- Is progressively losing the ability to practice nursing in the milieu of data collection.
- Cannot describe outcomes of nursing services.
- Is unable to describe or analyze practice consistently.

All countries in this region, but in particular Australia and New Zealand, are moving toward more seamless delivery of healthcare from hospital to community to minimize increasing costs and reduce waste. A multidisciplinary healthcare record would support this change by providing everyone with access to appropriate information about a patient. The danger is in the misinterpretation of information by different disciplines. Nursing language standards are required worldwide to prevent this confusion and to address the need to align with other medical languages as appropriate.[3]

Standards currently under development internationally through the Health Level 7 (HL7) ballot process may provide much of the world with a direction for development that will ensure the EHR is internationally understood in a consistent manner. Many countries of this region are actively involved in the HL7 movement, with Australia and New Zealand being early adopters of HL7 Standards. SNOMED CT has been adopted by Australia and New Zealand, and both countries are working together to develop an Australasian standard.

Australia is well-advanced in this region in the development of a national EHR. Fortunately, there are many collaborative networks already in place that mean developments in best practice and lessons learned from any country are quickly disseminated throughout the region. Presented next is an outline of the progress of developments in the EHR in Asia, Australia, New Zealand, and the South Pacific, and in particular, actual and potential nursing developments in the area of EHRs.

Asia

The development of medical and nursing informatics in Asian countries is unique and interesting in many ways. While some countries have very good healthcare infrastructures, others still lack enough necessary resources; these include two of the most populated countries, China and India. Even when promotion of medical or health informatics is not at the top of national healthcare reform policies, excellent national IT infrastructures still create a continuous and strong movement of developing and using the healthcare ICTs within the healthcare institutes, without emphasizing the terms of medical, health, or other healthcare-related informatics. Although there has been an economic downturn around the world which might constrain necessary development of medical or health informatics internationally, the recent success stories of economic development by two giant countries, China and India, brings about an interesting but challenging model of promoting medical and health informatics in a short time. This refers to the "Leapfrog" Model. These Asian patterns deserve marked attention from international health informatics communities to develop better strategies for successful

Table 19-1. The Nursing and Midwife Density per 1,000 Population for the Asian IMIA National Members[5]

Country	Nursing and Midwife Density per 1,000
China	1
India	1.3
Iran	1.6
Malaysia	1.8
Korea, South	1.9
Turkey	2.9
Saudi Arabia	3
Hong Kong	3.7
Singapore	4.4
Taiwan	5.2
Philippines	6.1
Israel	6.2
Japan	6.5
Kazakhstan	7.6

medical or health informatics reform and therefore improved health and cost-effective use of limited healthcare resources.

Generally speaking, most of the Asian countries do not have abundant healthcare resources, especially among clinical professionals. Large populations coupled with a low density of healthcare professionals in Asia might imply a difficult challenge for their national medical or health informatics professionals and organizations. Promoting nationwide medical informatics strategies is difficult when most of their healthcare colleagues have already suffered from the lack of medical and public health resources to better serve their people, not even considering healthcare ICTs. While Asia comprises one quarter of all global countries, it contains more than 60% of the world's population. There are currently 13 International Medical Informatics Association (IMIA) national members, including two of the most populated countries, China and India.[4] Based on the data published by the World Health Organization (WHO) in 2009, the nursing densities per 1000 population of all these 13 Asian IMIA national members range from 1 for China, 1.3 for India, to 6.5 for Japan and 7.6 for Kazakhstan, as shown in Table 19-1.[5] These numbers are smaller than those of many other IMIA national members, such as 9.4 for United States, 10.1 for Canada, 12.8 for the United Kingdom, together with many European countries.

However, the lack of sufficient numbers of healthcare professionals could imply an increased national interest in applying healthcare ICTs to improve the productivity of healthcare systems and people's health. This could become a stimulating factor for a rapid growth of medical or health informatics in some countries, such as China and India, which will be discussed in a later section.

However, it is interesting to see that many Asian countries have excellent national IT infrastructures to support the movement of medical or health informatics. Based on a report released by the Economist Intelligent Unit in 2008, among the top 20 countries with the best global IT competitiveness, 5 are in Asia: Taiwan (ranked 2nd), South Korea (8th, and 3rd in 2007), Singapore (9th), Japan (12th and 2nd in 2007) and Israel (16th).[6] These countries along with others such as Malaysia and Hong Kong (China) have developed excellent public

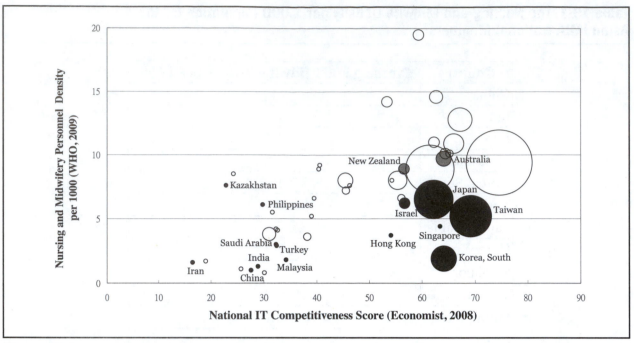

Figure 19-1. *The Publication of IMIA Asian vs. Non-Asian National Members in the NI2009 by Nursing Density[5] and by National IT Competitiveness[6]*

health and medical informatics projects and applications of their own kind in their countries. Among these, Singapore, Hong Kong (China), Malaysia, respectively, hosted the HIMSS Asia Pac starting in 2007; Korea hosted the MedInfo 1998 and Nursing Informatics, 2006; Taiwan hosted the Asia Pacific Association for Medical Informatics (APAMI), 2006; and Japan hosted the APAMI 2009. Many of them also hold their national medical informatics conferences annually. It is not uncommon that many local, highly-regarded medical institutes in these countries have developed their own institutional EHRs and applications of advanced ICTs for daily care services, without ever considering that they are undertaking medical informatics projects. In these cases, ICT projects are simply regarded as part of general hospital strategic projects.

The capability of these national IT infrastructures has a very interesting relationship with that of national medical or health informatics. For example, when we plot the data of national nursing density, national IT competitiveness scores, and national participation in the NI2009,[7] a very interesting pattern is seen, as shown in Figure 19-1. In Figure 19-1, the Asian national members are charted in black, the Australian and New Zealand members in grey, and other members in transparency. The size of the bubble relates to the number of papers published by that country in the NI2009, so that the larger the bubble, the more papers published. The Asian publications presented are mainly from three Asian countries: Taiwan, Japan, and South Korea. This pattern is quite consistent among those countries included on the list of top twenty countries with best global IT competitiveness. Among the Asian countries presented in the figure, Taiwan has the most papers presented. National IT competitiveness seems to be the factor that plays the most significant role in promoting medical or health informatics nationwide. In Asia, both Kazakhstan and the Philippines have a higher concentration of nursing professionals, and the latter even exports many of their nurses to other countries, such as Australia and Canada, but their performance in healthcare ICTs are a bit behind.

Another development in health informatics in Asia that deserves attention is the unique Leapfrog Model of promoting the health informatics developed in China and India since the mid-2000s. This is important because the model is implemented in the two most populated countries in the world and could have a positive impact on a great number of people. However, the Leapfrog Model also has a great risk in the implementation phase because the successful implementation of a quality healthcare ICT project requires time and patience, and is dependent on the implementation being overseen only by those who have experience and have been active in this area. This Leapfrog Model was proposed by China and India mainly due to their economic success. Brazil, Russia, India and China are called the BRIC countries, a term which refers to the rapid growth and future importance of these economic entities.[8] Their ambition and expectation of implementing healthcare ICTs to provide better health outcomes and services to their people are notably strong.[9,10]

Since 2006, a series of national policies has pushed public health and healthcare institutes to significantly increase annual investment and spending in healthcare ICTs by double digits.[9] In 2008-2009, China appeared to be one of very few countries not suffering from the global economic crisis that started in 2008; it still maintained a high economic growth rate. Much funding is poured into the healthcare sector to stimulate the economy and to improve healthcare quality. In mid-2009, the Chinese government announced its intention to allocate up to US $85 billion to healthcare systems in 2009 and 2010. US $2.5 billion will be directly invested in healthcare ICTs, including EHRs. Due to this significant investment in health informatics, the medical informatics associations in China, such as the China Medical Informatics Association (CMIA)[11] and the Chinese Hospital Information Management Association (CHIMA),[12] acted positively and proactively in 2009 to study and promote better use of these resources and look for a "leapfrog" in health informatics to catch up with other advanced countries. In 2008, NI special interest group was established inside CHIMA, and its members started to edit the first Chinese NI textbook in May 2009. Further, at the time of this writing, the first Chinese medical informatics textbook was expected to be published by the end of 2009. Currently, they are determined to make a successful leapfrog upgrade of healthcare ICTs in a short time.

In India, there has been a national medical informatics association operating since 1993,[13] but its member size is not sufficiently large, compared with its population size, to make great strides in the science and ICT industries. However, they joined the IMIA family as a national member in 2006 and are catching up. In India, they have experienced real needs for improved practices, knowledge management, evidence-based medicine, education for professionals and the public, communications, etc, which are all important factors to promote medical informatics in practical perspectives.[13] Therefore, it is not surprising that they are pursuing many avenues in modern health informatics, especially in HIS, e-learning, Tel-health, EHR, CDSS, etc.[10,14] A common EHR for standards and privacy was also recommended by their National Knowledge Commission.

The greatest challenge they face is the lack of infrastructure, including ICTs and necessary professionals' competency.[14] From its start in 2007, eHealth India has been the current most important national conference in promoting healthcare ICTs, technologies, and applications in India. It includes thousands of delegates, visitors, and hundreds of speakers and exhibitors.[15]

Australia

Australia's nursing workforce consists of registered and enrolled nurses whose scope of practice will vary based on education, levels of competence, and authorizations to perform specific duties/tasks. In 2001, the Australian nursing workforce comprised 228,230 nurses, 80% of whom were registered nurses and 20% were enrolled nurses.[16] Nurses in Australia enjoy some of the best working conditions in the region. For example, the state of Victoria requires that each nurse only be allocated four patients per shift. Considerable technologic infrastructure is available to the nurse, depending on the location. Some areas already have local versions of an EHR, some of which include nursing information.

Health*Connect* is an extensive project being run by the Central Department of Health and Aging in Canberra. Health*Connect* is Australia's proposed national health information network to facilitate the safe collection, storage, and exchange of consumer health information between authorized healthcare providers. Australia's national approach combines both centralized and decentralized components to create interoperable electronic health information and this infrastructure.[17]

Health*Connect* implementation aims to leverage existing e-health projects and infrastructure, and progress toward compliance with nationally agreed standards to improve the availability of information in the health sector.[18] Building on their experience from Health*Connect*, the Council of Australian Governments created the National E-Health Transition Authority (NEHTA).[19] NEHTA is a not-for-profit company limited by guarantee and jointly funded by all state, territorial, and national governments. To date, NEHTA has received $160 AUD million in funding.

Under Health*Connect*, health-related information about a consumer would be collected, subject to the consumer's consent, in a standard electronic format at the point of care. This could include a hospital or general practitioner's surgery. Health providers, again with the consumer's consent, would be able to access information for subsequent episodes of care, regardless of their location. Consumers would also have access to this information.

The information collected under Health*Connect* would be in the form of standardized "Health Event Summaries." Health Event Summaries would include information such as basic details about the results of health treatments, a hospital discharge report or referral, the results of pathology tests, or medications prescribed. They would not contain all of the clinical notes made by the provider. Health Event Summaries, when stored, form the basis of the Health*Connect* EHR. In the longer term, event summaries for the GP consultation, pathology, community healthcare, hospital, etc. must be defined and agreed on nationally. Local EHR systems have existed for some time now, and the Health*Connect* project aims to ensure interoperability across the various states of Australia. Several of the Health*Connect* projects have evolved from pilot studies to full implementation in the pilot sites.

Following a Health Ministers' Conference in 2003, the Health Informatics Society of Australia Nursing Informatics Special Interest Group has been funded to develop a strategic plan for nursing informatics capacity building and a plan for the nursing profession's engagement with the Australian government and its informatics agenda.[20] The provision of funding for such developments in Australia is likely to assist nursing informatics progress in Australia and internationally.

A recent review undertaken on behalf of the newly established National Health Information Group (NHIG)[21] and the Australian Health Information Council (AHIC)[22] identified the adoption of health informatics principles as an enabler of coordination between the many stakeholders. The review undertaken in early 2004 was a first step in the development of a revised national health information management and communications technology strategy. The trend is toward greater coordination between providers, with a strong emphasis on improving health outcomes.[23]

Many nurses in Australia are actively involved in various aspects of health informatics that may indirectly assist in the development of the Health*Connect* EHR model. In particular, nurses are involved in committees developing standards in health information. Nurses are working at all levels within the Health*Connect* projects, although they may not be specifically working in EHR nursing developments. There are also many nurses involved in health informatics organizations across Australia and have been for several years. Nursing Informatics Australia notes that:

> "Although nursing has had serendipitous involvement, and nurses have been engaged as trial managers and so on, *nursing* as a profession has not been the target of any research and development activity in Health*Connect*."[16]

Although there has been collaborative work undertaken in nursing informatics internationally, currently Australia lacks an infrastructure to do so nationally. Also lacking is the structure to harness greater professional nursing participation and to influence health informatics adoption and initiatives. In the survey of Nurses and IT undertaken in Australia, 52% stated they had never heard of Health*Connect*.[1]

Australia has emerged as a world leader in the sharing of clinical information between providers via the Health*Connect* program; however, it appears nursing has not been involved to the extent that it should. The program requires greater nursing participation and a structured program to support nursing and to ensure its success in nursing informatics capacity-building.[16,23]

The case study from our Australian colleagues associated with this chapter will examine these issues further.

New Zealand

The cornerstone of New Zealand's health system is public finance through taxes with access to health services based upon need. In 2000-2001, $9.884 billion was spent in New Zealand on health and disability support services (NZ$2601 per capita). The New Zealand government has been moving away from market-based structures by combining the healthcare purchaser and provider functions into community-focused District Health Boards (DHBs).

New Zealand is highly ranked in the development and application of patient management systems (PMS), second only to the United Kingdom in terms of primary care use of PMS within General Practice (52% of GPs versus 59%, respectively), double that achieved to date in Australia (25%) and triple that of the United States (17%). What is required now is the ability to share this electronic information, as work in this direction is underway.

The Health Information Strategy for New Zealand outlines the proposed development of a component-based EHR, whereby components are developed in isolation as stand alone applications, but all are compatible and interoperable in order to deliver data to the centrally and regionally held Health Event Summaries. The latest update from the Health Information Strategy Advisory Committee (HISAC) notes increased participation by healthcare consumers; healthcare providers having clearly defined roles when collecting, using, and sharing personal health information; and the focus on the delivery of quality healthcare through prioritised information improvement projects.[24] The HISAC vision states:

> "To achieve high quality healthcare and improve patient safety, by 2014 New Zealanders will have a core set of personal health information available electronically to them and their treatment providers regardless of the setting as they access health services."

- Information will be recorded in digital formats throughout the health system.
- Personal health information will be available, with appropriate access, across healthcare organizations.
- People will be more involved in the collection and use of their personal health information.
- Healthcare providers will have clearly defined roles when collecting, using, and sharing personal health information.
- Information improvements will be prioritized to enable clinicians to optimize their resources (time, facilities, and equipment) and focus on the delivery of quality healthcare.
  This vision is enabled by three principles:
1. Community understanding and support of the appropriate use of, and access to, electronically stored personal health information is ensured.
2. Clinicians are/will be integral to the development and ongoing use of personal health information solutions.
3. Electronic information will be centered on individual patient/consumer need.[24]

At this stage, there is no plan to include nursing information in Health Event Summaries at the central and regional level, and indeed this may not prove useful. However, it may be advantageous for nurses to investigate points at which their information needs overlap with the proposed EHR's components and ensure these needs are considered at the development phases. Locally held data on nursing care will provide extensive decision support to department managers and funders of care delivery. Further, the ability to "speak" to nursing colleagues and other disciplines through locally held EHRs will assist in the delivery of seamless care. It appears that now is the time to develop clear thinking within nursing in New Zealand toward what these information requirements are.

Historically, there has been no sector-wide approach to developing information systems in New Zealand. Over the past five years, however, the DHBs have been replacing isolated departmental and clinical systems with more integrated and dynamic network-based technologies that support a more connected delivery network.

New Zealand has had a National Health Index unique patient identifier (NHI) since 1977 and has a strong political will to develop comprehensive EHRs. Several components required to develop EHRs are already being tackled within New Zealand in response, in part, to strategic recommendations and from local initiatives to fill gaps in need.[24] The existing Health Network will provide access to Health Event Summaries that are available to all via a secure network, and in turn, increasing the usability of the Health Network, similar to Australia's Health*Connect* structure.

The ever-increasing workload of nurses in New Zealand means nurses themselves are searching for more efficient ways to deliver and record the care they give in an effort to reduce the amount of paperwork. While this is certainly not new or specific to New Zealand nurses, the added requirements of delivering care in sometimes isolated areas with few medical specialists available has meant New Zealand nurses have become extremely innovative. Particular attention has been paid to inputting data electronically at the point of care to reduce the re-work of transposing data from paper forms to electronic forms.[25] Data are required in primary care delivery to make claims against contracts for care delivery; without careful recording of these data, funding for services and nurses is at risk.

A recent media article highlighted the impact of nursing shortages in New Zealand, exacerbated by the movement of nurses internationally. The article notes, "Nurses are heading overseas to work because they are spending too much time 'massaging a keyboard' with the average nurse spending only one third of their time working with people."[26] This perhaps indicates that while nurses understand the importance of good information, time collecting and inputting must be balanced with the need to provide clinical care. New applications must take into account the limited time nurses have and wish to spend on administrative work.

There is considerable development toward a more collaborative approach to care delivery, with integrated patient notes found in many areas, particularly ICU and CCU. With staff shortages and the changing roles of both nursing and medicine, the overlap of information requirements is now considerable, making the shared record the most sensible approach and which supports the need for limiting the amount of time spent on administrative tasks.

At present, the standards required to share information across disciplines do not exist in New Zealand, particularly the requirement of a nursing language that is an accepted standard. This is probably the single biggest hurdle to the implementation of EHRs in New Zealand, as with most countries. Standards development in health is well-supported through the Health Information Standards Organisation (HISO) that endorses proposed standards following extensive stakeholder consultation and agreement. Currently, no nursing-specific standards are under consultation, development, or in HISO's prioritized work plan. Their most recent work is to develop the standards to require electronic referrals to other care providers and electronic laboratory orders and results.

The considerable expansion of the role of the nurse in New Zealand has been highlighted by recent changes to legislation to allow for Nurse Practitioners (nurses with a master's degree qualification in a particular area of nursing, for example rural nurses) with further education in pharmacology to enable limited nurse prescribing. Few nurses have thus far taken up the challenge. Those that have are mostly practicing in isolated locations where they are the only healthcare providers. EHRs and, in particular, access to effective electronic decision support would provide these isolated nurses with information at the time of prescribing. Other members of the care team at disparate locations would also have access to notes on the patient's progress and latest care plan.

Electronic prescribing is being implemented in many DHBs, at least at the hospital level, assisting in the improved safety of drug administration for nurses, particularly when noting the rate of errors that can be attributed to illegible handwriting on prescriptions.[24] Electronic discharge summaries from hospitals to GPs are also common; although these do not yet include a nursing discharge summary, there would be little work required to make this standard practice.

In primary care, considerable use is made of practice management systems. These systems have clinical components for prescribing, clinical notes, and some are now providing interactive disease management through decision support. At this stage, these systems are not used extensively by Practice Nurses to assist in care delivery. A 2001 study found that[25]

> "Nurses often lack buy-in towards information systems. They use them in a task orientated way and have not really invested in them due to lack of computer literacy and education on how to use systems extensively."

South Pacific

Healthcare provided in the South Pacific is public and free, or at least heavily subsidized. There are a number of private hospitals and clinics offering more services than available publicly for those that are able to pay or have insurance. A reduced population impacts most of the smaller island countries, with many young people leaving for Australia or New Zealand, where they have automatic rights to live and work. Life expectancy is considerably lower than most OECD countries, and diseases such as diabetes are prevalent. Local knowledge of prevalent disease is high, and preventative care is encouraged through WHO programs and support.

There are many barriers to implementing health informatics in developing countries, with the major barrier of financial constraints limiting communications infrastructure and information sharing, and the need for continuous training of health professionals limiting the introduction of new technologies. Further, state-owned telecommunications systems inhibit the rate of infrastructure distribution and reduce variation, innovation, and technology adoption.

The isolation encountered by physicians, nurses, and allied health workers working in remote South Pacific Island countries is considerable. For example, the northern group of the Cook Islands is a four-hour plane ride from the main island of Rarotonga. There is often only one health worker on each island. Low pay rates and recent political instability, particularly in Fiji, have increased the issues of recruitment and retention of qualified and experienced staff throughout the South Pacific.[27]

It may be that nurses are the ones most isolated and in need of better information. Nurses are situated on the most remote outposts, often covering scattered villages and a population of around 300 people on an entirely different island than ones having available medical assistance. Nurses are provided with radio or telephone contact with other nurses and medical staff at the local hospital ("local" may mean a journey of several hours by a small fishing boat). Many nurses note how difficult it is to adequately care for patients.[28]

Many nurses in the Pacific Islands undertake their nursing training locally. The training is based on the three-year New Zealand or Australian Nursing curriculum, with increased emphasis on Public Health. There are limited medical equipment and drugs on the smaller islands; many patients need to be moved to the local hospital for complex problems. Paper-based summaries of care provided prior to transfer are sent with the patient, and the nurse receives similar information back following discharge.

Many healthcare professionals in the South Pacific note the urgent need for distance consultation services to provide applicable healthcare advice between distant islands to larger healthcare centers or even to other countries with better specialization.

Ongoing education is also limited. Libraries, when available, are limited to a few mostly out-of-date books and journals. Nurses rarely have access to any journals, apart from those belonging to the main hospitals. Most health professionals express difficulties in gaining access to up-to-date medical information. Further, there is little opportunity for postgraduate education due to geography, cost, and low staffing levels.[27]

The development of the EHR in Australia and New Zealand may at some point impact on the Pacific Islands, particularly if the delivery of services using telehealth is included in the components of the EHR in these two countries. This is currently proposed in New Zealand and recent interest has increased to develop national policies, standards, and guidelines around telehealth, with consideration to Pacific countries' requirements. Health*Connect* in Australia also specifically outlines telehealth as a strategic initiative in their EHR.

Improvements to technology, particularly more affordable infrastructure and operational costs for connectivity between the islands, including more affordable basic equipment, is required before it would be feasible to implement even the most basic components of an EHR for nurses. In the meantime, it may be possible to include Pacific Island requirements in New Zealand or Australian developments in nursing standards to ensure the Pacific does not end up further behind in healthcare delivery advances. This would require changes to the curriculum of nurses in the South Pacific to include an outline of the EHR and a general overview of health informatics.

There are close links throughout the South Pacific with nursing institutions and representative organizations in Australia and New Zealand, with educational visits made possible through international aid funding and private grants. This provides nurses in the Pacific Islands with some exposure to healthcare technology. Although there are computers in the larger healthcare institutions in the South Pacific, many are not available to nurses or nurses are not provided with sufficient training to use them, as they are not seen as a "nursing tool."

The University of Otago[29] in New Zealand has recently commenced Health Informatics courses via distance learning, with access to computers with Internet access at the Fiji School of Medicine in Suva. Some nurses have already completed papers in this course. Close links with Ministries of Health throughout the South Pacific and Australasia also provide educational training opportunities for better management of centrally held healthcare data.

Summary

New Zealand and Australia propose a component-based EHR. It is therefore possible, particularly with the nursing informatics expertise found in this region, to develop effective EHR components for nurses that comply with the overall requirements of the EHR and other healthcare providers. It is unlikely there could be an EHR that meets everyone's needs, but individual components that are interoperable would allow the required flexibility for each discipline. Data would feed into a centrally managed Health Event Summary that includes multidisciplinary information for management and policy developers.

There is considerable potential for the EHR to capture nursing knowledge, and this is a great opportunity for nurses to be recognized for their impact on health outcomes. Nursing education and research would also benefit through the clear documentation of decision making at the bedside, with subsequent improved patient outcomes.

At present much of the South Pacific makes use of telehealth services providing for connectivity between major hospitals. Could this connectivity be utilized for other types of health communication around the Pacific? A component-based EHR has the potential to link health services provided via telehealth with the centrally held EHR to ensure all providers are aware of consultations provided via telehealth. While at present, it may not be feasible to implement a connected EHR in any country in the South Pacific, the opportunity to gain specific nursing knowledge of this population's needs may provide unforeseen benefits for all those caring for Pacific Islanders throughout Australasia.

In Asia, dramatic recent progress in all areas of e-health has taken place. The potential also for understanding the nursing needs of the very mobile Asian populations may provide Asian nurses with the impetus to continue to take part in new EHR developments.

It may not be feasible to expect the development of an EHR that meets everyone's requirements that is healthcare provider independent. Should nurses therefore work toward their own needs, taking into account the developments nationally and internationally? As a key contributor of data and most consistent user of an EHR, nurses are well-placed to be actively involved in the design evaluation to ensure the design meets their information needs. From a care integration perspective, design evaluation should consider the effectiveness of nursing contributions in meeting other stakeholder needs. In conjunction with design are the business and data aspects of the EHR. Only nurses can define the business context, information flow, and practices of what nursing information is required where, and only nurses can evaluate the effectiveness of this design component.[16] Nurses need not wait for central agencies to consider their needs but work on their own developments to ensure a nursing-led project with collaboration with central agencies when possible.

There is the danger of developing systems that do not meet nurses' needs, developed by IT specialists but unable to respond to the complexity and subtlety of the world of nursing and midwifery practice. It is in the best interests of nursing to remain involved at all levels of the development process. It is also important to be cognizant of the health needs of the whole of the Asia Pacific region in the development of the EHR as migration and tourism around the region grows dramatically, and we are increasingly nursing a multicultural population.

References

1. Hegney D, Buikstra E, Eley R, Fallon T, Gilmore V, Soar J. *Nurses and Information Technology.* 2007, Australian Nursing Federation. p. 123.
2. Kerr K, Cullen R, Duke J, et al, *Health Informatics Capability Development in New Zealand.* 2006, Tertiary Education Commission: Wellington. p. 102.
3. Coenen A. The International Classification for Nursing Practice (ICNP) Programme: Advancing a unifying framework for nursing. Online Journal of *Issues in Nursing,* 2003(3 April 2003).
4. IMIA National Member Societies. http://www.imia.org/members/national_list.lasso. Accessed June 30, 2009.
5. WHO. *World Health Statistics, 2009, Table 6. Health Workforce, Infrastructure, Essential Medicines.* http://www.who.int/whosis/whostat/EN_WHS09_Table6.pdf. Accessed June 30, 2009.
6. Economist Intelligent Unit, *How technology sectors grow? Benchmarking IT Industry Competitiveness 2008.* http://graphics.eiu.com/upload/BSA_2008.pdf. Accessed July 10.
7. IMIA-NI, *The Congress Program of the 10th International Congress on Nursing Informatics, Helsinki, Finland, 2009.* http://www.ni2009.org/mp/db/material_folder/x/IMG/31836:31355/file/NI_2009_program_vedos2.pdf. Accessed July 10, 2009.
8. The Economist, *Market View,* Apr 21, 2008. http://www.economist.com/finance/displaystory.cfm?story_id=11075147. Accessed July 10, 2009.
9. *Health Informatics in China,* 2006. http://en.wikipedia.org/wiki/Health_informatics_in_China. Accessed July 10, 2009.
10. *Health Informatics in India: Vision and Activities,* September 5, 2008, http://medinfo.cdac.in/resources/events/mig-symp-08/pdf/presentation/Ramakrishnan.pdf. Accessed July 10, 2009.
11. www.cmia.info. Accessed October 10, 2009.
12. www.chima.org. Accessed October 10, 2009.
13. *Indian Association for Medical Informatics,* http://www.iami.org.in/index.asp. Accessed July 10, 2009.
14. Bhandari N. *Three Points About Health Informatics in India.* December 30, 2008. http://blog.asian-hhm.com/?p=9. Accessed July 10, 2009.
15. *eHealth India* 2009. http://www.eindia.net.in/2009/ehealth/index.asp. Accessed July 10, 2009.
16. Conrick DM, Hovenga E, Cook R, Laracuente T, Morgan T. *A Framework for Nursing Informatics in Australia. A Strategic Paper.* 2004, Nursing Informatics Australia. p. 58.
17. Arnold S, Wieners W. 2008. *Electronic Health Records: A Global Perspective.* Healthcare Information and Management Systems Society (HIMSS). Enterprise Systems Steering Committee and the Global Enterprise Task Force.
18. Australian Government Department of Health and Ageing, *Health Connect.* 2008: Canberra. p. Overview of Health Connect.
19. www.nehta.gov.au. Accessed October 10, 2009.
20. Hovenga EJS, et al. *Pacific Rim.* 2005. Chapter 30.
21. www.aihw.gov.au. Accessed October 10, 2009.
22. www.health.gov.au. Accessed October 10, 2009.
23. Victoria Department of Human Services, *National E-Health Strategy Summary,* A.H.M. Conference, Editor. 2008: Melbourne.

24. Wilson S, Roy D. *KIWI Nurse: An Automated Documentation Solution for Nursing Education.* In: 8th International Congress in Nursing Informatics. 2003. Rio de Janeiro.

25. Ministry of Health, *Sharing Excellence in Health and Disability Information Management.* 2004, Wellington.

26. Boland MJ. Help me, nurse. I: *Listener.* 2009: 18-25.

27. Health Information Strategy Advisory Committee, *Vision.* 2009, Ministry of Health: Wellington.

28. Kerr K. *A Needs Assessment for Telehealth in the South Pacific.* In: Department of Medicine. 2002, Otago: Wellington. p.123.

29. www.otago.ac.nz. Accessed October 10, 2009.

Case Study 19A

The Nursing Informatics Renaissance in Taiwan

By Polun Chang, PhD

Introduction

In 2007 in Taiwan, approximately 182,000 healthcare professionals, 54% of whom were nurses, served in 530 hospitals, 23 of which were medical centers, with a total of 150,000 beds.[1] The practice rate for nurses was around 40%.[2] The history of nursing informatics (NI) development in Taiwan could be divided into four periods. The first is the Pre-Dawn period (before 2003) when NI-related activities were few, occurring mainly within the clinical settings in medical centers. The second is the Awakening period (2003-2006) when a series of NI promotion workshops were held nationwide, and the NI affiliation began being seriously noticed within a short time. During this period, the End-User Computer strategy was used to train hundreds of clinical nurses to better understand what IT tools could do for the nursing process. The third period is called the Growing-Up Phase (2006-2009) and is the beginning of our NI Renaissance, when the Taiwan Nursing Informatics Association (TNIA)[3] was established immediately after the Nursing Informatics 2006 conference in Seoul, Korea.[4] Many international distinguished NI leaders, such as Marion Ball, Suzanne Bakken, Robyn Carr, and others were invited to attend the first national Taiwan NI symposium.[4] Currently there are 400 active members in TNIA; nearly 350 are clinical nurses. The fourth period, which can be called the NI Renaissance, started in 2009, when almost all medical centers set up formal NI positions, a variety of NI applications, and relevant design development. We are eager to join international NI activities and willing to take the necessary responsibility to do so.

The Pre-Dawn Period, Before 2003

In the pre-dawn period, all key NI-related activities were mainly the responsibility of the Nursing Information Systems (NIS) in medical centers. The earliest one can be traced back to 1992, when the first mainframe and terminal-based institutional nursing planning system was implemented in the Taipei Veterans General Hospital. Then in the mid-1990s, there was early use of PDA bedside applications in other medical centers, such as Tri-Service General Hospital, Buddhist Tzu-Chi General Hospital, Shin-Kong Wu Ho-Su Memorial Hospital, Cathay General Hospital, and the Taipei Veterans General Hospital. When the NIS could be supported from the IT department, it could be scaled up quite quickly, such as those in the Chang-Gung Medical Foundation and Taipei Veterans General Hospital.

The Pre-Dawn NI activities were (1) focused on medical centers, (2) limited to some basic and practical nursing functions, (3) documentation-oriented, (4) under-prioritized, with very limited funding, (5) not-systematic and isolated to other parts of the hospital information system, and, most importantly, (5) not designed with the NI vision.

The Awakening Period, 2003-2006

This period started with the surprising observation that we had only one poster submitted to NI2003, and it failed to reflect our potential and capabilities in NI. Therefore, a series of NI workshops and training courses were held nationwide to "incubate" the clinical nurses who were interested in NI. Luckily, this NI initiative was endorsed by the Taiwan Medical Informatics Association and, especially, the National Yang-Ming University[5], which provided resources and support.

The Institute of Health Informatics and Decision Making, merged with the Institute of Bioinformatics to become the largest biomedical informatics institute in Asia—the Institute of Biomedical Informatics of the National Yang-Ming University (NYMU)[5]—and began to actively hold NI workshops and training programs in 2003. The training materials and teaching approaches have progressed a great deal since then. In the beginning, the courses were a general introduction to nursing informatics and experience-sharing among enrolled nurse members. There were also classes to teach computer skills, Excel, databases, PowerPoint, and multimedia applications at insignificant emphasis. However, to our surprise, the enrolled members expressed a high level of interest and discussed their needs in programming skills, especially VBA programming (Vital Basic for Applications) in Excel, so they could begin to design simple applications for themselves. The main reasons for the then 400 clinical nurses to learn Excel with VBA was not only because Excel was the tool with which they were familiar and VBA programming seemed easy to learn, but also because they had been seriously frustrated with the hitherto lack of sufficient IT support for their needs.[6] Thereafter, the main focus in training materials became building clinical nurses' capability in using Excel VBA to develop their own applications, and End-User Computing became our most critical strategy in promoting NI at this period.[7]

Using this strategy, a learning map, as seen in Figure 19A-1, was used to train the clinical nurses. The entire training lasted six days and was composed of three two-day sessions that lasted six hours each. The first two sessions were one week apart, and the last session occurred two weeks after the second session. The nurses were expected to pass through five stages. Stage I was designed to decide the Work Need on the morning of the first day. We covered general ideas in NI and how a good Request for Proposal (RFP) of a project should be prepared by combining the perspectives of IT, information management, and nursing professional objectives.

In Stage II, the various active roles nurses could take during the development of any application were discussed. Nurses do not need to be programmers to lead NIS projects, but they benefit a great deal from the hands-on training courses. The features of successful applications were discussed: they should be easy to use, easy to learn, practical and useful for work, compatible with current systems, project independent, and achievable with minimum resources. All key concepts were enhanced with simple Excel VBA samples.

In Stage III, which covered Samples and Practice, trainees were asked to personally run a demonstration case, such as a training satisfaction evaluation form, and explain how this application was operated within a concept of work flow, how data were collected through the form interface and saved to the worksheets as database, and the composition of codes. At Stage IV, a practical project was detailed, discussed, and practiced by each trainee, with a process of drilling down the demonstration project from its interface to the bottom codes, as seen in Figure 19A-2. Stage V began when nurses had a basic capability in programming knowledge and skills. We encouraged the trainees to work on their projects, and other supplementary training courses would be offered if needed. Some successful and interesting projects, which were not seen in the traditional NISs in Taiwan, were developed, such as a Handheld Application Kit (see Figure 19A-3)[8] and an Automatic Scheduling Support System (Figure 19A-4).[9]

Results of the Awakening Period are as follows: (1) for the first time, NI became the nationwide focus in medical informatics, (2) as many as 400 NI seeds of clinical nurses from various institutes were trained in the principles and vision of the potential and value of informatics in nursing, (3) many nursing departments from different institutes started to emphasize the importance of NIS and took a more active role in promoting NI inside hospitals, (4) there were close to 40 works submitted to and presented in the NI2006, and most importantly, (5) the Taiwan Nursing Informatics Association[3] was formally established.

The Growing-Up Period, 2006-2009

The first representative event in this period was the establishment of TNIA[3] in June 2006, with the aims of (1) serving the nursing clinical care, administration, education, quality control, and knowledge management needs of nurses in NI, (2) fostering collaboration among nurses and informatics-relative personnel who were interested in NI, (3) facilitating development in NI, (4) connecting to the international NI community, and (5) sharing knowledge, experiences, and ideas with nurses and healthcare providers worldwide. Nursing students can apply for student membership; clinical nurses are eligible for full membership. Any other informatics technicians interested in health informatics can join the association, and all organizations may apply for the organization membership. As of 2009, there are close to 400 active members.

The second characteristic of this period is the development of the NIS, which became a high-priority mission for the nursing departments in hospitals. The preliminary results of a survey to the medical centers in Taiwan show that as many as 75% have a working care plan subsystem, 62% have a MAR subsystem and Vital Sign and Flow Sheet subsystems, 71% have Nursing Assessment subsystems and, most interesting, all others without these functions will have their subsystems done in 2009. Some hospitals, such as the Taichung Veterans General Hospital, Chang-Gung Medical Foundation, Mackay Memorial Hospital, and Taiwan University Hospital, became very good benchmarks for others to successfully develop and implement the NIS.

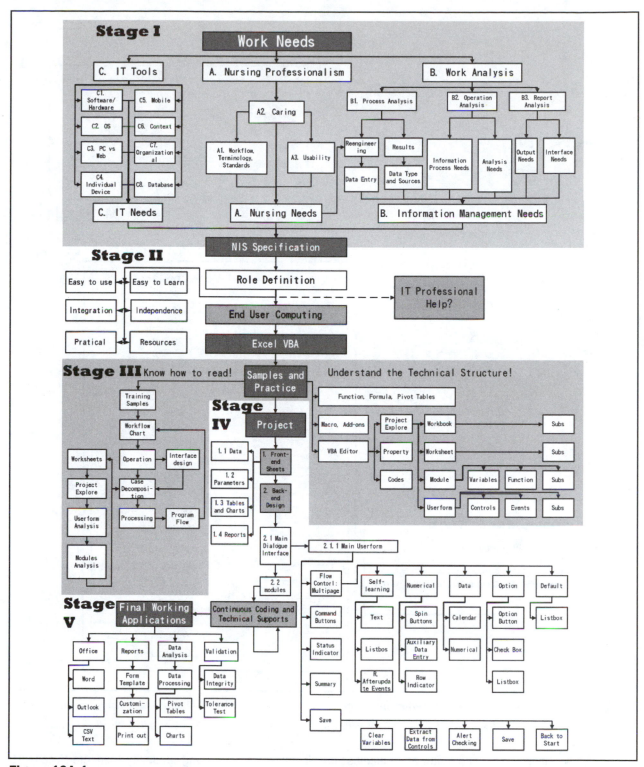

Figure 19A-1. *Learning Road Map for Excel VBA. Source: Research Institute of Nursing Science, Seoul National University.*

As many as 66% of medical centers design their own NIS in-house, and the most popular carriage device is computers on wheels (COW). The most encouraging achievement in this period is the recognition of the roles and importance of NI specialists; 58% of medical centers have assigned one or two full-time NI specialists to help coordinate nursing and informatics specialties to develop the NIS.

The third characteristic is that there are new NI faculty and graduate students joining the NI community in Taiwan. New faculty, specializing in NI, from the Columbia University, University of Maryland, and Utah

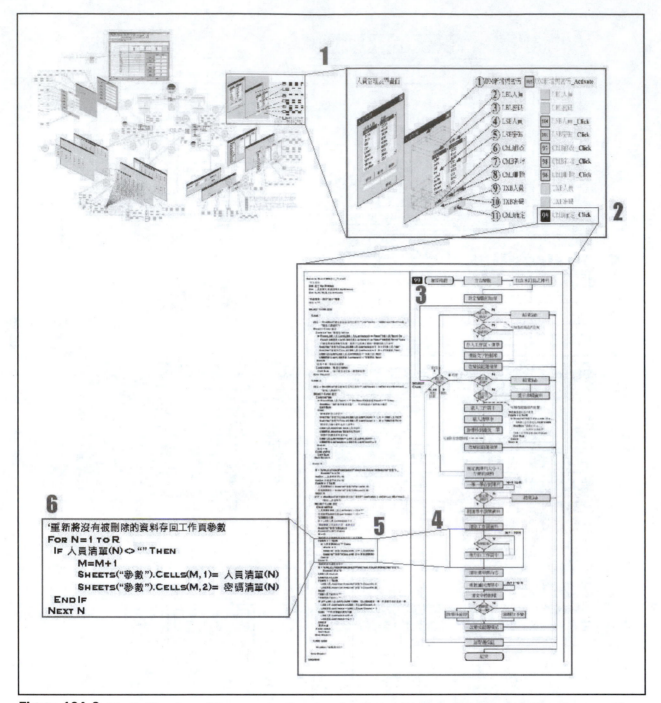

Figure 19A-2. *The Drilling-down of Programming from Interface Design (1), through Event, which Users Interact with System (2), to Flow-chart of Codes (3-6). Source: Research Institute of Nursing Science, Seoul National University.*

University have returned to Taiwan to increase our NI research and teaching capability. There are close to 10 NI PhD students trained locally, and an increasing number of nursing students are doing research in NI. Combined with many NI nurses in hospitals, the basic NI research momentum has been well-achieved. Studies in documentation, point of care, nursing terminology, end-user computing, and radio frequency identification have become quite common nowadays in our local nursing journals, such as the *Journal of Nursing Research* (http://www.lww.com/product/?1682-3141), *Journal of Taiwan Medical Management* (http://www.academic-journals.org/ojs2/index.php/tjom), and *Journal of Taiwan Society of Medical informatics.*[10]

The fourth characteristic is that much of the NI-related research and related projects outside the clinical settings deserve the same attention. For example, since 2006, the student health information systems for all school nurses, from primary schools to universities, were developed by the Wan-feng Primary School[11] and

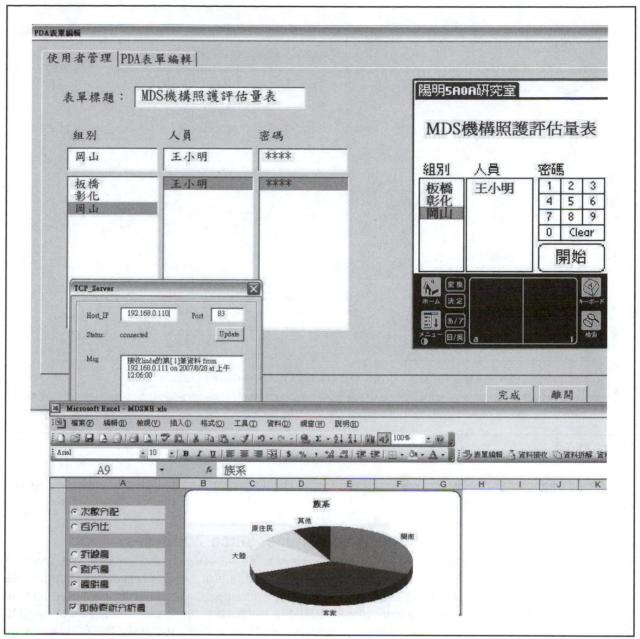

Figure 19A-3. *Snapshots of a Handheld Application Development Kit. Source: Research Institute of Nursing Science, Seoul National University.*

the National Yang-Ming University[12] with the support from the Ministry of Education (MOE).[13] In 2009, our MOE further decided to set up a national student data and policy center in the National Yang-Ming University to support 4,650 school nurses nationwide to benefit from IT in serving student health.

In the period 2002-2007, in terms of consumer health informatics, a national health Web site accreditation program was sponsored by the MOH to evaluate the quality of health information on the Web. Every year, there were approximately 300 Web sites enrolled in this program, but only 25 to 30 of the best ones were credited with a national quality logo. However, the impact of this program in terms of benefit to the people was not yet clear. One study showed that the winning Web sites failed to be easily located by using the two most popular search engines: Google and Yahoo.[14] The other example is the development of the point-of-care support system for long-term care institutes in which IT investment had been neglected. There is one study using the economic tools of PDA and Excel to develop cost-effective documentation systems for the nurses serving in these institutes.[15,16] There is another interesting project to study the nursing record corpus and lexicon in Mandarin in order to develop an effective speech recognition interface for our nurses. A nurs-

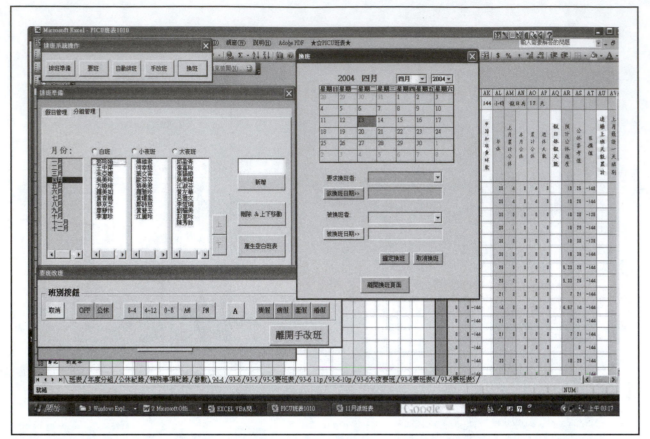

Figure 19A-4. *Snapshot of an Automatic Scheduling Support System*

ing corpus of 974 words were developed and found to be meaningful for potential improvements in speech recognition effectiveness.[17]

The NI Renaissance, Since 2009

The NI development in Taiwan since 2006 has been very active, full of variety, and well-balanced. There are still many domains not fairly covered in this short review, such as e-learning and evidence-based nursing. We currently not only keep working to develop more easy-to-use documentation tools for clinical nurses but have also started to introduce nursing terminology into the NIS. Without any doubt, more and more interesting NI projects and efforts in Taiwan will be proposed and initiated. Inspired by the successful NI2006 in Korea, we are determined to bid for the NI2015 to be held in Taiwan. There is even a great possibility that we might work with the NI community in China because of the special and improved relationship between us. We are excited with our growing NI momentum nationwide and are eager to take a more active role to join the international NI community.

Acknowledgment

I sincerely appreciate the assistance from the following NI colleagues to make this case lively: Che-Wei Liu, PhD Candidate, MS; Rung-Chuang Feng, PhD Candidate, MSN, RN; I-Ching Hou, PhD Candidate, RN; Fan-Ping Huang, MSN, RN; Ming-Hsiang Tu, MS, RN; Ming-Chuan Kuo, MS, RN, Li-Ping Fang, MS, RN; Chiao-Ling Hsu, MS, RN and Chuen-Xia Huang, MS, RN.

References

1. The Statistics Analysis of Medical Care, Institution's Status & Hospital's Utilization, 2007, http://www.doh.gov.tw/CHT2006/DM/DM2_2.aspx?now_fod_list_no=10293&class_no=440&level_no=4. Accessed June 1, 2009.

2. The National Union of Nurses Associations, R.O.C. http://www.nurse.org.tw/DataSearch/Manpower.aspx. Accessed June 1, 2009.

3. www.informaticsnurse.com. Accessed October 28, 2009.

4. http://www.people-x.com/previewni2006/asp/congress.asp. Accessed December 1, 2009.

5. www.ifs.sinica.edu. Accessed October 28, 2009.

6. I-Ching Hou, Che-Wei Liu, Chiao-Ling Hsu, Polun Chang. The evaluation of using road-map guided Excel VBA training to promote nursing informatics in Taiwan. *The 10th International Congress on Nursing Informatics (NI2009)*, Helsinki, Finland, 2009.

7. Chang P, Hsu CL, Hou IC, Tu MH, Liu CW. The end-user computing strategy of using Excel VBA in promoting nursing informatics in Taiwan. *Perspectives in Nursing Science*. The Research Institute of Nursing Science, Seoul National University, South Korea. 2008;5(1):45-58.

8. Hsu CL, Chang P. Developing an SDK of usability-engineered handheld evaluation aid. American Medical Informatics Association. 2007 Symposium, Chicago, IL, USA, 2007, p. 982.

9. Cheng ST, Wung SH, Chang P. The development of a heuristic-based excel scheduling support system for nurses. *The 9th International Congress on Nursing Informatics. (NI2006)*, Seoul, Korea, 2006, P792.

10. www.ncbi.nlm.nih.gov/journals. Accessed October 28, 2009.

11. www.szwanfeng.com. Accessed October 28, 2009.

12. www.nymu-e.web.ym.edu.tw/. Accessed October 28, 2009.

13. www.english.moe.gov.tw/. Accessed October 28, 2009.

14. Chang P, Hou IC, Hsu CL, Lai HF. *Are Google or Yahoo a Food Portal for Getting Quality Healthcare Web Information?* American Medical Informatics Association, 2006 Symposium, Washington, DC, USA, 2006.

15. Hsu CL, Kuo YY, Chang P. *Using PDA to Transform the Long MDS-HC Evaluation Form into a Favored System.* Medinfo 2007, Brisbane, Australia, August 20-24, 2007.

16. Chang P, Hsu CL, Lan CF. Is PDA good for complex documentation in healthcare? *The 10th International Congress on Nursing Informatics (NI2009)*, Helsinki, Finland, 2009.

17. Huang PJ, Chang P. The feasibility study of building a routine nursing records corpus, lexicon and its applications in the speech recognition. *The 10th International Congress on Nursing Informatics (NI2009)*, Helsinki, Finland, 2009.

Case Study 19B

Current Status and Evolution of Nursing Informatics in South Korea

By Hyeoun-Ae Park, PhD, RN; and Insook Cho, PhD

Introduction—Healthcare Services

South Korea has a total population of 47,008,000 and a very high population density of 473 people/km²; it is also one of the world's most rapidly aging countries. In 2005, elderly people made up just 9% of the population, compared with the developed country average of 15%. But with life expectancy rising and birthrates plummeting to record lows, Korea is about to undergo a stunning demographic transformation. According to the latest government projections, 38% of Korea's population will become part of the elderly population by 2050.

The entire Korean population has been insured by national health insurance programs—a compulsory social insurance system—since 1989. Its main sources of finance are contributions from the insured and government subsidy. When people receive healthcare services through the national health insurance program, copayments are applied according to the type of healthcare institution that they attend. The dominant method of payment/reimbursement is fee-for-service, with diagnosis-related groups currently also being investigated.

Healthcare delivery in Korea relies heavily on the private sector; only about 10% of hospitals are public. As of 2007, there were 2,238 general hospitals, 20,339 clinics (including long-term-care facilities), and 20,730 pharmacies.[1] However, the dealings of the health insurer with respect to, for example, the fee schedule, are the same, irrespective of whether a private or public hospital is used. Citizens can choose healthcare facilities or providers freely, since there is a very weak referral channel between the primary-care facilities and the secondary/tertiary healthcare facilities. The total healthcare expenditure of Korea is about US$22.9 billion, representing 6.4% of the GDP.

Information and Communication Technology

As a result of the rapid growth of its online and telecommunication sectors, Korea has developed into one of the most well-connected countries in the world. By the end of February 2009, there were 46 million mobile phone subscribers in Korea. According to statistics published by the Organization for Economic Co-operation and Development (OECD), there were more than 15 million broadband subscribers in Korea in June 2008, which translates to 31.2 subscribers per 100 inhabitants, ranking Korea seventh in the world. In terms of the broadband technology used, of the 31.2 subscribers per 100 inhabitants in Korea, 12.2 use fiber/LAN, 10.5 use cable, and 8.4 use DSL.[2]

As of October 2007, 94.1% of all households in Korea had broadband access, ranking Korea first in the world for this measure. The average broadband download speed advertised by Internet service providers is 43.301Mbit/s.

National Initiatives in e-health

Since 2004, the Korean government has been promoting a national e-health project to systemically build an integrated healthcare system, which is to be completed by 2010. The e-health project could realize EHRs, telemedicine, technology standardization, and technology interoperability by enabling the sharing of medical information and technology among hospitals. This could result in a total reform of the existing health and medical systems, with many positive outcomes, such as improvement in the healthcare system, increase in the patients' accessibility to medical care and satisfaction with it, enhancement in medical equality, improvement in medical quality, reduction in costs, and business rationalization of hospitals. From the national perspective, the project is anticipated to improve transparency by overcoming inequality within the healthcare system and to enhance accountability by providing well-structured health administrative services. However, to support the e-health project, it is necessary to resolve information security issues, such as protecting the privacy of personally identifiable health records and preventing discrimination based on genetic information.

Moreover, the policy priority should be to create a legal and institutional environment in order to establish sensible cooperation among medical and governmental organizations.

In 2000, the Korean Ministry for Health, Welfare, and Family Affairs (MOHW) began the process of developing a master plan for the implementation of National Healthcare Information and Communication Technology (NH-ICT). The vision of this program is to secure, by 2010, healthcare accessibility and efficiency anytime, anywhere, through the nationwide healthcare information system. Based on this program, two national committees and a research and development (R&D) center were established:[3] the Healthcare Information Privacy Protection Committee, the National Health Information Technology (HIT) Committee, and the Center of Interoperable EHR (CiEHR).[3] In addition, the MOHW initiated three projects in 2005: (1) to develop and implement a public health center information system, (2) to introduce electronic medical records (EMRs)/EHRs to public hospitals, and (3) to develop national health information standards. With these initiatives, Korean medical informatics academics, informatics experts, and industries have become involved and collaborated to stimulate the adoption of HIT in healthcare organizations.

The CiEHR[3] has long-term R&D plans to support the NH-ICT initiatives technically and strategically. The vision of CiEHR is to improve accessibility to EHRs and decision support anywhere and anytime in a secure way for all healthcare stakeholders, including patients and healthcare providers, by 2013. The first specific goal of the CiEHR is to achieve widespread adoption of EMRs by healthcare organizations to improve the quality, safety, and efficiency of care. Secondly, the CiEHR aims to establish a sharable lifetime EHR system to improve the quality of care and reduce the healthcare costs arising from redundant care in Korea.[4] To achieve these two goals, the CiEHR has been driving the implementation of EMRs throughout public hospitals and clinics, demonstrating the feasibility and benefits of adopting health IT. These efforts will be continued to facilitate the adoption of HIT in the private sector through various incentives such as financial and technical support. Simultaneous R&D activities ensuring standards for interoperability and essential reusable technologies for next-generation EMRs accompany the establishment of these EMR/EHR systems. The scope of R&D activities of the CiEHR is as follows:

- To design a conceptual logical interoperable EHR architecture.
- To stimulate compliance and harmonize EHR efforts with international standards.
- To facilitate health-information exchanges between health organizations.
- To develop a national healthcare terminology and common clinical content model.
- To develop clinical decision support services and core components for sharing encoded decision-support knowledge.
- To establish national guidelines for a privacy and security policy in healthcare organizations.

Since 2005, forty-two general hospitals, seven universities, and twenty-two companies in the healthcare industry have collaborated with the CiEHR and become involved in their research programs. From 2009, ten hospitals will participate voluntarily in pilot projects designed to demonstrate the feasibility and efficiency of the outcomes of these CiEHR research projects. These field trials are expected to further leverage the adoption of health IT in Korea. Many nursing informatics (NI) nurses, including the authors, have taken part in CiEHR initiatives and field trials as project manager, leader, and researcher.

Hospital Information Systems

Table 19B-1 presents the change in the rate of adoption of the hospital information system between 1999 and 2005 in Korea. In 2005, 97.6% of tertiary hospitals, 84.2% of general hospitals, and 62.2% of private clinics had computerized physician order entry (CPOE) systems. The high adoption rate is believed to have been initially driven by financial factors associated with medical claims. However, the focus has subsequently shifted to all areas of patient care, whereby clinicians have begun to use computers in their practices. Hospitals in South Korea are beginning to implement the paperless EMR system. The adoption rate of EMR systems in tertiary hospitals currently stands at more than 20%.

History of Nursing Informatics

The use of computers in South Korean healthcare began in the late 1970s in hospital finance and administration systems to expedite insurance reimbursements. When the national health insurance system expanded to cover the entire population in 1989, computers became a necessary tool in healthcare organizations.

Table 19B-1. Rate of Adoption of the Hospital Information System in Korea (1999–2005)[5]

HIS example	Hospital Category / Year	Tertiary Hospital 1999	Tertiary Hospital 2005	General Hospital 1999	General Hospital 2005	Private Clinics 1999	Private Clinics 2005
EMRs (%)		16.7	20.3	-	14.7	9.5	22.2
Picture archiving and communication system (%)		16.7	90.5	6.5	78.6	5.0	22.6
Computerized physician order entry system (%)		81.8	97.6	45.4	84.2	20.4	62.6
Laboratory information system (%)		83.3	97.6	50	86.7	23.8	54.1

The terms *medical informatics* and *nursing informatics* were first introduced in Korea when the Korean Society for Medical Informatics (KOSMI)[6] was founded in 1987. In contrast, computers were not used in nursing education and research until 1993, and NI was not taught in universities until 1994. In 1993, the NI special-interest group was organized as one of five in the KOSMI, and since then that NI group has held its own session at the biannual KOSMI conferences. Nursing has been highly visible in KOSMI through the presentation and publication of papers on the use of computers in nursing at these conferences and in the *Journal of KOSMI*.[7] The International Medical Informatics Association (IMIA) conference held in 1998 in Seoul, MEDINFO98,[8] provided an excellent opportunity for Korean nurses to become acquainted with NI.

Korean nurses have attended and participated in many international conferences promoted or supported by IMIA and IMIA-NI since 1989. Korean nurses represented the country at the IMIA-NI group[9] in 1995, and since then Korea has participated actively in developing and furthering NI. Korea hosted the IMIA-NI conference in 2006.[9] Of the 1,000 members of KOSMI, 400 are currently nurses.

Nursing Information Systems and Electronic Nursing Record Systems

The use of computers in clinical nursing practice in Korea began in the early 1980s. In the beginning, hospitals used computers mainly for administration and billing, as did most hospitals in other countries, but later, CPOE was introduced. This system allowed physicians to enter medical orders directly into the computer, and major ancillary departments such as clinical laboratories, pharmacies, and nutritional departments could receive requisitions, enter test results, fill prescriptions, or provide appropriate meals. The nurses' work list could be viewed on screen or printed so that the nurses did not need to copy medication schedules or care activities on the Kardex, or write paper messages. NI systems (NISs) proliferated in the mid-1990s when large tertiary teaching hospitals began to introduce unique nursing activities as part of CPOE, such as nursing assessment, nursing-care plans, and patient classification, in addition to nursing activities related to billing, managerial, and coordinating activities, and physician-delegated tasks.

The early forms of NIS have provided several templates of nursing records, but they are unstructured, allow free-text input, and do not involve the use of any nursing terminology or codes. NIS with standardized terminologies began to appear in Korea in the late 1990s. For example, Samsung Medical Center introduced an electronic nursing record (ENR) system based on recommendations of the North American Nursing Diagnosis Association (NANDA)[10] and the Nursing Interventions Classification (NIC), but again this system had neither an information model nor a code system.[11]

A terminology-based ENR system, covering the entire repertoire of nursing documentations at the enterprise level was first introduced in May 2002 at the Bundang Seoul National University Hospital,[12] a tertiary-care facility with more than 800 beds. The ENR system of this Bundang hospital was based on a concrete nursing information model and utilized a unified coding system that supports data items from all nursing records. The International Classification for Nursing Practice® (ICNP) was used as a nursing reference terminology, and a nursing data dictionary (NDD) that populated by combining terms from the ICNP was defined as an interface terms.[13,14] Other nursing classification systems such as NANDA, NIC, and Nursing Outcomes Classification (NOC) were integrated into the NDD at the aggregation level. The Bundang hospital demonstrated a high degree of acceptability and efficiency of an ICNP-based ENR system, which contributed to the following implementation of ENR systems in Korea. In October 2004, Seoul National University Hospital, one of Korea's largest facilities with more than 1,200 beds, also adopted the ICNP-based ENR system. Currently there are 12 tertiary hospitals in Korea that either use or are developing an ICNP-based ENR system: National Cancer Center, Korean VA Hospital, National Police Hospital, Catholic Medical Center, Busan University Hospital, Cheju University Hospital, SMG-SNU Boramae Medical Center, Gyeongsang National University Hospital, Dongkuk University Hospital, Dongkuk Ilsan Hospital, Konkuk University Hospital, and Kyung Hee University Medical Center.

Case Study: Evaluation of an Electronic Nursing Record System

The Bundang ENR system was evaluated by surveying user satisfaction and the time required to document nursing notes. Direct and indirect nursing-care times were measured with a time-and-motion study.[15]

We surveyed 230 nurses at 6 months after implementing the ENR system to establish how satisfied the nurses were with the new system. All of the nurses replied positively to most of the questions. They agreed that the system provides a high quality of care, prevents errors due to illegible handwriting, and improves the quality of nursing records. Furthermore, they replied that it is helpful for the nursing process, and that it has reduced the time taken to record nursing notes and vital signs. The nurses expressed their satisfaction by indicating that if they had a choice, they would like to use the system.

The time-and-motion study revealed that the mean direct nursing-care time increased after implementing the EMR system (before CPOE, 203.5 minutes; before EMR, 221.1 minutes; after EMR, 251.1 minutes). Conversely, the mean indirect nursing-care time decreased from 292.3 minutes before CPOE and 278.6 minutes before EMR, to 248.4 minutes after implementation of the EMR system. Among direct nursing-care items, the largest time increase was found for "measurement and observation," from 56.2 to 76.6 minutes, and "communication with patients," from 34.2 to 43.0 minutes, before compared with after EMR implementation. Among indirect nursing-care items, the largest time decrease was found for "indirect communication" from 49.3 minutes before EMR to 19.3 minutes after its implementation. With regard to where nurses document their nursing records, only 21.8% replied that they document nursing records at the nurse station, but approximately 60% replied that they document nursing records in the patient's room.

Case Study: Evaluation of the Expressiveness of ICNP-based Nursing Statements

The expressiveness of ICNP-based nursing statements in a computerized nursing record system was studied.[13] We identified to what extent ICNP-based statements are used in nursing-note data-entry events and determined the reasons for not using ICNP-based statements. In total, 530,218 entries of nursing notes that had been entered for patients hospitalized between May 2003 and July 2003 were retrieved from the EMR database and analyzed. Data coding was classified into three categories: (1) successful—when only the NDD was used, (2) suboptimal—when the NDD and free-text input were used, and (3) failed—when only free-text input was used. Free-text records were further analyzed and classified into four subcategories: (1) supplemental—when the free-text statement had no special meaning for nursing, (2) insufficient coverage—when the NDD did not contain a free-text statement, (3) usability problem—when users failed to find the statement in the NDD, and (4) context-specific – when the free-text statement described a specific care context.

Of the 530,218 entries, 75.7% were successful, 20.4% were optimal, and only 3.9% failed. Of the 20,543 failed entries, 7.8% were supplemental, 1.0% had insufficient coverage, 80.3% had usability problems, and 10.9% were context-specific. In summary, 510,695 (96.3%) input events were covered by the NDD, with more than 75% of successful input events being recorded using only the NDD. Further analysis of free-text input events revealed that it is necessary to supplement synonyms and abbreviations, improve the user interface, structure unstructured nursing documentation, and solve usability problems. However, the use of free text seems to be inevitable for documenting context-specific situations.

Case Study: Quality and Quantity of Electronic Nursing Record Systems

Nursing records made before and after the implementation of an ENR system were compared.[16] The paper-based nursing records and ENRs of 20 patients were analyzed according to the nursing process and compared in terms of quantity and quality. In terms of quantity, the average number of statements documented per patient per day increased by 2.4 times, from 10.3 to 25.6 statements, following the implementation of an ENR system. The average number of redundancies of a unique statement also increased by 67%, from 5.0 to 8.8. As for the content of nursing records, there are more patient-problem statements describing signs and symptoms, nursing observations, and patient status in paper-based nursing records than in ENRs, whereas ENRs contain more nursing-activity statements. In terms of quality, the proportion of nursing records that followed the patterns of the nursing process was greater in ENRs than in paper-based nursing records. Thus, the documentation was more detailed in ENRs than in paper-based nursing records.

Case Study: Use of the Electronic Nursing Record System

ENRs were used to explore practice variations in the care of pressure ulcers in a study conducted by the authors.[17] Selected portions of the database were downloaded from the Clinical Data Repository of Bundang Seoul National University Hospital using a query builder; the data were examined and further analyzed using graphical and statistical software. We reviewed the narrative nursing notes for 469 intensive-care patients who were discharged in 2007, which were documented at the point of care using standardized nursing statements from an NDD. We compared the frequencies of six nursing interventions carried out by nurses for pressure ulcer prevention and care, patient characteristics, and nurse characteristics between the two groups. We found that ulcer position change was the most popular nursing activity for pressure ulcer care, followed by skin assessment, wound care, nutritional assessment, use of devices, and sensory/mobility assessment. The frequencies of wound care and position change differed significantly between the two groups. The neurological, cardiovascular, and general surgery patients with ulcers had a significantly higher mean frequency of nursing interventions than the "no ulcer" patients. More nursing interventions were documented by those nurses who were younger, less experienced, and more educated.

Current Status of Nursing Information Systems and Electronic Nursing Record Systems

In 2007, there was a survey of the status of NIS implementation and the nurses' need for various NIS functionalities. NI nurses or nurses in charge of an NIS in 40 general hospitals in Seoul and Gyeonggi province were surveyed using a questionnaire developed by Choi and Park.[18] Table 19B-2 presents the survey results, which imply that there are three levels of NIS, according to the coverage of NIS functionality but that the NIS is evolving to support core components of nursing diagnoses, interventions, and outcomes using coded terminologies.

Nursing Informatics Education

NI was first taught in Korea in 1994 when the College of Nursing at Chonbuk University[19] offered an undergraduate NI course. As IT has become indispensable in healthcare, and its impact on the daily activities of healthcare professionals has become significant, nursing schools are beginning to realize the importance of NI education for nurses.

According to a telephone survey and Internet search conducted by the KOSMI Working Group on Medical Informatics Education[6] in 2003, 33 (28.7%) of 115 undergraduate nursing programs had incorporated NI into their curriculum. NI was offered mostly to the second- or third-year students with two or three credits. The second mailing survey querying the future directions and prospects of the NI curriculum revealed that more than half of institutions agreed that NI should be a mandatory course in undergraduate nursing education, even though they disagreed with the inclusion of NI in the registered nurse (RN) license examination.[14] The KOSMI Education Working Group developed a standard NI course with four main blocks through two rounds of the Delphi method, involving eleven NI experts. These four main blocks are (1) fundamentals of informatics, (2) fundamentals of NI, (3) application of NI, and (4) public health informatics/social aspects. They also recommended that 25 learning subjects with different weights should be added, depending on priorities to be covered in NI education.

NI was first introduced to graduate nursing programs of Seoul National University[20] in 1996. From the Internet search we conducted as part of this work, we found that 28 (66.7%) of 42 institutions with a graduate program in nursing offer NI as an elective course. Graduate programs specializing in NI were first introduced at Seoul National University in 2001. This program is the only one in Korea that awards master's and doctorate degrees in NI. The NI curriculum at Seoul National University offers courses in systems analy-

Table 19B-2. Recent Status of the NIS in Korea (N=40)[18]

Functionality of the NIS	Frequency (%)	
	Implemented	Not Implemented
CPOE Support Functions (e.g., order check, medication/treatment check)	33 (82.5)	7 (17.5)
Nursing Administrative Functions (e.g., scheduling, patient classification, meal management, unit statistics)	32 (80.0)	8 (20.0)
ENRs	12 (30.0)	28 (70.0)
Use of coded nursing terminology in ENRs	7 (58.3)	
-- ICNP	4 (57.1)	
-- NANDA + NIC + NOC	2 (28.6)	
-- NIC	1 (14.3)	

sis and design, project management, clinical databases, clinical decision support, healthcare standards, consumer informatics, and NI research seminars. It has three faculties with an NI background. More than twenty students have graduated from this program; some of these graduates are working as NI educators and researchers in universities, and others are working as researchers, systems analysts, and developers in health IT industries, health IT research centers and hospital information centers.

Nursing Informatics Research

The growing interest in information and technology has been reflected in nursing research in Korea. The number of NI-related papers published in Korea has increased dramatically over the past 15 years. We have reviewed the abstracts of oral and poster presentations at the KOSMI biannual conferences[6] and papers published in the *Journal of KOSMI*[7] to examine the research trend of NI in Korea. We included all of the abstracts and articles that were either written by a nurse researcher or had relevance or application to nursing. We reviewed 178 papers and grouped them into seven research areas: clinical practice; teaching and learning; decision support; public and consumer health informatics; patient-centered healthcare such as telemedicine and ubiquitous healthcare; standardization activities; and use of information technology for nursing research.

Early studies on the use of computers for clinical nursing practice in the late 1980s and 1990s focused on nurses' attitude toward CPOE, changes in attitude and information, nurses' job satisfaction, changes in direct and indirect nursing-care time, and changes in work flow after CPOE implementation. In the mid-2000s, terminology-based ENR systems with point-of-care systems were introduced. Direct and indirect nursing-care time, experience of nurses, and job satisfaction after ENRs were studied. Articles on the use of data stored in the clinical data repository warehouse have now begun to appear. Examples include analysis of quantity and quality of nursing records, use of nursing notes for pressure ulcers, clinical practice variation on pressure-ulcer care, and use of narrative nursing notes as a signal for adverse drug events. Other features that have been added to the EHR are patient safety programs, such as hospital incident (transfusion, medication, fall, medical equipment/devices) report systems.

Quite a few papers have been published on the use of IT as a tool for learning and education in Korea. Systems used for this have changed from stand-alone systems to networked systems with wired and wireless devices. The media used have changed from floppy diskettes to CD-ROM and the Internet. Target groups for computer-assisted instruction (CAI) and Web-based learning began with nursing students but now include nurses, patients, and also healthy populations.

Papers on the use of IT as a tool for student learning and education include topics such as CAI for intramuscular injection, CAI for potassium course, Web-based education for maternity nursing practice, interactive multimedia education and learning on aging, Web-based learning and education on growth and development for RN or Bachelor of Science in Nursing students, and Web-based learning and education of NI and research methodology for graduate students. Papers dealing with nurse education include computer literacy education of community-health nurse practitioners, Web-based continuing education on blood transfusion and medication errors, self-help programs for nursing diagnosis, multimedia education program for operating room nurses, Web-based education on open-heart surgery, and neurological nursing. Education and learning programs for patients and the healthy population include Web-based ostomy self-care, and health promotion for the elderly people and middle-aged women.

Another popular research area is decision support. In the late 1990s and early 2000s, most decision-support systems were limited to expert systems for nursing administration, such as nurse staffing and scheduling based on patient classification, and neural network and expert systems for nursing diagnosis and intervention. Since the late 2000s, disease management programs such as personal digital assistant (PDA)-based self-management programs for asthma patients, cancer-symptom management systems, and post-operative care for lumbar discectomy patients, have been introduced. Critical pathways and evidence-based clinical-practice guidelines have been developed and implemented as part of a decision-support system in the hospital setting. The use of decision support has recently been extended to community health nursing beyond the hospital setting. Examples are decision support for school nursing for primary school children, Web-based depression management systems, home-based hospice care, and hypertension management systems for home-visiting nurses.

Public- and consumer-health informatics have recently become the focus of health-informatics-related research. Studies on public-health informatics include topics such as Web-based health management of registered Health Maintenance Organization (HMO) members, Web-based information services for middle-aged women, nursing information services for nurses in cyberspace, community-based home care in health centers, home-care nursing for underprivileged citizens, Web-based nutrition programs for primary school children, Web-based exercise programs for chronically ill patients, and home hospice information systems using a PDA. Topics in consumer informatics include consumer behavior regarding information selection and use, effect of consumers' health knowledge on acceptability of the Web site and empowerment, consumer preference of health information on the Web, consumer attitude toward their personal health record, consumer vocabulary for health information, and patient perception of the effect of Internet-based health information on the patient–doctor relationship. There is also research evaluating how trustworthy health information is for citizens and patients. Examples include research on the development of a checklist for health and disease information on the Web, the acceptability of health information on the Web, and the evaluation of the management of various diseases and health promotion information, such as tobacco cessation information on the Web and Web sites related to asthma and diabetes mellitus.

With an aging population and increasing numbers of patients with chronic age-related diseases, there is a need for patient-centered healthcare, such as telemedicine. Many telemedicine systems have been tested over the past 10 years, one of which is a teleconsultation system that was initiated by the Korean government. Such a system allows, for example, a home-care nurse or visiting nurse at a home-care agency or health center to have a teleconsultation with a doctor at a remote hospital. Another type of patient-centered healthcare is ubiquitous healthcare. With hardware miniaturization and advances in ultralow power design and autonomic sensing devices, the use of ubiquitous computing in healthcare is being realized. Papers on these topics are beginning to appear in Korea, such as the role of nurses in ubiquitous healthcare, and the competencies and qualities nurses need to acquire for ubiquitous healthcare.

Standardization activities in Korea are widely published. They include work on standardization activities on nursing practice such as care plans, nursing practice guidelines and critical pathways, standardization of nursing document forms, use of Health Level Seven for nursing information exchange, a unified nursing language system, nursing minimum data set, uniform hospital discharge data set, use of nursing terminology in knowledge representation, development of Korean oriental nursing terminology, and use of nursing terminology for ENR systems.

Information technology has been used for research into nursing and for data analysis, not only for quantitative research, but also for qualitative research. The Internet has been used as a means of data collection for nursing research. For example, an e-mail survey was used for need assessment of the nursing research literature database. Systems were developed to store research data and measurement tools.

Summary

The use of IT in healthcare and NI has seen rapid progress in South Korea. Most Korean healthcare organizations were computerized following the introduction of the national health insurance system. Over recent decades, there have been exciting developments in EMR/ENR systems, health informatics education, and health informatics research. All of these developments have either directly or indirectly improved the productivity of healthcare professionals, the efficiency and effectiveness of the healthcare industry, and the education of healthcare professionals.

References

1. Health Insurance Review & Assessment Services. *Evidence and Value in Healthcare.* Seoul: Health Insurance Review & Assessment Service; 2008.
2. Organization for Economic Co-operation and Development. *OECD Broadband Portal.* www.oecd.org/sti/ict/broadband, Accessed April 28, 2009.
3. www.ehrkorea.org. Accessed October 20, 2009.
4. Kim Y, Cho I, Seo J, Kim I, Kim H, Choi Y. Research and development efforts aimed at implementing electronic health record systems with interoperability and patient safety. *Journal of Korean Society of Medical Informatics.* 2006;12(2):115-132.
5. Chae Y-M. *Report on HIT Adoptions in Healthcare Institutions.* Seoul: Health Insurance Review & Assessment Service; 2005.
6. www.imia.org. Accessed October 20, 2009.
7. www.journal.lww.com/cinjournal. Accessed October 20, 2009.
8. www.healthcare-informatics.com. Accessed October 20, 2009.
9. www2.amia.org/meetings. Accessed October 20, 2009.
10. www.nanda.org. Accessed October 20, 2009.
11. Sung Y-H Cho M-S, Hong M-S. User satisfaction of nursing information system. *Journal of the Korean Society of Medical Informatics.* 2006;12(3):227-238.
12. Find on en.wikipedia.org/bundang_seoul_national_university_hospital. Accessed October 20, 2009.
13. Cho I, Park H. Evaluation of the expressiveness of an ICNP-based nursing data dictionary in a computerized nursing record system. *Journal of the American Medical Informatics Association.* 2006;13(4):456-464.
14. Yom Y-H, Kim JE, Chun BC, et al. Development of standardized and competency-based curriculum in nursing informatics. *Journal of the Korean Society of Medical Informatics.* 2007;13(3):227-236.
15. Cho I, Park H, Chung E, Lee H. Formative evaluation of standard terminology-based electronic nursing record system in clinical setting. *Journal of the Korean Society of Medical Informatics.* 2003;9(4):413-422.
16. Lee I, Park H. Comparison of nursing records of open heart surgery patients before and after implementation of electronic nursing record. *Journal of the Korean Society of Medical Informatics.* 2009;15(1):83-92.
17. Park H, Cho I. Exploring practice variation in care of pressure ulcers using a Clinical Data Repository. 2009 (in review).
18. Choi H-W, Park H-A. Needs for nursing information system according to the level of nursing informatization in general hospitals. *Journal of the Korean Society of Medical Informatics.* 2008;14(4):405-416.
19. en.chobuk.ac.kr. Accessed October 20, 2009.
20. www.useoul.edu. Accessed October 20, 2009.

Case Study 19C

Nursing and the EHR in Thailand

By Kanittha Volrathongchai, PhD (Nursing), RN; and Rutja Phuphaibul, DNS, RN

Introduction

Thailand, located in Southeast Asia, covers an area of about 514,000 km[2]. As of 2007, the population of Thailand was 62.8 million. While the country's roots go back thousands of years, in the modern era, it has enjoyed a long history of continuous progress in healthcare development.[1]

Indicative of this progress, universal healthcare was established as part of the national health system reform in 2001. The purpose of this system was to ensure equitable healthcare access for every citizen, including those counted among the poorest. As a result, health insurance coverage has been steadily increasing, with 92.5% of the Thai population now covered.[1]

Currently, work is being undertaken on the 10th National Economic and Social Development Plan (2007-2011)[2]. While efforts are underway to enhance components of the health information system in furtherance of this goal, concurrent efforts are also underway to enhance current nursing information systems. This case study will explore how both efforts might be integrated to create a truly comprehensive, interoperable, health information system.

Health Information Systems in Thailand

Leading up to the 10th National Health Development Plan (2007-2011),[2] the 9th National Health Development Plan (2002-2006)[3] developed new guidelines that focused on well-being and integration efforts across the entire health system. One strategy within this plan was to develop basic factors for evaluating the program achievement of key national health indicators. Achieving this goal required the development of a nationwide health information system. Thus work commenced on the creation of health information systems to link relevant agencies and to provide opportunities for individuals or agencies to easily access and use the information and create a mechanism for the dissemination of relevant information to target populations on a timely basis. This resulted in the further utilization of information technology in support of health information systems.[4]

At the national level, the Ministry of Public Health (MoPH)[5] enhanced the existing disease surveillance system to collect and monitor communicable diseases and environmental occupational diseases. Other distinct surveillance systems were developed for certain domains, such as HIV/AIDS, tuberculosis, and accidental injuries. While this development was taking place at the national level, individual facilities were developing electronic medical record (EMR) systems and Routine Health Service Records.[6]

Currently, most medical records in hospitals are paper-based. However, many hospitals have implemented a limited form of EMR. Consequently a portion of these data are now being housed in electronic hospital databases unique to each hospital group. Many of these hospital databases have also been designed to provide electronic registration as a replacement of previous manual registry systems. Some standards have been incorporated into these EMR systems, including ICD-10 for diagnosis, ICD-9-CM for procedures, DRGs for reimbursement, and HL7 for electronic interchange of health information.[7]

To monitor and evaluate health services, the Minister of Public Health[5] identified standard datasets, established guidelines, and developed registering and reporting systems. The first standard data set, known as "standard 12 files," is a 12-file data set that includes outpatient data, inpatient data, diagnosis, procedures, and cost of service. This dataset comprises the data reporting requirements for hospitals.

Health centers and primary care units (PCUs) are required to report a different set of information to the MoPH. This newly developed approach is now being expanded for use in PCUs to gather required data at the community level, reduce duplication, and serve as a model for further development of registration and reporting systems. Thus a second standard data set, known as "standard 18 files," includes data regarding population, insurance, death, chronic disease, health service, diagnosis, surveillance, treatment, cost, Expanded Program on Immunization (EPI),[8] nutrition, family planning, maternal-child health and antenatal care. Software has been developed to ease maintenance and reporting of this second dataset, with the most common being the Health Center Information System (HCIS).[7]

Nursing Informatics in Thailand

While efforts to create a health information system (HIS) were underway, tremendous efforts were undertaken by visionary nurse leaders to create a Nursing Information System (NIS). The NIS was needed to enable evidence-based nursing, assure quality of nursing care together with improving outcomes. An effective NIS must not only assist nurses with the organization of data, but it must also describe and compare nursing practice across time and places. This latter goal was accomplished by deploying a standardized nursing terminology. Thus some of the earliest work in the area of nursing informatics was to identify a standardized, unified, nursing language.

This resulted in work being undertaken in 1998 to develop a Thai Nursing Minimum Data Set (NMDS) with support from the World Health Organization. The Thai NMDS was established through collaborative work done among the Center for Nursing Research at Ramathibodi School of Nursing, the Nurses' Association of Thailand and the Nursing Division of the MoPH.[9] The resulting Thai NMDS consists of three elements: nursing care elements, patient elements, and nursing services elements. Furthermore, the pertinence and validity of the alpha version of the ICNP in the Thai nursing environment was reviewed. Finally the Nurses' Association of Thailand received formal approval from the ICN to translate and publish an ICNP beta version in 2000.[10]

To assure the quality of nursing care, many hospitals have developed nursing information systems. For example, the Thai National Cancer Institute[10] successfully developed an ICNP-based nursing electronic record to be used in the In Patient Department (IPD). Maharaj Kakorn Chiang Mai Hospital[11] developed a beta version of an electronic ICNP database. The Bureau of Nursing developed ICNP-ER, an ICNP-based nursing information system for emergency departments, while, coincidentally, continuing their work on the ICNP - version 1. These successful pioneering works constitute exemplars that can be referenced for future development.

As the current healthcare environment continues to emphasize quality of care, the role of IT will continue to expand. To ensure continuous improvements, evaluations of nursing care quality; nursing standards criteria; and nursing quality assurance indices have been applied to the hospital accreditation process. This process requires a high level of documentation completeness to effectively monitor the quality over time, so IT was adopted to support these efforts. Many hospitals have also established pilot studies on how documentation standards might be leveraged to create an interoperable NIS.

Challenges

As work now progresses on the 10th National Health Development Plan,[2] significant challenges remain. This plan calls for people-centered development.[4] This requires an effective partnership between people and healthcare providers.[12] Thus the patient must be the central focus while working through the major technical concerns of system interoperability, integration, and data security. To successfully achieve this goal, the requirements of all stakeholders should be incorporated in future HIS development. To insure interoperability, the health information contained in the EHRs must be standardized and harmonized.

Summary

Significant progress has been made in bringing a standardized national EHR to fruition in Thailand. Standards have been gradually expanded to the national level (e.g., national health indicators have now been defined). Many facilities are working to rapidly implement newly adopted standards. The goal of a people-centered healthcare has already been identified. Going forward, attention must be given to ensuring that fully collaborative development processes are used, so that the person-centered focus is not lost in the transition to integrated standards and improved data security. The final measure of success in this endeavor will be how close we can come to the vision of a Healthy Thailand.

References

1. Bureau of Policy and Strategy, Ministry of Public Health. *Thailand Health Profile 2005-2007.* Bangkok: The War Veteran Organization of Thailand Press, 2007.

2. www.oecd.org. Accessed October 20, 2009.

3. www.thailandoutlook.com. Accessed October 20, 2009.

4. Bureau of Policy and Strategy, Minister of Public Health. *Health Policy in Thailand 2007.* Bangkok: The War Veteran Organization of Thailand Press, 2007.

5. http://eng.moph.go.th/. Accessed October 20, 2009.

6. Bureau of Policy and Strategy, Ministry of Public Health. *Thailand Health Profile 2001-2004.* Bangkok: Express Transportation Organization Press, 2004.

7. Thavichachart T, Kasitipradith N. *Thailand HIT Case Study.* http://pacifichealthsummit.org/downloads/HITCase Studies/Economy/ThailandHIT.pdf. Accessed April 20, 2009.

8. www.ncbi.nlm.nih.gov/. Accessed October 20, 2009.

9. lib.slc.ac.th/ebook/18102005165048.pdf. Accessed October 20, 2009.

10. Phuphaibul R., Kumpaliki S, Sriyaporn A, et al. The Royal Thai Government/The World Health Organization: *Nursing Minimum Data Set and Preliminary Nursing Classification Development.* Mahidol University Center of Nursing Research, Bangkok. 1999.

11. www.med.cmu.ac.th. Accessed October 20, 2009.

12. World Health Organization. *People-centered Health Care.* Geneva: WHO Press, 2007.

Case Study 19D

Australia: Developing the Electronic Health Record, A Continuing Nursing Challenge

By Robyn Cook, MBA, BBus, RN; and Joanne Foster, GradDipCIEdn, MEdTech, DipAppSc (NsgEd), BN, RN

Introduction—Australia's Health System

Australia's health system's structure reflects the country's model of governance, a complex combination of public and private service delivery models. The Commonwealth and state/territorial governments have overlapping responsibilities in providing health services. The Commonwealth Government's leadership role is in policymaking for national issues, such as public health, research, and national information management. The Commonwealth also funds most out-of-hospital medical services and health research.[1] In turn, the states are primarily responsible for service provision, although the Commonwealth influences this aspect. The six Australian states and two territories cover the delivery and management of public health services, as well as relationships with the health professionals.

Health services in Australia are a mix of Commonwealth- and state-funded public hospitals, community, aged care, and disability services. Universal access is provided through Medicare, a general taxation system. The Commonwealth exerts some control over the health agenda by directing state and territory funding of services through the Medicare Funding Agreement and offering incentive payments to them. However, this funding agreement is often criticized by the states because the agreements are renegotiated every five years and, according to the Commonwealth, meeting the financial pressure from the rising costs of and increasing demands for healthcare is always the responsibility of the states and territories. In 2006-2007, Australia spent $A94 billion on healthcare, which represents 9% of GDP.[2] This funding is divided across the Commonwealth, states and non-government sources. However, in some quarters, the current funding model is thought inadequate because of the cost of new drugs and technologies, rising wages, and increased demand for health services.[3] This complex funding leads to an equally complex arrangement for service provision.

Three key areas of service provision exist: community and private services; hospital and nursing home/aged care services; and public health services. Services are provided by either individual health professionals or by Commonwealth or state government healthcare organizations. Public hospitals are predominantly managed through state-based governments, while aged care or nursing home services are mostly provided through private organizations. Private sector and not-for-profit organizations are the major suppliers of nursing home/aged care beds, and the Commonwealth provides payments to the private providers to cover a percentage of the costs for residents, who often have to supplement the cost of their care. The private sector also offers a range of services and hospital beds. Although the system of joint governance over healthcare has been in place for some time, changes in demographics, escalating costs, a lack of clinical staff, and changes to the healthcare delivered, have led to the need for a more cohesive and integrated health service, delivered much more efficiently. Central to this goal is the use of IT.

Nursing and Primary, Secondary, and Tertiary Services

Nurses deliver care across all health sectors, often in very isolated settings throughout Australia. Nursing is dominant in the primary healthcare setting, but as in many other countries, general practitioners regard themselves as the gatekeepers of the system and claim to be primary healthcare givers, albeit in a very narrow sense. Nursing represents the largest group of health professionals in Australia, representing 55% of the workforce with 285,619 registered personnel.[4]

In the primary setting, nursing responsibilities range from early childhood monitoring and supporting child and family development to coordinating all aspects of individual healthcare and the broader population health programs in a rural or remote setting. Some nurse-led clinics are more than 600 kilometers from the nearest hospital or medical officer. At a secondary level, nurses are the core workforce needed for 24-hour, 7-day-a-week care and coordination in a range of settings. Nurse practitioners are gaining a greater role in healthcare, and nursing services that span hospital and community are becoming more common. Nurse practitioners prescribe medications, order diagnostic tests, and make referrals within approved guidelines. At a tertiary level, nurses provide extensive specialized nursing care.

Information Flow Challenges

As healthcare becomes more complex and the boundaries between the professions and health sectors (primary, secondary, and tertiary) become increasingly blurred, the ability to communicate effectively about patient care is essential. Information flow across all sectors of the healthcare system is less than satisfactory and does not support effective, efficient healthcare delivery.[5] Increasing pressure on the healthcare system, due to increasing costs and service demand, a shortage of healthcare workers,[6] and increasing demand by consumers to be more active in healthcare, requires a major review on the way information is gathered, documented, and shared across the system and with consumers. The complex structure creates artificial organizational boundaries, which reduces information flow. This challenge of information flow can only be effectively addressed by e-health capabilities.[7]

Another obstacle to information flow is the existing privacy policy frameworks in both Commonwealth and state jurisdictions that continue to be problematic, despite a number of task force reviews. While significant discussion and review of privacy policies has been undertaken in the last 10 years, changes still are required to achieve a standard that is applied consistently across all jurisdictions. The agreed on standard needs to support improved information flows within a consumer-agreed, consent model. A robust privacy and regulatory framework has yet to be established to support e-health initiatives in Australia.[7]

One of the greatest impediments to information flow in nursing is the lack of any standardization of data, leaving nurses unable to efficiently communicate across locations and geographic settings.[8] Changing community and clinical expectations about the management of data, and a growing expectation that health information should be available where it is needed, has also created an environment for change. While clinicians expect timely transfer of information to support care delivery, consumers are demanding it.

e-Health and the Individual Electronic Health Record

In 1999, a task force, under the auspices of Commonwealth and state health ministers, was established to provide a coordinated approach to the development of a national Australian electronic health record (EHR). The task force recommended the establishment of a health information network for Australia, and this was endorsed by the health ministers in 2000. This health policy act created Health*Connect* and a medications record (Medi*Connect*).[9] Health*Connect* was designed to provide an environment in which access to information can be used to support care delivery, improve health outcomes, and support care planning. In terms of supporting further research, Health*Connect* was to "improve the delivery of healthcare and provide better quality of care, consumer safety, and health outcomes for all Australians while enhancing the privacy and respecting the dignity of the health consumer."[10] The governance arrangements for Health*Connect* were to involve an integrated approach to planning, resourcing, and managing projects that involve sharing of costs and risks across jurisdictions and the private sector.[10] Unfortunately, the Health*Connect* Initiative only progressed to pilot projects in a few states. However, the majority of pilot projects demonstrated success and are still operational, e.g., The Northern Territory pilot project within the indigenous aboriginal community. Since 2005, the main national initiative has been the establishment of the National Electronic Health Transition Authority (NeHTA). NeHTA was created by the Commonwealth to focus on e-health informatics standards and integrating infrastructure. This standards development included the standards needed for the exchange of clinical information.

Entering into 2009, the national e-health agenda's focus is still limited to NeHTA standards development. In terms of implementing Information and Communication Technology (ICT) solutions, each state jurisdiction has undertaken a range of individual electronic health record projects. While these state initiatives contribute to the expansion of e-health at the local level, the lack of Commonwealth strategic vision at a national level has resulted in Australia's e-health agenda lacking direction, accountability, or shared goals across the country.[7] Since 2005, NeHTA has carried responsibility for standards development needed for a national approach to the individual electronic health record (IEHR). These standards pertain to event summaries, health identifiers, connectivity, and privacy policies regarding consent and access control. These components are the building blocks of what would be required for the IEHR available at a national level.

Nursing Involvement in e-Health Initiatives

Although nursing has fought for many years to be involved at the higher, decision-making levels of government, nursing representation at advisory levels[11] and standard-setting bodies have been limited to individual participation. This is especially the case within the NeHTA's scope of work. Nursing involvement in the Health-*Connect* trials was serendipitous, rather than a deliberate effort to have the nursing domain represented in these undertakings. NeHTA had not actively engaged nursing professional groups for their participation in their standards work until late 2008. This was in despite of NeHTA working on key standards projects, such as clinical terminology and SNOMED, event summaries, and other interoperability standards. Standards Australia has had a representative from the RCNA on its Health Informatics Committee (IT14) for many years. However, at a government advisory level and national standards level, no nursing representation has been sought nor nominated candidates accepted. It is anticipated that this will now be actively addressed with the appointment of the National Chief Nursing Officer in 2008.

Standard Initiatives to Support Individual Electronic Health Records

Standards. Standards underpin the effective operation of IEHRs, and it is generally acknowledged that the implementation of standards is essential to ensure the seamless movement of information across networks. Since 2005, the development of standards has accelerated and involves mainly the NeHTA, the Commonwealth government, and Standards Australia, with significant sharing of developments with the International Standards Organisation (ISO), European Committee for Standardisation (CEN), and Health Level 7 (HL7). These groups are developing standards for data security and authentication, messaging and communications, terminologies, coding, and classification systems.[12] Archetype development that underpins the open EHR architecture is also being pursued.[13]

    Event Summaries, Referrals and Other Content. Also vital to the development of e-health is the development of e-clinical information content for the health record. Defining clinical information content involves the development of a framework and model for determining clinical information capture and representation, prototype priority health event summaries, and prototype priority IEHR lists and views.[14] The overall objective is to enable information interchange from EHRs and to facilitate interoperability of clinical information across Australia.[14] Event summaries will contain only the information that is relevant to the future health and care of the consumer, rather than the comprehensive notes that a doctor may keep as a record of a consultation. An event summary may be retrieved and shared in a timely fashion via a secure network between authorized healthcare providers, with the consumer's consent. A number of state jurisdictions are developing event summaries and e-referrals; however, most of these are generic and do not contain specific nursing summaries or referrals. NeHTA's e-Discharge Summary and e-Referral programs are monitoring these developments and after evaluation will provide a blueprint for event summary standards and implementations.

Security and Confidentiality

The need for a secure system of identification is a significant issue for e-health, as Australia does not have a unique identification number for users of healthcare services or for providers. Consumer identification in a national record, however, is essential to ensure that a consumer's medical information is unambiguously linked to that person and that there is no uncertainty about the transfer of clinical information. NeHTA has published detailed standards for the development of Unique Identification services. These standards extend to the unique identification of healthcare providers that includes nurses, provider organizations, and individual health identifiers for consumers.[15]

    Under these models, providers and consumers will be assured that personal health information is adequately protected and that stringent access controls can be enforced. Consent will involve seeking the agreement of consumers to[1] record information on any EHR and to access that information in the future.

    In terms of consent and confidentiality NeHTA has developed a Privacy Management Framework.[16] This will work in conjunction with the identity management and secure messaging frameworks to ensure that consent is informed and voluntary. This Privacy Management also addresses the tension between consumer choice on who accesses the EHR and clinicians safely performing clinical care. New South Wales has been successful in implementing an "Opt Out" model, wherein consumer information is incorporated into the EHR and, through the process of registration, consumers then have the opportunity to choose the option of not participating in the system.

State-Based Implementations as Feeders to the Individual Electronic Health Record

A number of states are continuing to work toward the implementation of core clinical systems that will be used at the point of care. These systems will form the basis of the electronic clinical (patient) record (in contrast to the IEHR). Nursing will be a major contributor to the electronic clinical record as it will be the repository for all nursing documentation. Because these systems will feed summary data to the IEHR, it is important that they are implemented in the short to medium term. These local EHRs will need to align with IEHR implementations for the necessary data feeds to happen. Nurses are involved in many of the point-of-care clinical solution developments and implementations, particularly in the realm of clinical documentation.

In overall integration of e-health solutions into nursing practice, the Royal District Nursing Service in Melbourne, Victoria, a home healthcare provider, sets the Australian benchmark. Nurses document online, create electronic referrals, and operate using mobile technologies.[17]

Challenges for Nursing

IT supports clinicians by enabling much greater interaction and improvement in communication. If nurses in Australia are unable to engage because of incompatible work processes or the lack of a common language, identifiers, or interoperable systems, then nursing participation in the advancement of quality care, professional practice improvements, and significant members of the care team will be forfeited. Less than full participation in the e-health working environments translates into the potential that portions of the nursing community will remain isolated and nursing's communication within the health system inconsistent.[18] Australian nurses must also decide on a governance framework through which a group with delegated decision-making authority will direct nursing's collective efforts. Further insight into these and many others issues affecting the ability of nurses to embrace IT are contained in a 2004 report to the Commonwealth Government.[18] Some of the major issues from that report are discussed next.

The capacity of nursing in Australia to exploit IT is unknown, but anecdotal reports and generalized studies point to challenges in this area. Few education and training programs are available at either the undergraduate or postgraduate level, and indeed, there are very few informatics educators.[18] Nonetheless, it is essential that beginning practitioners have basic competencies in nursing informatics; in particular, they should understand the importance and use of clinical information systems. A national approach to the development of nursing informatics competencies and integration of these into the nursing curricula commenced in 2008.[19]

The standardization of nursing language presents quite a challenge. According to Conrick et al.,[18] Australian nurses will probably not agree on or find a single classification that covers a whole of nursing solution. A major problem is the lack of funding to initiate research into appropriate terminology that represents the spectrum of nursing practice. Utilizing foundation work done in Canada[20] and other parts of the world, a comprehensive report of nursing data sets and terminologies currently in use needs to be compiled, as does an evaluation of available data sets and terminologies to assess their ability to adequately represent nursing concepts and meet nurses' information needs at all levels in the health industry.[18]

A record architecture that is independent of particular language, such as an open EHR, may provide an answer. However, if the IEHR model adopts an open EHR, Australian nurses must develop archetypes to describe the concepts of their practice. As archetypes are not language specific, agreement on a particular data set would not be crucial. The Commonwealth Government's adoption of SNOMED and SNOMED's new international governance will help to alleviate these problems, but still much work is required. A study by Scott et al.[21] demonstrates the difficulties of content coverage when mapping three different classifications to raw patient data. Classification and terminologies for nursing is a critical area yet to be addressed by Australian nursing groups and nursing in the higher education sector.

As new technology is developed and implemented, personnel and organizations have to adjust, and sometimes the adjustment is major. As key participants and the largest stakeholder group in healthcare, nursing will be most affected by the introduction of technology, and change management will be crucial to its uptake. Nurse leaders and managers play vital roles to ensure the successful implementation of IT. If nurses are not involved and do not feel ownership in the early development of IT in Australia, future change management strategies may be at risk. Senior nursing personnel are aware and agree that information systems and technology are critical to improving clinical care. Consequently, nurse informaticians have a positive and receptive environment to partner with nursing leadership to raise the profile of nursing informatics and clinical information systems and to extol the benefits that technology can provide in supporting nursing practice.

Summary

In Australia, IT will significantly redefine professional boundaries in healthcare and support healthcare workers across vast geographical distances by providing access to quality, timely data and information. The EHR and supporting technologies open up new possibilities for the dissemination and use of information that enables improved performance and outcomes across the health sector. The explosion of mobile and Internet communication and information technologies and their uses in everyday life, means that their adoption into healthcare is inevitable. Australian nurses have the opportunity to be actively engaged, full partners in these developments; we can own our future, and it is ours for the taking.

Acknowledgments

Thank you to the following people for their contribution to this chapter:

- John Fletcher, Trial/Implementation Manager, Health*Connect* NT
- Sue Ashlin, Trial Manager, Tasmanian Health*Connect* Trial

References

1. Commonwealth of Australia. *The Australian Healthcare System: An Outline.* Canberra: Commonwealth Department of Health and Aged Care Financing and Analysis Branch, 2000.

2. Australian Institute of Health and Welfare. *Health Expenditure Australia 2006–07. Health and Welfare Expenditure Series no. 35.* Cat. no. HWE 42. Canberra: AIHW: 2008.

3. Menadue J. *Breaking the Commonwealth / State Impasse in Health.* Sydney: Whitlam Institute, University of Western Sydney, 2004.

4. Australian Institute of Health and Welfare. *Nursing and midwifery labour force 2005.* National Health Labour Force Series no. 39. Cat. no. HWL 40. Canberra: AIHW: 2008.

5. Conrick M. Introduction to information technology and information management. In: Conrick M, ed. *Health informatics: Transforming Healthcare with Technology.* Melbourne, Thompson Social Science Press: 2006.

6. Australian Health Ministers Conference. *National E Health Strategy Summary: December, 2008.* http://www.ahmac.gov.au/cms_documents/National%20E-Health%20Strategy.pdf. Accessed February 21, 2009.

7. Booz & Co. *E-Health Enabler for Australia's Health Reform - A discussion paper.* Booz Company, 2008. http://www.nhhrc.org.au/internet/nhhrc/publishing.nsf/Content/16F7A93D8F578DB4CA2574D7001830E9/$File/E-Health%20-%20Enabler%20for%20Australia's%20Health%20Reform,%20Booz%20&%20Company,%20November%202008.pdf. Accessed February 21, 2009.

8. Conrick M. *Nursing and the electronic health record.* In: Proceedings of Barnard A. *Nursing in a Technological World.* July 2003. Brisbane: Queensland University of Technology, 2003.

9. Commonwealth of Australia. Health*Connect.* Canberra: Department of Health and Ageing, 1999.

10. Commonwealth of Australia. *Report of the National Electronic Records Taskforce.* Canberra: Department of Health and Ageing, 2000.

11. Conrick M. Informatics Professional Roles and Governance. In: Conrick M, ed. *Health Informatics: Transforming Healthcare with Technology.* Melbourne: Thompson Social Science Press, 2006.

12. Walker S, Frean I, Scott P, Conrick M. *Classifications and Terminologies in Residential Aged Care: An Information Paper.* Canberra: The Ageing and Aged Care Division of the Commonwealth Department of Health and Ageing, 2004. http://www.niaonline.org.au. Accessed February 21, 2009.

13. Ocean Informatics. *Glossary.* 2007. https://wiki.oceaninformatics.com/confluence/display/ocean/Glossary. Accessed May 25, 2009.

14. Commonwealth of Australia. *Clinical Information Project.* http://www.healthconnect.gov.au/building/Building.htm#CIP. Accessed January 12, 2005.

15. NeHTA. *UHI Detailed Business Requirements.* Australian Government, 2007. http://www.NeHTA.gov.au/component/docman/doc_details/375-uhi-detailed-business-requirements-v20. Accessed May 21, 2009.

16. NeHTA. *Privacy Blueprint for the Individual Electronic Health Record.* Canberra: Australian Government. http://www.nehta.gov.au/component/docman/cat_view/49-publications/48-connecting-australia/163-privacy/164-general. Accessed May 21, 2009.

17. Royal District Nursing Service. *Information Technology.* Royal District Nursing Service Ltd. http://www.rdns.com.au/research_and_innovation/Initiatives/Pages/InformationTechnology.aspx Accessed May 21, 2009.

18. Conrick M, Hovenga E, Cook R, Laracuente T, Morgan T. *A Framework for Nursing Informatics in Australia: A Strategic Paper.* Health Informatics Society of Australia-Nursing Informatics Australia, Melbourne: Department of Health and Ageing, 2004.

19. Foster J, Bryce J. Australian Nursing Informatics Competency Project. Unpublished report; 2009.

20. Kaminski J. *Brief History of Nursing Informatics in Canada.* 2008. http://www.nursing-informatics.com/kwantlen/history.html. Accessed May 21, 2009.

21. Scott P, Jones L, Saad P, Conrick M, Foster J, Campbell M. Matching Residential Aged Care Terms to SNOMED CT, ICNP2Beta, and CATCH. In: Conrick M, Soar J, eds. Proceedings from ACCIC04. Brisbane: Health Informatics Society of Australia, 2004.

Case Study 19E

The New Zealand Approach to the Electronic Health Record

By Lucy Westbrooke, GDipBus (Health Informatics), DipNg, RCpN

Introduction

New Zealand, with its population of more than four million,[1] has traditionally embraced technology and is often at the forefront in the use of electronic systems. The use of technology has extended into the primary, secondary, and tertiary sectors of health. Electronic health records (EHRs) are recognized as improving healthcare outcomes. In line with many countries, New Zealand is aware that there is a need to improve the efficiency, safety, and quality of care, as well as information exchange between health service providers. New Zealand is in a good position to embrace EHRs, as much of the infrastructure needed to support the development and implementation of EHRs is already in place. The debate is currently around what the New Zealand EHR should look like.

New Zealand Health Sector

As illustrated in Figure 19E-1, New Zealand's health and disability services are delivered by a complex network of people and organizations.[2] More than three quarters of all healthcare is publicly funded. Within the public sector, the healthcare purchaser and provider functions are combined and delivered by 21 district health boards (DHBs). DHBs plan, purchase, manage, and provide services for the population of their district, including primary, secondary, and community care. Some DHBs also provide tertiary and quaternary services. This model has highlighted the need for information exchange and for a change to a sector-wide approach to the development and implementation of information systems.

Health Sector Strategies

Although there are more than 20 health-related strategies, the four major national health-related strategies published by the Ministry of Health that influence the direction of New Zealand healthcare are The New Zealand Health Strategy,[4] The New Zealand Disability Strategy,[5] The Korowai Oranga: Máori Health Strategy[6] and The Primary Health Care Strategy.[7]

Health information strategies have been developed to align with health strategies and promote the use of "information in innovative ways to improve the health and independence of New Zealanders." The first health information strategy, Health Information Strategy for the Year 2000, was released in 1996 followed by "From Strategy to Reality: The WAVE Project"[8] in 2001. The WAVE Project was developed through the collaboration of a range of health sector players, including government representatives, clinicians, healthcare managers, information technology managers, and system vendors. The publication of the Health Information Strategy for New Zealand 2005[9] (HIS-NZ) not only set the new strategy but also outlined the following 12 action zones required for the advancement of health information management:

1. National network strategy
2. National Health Index (NHI) promotion and enhancement
3. Health Provider Index (HPI) implementation
4. e-Pharmacy
5. e-Labs
6. Hospital discharge summaries
7. Chronic care and disease management
8. Electronic referrals
9. National outpatient collection
10. National primary and community care collection
11. National system access
12. Anchoring framework

A review of this strategy commenced in 2008 and will result in the publication of an updated strategy in 2009-2010.

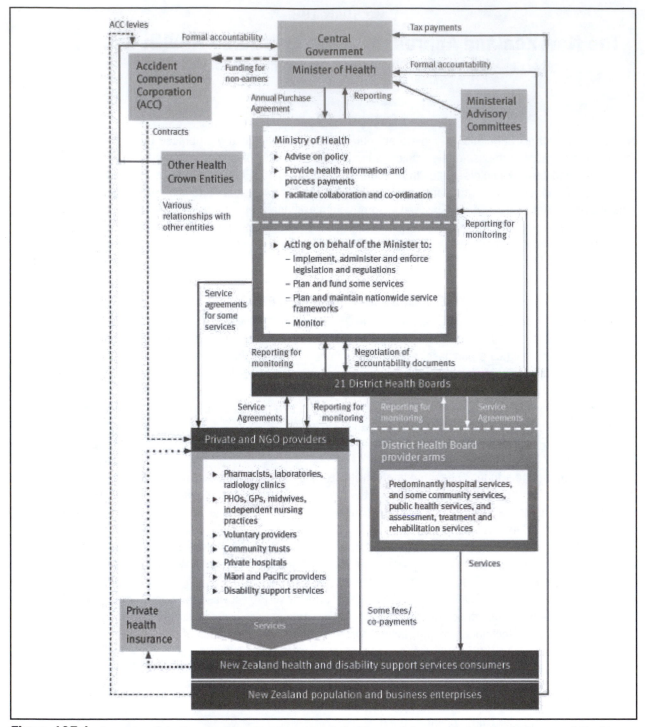

Figure 19E-1. *Structure of the New Zealand Health and Disability System.[3] Source: New Zealand Ministry of Health. Available at www.moh.govt.nz/moh.nsf/indexmh/healthsystem-overview.*

New Zealand's early recognition of the value of information systems in supporting improved health outcomes led to work on implementation of national infrastructure.

Electronic Health Record

From Strategy to Reality: the WAVE Project 2001[8] described an Electronic Health Record (EHR) as:

> An electronic longitudinal collection of health information, based on the individual patient, entered and accepted by healthcare professionals, which can be distributed over a number of sites and in a number of settings. The information is organized primarily in support of continu-

ing, efficient, and quality healthcare. The record (or records) is under the control of an agreed access policy. Information does not form part of the health record until a healthcare professional has taken responsibility for it and entered it into the record. The data is typically stored in a single clinical data repository at each site. An EHR exists when a healthcare provider accesses health information from a clinical data repository(s) or a single national server, or multiple distributed servers, where the health information is stored, for information on their patient's health history. A longitudinal history is incrementally created for the patient as more health information is provided to these servers.

The New Zealand EHR now aims for a distributed model wherein information residing in many individual repositories, local; regional; and national, can be linked to provide the appropriate information to support healthcare and achieve better health outcomes. The HIS-NZ strategy focuses on communication and connectivity to share the distributed information. Focusing on practical solutions and achieving results in the 12 action zone areas described in the HIS-NZ aims to deliver value for all stakeholders and move New Zealand closer to a distributed EHR.

Infrastructure Supporting EHRs

EHRs, by allowing providers access to clinical data about patients, can contribute to improved healthcare outcomes as well as efficiencies in healthcare delivery. New Zealand is fortunate that some of the core components have been long established, e.g., NHI. Work is in progress on other components through the action zones.

Legislation, such as the Privacy Act 1993,[10] governing the collection, storage, access, and use of personal information; the Health Information Privacy Code 1994,[11] applying the Privacy Act to the health sector; and the Official Information Act 1982,[12] providing controls on information, are well-established. Reviews ensure that they are amended to reflect changing practices and technology. The majority of the major health providers are covered by the Health Practitioners Competence Assurance Act 2003.[13] These pieces of legislation ensure that everyone who is dealing with health information knows what is acceptable and what compliance criteria is required.

Standards are recognized as critical to enable information to be shared effectively and efficiently. A standards group, under the direction of Health Information Strategy Advisory Committee (HISAC), plays a key co-ordination role in the development and implementation of information management and technology standards for the health sector. It works with other standards development groups, end-users, and key stakeholders to develop and/or ratify standards, e.g., HL7 – endorsement, primary practice management systems, NZ ethnicity protocols, LOINC – code set and business rules, Health Practitioner Index (HPI) code and data set, and interactive communications between patient management systems and external systems. Standardized coding sets such as the International Classification of Diseases version 10 - Australasian modified (ICD10AM) have been utilized for many years to code hospital events, and many primary care practices have used the READ codes. New Zealand is a now a charter member of International Health Terminology Standard Development Organization (IHTSDO),[14] which owns the SNOMED terminology set, and work is underway to explore how this terminology set can be utilized in the New Zealand health software.

The development of national networks continues to improve the infrastructure. The New Zealand Health Network consisting of two virtual provider networks, Telecom New Zealand and HealthLink,[15] form the backbone of the communications infrastructure providing a secure network for transfer of information.

Key data sets are now in place. The National Health Index, which provides a unique patient identifier, was established in 1993, and more recently, the Health Provider Index, which supplies a unique identifier for all healthcare providers, has been released. Identity management is a key requirement for many of our systems and, particularly for our EHR development.

There are more than 15 national data collections recording a range of information from patient demographic data, inpatient, outpatient, primary care, mental health, elective services, medical warnings, mortality, laboratory, pharmacy, maternity, newborn, cancer, hepatitis, immunization, as well as the workforce data from 13 health professional groups.

Stakeholders in EHRs

There are a number of parties participating in EHR initiatives in New Zealand: the IT Health Cluster,[16] which consists of health IT vendors and health informatics organizations such as Health Informatics New Zealand (HINZ),[17] and Health Information Association of New Zealand (HIANZ);[18] standards development group under HISAC; a range of professional organizations; and individual healthcare providers. The New Zealand government is taking a more active role in setting strategies for health information and is funding some initiatives that will support it. The approach focuses more on infrastructure and standards, leaving system implementations and change management to the local or regional levels. HINZ through its regular seminar program in 2008-2009, has provided a forum for the many stakeholders to explore and debate EHRs in the New Zealand context.

One of the major stakeholders in EHRs is the patient or consumer. There are few published New Zealand studies on this, but one by Ryan and Boustead[19] concluded that "there is a low level of awareness and many misconceptions amongst members of the lay public about e-health information and patient rights." National awareness campaigns are already underway to address this. As more clinical information is stored in wider health systems rather than an individual patient record, debate on access to the information arises and who is to authorize access. Many stakeholders believe that the consumer should be the one to determine access and trials have been undertaken looking at "patient audit" of access to their records.[20]

Initiatives with EHRs in New Zealand

The EHR is still seen as the "Holy Grail," but by using the philosophy of "not letting the perfect get in the way of the good," New Zealand has decided that having some of the components of an EHR is better than waiting for the ultimate solution, which may be financially out of reach. New Zealand is fortunate to have a number of health IT vendors and "healthcare" is the largest software export category for New Zealand. Some of the health IT vendors have worked with the health sector to provide an integrated view of information. Patient information is often held in a number of disparate systems, including patient management systems (PMS) (for registration; admission, discharge, and transfer (ADT); and outpatient scheduling), laboratory systems, radiology systems and clinical systems. For health professionals, there is a need to see a patient-centric view of this information.

In the secondary sector, companies such as Orion Systems International[21] and IBA[22] have products that allow a Web-based view of information from different systems, providing seamless access to patient-related information. Orion's Concerto product is a "Medical Applications Portal that is placed over multiple information systems to provide a single, seamless view of a patient's information" such as ADT, laboratory, radiology, clinical documents etc. The Soprano product provides "solutions for clinical notes, discharge summaries, and disease management. IBA's Clinician View™ and HealthViews™ and the new Lorenzo product create a comprehensive view of patient information.

Creation of template-based clinical documents such as discharge summaries, referral letters and clinical letters are used by a number of secondary providers. These documents are often pre-populated with selected information from other systems, e.g., visit details, diagnosis, laboratory, and radiology results. On completion, they can then be forwarded to other providers, e.g., general practitioners, using secure networks offered by HealthLink and the Telecom New Zealand. There are also initiatives underway in the areas of e-referrals, order entry, and e-prescribing. Information from these clinical transactions will then form part of the EHR of the future.

Community-based caregivers are also using computerized systems that integrate patient administration and clinical data to provide an EHR. Because nurses deliver much of the community care, they have significant input into information held in the EHR. The requirement for standardized terminology is urgent.

Nursing Initiatives

Nurses and midwives are traditionally patient-focused and therefore see the benefits of developing multi-disciplinary EHRs that are accessible from a range of places. Nurses and midwives are being utilized in the development of EHRs and through this utilization, are developing health informatics expertise. The initiatives in the EHR field involving nurses and midwives[23] are the maternity sector, mental health sector, primary and community sectors. There is still a big gap in electronic systems designed to address the specific nursing requirements to aid assessment, planning, implementation, and evaluation of care. The implementation of standard assessments for older people utilizing InterRAI[24] assessments is a more recent initiative which will involve many health professionals and nurses, in particular. Although the simple "contact assessment" can be completed in a paper-based format, the other assessments will require the use of electronic systems. The sharing of these data between multiple health professionals will be required to monitor the health status of the individual as well as to monitor the health status of our population and measure the effects of various health improvement programs.

Primary Care

The primary sector has had a high uptake of the use of electronic medical systems initially stimulated in the 1990s by the government requirement that all patients' registers and claims for service provision be submitted electronically and contain a unique patient identifier—the NHI number. The NHI number is now used on all health records, although private providers may also retain their own local number for their own use.

The use of information systems and technology has now reached 100% in the primary sector, and 75% use full clinical functionality,[25pt2,p189-193] including clinical note taking during patient encounters, generation of prescriptions, laboratory and radiology request forms and well as electronic receiving of results. Nurses working as practitioners in these areas are also contributing to the patient record. There is now a high use of clinical messaging exchange in General Practices.[25pt3,p285-290] The use of HL7 as the standard for messaging exchange has been of great benefit, as it is internationally recognized.

Mental Health

Mental Health is an area in which progress in the use of an EHR has also been made. The Auckland District Health Board (ADHB) has been utilizing a product called Health Care Community (HCC) from Intrahealth[26] for a number of years. The original implementation in the community has now been extended into the secondary sector. This allows access to a single EHR across both community and secondary sectors. The three district health boards in the Auckland Region sponsored the Auckland Regional Mental Health Information Technology (ARMHIT) project to extend the use of the one instance of HCC to the three DHBs. This allows access to one regional mental health record for a client. Through the interfacing of systems, each of the DHBs can utilize the one record that is interfaced to their own PMS.

Decision Support Systems

Decision support system (DSS) initiatives are also underway. One of these projects assists primary care practitioners with care planning and referral for chronic condition management, e.g., diabetes and cardiovascular disease, by utilizing the Predict product from Enigma.[27] These decision-support systems are integrated into some of the tertiary, secondary, and primary health systems.

Issues with EHRs

EHRs carry legal, privacy, and other risks but also have the potential for major benefits. For EHRs to be adopted, there must be a balance between the benefits and risks. Electronic solutions are not perfect but are probably less risky than the current combination of paper and electronic systems. To reach a high level of EHR compliance, the system must have well-structured authentication, confidentiality, integrity, and non-repudiation, while remaining user-friendly.

The New Zealand Privacy Act 1993 and the Health Information Privacy Code 1994 decree that patients have the right to the information retained about them. This, however, does not extend to ownership of the hardcopy or electronic documents. In the move toward EHRs, holders of such information need to consider, when a request is made, how to provide access to this electronically stored information. We are fortunate in that the New Zealand privacy legislation also considers criteria of "reasonable in the circumstances."[28] Although EHRs are on the increase, consumer access to these systems is trailing behind; however, discussion and debate are underway, and the use of Web-based technologies is reducing the barriers to access. We hope to see access in a secure manner to some of these systems granted to consumers, as well as practitioners in the future.

Unfortunately, under current New Zealand law, there are components that should form part of the EHR but still require paper, such as prescriptions. There are currently applications being tabled to the director general of health to consider electronic prescribing. Until this type of legislation changes, these requirements need to be accommodated. Electronic recording of prescriptions is allowed but not the electronic transmission of the prescription with a digital signature required to authorize dispensing.

With the large number of health IT projects going on in New Zealand, there is concern that patients are not well-informed and are putting their trust in healthcare and IT professionals to "get it right."[29] Some health professionals believe there is some information that should not be stored in an individual's EHR. These are some of areas needing further debate.

EHR's Future in the New Zealand Health Sector

Peer influence is a major factor influencing the development and uptake of anything new, and technology and the EHR are no exception. Particularly in the primary health sector, practitioners have been interested in technology, and their independence from some of the influences in the secondary sector has impacted positively on the uptake of new systems and services.

Many of the components required for an EHR are available, but New Zealand has yet to achieve a totally patient-centric EHR that is available to patients and a range of providers. New Zealand favors incremental steps toward EHRs, rather than the "big bang" approach to control costs and minimize disruption. The content of an EHR is currently under debate between health professionals, but this debate needs to be extended further to include consumers.

There continues to be work in the area of forms technology and the ability to transmit an increasing range of information.

The size of New Zealand and the work being done on health IT infrastructure, including the EHR component, does mean that we may, one day, be able to realize the dream of a national EHR for New Zealanders, but we still have a long way to go. The technology may be ready, but people, processes, and change management still require work.

Summary

New Zealand is beginning to capitalize on EHR initiatives. While effective use of IT is likely to play a significant role in the country's future success, the focus on building collaborative partnerships between government, clinicians, and patients is seen as the ultimate key to ensuring that the EHR becomes an integral part of improving patient care.

References

1. Statistics New Zealand. *QuickStats About New Zealand.* http://www.stats.govt.nz/census/census-outputs/quickstats/snapshotplace2.htm?id=9999999&type=region. Accessed April 11, 2009.
2. Ministry of Health. *New Zealand's Health and Disability System.* http://www.moh.govt.nz/moh.nsf/f872666357c511eb4c25666d000c8888/a4655bc724ee3809cc256ac0000d4bfa?OpenDocument. Accessed April 11, 2009.
3. Ministry of Health. *Health and Disability System Overview.* http://www.moh.govt.nz/moh.nsf/indexmh/healthsystem-overview#fast. Accessed April 11, 2009.
4. Ministry of Health. *The New Zealand Health Care Strategy.* 2000. http://www.moh.govt.nz/moh.nsf/pagesmh/2285/$File/newzealandhealthstrategy.pdf. Accessed April 11, 2009.
5. Ministry of Health. *The New Zealand Disability Strategy.* 2001. http://www.odi.govt.nz/documents/publications/nz-disability-strategy.pdf. Accessed April 11, 2009.
6. Ministry of Health. *He Korowai Oranga: Maori Health Strategy.* 2002. http://www.moh.govt.nz/moh.nsf/ea6005dc347e7bd44c2566a40079ae6f/8221e7d1c52c9d2ccc256a37007467df/$FILE/mhs-english.pdf. Accessed April 11, 2009.
7. Ministry of Health. *The Primary Health Care Strategy.* 2001. http://www.moh.govt.nz/moh.nsf/0/7BAFAD2531E04D92CC2569E600013D04/$File/PHCStrat.pdf. Accessed April 11, 2009.
8. Ministry of Health. *From Strategy to Reality: the WAVE Project.* 2001. http://www.moh.govt.nz/moh.nsf/0/F34F8959738E992CCC256AF400177998/$File/TheWAVEreport.pdf. Accessed April 11, 2009.
9. Ministry of Health. *Health Information Strategy for New Zealand.* 2005. http://www.moh.govt.nz/moh.nsf/0/1912064EEFEC8EBCCC2570430003DAD1/$File/health-information-strategy.pdf. Accessed April 11, 2009.

10. *New Zealand Government. Privacy Act 1993.* http://www.legislation.govt.nz/act/public/1993/0028/latest/DLM296639.html?search=ts_act_Privacy+act_resel&sr=1. Accessed April 11, 2009.

11. New Zealand Government. *Health Information Privacy Code 1994.* http://www.privacy.org.nz/assets/Files/Codes-of-Practice-materials/Health-Information-Privacy-Code-1994-including-Amendment.pdf. Accessed April 11, 2009.

12. New Zealand Government. *Official Information Act 1982.* http://www.legislation.govt.nz/act/public/1982/0156/latest/DLM64785.html. Accessed April 11, 2009.

13. New Zealand Government. *Health Practitioners Competence Assurance Act 2003.* http://www.legislation.govt.nz/act/public/2003/0048/latest/DLM203312.html?search=ts_act_Health+Practitioners+Act_resel&sr=1. Accessed April 11, 2009.

14. www.ihtsdo.org. Accessed October 10, 2009.

15. Healthlink. http://www.healthlink.net/. Accessed April 11, 2009.

16. Health IT Cluster. http://www.healthit.org.nz/. Accessed April 11, 2009.

17. Health Informatics New Zealand. http://www.hinz.org.nz. Accessed April 11, 2009.

18. Health Information Association of New Zealand. http://www.hianz.org.nz/. Accessed April 11, 2009.

19. Ryan KM, Boustead AJ. Universal electronic health records; a qualitative study of lay perspectives. *New Zealand Family Physician.* 2004;31:149-154.

20. Fletcher L. Managing Patient Privacy via Patient Centred Audit. *Proceedings of the HINZ Conference 2008.* http://www. Hinz.org.nz/uploads/file/2008conference/P20.pdf. Accessed April 11, 2009.

21. Orion Systems International. http://www.orionhealth.com. Accessed April 11, 2009.

22. IBA Health. http://www.ibahealth.com/html. Accessed April 11, 2009.

23. Hendry C. The challenge of developing an electronic health record for use by mobile community based health practitioners. *Proceedings of the HINZ Conference 2008.* http://www.hinz.org.nz/uploads/file/2008conference/P04.pdf. Accessed April 11, 2009.

24. InterRAI, http://www.interrai.org/section/view/. Accessed April 11, 2009.

25. Protti D, Bowden T, Johansen I. Adoption of information technology in primary care physician offices in New Zealand and Denmark, part 2: historical comparisons. *Informatics in Primary Care.* 2008;16:189-193, 285-290.

26. Intrahealth. http://www.intrahealth.com. Accessed April 11, 2009.

27. Enigma. http://www.enigma.co.nz. Accessed April 11, 2009.

28. Wigley & Company. Electronic health records: legal issues. Presentation at: NZ Electronic Health Records Summit; 28 June 2004; Auckland. http://www.wigleylaw.com/assets/_Attachments/ElectronicHealthRecords.pdf. Accessed April 11, 2009.

29. Hunter I. Patient attitudes to electronic medical records. Presentation at: The Privacy Forum; 28 March 2003; Wellington. http://www.privacy.org.nz/assets/Files/6257966.pdf. Accessed April 11, 2009.

Case Study 19F

Electronic Health Record National Strategies and Significance for Nursing (Singapore)

By Premarani Kannusamy, PhD, RN

Introduction—Overview of Singapore

Singapore is an island city-state in Southeast Asia, with a land area of 707 km². Singapore has a multi-ethnic resident population of approximately 4.8 million, comprising 75% Chinese, 13.7% Malay, 8.7% Indian, and 2.6% other ethnic origins.

Singapore's Healthcare System

There are well over 7,400 physicians, 1,360 dentists, and 22,340 nurses supporting the country's healthcare delivery system.[1] Singapore spends approximately 3–4% of its GDP on healthcare and was ranked 6th overall in the World Health Organization's ranking of the world's health systems.[2]

The public healthcare delivery system comprises seven acute care hospitals, six national specialty centers, three specialty institutes, and seventeen primary care polyclinics. Since 1985, every public hospital has been "restructured"—referring to the granting of autonomy in operational matters—so as to inject private sector efficiency and financial discipline but with the government retaining 100% ownership of the hospitals. The restructured hospitals underwent further reorganization in 2000, splitting into two vertically integrated clusters—the National Healthcare Group and Singapore Health Services. Both are owned by the government and partially funded through subsidies.

The private healthcare sector comprises 16 private hospitals and approximately 1,600 private medical clinics. Private General Practitioners, numbering more than 2,000, provide 80% of primary healthcare services, while government polyclinics provide the remaining 20%. For secondary and tertiary care, public hospitals provide 80% of the more costly hospital care, with the remaining 20% provided by private hospitals.

Intermediate and long-term healthcare services are mostly run by voluntary welfare organizations. There are six community hospitals that provide intermediate step-down care and more than 50 nursing homes and hospices that provide long-term care.

Healthcare in Singapore stresses an individual responsibility toward healthy living and medical expenses. Subsidized medical services are available at public hospitals and clinics. Patients have freedom of choice to choose any providers of care in the various sectors.

Challenges Facing Singapore's Healthcare System

Singapore has a fast growing aging population. It is envisaged that by 2030, one in five Singaporeans will be older than age 65. Besides a global shortage of healthcare professionals, Singapore's disease patterns are also evolving toward chronic lifestyle diseases, such as hypertension, diabetes, and cardiovascular diseases. The price for medical equipment and drugs are also on the rise. IT has the potential to enable solutions that will address these challenges.

Singapore's Information Technology Strategic Plan

Singapore has put in place an advanced and reliable infocomm infrastructure that has met the needs and demands of our economy and society. The development of the National Infocomm Infrastructure started as a key initiative of the IT 2000 Masterplan, with the building of a high-speed nationwide broadband network as a major milestone as part of its development. Singapore currently has a high household broadband penetration of over 80%.[3] In 2003, Singapore's incoming Minister of Health, Mr. Khaw Boon Wan identified one of his key priorities as "Exploit IT Maximally," with the aim of "One Singaporean, One Electronic Medical Record."[4] In 2006, the Infocomm Development Authority of Singapore (IDA) released the Intelligent Nation 2015 Masterplan, poised to look into the deployment of a seamless and intelligent infocomm infrastructure.[5] Such an infrastructure will contribute to the overall competitiveness of the infocomm sector and empower every individual and business in Singapore with the opportunity to engage in networked, infocomm-enabled services.

The IDA, in collaboration with the Ministry of Health, developed the iN2015 plan for the healthcare and biomedical sectors.[6] The goal of this plan is to "accelerate sectoral transformation through a personalized healthcare delivery system to achieve high quality care, service excellence, cost-effectiveness and strong clinical research."[6;p17] The plan is poised to achieve the following outcomes:

- Well-integrated and coordinated care that is enabled by a common information network;
- Cost-effective, consistent and evidence-based healthcare services through use of clinical decision-support systems;
- Greater ability of individuals to manage their health through home infocomm systems, such as an electronic personal health record;
- More effective and efficient integration between healthcare and advances in biomedical sciences.

Information Technology (IT) Deployment in the Singapore Healthcare System

By 2003, both public health clusters, National Healthcare Group and SingHealth, had already extensively implemented clinical IT systems. Electronic Medical Records (EMR) that contain digitized inpatient discharge summaries and laboratory and radiology results were implemented. For example, National University Hospital's Computerized Patient Support System enables an integrated view of patient data from multiple source systems, such as x-rays, laboratory results, surgical operating notes, discharge summaries, clinical results, and reports.[7]

Electronic medication prescriptions are also being widely used in the public health clusters. For instance, the National Healthcare Group uses iPharm, a patient-centric Web-based enterprise integrated pharmacy system that provides a fully automated workflow process between consultation rooms and the pharmacy. With e-prescription, orders are sent electronically to the pharmacies, which prepare the medications for dispensing while patients are on their way to the pharmacies. This not only means shorter waiting times for patients at pharmacies but also enables a more efficient and effective drug tracing process in the event of a drug recall, since all the data are available in a central database.

Both clusters are also working on deploying Computerized Physician Order Entries (CPOE) across their hospitals and polyclinics as an important step toward improving patient safety. The polyclinics have also been leveraging IT in healthcare through offshore outsourcing of teleradiology.[4] As a result, patients save time as return trips for results are no longer necessary. Figure 19F-1 summarizes the point at which we are now in terms of national deployment of IT initiatives.

As shown in Figure 19F-1, multiple EMR systems are in place at the cluster level, polyclinics and specialist clinics. However, there are minimal EMRs at the General Practitioner clinics and across Community Hospitals. To address the problems of interoperability between clusters, the Ministry of Health implemented the Electronic Medical Records (EMR) Exchange (EMRX) and Critical Medical Information Store (CMIS) systems in 2004 to enable secure health information exchange between clinicians in the public healthcare sector.[4] These systems provided basic capabilities in health information exchange between providers in the two clusters and among hospitals, polyclinics and some community hospitals. There are more than 100,000 clinical documents shared monthly through the EMRX.[8] The major types of clinical information shared through EMRX include hospital discharge summaries, laboratory test results and radiology reports, medication information, immunization records, drug allergy, medical alerts and adverse drug report, and operating theatre and endoscopy reports. However, test results, scans, and summaries compiled upon a patient's discharge from the hospital are still stored in separate files and inaccessible to private hospitals and clinics.

Along the way, other IT innovations are developed, tested, and implemented at the institution or at cluster level, which are primarily funded by the respective institution. Table 19F-1 provides some exemplars of IT innovations deployed in the public health care system.

National Electronic Health Record

In 2008, the National Electronic Health Record program was launched to address transition from document to standards-based data exchange and extend access to key clinical providers in the community and private sector. Anticipated to be a multi-year national initiative, the initial phases of this program will be implemented

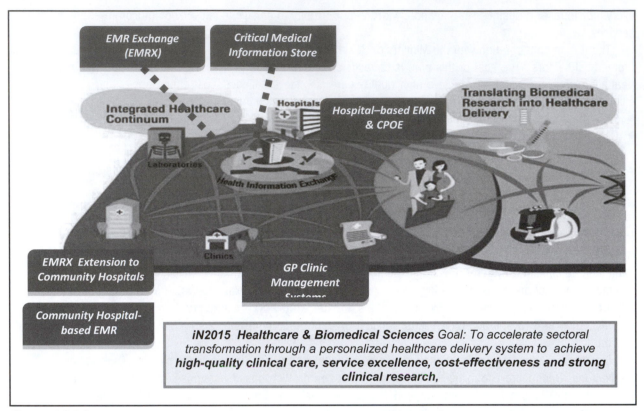

Figure 19F-1. *National IT and Related Initiatives. Source: Ministry of Health Holdings (2008).*

over the next two to three years. Singapore will be among the first in the world to implement such a system nationwide.

With the National EHR, patients' data can be shared across the continuum of care and across healthcare delivery organizations. Healthcare providers will be able to have a consolidated and longitudinal view of the patient's healthcare profile, medical condition, current medications, drug allergies, and test results across public and private care settings.

Over the medium to long term, the National EHR platform will potentially support a full spectrum of capabilities, as shown in Figure 19F-2.

The implementation of the EHR will be an iterative and phased implementation, targeting key clinical capabilities. When possible, it will leverage on existing systems and investments, as shown in Figure 19F-3.

Approach to EHR

A collaborative process and formal clinical engagement structure, consisting of a national Clinical Advisory Group and domain-specific task forces, have been put in place to ensure deeper clinician involvement in the planning and prioritization for the EHR and in aligning IT capability development with realizable clinical benefits.[12] The National EHR will encompass a broad range of participants across public and private sectors and care settings. In addition to clinician engagement, several independent teams were created to look into data standards, data stewardship, privacy and security and enterprise architecture.

In order to achieve semantic interoperability between diverse care settings, information systems and healthcare clusters, the following are planned:

1. Establish standards in the following ways, in order of preference:
   - Adopt existing standards when applicable.
   - Adapt existing standards with localization to meet national requirements.
   - Develop new standards through participation in established standards, development organizations, and processes.
2. Establish national Health Informatics standards with linkages to international standard bodies such as ISO, Health Level 7 (HL7)—Singapore launched the HL7 Affiliate in June 2008 to build up local expertise

Table 19F-1. Current Exemplars of IT Deployment

Electronic Documentation	The National Skin Centre uses electronic documentation to describe patients' conditions diagrammatically with precise location of the clinical findings. All annotated charts are integrated with the centre's Electronic Medical Record systems and are retrievable during consultations.
Bedside Mobile Workstation (BMW)	SingHealth implemented the BMW, a wireless notebook mounted on a height-adjustable trolley. Digital records including x-rays are easily accessible on the BMW, which can be wheeled to a patient's bedside. Doctors update records on-the-fly and place orders for medication and tests directly from the BMW.
Computer on Wheels (COWS)	COWS, a similar bedside mobile workstation, is also used in the hospitals within the National Healthcare Group.
Mobile Clinical Assistant[9]	Changi General Hospital implemented the MCA in its Accident & Emergency department. A lightweight, spill- and drop-tolerant mobile device that allows doctors and nurses to access patient data, such as lab results and medical histories, while on the move.
Community Care Management System[10]	This collaborative project between Singapore General Hospital, telecommunications SingTel and software firm HSA Global, uses computers and personal digital assistants to track patients following their discharge. Aside from ensuring patients get follow-up treatment, the Web-based project allows doctors and nurses to access and update patients' health records.
Wireless Temperature Monitoring	Tan Tock Seng hospital[11] used RFID technology to record patients' temperature readings automatically. The system allows patients to have more uninterrupted rest and nurses are alerted immediately once a fever is detected. RFID technology is also used in several public hospitals to track the movement of patients within the hospital.

Source: Ministry of Health Holdings (2008).

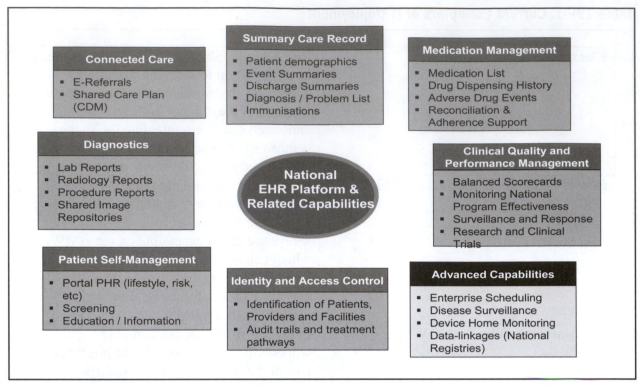

Figure 19F-2. *EHR Platform and Related Capabilities. Source: Ministry of Health Holdings (2008).*

in HL7 standards, and International Health Terminology Standards Development Organisation (IHTSDO)—Singapore joined IHTSDO as a national member and participates actively in SNOMED CT development internationally.

3. Develop a framework for the coordination of Health Informatics standards activities at the national level.
4. Standardisation of International Classification of Diseases (ICD) and Diagnosis-Related Groups (DRG).
5. Coordination of National Drug Dictionary for clinical purposes.
6. Implementation of Standards Program—data library, standards catalogue, conformance and capability.

Long-Term Objectives of EHR

For long-term planning, Ministry of Health Holdings[13] plans to use the EHR as a key enabler for clinical reform in achieving the following outcomes:

- Well-managed chronic illnesses
- Improved access to care
- Fewer unintended adverse drug events
- Better prescribing practices
- Reduced duplication of unnecessary tests
- Less risk of medical errors
- Reduced waiting times
- Increased patient participation in care
- Increased patient satisfaction

Significance of EHR for Nursing

The implementation of EHR represents a major investment of capital and human resources. As the largest single profession in the healthcare industry and the frontline of patient care, nursing is a critical component of successful EHR adoption. Working together, nurses can significantly impact the patient care agenda by getting involved in decision making, design, testing, implementation, and evaluation efforts, so that the EHR supports nursing functions.

To achieve this, we need to ensure that nurses have the required informatics competencies. According to Staggers et al.,[14] there are four levels of informatics competencies, from a beginner to an informatics innova-

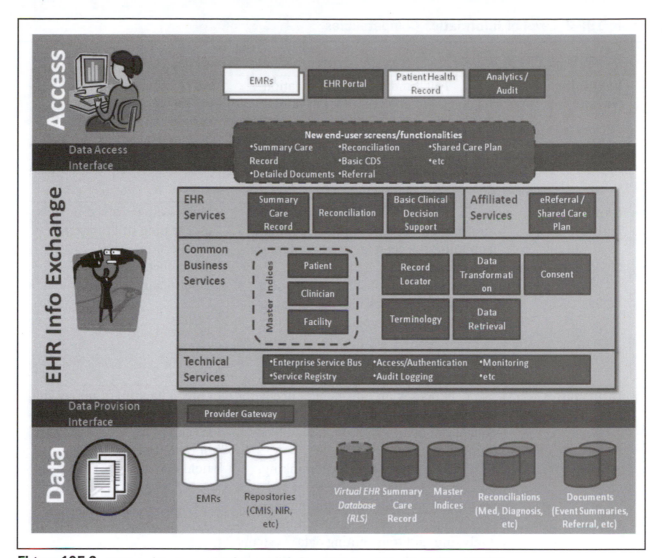

Figure 19F-3. *EHR Architecture and Solutioning. Source: Ministry of Health Holdings (2008).*

tor. Table 19F-2 presents the informatics competencies required for each of the four levels and where nurses in Singapore fit in to these competencies.

As shown in Table 19F-2, nurses in Singapore have, at the most, achieved Level 2 competencies. To enhance the competencies of nurses, there should be greater emphasis of Nursing Informatics in the undergraduate nursing curricula. Moreover, there is also a need for a Master of Nursing program with a major in Nursing Informatics that will prepare nurses with the appropriate informatics competencies. Nurse leaders also have a key role to play in establishing the vision for nursing informatics. Nurse leaders need to ask themselves the following questions:

- Do we have a nursing strategic plan in relation to IT?
- Have we set goals for how we want IT to assist nursing service delivery?
- Is there a plan for ensuring consistency of documentation throughout the entire institution?
- Have we investigated how our policies and procedures will change under automation?

It is imperative for nursing leaders to learn about current informatics issues from essential resources, including the literature, professional organizations, and education programs to develop successful strategies for innovation, collaboration, and implementation. More importantly, efforts need to be made to engage nurses in promoting a culture of innovation that goes beyond the technical hardware, to changing the work processes and how nursing care is delivered. The challenge now is for Singapore nurses to leverage EHR development plans in order to transform nursing care into care that is more satisfying, more research-based, and more visible, while yielding positive patient outcomes.

Table 19F-2. Level of Informatics Competencies

Level	Competencies	Where Singapore is Now
Beginning Nurse	• Has fundamental information management and computer technology skills • Uses existing information systems and available information to manage practice • Has computer and Web literacy	As IT systems are pervasive in the healthcare system, all nurses know how to use these systems.
Experienced Nurse	• Highly skilled in using information management and computer technology skills to support own major area of practice • Sees relationships among data elements and makes judgments based on trends and patterns within these data. • Uses current information systems but collaborates with informatics to suggest improvements to systems	Nurses are involved in end-user testing of IT systems to determine user preferences and the functionality of the system.
Informatics Nurse Specialist	• Focuses on information needs for the practice of nursing, which includes education, administration, research and clinical practice. • Uses tools of critical thinking, process skills, data management skills (including identifying, acquiring, preserving, retrieving, aggregating, analyzing and transmitting data) systems development life cycle and computer skill	Only a handful of nurses in Singapore are truly at this level. A few have ventured into the Healthcare IT field.
Informatics Innovator	• Leads the advancement of informatics practice and research • Functions with ongoing existing data management practices and is creative in developing solutions • Possesses a sophisticated level of understanding and skills in information management and computer technology • Understands the interdependence of systems, disciplines, & outcomes and can finesse situations to maximize outcomes	Currently, there is none in Singapore who fit this level.

Source: Ministry of Health Holdings (2008).

References

1. Ministry of Health (2007). *Health Manpower.* http://www.moh.gov.sg/mohcorp/statistics.aspx?id=5966. Accessed June 18, 2009.

2. World Health Organisation (2000). *The World Health Report 2000 - Health Systems: Improving Performance.* http://www.who.int/whr/2000/en/index.html. Accessed June 18, 2009.

3. Infocomm Development Authority of Singapore (2008). *Infrastructure.* http://www.ida.gov.sg/Infrastructure/20060411230420.aspx. Accessed June 18, 2009.

4. Lee CH, Lim BK, Tan CSP. *Singapore HIT Case Study.* Washington: The National Bureau of Asian Research, 2007; p. 65-70.

5. Infocomm Development Authority of Singapore (2006a). *Innovation. Integration. Internationalisation.* Report by the iN2015 Steering Committee. Singapore: Infocomm Development Authority of Singapore.

6. Infocomm Development Authority of Singapore (2006b). *Integrating Healthcare, Empowering Patients.* Report by the iN2015 Healthcare and Biomedical Sciences Sub-Committee. Singapore: Infocomm Development Authority of Singapore.

7. Computer Times (2003, Nov 26). *A Connected Hospital for Improved Patient Care.* http://computertimes.asiaone.com.sg/people/story/0,5104,1624,00.html. Accessed June 18, 2009.

8. Muttitt S. (2008) *Towards a National Electronic Health Record.* HIMSS Asiapac 2008 conference lecture. Hong Kong. http://www.himssasiapac.org/2008/docs/presentations/32_Muttitt.pdf. Accessed June 18, 2009.

9. Chan I. (2007, May 10) S'pore hospital to use tablet-like PC. ZDNet Asia

10. Khalik S. (2009, February 17). SGH Expands New Patient Care. *The Straits Times.* http://www.straitstimes.com/Breaking%2BNews/Singapore/Story/STIStory_339526.html. Accessed June 18, 2009.

11. Friedlos D. (2009). Tan Tock Seng Hospital uses RFID to take patient temperatures. *RFID Journal.* http://www.rfidjournal.com/article/print/4560. Accessed June 18, 2009.

12. Ministry of Health Holdings (2008). *EHR Country Status White Paper.* Singapore: Ministry of Health Holdings.

13. Ministry of Health Holdings (2008). Presentation on *Creating a National Health Record in Singapore.* Walter Lim. Singapore: Ministry of Health Holdings.

14. Staggers N, Gassert CA, Curran C. (2001) Informatics competencies for nurses at four levels of practice. *J Nurs Educ.* 2001;40:303–316.

Case Study 19G

Health and Nursing Informatics in Indian Context: A Futuristic Perspective of e-Healthcare

By Ratna Prakash, PhD, MSc, BSc, BScN, PG DH.Ed;
and Nagendra Prakash Mattur, PhD, MA, M.Phil

Introduction—Background

The prospects of growth for any technology depend on its economic status and socio-cultural environment that emphasizes the IT potential of the country. India is one of the largest democracies, with a population of 1.1 billion, which is growing at a rate of 1.80. The country has a wide diversity in its socio-economic characteristics. There are 6,400 casts and sub-casts, 1,600 minor dialects, 6 major religions, 52 major tribes, and a predominant rural population. The impact of the rural social-cultural systems pervades the urban society and its systems as well.

The Indian economy is diverse, fast-growing, and considered to be the largest economy in the world. Agriculture is the major source of economy, and 65% of the population earns a livelihood from it. Major sectors include manufacturing industries, textiles, handicraft, and services. The service sector is expanding and plays an important role in the country's development. The recent trends in India have been a remarkable advancement in numerous information technology services and progress in the export of these services.

Prospects of Expansion

Currently ranked by the exchange rates of the United States dollar, the Indian economy is the 12th largest in the world. The growing manufacturing sector, information and communication system, education at all levels, and advancement in science and technology provide a tremendous potential for the development and use of IT. The expansion in the education sector is providing a skill-based human resource to meet the requirement in all other sectors. The expansion of these sectors has set the economy on the fast track for growth.

Among the various sectors that have a steady growth rate and major contributions to GDP, the service sector and industrial sector have significant roles. The contribution of both the sectors in the country's GDP is 53% and 29%, respectively.

The potential of the country's economy is well-sustained in high investment and saving rate. The gross saving rate, proportional to the GDP, rose from 23.5% to 34.8% during 2007. The gross capital in GDP showed a rise from 22.8% during 2001 to 35.9% by 2006. From the point of overall performance and growth, the economy is leading toward steady growth and promising further scope of expansion in the IT industry, manufacturing, and the service sector.

Health Infrastructure

The government has a great responsibility to provide healthcare free of cost to the large dependent rural population, with its low purchasing power. However, the private healthcare industry is rapidly expanding at all levels and is important in serving people's health needs.

The Indian healthcare services industry is composed of both public and private organizations. The Union of Health and Family Planning is the apex body that formulates policies and implements various health programs. The Director General of Health Services (Union Government) provides technical advice on all health matters and implementation of health services. The organization of Public and Private sectors are briefly presented next.

Public Health as Managed by the Government

Public health in India is managed by five sectors: Public Health Sector, Private Health Sector, Indigenous Health Systems, Voluntary Health agencies, and National Health Programs. Each of these operates at different levels. The organizational structure of the public health system from the village level to the district level is presented in Figure 19G-1.

A brief description of the areas mentioned in Figure 19G-1 is provided next.

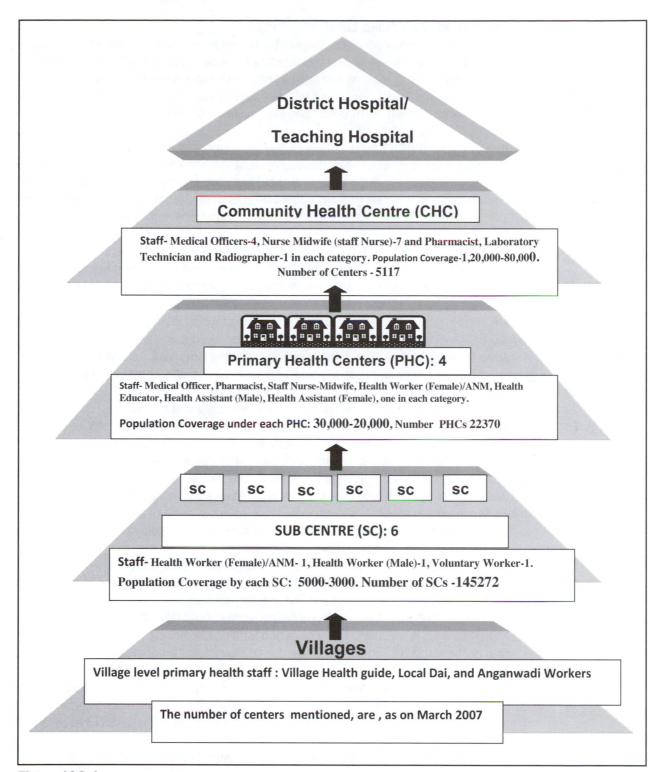

Figure 19G-1. *Rural Healthcare System in India. Adapted from www.nrhmcommunityaction.org.*

Each health center is established according to the population it is expected to cover. Compared with the centers in the general/plain regions, these centers are established for a smaller population in the tribal regions, hilly areas, and backward regions. For example, a sub centre exists for every 3,000 population in the backward/hilly regions. In plain regions, there is a center for every 5,000 population. Likewise, in primary health centers and community health centers, the development of the region is taken into consideration in providing primary care services.

Healthcare Providers at the Village Level

Public health service is provided at the micro-level village by the trained female Village Health Guide (VHG), the local Dais, and Anganwadies. The services consist of conducting home deliveries, immunizations, non-formal pre-school education, nutritional supplements and referral services to mothers and pre-school children.

1. **Sub-Center (SC).** This is a peripheral outpost of healthcare delivery and renders maternal and child care, family planning, and immunization. Each center has two multipurpose health workers and two health assistants.

2. **The Primary Health Center (PHC).** The PHC covers all the eight elements of primary care. Under the basic requirements, it provides services such as safe drinking water, health education, basic sanitation, and the prevention and control of diseases. PHCs perform surgical procedures, vasectomy, tubectomy, titanium joint replacement surgery, and minor surgical procedures. Other functions include referral services to community health centers, implementing national health programs, registering and maintaining vital health statistics.

   - *Community Health Center (CHC).* The CHCs were created by upgrading PHCs. Their population coverage is 80,000 to 100,000, with a bed strength of thirty and specialists in surgery, medicine, OBG and pediatrics. The centers have laboratory and x-ray facilities. The specialists in the CHC may refer patients to the District level Hospital or to the nearest Medical College Hospital.

3. **Rural Hospitals.** There is no specific center at which the rural hospital is situated. Usually these are located in the taluk/sub-divisional headquarters and each Rural Hospital covers a population of 500,000.

4. **District Hospitals/Health Centers/Specialty Hospitals/Teaching Hospitals.** All district hospitals are usually general hospitals or teaching hospitals and may be located at the district headquarters or in capitols of states within India. The hospitals located at the capitals are the medical college hospitals. The government medical college hospitals are established in different regions of the country.

5. **ESI Hospitals.** These hospitals are managed by the ESI Corporation of the Labor Ministry of India. The corporation provides all types of secondary and tertiary services free of cost to all employees insured under the ESI Act. In 2002, this included 183 hospitals and 1,453 dispensaries.

6. **CGHS Hospitals.** These hospitals are managed by Central Government Health Service and provide all types of healthcare, including specialized care. The plan is based on a cooperative effort by the employers and employees. There are 320 hospitals and dispensaries in various systems of medicine, which provide services to 4.27 million beneficiaries. The ESI and the CGHS schemes cover the two largest groups, state government and central government employees.

7. **Defense Hospitals.** Defense Hospitals provide health services to the defense personnel.

8. **Railway Hospitals.** The Railway Hospitals are for the Railway employees and are situated at the regional headquarters of the railways. They provide general and specialty services.

9. **Indigenous Systems of Medicine.** There are separate government hospitals for indigenous systems of medicine, such as Ayurveda, Homeopathy, Unani, Yoga and Naturopathy. However, the main public health strategy is based on the Allopathic system. The Indigenous health systems are not yet well-integrated into rural healthcare organizational structure.

The private sector has a greater role than the Public sector in Healthcare Education and Service. The private role ranges from small clinics, owned by the General Practitioners, to the large-scale corporate and research institutes. But the healthcare service facility is highly concentrated in the district headquarters, major towns, state capitals, and metropolitan cities.

As depicted in Figure 19G-2, the healthcare delivery system, which is managed by the government, is a massive industry in India, having outreach programs at the grass-root level and specialty and teaching hospitals at the Districts and State Capitals.

The number of health-related institutions and the education of healthcare providers appears to present a picture of equity in the distribution of healthcare delivery (see Table 19G-1). In reality, there is wide disparity in the distribution of various health system institutions between rural and urban areas, with most hospitals of all types of health specialties and 70% of providers located in urban areas. The Ayurvedic, Homoeopathic, and Unani practitioners provide a major part of healthcare in rural areas. In short, 70% of the rural population is deprived of healthcare employment and education accessibility. The private health sector delivers health services through Allopathic, Ayurvedic, Unani, Siddha, and Homoeopathic (AYUSH) professionals. This

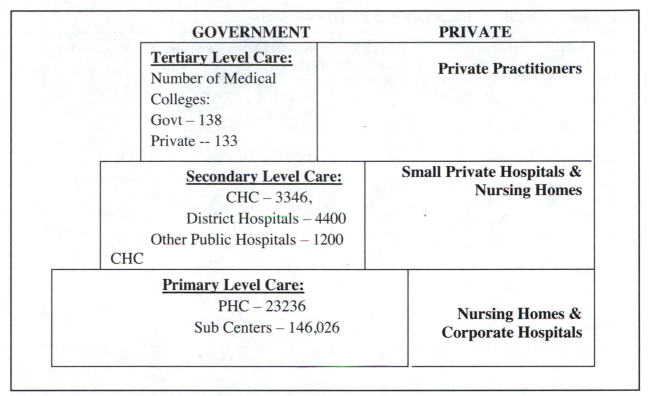

Figure 19G-2. *India's Healthcare Delivery System at a Glance*

accounts for 82% of overall healthcare expenditure, compared with the public sector. Healthcare facilities range from 1 to 10 bed Nursing Homes to Corporate Hospitals with Multi-Specialty and Super-Specialty treatment facilities. The Healthcare Sector employs approximately 4 million people.

As of March 2008, there were 1.28 million nurses in India and accordingly the nurse - population ratio is 1:859. Table 19G-2 includes a total of more than 2,100 educational programs preparing more than 30,000 graduates a year; there are an expanding number of graduates each year to meet workforce needs. This massive manpower can be used optimally to provide healthcare at all levels. The significance of informatics, if applied properly, can release the potential of nursing professionals to liberate the Indian subcontinent from major health issues.

Healthcare Expenditure

The total national expenditure on healthcare in 2006 was nearly 5.3% of GDP ($45 billion), out of which private spending was 82% and government share was 18% (1.3 of GDP). A major part of healthcare expenditure is borne by the individual household followed by government spending and a very small amount is covered by the Insurance Sector. The individual households bear 70 – 75% of the healthcare cost. The problem with healthcare expenditure is that the Health Insurance is not well utilized by people due to lack of awareness. The growth of health insurance will promote IT progress in healthcare.

In 2002, the contribution of the healthcare industry to the GDP was 5%, with a projected increased contribution by 2012 of 8.5%. The healthcare expenditure is expected to double over ten years, whereas in the orivate healthcare sector, contribution in this expenditure is supposed to increase from 14.8 billion US dollars to 33.6 billion dollars.

The infrastructure, escalating healthcare expenditure, and increasing contribution of health industry in GDP indicate a positive prospect for expanding the IT application in the health sector and points to the significant role IT has in enhancing the potential healthcare industry to contribute a larger share in the country's GDP. India is a destination of Medical Tourism.

Table 19G-1. Healthcare Education and Hospitals in India

Medical Systems	Number of Colleges	Annual Number of Graduates	Registered Practitioners	Hospitals: Government & Private, including CHCs	Dispensaries
Allopathy	422	12000	725190*	8202	-
Ayurveda	240	3763	5,00,000	2398	1391
Homeopathy	183	3490	2,17,850	235	5836
Unani	39	785	46,558	267	1010
Siddha	7	150	6,381	277	464
Naturopathy	10	----	888	170	56
Yoga	----	----	----	12	71
Dental	146		73057		
Total	911	20,188	1,271,677	11,405	8,828

*Data - March 2008

Adapted from: Park K, *Park's Textbook of Preventive and Social Medicine.* Jabalpur, India: M/s Banarsidas Bhanot Publishers, 2002, p. 655. Available at www.indiannursingcouncil.org.

Table 19G-2. Nursing Educational Institutions and Nursing Manpower in India

Institutions of Nursing Education and Manpower			
Types of Nursing Institutions	Number of Schools and Colleges	Annual Production of Graduates	Registered Nurse Practitioners
Auxiliary Nurse Midwife Schools	271	-	5,50,958
General Nurse Midwife schools	1112	-	
Basic B.Sc nursing	586	30,000	9,93,256
Post Basic B.Sc nursing	62		
M.Sc Nursing	71		
Total	2,102		

Adapted from: Park K, *Park's Textbook of Preventive and Social Medicine.* Jabalpur, India: M/s Banarsidas Bhanot Publishers, 2002, p. 655. Available at www.indiannursingcouncil.org.

India's Health IT Scenario

From the year 2000, India has ascended as the hub of IT and IT-enabled services. It has become the world's leading destination in IT and related services. While pockets of extraordinary innovation do exist, its national health IT infrastructure and basic infrastructure continue to lag behind other countries. The expenditure for health IT by large corporate hospitals is even below 1% of their entire operating budget for IT, whereas the expenditure in the West is 3%, even though the West outsources IT services to India and other countries.

The Central Bureau of Health Intelligence (CBHI), a national institute established in 1961, is the national nodal institution for health statistics in the country. The directorates of health services of states and union

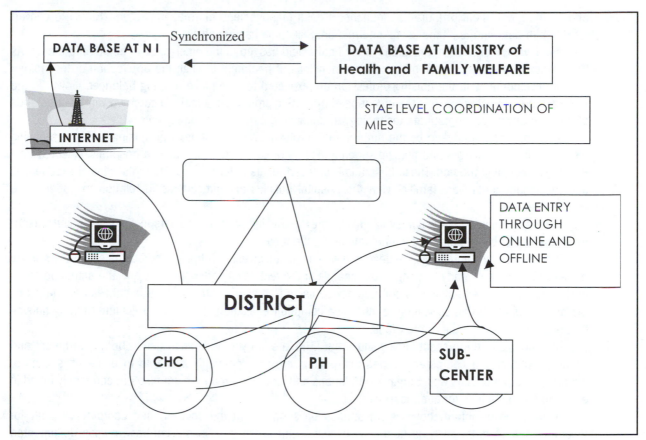

Figure 19G-3. *Work Process for Management Information and Evaluation System*

territories are the primary sources for transmission of health data to the central level. The concept map in Figure 19G-3 shows the process of information flow from bottom to top.

E-health in India is limited to medical transcription and health awareness through portals, telemedicine, hospital management systems, customer service using Internet, and electronic medical record and hospital information and management systems in corporate hospitals and academic medical institutions. The first computerized Health Information System (HIS) in India was established in Sanjay Gandhi PG Institute, Lucknow in 1998.

At present, there are more than 400 Telemedicine platforms in India. National E-Governance Action Plan Initiative includes 100,000 common service centers rendering 80 services, ranging from Mother & Child Care, Immunization, Family Welfare, Manpower Database, Diagnosis & Treatment to Material Management, Medical Research, etc. The private sectors have their own telemedicine centers, e.g., Apollo group of hospitals has 26 centers for rural healthcare. Statewide telemedicine networks have begun in three of the twenty-eight States and seven Union Territories. Government of India Initiative also plans to establish Village Resource Centers in 600,000 villages, with Communication and Remote Sensing Satellite provided by ISRO, to provide information on agriculture, health, education, and natural resources. ISRO Telemedicine Network is established so far in 205 District/Rural Hospitals and 40 Super-Specialty Hospitals. The National Infrastructure and Standardization, Government of India (GOI) has developed guidelines and standards for the practice of telemedicine in India and infrastructure for the national telemedicine grid. The grid connects patient to physician from the time of registration; the physician relates directly to all diagnostic processes. The nurse appears in the network after the patient is admitted to hospital and remains connected at various phases of the patient's treatment, recovery, and discharge or death and last rights. Networking facility for networking of national medical institutes and e-learning in health services facility has been created. More than nine giant IT agencies are engaged in research and development in medical technologies and diagnostics.

The Telemedicine Society of India (http://www.telemedicineindia.org), The Indian Association of Medical Informatics (http://www.iami.org), CBHI, and HS-PROD under the Ministry of Health and Family Welfare, Networking collaborations and projects with IBM, Apollo Group, all are striving to take the health informatics ahead. The government of India has launched Health Management Information System (HMIS) to convert local health data into real time useful information. Still, India has a long way to go.

The development in IT applications in the health field has led to the emergence of health informatics. As the medical profession is promoting newer dimensions of treatment through the application of technology, similar developments in the nursing profession are expected to take place to bring balanced growth in the management of healthcare. It is the urgent need of nursing profession in India to catch up with the demands of the time and apply appropriate technology to enhance the quality of nursing care.

A survey was undertaken by the authors that involved 37 administrators of nursing colleges, teaching faculty of nursing colleges and nursing superintendents of government and private hospitals, selected by a Purposive Sampling method. These hospitals were used regularly for Nursing Students' clinical experiences and the respondents were familiar with the hospital policies and procedures in relation to patient care documentations.

The major objective of the survey was to explore the existing practice and perspectives of nursing personnel in the use of computers for documentation of patient care.

This case study summarizes the degree to which the nurses use electronic records, the extent the nursing profession in India is ready to bring about change in the technology of healthcare, and the actual potential of the profession in enhancing its competency by using IT. It also summarizes the initiatives undertaken by the promoters of nursing education to introduce computer education in nursing curriculum to bring nursing that is on par with the other professions.

The findings of the present survey show that EHRs are not yet in common use in both government and private hospitals and computer-assisted instructions are not commonly available to either physicians or nurses and to patients as well. Surgical simulations and virtual environment are also not commonly found in educational institutions for healthcare professionals.

Observation on information system application showed that the doctors used computers mainly for recording patient data, such as health assessment and prognosis. On the contrary, nurses documented medications, lab results, patient requests, and equipment and supplies.

In 80% of the government hospitals and 55% of the private hospitals, nurses used computers to enter medications administered, whereas very few entered patients' baseline information.

It was found that in most of the hospitals, trauma centers, general wards, private wards and ICUs, nurses made use of computer to enter data on a larger scale, compared with the physicians, while in areas for which nurses were not involved in direct patient care, such as, OPD, Operating Rooms, and Clinical Labs, the computer entry of patient information by nurses was minimal. These differences are obviously related to the nature of responsibility of health professionals in the patient care arena.

The survey respondents' opinions on the implications of nursing informatics were manifold. Much required changes in both undergraduate and graduate education curricula needed to make curricula healthcare-focused, which in turn can promote an atmosphere of evidence-based nursing practice at all levels, thus adding quality to both education and practice. They also expressed that innovation was required in developing nursing care protocols, procedures, and modules using technology for developing nursing informatics and bringing awareness among Indian nurses about its importance. They emphasized that the HIS packages currently used in hospitals must include components supporting nursing process.

As the number of beds increases, handling data becomes more and more complex. The use of the EHR would be most beneficial in such situations. It saves time and resources. It can make healthcare cost-effective in terms of saving manpower, money, and time, as well as providing accuracy and accessibility to voluminous data. The use of computers by physicians in hospitals is considered an indication of the prospects of computer usage in all healthcare service sectors. It also gives an idea of the possibility of its application in nursing care. Nursing care process and decision making for nursing in India are still dependent on the decisions of the medical superintendents and the medical profession.

A critical view of the existing HIS role in India illustrates the extent to which facilities and practices are utilized. In advanced healthcare set-up, HIS plays a vital role in decision making in all areas of functioning. Documented research findings show that in India, healthcare professionals are becoming aware of its appropriate utilization and significant outcome.

Study findings of a 1,200 bed tertiary care hospital showed that the overall opinion of managers, physicians, and patients about the existing HIS application was satisfactory (80%). The majority (85%) opined that non-existence of ward computers was affecting patient care; however, 80% expressed that installation of HIS was delaying the OPD consultation.

In another study, investigators observed that patient care management had fully utilized the power of computers in Medicare, whereby the network of integrated systems maintaining the database for hospital services in the areas of Pathology, Radiology, In-Patient admissions and Billing, Medical Research, Medical stores and Pharmacy are operational. The implementation of these modules have evolved user-friendly computerized systems which are loved and cared by all, as they help to provide quality services.

From a literature search, a generally grim picture of the extent to which the HIS in India is developed and applied is observed. In major hospitals in the cities and state capitals, doctors, nurses and lab technicians enter patient data. However, the EHRs which are being used for research projects do not have complete information regarding treatment and nursing care. Computer-assistance instructions to doctors and nurses are not present. Also the computer-assisted imaging and surgery facility is available only in a few super-specialty hospitals. There is a lack of evidence of sharing best practices.

At the government institutional level, the practice of paper entry still continues; records are carried manually from level to level, and there is no evidence of improvement in quality of care by way of feedback from healthcare functionaries and patients.

Nursing manpower is the largest manpower in the healthcare industry in India. The number of nursing educational institutions is also the largest, compared with other institutions in the healthcare professions. This promises a great future for nursing informatics; from the point of view of human resource and skills, the potential in the nursing profession is enormous. This potential needs to be combined with awareness to apply IT to promote professional skill and competency. A strong professional identity has to emerge among the nurses, so that empowerment of nurses leads the era of change. Only by empowering nurses will the technology of care develop, which can be called caring information technology (CIT). Empowerment alone holds the key for nursing informatics in India.

A concept plan is presented next to highlight how the empowerment of nurses can release the potential for optimum health of the entire population.

Model of People-Nurse Empowerment

The existing model of nursing does not encourage the scope of integrating and accessing data from the sources presented in the earlier model. This is related to the job descriptions and the attitude of policy makers in designing the role of a nurse/public health nurse. Based on the model shown in Figure 19G-4, nursing can be optimized in the service of public health.

Summary

Nursing professional knowledge by virtue of multidisciplinary integration has developed into a trans-disciplinary science. Among the healthcare professions, no other field is more holistic than nursing in terms of its philosophy and objectives. The nursing practice alone explores various knowledge practices available in knowledge systems, compared with the medical field. This quality of nursing is derived from the professional experience working at the grass-roots level to the top. The professional functioning from bottom to top or from grass-roots to the top-level of the profession is the essence of a collaborative role exclusive to nursing. Hence, the nurse is a knowledge and skill data bank of all dimensions of health, as well a community resource.

The system design in healthcare has limited the nurses' freedom in functioning. The empowerment of nursing has to take place by extending greater freedom of decision making and extending greater authority; only then will the maximization of potential and competency of functioning be possible. When this happens, innovations in nursing and the application of those innovations will take place.

In the Indian context, the expansion of IT in the health sector needs to focus on the health of the people. Currently, IT expansion is focused on technology of treatment only. The application of technology with a focus on people is possible by expanding IT in nursing care.

In the hospital context, nursing informatics can promote complementary and alternative therapies. In the rural community, integrating IT has to take place by enabling data generation and integration of all sectors. In this mission, nurses can become the central figures to perform this function. The data integration generates virtual knowledge. This virtual knowledge is derived by the nurses' collaborative role. The areas of

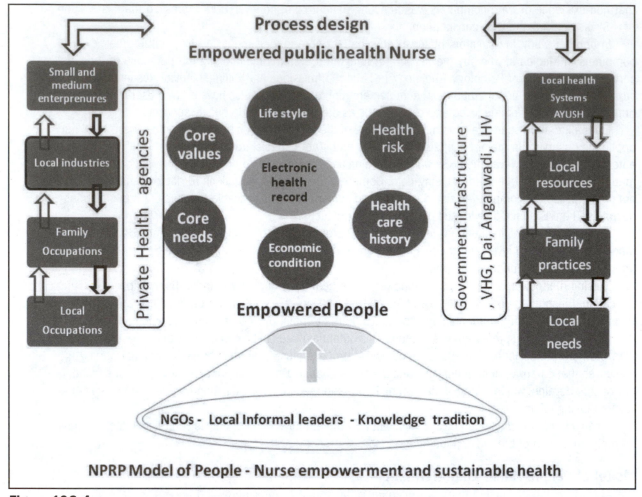

Figure 19G-4. *NPRP Model of People–Nurse Empowerment and Sustainable Health*

knowledge input are grass-roots level contact, knowledge tradition, NGOs, indigenous medical systems, local occupations, and local industries. The electronic input derived from these sources enables the public health nurse to design Public Health Process at the micro level. It will be possible to combine local needs, local resources, and formal knowledge. This synthesis leads to innovation and promotes real knowledge management of healthcare, appropriate to local needs and economic endurance. Sustainable health will be possible through this mechanism.

Two major drawbacks have circumscribed nursing from achieving this goal:

1. Nursing care regulated by an allopathic model
2. Lack of recognition of knowledge generated by the nursing profession

The issues of public health will continue to threaten societies until the link between the grass-roots and the top-level are integrated and the public health nurse is empowered and well-trained.

Bibliography

Ball MJ, Morris CF. *Aspects of the Computer-based Patient Record.* New York: Springer-Verlag, 1992.

Bansal M. *Medical Informatics: A Premier.* New Delhi: Tata McGraw-Hill Publishing Company Limited, 2003.

Burke L, Weill B. *Information Technology for the Health Professions.* New Jersey: Upper Saddle River, Pearson Education, Inc. (Prentice Hall), 2005.

Datanet India Pvt. Ltd. http://www.indiastat.com/default.aspx. Accessed December 1, 2009.

Department of Indian Systems of Medicine and Homoeopathy (ISM&H). http://www.indianmedicine.nic.in. Accessed October 20, 2009.

Mahanty R, Rana SD, Kolay SK. *HIS in Medicare: An experience at Tata Main Hospital, Jamshedpur.* Indian Jr. of Occupational and Environmental Medicine. October-December, 1999;3(4):187-190.

McLachlan G, Shegog RA, eds. *Computers in the Service of Medicine: Essays on current research and applications.* Volume 1. London, New York, Published for the Nuffield Provincial Hospitals Trust by the Oxford University Press; 1969.

Naik P, Sarkar P. *J Med Infor* 2004;1:.2.

National Health Information Infrastructure and Standardization. www.mit.gov.in http://www.Telemedindia.org./original_articles. pdf. Accessed October 20, 2009.

Pacific Health Summit – HIT Case Studies. http://pacific health summit.org. Accessed October 20, 2009.

Park K. *Park's textbook of preventive and social medicine.* Jabalpur, India: M/s Banarsidas Bhanot Publishers, 2002; 655. http://www.indiannursingcouncil.org.

Praveen KA, Gomes LA. *A study of the HIS in Medical Records Dept. of a Tertiary Teaching Hospital.* Jr. Academy of Hospital Administration, 2006;18;1:1-12.

Sanjay Gandhi Postgraduate Institute of Medical Sciences Lucknow School of Telemedicine. www.sgpgi-telemedicine.org. Accessed October 20, 2009.

Virk P, Khan S, Kumar V: *The WHO Country Report.* Geneva; 2006.

Virk P, Khan S, Kumar V. *India HIT Case Study.* NBR Center for Health and Aging, Health Information Technology and Policy Lab. The National Bureau of Asian Research. The Indian Brand Equity Foundation. The Health Sector Report; 2006, www.ibef.org.

Weaver CA, Delaney CW, Weber P, Carr RL. *Nursing and Informatics for the 21st Century.* Chicago: HIMSS, 2006.

Case Study 19H

Health and Nursing Information Technology: A Case Study of Pakistan

By Rafat Jan, PhD, RN; Arusa Lakhani, MScN, BScN, RN, RM; and Nighat Ijaz Durrani, MPH(PAK), Dip in Administration & Teaching, Opthlamic Nursing UK, RN, RM

Introduction

Pakistan

Pakistan is situated in a strategic geographical location connecting world economic giants India and China on one side and developing economies, such as Afghanistan and Iran on the other. Pakistan also includes a large costal area with the Arabian Sea to the south, complemented by the northern and western highlands featuring the towering Karakoram and Pamir mountain ranges, which include some of the world's highest peaks: K2 (28,250 ft; 8,611 m) and Nanga Parbat (26,660 ft; 8,126 m).

In 1947, British rule came to an end in the Asian subcontinent and, as events unfolded, Pakistan and India were created. Pakistan, located in south Asia, has a population of approximately 1.6 million. It has four provinces: Sind, Punjab, Baluchistan and the North West Frontier Province (NWFP); and disputed territories of Federally Administered Tribal Areas (FATA); part of Kashmir; and northern areas of Pakistan.

Pakistan is a multilingual country with more than 60 languages spoken. Urdu is the national language of Pakistan, while English is the official language. The internal security and border patrol are carried out by three main services including the Army, Air Force and Navy. Pakistani society is largely hierarchical and regarded as a patriarchal society. Most of the urban families choose to stay in a nuclear family system due to socio-economic limitations. Approximately 20% of the population live below the international poverty line of US $1.5 a day. The Pakistan economy has changed from a mainly agricultural base to a powerful service base structure. In today's era, the service sector accounts for approximately 52% of the GDP. The education system in Pakistan is divided into five levels: (a) primary (grades one through five), (b) secondary (grades six through eight), (c) high (grades nine and ten), (d) intermediate (grades eleven and twelve) and (e) university (graduate and advance studies).

Pakistan has witnessed a strong growth in information technology (IT) and telecommunications in the last few years. The IT market was estimated to be $1billion by the end of 2008. On the other hand, Pakistan's telecom market has seen a huge growth mainly because of cellular companies. This sector is growing at 170% annually and is contributing 2% to the GDP. There are many best international IT companies now operating in Pakistan. Fiber optics connections are available in major cities of Pakistan.

Pakistan has developed expertise in various IT areas, including mobile technologies; Web development; call centers; medical transcription; telesales and telemarketing; document management; accounting and billing services; HR hiring and administration; and software and solution development. The government of Pakistan has a keen interest in the IT industry. As a result, the Higher Education Commission has video conferencing and a digital library connected to major national universities libraries. Further, government is also supporting some initiatives in telemedicine.

Overview of Healthcare and the Health System

The healthcare system of Pakistan comprises the Federal Ministry of Health, Directorate of Health, provincial health systems, and districts and city governments. Both at the federal and province level, the Department of Health of Pakistan is structured in two main areas: (1) the Health Secretariat, and (2) the Directorate General Health Services Each province is divided into districts or towns that further divide into a *tehsil* or *taluka*. Under the Pakistani constitution, the primary responsibility for healthcare services lies with the provincial government, while the federal government engages in planning and formulating policy. The healthcare system of Pakistan has both private and public health facilities. There are 796 hospitals, 93,907 hospital beds, 5,171 basic health units, 531 rural health centers, and 856 maternity and child health centers. In addition to these facilities, people also approach homeopaths, hakeems (traditional physicians), traditional/spiritual healers, and Unani (Greco-Arabic) healers.

The federal health department has the one major responsibility of developing human resource planning through a variety of training programs, such as medical education, tertiary medical care, specialized medical treatments, nursing, midwifery, and Lady Health Visitor (LHV) programs, as well as allied and para-medical programs. Healthcare workers include 91,823 physicians, 37,623 nurses, 4,175 dentists, 22,528 paramedics, and 5,619 female health workers. Pakistan is a signatory to the UN Millennium Development Goals (MDG), 2000-2015. Three of the eight MDGs, with four targets and sixteen indicators, are directly related to the health sector. Some of the federally funded programmes to improve the health of the Pakistani people are: Lady Health Worker Programme; National Maternal and Child Health Programme, the Expanded Programme on Immunization, Malaria Control Programme, Tuberculosis and HIV/AIDS Control Programme, Cancer Treatment Programme, Food and Nutrition Programme, and the Preventive Programme for Control of Hepatitis A & B. Due to the scattered geography, it is imperative to use ITs in the health field.

Because nurses, midwives, and LHVs play major roles in providing health care services across Pakistan, it is important to know about their education and the regulatory body that supports them in their role in the technology world.

Nursing/Midwifery/LHV Education

Pakistan recognized nursing and midwifery as healthcare professions in the early 1900s. Today there are 109 schools of nursing, 144 schools of midwifery, 28 public health schools, and 9 colleges of nursing. The schools of nursing and midwifery provide basic diploma and degree education, while colleges of nursing provide an advanced level of education. Several kinds of diplomas in nursing and midwifery education with various duration are available in Pakistan including: (1) three years general nursing education for a diploma in RN, (2) one year midwifery and one year in public health school for diploma in Lady Health Visitor, (3) 15 months midwifery education for RM diploma, (4) and 18 months midwifery education for the diploma in community midwifery (CMW). Recently, Pakistan has embarked on degree education including: (1) four years of nursing education for Baccalaureates in Nursing degree with RN license, (2) two years for a Post RN Baccalaureate in Nursing education, and (3) two years for the Master's in Nursing degree. According to recent statistics from the Pakistan Nursing Council database (2009), there are 47,200 nurses, 4,752 LHVs, 3,162 midwives, and 158 Dias (Traditional Birth attendants) in the existing healthcare workforce.

The Pakistan Nursing Council

The Pakistan Nursing Council (PNC) is the regulatory body for education and licensing for nurses, midwives, and LHVs in Pakistan (PNC Act 1972). PNC was established in Karachi, Pakistan under the Central Nursing Ordinance Act 1948. The National Assembly passed the Act of PNC in 1952, making the PNC a legal regulatory body to oversee a uniform system of training for nurses, midwives, LHVs, and Nursing Auxiliaries. A further streamlining of training was done in 1973. All the nursing and midwifery graduates are now expected to register themselves with the PNC after passing their examination, which is administered by nursing examination boards.

Overview of Health Information Technology

Mobile and e-technology are the fastest growing technology areas in Pakistan. The web of fiber optics lines and wireless technologies has proliferated the urban centers. All technologies in cities have broadband availability. However, rural areas of Pakistan do not have broadband and have few technology resources and other facilities, such as education, economic opportunities, and effective health facilities.

Although many medical doctors graduate in Pakistan each year, very few choose to serve the rural population. Therefore, nurses and midwives or other auxiliaries provide healthcare services in rural areas. During the last couple of years, efforts been made to connect rural Pakistanis to physicians in the city. However, this effort has had limited success and has not affected the general population. There is some work being done in the area of Medi-Connect to create a centralized database of healthcare facilities in Pakistan.

With the poor indicators of health, especially high maternal and neonate mortality and morbidity rates, the government is now investing more to develop midwives and nurses who can serve in rural areas. Such gaps and disparities in healthcare availability, lack of quality of healthcare, and lack of effectively trained human resources are seen as poor indicators. As a result, like many developing countries and in line with WHO objectives, many experts feel that e-health and e-education will be solutions for developing world populations. WHO highlights that e-health has three main areas including: (1) delivery of health information for both health professionals and health consumers via the Internet and telecommunications; (2) using IT and e-commerce for improvement of public health services through capacity building of health force; and (3) using e-commerce and e-business practices for health systems management.

Congruent with the WHO vision, many developing countries including Pakistan launched sporadic initiatives of telemedicine for physicians, supported by the government and international funding agencies. Several institutions in Pakistan currently offer telemedicine emanating from high resource urban areas to low resource rural areas. There are several projects funded by U.S. universities and software companies and USAID to assist Pakistani medical professionals to build capacity in telemedicine and provide services through telemedicine. Several individual universities are involved in telemedicine training and services. One of the hospitals has initiated a project on an Alert System for Child Pneumonia with NOKIA, in collaboration with MIT and Johns Hopkins.

An additional example of telemedicine application is the Pakistan Space and Upper Atmosphere Research Commission (SUPARCO), the country's national space agency. It is responsible for the execution of the space science and technology programs in the country, as approved by the government of Pakistan.

SUPARCO has now embarked in telemedicine initiatives by launching Pakistan's first satellite-based network. It has connected Jinnah Post Medical Centre hospital in Karachi with a remote medical center at Shikarpur for patient evaluation and consultation. This network has been established in Sindh province. The next step is development of satellite-based telemedicine centers at the Holy Family Hospital, Rawalpindi in Punjab province, and primary care centers in Muzaffarabad. This project exemplifies the role space technology can play in the geographical isolation of northern areas and healthcare inaccessible areas. Mostly institutional projects are tele-consultation based on storing and forwarding information and/or real-time consultation.

Very recently, through Rockefeller Foundation funding, the e-Health Association for Pakistan (eHAP) initiated the promotion and adoption of evidence-based, informed, and integrated e-health as a main component of health services and education in Pakistan. At the national level, the Ministry of Science and Technology established the National Telemedicine Forum in September 2001, with the main objective of developing and enhancing collaboration among IT and medicine for telemedicine initiatives. This forum will also support increasing awareness about telemedicine in the country.

While the country has been advancing e-health and e-technology, nurses are struggling to become part of these initiatives. There are very few hospitals in which nurses are using IT and e-technologies to develop their capacity. One of these few hospitals is Aga Khan University Hospital (AKUH) where nurses are given complete information and computer training for use in patient care areas. Nurses use IT for entering patient clinical data in EHRs. Nurses usually enter patient assessment, medication entry, request entry, etc.

Nurses at the Aga Khan University are also using synchronous and asynchronous technology to build their capacity for tele-teaching, tele-meetings, and tele-consultations. The e-learning team of the university also conducts needs assessment of nurses for using e-learning and informational technologies. Almost all nurses demonstrate keen interest in using e-learning and IT. Nurses, midwives, and LHVs note that due to culture restrictions and family demands, it is imperative to use information technologies, e-health, and e-tools to provide quality clinical care to society and to maintain continuing education and research initiatives.

Some nursing documentation is stored at the AKUH as part of patient records. This includes data related to admission discharge and transfer of patients, outpatient management, nutrition care management, vital signs, immunization record, clinical pathways, critical care management, electronic medication administration, and online nursing documentation. Nurses realize the importance of standardized nursing languages, and they are keen to initiate them.

While nurses are moving toward advanced informational technologies in healthcare, they are farther ahead in maintaining automated health human resource data called the Nursing Registration System of Pakistan. This database is administratively managed by the Pakistan Nursing Council (PNC). This database can benefit future plans for human resource planning and development and training of nurses and midwives in Pakistan and in other developing countries.

The purpose of the registration is to provide legal support for the nursing practice, ensure accuracy in registration data and recordkeeping, provide professional accountability, and assign responsibilities for all nursing interventions. In addition, it contributes toward planning and human resource development for the health sector (in general) and nursing (in particular) and maintains an accurate profile of the nursing personnel that are active in the healthcare system. Until 1996, PNC had graduate nursing data that was paper-based. The nurses and midwives completed paper applications and mailed them to the PNC. The clerks at the PNC then transferred the written information into registers and stored the application forms into binders. The challenges of a paper-driven database were numerous, such as papers lost, absence of uniformity in records, related financial burden and time-consuming paperwork, no tracking system, and non-availability of aggregated reports. Information was difficult to retrieve and use when required for statistics on the number and type of practicing nurses and midwives was needed.

The outcomes of the computerized nursing management system database included accurate data with timely retrieval, tracking nursing and midwifery workforces, standardized and uniform documentation; easy storage and retrieval of HRH data; projecting future trends for HRH; validating licenses in a timely manner; and further aggregating data according to the needs of various health departments. In addition, assisting in generating reports for human resource policy decision making was a capability of the new system.

But perhaps one of the most significant advances to propel IS and the EHR in Pakistan was the creation of the Health Management Information System (HIMS) of Pakistan in the early 1990s. HIMS is based on the need for timely and accurate health management and serves as the backbone of evidence-based planning and decision making for health personnel and service provision.

Federal and provincial health officials decided that routine reporting systems at the government-managed first-level care facilities (FLCF) must change into a comprehensive and integrated health management information system. Hence, HIMS' birth took place through a consensus-based conference in each province to develop data items.

The objectives of HIMS were two-fold: (a) record information, and (b) monitor the availability of basic items of FLCFs, including Basic Health Units (BHU), Rural Health Centers (RHC), Maternity homes, and dispensaries. The monitoring includes availability of drugs, contraceptives, functionality of equipment, repair and maintenance of facilities and utilities.

The information in HIMS includes preventive care for mothers (with number of deliveries and antenatal visits) and children younger than five years, referrals, immunization, epidemic diseases, 18 priority health problems, drug supply and distribution, and information related to status of instruments and equipment. As a result, a comparison among districts made for improved healthcare delivery and availability of supplies.

HMIS data flow from FLCF to the District Computer Centers, then to the Provincial Computer Centers. Ultimately, the information arrives at the National HMIS division on computer diskettes. The data are then synthesized and analyzed via Statistical Package of Social Sciences (SPSS) software. The quarterly reports are then distributed to various stakeholders.

There are several benefits of the HIMS system in Pakistan: (a) the information flows from FLFC to district and provincial levels to the national level, (b) nearly 117 of 120 districts provide data, hence coverage and range of information are very wide, and (c) all districts participate in data collection.

There are several challenges for HIMS. One of the major challenges is that HIMS has limited information up to FLCF; it does not include any tertiary care facility in the government or private sectors. This is perhaps because HIMS' major goal is data collection at primary care facilities rather than from tertiary level hospitals. As a result, to date hospitals do not have EHRs for patients at the individual level, and none of the indicators submitted to national level. Consequently, monitoring of institutions is not possible.

The second most concerning challenge is that at the FLCF level, there are other programmes, such as the Expanded Programme on Immunization (EPI), Malaria Control Program, National AIDS Prevention and Control Programme, National ARI Control Programme, Tuberculosis Control Programme, and the National Leprosy Control Programme that collect parallel data for specific needs. As a result, duplication and redundancy exist in HIMS data, because data collectors submit several data and some data is submitted late. Reports are generated; however, no feedback is incorporated from the grassroots level.

Consequently, health planners and policy makers do not use HIMS data because of the lack of timely data reporting and feedback and the availability of too many different databases. Therefore, no plan is currently in development on evidence in healthcare. By 2009, Pakistan has become one of fastest growing in mobile technology, along with fiber optics and easy access to computer centers and cafés. It is imperative to expand HIMS to all levels, especially the tertiary level. HIMS must include hospital information, and this may expedite the move toward EHRs.

Summary

Due to family demands, cultural expectation, and lack of mobility of women in general and particularly for nurses and midwives, informational technologies, telenursing and midwifery, and other e-tools for patient care and continuing education will be the answer for empowering nurses and nursing. It has been highlighted that Pakistan is the fastest growing country in informational and mobile technologies. Some current examples in this case study provide clear evidence of telemedicine and other informational technologies that provide communication, networking, and quality of patient care from high-resource areas to low-resource areas and are working well even in disaster areas. These technologies are used by nurses and midwives who are the major healthcare providers in the rural areas of Pakistan.

Acknowledgment

The authors would like to thank Karen Bashir for her contribution to this case study.

Bibliography

Aga Khan University. http://aku.edu. Accessed October 20, 2009.

Aga Khan University School of Nursing. http://aku.edu/SON/. Accessed October 20, 2009.

Ali M, Horikoshi Y. Situation analysis of health management information system in Pakistan. *Pakistan Journal of Medical Research.* 2002;41(2).

Amarsi Y. *Key Stakeholders Perceptions of Nursing Human Resource Development in Pakistan: A situational analysis.* Unpublished dissertation, McMaster University Hamilton, Ontario. 1998.

Assessing the Impact of Devolution on Healthcare and Education in Pakistan. http://www.urban.org/UploadedPDF/411318_pakistan_project.pdf. Accessed April 20, 2009.

Capacity Project. Global HRIS strengthening [Web site]. Chapel Hill, NC: Capacity Project, 2008. http://www.capacityproject.org/hris/. Accessed April 14, 2009.

Decentralization support programmes. http://www.decentralization.org.pk/index.asp. Accessed April 14, 2009.

Djibuti M, Gotsadze G, Mataradze G, Menabde G. Human resources for health challenges of public health system reform in Georgia. *Human Resources for Health* 2008;6:8

eHealth Association of Pakistan. http://www.ehap.net.pk/. Accessed August 18, 2009.

eHealth. http://www.euro.who.int/telemed. Accessed August 24, 2009.

Gupta N, Dal Poz MR. Assessment of human resources for health using cross-national comparison of facility surveys in six countries. *Human Resources for Health.* 2009;7:22

Higher Education Commission Pakistan. http://www.hec.gov.pk/ Accessed April 28, 2009.

Homedes N, Ugalde A. Human resources: the Cinderella of health sector reform in Latin America. *Human Resources for Health.* 2005;3:1.

Islam A. Health sector reform in Pakistan: Future directions. *J Pak Med Assoc.* 2002;52,174.

Kabene SM, Orchard C, Howard JM, Soriano MA, Leduc R. The importance of human resources management in health care: a global context. *Human Resources for Health.* 2006;4:20.

Khowaja K. Healthcare Systems and Care Delivery in Pakistan. *J Nurs Adm.* 2009;39(6):263-265.

Lincoln Chen, et al. Human resources for health: overcoming the crisis. *Lancet.* 2004;364:1984–1990.

Government of Paksitan: Ministry of Health. http://www.health.gov.pk/. Accessed July 24, 2009.

Pakistan Nursing Council. http://www.pnc.org.pk/. Accessed July 12, 2009.

Pakistan Space and Upper Atmosphere Research Commission (SUPARCO). *Tele-Medicine Pilot Project.* http://www.suparco.gov.pk/pages/tele-medicine.asp?telelinksid=1. Accessed August 24, 2009.

Paracha SA. *Devolution Plan: Context, implementation and issues.* Budapest, Hungary: Open Society Institute, 2003.

Riley PL, Vindigni SM, Arudo J, et al. Developing a Nursing Database System in Kenya. *Health Research and Educational Trust.* [Serial Number] 2007.

Role of information technology in the development of Pakistan. http://www.khwarzimic.org/takveen/infotech_pakistan.pdf. Accessed August 18, 2009.

Telemedicine in Pakistan. http://www.telmedpak.com/Telemedicine/. Accessed August 23, 2009.

Werley HH, Lang NM. *Identification of the nursing minimum data set.* New York: Springer, 1988.

Werley HH, Lang N. The consensually derived nursing minimum data set elements and definitions. In: Werley HH, Lang N, eds. *Identification of the Nursing Minimum Dataset,* New York: Springer, 1988:402-411.

Werley HH, Devine EC, Zorn CR, Ryan P, Westra BL. The nursing minimum data set: abstraction tool for standardized, comparable, essential data. *Am J Pub Health.* 1991;81:421-426.

The Near Future and Nursing

SECTION V

Introduction

By Charlotte A. Weaver, PhD, MSPH, RN, FHIMSS

Chapter 20, written by the four book editors (Weaver, Delaney, Weber, and Carr), is a book-end to Angela McBride's opening chapter. Starting with the international definition of nursing, Chapter 20 traces the imperatives being pushed by health reforms: new communications (Internet) and information technologies and the growing segment of chronically ill patients, including the aged, in our nations' populations. These imperatives are linked to an examination of opportunities and challenges in current day nursing practice and science and call out the contributions and the role of nursing informatics within our present state. The authors emphasize the critical contributions from nursing informaticians' work over the past three decades for achieving international standards for the nursing minimum dataset (iNMDS) and a reference terminology (ICNP®).

The synergies of the EHR era, with nursing positioned to collect a standard set of data using a structured terminology, represent a pivotal turning point in nursing history. Having a standardized nursing reference terminology holds the promise of being able to harmonize the multiple nursing terminologies in use throughout the world. Consequently, not only is research supported at an organizational, local, and national level, but a common terminology base will also allow for comparative nursing research across countries. Increasingly, as countries automate the core clinical processes of nurses and other members of the healthcare team across primary, community, and acute care settings, nurses will have their care delivery captured in structured, electronic databases. The significance of this milestone for nursing is that the medium for discovering nursing's contribution to outcomes will be fully developed as the base for all current and future nursing efforts. Additionally, this rich research database will be available to nursing science for generating new knowledge and determining best practices. Nursing stands to benefit the most from this new world. As McBride points out, our "invisibility" will disappear and in its place will be opportunity for independent practice, accountability, and interprofessional collaboration for a position of strength.

Weaver and colleagues relate this potential to their projection for a "preferred future" vision for nursing. Additionally, the demographic and financial pressures in play across our societies today are forcing new economic models that have as a common theme "individual empowerment" with accountability for prevention, wellness, and self-management. And these new care models hold rich new areas for nursing in primary and home healthcare as coaches and facilitators to individuals in their self-management and empowerment. However, embracing this preferred future vision means that nursing integrates information and communication technology competencies into their practice, education, science, and leadership/management. As we step across this threshold into the second decade of the 21st century, we too pose McBride's question: "What will nurses do with this opportunity?" As we reflect on the work reported in this 2nd edition, we are very optimistic that nursing will fully embrace these new opportunities in practice, education, and research to firmly come into its own as a discipline grounded in independent science. This is our preferred future vision for nursing!

CHAPTER 20

Nursing and Nursing Informatics: Current Context To Preferred Future

By Charlotte A. Weaver, PhD, MSPH, RN, FHIMSS; Connie White Delaney, PhD, RN, FAAN, FACMI; Patrick Weber, MA, RN; and Robyn L. Carr, RGON

Introduction

Nursing and other health professions have a social mandate to serve the world's population, now numbered at 6,792,797,015 as of 18:45 UTC (EST+5) on October 25, 2009.[1] When contemplating this obligation from a futurist perspective, one usually first asks: "What is the current context of healthcare?" and "What do we as nurses and nursing bring to present healthcare systems?" Bridging the answers to these two questions helps to frame an understanding of the changes occurring in our healthcare systems and the opportunities that these changes hold for nursing. Answering these questions invariably brings one to the bold call to action for mobilizing technologies and the expert knowledge of informatics to address these opportunities.

As we close this first decade of the 21st century, the forces driving change are scientific advancements, new synergies in information and communication technologies (ICT), and a near global imperative for containing healthcare costs. Within the cost containment imperative resides quality outcomes and expanding access to safe quality care. In this closing chapter, we use this framework to describe our vision of a preferred future that intensely integrates nursing and nursing informatics within a person-centered, care delivery model. This person-centered, care delivery model encompasses population health, self-management in chronic disease, patient empowerment, the healthcare home, and personalized care through genomics.

Demographics Pushing Health Policy

Understanding the current healthcare context also requires understanding the backdrop of two important movements within policymakers' mindsets and worldview. One cultural trend is the ethical and social perspective of equity in access to care, which is discussed next. The second factor is driven by policymakers' awareness of the increasing percentages of older adults in their societies. In the case of the latter, the 2005 U.S. Census cites statistics that show a near doubling in the percentage of population aged 65 years and older between 2005 and 2030.[2] Increased life expectancy and decreased reproduction rates throughout many of the industrialized countries account for the marked growth in the increased percentage of older adults in our societies today.

The aging populations and increased life expectancies of 12 countries are shown in Table 20-1.[3] Japan, France, Norway, Iceland, and Sweden comprise the top five countries with life expectancy at birth exceeding 80 years of age. Life expectancy is increasing in all the industrialized countries, with the older-than-80 years portion of the elderly population increasing the fastest. Table 20-2 illustrates the percentage growth of the older-than-65 years population in the Eurostat reported countries as of 2008.[4] While the average percentage of total population that is 65 years and older for the 27 countries in the European Union is 17% in 2008, Germany, Italy, Sweden, and Belgium all have country averages that exceed this number. Germany shows the fastest growth in its 65 and older population, moving from 15.7% in 1997 to 19.9% in 2008, an increase of 4.2%.[4]

Table 20-1. Growing Life Expectancy in Selected Countries[3].

Life expectancy at birth. Selected countries. 2006

Reprinted with permission from the World Health Organization (WHO), *World Health Statistics 2008,* available at http://www.who.int/whosis/whostat/2008/en/.

These demographics reflect both increased growth in our 65 years and older population but also an increased growth in life expectancy within our aged population. For healthcare utilization and costs, this demographic trend in our elderly population equates to increased use and expenditures because elderly populations have higher incidence and prevalence rates for chronic diseases, as well as prevalence of multiple chronic conditions.[5] According to the Institute of Medicine's (IOM's) 2008 report on the aged population in the United States, the prevalence and number of chronic conditions for Medicare beneficiaries (older than 65 years) is striking.[5p.43] As shown in Table 20-3, within the U.S. aged population, 65% had two or more chronic conditions, and expenditures doubled for each additional chronic condition with the exception of the "four or more" category for which expenditures more than tripled. When looked at in conjunction with the growing percentages of elderly populations within each country, these demographics portray dramatic increases in healthcare utilization and costs unless marked changes are made in care delivery modalities. The health economics of the aging populations brings an urgency to nations' health reforms that care delivery move away from acute and long term care into community and home. Health policies mirror this shift through an emphasis on self-management and optimum wellness in life style and healthy living practices.

Healthcare Reform and Social Equity

Healthcare reform has been one of the top policy initiatives of most industrialized countries since the mid-1980s. Health reform is currently occurring in nearly every Organization for Economic Co-operation & Development (OECD) country in direct response to concerns over growing health expenditures. Government is the primary payer in most of the OECD countries, the Commonwealth countries and, increasingly, the United States. And consequently, there has been particular concern as countries, have experienced growth in their healthcare expenditures as a percentage of their gross domestic product (GDP).[6] Added to this concern is the prospect of an aging population with a high utilization rate, as well as expectations related to the satisfaction of their healthcare needs and wants. Policymakers in all jurisdictions have also become increasingly aware of a body of economic literature that emphasizes scant evidence of the cost-effectiveness or even effectiveness of many healthcare services.[7,8] A general

Table 20-2. Proportion of Population Aged 65 and Older for Selected Countries 1997 – 2008 [EUROSTAT Oct 28, 2009]

	1997	1998	1999	2000	2001	2002	2003	2004	2005	2006	2007	2008
European Union (27 countries)	15.1	15.3	15.4	15.6	15.8	16.0	16.2	16.4	16.6	16.8	16.9	17.0
Belgium	16.3	16.5	16.6	16.8	16.9	16.9	17.0	17.1	17.2	17.2	17.1	17.1
Denmark	15.0	14.9	14.9	14.8	14.8	14.8	14.8	14.9	15.0	15.2	15.3	15.6
Germany (including ex-GDR from 1991)	15.7	15.8	15.9	16.2	16.6	17.1	17.5	18.0	18.6	19.3	19.8	19.9
Greece	15.6	15.9	16.2	16.5	16.8	17.2	17.5	17.8	18.1	18.5	18.6	18.6
Spain	15.8	16.2	16.5	16.7	16.9	17.0	16.9	16.9	16.8	16.7	16.7	16.6
France	15.3	15.5	15.7	15.8	15.9	16.0	16.1	16.1	16.2	16.2	16.2	16.3
Italy	17.2	17.5	17.8	18.1	18.4	18.7	19.0	19.2	19.5	19.7	19.9	20.0
Netherlands	13.4	13.5	13.5	13.6	13.6	13.7	13.7	13.8	14.0	14.3	14.5	14.7
Poland	11.5	11.7	11.9	12.1	12.4	12.6	12.8	13.0	13.1	13.3	13.4	13.5
Finland	14.5	14.6	14.7	14.8	15.0	15.2	15.3	15.6	15.9	16.0	16.5	16.5
Sweden	17.4	17.4	17.4	17.3	17.2	17.2	17.2	17.2	17.2	17.3	17.4	17.5
United Kingdom	15.9	15.9	15.8	15.8	15.8	15.9	15.9	16.0	16.0	16.0	16.0	16.1
Norway	15.8	15.7	15.5	15.3	15.1	14.9	14.8	14.7	14.7	14.7	14.6	14.6
Switzerland	14.9	15.0	15.2	15.3	15.4	15.6	15.6	15.7	15.8	16.0	1.62	16.4

Source of Data: Eurostat
Last Update: 20.10.2009
Date of extraction: 28 Oct 2009 17:09:09 GMT
General Disclaimer of the EC: http://europa.eu/geninfo/legal_notice_en.htm

© European Communities, 2009

Table 20-3. Chronic Disease Prevalence, Cost, and Physician Use Among Medicare Beneficiaries

	Number of Chronic Conditions				
	0	1	2	3	4 or more
Percent of Medicare beneficiaries, 1999	18%	17%	22%	19%	24%
Average Medicare expenditures, 1999	$211	$1,154	$2,394	$4,701	$13,973
Percent that sees more than 10 different physicians per year, 2003	6%	18%	40%	61%	Not available

Source: MedPAC, 2006; Wolff et al., 2002.
Obtained from IOM2008[5]

Reprinted with permission from the National Academies Press, Copyright 2008, National Academy of Sciences

concern is that prioritization of healthcare needs and the supply of healthcare services has unduly emphasized acute care and expensive technologies over primary and preventive care.[9]

Over the past decade, health reform has assumed an added focus on enabling competition to more efficiently achieve those social justice ends of equality in care delivery and equity in care access.[10] Reform efforts spanning the United Kingdom, the United States, New Zealand, and the Netherlands are exploring the care delivery models that best solve the complex optimization problem of how to strike a balance between individual needs and societal interests, and more generally, between equity and efficiency.[9]

There is a widespread geographical goal to address healthcare reform. This manifests itself within single nations—Great Britain,[11] Canada,[12] United States,[13] Germany,[14] Australia,[15] South Africa,[16] and Japan[17] but also has pan-continental commonality across the constituent countries of Latin America[18] in which globalization and health reform permeate current top policy concerns. After an initial wave of economic liberalization in response to the debt crisis of the 1980s, most countries moved on to a second stage of reform meant to address the profound deterioration of public social services, particularly in areas such as healthcare. Transnational alliances between domestic officials and international development institutions often led the formulation and implementation of such policies.[18]

Against this geopolitical and health policy backdrop, we will provide a global view of the current context of healthcare throughout the world and draw on many of the chapters and case studies in this book as references for this synthesis. We conclude with a projection of the opportunities and options facing nursing and link these to a preferred future vision for nursing and nursing informatics.

Current Global Healthcare Context

Seismic changes in national and international healthcare environments have occurred over the past decade, reflecting huge shifts in nations' health policies. Globally, several common themes are evident in countries' national health policies and underpin the transformative changes in present day healthcare systems throughout most of the world. These themes include:

- A focus on population health, with services and technologies to support wellness and disease prevention.
- Self-management for those with chronic diseases and transitioning resources and services from acute care to community and home.
- A person-centric focus in care delivery and services for patient empowerment.
- Healthcare system reform using electronic health records technologies that extend across all levels of services and care settings, including the person's home.
- Resource demands including capacity, as well as challenges in the healthcare workforce's skills and preparedness for this new work environment.

Population Health, Wellness, and Self-Management

The consumer empowerment trend and prevention/wellness focus can be seen on most governments' health policy Web pages today.[19-25] The policy shifts are not solely due to financial imperatives to reduce costs. These policy changes also coincide with advancements in today's ICT that make engaging consumers to be active participants in their health management possible. Just nine short years ago at the turn of the 21st century, this "ask" of citizenry would not have been technically feasible. But in 2009, Internet use, Internet connected mobile phone adoption, and the explosion of Web-connected entities and organizations combine to make this era of engagement and consumerism feasible.

Importantly, the move toward the individual as an active participant in his or her care is supported as "best practice" by a growing body of literature. Recent reviews of the literature reveal a solid body of research evidence that show a strong correlation between patient engagement and participation in care decisions to improved health outcomes, quality, and costs.[26-28] Thus, aside from economic imperatives, the engaged consumer shift in health policy is based on best practice evidence. And today, countries such as Canada, Scotland, Great Britain, and the United States have defined "self management" and person-centered healthcare as being at the very core of their national health policy strategies.[19-23] Countries are fostering this "personal health management" trend as a way to achieve better outcomes and more cost-effective care delivery through consumer-centered, health ICT initiatives.[23-25] Concurrently, nations are working to raise the health literacy levels of their citizens and use of the Internet and electronic records technologies. These technologies will enable citizens to be informed and engaged in their healthcare as active participants in their care decisions, as well as in the management of their health and/or disease state.[29-32]

Transitions and Shifting to Community and Home

As countries work to put system reforms and full use of electronic health record systems (EHRs) in place, self-management also becomes a person's best defense against the continued challenge of fragmentation in the healthcare of elderly and chronically ill people. Evidence bears out that, regardless of the country, the engaged consumer is actually the first line of defense against the fragmentation of our industrialized countries' medical systems. A recent survey examined care characteristics for chronically ill adults in eight countries: Australia, Canada, France, Germany, the Netherlands, New Zealand, the United Kingdom and the United States.[33] Results showed that all eight countries shared a pattern of chronically ill adults using multiple providers across different care settings at high risk of medical errors, poorly coordinated care, and disproportionate costs.[33] Specifically, in all eight countries, the study's authors reported that deficits in care management occurred in the context of hospital discharge or when seeing multiple doctors. The researchers noted that even in the Netherlands, with its strong primary care system, fragmentation still occurred in this space of acute care transitioning and when multiple specialists were involved in care.[33]

In the United States, consumers are only too aware of the fragmentation of the current healthcare system. According to a 2007 Wall Street Journal/Harris Interactive poll, "only one third (33%) of adults are very confident in their physicians and other healthcare providers having a complete and accurate picture of their medical history."[34] In fact, many errors occur because individual professionals are not fully aware of all the therapies that the patient is receiving or has received.[35] As a result, U.S. health policy is promoting use of personal health records (PHR) and a high health literacy in its citizens.[19,30] A comprehensive personal health record maintained and made accessible by the patient is seen as another defense in a fragmented healthcare system.[36-38] Significantly, most European Community (EU) countries are adopting the use of some form of summarized health information that individuals carry with them for emergent situations, as well as to minimize fragmentation. These strategies range from health cards, flash drive pocket devices, and electronic access to an individual's PHR. In instances of travel to foreign countries or in emergent care situations in which the individual is unable to communicate, a personally carried PHR abstract that describes allergies, current diagnoses, and medications can make the difference between life and death.[38]

People-Centric Healthcare

Recent studies indicate that individuals are ready to accept more responsibility for their care management and are asking for increased engagement in their care decisions. In the United States, two recent surveys show that people make decisions about their own health and want to be more engaged in their own self-care.[39,40] In another example, New Zealand's Ministry of Health commissioned the Synergia research group to study New Zealanders' wishes regarding the extent to which they want to participate in their healthcare and the primary care sector's readiness for people's active participation.[41] Synergia explored people's experience of long-term health conditions (such as diabetes, cardiovascular disease, and asthma), the impact of their social and family environments, and the interventions that support effective self-care. Findings concluded that a wide range of information innovations exist that can assist individuals and families with self-care, from devices and technologies to complex, tailored initiatives spanning the patient and the primary care practice team. Furthermore, the mix of three major ethnic cultures: Maori, Pacific Island, and European, has resulted in the emergence of patient self-care, especially within the first two groups for which family beliefs and traditional, historic treatments and social networks are re-emerging as current concepts. Based on these key findings of the potential value of a more culturally tailored approach to the different cultural groups in New Zealand's population, Synergia recommended that primary care providers engage with individuals from a starting point that is mindful of their specific cultural beliefs and attitudes. Concluding that primary healthcare needs to move away from a "one-size fits all" response to chronic illnesses, the study advised that primary care providers seek to understand the wider context of people's conditions and build on opportunities to engage with families as a whole.[41]

Conversely, from the health systems side, some of this change has already occurred as seen in health literature that is permeated by descriptions of the change from a health system focus to a people-centric, healthcare focus. One notable example from Chapter 3 is the work that Finland is doing with its elderly population. As Kouri reports in this chapter, Finland is taking a multidimensional approach to address the needs of elderly people to achieve better continuity of care after discharge from an acute hospital stay. In the "Going Home" demonstration project, elderly people are supported through a combination of technology services that involves aspects of the "medical home," telemonitoring, and assistance in self-management. "Going Home" includes interactive "CaringTV" programs delivered through three unique subprojects that were each created with user involvement (see http://kotiin.laurea.fi).[42]

Enabling Technologies and National Health IT Strategies

A major strategy in national health policy is to heavily invest in ICT. Importantly, this ICT investment extends beyond the acute care sector and physician practices into the community and the home. Citizens need the tools to access their health information, to communicate directly with providers, and to seek out reliable health information. Section IV richly describes ICT and EHR initiatives across the globe. Some of the associated country case studies that reflect the people-centric healthcare focus in their ICT national strategies are the United Kingdom, Iceland, Canada, Sweden, Norway, and Finland. More evolved strategies have moved to use of electronic personal health records and data exchange between individuals and providers or health entities, such as pharmacies, medical laboratories, and local clinics.[43] Consolidating all the health information held by diverse provider entities across the healthcare system into one place that is accessible by consumers will be essential for realizing the full potential of consumer empowerment. Countries that reach this technologic milestone will greatly help their citizens to be informed, engaged, active participants in their care and self-management. As shown throughout the chapters and country case studies in Section IV, nations are indeed rapidly addressing consolidation of health information in strategies that involve some sort of EHR repository with consumer access through health cards, Internet portals and/or by electronic personal health records.[23-25,31,44-46]

Finland's national health technology strategy offers a marked contrast to larger countries, such as the United States, the United Kingdom, Australia, and Canada, in the speed with which they have moved to a person-centered healthcare system. Similar to Denmark, Finland's rapid advancement in transforming their country (2002 to 2009) to an EHR that extends to community and into the home at a national level is striking. Both Finland and Denmark have populations of approximately 5 million and within their societies they have marked cultural and linguistic variation.[47,48] However, their respective governments' health IT strategy has accommodated their cultural diversity, so that it does not obstruct national adoption of hospital-to-home EHRs. While the implementation of these layered initiatives is still in process in Finland, the important point is that their national strategy is committed to EHR adoption and use throughout their healthcare system into communities and directly into the home (see Finland's case study 16B in Section IV). Technology advancement and new care delivery models, such as those being tested in Finland, Sweden, and Norway, will continue to enable more consumer engagement, better PHR tools, and national connectedness between EHRs and PHRs. This technology infrastructure will also enable more primary care delivered in the home that involves multidisciplinary teams and new roles and opportunities for nurses.

Throughout the world, increasing arrays of health-enabling technologies are being introduced to support consumer empowerment and self-management of wellness and disease.[36,39] Policymakers define these enabling technologies as providing the potential to improve clinical excellence, the care experience, and the continuity and affordability of care.[19,30,39,49] The personal health record is emerging as a clear technology leader in this exploration, and its related technologies are seen as tools that give people more control over their care and allow them to be participants in their care management decisions.[30,34,39,50] The TIGER PHR/Consumer Empowerment Collaborative team summarized the major benefits of PHR use in a 2010 state-of-the-art review paper.[51] The TIGER team noted that, in addition to enabling individuals to collect and trend their own health and disease management information, the electronic PHR allows for easy data exchange with health providers and, thus, more timely response to "red flag" events in chronic disease management. It is this feature of timely data exchange controlled by the individual that helps to empower consumers through improved patient safety with the use of timely reminders or interventions, access to their personal health information and general health information, and communication with their care providers.

In response to this international demand for ICT solutions that extend the reach of the EHR to the individual within the home, ICT businesses are addressing the voice of the people as well. In the mid-1990s, Kaiser Permanente, the largest, non-profit health maintenance organization in the United States, began offering its members the ability to ask health questions to nurses over the Web. Kaiser has been on a "patient empowerment" journey for its clients over the past few years, using technology as a primary enabling strategy. Kaiser has developed its Web-based *My Health Manager* PHR to allow patients to make appointments, send e-mail questions to doctors, and place prescription orders online. In June 2008, Kaiser announced a partnership with Microsoft to use Microsoft's Health Vault, a consumer-controlled, personal health service for its 156,000 employees and 8.7 million members.[50] In addition to Kaiser, Microsoft is also partnering with the Mayo Clinic, and New York-Presbyterian Hospital for use of its Health Vault PHR service.

Entering the PHR market just a few months after Microsoft, Google introduced its Google Health solution. Google Health is also a consumer-controlled PHR with functions that allow individuals to build a health profile; import medical records from physicians, hospitals, and pharmacies; share their record; and utilize the online health service directory.[52] Google Health is also working with the Cleveland Clinic and Beth Israel Deaconess Medical Center.

Despite more than 200 PHR solution offerings in the U.S. marketplace in 2008, adoption and sustained use is estimated to have occurred between 1% and 3% of the population.[37] Obstacles to wider adoption and active use by people with chronic conditions, who have the greatest need of self management support, revolve around usability value delivered and, most importantly, peoples' concern over privacy security and control over access.[36,37,40] The majority of the PHR products in the marketplace are tethered to the EHR systems of providers, employers, or health insurance companies and are neither portable nor consumer controlled. Thus, while there are many companies offering a personal health record solution on the Web, the entry of Microsoft and Google into this space with a consumer controlled offering, created in partnership with leading healthcare organizations, is seen as potentially hastening the adoption of EHRs.

Health Workforce Challenges

The healthcare context also means dealing with workforce issues worldwide, as well. In 2008, the IOM under the auspices of the National Academies released an urgent press release entitled *Health Care Work Force Too Small, Unprepared For Aging Baby Boomers; Higher Pay, More Training, and Changes In Care Delivery Needed To Avert Crisis.*[53] In this release, the IOM noted that as the first of the United States' 78 million baby boomers begin to reach age 65 in 2011, the country will face a healthcare workforce that is too small and woefully unprepared to meet their specific health needs. In the IOM's subsequent 2008 report, *Retooling for an Aging America: Building the Health Care Workforce,* the committee called for bold initiatives to immediately start training all healthcare providers in the basics of geriatric care and to prepare family members and other informal caregivers who currently receive little or no training in how to tend to their aging loved ones.[54] The IOM Committee set a target date of 2030 for the necessary reforms to take place—the year in which all baby boomers will have turned 65 years or older.[54]

As discussed earlier in this chapter, the "graying populations" of industrialized countries is a general trend that makes the nursing workforce shortage and its lack of geriatrics training a common challenge. Not only is there a worldwide crisis in available numbers of healthcare professionals, there is also a crisis in terms of the competencies of the workforce. Pruitt and Epping-Jordan[55] note that to meet the growing global demands of caring for the increasing numbers of patients with chronic conditions, we need to develop a new approach to training. It is important to note that chronicity is not solely the domain of the aged. HIV and AIDS have exacted a devastating toll throughout the African continent, with such a heavy burden to their population's health that the disease presents the number one health threat to their economies and standard of living. South Africa now has more HIV-infected people and annual AIDS deaths than any other country in the world.[56] With their death rate increasing to approximately 756,000 in 2008 from 536,000 in 2007, President Jacob Zuma recently reflected that South Africa's death rate may soon outpace their birth rate.[56] And while African countries have been the hardest hit by HIV/AIDS, incidence and prevalence rates are also increasing throughout-Southeast Asian countries.[57] So, chronicity may present as the major health challenge in every country, but the age demographics vary from predominantly the aged in developed countries to young adults, children, and newborns in developing countries.

While the world is experiencing a rapid transition from acute diseases to chronic health problems, training of the healthcare workforce relies on early 20th century models that continue to emphasize diagnosis and treatment of acute diseases. Educational leaders, health professional bodies, and the World Health Organization (WHO) recognize such models as inadequate for health workers caring for a growing population of patients with health problems that persist across decades or lifetimes. The WHO listed core competencies for delivering effective healthcare for patients with chronic conditions which included patient-centered care and partnering.[58]

Nursing shortages in health systems around the world are creating negative impacts on the health and well-being of populations because of the lack of sufficient numbers to cover their care delivery needs.[55,58-61] The shortage in available health professionals poses unprecedented challenges for policy makers and planners in high- and low-income countries alike. Inadequate human resources planning and management, poor deployment practices, internal and external migration, high attrition (due to poor work environments, low professional satisfaction, and inadequate remuneration), and the impact of HIV and AIDS are just some of the critical issues driving nursing shortages worldwide. The International Council of Nurses and the Florence Nightingale International Foundation undertook a Global Nursing Review Initiative: Policy Options and Solutions. The ensuing 2006 report, *The Global Nursing Shortage: Priority Areas for Intervention,* emerged from the two-year process and summarizes key issues in nursing shortages.[61] The 2006 World Health Assembly Resolution called for nursing and midwifery skills and services to be strengthened. This resolution recognizes the importance of these health professionals in attaining global health goals. A workforce that is not only adequate in numbers but also in competencies is a critical need worldwide.[61]

The TIGER Collaborative's Impact on Nursing in the United States

In July 2004, David J. Brailer, MD, PhD, the then newly appointed director of the Office of the National Coordinator, was holding discovery meetings on the numbers of informatics health professionals needed to support national EHR adoption.[62] Nursing was represented at these meetings by a physician. Subsequently, a small group of nurse leaders met to plan steps to ensure that this exclusion from self-representation in health policy never happened again. From those initial discussions, and under the tenacious and gracious leadership of Marion Ball, this group grew into the powerful collaboration called TIGER (Technology Informatics Guiding Education Reform). The approach and strategy adopted by the TIGER leadership grew out of recognition that the U.S. nursing workforce largely lacked informatics competencies and that there was an absence of informatics integrated into nursing students' curriculum, as well as a near void of nursing faculty with sufficient informatics skills to be able to teach the next generation. With the goal of accomplishing a rapid transformation of nursing practice, education, and administration, the TIGER leadership convened invitational summits in 2005 and 2006 to map out strategic steps.[63,64] Emerging from the 2006 summit, nine collaborative teams were formed to produce demonstration projects, wide-spread education efforts, and white papers on state-of-the-art/science in the following: standards and interoperability; national health IT agenda; informatics competencies; education and faculty development; staff development; usability and clinical application design; virtual demonstration center; leadership development; and consumer empowerment and PHRs.[65]

Since the 2006 Invitational Summit, the TIGER collaborative has galvanized nursing in the United States. An important principle was to involve all the major nursing professional organizations and specialties and to avoid having the "call to action" be a conversation that just occurs between nurse informaticists. More than 70 professional nursing organizations engaged in the 2006 summit and more than 400 volunteers participated in the subsequent nine collaborative teams as they completed their assigned commitments between 2006 and 2009.[63-65] This inspection into the state of nursing created a sense of urgency around integrating informatics into our practice, education, and science. The collaboration achieved in the initial 2006 Invitational Summit drew the focus and commitment of national nursing entities, such as the National League for Nursing, Health Resources and Services Administration, National Institute for Nursing Research, and the American Nurses Association. The collaborations that TIGER has been able to bring to address the informatics skills needs of our nursing profession is reflected in the work reported on by Skiba and colleagues in Chapter 5, Connors in Chapter 7, and Warren et al. in Chapter 9. In addition to DuLong and Ball's TIGER overview in Chapter 2, the work of the nine collaborative teams is available on the TIGER Web site (www.tigersummit.com).[63] The white papers from all nine teams will be published in the upcoming *Nursing Informatics: Where Caring and Technology Meet, 4th edition.*[65]

Nursing and Nursing Informatics: Current Context

Nursing Today

Environmental, political, economic, and professional forces influence nursing's domain. Nursing's practice and science are shaped by populations' healthcare needs and nurses' ability to influence them. Changes in healthcare needs have been influenced by emerging concepts of health and illness, technology and science advancements, disease patterns, population structures, and our growing ability to meet care delivery needs through new healthcare technologies and knowledge. The demand for healthcare has increased exponentially, although the economic and political status of each country has determined the extent and degree of health services offered.[11-18] In countries with government purchased healthcare, for example, escalating costs resulted in a need to scrutinize how taxpayers' money was being used. As a trend that crossed many industrialized countries in the 1990s, healthcare organizations became accountable to the tax-paying public and consumers for efficient and effective healthcare services and for ensuring value for cost. In the United Kingdom specifically, political recognition of the need to be accountable to taxpayers and healthcare consumers led to a number of government inquiries and initiatives which in turn recognized the importance of having thorough and accurate information to manage healthcare resources. Without data to show the added value of nursing care to outcomes and costs, historically, nursing has been vulnerable to budget cuts, restructuring, and reductions as governments look to contain health costs. As the biggest cost component of healthcare, nursing has tended to be the primary target when efficiencies are examined. These wide-ranging issues influenced not only nursing informatics but the entire nursing profession. Reporting demands required nurse managers and informaticians to focus on nursing-specific information and to define what should and could be collected, how to analyze it, and how it should be used to promote greater efficiency and effectiveness of healthcare and improve the populations' health.

Nursing and the Empowered Consumer

The phenomenon of the Internet-empowered "informed patient" has enabled health consumerism and has led to redefining the power relationship between patient and clinician toward that of "equal partner" in decision-making and care management. In 2010, pervasive information availability is a global reality made possible by advances in Internet search engine technologies, online journals and latest clinical studies, and near universal availability of broadband access. Consequently, expert clinical knowledge is no longer the sole domain of the health professional. Today, the informed consumer may have as much knowledge for their particular health concern as does the general practitioner or specialist. This dynamic has caused profound cultural change in the traditional patient role and has leveled the power dynamic between provider and patient.[39,66,67] The transition in our societies from a patient orientation to a consumer orientation also has ramifications in terms of what people want from their providers, health organizations, and health systems. As nurses, we will want to be aware of health policy that advocates for informed and participatory consumerism, as well as the latest trends in consumer behaviors and expectations, so that we can appropriately tailor our care delivery approaches to these culturally different consumer populations.

Nursing Informatics Today

Nursing informatics has developed in tandem with the advancement of science, ICT technologies, and nursing practice as reflected in the 2009 definition of nursing informatics adopted by the International Medical Informatics Association-Nursing Informatics special interest group (IMIA-NI):

> "Nursing informatics' science and practice integrates nursing, its information and knowledge and their management with information and communication technologies to promote the health of people, families and communities worldwide."[68]

Nursing informatics' focus is on the collection, analysis, and use of nursing information to improve health outcomes and advance nursing knowledge and science. From its beginnings in the late 1970s, the early pioneers focused their efforts on the need to use data and information to support nurses' clinical decision making and to show the value of nursing to improved outcomes within clinical information systems. Nurse informaticians defined the concept of "nursing information" as that information that is specific and necessary for nursing practice and research on nursing practice.[69,70]

Nursing informatics in the United States emerged within this traditional framework and is consequently supported by educational programs within the higher education model, both in terms of master's and doctoral study, and integrated within other specialties, e.g., nursing administration and gerontological nursing. Nursing informatics as a specialty itself now has master's and doctoral degrees in nursing and health informatics.[71,72] Moreover, the nursing informatics specialty has also emerged within both professional organizations, such as the American Nurses Association (ANA); nursing accreditation organizations in the form of the Commission on Collegiate Nursing Education (CCNE); and the National League for Nursing (NLN), and research organizations, such as the Midwest Nursing Research Society (MNRS) and the National Institute for Nursing Research (NINR). In 2008, the ANA issued its second edition of *Scope and Standards of Nursing Informatics Practice*. This updated version makes explicit references to patients' use of technology for managing their health and in decision making and the role of nursing informatics specialists in supporting that function.[73]

Internationally, as is demonstrated throughout the country case studies in Section IV, there are sophisticated examples of nursing's leadership and participation in documentation and terminology standardization initiatives. The reader is referred to the case studies on Spain, Germany, Sweden, Norway, Finland, and Iceland as just a few examples that show marked progress between the 1ˢᵗ and 2ⁿᵈ editions. While the degree of integration of nursing and informatics is high throughout these European countries and is emerging in South American countries, few countries have embraced informatics within their definition of the scope and practice standards of nursing with informatics as a recognized nursing specialty. However, many countries are moving in this direction as can be seen in the European country case studies included in Section IV.

At the other end of this continuum, Anne Casey notes in her overview on the United Kingdom in Chapter 15 that while tremendous growth in the integration of informatics competencies into nursing practice has occurred over the past five years, "informatics is still not regarded as a speciality by the nursing profession in the UK and Ireland," and warns that "those nurses who wish to move into the informatics field may limit their career opportunities in nursing."[74] This reluctance of the professional nursing bodies and national leadership to embrace informatics within nursing practice and science in the UK is paradoxical, given this country's formative leadership in the field from the early 1980s onward. Under Maureen Scholes' leadership, then director of nursing at The London Hospital, the Nursing Informatics Special Interest Group (NI-SIG) was formed within the International Medical Informatics Group in 1983.[69]

Nursing's Voice in Health Policy

The immense and extensive developments of nursing informatics within nursing and the interdisciplinary context in the United States set the stage for dramatic and revolutionary changes in nursing and healthcare—a 21ˢᵗ century synergy. However, to capitalize on these opportunities, nursing leadership needed to organize to gain a unified voice in health policy and to be included in national research agendas. Key health policy areas in which this unified nursing informatics voice was needed included IT standards development, shared communication and networking opportunities, development of a consistent core curricula and certification process, and promotion of collaborative research initiatives. Importantly for the advancement of nursing informatics, there is a need to establish a nursing informatics research agenda in collaboration with multidisciplinary research initiatives and governmental and non-governmental funding sources.

In the U.S., the opportunity to coalesce this talent, energy, and membership into a single alliance was spearheaded by nurse leaders in the AMIA and HIMSS organizations. Importantly, these two informatics organizations' infrastructure and staff provided the support needed to establish a collaborative entity for all U.S. nursing informatics in late 2004. Named the Alliance for Nursing Informatics (ANI), this umbrella entity now represents more than 3,500 nurses with informatics expertise from more than 25 nursing informatics groups in the United States.[75] The importance of the ANI for U.S. nursing informatics is that it allows nursing to speak with a single, unified voice on health policy, standards, and relevant professional issues. As the U.S. government under the Obama administration pushes major health reform and funded mandates for EHR adoption by 2014,[13] ANI gives the entire nursing informatics community a voice that can respond to and participate in policy discussions and standards developments. Fortunately, for integration of nursing informatics into the broader nursing professional community, ANA assisted in the initial development of the Alliance and is an ad hoc member of all ANI activities. The contribution that nursing plays in the consumer-centric, information-rich EHR initiatives currently happening in the United States will benefit from the plethora of nursing education, research, and practice knowledge given a voice through the Alliance.[75]

Terminology and Minimum Database Standards

To ensure that nursing develops to benefit people, nursing must be able to "name" its unique knowledge base in order to measure and evaluate its impact.[76] At present, universally agreed terminology to describe nursing is just becoming available. This pursuit has been a journey of almost three decades involving numerous international nurse informaticians, research teams, and professional organizations.[70,77-86] All of these referenced nurse researchers have worked to develop a standardized nursing reference terminology that could serve as an international standard.[77-86] Harriet Werley, PhD, RN, first presented this nursing information concept as the "Nursing Minimum Data Set" in 1982.[70] Dr. Werley defined a set of 16 data elements that cover who the patient is as a socio-cultural person, problems assessed, interventions used, and goals/outcomes and the care context.[70,87] This informatics approach to defining nursing practice put quantifiable form and structure into the evolving, yet sometimes invisible, science of nursing.

Werley's minimum data set defined the data elements needed to capture the essence of nursing in a care delivery context. Importantly, it gave nursing the data and information to leverage the qualitative and quantitative scientific methods and technology tools to look at itself in an increasingly sophisticated scientific light. Not only did the nursing minimum data set (NMDS) allow nursing to discover what it is that nursing does, these same informatics tools provided the means to begin to demonstrate to other health professionals, and to society, nursing's contribution to patient outcomes, costs, and satisfaction measures. Efforts to operationalize the NMDS immediately called into question the need for nursing to have a standardized language. In contrast to medicine, nursing evolved without a language and lacked a coded standardized terminology system to be able to name what it is that nurses do that is unique to nursing.

An international version of the NMDS, termed *i*NMDS, has been in development over the past decade under the auspices of the International Council of Nurses (ICN) and the International Medical Informatics Association's Nursing Informatics Special Interest Group (NI-SIG).[88,89] Building on the nursing minimum data set work of Werley and Lang from 1988, the *i*NMDS expanded to encompass work that was already underway in individual countries and to use the ICNP concepts. In addition to capturing nursing care delivery and outcomes, *i*NMDS allows for reuse of data for resource consumption analysis, performance improvement, best practices, and population health.[89] Given its international baseline, the *i*NMDS can be used to coordinate international data collection to support the description, study, and improvement of nursing practice.[89]

As Coenen and Bartz describe in Chapter 11, we have finally built an international reference terminology standard that can name what it is that nursing does, can now link these interventions for patient health to nurse-sensitive outcomes, and can analyse these data on large, aggregated, population-based, clinical databases generated from EHRs. As program directors over the International Classification of Nursing Practice Program, Coenen and Bartz have contributed to international standards in the form of developing five versions of ICNP® with the release of Version 2 in 2009. Importantly in 2008, ICNP was approved for inclusion in the WHO Family of International Classifications (WHO-FIC), the core of which is the International Classification of Diseases (ICD). The WHO-FIC is a suite of classification products that may be used in an integrated fashion to compare health information internationally as well as nationally.[90] As a related classification and member of the WHO-FIC, ICNP represents the domain of nursing practice worldwide. Also, the development of SNOMED CT® as an international terminology[91,92] and ongoing harmonization efforts with ICNP Version 2 means that nursing has mature terminology international standards that are emerging for use in clinical systems to support nursing documentation.[92]

The significance of this development—that of international standardized nursing terminologies that are available for use within clinical information systems—has profound importance for nursing practice and science. At the most basic level, nursing will be in a position for the first time in its modern history to capture, in a quantitative way through codified data, what nursing does that is uniquely nursing and what impact this has on patient outcomes. Given the large population-based databases that are generated with EHRs, nurse researchers will have a natural laboratory to support the most rigorous of quantitative research methodologies to generate new nursing knowledge and to evaluate effectiveness of current best practices. Nursing has never before had these research tools available to support its science and practice. We stand on this threshold, poised for advances to happen quickly once a critical mass in EHR adoption occurs within and across nations in which standardized nursing terminology for nursing documentation is included.

Throughout the world, nurse informaticians have been leaders among nurses, adopting many of the attributes of an advanced practitioner.[76] Nurses come into the informatician role already experts in nursing. These nurses have taken theories, models, and principles from information and computer science and applied them to nursing theory and practice. In doing so, these nurse leaders have recognized the complexities of the nature of nursing knowledge and its use in decision making. Nurse informaticians have embraced both the art and science of nursing by using technology with a human interface. Their informatics focus extends to examining what nurses do, how they make decisions, and with what results. Their body of work has supported the development of nursing practice and enhanced the quality of care and supported educational strategies. Nurse informaticians recognize their accountability to the patient and the need to ensure efficient use of limited resources. Collaboration and working as part of multidisciplinary teams has been a consistent theme in NI professional organizations as well as the work setting. And finally, in their leadership roles within the informatics teams, they have supported the management of change and promoted evaluation of the impact of technology on healthcare and patients.

Nursing and Nursing Informatics: A Preferred Vision

Nursing Looking Forward

The ICN Definition of Nursing reminds us of our social call to action:

> Nursing encompasses autonomous and collaborative care of individuals of all ages, families, groups and communities, sick or well and in all settings. Nursing includes the promotion of health, prevention of illness, and the care of ill, disabled and dying people. Advocacy, promotion of a safe environment, research, participation in shaping health policy and in patient and health systems management, and education are also key nursing roles.[93]

National and international anchoring in a common nursing body emphasizes that nursing's fundamental commitment to individuals, families, and communities, and their health and chronic care is clear. The acknowledgement of excellent educational programs to support the preparation of the nursing workforce is clear. The importance of nursing research and scholarship to inform education and the practice of nursing is unequivocal. And the inter-relationships of these roles and functions is widely accepted. *Nursing and Informatics for the 21ˢᵗ Century,* 2nd edition, shares a wealth of nursing expertise, creativity, and boldness in addressing the need for nursing's participation within healthcare systems' transformation. Nursing and nursing informatics bring a wealth of expertise and proven initiatives to the current healthcare challenges.

Integrating Nursing and Nursing Informatics Competencies

While advocacy, education, and support of the patient are core nursing functions that cross all care settings and national boundaries, 21ˢᵗ century practice also carries a requirement for nurses to know about an array of technologies and learning modalities. Nurses' efforts to assist individuals to engage fully in the self-management of their health and care decisions will require that they instruct individuals on how to use the technology resources available to them in their home, community, and country. Nurses will need to be able to teach their patients how to use health-enabling technologies, such as a personal health record; how to access trusted health information sites; and, how to use tools interactively to communicate with health resources and clinical providers. Having informatics competencies is rapidly becoming no longer an optional choice for nurses but rather a core skill set for nurses—in any role in any country in this second decade of the 21ˢᵗ century. Basic to our ability to be educators and advocates for our patients is the ability to use and demonstrate to others the use of health-enabling technologies; knowledge of health information sites; the ability to handle e-mail and document exchange; the ability to show patients how to use appropriate social networks; and the ability to work with wireless monitoring patient data.[94] The rate at which new transformative technologies are being developed and introduced into the marketplace is also a reality that calls for the ongoing need for continuing education in ICT for healthcare. Just reviewing the technologies being presented in the 5th Annual World Healthcare Innovation and Technology Congress program confirms the need for refreshing the workforce with technology knowledge and the evolution of healthcare organizations in this ever-changing information age.[95]

Approximately 20 years ago, the international community embarked on a project to bring healthcare to everyone by the year 2000 and featured technologies that were known to be effective and economical. The commitment is still there.[96] For example, technological advances in sensing, computation, storage, and communications will turn the near-ubiquitous mobile phone into a global mobile sensing device. People-centric sensing will help drive this trend by enabling a different way to sense, learn, visualize, and share information about ourselves, friends, communities, the way we live, and the world we live in.[97]

Nursing and Health Literacy in Patient Education

Patient education in this new context of person empowerment and technology must take on the added nuance of health literacy—teaching people how and where to find information, how to use this information for their own health management, and how to navigate the health system. While all care settings carry responsibility for teaching and education, we know that individuals have the least ability to learn in acute care settings. Ambulatory settings are somewhat better, but the person's home is the optimum setting.[54] Therefore, as nurses consider how best to tailor teaching and materials to fit the individual's ability to learn, acute care discharge planning should include transitioning to community and home healthcare for patient teaching and to support learning skills that increase their health literacy proficiency.

Nursing in the Era of Self-Management

The shift to self-management and active participation highlights a pivotal role for the nurse as the only member of the interdisciplinary team that is in constant contact with the patient in acute care and who coordinates care across all venues from hospital to home. Care transitions from the acute care segment to community and home is the point at which fragmentation of care occurs.[33] In governments' efforts to eliminate the waste that happens with fragmentation, nurses are positioned to step into this new health services focus. In this role of assisting care transitions across care venues, but especially in home health settings, nurses will be required to act as knowledge facilitators, translators, and interpreters of scientific information to support patient preference and the development of individualized care pathways for optimal health outcomes. Working throughout the community in such virtual and decentralized ways means that ICT technologies can be powerful tools for efficient and best care practices. Not only does the ICT support the nurse in managing information and knowledge but also for care delivery in new telehealth modes and for educating the consumer/patient in self-management.

In the context of the care of elderly populations, chronic illness and life-long disabilities, care management is a long-term relationship between individual and nurse. Long-term, person-centered relationships are mostly developed in the context of primary care in the community and in the home. As industrialized countries push self-management for their citizens' health and disease maintenance, this opens up great opportunity for nurses at all levels of practice. The extent to which individuals are empowered to be fully engaged in their healthcare is largely in the domain of nursing practice. It is a challenge for us to accept, but the question is, will we?

Universities and Colleges—Key Players

Nursing has been proactive in developing educational programs to prepare an informatics-literate nursing workforce, as well as to increase the support of nursing informatics specialists, as noted by Skiba et al. in Chapter 5. Regardless of the status of informatics as a recognized nursing specialty or not, in the immediate and near future, all nursing education programs need to be able to teach informatics competencies to nursing students. There are many opportunities for nursing education with simulation labs to develop informatics skills with clinical skills in venues using EHRs and associated technologies. Nursing workforce and nursing students will increasingly encounter this new emphasis on technology-assisted communication in care delivery approaches as an important technique to support continuity and care coordination. The pervasiveness of Internet technologies and broad use adoption into all aspects of daily life by the world's populations are also extending into healthcare. The tools to access reliable health information and expert knowledge databases are available in every country throughout the world. Today, informed and engaged consumers are a reality, and all indications point to this as the developing norm in our Internet-empowered societies. Thus, nurses' approach to patient education will be teaching the individual how to acquire information—the difference between fishing for someone versus teaching the person to fish.

Nursing education and practice has the urgent challenge of embracing these new skills and knowledge within ICT health technologies. It will require a cultural shift and embracing of the new. If nursing can affect this transformative change, the opportunity to expand nursing roles into new realms and make significant contributions in primary care, consumer empowerment, and self-management will be our rewards. The alternative is that nursing is unable to adapt to these rapid changes and other or new disciplines step in to the address the void. The consequence of this alternative outcome could well be a narrowing of nursing domain and role functions and care delivery venues.

Specialties for Nurses Who Work Outside of Acute Care Facilities

Nurses who enjoy using the technology to support nursing care can find new niche roles for themselves in telehealth, home care, case management, and population health using ePHR and communication technologies. While patient education, empowerment, and support of self-management through enabling technologies are the new and future arenas for nursing and nursing informatics, there is an evolving specialty field that deals with technologies that support individual's knowledge and participation in their healthcare, termed "consumer health informatics." Consumer health informatics is defined as "the use of communication and information technologies to support consumers in obtaining information, analyzing their unique healthcare needs, and helping them make decisions about their own health."[98] This developing application offers new opportunities to nurses who have a vital role to play in this arena. If nurses will take up this opportunity, they will be uniquely positioned to expand into this domain due to their clinical knowledge and focus on patient education, empowerment, and advocacy.

Summary

Nurses are at the leading edge of the transformation of our healthcare systems worldwide. This is demonstrated by the wide range of new and extended roles that have been adopted and continue to be developed by nurses in recent years to meet the challenges of delivering safe, sustainable, effective, and efficient healthcare consistently. Nursing is in a state of rapid change and now, as never before, the possibilities exist for nurses to develop their careers in response to service demands, professional aspirations, policy drivers and, most importantly, patients' needs.

In closing, we would like to note the extensive progress made in the adoption of EHRs in countries profiled in the first and now this second edition. Over this five-year period, EHRs have grown in depth and breadth, and national EHR roadmaps are driving the early adoption or refinement of existing EHRs. Interoperability and terminology standards have matured considerably, both at the national and international levels. The advantages of these standards also extend to the functionality of existing EHRs as vendors commit to meeting new requirements for data structures, terminology, and interoperability. The tipping point has been reached. Our discussions on whether there is a role for informatics in nursing practice, education, and research will be a given reflected in our everyday reality. That we have had this two-decade conversation will be remembered only as a bookmark in nursing's history.

References

1. World Census by the Clock. http://www.census. gov/main/www/popclock.html, Accessed October 25, 2009.
2. US Census. 2005. http://www.census.gov/population/www/projections/projectionsagesex.html. Accessed October 30, 2009.
3. http://www.who.int/whosis/whostat/2008/en/.
4. Eurostat (EC). 2009. http://europa.eu/geninfo/legal_notice_en.htm. Last Update: October 20, 2009. Accessed October 28-November 10, 2009.
5. Institute of Medicine. *Retooling for An Aging America. Building the Healthcare Workforce.* Washington, DC: The National Academies Press; 2008.
6. Anderson GF, Frogner BK. Health spending in OECD countries: Obtaining value per dollar. *Hlt Aff.* 2008;27(6)1718-1727.
7. Wagner EH, Austin BT, Davis C, et al. Improving chronic illness care: translating evidence into action. *Hlt Aff* (Millwood). 2001; 20:64-78.
8. Institute of Medicine. *To Err is Human.* Washington, DC: The National Academies Press, 2000.
9. Flood C. *International Health Care Reform: A Legal, Economic, and Political Analysis.* Routledge, 2000.
10. Institute of Medicine. *Crossing the Quality Chasm. A New Health System for the 21ˢᵗ Century.* Washington, DC: The National Academies Press, 2001.
11. National Health Service. *Health Reform.* http://www.dh.gov.uk/en/Managingyourorganisation/Healthreform/index.htm. Accessed October 24, 2009.
12. *Canadian Health Care Policy Reform.* http://www.lib.sfu.ca/help/subject-guides/health-sciences/healthcare-reform. Accessed October 24, 2009.
13. *American Recovery and Reinvestment Act of 2009.* http://www.recovery.gov/. Accessed May 6, 2009.
14. *Germany Health Care Reform.* http://www.dw-world.de/dw/article/0,2144,2117345,00.html, Accessed October 24, 2009.
15. Van Der Weyden M. Australian healthcare reform: ailments and cures. *Med J Aust.* 2003;179(7):336-337.
16. Gilson L, Doherty J, Lake S, McIntyre D, Mwikisa C, Thomas S. The SAZA Study: implementing health financing reform in South Africa and Zambia. *Health Policy and Planning.* 2003;18(1):31-46.
17. *Japan Health Care Reform.* http://content.healthaffairs.org/cgi/content/full/23/3/26. Accessed October 24, 2009.
18. *Latin America Health Reform.* http://www.allacademic.com/meta/p_mla_apa_research_citation/0/7/0/1/8/p70186_index.html. Accessed October 24, 2009.
19. Office of Disease Prevention and Health Promotion. U.S. Department of Health and Human Services. *Healthy People 2010,* Chapter 11, Health Communication 2000. http://www.healthypeople.gov/document/html/volume1/11healthcom.htm. Accessed July 11, 2009.
20. National Health Services. *NHS Choices: Your Health, Your Choices.* http://www.nhs.uk/choiceintheNHS/Yourchoices/Pages/Yourchoices.aspx. Accessed August 30, 2009.
21. Department of Health. The NHS Constitution for England. January 2009. http://www.dh.gov.uk/en/Publicationsandstatistics/Publications/PublicationsPolicyAndGuidance/DH_093419. Accessed August 30, 2009.
22. Canada Health Infoway. *Making health information work better for Canadians.* Corporate Business Plan 2009/2010. http://www2.infoway-inforoute.ca/Documents/bp/Business_Plan_2009-2010_en.pdf. Accessed August 30, 2009.
23. NNS Scotland. *Patient Focus and Public Involvement.* www.scotland.gov.uk/Resource/Doc/158744/0043087.pdf. Accessed June 22, 2009.
24. Department of Health and Ageing. Australian Government. 2009. *A healthier Future for all Australians—final report,* June 2009. http://www.health.gov.au/internet/main/publishing.nsf/Content/nhhrc-report. Accessed August 30, 2009.
25. *The Finnish Health Care System: A Value-Based Perspective.* 2009. http://www.sitra.fi/fi/Julkaisut/OhjelmienJulkaisut/teho/terveydenhuolto.htm. Accessed May 5, 2009.
26. Adams K, Greiner AC, Corrigan JM, eds. First annual Crossing the Quality Chasm Summit. Washington, DC: The National Academies Press, 2004.
27. Lynn NB, Panzer AM, Kindig DA, eds. Committee on Health Literacy, *Institute of Medicine.* Health Literacy: A Prescription to End Confusion. Washington, DC: The National Academies Press, 2004.
28. Berkman ND, DeWalt DA, Pignone MP, et al. *Literacy and Health Outcomes.* Evidence Report/Technology Assessment #87. AHRQ Publication No04-E007-1. 2004. www.ahrq.gov/clinic/epcsums/litsum.pdf. Accessed July 3, 2009.
29. Duodecim. *Finland's Health Library.* 2009. www.terveyskirjasto.fi. Accessed May 5, 2009.

30. Office of Disease Prevention and Health Promotion. *Healthy People 2010*. Progress review on Focus 11, April 19 2007. Department of Health and Human Services, 2007. www.healthypeople. gov/data/2010prog/focus11. Accessed July 11, 2009.

31. Department of Health and Ageing. Australian Government. Health Connect. 2009 e-Health: *Overview of Health Connect*. http://www.health. gov.au/healthconnect. Accessed August 30, 2009.

32. Barlow JH, et al. Self management approaches for people with chronic conditions: A review. *Patient Ed Couns*. 2002;48:177-187.

33. Schoen C, Osborn R, How SKH, Doty MM, JP. In chronic condition: Experiences of patients with complex healthcare needs in eight countries. 2008. *Health Aff*. 2009;28(1):w1-w16.

34. Harris Interactive (2007). US adults not very confident that physicians have the complete picture, according to a new WSJ.com/Harris Interactive Survey: December 5, 2007. Harris Interactive Inc. All rights reserved. http://www.harrisinteractive. com/news/printerfriend/index.asp?NewsID=1264. Accessed July 16, 2009.

35. Ghandi TK, Weingart SN, Borus J, et al. Adverse drug events in ambulatory care. *N Engl J Med*. 2003;348:1556-1564.

36. Cain C, Clancy C. Commentary: Patient-Centered Health Information Technology. *Am J Med Qual*. 2005;20(3):164-165.

37. Tang P, Ash J, Bates DW, et al. Personal Health Records: Definitions, benefits, and strategies for overcoming barriers to adoption. *JAMIA*. 2006;13(2):121-126.

38. Wolter J, Friedman B. 2005 Health records for the people: Touting the benefits of the consumer-based Personal Health Record. *JAMIA*. 2005;76(10):28-32. http://library.ahima.org/xpedio/ groups/public/documents/ahima/bok1_028385. hcsp?dDocName=bok1_028385. Accessed 16 July 16, 2009.

39. Deloitte 2008. *Many Consumers Want Major Changes in Health Care Design, Delivery*. Deloitte LLP. http://www.deloitte.com/dtt/article/ 0,1002,cid%253D192717,00.html. Accessed July 16, 2009.

40. Seidman J, Eytan T. (2008) Helping Patients Plug In: *Lessons in the Adoption of Online Consumer Tools*. California Healthcare Foundation. www.chcf.org/documents/chronicdisease/ HelpingPatientsPlugIn.pdf. Accessed July 3, 2009.

41. *Synergia Study*. http://www.synergia.co.nz/page/ case-studies-health-sector-people-centric-self-care, Accessed October 23, 2009.

42. http://kotiin.laurea.fi. Accessed October 20, 2009.

43. Annakaisa Iivari, Pekka Ruotsalainen: *eHealth Roadmap – Finland*. Ministry of Social Affairs and Health's Reports 2007:15. http://www.stm. fi/en/publications/publication/_julkaisu/1056833. Accessed July 16, 2009.

44. Microsoft. *TELUS licenses Microsoft HealthVault to launch TELUS Health Space*, Canada's first consumer e-health platform. May 6, 2009. http://www. microsoft.com/presspass/events/healthvault/docs/ HealthSpacePR.doc. Accessed August 9, 2009.

45. Donnelly L. *Patients to be given Google health records under Tories*. Telegraph.co.uk. 09 August 2009. http://www.telegraph.co.uk/news/ newstopics/politics/conservative/5995382/Patients- to-be-given-Google-health-records-under-Tories. html. Access August 9, 2009.

46. In EK. Elektronische Fallakte. http://www.fallakte. de/index.html. Accessed August 30, 2009.

47. http://www.denmark.dk/en/menu/About- Denmark/Denmark-In-Brief/. Accessed November 9, 2009.

48. http://www.stat.fi/tup/suoluk/suoluk_vaesto_ en.html. Accessed October 20, 2009.

49. Office of the Surgeon General. *Proceedings of Surgeon General's Workshop on Improving Health Literacy*. NIH: Bethesda, September 7, 2006: http:// www.surgeongeneral.gov/topics/healthliteracy/ pdf/proceedings120607.pdf. Accessed July 5, 2009.

50. Lohr S. Kaiser backs Microsoft patient-data plan. *NY Times*, June 10, 2008. http://www.nytimes. com/2008/06/10/business/10kaiser.html. Accessed July 6, 2009.

51. Weaver C, Zeildorff R. TIGER Collaborative 9. Consumer empowerment, health literacy and Personal Health Records. In: Ball M, Hinton Walker P, Douglas J, et al (eds). *Nursing Informatics: Where Technology and Caring Meet*. 4th edition. New York: Springer Science and Business Media, L.L.C, in press summer 2010.

52. *Google Health*. 2008: http://www.google.com/intl/ en-US/health/about/. Accessed September 6, 2009.

53. Institute of Medicine. Press Release, April 14 2008. Health Care Workforce Too Small: Unprepared for Aging Baby Boombers. http://www8. nationalacademies.org/onpinews/newsitem. aspx?RecordID=12089. Accessed November 25, 2009.

54. Institute of Medicine. *Retooling for an Aging America: Building the Health Care Workforce*. Washington, DC: The National Academies Press, 2008.

55. Pruitt S, Epping-Jordan J. Preparing the 21st century global healthcare workforce. *BMJ*. 2005;330:637-639.

56. Dugger CW. South African leader, rejecting predecessor's stance, rallies nation to fight AIDS. *NY Times*. Nov 1, 2009:A16.

57. WHO. Data 2008. http://www.who.int/hiv/countries/en/. Accessed November 10, 2009.

58. WHO. 2005. Preparing a Health Care Workforce for the 21st Century: The Challenge of Chronic Conditions. http://apps.who.int/bookorders/anglais/ detart1.jsp?sesslan=1&codlan=1&codcol=15&co dcch=621. Accessed November 9, 2009.

59. Skinner J, Staiger D. NBER Working Paper No. 14865. http://www.nber.org/papers/w14865. Accessed October 24, 2009.

60. International Council Nurses. Global Nursing Shortage: Priority Areas for Intervention. A Report from ICN/FNIF. International Council of Nurses, Florence Nightingale International Foundation, Burdett Trust for Nursing. *Global Nursing Review Initiative 2006*. http://www.hrhresourcecenter.org/node/420. Accessed November 8, 2009.

61. Nursing Workforce. http://www.eldis.org/go/topics/dossiers/human-resources-for-health/strengthening-capacity/nursing-workforce. Accessed October 25, 2009.

62. Thompson TG, Brailer DJ. *The Decade of Health Information Technology: Delivering Consumer-centric and Information-rich Health Care. Framework for Strategic Action*. Washington, DC: Department of Health and Human Services, 2004.

63. Technology Informatics Guiding Education Reform. Evidence and Informatics Transforming Nursing: 3-Year Action Steps toward a 10-Year Vision. http://www.tigersummit.com. And TIGER. (www.tigersummit.com/participants). Accessed April 21, 2009.

64. Technology Informatics Guiding Education Reform. *Collaborating to Integrate Evidence and Informatics into Nursing Practice and Education: An Executive Summary*. http://www.tigersummit.com. Accessed April 21, 2009.

65. Ball M, Hinton Walker P, Douglas J, et al. *Nursing Informatics: Where Technology and Caring Meet*. 4th edition. New York: Springer Science and Business Media, L.L.C, in press summer 2010.

66. Balint M. The Doctor, His Patient and the Illness. New York: International Universities Press, 1957.

67. Dickerson SS, Brennan PF. The Internet as a catalyst for shifting power in provider-patient relationship. *Nurs Outlook*. 2002;50:195-203.

68. General Assembly IMIA NI. *Nursing Informatics Definition*. www.imiani.org. Accessed September 20, 2009.

69. Scholes M, Bryant Y, Barber B, eds. *The impact of computers in nursing: an international review*. North Holland: Elsevier Science Publishers BV, 1983.

70. Werley HH, Lang NM, eds. *Identification of the Nursing Minimum Data Set*. New York: Springer, 1988.

71. AMIA. (2005) Nursing Informatics-Working Group. *Nursing Informatics programs available in the United States*. http://www.amia.org/mbrcenter/wg/ni/education.asp. Accessed September 23, 2005.

72. Skiba DJ, Carty B, Nelson R. Growth in nursing informatics education programs: Skills and competencies. In: Weaver CA, Delaney CW, Weber P, Carr R, eds. *Nursing and Informatics for the 21st Century: An International Look at Practice, Trends and the Future*. Chicago: HIMSS, 2006; 35-44

73. American Nurses Association. *Nursing Informatics: Scope and Standards of Practice*. Silver Spring, MD: http://www.Nursesbooks.org. Accessed October 10, 2009.

74. Casey A. Information technology strategies in the United Kingdom and Ireland. In: Weaver CA, Delaney CW, Weber P, Carr RL, eds. *Nursing and Nursing Informatics for the 21st Century, 2nd ed*. Chicago: HIMSS, 2010, in process.

75. Alliance for Nursing Informatics. http://www.allianceni.org. Accessed September 23, 2005.

76. Clark J, Lang N. Nursing's next advance: an international classification for nursing practice. *Int Nurs Rev*. 1992;39(4):109-112.

77. Saba VK. The classification of home health care nursing diagnoses and interventions. *Caring*. 1992;11(3):50-57.

78. Saba VK. Home Health Care Classification (HHCC) System two terminologies: HHCC of nursing diagnoses and HHCC of nursing interventions with 20 care components. Appendix A, In: Saba VK, McCormick KA, eds. *Essentials of Computers for Nurses*, New York: McGraw-Hill; 1999. 3rd ed, pp 529-533. http://www.dml.georgetown.edu/research/hhcc. Accessed October 20, 2009.

79. Martin KS, Scheet NJ. *The Omaha System: Applications for Community Health Nursing*. Philadelphia: WB Saunders, 1992.

80. McCloskey JC, Bulechek GM. *Nursing Interventions Classification*, 2nd ed. St. Louis: Mosby, 1996.

81. Johnson M, Maas M. Nursing Outcome Classification. St. Louis: Mosby, 1997.

82. Ozbolt JG. From minimum data to maximum impact. Using clinical data to strengthen patient care. *Adv Pract Nurs Q*. 1997;1:62-69.

83. International Council of Nurses. *Nursing's Next Advance: Development of an International Classification for Nursing Practice: A Working Paper*. Geneva; ICN, 1993.

84. International Council of Nurses. *The International classification for Nursing Practice: A Unifying Framework*: The Alpha Version. Geneva: ICN, 1996.

85. Casey A. Standard terminology for nursing: results of the nursing, midwifery and health visiting terms project. *Health Inform*. 1995;1(2):41-43.

86. Gliddon T, Weaver C. The community nursing minimum data set Australia: from definition to the real world. In: Grobe SJ, Pluyter-Wenting ESP, eds. *Nursing Informatics: An International Overview for Nursing in a Technological Era*. Amsterdam: Elsevier, 1994.

87. Werley HH, Devine EC, Zorn CR. *Nursing Minimum Data Set*. Collection Manual, Milwaukee, WI: University of Wisconsin, Milwaukee, School of Nursing; 1990.

88. Goossen W, Delaney C, Sermeus W, et al. (2004). Preliminary Results of a Pilot of the International Nursing Minimum Data Set (iNMDS) [Abstract] In: *Proceedings of MedInfo 11th World Congress on Medical Informatics of the International Medical Informatics Association*. S103.

89. Goossen W, Delaney C, Coenen A, et al. The International Nursing Minimum Data Set: iNMDS. In: Weaver CA, Delaney CW, Weber P, Carr R, eds. *Nursing and Informatics for the 21st Century: An International look at Practice, Trends and the Future.* Chicago: HIMSS Publishing; 2006. Chapter 24.

90. WHO (2009). http://www.who.int/classifications/en/. Accessed June 2, 2009.

91. IHTSDO (2009). http://www.ihtsdo.org/. Accessed June 2, 2009.

92. Park H, Lundberg C, Coenen A. (2008) Making connections: SNOMED-CT and ICNP. Unpublished presentation, Summer Institute in Nursing Informatics, Baltimore, MD.

93. *ICN Definition of Nursing.* http://www.icn.ch/definition.htm. Accessed October 25, 2009.

94. Gugerty B. (chair) TIGER Informatics Competencies Collaborative final report. http://tigercompetencies.pbworks.com/FrontPage. Accessed November 25, 2009.

95. *5th Annual World Healthcare Innovation and Technology Congress.* http://www.worldcongress.com/events/HL09010/. Accessed October 25, 2009.

96. *Design of Health Care Technologies for the Developing World.* http://arjournals.annualreviews.org/doi/abs/10.1146/annurev.bioeng.9.060906.151913. Accessed October 25, 2009.

97. Campbell A, Eisenman S, Lane N, et al. *The Rise of People-Centric Sensing, IEEE Internet Computing.* 2008;12,4:12-21.

98. McDaniel AM, Schutte DL, Keller LO. Consumer health informatics: From genomics to population health. *Nur Outlook.* 2008;56:216-223.

Index

t = table entry
f = figure entry